Microsoft® Office

Excel 2003

COMPREHENSIVE

Microsoft® Office

Excel 2003

COMPREHENSIVE

ROBERT T.
GRAUER
UNIVERSITY OF MIAMI

MARYANN
BARBER
UNIVERSITY OF MIAMI

PEARSON
Prentice
Hall

Upper Saddle River,
New Jersey 07458

Library of Congress Cataloging-in-Publication Data

Grauer, Robert T.
Microsoft Office Excel 2003 / Robert T. Grauer, Maryann Barber.
p. cm. -- (The exploring Office series)
Includes index.
ISBN 0-13-143483-7
1. Microsoft Excel (Computer file) 2. Business--Computer programs. 3. Electronic spread sheets. I. Barber, Maryann M. II. Title. III. Series.
HF5548.4.M523G725 2004
005.54--dc22 2003064809

Executive Acquisitions Editor: Jodi McPherson
VP/ Publisher: Natalie E. Anderson
Associate Director of IT Product Development: Melonie Salvati
Senior Project Manager, Editorial: Eileen Clark
Project Manager: Melissa Edwards
Editorial Assistants: Jodi Bolognese and Jasmine Slowik
Media Project Manager: Cathleen Profitko
Marketing Manager: Emily Williams Knight
Marketing Assistant: Nicole Beaudry
Production Manager: Gail Steier de Acevedo
Project Manager, Production: Lynne Breitfeller
Production Editor: Greg Hubit
Associate Director, Manufacturing: Vincent Scelta
Manufacturing Buyer: Lynne Breitfeller
Design Manager: Maria Lange
Interior Design: Michael J. Fruhbeis
Cover Design: Michael J. Fruhbeis
Cover Printer: Phoenix Color
Composition and Project Management: The GTS Companies
Printer/Binder: Banta Menasha

10 9 8 7 6 5 4 3 2 1
ISBN 0-13-143483-7 spiral
ISBN 0-13-145183-9 adhesive

To Marion —
my wife, my lover, and my best friend

Robert Grauer

To Frank —
I love you

To Holly —
for being my friend

Maryann Barber

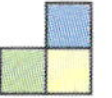

What does this logo mean?

It means this courseware has been approved by the Microsoft® Office Specialist Program to be among the finest available for learning **Microsoft Excel 2003**. It also means that upon completion of this courseware, you may be prepared to take an exam for Microsoft Office Specialist qualification.

What is a Microsoft Office Specialist?

A Microsoft Office Specialist is an individual who has passed exams for certifying his or her skills in one or more of the Microsoft Office desktop applications such as Microsoft Word, Microsoft Excel, Microsoft PowerPoint, Microsoft Outlook, Microsoft Access, or Microsoft Project. The Microsoft Office Specialist Program typically offers certification exams at the "Specialist" and "Expert" skill levels.* The Microsoft Office Specialist Program is the only program approved by Microsoft for testing proficiency in Microsoft Office desktop applications and Microsoft Project. This testing program can be a valuable asset in any job search or career advancement.

More Information:

To learn more about becoming a Microsoft Office Specialist, visit www.microsoft.com/officespecialist

To learn about other Microsoft Office Specialist approved courseware from Pearson Education visit www.prenhall.com

---

*The availability of Microsoft Office Specialist certification exams varies by application, application version, and language. Visit www.microsoft.com/officespecialist for exam availability.

Contents

MICROSOFT® OFFICE EXCEL 2003

one

Introduction to Excel: What Is a Spreadsheet? 1

two

Gaining Proficiency: The Web and Business Applications 65

three

Graphs and Charts: Delivering a Message 109

four

Using Spreadsheets in Decision Making: What If? 159

five

Consolidating Data: Worksheet References and File Linking 217

A Financial Forecast: Auditing, Protection, and Templates 261

seven

List and Data Management: Converting Data to Information 307

eight

Automating Repetitive Tasks: Macros and Visual Basic for Applications 367

nine

A Professional Application: VBA and Date Functions 431

ten

Extending VBA: Processing Worksheets and Workbooks 491

MICROSOFT® WINDOWS® XP

Getting Started with Microsoft® Windows® XP

GETTING STARTED WITH VBA

Getting Started with VBA: Extending Microsoft® Office 2003 1

Preface

THE EXPLORING OFFICE SERIES FOR 2003

Continuing a tradition of excellence, Prentice Hall is proud to announce the new ***Exploring Microsoft Office 2003*** series by Robert T. Grauer and Maryann Barber. The hands-on approach and conceptual framework of this comprehensive series helps students master all aspects of the Microsoft Office 2003 software, while providing the background necessary to transfer and use these skills in their personal and professional lives.

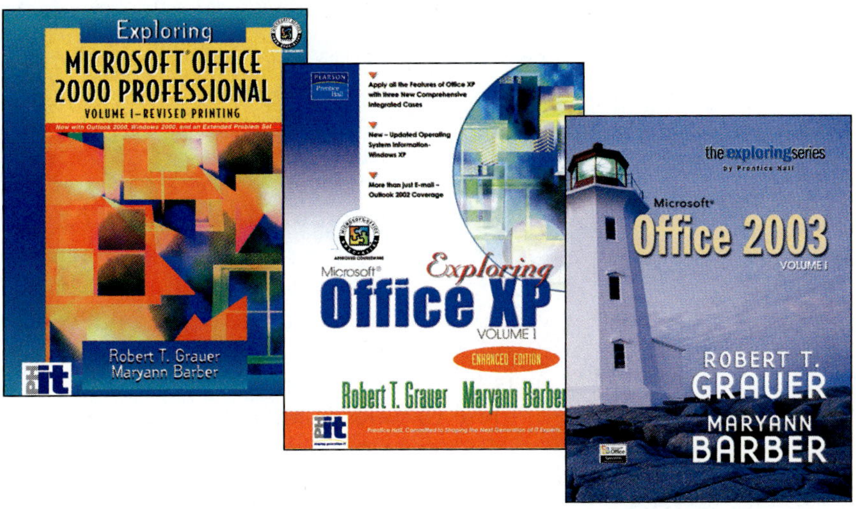

The entire series has been revised to include the new features found in the Office 2003 Suite, which contains Word 2003, Excel 2003, Access 2003, PowerPoint 2003, Publisher 2003, FrontPage 2003, and Outlook 2003.

In addition, this edition includes fully revised end-of-chapter material that provides an extensive review of concepts and techniques discussed in the chapter. Each chapter now begins with an ***introductory case study*** to provide an effective overview of what the reader will be able to accomplish, with additional ***mini cases*** at the end of each chapter for practice and review. The conceptual content within each chapter has been modified as appropriate and numerous end-of-chapter exercises have been added.

The new ***visual design*** introduces the concept of ***perfect pages***, whereby every step in every hands-on exercise, as well as every end-of-chapter exercise, begins at the top of its own page and has its own screen shot. This clean design allows for easy navigation throughout the text.

Continuing the success of the website provided for previous editions of this series, Exploring Office 2003 offers expanded resources that include online, interactive study guides, data file downloads, technology updates, additional case studies and exercises, and other helpful information. Start out at www.prenhall.com/grauer to explore these resources!

Organization of the Exploring Office 2003 Series

The new Exploring Microsoft Office 2003 series includes four combined Office 2003 texts from which to choose:

- ***Volume I*** is Microsoft Office Specialist certified in each of the core applications in the Office suite (Word, Excel, Access, and PowerPoint). Five additional modules (*Essential Computing Concepts, Getting Started with Windows XP, The Internet and the World Wide Web, Getting Started with Outlook,* and *Integrated Case Studies*) are also included.
- ***Volume II*** picks up where Volume I leaves off, covering the advanced topics for the individual applications. A *Getting Started with VBA* module has been added.
- The ***Brief Microsoft Office 2003*** edition provides less coverage of the core applications than Volume I (a total of 10 chapters as opposed to 18). It also includes the *Getting Started with Windows XP* and *Getting Started with Outlook* modules.
- ***Getting Started with Office 2003*** contains the first chapter from each application (Word, Excel, Access, and PowerPoint), plus three additional modules: *Getting Started with Windows XP, The Internet and the World Wide Web,* and *Essential Computing Concepts.*

Individual texts for Word 2003, Excel 2003, Access 2003, and PowerPoint 2003 provide complete coverage of the application and are Microsoft Office Specialist certified. For shorter courses, we have created brief versions of the Exploring texts that give students a four-chapter introduction to each application. Each of these volumes is Microsoft Office Specialist certified at the Specialist level.

This series has been approved by Microsoft to be used in preparation for Microsoft Office Specialist exams.

The Microsoft Office Specialist program is globally recognized as the standard for demonstrating desktop skills with the Microsoft Office suite of business productivity applications (Microsoft Word, Microsoft Excel, Microsoft PowerPoint, Microsoft Access, and Microsoft Outlook). With a Microsoft Office Specialist certification, thousands of people have demonstrated increased productivity and have proved their ability to utilize the advanced functionality of these Microsoft applications.

By encouraging individuals to develop advanced skills with Microsoft's leading business desktop software, the Microsoft Office Specialist program helps fill the demand for qualified, knowledgeable people in the modern workplace. At the same time, Microsoft Office Specialist helps satisfy an organization's need for a qualitative assessment of employee skills.

Instructor and Student Resources

The **Instructor's CD** that accompanies the Exploring Office series contains:

- Student data files
- Solutions to all exercises and problems
- PowerPoint lectures
- Instructor's manuals in Word format that enable the instructor to annotate portions of the instructor manuals for distribution to the class

- Instructors may also use our ***test creation software***, TestGen and QuizMaster.

TestGen is a test generator program that lets you view and easily edit testbank questions, transfer them to tests, and print in a variety of formats suitable to your teaching situation. The program also offers many options for organizing and displaying testbanks and tests. A random number test generator enables you to create multiple versions of an exam.

QuizMaster, also included in this package, allows students to take tests created with TestGen on a local area network. The QuizMaster Utility built into TestGen lets instructors view student records and print a variety of reports. Building tests is easy with TestGen, and exams can be easily uploaded into WebCT, BlackBoard, and CourseCompass.

Prentice Hall's Companion Website at www.prenhall.com/grauer offers expanded IT resources and downloadable supplements. This site also includes an online study guide for students containing true/false and multiple choice questions and practice projects.

WebCT www.prenhall.com/webct

Gold level customer support available exclusively to adopters of Prentice Hall courses is provided free-of-charge upon adoption and provides you with priority assistance, training discounts, and dedicated technical support.

Blackboard www.prenhall.com/blackboard

Prentice Hall's abundant online content, combined with Blackboard's popular tools and interface, result in robust Web-based courses that are easy to implement, manage, and use—taking your courses to new heights in student interaction and learning.

CourseCompass www.coursecompass.com

CourseCompass is a dynamic, interactive online course management tool powered by Blackboard. This exciting product allows you to teach with marketing-leading Pearson Education content in an easy-to-use, customizable format.

Training and Assessment www2.phgenit.com/support

Prentice Hall offers Performance Based Training and Assessment in one product, Train&Assess IT. The Training component offers computer-based training that a student can use to preview, learn, and review Microsoft Office application skills. Web or CD-ROM delivered, Train IT offers interactive multimedia, computer-based training to augment classroom learning. Built-in prescriptive testing suggests a study path based not only on student test results but also on the specific textbook chosen for the course.

The Assessment component offers computer-based testing that shares the same user interface as Train IT and is used to evaluate a student's knowledge about specific topics in Word, Excel, Access, PowerPoint, Windows, Outlook, and the Internet. It does this in a task-oriented, performance-based environment to demonstrate proficiency as well as comprehension on the topics by the students. More extensive than the testing in Train IT, Assess IT offers more administrative features for the instructor and additional questions for the student.

Assess IT also allows professors to test students out of a course, place students in appropriate courses, and evaluate skill sets.

Opening Case Study

New! Each chapter now begins with an introductory case study to provide an effective overview of what students will accomplish by completing the chapter.

CHAPTER 1

Getting Started with Microsoft® Windows® XP

OBJECTIVES

After reading this chapter you will:

1. Describe the Windows desktop.
2. Use the Help and Support Center to obtain information.
3. Describe the My Computer and My Documents folders.
4. Differentiate between a program file and a data file.
5. Download a file from the Exploring Office Web site.
6. Copy and/or move a file from one folder to another.
7. Delete a file, and then recover it from the Recycle Bin.
8. Create and arrange shortcuts on the desktop.
9. Use the Search Companion.
10. Use the My Pictures and My Music folders.
11. Use Windows Messenger for instant messaging.

hands-on exercises

1. WELCOME TO WINDOWS XP
   Input: None
   Output: None
2. DOWNLOAD PRACTICE FILES
   Input: Data files from the Web
   Output: Welcome to Windows XP (a Word document)
3. WINDOWS EXPLORER
   Input: Data files from exercise 2
   Output: Screen Capture within a Word document
4. INCREASING PRODUCTIVITY
   Input: Data files from exercise 3
   Output: None
5. FUN WITH WINDOWS XP
   Input: None
   Output: None

CASE STUDY
UNFORESEEN CIRCUMSTANCES

Steve and his wife Shelly have poured their life savings into the dream of owning their own business, a "nanny" service agency. They have spent the last two years building their business and have created a sophisticated database with numerous entries for both families and nannies. The database is the key to their operation. Now that it is up and running, Steve and Shelly are finally at a point where they could hire someone to manage the operation on a part-time basis so that they could take some time off together.

Unfortunately, their process for selecting a person they could trust with their business was not as thorough as it should have been. Nancy, their new employee, assured them that all was well, and the couple left for an extended weekend. The place was in shambles on their return. Nancy could not handle the responsibility, and when Steve gave her two weeks' notice, neither he nor his wife thought that the unimaginable would happen. On her last day in the office Nancy "lost" all of the names in the database—the data was completely gone!

Nancy claimed that a "virus" knocked out the database, but after spending nearly $1,500 with a computer consultant, Steve was told that it had been cleverly deleted from the hard drive and could not be recovered. Of course, the consultant asked Steve and Shelly about their backup strategy, which they sheepishly admitted did not exist. They had never experienced any problems in the past, and simply assumed that their data was safe. Fortunately, they do have hard copy of the data in the form of various reports that were printed throughout the time they were in business. They have no choice but to manually reenter the data.

Your assignment is to read the chapter, paying special attention to the information on file management. Think about how Steve and Shelly could have avoided the disaster if a backup strategy had been in place, then summarize your thoughts in a brief note to your instructor. Describe the elements of a basic backup strategy. Give several other examples of unforeseen circumstances that can cause data to be lost.

1

New! A listing of the input and output files for each hands-on exercise within the chapter. Students will stay on track with what is to be accomplished.

PERFECT PAGES

hands-on exercise

1 Welcome to Windows XP

Objective To log on to Windows XP and customize the desktop; to open the My Computer folder; to move and size a window; to format a floppy disk and access the Help and Support Center. Use Figure 7 as a guide.

Step 1: **Log On to Windows XP**

- Turn on the computer and all of the peripheral devices. The floppy drive should be empty prior to starting your machine.
- Windows XP will load automatically, and you should see a login screen similar to Figure 7a. (It does not matter which version of Windows XP you are using.) The number and names of the potential users and their associated icons will be different on your system.
- Click the icon for the user account you want to access. You may be prompted for a password, depending on the security options in effect.

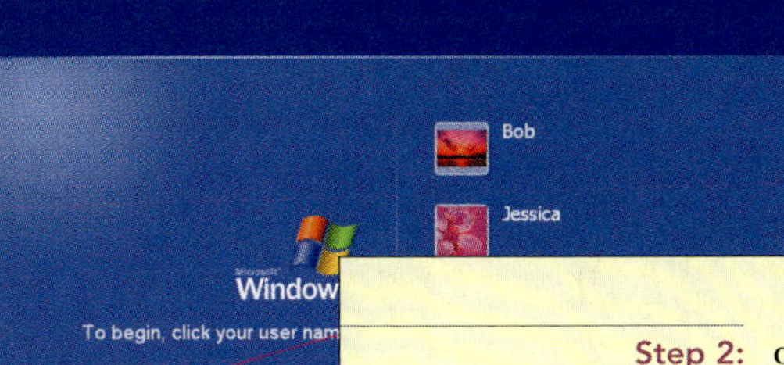

(a) Log On to Windows XP (step 1)

FIGURE 7 Hands-on Exercise 1

USER ACCOUNTS

The available user names are cr Windows XP, but you can add or d click Control Panel, switch to the Ca the desired task, such as creating a then supply the necessary informati user accounts in a school setting.

Each step in the hands-on exercises begins at the top of the page to ensure that students can easily navigate through the text.

Step 2: **Choose the Theme and Start Menu**

- Check with your instructor to see if you are able to modify the desktop and other settings at your school or university. If your network administrator has disabled these commands, skip this step and go to step 3.
- Point to a blank area on the desktop, click the **right mouse button** to display a context-sensitive menu, then click the **Properties command** to open the Display Properties dialog box. Click the **Themes tab** and select the **Windows XP theme** if it is not already selected. Click **OK**.
- We prefer to work without any wallpaper (background picture) on the desktop. **Right click** the desktop, click **Properties**, then click the **Desktop tab** in the Display Properties dialog box. Click **None** as shown in Figure 7b, then click **OK**. The background disappears.
- The Start menu is modified independently of the theme. **Right click** a blank area of the taskbar, click the **Properties command** to display the Taskbar and Start Menu Properties dialog box, then click the **Start Menu tab**.
- Click the **Start Menu option button**. Click **OK**.

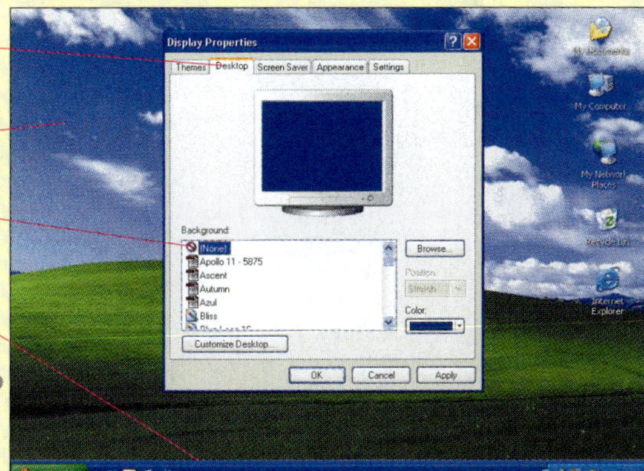

(b) Choose the Theme and Start Menu (step 2)

FIGURE 7 Hands-on Exercise 1 *(continued)*

New! Larger screen shots with clear callouts.

Boxed tips provide students with additional information.

IMPLEMENT A SCREEN SAVER

A screen saver is a delightful way to personalize your computer and a good way to practice with basic commands in Windows XP. Right click a blank area of the desktop, click the Properties command to open the Display Properties dialog box, then click the Screen Saver tab. Click the down arrow in the Screen Saver list box, choose the desired screen saver, then set the option to wait an appropriate amount of time before the screen saver appears. Click OK to accept the settings and close the dialog box.

Mini Cases and Practice Exercises

New!

We've added mini cases at the end of each chapter for expanded practice and review.

MINI CASES

The Financial Consultant

A friend of yours is in the process of buying a home and has asked you to compare the payments and total interest on a 15- and 30-year loan at varying interest rates. You have decided to analyze the loans in Excel, and then incorporate the results into a memo written in Microsoft Word. As of now, the principal is $150,000, but it is very likely that your friend will change his mind several times, and so you want to use the linking and embedding capability within Windows to dynamically link the worksheet to the word processing document. Your memo should include a letterhead that takes advantage of the formatting capabilities within Word; a graphic logo would be a nice touch.

Fun with the If Statement

Open the *Chapter 4 Mini Case—Fun with the If Statement* workbook in the Exploring Excel folder, then follow the directions in the worksheet to view a hidden message. The message is displayed by various If statements scattered throughout the worksheet, but the worksheet is protected so that you cannot see these formulas. (Use help to see how to protect a worksheet.) We made it easy for you, however, because you can unprotect the worksheet since a password is not required. Once the worksheet is unprotected, pull down the Format menu, click the Cells command, click the Protection tab, and clear the Hidden check box. Prove to your professor that you have done this successfully, by changing the text of our message. Print the completed worksheet to show both displayed values and cell formulas.

The Lottery

Many states raise money through lotteries that advertise prizes of several million dollars. In reality, however, the actual value of the prize is considerably less than the advertised value, although the winners almost certainly do not care. One state, for example, recently offered a twenty million dollar prize that was to be distributed in twenty annual payments of one million dollars each. How much was the prize actually worth, assuming a long-term interest rate of five percent? Use the PV (Present Value) function to determine the answer. What is the effect on the answer if payments to the recipient are made at the beginning of each year, rather than at the end of each year?

A Penny a Day

What if you had a rich ur
salary each day for the n
prised at how quickly th
use the Goal Seek comm
(if any) will your uncle p
uncle pay you on the 31s

The Rule of 72

Delaying your IRA for or
on when you begin. Tha
a calculator, using the "R
long it takes money to
money earning 8% annu
money doubles again in
your IRA at age 21, rathe
initial contribution. Use
lose, assuming an 8% ra
determine the exact am

New!

Each project in the end-of-chapter material begins at the top of a page—now students can easily see where their assignments begin and end.

PRACTICE WITH EXCEL

1. **Theme Park Admissions:** A partially completed version of the worksheet in Figure 3.13 is available in the Exploring Excel folder as *Chapter 3 Practice 1*. Follow the directions in parts (a) and (b) to compute the totals and format the worksheet, then create each of the charts listed below.
   a. Use the AutoSum command to enter the formulas to compute the total number of admissions for each region and each quarter.
   b. Select the entire worksheet (cells A1 through F8), then use the AutoFormat command to format the worksheet. You do not have to accept the entire design, nor do you have to use the design we selected. You can also modify the design after it has been applied to the worksheet by changing the font size of selected cells and/or changing boldface and italics.
   c. Create a column chart showing the total number of admissions in each quarter as shown in Figure 3.13. Add the graphic shown in the figure for emphasis.
   d. Create a pie chart that shows the percentage of the total number of admissions in each region. Create this chart in its own chart sheet with an appropriate name.
   e. Create a stacked column chart that shows the total number of admissions for each region and the contribution of each quarter within each region. Create this chart in its own chart sheet with an appropriate name.
   f. Create a stacked column chart showing the total number of admissions for each quarter and the contribution of each region within each quarter. Create this chart in its own chart sheet with an appropriate name.
   g. Change the color of each of the worksheet tabs.
   h. Print the entire workbook, consisting of the worksheet in Figure 3.13 plus the three additional sheets that you create. Use portrait orientation for the Sales Data worksheet and landscape orientation for the other worksheets. Create a custom header for each worksheet that includes your name, your course, and your instructor's name. Create a custom footer for each worksheet that includes the name of the worksheet. Submit the completed assignment to your instructor.

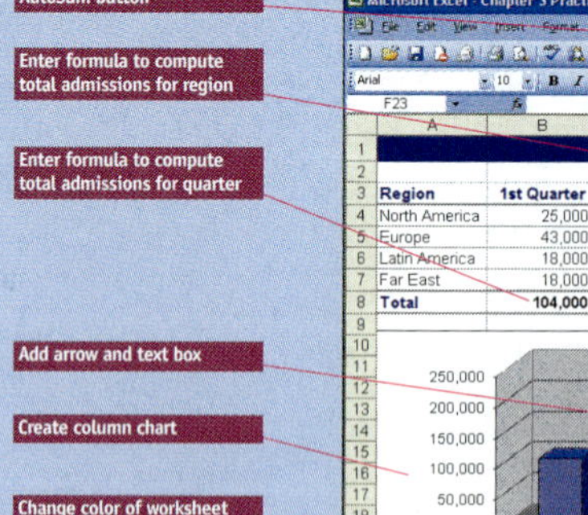

FIGURE 3.13 Theme Park Admissions (exercise 1)

Integrated Case Studies

New!

Each case study contains multiple exercises that use Microsoft Office applications in conjunction with one another.

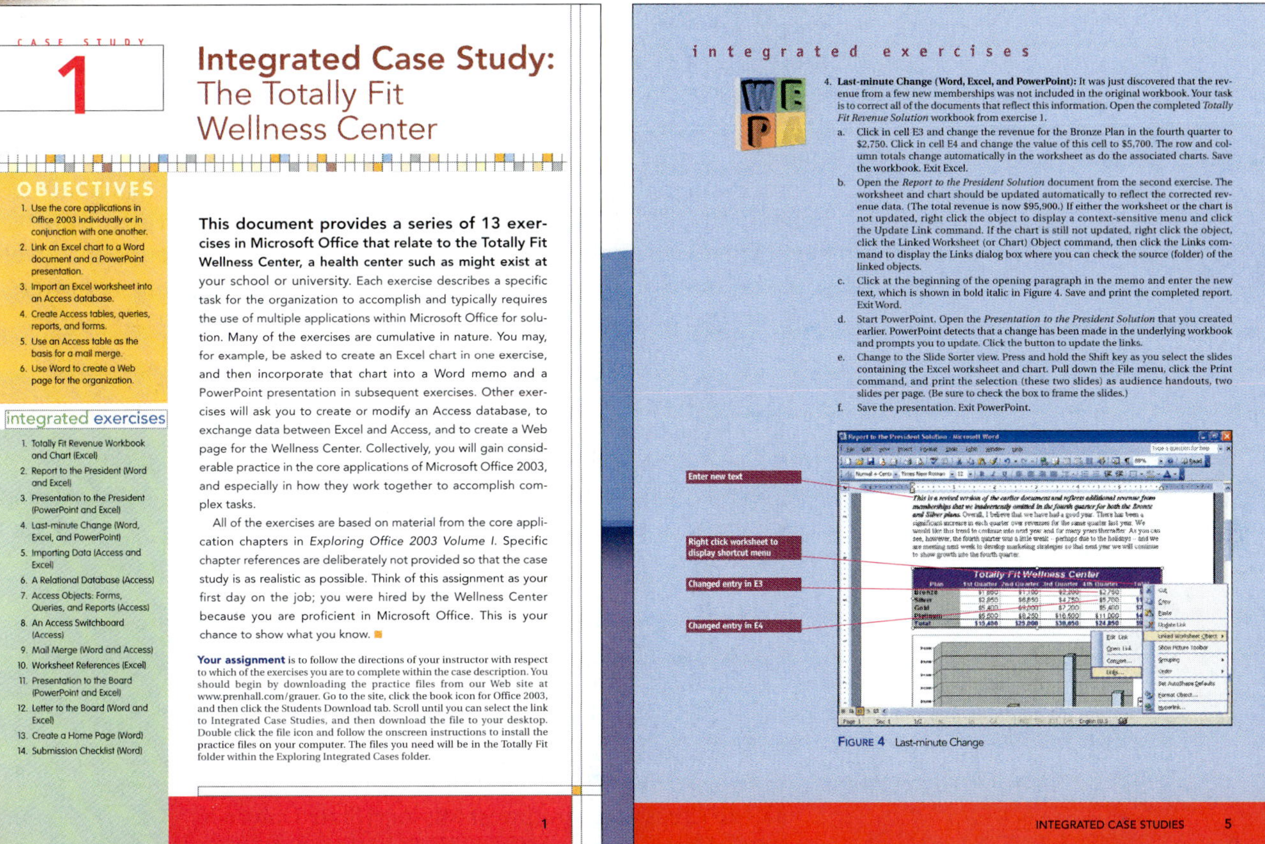

CASE STUDY 1

Integrated Case Study: The Totally Fit Wellness Center

OBJECTIVES

1. Use the core applications in Office 2003 individually or in conjunction with one another.
2. Link an Excel chart to a Word document and a PowerPoint presentation.
3. Import an Excel worksheet into an Access database.
4. Create Access tables, queries, reports, and forms.
5. Use an Access table as the basis for a mail merge.
6. Use Word to create a Web page for the organization.

integrated exercises

1. Totally Fit Revenue Workbook and Chart (Excel)
2. Report to the President (Word and Excel)
3. Presentation to the President (PowerPoint and Excel)
4. Last-minute Change (Word, Excel, and PowerPoint)
5. Importing Data (Access and Excel)
6. A Relational Database (Access)
7. Access Objects: Forms, Queries, and Reports (Access)
8. An Access Switchboard (Access)
9. Mail Merge (Word and Access)
10. Worksheet References (Excel)
11. Presentation to the Board (PowerPoint and Excel)
12. Letter to the Board (Word and Excel)
13. Create a Home Page (Word)
14. Submission Checklist (Word)

This document provides a series of 13 exercises in Microsoft Office that relate to the Totally Fit Wellness Center, a health center such as might exist at your school or university. Each exercise describes a specific task for the organization to accomplish and typically requires the use of multiple applications within Microsoft Office for solution. Many of the exercises are cumulative in nature. You may, for example, be asked to create an Excel chart in one exercise, and then incorporate that chart into a Word memo and a PowerPoint presentation in subsequent exercises. Other exercises will ask you to create or modify an Access database, to exchange data between Excel and Access, and to create a Web page for the Wellness Center. Collectively, you will gain considerable practice in the core applications of Microsoft Office 2003, and especially in how they work together to accomplish complex tasks.

All of the exercises are based on material from the core application chapters in *Exploring Office 2003 Volume I*. Specific chapter references are deliberately not provided so that the case study is as realistic as possible. Think of this assignment as your first day on the job; you were hired by the Wellness Center because you are proficient in Microsoft Office. This is your chance to show what you know.

Your assignment is to follow the directions of your instructor with respect to which of the exercises you are to complete within the case description. You should begin by downloading the practice files from our Web site at www.prenhall.com/grauer. Go to the site, click the book icon for Office 2003, and then click the Students Download tab. Scroll until you can select the link to Integrated Case Studies, and then download the file to your desktop. Double click the file icon and follow the onscreen instructions to install the practice files on your computer. The files you need will be in the Totally Fit folder within the Exploring Integrated Cases folder.

1

integrated exercises

4. **Last-minute Change (Word, Excel, and PowerPoint):** It was just discovered that the revenue from a few new memberships was not included in the original workbook. Your task is to correct all of the documents that reflect this information. Open the completed *Totally Fit Revenue Solution* workbook from exercise 1.
   a. Click in cell E3 and change the revenue for the Bronze Plan in the fourth quarter to $2,750. Click in cell E4 and change the value of this cell to $5,700. The row and column totals change automatically in the worksheet as do the associated charts. Save the workbook. Exit Excel.
   b. Open the *Report to the President Solution* document from the second exercise. The worksheet and chart should be updated automatically to reflect the corrected revenue data. (The total revenue is now $95,900.) If either the worksheet or the chart is not updated, right click the object to display a context-sensitive menu and click the Update Link command. If the chart is still not updated, right click the object, click the Linked Worksheet (or Chart) Object command, then click the Links command to display the Links dialog box where you can check the source (folder) of the linked objects.
   c. Click at the beginning of the opening paragraph in the memo and enter the new text, which is shown in bold italic in Figure 4. Save and print the completed report. Exit Word.
   d. Start PowerPoint. Open the *Presentation to the President Solution* that you created earlier. PowerPoint detects that a change has been made in the underlying workbook and prompts you to update. Click the button to update the links.
   e. Change to the Slide Sorter view. Press and hold the Shift key as you select the slides containing the Excel worksheet and chart. Pull down the File menu, click the Print command, and print the selection (these two slides) as audience handouts, two slides per page. (Be sure to check the box to frame the slides.)
   f. Save the presentation. Exit PowerPoint.

FIGURE 4 Last-minute Change

INTEGRATED CASE STUDIES 5

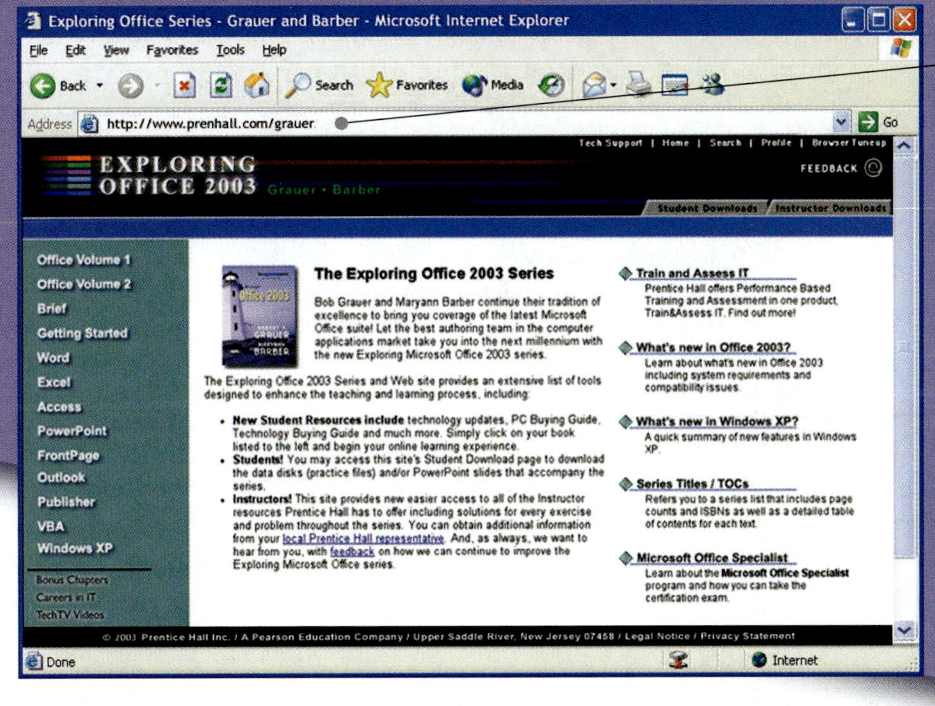

Companion Web site

New!

Updated and enhanced Companion Web site. Find everything you need—student practice files, PowerPoint lectures, online study guides, and instructor support (solutions)!

www.prenhall.com/grauer

Acknowledgments

We want to thank the many individuals who have helped to bring this project to fruition. Jodi McPherson, executive acquisitions editor at Prentice Hall, has provided new leadership in extending the series to Office 2003. Cathi Profitko did an absolutely incredible job on our Web site. Shelly Martin was the creative force behind the chapter-opening case studies. Emily Knight coordinated the marketing and continues to inspire us with suggestions for improving the series. Greg Hubit has been masterful as the external production editor for every book in the series from its inception. Eileen Clark coordinated the myriad details of production and the certification process. Lynne Breitfeller was the project manager and manufacturing buyer. Lori Johnson was the project manager at The GTS Companies and in charge of composition. Chuck Cox did his usual fine work as copyeditor. Melissa Edwards was the supplements editor. Cindy Stevens, Tom McKenzie, and Michael Olmstead wrote the instructor manuals. Michael Fruhbeis developed the innovative and attractive design. We also want to acknowledge our reviewers who, through their comments and constructive criticism, greatly improved the series.

Lynne Band, Middlesex Community College
Don Belle, Central Piedmont Community College
Stuart P. Brian, Holy Family College
Carl M. Briggs, Indiana University School of Business
Kimberly Chambers, Scottsdale Community College
Jill Chapnick, Florida International University
Alok Charturvedi, Purdue University
Jerry Chin, Southwest Missouri State University
Dean Combellick, Scottsdale Community College
Cody Copeland, Johnson County Community College
Larry S. Corman, Fort Lewis College
Janis Cox, Tri-County Technical College
Douglass Cross, Clackamas Community College
Martin Crossland, Southwest Missouri State University
Bill Daley, University of Oregon
Paul E. Daurelle, Western Piedmont Community College
Shawna DePlonty, Sault College of Applied Arts and Technology
Carolyn DiLeo, Westchester Community College
Judy Dolan, Palomar College
David Douglas, University of Arkansas
Carlotta Eaton, Radford University
Judith M. Fitspatrick, Gulf Coast Community College
James Franck, College of St. Scholastica
Raymond Frost, Central Connecticut State University
Susan Fry, Boise State University
Midge Gerber, Southwestern Oklahoma State University
James Gips, Boston College
Vernon Griffin, Austin Community College
Ranette Halverson, Midwestern State University
Michael Hassett, Fort Hays State University
Mike Hearn, Community College of Philadelphia
Wanda D. Heller, Seminole Community College

Bonnie Homan, San Francisco State University
Ernie Ivey, Polk Community College
Walter Johnson, Community College of Philadelphia
Mike Kelly, Community College of Rhode Island
Jane King, Everett Community College
Rose M. Laird, Northern Virginia Community College
David Langley, University of Oregon
John Lesson, University of Central Florida
Maurie Lockley, University of North Carolina at Greensboro
Daniela Marghitu, Auburn University
David B. Meinert, Southwest Missouri State University
Alan Moltz, Naugatuck Valley Technical Community College
Kim Montney, Kellogg Community College
Bill Morse, DeVry Institute of Technology
Kevin Pauli, University of Nebraska
Mary McKenry Percival, University of Miami
Marguerite Nedreberg, Youngstown State University
Jim Pruitt, Central Washington University
Delores Pusins, Hillsborough Community College
Gale E. Rand, College Misericordia
Judith Rice, Santa Fe Community College
David Rinehard, Lansing Community College
Marilyn Salas, Scottsdale Community College
Herach Safarian, College of the Canyons
John Shepherd, Duquesne University
Barbara Sherman, Buffalo State College
Robert Spear, Prince George's Community College
Michael Stewardson, San Jacinto College—North
Helen Stoloff, Hudson Valley Community College
Margaret Thomas, Ohio University
Mike Thomas, Indiana University School of Business
Suzanne Tomlinson, Iowa State University
Karen Tracey, Central Connecticut State University
Antonio Vargas, El Paso Community College
Sally Visci, Lorain County Community College
David Weiner, University of San Francisco
Connie Wells, Georgia State University
Wallace John Whistance-Smith, Ryerson Polytechnic University
Jack Zeller, Kirkwood Community College

A final word of thanks to the unnamed students at the University of Miami who make it all worthwhile. Most of all, thanks to you, our readers, for choosing this book. Please feel free to contact us with any comments and suggestions.

Robert T. Grauer
rgrauer@miami.edu
www.prenhall.com/grauer

Maryann Barber
mbarber@miami.edu

Microsoft® Office

Excel 2003

COMPREHENSIVE

CHAPTER 1

Introduction to Excel: What Is a Spreadsheet?

OBJECTIVES

After reading this chapter you will:

1. Describe several potential spreadsheet applications.
2. Distinguish among a constant, a formula, and a function.
3. Distinguish between a workbook and a worksheet.
4. Explain how the rows and columns in a worksheet are labeled.
5. Download the practice files for use in hands-on exercises.
6. Insert or delete rows and columns in a worksheet.
7. Print a worksheet to show displayed values or cell contents.
8. Distinguish between relative and absolute references.
9. Copy and/or move cell formulas within a worksheet.
10. Format a worksheet; use borders and shading; change fonts and alignment.

hands-on exercises

1. INTRODUCTION TO EXCEL
   Input: Grade Book
   Output: Grade Book Solution
2. MODIFYING A WORKSHEET
   Input: Grade Book Solution (from exercise 1)
   Output: Grade Book Solution (additional modifications)
3. CREATING A WORKBOOK
   Input: None
   Output: Better Grade Book Solution
4. FORMATTING A WORKSHEET
   Input: Better Grade Book Solution (from exercise 3)
   Output: Better Grade Book Solution (additional modifications)

CASE STUDY
THE CLARK SCHOOL

The Clark School has been severely impacted by a statewide cutback in funding for extracurricular activities. The school needs money badly and has settled on a door-to-door sale of food items by its students as the initial fund-raiser. The goal is to raise $5,000 for the purchase of new instruments for the music program. The plan is for students to present a catalog to their parents and other potential customers, who are asked to indicate their choices and provide immediate payment.

Melissa Edwards, the individual in charge of fund-raising, has settled on cookie dough as the featured product. Melissa has contracted with an organization that offers ten flavors of the dough, each in a two-pound tub that sells for $8.00 to $10.00 per tub. The school keeps a specified percentage of the selling price (50% in this instance) as profit. The students take the orders and collect the money. The organization delivers the cookie dough to the school, and the students deliver the cookie dough to their customers.

The principal has asked for a progress report midway through the fund-raiser. He wants to know whether the $5,000 goal has been met, and if not, how far the school is from meeting its goal. ■

Your assignment is to read the chapter, paying special attention to Hands-on Exercises 3 and 4, which describe how to create and format a spreadsheet. You will put yourself in Melissa's place and open the workbook, *Chapter 1 Case Study—The Clark School,* which contains the sales data through day 15 of the fund-raiser. Your task is to complete the worksheet by adding the formulas to compute the profit to date, check the profit against the intended goal, and finally, format the spreadsheet in an attractive fashion for presentation to the principal. Print the completed worksheet to show both displayed values and cell formulas.

INTRODUCTION TO SPREADSHEETS

The spreadsheet is the PC application that is used most frequently by managers and executives. This chapter provides a broad-based introduction to spreadsheets in general and to Microsoft Excel in particular. A spreadsheet (also called a worksheet) is stored within a workbook, which in turn may contain multiple worksheets.

The illustrations in this chapter are set in the context of an accountant's ledger and a professor's grade book, with the latter implemented on the computer. You will learn how students can be inserted into or removed from the worksheet and how changing a student's grade automatically recalculates the dependent values in the worksheet.

The Accountant's Ledger

A ***spreadsheet*** is the computerized equivalent of an accountant's ledger. As with the ledger, it consists of a grid of rows and columns that enables you to organize data in a readily understandable format. Figures 1.1a and 1.1b show the same information displayed in ledger and spreadsheet format, respectively.

"What is the big deal?" you might ask. The big deal is that after you change an entry (or entries), the spreadsheet will, automatically and almost instantly, recompute all of the formulas. Consider, for example, the profit projection spreadsheet shown in Figure 1.1b. As the spreadsheet is presently constructed, the unit price is \$20 and the projected sales are 1,200 units, producing gross sales of \$24,000 (\$20/unit × 1,200 units). The projected expenses are \$19,200, which yields a profit of \$4,800 (\$24,000 – \$19,200). If the unit price is increased to \$22 per unit, the spreadsheet recomputes the formulas, adjusting the values of gross sales and net profit. The modified spreadsheet of Figure 1.1c appears automatically.

With a calculator and bottle of correction fluid or a good eraser, the same changes could also be made to the ledger. But imagine a ledger with hundreds of entries and the time that would be required to make the necessary changes to the ledger by hand. The same spreadsheet will be recomputed automatically by the computer. And the computer will not make mistakes. Herein lie the advantages of a spreadsheet—the ability to make changes, and to have the computer carry out the recalculation faster and more accurately than could be accomplished manually.

Initials Date
Prepared by:
Approved by:

		1	2	3	4	5	6	
1	UNIT PRICE		20					1
2	UNIT SALES		1,200					2
3	GROSS PROFIT		24,000					3
4								4
5	EXPENSES							5
6	PRODUCTION		10,000					6
7	DISTRIBUTION		1,200					7
8	MARKETING		5,000					8
9	OVERHEAD		3,000					9
10	TOTAL EXPENSES		19,200					10
11								11
12	NET PROFIT		4,800					12

(a) The Accountant's Ledger

FIGURE 1.1 The Accountant's Ledger

Unit price is $20

Gross sales calculated automatically

Net profit calculated automatically

	A	B
1	Profit Projection	
2		
3	Unit Price	$20
4	Unit Sales	1,200
5	Gross Sales	$24,000
6		
7	Expenses	
8	Production	$10,000
9	Distribution	$1,200
10	Marketing	$5,000
11	Overhead	$3,000
12	Total Expenses	$19,200
13		
14	Net Profit	$4,800

(b) Original Spreadsheet

Gross sales are recalculated

Unit price increased to $22

Net profit is recalculated

	A	B
1	Profit Projection	
2		
3	Unit Price	$22
4	Unit Sales	1,200
5	Gross Sales	$26,400
6		
7	Expenses	
8	Production	$10,000
9	Distribution	$1,200
10	Marketing	$5,000
11	Overhead	$3,000
12	Total Expenses	$19,200
13		
14	Net Profit	$7,200

(c) Modified Spreadsheet

FIGURE 1.1 The Accountant's Ledger (*continued*)

The Professor's Grade Book

A second example of a spreadsheet, one with which you can easily identify, is that of a professor's grade book. The grades are recorded by hand in a notebook, which is nothing more than a different kind of accountant's ledger. Figure 1.2 contains both manual and spreadsheet versions of a grade book.

Figure 1.2a shows a handwritten grade book as it has been done since the days of the little red schoolhouse. For the sake of simplicity, only five students are shown, each with three grades. The professor has computed class averages for each exam, as well as a semester average for every student. The final counts *twice* as much as either test; for example, Adams's average is equal to (100+90+81+81)/4 = 88. This is the professor's grading scheme, and it is incorporated into the manual grade book and equivalent spreadsheet.

Figure 1.2b shows the grade book as it might appear in a spreadsheet, and is essentially unchanged from Figure 1.2a. Walker's grade on the final exam in Figure 1.2b is 90, giving him a semester average of 85 and producing a class average on the final of 75.2 as well. Now consider Figure 1.2c, in which the grade on Walker's final has been changed to 100, causing Walker's semester average to change from 85 to 90, and the class average on the final to go from 75.2 to 77.2. As with the profit projection, a change to any entry within the grade book automatically recalculates all other dependent formulas as well. Hence, when Walker's final exam was regraded, all dependent formulas (the class average for the final as well as Walker's semester average) were recomputed.

As simple as the idea of a spreadsheet may seem, it provided the first major reason for managers to have a personal computer on their desks. Essentially, anything that can be done with a pencil, a pad of paper, and a calculator can be done faster and far more accurately with a spreadsheet. The spreadsheet, like the personal computer, has become an integral part of every type of business. Indeed, it is hard to imagine that these calculations were ever done by hand. The spreadsheet has become an integral part of corporate culture.

Final counts twice so average is computed as (100+90+81+81)/4

	TEST 1	TEST 2	FINAL	AVERAGE
ADAMS	100	90	81	88
BAKER	90	76	87	85
GLASSMAN	90	78	78	81
MOLDOF	60	60	40	50
WALKER	80	80	90	85
CLASS AVERAGE	84.0	76.8	75.2	
NOTE: FINAL COUNTS DOUBLE				

(a) The Professor's Grade Book

Walker's original grade is 90

	A	B	C	D	E
1	Student	Test 1	Test 2	Final	Average
2					
3	Adams	100	90	81	88.0
4	Baker	90	76	87	85.0
5	Glassman	90	78	78	81.0
6	Moldof	60	60	40	50.0
7	Walker	80	80	90	85.0
8					
9	Class Average	84.0	76.8	75.2	

(b) Original Grades

Grade on Walker's final is changed to 100

Formulas recompute automatically

	A	B	C	D	E
1	Student	Test 1	Test 2	Final	Average
2					
3	Adams	100	90	81	88.0
4	Baker	90	76	87	85.0
5	Glassman	90	78	78	81.0
6	Moldof	60	60	40	50.0
7	Walker	80	80	100	90.0
8					
9	Class Average	84.0	76.8	77.2	

(c) Modified Spreadsheet

FIGURE 1.2 The Professor's Grade Book

Row and Column Headings

A spreadsheet is divided into rows and columns, with each row and column assigned a heading. Rows are given numeric headings ranging from 1 to 65,536 (the maximum number of rows allowed). Columns are assigned alphabetic headings from column A to Z, then continue from AA to AZ and then from BA to BZ and so on, until the last of 256 columns (column IV) is reached.

The intersection of a row and column forms a ***cell***, with the number of cells in a spreadsheet equal to the number of rows times the number of columns. The professor's grade book in Figure 1.2, for example, has 5 columns labeled A through E, 9 rows numbered from 1 to 9, and a total of 45 cells. Each cell has a unique ***cell reference***; for example, the cell at the intersection of column A and row 9 is known as cell A9. *The column heading always precedes the row heading in the cell reference.*

Formulas and Constants

Figure 1.3 is an alternate view of the professor's grade book that shows the cell contents rather than the computed values. Cell E3, for example, does not contain the number 88 (Adams's average for the semester), but rather the formula to compute the average from the exam grades. Indeed, it is the existence of the formula that lets you change the value of any cell containing a grade for Adams (cells B3, C3, or D3), and have the computed average in cell E3 change automatically.

To create a spreadsheet, one goes from cell to cell and enters either a constant or a formula. A ***constant*** is an entry that does not change. It may be a number, such as a student's grade on an exam, or it may be descriptive text (a label), such as a student's name. A ***formula*** is a combination of numeric constants, cell references, arithmetic operators, and/or functions (described below) that displays the result of a calculation. You can ***edit*** (change) the contents of a cell by returning to the cell and reentering the constant or formula.

A formula always begins with an equal sign. Consider, for example, the formula in cell E3, =(B3+C3+2*D3)/4, which computes Adams's semester average. The formula is built in accordance with the professor's rules for computing a student's semester average, which counts the final twice as much as the other tests. Excel uses symbols +, –, *, /, and ^ to indicate addition, subtraction, multiplication, division, and exponentiation, respectively, and follows the normal rules of arithmetic precedence. Any expression in parentheses is evaluated first, then within an expression exponentiation is performed first, followed by multiplication or division in left to right order, then finally addition or subtraction.

The formula in cell E3 takes the grade on the first exam (in cell B3), plus the grade on the second exam (in cell C3), plus two times the grade on the final (in cell D3), and divides the result by four. Thus, should any of the exam grades change, the semester average (a formula whose results depend on the individual exam grades) will also change. This, in essence, is the basic principle behind the spreadsheet and explains why, when one number changes, various other numbers throughout the spreadsheet change as well.

A formula may also include a ***function***, or predefined computational task, such as the AVERAGE function in cells B9, C9, and D9. The function in cell B9, for example, =AVERAGE(B3:B7), is interpreted to mean the average of all cells starting at cell B3 and ending at cell B7 and is equivalent to the formula =(B3+B4+B5+B6+B7)/5. You can appreciate that functions are often easier to use than the corresponding formulas, especially with larger spreadsheets (and classes with many students). Excel contains a wide variety of functions that help you to create very powerful spreadsheets. Financial functions, for example, enable you to calculate the interest payments on a car loan or home mortgage.

Constant (entry that does not change)

Function (predefined computational task)

Formula (mathematical expression)

	A	B	C	D	E
1	Student	Test 1	Test 2	Final	Average
2					
3	Adams	100	90	81	=(B3+C3+2*D3)/4
4	Baker	90	76	87	=(B4+C4+2*D4)/4
5	Glassman	90	78	78	=(B5+C5+2*D5)/4
6	Moldof	60	60	40	=(B6+C6+2*D6)/4
7	Walker	80	80	90	=(B7+C7+2*D7)/4
8					
9	Class Average	=AVERAGE(B3:B7)	=AVERAGE(C3:C7)	=AVERAGE(D3:D7)	

FIGURE 1.3 The Professor's Grade Book (cell formulas)

Figure 1.4 displays the professor's grade book as it is implemented in Microsoft Excel. Microsoft Excel is a Windows application, and thus shares the common user interface with which you are familiar. (It's even easier to learn Excel if you already know another Office application such as Microsoft Word.) You should recognize, therefore, that the desktop in Figure 1.4 has two open windows—an application window for Microsoft Excel and a document window for the workbook.

Each window has its own Minimize, Maximize (or Restore), and Close buttons. Both windows have been maximized and thus the title bars have been merged into a single title bar that appears at the top of the application window. The title bar reflects the application (Microsoft Excel) as well as the name of the workbook (Grade Book) on which you are working. A menu bar appears immediately below the title bar. Two toolbars, which are discussed in depth on page 8, appear below the menu bar. Vertical and horizontal scroll bars appear at the right and bottom of the document window.

The ***Ask a Question box*** appears to the right of the menu bar and provides instant access to the Help facility. The ***task pane*** at the right of the window provides access to several basic tasks in Excel. Different task panes are displayed at different times, depending on what you want to accomplish. The Getting Started task pane is the one you see when Excel is started initially. It lists the last several workbooks that were opened and also provides access to help. The Help task pane is shown in Figure 1.4.

The terminology is important, and we distinguish among spreadsheet, worksheet, and workbook. Excel refers to a spreadsheet as a ***worksheet***. Spreadsheet is a generic term; *workbook* and *worksheet* are unique to Excel. An Excel ***workbook*** contains one or more worksheets. The professor's grades for this class are contained in the CIS120 worksheet within the Grade Book workbook. This workbook also contains additional worksheets (CIS223 and CIS316) as indicated by the worksheet tabs at the bottom of the window. These worksheets contain the professor's grades for other courses that he or she is teaching this semester.

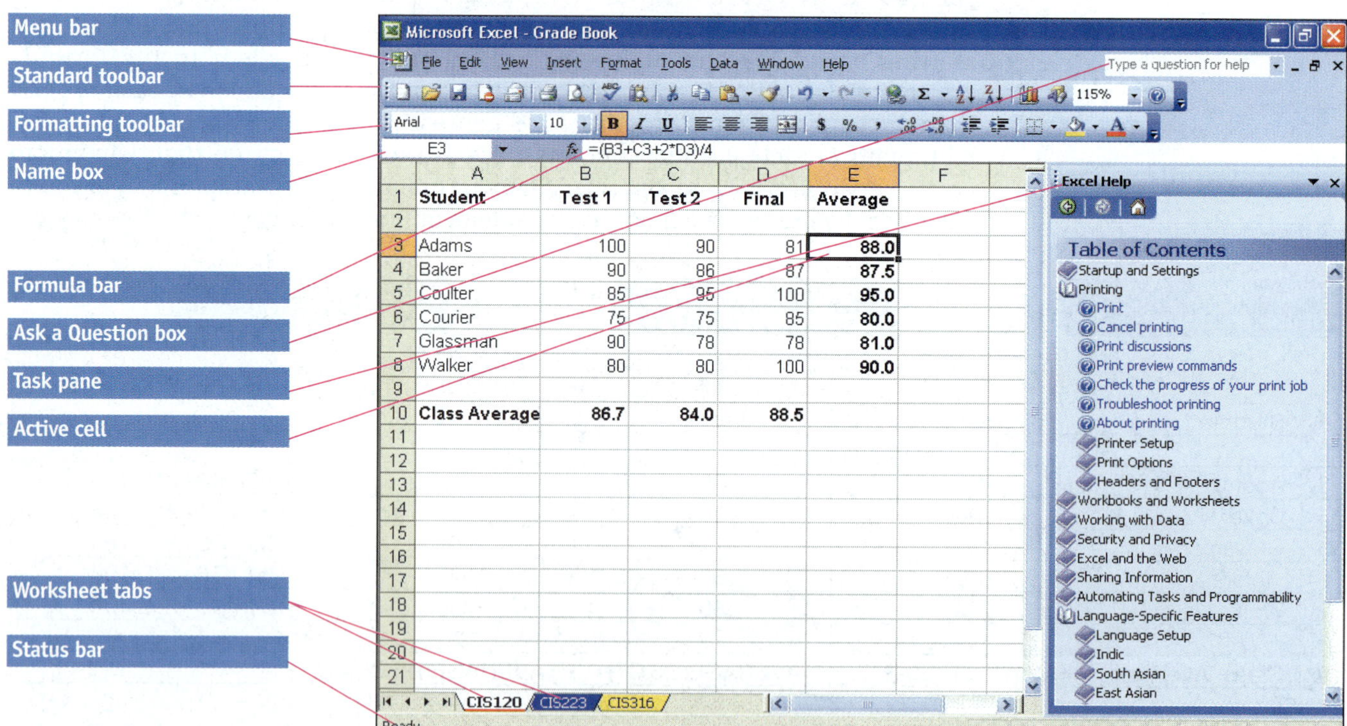

FIGURE 1.4 The Professor's Grade Book

Figure 1.4 resembles the grade book shown earlier, but it includes several other elements that enable you to create and/or edit the worksheet. The heavy border around cell E3 indicates that it (cell E3) is the ***active cell***. (The row and column headings are also highlighted to indicate the active cell.) Any entry made at this time is made into the active cell, and any commands that are executed affect the contents of the active cell. The active cell can be changed by clicking a different cell, or by using the arrow keys to move to a different cell.

The displayed value in cell E3 is 88.0, but as indicated earlier, the cell contains a formula to compute the semester average rather than the number itself. The contents of the active cell, =(B3+C3+2*D3)/4, are displayed in the ***formula bar*** near the top of the worksheet. The cell reference for the active cell, cell E3 in Figure 1.4, appears in the ***Name box*** at the left of the formula bar. The essence of Excel is the automatic recalculation of the formulas in a workbook; i.e., change a value in any cell and the entire workbook is recalculated. Change Adams's grade on the final exam, for example, and the displayed values for his semester average in cell E3, as well as the class average in cell D10, are updated automatically.

The ***status bar*** at the bottom of the worksheet keeps you informed of what is happening as you work within Excel. It displays information about a selected command or an operation in progress.

THE EXCEL WORKBOOK

An Excel workbook is the electronic equivalent of the three-ring binder. A workbook contains one or more worksheets (or chart sheets), each of which is identified by a tab at the bottom of the workbook. The worksheets in a workbook are normally related to one another; for example, each worksheet may contain the sales for a specific division within a company. The advantage of a workbook is that all of its worksheets are stored in a single file, which is accessed as a unit.

Toolbars

Excel provides several different ways to accomplish the same task. Commands may be accessed from a pull-down menu, from a shortcut menu (which is displayed by pointing to an object and clicking the right mouse button), and/or through keyboard equivalents. Commands can also be executed from one of many ***toolbars*** that appear immediately below the menu bar. The Standard and Formatting toolbars are displayed by default. The toolbars appear initially on the same line, but can be separated as described in the hands-on exercise that follows.

The ***Standard toolbar*** contains buttons corresponding to the most basic commands in Excel—for example, opening and closing a workbook, printing a workbook, and so on. The icon on the button is intended to be indicative of its function (e.g., a printer to indicate the Print command). You can also point to the button to display a ***ScreenTip*** showing the name of the button.

The ***Formatting toolbar*** appears under the Standard toolbar and provides access to common formatting operations such as boldface, italics, or underlining. It also enables you to change the alignment of entries within a cell and/or change the font or color. The easiest way to master the toolbars is to view the buttons in groups according to their general function, as shown in Figure 1.5.

The toolbars may appear overwhelming at first, but there is absolutely no need to memorize what the individual buttons do. That will come with time. Indeed, if you use another Office application such as Microsoft Word, you may already recognize many of the buttons on the Standard and Formatting toolbars. Note, too, that many of the commands in the pull-down menus are displayed with an image that corresponds to a button on a toolbar.

Opens a new workbook; opens an existing workbook; saves a workbook; prevents a workbook from being copied or edited; sends a workbook via e-mail

Prints the workbook; previews the workbook prior to printing

Checks the spelling; opens Research in the task pane

Cuts or copies the selecton to the clipboard; pastes the clipboard contents; copies the formatting of the selected cells

Undoes or redoes a previously executed command

Inserts a hyperlink; sums the suggested range; performs an ascending or descending sort

Starts the Chart Wizard; displays the Drawing toolbar

Changes the magnification

Opens Help in the task pane

(a) The Standard Toolbar

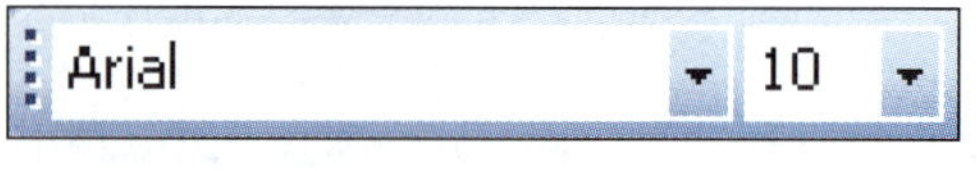

Changes the font or point size

Toggles boldface, italic, and underline on and off

Aligns left, center, right; merges cells and centers

Applies accounting, percentage, or comma formatting; increases or decreases the number of decimals

Decreases or increases the indent

Applies a border; applies a background color; applies a font color

(b) The Formatting Toolbar

FIGURE 1.5 Toolbars

THE FILE MENU

The ***File menu*** is a critically important menu in virtually every Windows application. It contains the Save and Open commands to save a workbook on disk, then subsequently retrieve (open) that workbook at a later time. The File menu also contains the ***Print command*** to print a workbook, the ***Close command*** to close the current workbook but continue working in the application, and the ***Exit command*** to quit the application altogether.

The ***Save command*** copies the workbook that you are working on (i.e., the workbook that is currently in memory) to disk. The command functions differently the first time it is executed for a new workbook, in that it displays the Save As dialog box as shown in Figure 1.6a. The dialog box requires you to specify the name of the workbook, the drive (and an optional folder) in which the workbook is to be stored, and its file type. All subsequent executions of the command save the workbook under the assigned name, replacing the previously saved version with the new version.

The ***file name*** (e.g., My First Spreadsheet) can contain up to 255 characters including spaces, commas, and/or periods. (Periods are discouraged, however, since they are too easily confused with DOS extensions.) The Save In list box is used to select the drive (which is not visible in Figure 1.6a) and the optional folder (e.g., Exploring Excel). The ***Places bar*** provides shortcuts to any of its folders without having to search through the Save In list box. Click the Desktop icon, for example, and the file is saved on the Windows desktop. You can also use the My Documents folder, which is accessible from every application in Microsoft Office.

The ***file type*** defaults to an Excel workbook. You can, however, choose a different format to maintain compatibility with earlier versions of Microsoft Excel. You can also save any Excel workbook as a Web page.

The ***Save As command*** saves a copy of an existing workbook under a different name, and/or a different file type, and is useful when you want to retain a copy of the original workbook. The command results in two copies of the workbook. The original workbook is kept on disk under the original name. A copy of the workbook is saved on disk under the new name and remains in memory. The Save As command also lets you save a workbook in a different file format such as text or CSV (comma-separated values) in order to convert the Excel data to a format required by another application.

The ***Open command*** is the opposite of the Save command as it brings a copy of an existing workbook into memory, enabling you to work with that workbook. The Open command displays the Open dialog box in which you specify the file name, the drive (and optionally the folder) that contains the file, and the file type. Microsoft Excel will then list all files of that type on the designated drive (and folder), enabling you to open the file you want.

The Save and Open commands work in conjunction with one another. The Save As dialog box in Figure 1.6a, for example, saves the file My First Spreadsheet in the Exploring Excel folder. The Open dialog box in Figure 1.6b loads that file into memory so that you can work with the file, after which you can save the revised file for use at a later time.

The toolbars in the Save As and Open dialog boxes have several buttons in common that facilitate the execution of either command. The Views button lets you display the files in many different views. The Details view shows the file size as well as the date and time a file was last modified. The Preview view shows the beginning of a workbook, without having to open the workbook. The List view displays only the file names, and thus lets you see more files at one time. The Properties view shows information about the workbook, including the date of creation and number of revisions. Other buttons provide limited file management without having to go to My Computer or Windows Explorer. You can, for example, delete a file, create a new folder, or start your Web browser from either dialog box.

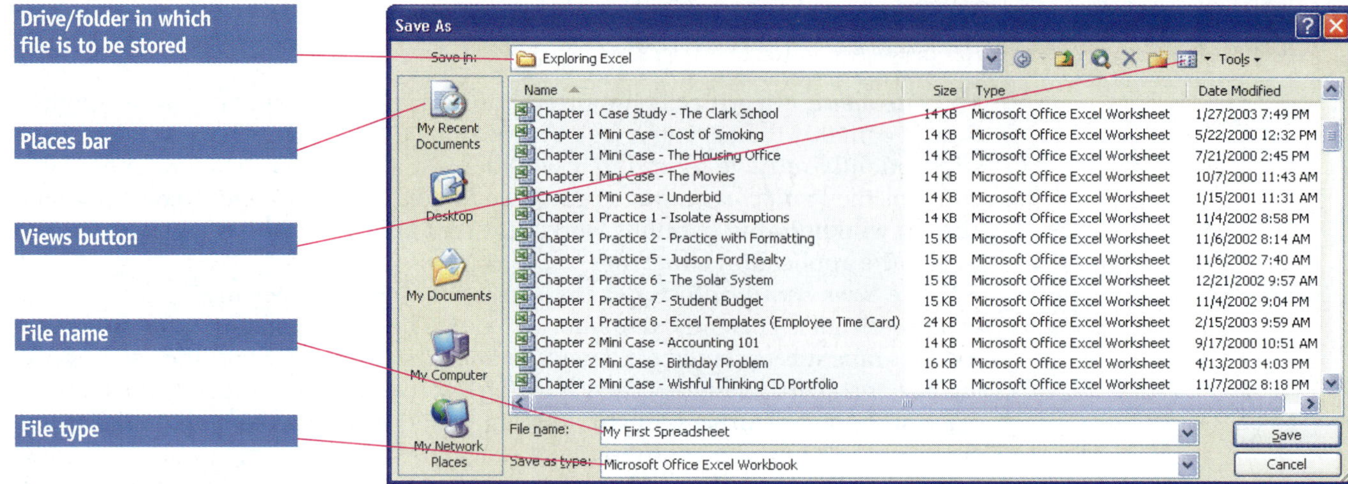

(a) Save As Dialog Box (Details View)

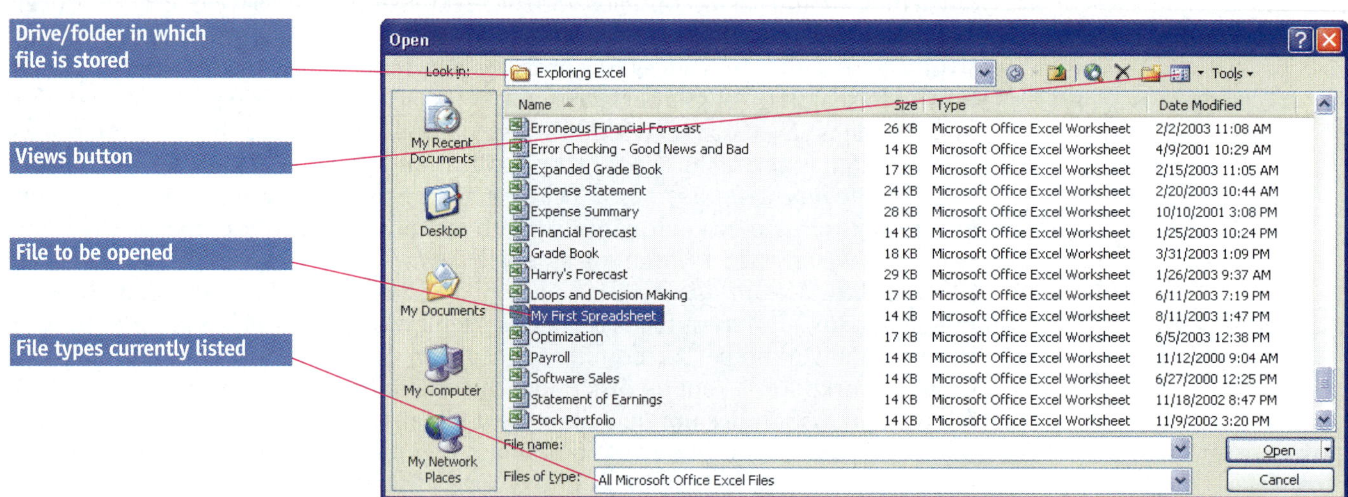

(b) Open Dialog Box (Details View)

FIGURE 1.6 The Save and Open Commands

FILE MANAGEMENT AT YOUR FINGERTIPS

Use the toolbar in the Open and/or Save As dialog box to perform basic file management within any Office application. You can select any existing file or folder, and delete it or rename it. You can also create a new folder, which is very useful when you begin to work with a large number of documents. You can also use the Views button to change the way the files are listed within the dialog box.

hands-on exercise

1 Introduction to Microsoft Excel

Objective To start Microsoft Excel; to open, modify, and print an existing workbook. Use Figure 1.7 as a guide in the exercise.

Step 1: Log On to Windows XP

- Turn on the computer and all of its peripherals. The floppy drive should be empty prior to starting your machine.
- Your system will take a minute or so to get started, after which you should see a logon screen similar to Figure 1.7a. Do not be concerned if the appearance of your desktop is different from ours.
- Click the icon for the user account you want to access. You may be prompted for a password, depending on the security options in effect.
- You should be familiar with basic file management and very comfortable moving and copying files from one folder to another. If not, you may want to review the material in the Windows XP section of this text.

Click icon for your user account

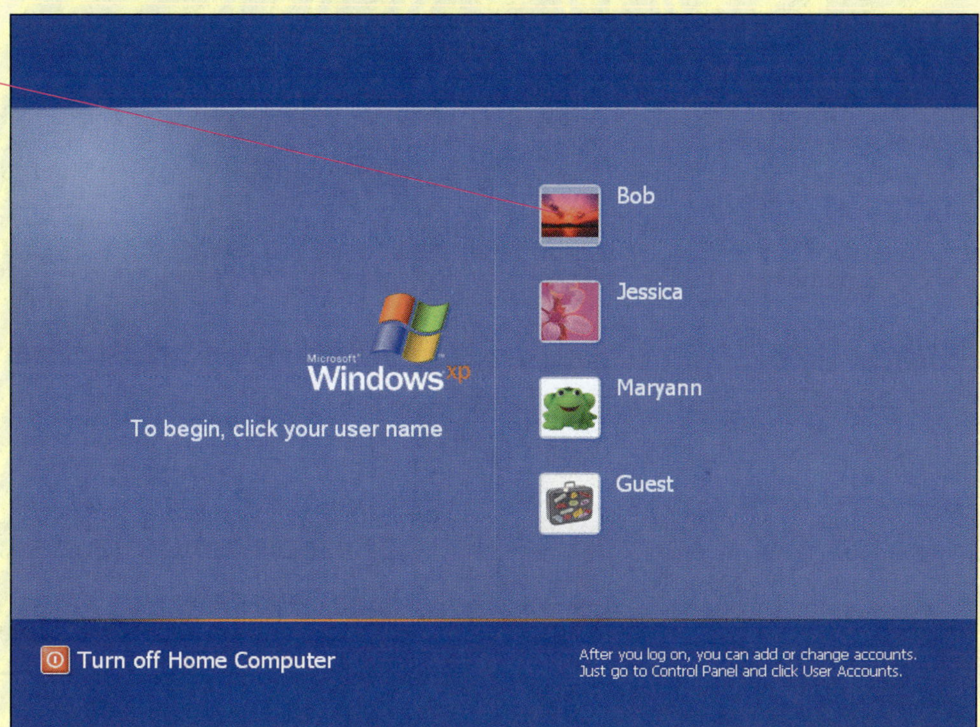

(a) Log On to Windows XP (step 1)

FIGURE 1.7 Hands-on Exercise 1

USER ACCOUNTS

The available user names are created automatically during the installation of Windows XP, but you can add or delete users at any time. Click the Start button, click Control Panel, switch to the Category view, and select User Accounts. Choose the desired task, such as creating a new account or changing an existing account, then supply the necessary information. Do not expect, however, to be able to modify accounts in a school setting.

Step 2: **Download the Practice Files**

- Start Internet Explorer and go to **www.prenhall.com/grauer**. Click the book for **Office 2003**, which takes you to the Office 2003 home page. Click the **Student Downloads tab** to go to the Student Download page as shown in Figure 1.7b.
- Select the appropriate file to download.
  - Choose **Exploring Excel** (or **Excel Volume I**) if you are using a stand-alone Excel text, as opposed to an Office text with multiple applications.
  - Choose **Office 2003 Volume I** (or **Office 2003 Brief**) with an Office text.
- Click the link to download the file. You will see the File Download box asking what you want to do. Click the **Save button**. The Save As dialog box appears.
- Click the **down arrow** in the Save In list box and select the drive and folder where you want to save the file. Click **Save**.
- Start Windows Explorer to select the drive and folder where you saved the file, then double click the file and follow the onscreen instructions. Check with your instructor for additional information.

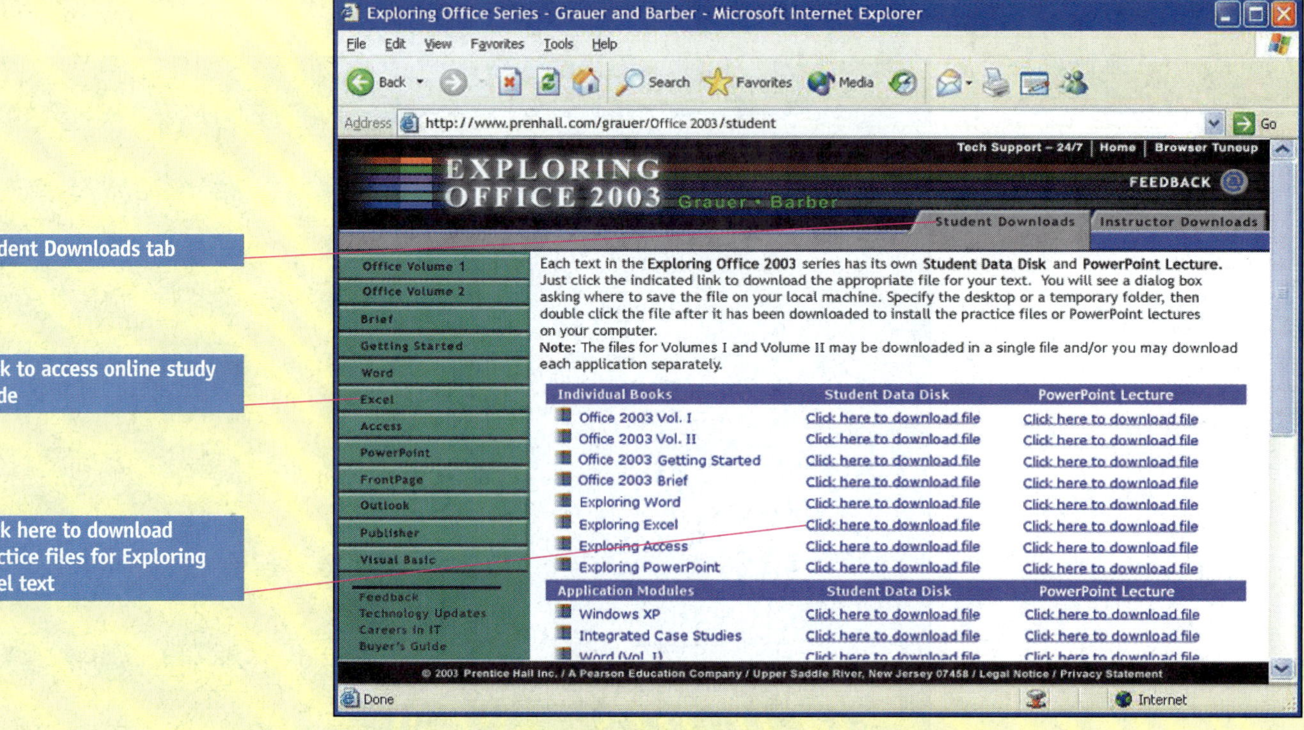

(b) Download the Practice Files (step 2)

FIGURE 1.7 Hands-on Exercise 1 (*continued*)

EXPLORE OUR WEB SITE

The Exploring Office Series Web site offers an online study guide (multiple-choice, true/false, and matching questions) for each individual textbook to help you review the material in each chapter. You can take practice quizzes by yourself and/or e-mail the results to your instructor. These online study guides are available via the tabs in the left navigation bar. You can return to the Student Download page at any time by clicking the tab toward the top of the window and/or you can click the link to Home to return to the home page for the Office 2003 Series. And finally, you can click the Feedback button at the top of the screen to send a message directly to Bob Grauer.

Step 3: Start Excel

- Click the **Start button** to display the Start menu. Click (or point to) the **All Programs button**, click **Microsoft Office**, then click **Microsoft Excel 2003** to start the program.
- Right click the Office Assistant if it appears. Click the **Hide command**.
- If necessary, click the **Maximize button** in the application window so that Excel takes the entire desktop as shown in Figure 1.7c. Click the **Maximize button** in the document window (if necessary) so that the document window is as large as possible.
- Pull down the **View menu** and click the **Task Pane command** to display (hide) the task pane. The command functions as a toggle switch; that is, execute the command and the task pane is open. Execute the command a second time and the task pane is closed.
- The Getting Started task pane appears initially. Click the down arrow in the task pane to see what other panes are available. The Help task pane is shown in Figure 1.7c. Close the task pane by clicking its **Close button**.

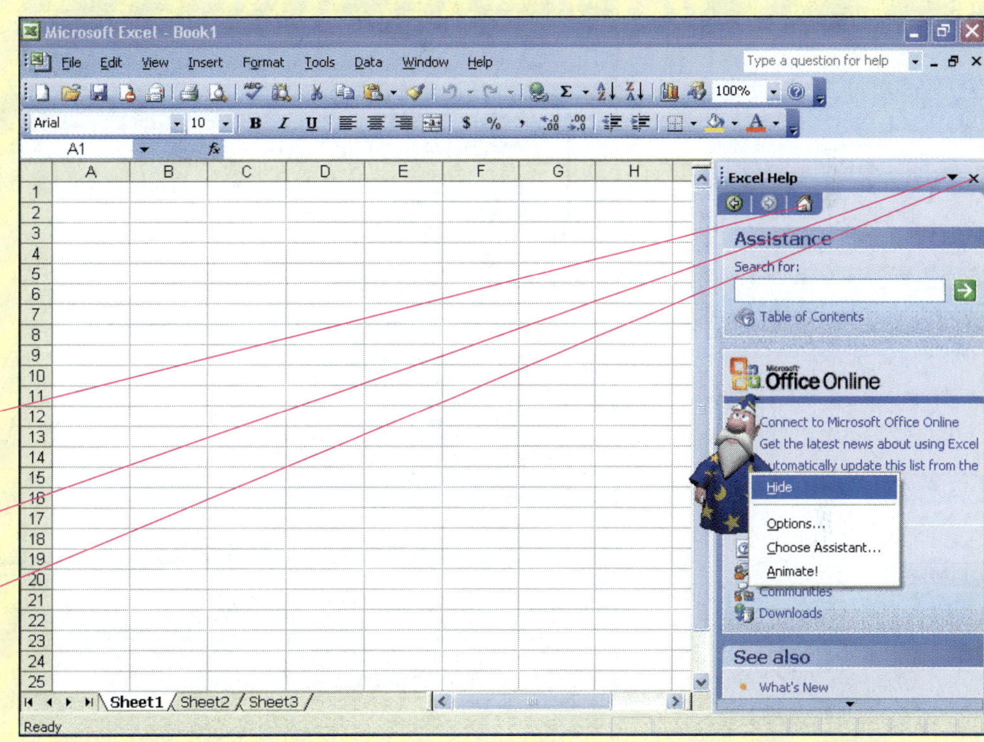

(c) Start Excel (step 3)

FIGURE 1.7 Hands-on Exercise 1 (*continued*)

SEPARATE THE TOOLBARS

You may see the Standard and Formatting toolbars displayed on one row to save space within the application window. If so, we suggest that you separate the toolbars, so that you see all of the buttons on each. Click the down arrow at the end of any visible toolbar to display toolbar options, then click the option to show the buttons on two rows. Click the down arrow a second time to show the buttons on one row if you prefer this configuration.

Step 4: Open the Workbook

- Pull down the **File menu** and click **Open** (or click the **Open button** on the Standard toolbar). You should see a dialog box similar to the one in Figure 1.7d.
- Click the **drop-down arrow** on the Views button, then click **Details** to change to the Details view. Click and drag the vertical border between two columns to increase (or decrease) the size of a column.
- Click the **drop-down arrow** on the Look In list box. Click the appropriate drive, drive C or drive A, depending on the location of your data.
- Double click the **Exploring Excel folder** to make it the active folder (the folder from which you will retrieve and into which you will save the workbook).
- Click the **down scroll arrow** if necessary in order to click **Grade Book** to select the professor's grade book. Click the **Open command button** to open the workbook and begin the exercise.

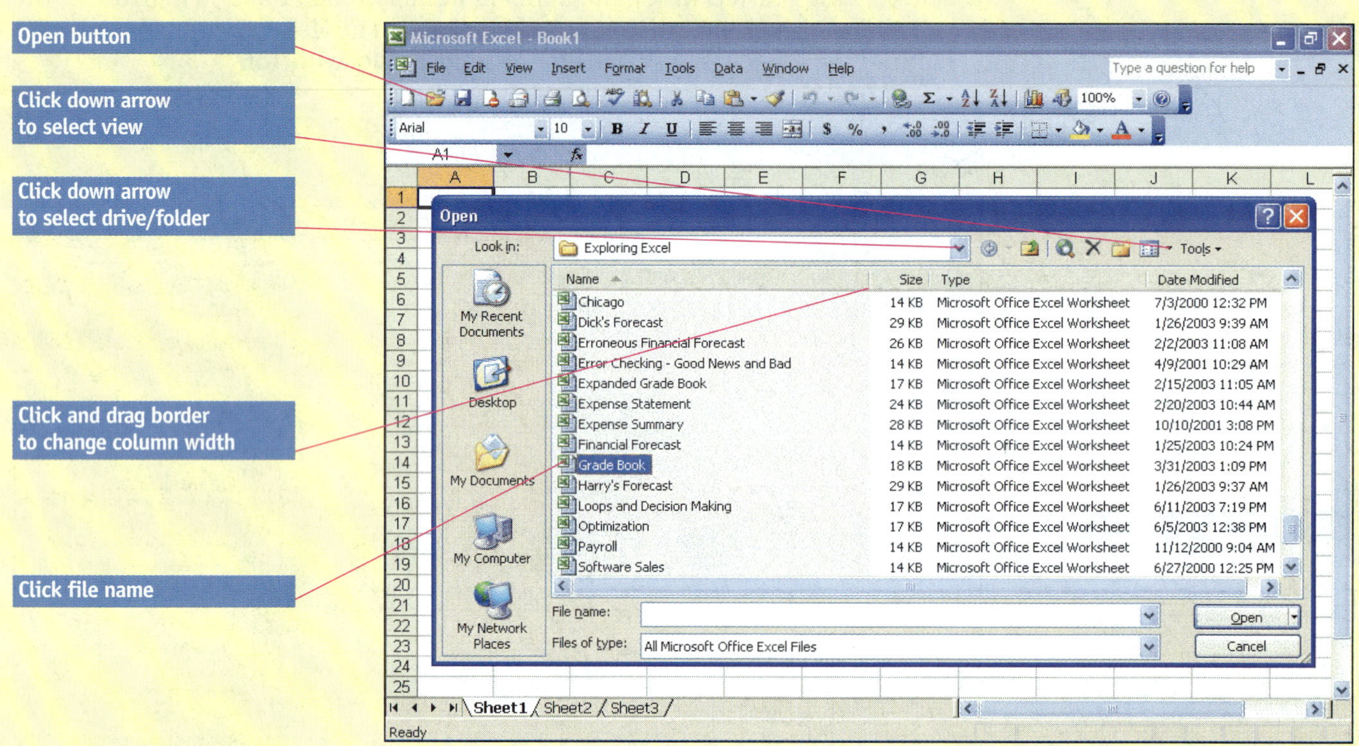

(d) Open the Workbook (step 4)

FIGURE 1.7 Hands-on Exercise 1 (*continued*)

THE MENUS MAY CHANGE

Microsoft Office gives you the option of displaying short menus (ending in a double arrow to show additional commands), as opposed to complete menus with all commands. We prefer the complete menus because that is the way you learn an application, but the settings may be different on your system. Pull down the Tools menu, click the Customize command to display the Customize dialog box, click the Options tab, and check the box to always show full menus.

Step 5: The Save As Command

- Pull down the **File menu**. Click **Save As** to display the dialog box shown in Figure 1.7e.
- Enter **Grade Book Solution** as the name of the new workbook. (A file name may contain up to 255 characters. Spaces and commas are allowed in the file name.)
- Click the **Save button**. Press the **Esc key** or click the **Close button** if you see a Properties dialog box.
- There are now two identical copies of the file on disk: "Grade Book" and "Grade Book Solution," which you just created. The title bar shows the latter name, which is the workbook currently in memory.
- You will work with "Grade Book Solution" but can always return to the original "Grade Book" if necessary.

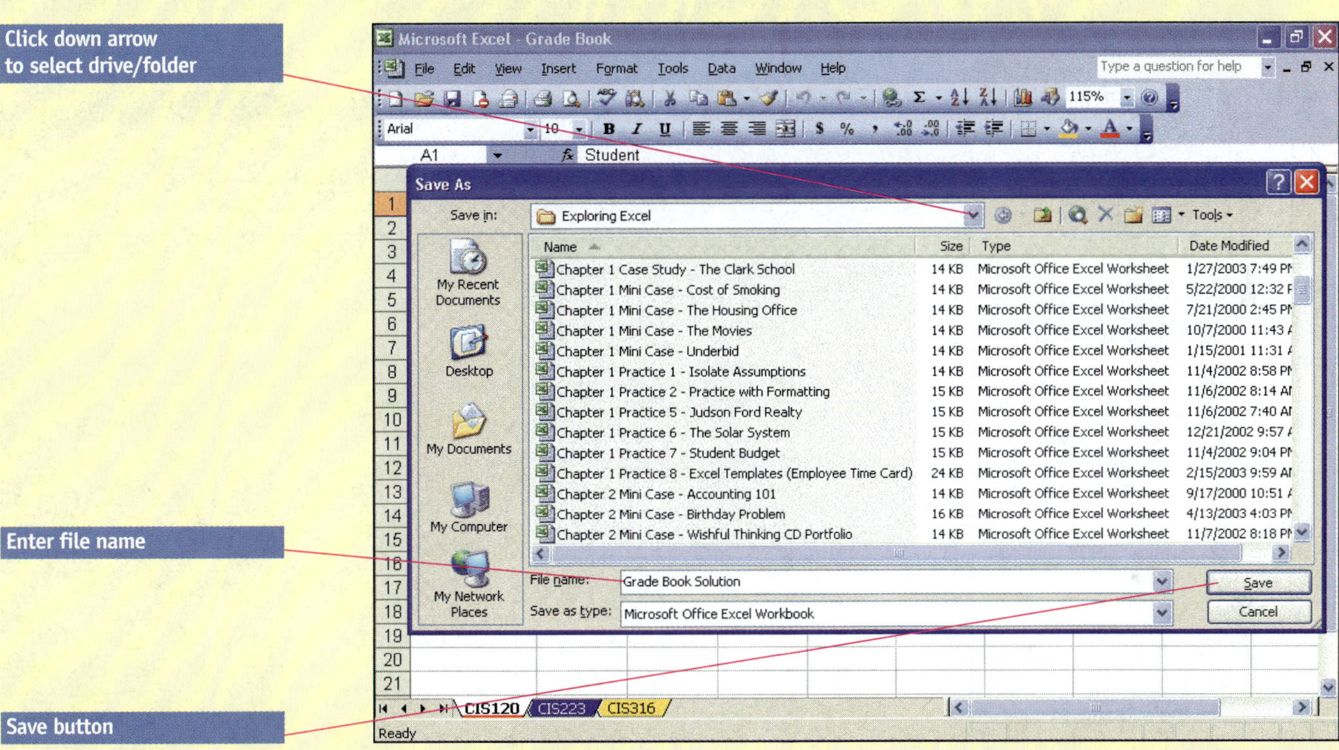

(e) The Save As Command (step 5)

FIGURE 1.7 Hands-on Exercise 1 (*continued*)

QUIT WITHOUT SAVING

There will be times when you do not want to save the changes to a workbook—for example, when you have edited it beyond recognition and wish you had never started. Pull down the File menu and click the Close command, then click No in response to the message asking whether to save the changes. Pull down the File menu, click the file's name at the bottom of the menu to reopen the file, then begin all over.

Step 6: The Active Cell, Formula Bar, and Worksheet Tabs

- You should see the workbook in Figure 1.7f. Click in **cell B3**, the cell containing Adams's grade on the first test. Cell B3 is now the active cell and is surrounded by a heavy border. The Name box indicates that cell B3 is the active cell, and its contents are displayed in the formula bar.
- Click in **cell B4** (or press the **down arrow key**) to make it the active cell. The Name box indicates cell B4 while the formula bar indicates a grade of 90.
- Click in **cell E3**, the cell containing the formula to compute Adams's semester average; the worksheet displays the computed average of 88.0, but the formula bar displays the formula, =(B3+C3+2*D3)/4, to compute that average based on the test grades.
- Click the **CIS223 tab** to view a different worksheet within the same workbook. This worksheet contains the grades for a different class.
- Click the **CIS316 tab** to view this worksheet. Click the **CIS120 tab** to return to this worksheet and continue with the exercise.

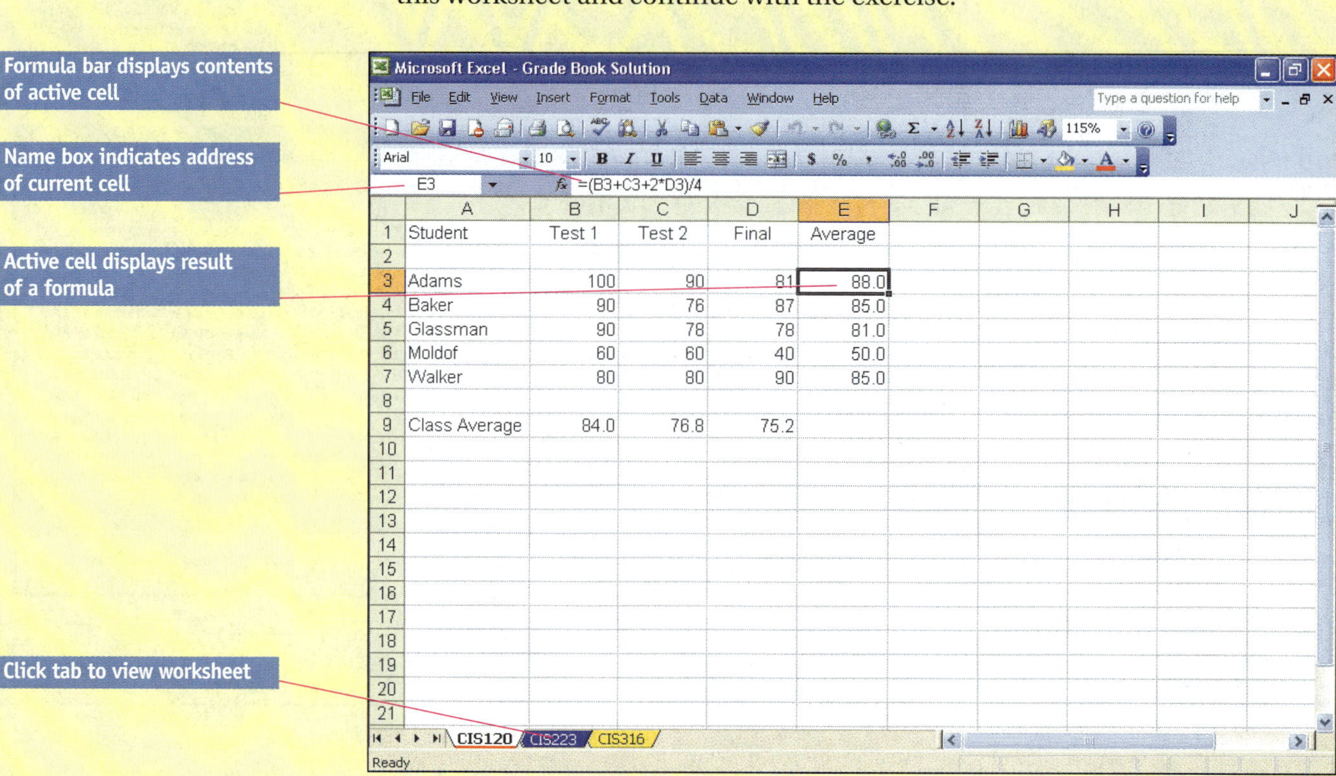

	A	B	C	D	E
1	Student	Test 1	Test 2	Final	Average
2					
3	Adams	100	90	81	88.0
4	Baker	90	76	87	85.0
5	Glassman	90	78	78	81.0
6	Moldof	60	60	40	50.0
7	Walker	80	80	90	85.0
8					
9	Class Average	84.0	76.8	75.2	

(f) The Active Cell, Formula Bar, and Worksheet Tabs (step 6)

FIGURE 1.7 Hands-on Exercise 1 (*continued*)

ADD COLOR TO THE WORKSHEET TABS

Select (click) the worksheet tab for which you want to change the tab color. (If you don't see the worksheet you want, click the tab scrolling buttons to display the tab, and then click the tab.) Pull down the Format menu, click the Sheet command, then click Tab Color to display a color palette. Click the color you want, and then click OK. You can also right click a worksheet tab to display a context-sensitive menu, and change the color from there.

Step 7: Experiment (What If?)

- Click in **cell C4**, the cell containing Baker's grade on the second test. Enter a corrected value of **86** (instead of the previous entry of 76). Press **Enter** (or click in another cell).
- The effects of this change ripple through the worksheet, automatically changing the computed value for Baker's average in cell E4 to 87.5. The class average on the second test in cell C9 changes to 78.8.
- Change Walker's grade on the final from 90 to **100**. Press **Enter** (or click in another cell). Walker's average in cell E7 changes to 90.0, while the class average in cell D9 changes to 77.2.
- Your worksheet should match Figure 1.7g. Save the workbook.

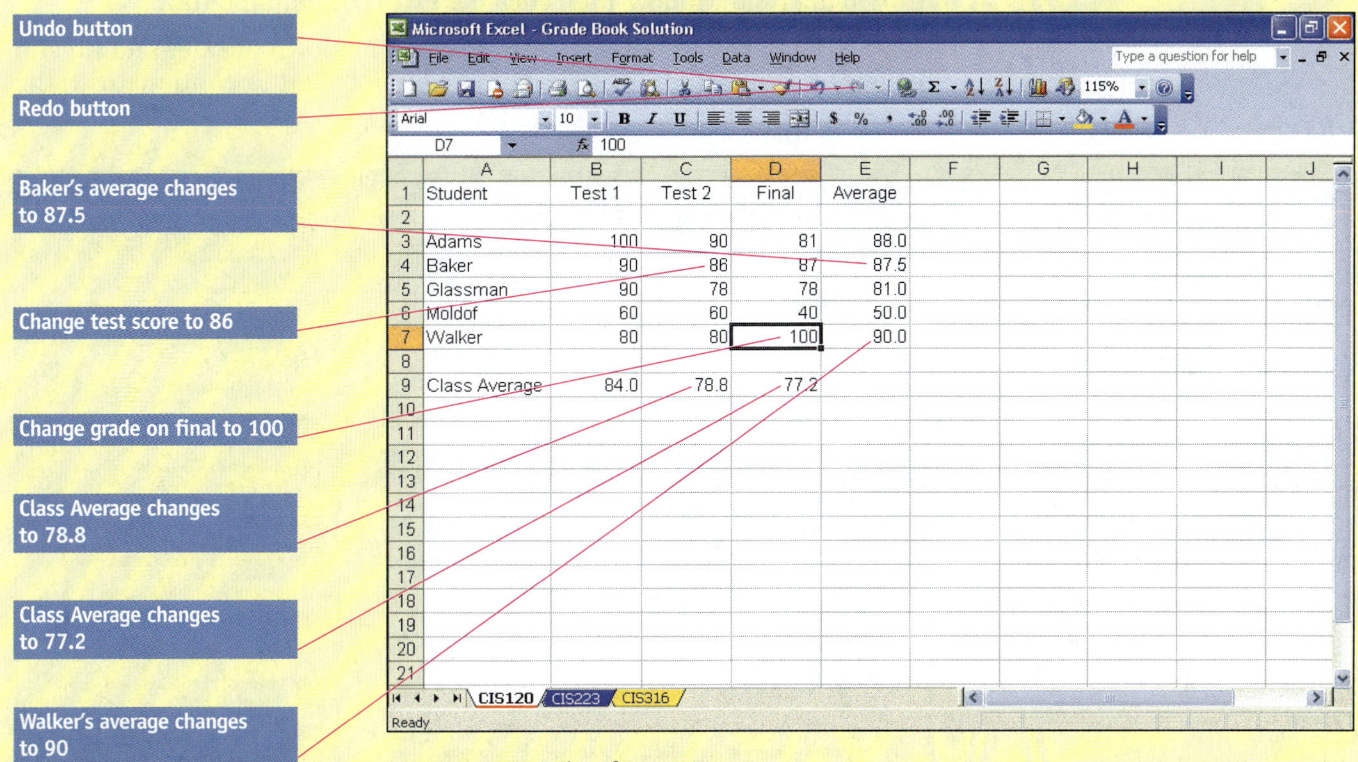

(g) Experiment (What If?) (step 7)

FIGURE 1.7 Hands-on Exercise 1 (*continued*)

THE UNDO AND REDO COMMANDS

The Undo command lets you undo the last several changes to a workbook. Click the down arrow next to the Undo button on the Standard toolbar to display a reverse-order list of your previous commands, then click the command you want to undo, which also cancels all of the preceding commands. Undoing the fifth command in the list, for example, will also undo the preceding four commands. The Redo command redoes (reverses) the last command that was undone. It, too, displays a reverse-order list of commands, so that redoing the fifth command in the list will also redo the preceding four commands.

Step 8: Help with Excel

- There are several different ways to request help, but in any event, the best time to obtain help is when you don't need any. Try either of the following:
  - ❑ Pull down the **Help menu** and click the command to **Show the Office Assistant**. Click the Assistant, then enter the question, "**How do I undo a command?**" in the Assistant's balloon and click **Search**, or
  - ❑ Type the question directly in the **Ask a Question list box** in the upper right of the Excel window and press **Enter**.
- Excel will display a message indicating that it is searching the Office Web site. You should see a task pane with the results as shown in Figure 1.7h.
- Click the link that is most appropriate, for example, **Undo or redo an action**. A new window opens containing the detailed help information. Click the **Print button** in the Help window, then click the **Print command button**.
- Close the Help window. Close the task pane. Pull down the **Help menu** and hide the Office Assistant. Exit Excel if you do not want to continue with the next exercise at this time.

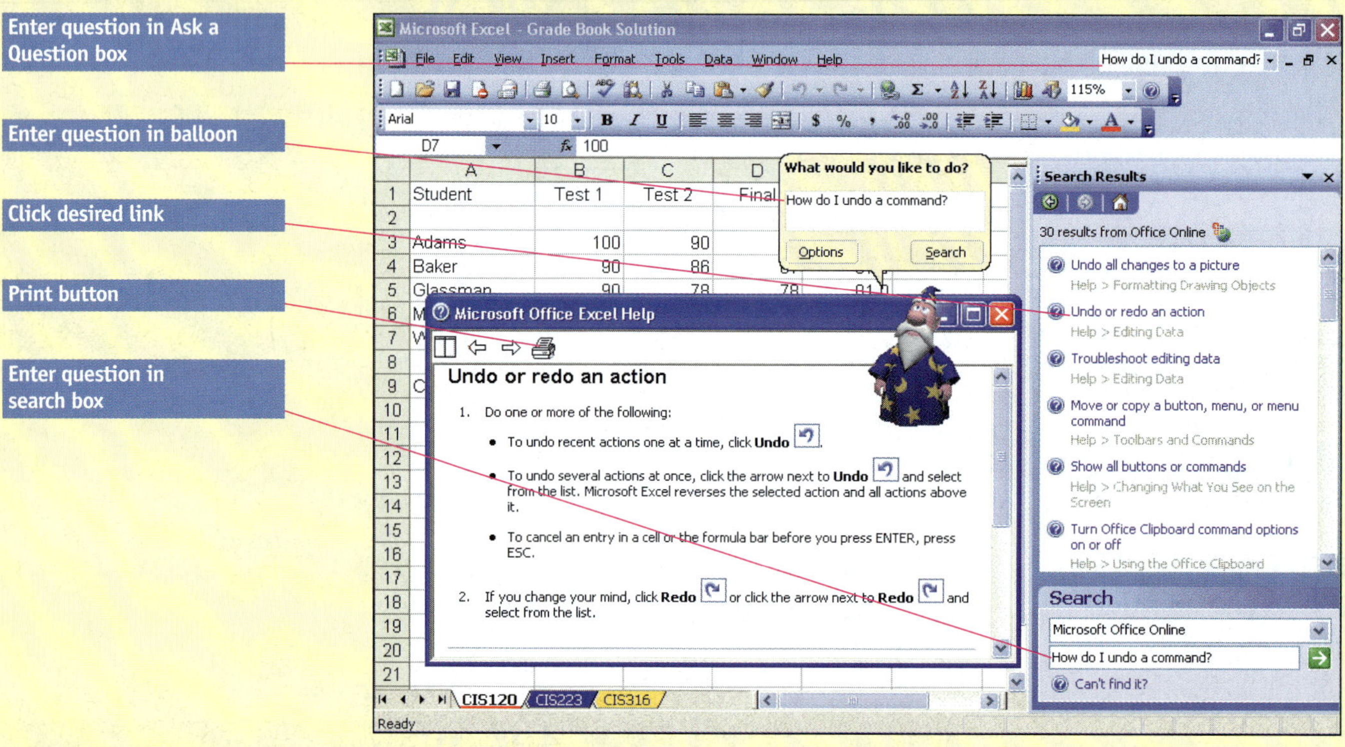

(h) Help with Excel (step 8)

FIGURE 1.7 Hands-on Exercise 1 (*continued*)

ABOUT MICROSOFT EXCEL

Pull down the Help menu and click About Microsoft Excel to display the specific release number as well as other licensing information, including the Product ID. This Help screen also contains two very useful command buttons, System Info and Technical Support. The first button displays information about the hardware installed on your system, including the amount of memory and available space on the hard drive. The Technical Support button provides information on obtaining technical assistance.

MODIFYING A WORKSHEET

We trust that you completed the hands-on exercise without difficulty and that you are more confident in your ability than when you first began. The exercise was not complicated, but it did accomplish several objectives and set the stage for a second exercise, which follows shortly.

Consider now Figure 1.8, which contains a modified version of the professor's grade book. Figure 1.8a shows the grade book at the end of the first hands-on exercise and reflects the changes made to the grades for Baker and Walker. Figure 1.8b shows the worksheet as it will appear at the end of the second exercise. Several changes bear mention:

1. One student has dropped the class and two other students have been added. Moldof appeared in the original worksheet in Figure 1.8a, but has somehow managed to withdraw; Coulter and Courier did not appear in the original grade book but have been added to the worksheet in Figure 1.8b.
2. A new column containing the students' majors has been added.

The implementation of these changes is accomplished through a combination of the ***Insert command*** (to add individual cells, rows, or columns) and/or the ***Delete command*** (to remove individual cells, rows, or columns). Execution of either command automatically adjusts the cell references in existing formulas to reflect the insertion or deletion of the various cells. The Insert and Delete commands can also be used to insert or delete a worksheet. The professor could, for example, add a new sheet to a workbook to include grades for another class and/or delete a worksheet for a class that was no longer taught. We focus initially, however, on the insertion and deletion of rows and columns within a worksheet.

Moldof will be dropped from class

	A	B	C	D	E
1	Student	Test 1	Test 2	Final	Average
2					
3	Adams	100	90	81	88.0
4	Baker	90	86	87	87.5
5	Glassman	90	78	78	81.0
6	Moldof	60	60	40	50.0
7	Walker	80	80	100	90.0
8					
9	Class Average	84.0	78.8	77.2	

(a) After Hands-on Exercise 1

A new column has been added (Major)

Two new students have been added

Moldof has been deleted

	A	B	C	D	E	F
1	Student	Major	Test 1	Test 2	Final	Average
2						
3	Adams	CIS	100	90	81	88.0
4	Baker	MKT	90	86	87	87.5
5	Coulter	ACC	85	95	100	95.0
6	Courier	FIN	75	75	85	80.0
7	Glassman	CIS	90	78	78	81.0
8	Walker	CIS	80	80	100	90.0
9						
10	Class Average		86.7	84.0	88.5	

(b) After Hands-on Exercise 2

FIGURE 1.8 The Modified Grade Book

Figure 1.9 displays the cell formulas in the professor's grade book and corresponds to the worksheets in Figure 1.8. The "before" and "after" worksheets reflect the insertion of a new column containing the students' majors, the addition of two new students, Coulter and Courier, and the deletion of an existing student, Moldof.

Let us consider the formula to compute Adams's semester average, which is contained in cell E3 of the original grade book, but in cell F3 in the modified grade book. The formula in Figure 1.9a referenced cells B3, C3, and D3 (the grades on test 1, test 2, and the final). The corresponding formula in Figure 1.9b reflects the fact that a new column has been inserted, and references cells C3, D3, and E3. The change in the formula is made automatically by Excel, without any action on the part of the user other than to insert the new column. The formulas for all other students have been adjusted in similar fashion.

Some students (all students below Baker) have had a further adjustment to reflect the addition of the new students through insertion of new rows in the worksheet. Glassman, for example, appeared in row 5 of the original worksheet, but appears in row 7 of the revised worksheet. Hence the formula to compute Glassman's semester average now references the grades in row 7, rather than in row 5 as in the original worksheet.

Finally, the formulas to compute the class averages have also been adjusted. These formulas appeared in row 9 of Figure 1.9a and averaged the grades in rows 3 through 7. The revised worksheet has a net increase of one student, which automatically moves these formulas to row 10, where the formulas are adjusted to average the grades in rows 3 through 8.

	A	B	C	D	E
1	Student	Test1	Test2	Final	Average
2					
3	Adams	100	90	81	=(B3+C3+2*D3)/4
4	Baker	90	86	87	=(B4+C4+2*D4)/4
5	Glassman	90	78	78	=(B5+C5+2*D5)/4
6	Moldof	60	60	40	=(B6+C6+2*D6)/4
7	Walker	80	80	100	=(B7+C7+2*D7)/4
8					
9	Class Average	=AVERAGE(B3:B7)	=AVERAGE(C3:C7)	=AVERAGE(D3:D7)	

Function references grades in rows 3–7

Formula references grades in B3, C3, and D3

(a) Before

	A	B	C	D	E	F
1	Student	Major	Test1	Test2	Final	Average
2						
3	Adams	CIS	100	90	81	=(C3+D3+2*E3)/4
4	Baker	MKT	90	86	87	=(C4+D4+2*E4)/4
5	Coulter	ACC	85	95	100	=(C5+D5+2*E5)/4
6	Courier	FIN	75	75	85	=(C6+D6+2*E6)/4
7	Glassman	CIS	90	78	78	=(C7+D7+2*E7)/4
8	Walker	CIS	80	80	100	=(C8+D8+2*E8)/4
9						
10	Class Average		=AVERAGE(C3:C8)	=AVERAGE(D3:D8)	=AVERAGE(E3:E8)	

Function changes to reference grades in rows 3–8 (due to addition of 2 new students and deletion of 1)

Formula changes to reference grades in C3, D3, and E3 due to addition of new column

(b) After

FIGURE 1.9 The Insert and Delete Commands

THE PAGE SETUP COMMAND

The ***Page Setup command*** gives you complete control of the printed worksheet as illustrated in Figure 1.10. Many of the options may not appear important now, but you will appreciate them as you develop larger and more complicated worksheets later in the text.

The Page tab in Figure 1.10 determines the orientation and scaling of the printed page. ***Portrait orientation*** (8½ × 11) prints vertically down the page. ***Landscape orientation*** (11 × 8½) prints horizontally across the page and is used when the worksheet is too wide to fit on a portrait page. The option buttons indicate mutually exclusive items, one of which *must* be selected; that is, a worksheet must be printed in either portrait or landscape orientation. Option buttons are also used to choose the scaling factor. You can reduce (enlarge) the output by a designated scaling factor, or you can force the output to fit on a specified number of pages. The latter option is typically used to force a worksheet to fit on a single page.

The Margins tab not only controls the margins, but will also center the worksheet horizontally and/or vertically. The Margins tab also determines the distance of the header and footer from the edge of the page.

The Header/Footer tab lets you create a header (and/or footer) that appears at the top (and/or bottom) of every page. The pull-down list boxes let you choose from several preformatted entries, or alternatively, you can click the appropriate command button to customize either entry.

The Sheet tab offers several additional options. The Gridlines option prints lines to separate the cells within the worksheet. The Row and Column Headings option displays the column letters and row numbers. Both options should be selected for most worksheets. Information about the additional entries can be obtained by clicking the Help button.

The Print Preview command button is available from all four tabs within the Page Setup dialog box. The command shows you how the worksheet will appear when printed and saves you from having to rely on trial and error.

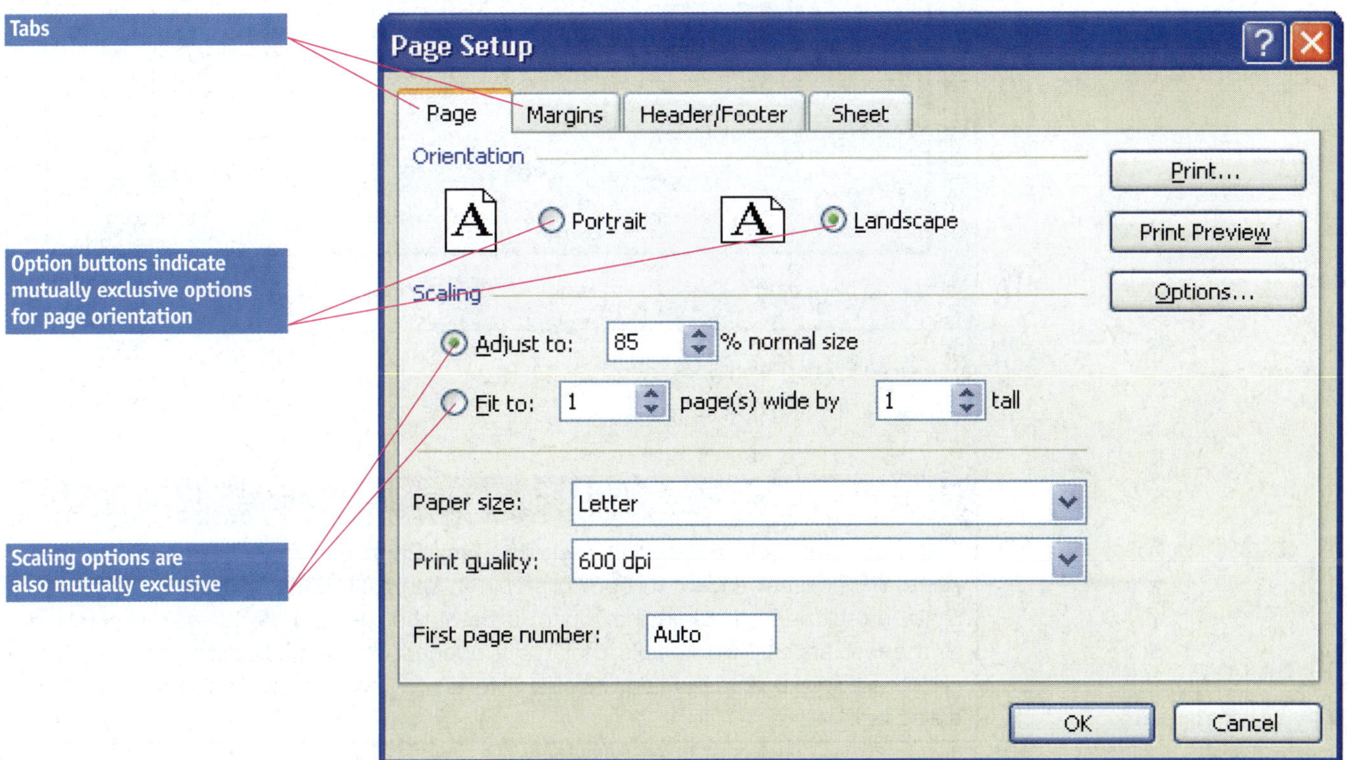

FIGURE 1.10 The Page Setup Command

hands-on exercise

2 Modifying a Worksheet

Objective To open an existing workbook; to insert and delete rows and columns of a worksheet; to print cell formulas and displayed values; to use the Page Setup command. Use Figure 1.11 as a guide.

Step 1: Open an Existing Workbook

- Start Excel. Click the **Open button** on the Standard toolbar. You should see a dialog box similar to the one in Figure 1.11a. Click the **drop-down arrow** on the Views button and click **Details** to change to the Details view.
- Click the **drop-down arrow** on the Look In list box and select drive C or drive A, depending on the location of your data. Double click the **Exploring Excel folder** to make it the active folder.
- Scroll until you can open (double click) the **Grade Book Solution** workbook from the previous exercise.

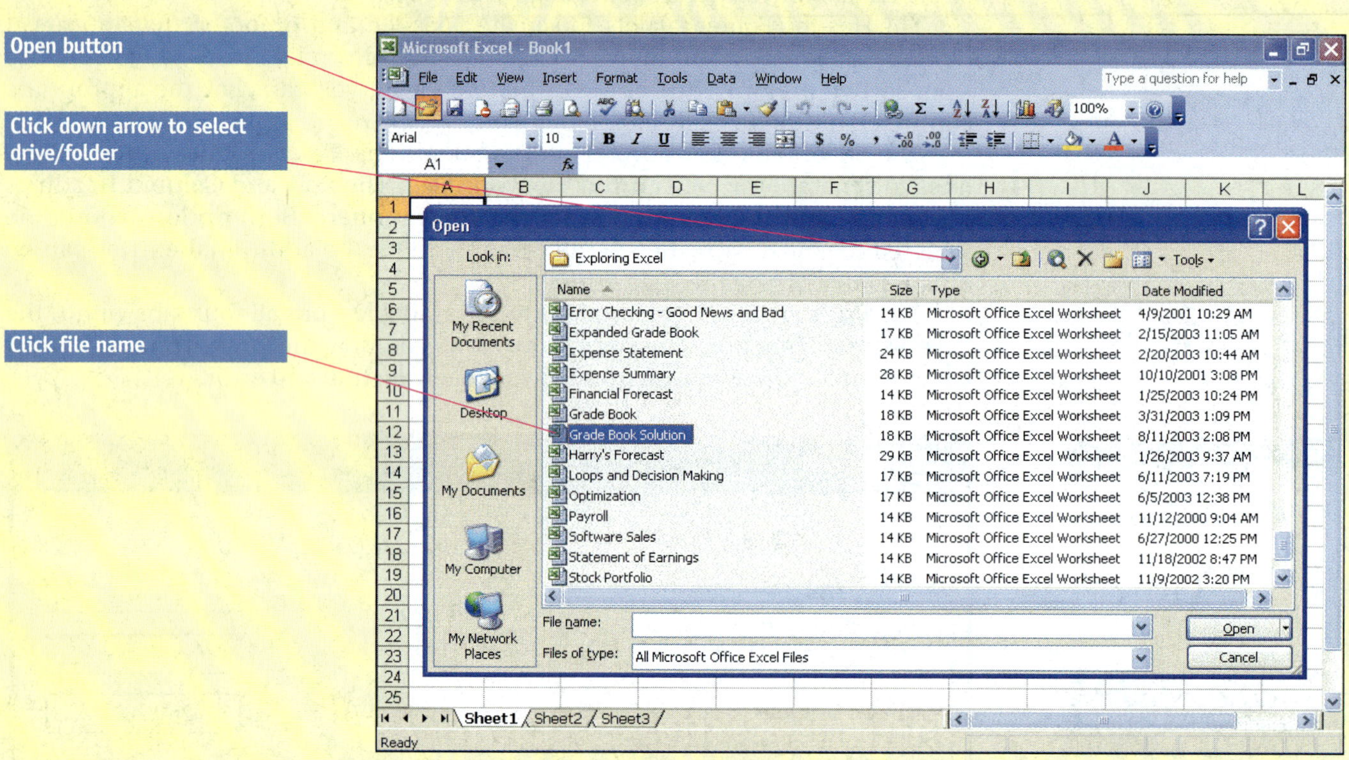

(a) Open an Existing Workbook (step 1)

FIGURE 1.11 Hands-on Exercise 2

THE GETTING STARTED TASK PANE

Pull down the View menu and click the Task Pane command to open the task pane. If necessary, click the down arrow in the task pane to select the Getting Started task pane. Look in the "Open" area of the task pane and you will see links to the last several workbooks that were opened in the application. You can also click the link to the open folder labeled "More . . . ", which will display the File Open dialog box.

Step 2: Delete a Row

- Click any cell in **row 6** (the row you will delete). Pull down the **Edit menu**. Click **Delete** to display the dialog box in Figure 1.11b. Click **Entire row**. Click **OK** to delete row 6.
- Moldof has disappeared from the grade book, and the class averages (now in row 8) have been updated automatically.
- You can restore the row you just deleted if you made a mistake. Pull down the **Edit menu** and click **Undo Delete** (or click the **Undo button** on the Standard toolbar) to reverse the last command.
- The row for Moldof has been put back into the worksheet.
- Click any cell in **row 6**, and this time delete the entire row for good.
- Save the workbook.

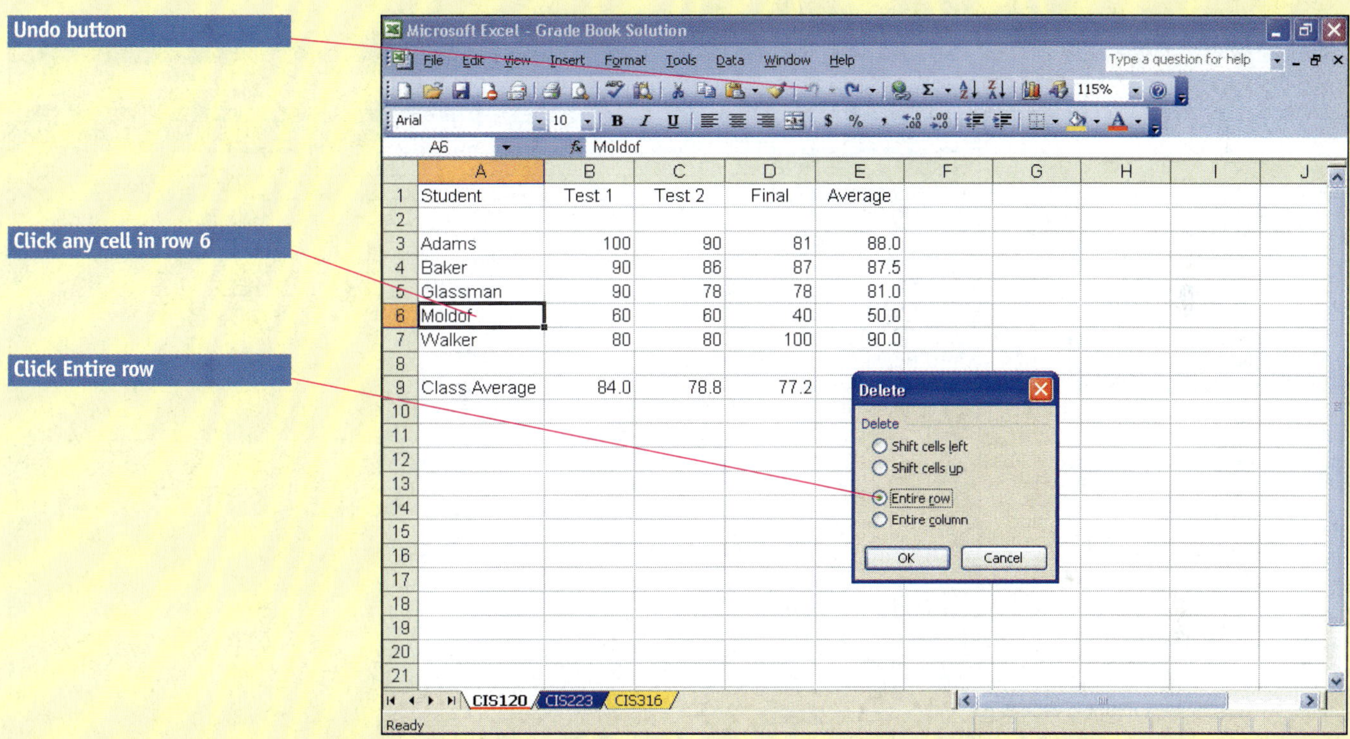

(b) Delete a Row (step 2)

FIGURE 1.11 Hands-on Exercise 2 (*continued*)

INSERT COMMENT COMMAND

You can add a comment, which displays a ScreenTip when you point to the cell, to any cell in a worksheet to explain a formula or other piece of information associated with that cell. Click in the cell that is to hold the comment, pull down the Insert menu, and click Comment to display a box in which you enter the comment. Click outside the box when you have completed the entry. Point to the cell (which should have a tiny red triangle) and you will see the comment you just created.

Step 3: Insert a Row

- Click any cell in **row 5** (the row containing Glassman's grades). Pull down the **Insert menu**. Click **Rows** to add a new row above the current row.
- A new row is inserted into the worksheet with the same formatting as in the row above. (Thus you can ignore the Format Painter button, which allows you to change the formatting.) Row 5 is now blank, and Glassman is now in row 6.
- Enter the data for the new student in row 5 as shown in Figure 1.11c. Click in **cell A5**. Type **Coulter**. Press the **right arrow key** or click in **cell B5**. Enter the test grades of 85, 95, 100 in cells B5, C5, and D5, respectively.
- Enter the formula to compute the semester average, **=(B5+C5+2*D5)/4**. Be sure to begin the formula with an equal sign. Press **Enter**.
- Click the **Save button** on the Standard toolbar, or pull down the **File menu** and click **Save** to save the changes made to this point.

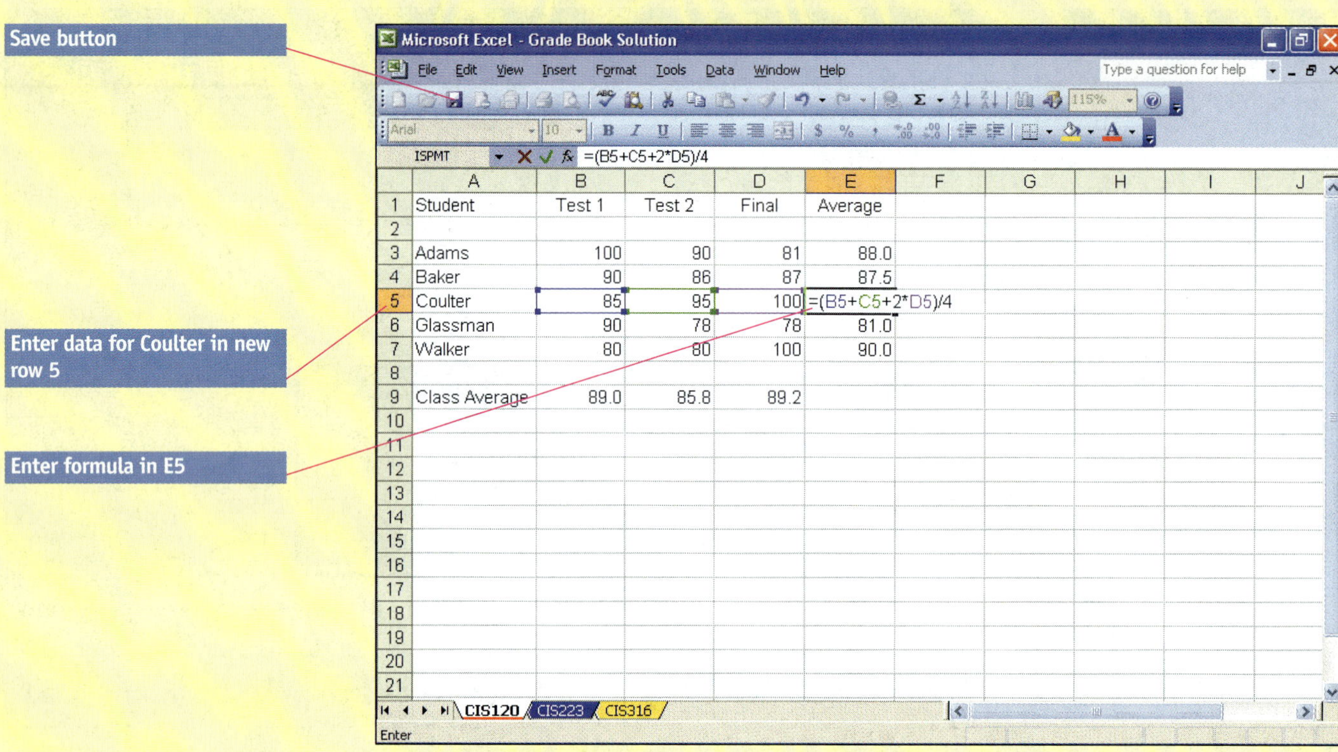

(c) Insert a Row (step 3)

FIGURE 1.11 Hands-on Exercise 2 (*continued*)

CORRECTING MISTAKES

The fastest way to change the contents of an existing cell is to double click in the cell in order to make the changes directly in the cell rather than on the formula bar. Use the mouse or arrow keys to position the insertion point at the point of correction. Press the Ins key to toggle between insert and overtype and/or use the Backspace or Del key to erase a character. Press the Home and End keys to move to the first and last characters in the cell, respectively. (If this feature does not work, pull down the Tools menu, click the Options command, select the Edit tab, and check the box to Edit directly in a cell.)

Step 4: The AutoComplete Feature

- Point to the row heading for **row 6** (which now contains Glassman's grades), then click the **right mouse button** to select the row and display a shortcut menu.
- Click **Insert** to insert a new row 6, which moves Glassman to row 7 as shown in Figure 1.11d.
- Click in **cell A6**. Type **C**, the first letter in "Courier," which also happens to be the first letter in "Coulter," a previous entry in column A. If the AutoComplete feature is on (see boxed tip), Coulter's name will be automatically inserted in cell A6 with "oulter" selected.
- Type **ourier** (the remaining letters in "Courier," which replace "oulter."
- Enter Courier's grades in the appropriate cells (75, 75, and 85 in cells B6, C6, and D6, respectively). Click in **cell E6**. Enter the formula to compute the semester average, **=(B6+C6+2*D6)/4**. Press **Enter**.
- Save the workbook.

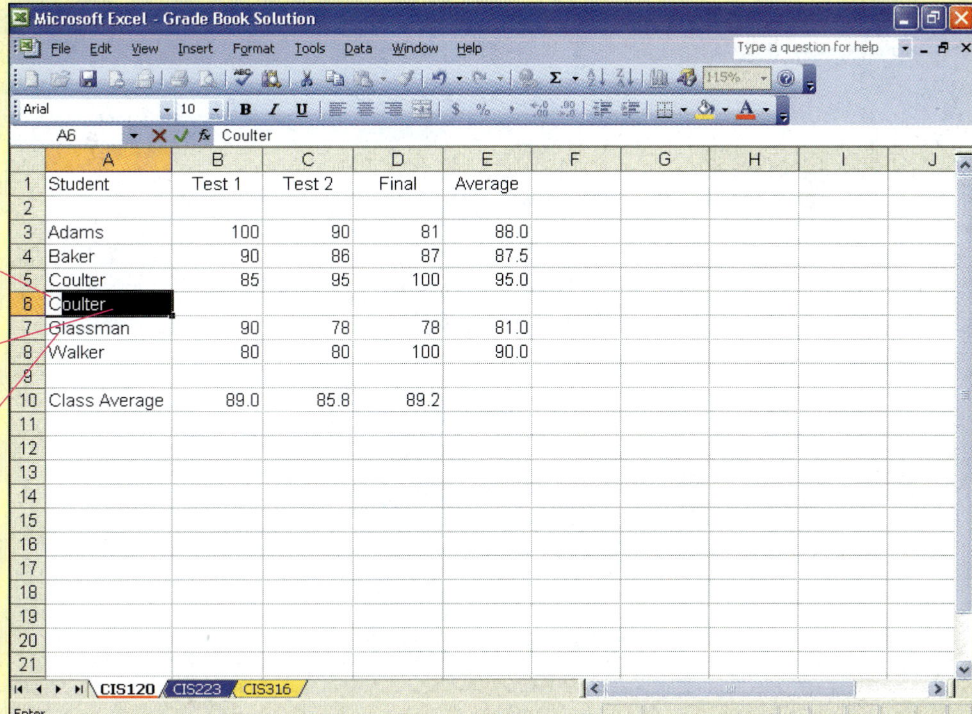

(d) The AutoComplete Feature (step 4)

FIGURE 1.11 Hands-on Exercise 2 (*continued*)

AUTOCOMPLETE

As soon as you begin typing a label into a cell, Excel searches for and (automatically) displays any other label in that column that matches the letters you typed. It's handy if you want to repeat a label, but it can be distracting if you want to enter a different label that just happens to begin with the same letter. To turn the feature on (off), pull down the Tools menu, click Options, then click the Edit tab. Check (clear) the box to enable (disable) the AutoComplete feature.

Step 5: Insert a Column

- Point to the column heading for column B, then click the **right mouse button** to display a shortcut menu as shown in Figure 1.11e.
- Click **Insert** to insert a new column, which becomes the new column B. All existing columns have been moved to the right.
- Click in **cell B1**. Type **Major**.
- Click in **cell B3**. Enter **CIS** as Adams's major. Press the **down arrow** to move automatically to the major for the next student.
- Type **MKT** in cell B4. Press the **down arrow**. Type **ACC** in cell B5. Press the **down arrow**. Type **FIN** in cell B6.
- Press the **down arrow** to move to cell B7. Type **C** (AutoComplete will automatically enter "IS" to complete the entry). Press the **down arrow** to move to cell B8. Type **C** (the AutoComplete feature again enters "IS"), then press **Enter** to complete the entry.

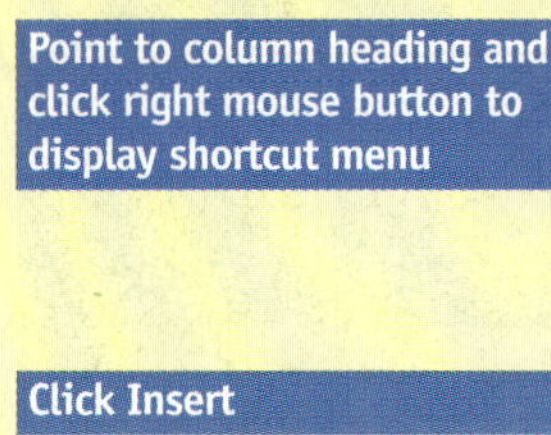

Click Insert

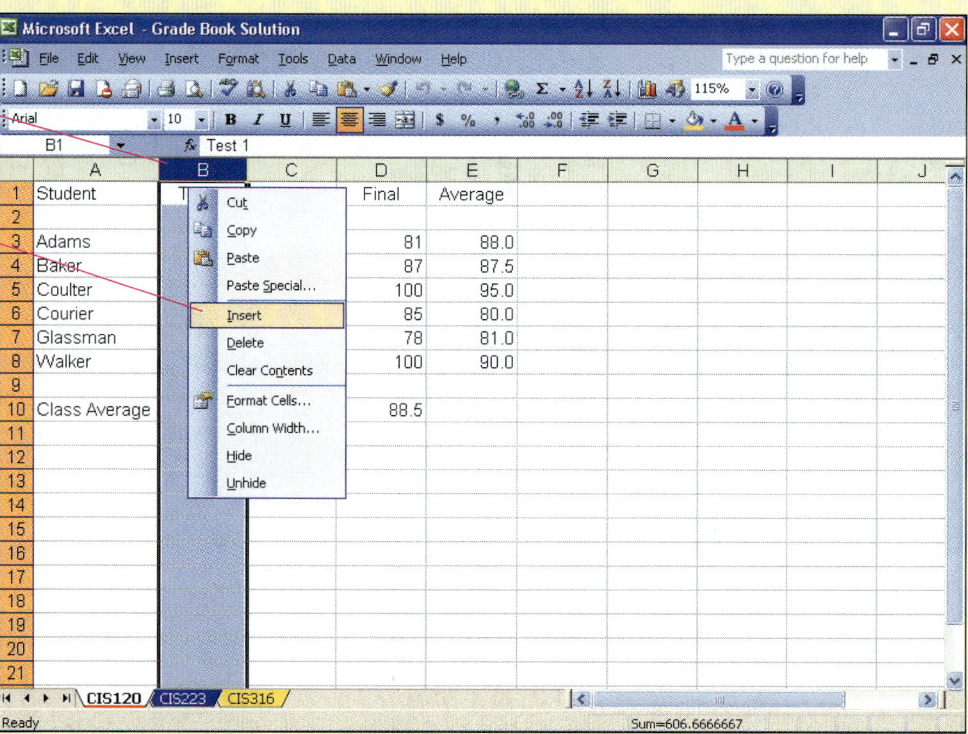

(e) Insert a Column (step 5)

FIGURE 1.11 Hands-on Exercise 2 (*continued*)

INSERTING AND DELETING INDIVIDUAL CELLS

You can insert and/or delete individual cells, as opposed to an entire row or column. To insert a cell, click in the cell where you want the new cell to go, pull down the Insert menu, then click Cells to display the Insert dialog box. Click the appropriate option button to shift cells right or down and click OK. To delete a cell or cells, select the cell(s), pull down the Edit menu, click the Delete command, then click the option button to shift cells left or up.

Step 6: Display the Cell Formulas

- Pull down the **Tools menu**. Click **Options** to display the Options dialog box. Click the **View tab**. Check the box for **Formulas**. Click **OK**. (You can also press **Ctrl+~** to toggle between cell formulas and displayed values.)
- The worksheet should display the cell formulas as shown in Figure 1.11f. The Formula Auditing toolbar is displayed automatically.
- If necessary, click the **right scroll arrow** on the horizontal scroll bar until column F, the column containing the formulas to compute the semester averages, comes into view.
- If necessary (i.e., if the formulas are not completely visible), double click the border between the column headings for columns F and G. This increases the width of column F to accommodate the widest entry in that column.

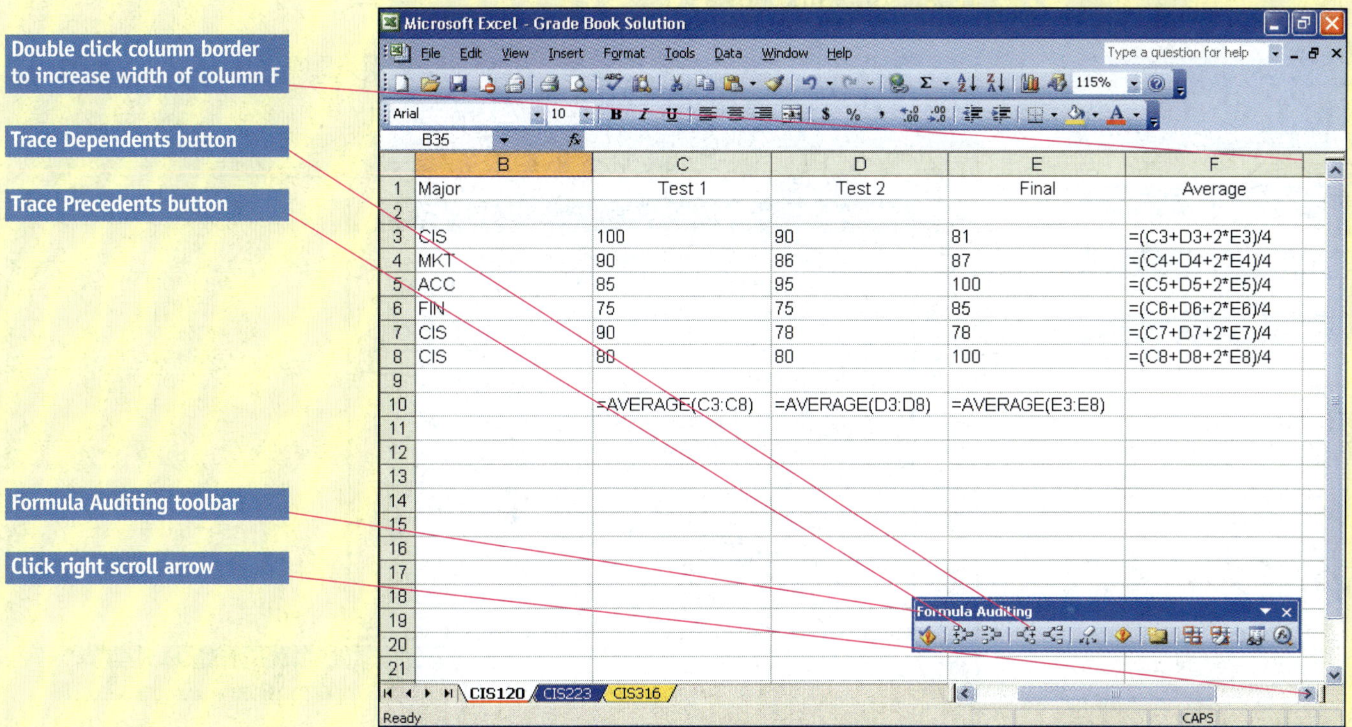

(f) Display the Cell Formulas (step 6)

FIGURE 1.11 Hands-on Exercise 2 (*continued*)

THE FORMULA AUDITING TOOLBAR

The Formula Auditing Toolbar appears automatically any time the display is changed to show cell formulas rather than displayed values. The toolbar is designed to help you detect and correct errors in cell formulas. Click in any cell containing a formula, then click the Trace Precedents button to show the cells that are used in calculating the formula in the selected cell. You can also click in any cell displaying a value and use the Trace Dependents button to show those cells whose formula references the selected cell. Click the Remove All Arrows button to erase the arrows from the display.

Step 7: The Page Setup Command

- Pull down the **File menu**. Click the **Page Setup command** to display the Page Setup dialog box as shown in Figure 1.11g.
- Click the **Page tab**. Click the **Landscape option button**. Click the option button to **Fit to 1 page**.
- Click the **Margins tab**. Check the box to center the worksheet horizontally.
- Click the **Sheet tab**. Check the boxes to print Row and Column Headings and Gridlines.
- Click the **Header/Footer tab**. Click the **drop-down arrow** on the Footer list box and select **CIS120**, which corresponds to the worksheet name.
- Click **OK** to exit the Page Setup dialog box.
- Save the workbook.

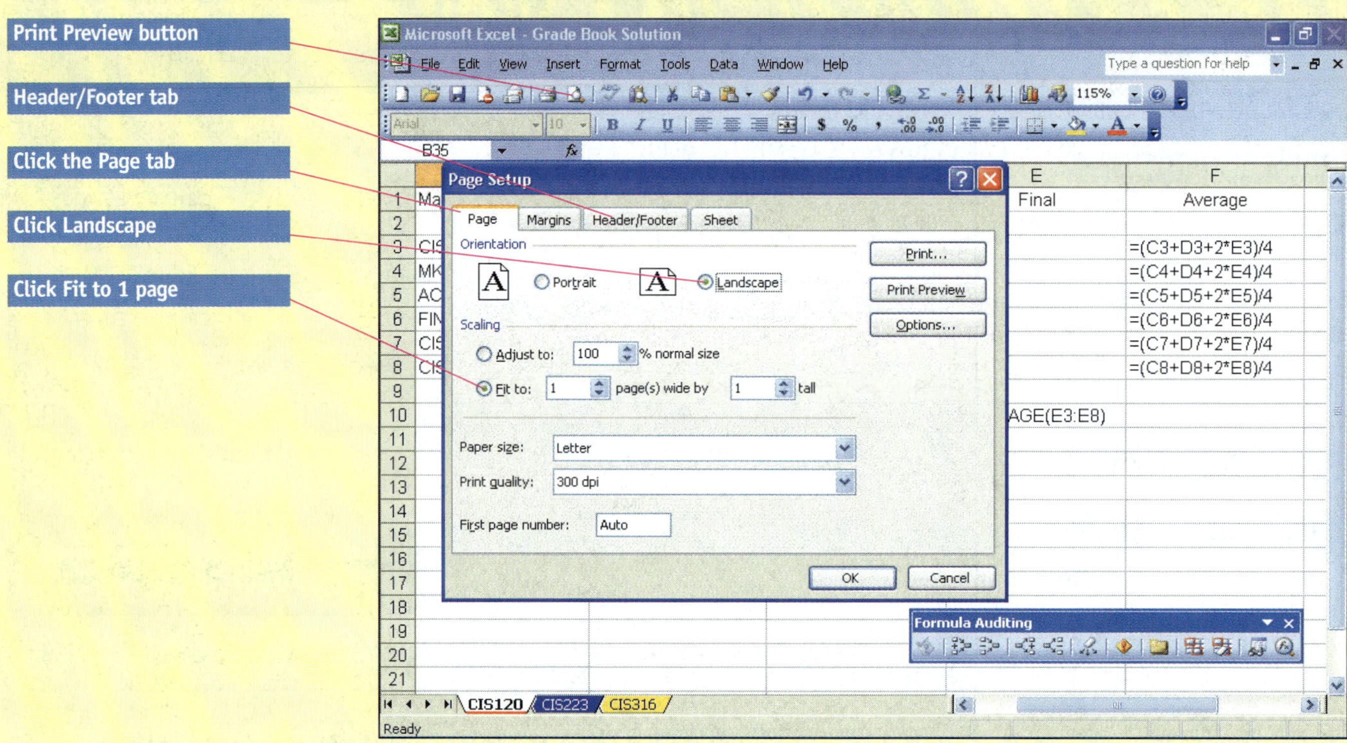

(g) The Page Setup Command (step 7)

FIGURE 1.11 Hands-on Exercise 2 (*continued*)

KEYBOARD SHORTCUTS—THE DIALOG BOX

Press Tab or Shift+Tab to move forward (backward) between fields in a dialog box, or press the Alt key plus the underlined letter to move directly to an option. Use the space bar to toggle check boxes on or off and the up (down) arrow keys to move between options in a list box. Press Enter to activate the highlighted command button and Esc to exit the dialog box without accepting the changes. These are universal shortcuts and apply to any Windows application.

Step 8: The Print Preview Command

- Pull down the **File menu** and click **Print Preview** (or click the **Print Preview button** on the Standard toolbar).
- Click the **Margins button** to toggle the margin lines on and off. (You can click and drag any margin line to change the position of the worksheet on the page and/or to change the column widths.)
- Your monitor should match the display in Figure 1.11h. (The Page Setup dialog box is also accessible from this screen.)
- Click the **Print command button** to display the Print dialog box, then click **OK** to print the worksheet.
- Press **Ctrl+~** to switch to displayed values rather than cell formulas. Click the **Print button** on the Standard toolbar to print the worksheet without displaying the Print dialog box.

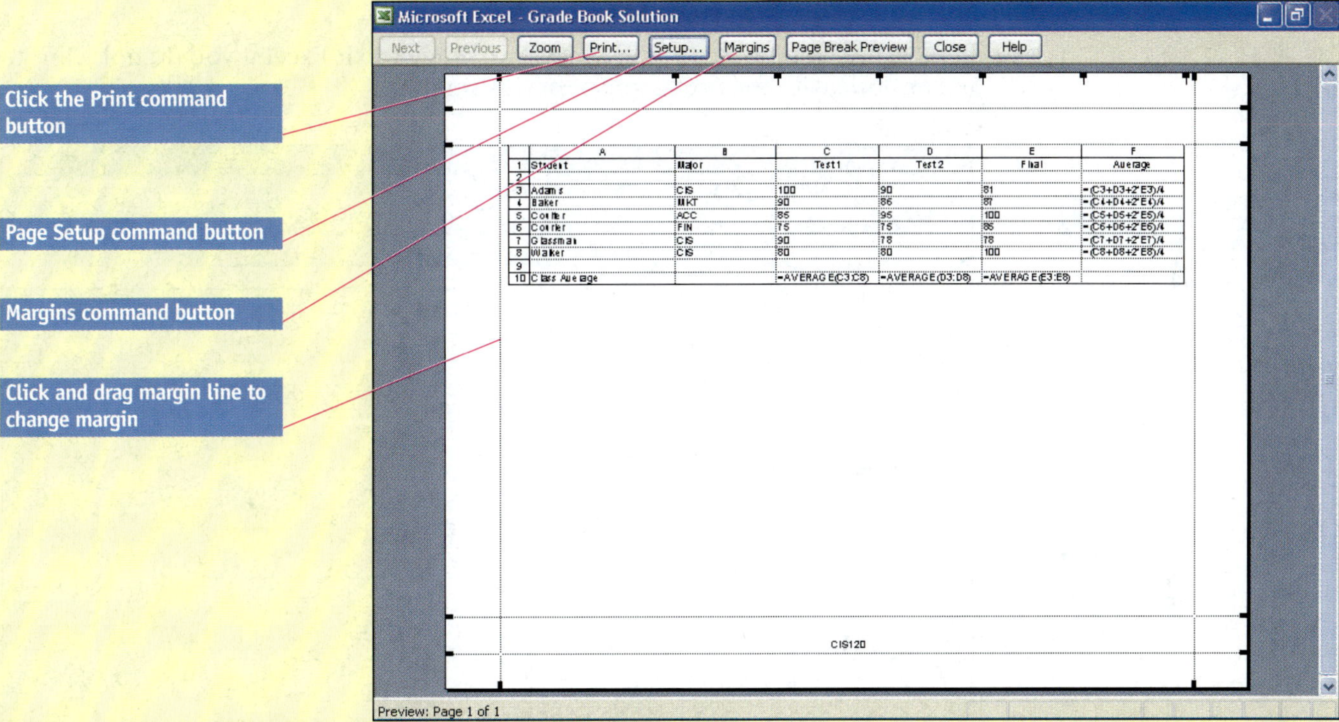

(h) The Print Preview Command (step 8)

FIGURE 1.11 Hands-on Exercise 2 (*continued*)

IDENTIFY YOUR WORKSHEETS

Use the Page Setup command to create a custom header and/or footer to identify your worksheets. Pull down the File menu, click the Page Setup command, and click the Header/Footer tab, then click the Custom Header or Custom Footer button. You can insert your own text in any desired font, as well as the date and time the worksheet was printed. You can also specify the folder, file name, and/or the worksheet name. All of the buttons are clearly marked with instructions within the dialog box.

Step 9: Insert and Delete a Worksheet

- Pull down the **Insert menu** and click the **Worksheet command** to insert a new worksheet. The worksheet is inserted as Sheet1.
- Click in **cell A1**, type **Student**, and press **Enter**. Enter the labels and student data as shown in Figure 1.11i. Enter the formulas to calculate the students' semester averages in column D. (The midterm and final count equally.)
- Enter the formulas in row 7 to compute the class averages on each exam. If necessary, click and drag the column border between the column headings for columns A and B to widen column A.
- Double click the name of the worksheet (Sheet1) to select the name. Type a new name, **CIS101**, to replace the selected text and press **Enter**. If necessary, click and drag the worksheet tab to the beginning of the workbook.
- Click the worksheet tab for **CIS223**. Pull down the **Edit menu** and click the **Delete Sheet command**. Click **Delete** when you are warned that the worksheet will be permanently deleted.
- Save the workbook. Print the new worksheet. Exit Excel if you do not want to continue with the next exercise at this time.

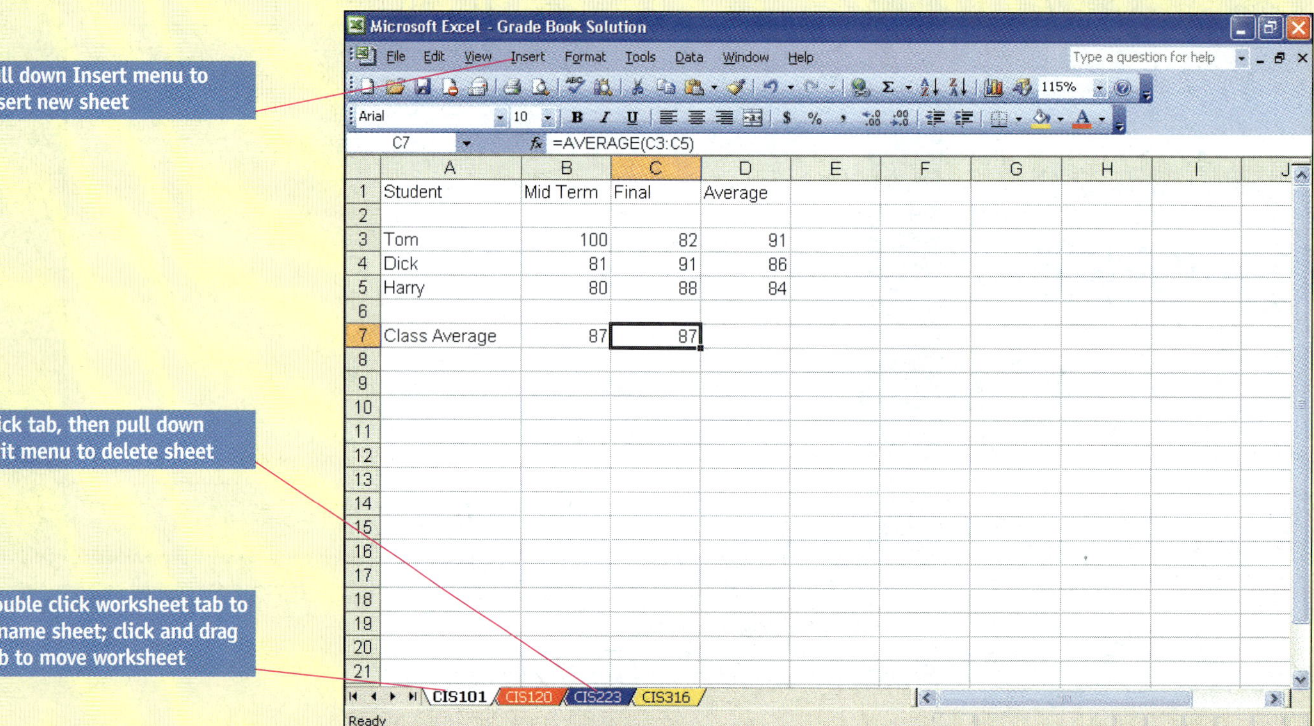

(i) Insert and Delete a Worksheet (step 9)

FIGURE 1.11 Hands-on Exercise 2 (*continued*)

MOVING, COPYING, AND RENAMING WORKSHEETS

The fastest way to move a worksheet is to click and drag the worksheet tab. You can copy a worksheet in similar fashion by pressing and holding the Ctrl key as you drag the worksheet tab. To rename a worksheet, double click its tab to select the current name, type the new name, and press the Enter key.

A BETTER GRADE BOOK

Figure 1.12 contains a much improved version of the professor's grade book. The most *obvious* difference is in the appearance of the worksheet, as a variety of formatting commands have been used to make it more attractive. The exam scores and semester averages are centered under the appropriate headings. The exam weights are formatted with percentages, and all averages are displayed with exactly one decimal point. Boldface and italics are used for emphasis. Shading and borders are used to highlight various areas of the worksheet. The title has been centered over the worksheet and is set in a larger typeface.

The most *significant* differences, however, are that the weight of each exam is indicated within the worksheet, and that the formulas to compute the students' semester averages reference these cells in their calculations. The professor can change the contents of the cells containing the exam weights and see immediately the effect on the student averages.

The isolation of cells whose values are subject to change is one of the most important concepts in the development of a spreadsheet. This technique lets the professor explore alternative grading strategies. He or she may notice, for example, that the class did significantly better on the final than on either of the first two exams. The professor may then decide to give the class a break and increase the weight of the final relative to the other tests. But before the professor says anything to the class, he or she wants to know the effect of increasing the weight of the final to 60%. What if the final should count 70%? The effect of these and other changes can be seen immediately by entering the new exam weights in the appropriate cells at the bottom of the worksheet.

Title is centered in larger font size; it is also in boldface and italics

Formatting includes boldface, shading, and borders

Exam weights are used to calculate the semester average

	A	B	C	D	E
1		***CIS120 - Spring Semester***			
2					
3	**Student**	**Test 1**	**Test 2**	**Final**	**Average**
4	Costa, Frank	70	80	90	82.5
5	Ford, Judd	70	85	80	78.8
6	Grauer, Jessica	90	80	98	91.5
7	Howard, Lauren	80	78	98	88.5
8	Krein, Darren	85	70	95	86.3
9	Moldof, Adam	75	75	80	77.5
10					
11	**Class Averages**	**78.3**	**78.0**	**90.2**	
12					
13	**Exam Weights**	**25%**	**25%**	**50%**	

FIGURE 1.12 A Better Grade Book

ISOLATE ASSUMPTIONS

The formulas in a worksheet should always be based on cell references rather than on specific values—for example, B13 or $B$13 rather than .25. The cells containing these values should be clearly labeled and set apart from the rest of the worksheet. You can then vary the inputs (or assumptions on which the worksheet is based) to see the effect within the worksheet. The chance for error is also minimized because you are changing the contents of a single cell rather than changing the multiple formulas that reference those values.

CELL RANGES

Every command in Excel operates on a rectangular group of cells known as a ***range***. A range may be as small as a single cell or as large as the entire worksheet. It may consist of a row or part of a row, a column or part of a column, or multiple rows and/or columns. The cells within a range are specified by indicating the diagonally opposite corners, typically the upper-left and lower-right corners of the rectangle. Many different ranges could be selected in conjunction with the worksheet of Figure 1.12. The exam weights, for example, are found in the range B13:D13. The students' semester averages are found in the range E4:E9. The student data is contained in the range A4:E9.

The easiest way to select a range is to click and drag—click at the beginning of the range, then press and hold the left mouse button as you drag the mouse to the end of the range where you release the mouse. Once selected, the range is highlighted and its cells will be affected by any subsequent command. The range remains selected until another range is defined or until you click another cell anywhere on the worksheet.

COPY COMMAND

The ***Copy command*** duplicates the contents of a cell, or range of cells, and saves you from having to enter the contents of every cell individually. Figure 1.13 illustrates how the command can be used to duplicate the formula to compute the class average on the different tests. The cell that you are copying from, cell B11, is called the ***source range***. The cells that you are copying to, cells C11 and D11, are the ***destination range***. The formula is not copied exactly, but is adjusted as it is copied, to compute the average for the pertinent test.

The formula to compute the average on the first test was entered in cell B11 as =AVERAGE(B4:B9). The range in the formula references the cell seven rows above the cell containing the formula (i.e., cell B4 is seven rows above cell B11) as well as the cell two rows above the formula (i.e., cell B9). When the formula in cell B11 is copied to C11, it is adjusted so that the cells referenced in the new formula are in the same relative position as those in the original formula; that is, seven and two rows above the formula. The formula in cell C11 becomes =AVERAGE(C4:C9). The formula in cell D11 becomes =AVERAGE(D4:D9).

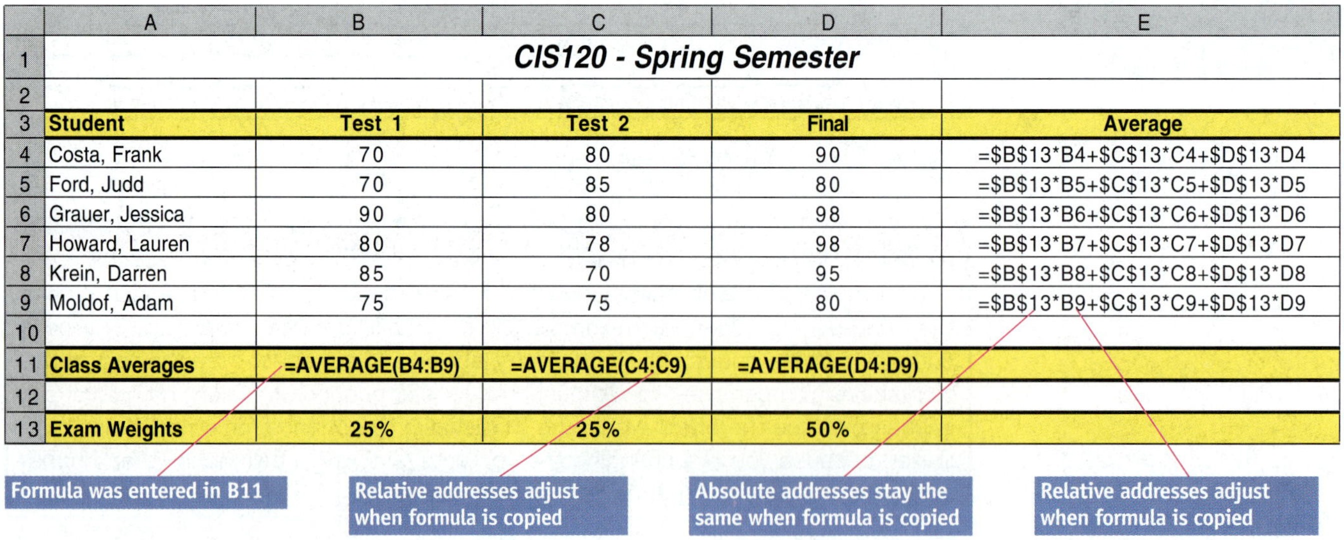

	A	B	C	D	E
1	CIS120 - Spring Semester				
2					
3	Student	Test 1	Test 2	Final	Average
4	Costa, Frank	70	80	90	=$B$13*B4+$C$13*C4+$D$13*D4
5	Ford, Judd	70	85	80	=$B$13*B5+$C$13*C5+$D$13*D5
6	Grauer, Jessica	90	80	98	=$B$13*B6+$C$13*C6+$D$13*D6
7	Howard, Lauren	80	78	98	=$B$13*B7+$C$13*C7+$D$13*D7
8	Krein, Darren	85	70	95	=$B$13*B8+$C$13*C8+$D$13*D8
9	Moldof, Adam	75	75	80	=$B$13*B9+$C$13*C9+$D$13*D9
10					
11	Class Averages	=AVERAGE(B4:B9)	=AVERAGE(C4:C9)	=AVERAGE(D4:D9)	
12					
13	Exam Weights	25%	25%	50%	

Formula was entered in B11

Relative addresses adjust when formula is copied

Absolute addresses stay the same when formula is copied

Relative addresses adjust when formula is copied

FIGURE 1.13 The Copy Command

Figure 1.13 also illustrates how the Copy command is used to copy the formula for a student's semester average, from cell E4 (the source range) to cells E5 through E9 (the destination range). This is slightly more complicated than the previous example because the formula is based on a student's grades, which vary from one student to the next, and on the exam weights, which do not. The cells referring to the student's grades should adjust as the formula is copied, but the addresses referencing the exam weights should not.

The distinction between cell references that remain constant versus cell references that change is made by means of a dollar sign. An ***absolute reference*** remains constant throughout the copy operation and is specified with a dollar sign in front of the column and row designation, for example, $B$13. A ***relative reference***, on the other hand, adjusts during a copy operation and is specified without dollar signs, for example, B4. (A ***mixed reference*** uses a single dollar sign to make the column absolute and the row relative, for example, $A5. Alternatively, you can make the column relative and the row absolute as in A$5.)

Consider, for example, the formula to compute a student's semester average as it appears in cell E4 of Figure 1.13:

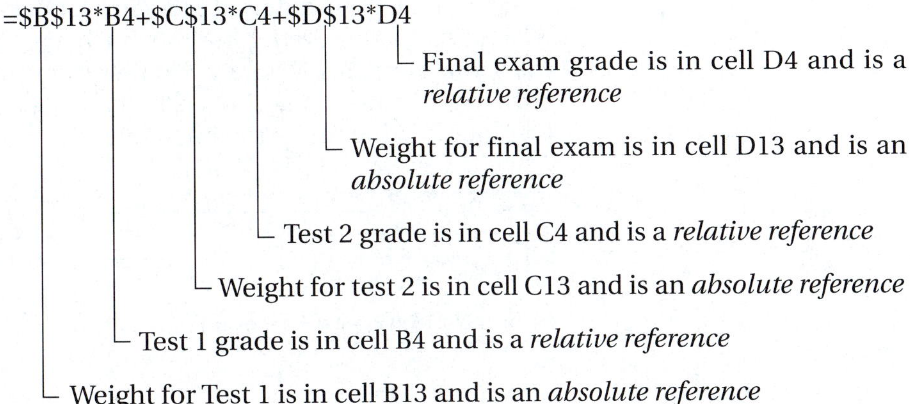

The formula in cell E4 uses a combination of relative and absolute addresses to compute the student's semester average. Relative addresses are used for the exam grades (found in cells B4, C4, and D4) and change automatically when the formula is copied to the other rows. Absolute addresses are used for the exam weights (found in cells B13, C13, and D13) and remain constant.

The copy operation is implemented by using the ***clipboard*** common to all Windows applications and a combination of the Copy and Paste commands from the Edit menu. (Office 2002 also supports the Office Clipboard that can hold 24 separate items. All references to the "clipboard" in this chapter, however, are to the Windows clipboard.) The contents of the source range are copied to the clipboard, from where they are pasted to the destination range. The contents of the clipboard are replaced with each subsequent Copy command but are unaffected by the Paste command. Thus, you can execute the Paste command several times in succession to paste the contents of the clipboard to multiple locations.

MIXED REFERENCES

Most spreadsheets can be developed using only absolute or relative references such as $A1$1 or A1 respectively. Mixed references, where only the row ($A1) or column (A$1) changes, are more subtle, and thus are typically not used by beginners. Mixed references are necessary in more sophisticated worksheets and add significantly to the power of Excel.

MOVE OPERATION

The ***move operation*** is not used in the grade book, but its presentation is essential for the sake of completeness. The move operation transfers the contents of a cell (or range of cells) from one location to another. After the move is completed, the cells where the move originated (that is, the source range) are empty. This is in contrast to the Copy command, where the entries remain in the source range and are duplicated in the destination range.

A simple move operation is depicted in Figure 1.14a, in which the contents of cell A3 are moved to cell C3, with the formula in cell C3 unchanged after the move. In other words, the move operation simply picks up the contents of cell A3 (a formula that adds the values in cells A1 and A2) and puts it down in cell C3. The source range, cell A3, is empty after the move operation has been executed.

Figure 1.14b depicts a situation where the formula itself remains in the same cell, but one of the values it references is moved to a new location; that is, the entry in A1 is moved to C1. The formula in cell A3 is adjusted to follow the moved entry to its new location; that is, the formula is now =C1+A2.

The situation is different in Figure 1.14c as the contents of all three cells—A1, A2, and A3—are moved. After the move has taken place, cells C1 and C2 contain the 5 and the 2, respectively, with the formula in cell C3 adjusted to reflect the movement of the contents of cells A1 and A2. Once again the source range (A1:A3) is empty after the move is completed.

	A	B	C
1	5		
2	2		
3	=A1+A2		

	A	B	C
1	5		
2	2		
3			=A1+A2

Source range is empty after move

(a) Example 1 (only cell A3 is moved)

	A	B	C
1	5		
2	2		
3	=A1+A2		

	A	B	C
1			5
2	2		
3	=C1+A2		

Cell reference is adjusted to follow moved entry

(b) Example 2 (only cell A1 is moved)

	A	B	C
1	5		
2	2		
3	=A1+A2		

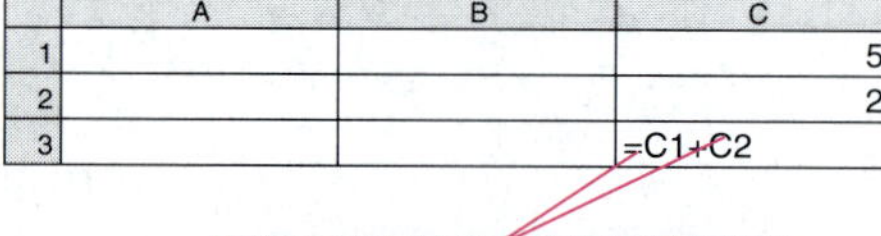

Both cell references adjust to follow moved entries

(c) Example 3 (all three cells in column A are moved)

FIGURE 1.14 The Move Command

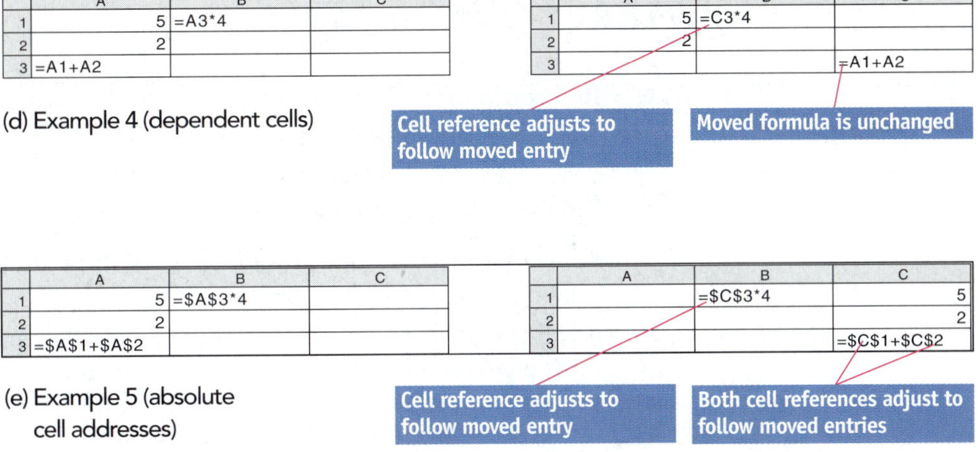

(d) Example 4 (dependent cells)

(e) Example 5 (absolute cell addresses)

FIGURE 1.14 The Move Command (*continued*)

Figure 1.14d contains an additional formula in cell B1, which is *dependent* on cell A3, which in turn is moved to cell C3. The formula in cell C3 is unchanged after the move because *only* the formula was moved, *not* the values it referenced. The formula in cell B1 changes because cell B1 refers to an entry (cell A3) that was moved to a new location (cell C3).

Figure 1.14e shows that the specification of an absolute reference has no meaning in a move operation, because the cell addresses are adjusted as necessary to reflect the cells that have been moved. Moving a formula that contains an absolute reference does not adjust the formula. Moving a value that is specified as an absolute reference, however, adjusts the formula to follow the cell to its new location. Thus all of the absolute references in Figure 1.14e are changed to reflect the entries that were moved.

The move operation is a convenient way to improve the appearance of a worksheet after it has been developed. It is subtle in its operation, and we suggest you think twice before moving cell entries because of the complexities involved.

The move operation is implemented by using the Windows clipboard and a combination of the Cut and Paste commands from the Edit menu. The contents of the source range are transferred to the clipboard, from which they are pasted to the destination range. (Executing a Paste command after a Cut command empties the clipboard. This is different from pasting after a Copy command, which does not affect the contents of the clipboard.)

LEARNING BY DOING

As we have already indicated, there are many different ways to accomplish the same task. You can execute commands using a pull-down menu, a shortcut menu, a toolbar, or the keyboard. In the exercise that follows we emphasize pull-down menus (the most basic technique) but suggest various shortcuts as appropriate.

Realize, however, that while the shortcuts are interesting, it is far more important to focus on the underlying concepts in the exercise, rather than specific key strokes or mouse clicks. The professor's grade book was developed to emphasize the difference between relative and absolute cell references. The grade book also illustrates the importance of isolating assumptions so that alternative strategies (e.g., different exam weights) can be considered.

hands-on exercise

3 Creating a Workbook

Objective To create a new workbook; to copy formulas containing relative and absolute references. Use Figure 1.15 as a guide in doing the exercise.

Step 1: Create a New Workbook

- Start Excel. A blank workbook should appear automatically in the application window. Close the task pane.
- If necessary, separate the Standard and Formatting toolbars. Pull down the **View menu**, click **Toolbars**, click **Customize**, and click the **Options tab**. Check the box that indicates the Standard and Formatting toolbars should be displayed on two rows. Close the dialog box.
- Click in **cell A1**. Enter the title of the worksheet, **CIS120 - Spring Semester**.
- Enter the column headings in row 3 as in Figure 1.15a. Click in **cell A3** and type **Student**, then press the **right arrow key** to move to **cell B3**. Type **Test 1**.
- Press the **right arrow key** to move to **cell C3**. Type **Test 2**. Enter the words **Final** and **Average** in cells D3 and E3, respectively.

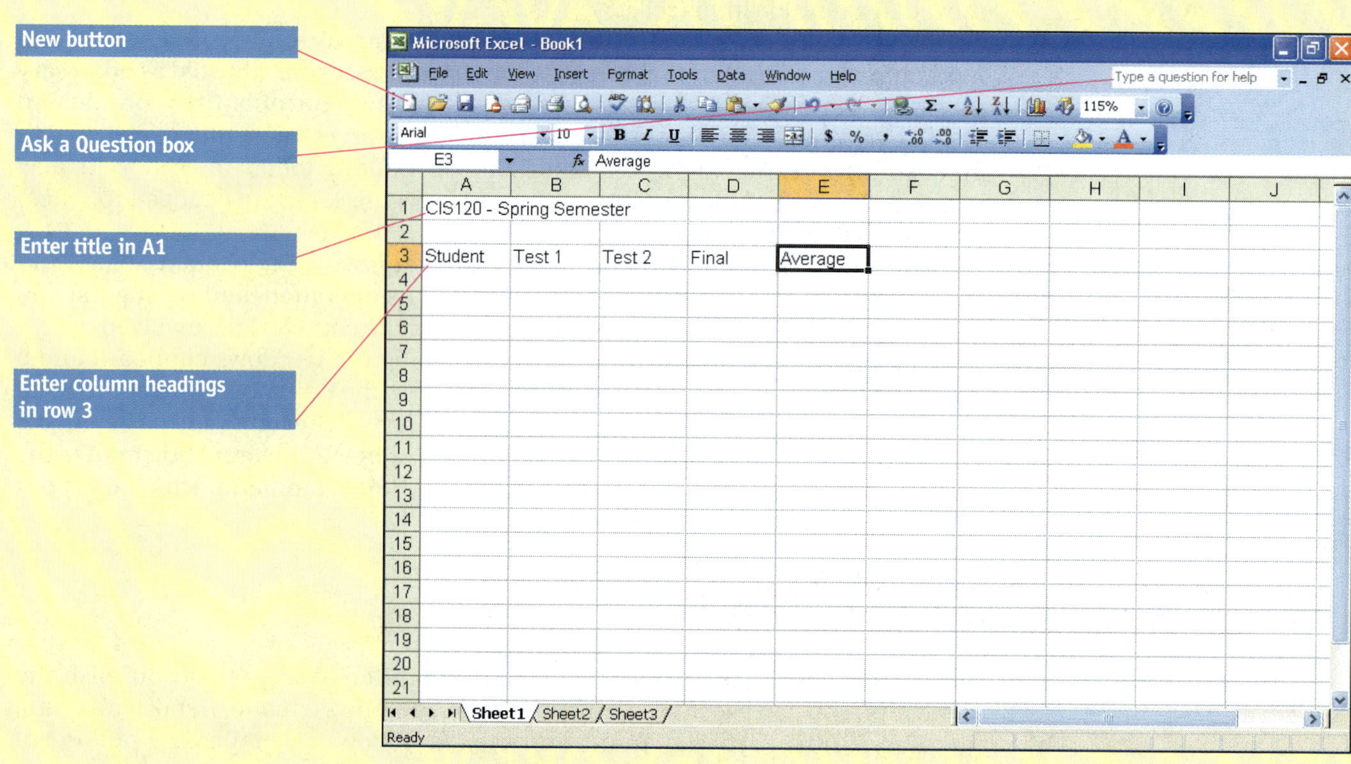

(a) Create a New Workbook (step 1)

FIGURE 1.15 Hands-on Exercise 3

ASK A QUESTION

Click in the "Ask a Question" list box to the right of the menu bar, type a question, press enter, and Excel returns a list of Help topics. Click any topic that appears to open the Help window with detailed information. You can ask multiple questions during an Excel session, then click the down arrow in the list box to return to an earlier question, which will return you to the Help topics.

Step 2: Save the Workbook

- Pull down the **File menu** and click **Save** (or click the **Save button** on the Standard toolbar) to display the Save As dialog box as shown in Figure 1.15b. (The Save As dialog box always appears the first time you save a workbook, so that you can give the workbook a name.)
- Click the **drop-down arrow** on the Save In list box. Click the appropriate drive, drive C or drive A, depending on where you are saving your Excel workbooks.
- Double click the **Exploring Excel folder** to make it the active folder (the folder in which you will save the document).
- Click and drag **Book1** (the default entry) in the File name text box to select it, then type **Better Grade Book** as the name of the workbook.
- Click the **Save button** in the Save As dialog box or press the **Enter key**. The title bar changes to reflect the name of the workbook.

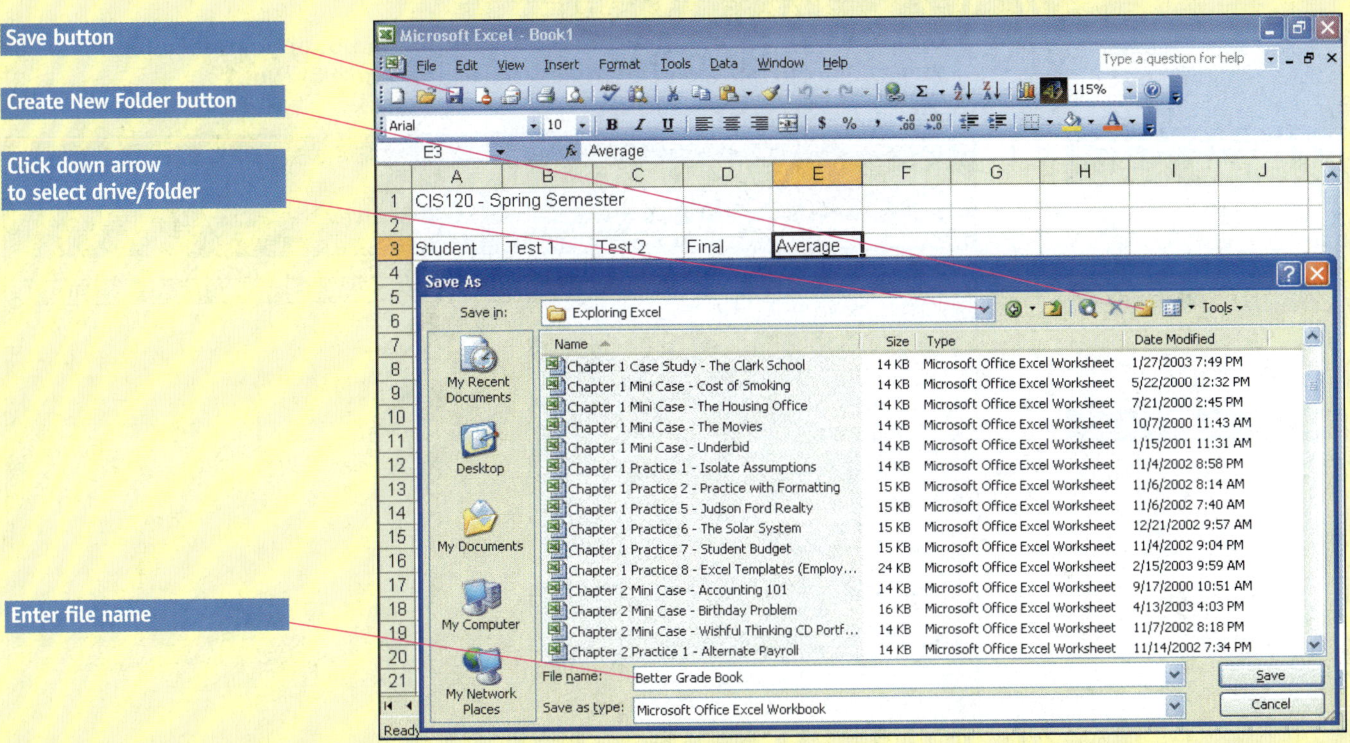

(b) Save the Workbook (step 2)

FIGURE 1.15 Hands-on Exercise 3 (*continued*)

CREATE A NEW FOLDER

Do you work with a large number of different workbooks? If so, it may be useful to store those workbooks in different folders, perhaps one folder for each subject you are taking. Pull down the File menu, click the Save As command to display the Save As dialog box, then click the Create New Folder button to display the associated dialog box. Enter the name of the folder, then click OK. Once the folder has been created, use the Look In box to change to that folder the next time you open that workbook.

Step 3: Enter Student Data and Literal Information

- Click in **cell A4** and type **Costa, Frank**, then enter Frank's grades on the two tests and the final as shown in Figure 1.15c. Do *not* enter Frank's semester average in cell E4 as that will be entered as a formula.
- If necessary, click and drag the border between columns A and B so that you can read Frank Costa's complete name. Check that you entered the data for this student correctly. If you made a mistake, return to the cell and retype the entry.
- Enter the names and grades for the other students in rows 5 through 9. Do *not* enter the student averages.
- Complete the entries in column A by typing **Class Averages** and **Exam Weights** in **cells A11** and **A13**, respectively.
- Enter the exam weights in row 13. Click in **cell B13** and enter **.25**, press the **right arrow key** to move to **cell C13** and enter **.25**, then press the **right arrow key** to move to **cell D13** and enter **.5**. Press **Enter**.
- Do *not* be concerned that the exam weights do not appear as percentages as they will be formatted in a later exercise. Save the workbook.

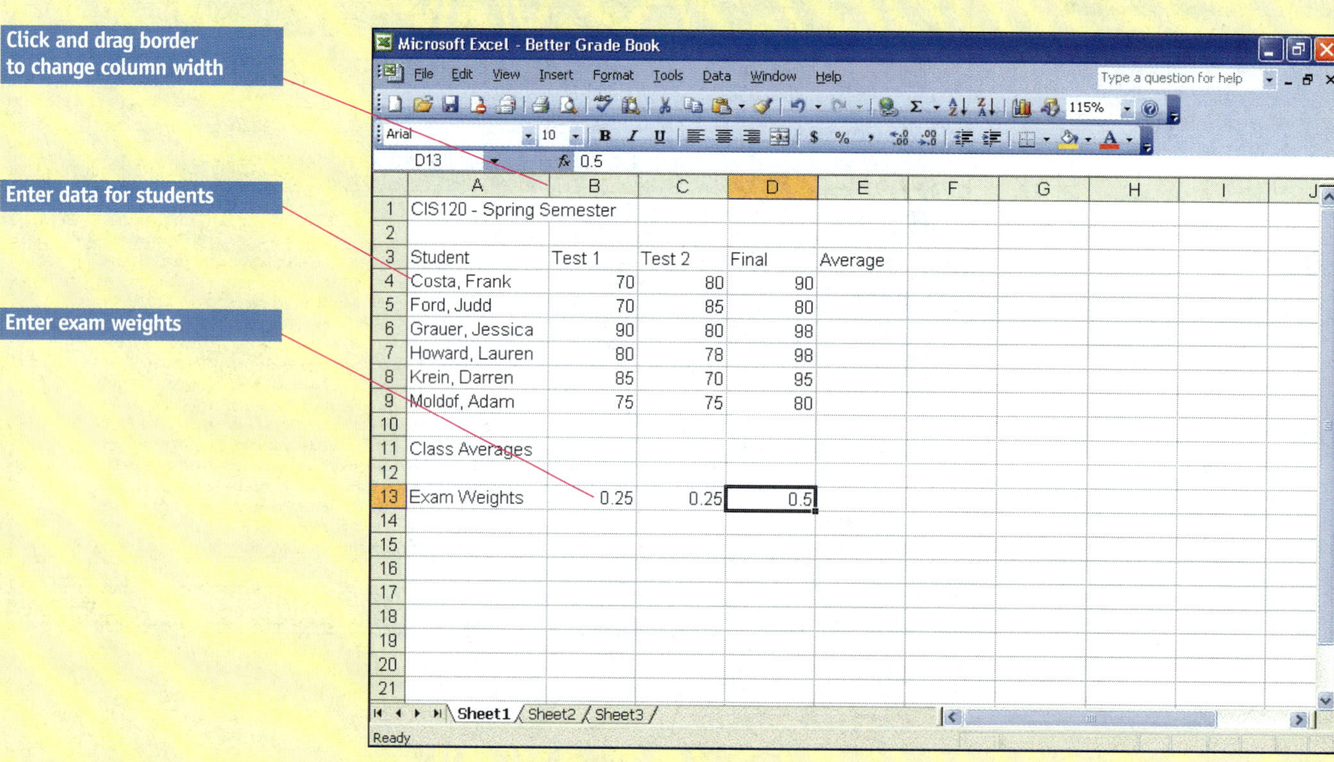

(c) Enter Student Data and Literal Information (step 3)

FIGURE 1.15 Hands-on Exercise 3 (*continued*)

COLUMN WIDTHS AND ROW HEIGHTS

Drag the border between column headings to change the column width; for example, to increase (decrease) the width of column A, drag the border between column headings A and B to the right (left). Double click the right boundary of a column heading to change the column width to accommodate the widest entry in that column. Use the same techniques to change the row heights. See practice exercise 2 at the end of the chapter.

Step 4: Compute the Student Semester Averages

- Click in **cell E4** and type the formula **=$B$13*B4+$C$13*C4+$D$13*D4** to compute the semester average for the first student. Press **Enter**. Check that the displayed value in cell E4 is 82.5 as shown in Figure 1.15d.
- Click in **cell E4** to make this the active cell, then click the **Copy button** on the Standard toolbar. A moving border will surround cell E4, indicating that its contents have been copied to the clipboard.
- Click and drag to select **cells E5** through **E9** as the destination range. Click the **Paste button** to copy the contents of the clipboard to the destination range. Ignore the Paste Options button that appears automatically any time the Paste command is executed.
- Press **Esc** to remove the moving border around cell E4. The Paste Options button also disappears.
- Click in **cell E5** and look at the formula. The cells that reference the grades have changed to B5, C5, and D5. The cells that reference the exam weights—$B$13, $C$13, and $D$13—are the same as in cell E4.
- Save the workbook.

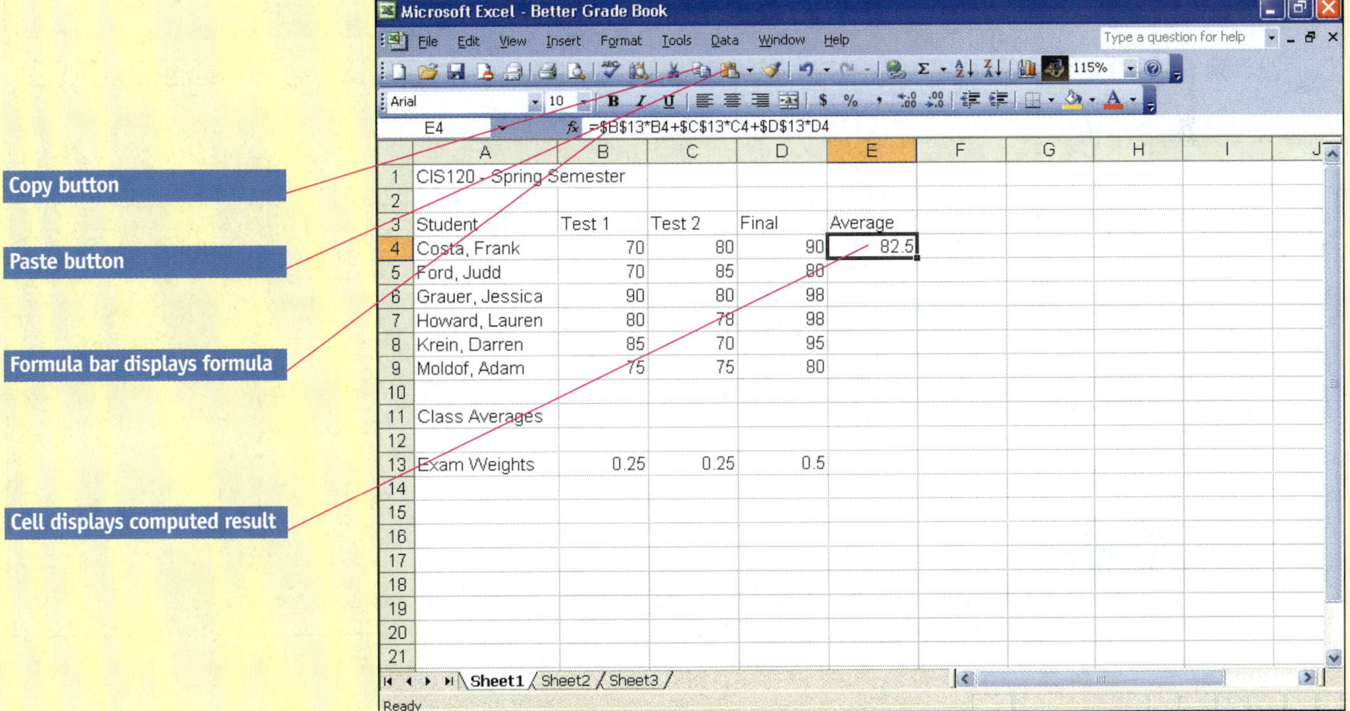

(d) Compute the student Semester Averages (step 4)

FIGURE 1.15 Hands-on Exercise 3 (*continued*)

THE PASTE OPTIONS BUTTON

The Paste Options button (includes options from the Paste Special command and) provides flexibility when you paste the contents of the clipboard into a worksheet. Press Esc to ignore the options and you automatically paste both the cell formulas and associated formatting. Alternatively, you can click the down arrow to display options to copy values rather than formulas with or without formatting, Formatting is discussed in detail later in the chapter.

Step 5: Compute the Class Averages

- Click in **cell B11** and type the formula **=AVERAGE(B4:B9)** to compute the class average on the first test. Press the **Enter key** when you have completed the formula.
- Point to cell B11, then click the **right mouse button** to display a context-sensitive menu, then click the **Copy command**. You should see a moving border around cell B11, indicating that the contents of this cell have been copied to the clipboard.
- Click and drag to select **cells C11** and **D11** as shown in Figure 1.15e. Click the **Paste button** on the standard toolbar to copy the contents of the clipboard to the destination range. Press **Esc** to remove the moving border.
- Click anywhere in the worksheet to deselect cells C11 through D11. Cells C11 and D11 should contain 78 and 90.16667, the class averages on Test 2 and the Final, respectively. Do not worry about formatting at this time.
- Save the workbook.

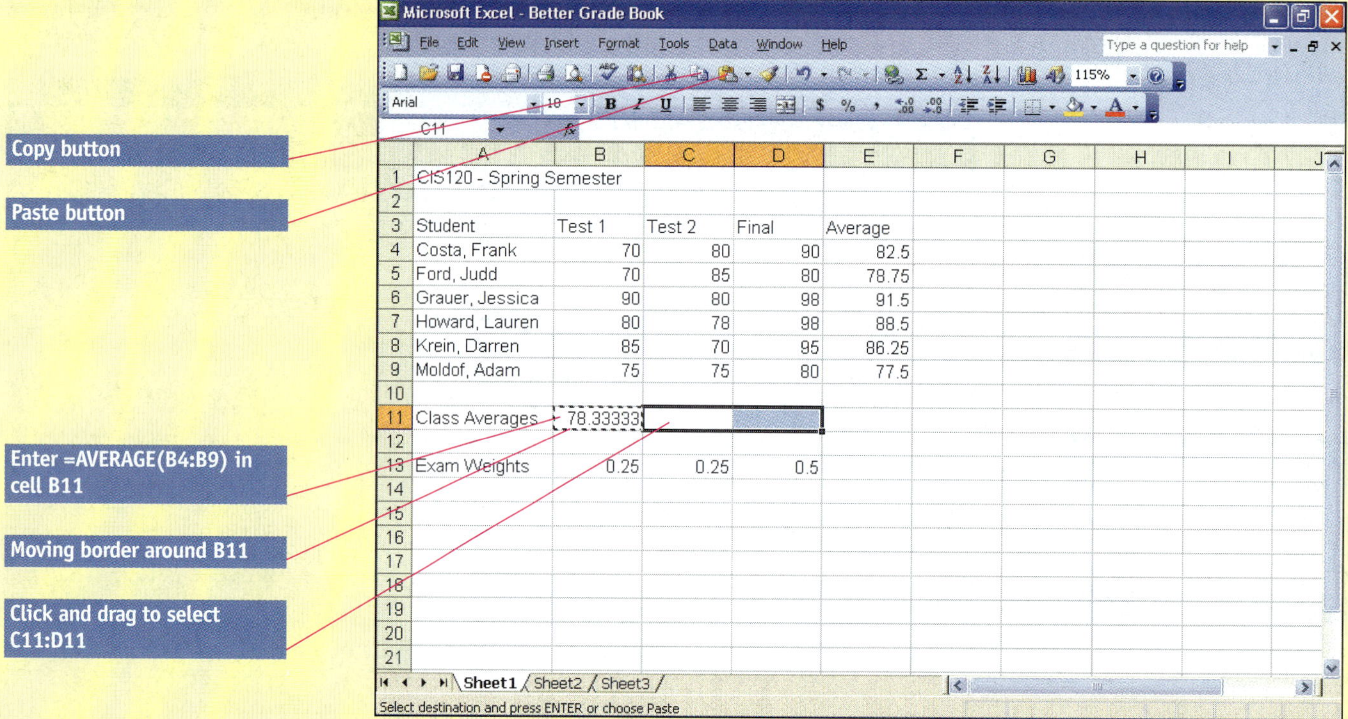

(e) Compute the Class Averages (step 5)

FIGURE 1.15 Hands-on Exercise 3 (*continued*)

TWO DIFFERENT CLIPBOARDS

The Office clipboard holds a total of up to 24 objects from multiple applications, as opposed to the Windows clipboard, which stores only the results of the last Cut or Copy command. Thus, each time you execute a Cut or Copy command, the contents of the Windows clipboard are replaced, whereas the copied object is added to the objects already in the Office clipboard. To display the Office clipboard, open the task pane, click the down arrow, and select clipboard. Leave the clipboard open as you execute multiple cut and copy operations to observe what happens.

Step 6: Change the Exam Weights

- Change the entries in **cells B13** and **C13** to **.20** and the entry in **cell D13** to **.60**. The semester average for every student changes automatically; for example, Costa and Moldof change to 84 and 78, respectively, as shown in Figure 1.15f.
- The professor decides this does not make a significant difference and wants to go back to the original weights. Click the **Undo button** three times to reverse the last three actions. You should see .25, .25, and .50 in cells B13, C13, and D13, respectively.
- Click in **cell A15** and type the label **Grading Assistant**. Press **Enter**. Type your name in **cell A16**, so that you will get credit for this assignment.
- Save the workbook. You do not need to print the workbook yet, since we will do that at the end of the next exercise, after we have formatted the workbook.
- Exit Excel if you are not ready to begin the next exercise at this time.

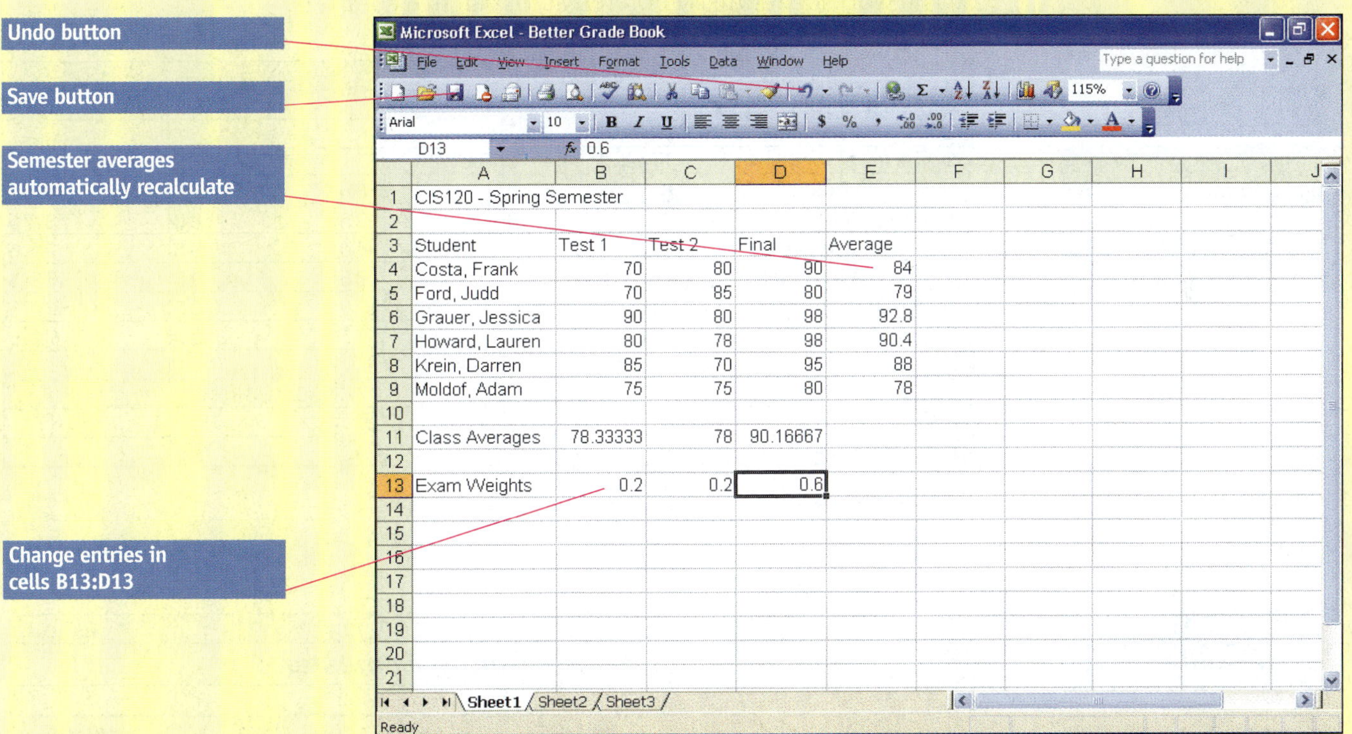

(f) Change the Exam Weights (step 6)

FIGURE 1.15 Hands-on Exercise 3 (*continued*)

CHANGE THE ZOOM PERCENTAGE

You can increase or decrease the size of a worksheet as it appears on the monitor by clicking the down arrow on the zoom box and selecting an appropriate percentage. If you are working with a large spreadsheet and cannot see it at one time on the screen, choose a number less than 100%. Conversely, if you find yourself squinting because the numbers are too small, select a percentage larger than 100%. Changing the magnification on the screen does not affect printing; that is, worksheets are always printed at 100% unless you change the scaling within the Page Setup command.

FORMATTING

Figure 1.16a shows the grade book as it exists at the end of the third hands-on exercise, without concern for its appearance. Figure 1.16b shows the grade book as it will appear at the end of the next exercise after it has been formatted. The differences between the two are due entirely to formatting. Consider:

- The exam weights are formatted as percentages in Figure 1.16b, as opposed to decimals in Figure 1.16a.
- The class and semester averages are displayed with a single decimal place in Figure 1.16b as opposed to a variable number of places in Figure 1.16a.
- Boldface and italic are used for emphasis, as are shading and borders.
- Exam grades and computed averages are centered under their respective headings, as are the exam weights.
- The worksheet title is centered across all five columns.

Class Averages are not uniformly formatted

Percentages are not formatted

	A	B	C	D	E
1	CIS120 - Spring Semester				
2					
3	Student	Test 1	Test 2	Final	Average
4	Costa, Frank	70	80	90	82.5
5	Ford, Judd	70	85	80	78.75
6	Grauer, Jessica	90	80	98	91.5
7	Howard, Lauren	80	78	98	88.5
8	Krein, Darren	85	70	95	86.25
9	Moldof, Adam	75	75	80	77.5
10					
11	Class Averages	78.33333333	78	90.16666667	
12					
13	Exam Weights	0.25	0.25	0.5	

(a) At the End of Hands-on Exercise 3

Title is centered across columns; font is larger and both bold and italic

Shading, borders, and boldface are used for emphasis

Test grades are centered in columns

Uniform number of decimal places

Percent formatting has been applied

	A	B	C	D	E
1	***CIS120 - Spring Semester***				
2					
3	**Student**	**Test 1**	**Test 2**	**Final**	**Average**
4	Costa, Frank	70	80	90	82.5
5	Ford, Judd	70	85	80	78.8
6	Grauer, Jessica	90	80	98	91.5
7	Howard, Lauren	80	78	98	88.5
8	Krein, Darren	85	70	95	86.3
9	Moldof, Adam	75	75	80	77.5
10					
11	**Class Averages**	**78.3**	**78.0**	**90.2**	
12					
13	**Exam Weights**	**25%**	**25%**	**50%**	

(b) At the End of Hands-on Exercise 4

FIGURE 1.16 Developing the Grade Book

FORMAT CELLS COMMAND

The ***Format Cells command*** controls the formatting for numbers, alignment, fonts, borders, and patterns (color). Execution of the command produces a tabbed dialog box in which you choose the particular formatting category, then enter the desired options. All formatting is done within the context of ***select-then-do***. You select the cells to which the formatting is to apply, then you execute the Format Cells command (or click the appropriate button on the Formatting toolbar).

Once a format has been assigned to a cell, the formatting remains in the cell and is applied to all subsequent values that are entered into that cell. You can, however, change the formatting by executing a new formatting command. You can also remove the formatting by using the Clear command in the Edit menu. Note, too, that changing the format of a number changes the way the number is displayed, but does not change its value. If, for example, you entered 1.2345 into a cell, but displayed the number as 1.23, the actual value (1.2345) would be used in all calculations involving that cell. The numeric formats are shown in Figure 1.17a and described below.

- ***General format*** is the default format for numeric entries and displays a number according to the way it was originally entered. Numbers are shown as integers (e.g., 123), decimal fractions (e.g., 1.23), or in scientific notation (e.g., 1.23E+10) if the number exceeds 11 digits.
- ***Number format***, which displays a number with or without the 1000 separator (e.g., a comma) and with any number of decimal places. Negative numbers can be displayed with parentheses and/or can be shown in red.
- ***Currency format***, which displays a number with the 1000 separator and an optional dollar sign (which is placed immediately to the left of the number). Negative values can be preceded by a minus sign or displayed with parentheses and/or can be shown in red.
- ***Accounting format***, which displays a number with the 1000 separator, an optional dollar sign (at the left border of the cell, vertically aligned within a column), negative values in parentheses, and zero values as hyphens.
- ***Date format***, which displays the date in different ways, such as March 14, 2001, 3/14/01, or 14-Mar-01.
- ***Time format***, which displays the time in different formats, such as 10:50 PM or the equivalent 22:50 (24-hour time).
- ***Percentage format***, whereby the number is multiplied by 100 for display purposes only, a percent sign is included, and any number of decimal places can be specified.
- ***Fraction format***, which displays a number as a fraction, and is appropriate when there is no exact decimal equivalent. A fraction is entered into a cell by preceding the fraction with an equal sign—for example, = ⅓.
- ***Scientific format***, which displays a number as a decimal fraction followed by a whole number exponent of 10; for example, the number 12345 would appear as 1.2345E+04. The exponent, +04 in the example, is the number of places the decimal point is moved to the left (or right if the exponent is negative). Very small numbers have negative exponents.
- ***Text format***, which left aligns the entry and is useful for numerical values that have leading zeros and should be treated as text, such as ZIP codes.
- ***Special format***, which displays a number with editing characters, such as hyphens in a Social Security number.
- ***Custom format***, which allows you to develop your own formats.

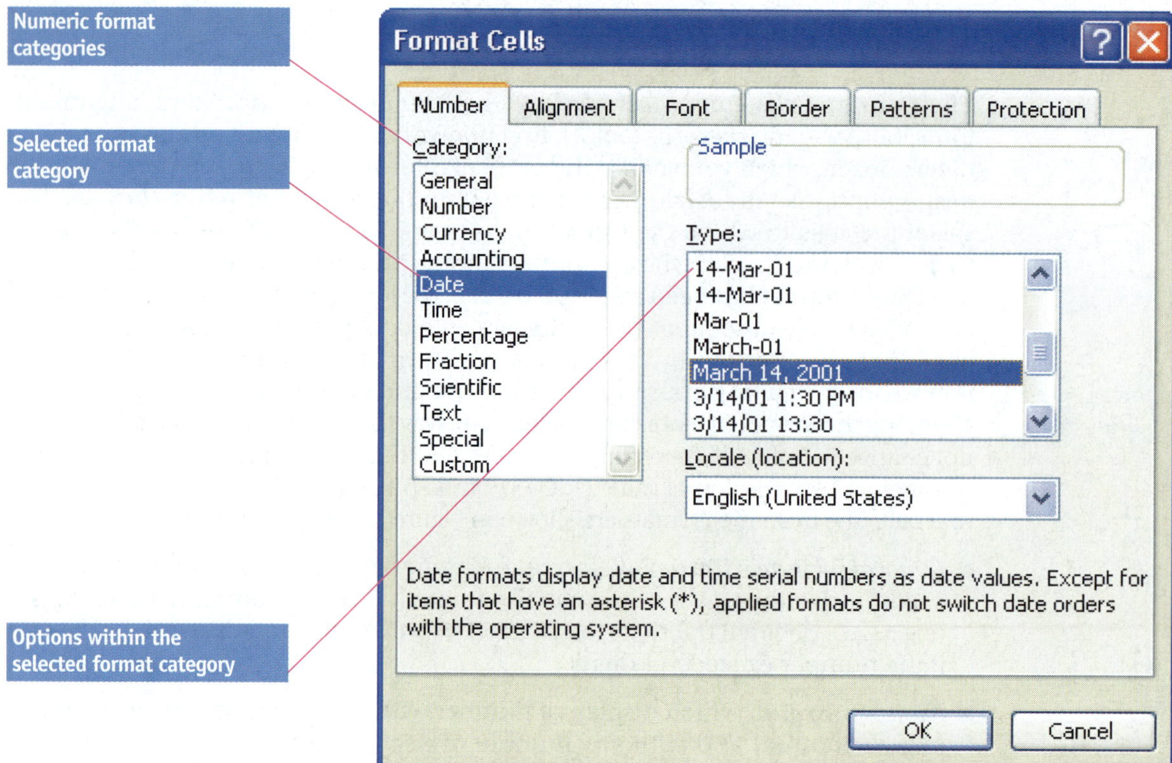

(a) The Number Tab

FIGURE 1.17 The Format Cells Command

Alignment

The contents of a cell (whether text or numeric) may be aligned horizontally and/or vertically as indicated by the dialog box of Figure 1.17b. The default horizontal ***alignment*** is general, which left-aligns text and right-aligns date and numbers. You can also center an entry across a range of selected cells (or ***merge cells***), as in the professor's grade book, which centered the title in cell A1 across columns A through E. Clear the box to merge cells if you want to ***split cells*** that have been previously merged. The Fill option under Horizontal alignment distributes the characters in the cell across the entire width of that cell.

Vertical alignment is important only if the row height is changed and the characters are smaller than the height of the row. Entries may be vertically aligned at the top, center, or bottom (the default) of a cell.

It is also possible to wrap the text within a cell to emulate the word wrap of a word processor. You select multiple cells and merge them together. And finally, you can achieve some interesting effects by rotating text up to 90° in either direction.

Fonts

You can use the same fonts in Excel as you can in any other Windows application. All fonts are WYSIWYG (What You See Is What You Get), meaning that the worksheet you see on the monitor will match the printed worksheet.

Any entry in a worksheet may be displayed in any font, style, or point size as indicated by the dialog box of Figure 1.17c. The example shows Arial, Bold Italic, and 14 points, and corresponds to the selection for the worksheet title in the improved grade book. Special effects, such as subscripts or superscripts, are also possible. You can even select a different color, but you will need a color printer to see the effect on the printed page.

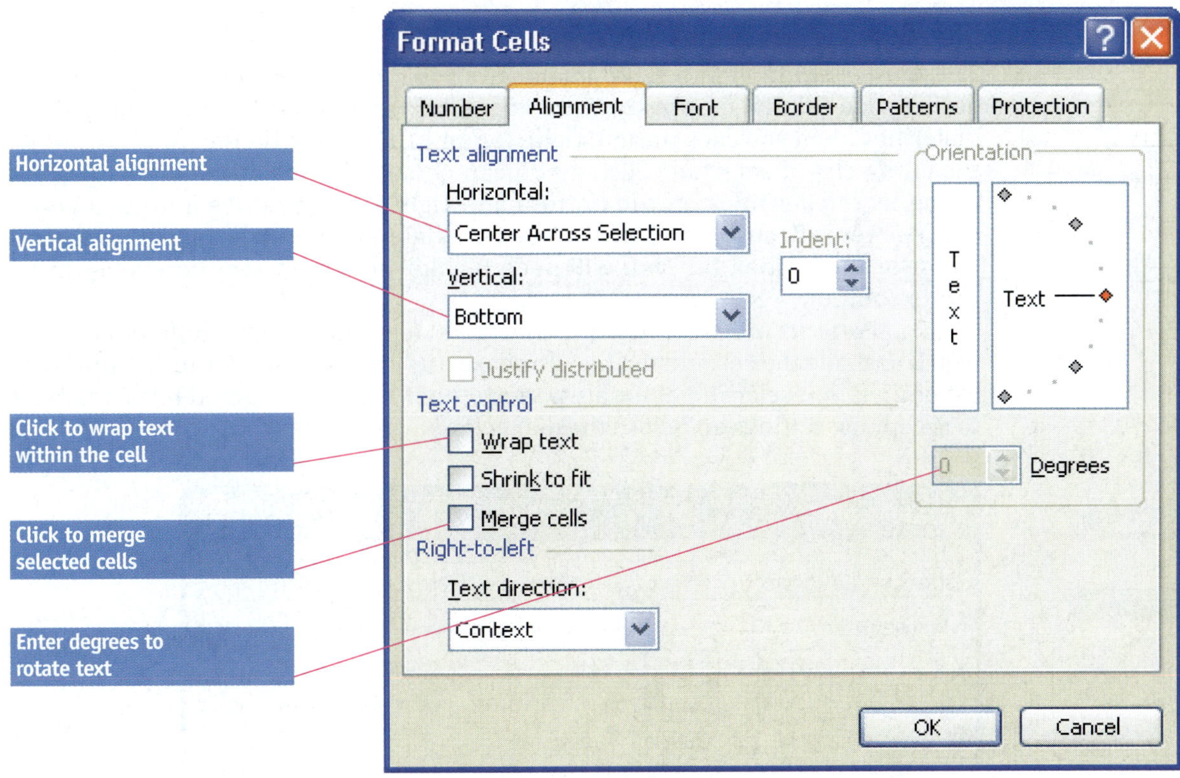

(b) The Alignment Tab

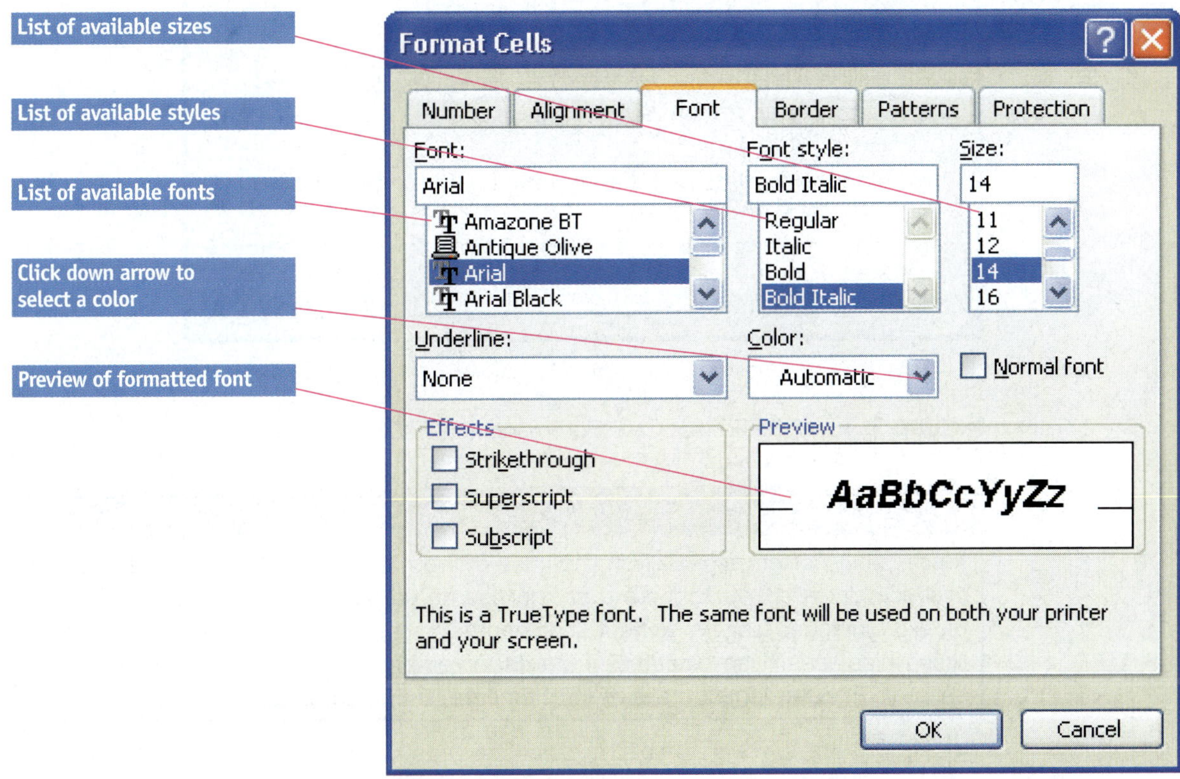

(c) The Font Tab

FIGURE 1.17 The Format Cells Command (*continued*)

Borders, Patterns, and Shading

The ***Border tab*** in Figure 1.17d enables you to create a border around a cell (or cells) for additional emphasis. You select (click) the line style at the right of the dialog box, then you click the left, right, top, and/or bottom border. You can outline the entire cell or selected cells, or you can choose the specific side or sides; for example, thicker lines on the bottom and right sides produce a drop shadow, which is very effective. You can also specify a different line style and/or a different color for the border, but you will need a color printer to see the effect on the printed output.

The ***Patterns tab*** (not shown in the figure) lets you choose a different color in which to shade the cell and further emphasize its contents. The Pattern drop-down list box lets you select an alternate pattern, such as dots or slanted lines. Click OK to accept the settings and close the dialog box.

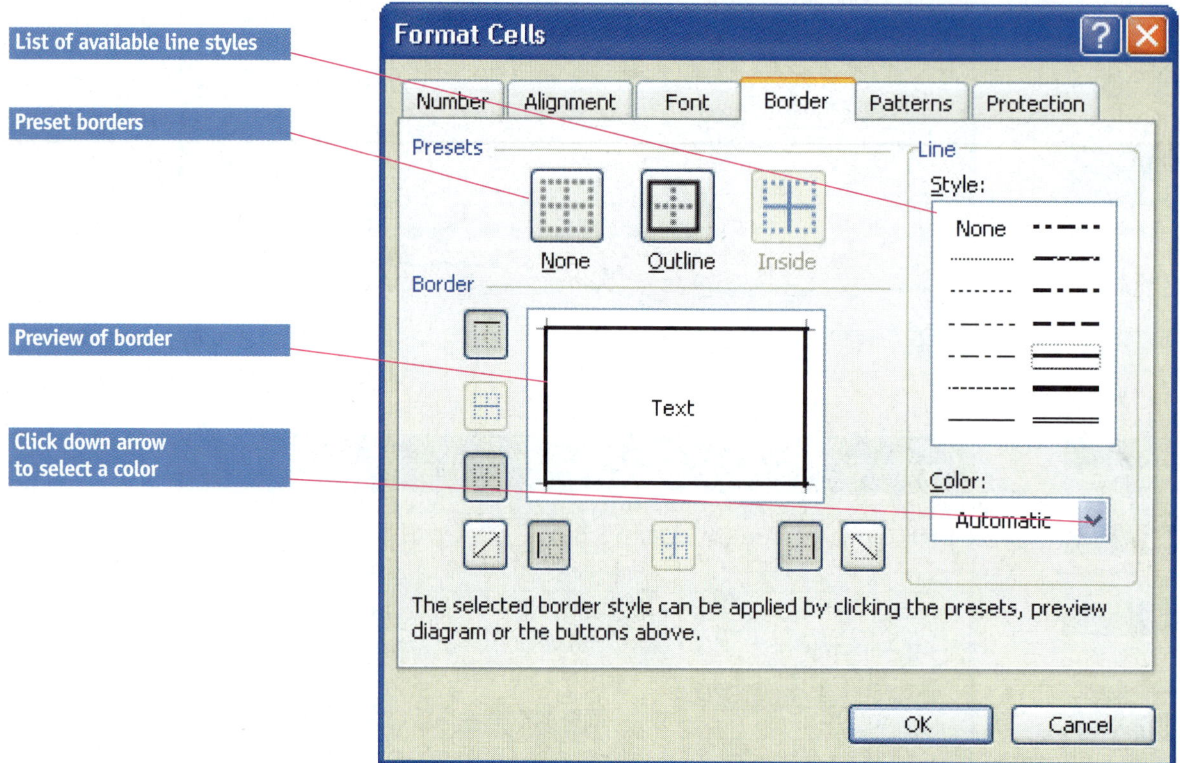

(d) The Border Tab

FIGURE 1.17 The Format Cells Command (*continued*)

> **USE RESTRAINT**
>
> More is not better, especially in the case of too many typefaces and styles, which produce cluttered worksheets that impress no one. Limit yourself to a maximum of two typefaces per worksheet, but choose multiple sizes and/or styles within those typefaces. Use boldface or italics for emphasis, but do so in moderation, because if you emphasize too many elements, the effect is lost.

hands-on exercise

4 Formatting a Worksheet

Objective To format a worksheet using boldface, italic, shading, and borders; to change the font and/or alignment of a selected entry. Use Figure 1.18 as a guide in the exercise.

Step 1: Center the Title

- Open **Better Grade Book** from the previous exercise. Click in **cell A1** to select the cell containing the title of the worksheet. Click the **Bold button** on the Formatting toolbar to boldface the title. Click the **Italic button** to italicize the title.
- Click in **cell A15** and click the **Bold button**. Click the **Bold button** a second time, and the boldface disappears. Click the **Bold button** again, and you are back to boldface. The same is true of the Italic button; that is, the Bold and Italic buttons function as toggle switches.
- Click in **cell A1**. Click the **down arrow** on the Font size list box and change the size to **14** to further accentuate the title.
- Click and drag to select **cells A1** through **E1**, which represents the width of the entire worksheet. Click the **Merge and Center button** on the Formatting toolbar as shown in Figure 1.18a to center the title across the width of your worksheet.
- Save the workbook.

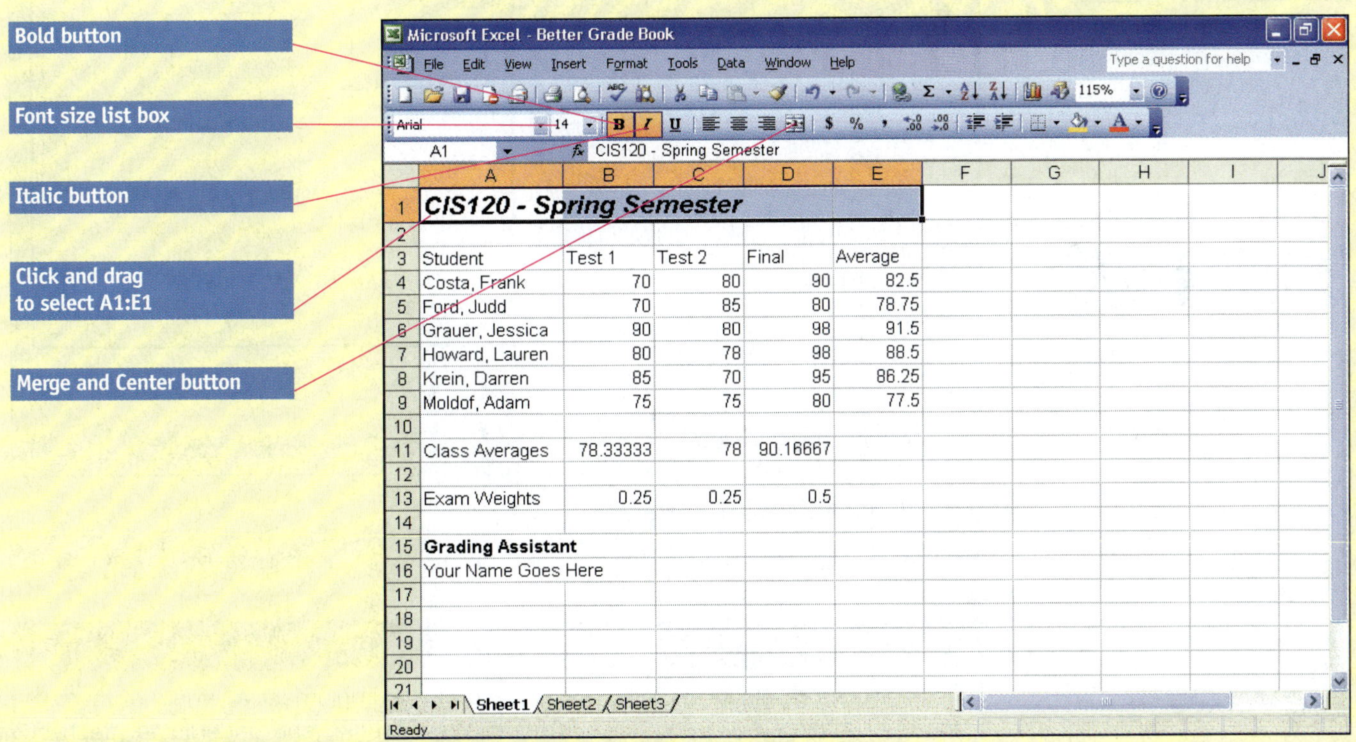

(a) Center the Title (step 1)

FIGURE 1.18 Hands-on Exercise 4

Step 2: Format the Exam Weights

- Click and drag to select **cells B13** through **D13**. Pull down the **Format menu**, then click the **Cells command** to display the dialog box in Figure 1.18b.
- If necessary, click the **Number tab**. Click **Percentage** in the Category list box. Click the **down spin arrow** in the Decimal Places box to select **zero decimals**, then click **OK**. The exam weights are displayed with percent signs and no decimal places.
- You can also use the buttons on the Formatting toolbar to accomplish the same formatting. First remove the formatting by clicking the **Undo button** on the Standard toolbar to cancel the formatting command.
- Check that cells B13 through D13 are still selected. Click the **Percent Style button** on the Formatting toolbar. (You can also pull down the **Format menu**, click the **Style command**, then choose the **Percent Style** from the Style Name list box.) Once again cells B13 through D13 are displayed in percent format.
- Save the workbook.

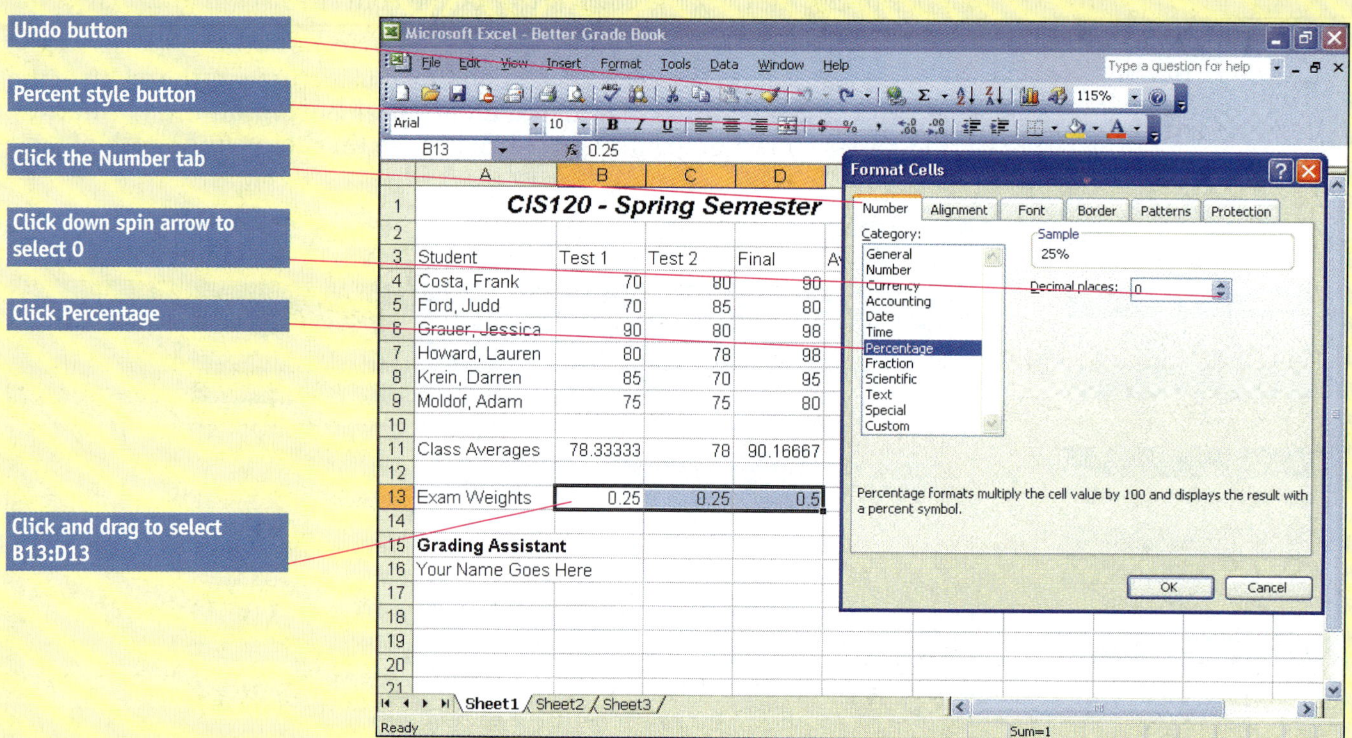

(b) Format the Exam Weights (step 2)

FIGURE 1.18 Hands-on Exercise 4 (*continued*)

THE MENU OR THE TOOLBAR

The Formatting toolbar is often the easiest way to implement a variety of formatting operations. There are buttons for boldface, italic, and underlining (each of which functions as a toggle switch). There are also buttons for alignment (including merge and center), currency, percent, and comma formats, together with buttons to increase or decrease the number of decimal places. You can find various buttons to change the font, point size, color, and borders.

Step 3: Format the Class Averages

- Click and drag to select **cells B11** through **D11**. Now press and hold the **Ctrl key** as you click and drag to select **cells E4** through **E9**. Using the Ctrl key in this way allows you to select noncontiguous (nontouching) cells as shown in Figure 1.18c.
- Format the selected cells using the Formatting toolbar or the Format menu:
  - ❑ To use the Format menu, pull down the **Format menu**, click **Cells**, click the **Number tab**, then click **Number** in the Category list box. Click the **down spin arrow** in the Decimal Places text box to reduce the decimal places to one. Click **OK**.
  - ❑ To use the Formatting toolbar, click the appropriate button repeatedly to increase or decrease the number of decimal places to one.
- Click and drag to select **cells B3** through **E13**. Click the **Center button** to center the numeric data in the worksheet under the respective column headings.
- Save the workbook.

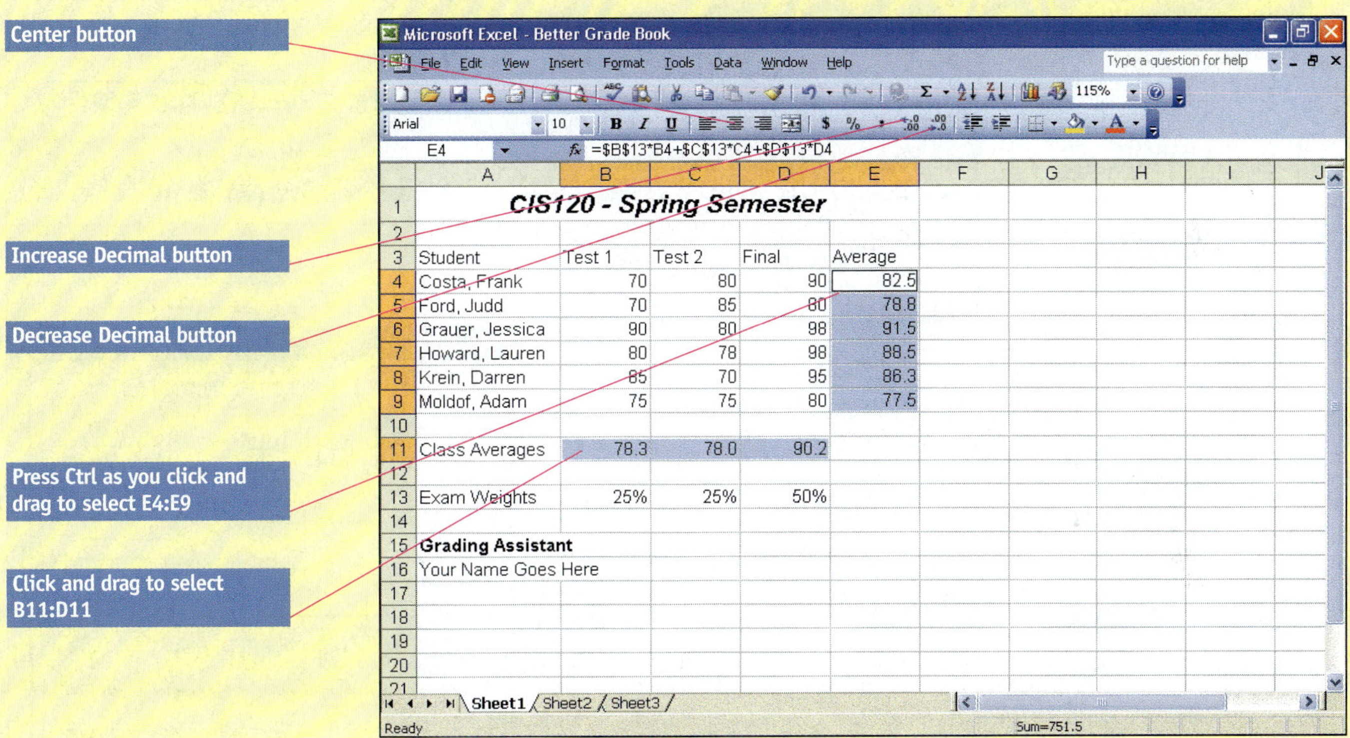

(c) Format the Class Averages (step 3)

FIGURE 1.18 Hands-on Exercise 4 (*continued*)

CLEAR THE FORMATS, BUT KEEP THE CONTENTS

You can clear the formatting in a cell and retain the contents, and/or you can clear contents but retain the formatting. Click and drag over the cell(s) for which the command is to apply, then pull down the Edit menu, click the Clear command, and choose the appropriate option—for example, the option to clear Formats. Click the tiny square immediately below the name box (to the left of the header for column A) to select the entire worksheet, then clear the formats for the worksheet. You can then repeat the steps in this exercise to practice the various formatting commands.

Step 4: Borders and Color

- Click and drag to select **cells A3** through **E3**. Press and hold the **Ctrl key** as you click and drag to select the range **A11:E11**.
- Continue to press the **Ctrl key** as you click and drag to select **cells A13:E13**. All three cell ranges should be selected, which means that any formatting command you execute will apply to all of the selected cells.
- Pull down the **Format menu** and click **Cells** (or point to any of the selected cells and click the **right mouse button** to display a shortcut menu, then click **Format Cells**). Click the **Border tab** to display the dialog box in Figure 1.18d.
- Choose a line width from the Style section. Click the **Top** and **Bottom** boxes in the Border section. Click **OK** to exit the dialog box.
- Check that all three ranges are still selected (A3:E3, A11:E11, *and* A13:E13). Click the **down arrow** on the **Fill Color button** on the Formatting toolbar. Click **yellow** (or whatever color appeals to you).
- Click the **Bold button** on the Formatting toolbar. Click outside the selected cells to see the effects of the formatting change. Save the workbook.

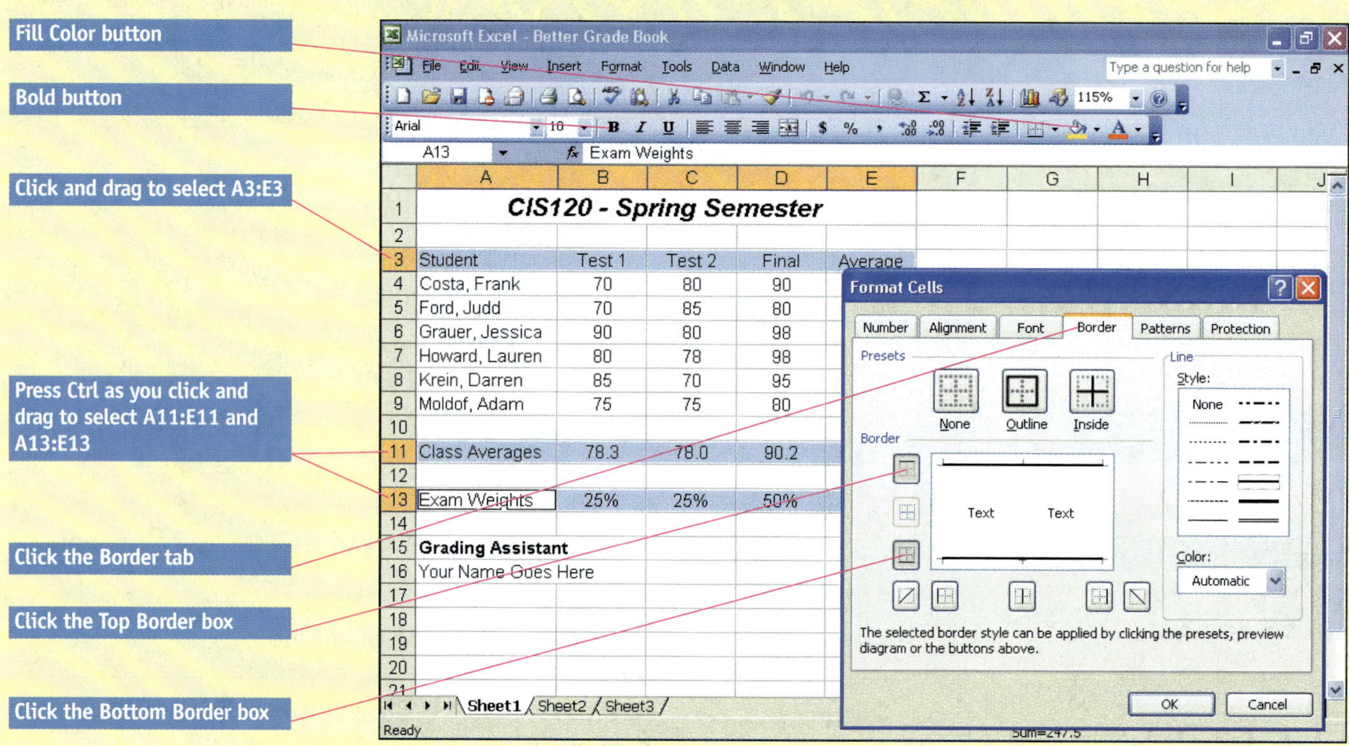

(d) Borders and Color (step 4)

FIGURE 1.18 Hands-on Exercise 4 (*continued*)

USE A PEN TO DRAW THE BORDER

You can draw borders of any thickness or color around the cells in a worksheet using a "pen," as opposed to a menu command. Click the down arrow on the Borders button on the Standard toolbar, then click the Draw Borders command to change the mouse pointer to a pen and simultaneously display the Borders toolbar. Click the Line Color or Line Style buttons to change the appearance of the border, then draw the borders directly in the worksheet. Close the Borders toolbar when you are finished.

Step 5: The Completed Worksheet

- Check that your worksheet matches ours as shown in Figure 1.18e. Pull down the **File menu**. Click **Page Setup** to display the Page Setup dialog box.
  - Click the **Margins tab**. Check the box to center the worksheet horizontally.
  - Click the **Sheet tab**. Check the boxes to print **Row and Column Headings** and **Gridlines**.
  - Click the **Header/Footer tab**. If necessary, click the **drop-down arrow** on the Header list box. Scroll to the top of the list and click **(none)** to remove the header. Click the **drop-down arrow** on the Footer list box. Scroll to the top of the list and click **(none)** to remove the footer. Click **OK**.
- Click the **Print Preview button** to preview the worksheet before printing:
  - If you are satisfied with the appearance of the worksheet, click the **Print button** within the Preview window, then click **OK** to print the worksheet.
  - If you are not satisfied with the appearance of the worksheet, click the **Setup button** within the Preview window to make the necessary changes.
- Save the workbook.

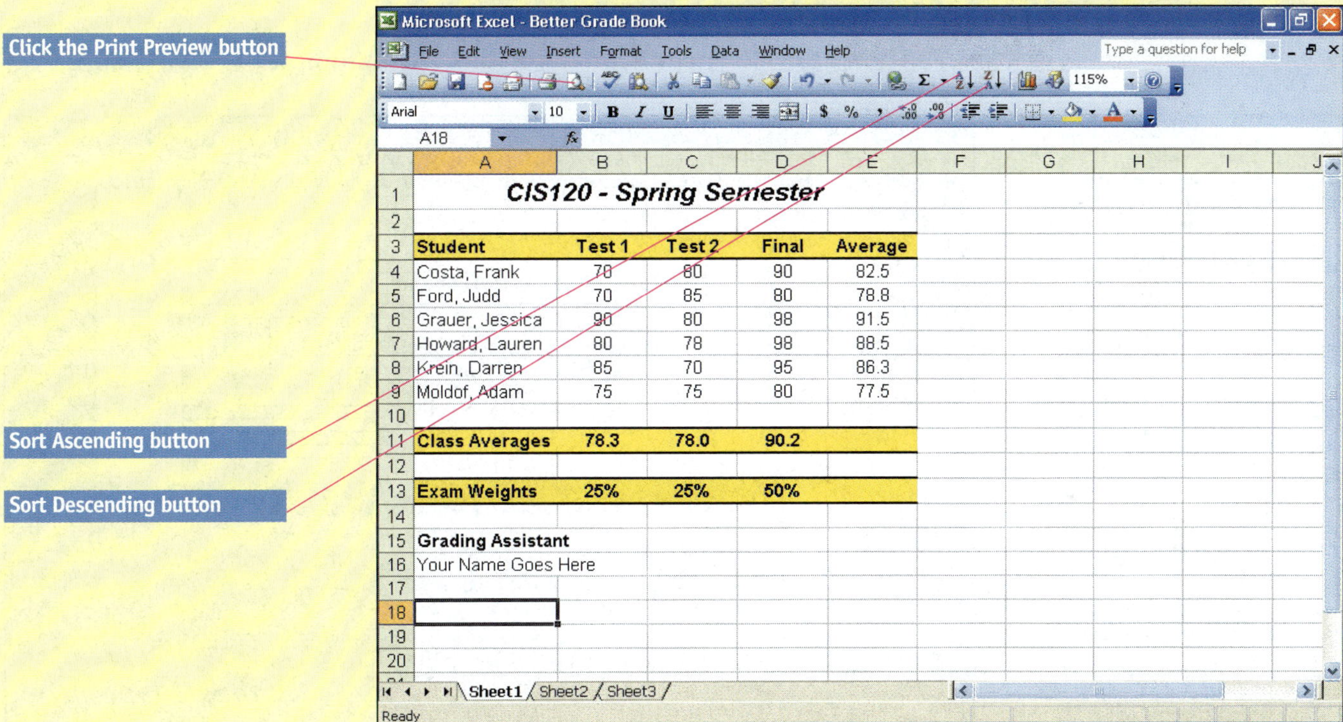

(e) The Completed Worksheet (step 5)

FIGURE 1.18 Hands-on Exercise 4 (*continued*)

SORT THE STUDENTS

The students are listed on the worksheet in alphabetical order, but you can rearrange the list according to any other field, such as the average or the result of a specific exam. Click on a single cell containing the student data in the column on which you want to sort, then click the Sort Ascending or Sort Descending button on the Standard toolbar. Click the Undo button if the result is different from what you intended.

Step 6: Print the Cell Formulas

- Pull down the **Tools menu**, click **Options**, click the **View tab**, check the box for **Formulas**, then click **OK**. You should see the cell formulas.
- Pull down the **File menu**. Click **Page Setup** to display the Page Setup dialog box. Click the **Page tab**. Click the **Landscape Orientation button**. Click the option button to **Fit to 1 Page**. Click **OK** to exit the Page Setup dialog box.
- Click the **Print Preview button** to preview the worksheet before printing.
  - Click the **Margins button** to display gridlines within the Print Preview window. Click and drag the column indicators to widen columns as necessary so that the cell formulas are completely visible.
  - Click the **Setup button** to display the Page Setup dialog box. Click the **Header/Footer tab**. Click the button to create a **Custom Header**.
  - Click in the **left section** and enter your name. Click in the **center section** and enter your course and your instructor's name.
  - Click in the **right section**. Click the **Date button**, press the **space bar**, then click the **Time button** to complete the custom header as shown in Figure 1.18f. Click **OK** to close the Header dialog box, then click **OK** to close the Page Setup dialog box. Print the worksheet.
- Pull down the **File menu**. Click **Exit**. Click **No** if prompted to save changes.

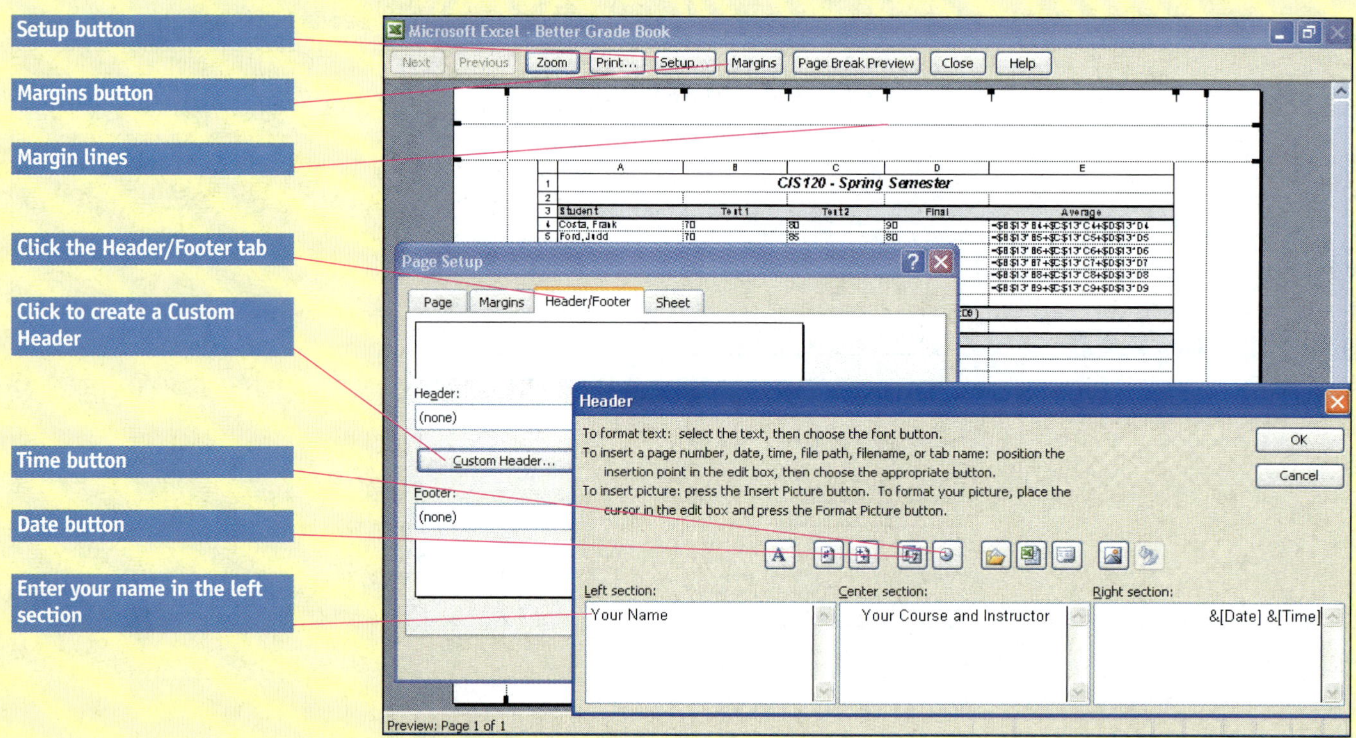

(f) Print the Cell Formulas (step 6)

FIGURE 1.18 Hands-on Exercise 4 (*continued*)

FIND AND REPLACE

Anyone familiar with a word processor takes the Find and Replace command for granted, but many people are surprised to learn that the same commands are also found in Excel. The commands are found in the Edit menu and provide the same options as in Microsoft Word. You can replace text and/or formatting throughout a worksheet. See practice exercise 5 at the end of the chapter.

SUMMARY

A spreadsheet is the computerized equivalent of an accountant's ledger. It is divided into rows and columns, with each row and column assigned a heading. The intersection of a row and column forms a cell. Spreadsheet is a generic term. Workbook and worksheet are Excel specific. An Excel workbook contains one or more worksheets.

Every cell in a worksheet (spreadsheet) contains either a formula or a constant. A formula begins with an equal sign and is a combination of numeric constants, cell references, arithmetic operators, and/or functions. A constant is an entry that does not change and may be numeric or descriptive text.

The Insert and Delete commands add or remove individual cells, rows, or columns of a worksheet. The commands are also used to insert or delete worksheets within a workbook. The Open command brings a workbook from disk into memory. The Save command copies the workbook in memory to disk.

The Page Setup command provides complete control over the printed page, enabling you to print a worksheet with or without gridlines or row and column headings. The Page Setup command also controls margins, headers and footers, centering the worksheet on a page, and orientation. The Print Preview command shows the worksheet as it will print and should be used prior to printing.

All worksheet commands operate on a cell or group of cells known as a range. A range is selected by dragging the mouse to highlight the range; the range remains selected until another range is selected or you click another cell in the worksheet. Noncontiguous (nonadjacent) ranges may be selected in conjunction with the Ctrl key.

The formulas in a cell or range of cells may be copied or moved anywhere within a worksheet. An absolute reference remains constant throughout a copy operation, whereas a relative address is adjusted for the new location. Absolute and relative references have no meaning in a move operation.

Formatting is done within the context of select-then-do; that is, select the cell or range of cells, then execute the appropriate command. The Format Cells command controls the formatting for numbers, alignment, font, borders, and patterns (colors). The Formatting toolbar simplifies the formatting process.

KEY TERMS

MULTIPLE CHOICE

1. Which of the following is true?
   (a) A worksheet contains one or more workbooks
   (b) A workbook contains one or more worksheets
   (c) A spreadsheet contains one or more worksheets
   (d) A worksheet contains one or more spreadsheets

2. The cell at the intersection of the second column and third row is cell:
   (a) B3
   (b) 3B
   (c) C2
   (d) 2C

3. What is the effect of typing F5+F6 into a cell *without* a beginning equal sign?
   (a) The entry is equivalent to the formula =F5+F6
   (b) The cell will display the contents of cell F5 plus cell F6
   (c) The entry will be treated as a text entry and display F5+F6 in the cell
   (d) The entry will be rejected by Excel, which will signal an error message

4. The Open command:
   (a) Brings a workbook from disk into memory
   (b) Brings a workbook from disk into memory, then erases the workbook on disk
   (c) Stores the workbook in memory on disk
   (d) Stores the workbook in memory on disk, then erases the workbook from memory

5. The Save command:
   (a) Brings a workbook from disk into memory
   (b) Brings a workbook from disk into memory, then erases the workbook on disk
   (c) Stores the workbook in memory on disk
   (d) Stores the workbook in memory on disk, then erases the workbook from memory

6. In the absence of parentheses, the order of operation is:
   (a) Exponentiation, addition or subtraction, multiplication or division
   (b) Addition or subtraction, multiplication or division, exponentiation
   (c) Multiplication or division, exponentiation, addition or subtraction
   (d) Exponentiation, multiplication or division, addition or subtraction

7. Cells A1, A2, and A3 contain the values 10, 20, and 40, respectively. What value will be displayed in a cell containing the cell formula =A1/A2*A3+1?
   (a) 1.125
   (b) 21
   (c) 20.125
   (d) Impossible to determine

8. The entry =AVERAGE(A4:A6):
   (a) Is invalid because the cells are not contiguous
   (b) Computes the average of cells A4 and A6
   (c) Computes the average of cells A4, A5, and A6
   (d) None of the above

9. Which of the following was suggested with respect to printing a workbook?
   (a) Print the displayed values only
   (b) Print the cell formulas only
   (c) Print both the displayed values and cell formulas
   (d) Print neither the displayed values nor the cell formulas

10. Which options are mutually exclusive in the Page Setup menu?
    (a) Portrait and landscape orientation
    (b) Cell gridlines and row and column headings
    (c) Left and right margins
    (d) All of the above

... continued

multiple choice

11. If cells A1, A2, and A3 contain the values 1, 2, and 5, respectively, what value will be displayed in a cell containing the formula =(A3-A1)/A2^2+A2?

(a) 1
(b) 3
(c) .0625
(d) .4

12. Which of the following best describes the formula used to compute a student's semester average, when the weights of each exam are isolated at the bottom of a spreadsheet?

(a) The student's individual grades are entered as absolute references and the exam weights are entered as relative references
(b) The student's individual grades are entered as relative references and the exam weights are entered as absolute references
(c) All cell references are relative
(d) All cell references are absolute

13. Cell B11 contains the formula, =SUM (B3:B9). What will the contents of cell C11 be if the formula in cell B11 is copied to cell C11?

(a) =SUM (C3:C9)
(b) =SUM (B3:B9)
(c) =SUM ($B$3:$B$9)
(d) =SUM ($C$3:$C$9)

14. Given that cell E6 contains the formula =B6*$B$12+C6*$C$12+D6*$D$12. What will be the formula in cell E7 if the contents of cell E6 are copied to that cell?

(a) =B7*$B$12+C7*$C$12+D7*$D$12
(b) =B7*$B$13+C7*$C$13+D7*$D$13
(c) =B6*$B$13+C6*$C$13+D6*$D$13
(d) None of the above

15. A formula containing the reference =D$5 is copied to a cell one column over and two rows down. How will the entry appear in its new location?

(a) =E5
(b) =E$5
(c) =E$6
(d) =$E5

16. The formula =B3+C4 is stored in cell D5. What will the formula be if row two is deleted from the worksheet?

(a) =B2+C4
(b) =B3+C3
(c) =B3+C4
(d) =B2+C3

17. You are creating a sales forecast, and have entered the sales for 2002 in cell B4. The expected rate of increase is in cell C2. What formula would you enter in cell C4 to compute the sales for 2003, given that you will copy that formula to cells D4:E4 to calculate the forecast for 2004 and 2005?

(a) =B4+B4*C2
(b) =$B$4+$B$4*C2
(c) =B4*(1+$C$2)
(d) None of the above

18. What is the end result of clicking in a cell, then clicking the Italic button on the Formatting toolbar twice in a row?

(a) The cell contents are displayed in italic
(b) The cell contents are displayed in ordinary (nonitalicized) type
(c) The cell contents are unchanged and appear exactly as they did prior to clicking the Italic button twice in a row
(d) Impossible to determine

ANSWERS

1. b	**7.** b	**13.** a
2. a	**8.** c	**14.** a
3. c	**9.** c	**15.** b
4. a	**10.** a	**16.** d
5. c	**11.** b	**17.** c
6. d	**12.** b	**18.** c

PRACTICE WITH EXCEL

1. **Isolate Assumptions:** Figure 1.19 displays a new grade book with a different grading scheme. Students take three exams worth 100 points each, submit a term paper and various homework assignments worth 50 points each, then receive a grade for the semester based on their total points. The maximum number of points (the point threshold) is 400. A student's semester average is computed by dividing his or her total points by the point threshold. Open the partially completed workbook in *Chapter 1 Practice 1* in the Exploring Excel folder and proceed as follows:
   a. Click in cell G4 and enter a formula to compute Anderson's total points. Click in cell H4 and enter a formula that will compute Anderson's semester average. Be sure this formula includes an absolute reference to cell B16.
   b. Click and drag to select the formulas in cells G4 and H4, then copy these formulas to cells G5 through H12.
   c. Click in cell B14 and enter a formula that will compute the class average on the first exam. Copy this formula to cells C14 to H14.
   d. Format the worksheet appropriately, but you need not match our formatting exactly. Note, too, that we have wrapped the text in cells B3 through H3 in order to use a narrower column width. (Select the cells, pull down the Format Cells command, click the Alignment tab, then check the box to wrap text.)
   e. Add your name as the grading assistant, then print the worksheet twice, once to show displayed values and once to show the cell formulas. Use landscape printing and be sure that the worksheet fits on one sheet of paper.
   f. The professor is concerned about the grades being too low and wants to introduce a curve. He does this by reducing the point threshold on which the students' semester averages are based. Click in cell B16 and change the threshold to 350, which automatically raises the average of every student.
   g. Print the displayed values that reflect the change in part (e). Can you see the value of isolating the assumptions within a worksheet?
   h. Add a cover page, then submit the complete assignment (four pages in all, counting the cover page) to your instructor as proof that you did this exercise.

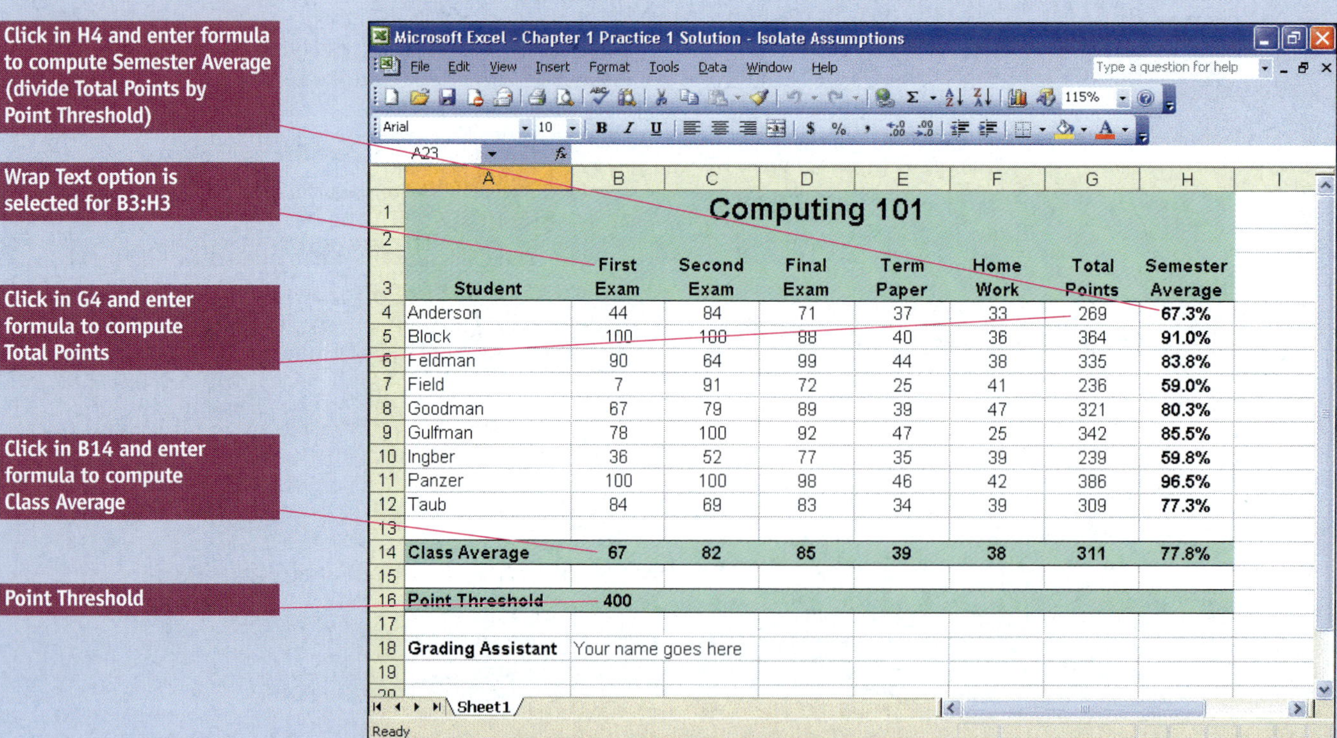

	A	B	C	D	E	F	G	H
1	Computing 101							
2								
3	Student	First Exam	Second Exam	Final Exam	Term Paper	Home Work	Total Points	Semester Average
4	Anderson	44	84	71	37	33	269	67.3%
5	Block	100	100	88	40	36	364	91.0%
6	Feldman	90	64	99	44	38	335	83.8%
7	Field	7	91	72	25	41	236	59.0%
8	Goodman	67	79	89	39	47	321	80.3%
9	Gulfman	78	100	92	47	25	342	85.5%
10	Ingber	36	52	77	35	39	239	59.8%
11	Panzer	100	100	98	46	42	386	96.5%
12	Taub	84	69	83	34	39	309	77.3%
13								
14	Class Average	67	82	85	39	38	311	77.8%
15								
16	Point Threshold	400						
17								
18	Grading Assistant	Your name goes here						

FIGURE 1.19 Isolate Assumptions (exercise 1)

2. **Practice with Formatting:** The workbook in Figure 1.20 provides practice with formatting and basic cell operations. Open the partially completed workbook in *Chapter 1 Practice 2*, and then format the workbook using the instructions in each cell. The formatting is very straightforward, but inserting and deleting cells is a little trickier since it can affect cells that have been merged together. You will find it easier therefore if you start in cell A1 and work your way down the worksheet, one row at a time. Proceed as follows:
   a. Click in cell A1 and enter your name, then change the formatting to 16 point white text on a blue background as shown in the figure.
   b. Move to cell A3 and format the text as indicated. You can use the Format Cells command and/or the various tools on the Formatting toolbar as you see fit. Move to cell B3 and italicize the text in green. Format cells A4 through B7 in similar fashion. Follow the instructions in cell B5 to change the width of column B.
   c. Follow the instructions in cells A8 to A12 to format the contents of cells B8 to B12, respectively. (No additional formatting is required for cells A8 to A12 at this time.)
   d. Click in cell A13, then click the Merge and Center button to split the merged cell into two cells. (The Merge and Center button functions as a toggle switch: Click it once, the selected cells are merged; click it a second time, and the merged cell is split.) Follow the instructions in the cell to change the row height and other formatting. Cell B13 should be blank when you are finished.
   e. Click in cell A14, click the Format Painter tool, and then click and drag cells A8 through A12 to apply the formatting from cell A14.
   f. Right click the row indicator for row 15 and insert a new row, and then move the contents of cell A20 to the newly inserted cell A15.
   g. Change the width of column A to 55, merge cells A16 and B16, then complete the indicated formatting for the merged cell.
   h. Print the completed workbook for your instructor. Use the Page Setup command to display gridlines and row and column headings. Change to landscape printing and center the worksheet horizontally on the page. Create a custom header that contains your name, your school, and your instructor's name. Add a custom footer that contains the name of the workbook, and the date and time you completed the assignment.

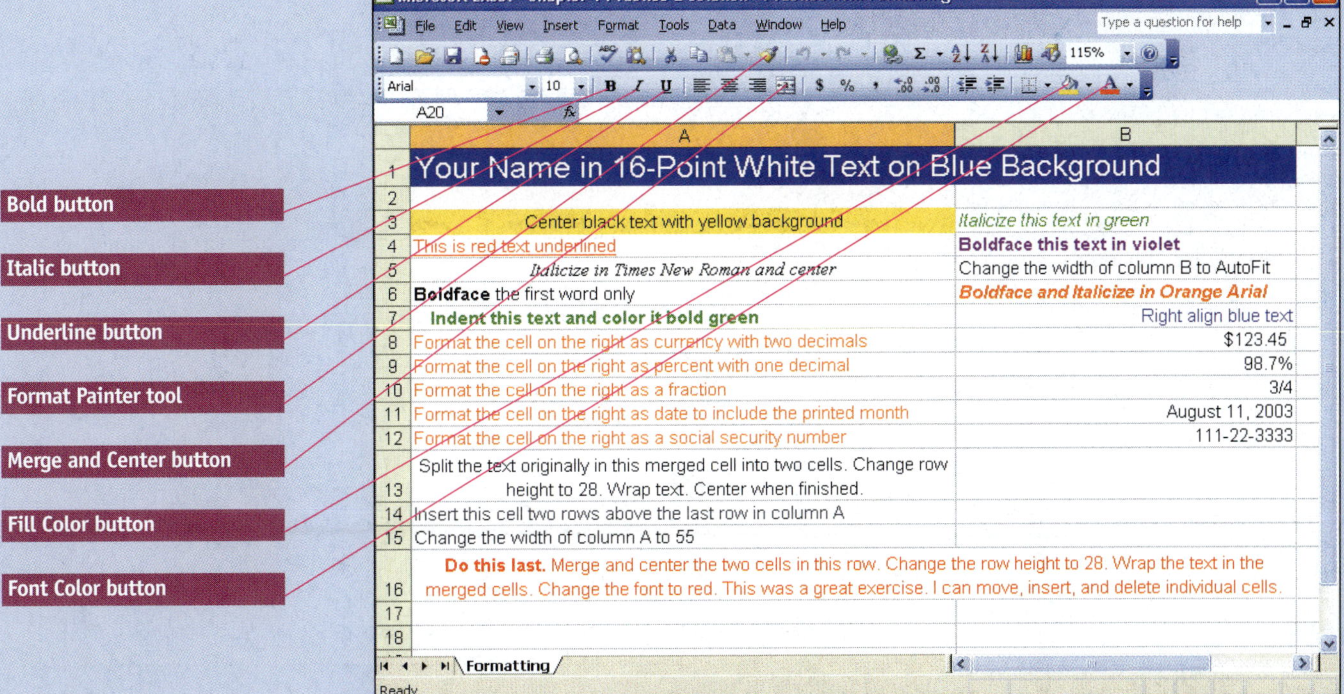

FIGURE 1.20 Practice with Formatting (exercise 2)

3. **The Calendar:** There are many way to create a calendar within Microsoft Office. The most important step, however, is to design the calendar with the computer off, then once you know the type of calendar (e.g., weekly or monthly) and the desired look, it is relatively easy to create regardless of the application.
   a. Start a new workbook. Click and drag to select cells D1 through F1, click the Merge and Center button, then change the format of the merged cells to text. Enter the month for which you will create the calendar—for example, October 2003 as shown in Figure 1.21. Click and drag to merge cells D2 through F2 in similar fashion, and enter your name. Change the row height, column width, font size, and color as appropriate.
   b. Click in cell B3 and enter "Sunday", the day on which our calendar will begin. Click and drag the fill handle to cells C3 to H3 to automatically enter the remaining days of the week (using the AutoFill capability within Excel).
   c. Click and drag to select cells B3 through H3 and click the Bold button. Pull down the Format menu, click the Cells command, click the Alignment tab, and then choose Center for the Vertical Alignment. Increase the row height to see the vertical alignment. Change the formatting of the text as desired.
   d. Click in the appropriate cell in row four (cell E4 in our figure) and enter 1 for the first day of the month. Enter the remaining days of the month in rows four through eight as appropriate, then increase the row height in rows 4 through 7 so that the calendar fills the page. (We specified a row height of 65.) Change the vertical alignment to the top of each cell and format the text as appropriate, for example, 14 point bold.
   e. Use the Insert Picture command to insert an appropriate piece of clip art. Complete the formatting by changing the fill color in cells B3 through H3, B3 through B8, and H3 through H8.
   f. Insert a second worksheet and create a weekly calendar. The calendar should show the days of the week going across the top, and the times of the day down the side. The rest of the design is up to you.
   g. Use the Page Setup command to change to landscape printing, then print both calendars for your instructor.

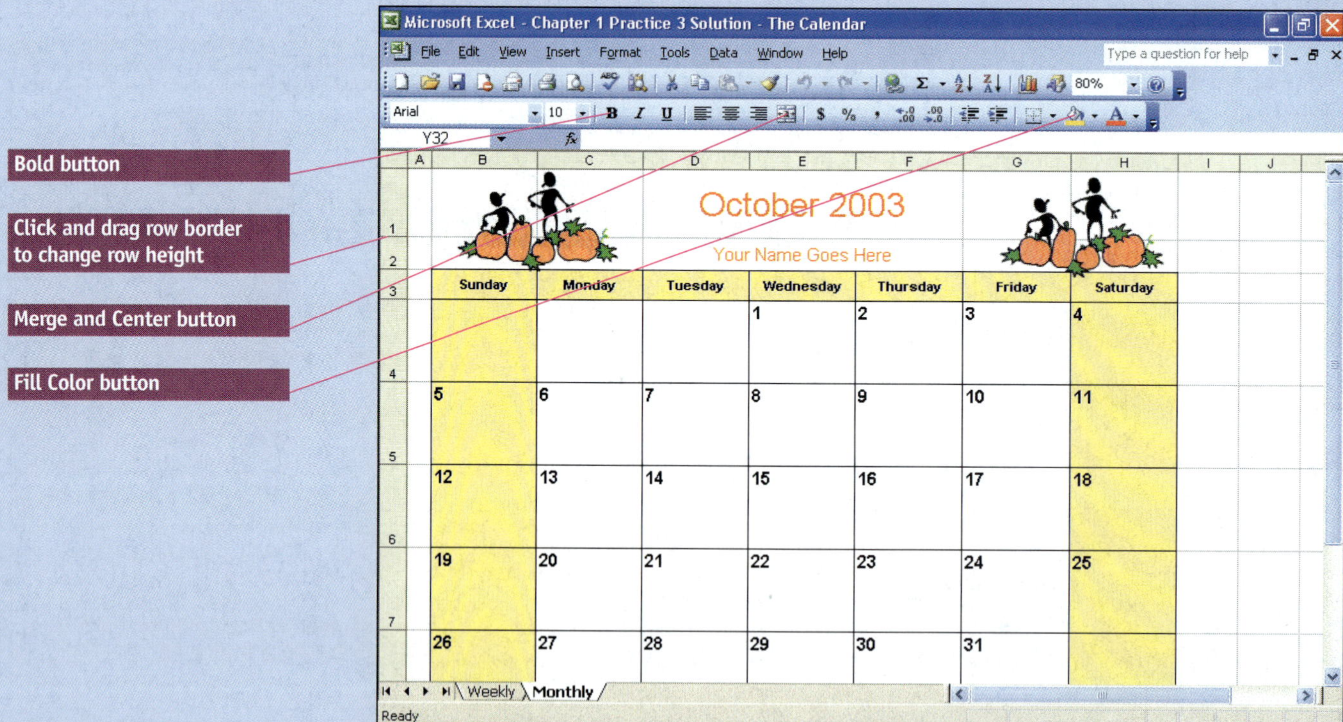

FIGURE 1.21 The Calendar (exercise 3)

4. **The Checkbook:** Figure 1.22 displays a worksheet that can be used to balance your checkbook. Your assignment is to create a similar worksheet using real or hypothetical data. Proceed as follows:
   a. Start Excel. If necessary, click the New button on the Standard toolbar to display a blank workbook. Click in cell A1 and enter the title with your name as shown. Enter the labels for cells A2 through F2. Do not worry about formatting at this time.
   b. Enter the initial balance in cell F3. Enter the data for your first check in row 4. To enter a date, just type the date without an equal sign; e.g., type 6/2 to display June 2 of the current year. Do not worry about the precise formatting at this time.
   c. Click in cell F4 and enter the formula to compute the balance. The formula should be entered in such a way that the balance is computed correctly, regardless of whether the transaction is a check (withdrawal) or deposit.
   d. Enter data for at least 6 additional transactions in cells A through E of the appropriate rows. Copy the formula to compute the balance for these transactions from cell F4.
   e. Skip one row after the last transaction, then enter the formulas to verify that the balance is correct. The formula for cell F18 (in our worksheet) is the initial balance, minus the sum of all checks and withdrawals, plus the sum of all deposits. The displayed value should equal the balance after the last transaction. Pull down the Insert menu and click the Comment command to enter a comment in that cell that explains the formula in cell F18.
   f. Format the completed worksheet as shown in Figure 1.22. You do not have to duplicate our formatting exactly, but you are to use date and currency formatting in the appropriate cells.
   g. Print the completed workbook to show both displayed values and cell formulas. Use the Page Setup command to display gridlines and row and column headings. Center the worksheet horizontally on the page. Create a custom header that contains your name, your school, and your instructor's name. Add a custom footer that contains the name of the workbook, and the date and time you completed the assignment.

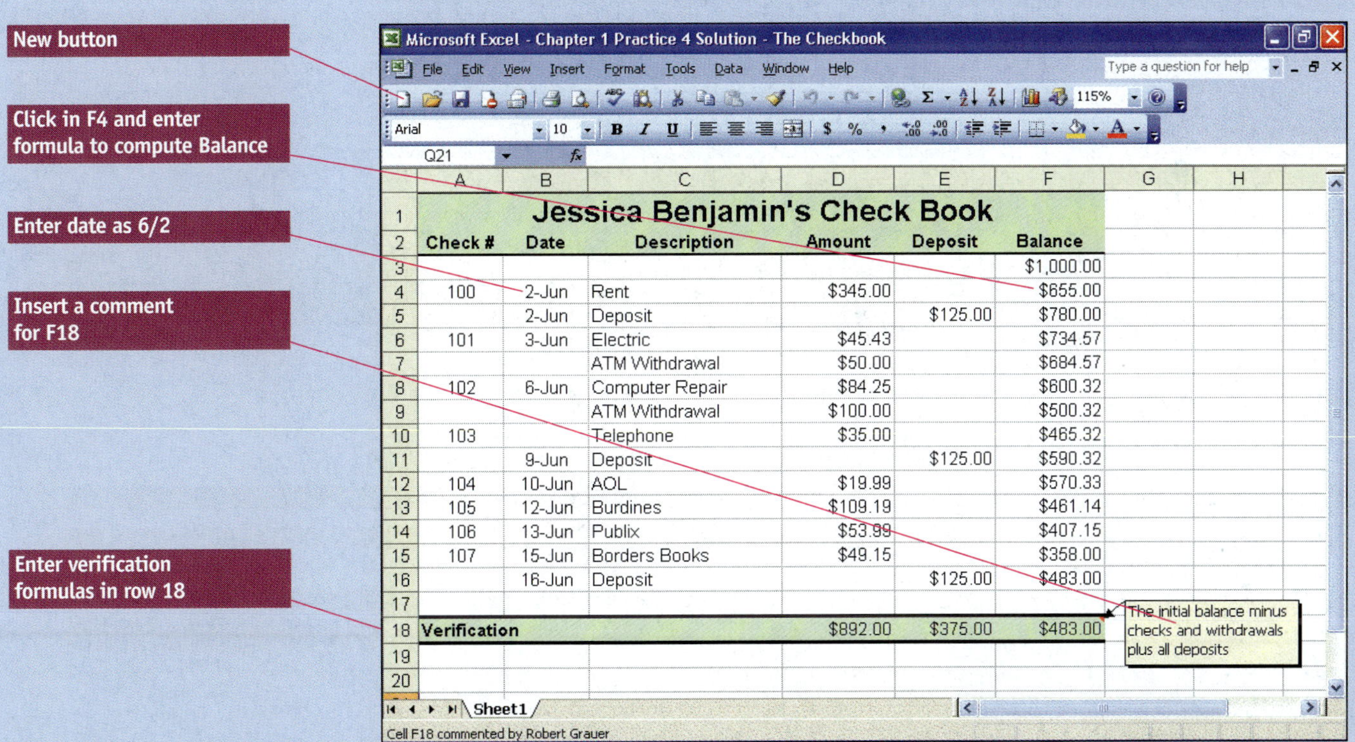

	A	B	C	D	E	F
1	Jessica Benjamin's Check Book					
2	Check #	Date	Description	Amount	Deposit	Balance
3						$1,000.00
4	100	2-Jun	Rent	$345.00		$655.00
5		2-Jun	Deposit		$125.00	$780.00
6	101	3-Jun	Electric	$45.43		$734.57
7			ATM Withdrawal	$50.00		$684.57
8	102	6-Jun	Computer Repair	$84.25		$600.32
9			ATM Withdrawal	$100.00		$500.32
10	103		Telephone	$35.00		$465.32
11		9-Jun	Deposit		$125.00	$590.32
12	104	10-Jun	AOL	$19.99		$570.33
13	105	12-Jun	Burdines	$109.19		$461.14
14	106	13-Jun	Publix	$53.99		$407.15
15	107	15-Jun	Borders Books	$49.15		$358.00
16		16-Jun	Deposit		$125.00	$483.00
17						
18	Verification			$892.00	$375.00	$483.00

FIGURE 1.22 The Checkbook (exercise 4)

5. **Judson Ford Realty:** The worksheet in Figure 1.23 displays the sales for Judson Ford Realty for the month of October. You can open a partially completed version of this worksheet in *Chapter 1 Practice 5*, but it is up to you to complete the worksheet so that it matches Figure 1.23. The notes in the worksheet and/or the column headings should be self-explanatory with respect to entering the various formulas, but the information is repeated below.
   a. The percentage of the asking price in cell E4 is the sales price divided by the asking price. Format the result as a percent with one decimal place.
   b. The price per square foot in cell F4 is the selling price divided by the number of square feet.
   c. The realtor's commission in cell G4 is a percentage of the selling price and is based on the commission percentage in cell B14.
   d. The net to the homeowner in cell H4 is the selling price minus the commission to the realtor.
   e. Copy the formulas in row 4 to the remaining rows in the worksheet.
   f. Format the worksheet in an appropriate fashion, but you need not match our formatting exactly. Note, too, that we have wrapped the text in row 3 in order to use a narrower column width. (Select cells A3 through H3, pull down the Format Cells command, click the Alignment tab, then check the box to wrap text.)
   g. Compute the agency statistics as shown in row 12. Use the Average, Max, and Min functions in cells H17 through H19 to display these values for the properties that were sold during the month.
   h. Use the Find and Replace command to change the text in the various addresses. Change all occurrences of "Str" to "Street", "Rd" to "Road", and "Ave" to "Avenue". You also need to replace the Courier New font with Arial throughout the worksheet.
   i. Add your name in cell G14, then print the worksheet to show both displayed values and cell formulas. Change to landscape printing and add a custom header and/or a custom footer.
   j. Create a cover sheet, then submit the assignment to your instructor.

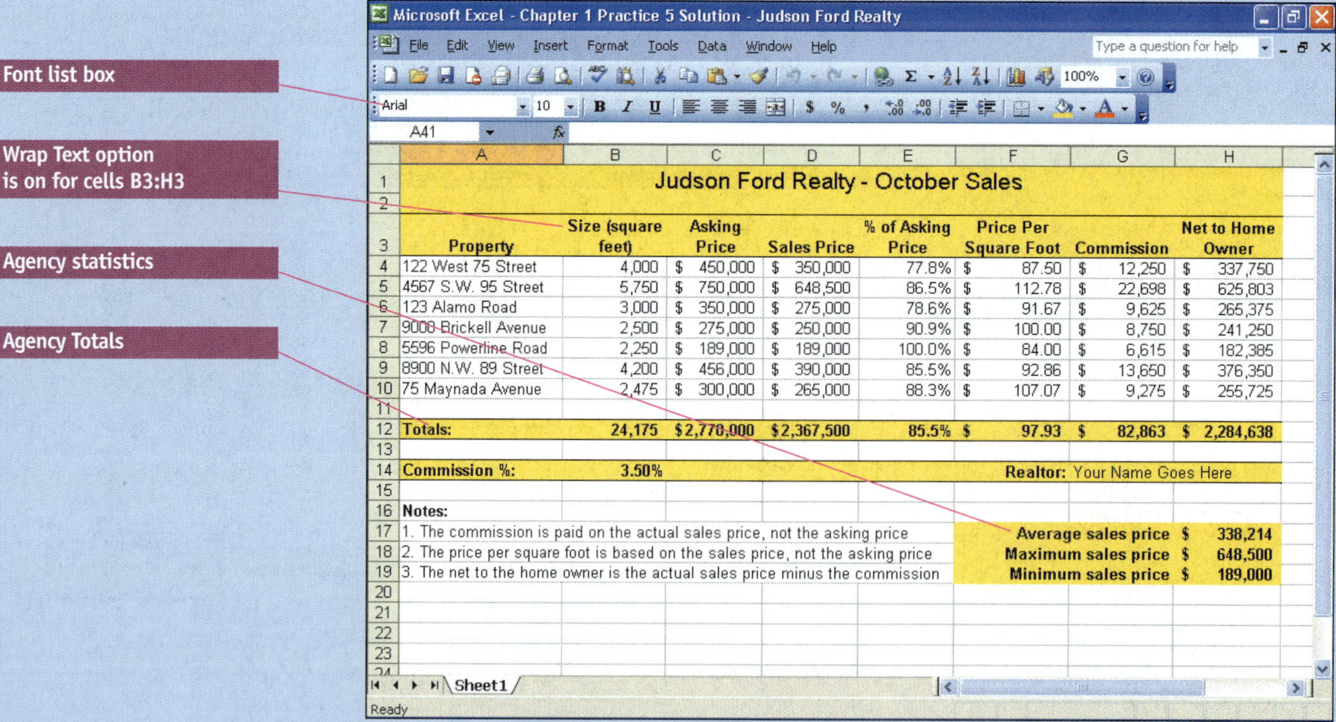

	A	B	C	D	E	F	G	H
1	Judson Ford Realty - October Sales							
2								
3	Property	Size (square feet)	Asking Price	Sales Price	% of Asking Price	Price Per Square Foot	Commission	Net to Home Owner
4	122 West 75 Street	4,000	$ 450,000	$ 350,000	77.8%	$ 87.50	$ 12,250	$ 337,750
5	4567 S.W. 95 Street	5,750	$ 750,000	$ 648,500	86.5%	$ 112.78	$ 22,698	$ 625,803
6	123 Alamo Road	3,000	$ 350,000	$ 275,000	78.6%	$ 91.67	$ 9,625	$ 265,375
7	9000 Brickell Avenue	2,500	$ 275,000	$ 250,000	90.9%	$ 100.00	$ 8,750	$ 241,250
8	5596 Powerline Road	2,250	$ 189,000	$ 189,000	100.0%	$ 84.00	$ 6,615	$ 182,385
9	8900 N.W. 89 Street	4,200	$ 456,000	$ 390,000	85.5%	$ 92.86	$ 13,650	$ 376,350
10	75 Maynada Avenue	2,475	$ 300,000	$ 265,000	88.3%	$ 107.07	$ 9,275	$ 255,725
11								
12	**Totals:**	**24,175**	**$2,770,000**	**$2,367,500**	**85.5%**	**$ 97.93**	**$ 82,863**	**$ 2,284,638**
13								
14	**Commission %:**	**3.50%**					**Realtor:**	Your Name Goes Here
15								
16	**Notes:**							
17	1. The commission is paid on the actual sales price, not the asking price						**Average sales price**	**$ 338,214**
18	2. The price per square foot is based on the sales price, not the asking price						**Maximum sales price**	**$ 648,500**
19	3. The net to the home owner is the actual sales price minus the commission						**Minimum sales price**	**$ 189,000**

FIGURE 1.23 Judson Ford Realty (exercise 5)

6. **The Solar System:** The potential uses of a spreadsheet are limited only by your imagination as can be seen by Figure 1.24, which displays a spreadsheet with information about our solar system. Open the partially completed version of the workbook in *Chapter 1 Practice 6*, then complete the worksheet by developing the formulas for the first planet, copying those formulas to the remaining rows in the worksheet, then formatting appropriately.
   a. Click in cell C15 and enter your weight on Earth. You can specify your weight in pounds rather than kilograms.
   b. Click in cell C16 and enter the function =Pi() as shown in Figure 1.23. The displayed value for the cell shows the value of Pi to several decimal places. The contents of the cell, however, contain the indicated function as can be seen in the formula bar.
   c. Click in cell D4 and enter the formula to compute the diameter of the first planet (Mercury). The diameter of a planet is equal to twice its radius.
   d. Click in cell E4 and enter the formula to compute the circumference of a planet. The circumference is equal to the diameter times the constant Pi.
   e. Click in cell F4 and enter the formula to compute the surface area, which is equal to four times Pi times the radius squared. (This is the formula to compute the surface area of a sphere, which is different from the formula to compute the area of a circle.)
   f. Click in cell G4 and enter the formula to compute your weight on Mercury, which is your weight on Earth times the relative gravity of Mercury compared to that of Earth.
   g. Copy the formulas in row 4 to the remainder of the worksheet, then format the worksheet appropriately. You need not copy our formatting exactly. Add your name in cell E15 as indicated.
   h. The worksheet contains a hyperlink to a Web site by Bill Arnett, which has additional information about the planets. If you click the hyperlink within Excel, your browser will open automatically, and you will be connected to the site, provided you have an Internet connection.
   i. Print the worksheet two ways, once with displayed values, and once to show the cell contents. Use landscape orientation and appropriate scaling so that the worksheet fits on a single page.

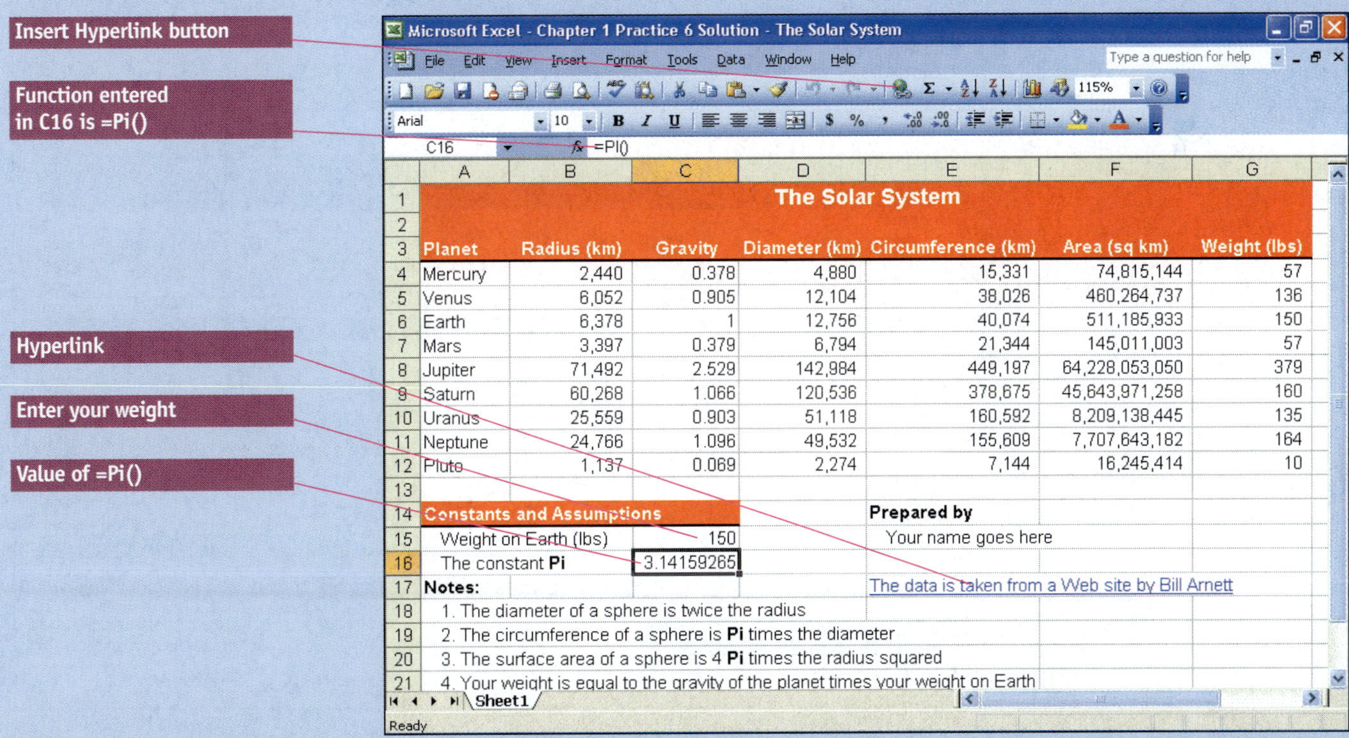

Planet	Radius (km)	Gravity	Diameter (km)	Circumference (km)	Area (sq km)	Weight (lbs)
Mercury	2,440	0.378	4,880	15,331	74,815,144	57
Venus	6,052	0.905	12,104	38,026	460,264,737	136
Earth	6,378	1	12,756	40,074	511,185,933	150
Mars	3,397	0.379	6,794	21,344	145,011,003	57
Jupiter	71,492	2.529	142,984	449,197	64,228,053,050	379
Saturn	60,268	1.066	120,536	378,675	45,643,971,258	160
Uranus	25,559	0.903	51,118	160,592	8,209,138,445	135
Neptune	24,766	1.096	49,532	155,609	7,707,643,182	164
Pluto	1,137	0.069	2,274	7,144	16,245,414	10

Constants and Assumptions
Weight on Earth (lbs) 150
The constant **Pi** 3.14159265

Prepared by
Your name goes here

Notes:
1. The diameter of a sphere is twice the radius
2. The circumference of a sphere is **Pi** times the diameter
3. The surface area of a sphere is 4 **Pi** times the radius squared
4. Your weight is equal to the gravity of the planet times your weight on Earth

The data is taken from a Web site by Bill Arnett

FIGURE 1.24 The Solar System (exercise 6)

7. **Student Budget:** Figure 1.25 displays a hypothetical budget for a nine-month academic year. You can use the partially completed version of this worksheet in the *Chapter 1 Practice 7* workbook, or you can create your own budget. If you use our file, then the totals in your worksheet should correspond exactly to those in Figure 1.25, whereas if you create your own budget, the numbers will differ. The worksheet is straightforward, but we want to call your attention to the following:
   a. Enter the data (the labels for the various income and expense categories as well as the specific amounts) in the body of the worksheet.
   b. Use the Sum function in cell K4 to compute the total for the first income source for the academic year. Copy this formula to the remaining cells in this column.
   c. Use the Sum function in cell B8 to compute the total income for September. Copy this formula to the remaining cells in this row. (The total income for the year can be obtained by summing either cells K4 through K7 or cells B8 through J8.) Use a similar approach to determine the total expenses for each month in row 18.
   d. Compute the deficit or surplus for each month in row 20. If necessary, adjust your numbers to show at least one month where you run a deficit. Negative numbers should be formatted in red and be enclosed in parentheses.
   e. Compute the minimum and maximum monthly expense in cells B22 and B23, respectively.
   f. Merge and center the cells in row 1, and enter your name to identify the worksheet as your own. Format it appropriately. Print the worksheet two ways, to show both displayed values and cell formulas, then submit both pages to your instructor. Be sure to use the Page Setup command to specify landscape printing, and appropriate scaling so that the entire worksheet fits on a single page.
   g. Extend the exercise by exploring potential sources for financial aid. Your school or university may offer scholarships or work study programs of which you are currently unaware. Outside agencies may provide similar help. Summarize your findings and bring them to class for discussion.

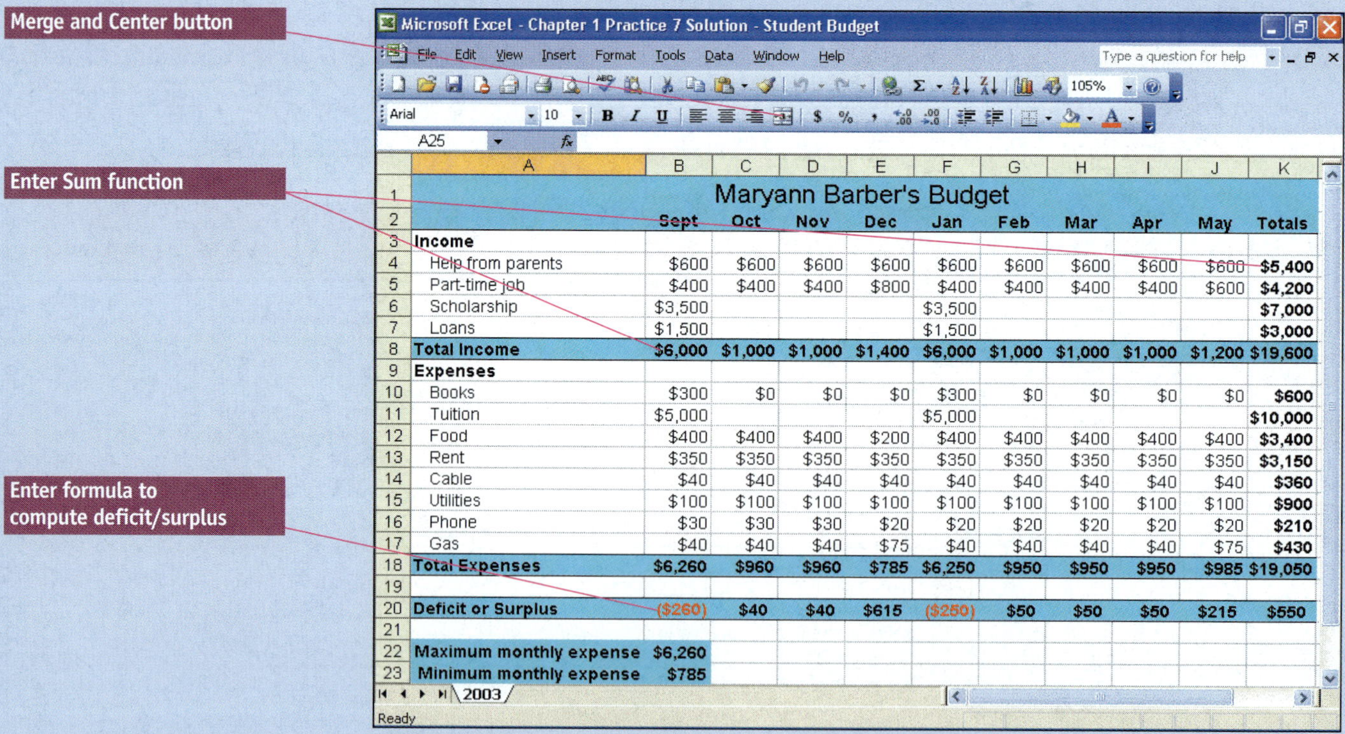

Merge and Center button

Enter Sum function

Enter formula to compute deficit/surplus

Microsoft Excel - Chapter 1 Practice 7 Solution - Student Budget

File Edit View Insert Format Tools Data Window Help

A25

	A	B	C	D	E	F	G	H	I	J	K
1	Maryann Barber's Budget										
2		Sept	Oct	Nov	Dec	Jan	Feb	Mar	Apr	May	Totals
3	Income										
4	Help from parents	$600	$600	$600	$600	$600	$600	$600	$600	$600	$5,400
5	Part-time job	$400	$400	$400	$800	$400	$400	$400	$400	$600	$4,200
6	Scholarship	$3,500				$3,500					$7,000
7	Loans	$1,500				$1,500					$3,000
8	Total Income	$6,000	$1,000	$1,000	$1,400	$6,000	$1,000	$1,000	$1,000	$1,200	$19,600
9	Expenses										
10	Books	$300	$0	$0	$0	$300	$0	$0	$0	$0	$600
11	Tuition	$5,000				$5,000					$10,000
12	Food	$400	$400	$400	$200	$400	$400	$400	$400	$400	$3,400
13	Rent	$350	$350	$350	$350	$350	$350	$350	$350	$350	$3,150
14	Cable	$40	$40	$40	$40	$40	$40	$40	$40	$40	$360
15	Utilities	$100	$100	$100	$100	$100	$100	$100	$100	$100	$900
16	Phone	$30	$30	$30	$20	$20	$20	$20	$20	$20	$210
17	Gas	$40	$40	$40	$75	$40	$40	$40	$40	$75	$430
18	Total Expenses	$6,260	$960	$960	$785	$6,250	$950	$950	$950	$985	$19,050
19											
20	Deficit or Surplus	($260)	$40	$40	$615	($250)	$50	$50	$50	$215	$550
21											
22	Maximum monthly expense	$6,260									
23	Minimum monthly expense	$785									

2003

Ready

FIGURE 1.25 Student Budget (exercise 7)

8. **Excel Templates:** This chapter introduced you to the basics of Excel and showed you how to create your own spreadsheets. It is often convenient, however, to use a workbook that was created by someone else that is tailored to a specific application. This type of workbook is called a template and it contains text, formulas, and formatting, but no specific data. Proceed as follows:
   a. Start Excel. Pull down the View menu to display the task pane, then click the down arrow in the task pane to display the New Workbook task pane. Look in the Other templates area and click the link to On My Computer to display the Templates dialog box. Click the Spreadsheet Solutions tab.
   b. You should see several templates that were installed locally with the installation of Microsoft Office. Select the *Timecard* template and click OK. (You can open the *Chapter 1 Practice 8* workbook in the Exploring Excel folder if this template is not available on your system.)
   c. Click in cell E10, type your name, and press the Tab key to move to cell I10. Enter your student number (do not be concerned that the worksheet asks for an employee number rather than a student number). Press the Tab key to move to cell M9 where you enter the note in Figure 1.26.
   d. Click in cell D20 and type the name of the first course you are taking. Use the Tab key to move across the row to enter your study hours for the week. You cannot, however, move to column Q because the total is calculated automatically. Click in cell D22 and start to enter the data for your second course. Enter the data for your remaining courses in similar fashion.
   e. The worksheet is currently protected, which means you cannot change the contents of the cells containing labels and formulas. Pull down the Tools menu, click Protection, and then click the Unprotect Sheet command. (A password is not required.) You can now modify the worksheet to fit your specific application, for example, logging study hours instead of an employee worksheet. Click in cell P5 and enter Study Hours. Make additional modifications as you see fit. (We changed the name of the worksheet tab to Study Schedule.) Print the completed worksheet for your instructor. Save the workbook as *Chapter 1 Practice 8 Solution—Study Schedule.*

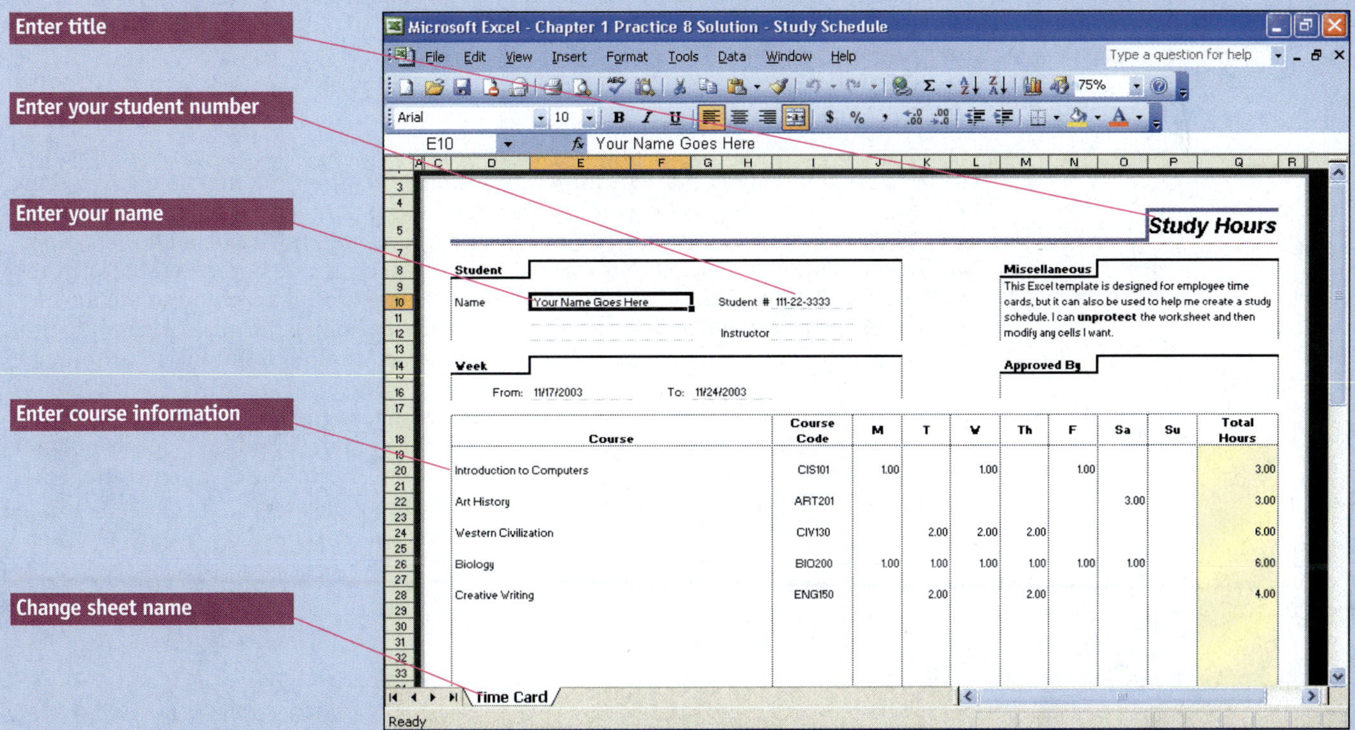

FIGURE 1.26 Excel Templates (exercise 8)

MINI CASES

The Movies

The partially completed *Chapter 1 Mini Case—The Movies* workbook in the Exploring Excel folder is intended to compute the weekly revenue for a chain of movie theatres. The revenue includes income from day and evening tickets as well as the food concession. Complete the workbook by using the appropriate combination of relative and absolute references in your cell formulas so that you can copy the formulas from the first theatre to the remaining rows in the worksheet. If you do the assignment correctly, your worksheet should display total revenue of $455,625. Format the completed worksheet as appropriate. Place your name somewhere in the worksheet, then print the worksheet two ways, to show both displayed values and cell formulas, then submit both pages to your instructor. Be sure to use the Page Setup command to specify landscape printing, and appropriate scaling so that the entire worksheet fits on a single page.

The Cost of Smoking

Smoking is hazardous to your health as well as your pocketbook. A one-pack-a-day habit, at $3/pack, will cost you more than $1000 per year. For the same money you could buy 20 concert tickets at $50 each, or more than 700 gallons of gas at $1.50 per gallon. Open the partially completed *Chapter 1 Mini Case—Cost of Smoking* workbook and compute the number of various items that you could buy over the course of a year in lieu of cigarettes. We have entered approximate prices, but you need not use our numbers and/or you can substitute additional items of your own.

Accuracy Counts

The *Chapter 1 Mini Case—Underbid* workbook in the Exploring Excel folder was the last assignment completed by your predecessor prior to his unfortunate dismissal. The worksheet contains a significant error, which caused your company to underbid a contract and assume a subsequent loss of $100,000. As you look for the error, don't be distracted by the attractive formatting. The shading, lines, and other touches are nice, but accuracy is more important than anything else. Write a memo to your instructor describing the nature of the error. Include suggestions in the memo on how to avoid mistakes of this nature in the future.

The Housing Office

The partially completed *Chapter 1 Mini Case—Housing Office* workbook in the Exploring Excel folder is intended to compute the revenue for the dorms on campus. The revenue includes the income from single rooms, double rooms, and the associated meal plans. Your assignment is to complete the workbook. If you do the assignment correctly, the total revenue for Lincoln Hall should be $4,392,500. Pay special attention to the formula for the meal plan revenue (cell G4 for the first residence hall), which uses a combination of relative and absolute addresses. Note, too, that each double room has two students, each of whom is required to pay for the meal plan. Format the completed worksheet as appropriate. Place your name somewhere in the worksheet, then print the worksheet two ways, to show both displayed values and cell formulas, then submit both pages to your instructor. Be sure to use the Page Setup command to specify landscape printing, and appropriate scaling so that the entire worksheet fits on a single page.

CHAPTER

2

Gaining Proficiency: The Web and Business Applications

OBJECTIVES

After reading this chapter you will:

1. Gain proficiency in using relative and absolute references to create a worksheet.
2. Explain the importance of isolating assumptions in a worksheet.
3. Use the fill handle to copy a formula to adjacent cells.
4. Use pointing to enter a formula.
5. Insert a hyperlink into a worksheet.
6. Save a worksheet as a Web page, and then view the page in a Web browser.
7. Import data from a Web query into a workbook; refresh the query to obtain current information.
8. Describe the Today() function and its use in date arithmetic.

hands-on exercises

1. PAYROLL
   Input: Payroll
   Output: Payroll Solution
2. CREATING A WEB PAGE
   Input: Statement of Earnings
   Output: Statement of Earnings Solution (workbook and MHT document)
3. WEB QUERIES
   Input: Stock Portfolio
   Output: Stock Portfolio Solution

CASE STUDY

THE PROPER TIP

There is no perfect answer to the question, "how much to tip." It helps to realize, however, that the word "tip" is an acronym for the phrase "to insure promptness." One should focus, therefore, on the server's ability to meet your requests: did he or she hustle and try to please you; was the server professional; did he or she try to rectify a bad situation if there was one? It is truly impolite to omit a tip even if the service was poor, but there is a range of amounts that sends a clear message to your server. This is generally accepted to be between 10% and 20% of the pretax total of the meal.

Lynne Breitfeller has decided to make the calculation easy for herself by creating a simple worksheet that will calculate the appropriate tip, based on the amount of the meal and the level of service. Lynne intends to make the worksheet completely general; she wants to be able to vary the suggested percentages and/or the amount of the bill and see the recommended tip. This is an unusual application, but it is intended to show that Excel can be applied to virtually any numeric calculation. ■

Your assignment is to read the chapter, paying special attention to Hands-on Exercises 1 and 2, which explain how to use relative and absolute references, and how to save and edit a Web page. You will then put yourself in Lynne's place and create a new workbook that calculates the suggested tip for poor, average, and excellent service on bills ranging from $10 to $200 in increments of $5. Use 10%, 15%, and 20% as the percentages for the different levels of service. Isolate all of the assumptions so that you can change the amount of the bill and/or the suggested percentages. Add a hyperlink to your favorite restaurant or dining etiquette Web site on the worksheet, then save the worksheet as a Web page. Print a copy of the completed worksheet to show both the displayed values and cell formulas. Print a second copy of the worksheet from your Internet browser.

This chapter introduces several new capabilities to increase your proficiency in Excel. We begin with pointing, which is a preferred way to enter a cell formula. We present the fill handle to facilitate copying a formula to other rows or columns within a worksheet. We introduce the Today() function and the use of date arithmetic. We also discuss the various Web capabilities that are built into Excel. You will learn how to add a hyperlink to a worksheet and how to save a worksheet as a Web page for viewing in a browser such as Internet Explorer or Netscape Navigator. You will also learn how to create a Web query to download information from the Web directly into an Excel worksheet.

The spreadsheet in Figure 2.1 shows how Excel can be used to compute a simple payroll. Figure 2.1a shows the displayed values and Figure 2.1b contains the underlying formulas. The concepts necessary to develop the spreadsheet were presented in the previous chapter. The intent here is to reinforce the earlier material, with emphasis on the use of ***relative*** and ***absolute references*** in the various cell formulas.

The calculation of an individual's gross pay depends on the employment practices of the organization. The formula used in the worksheet is simply an algebraic statement of how employees are paid, in this example, straight time for regular hours, and time-and-a-half for each hour of overtime. The first employee, Adams, earns $400 for 40 regular hours (40 hours at $10/hour) plus $60 for overtime (4 overtime hours × $10/hour × 1.5 for overtime). The formula to compute Adams's gross pay is entered into cell E2 as follows:

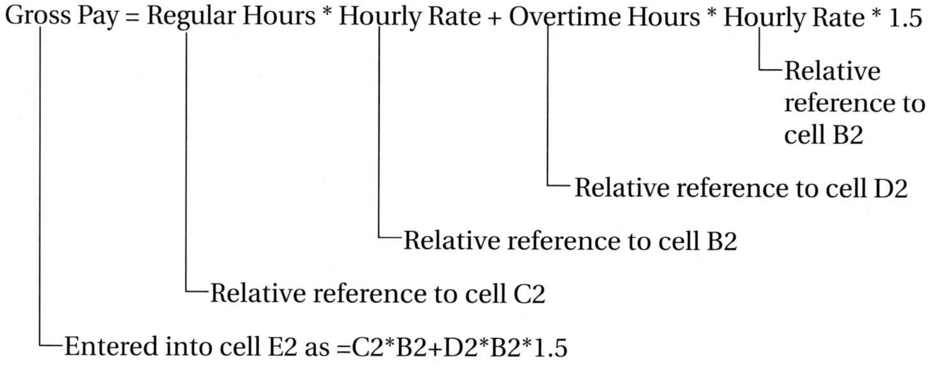

The cell references in the formula are relative references, which means that they will change when copied to another cell. Thus, you can copy the formula in cell E2 to the other rows in column E to compute the gross pay for the other employees. The formula in cell E3, for example, becomes =C3*B3+D3*B3*1.5, as can be seen from the displayed formulas in Figure 2.1b.

The withholding tax is computed by multiplying an individual's gross pay by the withholding tax rate. (This is an approximate calculation because the true withholding tax rate is implemented on a sliding scale; that is, the more an individual earns, the higher the tax rate. We use a uniform rate, however, to simplify the example.) The formula in cell F2 to compute the withholding tax uses a combination of relative and absolute references as follows:

Withholding Tax = Gross Pay * Withholding Rate

Absolute reference to cell C11

Relative reference to cell E2

Entered into cell F2 as =E2*$C$11

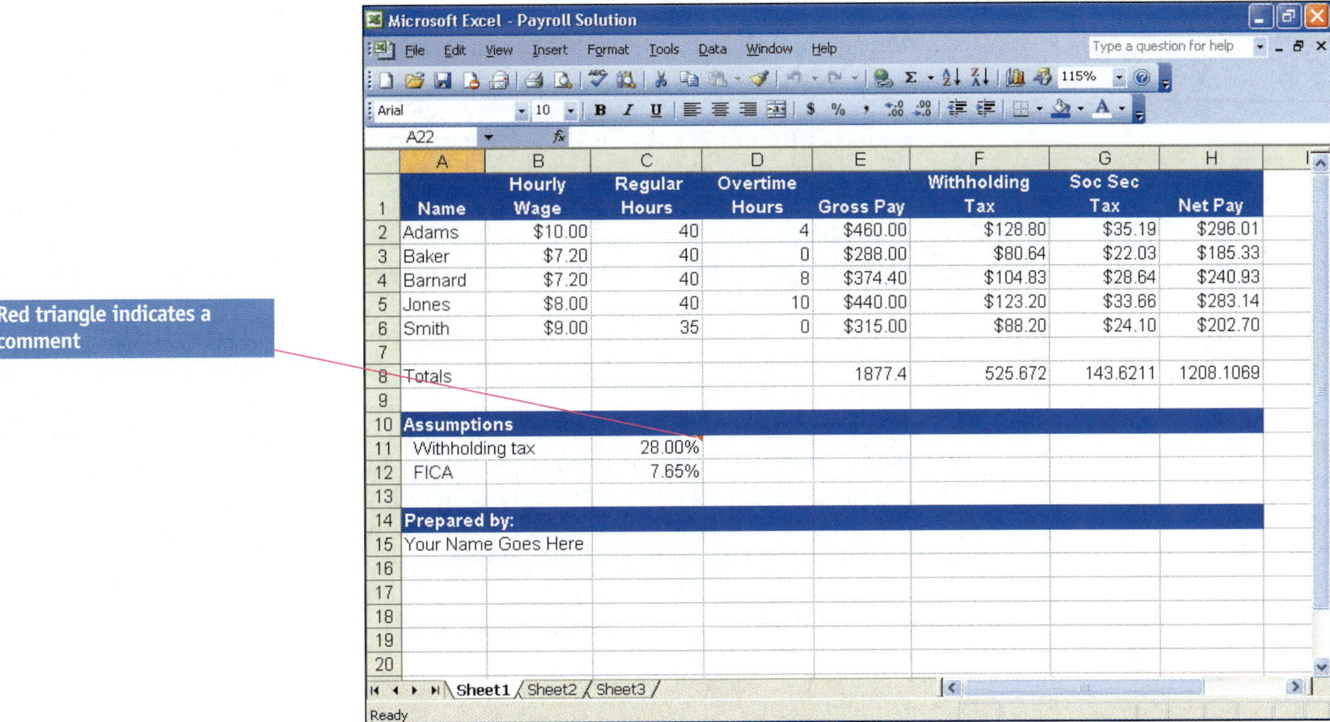

(a) Displayed Values

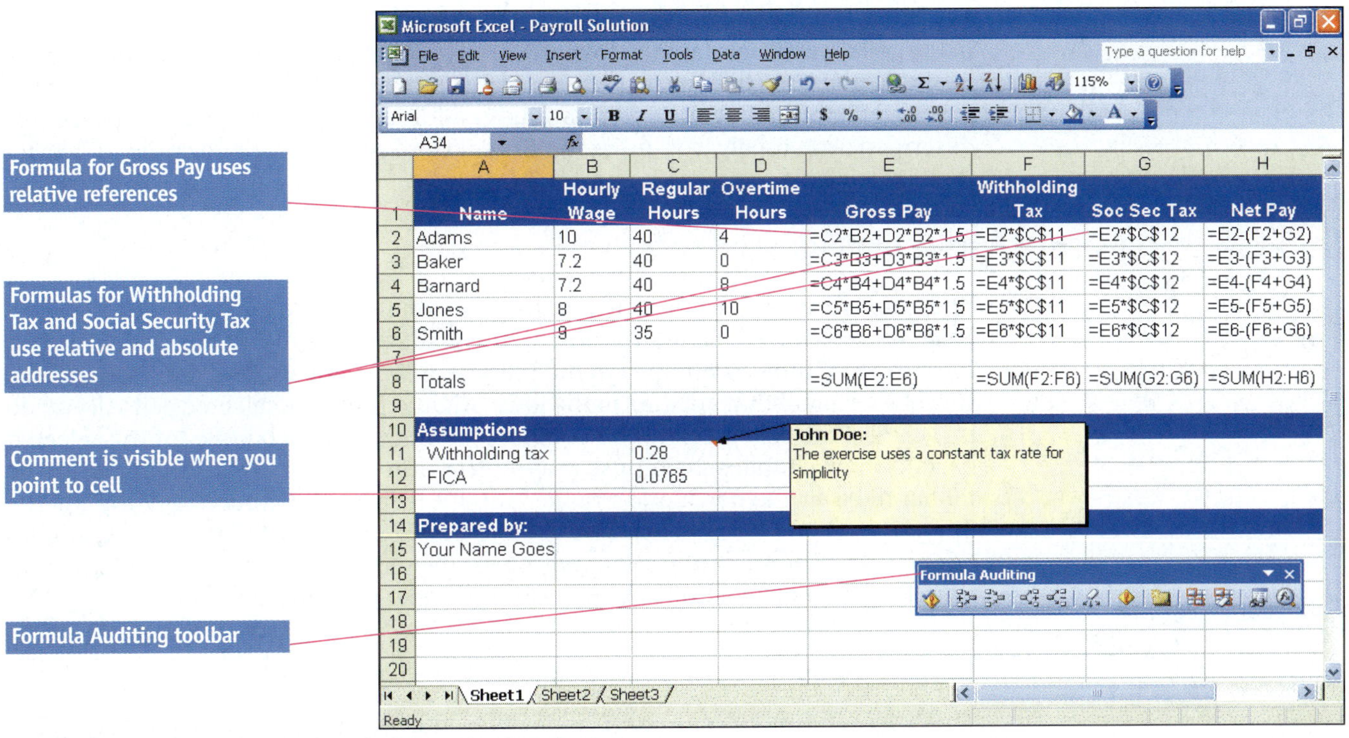

(b) Cell Formulas

FIGURE 2.1 Payroll

It is important to emphasize that the formula to compute the withholding tax contains an absolute reference to the tax rate (cell C11), as opposed to the actual constant (.28 in this example). The distinction may seem trivial, but most assuredly it is not, as two important objectives are achieved. First, the user sees those factors that affect the results of the spreadsheet in a separate assumption area (e.g., the withholding rate). Second, the user can change the value in one place, cell C11, then have the change automatically reflected in the calculations for all of the employees. The calculation of the employee's Social Security tax in cell G2 is performed in similar fashion and includes an absolute reference to cell C12.

The remaining formulas in the worksheet are also straightforward. An employee's net pay is computed by subtracting the deductions (the withholding tax and the Social Security tax) from the gross pay. Thus the net pay for the first employee is entered in cell H2 using the formula =E2–(F2+G2). The cell references are relative, which enables us to copy the formula to the remaining rows in column H, and thus calculate the net pay for the other employees.

The employee totals for gross pay, withholding tax, social security tax, and net pay are computed using the SUM function in the appropriate cells in row 8. The formula to compute the gross pay, =SUM(E2:E6), is entered into cell E8, after which it is copied to the remaining cells in row 8.

Pointing

Any cell reference can be entered into a formula by typing the address explicitly into a cell. Entering addresses in this way is not recommended, however, because it is all too easy to make a mistake, such as typing A40 when you really mean A41. ***Pointing*** to the cell is a more accurate method, since you use the mouse (or arrow keys) to select the cell directly when you build the formula. In essence you (1) Click in the cell that will contain the formula, (2) Type an equal sign to begin entering the formula, and (3) Click in the cell you want to reference. You then type any arithmetic operator, then continue pointing to additional cells using the steps we just described. And finally, you press the Enter key to complete the formula. It's easier than it sounds, and you get to practice in our next exercise.

The Fill Handle

There are several ways to copy the contents of a cell. You can use the Copy and Paste buttons on the Standard toolbar, the associated keyboard shortcuts, and/or the corresponding commands in the Edit menu. You can also use the ***fill handle,*** a tiny black square that appears in the lower-right corner of a selected cell. All you do is (1) Select the cell or cells to be copied, (2) Point to the fill handle for the selected cell(s), which changes the mouse pointer to a thin crosshair, (3) Click and drag the fill handle over the destination range, and (4) Release the mouse to complete the operation. (The fill handle can be used to copy only to adjacent cells.) Again, it's easier than it sounds, and as you may have guessed, it's time for our next hands-on exercise, in which you build the payroll worksheet in Figure 2.1.

Comments

The ***Insert Comment command*** creates the equivalent of a ScreenTip that displays information about the worksheet. Cell C11 in Figure 2.1a contains a tiny red triangle to indicate the presence of a comment, which appears as a ScreenTip when you point to the cell, as shown in Figure 2.1b. (An option can be set to display the comment permanently, but most people opt for just the triangle.) Comments may be subsequently edited, or deleted altogether if they are no longer appropriate.

hands-on exercise

1 Payroll

Objective Develop a spreadsheet for a simplified payroll to illustrate relative and absolute references. Use pointing to enter formulas and the fill handle to copy formulas. Use Figure 2.2 as a guide in the exercise.

Step 1: Compute the Gross Pay

- Start Excel. Open the **Payroll workbook** in the **Exploring Excel folder** to display the worksheet in Figure 2.2a.
- Save the workbook as **Payroll Solution** so that you may return to the original workbook if necessary.
- Click in **cell E2,** the cell that contains the gross pay for the first employee. Press the **equal sign** on the keyboard to begin pointing, click in **cell C2** (which produces a moving border around the cell), press the **Asterisk key**, then click in **cell B2**. You have entered the first part of the formula to compute an employee's gross pay.
- Press the **plus sign**, click in **cell D2**, press the **Asterisk**, click in **cell B2**, press the **Asterisk**, type **1.5**, then press **Enter**. You should see 460 as the displayed value for cell E2.
- Click in **cell E2**, then check to be sure that the formula you entered matches the formula in the formula bar in Figure 2.2a. If necessary, click in the formula bar and make the appropriate changes so that you have the correct formula in cell E2.
- Enter your name in cell A15. Save the workbook.

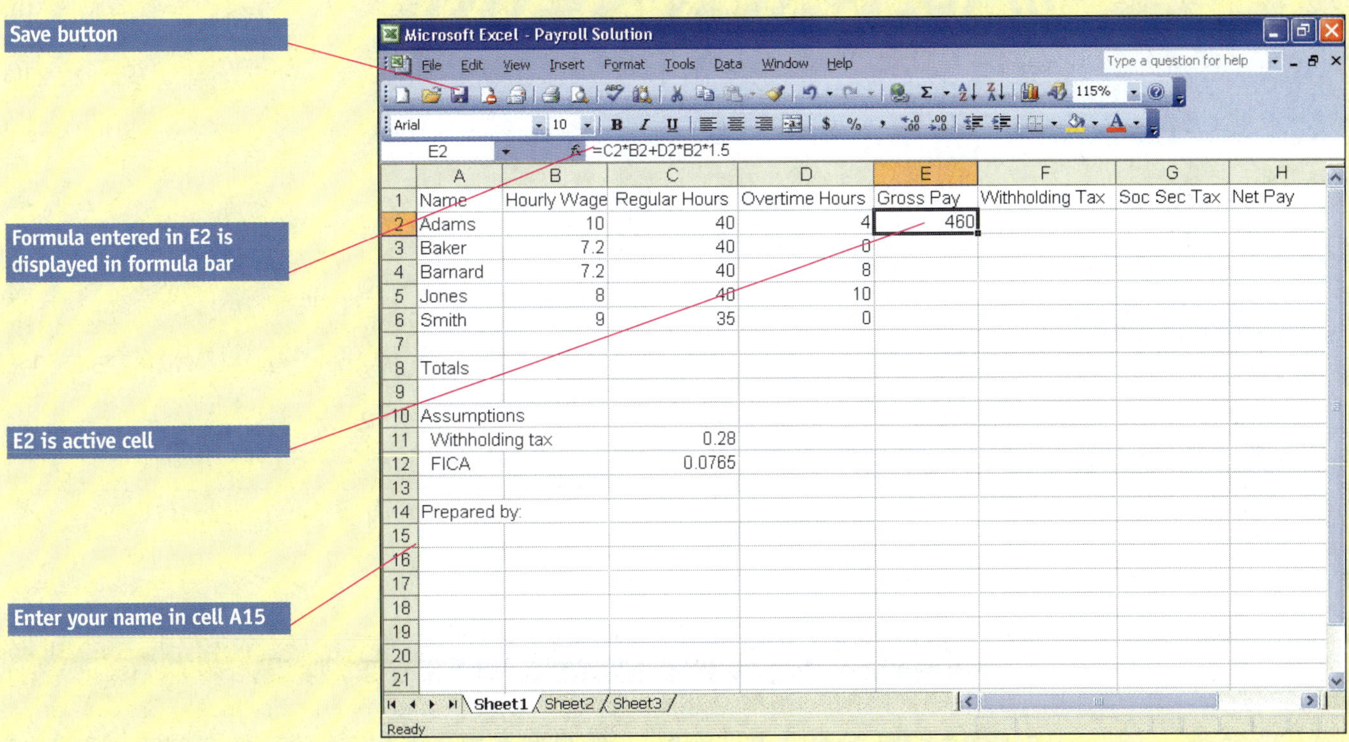

(a) Compute the Gross Pay (step 1)

FIGURE 2.2 Hands-on Exercise 1

Step 2: Complete the Calculations

- Click in **cell F2**, the cell that contains the withholding tax for the first employee. Press the **equal sign** on the keyboard to begin pointing, then click in **cell E2**, the cell that contains the employee's gross pay.
- Press the **Asterisk key**, then click in **cell C11**, the cell that contains the withholding tax. Cell F2 should now contain the formula, =E2*C11, but this is not quite correct.
- Check that the insertion point (the flashing vertical line) is within (or immediately behind) the reference to cell C11, then press the **F4 key** to change the cell reference to $C$11 as shown in Figure 2.2b.
- Press **Enter**. The displayed value in cell F2 should be 128.8, corresponding to the withholding tax for this employee.
- Use pointing to enter the remaining formulas for the first employee. Click in **cell G2**, then enter the formula **=E2*$C$12**. The displayed value is 35.19, corresponding to the Social Security Tax.
- Click in **cell H2**, and enter the formula **=E2–(F2+G2)**. The displayed value is 296.01, corresponding to the net pay for this individual.
- Save the workbook.

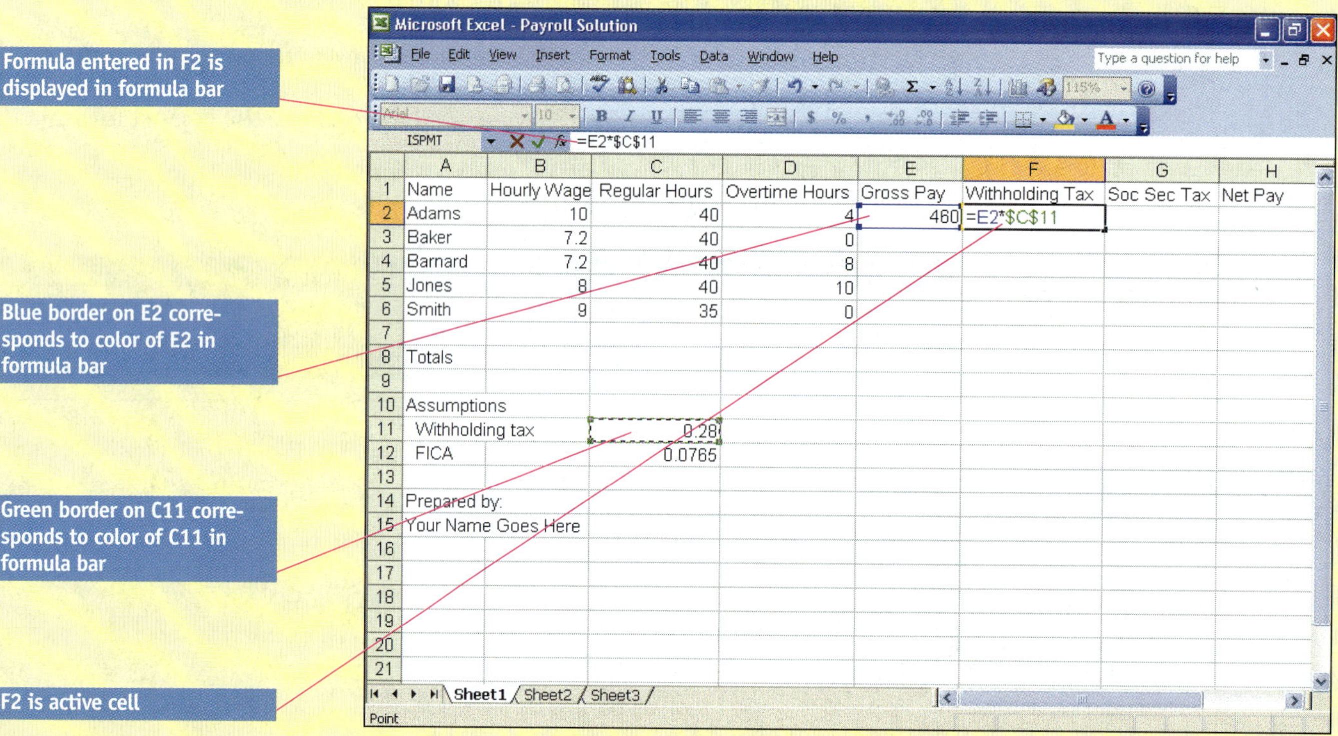

(b) Complete the Calculations (step 2)

FIGURE 2.2 Hands-on Exercise 1 (*continued*)

THE F4 KEY

The F4 key cycles through relative, absolute, and mixed references. Click on any reference within the formula bar; for example, click on A1 in the formula =A1+A2. Press the F4 key once, and it changes to an absolute reference. Press the F4 key a second time, and it becomes a mixed reference, A$1; press it again, and it is a different mixed reference, $A1. Press the F4 key a fourth time, and return to the original relative reference, A1.

Step 3: Copy the Formulas

- Click in **cell E2**, then click and drag to select **cells E2:H2**, as shown in Figure 2.2c. Point to the **fill handle** in the lower-right corner of cell H2. The mouse pointer changes to a thin crosshair.
- Drag the **fill handle** to cell H6 (the lower-right cell in the range of employee calculations). A dim border appears as you drag the fill handle as shown in Figure 2.2c.
- Release the mouse to complete the copy operation. The formulas for the first employee have been copied to the corresponding rows for the other employees.
- Click in **cell E3**, the cell containing the gross pay for the second employee. You should see the formula =C3*B3+D3*B3*1.5. Now click in **cell F3**, the cell containing the withholding tax for the second employee.
- You should see the formula =E3*$C$11, which contains a relative reference (cell E3) that is adjusted from one row to the next, and an absolute reference (cell $C$11) that remains constant from one employee to the next.
- Save the workbook.

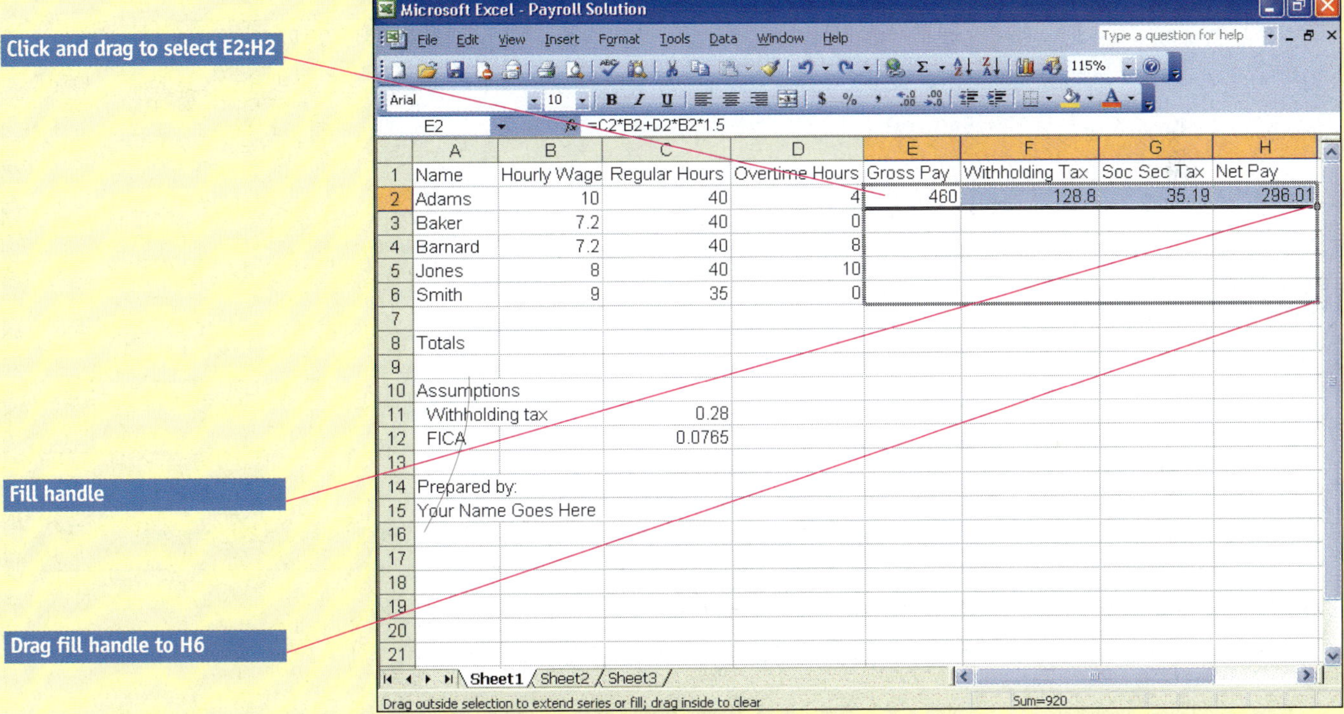

(c) Copy the Formulas (step 3)

FIGURE 2.2 Hands-on Exercise 1 (*continued*)

IT'S ONLY ALGEBRA

There are several ways to enter the formula to compute an employee's gross pay. You could, for example, factor out the hourly rate and enter the formula as =B3*(C3+D3*1.5). It doesn't matter how you enter the formula as long as the results are algebraically correct. What is important is the combination of relative and absolute references, so that the formula is copied correctly from one row to the next.

Step 4: Compute the Totals

- Click in **cell E8**, the cell that is to contain the total gross pay for all employees. Type the **=sign**, type **SUM(**, then click and drag over **cells E2** through **E6**.
- Type a **closing parenthesis**, and then press **Enter** to complete the formula. Cell E8 should display the value 1877.4. Now click in **cell E8** and you should see the function, =SUM(E2:E6).
- Click and drag the **fill handle** in cell E8 to the remaining cells in this row (cells F8 through H8). Release the mouse to complete the copy operation.
- You should see 1208.1069 in cell H8, corresponding to the total net pay for all employees. Click in **cell H8** to view the formula, =SUM(H2:H6), which results from the copy operation.
- Save the workbook.

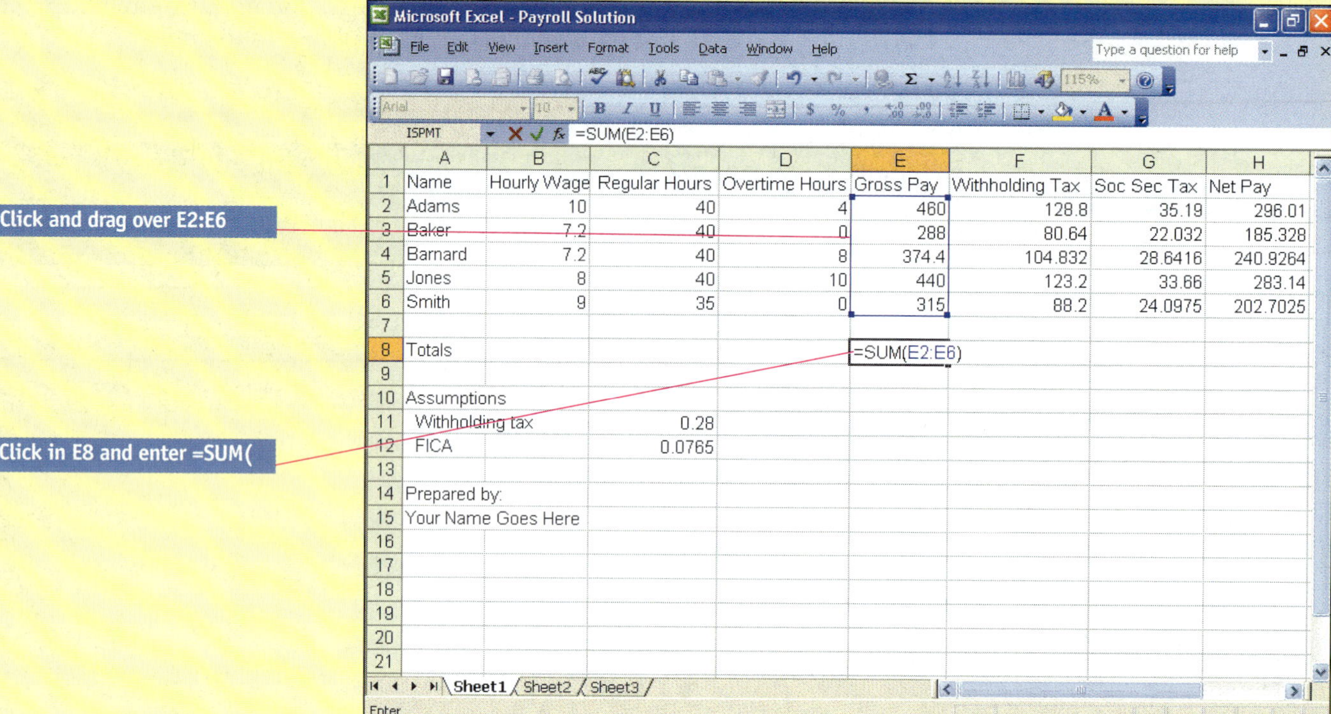

(d) Compute the Totals (step 4)

FIGURE 2.2 Hands-on Exercise 1 (*continued*)

FORMULAS VERSUS FUNCTIONS

There are in essence two ways to compute the total gross pay for all employees, using the SUM function, or the equivalent formula (e.g., =E2+E3+E4+E5+E6). The function is preferable for two reasons. First, it's easier to enter, and therefore less prone to error. Second, the function adjusts automatically to include any additional employees that will be entered within the cell range. Try inserting a new employee between the existing employees in rows 3 and 4, then observe how the values for this employee will be included automatically in the computed totals. The function also adjusts for deleted rows, whereas the formula does not.

Step 5: Format the Spreadsheet

- Click in **cell B2**, then click and drag to select **cells B2** through **B6**. Press and hold the **Ctrl key** as you click and drag to select cells **E2** through **H8** (in addition to the previously selected cells).
- Pull down the **Format menu** and click the **Cells command** to display the Format Cells dialog box in Figure 2.2e. Click the **Number tab** and choose **Currency** from the Category list box. Specify **2** as the number of decimal places.
- If necessary, choose the **$ sign** as the currency symbol. (Note, too, that you can select a variety of alternative symbols such as the British Pound or the Euro symbol for the European Community.) Click **OK** to accept the settings and close the dialog box.
- Click and drag to select **cells C11** and **C12**, then click the **Percent Style button** on the Formatting toolbar. Click the **Increase/Decrease Decimals buttons** to format each number to two decimal places.
- Save the workbook.

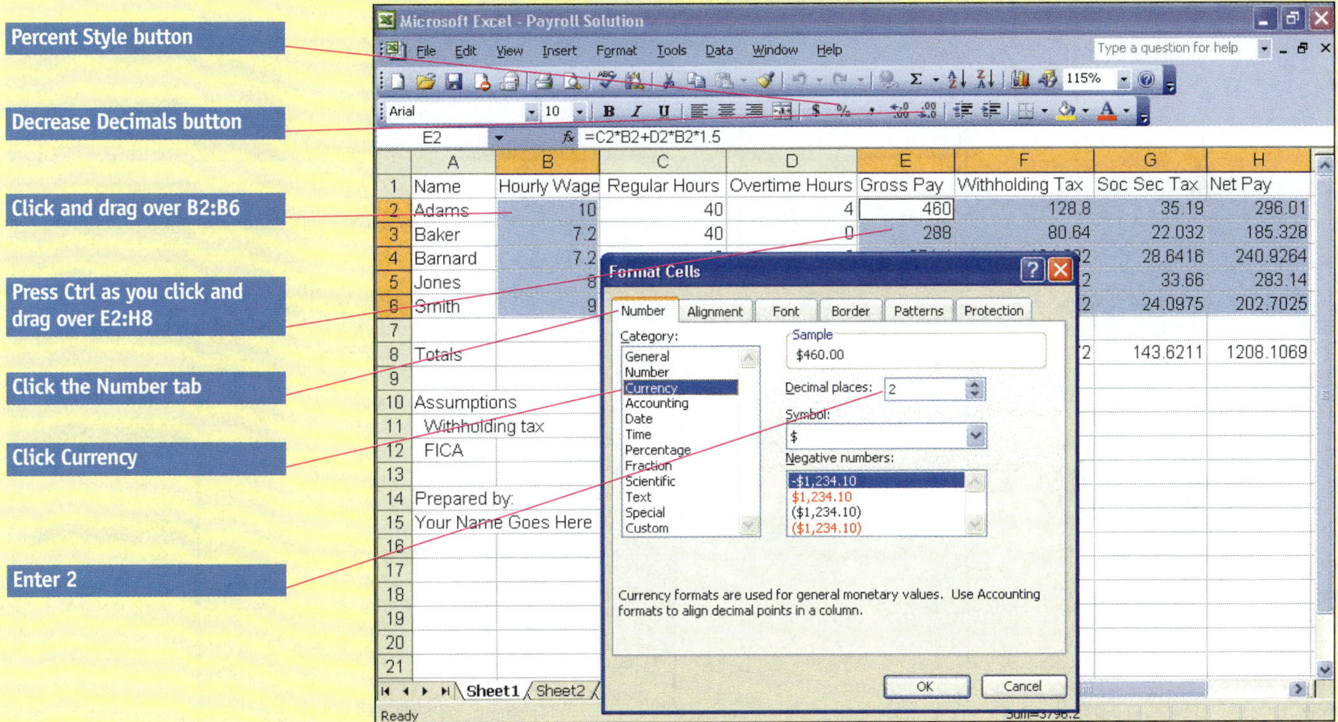

(e) Format the Spreadsheets (step 5)

FIGURE 2.2 Hands-on Exercise 1 (*continued*)

THE FORMAT STYLE COMMAND

A style is a collection of formats such as the font, alignment, and number of decimal places. Common styles, such as percent or currency, are represented by buttons on the Formatting toolbar and are most easily applied by clicking the appropriate tool. You can also apply the style by pulling down the Format menu, clicking the Style command, and selecting the style from the Style Name list box. The latter allows you to modify the definition of existing styles and/or to create a new style.

Step 6: Complete the Formatting

- Click and drag to select **cells A1** through **H1**. Press and hold the **Ctrl key**, then click and drag to select **cells A10** through **H10** in addition to the cells in row 1. Continue to press and hold the **Ctrl key**, then click and drag to select cells **A14** through **H14**.
- Click the **Fill Color arrow** on the Formatting toolbar, then select **blue** as the fill color. Click the **Font Color arrow** on the Formatting toolbar, then select **white** as the color for the text. Click the **Bold button** so that the text stands out from the fill color.
- Click and drag to select **cells A1** through **H1** (which also deselects the cells in rows 10 and 14). Click the **Right mouse button** to display a context-sensitive menu, then click the **Format Cells command** to display the dialog box in Figure 2.2f.
- Click the **Alignment tab,** then check the box to **Wrap text** in a cell. Click **OK** to accept the settings and close the dialog box.
- Click the **Center button** to center the text as well. Reduce the width of columns C and D. Save the workbook.

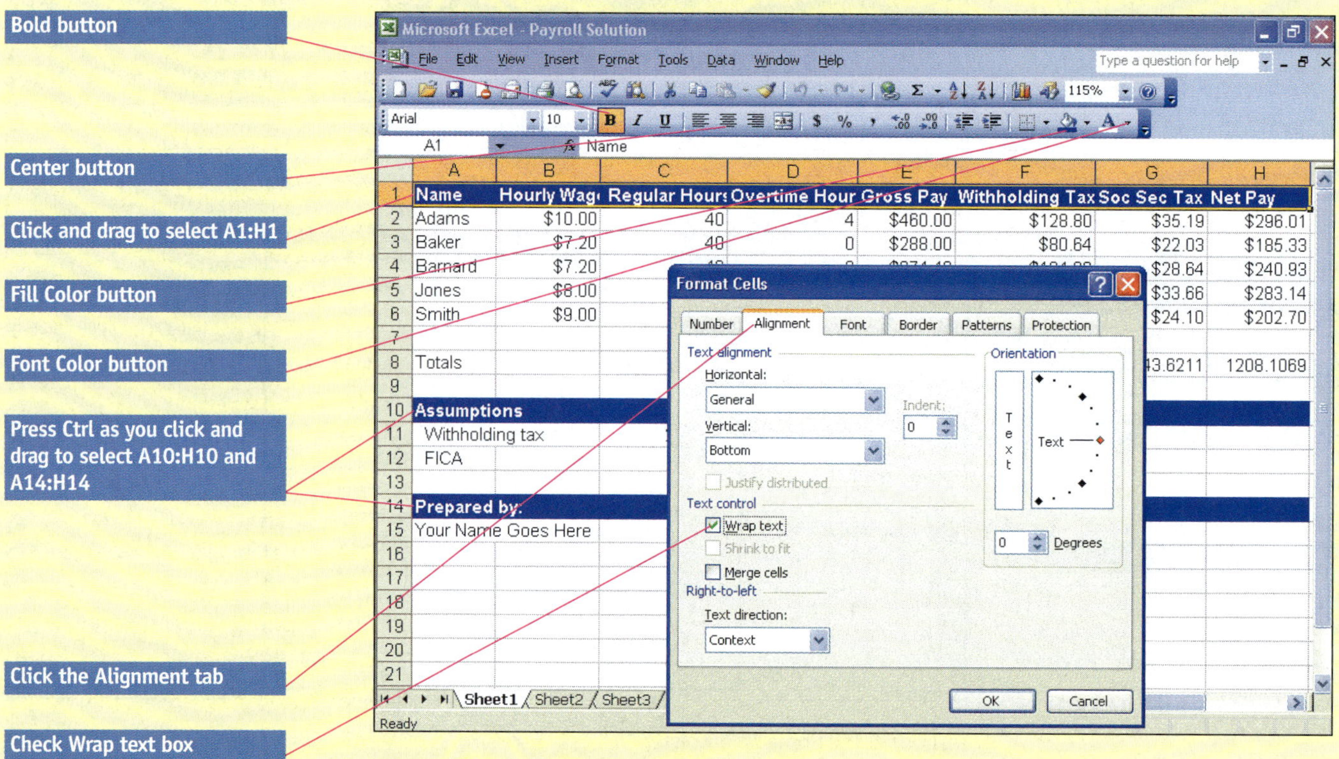

(f) Complete the Formatting (step 6)

FIGURE 2.2 Hands-on Exercise 1 (*continued*)

SORT THE EMPLOYEE LIST

The employees are listed on the worksheet in alphabetical order, but you can rearrange the list according to any other field, such as the net pay. Click a single cell containing employee data in the column on which you want to sort, then click the Sort Ascending or Sort Descending button on the Standard toolbar. Click the Undo button if the result is different from what you intended.

Step 7: The Completed Workbook

- Click in **cell C11**. Pull down the **Insert menu** and click **Comment**, then insert the text of the comment as shown in Figure 2.2g. (The name that appears in the comment box will be different on your system.)
- Click in any other cell when you have finished inserting the comment. The text of the comment is no longer visible, but you should still see the tiny triangle. Now point to cell C11 and you see the text of the comment.
- Pull down the **File menu** and click the **Page Setup command** to display the Page Setup dialog box. Click the **Page tab**. Click the **Landscape Option button**. Click the option to **Fit to 1 page**.
- Click the **Margins tab**. Check the box to center the worksheet horizontally. Click the **Sheet tab**. Check the boxes to print **Row and Column Headings** and **Gridlines.** Click **OK**. Print the worksheet.
- Save the workbook. Press **Ctrl+~** to show the cell formulas rather than the displayed values. Adjust the column widths as necessary, then print the worksheet a second time.
- Close the workbook. Exit Excel if you do not want to continue with the next exercise at this time.

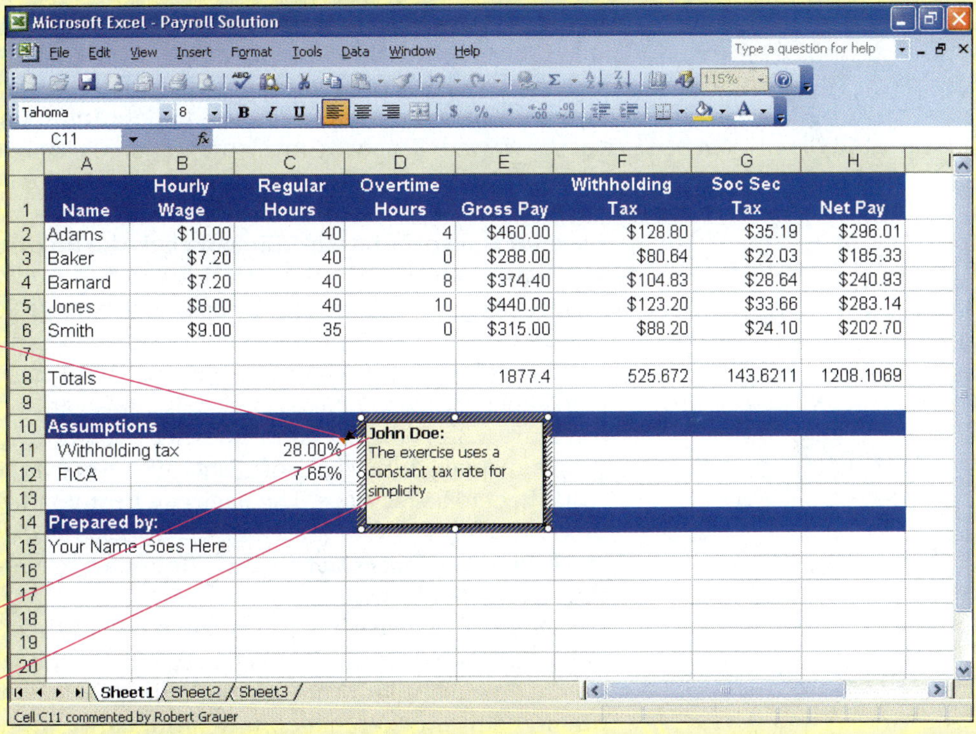

	A	B	C	D	E	F	G	H
1	Name	Hourly Wage	Regular Hours	Overtime Hours	Gross Pay	Withholding Tax	Soc Sec Tax	Net Pay
2	Adams	$10.00	40	4	$460.00	$128.80	$35.19	$296.01
3	Baker	$7.20	40	0	$288.00	$80.64	$22.03	$185.33
4	Barnard	$7.20	40	8	$374.40	$104.83	$28.64	$240.93
5	Jones	$8.00	40	10	$440.00	$123.20	$33.66	$283.14
6	Smith	$9.00	35	0	$315.00	$88.20	$24.10	$202.70
7								
8	Totals				1877.4	525.672	143.6211	1208.1069
9								
10	Assumptions							
11	Withholding tax		28.00%					
12	FICA		7.65%					
13								
14	Prepared by:							
15	Your Name Goes Here							

(g) The Completed Workbook (step 7)

FIGURE 2.2 Hands-on Exercise 1 (*continued*)

EDIT AND DELETE COMMENTS

Point to any cell that contains a comment, then click the right mouse button to display a context-sensitive menu with commands to edit or delete a comment. (The menu also contains the option to show or hide the comment.) The name that appears within the comment box corresponds to the user name set during installation. Pull down the Tools menu, click the Option command, click the General tab, then go to the User Name area to modify this information.

EXCEL AND THE INTERNET

The ***Internet*** is closely tied to Microsoft Excel through three basic capabilities. First, you can insert a ***hyperlink*** (a reference to another document) into any Excel worksheet, then view the associated document by clicking the link without having to start your Web browser manually. Second, you can save any Excel workbook as a ***Web page*** (or ***HTML document***), which in turn can be displayed through a Web browser. And finally, you can download information from a Web server directly into an Excel workbook through a ***Web query*** (a capability that we illustrate later in the chapter).

Consider, for example, Figure 2.3a, which contains an Excel worksheet that displays a consolidated statement of earnings for a hypothetical company. The information in this worksheet is typical of what companies publish in their annual report, a document that summarizes the financial performance of a corporation. Every public corporation is required by law to publish this type of information so that investors may evaluate the strength of the company. The annual report is mailed to the shareholders, and it is typically available online as well.

The worksheet in Figure 2.3a is easy to create, and you do not have to be a business major to understand the information. Indeed, if you have any intention of investing in the stock market, you should be able to analyze the data in the worksheet, which conveys basic information about the financial strength of a company to potential investors. In essence, the worksheet shows the sales for the company in the current year, subtracts the expenses to obtain the earnings before taxes, displays the income taxes that were paid, then arrives at the net earnings after taxes.

The worksheet also contains a calculation that divides the net earnings for the company by the number of shares to determine the earnings per share (a number that is viewed closely by investors). There is also comparable information for the previous year to show the increase or decrease for each item. And finally, the worksheet contains a hyperlink or reference to a specific Web site, such as the home page for the corporation. You can click the link from within Excel, and provided you have an Internet connection, your Web browser will display the associated page. Once you click the link, its color will change, just as it would if you were viewing the page in Netscape Navigator or Internet Explorer.

The Web page in Figure 2.3b is, for all intents and purposes, identical to the worksheet in Figure 2.3a. Look closely, however, and you will see that the Web page in Figure 2.3b is displayed in Internet Explorer, whereas the worksheet in Figure 2.3a is displayed in Microsoft Excel. The ***Save as Web Page command*** converts a worksheet to a Web page. The page can be uploaded to the Internet, but it can also be viewed from a PC or local area network, as was done in Figure 2.3b. Use the ***Web Page Preview command*** in the File menu to view the page, or open the page directly in your browser.

Our next exercise has you create the worksheet in Figure 2.3a, after which you create the Web document in Figure 2.3b. All applications in Microsoft Office incorporate a concept known as ***round trip HTML***, which means that you can subsequently edit the Web page in the application that created it originally. In other words, you start with an Excel worksheet, save it as a Web page, then you can open the Web page and return to Excel to edit the document.

SINGLE FILE WEB PAGES

Web documents are written in HTML or HyperText Markup Language. The newest version of Microsoft Office also recognizes the Single File Web Page (MHTML) format, in which all of the elements of a Web page (text and graphics) are saved as a single file. The address bar of a Web browser displays the document name and extension, which may appear as htm (or html) or mht, depending on how the Web page was created initially.

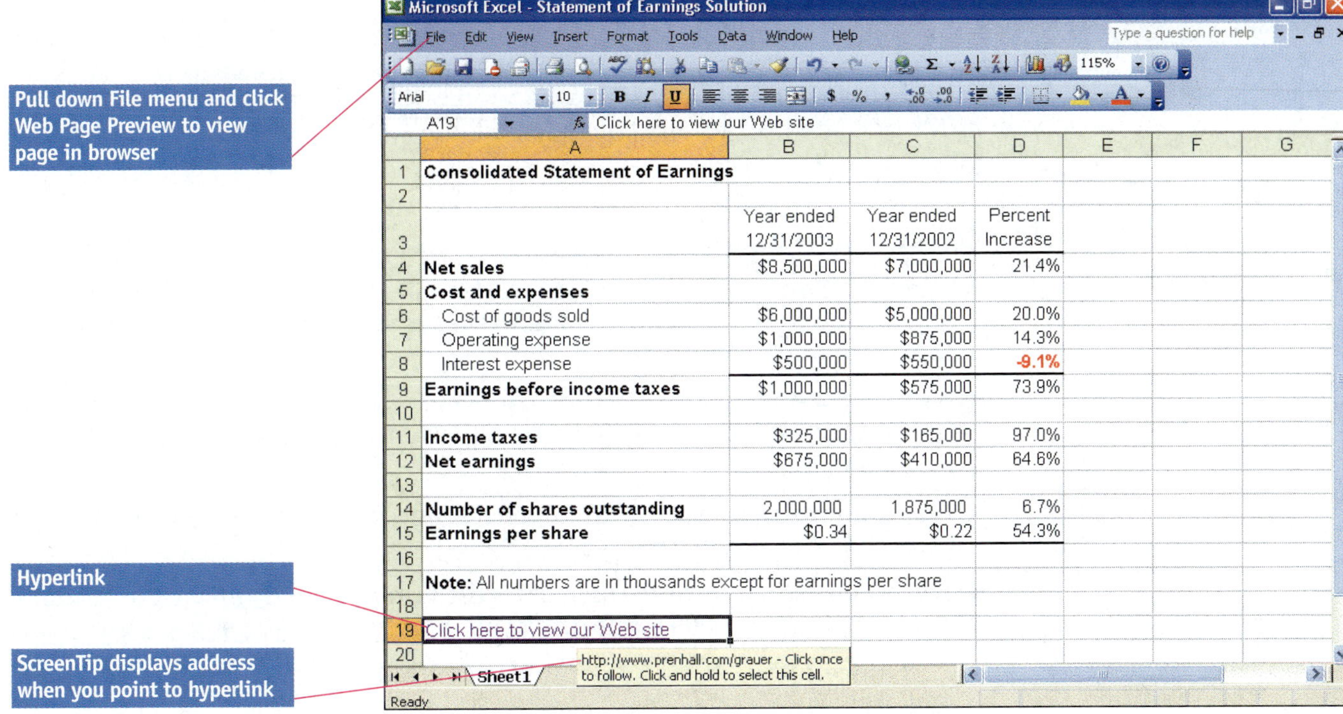

(a) Excel Worksheet

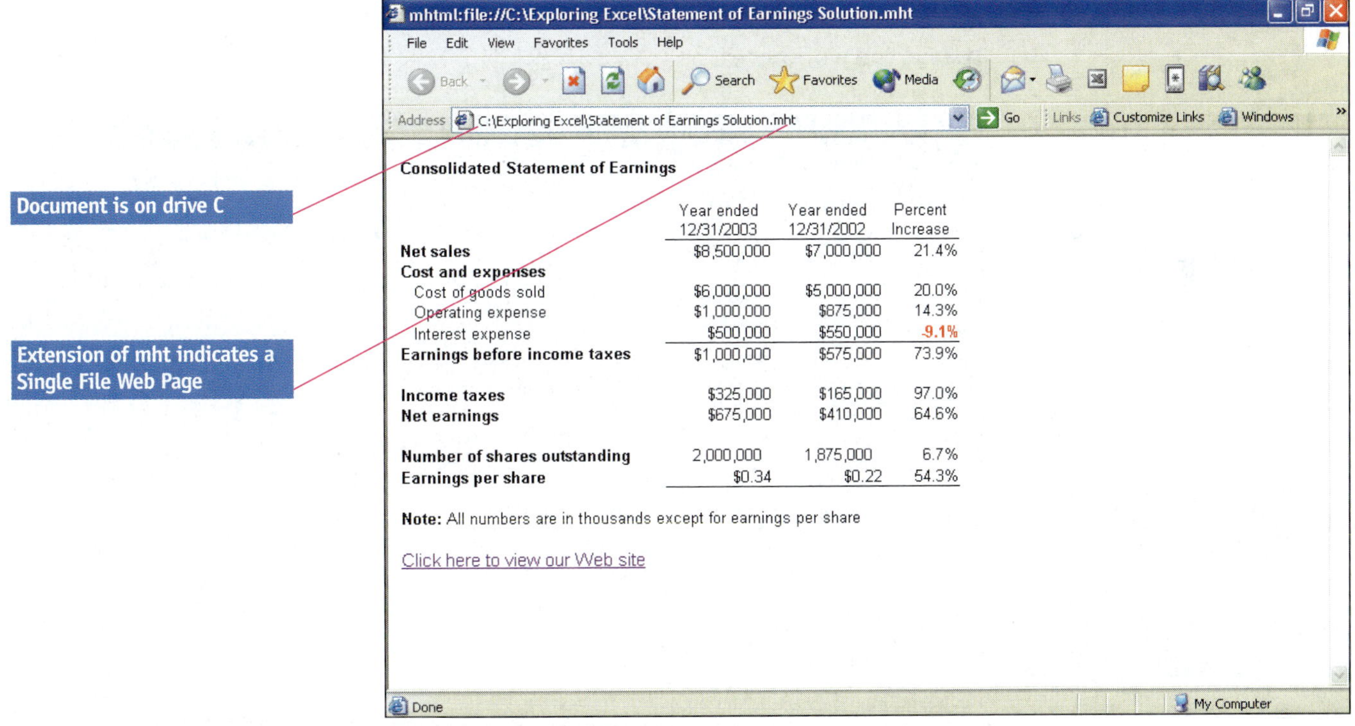

(b) Web Page

FIGURE 2.3 Consolidated Statement of Earnings

hands-on exercise

2 Creating a Web Page

Objective To insert a hyperlink into an Excel workbook; to save a workbook as an HTML document, then subsequently edit the Web page. Use Figure 2.4 as a guide in the exercise.

Step 1: Compute the Net Earnings

- Open the **Statement of Earnings workbook** in the **Exploring Excel folder**. Save the workbook as **Statement of Earnings Solution** so that you can always go back to the original workbook if necessary.
- We have entered the labels and data for you, but you have to create the formulas. Click in **cell B9**. Type an **equal sign**, then click in **cell B4** to begin the pointing operation.
- Type a **minus sign**, type **SUM(**, then click and drag to select **cells B6** through **B8** as shown in Figure 2.4a.
- Type a **closing parenthesis**, then press the **Enter key** to complete the formula. You should see 1000000 as the displayed value in cell B9.
- Click in **cell B12**, then use pointing to enter the formula for net earnings, **=B9–B11**.
- Click in **cell B15**, then use pointing to enter the formula for earnings per share, **=B12/B14**.
- Copy the formulas in cells B9, B12, and B15 to the corresponding cells in column C. You have to copy the formulas one at a time.
- Save the workbook.

Click in B4 to enter B4 in formula, then type –SUM(

Click and drag over B6:B8, then type)

Click in B9 and type = to begin formula

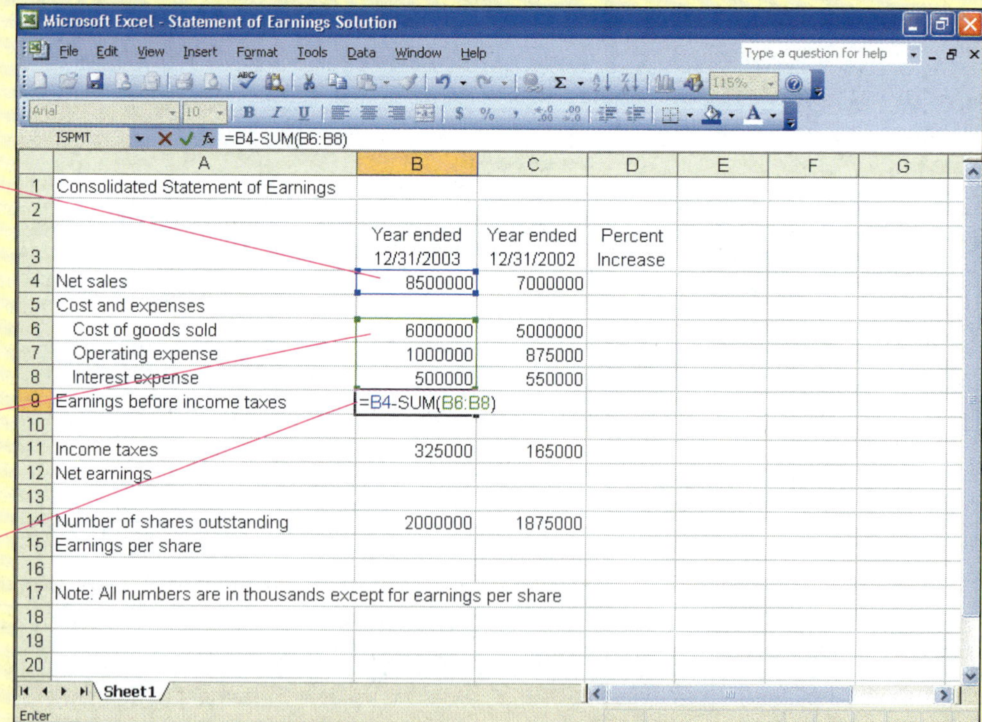

(a) Compute the Net Earnings (step 1)

FIGURE 2.4 Hands-on Exercise 2

Step 2: Compute the Percent Increase

- Click in **cell D4**, then enter the formula to compute the percent increase from the previous year. Use pointing to enter the formula, **=(B4-C4)/C4**.
- You should see .214286 as the displayed value in cell D4 as shown in Figure 2.4b. Do not worry about formatting at this time.
- Click in **cell D4**. Click the **Copy button** on the Standard toolbar (or use the **Ctrl+C** keyboard shortcut) to copy the contents of this cell to the clipboard. You should see a moving border around cell D4.
- Press and hold the **Ctrl key** to select **cells D6** through **D9**, **D11**, and **D12**, and **D14** and **D15** as shown in Figure 2.4b. (We have selected a noncontiguous range of cells, because we do not want to copy the formula to cells D10 or D13.)
- Click the **Paste button** on the Standard toolbar (or use the **Ctrl+V** keyboard shortcut) to paste the contents of cell D4 into these cells. Ignore the Paste Options button if it appears.
- Press the **Esc key** to remove the moving border around cell D4.

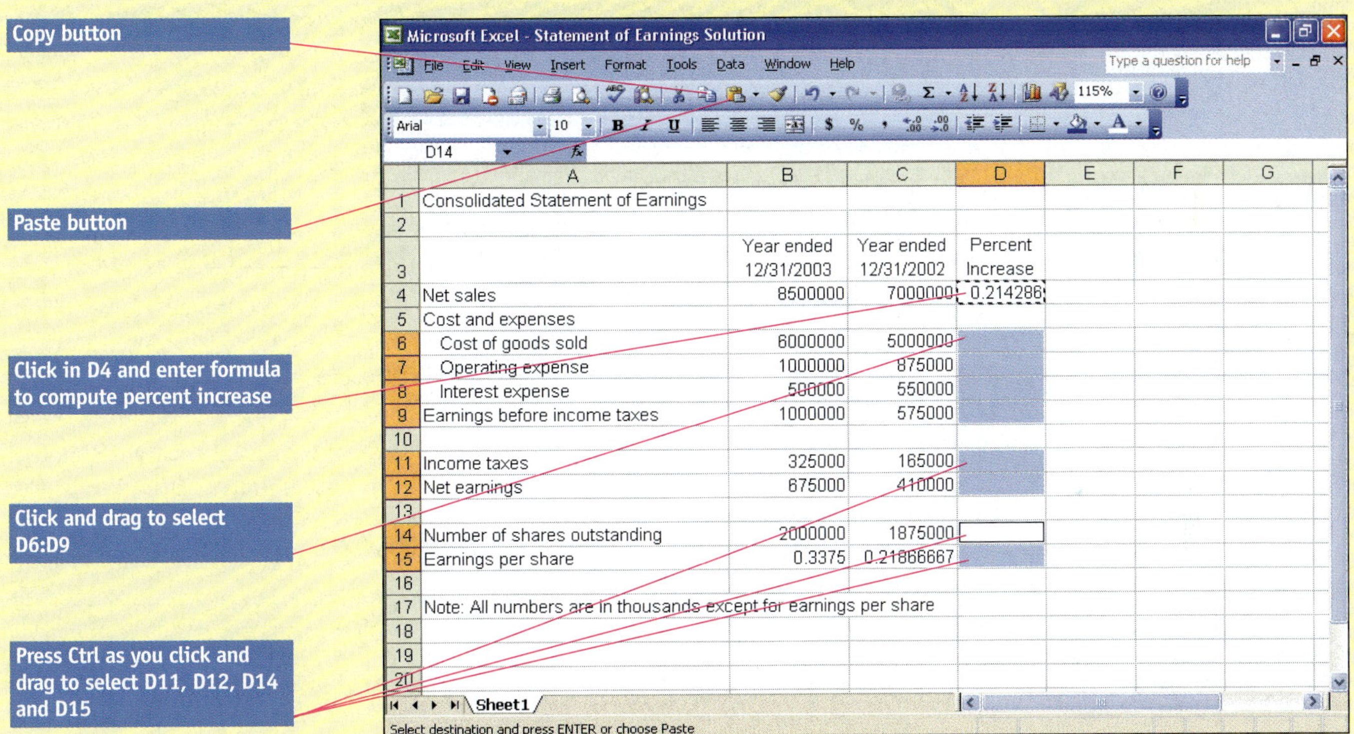

(b) Compute the Percent Increase (step 2)

FIGURE 2.4 Hands-on Exercise 2 (*continued*)

USE POINTING TO ENTER CELL FORMULAS

A cell reference can be typed directly into a formula, or it can be entered more easily through pointing. The latter is also more accurate as you use the mouse or arrow keys to reference cells directly. To use pointing, select (click) the cell to contain the formula, type an equal sign to begin entering the formula, click (or move to) the cell containing the reference, then press the F4 key as necessary to change from relative to absolute references. Type any arithmetic operator to place the cell reference in the formula, then continue pointing to additional cells. Press the Enter key to complete the formula.

Step 3: Format the Worksheet

- Format the worksheet as shown in Figure 2.4c. Click in **cell A1**, then press and hold the **Ctrl key** to select **cells A4, A5, A9, A11, A12, A14**, and **A15**. Click the **Bold button** on the Formatting toolbar (or use the **Ctrl+B** keyboard shortcut).
- Double click in **cell A17**, then click and drag over **Note**: within the cell to select this portion of the label. Press **Ctrl+B** to boldface the selected text.
- Remember that boldfacing the contents of a cell functions as a toggle switch; that is, click the Boldface button and the text is bold. Click the button a second time and the boldface is removed.
- Select **cells B3** through **D3, B8** through **D8**, and **B15** through **D15** as shown in Figure 2.4c. Click the **down arrow** on the Borders button on the Formatting toolbar to display the available borders. Click the bottom border icon to implement this formatting in the selected cells.
- Complete the formatting in the remainder of the worksheet by using currency, comma, and percent formats as appropriate. Save the workbook.

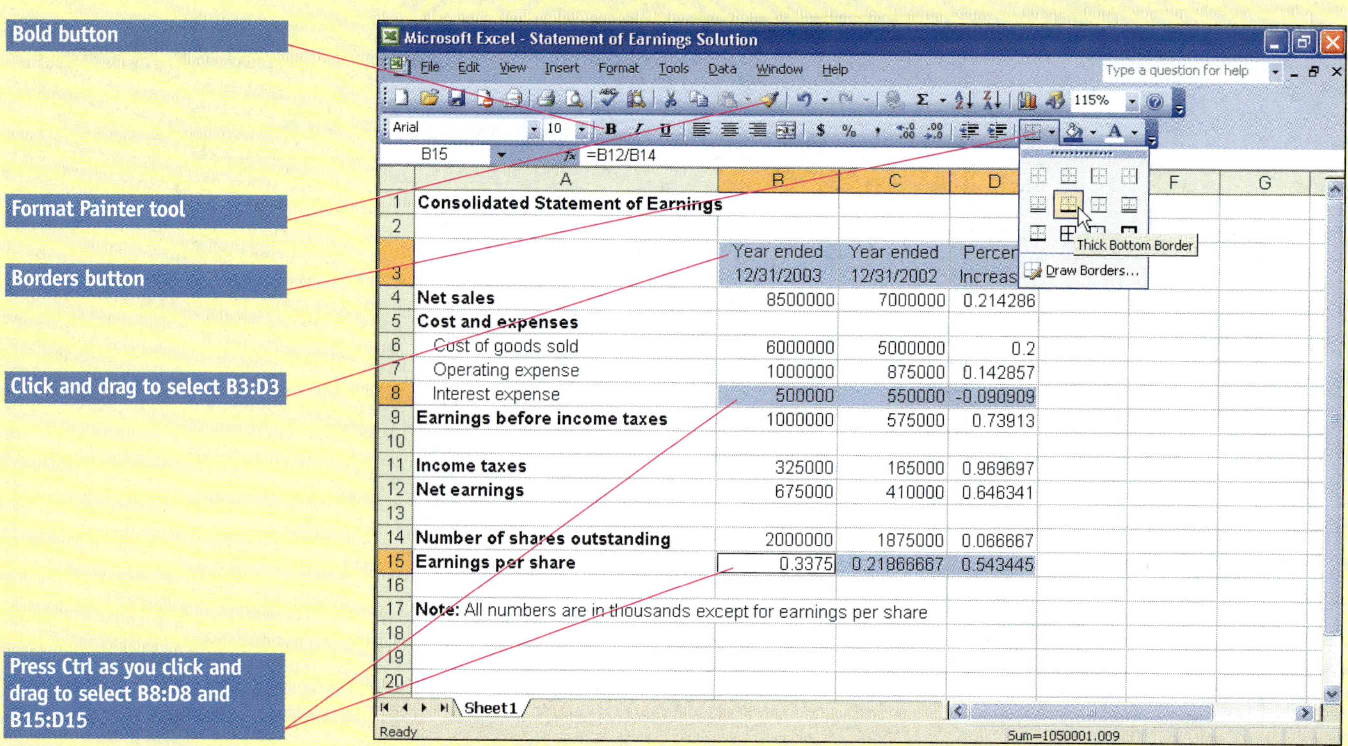

(c) Format the Worksheet (step 3)

FIGURE 2.4 Hands-on Exercise 2 (*continued*)

THE FORMAT PAINTER

The Format Painter copies the formatting of the selected cell to other cells in the worksheet. Click the cell whose formatting you want to copy, then double click the Format Painter button on the Standard toolbar. The mouse pointer changes to a paintbrush to indicate that you can copy the current formatting; just click and drag the paintbrush over the cells that you want to assume the formatting of the original cell. Repeat the painting process as often as necessary, then click the Format Painter button a second time to return to normal editing.

Step 4: Conditional Formatting

- Click and drag to select **cells D4** through **D15**, the cells that contain the percentage increase from the previous year.
- Pull down the **Format menu** and click the **Conditional Formatting command** to display the Conditional Formatting dialog box.
- Check that the Condition 1 list box displays Cell Value Is. Click the **down arrow** in the relationship list box and choose **less than**. Press **Tab** to move to the next list box and enter a **zero** as shown in Figure 2.4d.
- Click the **Format button** to display the Format Cells dialog box. Click the **Font tab**, click the **down arrow** on the Color list box and choose **Red**. Choose Bold as the Font style. Click **OK** to close the Format Cells dialog box.
- Click **OK** to close the Conditional Formatting dialog box. The decrease in the interest expense should be displayed in bold red as –9.1%.
- Save the workbook.

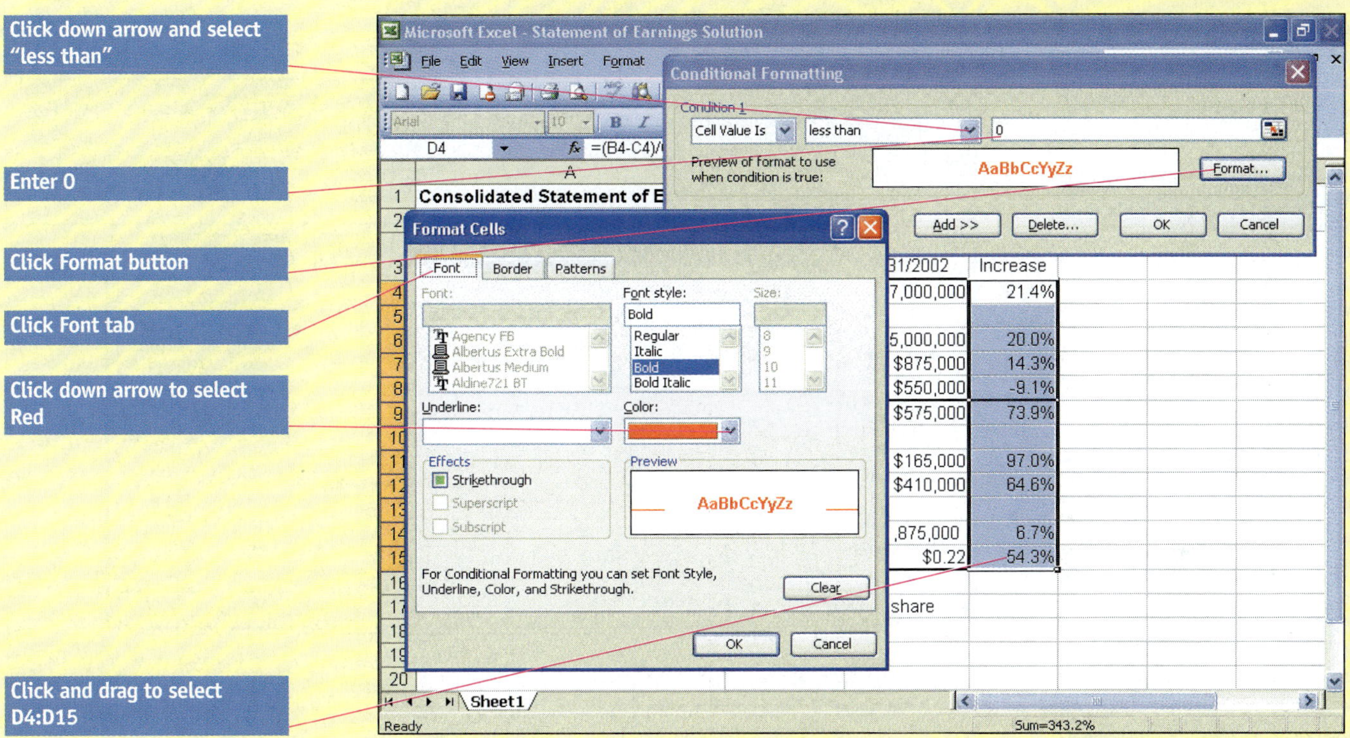

(d) Conditional Formatting (step 4)

FIGURE 2.4 Hands-on Exercise 2 (*continued*)

ADDING MULTIPLE CONDITIONS

Use the Conditional Formatting command to impose additional conditions with alternative formats depending on the value within a cell. You can, for example, display negative values in red (as was done in this example) and positive values (above a certain number) in blue. Pull down the Format menu and click the Conditional Formatting command, then click the Add button within the dialog box to add the additional conditions. Conditional formatting is a lesser-known feature that adds significantly to the appearance of a worksheet.

Step 5: Insert the Hyperlink

- Click in **cell A19**. Pull down the **Insert menu** and click the **Hyperlink command** (or click the **Insert Hyperlink button** on the Standard toolbar) to display the Insert Hyperlink dialog box in Figure 2.4e. Click in the **Text to display** text box and enter **Click here to view our Web site**.
- Click **Existing File or Web Page**, then click the button for **Browsed Pages**, then click in the Address text box (toward the bottom of the dialog box) and enter the Web address such as **www.prenhall.com/grauer** (the http:// is assumed). Click **OK** to accept the settings and close the dialog box.
- The hyperlink should appear as an underlined entry in the worksheet. Point to the hyperlink (the Web address should appear as a ScreenTip), then click the link to start your browser and view the Web page. You need an Internet connection to see the actual page.
- You are now running two applications, Excel and the Web browser, each of which has its own button on the Windows taskbar. Click the **Excel button** to continue working (and correct the hyperlink if necessary).
- Save the workbook.

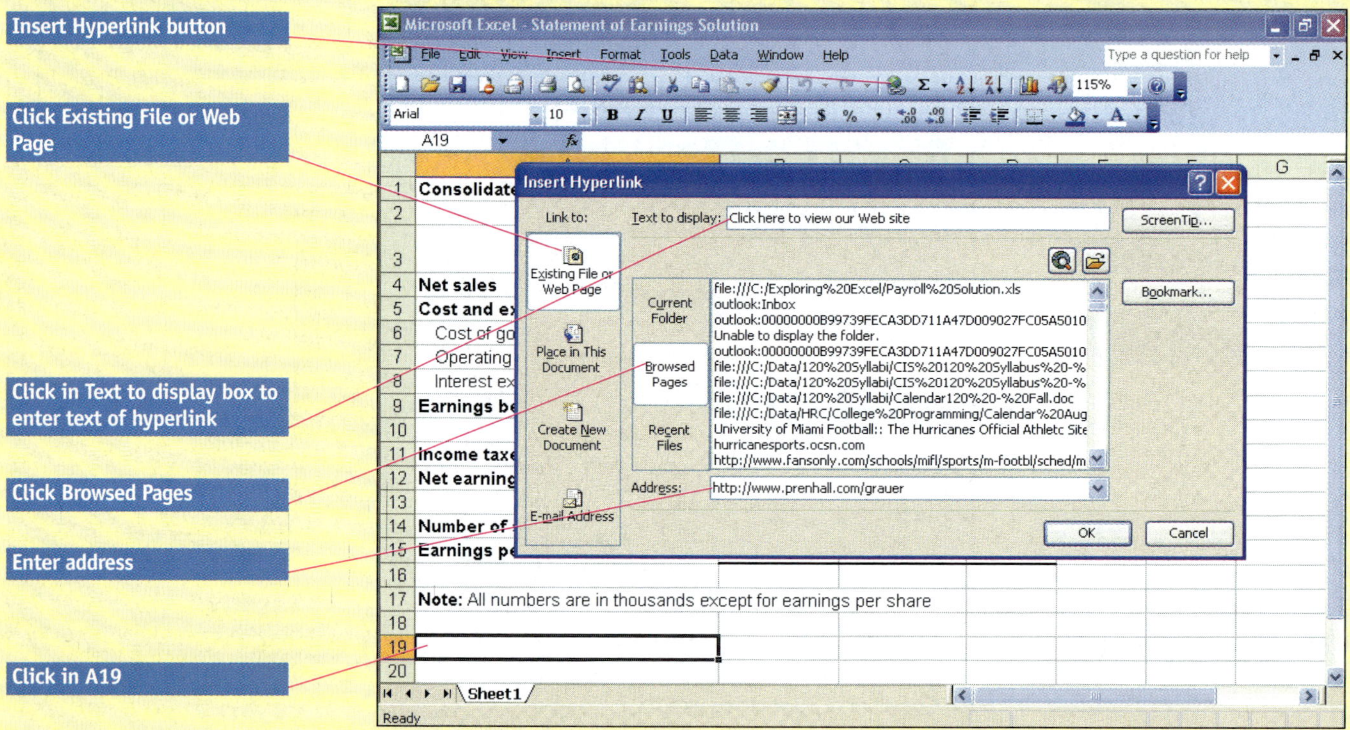

(e) Insert the Hyperlink (step 5)

FIGURE 2.4 Hands-on Exercise 2 (*continued*)

SELECTING (EDITING) A HYPERLINK

In an ideal world you will enter all the information for a hyperlink correctly on the first attempt. But what if you make a mistake and need to edit the information? You cannot select a hyperlink by clicking it, because that displays the associated Web page. You can, however, right click the cell containing the hyperlink to display a context-sensitive menu, then click the Edit Hyperlink command to display the associated dialog box in which to make the necessary changes. (The menu also enables you to remove the hyperlink.)

Step 6: Save the Web Page

- Pull down the **File menu** and click the **Save as Web Page command** to display the Save As dialog box in Figure 2.4f. Note the following:
  - The **Exploring Excel folder** is entered automatically as the default folder, since that is the location of the original workbook.
  - **Statement of Earnings Solution** is entered automatically as the name of the Web page, corresponding to the name of the workbook, Statement of Earnings Solution.
  - The default file type is **Single File Web Page**, as opposed to HTML.
  - It does not matter whether you save the entire workbook or a single sheet, since the workbook contains only a single sheet. However, you need to specify a single sheet if and when you want to add interactivity (i.e., Excel functionality) when the page is opened through a Web browser.
- Click the **Save button**. There are now two versions of the workbook on disk, both with the same name (Statement of Earnings Solution), but with different extensions, corresponding to a Web page and Excel workbook.
- Close Microsoft Excel. (We will restart the application later in the exercise.)

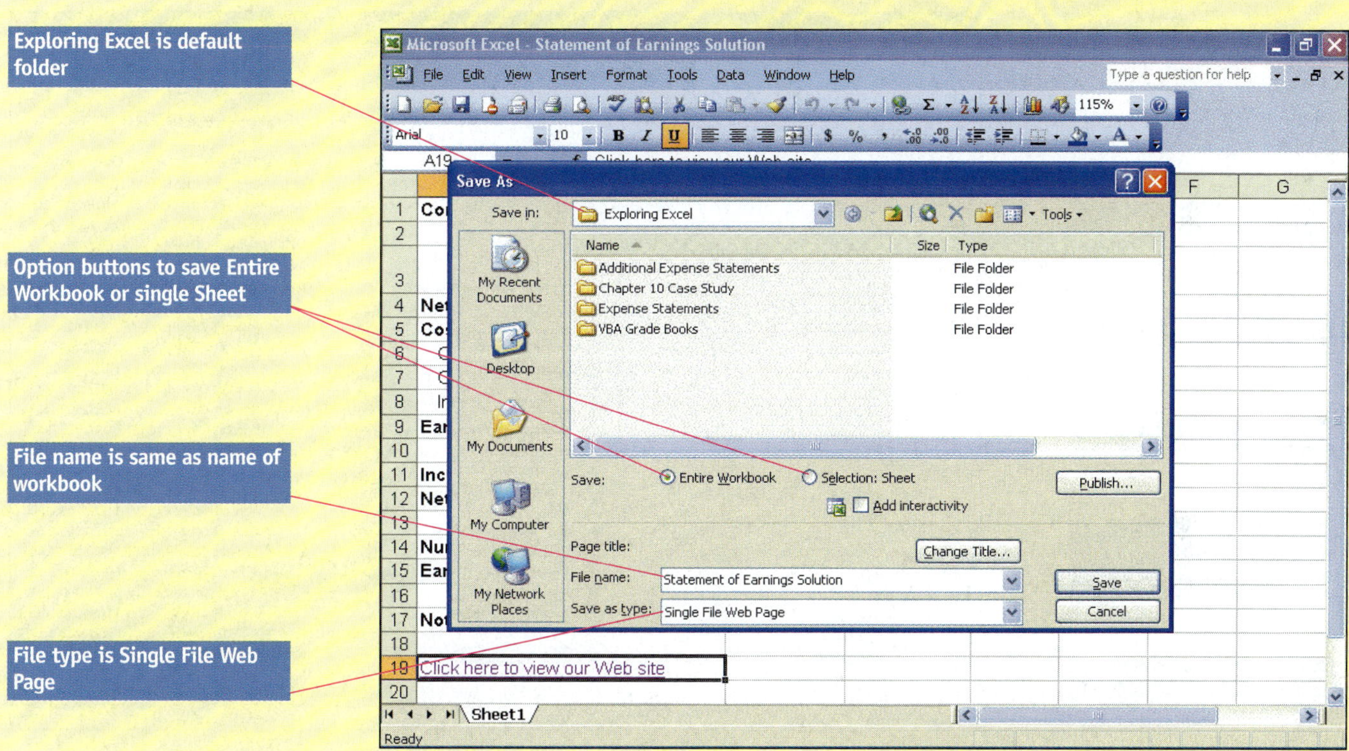

(f) Save the Web Page (step 6)

FIGURE 2.4 Hands-on Exercise 2 (*continued*)

CHANGE THE DEFAULT FILE LOCATION

The default file location is the folder Excel uses to open and save a workbook unless it is otherwise instructed. To change the default location, pull down the Tools menu, click Options, and click the General tab. Enter the name of the new folder (e.g., C:\Exploring Excel) in the Default File Location text box, then click OK. The next time you access the Open or Save command from the File menu, the Look In text box will reflect the change.

Step 7: Start Windows Explorer

- Click the **Start button,** start **Windows Explorer**, then change to the Exploring Excel folder. The location of this folder depends on whether you have your own computer.
  - ❑ If you are working from a floppy disk, select drive A in the left pane.
  - ❑ If you are working on your own computer, expand drive C in the left pane, then scroll until you can select the Exploring Excel folder.
- Either way, you should see the contents of the Exploring Excel folder in the right pane as shown in Figure 2.4g. As indicated, there are two versions of the Statement of Earnings Solution with different icons and file types.
- Right click the file with the Excel icon and file type to display a shortcut menu, then click the **Delete command** to delete this file. You do not need the Excel workbook any longer because you can edit the workbook from the Web page through the concept of round trip HTML.
- Double click the Web page version of the earnings statement to view the document in your default browser.

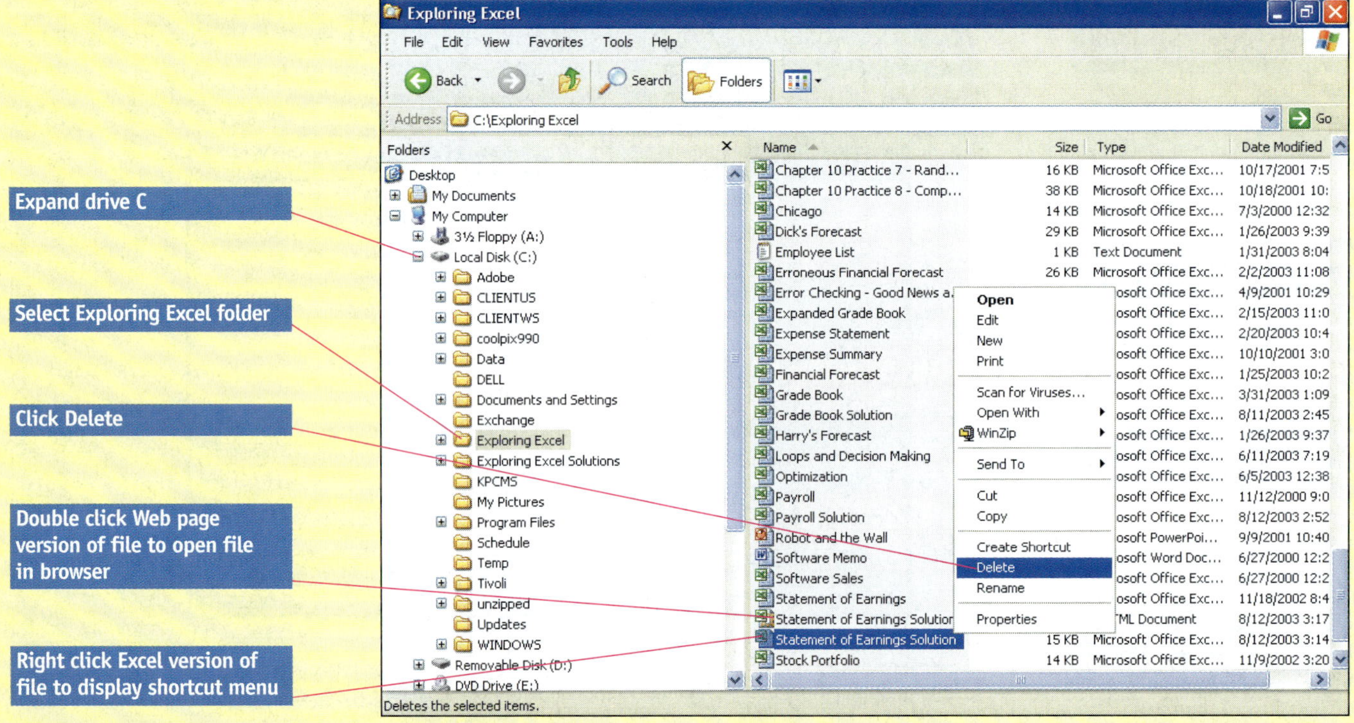

(g) Start Windows Explorer (step 7)

FIGURE 2.4 Hands-on Exercise 2 (*continued*)

ROUND TRIP HTML

Each application in Microsoft Office lets you open an HTML document in both Internet Explorer and the application that created the Web page initially. In other words, you can start with an Excel worksheet and use the Save as Web Page command to convert the document to a Web page, then view that page in a Web browser. You can then reopen the Web page in Excel (the application that created it initially) with full access to all Excel commands in order to edit the document.

Step 8: View the Web Page

- You should see the Statement of Earnings Solution displayed within Internet Explorer (or Netscape Navigator) as shown in Figure 2.4h. The Web page looks identical to the worksheet that was displayed earlier in Excel.
- Click the hyperlink that was inserted through the Insert Hyperlink command to view the Web site. You should see our Web site (**www.prenhall.com/grauer**), if that was the address you used earlier.
- Click the **Back button** on the Standard Buttons toolbar to return to the Statement of Earnings Solution Web page. Look carefully at the Address bar and note that unlike other Web documents, this page is displayed from your local system (drive C or drive A), depending on the location of the file.
- Click the **Edit with Microsoft Excel button** on the Standard Buttons toolbar to start Excel in order to modify the Web page.
- Both applications, Internet Explorer and Microsoft Excel, are open as can be seen by the taskbar, which contains buttons for both.

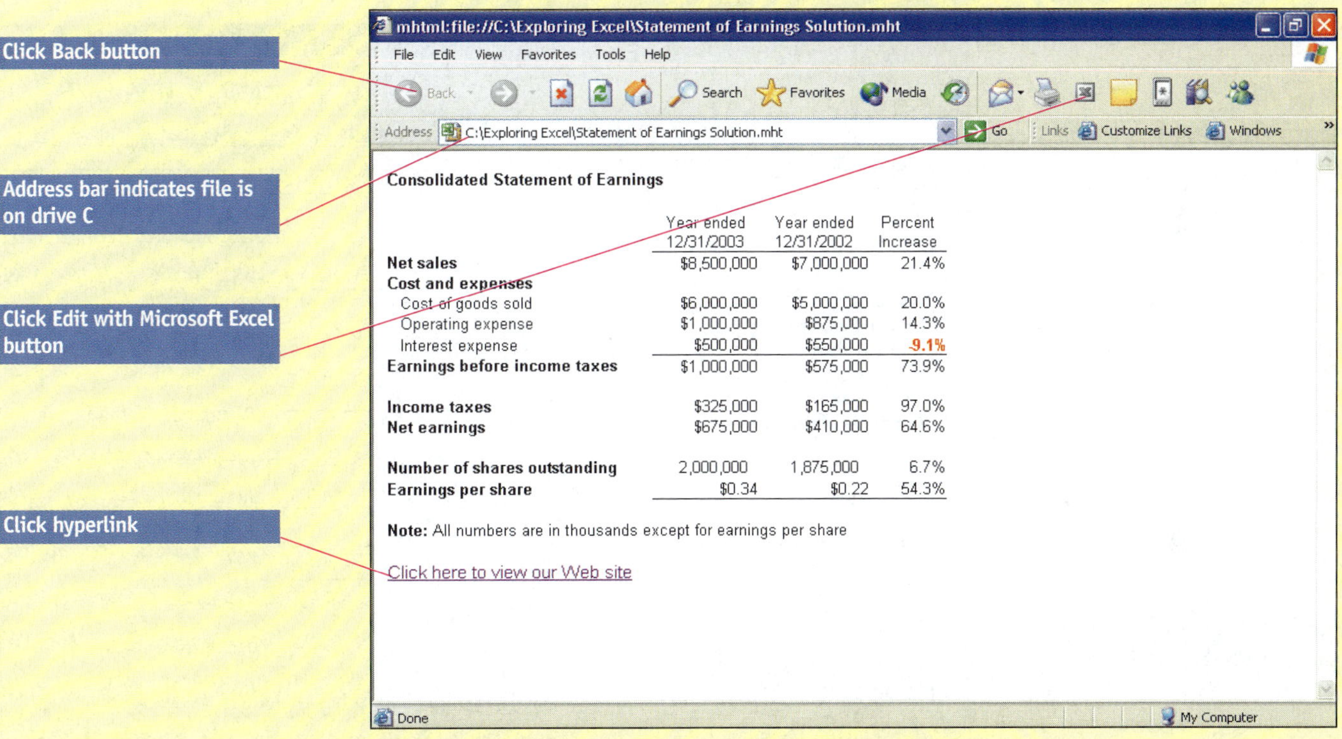

	Year ended 12/31/2003	Year ended 12/31/2002	Percent Increase
Net sales	$8,500,000	$7,000,000	21.4%
Cost and expenses			
Cost of goods sold	$6,000,000	$5,000,000	20.0%
Operating expense	$1,000,000	$875,000	14.3%
Interest expense	$500,000	$550,000	-9.1%
Earnings before income taxes	$1,000,000	$575,000	73.9%
Income taxes	$325,000	$165,000	97.0%
Net earnings	$675,000	$410,000	64.6%
Number of shares outstanding	2,000,000	1,875,000	6.7%
Earnings per share	$0.34	$0.22	54.3%

(h) View the Web Page (step 8)

FIGURE 2.4 Hands-on Exercise 2 (*continued*)

MULTITASKING

Multitasking, the ability to run multiple applications at the same time, is one of the primary advantages of the Windows environment. Minimizing an application is different from closing it, and you want to minimize, rather than close, an application to take advantage of multitasking. Closing an application removes it from memory so that you have to restart the application if you want to return to it later in the session. Minimizing, however, leaves the application open in memory, but shrinks its window to a button on the Windows taskbar.

Step 9: Edit the Web Page

- You should be back in Microsoft Excel as shown in Figure 2.4i. Click in **cell A21** and enter the label, **Prepared by**, followed by your name.
- Save the worksheet.
- Click the **Internet Explorer button** on the taskbar to return to your browser. The change you made (the addition of your name) is not yet visible because the browser displays the previous version of the page.
- Click the **Refresh button** on the Standard Buttons toolbar to bring in the most current version of the worksheet. Your changes should now be visible.(You may, however, have to close, then reopen Internet Explorer to see the change.)
- Pull down the **File menu** (within Internet Explorer) and click the **Print command,** then click the **Print command button** to print the Web page for your instructor.
- Close Internet Explorer. Exit Excel if you do not wish to continue with the next exercise at this time.

Click in A21 and enter your name

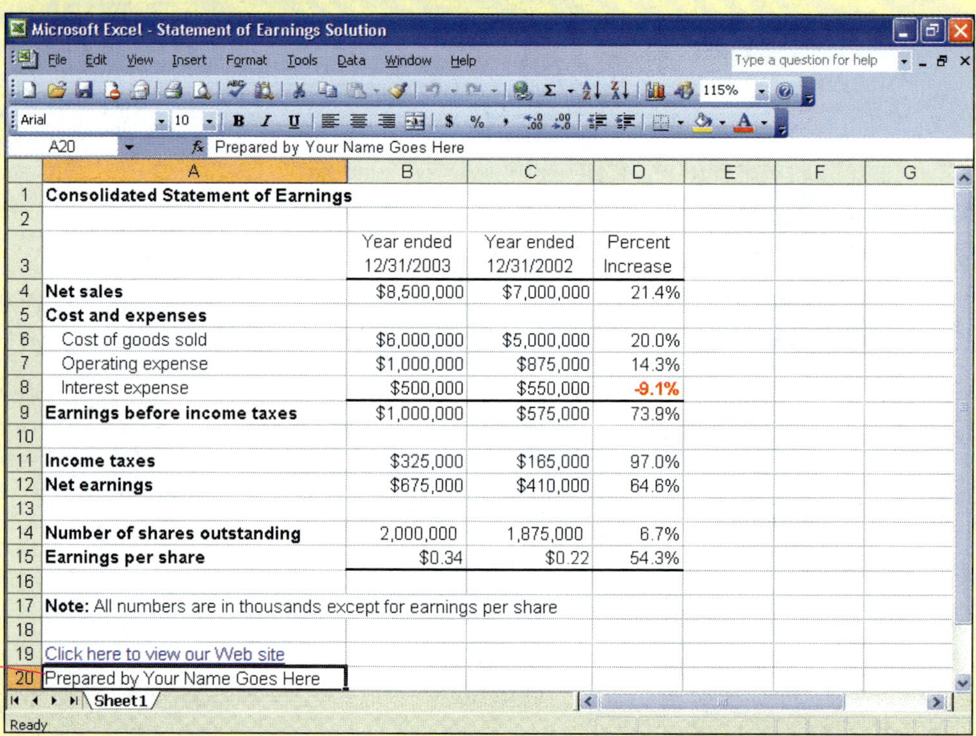

(i) Edit the Web Page (step 9)

FIGURE 2.4 Hands-on Exercise 2 (*continued*)

USE A TEMPLATE

A template is a partially completed workbook that is used to create other workbooks. It typically contains formulas and formatting but no specific data. Thus you open a template and enter the information that is specific to your application, then you save the template as an ordinary workbook. Excel provides several business templates.

Our next example is a worksheet to maintain a stock portfolio and compute the gain or loss associated with investment. The worksheet in Figure 2.5 lists several stocks, each with its recognized symbol, and records the purchase price, number of shares, and date of purchase of each investment. This information is "fixed" for each stock at the time of purchase. The worksheet then uses the current (today's) price to determine the gain or loss. It also uses today's date to compute the length of time the investment was held. The interesting thing about the worksheet is that the current price is obtained via a ***Web query***, a capability that enables Excel to go to a specific site on the Web to retrieve the information. The worksheet is time-sensitive and thus the values you see on your computer will be different from those in Figure 2.5.

The top half of the worksheet is typical of the worksheets we have studied thus far. The bottom portion (from row 14 down) represents the result of the Web query, which is entered into the worksheet via the ***Import External Data command***. Execution of this command prompts you for the location of the result (e.g., cell A14 in Figure 2.5) and the location of the parameters (or stock symbols), for which you want to determine the price (cells A5 through A10 in this example). Excel does the rest and places the results of the query into the worksheet. The results of the query can be continually updated through the ***Refresh command***, which is represented by the Exclamation Point button on the ***External Data toolbar***.

The worksheet in Figure 2.5 also illustrates the use of ***date arithmetic*** to determine the length of time an investment is held. (This is an important consideration for investors who can reduce their tax liability through a capital gains tax break on investments held for more than one year.) Date arithmetic is made possible through a simple concept by which Excel stores all dates as integers (serial numbers) beginning with January 1, 1900. Thus, January 1, 1900 is stored as the number 1, January 2, 1900 as the number 2, and so on.

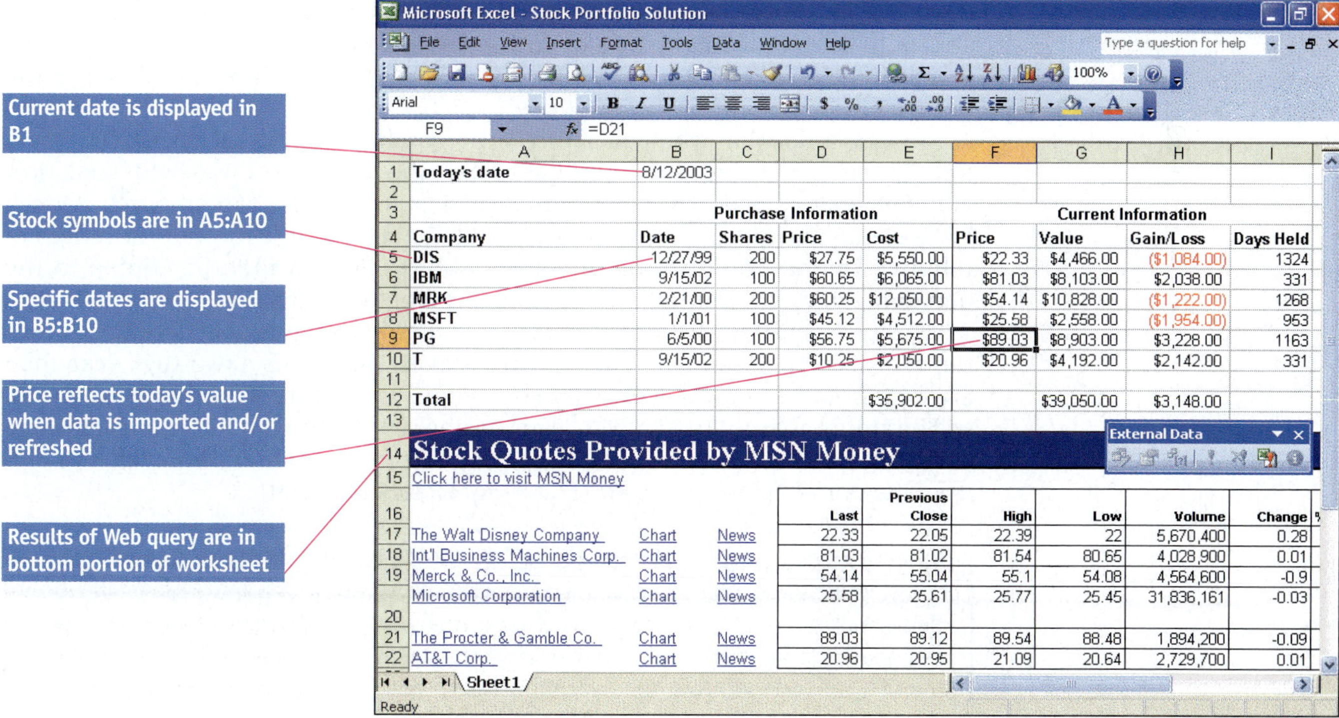

	A	B	C	D	E	F	G	H	I
1	Today's date	8/12/2003							
2									
3			Purchase Information				Current Information		
4	Company	Date	Shares	Price	Cost	Price	Value	Gain/Loss	Days Held
5	DIS	12/27/99	200	$27.75	$5,550.00	$22.33	$4,466.00	($1,084.00)	1324
6	IBM	9/15/02	100	$60.65	$6,065.00	$81.03	$8,103.00	$2,038.00	331
7	MRK	2/21/00	200	$60.25	$12,050.00	$54.14	$10,828.00	($1,222.00)	1268
8	MSFT	1/1/01	100	$45.12	$4,512.00	$25.58	$2,558.00	($1,954.00)	953
9	PG	6/5/00	100	$56.75	$5,675.00	$89.03	$8,903.00	$3,228.00	1163
10	T	9/15/02	200	$10.25	$2,050.00	$20.96	$4,192.00	$2,142.00	331
11									
12	Total				$35,902.00		$39,050.00	$3,148.00	
13									
14	Stock Quotes Provided by MSN Money								
15	Click here to visit MSN Money								

				Last	Previous Close	High	Low	Volume	Change
17	The Walt Disney Company	Chart	News	22.33	22.05	22.39	22	5,670,400	0.28
18	Int'l Business Machines Corp.	Chart	News	81.03	81.02	81.54	80.65	4,028,900	0.01
19	Merck & Co., Inc.	Chart	News	54.14	55.04	55.1	54.08	4,564,600	-0.9
20	Microsoft Corporation	Chart	News	25.58	25.61	25.77	25.45	31,836,161	-0.03
21	The Procter & Gamble Co.	Chart	News	89.03	89.12	89.54	88.48	1,894,200	-0.09
22	AT&T Corp.	Chart	News	20.96	20.95	21.09	20.64	2,729,700	0.01

(a) The Excel Worksheet

FIGURE 2.5 Web Queries

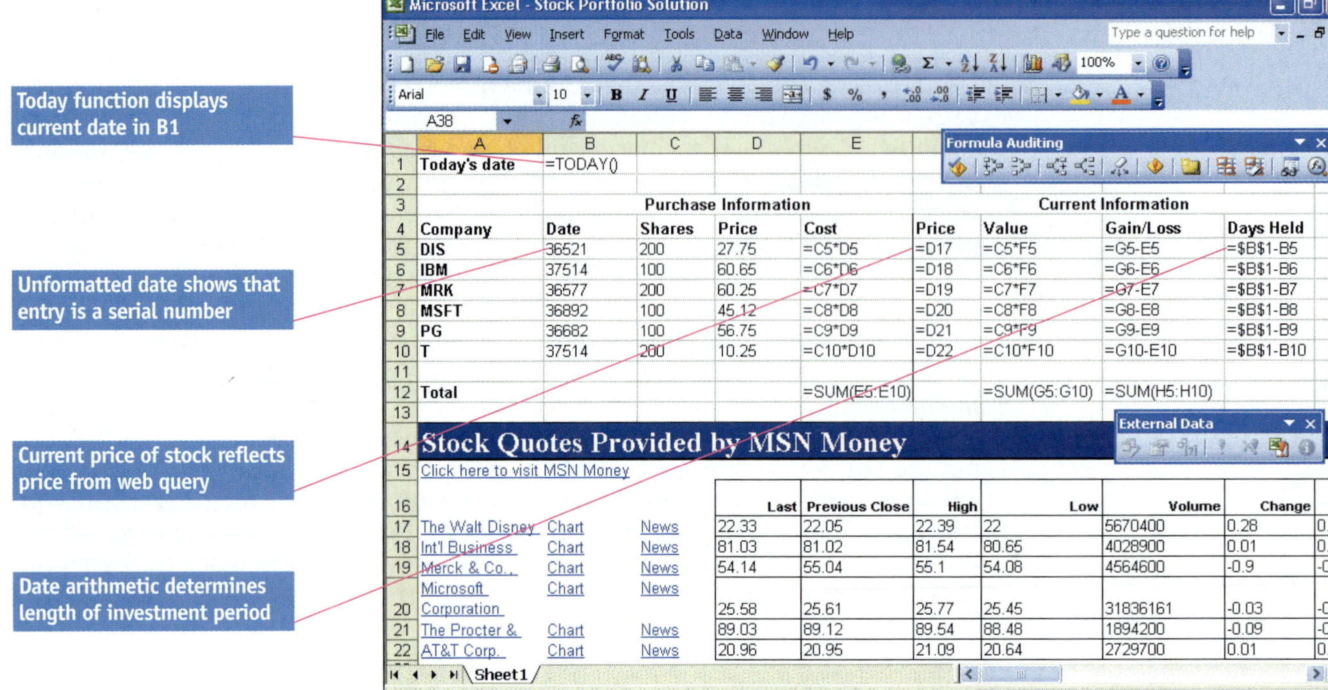

	A	B	C	D	E	F	G	H	I
1	Today's date	=TODAY()							
2									
3		Purchase Information				Current Information			
4	Company	Date	Shares	Price	Cost	Price	Value	Gain/Loss	Days Held
5	DIS	36521	200	27.75	=C5*D5	=D17	=C5*F5	=G5-E5	=$B$1-B5
6	IBM	37514	100	60.65	=C6*D6	=D18	=C6*F6	=G6-E6	=$B$1-B6
7	MRK	36577	200	60.25	=C7*D7	=D19	=C7*F7	=G7-E7	=$B$1-B7
8	MSFT	36892	100	45.12	=C8*D8	=D20	=C8*F8	=G8-E8	=$B$1-B8
9	PG	36682	100	56.75	=C9*D9	=D21	=C9*F9	=G9-E9	=$B$1-B9
10	T	37514	200	10.25	=C10*D10	=D22	=C10*F10	=G10-E10	=$B$1-B10
11									
12	Total				=SUM(E5:E10)		=SUM(G5:G10)	=SUM(H5:H10)	
13									
14	Stock Quotes Provided by MSN Money								
15	Click here to visit MSN Money								
16				Last	Previous Close	High	Low	Volume	Change
17	The Walt Disney	Chart	News	22.33	22.05	22.39	22	5670400	0.28
18	Int'l Business	Chart	News	81.03	81.02	81.54	80.65	4028900	0.01
19	Merck & Co.,	Chart	News	54.14	55.04	55.1	54.08	4564600	-0.9
20	Microsoft Corporation	Chart	News	25.58	25.61	25.77	25.45	31836161	-0.03
21	The Procter &	Chart	News	89.03	89.12	89.54	88.48	1894200	-0.09
22	AT&T Corp.	Chart	News	20.96	20.95	21.09	20.64	2729700	0.01

(b) Cell Formulas

FIGURE 2.5 Web Queries (*continued*)

The ***Today( ) function*** returns the current date (i.e., the date on which the spreadsheet is opened). If, for example, you entered the Today( ) function into a spreadsheet that was created on May 14, and you opened the spreadsheet a month later, the value of the function would be automatically updated to June 14. The fact that dates are stored as integers enables you to add or subtract two different dates and/or to use a date in any type of arithmetic computation. A person's age can be computed by subtracting the date of birth from today's date, and dividing the result by 365.

In similar fashion, you can subtract the purchase date of an investment from today's date to determine the number of days the investment was held. Look now at the formula in cell I5 of Figure 2.5b, which subtracts the date of purchase (cell B5) from an absolute reference to today's date (cell B1) to compute the length of the investment. The formula in cell I5 (=$B$1–B5) can then be copied to the remaining rows in column I to determine the length of each investment.

A date is entered in different ways, most easily by typing the date in conventional fashion such as 12/31/99 or 12/31/1999. If you specify a two-digit year, then any year from 00 to 29, is assumed to be in the 21st century; for example, 1/21/00, will be stored as January 21, 2000. (The number 29 is arbitrary and you will have to ask Microsoft why it was chosen.) To avoid confusion, you should enter all four digits of the year—for example, 10/31/2001 for October 31, 2001.

YOU MUST UNDERSTAND THE PROBLEM

The formulas to compute the cost of an investment, its current value, the associated gain or loss, and the number of days the investment was held have nothing to do with Excel per se. Neither did the formulas to compute the gross pay, net pay, and so on in the payroll example. In other words, Excel is a means to an end, rather than an end unto itself, and you must understand the underlying problem.

hands-on exercise

3 Web Queries

Objective Include a Web query into a worksheet to retrieve current stock prices from the Internet. (The exercise requires an Internet connection.) Use the Today() function to illustrate the use of date arithmetic. Use Figure 2.6 as a guide in the exercise.

Step 1: Open the Stock Portfolio

- Open the **Stock Portfolio workbook** in the **Exploring Excel folder** to display the worksheet in Figure 2.6a.
- Save the workbook as **Stock Portfolio Solution** so that you can return to the original workbook if necessary.
- Cell B1 displays today's date 8/12/2003 in our figure, but a different date on your machine. If necessary, click in **cell B1**, and note that it contains the function, **=Today()**. Thus the displayed value in cell B1 will always reflect the current date.
- Click in **cell B5**, the cell containing the date on which the shares in DIS were purchased. The contents of cell B5 are 12/27/1999 (there is no equal sign). This is a "fixed" date, and its value will not change from one day to the next.
- Pull down the **Data menu**, click **the Import External Data command**, then choose **Import Data command** to display the Select Data Source dialog box in Figure 2.6a.
- Choose the **MSN MoneyCentral Investor Stock Quotes** query, then click the **Open button**.

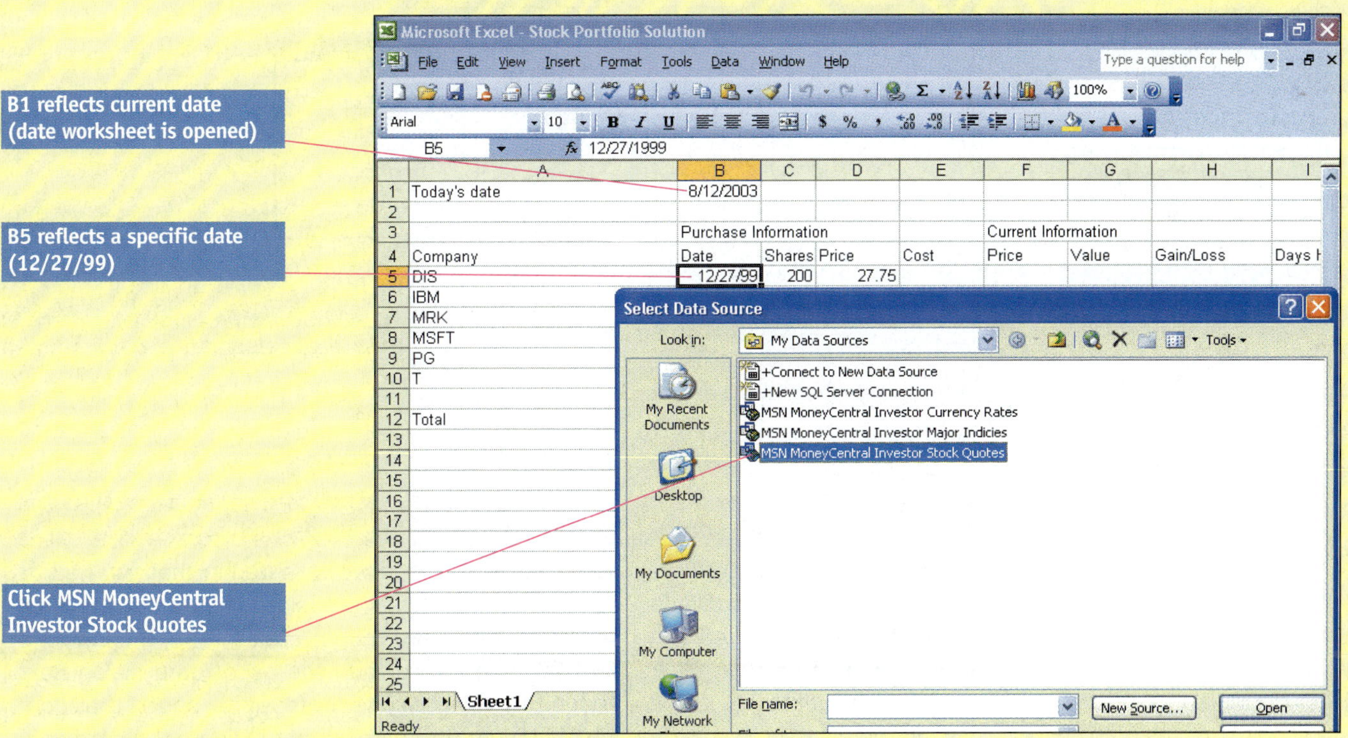

(a) Open the Stock Portfolio (step 1)

FIGURE 2.6 Hands-on Exercise 3

Step 2: Complete the Web Query

- The Import Data dialog box opens and prompts you for information about the Web query. Click the option button to put the data into the existing worksheet, then click in **cell A14** to indicate the location within the current worksheet. Click **OK**.
- Click and drag to select **cells A5** through **A10**, as the cells containing the stock symbols as shown in Figure 2.6b. Check the box to use this value reference for future refreshes. Click **OK**.
- Your system will pause as Excel goes to the Web to retrieve the information, provided you have an Internet connection. You should then see the stock quotes provided by MSN Money Central Investor.
- Do not be concerned if the column widths change as a result of the query. (You can widen them later.)
- Save the workbook.

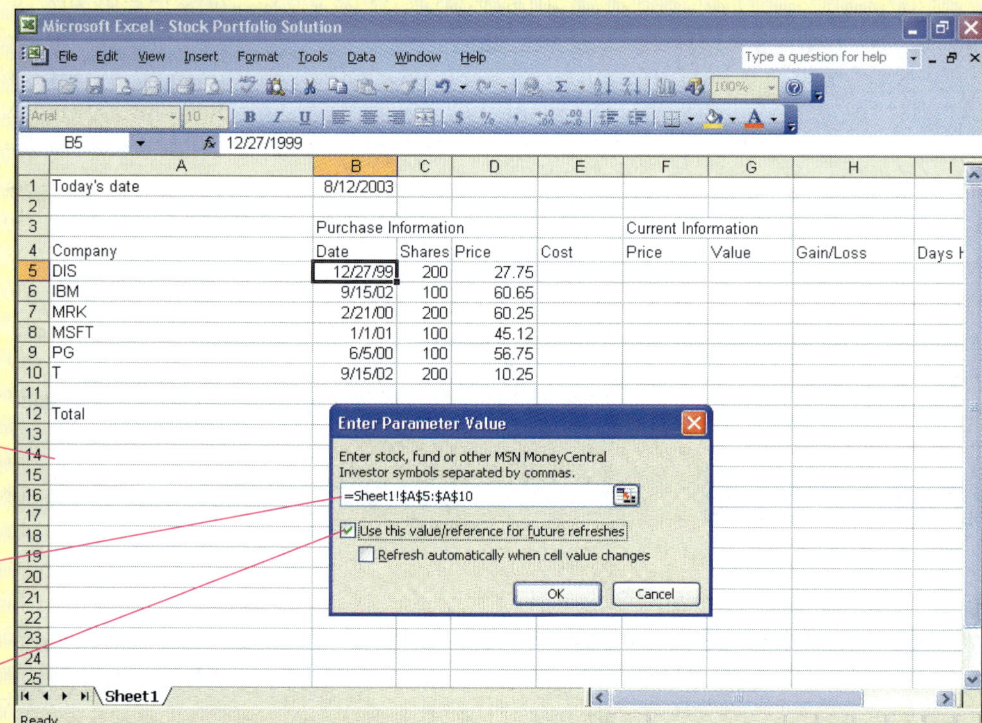

(b) Complete the Web Query (step 2)

FIGURE 2.6 Hands-on Exercise 3 (*continued*)

CREATE A NEW WEB QUERY

Web queries in earlier versions of Microsoft Office were limited in that you had to use existing queries. Office 2003, however, makes it easy to create new queries from virtually any Web page. Pull down the Data menu, click the Import External Data command, then click New Web query to display the associated dialog box. Enter the address of any Web page (try your favorite professional sport) that contains the data you want, then look for the yellow arrows that indicate the data may be imported. See problem 9 at the end of the chapter.

Step 3: Compute the Gain/Loss

- You should see the information that was obtained via the Web query as shown in Figure 2.6c. Use pointing to enter the cell references to complete the formulas for the first investment.
  - Click in **cell E5** (the cell that contains the cost of the investment) and enter the formula, **=C5*D5**.
  - Click in **cell F5** (the cell that contains today's price), and enter the formula **=D17**, which references the cell that contains the current price of **DIS**.
  - Click in **cell G5** (the cell that contains today's value of the investment) and enter the formula, **=C5*F5**.
  - Click in **cell H5** (the cell that contains the gain or loss) and enter the formula, **=G5–E5**, corresponding to today's value minus the cost.
  - Click in **cell I5** (the cell that contains the days held) and enter the formula, **=$B$1–B5**.
- If necessary, change the format in cell I5 to reflect a number, rather than a date. Click in **cell I5**, pull down the **Format menu**, click the **Cells command**, click the **Number tab**, choose **Number** as the category, and specify **zero decimal places**. Click **OK**.
- Save the workbook.

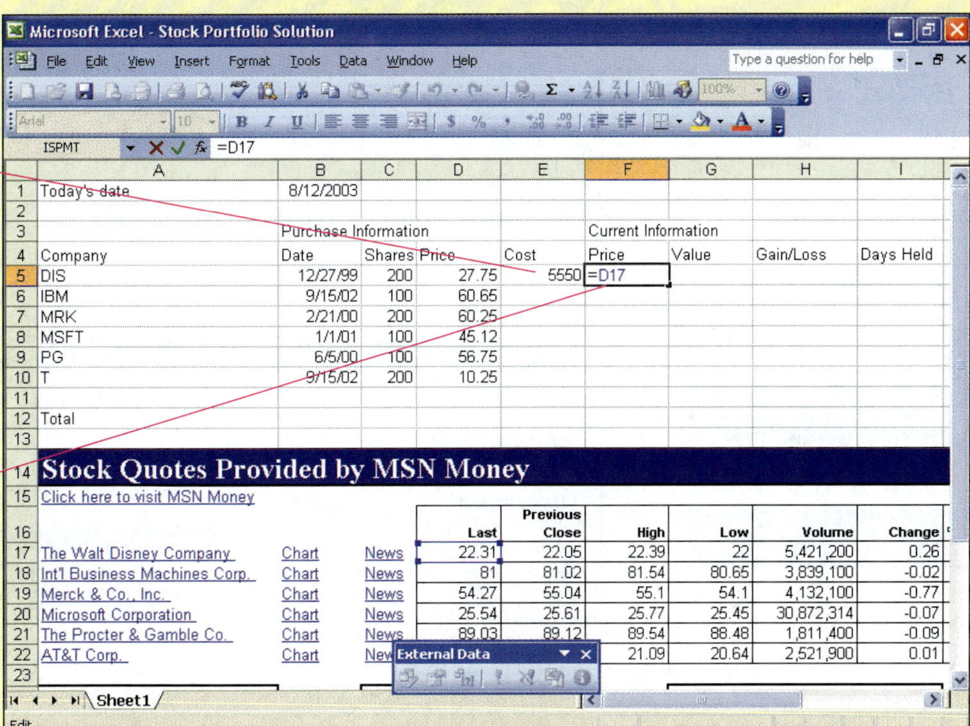

(c) Compute the Gain/Loss (step 3)

FIGURE 2.6 Hands-on Exercise 3 (*continued*)

NUMBERS, DATES, AND FORMATS

Any cell that contains a numeric value may be formatted in a variety of styles: date, number, percentage, currency, and so on. Excel does not know which format to use, and thus it is up to the user to select the cell, pull down the Format menu, click the Cells command to display the Format cells dialog box, click the Number tab, then choose the appropriate category.

Step 4: Copy the Formulas

- Click and drag to select **cells E5** through **I5**, the cells containing the formulas associated with the first investment, as shown in Figure 2.6d.
- Point to the fill handle in the lower-right corner of cell I5, then click and drag the fill handle to copy the formulas in row 5 to rows 6 through 10. Release the mouse to complete the copy operation.
- Click in **cell E12**, the cell that contains the total cost of your investments. Type **=SUM(** then click and drag to select **cells E5:E10**.
- Type a **closing parenthesis**, then press the **Enter key**. Cell E12 should contain the formula **=SUM(E5:E10)**.
- Copy the formula in cell E12 to **cells G12** and **H12**. The displayed value in cell E12 should be 35902. The displayed values in cells G12 and H12 depend on the current stock prices. The value of your portfolio will be very different from ours.
- Save the workbook.

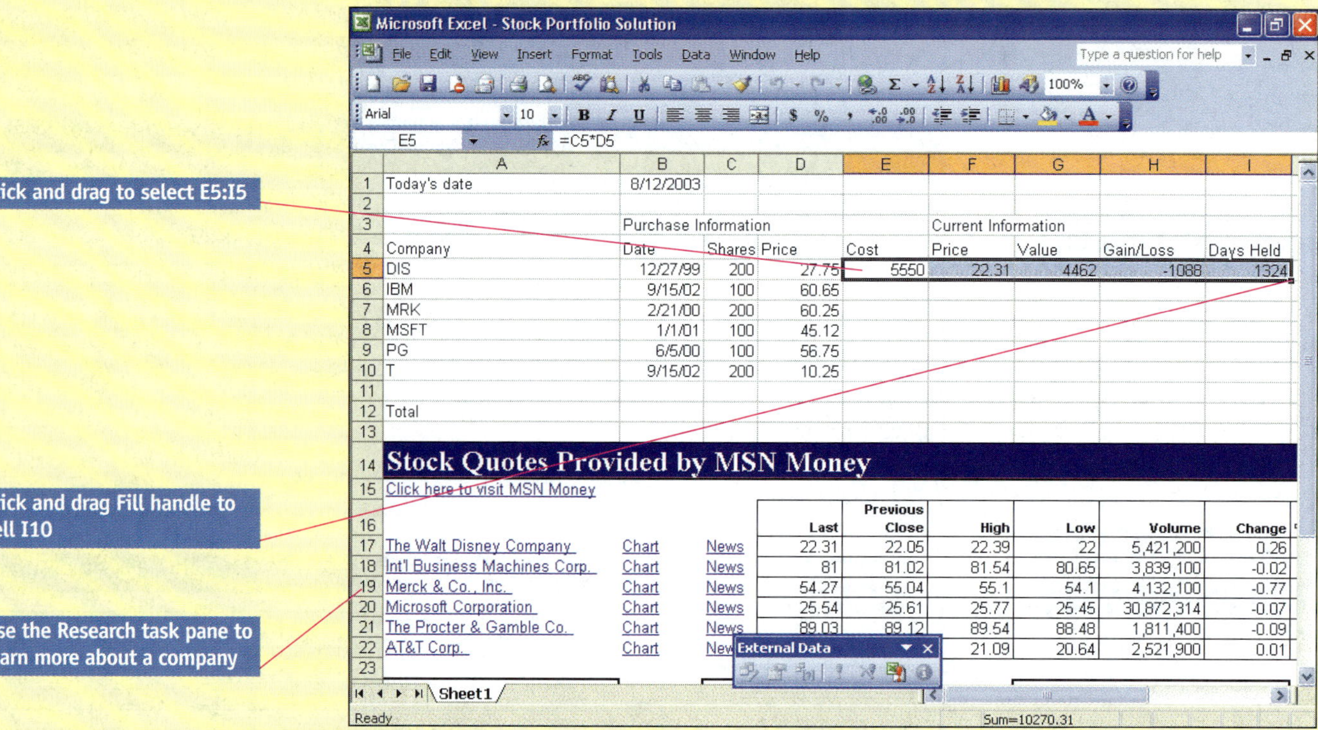

(d) Copy the Formulas (step 4)

FIGURE 2.6 Hands-on Exercise 3 (*continued*)

THE RESEARCH TASK PANE

Microsoft Office Excel 2003 introduces a research pane that connects you directly to various research tools on the Web. Pull down the Tools menu and click the Research command to display the Research task pane. Enter the name of the company for which you want information in the Search for text box, click the down arrow in the Reference Books list box, and then select Gale Company Profiles. Excel retrieves basic corporate information such as the company's address, phone, ticker symbol, and revenue, and displays the results in the task pane. Close the task pane when you are finished reading the information.

Step 5: Format the Worksheet

- Click and drag to select **cells D5** through **H12**, the cells that contain dollar amounts. Pull down the **Format menu**, click the **Cells command** to display the Format Cells dialog box, then click the **Number tab**. Format these cells in **Currency format,** with **two decimal places**. Display negative values in **red** and enclosed in **parentheses**. Click **OK**.
- Select all of the cells that contain a label (**cell A1**, **cells A3** through **I4**, **A5** through **A10**, and **cell A12**). Click the **Bold button** to boldface this information.
- Click and drag to select cells **B3** through **E3**, then click the **Merge and Center button**. Merge **cells F3** through **I3** in similar fashion.
- Click and drag to select **cells E4** through **E12.** Click the **down arrow** on the Borders button on the Formatting toolbar, then click the **right border icon** as shown in Figure 2.6e. Click **cell A1** (to deselect these cells). You should see a vertical line separating the purchase information from the current values.
- Adjust the column widths if necessary. Save the workbook.

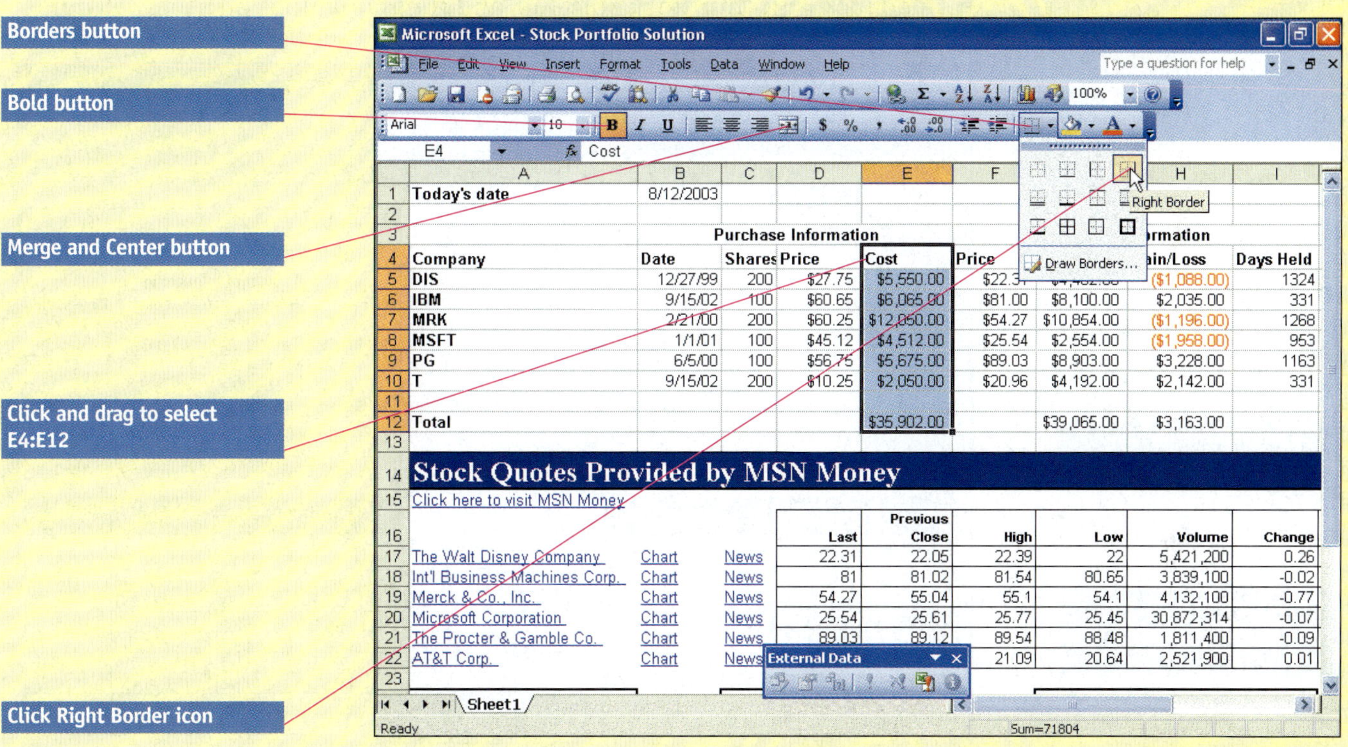

(e) Format the Worksheet (step 5)

FIGURE 2.6 Hands-on Exercise 3 (*continued*)

CAPITAL GAINS AND CONDITIONAL FORMATTING

The Internal Revenue Service offers a significant tax break on stock transactions that are considered a "long term" capital gain (more than one year under today's tax code). Click and drag to select cells I5 through I10, the cells that show how long a stock has been held. Pull down the Format menu, click the Conditional Formatting command, then enter the condition as cell value is >365. Click the Format button, click the Font tab, then choose a different color (e.g., blue) to highlight those investments that qualify for this consideration.

Step 6: **Refresh the Query**

- Right click anywhere within the Web query (i.e., within cells A14 to I22) to display the context-sensitive menu in Figure 2.6f. Click the **Refresh External Data command** to retrieve the current prices from the Web. Click **OK**.
- The numbers in your worksheet will change, provided you have an Internet connection and the stock market is open. The column widths may also change since the Web query automatically adjusts the width of its columns (see boxed tip).
- Adjust the column widths if necessary. (Remember, the value of your portfolio will be very different from ours.)
- Save the workbook a final time. Print the workbook twice, once to show the displayed values, and once to show the cell contents.
- Now that you have completed this exercise, you can experiment further with the various links within the Web query. Scroll to the bottom of the query, for example, then click the link for Symbol Lookup to find the symbol for your favorite stock or index.
- Good luck with your stock portfolio, and congratulations on a job well done.

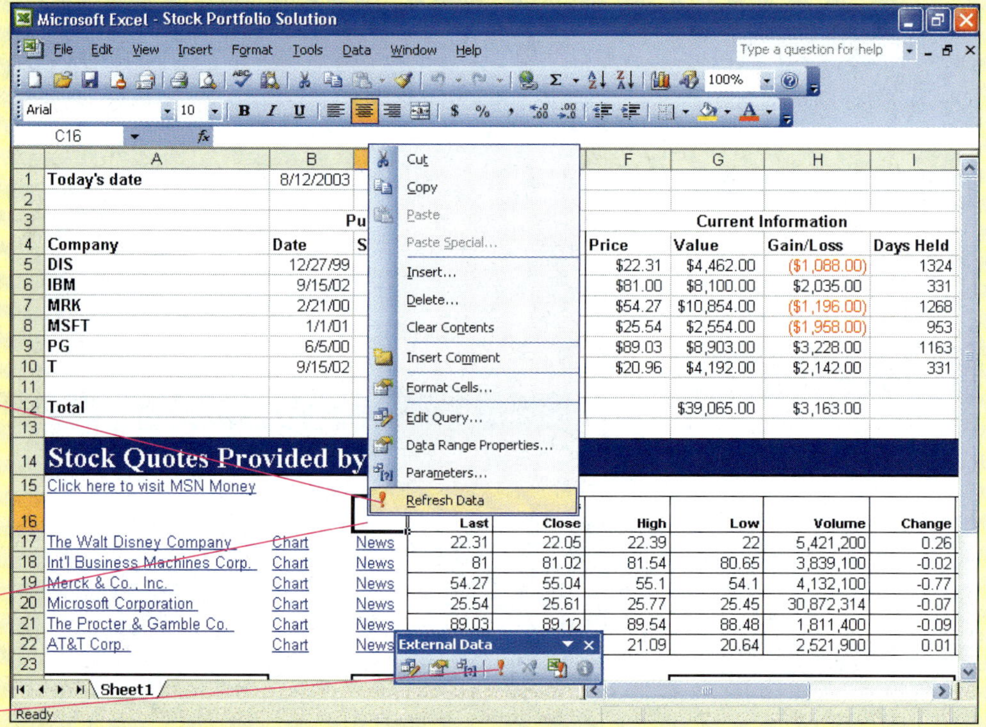

(f) Refresh the Query (step 6)

FIGURE 2.6 Hands-on Exercise 3 (*continued*)

DATA RANGE PROPERTIES

The Web query associated with MSN Stock quotes will, by default, change the column widths in the entire worksheet each time the query is refreshed. You can prevent this from happening by right clicking in the query area, then clicking the Data Range Properties command to display the associated dialog box. Clear the check box to Adjust column width, then click OK to accept the settings and close the dialog box. The next time you refresh the query, the column widths will not change.

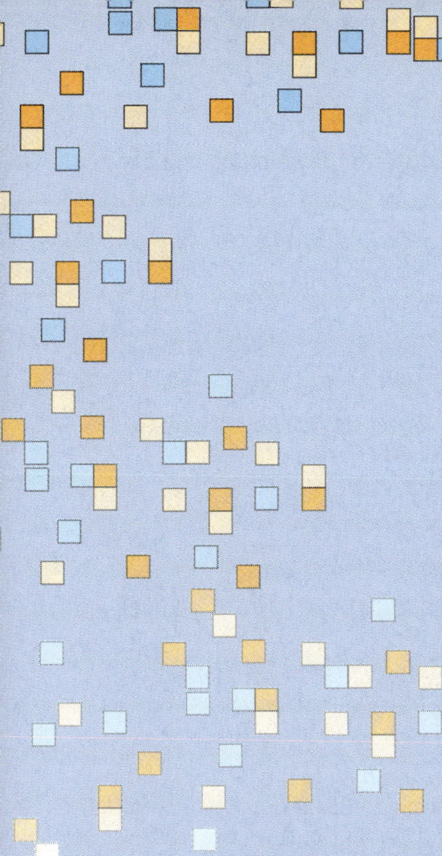

SUMMARY

The distinction between relative, absolute, and mixed references, coupled with the importance of isolating the assumptions on which a worksheet is based, are basic concepts in spreadsheet design. A relative reference (such as A1) changes both the row and column, when the cell containing the reference is copied to other cells in the worksheet. An absolute reference (such as $A$1) remains constant throughout the copy operation. A mixed reference, either $A1 or A$1, modifies the row or column, respectively. Most spreadsheets can be built through combinations of relative and absolute addresses. Mixed references are required for more advanced spreadsheets.

The initial conditions and/or assumptions on which a spreadsheet is based should be isolated so that their values can be easily changed. The formulas in the main body of the spreadsheet typically contain absolute references to these assumptions. The placement of the assumptions and initial conditions is not a requirement of Excel per se, but is crucial to the development of accurate and flexible worksheets. The Insert Comment command creates the equivalent of a screen tip that displays information about the worksheet.

Pointing and the fill handle are two techniques that facilitate the development of a spreadsheet. Although any cell reference can be entered into a formula by typing the reference directly, it is easier and more accurate to enter the reference through pointing. In essence you click in the cell that contains the formula, type an equal sign to begin the formula, then use the mouse (or arrow keys) to enter the various cell references as you build the formula.

The fill handle, a tiny black square in the lower-right corner of the selected cell(s), is the easiest way to copy a cell formula to adjacent cells. Just select the cell or cells to be copied, point to the fill handle for the selected cell(s), click and drag the fill handle over the destination range, and release the mouse.

A hyperlink can be inserted into any Excel worksheet, then the associated page viewed by clicking the link, without having to start the Web browser manually. Any worksheet or workbook can be saved as a Web page, which in turn can be stored on a Web server and displayed through a Web browser. Microsoft Office now recognizes the Single File Web Page format, which stores all of the elements on a Web page (text and graphics) as a single file.

Information from the Web can also be downloaded and inserted directly into an Excel workbook through a Web query. Office 2003 enables you to create your own Web queries from virtually any Web page.

Dates are entered into a worksheet by typing the date in conventional fashion such as 11/24/2000 or December 24, 2000. Either way all dates are stored as integers, beginning with January 1, 1900; that is January 1, 1900 is stored as the number 1. This simple concept enables date arithmetic, whereby calculations can be made between two dates to determine the number of days that have elapsed. The Today() function always returns the current date and is used in conjunction with date arithmetic.

KEY TERMS

Absolute reference 66
Conditional formatting 81
Date arithmetic 87
External Data toolbar 87
Fill handle 68
HTML document 76
Hyperlink 76
Import External Data
command 87
Insert Comment
command 68
Insert Hyperlink
command 82
Internet 76
Pointing 68
Refresh command 87
Relative reference 66
Research task pane 92
Round trip HTML 76
Save as Web Page
command 76
Single File Web Page 76
Template 86
Today() function 88
Web page 76
Web Page Preview
command 76
Web query 87

MULTIPLE CHOICE

1. The formula to compute the gross pay of an employee in the payroll example that was developed in this chapter uses:
   (a) Absolute references for hourly wage, regular hours, and overtime hours
   (b) Relative references for hourly wage, regular hours, and overtime hours
   (c) Mixed references for hourly wage, regular hours, and overtime hours
   (d) Impossible to determine

2. Which of the following best describes the formula to compute the withholding tax of an employee in the payroll example that was developed in this chapter?
   (a) It contains a relative reference to gross pay and an absolute reference to the withholding rate
   (b) It contains an absolute reference to gross pay and a relative reference to the withholding rate
   (c) It contains absolute references to both the gross pay and withholding tax
   (d) It contains relative references to both the gross pay and withholding tax

3. Cell D12 contains the formula, =SUM (A12:C12). What will the contents of cell D13 be, if the formula in cell D12 is copied to cell D13?
   (a) =SUM (A12:C12)
   (b) =SUM (A13:C13)
   (c) =SUM (A12:C13)
   (d) =SUM (A13:C12)

4. A formula containing the entry =$B$3 is copied to a cell one column over and two rows down. How will the entry appear in its new location?
   (a) =$C$5
   (b) =$B$3
   (c) =B3
   (d) =C5

5. How do you insert a hyperlink into a workbook?
   (a) Pull down the Insert menu and click the Hyperlink command
   (b) Click the Insert Hyperlink button on the Standard toolbar
   (c) Right click a cell and click the Hyperlink command
   (d) Any of the above

6. A Web browser such as Internet Explorer can display a page from:
   (a) A local drive such as drive A or drive C
   (b) A drive on a local area network
   (c) The World Wide Web
   (d) All of the above

7. What is the best way to enter the current price of a stock into an Excel worksheet?
   (a) Copy the price directly from today's copy of *The Wall Street Journal*
   (b) Save the worksheet as a Web page
   (c) Create a Web query, then refresh the query to obtain the current price
   (d) Use Internet Explorer to locate a Web page that contains the current price

8. The estimated sales for the first year of a financial forecast are contained in cell B3. The sales for year two are assumed to be 10% higher than the first year, with the rate of increase (10%) stored in cell C23 at the bottom of the spreadsheet. Which of the following is the best way to enter the sales for year two?
   (a) =B3+B3*.10
   (b) =B3+B3*C23
   (c) =B3+B3*$C$23
   (d) All of the above are equivalent entries

9. Which of the following requires an Internet connection?
   (a) Using Internet Explorer to view a Web page that is stored locally
   (b) Updating the values that are obtained through a Web query
   (c) Clicking a hyperlink that references a document that is stored on drive C
   (d) All of the above

10. Cell F6 contains the formula =AVERAGE(B6:D6). What will be the contents of cell F7 if the entry in cell F6 is *moved* to cell F7?
    (a) =AVERAGE(B6:D6)
    (b) =AVERAGE(B7:D7)
    (c) =AVERAGE($B$6:$D$6)
    (d) =AVERAGE($B$7:$D$7)

... continued

multiple choice

11. What will be stored in a cell if 2/5 is entered in it?

(a) 2/5
(b) .4
(c) The date value February 5 of the current year
(d) 2/5 or .4, depending on the format in effect

12. You type 11/24/00 into a cell, press the Enter key, and expect to see Nov 24, 2000. Instead you see the value 36854. Which of the following is the most likely explanation?

(a) Something is radically wrong with the date function
(b) The cell is formatted to display a numeric value rather than a date
(c) You should have used an equal sign to enter the date
(d) None of the above makes any sense at all

13. Which of the following formulas can be used to compute an individual's age, given that the individual's birth date is stored in cell A4?

(a) =(Today( )–A4)/365
(b) =(Today–A4)/365
(c) =(A4–Today)/365
(d) =(A4–Today( ))/365

14. Microsoft Excel and Internet Explorer are both open and display the "same" worksheet. You make a change in the Excel file that is not reflected in the Web page. What is the most likely explanation?

(a) The two files are not linked to one another
(b) The files are stored locally, as opposed to a Web server
(c) You did not refresh the Web page in Microsoft Excel
(d) You did not refresh the Web page in Internet Explorer

15. You notice that the values in a specific column are displayed in three different colors, red for values less than zero, blue for values greater than $100,000, and black otherwise. How is this possible?

(a) The colored formatting is automatically built into every Excel worksheet
(b) A Web query was used to implement the red and blue formatting
(c) Conditional formatting was applied to the column
(d) It is not possible; that is, the question is in error

16. A formula containing the cell reference A$4 is copied to a cell one column over and two rows down. How will the reference appear in its new location?

(a) Both the row and column will change
(b) Neither the row nor column will change
(c) The row will change but the column will remain the same
(d) The column will change but the row will remain the same

17. The formula =B3+C4 is stored in cell D5. What will the formula be if a row is inserted above the second row?

(a) =B3+C4
(b) =B4+C5
(c) =C3+D4
(d) =B2+C3

18. You want to add the contents of cells C1, C2, C3, and C4 but expect that additional values may be inserted within the column of numbers at a later time. Which formula automatically adjusts to *include* the additional entries?

(a) =C1+C2+C3+C4
(b) =SUM(C1:C4)
(c) Both entries will automatically adjust
(d) Neither entry will adjust if rows are inserted

ANSWERS

1. b	**7.** c	**13.** a
2. a	**8.** c	**14.** d
3. b	**9.** b	**15.** c
4. b	**10.** a	**16.** d
5. d	**11.** c	**17.** b
6. d	**12.** b	**18.** b

PRACTICE WITH EXCEL

1. **Alternate Payroll:** Figure 2.7 contains an alternate version of the payroll that was created in the first hands-on exercise in the chapter. The new spreadsheet includes the number of dependents for each employee and a fixed deduction per dependent, which combine to reduce an individual's taxable income. An employee with two dependents, for example, would have his or her taxable income reduced by $100 ($50 per dependent). The revised spreadsheet also isolates the overtime rate as an assumption at the bottom of the worksheet, which enables the user to change the overtime rate in a single place should that become necessary.
   a. Open the *Chapter 2 Practice 1* workbook, and then complete the spreadsheet so that the displayed values match ours. Use the appropriate combination of relative and absolute references in row 4, so that you can copy the formulas in this row to the remaining rows in the worksheet.
   b. Click in cell F12 and enter the appropriate Sum function to compute the total gross pay for all employees. Copy this formula to the remaining cells in this row.
   c. Format the worksheet in an attractive fashion. You do not have to match our formatting exactly, but you are to display all dollar amounts with the currency symbol and two decimal places.
   d. Substitute your name for the employee named "Grauer", then sort the worksheet so that the employees appear in alphabetical order. (Click anywhere within column A and click the Sort Ascending button on the Standard toolbar. Note, too, that there must be a blank row above the total row, or else it will be sorted with the other rows.) Shade the row containing your name.
   e. Print the completed worksheet twice, once with displayed values, and once to show the cell formulas. Use the Page Setup command to switch to landscape printing and force the output onto one page. Print gridlines and row and column headings. Change the column widths as appropriate.
   f. Change the overtime rate in cell E14 to 2.00; that is, an employee is paid double time for each overtime hour. Change the withholding rate in cell E16 to 25%. Print the displayed values to reflect these changes.

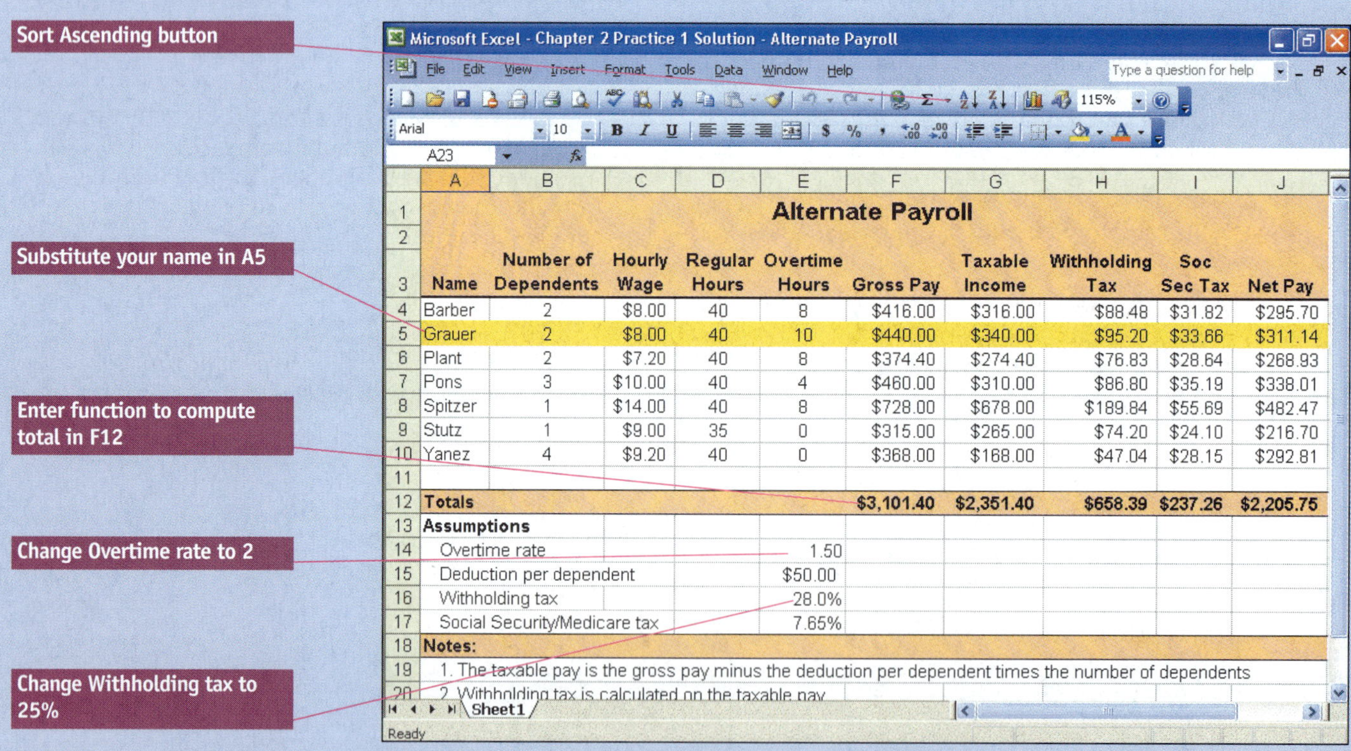

Alternate Payroll

Name	Number of Dependents	Hourly Wage	Regular Hours	Overtime Hours	Gross Pay	Taxable Income	Withholding Tax	Soc Sec Tax	Net Pay
Barber	2	$8.00	40	8	$416.00	$316.00	$88.48	$31.82	$295.70
Grauer	2	$8.00	40	10	$440.00	$340.00	$95.20	$33.66	$311.14
Plant	2	$7.20	40	8	$374.40	$274.40	$76.83	$28.64	$268.93
Pons	3	$10.00	40	4	$460.00	$310.00	$86.80	$35.19	$338.01
Spitzer	1	$14.00	40	8	$728.00	$678.00	$189.84	$55.69	$482.47
Stutz	1	$9.00	35	0	$315.00	$265.00	$74.20	$24.10	$216.70
Yanez	4	$9.20	40	0	$368.00	$168.00	$47.04	$28.15	$292.81
Totals					$3,101.40	$2,351.40	$658.39	$237.26	$2,205.75
Assumptions									
Overtime rate				1.50					
Deduction per dependent				$50.00					
Withholding tax				28.0%					
Social Security/Medicare tax				7.65%					
Notes:									
1. The taxable pay is the gross pay minus the deduction per dependent times the number of dependents									
2. Withholding tax is calculated on the taxable pay									

FIGURE 2.7 Alternate Payroll (exercise 1)

2. **The Sports Statistician:** Figure 2.8 illustrates how Excel can be used to tabulate statistics for a hypothetical softball league. Open the partially completed worksheet in *Chapter 2 Practice 2* workbook, and proceed as follows:
   a. An individual batting average is computed by dividing the number of hits by the number of at bats (e.g., 30/80 or .375 for Maryann Barber). The batting average should be formatted to three decimal places. (Create the Custom format .000 to eliminate the 0 before the batting average to display .375, rather than the default numerical format of 0.000.)
   b. Compute the total bases for an individual by multiplying the number of singles by one, the number of doubles by two, the number of triples by three, and the number of home runs by four, then adding the results.
   c. The slugging percentage is computed by dividing the total bases by the number of at bats (e.g., 48/80 or .600 for Maryann Barber). The slugging average should be formatted to three decimal places.
   d. The team totals for all columns except batting average and slugging percentage are determined by summing the appropriate values. The team batting average and slugging percentage are computed by dividing the number of hits and total bases, respectively, by the number of at bats.
   e. Substitute your name for Jessica Grauer (our league is coed), sort the players in alphabetical order, then format the worksheet so that it matches Figure 2.8.
   f. Add an appropriate clip art image somewhere in the worksheet using the same technique as in any Office application. Pull down the Insert menu, click (or point to) Picture, then click Clip Art to open the task pane. Click in the Search text box. Enter "baseball" to search for any clip art image that is described with this keyword and click the Go button.
   g. Print the completed worksheet twice, once with displayed values, and once to show the cell formulas. Use the Page Setup command for the cell formulas to switch to landscape printing and force the output onto one page. Print gridlines and row and column headings. Add a cover sheet, then submit all three pages (cover sheet, displayed values, and cell formulas) to your instructor.

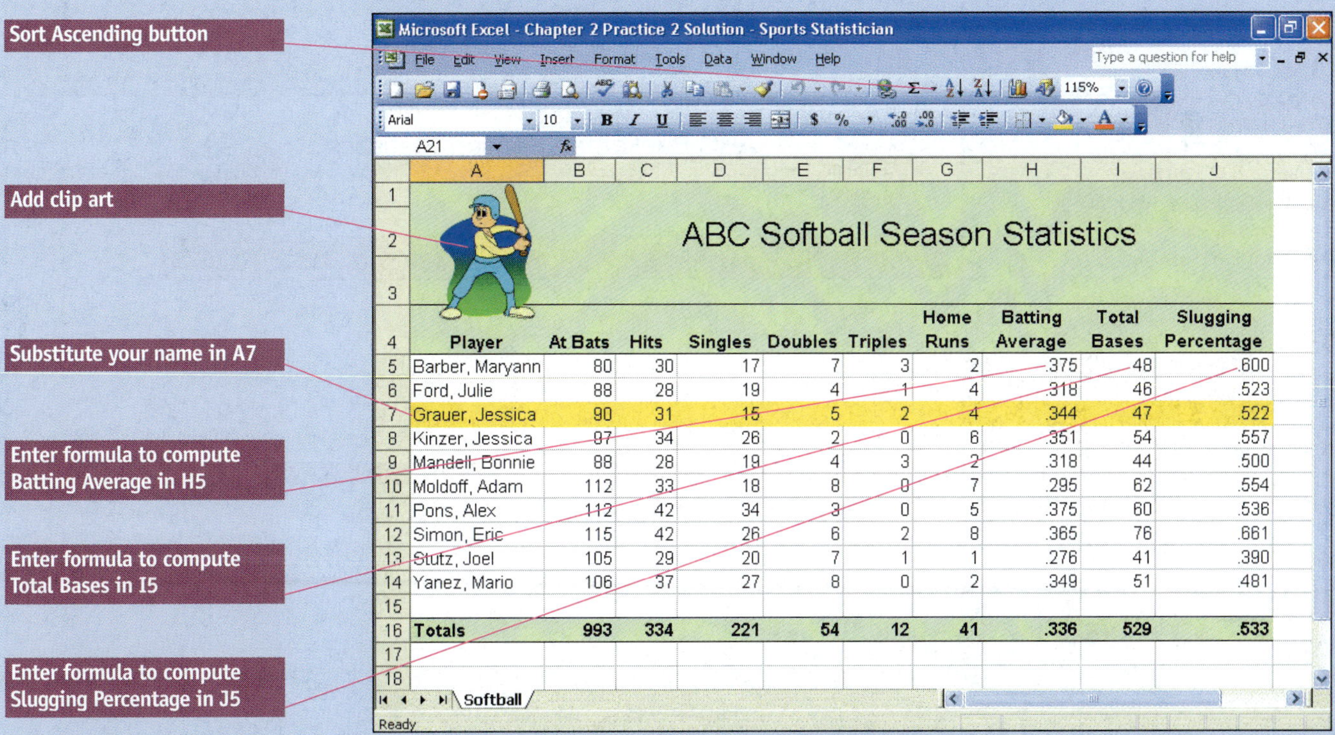

Player	At Bats	Hits	Singles	Doubles	Triples	Home Runs	Batting Average	Total Bases	Slugging Percentage
Barber, Maryann	80	30	17	7	3	2	.375	48	.600
Ford, Julie	88	28	19	4	1	4	.318	46	.523
Grauer, Jessica	90	31	15	5	2	4	.344	47	.522
Kinzer, Jessica	97	34	26	2	0	6	.351	54	.557
Mandell, Bonnie	88	28	19	4	3	2	.318	44	.500
Moldoff, Adam	112	33	18	8	0	7	.295	62	.554
Pons, Alex	112	42	34	3	0	5	.375	60	.536
Simon, Eric	115	42	26	6	2	8	.365	76	.661
Stutz, Joel	105	29	20	7	1	1	.276	41	.390
Yanez, Mario	106	37	27	8	0	2	.349	51	.481
Totals	**993**	**334**	**221**	**54**	**12**	**41**	**.336**	**529**	**.533**

FIGURE 2.8 The Sports Statistician (exercise 2)

3. **Web Pages and Hyperlinks:** The Web page in Figure 2.9 is based on the partially completed *Chapter 2 Practice 3* workbook in the Exploring Excel folder. Your assignment is to complete the workbook in Excel, then save the workbook as a Web page. (You can view the Web page locally as in Figure 2.9, without loading it onto a Web server.) Proceed as follows:
   a. Compute the total points for each player by multiplying the number of free throws, 2-point field goals, and 3-point field goals by 1, 2, and 3, respectively.
   b. Compute the points per game for each player by dividing the total points by the number of games. Display the result to one decimal point. Compute the rebounds per game in similar fashion.
   c. Add clip art as you see fit. We used the same image twice to bracket the title of the worksheet, but feel free to improve on our design. Format your page to match ours.
   d. Add your name as the statistician in the bottom of the worksheet. Instead of merely typing your name, however, add your name as a hyperlink that points to your home page if you have one. If you do not have a home page, use any Web address that is appropriate, such as www.nba.com for the National Basketball Association. In any event, the text should say, "Click here for John Doe's (substitute your name) Home Page".
   e. Print the completed workbook from Excel to show both displayed values and cell formulas. Use the Page Setup command to display gridlines and row and column headings.
   f. Save the workbook as a Web page, then open the workbook in Internet Explorer. How does the printed Web page compare to the printed workbook?
   g. This exercise demonstrates how easy it is to create a Web page from an Excel worksheet and view it locally within Internet Explorer. To place a page on the Web, you will need Internet access, and further, you will need storage space on a Web server. Check with your instructor to see if these resources are available to you, and if so, find out the steps necessary to upload your page to the server. Send a note to your instructor that contains the Web address where he or she may view your Web page.

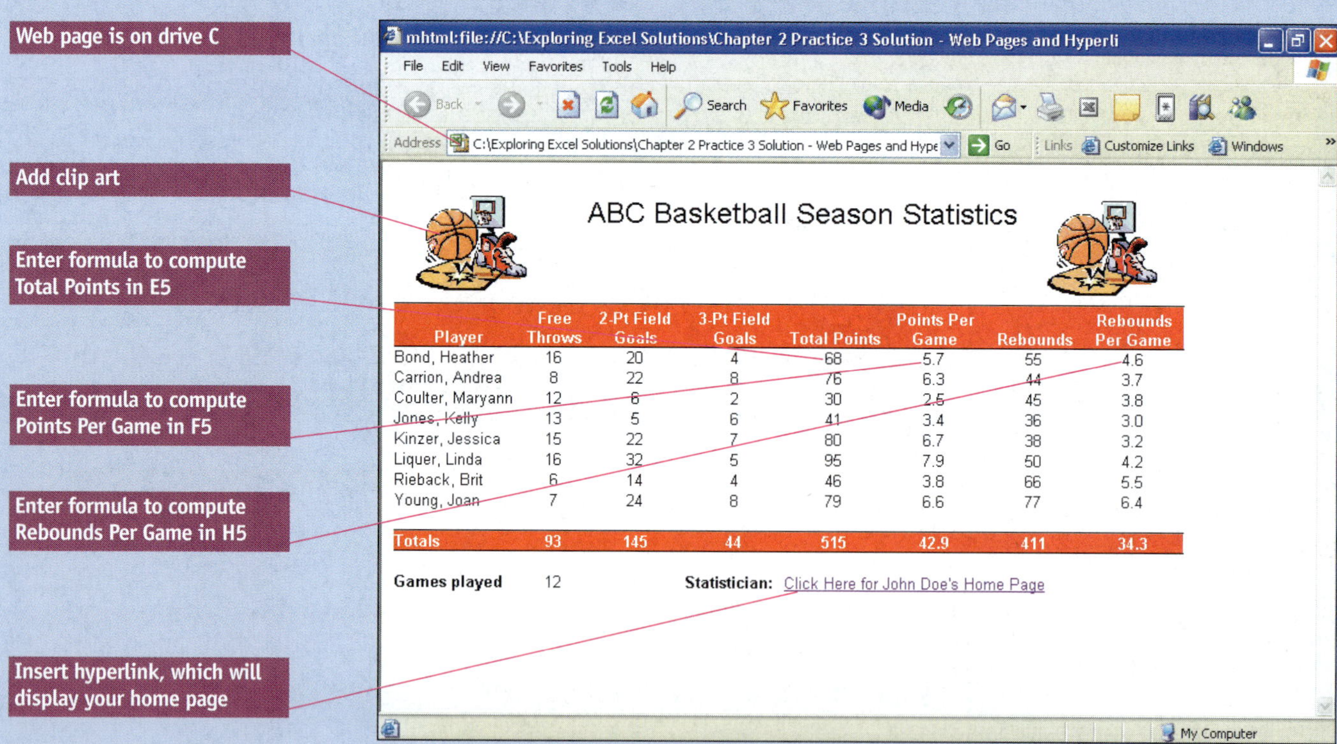

Player	Free Throws	2-Pt Field Goals	3-Pt Field Goals	Total Points	Points Per Game	Rebounds	Rebounds Per Game
Bond, Heather	16	20	4	68	5.7	55	4.6
Carrion, Andrea	8	22	8	76	6.3	44	3.7
Coulter, Maryann	12	6	2	30	2.5	45	3.8
Jones, Kelly	13	5	6	41	3.4	36	3.0
Kinzer, Jessica	15	22	7	80	6.7	38	3.2
Liquer, Linda	16	32	5	95	7.9	50	4.2
Rieback, Brit	6	14	4	46	3.8	66	5.5
Young, Joan	7	24	8	79	6.6	77	6.4
Totals	93	145	44	515	42.9	411	34.3

FIGURE 2.9 Web Pages and Hyperlinks (exercise 3)

4. **The Workout Schedule:** The worksheet in Figure 2.10 is essentially an exercise in formatting, but it also tests your ability to copy efficiently within a worksheet. You do not have to duplicate our document exactly, but you are required to have the equivalent functionality. You can create the document entirely on your own, or you can follow our suggested procedure.
   a. Open a new workbook. Click in cell B4 and enter "Day". Click in cell C4 and type "Monday". Click and drag to select cells C4 through E4, click the Merge and Center button to create a single cell, then use the Borders button to place a border around the merged cell. Drag the fill handle of this cell to enter the remaining days of the week in row 4.
   b. Enter "EXERCISE" and "SET" in cells A5 and B5, respectively. Select both cells, change the fill color to black and the text color to white. Center the text. Click the Bold button so that the text stands out.
   c. Enter 1, 2, and 3 in cells C5, D5, and E5, respectively. Click in cell B5, click the Format Painter button, and copy the formatting to cells C5 through E5. Copy these cells to the remaining cells in this row.
   d. Center "Pounds" and "Reps" in cells B6 and B7, respectively. Change the fill color in cell B7. Place a border around cells B6 and B7, then copy the formatting to the remaining cells in rows 6 and 7. (You can use the Format Painter and/or the Paste Special command, after which you choose formats.)
   e. Adjust the width of column A. Add the appropriate border around the merged cell in A6. Copy rows 6 and 7 to the remaining rows in the worksheet.
   f. Merge cells B1 through Q1 to enter the title of the worksheet. Merge cells B2 through Q2 and enter your name. Change the row height in rows 1 to 4 as appropriate, and then insert an appropriate logo in the upper-left portion of the worksheet.
   g. Print the completed worksheet in landscape mode. Be sure the worksheet fits on a single sheet of paper. Use the Page Setup command to add a footer that shows the name of the worksheet (i.e., the week of the workout).
   h. Copy the completed worksheet to two additional worksheets within the workbook. Rename all three worksheets to indicate the week of the workout.

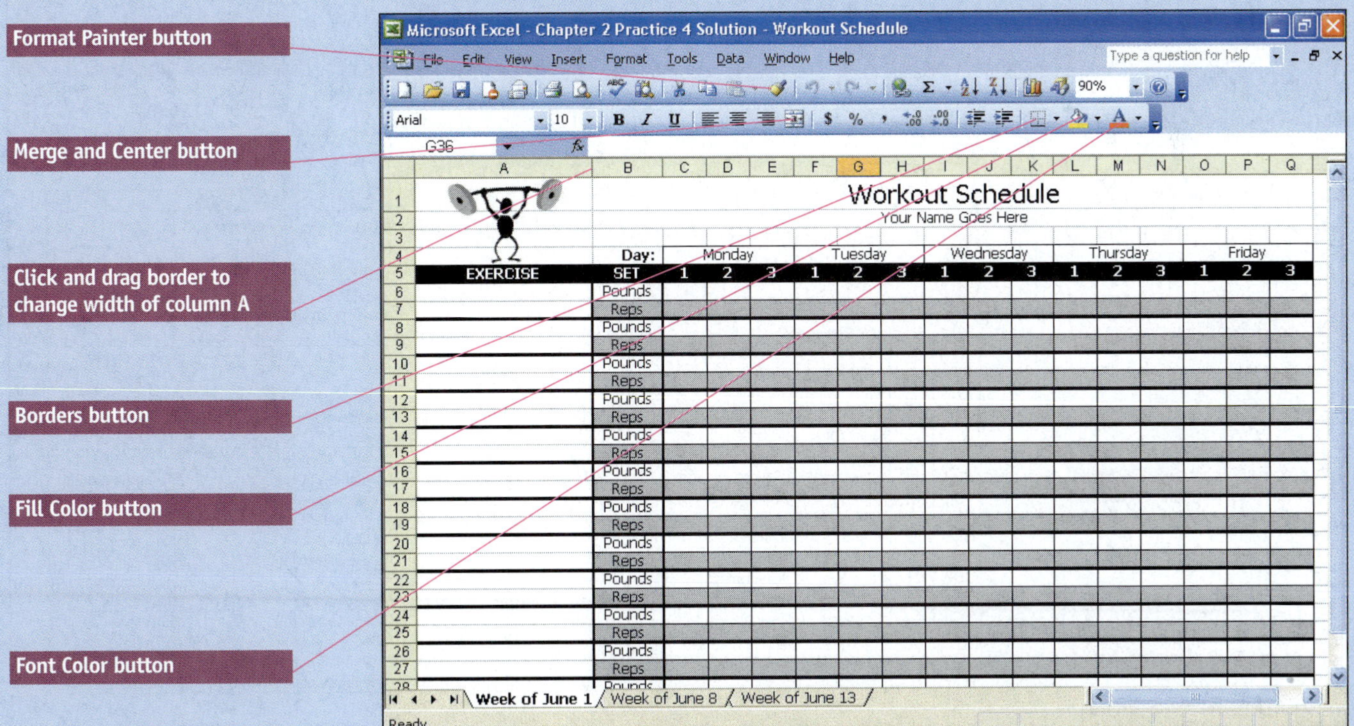

FIGURE 2.10 The Workout Schedule (exercise 4)

5. **An Exercise in Conversion:** The worksheet in Figure 2.11 displays a series of common conversion factors and the associated set of equivalent values. Open the partially completed workbook in *Chapter 2 Practice 5,* and then complete the workbook to match Figure 2.11. You do not have to match our formatting exactly, nor do you have to enter the identical values in column G.
   a. Click in cell E8 and enter the formula, =1/E7. (Cell E7 contains the value to convert inches to centimeters; the reciprocal of that value will convert centimeters to inches.) Enter the appropriate formula in cell E19 to convert kilograms to pounds.
   b. A kilobyte is mistakenly thought of as 1,000 bytes, whereas it is actually 1,024 (2^{10}) bytes. In similar fashion, a megabyte and a gigabyte are 2^{20} and 2^{30} bytes, respectively. Use this information to enter the appropriate formulas to display the conversion factors in cells E21, E22, and E23.
   c. Enter the formulas for the first conversion in row 7. Click in cell H7 and enter =C7. Click in cell J7 and enter =E7*G7. Click in cell K7 and enter =D7. Copy the formulas in row 7 to the remaining rows in the worksheet. (The use of formulas for columns H through K builds flexibility into the worksheet; that is, you can change any of the conversion factors on the left side of the worksheet, and the right side will be updated automatically.)
   d. Enter a set of values in column G for conversion; for example, enter 12 in column G7 to convert 12 inches to centimeters. The result should appear automatically in cell J7. Shade cells G7 through G23.
   e. Convert the entry in cell B3 to a hyperlink for www.onlineconversion.com.
   f. Use the Merge and Center command as necessary throughout the worksheet to approximate the formatting in Figure 2.11. Change the orientation in Column B so that the various labels are displayed as indicated.
   g. Display a border around groups of cells as shown in Figure 2.11. The easiest way to do this is to select the cells, then click the down arrow on the Borders tool on the Formatting toolbar to choose the appropriate border.
   h. Print the displayed values and the cell formulas for your instructor. Be sure to show the row and column headings as well as the gridlines. Use landscape printing to be sure the worksheet fits on a single sheet of paper.

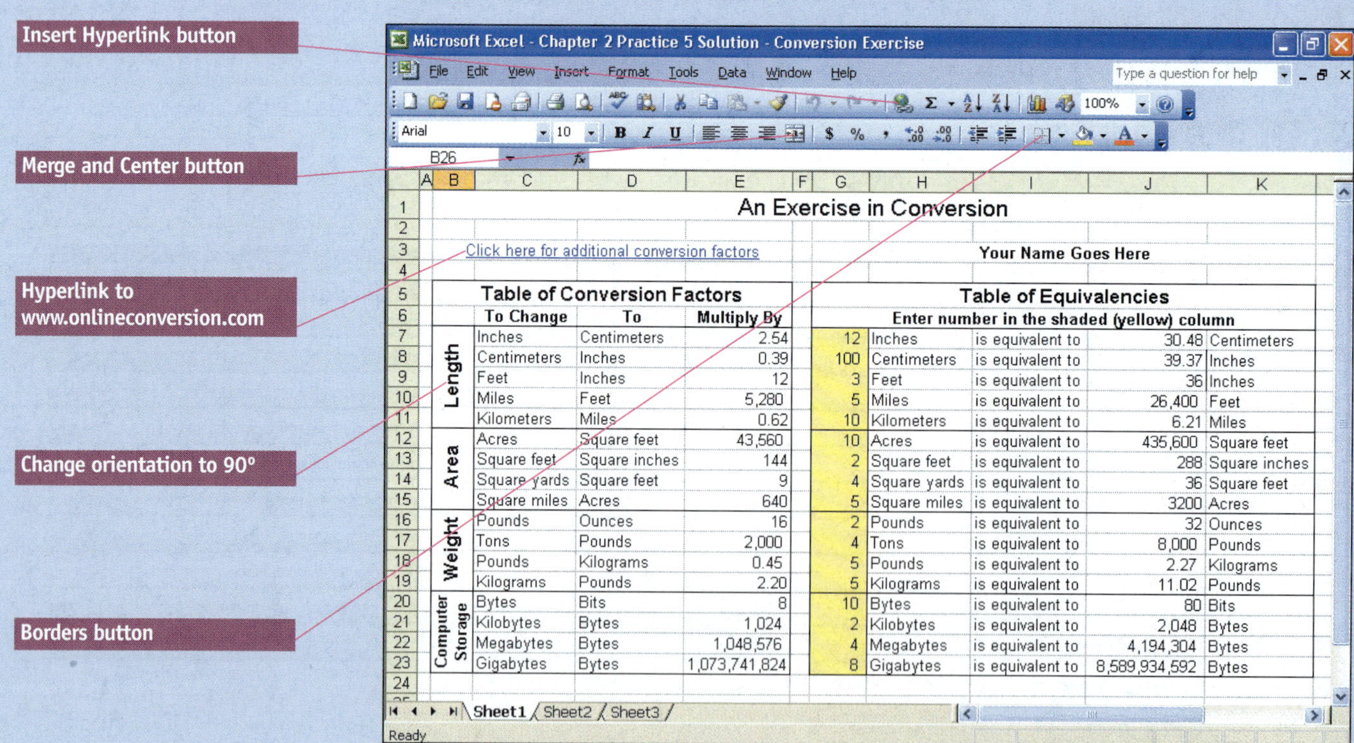

	Table of Conversion Factors				Table of Equivalencies			
	To Change	To	Multiply By		Enter number in the shaded (yellow) column			
Length	Inches	Centimeters	2.54	12	Inches	is equivalent to	30.48	Centimeters
	Centimeters	Inches	0.39	100	Centimeters	is equivalent to	39.37	Inches
	Feet	Inches	12	3	Feet	is equivalent to	36	Inches
	Miles	Feet	5,280	5	Miles	is equivalent to	26,400	Feet
	Kilometers	Miles	0.62	10	Kilometers	is equivalent to	6.21	Miles
Area	Acres	Square feet	43,560	10	Acres	is equivalent to	435,600	Square feet
	Square feet	Square inches	144	2	Square feet	is equivalent to	288	Square inches
	Square yards	Square feet	9	4	Square yards	is equivalent to	36	Square feet
	Square miles	Acres	640	5	Square miles	is equivalent to	3200	Acres
Weight	Pounds	Ounces	16	2	Pounds	is equivalent to	32	Ounces
	Tons	Pounds	2,000	4	Tons	is equivalent to	8,000	Pounds
	Pounds	Kilograms	0.45	5	Pounds	is equivalent to	2.27	Kilograms
	Kilograms	Pounds	2.20	5	Kilograms	is equivalent to	11.02	Pounds
Computer Storage	Bytes	Bits	8	10	Bytes	is equivalent to	80	Bits
	Kilobytes	Bytes	1,024	2	Kilobytes	is equivalent to	2,048	Bytes
	Megabytes	Bytes	1,048,576	4	Megabytes	is equivalent to	4,194,304	Bytes
	Gigabytes	Bytes	1,073,741,824	8	Gigabytes	is equivalent to	8,589,934,592	Bytes

FIGURE 2.11 An Exercise in Conversion (exercise 5)

6. **Web Queries:** Microsoft Office includes a Web query to determine the exchange rates for popular currencies as can be seen in Figure 2.12. The worksheet contains formulas for two parallel sets of conversions, from British pounds to dollars, and from dollars to British pounds. Open the partially completed workbook in *Chapter 2 Practice 6*, then proceed as follows:
   a. Use the Import External Data command to enter the Web query (MS MoneyCentral Investor Currency Rates) in the worksheet, starting in cell A13. Click in cell B11 and enter the appropriate cell reference within the query (cell B24 in our example, which is not visible in Figure 2.12) to obtain the current value of the conversion factor. Use the value in cell B11 to convert the amounts in British pounds to the equivalent dollar amounts. Note that Microsoft is continually changing the content of its queries to include different currencies, so you may have to enter a different cell address.
   b. Click in cell E11 and enter the conversion factor to convert dollars to pounds. (This is the reciprocal of the value in cell B11.) Complete the entries in column E, which convert dollars to the equivalent amount in British pounds.
   c. Format the worksheet to match Figure 2.12. Be sure to use the appropriate currency symbols for dollars and pounds. Add your name and today's date as shown.
   d. Click the tab for the Euro (European Currency) worksheet and enter the formulas for the appropriate conversion from Euros to dollars and vice versa. You do not have to enter the query on this worksheet, because you can reference the values in the existing query. The entry in cell B11 of the Euro worksheet is Pounds!B34 on our worksheet (remember, the query changes continually so you may have to adjust the cell reference). Click in cell B11 of the Euro worksheet, type an equal sign to begin pointing, click the Pounds worksheet, and click in the cell containing the appropriate conversion, then click Enter to finish the formula.
   e. Format the Euro worksheet and include the European Currency Symbol as appropriate. Print both worksheets for your instructor.

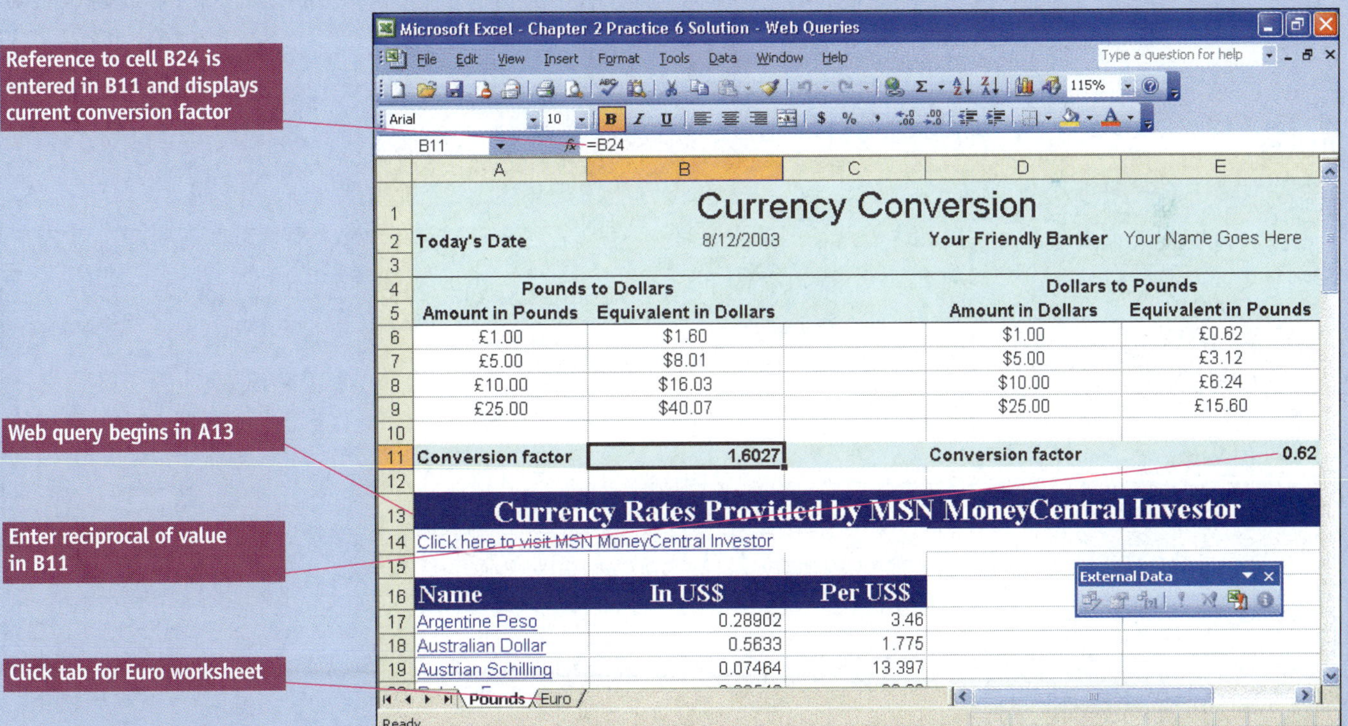

FIGURE 2.12 Web Queries (exercise 6)

7. **Buying a PC:** The worksheet in Figure 2.13 is intended to help you evaluate PC configurations from different vendors. The technical specifications for a PC are continually changing, so the minimum requirements in our worksheet may no longer be appropriate. Still, the partially completed worksheet in *Chapter 2 Practice 7* is a good starting place for your research. Open the workbook and proceed as follows:
   a. Enter the names of three vendors you would consider in cells C3, D3, and E3, respectively. Enter the associated Web sites in cells C4, D4, and E4. Visit the Web site of each vendor to determine an appropriate configuration that the vendor is currently offering. Specifications change all the time, and our minimum specifications in column B may be out of date. Thus, adjust the entries in column B as you see fit. Highlight any cell where you have modified the specification.
   b. Enter the costs associated with each system selected in part (a) in row 6. Your system will include some or all of the specifications at no additional charge. Enter the dollar amount of any item that is not included in the bundled price in the appropriate cell in the body of the worksheet.
   c. Software is probably extra. The vendor may include a basic version of the operating system; e.g., Windows XP Home edition, but there will (most likely) be a charge if you want to upgrade. The same is true for Microsoft Office; that is, you have to purchase the version of the Office suite that contains the four major applications.
   d. Enter the appropriate Sum function in cell C25. You also need to enter the shipping, sales tax, and formula for the grand total in the appropriate cells in column C. Copy the formulas for the cells in column C to the corresponding cells in columns D and E.
   e. Enter your name in cell B3 as indicated. Enter a function to determine today's date in cell B4. Insert an appropriate piece of clip art in the upper left portion of the worksheet.
   f. Format the completed worksheet. You do not have to match our formatting exactly, but you are to display dollar amounts with the currency symbol and no decimal places.
   g. Print the completed worksheet two ways, once with displayed values and once with cell formulas. Be sure the worksheet fits on one page and that you display gridlines and row and column headings.

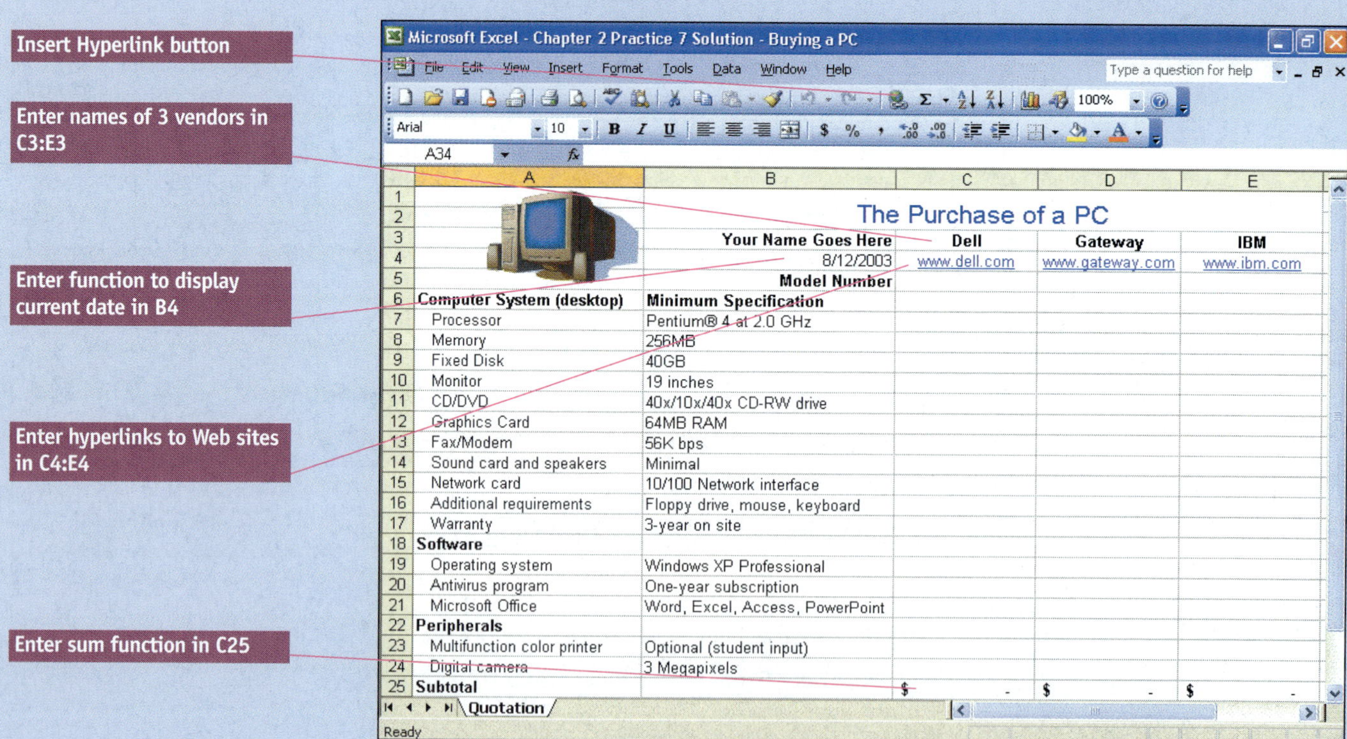

FIGURE 2.13 Buying a PC (exercise 7)

8. **Mixed References:** Most spreadsheets can be developed using a combination of relative and absolute references. Occasionally, however, you will need to incorporate mixed references as in a multiplication table. This assignment asks you to create a worksheet similar to the one in Figure 2.14. You can extend the range of the table and/or use different formatting. You are required, however, to use a formula containing mixed references in the first cell of the table (cell B4 in our figure) that can be copied to the remaining entries in this row, after which the entire row can be copied to the remaining rows in the worksheet.
   a. Enter the row and column headings in row 3 and column A, respectively. One way to create these values is through the AutoFill feature. Simply enter 1 and 2 in the first two cells for the row headings, select both of these cells, then drag the fill handle to continue the series in the remaining cells. Repeat the process to enter the column headings.
   b. The interesting part of this problem is the initial formula in the body of the worksheet (we don't want you to enter the results manually); that is, you need mixed references for the formula in cell B4. The formula is easy if you ask yourself the right questions. The product in cell B4 multiplies the value in cell A4 by the value in cell B3. Ask yourself questions to what happens to the formula when it is copied to the remaining rows and columns in the worksheet. Will the first number always come from column A? (Yes.) Will it always come from row 4? (No.) Will the second number always come from column B? (No.) Will it always come from row 3? (Yes.) The answers tell you how to create the mixed references.
   c. Copy the formula in cell B4 to the remaining columns in this row. Now copy row 4 to the remaining rows in the worksheet. Verify that the worksheet is correct by checking the displayed value at the bottom right of the table (144 in our example.)
   d. Add your name to the worksheet and submit it to your instructor. Remember, this worksheet is for a young person, so formatting is important. Print the cell formulas as well so that you can see how the mixed reference changes throughout the worksheet. Submit the complete assignment to your instructor. Using mixed references correctly is challenging, but once you arrive at the correct solution, you will have learned a lot about this very powerful spreadsheet feature.

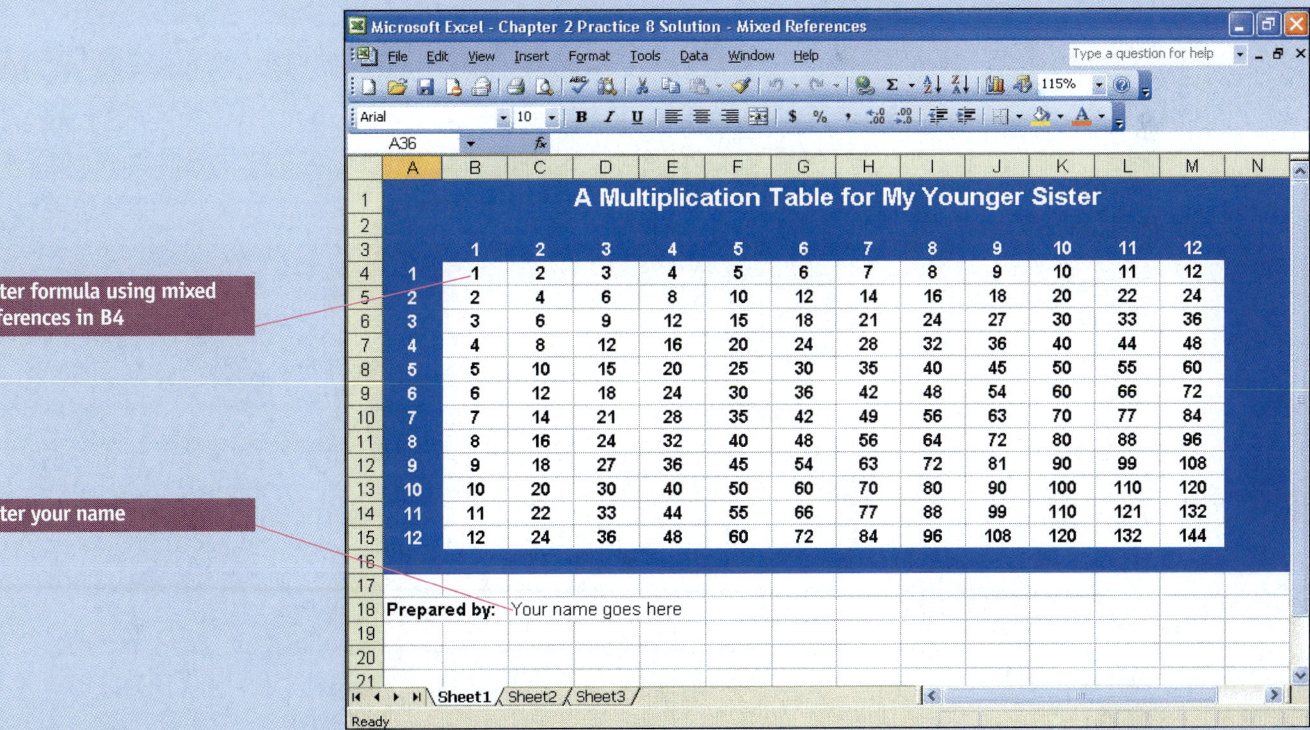

FIGURE 2.14 Mixed References (exercise 8)

9. **Create a New Web Query:** You can create a new Web query to obtain data from almost any site and then use that data as the basis of calculations within an Excel workbook. Use Internet Explorer to locate a Web site containing data you wish to import before you start Excel, then proceed as follows:
   a. Start a new workbook, pull down the Data menu, click the Import External Data command, and then click New Web query to display New Web Query dialog box as shown in Figure 2.15. Enter the address of the site containing the data. We chose the National Basketball Association at http://www. nba.com/statistics.
   b. Click the Go button to display the site that you selected. The site must contain one or more yellow arrows to indicate that data from the site can be imported via a Web query. Click the arrow next to the table you want to import; in our example this is the 2002–2003 regular season leaders in the NBA. The arrow changes to a green check to indicate the data has been selected.
   c. Click the Import button, and then click OK. The data should appear in your worksheet (in similar fashion to the stock query that was developed in the chapter). Continue to develop the worksheet using formulas that reference the data that was imported by the query.
   d. Print the worksheet containing the query for your instructor to show you completed the exercise. Save the workbook. Exit Excel.
   e. Open your workbook the next day, click anywhere within the Web query on the worksheet, then click the Refresh External Button on the External Data toolbar. The data in the query should be updated automatically. Print the worksheet containing the new values for your instructor.
   f. Add a cover sheet then submit both worksheets to your instructor. Were you successful immediately; i.e., did your initial site permit you to create a Web query, or did you have to search multiple sites? Were you able to build a useful worksheet from the query that you created?

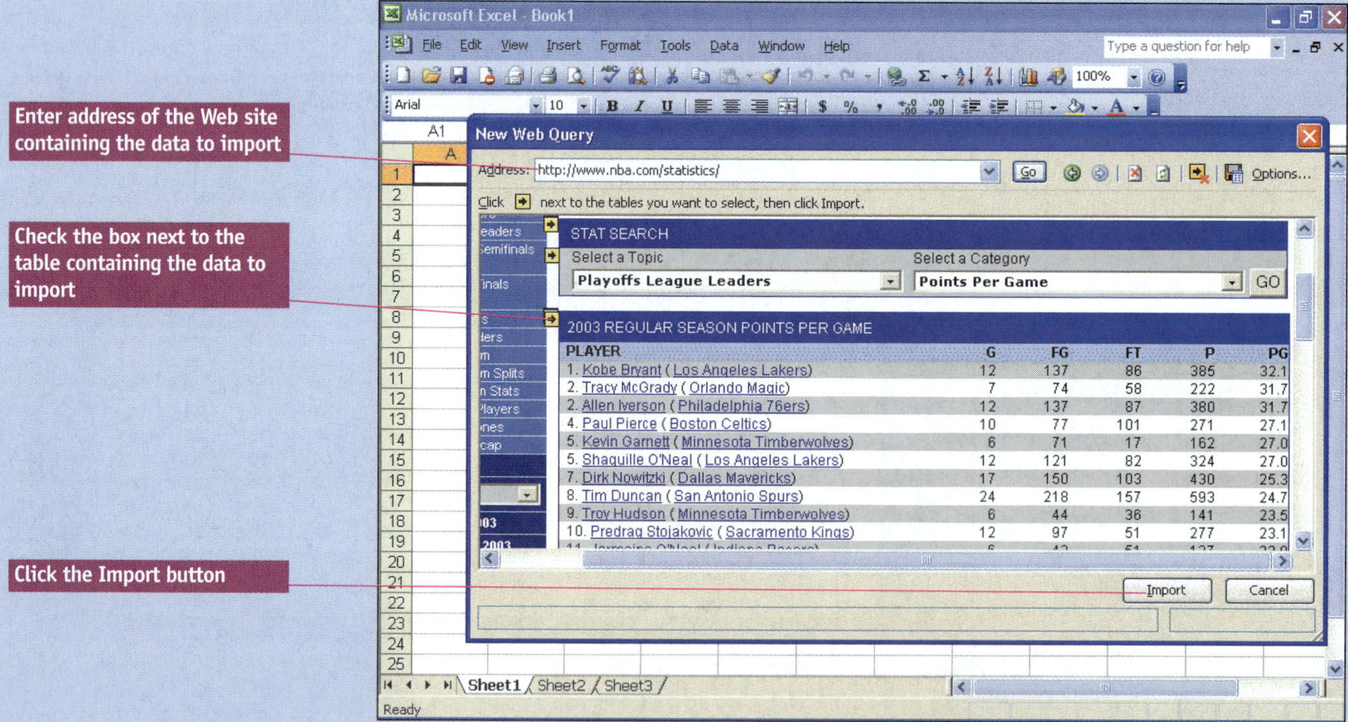

FIGURE 2.15 Create a New Web Query (exercise 9)

10. **Financial Forecast:** Financial planning and budgeting is one of the most common business applications of spreadsheets. Figure 2.16 depicts one such illustration, in which the income and expenses of Get Rich Quick Enterprises are projected over a six-year period. You don't have to be a business major to do the assignment. You do, however, need to follow a logical approach to develop the worksheet. We have entered the text in column A and the assumptions in the bottom of the partially completed workbook, *Chapter 2 Practice 10,* in the Exploring Excel folder. Open the workbook and proceed as follows.
    a. Develop the formulas for the first year of the forecast based on the initial conditions at the bottom of the spreadsheet. The projected income for the first year of the forecast (cell B7) is $225,000, based on sales of 75,000 units at a price of $3.00 per unit. The overhead (fixed costs) consists of the production facility at $50,000 and administrative expenses of $25,000. The variable costs for the same year are broken down into manufacturing of $75,000 (75,000 units at $1.00 per unit) and sales of $15,000 (75,000 units at $.20 per unit). Subtracting the total expenses from the estimated income yields a net income before taxes of $75,000. The income tax is subtracted from this amount, leaving net earnings of $38,400 in the first year.
    b. Develop the formulas for the second year, based on the values in year 1 and the assumed rates of increase at the bottom of the worksheet. Use an appropriate combination of relative and absolute references so that these formulas can be copied to the remaining columns in the worksheet. We suggest you use pointing to enter the formulas in column C.
    c. Copy the formulas for year 2 (in column C) to the remaining years of the forecast (columns D through G). Check that your worksheet is correct by comparing the displayed values to Figure 2.16.
    d. Format the completed worksheet. You do not have to match our formatting exactly, but you are to display dollar amounts with the currency symbol and appropriate decimal places.
    e. Add your name somewhere in the worksheet. Print the completed worksheet two ways, once with displayed values and once with cell formulas. Use landscape printing and force the worksheet to one page. Display gridlines and row and column headings.

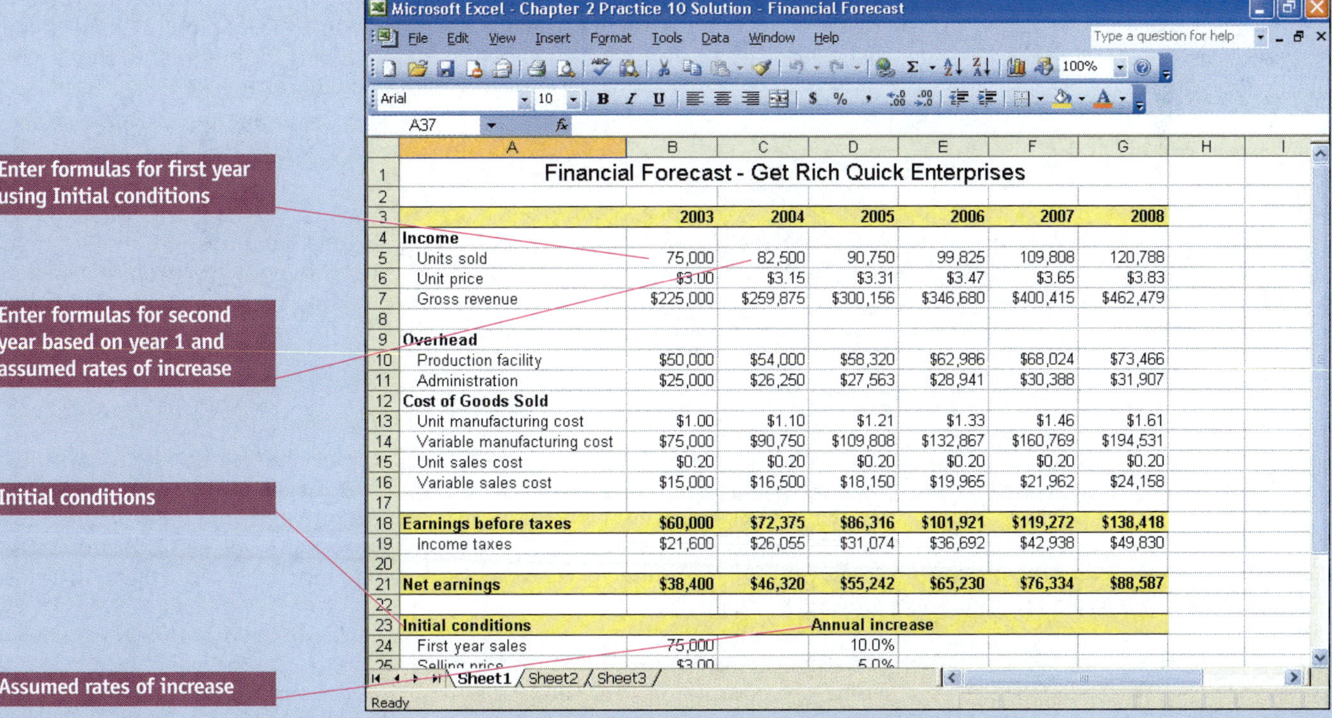

	A	B	C	D	E	F	G
1	Financial Forecast - Get Rich Quick Enterprises						
2							
3		2003	2004	2005	2006	2007	2008
4	**Income**						
5	Units sold	75,000	82,500	90,750	99,825	109,808	120,788
6	Unit price	$3.00	$3.15	$3.31	$3.47	$3.65	$3.83
7	Gross revenue	$225,000	$259,875	$300,156	$346,680	$400,415	$462,479
8							
9	**Overhead**						
10	Production facility	$50,000	$54,000	$58,320	$62,986	$68,024	$73,466
11	Administration	$25,000	$26,250	$27,563	$28,941	$30,388	$31,907
12	**Cost of Goods Sold**						
13	Unit manufacturing cost	$1.00	$1.10	$1.21	$1.33	$1.46	$1.61
14	Variable manufacturing cost	$75,000	$90,750	$109,808	$132,867	$160,769	$194,531
15	Unit sales cost	$0.20	$0.20	$0.20	$0.20	$0.20	$0.20
16	Variable sales cost	$15,000	$16,500	$18,150	$19,965	$21,962	$24,158
17							
18	**Earnings before taxes**	**$60,000**	**$72,375**	**$86,316**	**$101,921**	**$119,272**	**$138,418**
19	Income taxes	$21,600	$26,055	$31,074	$36,692	$42,938	$49,830
20							
21	**Net earnings**	**$38,400**	**$46,320**	**$55,242**	**$65,230**	**$76,334**	**$88,587**
22							
23	**Initial conditions**			**Annual increase**			
24	First year sales	75,000		10.0%			
25	Selling price	$3.00		5.0%			

FIGURE 2.16 Financial Forecast (exercise 10)

MINI CASES

Accounting 101—Straight Line Depreciation

Every asset depreciates (loses value) over time. It's similar to the value of your car, which loses value with every mile you drive. The straight line method of depreciation assumes that an asset depreciates at a uniform rate over its projected life. The amount of value that the asset loses each year is the depreciation expense for that year. To determine the depreciation amount for each year, take the cost of the asset, subtract its residual (salvage) value, and then divide the result by the number of years the asset will be used. Assume, for example, that an asset cost $25,000 new, that it will last for 8 years, at the end of which time it will have a $5,000 salvage value. The annual depreciation expense for this asset is ($25,000–$5,000)/8 or $2,500.

Your assignment is to open the *Chapter 2 Mini Case—Accounting 101* workbook in the Exploring Excel folder in order to enter the necessary formulas to compute the annual depreciation expense. You also have to determine the accumulated deprecation for each year (the sum of all depreciation taken so far, including the current year) as well as the value of the asset (its cost minus the accumulated depreciation). Add your name to the worksheet, enter today's date and the appropriate formatting, then print the worksheet twice, once with displayed values, and once to show the cell formulas.

Wishful Thinking CD Portfolio

It must be nice to have a portfolio of CDs (Certificates of Deposit) where all you do is collect the interest. Your assignment is to open the *Chapter 2 Mini Case—Wishful Thinking CD Portfolio* workbook to determine the total interest earned by the portfolio. The formulas should be straightforward. The maturity date is computed by adding the term (converted to days) to the purchase date. Determine the days until maturity by subtracting today's date from the maturity date. The annual income is determined by multiplying the amount of the CD times its interest rate. The estimated tax is found by multiplying the annual income by the tax rate. The net income is the annual income minus the estimated tax. If you do the exercise correctly, the net income should be almost $18,000.

Format the completed worksheet in an attractive fashion. Add your name in cell A19. Print the worksheet twice, once with displayed values, and once to show the cell formulas. You might also do a little research on the Web to see what the current interest rates on CDs of varying term are. What is the FDIC? Is the investment in a CD insured to its full value? Add a cover sheet, then submit all three pages, together with the answers to the discussion questions, to your instructor as proof you completed this exercise.

Your Net Worth

Your net worth is the sum of all your assets (such as cash, mutual funds, the value of your home and furniture, and so on) minus the sum of all your liabilities (credit card debt, home mortgages, taxes, etc.) Create a simple worksheet that could be used to calculate your net worth, and then complete the worksheet by adding hypothetical data. *Wishful thinking is encouraged.* Submit the completed worksheet to your instructor.

The Birthday Problem

How much would you bet *against* two people in your class having the same birthday? Don't be too hasty, for the odds of two classmates sharing the same birthday (month and day) are much higher than you would expect: There is a fifty percent chance (.5063) in a class of 23 students that two people will have been born on the same day. The probability jumps to seventy percent (.7053) in a class of thirty, and to ninety percent (.9025) in a class of forty-one.

Open the partially completed *Chapter 2 Mini Case—The Birthday Problem* workbook, which contains the basic formula you will need to determine the probabilities. Your assignment is to complete the workbook by copying the formulas we provide to the remaining rows in the worksheet. Print the completed worksheet for your instructor, and then see whether the probabilities hold in your class.

CHAPTER 3

Graphs and Charts: Delivering a Message

OBJECTIVES

After reading this chapter you will:

1. Describe how a chart can be used to deliver a message.
2. List several types of charts and describe the purpose of each.
3. Distinguish between an embedded chart versus a chart in its own chart sheet.
4. Use the Chart Wizard to create and modify a chart.
5. Use the Drawing toolbar to enhance a chart by adding lines and objects.
6. Distinguish between data series in rows versus columns.
7. Differentiate between a stacked-column chart versus a side-by-side column chart.
8. Create a Word document that is linked to a worksheet and an associated chart.

hands-on exercises

1. THE CHART WIZARD
   Input: Software Sales
   Output: Software Sales Solution
2. MULTIPLE DATA SERIES
   Input: Software Sales Solution (from first exercise)
   Output: Software Sales Solution (additional modifications)
3. OBJECT LINKING AND EMBEDDING
   Input: Software Sales Solution (from second exercise)
   Output: Software Sales Solution (additional modifications); Software Memo Solution (Word document)

CASE STUDY

TAX CUTS AND DINNER

What if people split a dinner check using the principles of the progressive income tax that is central to our tax code? Five lifelong friends of various means meet once a week for dinner and split the $100 check according to their ability to pay. Tom, Dick, and Harry are of relatively modest means and pay $1, $4, and $9, respectively. Ben and Ken are far more prosperous and pay $18 and $68, respectively.

The friends were quite satisfied with the arrangement until the owner offered a rebate. "You are excellent customers, and I will reduce the cost of your meal by $15." The question became how to divide the $15 windfall in order to give everyone his fair share? The proprietor suggested that they allocate the savings according to the amount each contributed to the original check. He made a quick calculation, and then rounded each person's share to an integer; e.g., Tom's new bill should have been 85 cents, but it was decided he would eat for free. In similar fashion, Dick now owes $3, Harry $7, Ben $15, and Ken $60. (Ken, the most prosperous individual, made up the difference with respect to the cents that were dropped.) The new total is $85 and everyone saves money.

Once outside the restaurant the friends began to compare their savings. Tom and Dick each complained that they saved only $1. Harry grumbled that he saved only $2. Ben thought it unfair that Ken saved more than the other four friends combined. Everyone continued to pick on Ken. The next week Ken felt so uncomfortable that he did not show up, so his former friends ate without him. But when the bill came they were $60 short. ■

Your assignment is to create a simple worksheet and associated set of charts that shows the amounts the friends pay before and after the rebate. The numbers in the case are not contrived; that is, they represent the proportion of income taxes that are paid by five different income groups. The 20% of families that represent the lowest income group pay approximately 1% of the total tax bill. The second 20% pays 4%, the third 20% pays 18%, and the upper 20% pays 68%. This example was inspired by an anonymous e-mail message.

CHART TYPES

Business has always known that the graphic representation of data is an attractive, easy-to-understand way to convey information. Indeed, business graphics has become one of the most exciting Windows applications, whereby charts (graphs) are easily created from a worksheet, with just a few simple keystrokes or mouse clicks.

The chapter begins by emphasizing the importance of determining the message to be conveyed by a chart. It describes the different types of charts available within Excel and how to choose among them. It explains how to create a chart using the Chart Wizard, how to embed a chart within a worksheet, and how to create a chart in a separate chart sheet. It also describes how to use the Drawing toolbar to enhance a chart by creating lines, objects, and 3-D shapes.

The second half of the chapter explains how one chart can plot multiple sets of data, and how several charts can be based on the same worksheet. It also describes how to create a compound document, in which a chart and its associated worksheet are dynamically linked to a memo created by a word processor. All told, we think you will find this to be one of the most enjoyable chapters in the text.

A ***chart*** is a graphic representation of data in a worksheet. The chart is based on descriptive entries called ***category labels***, and on numeric values called ***data points***. The data points are grouped into one or more ***data series*** that appear in row(s) or column(s) on the worksheet. In every chart there is exactly one data point in each data series for each value of the category label.

The worksheet in Figure 3.1 will be used throughout the chapter as the basis for the charts we will create. Your manager believes that the sales data can be understood more easily from charts than from the strict numerical presentation of a worksheet. You have been given the assignment of analyzing the data in the worksheet and are developing a series of charts to convey that information.

The sales data in the worksheet can be presented several ways—for example, by city, by product, or by a combination of the two. Ask yourself which type of chart is best suited to answer the following questions:

- What percentage of the total revenue comes from each city? What percentage comes from each product?
- What is the dollar revenue produced by each city? What is the revenue produced by each product?
- What is the rank of each city with respect to sales?
- How much revenue does each product contribute in each city?

In every instance, realize that a chart exists only to deliver a message, and that *you cannot create an effective chart unless you are sure of what that message is.* The next several pages discuss various types of business charts, each of which is best suited to a particular type of message. After you understand how charts are used conceptually, we will create various charts in Excel.

	A	B	C	D	E	F
1	**Superior Software Sales**					
2						
3		**Miami**	**Denver**	**New York**	**Boston**	**Total**
4	**Word Processing**	$50,000	$67,500	$9,500	$141,000	**$268,000**
5	**Spreadsheets**	$44,000	$18,000	$11,500	$105,000	**$178,500**
6	**Database**	$12,000	$7,500	$6,000	$30,000	**$55,500**
7	**Total**	**$106,000**	**$93,000**	**$27,000**	**$276,000**	**$502,000**

FIGURE 3.1 Superior Software

Pie Charts

A ***pie chart*** is the most effective way to display proportional relationships. It is the type of chart to select whenever words like *percentage* or *market share* appear in the message to be delivered. The pie, or complete circle, denotes the total amount. Each slice of the pie corresponds to its respective percentage of the total.

The pie chart in Figure 3.2a divides the pie representing total sales into four slices, one for each city. The size of each slice is proportional to the percentage of total sales in that city. The chart depicts a single data series, which appears in cells B7 through E7 on the associated worksheet. The data series has four data points corresponding to the total sales in each city.

To create the pie chart, Excel computes the total sales ($502,000 in our example), calculates the percentage contributed by each city, and draws each slice of the pie in proportion to its computed percentage. Boston's sales of $276,000 account for 55 percent of the total, and so this slice of the pie is allotted 55 percent of the area of the circle.

An ***exploded pie chart***, as shown in Figure 3.2b, separates one or more slices of the pie for emphasis. Another way to achieve emphasis in a chart is to choose a title that reflects the message you are trying to deliver. The title in Figure 3.2a, for example, *Revenue by Geographic Area*, is neutral and leaves the reader to develop his or her own conclusion about the relative contribution of each area. By contrast, the title in Figure 3.2b, *New York Accounts for Only 5% of Revenue*, is more suggestive and emphasizes the problems in this office. Alternatively, the title could be changed to *Boston Exceeds 50% of Total Revenue* if the intent were to emphasize the contribution of Boston.

Three-dimensional pie charts may be created in exploded or nonexploded format as shown in Figures 3.2c and 3.2d, respectively. Excel also enables you to add arrows and text for emphasis.

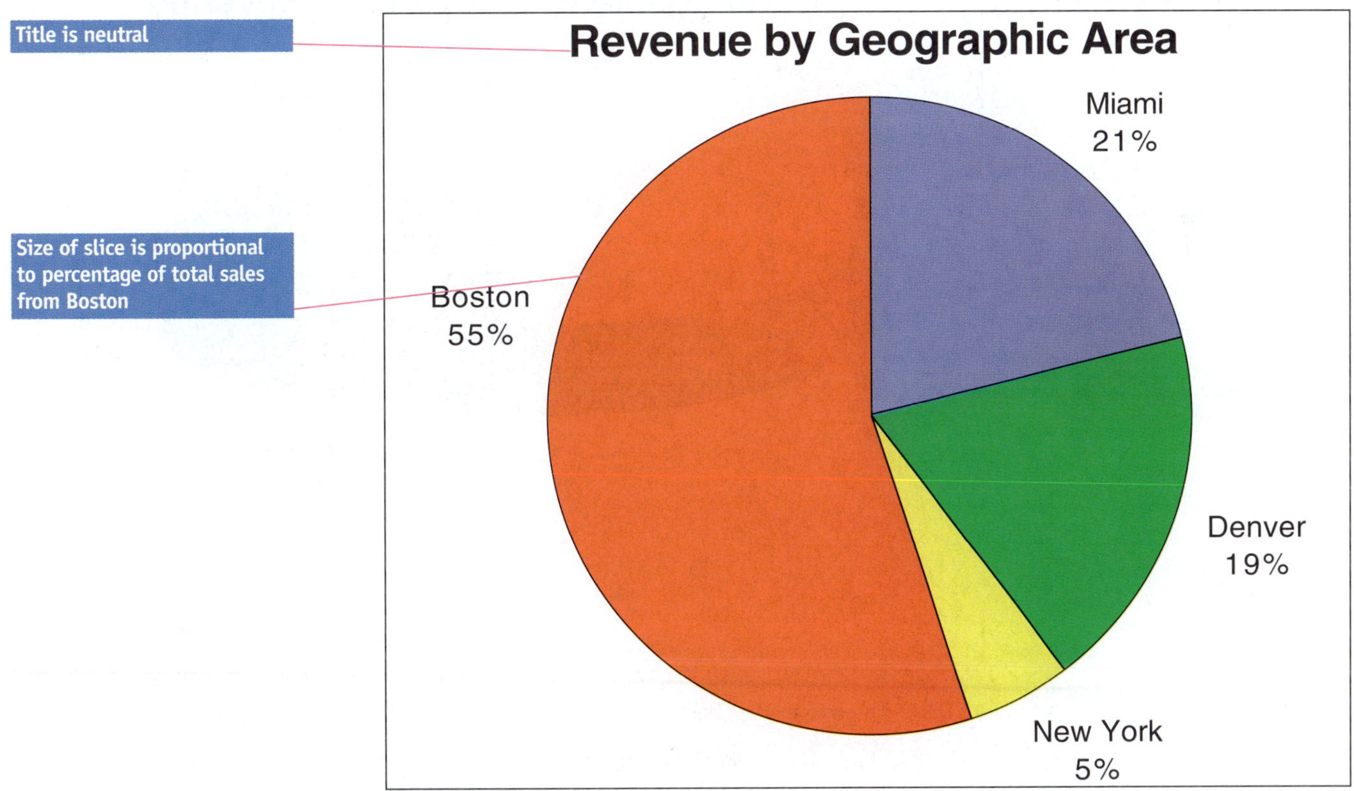

(a) Simple Pie Chart

FIGURE 3.2 Pie Charts

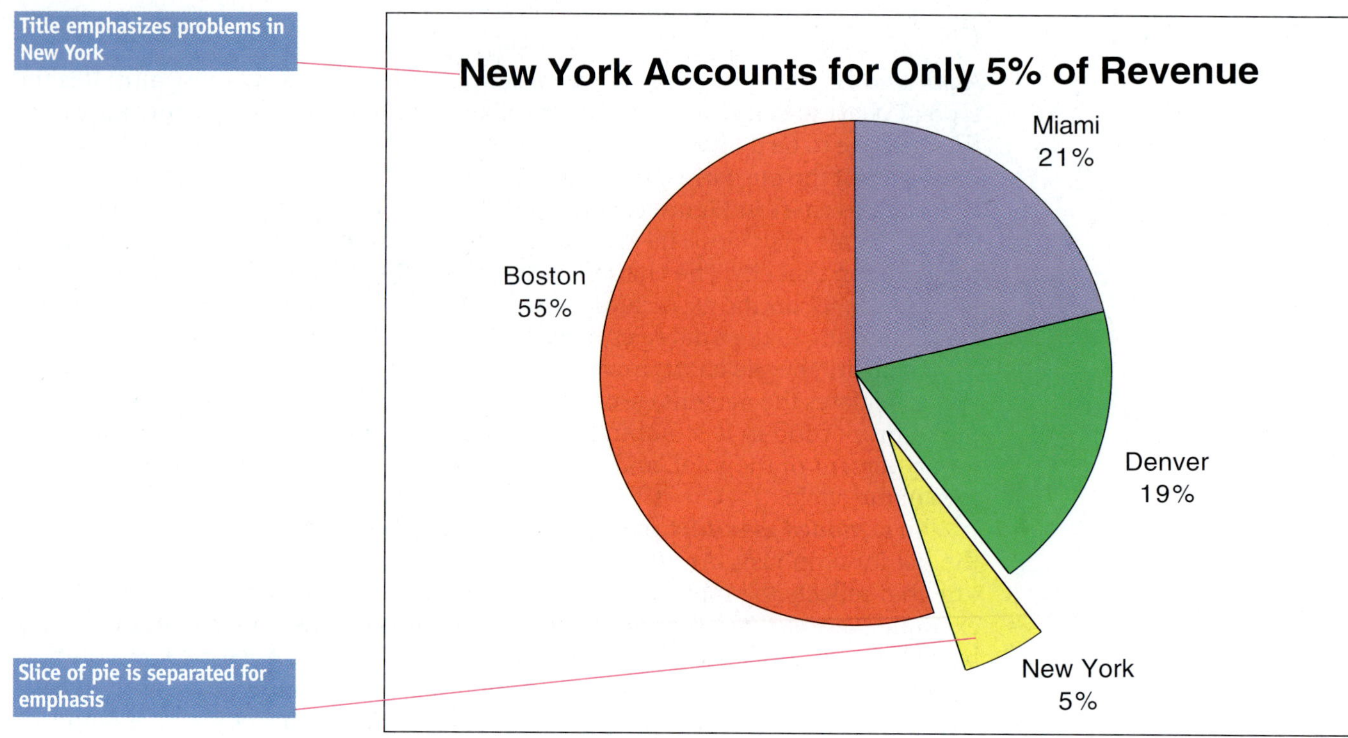

(b) Exploded Pie Chart

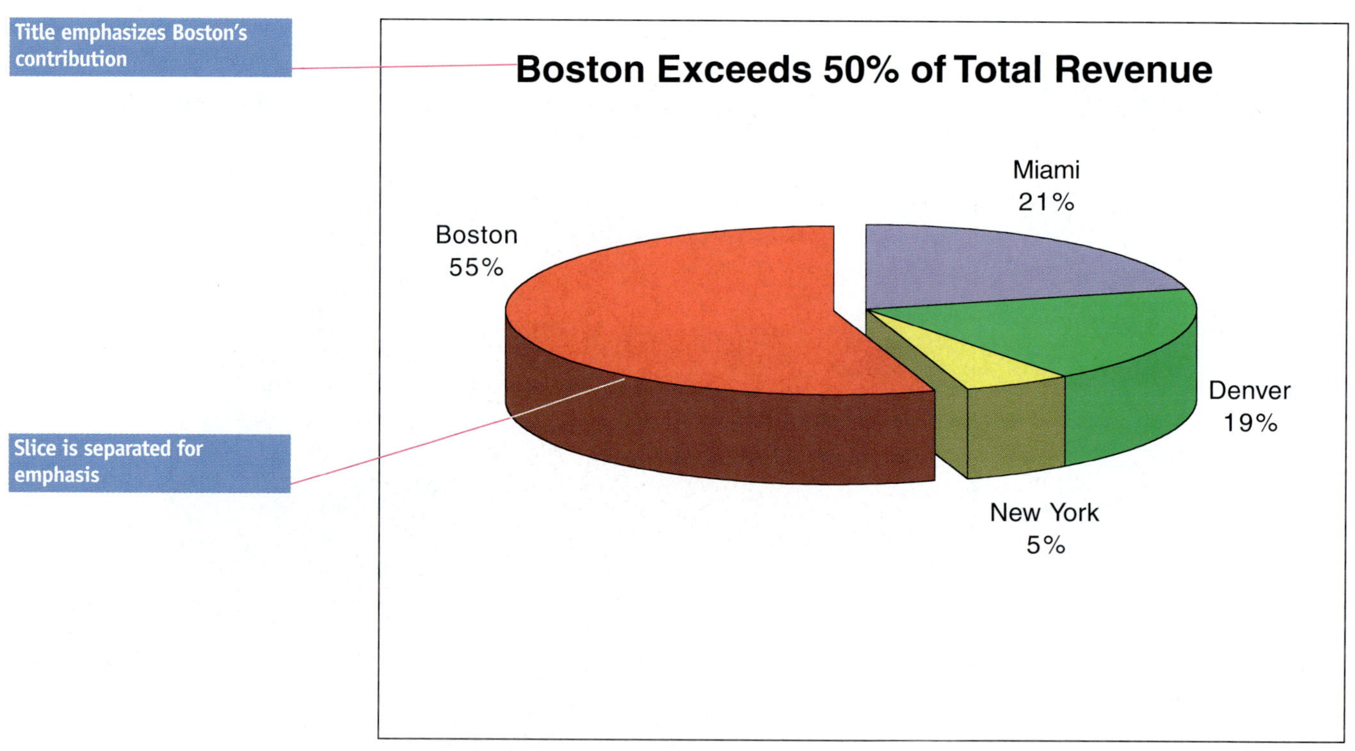

(c) Three-dimensional Pie Chart

FIGURE 3.2 Pie Charts (*continued*)

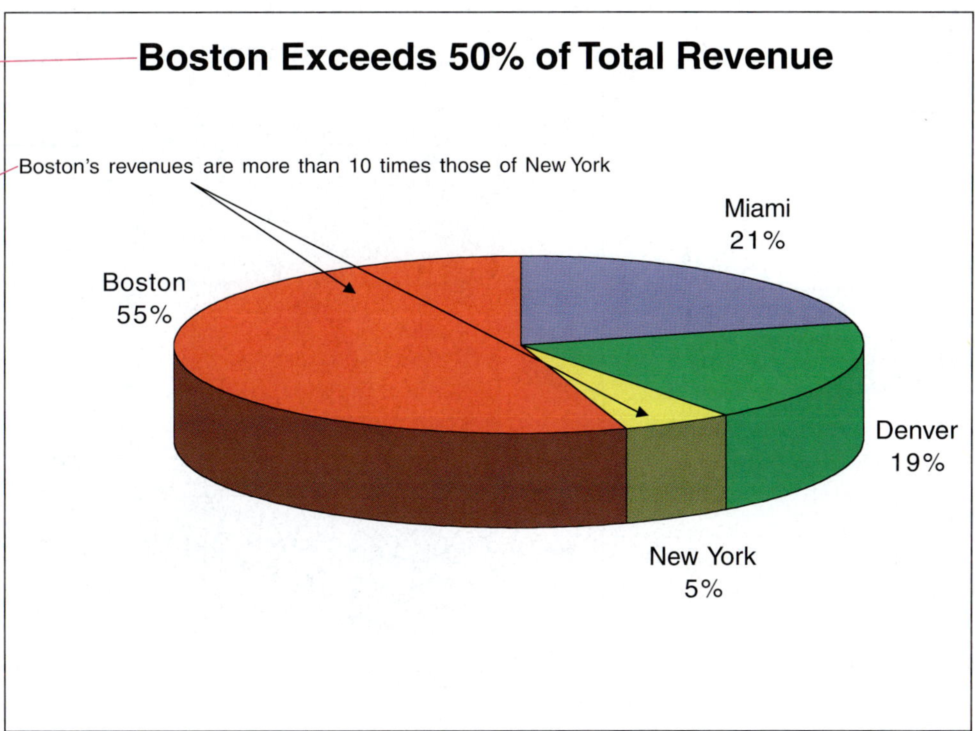

(d) Enhanced Pie Chart

FIGURE 3.2 Pie Charts (*continued*)

A pie chart is easiest to read when the number of slices is limited (i.e., not more than six or seven), and when small categories (percentages less than five) are grouped into a single category called "Other."

Column and Bar Charts

A ***column chart*** is used when there is a need to show actual numbers rather than percentages. The column chart in Figure 3.3a plots the same data series as the earlier pie chart, but displays it differently. The category labels (Miami, Denver, New York, and Boston) are shown along the ***X*** (horizontal) ***axis***. The data points (monthly sales) are plotted along the ***Y*** (vertical) ***axis***, with the height of each column reflecting the value of the data point.

A column chart can be given a horizontal orientation and converted to a ***bar chart*** as in Figure 3.3b. Some individuals prefer the bar chart over the corresponding column chart because the longer horizontal bars accentuate the difference between the items. Bar charts are also preferable when the descriptive labels are long, to eliminate the crowding that can occur along the horizontal axis of a column chart. As with the pie chart, a title can lead the reader and further emphasize the message, as with *Boston Leads All Cities* in Figure 3.3b.

KEEP IT SIMPLE

Keep it simple. This rule applies to both your message and the means of conveying that message. Excel makes it almost too easy to change fonts, styles, the shape of columns, type sizes, and colors, but such changes will often detract from, rather than enhance, a chart. More is not necessarily better, and you do not have to use a feature just because it is there. Remember that a chart must ultimately succeed on the basis of content, and content alone.

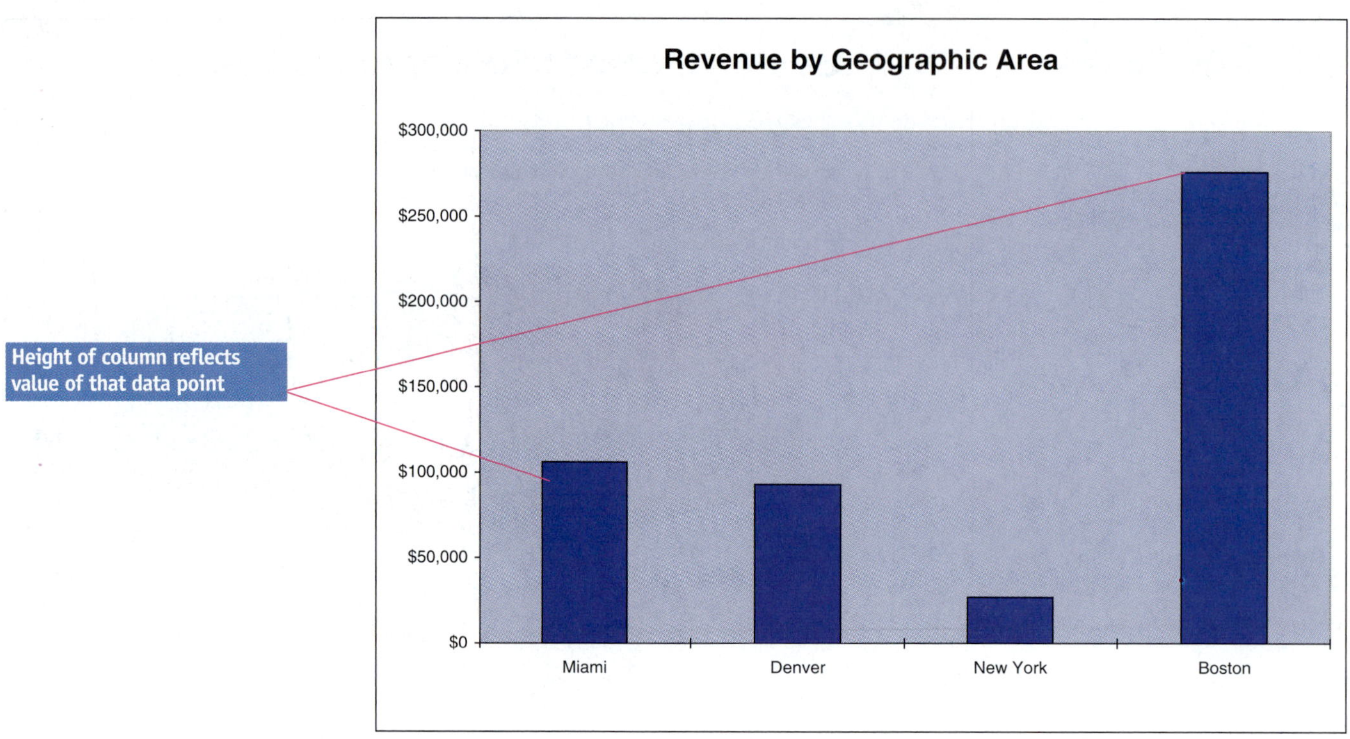

(a) Column Chart

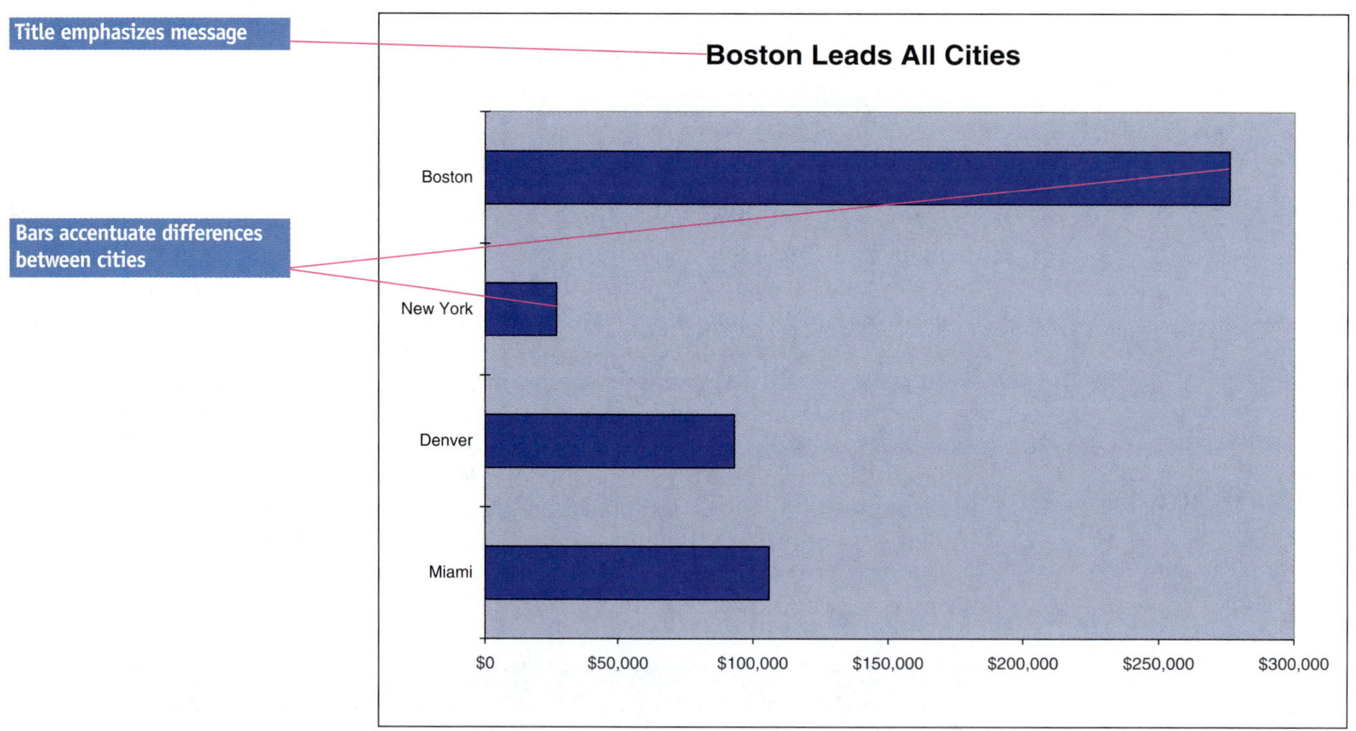

(b) Horizontal Bar Chart

FIGURE 3.3 Column/Bar Charts

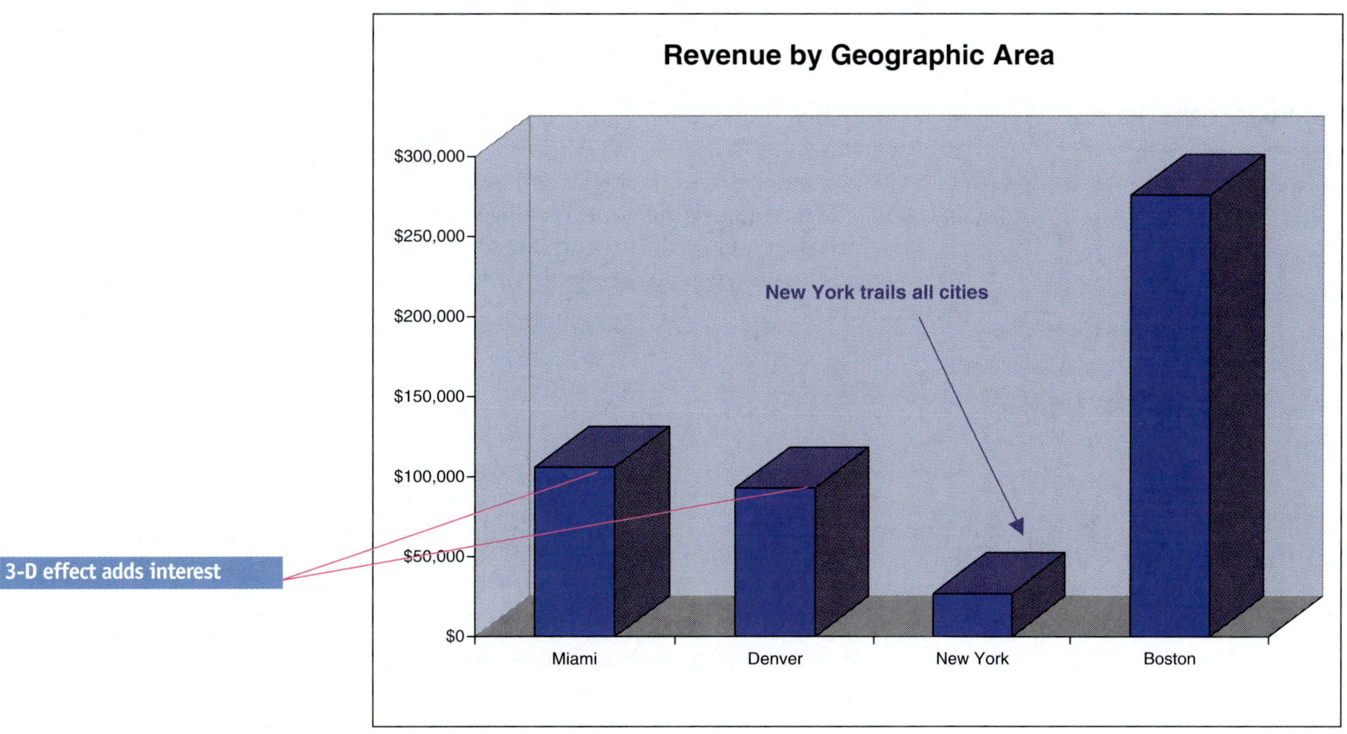

(c) Three-dimensional Column Chart

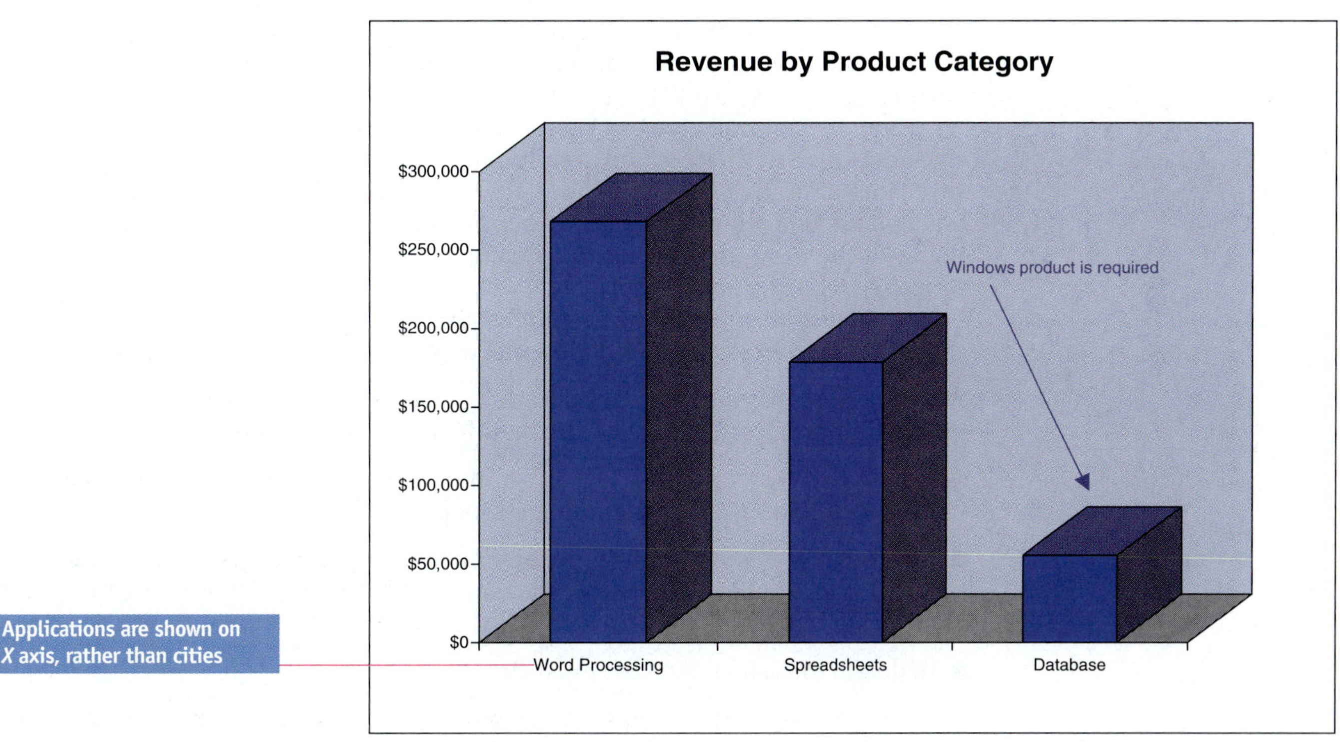

(d) Alternate Column Chart

FIGURE 3.3 Column/Bar Charts (*continued*)

The special effect of a ***three-dimensional column chart*** can produce added interest as shown in Figures 3.3c and 3.3d. Figure 3.3d plots a different set of numbers than we have seen so far (the sales for each product, rather than the sales for each city). The choice between the charts in Figures 3.3c and 3.3d depends on the message you want to convey—whether you want to emphasize the contribution of each city or each product. The title can be used to emphasize the message. Arrows, text, and 3-D shapes can be added to either chart to enhance the message.

As with a pie chart, column and bar charts are easiest to read when the number of categories is relatively small (seven or fewer). Otherwise, the columns (bars) are plotted so close together that labeling becomes impossible.

CREATING A CHART

There are two ways to create a chart in Excel. You can *embed* the chart in a worksheet, or you can create the chart in a separate ***chart sheet***. Figure 3.4a displays an embedded column chart. Figure 3.4b shows a pie chart in its own chart sheet. Both techniques are valid. The choice between the two depends on your personal preference.

Regardless of where it is kept (embedded in a worksheet or in its own chart sheet), a chart is linked to the worksheet on which it is based. The charts in Figure 3.4 plot the same data series (the total sales for each city). Change any of these data points on the worksheet, and both charts will be updated automatically to reflect the new data.

Both charts are part of the same workbook (Software Sales) as indicated in the title bar of each figure. The tabs within the workbook have been renamed to indicate the contents of the associated sheet. Additional charts may be created and embedded in the worksheet and/or placed on their own chart sheets. And, as previously stated, if you change the worksheet, the chart (or charts) based upon it will also change.

Study the column chart in Figure 3.4a to see how it corresponds to the worksheet on which it is based. The descriptive names on the *X* axis are known as category labels and match the entries in cells B3 through E3. The quantitative values (data points) are plotted on the *Y* axis and match the total sales in cells B7 through E7. Even the numeric format matches; that is, the currency format used in the worksheet appears automatically on the scale of the *Y* axis.

The ***sizing handles*** on the ***embedded chart*** indicate it is currently selected and can be sized, moved, or deleted the same way as any other Windows object:

- To size the selected chart, point to a sizing handle (the mouse pointer changes to a double arrow), then drag the handle in the desired direction.
- To move the selected chart, point to the chart (the mouse pointer is a single arrow), then drag the chart to its new location.
- To copy the selected chart, click the Copy button to copy the chart to the clipboard, click in the workbook where you want the copied chart to go, then click the Paste button to paste the chart at that location.
- To delete the selected chart, press the Del key.

The same operations apply to any of the objects within the chart (such as its title), as will be discussed in the next section on enhancing a chart. Note, too, that both figures contain the chart toolbar that enables you to modify a chart after it has been created.

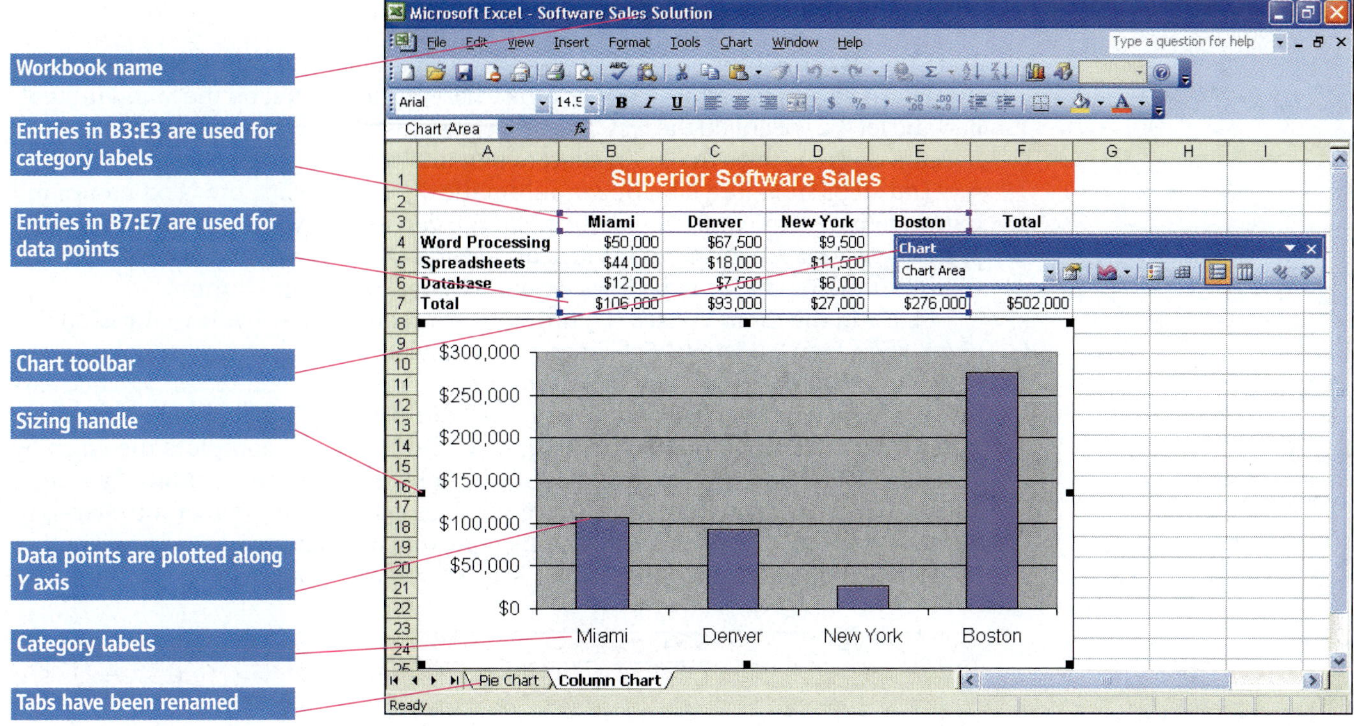

(a) Embedded Chart

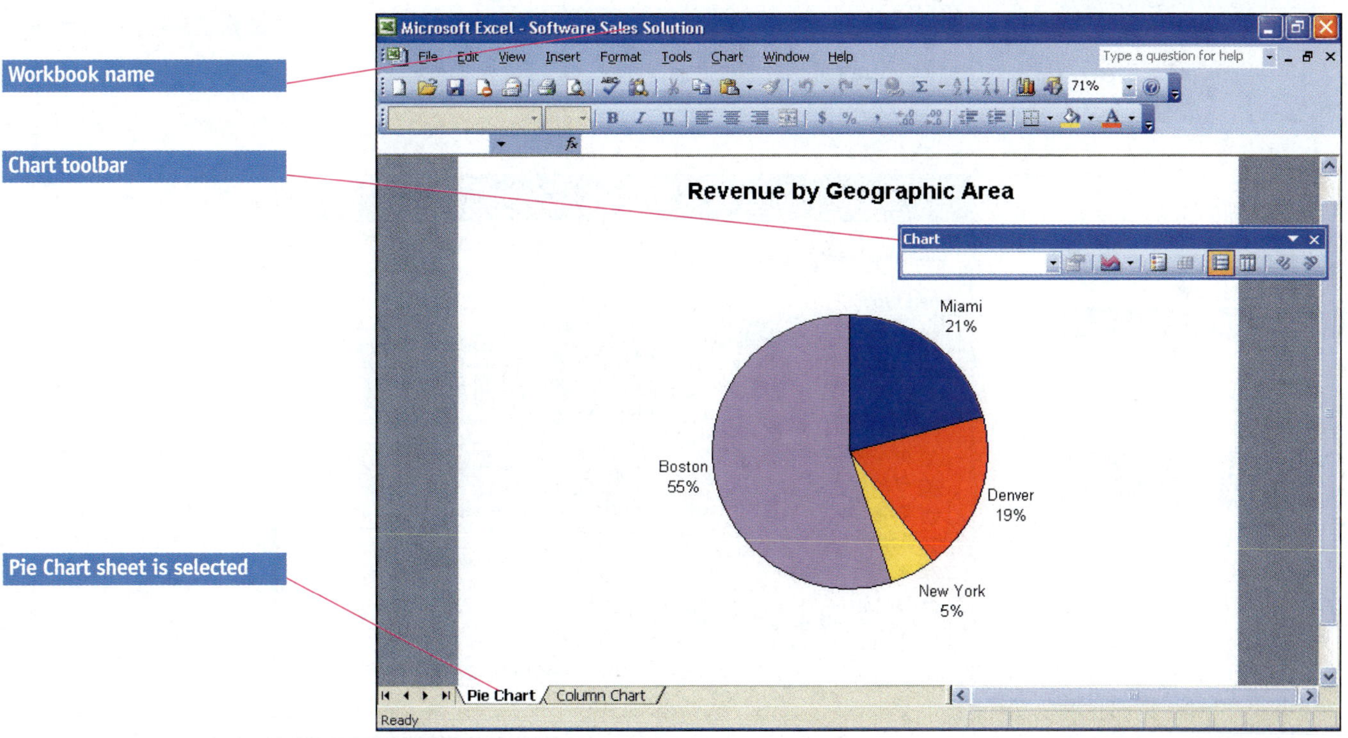

(b) Chart Sheet

FIGURE 3.4 Creating a Chart

The Chart Wizard

The ***Chart Wizard*** is the easiest way to create a chart. Just select the cells that contain the data as shown in Figure 3.5a, click the Chart Wizard button on the Standard toolbar, and let the wizard do the rest. The process is illustrated in Figure 3.5, which shows how the wizard creates a column chart to plot total sales by geographic area (city).

The steps in Figure 3.5 appear automatically as you click the Next command button to move from one step to the next. You can retrace your steps at any time by pressing the Back command button, access the Office Assistant for help with the Chart Wizard, or abort the process with the Cancel command button.

Step 1 in the Chart Wizard (Figure 3.5b) asks you to choose one of the available ***chart types***. Step 2 (Figure 3.5c) shows you a preview of the chart and enables you to confirm (and, if necessary, change) the category names and data series specified earlier. (Only one data series is plotted in this example. Multiple data series are illustrated later in the chapter.) Step 3 (Figure 3.5d) asks you to complete the chart by entering its title and specifying additional options (such as the position of a legend and gridlines). And finally, step 4 (Figure 3.5e) has you choose whether the chart is to be created as an embedded chart (an object) within a specific worksheet, or whether it is to be created in its own chart sheet. The entire process takes but a few minutes.

Selected cells (B3:E3 and B7:E7)

	A	B	C	D	E	F
1	Superior Software Sales					
2						
3		Miami	Denver	New York	Boston	Total
4	Word Processing	$50,000	$67,500	$9,500	$141,000	$268,000
5	Spreadsheets	$44,000	$18,000	$11,500	$105,000	$178,500
6	Database	$12,000	$7,500	$6,000	$30,000	$55,500
7	Total	$106,000	$93,000	$27,000	$276,000	$502,000

(a) The Worksheet

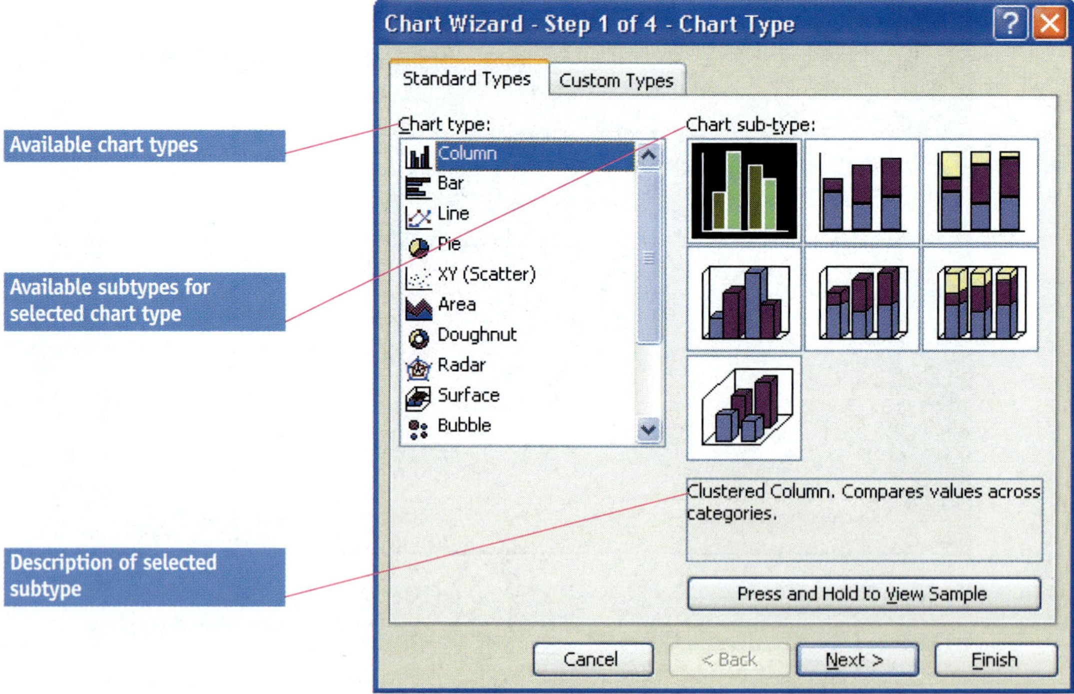

(b) Select the Chart Type (step 1)

FIGURE 3.5 The Chart Wizard

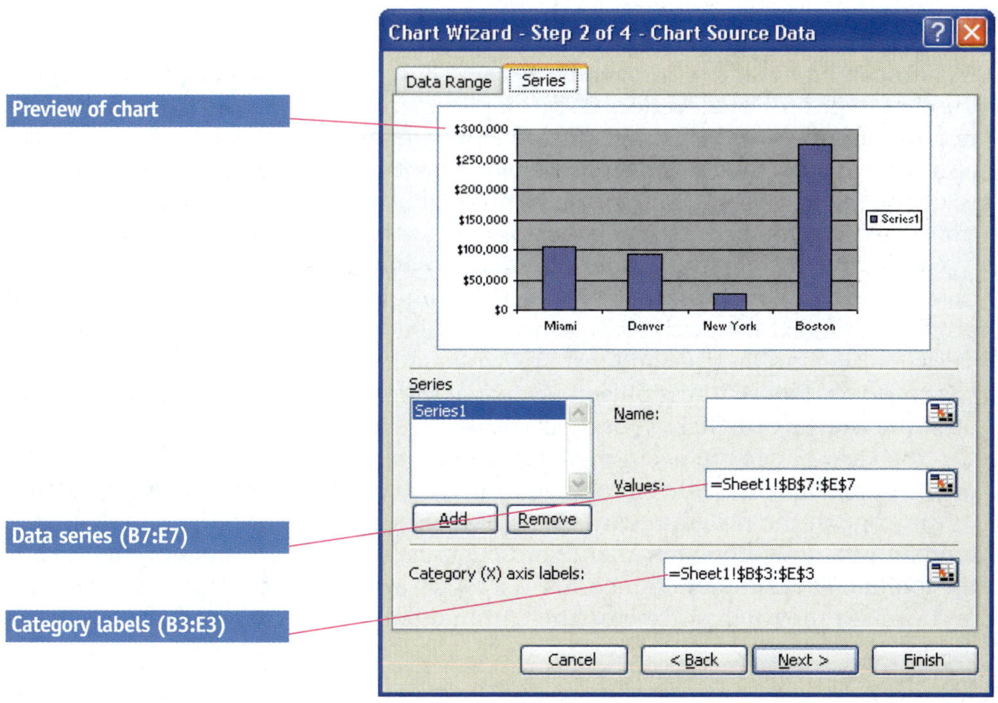

(c) Check the Data Series (step 2)

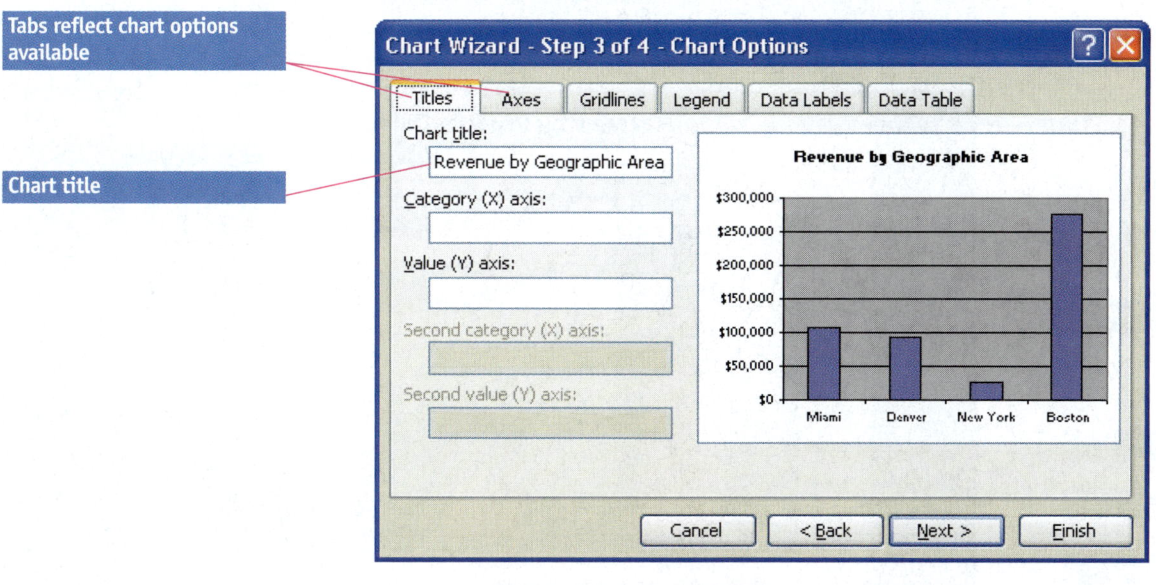

(d) Complete the Chart Options (step 3)

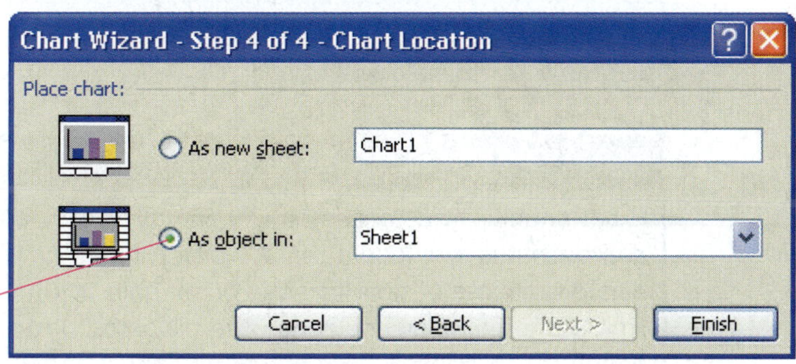

(e) Choose the Location (step 4)

FIGURE 3.5 The Chart Wizard (*continued*)

Modifying a Chart

A chart can be modified in several ways after it has been created. You can change the chart type and/or the color, shape, or pattern of the data series. You can add (or remove) gridlines and/or a legend. You can add labels to the data series. You can also change the font, size, color, and style of existing text anywhere in the chart by selecting the text, then changing its format. All of these features are implemented from the Chart menu or by using the appropriate button on the ***Chart toolbar***.

You can also use the ***Drawing toolbar*** to add text boxes, arrows, and other objects for added emphasis. Figure 3.6, for example, contains a three-dimensional arrow with a text box within the arrow to call attention to the word processing sales. It also contains a second text box with a thin arrow in reference to the database product. Each of these objects is created separately using the appropriate tool from the Drawing toolbar. It's easy, as you will see in our next exercise.

You can change the position of any toolbar by dragging the move handle of a docked toolbar or the title bar of a floating toolbar. (If you drag a floating toolbar to the edge of the program window, it becomes a docked toolbar.) To display a toolbar, pull down the View menu and click the Toolbars command, then check the toolbar. The command functions as a toggle switch; i.e., execute the command and you see the toolbar. Execute the command a second time and the toolbar is hidden.

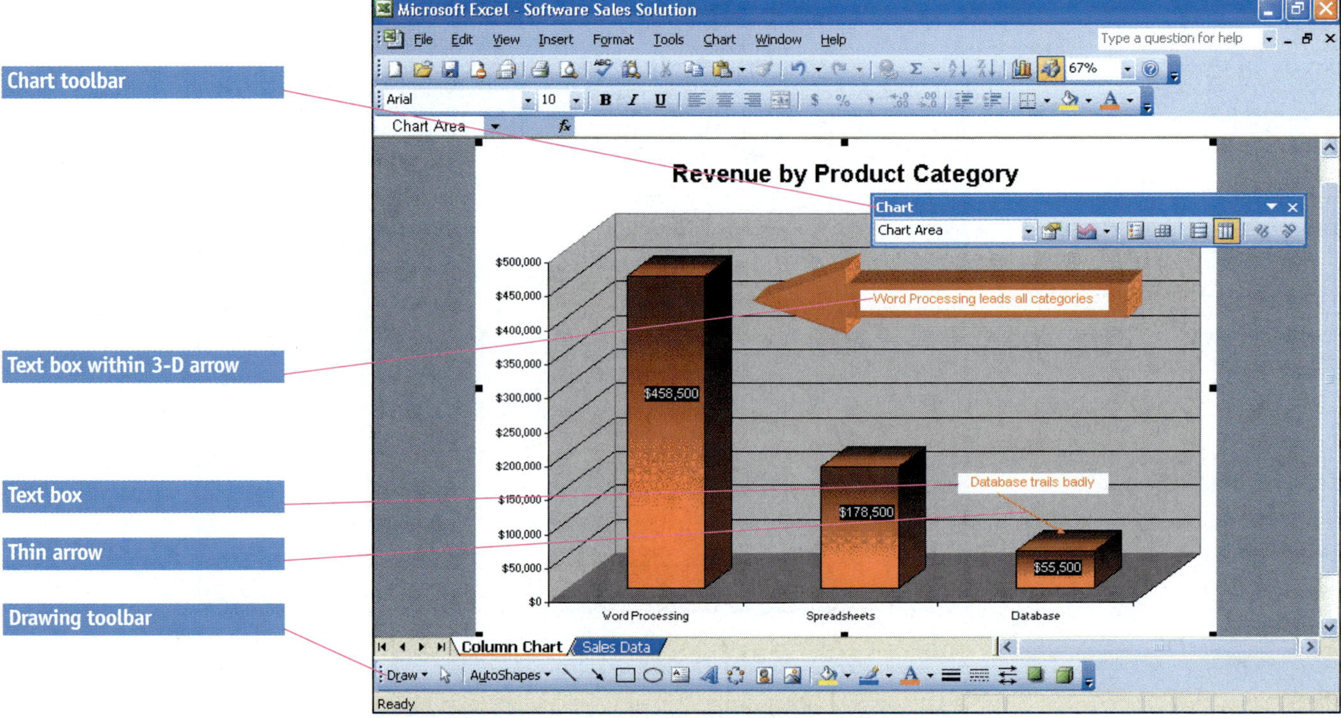

FIGURE 3.6 Enhancing a Chart

SET A TIME LIMIT

Excel enables you to customize virtually every aspect of every object within a chart. That is the good news. It's also the bad news, because you can spend inordinate amounts of time for little or no gain. It's fun to experiment, but set a time limit and stop when you reach the allocated time. The default settings are often adequate to convey your message, and further experimentation might prove counterproductive.

hands-on exercise

1 The Chart Wizard

Objective To create and modify a chart by using the Chart Wizard; to embed a chart within a worksheet; to enhance a chart to include arrows and text. Use Figure 3.7 as a guide in the exercise.

Step 1: The AutoSum Command

- Start Excel. Open the **Software Sales workbook** in the **Exploring Excel folder**. Save the workbook as **Software Sales Solution**.
- Click and drag to select **cells B7** through **E7** (the cells that will contain the total sales for each location). Click the **AutoSum button** on the Standard toolbar to compute the total for each city.
- The totals are computed automatically as shown in Figure 3.7a. The formula bar shows that Cell B7 contains the Sum function to total all of the numeric entries immediately above the cell.
- Click and drag to select **cells F4** through **F7**, then click the **AutoSum button**. The Sum function is entered automatically into these cells to total the entries to the left of the selected cells.
- Click and drag to select **cells B4** through **F7** to format these cells with the currency symbol and no decimal places.
- **Boldface** the row and column headings and the totals. Center the entries in **cells B3** through **F3**.
- Save the workbook.

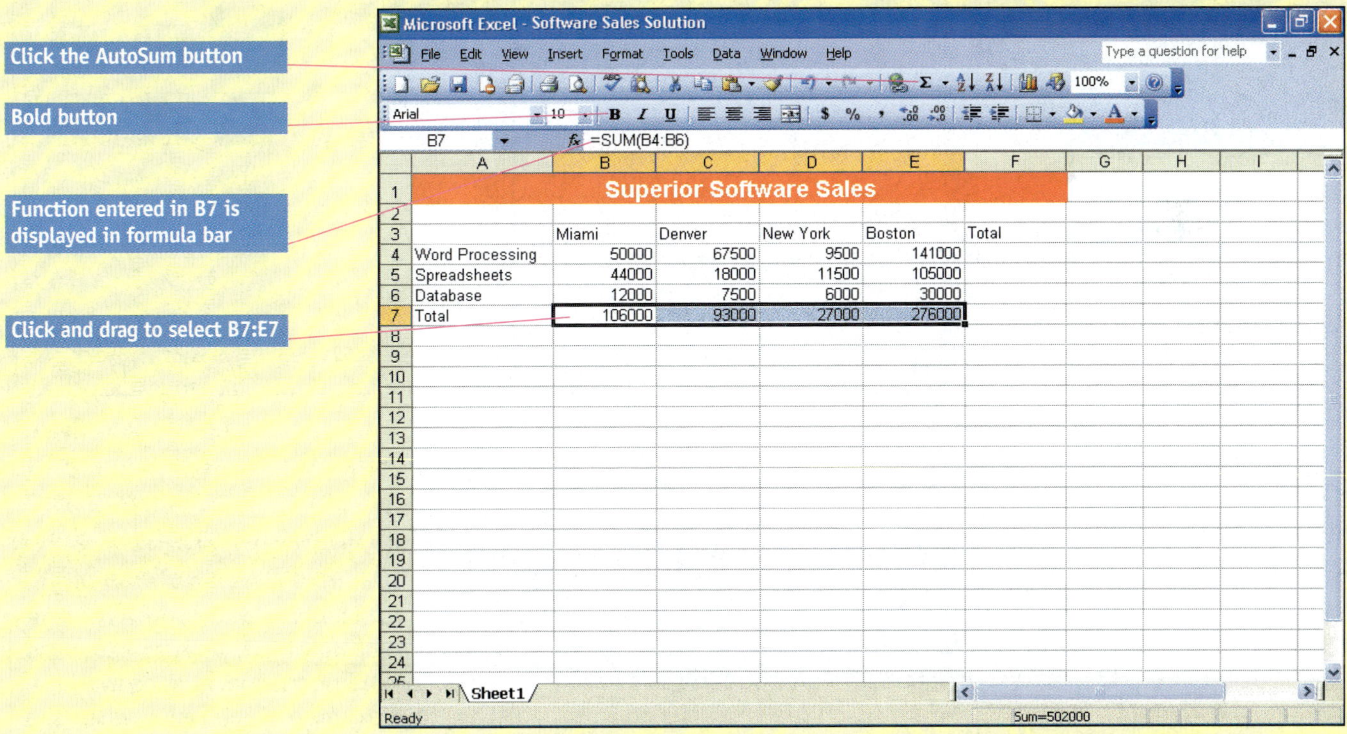

(a) The AutoSum Command (step 1)

FIGURE 3.7 Hands-on Exercise 1

Step 2: Start the Chart Wizard

- Separate the toolbars if they occupy the same row. Pull down the **Tools menu**, click the **Customize command**, click the **Options tab**, then check the box that displays the toolbars on two rows.
- Drag the mouse over **cells B3** through **E3** to select the category labels (the names of the cities). Press and hold the **Ctrl key** as you drag the mouse over **cells B7** through **E7** to select the data series (the cells containing the total sales for the individual cities).
- Check that cells B3 through E3 and B7 through E7 are selected. Click the **Chart Wizard button** on the Standard toolbar to start the wizard. If you don't see the button, pull down the **Insert menu** and click the **Chart command**.
- You should see the dialog box for step 1 of the Chart Wizard as shown in Figure 3.7b. The **Column** chart type and **Clustered column** subtype are selected.
- Click (and hold) the button to see a sample chart. Click **Next**.

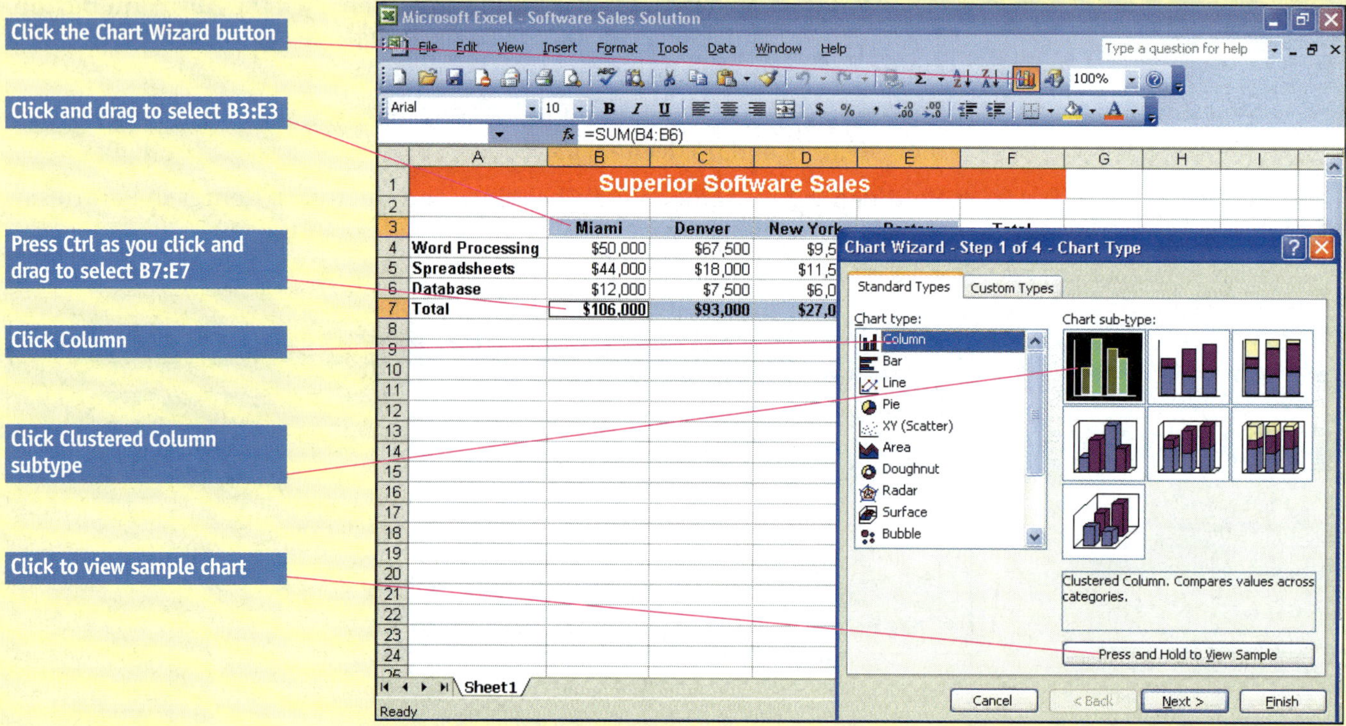

(b) Start the Chart Wizard (step 2)

FIGURE 3.7 Hands-on Exercise 1 (*continued*)

RETRACE YOUR STEPS

The Chart Wizard guides you every step of the way, but what if you make a mistake or change your mind? Click the Back command button at any time to return to a previous screen to enter different information, then continue working with the wizard. Click the Next button to proceed to the next step. Click Finish when the chart is complete.

Step 3: The Chart Wizard (continued)

- You should see step 2 of the Chart Wizard. Click the **Series tab** in the dialog box so that your screen matches Figure 3.7c.
- The values (the data being plotted) are in cells B7 through E7. The Category labels for the *X* axis are in cells B3 through E3. Click **Next** to continue.
- You should see step 3 of the Chart Wizard. If necessary, click the **Titles tab**, then click in the text box for the Chart title.
- Type **Revenue by Geographic Area**. Click the **Legend tab** and clear the box to show a legend. Click **Next**.
- You should see step 4 of the Chart Wizard. If necessary, click the option button to place the chart **As object** in Sheet1 (the name of the worksheet in which you are working).
- Click **Finish**.

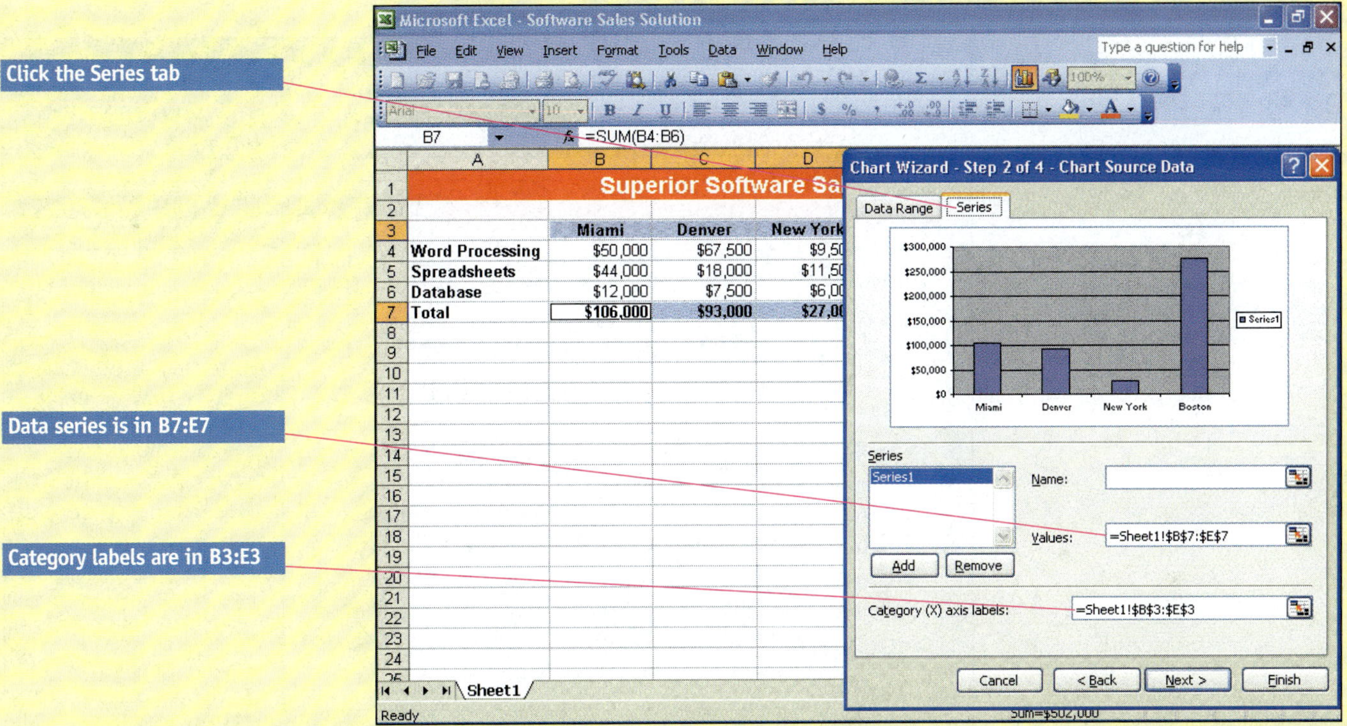

(c) The Chart Wizard (continued) (step 3)

FIGURE 3.7 Hands-on Exercise 1 (*continued*)

THE F11 KEY

The F11 key is the fastest way to create a chart in its own sheet. Select the data, including the legends and category labels, then press the F11 key to create the chart according to the default format built into the Excel column chart. After the chart has been created, you can use the menu bar, Chart toolbar, or shortcut menus to choose a different chart type and/or customize the formatting.

Step 4: Move and Size the Chart

- You should see the completed chart as shown in Figure 3.7d. The sizing handles indicate that the chart is selected and will be affected by subsequent commands. The Chart toolbar is displayed automatically whenever a chart is selected.
- Move and/or size the chart just as you would any other Windows object:
  - To move the chart, click the chart (background) area to select the chart (a ScreenTip, "Chart Area," is displayed), then click and drag (the mouse pointer changes to a four-sided arrow) to move the chart.
  - To size the chart, drag a corner handle (the mouse pointer changes to a double arrow) to change the length and width of the chart simultaneously, keeping the chart in proportion as it is resized.
- Click outside the chart to deselect it. The sizing handles disappear and the Chart toolbar is no longer visible.
- Save the workbook.

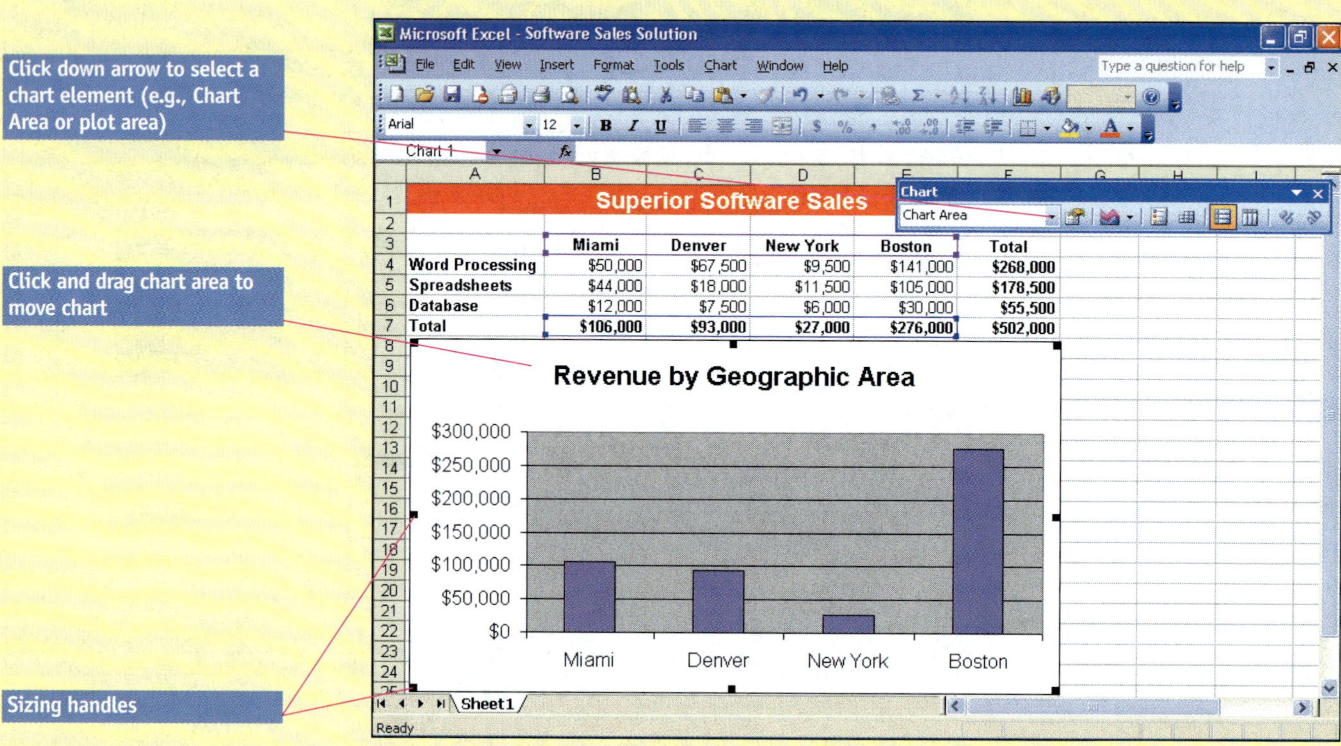

(d) Move and Size the Chart (step 4)

FIGURE 3.7 Hands-on Exercise 1 (*continued*)

EMBEDDED CHARTS

An embedded chart is treated as an object that can be moved, sized, copied, or deleted just as any other Windows object. To move an embedded chart, click the background of the chart to select the chart, then drag it to a new location in the worksheet. To size the chart, select it, then drag any of the eight sizing handles in the desired direction. To delete the chart, select it, then press the Del key. To copy the chart, select it, click the Copy button on the Standard toolbar to copy the chart to the clipboard, click elsewhere in the workbook where you want the copied chart to go, then click the Paste button.

Step 5: Change the Worksheet

- Any changes in a worksheet are automatically reflected in the associated chart. Click in **cell B4**, change the entry to **$400,000**, and press the **Enter key**.
- The total sales for Miami in cell B7 change automatically to reflect the increased sales for word processing, as shown in Figure 3.7e. The column for Miami also changes in the chart and is now larger than the column for Boston.
- Click in **cell B3**. Change the entry to **Chicago**. Press **Enter**. The category label on the *X* axis changes automatically.
- Click the **Undo button** to change the city back to Miami. Click the **Undo button** a second time to return to the initial value of $50,000. The worksheet and chart are restored to their earlier values.
- Save the workbook.

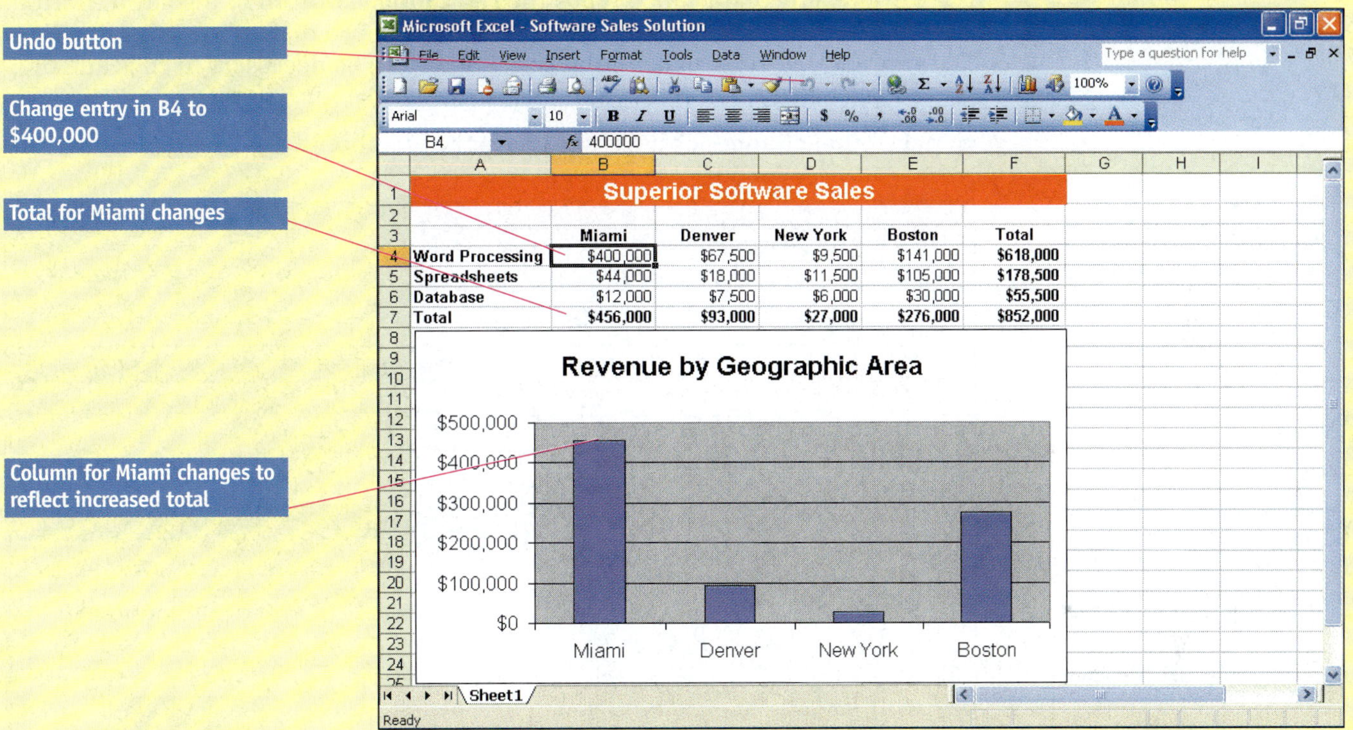

(e) Change the Worksheet (step 5)

FIGURE 3.7 Hands-on Exercise 1 (*continued*)

THE AUTOFORMAT COMMAND

The AutoFormat command does not do anything that could not be done through individual formatting commands, but it does provide inspiration by suggesting several attractive designs. Select the cells you want to format, pull down the Format menu, and click the AutoFormat command to display the AutoFormat dialog box. Select (click) a design, then click the Options button to determine the formats to apply (font, column width, patterns, and so on). Click OK to close the dialog box and apply the formatting. Click the Undo button if you do not like the result. See practice exercise 1 at the end of the chapter.

Step 6: Change the Chart Type

- Click the **chart** (background) **area** to select the chart, click the **drop-down arrow** on the Chart type button on the Chart toolbar, then click the **3-D Pie Chart icon**. The chart changes to a three-dimensional pie chart.
- Point to the chart area, click the **right mouse button** to display a shortcut menu, then click the **Chart Options command** to display the Chart Options dialog box shown in Figure 3.7f.
- Click the **Data Labels tab**, then click the check boxes for Category name and Percentage. Click **OK** to accept the settings and close the dialog box.
- The pie chart changes to reflect the options you just specified. Modify each component as necessary:
  - ❏ Select (click) the (gray) **Plot area**. Click and drag the sizing handles to increase the size of the plot area within the embedded chart.
  - ❏ Point to any of the labels, click the **right mouse button** to display a shortcut menu, and click **Format Data Labels** to display a dialog box. Click the **Font tab**, and select a smaller point size. It may also be necessary to click and drag each label away from the plot area.
- Make other changes as necessary. Save the workbook.

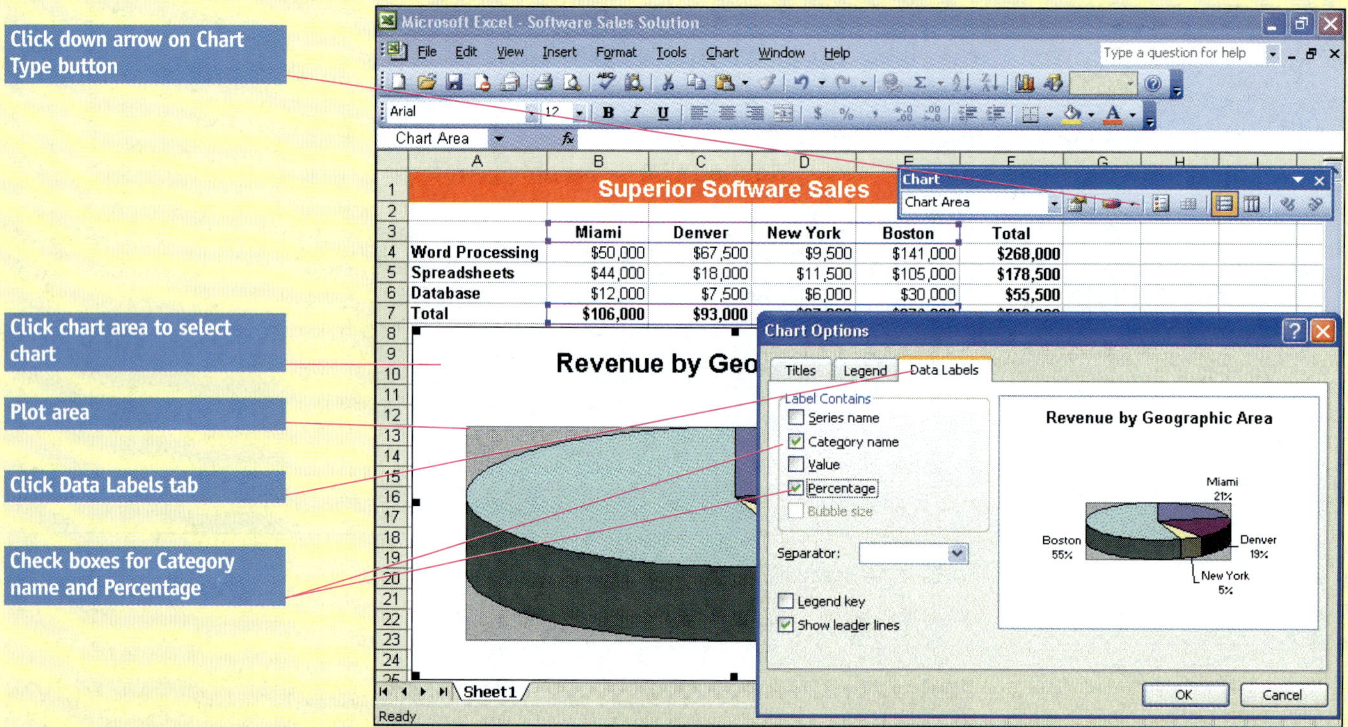

(f) Change the Chart Type (step 6)

FIGURE 3.7 Hands-on Exercise 1 (*continued*)

ADDITIONAL CHART TYPES

Excel offers multiple chart types, each with several formats. Line charts are best to display time-related information such as a five-year trend of sales or profit data. A combination chart uses two or more chart types to display different kinds of data or when different scales are required for multiple data series. See practice exercise 6 at the end of the chapter.

Step 7: Create a Second Chart

- Click and drag to select **cells A4** through **A6** in the worksheet. Press and hold the **Ctrl key** as you drag the mouse to select **cells F4** through **F6**.
- Click the **Chart Wizard button** on the Standard toolbar to start the Chart Wizard and display the dialog box for step 1 as shown in Figure 3.7g. The Column Chart type is already selected. Click the **Clustered column with a 3-D visual effect subtype**. Press and hold the indicated button to preview the chart with your data. Click **Next**.
- Click the **Series tab** in the dialog box for step 2 to confirm that you selected the correct data points. The values for Series1 should consist of cells F4 through F6. The Category labels for the *X* axis should be cells A4 through A6. Click **Next**.
- You should see step 3 of the Chart Wizard. Click the **Titles tab**, then click in the text box for the Chart title. Type **Revenue by Product Category**. Click the **Legend tab** and clear the box to show a legend. Click **Next**.
- You should see step 4 of the Chart Wizard. Select the option button to create the chart **As new sheet** (Chart1). Click **Finish**.
- The 3-D column chart has been created in the chart sheet labeled Chart1.

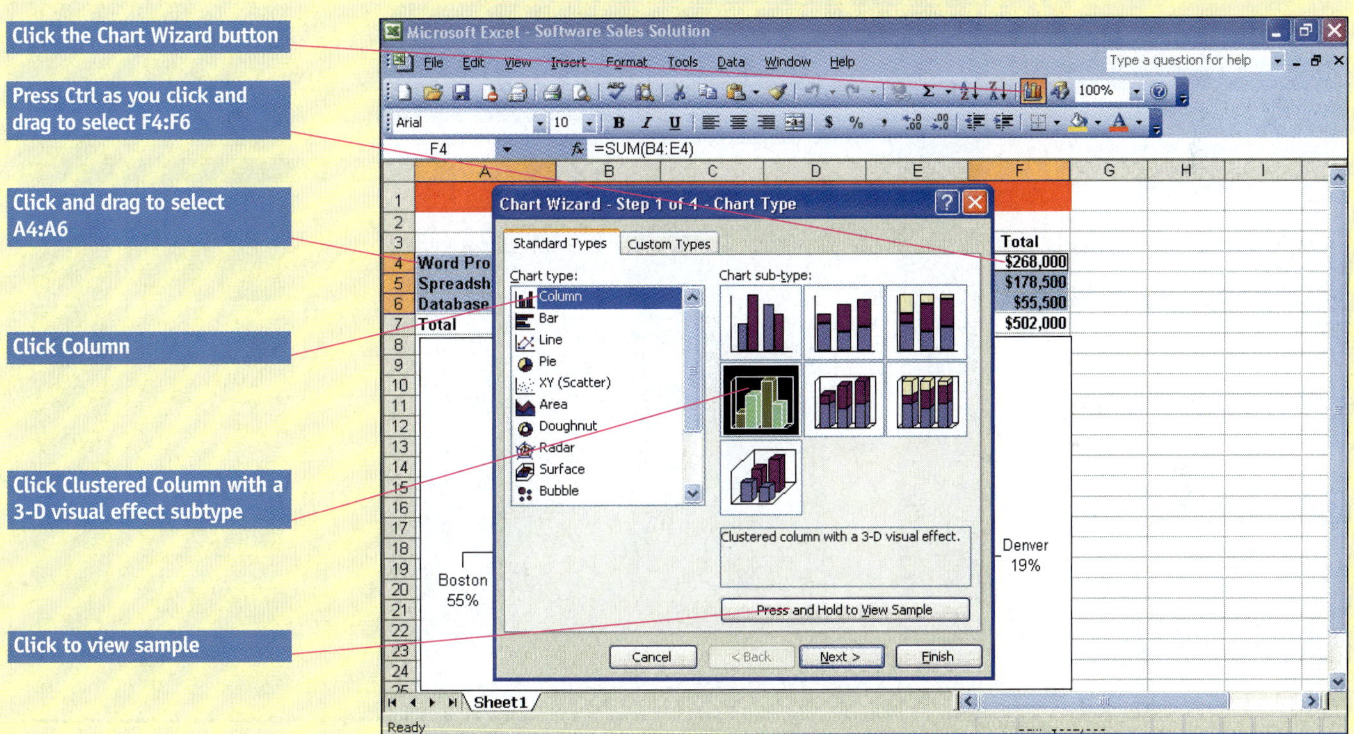

(g) Create a Second Chart (step 7)

FIGURE 3.7 Hands-on Exercise 1 (*continued*)

ANATOMY OF A CHART

A chart is composed of multiple components (objects), each of which can be selected and changed separately. Point to any part of a chart to display a ScreenTip indicating the name of the component, then click the mouse to select that component and display the sizing handles. You can then click and drag the object within the chart and/or click the right mouse button to display a shortcut menu with commands pertaining to the selected object.

Step 8: Add a Text Box

- Point to any visible toolbar, click the **right mouse button** to display a shortcut menu listing the available toolbars, then click **Drawing** to display the Drawing toolbar as shown in Figure 3.7h.
- Click the **Text Box button** on the Drawing toolbar. Click in the chart (the mouse pointer changes to a thin crosshair), then click and drag to create a text box. Release the mouse, then enter the text, **Word Processing leads all categories**.
- Point to the thatched border around the text box, then right click the border to display a context-sensitive menu. Click **Format Text Box** to display the Format Text dialog box. Click the **Font tab** and change the font to **12 point bold**. Choose **Red** as the font color.
- Click the **Colors and Lines tab** and select **white** as the fill color. Click **OK**. You should see red text on a white background. If necessary, size the text box so that the text fits on one line. Do not worry about the position of the text box.
- Click the title of the chart. You will see sizing handles around the title to indicate it has been selected. Click the **drop-down arrow** in the Font Size box on the Formatting toolbar. Click **22** to increase the size of the title. Save the workbook.

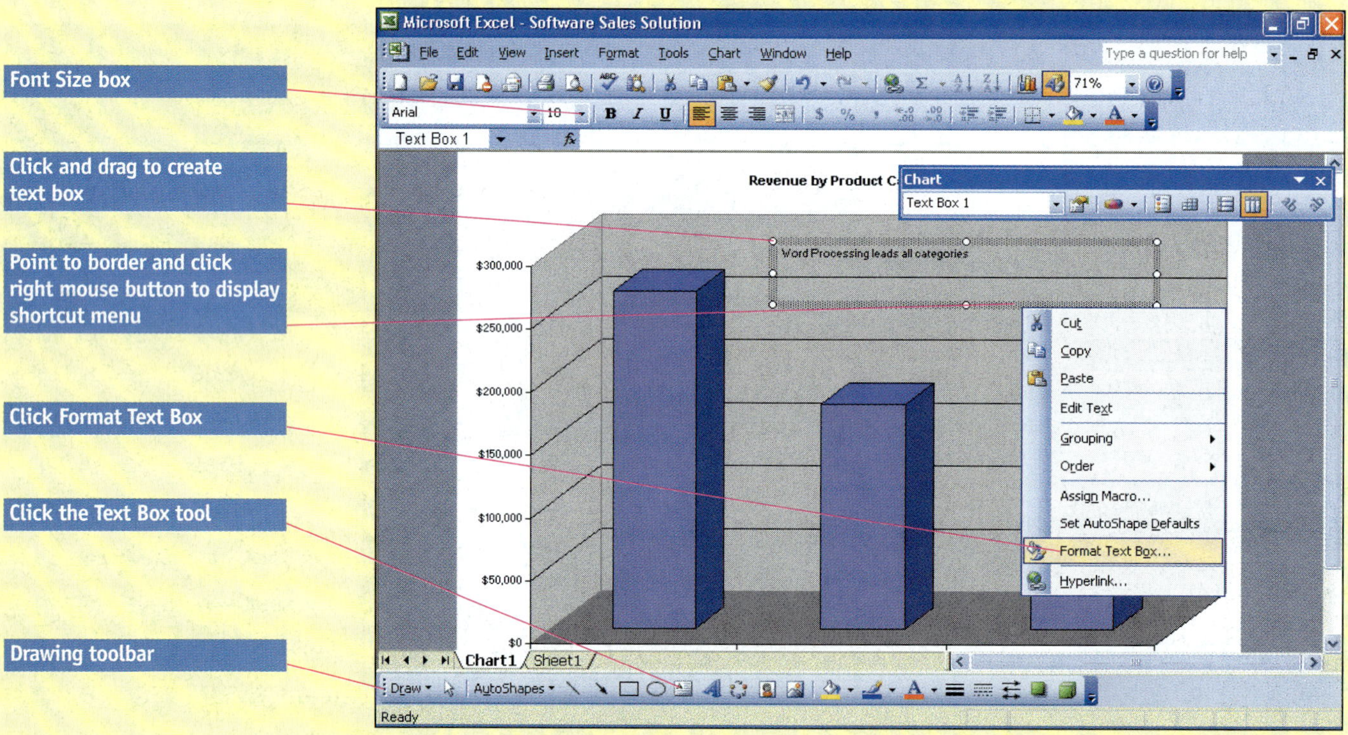

(h) Add a Text Box (step 8)

FIGURE 3.7 Hands-on Exercise 1 (*continued*)

FLOATING TOOLBARS

Any toolbar can be docked along the edge of the application window, or it can be displayed as a floating toolbar within the application window. To move a docked toolbar, drag the move handle. To move a floating toolbar, drag its title bar. To size a floating toolbar, drag any border in the direction you want to go. Double click the title bar of any floating toolbar to dock it. A floating toolbar will dim and disappear if it is not used.

Step 9: Create a 3-D Shape

- Click on the **AutoShapes button** and, if necessary, click the double arrow to display additional commands. Click **Block Arrows**. Select an arrow style.
- Click in the chart (the mouse pointer changes to a thin crosshair), then click and drag to create an arrow. Release the mouse.
- Click the **3-D button** on the drawing toolbar and click **3-D Style 1** as shown in Figure 3.7i. Right click the arrow and click the **Format AutoShape command** to display the Format AutoShape dialog box. Click the **Colors and Lines tab**. Choose **Red** as the fill color. Click **OK**, then size the arrow.
- Select (click) the text box you created in the previous step, then click and drag the text box out of the way. Select (click) the **3-D arrow** and position it next to the word processing column.
- Click and drag the text box on top of the arrow. If you do not see the text, right click the arrow, click the **Order command**, and click **Send to Back**.
- Save the workbook, but do not print it at this time. Exit Excel if you do not want to continue with the next exercise at this time.

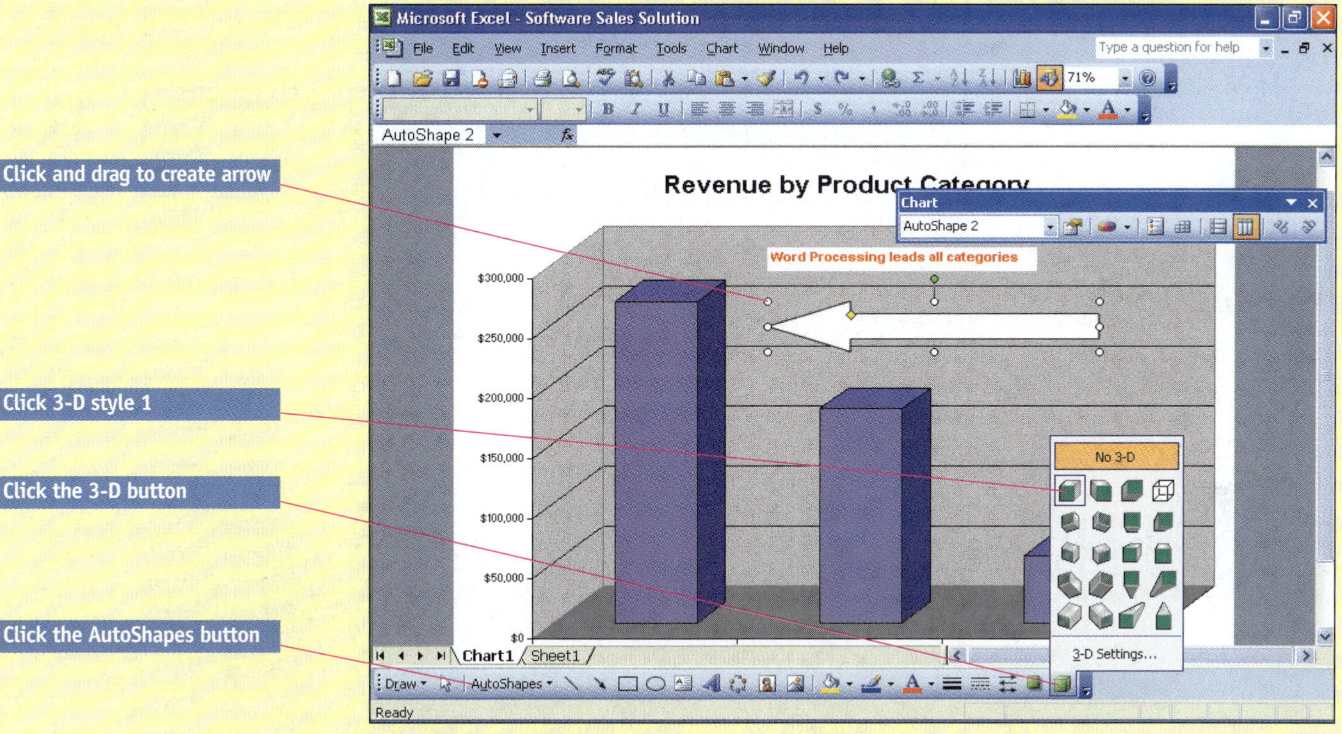

(i) Create a 3-D Shape (step 9)

FIGURE 3.7 Hands-on Exercise 1 (*continued*)

FORMAT THE DATA SERIES

Use the Format Data Series command to change the color, shape, or pattern of the columns within the chart. Right click any column to select the data series (be sure that all three columns are selected), then click Format Data Series to display the Format Data Series dialog box. Experiment with the various options, especially those on the Shape and Patterns tabs within the dialog box. Click OK when you are satisfied with the changes.

MULTIPLE DATA SERIES

The charts presented so far displayed only a single data series such as the total sales by location or the total sales by product category. Although such charts are useful, it is often more informative to view ***multiple data series*** on the same chart. Figure 3.8a displays the worksheet we have been using throughout the chapter. Figure 3.8b displays a side-by-side column chart that plots multiple data series that exist as rows (B4:E4, B5:E5, and B6:E6) within the worksheet. Figure 3.8c displays a chart based on the same data when the series are in columns (B4:B6, C4:C6, D4:D6, and E4:E6).

Both charts plot a total of twelve data points (three product categories for each of four locations), but they group the data differently. Figure 3.8b displays the data by city in which the sales of three product categories are shown for each of four cities. Figure 3.8c is the reverse and groups the data by product category. This time the sales in the four cities are shown for each of three product categories. The choice between the two charts depends on your message and whether you want to emphasize revenue by city or by product category. It sounds complicated, but it's not; Excel will create either chart for you according to your specifications.

A3:E6 is selected

	A	B	C	D	E	F
1	Superior Software Sales					
2						
3		Miami	Denver	New York	Boston	Total
4	Word Processing	$50,000	$67,500	$9,500	$141,000	$268,000
5	Spreadsheets	$44,000	$18,000	$11,500	$105,000	$178,500
6	Database	$12,000	$7,500	$6,000	$30,000	$55,500
7	Total	$106,000	$93,000	$27,000	$276,000	$502,000

(a) Worksheet Data

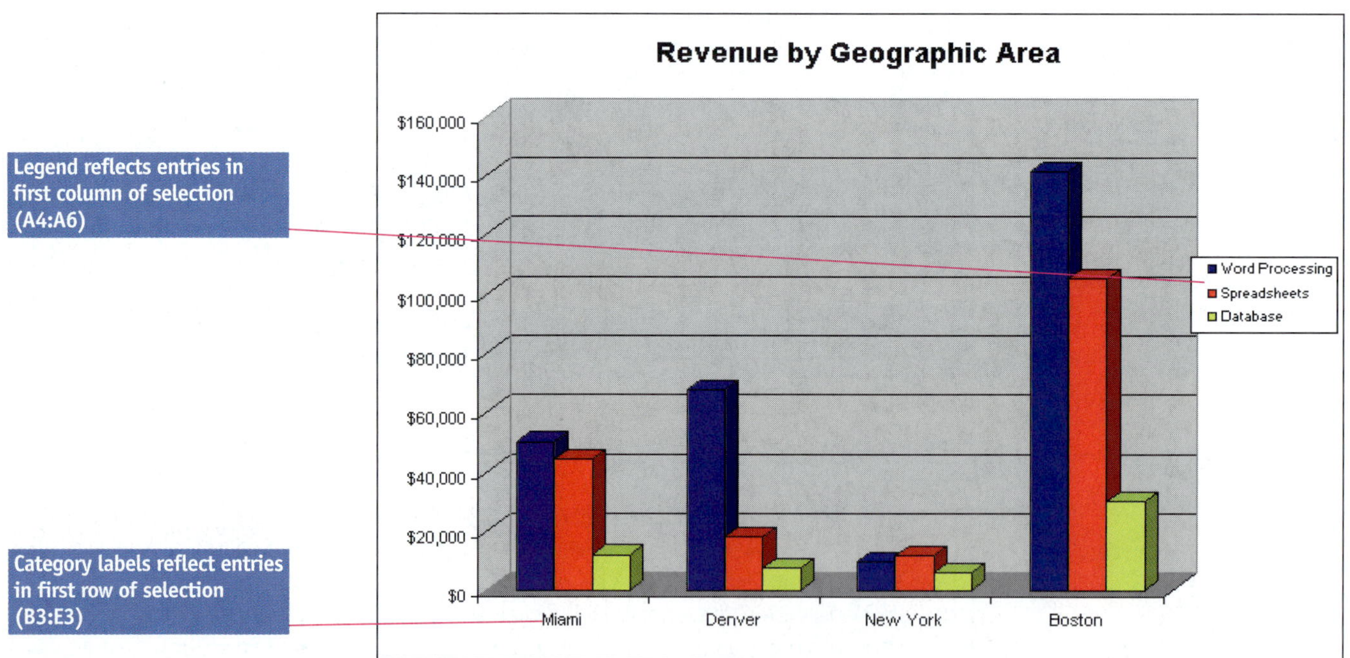

(b) Data in Rows

FIGURE 3.8 Side-by-Side Column Charts

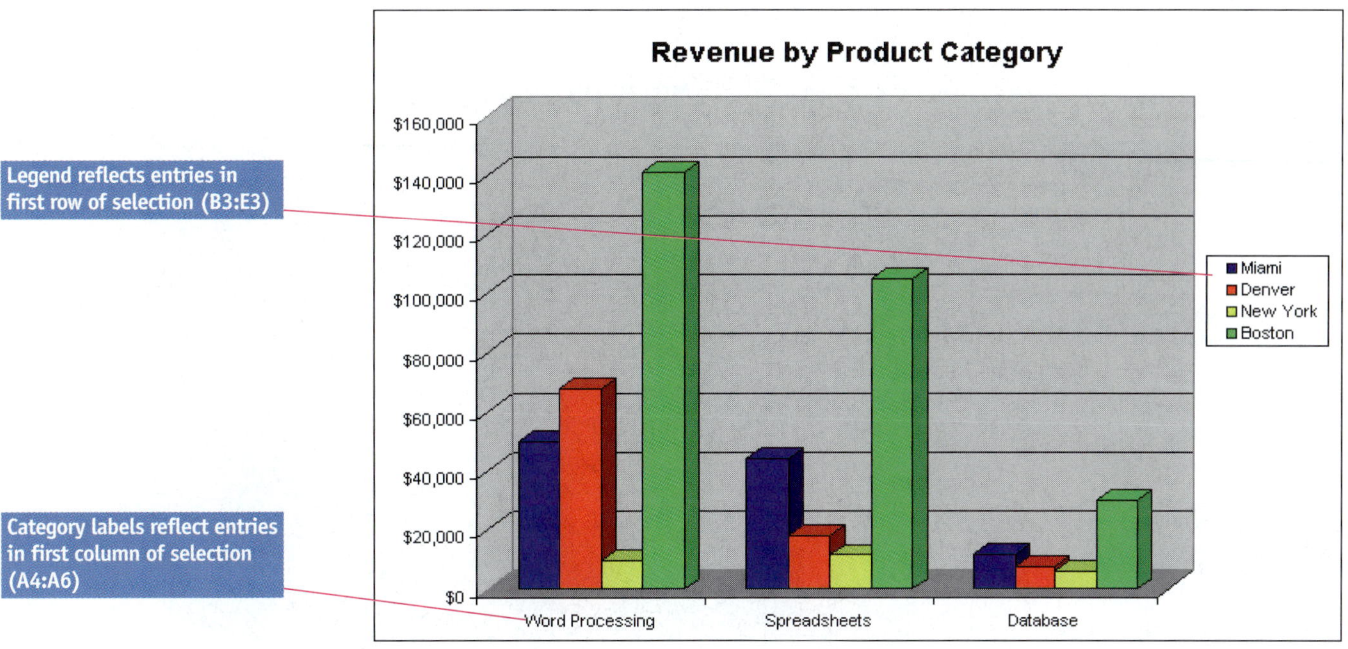

(c) Data in Columns

FIGURE 3.8 Side-by-Side Column Charts (*continued*)

- If you specify that the data series are in rows (Figure 3.8b), the wizard will:
  - Use the first row (cells B3 through E3) for the category labels
  - Use the remaining rows (rows four, five, and six) for the data series
  - Use the first column (cells A4 through A6) for the legend text
- If you specify the data series are in columns (Figure 3.8c), the wizard will:
  - Use the first column (cells A4 through A6) for the category labels
  - Use the remaining columns (columns B, C, D, and E) for the data series
  - Use the first row (cells B3 through E3) for the legend text

Stacked Column Charts

The next decision is the choice between ***side-by-side column charts*** versus ***stacked column charts*** such as those shown in Figure 3.9. Stacked column charts also group data in one of two ways, in rows or in columns. Thus Figure 3.9a is a stacked column chart with the data in rows. Figure 3.9b is also a stacked column chart, but the data is in columns.

The choice of side-by-side versus stacked column charts depends on the intended message. If you want the audience to see the individual sales in each city or product category, then the side-by-side columns in Figure 3.8 are more appropriate. If, on the other hand, you want to emphasize the total sales for each city or product category, the stacked columns are preferable. The advantage of the stacked column is that the totals are clearly shown and can be easily compared. The disadvantage is that the segments within each column do not start at the same point, making it difficult to determine the actual sales for the individual categories.

Note, too, that the scale on the *Y* axis is different for charts with side-by-side columns versus charts with stacked columns. The side-by-side columns in Figure 3.8 show the sales of each product category and so the *Y* axis goes only to $160,000. The stacked columns in Figure 3.9, however, reflect the total sales for all products in each city and thus the scale goes to $300,000. Realize, too, that for a stacked column chart to make sense, its numbers must be additive. You would not, for example, convert a column chart that plots units and dollar sales side by side to a stacked column chart, because units and dollars are not additive.

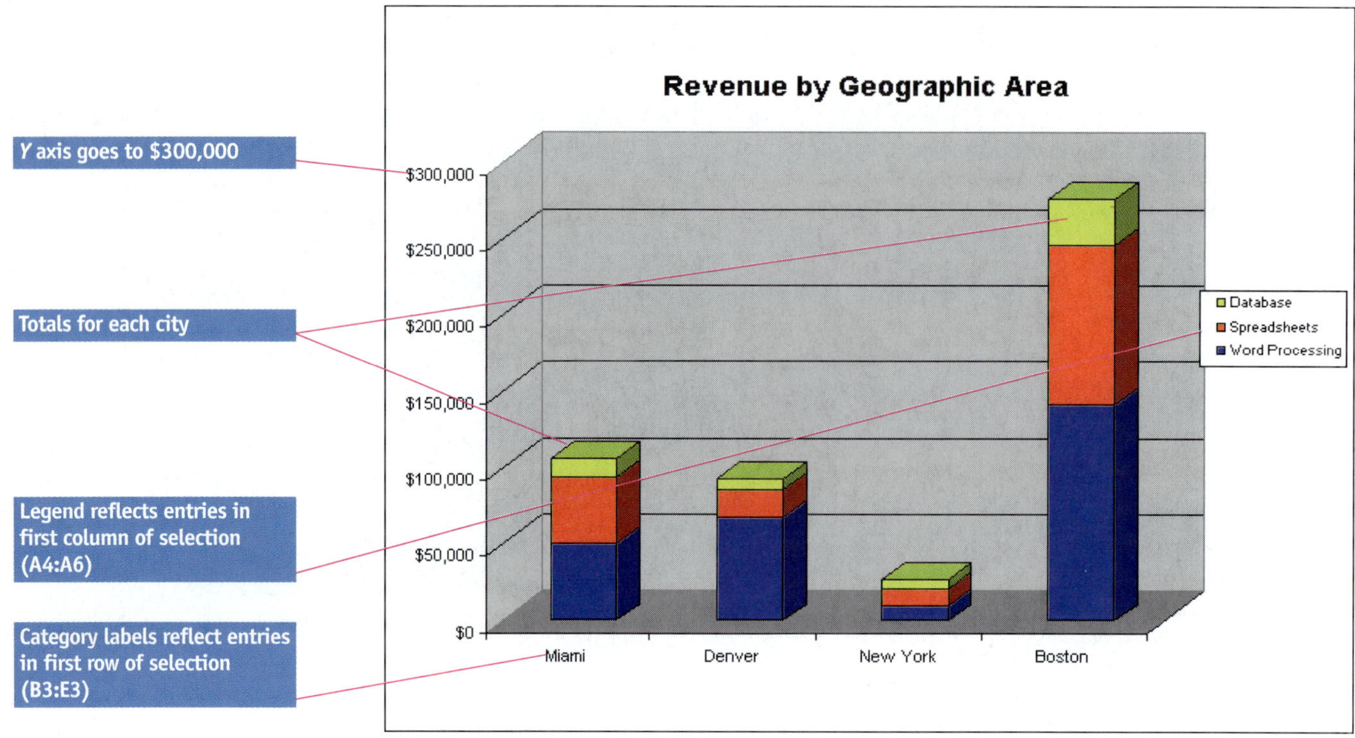

(a) Data in Rows

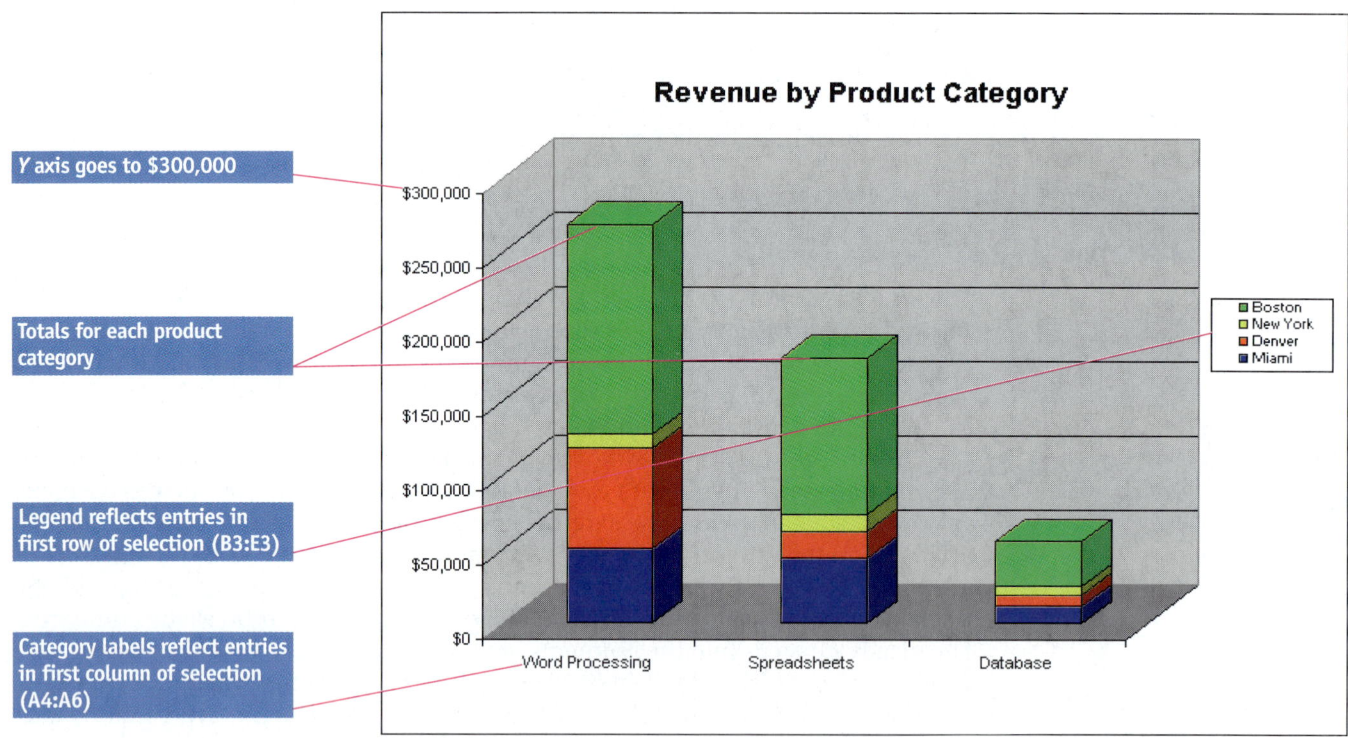

(b) Data in Columns

FIGURE 3.9 Stacked Column Charts

hands-on exercise

2 Multiple Data Series

Objective To plot multiple data series in the same chart; to differentiate between data series in rows and columns. Use Figure 3.10 as a guide.

Step 1: Rename the Worksheets

- Open the **Software Sales Solution workbook** from the previous exercise as shown in Figure 3.10a.
- Point to the workbook tab labeled **Sheet1**, click the **right mouse button** to display a shortcut menu, then click the **Rename command**. The name of the worksheet (Sheet1) is selected.
- Type **Sales Data** to change the name of the worksheet to the more descriptive name. Press the **Enter key**. Right click the worksheet tab a second time, click the **Tab Color command**, then change the color to **blue**. Click **OK**.
- Change the name of the Chart1 sheet to **Column Chart**. Change the tab color to **red**. Close the Drawing toolbar. Save the workbook.

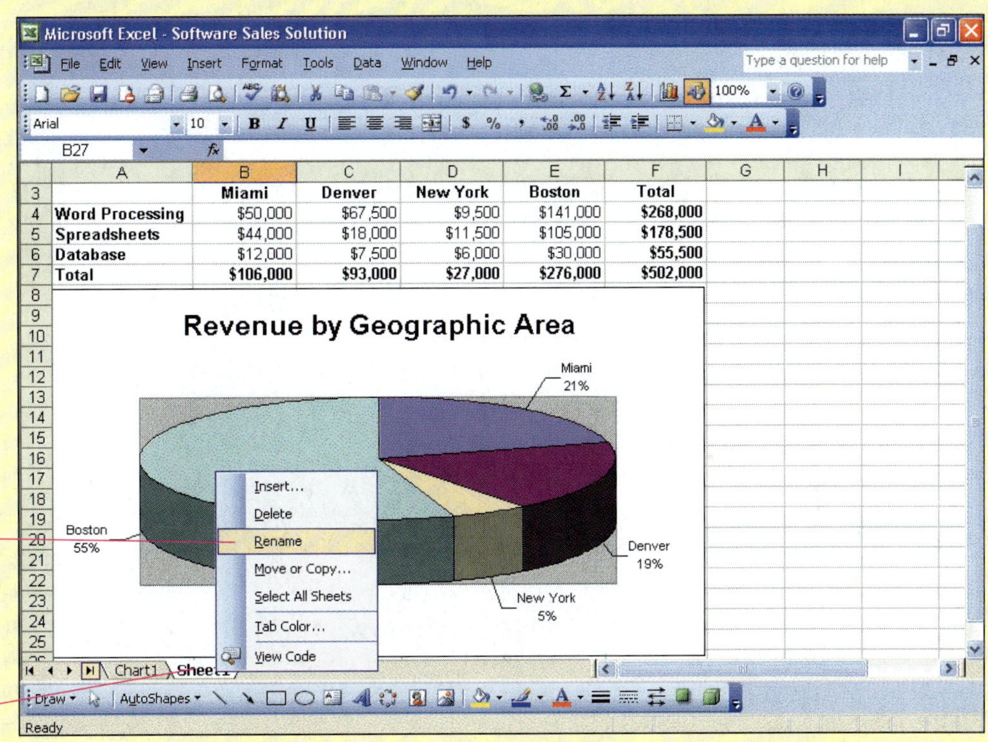

	Miami	Denver	New York	Boston	Total
Word Processing	$50,000	$67,500	$9,500	$141,000	$268,000
Spreadsheets	$44,000	$18,000	$11,500	$105,000	$178,500
Database	$12,000	$7,500	$6,000	$30,000	$55,500
Total	$106,000	$93,000	$27,000	$276,000	$502,000

(a) Rename the Worksheets (step 1)

FIGURE 3.10 Hands-on Exercise 2

HIDING AND UNHIDING A WORKSHEET

A chart delivers a message more effectively than the corresponding numeric data, and thus it may be convenient to hide the associated worksheet on which the chart is based. Click the tab of the worksheet you want to hide, pull down the Format menu, click Sheet, and then click the Hide command. (Reverse the process to unhide the worksheet. Pull down the Format menu, click Sheet, click the Unhide command, and then click the name of the worksheet you want to see.)

Step 2: The Chart Wizard

- Click the **Sales Data tab**, then click and drag to select **cells A3** through **E6**. Click the **Chart Wizard button** on the Standard toolbar to start the wizard.
- Select **Column** as the chart type and **Clustered column with a 3-D visual effect** as the subtype. Click **Next** to continue with the Chart Wizard.
- You should see step 2 of the Chart Wizard as shown in Figure 3.10b. The data range should be specified as **Sales Data!$A$3:$E$6**. The option button for **Series in Rows** should be selected. Click **Next**.
- You should see step 3 of the Chart Wizard. Click the **Titles tab**. Click the text box for Chart title. Type **Revenue by City**. Click **Next**.
- You should see step 4 of the Chart Wizard. Click the option button for **As new sheet**. Type **Revenue by City** in the associated text box. Click **Finish**.
- Excel creates the new chart in its own sheet named Revenue by City. Change the tab color of the chart sheet to **red**. Save the workbook.

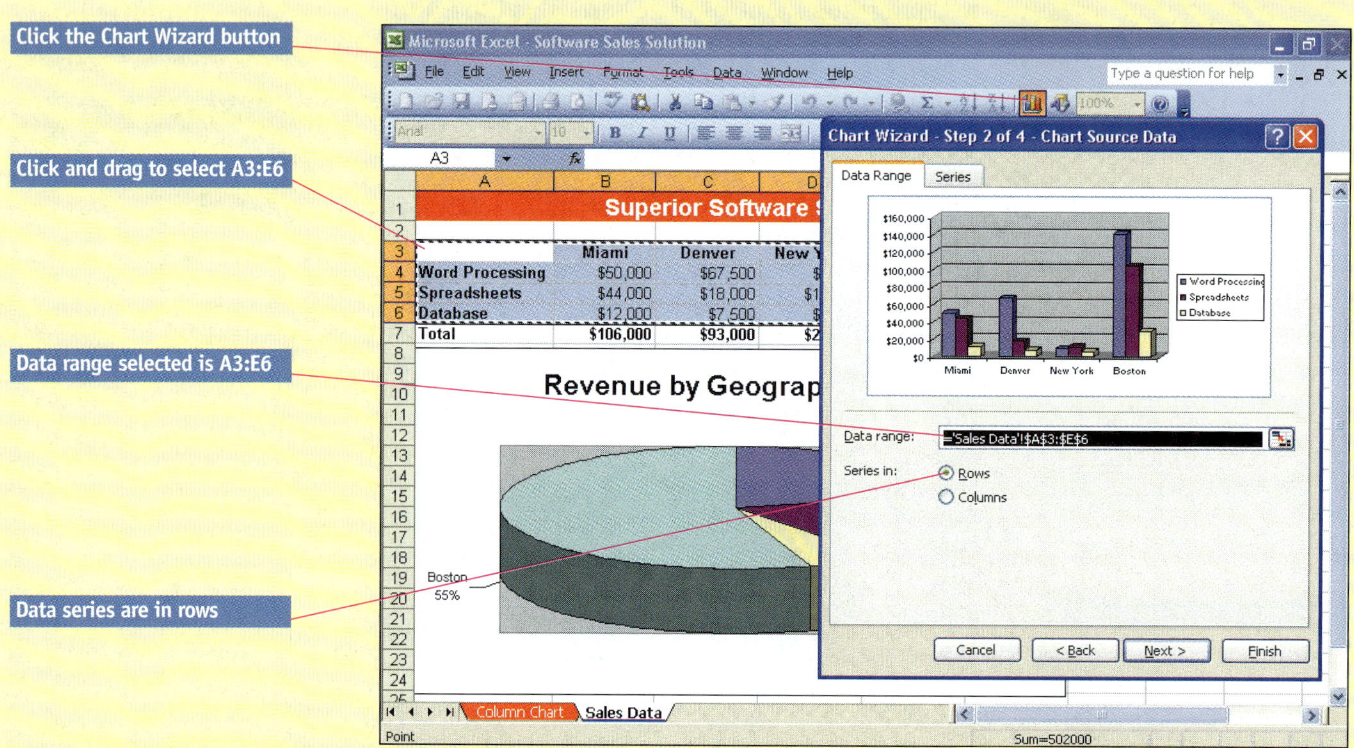

(b) The Chart Wizard (step 2)

FIGURE 3.10 Hands-on Exercise 2 (*continued*)

DATA IN ROWS VERSUS COLUMNS

The choice between data series in rows versus columns depends on the message you want to convey. If the data series are in rows (as in this example), the contribution of each city is emphasized. The first row in the selected range from the worksheet (cells A3 through E6) appears on the *X* axis, and the first column is used as the legend. To view the individual data series, pull down the Chart menu, click the Source Data command to display the associated dialog box, then click the Series tab. You will find three data series (Word processing, Spreadsheets, and Database), each with four data points.

Step 3: Copy the Chart

- Click anywhere in the chart title to select the title. Click the **Font Size list box** and change to **18 point** type to enlarge the title.
- Point to the tab named **Revenue by City**. Click the **right mouse button**. Click **Move or Copy** to display the dialog box in Figure 3.10c.
- Click **Sales Data** in the Before Sheet list box. Check the box to **Create a Copy**. Click **OK**.
- A duplicate worksheet called Revenue by City(2) is created and appears before (to the left of) the Sales Data worksheet. (You can also press and hold the Ctrl key as you drag the worksheet tab to create a copy of the worksheet.)
- Double click the newly created worksheet tab to select the name. Enter **Revenue by Product** as the new name.
- Save the workbook.

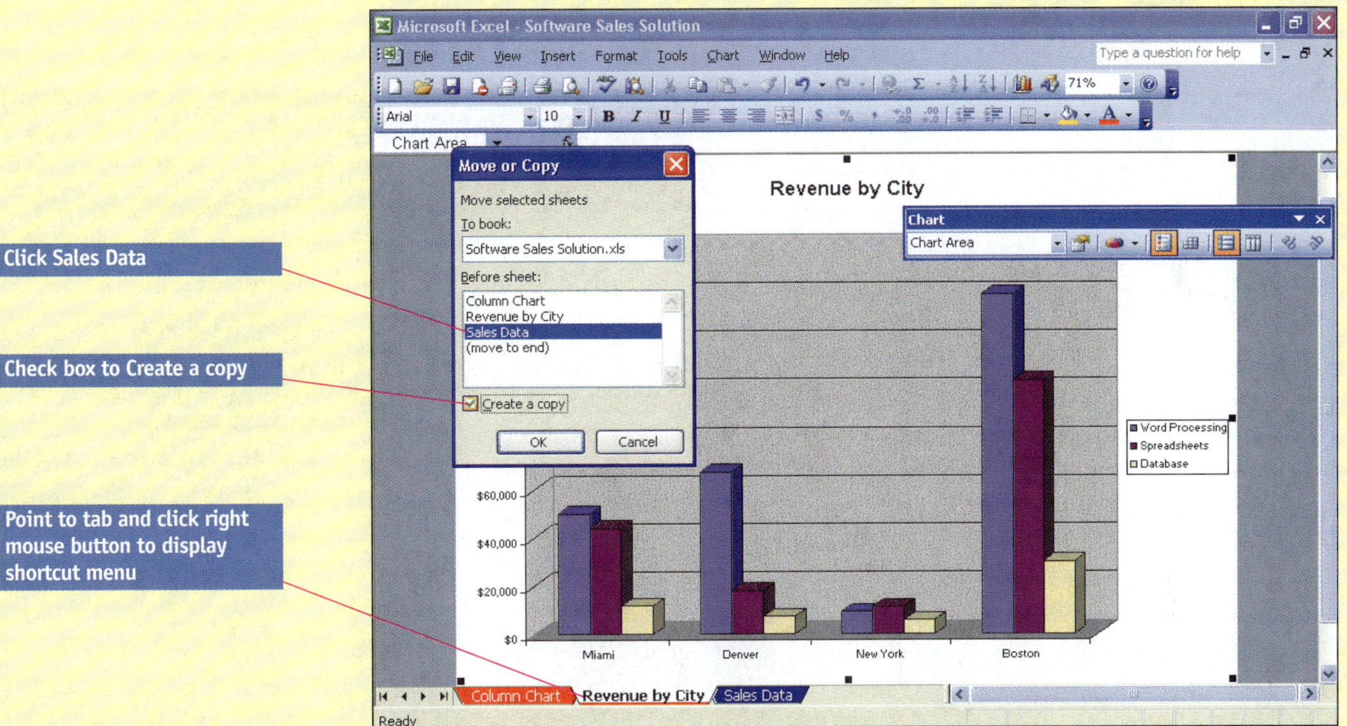

(c) Copy the Chart (step 3)

FIGURE 3.10 Hands-on Exercise 2 (*continued*)

MOVING AND COPYING A WORKSHEET

The fastest way to move or copy a chart sheet is to drag its tab. To move a sheet, point to its tab, then click and drag the tab to its new position. To copy a sheet, press and hold the Ctrl key as you drag the tab to the desired position for the second sheet. Rename the copied sheet (or any sheet for that matter) by double clicking its tab to select the existing name. Enter a new name for the worksheet, then press the Enter key. You can also right click the worksheet tab to change its color. See practice exercise 1 at the end of the chapter.

Step 4: Change the Source Data

- Click the **Revenue by Product tab** to make it the active sheet. Click anywhere in the title of the chart, drag the mouse over the word **City** to select the text, then type **Product Category** to replace the selected text. Click outside the title to deselect it.
- Pull down the **Chart menu**. If necessary, click the double arrow to see more commands, click **Source Data** and click the **Data Range tab** (you will see the Sales Data worksheet). Click the **Columns option button** so that your screen matches Figure 3.10d.
- Click the **Series tab** and note the following:
  - The original chart plotted the data in rows. There were three data series (one series for each product).
  - The new chart (shown in the dialog box) plots the data in columns. There are four data series (one for each city as indicated in the Series list box).
- Click **OK** to close the Source Data dialog box.
- Save the workbook.

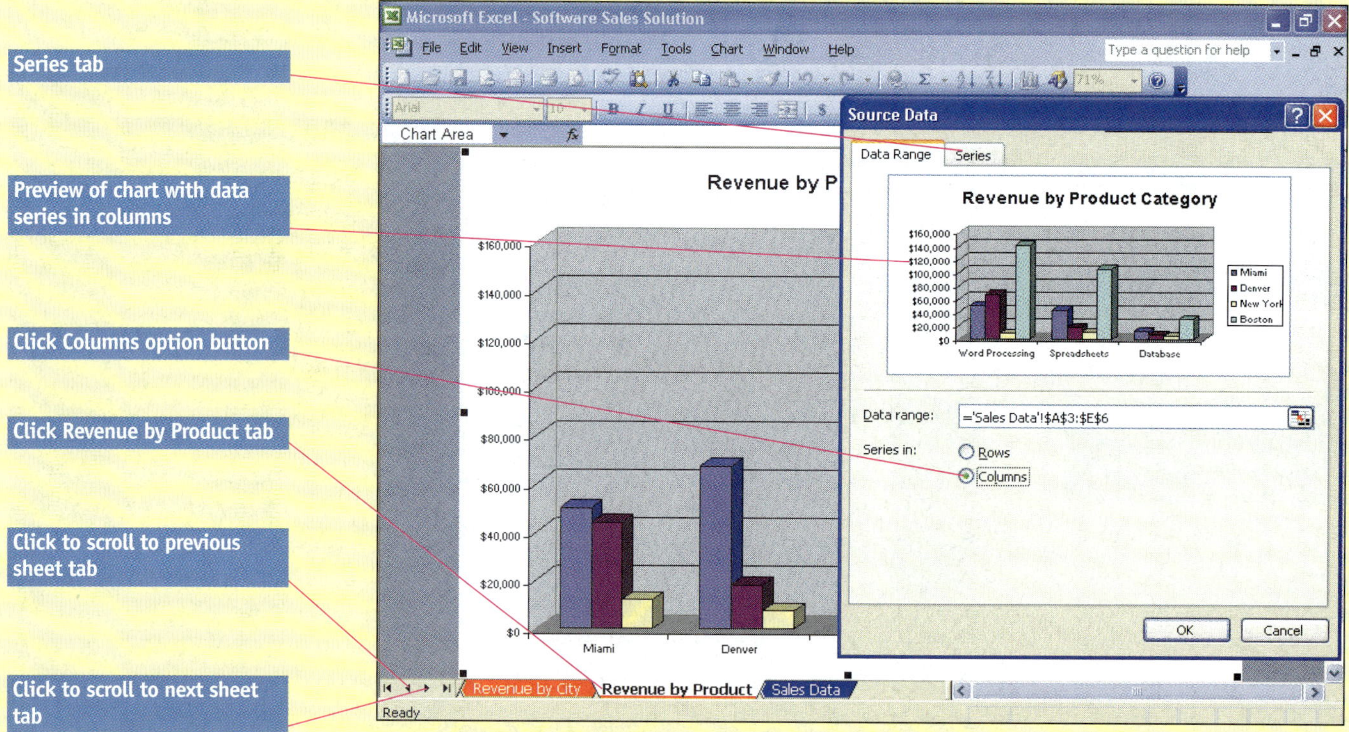

(d) Change the Source Data (step 4)

FIGURE 3.10 Hands-on Exercise 2 (*continued*)

THE HORIZONTAL SCROLL BAR

The horizontal scroll bar contains four scrolling buttons to scroll through the sheet tabs in a workbook. Click ◀ or ▶ to scroll one tab to the left or right. Click |◀ or ▶| to scroll to the first or last tab in the workbook. Once the desired tab is visible, click the tab to select it. Change the color of any tab by right clicking the tab and selecting Tab Color from the context-sensitive menu. See practice exercise 1 at the end of the chapter.

Step 5: Change the Chart Type

- Pull down the **Chart menu** and click the **Chart Type command** to display the associated dialog box.
- Select the **Stacked Column with a 3-D visual effect** chart (the middle entry in the second row). Click **OK**. The chart changes to a stacked column chart.
- Pull down the **Chart menu** and click the **Chart Options command** to display the associated dialog box. Click the **Legend tab** and check the option button to display the legend at the **bottom** of the chart.
- Click the **Data Labels tab**. Check the box to display the **Value** of each chart component as shown in Figure 3.10e.
- Experiment further with the various options that are available. Click the **Data Table tab**, then check the box to show the data table. We think the table is cluttered in this example, and thus we clear the box to show the table.
- Click **OK** to accept the existing settings and close the Chart Options dialog box. Save the workbook.

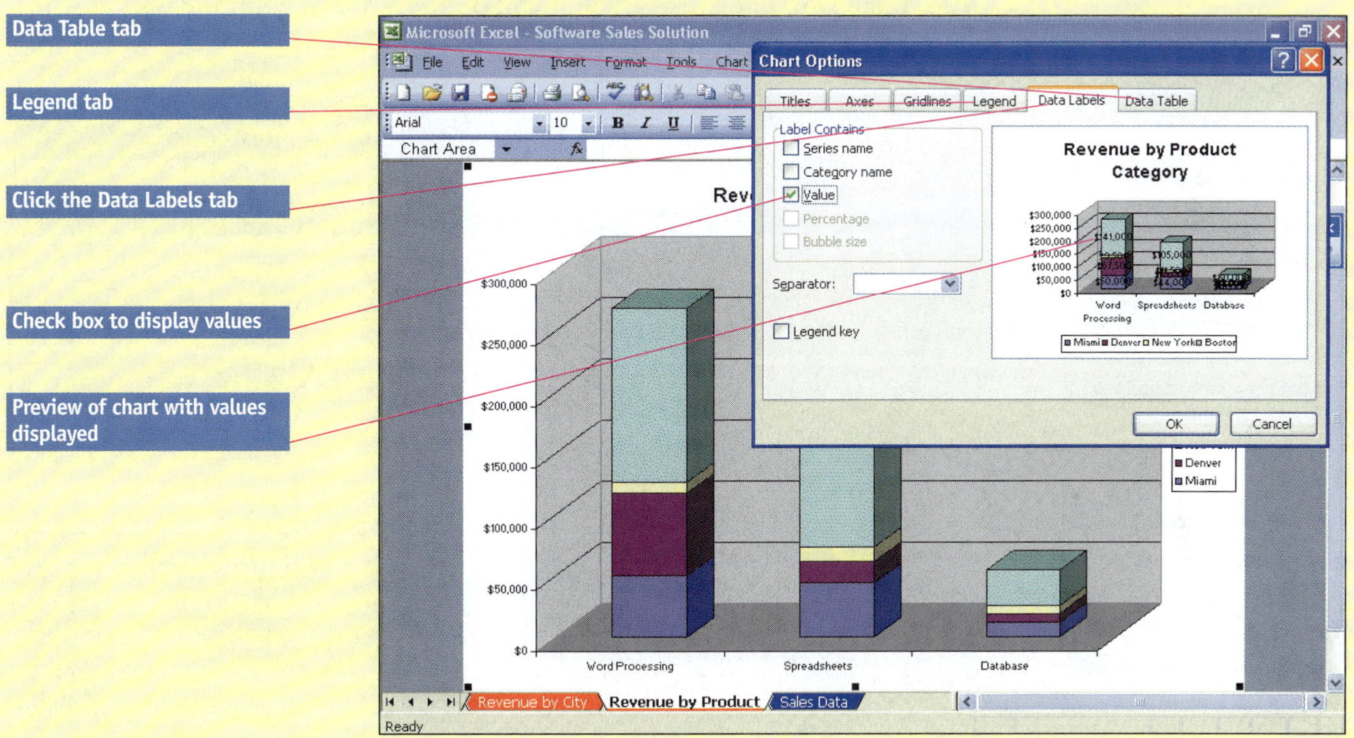

(e) Change the Chart Type (step 5)

FIGURE 3.10 Hands-on Exercise 2 (*continued*)

THE RIGHT MOUSE BUTTON

Point to a cell (or group of selected cells), a chart or worksheet tab, a toolbar, or chart (or a selected object on the chart), then click the right mouse button to display a shortcut menu. All shortcut menus are context-sensitive and display commands appropriate for the selected item. Right clicking a toolbar, for example, enables you to display (hide) additional toolbars. Right clicking a sheet tab enables you to rename, move, copy, or delete the sheet.

Step 6: Print the Workbook

- Click the **Print Preview button** on the Standard toolbar to display the Print Preview screen. Click the **Margins button** on the Print Preview toolbar to toggle the (display of the) margins on and off.
- Click the **Setup button** to display the Page Setup dialog box. Click the **Page tab** in the Page Setup dialog box. Click the option button for **landscape**.
- Click the **Header/Footer tab** in the Page Setup dialog box, then click the button to create a **Custom Footer** to display the Footer dialog box as shown in Figure 3.10f.
- Click the text box for the left section and **enter your name**. Click the text box for the center section and **enter your instructor's name**.
- Click the text box for the right section. Click the **Date button**, press the **space bar**, and then click the **Time button**. Click **OK** to accept these settings and close the Footer dialog box. Click **OK** to close the Page Setup dialog box.
- Print the completed chart for your instructor. Use the **Page Setup command** as appropriate prior to printing the other charts in the workbook.
- Save the workbook. Exit Excel if you do not want to continue with the next exercise at this time.

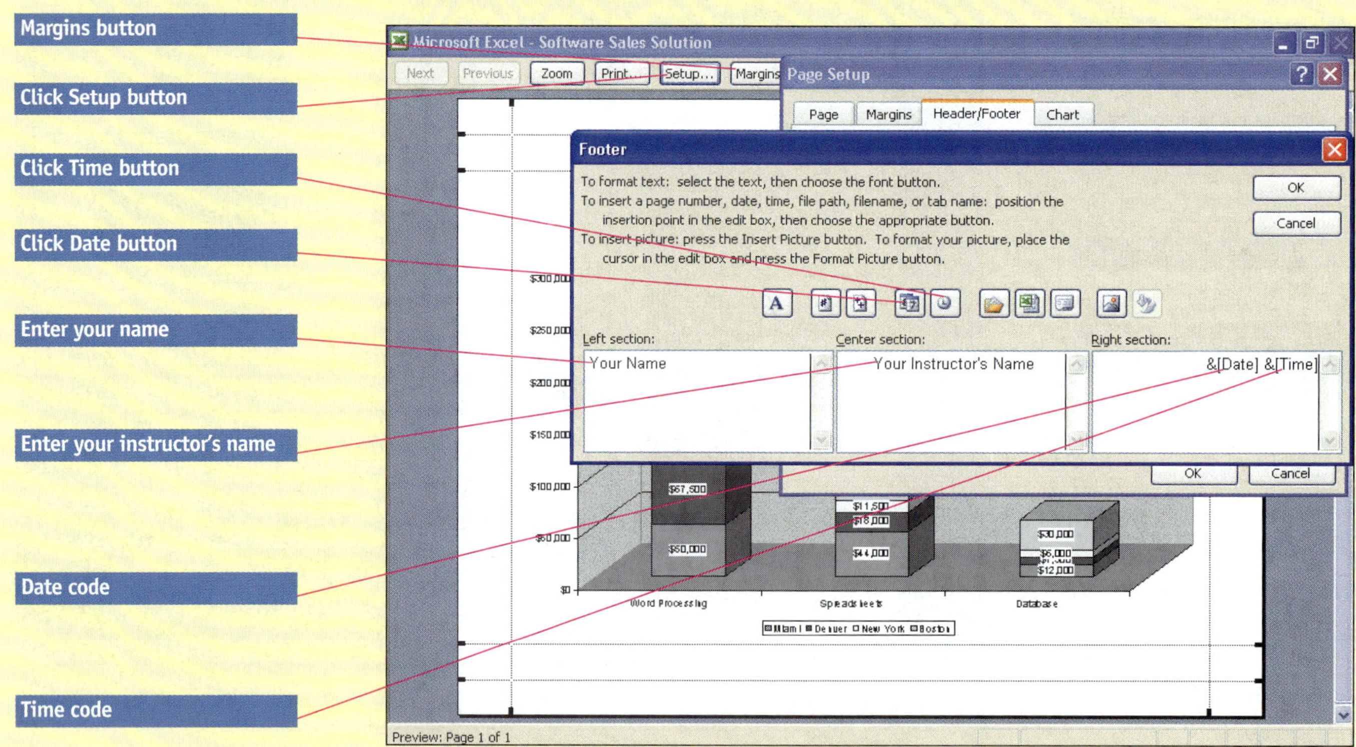

(f) Print the Workbook (step 6)

FIGURE 3.10 Hands-on Exercise 2 (*continued*)

PRINT ONLY WHAT YOU NEED

Why print an entire workbook if you need only a single worksheet? Press and hold the Ctrl key as you click the tab(s) of the worksheet(s) that you want to print. Pull down the File menu, click the Print command, click the option button for Active Sheet(s) in the Print What area, then click OK. (You can also print selected cells within a worksheet by selecting the cells, then clicking the Selection option button.)

OBJECT LINKING AND EMBEDDING

The applications within Microsoft Office enable you to create a document in one application that contains data (objects) from another application. The memo in Figure 3.11, for example, was created in Microsoft Word, and it contains ***objects*** (a worksheet and a chart) that were developed in Microsoft Excel. The Excel objects are linked to the Word document, so that any changes to the Excel workbook are automatically reflected in the Word document.

The following exercise uses ***Object Linking and Embedding (OLE)*** to create a Word document containing an Excel worksheet and chart. As you do the exercise, both applications (Word and Excel) will be open, and it will be necessary to switch back and forth between them. This in turn demonstrates the ***multitasking*** capability within Windows and the use of the ***taskbar*** to switch between the open applications.

Superior Software

To: Mr. White
Chairman, Superior Software

From: Heather Bond
Vice President, Marketing

Subject: May Sales Data

The May sales data clearly indicate that Boston is outperforming our other geographic areas. It is my feeling that Ms. Brown, the office supervisor, is directly responsible for its success and that she should be rewarded accordingly. In addition, we may want to think about transferring her to New York, as they are in desperate need of new ideas and direction. I will be awaiting your response after you have time to digest the information presented.

Superior Software Sales

	Miami	Denver	New York	Boston	Total
Word Processing	$50,000	$67,500	$200,000	$141,000	**$458,500**
Spreadsheets	$44,000	$18,000	$11,500	$105,000	**$178,500**
Database	$12,000	$7,500	$6,000	$30,000	**$55,500**
Total	**$106,000**	**$93,000**	**$217,500**	**$276,000**	**$692,500**

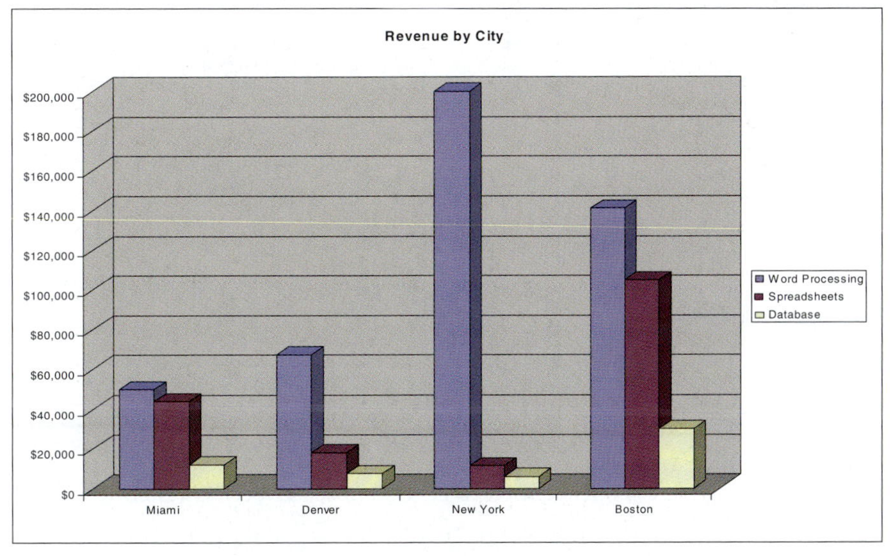

FIGURE 3.11 Object Linking and Embedding

hands-on exercise

3 Object Linking and Embedding

Objective To create a compound document consisting of a memo, worksheet, and chart. Use Figure 3.12 as a guide in the exercise.

Step 1: Open the Software Sales Document

- Click the **Start button**, click **All Programs**, click **Microsoft Office**, then click **Microsoft Office Word 2003** to start Word. Hide the Office Assistant if it appears.
- If necessary, click the **Maximize button** in the application window so that Word takes the entire desktop as shown in Figure 3.12a. (The Open dialog box is not yet visible.)
- Pull down the **File menu** and click **Open** (or click the **Open button** on the Standard toolbar).
  - Click the **drop-down arrow** in the Look In list box. Click the appropriate drive, drive C or drive A, depending on the location of your data.
  - Double click the **Exploring Excel folder** (we placed the Word memo in the Exploring Excel folder) to open the folder. Double click the **Software Memo** to open the document.
  - Save the document as **Software Memo Solution**.
- Pull down the **View menu**. Click **Print Layout** to change to the Print Layout view. Pull down the **View menu**. Click **Zoom**. Click **Page Width**. Click **Ok**.
- The software memo is open on your desktop.

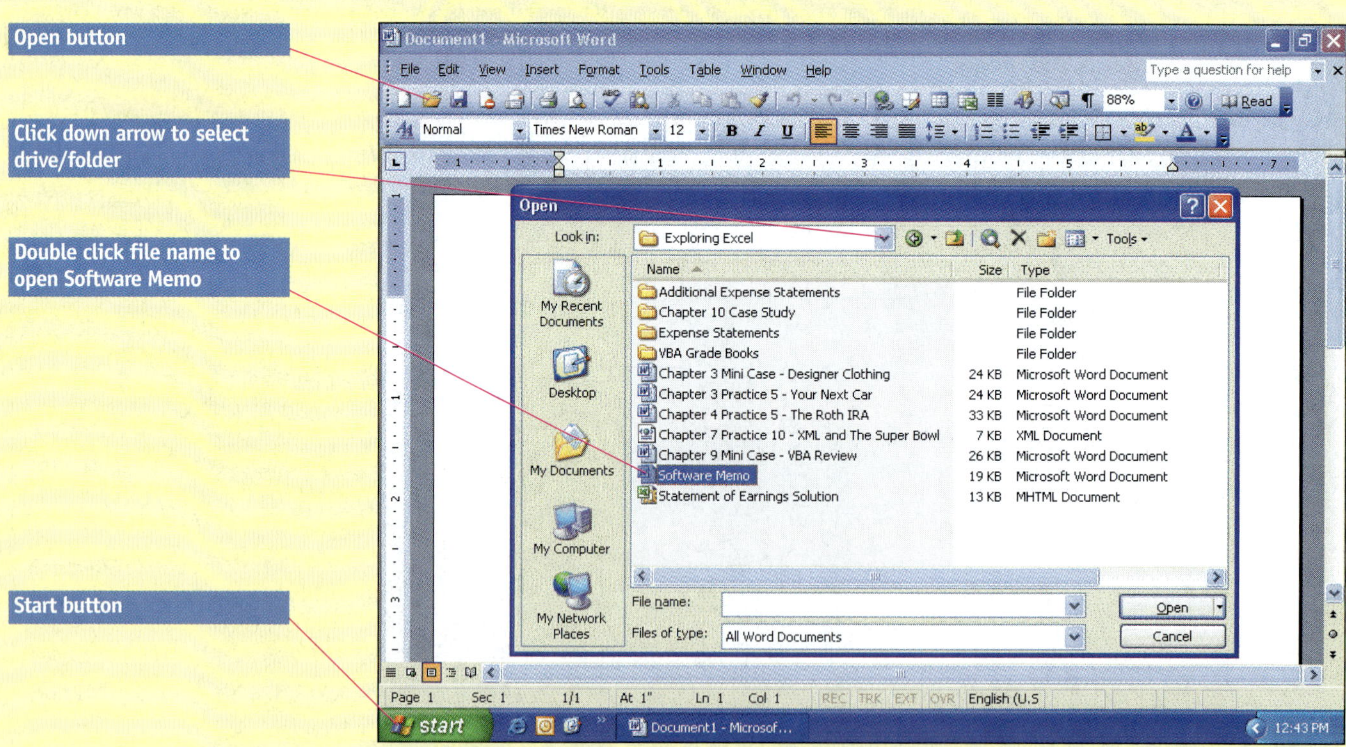

(a) Open the Software Sales Document (step 1)

FIGURE 3.12 Hands-on Exercise 3

Step 2: Copy the Worksheet

- Open the **Software Sales Solution workbook** from the previous exercise.
  - If you did not close Microsoft Excel at the end of the previous exercise, you will see its button on the taskbar. Click the **Microsoft Excel button** to return to the Software Sales Solution workbook.
  - If you closed Microsoft Excel, click the **Start button** to start Excel, then open the Software Sales Solution workbook.
- The taskbar should now contain a button for both Microsoft Word and Microsoft Excel. Click either button to move back and forth between the open applications. End by clicking the **Microsoft Excel button**.
- Click the tab for **Sales Data**. Click and drag to select **A1** through **F7** to select the entire worksheet as shown in Figure 3.12b.
- Point to the selected area and click the **right mouse button** to display the shortcut menu. Click **Copy**.
- A moving border appears around the entire worksheet, indicating that it has been copied to the clipboard.

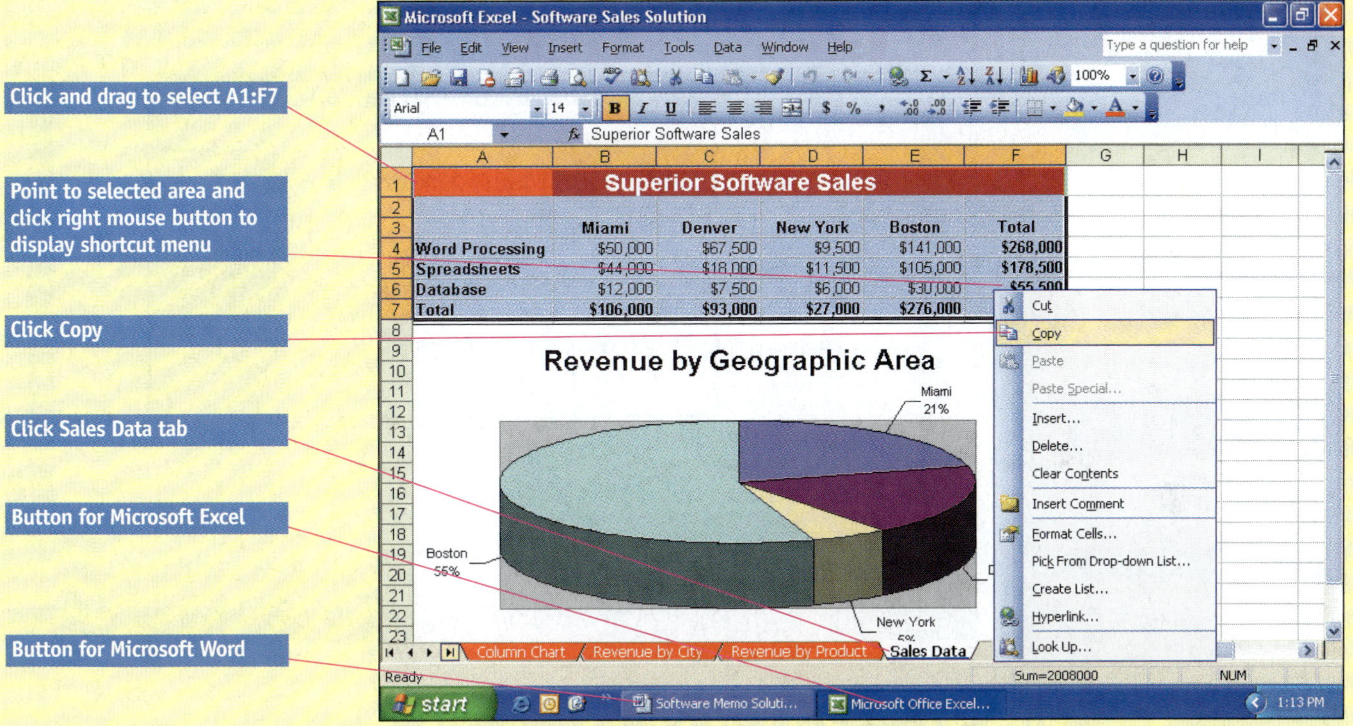

(b) Copy the Worksheet (step 2)

FIGURE 3.12 Hands-on Exercise 3 (*continued*)

THE WINDOWS TASKBAR

Multitasking, the ability to run multiple applications at the same time, is one of the primary advantages of the Windows environment. Each button on the taskbar appears automatically when its application or folder is opened, and disappears upon closing. (The buttons are resized automatically according to the number of open windows.) The taskbar can be moved to the left or right edge of the desktop, or to the top of the desktop, by dragging a blank area of the taskbar to the desired position.

Step 3: Create the Link

- Click the **Microsoft Word button** on the taskbar to return to the memo as shown in Figure 3.12c. Press **Ctrl+End** to move to the end of the memo, which is where you will insert the Excel worksheet.
- Pull down the **Edit menu**. If necessary, click the **double arrow** to see more commands, then click **Paste Special** to display the dialog box in Figure 3.12c.
- Click **Microsoft Excel Worksheet Object** in the As list. Click the **Paste link option button**. Click **OK** to insert the worksheet into the document.
- Right click the worksheet to display a context-sensitive menu, click **Format Object** to display the associated dialog box, and click the **Layout tab**.
- Choose **Square** in the Wrapping Style area, then click the option button to **Center** the object. Click **OK** to accept the settings and close the dialog box.
- Save the memo.

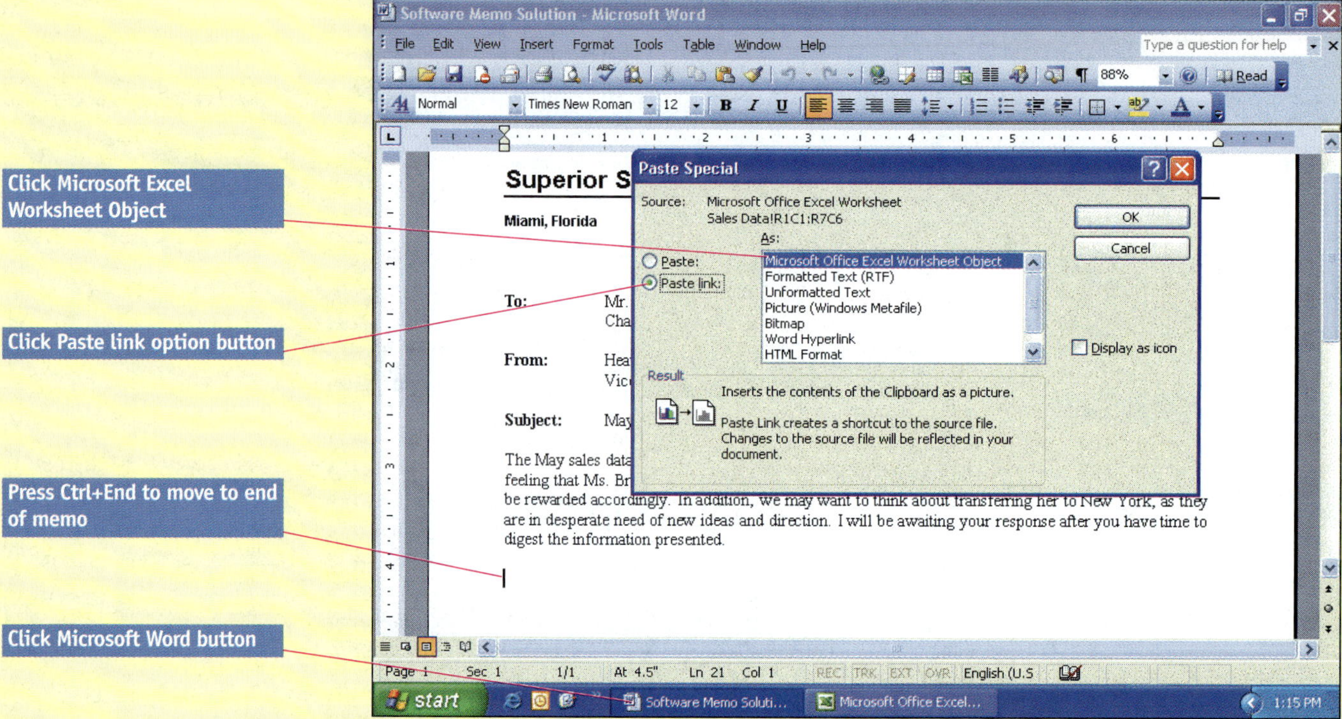

(c) Create the Link (step 3)

FIGURE 3.12 Hands-on Exercise 3 (*continued*)

THE COMMON USER INTERFACE

The common user interface provides a sense of familiarity from one Office application to the next. The applications share a common menu structure with consistent ways to execute commands from those menus. The Standard and Formatting toolbars are present in both applications. Many keyboard shortcuts are also common, such as Ctrl+Home and Ctrl+End to move to the beginning and end of a document, respectively.

Step 4: Copy the Chart

- Click the **Microsoft Excel button** on the taskbar to return to the worksheet.
- Click outside the selected area (cells A1 through F7) to deselect the cells. Press **Esc** to remove the moving border.
- Click the **Revenue by City tab** to select the chart sheet. Point to the chart area, then click the left mouse button to select the chart.
- Be sure you have selected the entire chart and that you see the same sizing handles as in Figure 3.12d.
- Pull down the **Edit menu** and click the **Copy command** (or click the **Copy button** on the Standard toolbar).
- A moving border appears around the entire chart, indicating that the chart has been copied to the clipboard. You can now link the chart to the Word document.

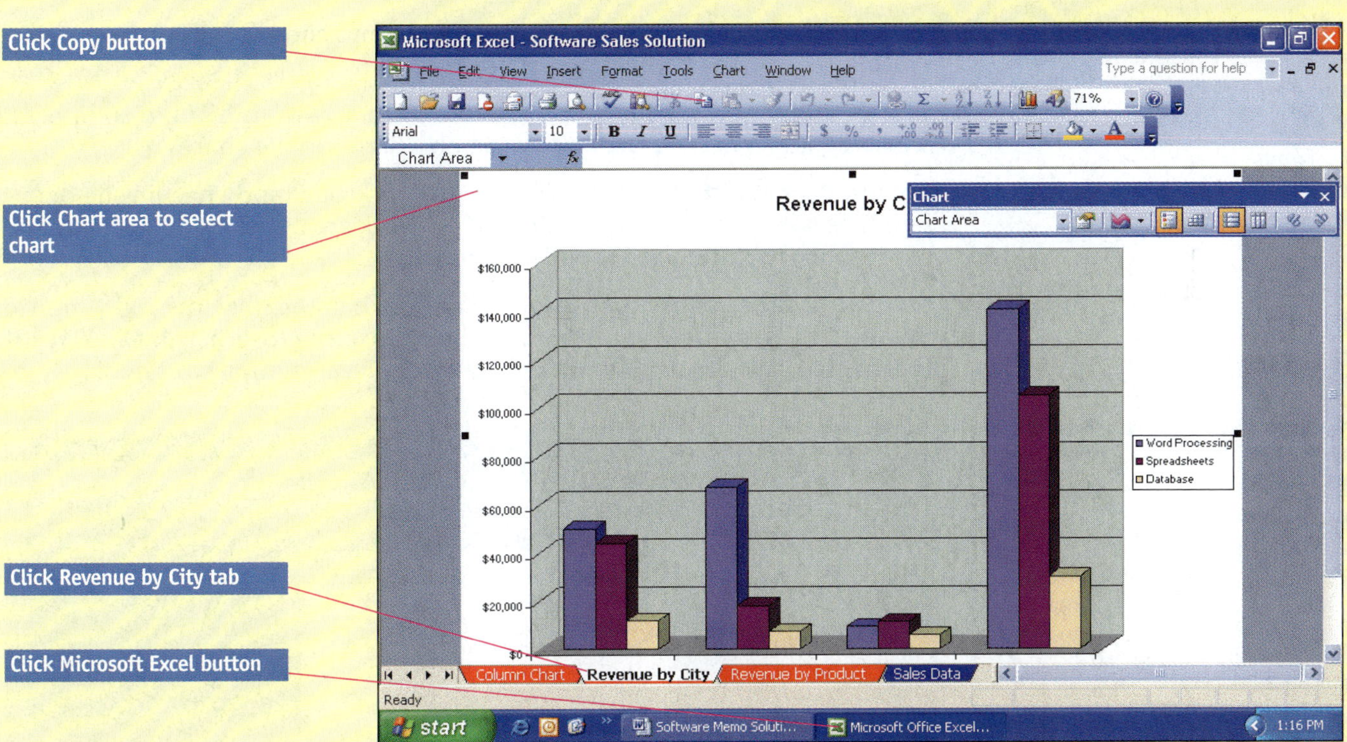

(d) Copy the Chart (step 4)

FIGURE 3.12 Hands-on Exercise 3 (*continued*)

ALT+TAB STILL WORKS

Alt+Tab was a treasured shortcut in the first version of Windows that enabled users to switch back and forth between open applications. The shortcut also works in all subsequent versions of Windows. Press and hold the Alt key while you press and release the Tab key repeatedly to cycle through the open applications, whose icons are displayed in a small rectangular window in the middle of the screen. Release the Alt key when you have selected the icon for the application you want.

Step 5: Add the Chart

- Click the **Microsoft Word button** on the taskbar to return to the memo. Double click below the worksheet to set the insertion point.
- Pull down the **Edit menu**. Click **Paste Special**. Click the **Paste link option button**. If necessary, click **Microsoft Excel Chart Object**. Click **OK** to insert the chart into the document.
- Right click the chart to display a context-sensitive menu, click **Format Object**, click the **Layout tab**, and choose **Square** in the Wrapping Style area. Click **OK**.
- Zoom to **Whole Page** to facilitate moving and sizing the chart. You need to reduce its size so that it fits on the same page as the memo. Thus scroll to the chart and click the chart to select it. This displays the sizing handles as shown in Figure 3.12e.
- Click and drag a corner sizing handle inward to make the chart smaller. Move the chart to the first page and center it on the page below the spreadsheet.
- Select the chart. Pull down the **Format menu**, and click the **Object command** to display the Format Object dialog box.
- Click the **Colors and Lines tab**. Click the **down arrow** in the Line color area, choose a color, and click **OK** to place a border around the chart.
- Zoom to **Page Width**. Look carefully at the worksheet and chart in the document. The sales for Word Processing in New York are currently $9,500, and the chart reflects this amount. Save the memo.
- Point to the **Microsoft Excel button** on the taskbar and click the **right mouse button** to display a shortcut menu. Click **Close** to close Excel. Click **Yes** if prompted to save the changes to the Software Sales Solution workbook.

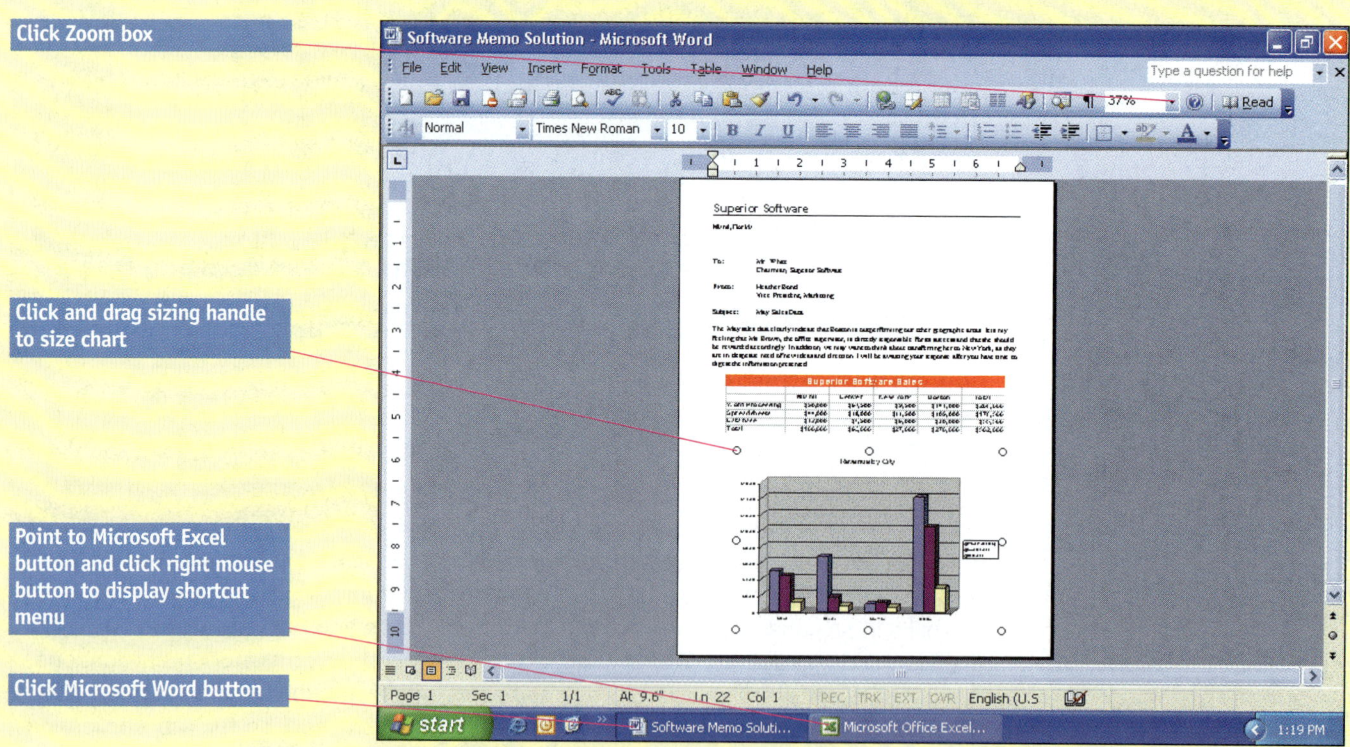

(e) Add the Chart (step 5)

FIGURE 3.12 Hands-on Exercise 3 (*continued*)

Step 6: Modify the Worksheet

- Click anywhere in the worksheet to select the worksheet and display the sizing handles as shown in Figure 3.12f.
- The status bar indicates that you can double click to edit the worksheet. Thus, double click anywhere within the worksheet to start Excel, the application that created the chart originally, in order to change the data.
- The system pauses as it loads Excel and reopens the Software Sales Solution workbook. If necessary, click the **Maximize button** to maximize the Excel window. Hide the Office Assistant if it appears.
- If necessary, click the **Sales Data tab** within the workbook. Click in **cell D4**. Type **$200,000**. Press **Enter**.
- Click the **|◀ button** to scroll to the first tab. Click the **Revenue by City tab** to select the chart sheet. The chart has been modified automatically and reflects the increased sales for New York.
- Save the workbook.

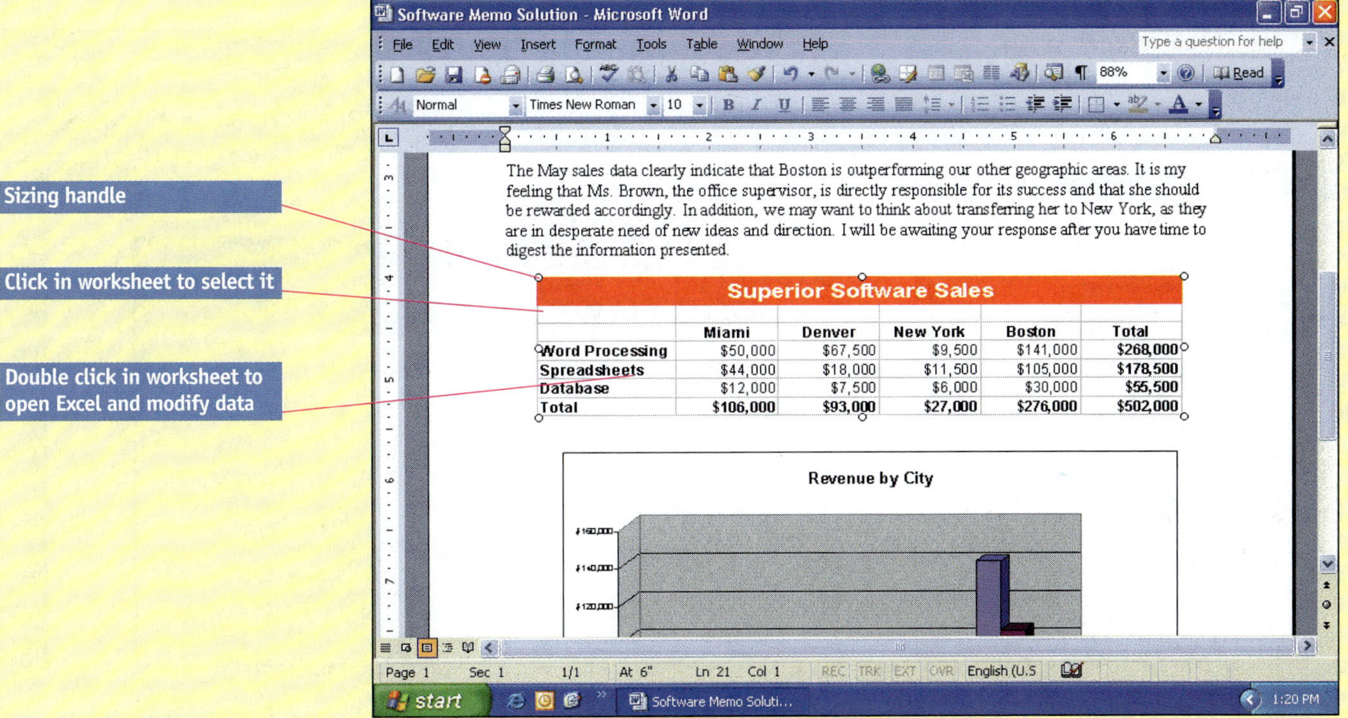

	Miami	Denver	New York	Boston	Total
Word Processing	$50,000	$67,500	$9,500	$141,000	$268,000
Spreadsheets	$44,000	$18,000	$11,500	$105,000	$178,500
Database	$12,000	$7,500	$6,000	$30,000	$55,500
Total	$106,000	$93,000	$27,000	$276,000	$502,000

(f) Modify the Worksheet (step 6)

FIGURE 3.12 Hands-on Exercise 3 (*continued*)

LINKING VERSUS EMBEDDING

A linked object maintains its connection to the source file. An embedded object does not. Thus, a linked object can be placed in any number of destination files, each of which maintains a pointer (link) to the same source file. Any change to the object in the source file is reflected automatically in every destination file containing that object.

Step 7: Update the Links

- Click the **Microsoft Word button** on the taskbar to return to the Software Memo. The worksheet and chart should be updated automatically. If not:
  - Pull down the **Edit menu**. Click **Links** to display the Links dialog box in Figure 3.12g.
  - Select the link(s) to update. (You can press and hold the **Ctrl key** to select multiple links simultaneously.)
  - Click the **Update Now button** to update the selected links.
  - Close the Links dialog box.
- The worksheet and chart should both reflect $200,000 for word processing sales in New York.
- Zoom to the **Whole Page** to view the completed document. Click and drag the worksheet and/or the chart within the memo to make any last-minute changes. Save the memo a final time.
- Print the completed memo and submit it to your instructor. Exit Word. Exit Excel. Save the changes to the Software Sales Solution workbook if you are prompted to do so.

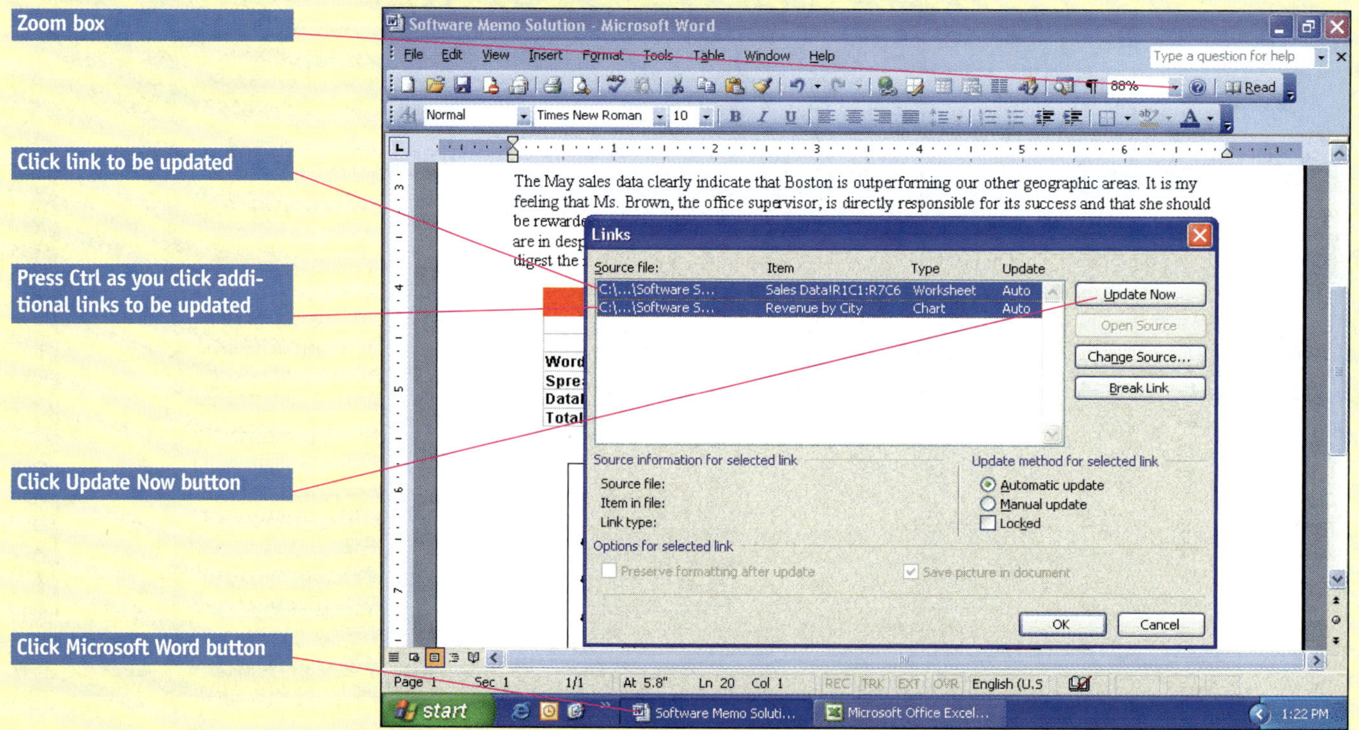

(g) Update the Links (step 7)

FIGURE 3.12 Hands-on Exercise 3 (*continued*)

LINKING WORKSHEETS

A Word document can be linked to an Excel chart and/or worksheet; that is, change the chart in Excel, and the Word document changes automatically. The chart itself is linked to the underlying worksheet; change the worksheet, and the chart changes. Worksheets can also be linked to one another; for example, a summary worksheet for the corporation as a whole can reflect data from detail worksheets for individual cities. See practice exercises 7 and 8 at the end of the chapter.

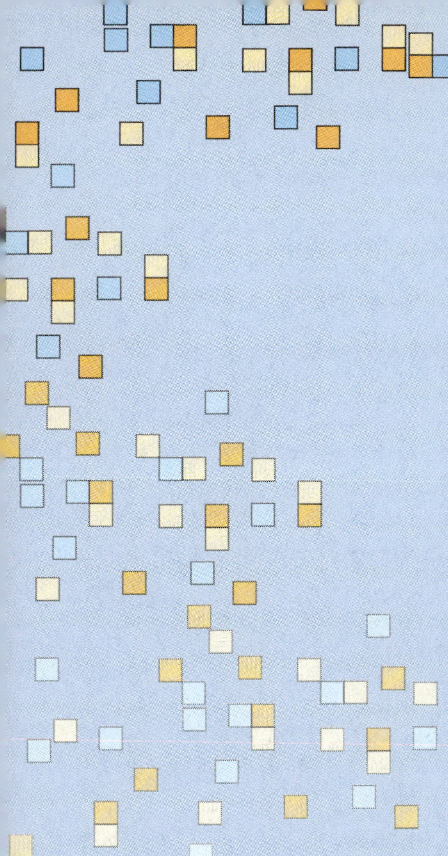

SUMMARY

A chart is a graphic representation of data in a worksheet. The type of chart chosen depends on the message to be conveyed. A pie chart is best for proportional relationships. A column or bar chart is used to show actual numbers rather than percentages. A line chart is preferable for time-related data. A combination chart uses two or more chart types when different scales are required for different data series.

The title of a chart can help to convey the message. A neutral title such as "Revenue by City" leaves the reader to draw his or her own conclusion. Using a different title such as "Boston Leads All Cities" or "New York is Trailing Badly" sends a very different message.

The Chart Wizard is an easy way to create a chart. Once created, a chart can be enhanced with arrows and text boxes found on the Drawing toolbar. These objects can be moved or sized and/or modified with respect to their color and other properties. The chart itself can also be modified using various commands from the Chart menu or tools on the Chart toolbar. A toolbar may be docked along the edge of a window or it may be floating within the window. All toolbars are displayed or hidden using the Toolbar command in the View menu.

A chart may be embedded in a worksheet or created in a separate chart sheet. An embedded chart may be moved within a worksheet by selecting it and dragging it to its new location. An embedded chart may be sized by selecting it and dragging any of the sizing handles in the desired direction.

Multiple data series may be specified in either rows or columns. If the data is in rows, the first row is assumed to contain the category labels, and the first column is assumed to contain the legend. Conversely, if the data is in columns, the first column is assumed to contain the category labels, and the first row the legend. The Chart Wizard makes it easy to switch from rows to columns and vice versa.

The choice between a side-by-side and a stacked column chart depends on the intended message. A side-by-side chart shows the contribution of each data point, but the total for each series is not as clear as with a stacked column chart. The stacked column chart, on the other hand, shows the totals clearly, but the contribution of the individual data points is obscured since the segments do not start at zero. It is important that charts are created accurately and that they do not mislead the reader. Stacked column charts should not add dissimilar quantities such as units and dollars.

Object Linking and Embedding enables the creation of a compound document containing data (objects) from multiple applications. The essential difference between linking and embedding is whether the object is stored within the compound document (embedding) or in its own file (linking). An embedded object is stored in the compound document, which in turn becomes the only user (client) of that object. A linked object is stored in its own file, and the compound document is one of many potential clients of that object. The same chart can be linked to a Word document and a PowerPoint presentation.

KEY TERMS

MULTIPLE CHOICE

1. Which type of chart is best to portray proportion or market share?
   (a) Pie chart
   (b) Line
   (c) Column chart
   (d) Combination chart

2. Which of the following is a true statement about the Chart Wizard?
   (a) It is accessed via a button on the Standard toolbar
   (b) It enables you to choose the type of chart you want as well as specify the location for that chart
   (c) It enables you to retrace your steps via the Back command button
   (d) All of the above

3. Which of the following chart types is *not* suitable to display multiple data series?
   (a) Pie chart
   (b) Horizontal bar chart
   (c) Column chart
   (d) All of the above are equally suitable

4. Which of the following is best to display additive information from multiple data series?
   (a) A column chart with the data series stacked one on top of another
   (b) A column chart with the data series side by side
   (c) Both (a) and (b) are equally appropriate
   (d) Neither (a) nor (b) is appropriate

5. A workbook must contain:
   (a) A separate chart sheet for every worksheet
   (b) A separate worksheet for every chart sheet
   (c) Both (a) and (b)
   (d) Neither (a) nor (b)

6. Which of the following is true regarding an embedded chart?
   (a) It can be moved elsewhere within the worksheet
   (b) It can be made larger or smaller
   (c) Both (a) and (b)
   (d) Neither (a) nor (b)

7. Which of the following will produce a shortcut menu?
   (a) Pointing to a workbook tab and clicking the right mouse button
   (b) Pointing to an embedded chart and clicking the right mouse button
   (c) Pointing to a selected cell range and clicking the right mouse button
   (d) All of the above

8. Which of the following is done *prior* to invoking the Chart Wizard?
   (a) The data series are selected
   (b) The location of the embedded chart within the worksheet is specified
   (c) Both (a) and (b)
   (d) Neither (a) nor (b)

9. Which of the following will display sizing handles when selected?
   (a) An embedded chart
   (b) The title of a chart
   (c) A text box or arrow
   (d) All of the above

10. How do you switch between open applications?
    (a) Click the appropriate button on the taskbar
    (b) Use Alt+Tab to cycle through the applications
    (c) Both (a) and (b)
    (d) Neither (a) nor (b)

... continued

multiple choice

11. A Word document is linked to an Excel worksheet and associated chart. Which of the following best describes the way the documents are stored on disk?

(a) A single file contains the Word document, the worksheet, and the associated chart
(b) There are two files—one for the Word document and one for the Excel workbook, which contains both the worksheet and associated chart
(c) There are three files—one for the Word document, one for the Excel worksheet, and one for the Excel chart
(d) None of the above

12. To represent multiple data series on the same chart:

(a) The data series must be in rows and the rows must be adjacent to one another on the worksheet
(b) The data series must be in columns and the columns must be adjacent to one another on the worksheet
(c) The data series may be in rows or columns so long as they are adjacent to one another
(d) The data series may be in rows or columns with no requirement to be next to one another

13. If multiple data series are selected and rows are specified:

(a) The first row will be used for the category labels
(b) The first column will be used for the legend
(c) Both (a) and (b)
(d) Neither (a) nor (b)

14. If multiple data series are selected and columns are specified:

(a) The first column will be used for the category (*X* axis) labels
(b) The first row will be used for the legend
(c) Both (a) and (b)
(d) Neither (a) nor (b)

15. Which of the following is true about the scale on the *Y* axis in a column chart that plots multiple data series side-by-side versus one that stacks the values one on top of another?

(a) The scale for the stacked columns chart contains larger values than the side-by-side chart
(b) The scale for the side-by-side columns contains larger values than the stacked columns
(c) The values on the scale will be the same for both charts
(d) The values will be different but it is not possible to tell which chart has higher values

16. A workbook includes a revenue worksheet with two embedded charts. The workbook also includes one chart in its own worksheet. How many files does it take to store this workbook?

(a) 1
(b) 2
(c) 3
(d) 4

17. Assume that cells A1 through E5 have been selected, after which the Chart Wizard is used to create a side-by-side column chart. Which of the following is true, given that the data are plotted in rows?

(a) The category names are in cells B1 through E1
(b) The legends are in cells A2 through A5
(c) Both (a) and (b)
(d) Neither (a) nor (b)

18. Which of the following creates a dynamic link between a workbook and a word processing memo?

(a) Copy, Paste Special, and Paste Link
(b) Copy and Paste
(c) Cut, Paste Special, and Paste Link
(d) Cut and Paste

ANSWERS

1. a	**7.** d	**13.** c
2. d	**8.** a	**14.** c
3. a	**9.** d	**15.** a
4. a	**10.** c	**16.** a
5. d	**11.** b	**17.** c
6. c	**12.** d	**18.** a

PRACTICE WITH EXCEL

1. **Theme Park Admissions:** A partially completed version of the worksheet in Figure 3.13 is available in the Exploring Excel folder as *Chapter 3 Practice 1*. Follow the directions in parts (a) and (b) to compute the totals and format the worksheet, then create each of the charts listed below.
   a. Use the AutoSum command to enter the formulas to compute the total number of admissions for each region and each quarter.
   b. Select the entire worksheet (cells A1 through F8), then use the AutoFormat command to format the worksheet. You do not have to accept the entire design, nor do you have to use the design we selected. You can also modify the design after it has been applied to the worksheet by changing the font size of selected cells and/or changing boldface and italics.
   c. Create a column chart showing the total number of admissions in each quarter as shown in Figure 3.13. Add the graphic shown in the figure for emphasis.
   d. Create a pie chart that shows the percentage of the total number of admissions in each region. Create this chart in its own chart sheet with an appropriate name.
   e. Create a stacked column chart that shows the total number of admissions for each region and the contribution of each quarter within each region. Create this chart in its own chart sheet with an appropriate name.
   f. Create a stacked column chart showing the total number of admissions for each quarter and the contribution of each region within each quarter. Create this chart in its own chart sheet with an appropriate name.
   g. Change the color of each of the worksheet tabs.
   h. Print the entire workbook, consisting of the worksheet in Figure 3.13 plus the three additional sheets that you create. Use portrait orientation for the Sales Data worksheet and landscape orientation for the other worksheets. Create a custom header for each worksheet that includes your name, your course, and your instructor's name. Create a custom footer for each worksheet that includes the name of the worksheet. Submit the completed assignment to your instructor.

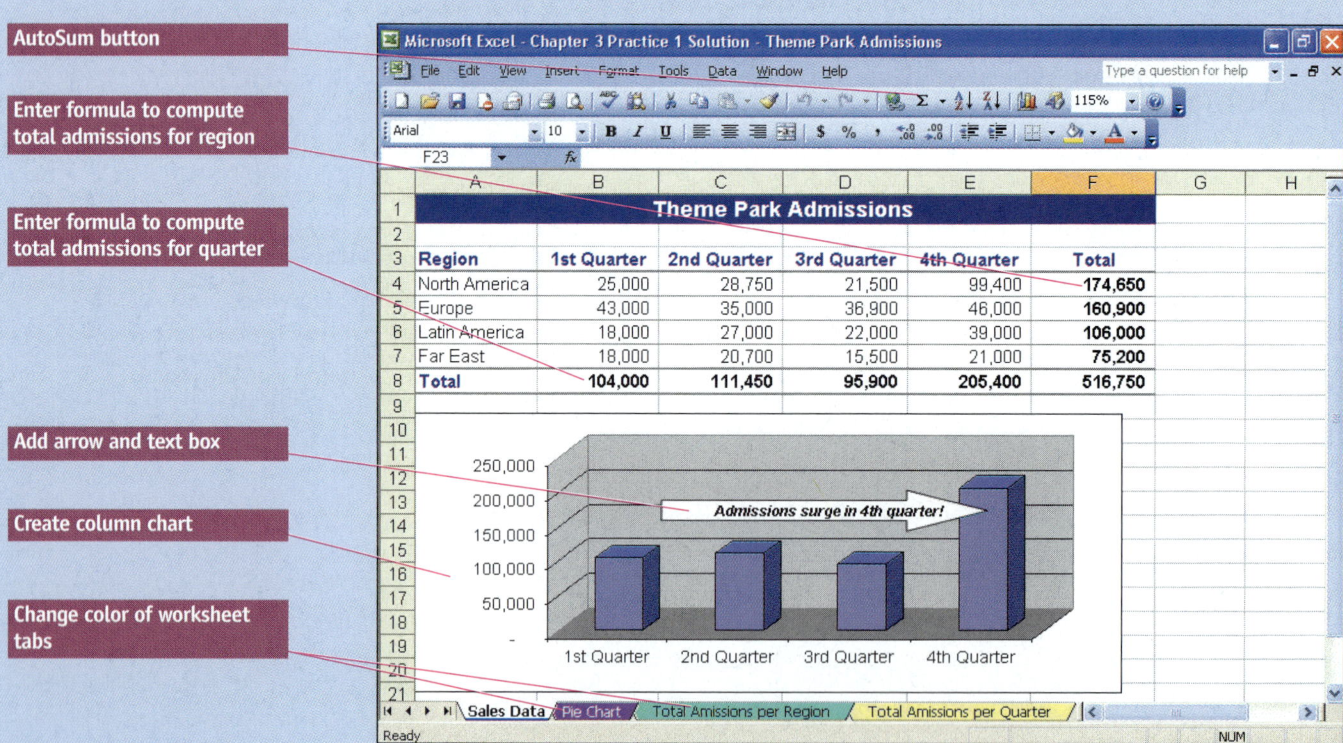

FIGURE 3.13 Theme Park Admissions (exercise 1)

2. **Rows versus Columns:** Figure 3.14 displays the Page Preview view of a worksheet with two similar charts, one that plots data by rows and the other by columns. The distinction depends on the message you want to deliver. Both charts are correct. Your assignment is to open the partially completed worksheet in the *Chapter 3 Practice 2* workbook and proceed as follows.
    a. Use the AutoSum command to compute the total number of visits for each pet category and for each quarter. Format the completed worksheet in an attractive manner. You do not have to duplicate our formatting exactly.
    b. Create each of the charts in Figure 3.14 as an embedded chart on the current worksheet. The first chart specifies that the data series are in columns. The second chart specifies the data series are in rows.
    c. Use the Page Setup command to change to landscape orientation when the chart is printed. Create a custom header that includes your name, your course, and your instructor's name. Create a custom footer with the name of the worksheet, today's date, and the current time. Specify that the worksheet will be printed at 110% to create a more attractive printed page. Be sure, however, that the worksheet and associated charts fit on a single page.
    d. Right click the Worksheet tab, click the Move or Copy command, then check the box to copy the worksheet. Double click the Worksheet tab and change the name of the duplicate worksheet to Stacked Columns.
    e. Select the first chart in the newly created Stacked Columns worksheet. Change the chart type to Stacked Columns. Check the box to use the default formatting for the chart. Change the chart type of the second chart to stacked columns as well.
    f. Print the completed workbook (both worksheets) for your instructor. Add a short note that summarizes the difference between plotting data in rows versus columns, and between side-by-side column charts and stacked column charts.

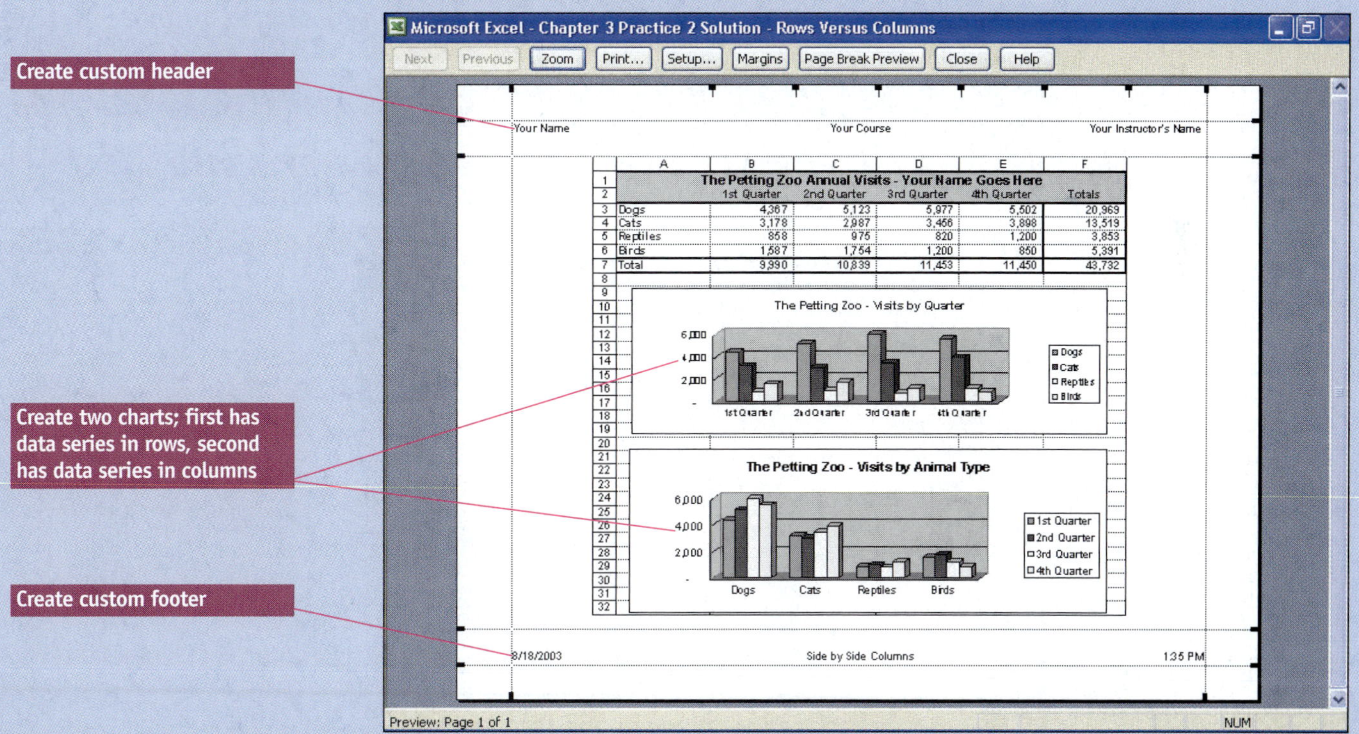

The Petting Zoo Annual Visits - Your Name Goes Here	1st Quarter	2nd Quarter	3rd Quarter	4th Quarter	Totals
Dogs	4,367	5,123	5,977	5,502	20,969
Cats	3,178	2,987	3,456	3,898	13,519
Reptiles	858	975	820	1,200	3,853
Birds	1,587	1,754	1,200	850	5,391
Total	9,990	10,839	11,453	11,450	43,732

FIGURE 3.14 Rows versus Columns (exercise 2)

3. **Flexibility in Charting:** The worksheet in Figure 3.15 displays the second quarter revenues for each salesperson in TalkAway, Inc., a local cellular company. Open the partially completed workbook in *Chapter 3 Practice 3* to complete the worksheet, then create the chart in Figure 3.15. The intent of this exercise is to show you several formatting options that are available in conjunction with charts. It's fun to experiment, but set a reasonable time limit.
   a. Use the AutoSum command to enter the formulas to compute the total sales for each month and for each salesperson.
   b. Format the worksheet in attractive fashion. You do not have to duplicate our formatting exactly, but you are to highlight the data in row four. In addition, use boldface to emphasize the totals for each salesperson and each month.
   c. Use the Chart wizard to create a column chart that displays the total sales for each salesperson for the second quarter.
   d. Right click any column (data series) within the chart to display a context-sensitive menu, then click the Format Data Series command. Click the Shape tab within the dialog box to change the shape of each column. Click the Data Labels tab to display the dollar value for each salesperson.
   e. Click the second column to select just this column. Click the right mouse button, click the Format Data Point command, click the Pattern tab in the associated dialog box, then change the color of this column.
   f. Click in Cell A4 and enter your name instead of Grauer. The value on the *X* axis changes automatically to reflect the entry in cell A4.
   g. Click the AutoShapes button on the Drawing toolbar to add a callout indicating that this column represents your sales data. Right click the border of the AutoShape, click the Format AutoShape command, click the Colors and Lines tab, and add a fill color.
   h. Right click the border of the chart, click the Format Chart Area command, then change the border to include rounded corners with a shadow effect.
   i. Print the completed worksheet for your instructor.

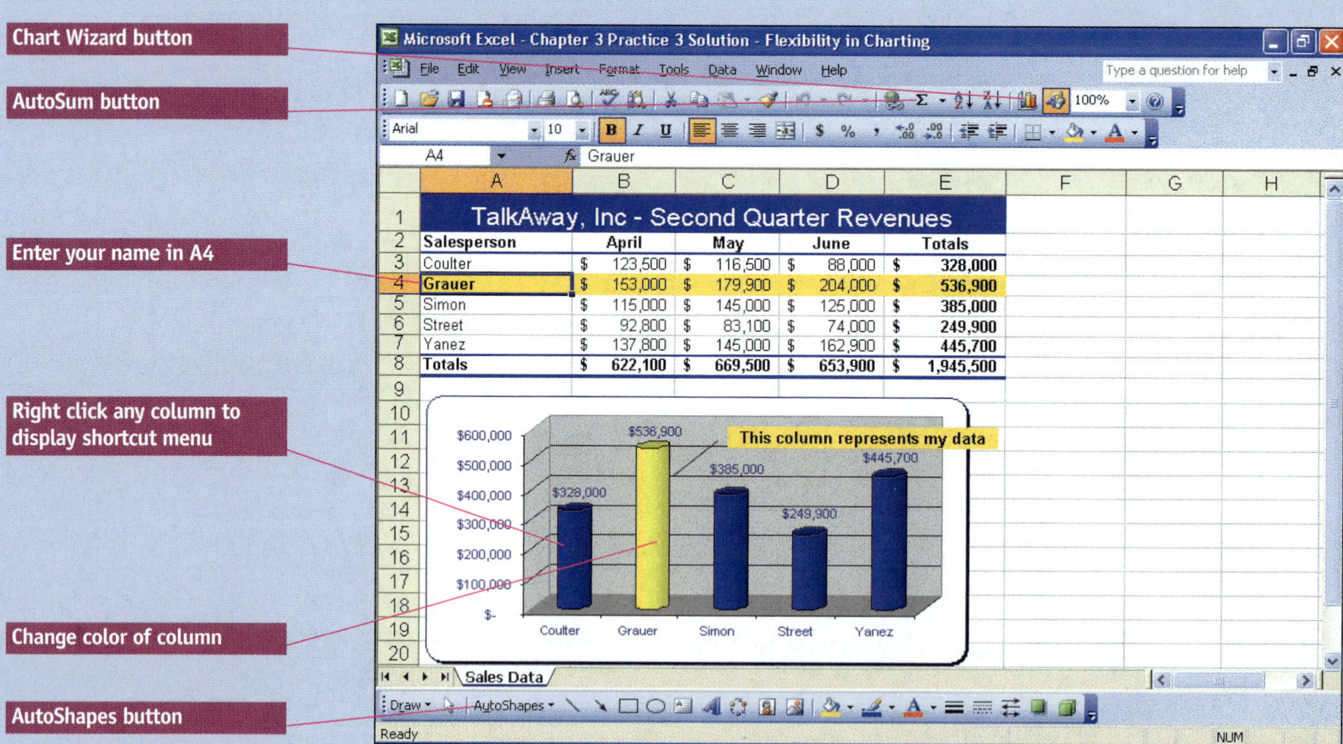

Salesperson	April	May	June	Totals
Coulter	$ 123,500	$ 116,500	$ 88,000	$ **328,000**
Grauer	$ 153,000	$ 179,900	$ 204,000	$ **536,900**
Simon	$ 115,000	$ 145,000	$ 125,000	$ **385,000**
Street	$ 92,800	$ 83,100	$ 74,000	$ **249,900**
Yanez	$ 137,800	$ 145,000	$ 162,900	$ **445,700**
Totals	$ **622,100**	$ **669,500**	$ **653,900**	$ **1,945,500**

FIGURE 3.15 Flexibility in Charting (exercise 3)

4. **Page Break Preview:** Open the partially completed workbook in *Chapter 3 Practice 4* and create the four charts shown in Figure 3.16. Use the AutoSum and AutoFormat commands to complete the worksheet. Select cells A2 through E6 as the basis for each of the four charts in the figure. The charts should appear as embedded objects on the worksheet, but do not be concerned about the placement of each chart until you have completed all four charts.
   a. The first chart is a side-by-side column chart that emphasizes the sales in each city (the data is in rows).
   b. The second chart is a stacked column version of the chart in part (a).
   c. The third chart (that begins in column H of the worksheet) is a side-by-side column chart that emphasizes the sales in each product line (the data is in columns).
   d. The last chart is a stacked column version of the chart in part (c).
   e. Pull down the View command, then change to the Page Break Preview view as shown in Figure 3.16. You will see one or more dotted lines that show where the page breaks will occur. You will also see the message in Figure 3.16 indicating that you can change the location of the page breaks. Click OK after you have read the message.
   f. Remove any existing page breaks by clicking and dragging the solid blue line that indicates the break. (You can insert horizontal or vertical page breaks by clicking the appropriate cell, pulling down the Insert menu, and selecting Page Break.) Pull down the View menu and click Normal view to return to the normal view.
   g. Add your name to the completed worksheet, then print the worksheet and four embedded charts on one page. If necessary, change to landscape printing for a more attractive layout. Use the Page Setup command to create a custom header with your name, your course, and your instructor's name. Create a custom footer that contains today's date, the name of the workbook, and the current time.
   h. Write a short note to your instructor that describes the differences between the charts. Suggest a different title for one or more charts that helps to convey a specific message.

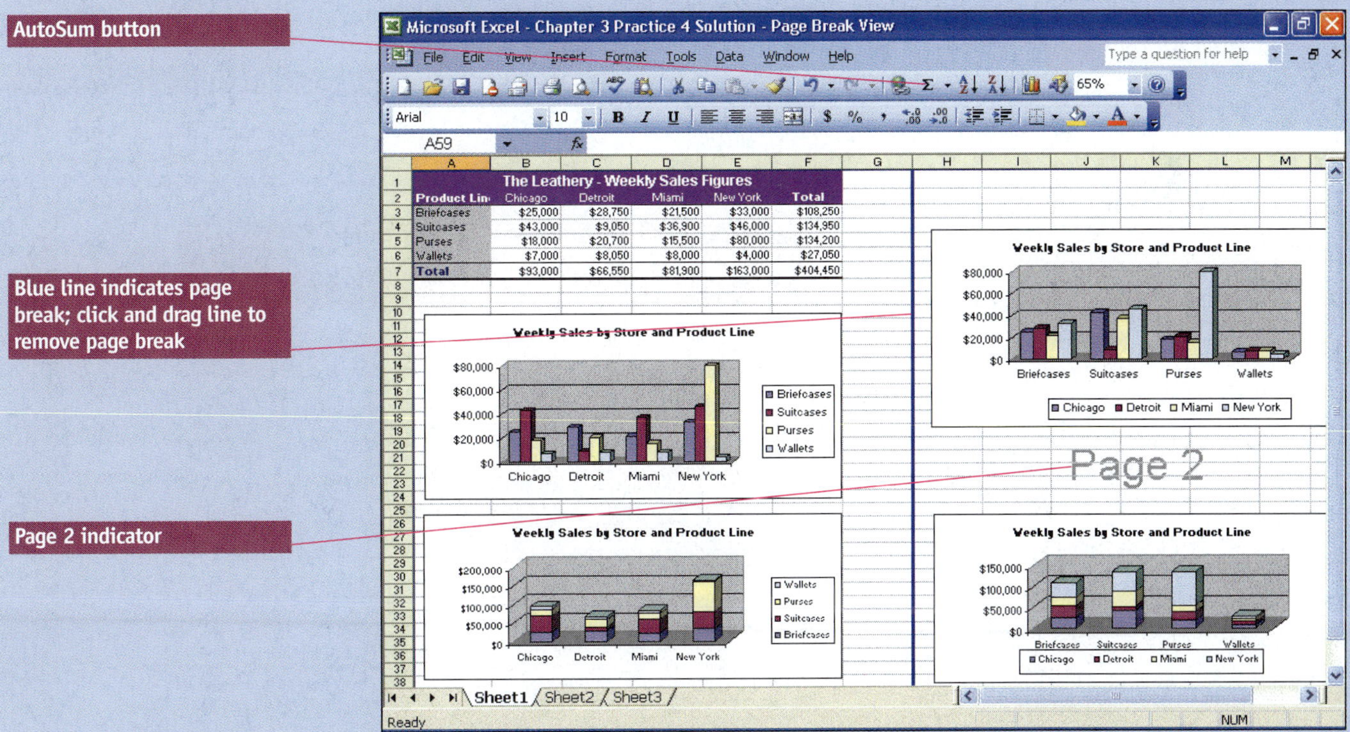

FIGURE 3.16 Page Break Preview (exercise 4)

5. **Your Next Car:** The Word document in Figure 3.17 displays descriptive information about a car you are interested in, a picture of the car, and a hyperlink to the Web site where the information was obtained. In addition, the document is linked to an Excel workbook that computes the car payment for you, based on the loan parameters that you provide. Your assignment is to create a similar document based on any car you choose. Proceed as follows:
   a. Use your favorite search engine to locate a Web site that contains information about the car you are interested in. You can go to the Web site of the manufacturer and/or you can go to a general site such as carpoint.msn.com, which contains information about all makes and models. Select the car you want and obtain the retail price of the car.
   b. Open the *Chapter 3 Practice 5* workbook in the Exploring Excel folder. Enter the price of the car, a hypothetical down payment, the interest rate of the car loan, and the term of the loan in the indicated cells. The monthly payment will be determined automatically by the PMT function that is stored in the workbook. (The PMT function is covered in detail in Chapter 4.) Save the workbook.
   c. Click and drag to select cells A3 through B9 (the cells that contain the information you want to insert into the Word document). Click the Copy button.
   d. Open the partially completed Word document, *Chapter 3 Practice 5,* that is stored in the Exploring Excel folder. Pull down the Edit menu, click the Paste Special command, and then choose the option to link the worksheet data to the Word document. Move and size the inserted worksheet to its approximate position in the document. Save the Word document.
   e. Use the taskbar to return to the Excel workbook. Change the amount of the down payment and/or the interest rate for your loan. Save the workbook. Close Excel. Return to the Word document, which should reflect the updated loan information.
   f. Return to the Web page that contains the information about your car. Right click the picture of the car that appears within the Web page, and click the Save As command to save the picture of the car to your computer. Use the Insert Picture command to insert the picture that you just obtained.
   g. Complete the Word document by inserting some descriptive information about your car. Print the completed document for your instructor.

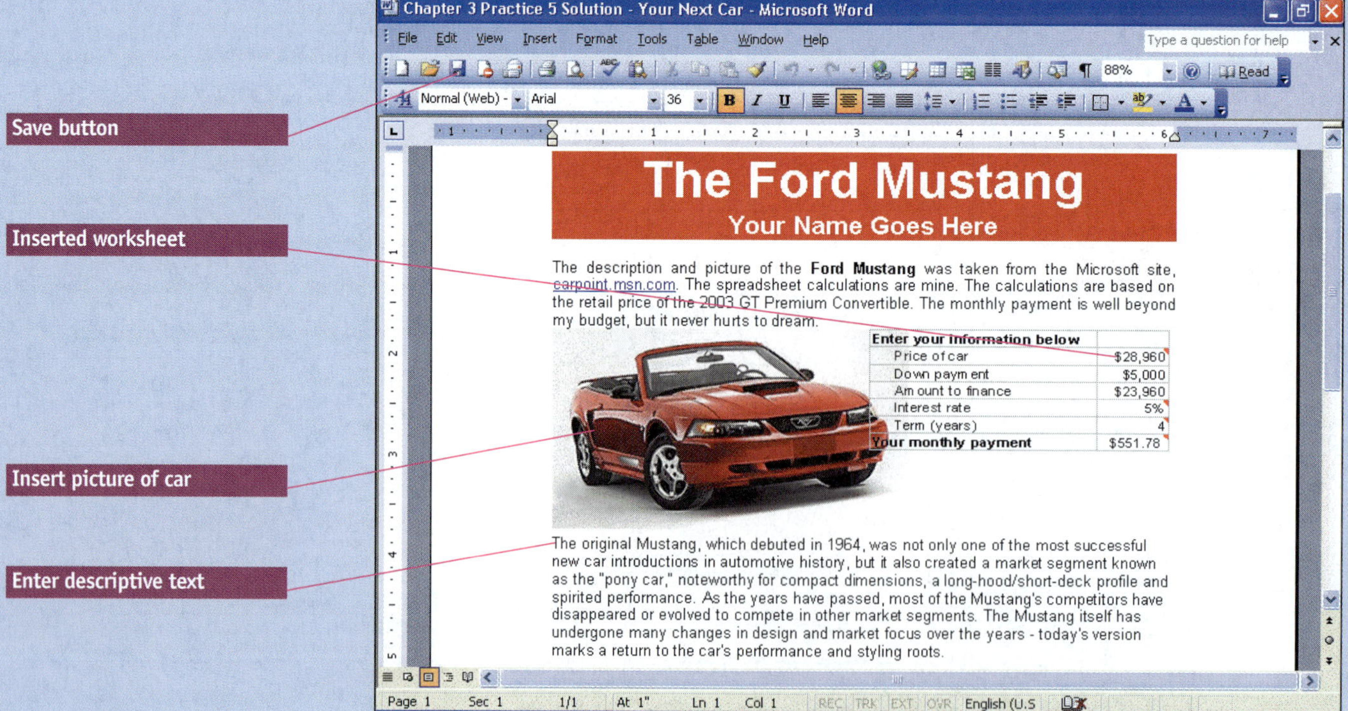

FIGURE 3.17 Your Next Car (exercise 5)

6. **Irrational Exuberance:** Figure 3.18 contains a combination chart to display different kinds of information on different scales for multiple data series. A column chart is specified for the revenue and profits, while a line chart is used for the stock price. Two different scales are necessary because the magnitudes of the numbers differ significantly.
   a. Open the partially completed workbook in *Chapter 3 Practice 6* and format the worksheet appropriately.
   b. Select the entire worksheet (cells A1 through F4), then invoke the Chart Wizard. Click the Custom Types tab in step 1 of the Chart Wizard, choose Line-Column on 2 Axes as the chart type, then in step 2 specify the data in rows. The Chart Wizard will do the rest.
   c. Modify the completed chart so that its appearance is similar to our figure. We made the chart wider and moved the legend to the bottom. (Right click the legend, click the Format Legend command, click the Placement tab, then click the Bottom option button.)
   d. Customize the border around the chart. Right click the completed chart, choose the Format Chart Area command, click the Patterns tab, then choose the style, thickness, and color of the border.
   e. Insert your name somewhere in the worksheet, then print the completed worksheet for your instructor. Use the Page Setup command to change to landscape orientation. Center the worksheet and chart horizontally on the page.
   f. Create a custom header for the worksheet that includes your name, your course, and your instructor's name. Create a custom footer that contains the name of the file in which the worksheet is contained, today's date, and the current time.
   g. What do you think should be the more important factor influencing a company's stock price, its revenue (sales) or its profit (net income)? Could the situation depicted in the worksheet occur in the real world? Summarize your thoughts in a brief note to your instructor.

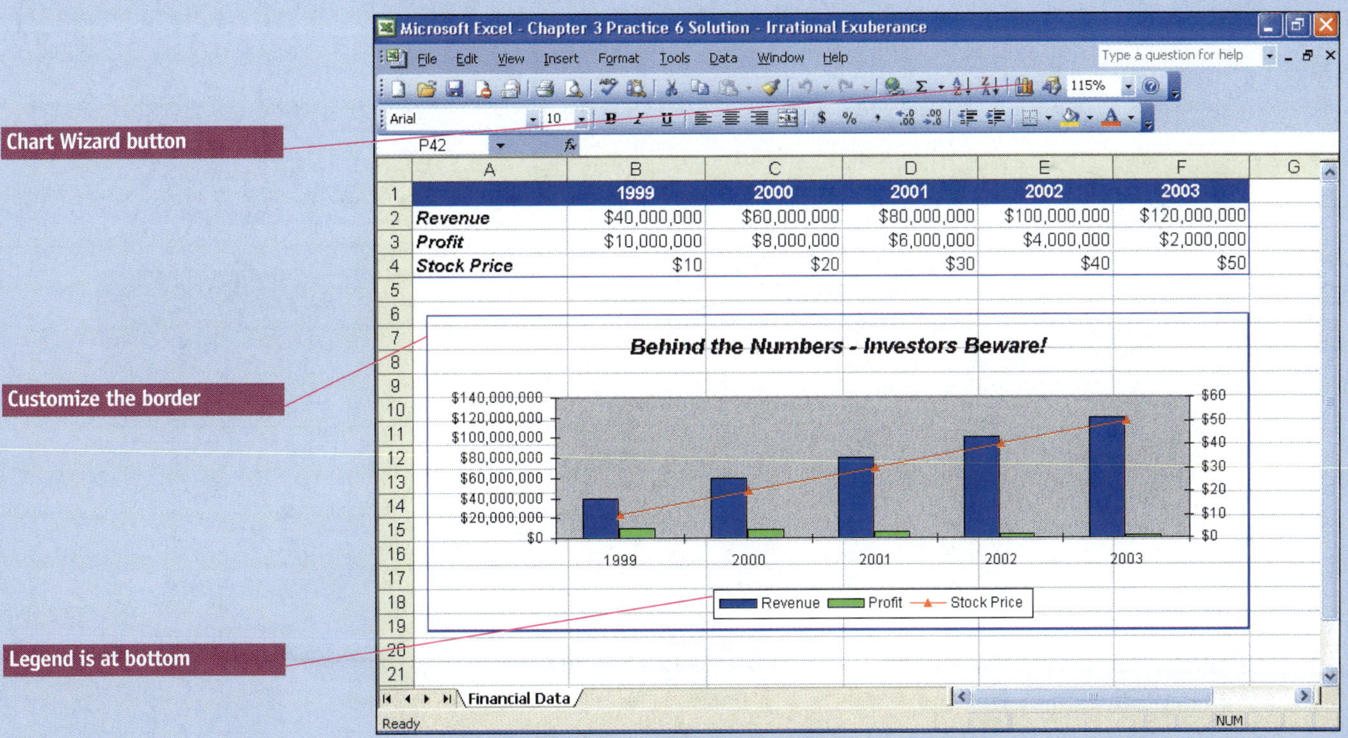

FIGURE 3.18 Irrational Exuberance (exercise 6)

7. **Worksheet References:** The worksheet in Figure 3.19 appears similar to the example that was used throughout the chapter. Look closely, however, and you will see that the workbook contains individual worksheets for each city, in addition to a worksheet for the corporation as a whole. The formulas in the corporate worksheet reference cells in the worksheets of the individual cities. For example, the entry in cell B3 of the Corporate worksheet contains the formula =Phoenix!F2 to indicate that the entry comes from cell F2 in the Phoenix worksheet. Other cells in the table reference other cells in the Phoenix worksheet as well as cells in the other worksheets.
   a. Open the *Chapter 3 Practice 7* workbook in the Exploring Excel folder. Select the Corporate worksheet by clicking the Worksheet tab. (The color of the tab for this worksheet is different from the tabs for the individual cities.) You can enter the formulas in this worksheet explicitly, but it is easier to use pointing, especially when referencing cells in other worksheets.
   b. Click (select) cell B3 in the Corporate worksheet. Type an = sign, click the Phoenix worksheet tab, click in cell F2 of this worksheet, and press the Enter key. Click in cell C3, type an = sign, click the Minneapolis tab, click in cell F2 of that worksheet, and press Enter. Repeat the process to enter the sales for San Francisco and Los Angeles.
   c. Select cells B3 through E3, then drag the fill handle to row 5 to copy the formulas for the other product lines. The copy operation works because the worksheet references are absolute, but the cell references are relative.
   d. Use the AutoSum button to compute the totals for the corporation as a whole in column F.
   e. Use the AutoFormat command to format the worksheet in an attractive fashion. (You do not have to duplicate our formatting exactly.)
   f. Use the completed worksheet as the basis for a stacked column chart with the data plotted in rows.
   g. Use the Page Setup command to display gridlines and row and column headings for each worksheet. Create a custom footer that contains your name, the name of the worksheet, and today's date. Print the entire workbook and submit the completed assignment to your instructor.

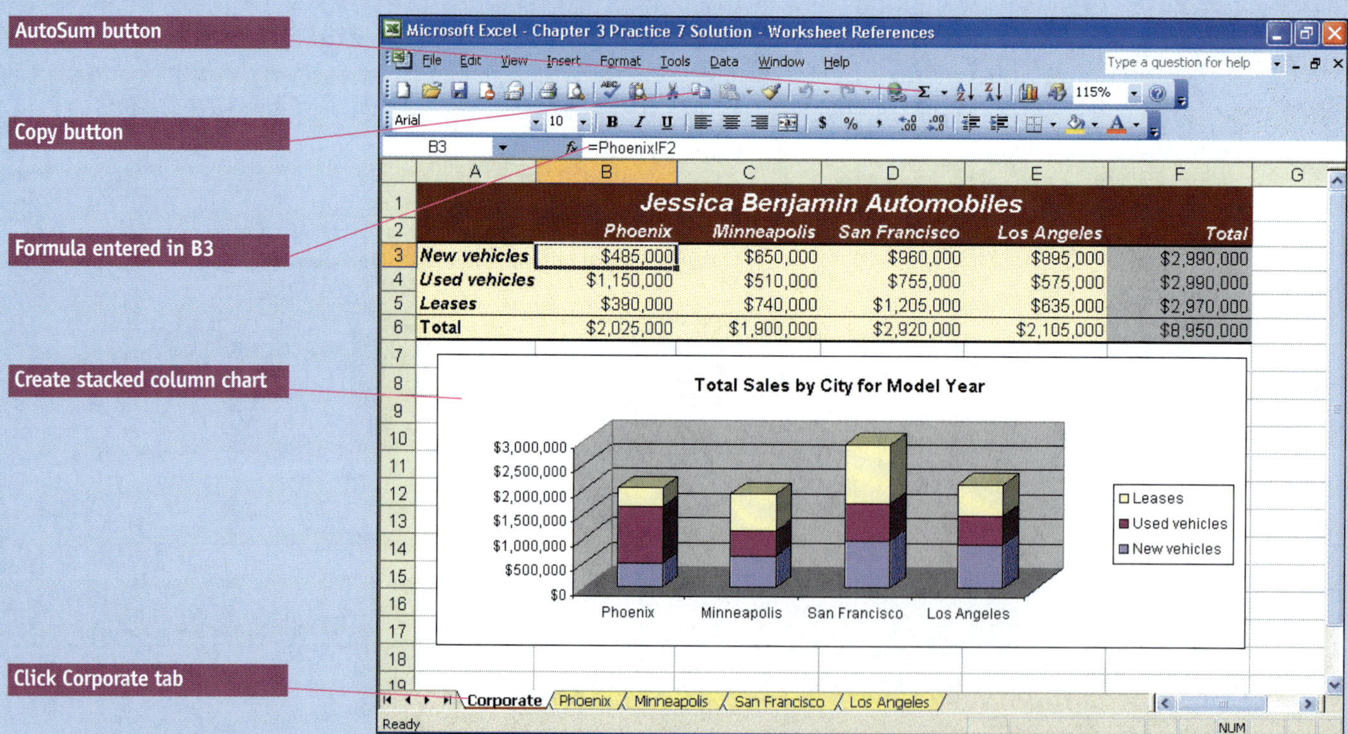

FIGURE 3.19 Worksheet References (exercise 7)

8. **Additional Practice:** The worksheet in Figure 3.20 contains a year-to-year comparison of sales data in both graphical and tabular form. Open the partially completed workbook in *Chapter 3 Practice 8* and proceed as follows:
   a. Select the Year to Year Comparison worksheet. Click in cell B3 of this worksheet, type an equal sign, click the worksheet tab labeled Previous Year, click in cell B8 of this worksheet, and press Enter. The formula for cell B3 should appear in the formula bar as ='Previous Year'!B8, indicating that the value for this cell is obtained from another worksheet in the same workbook. Copy the formula in cell B3 to cells C3 through E3.
   b. Click in cell C4 and use the same technique as in part (a) to obtain the sales for the first quarter for the current year. Copy this formula to cells C4 through E4.
   c. Use the AutoSum command to compute the total sales for the previous year (cell F3 in this worksheet). Compute the total sales for the current year in cell F4.
   d. Enter the formulas to compute the dollar increase for the first quarter in cell B5. Copy the formula in cell B5 to cells D5 through F5.
   e. Format the worksheet as shown in Figure 3.20. Try to duplicate our formatting. Use the Chart Wizard to create a side-by-side column chart that compares the sales in the current year to those in the previous year for each quarter. Display a legend at the bottom of the chart.
   f. Right click each data series individually within the chart, select the Format Data Series command, and then change the colors of the current and previous years to green and white, respectively.
   g. Use the AutoShapes button on the Drawing toolbar to create the arrow in the figure. Enter the indicated text as shown.
   h. Add your name to the title of the worksheet in cell A1. Print the completed worksheet for your instructor. Be sure to show gridlines and row and column headings.

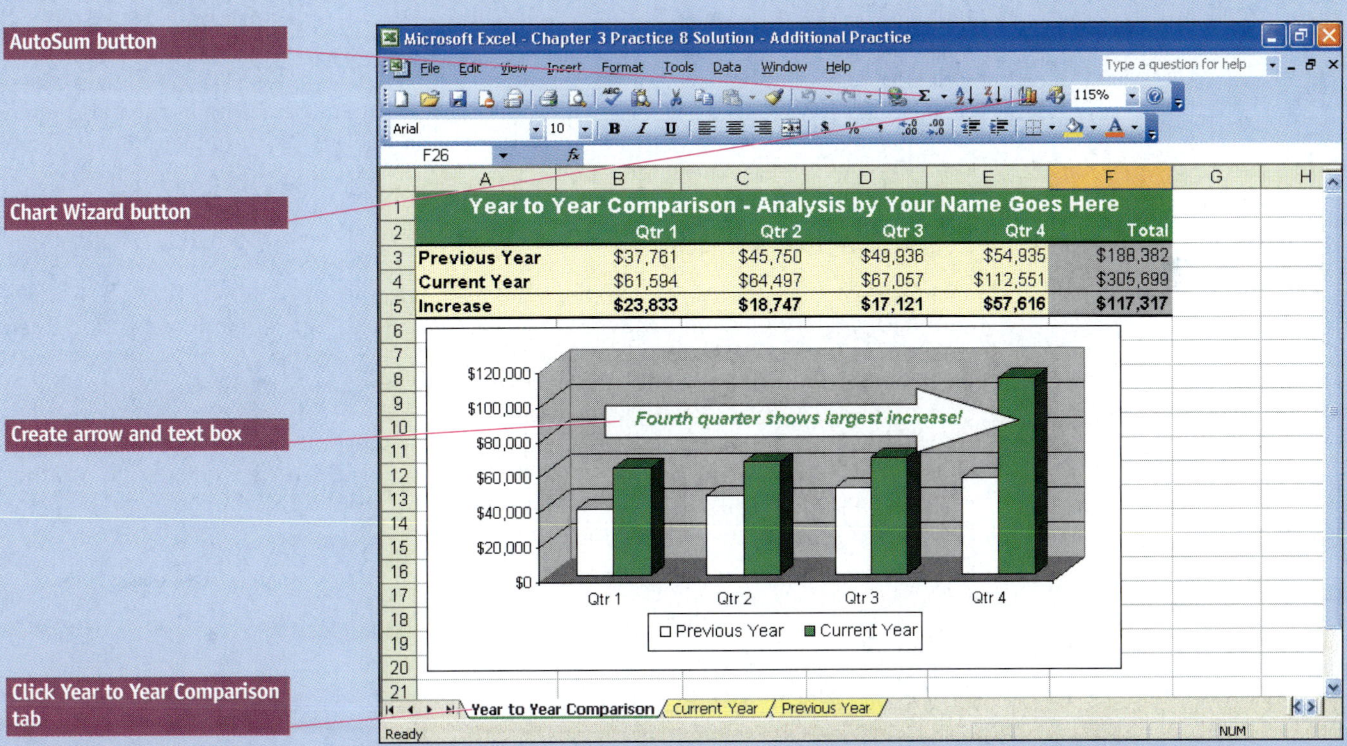

FIGURE 3.20 Additional Practice (exercise 8)

MINI CASES

The Convention Planner

Your first task as a convention planner is to evaluate the hotel capacity for the host city in order to make recommendations as to which hotels should host the convention. The data can be found in the *Chapter 3 Mini Case—Convention Planner* workbook, which contains a single worksheet showing the number of rooms in each hotel, divided into standard and deluxe categories, together with the associated room rates. Complete the worksheet by computing the total number of rooms in each category. Format the worksheet in an attractive way. Create a stacked column chart that shows the total capacity for each hotel. Create a second chart that shows the percentage of total capacity for each hotel. Store each chart in its own worksheet, and then print the entire workbook for your instructor.

Designer Clothing

This assignment asks you to complete a worksheet and associated chart for a Designer Clothing boutique, and then link these Excel objects to an appropriate memo. Open the partially completed *Chapter 3 Mini Case—Designer Clothing* workbook; compute the sales totals for each individual salesperson as well as the totals for each quarter, then format the resulting worksheet in an attractive fashion. Include your name in the title of the worksheet (cell A1). We have started the memo for you and have saved the text in the *Chapter 3 Mini Case—Designer Clothing* Word document. Open the Word document, and then link the Excel worksheet to the Word document. Repeat the process to link the Excel chart to the Word document. Print the completed document for your instructor.

PowerPoint Presentations

The chapter described how to link an Excel chart and/or worksheet to a Word document, but you can use the same technique to link these objects to a PowerPoint presentation. Open the *Chapter 3 Mini Case—Theme Park Admissions* PowerPoint presentation that is found in the Exploring Excel folder. Now open your solution to the *Chapter 3 Practice 1—Theme Park Admissions* exercise, and link the worksheet and charts in the completed workbook to the appropriate slides in the presentation. Print the completed presentation (six slides per page) for your instructor.

Exploded Pie Charts

The *Chapter 3 Mini Case—Exploded Pie Chart* workbook contains a worksheet with summary data for the Tom Laquer Men's Wear Boutique. There are four stores and three categories of sales. Your assignment is to complete the worksheet to show the summary data, using the AutoSum and AutoFormat commands as appropriate. Once this is accomplished, you can create the two required charts. The first chart is an exploded pie chart that shows the percentage of total sales that is attributed to each city. The second chart is also a pie chart that shows the percentage of sales attributed to each product line. Replace "Tom Laquer" with your name, and then print the completed workbook for your instructor.

CHAPTER

4

Using Spreadsheets in Decision Making: What If?

OBJECTIVES

After reading this chapter you will:

1. Use the PMT function to calculate the payment of a car loan or mortgage.
2. Use the FV function to determine the future value of a retirement account.
3. Explain how the Goal Seek command facilitates the decision-making process.
4. Use mixed references to vary two parameters in a table.
5. Use the AVERAGE, MAX, MIN, and COUNT functions.
6. Use the IF and VLOOKUP functions to implement decision making.
7. Freeze, unfreeze, hide, and unhide rows and columns in a worksheet.
8. Use the AutoFilter command to display selected records in a list.
9. Describe the options in the Page Setup command used with large worksheets.

hands-on exercises

1. BASIC FINANCIAL FUNCTIONS
   Input: None
   Output: Basic Financial Functions
2. ADVANCED FINANCIAL FUNCTIONS
   Input: None
   Output: Advanced Financial Functions
3. THE EXPANDED GRADE BOOK
   Input: Expanded Grade Book
   Output: Expanded Grade Book Solution

CASE STUDY

VACATION TIME

Emily Knight is the office manager for a regional office of a large, multinational corporation. As office manager, she handles some extremely confidential employee information, including Social Security number, salary, and bonus information. It is also her responsibility to monitor the amount of vacation time each employee has accrued, and how much of that they have used thus far this year.

The Human Resources department has asked Emily to prepare a worksheet for a selected set of employees that will show the weeks of vacation granted to each employee, the number of days already used, and the number of days remaining. The amount of vacation is based on the employee's years of service, which changes continually; that is, the worksheet must reference today's date when computing the amount of vacation time. The worksheet should also contain summary statistics for the group of employees that shows the average number of days used, as well as the maximum and minimum number of days remaining. Your predecessor began the worksheet but left unexpectedly. Emily has asked you to step in and complete the worksheet as quickly as possible. ■

Your assignment is to read the chapter, paying special attention to Hands-on Exercise 3, which describes the use of statistical and logical functions. You will then open the *Chapter 4 Case Study—Vacation Time* workbook, which contains the employee data for the regional sales office, and complete the worksheet. Use the VLOOKUP function to determine the vacation time for each employee by referencing the table at the bottom of the worksheet. You will also need the IF function to display the number of days remaining. And finally, you will have to enter the formulas for the summary statistics table at the bottom of the worksheet. Print the completed worksheet for your instructor. Print the worksheet twice to show both displayed values and cell formulas. Use the Page Setup command to create a custom footer that contains your name.

SPREADSHEETS IN DECISION MAKING

Excel is a truly fascinating program, but it is only a means to an end. A spreadsheet is first and foremost a tool for decision making, and the objective of this chapter is to show you just how valuable that tool can be. Decisions typically involve money, and so we begin by introducing two financial functions, PMT and FV, either of which is entered directly into a worksheet.

The PMT (Payment) function calculates the periodic payment on a loan, such as one you might incur with the purchase of an automobile. The FV (Future Value) function determines the future value of a series of periodic payments, such as annual contributions to a retirement account. Either function can be used in conjunction with the Goal Seek command that lets you enter the desired end result (such as the monthly payment on a car loan) and from that, determines the input (e.g., the price of the car) to produce that result.

The second half of the chapter presents an expanded version of the professor's grade book that uses several commands associated with large spreadsheets. We describe scrolling and explain how its effects are modified by freezing and/or hiding rows and columns in a worksheet. We describe various statistical functions such as MAX, MIN, COUNT, and COUNTA as well as the IF and VLOOKUP functions that provide decision making within a worksheet. We also review the important concepts of relative and absolute cell references, as well as the need to isolate the assumptions and initial conditions in a worksheet.

Analysis of a Car Loan

Figure 4.1 shows how a worksheet might be applied to the purchase of a car. In essence you need to know the monthly payment, which depends on the price of the car, the down payment, and the terms of the loan. In other words:

- Can you afford the monthly payment on the car of your choice?
- What if you settle for a less expensive car and receive a manufacturer's rebate?
- What if you work next summer to earn money for a down payment?
- What if you extend the life of the loan and receive a better interest rate?
- Have you accounted for additional items such as insurance, gas, and maintenance?

The answers to these and other questions determine whether you can afford a car, and if so, which car, and how you will pay for it. The decision is made easier by developing the worksheet in Figure 4.1, and then by changing the various parameters as indicated.

Figure 4.1a contains the ***template***, or "empty" worksheet, in which the text entries and formulas have already been entered, the formatting has already been applied, but no specific data has been input. The template requires that you enter the price of the car, the manufacturer's rebate, the down payment, the interest rate, and the length of the loan. The worksheet uses these parameters to compute the monthly payment. (Implicit in this discussion is the existence of a PMT function within the worksheet program, which is explained in the next section.)

The availability of the worksheet lets you consider several alternatives, and therein lies its true value. You quickly realize that the purchase of a $14,999 car as shown in Figure 4.1b is prohibitive because the monthly payment is almost $500. Settling for a less expensive car, coming up with a substantial down payment, and obtaining a manufacturer's rebate in Figure 4.1c help considerably, but the $317 monthly payment is still too steep. Extending the loan to a fourth year at a lower interest rate in Figure 4.1d reduces the monthly payment to (a more affordable) $244.

No specific data has been input

	A	B
1	Price of car	
2	Manufacturer's rebate	
3	Down payment	
4	Amount to finance	=B1-(B2+B3)
5	Interest rate	
6	Term (in years)	
7	Monthly payment	=PMT(B5/12,B6*12,-B4)

(a) The Template

Data entered

	A	B
1	Price of car	$14,999
2	Manufacturer's rebate	
3	Down payment	
4	Amount to finance	$14,999
5	Interest rate	9%
6	Term (in years)	3
7	Monthly payment	$476.96

(b) Initial Parameters

Less expensive car

Rebate

Down payment made

	A	B
1	Price of car	$13,999
2	Manufacturer's rebate	$1,000
3	Down payment	$3,000
4	Amount to finance	$9,999
5	Interest rate	9%
6	Term (in years)	3
7	Monthly payment	$317.97

(c) Less Expensive Car with Down Payment and Rebate

Lower interest rate

Longer term

	A	B
1	Price of car	$13,999
2	Manufacturer's rebate	$1,000
3	Down payment	$3,000
4	Amount to finance	$9,999
5	Interest rate	8%
6	Term (in years)	4
7	Monthly payment	$244.10

(d) Longer Term and Better Interest Rate

FIGURE 4.1 Spreadsheets in Decision Making

PMT Function

A ***function*** is a predefined formula that accepts one or more ***arguments*** as input, performs the indicated calculation, then returns another value as output. Excel has more than 100 different functions in various categories. Financial functions, such as the PMT function we are about to study, are especially important in business.

The ***PMT function*** requires three arguments (the interest rate per period, the number of periods, and the amount of the loan), from which it computes the associated payment on a loan. The arguments are placed in parentheses and are separated by commas. Consider the PMT function as it might apply to Figure 4.1b:

=PMT(.09/12,36,–14999)

- Amount of loan (as a *negative* amount)
- Number of periods (3 years × 12 months/year)
- Interest rate per period (annual rate divided by 12)

Instead of using specific values, however, the arguments in the PMT function are supplied as cell references, so that the computed payment can be based on values supplied by the user elsewhere in the worksheet. Thus, the PMT function is entered as =PMT(B5/12,B6*12,–B4) to reflect the terms of a specific loan whose arguments are in cells B4, B5, and B6. (The principal is entered as a negative amount so that the worksheet will display a positive value.)

FV Function

The ***FV function*** returns the future value of an investment based on constant periodic payments and a constant interest rate. It can be used to determine the future value of a retirement plan such as an IRA (Individual Retirement Account) or 401K, two plans that are very popular in today's workplace. Under either plan, an individual saves for his or her retirement by making a fixed contribution each year. The money is allowed to accumulate tax-free until retirement, and it is an excellent way to save for the future.

Assume, for example, that you plan to contribute $3,000 a year to an IRA, that you expect to earn 7% annually, and that you will be contributing for 40 years (i.e., you began contributing at age 25 and will continue to contribute until age 65). The future value of that investment—the amount you will have at age 65—would be $598,905! All told, you would have contributed $120,000 ($3,000 a year for 40 years). The difference, more than $470,000, results from compound interest over the life of your investment.

The FV function is entered into a worksheet in similar fashion to the PMT function. There are three arguments—the interest rate (also called the rate of return), the number of periods, and the periodic investment. The FV function corresponding to our earlier example would be:

Amount at retirement = FV(Rate of return, Term, Periodic payment)

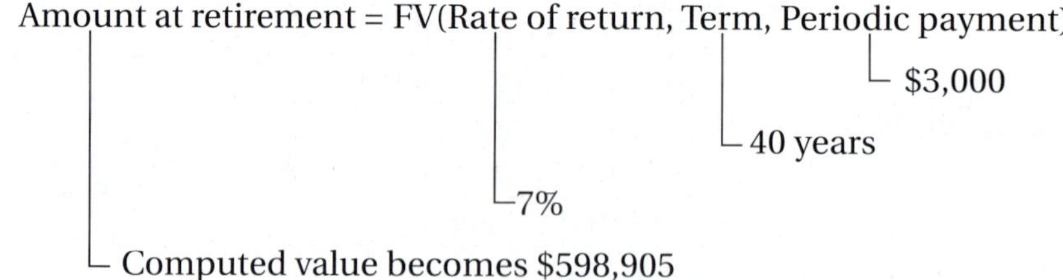

It's more practical, however, to enter the values into a worksheet, then use cell references within the FV function. If, for example, cells A1, A2, and A3 contained the rate of return, term, and annual contribution, respectively, the resulting FV function would be =FV(A1, A2, –A3). The periodic payment is preceded by a minus sign, just as the principal in the PMT function.

Inserting a Function

The ***Insert Function command*** places a function into a worksheet. You can select a function from a category as was done in Figure 4.2a, or you can enter a brief description of the function you are searching for. The Function Arguments dialog box in Figure 4.2b appears after you choose the function and is where you enter the various arguments. (Only the first three arguments are required for the Future Value function.) Excel displays the calculated value of each argument as well as the value of the function within the dialog box.

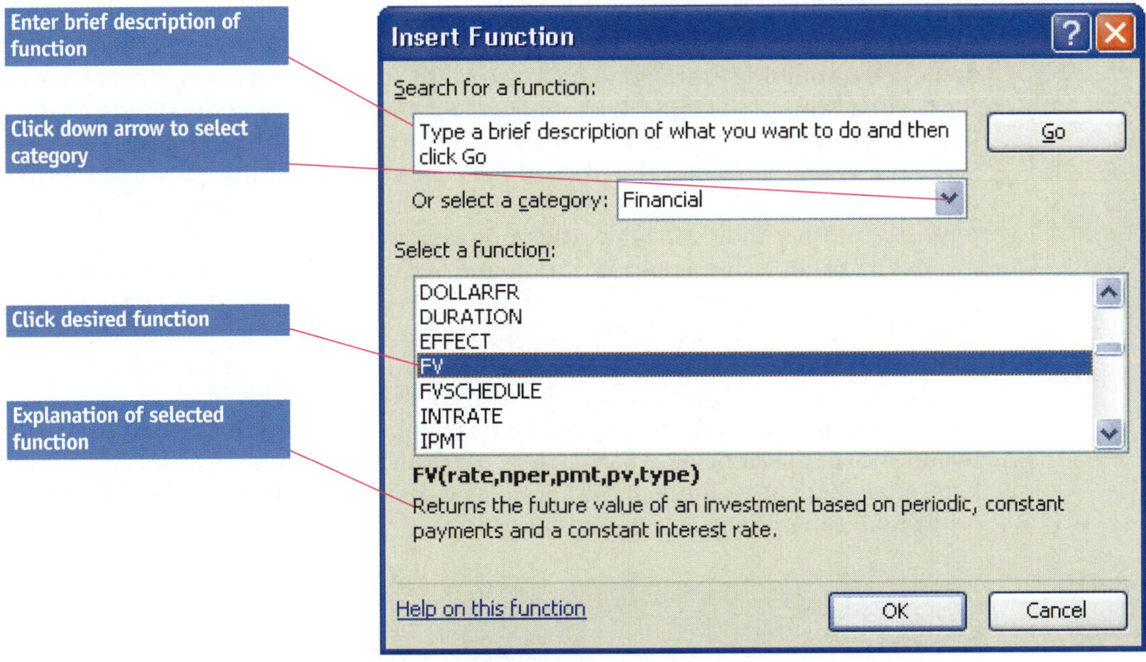

(a) Select the Function

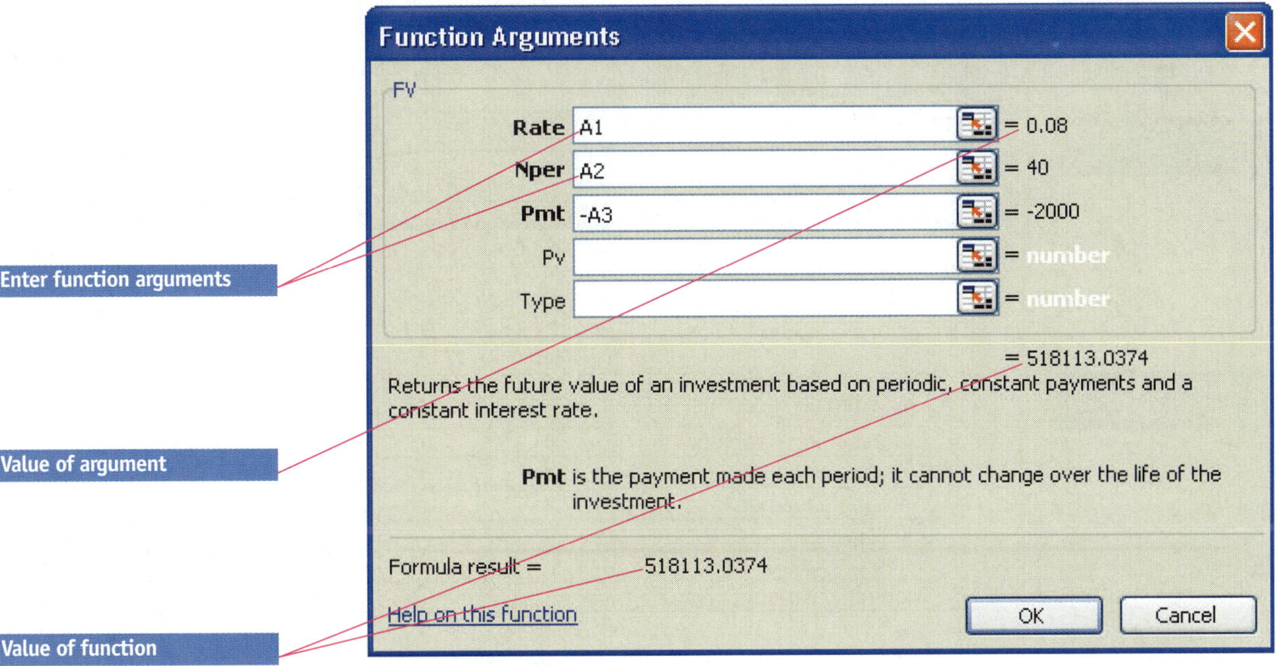

(b) Enter the Argument

FIGURE 4.2 Inserting a Function

The Goal Seek Command

The analysis in Figure 4.1 enabled us to reduce the projected monthly payment from $476 to a more affordable $244. What if, however, you can afford a payment of only $200, and you want to know the maximum you can borrow in order to keep the payment to the specified amount? The ***Goal Seek command*** is designed to solve this type of problem, as it enables you to set an end result (such as the monthly payment) in order to determine the input (the price of the car) to produce that result. Only one input (the price of the car, the interest rate, or the term) can be varied at a time.

Figure 4.3 extends our earlier analysis to illustrate the Goal Seek command. You create the spreadsheet as usual, then you pull down the Tools menu, and select the Goal Seek command to display the dialog box in Figure 4.3a. Enter the address of the cell containing the dependent formula (the monthly payment in cell B7) and the desired value of this cell ($200). Indicate the cell whose contents should be varied (the price of the car in cell B1), then click OK to execute the command. The Goal Seek command then varies the price of the car until the monthly payment returns the desired value of $200. (Not every problem has a solution, in which case Excel returns a message indicating that a solution cannot be found.)

In this example, the Goal Seek command is able to find a solution and returns a purchase price of $12,192 as shown in Figure 4.3b. You now have all the information you need. Find a car that sells for $12,192 (or less), hold the other parameters to the values shown in the figure, and your monthly payment will be (at most) $200.

The analysis in Figure 4.3 illustrates how a worksheet is used in the decision-making process. An individual defines a problem, then develops a worksheet that includes all of the associated parameters. He or she can then plug in specific numbers, changing one or more of the variables until a decision can be reached. Excel is invaluable in arriving at the solution.

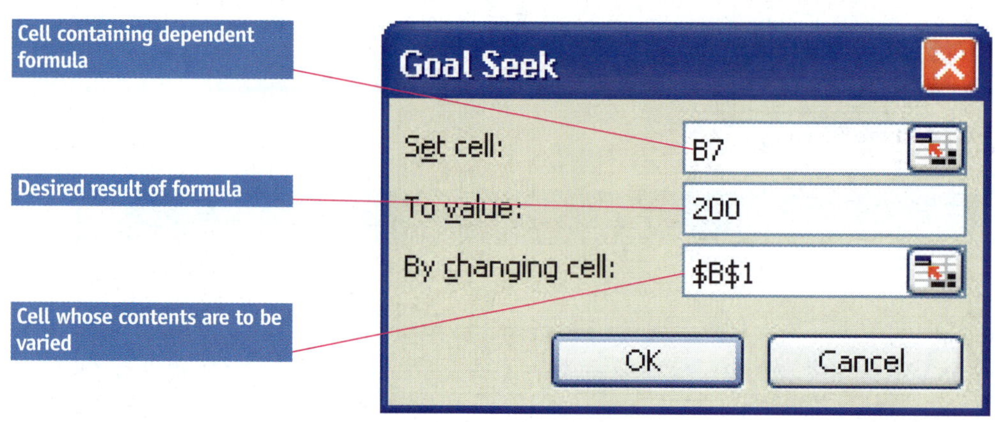

(a) Set the Maximum Payment

Required purchase price for a $200 monthly payment

	A	B
1	Price of car	$12,192
2	Manufacturer's rebate	$1,000
3	Down payment	$3,000
4	Amount to finance	$8,192
5	Interest rate	8%
6	Term (in years)	4
7	Monthly payment	$200.00

(b) Solution

FIGURE 4.3 The Goal Seek Command

hands-on exercise

1 Basic Financial Functions

Objective To illustrate the PMT and FV functions; to illustrate the Goal Seek command. Use Figure 4.4 as a guide in the exercise.

Step 1: Enter the Descriptive Labels

- Start Excel. If necessary, click the **New button** on the Standard toolbar to open a new workbook as shown in Figure 4.4a.
- Click in **cell A1**, type the label **Basic Financial Functions**, then press the **Enter key** to complete the entry. Enter the remaining labels for column A.
- Click and drag the column border between columns A and B to increase the column width of column A to accommodate the widest entry in column A (other than cell A3).
- Click in **cell B4** and type **$14,999** corresponding to the price of the automobile you hope to purchase. Be sure to include the dollar sign as you enter the data to format the cell automatically.
- Enter **$1,000** and **$3,000** in **cells B5** and **B6**, respectively, corresponding to the manufacturer's rebate and down payment, respectively.
- Click in **cell B7**. Use pointing to enter the formula **=B4–(B5+B6)**, which calculates the amount to finance (i.e., the principal of the loan).
- Enter **9%** and **3** in **cells B8** and **B9**. (If necessary, click in **cell B9**, pull down the **Edit menu**, select the **Clear command**, and choose the **Format command** to remove the dollar sign.)
- All of the loan parameters have been entered.

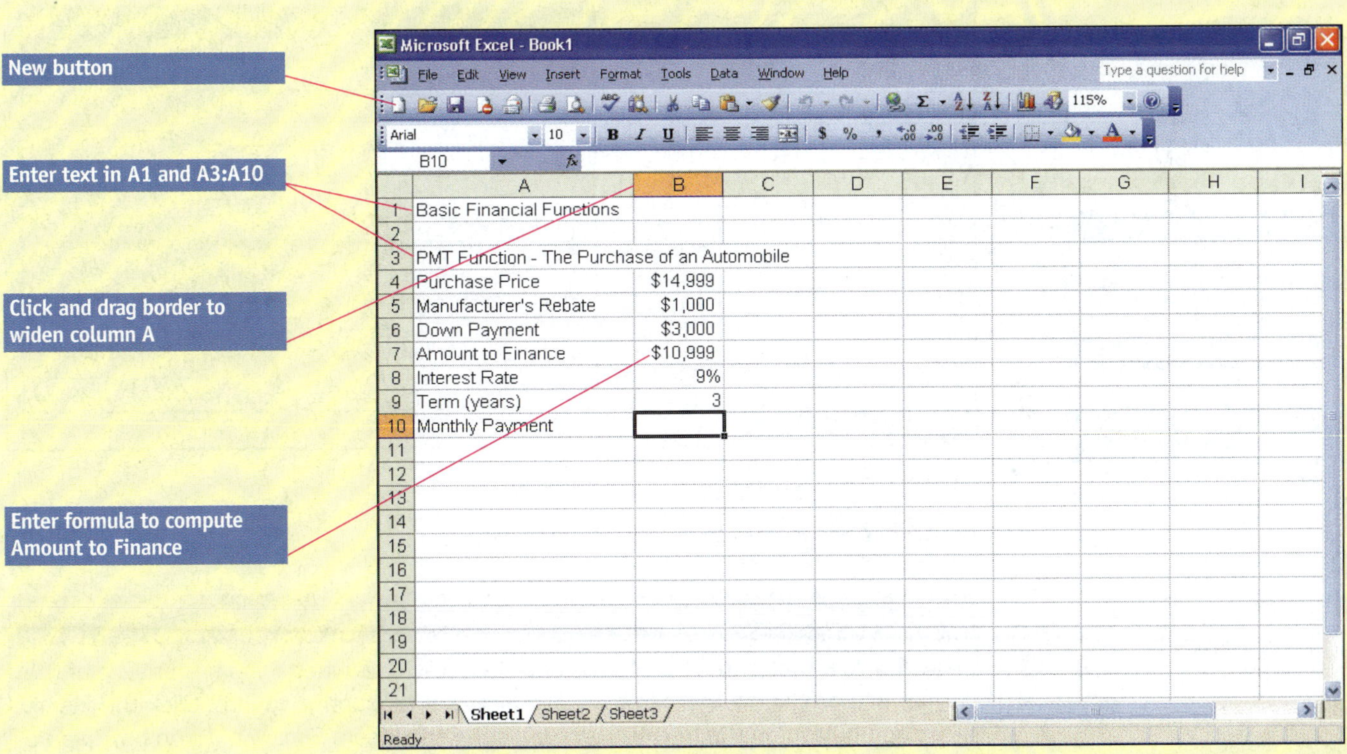

(a) Enter the Descriptive Labels (step 1)

FIGURE 4.4 Hands-on Exercise 1

Step 2: Insert a Function

- Click in **cell B10**. Pull down the **Insert menu** and click the **Function command** (or click the **Insert Function button** on the formula bar) to display the Insert Function dialog box.
- Click the **down arrow** in the Select a Category list box and select **Financial**, select the **PMT function** and click **OK** to display the Function Arguments dialog box in Figure 4.4b.
- Click the **Rate text box** and use pointing to enter the rate. Click in **cell B8** of the worksheet, then type **/12**, so that the text box contains the entry B8/12.
- Click the **Nper text box** and use pointing to enter the number of periods. Click in **cell B9**, then type ***12**, so that the formula bar contains the entry B9*12.
- Click the **Pv text box**. Type a – sign, then click in **cell B7**. You should see 349.7652595 as the value for the PMT function. Click **OK** to close the Function Arguments dialog box.
- Pull down the **File menu** and click the **Save command** (or click the **Save button** on the Standard toolbar) to display the Save As dialog box, then save the workbook as **Basic Financial Functions** in the **Exploring Excel** folder.

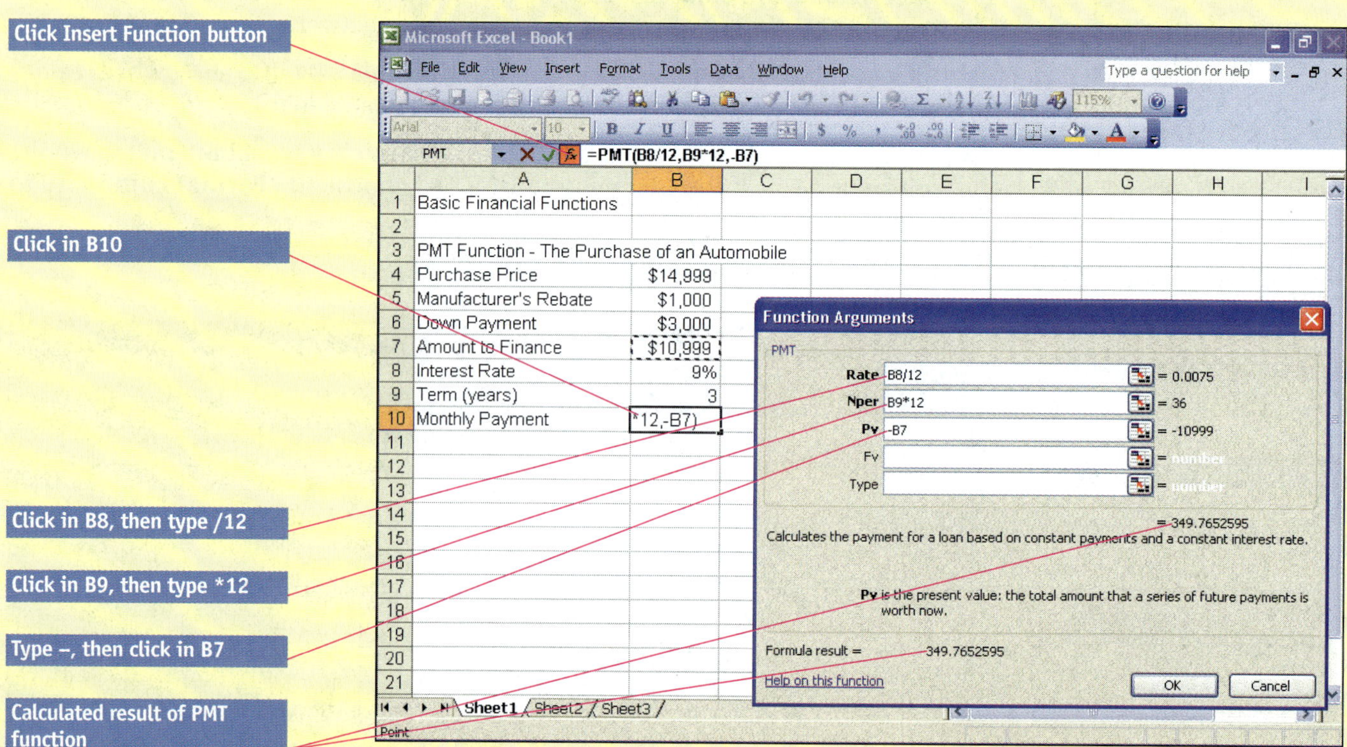

(b) Insert a Function (step 2)

FIGURE 4.4 Hands-on Exercise 1 (*continued*)

SEARCH FOR THE FUNCTION

It's easy to select a function if you know its name, but what if you are unsure of the name or don't know the category in which the function is found? Click the Insert Function button on the formula bar to display the Insert Function dialog box, type a keyword such as "payment" in the Search text box, then click the Go button. Excel returns nine functions in this example, one of which is the PMT function that you are looking for.

Step 3: The Goal Seek Command

- You can reduce the monthly payment in various ways. Click in **cell B4** and change the price of the car to **$13,999**. The monthly payment drops to $317.97.
- Change the interest rate to **8%** and the term of the loan to **4** years. The payment drops to $244.10.
- You can reduce the payment still further by using the Goal Seek command to fix the payment at a specified level. Click in **cell B10**, the cell containing the formula for the monthly payment.
- Pull down the **Tools menu**. Click **Goal Seek** to display the dialog box in Figure 4.4c. Click in the **To value** text box. Type **200** (the desired payment).
- Click in the **By changing cell** text box. Type **B4**, the cell containing the price of the car. This is the cell whose value will be determined. Click **OK**.
- The Goal Seek command returns a successful solution consisting of $12,192 and $200 in cells B4 and B10, respectively. Click **OK** to accept the solution and close the Goal Seek dialog box.
- Save the workbook.

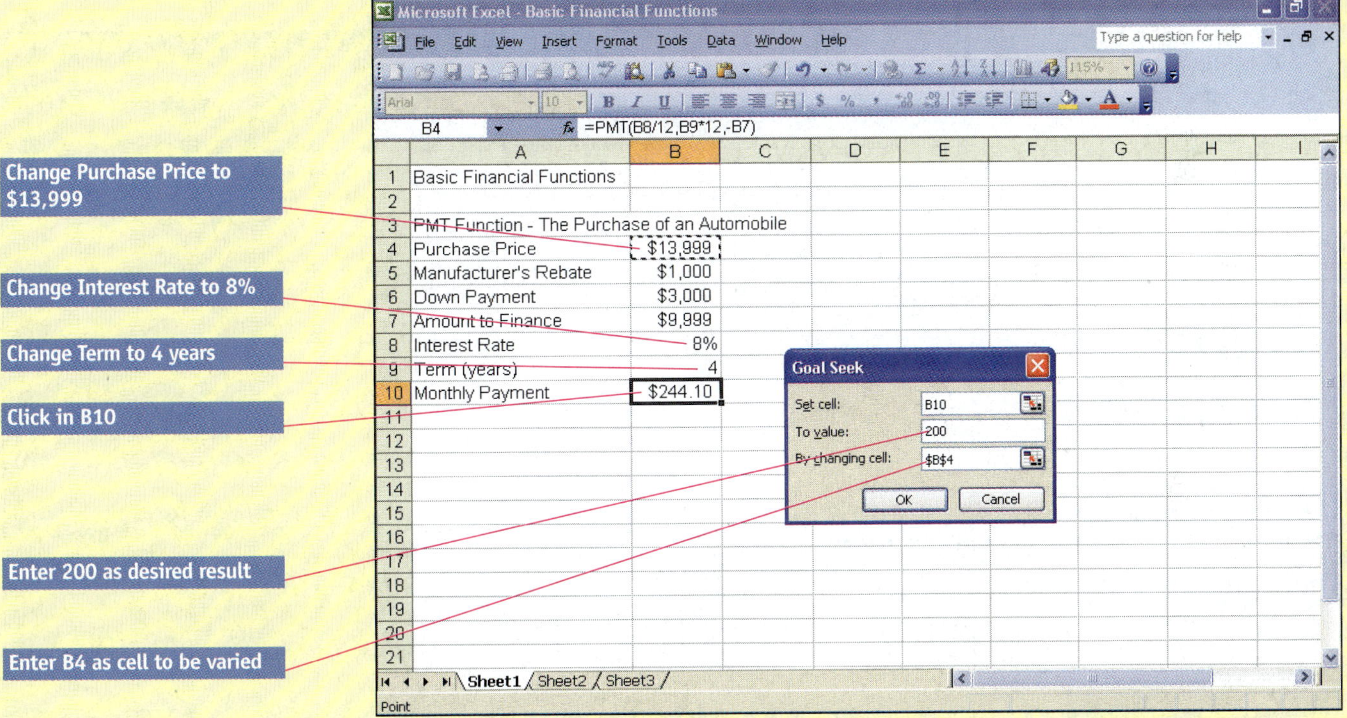

(c) The Goal Seek command (step 3)

FIGURE 4.4 Hands-on Exercise 1 (*continued*)

THE FORMATTING IS IN THE CELL

Once a number format has been assigned to a cell, either by including the format as you entered a number, or through execution of a formatting command, the formatting remains in the cell. Thus, to change the contents in a formatted cell, all you need to do is enter the new number without the formatting. Entering 5000, for example, into a cell that was previously formatted as currency will display the number as $5,000. To remove the formatting, pull down the Edit menu, select the Clear command, then choose Format.

Step 4: The Future Value Function

- Check your work carefully to be sure that your worksheet matches the top half of Figure 4.4d. Make corrections as necessary.
- Enter the labels in **cells A13** through **A17** as shown in the figure. Click in **cell B14** and type **$3,000** corresponding to the annual contribution. Be sure to include the dollar sign.
- Enter **7%** (type the percent sign) and **40** in **cells B15** and **B16**, respectively.
- Click in **cell B17**, type **=FV(**. You will see a ScreenTip that shows the arguments in the FV function. There are five arguments, but only the first three (rate, nper, and pv) are required. (The last two arguments are enclosed in square brackets to indicate they are optional.)
- Use pointing to complete the function, which is **=FV(B15,B16,–B14)**. Press **Enter** when you have finished.
- You should see $598,905.34 in cell B17. This is the amount you will have at retirement, given that you save $3,000 a year for 40 years and earn 7% interest over the life of your investment.
- Save the workbook.

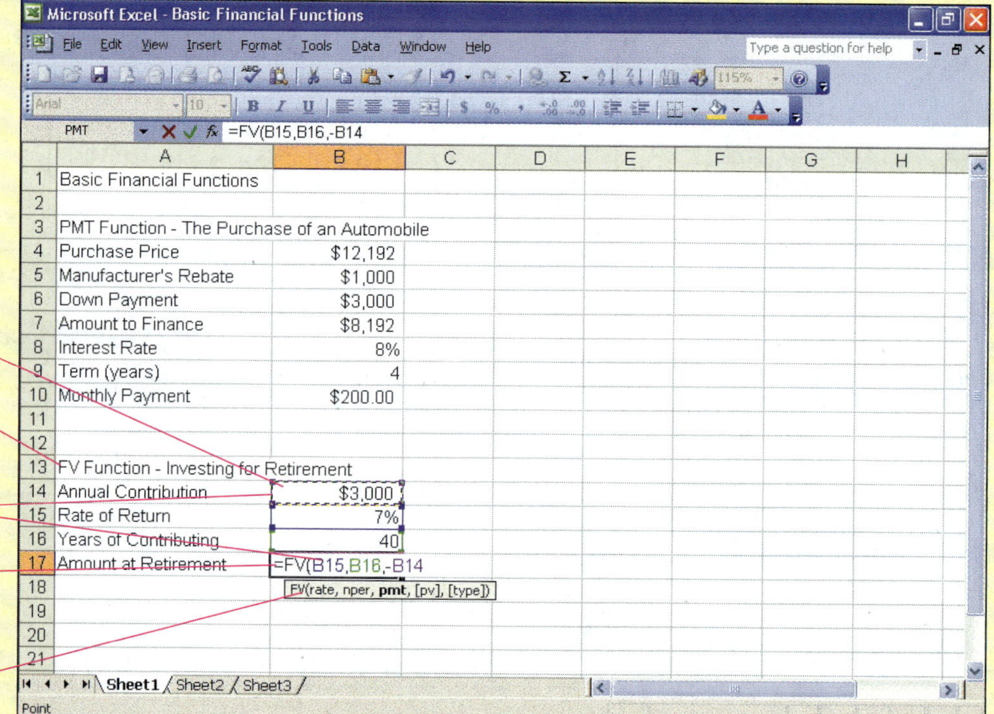

(d) The Future Value (FV) Function (step 4)

FIGURE 4.4 Hands-on Exercise 1 (*continued*)

IT'S COLOR CODED

Double click in the cell that contains the FV function, then look closely at the arguments within the function to see that each argument is a different color. Each color corresponds to the border color of the referenced cell. You can change any reference in the function (e.g., from B15 to C15) by dragging the color-coded border surrounding cell B15 (the reference you want to change) to cell C15 (the new reference).

Step 5: Format the Worksheet

- Your workbook should match Figure 4.4e except for the formatting. Click and drag **cells A1** and **B1**, then click the **Merge and Center button**.
- Click the **down arrow** on the Font Size list box to change the font size to **12**. Click the **Bold button** to boldface the title.
- Click **cell A3**. Press and hold the **Ctrl key** as you click cells **A10:B10, A13**, and **A17:B17** to select all of these cells. Click the **Bold button** to boldface the contents of these cells.
- Click and drag to select **cells A4** through **A9**. Press and hold the **Ctrl key** as you click and drag to select **cells A14** through **A16** (in addition to cells A4 through A9).
- Click the **Increase Indent button** on the Formatting toolbar to indent the labels as shown in Figure 4.4e.
- Click in **cell A19** and enter your name, then click the **Bold button** to boldface the type.
- Save the workbook.

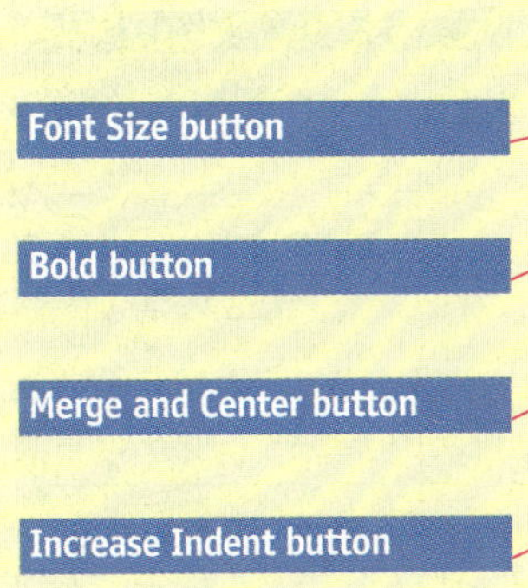

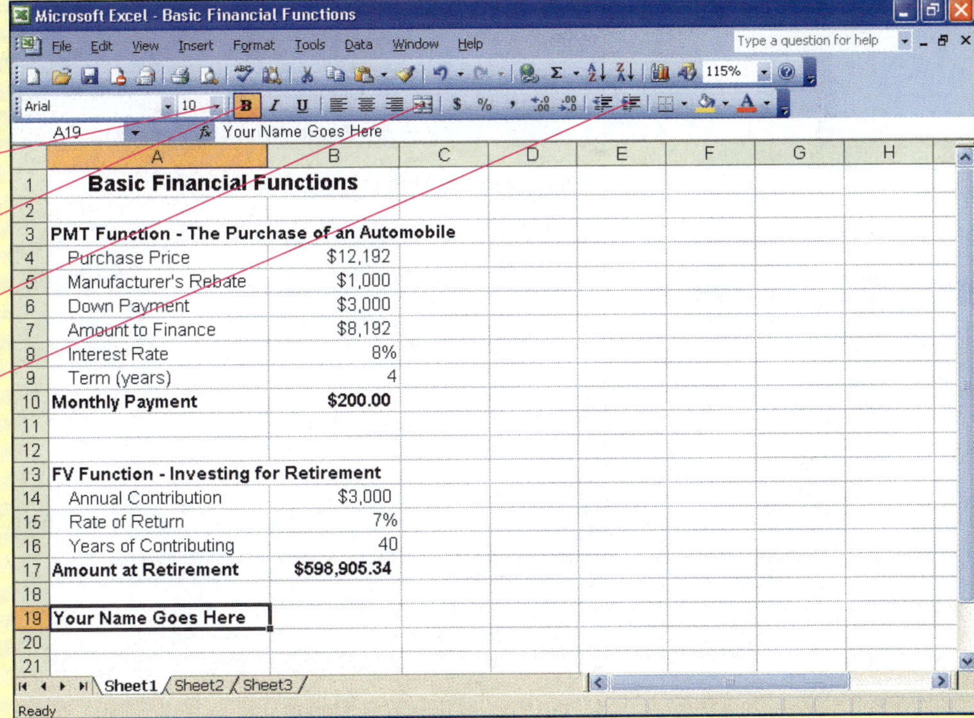

(e) Format the Worksheet (step 5)

FIGURE 4.4 Hands-on Exercise 1 (*continued*)

SELECTING NONCONTIGUOUS RANGES

You can apply the same formatting to noncontiguous (nonadjacent) cells within a worksheet by using the Ctrl key to select the cells. Click and drag to select the first cell range, then press and hold the Ctrl key as you select a second range. Continue to press the Ctrl key to select additional ranges, then format all of the selected cells with a single command. Click anywhere in the worksheet to deselect the cells.

Step 6: Print the Cell Formulas

- Pull down the **File menu** and click the **Page Setup command** to display the Page Setup dialog box. Click the **Sheet tab**, then check the boxes to print gridlines and row and column headings.
- Click the **Margins tab** and check the box to center the worksheet horizontally. Click **OK** to accept the settings and close the dialog box.
- Save the workbook. Click the **Print Preview button** on the Standard toolbar to be sure you are satisfied with the appearance of the workbook. Click the **Print button**, then click **OK** to print the worksheet.
- Press **Ctrl+`** to display the cell contents, as opposed to the displayed values. Preview the worksheet in this format, then print it when you are satisfied with its appearance. Press **Ctrl+`** to return the worksheet to displayed values.
- Submit printouts—the displayed values and the cell formulas—to your instructor as proof that you did this exercise.
- Exit Excel if you do not want to continue with the next exercise at this time.

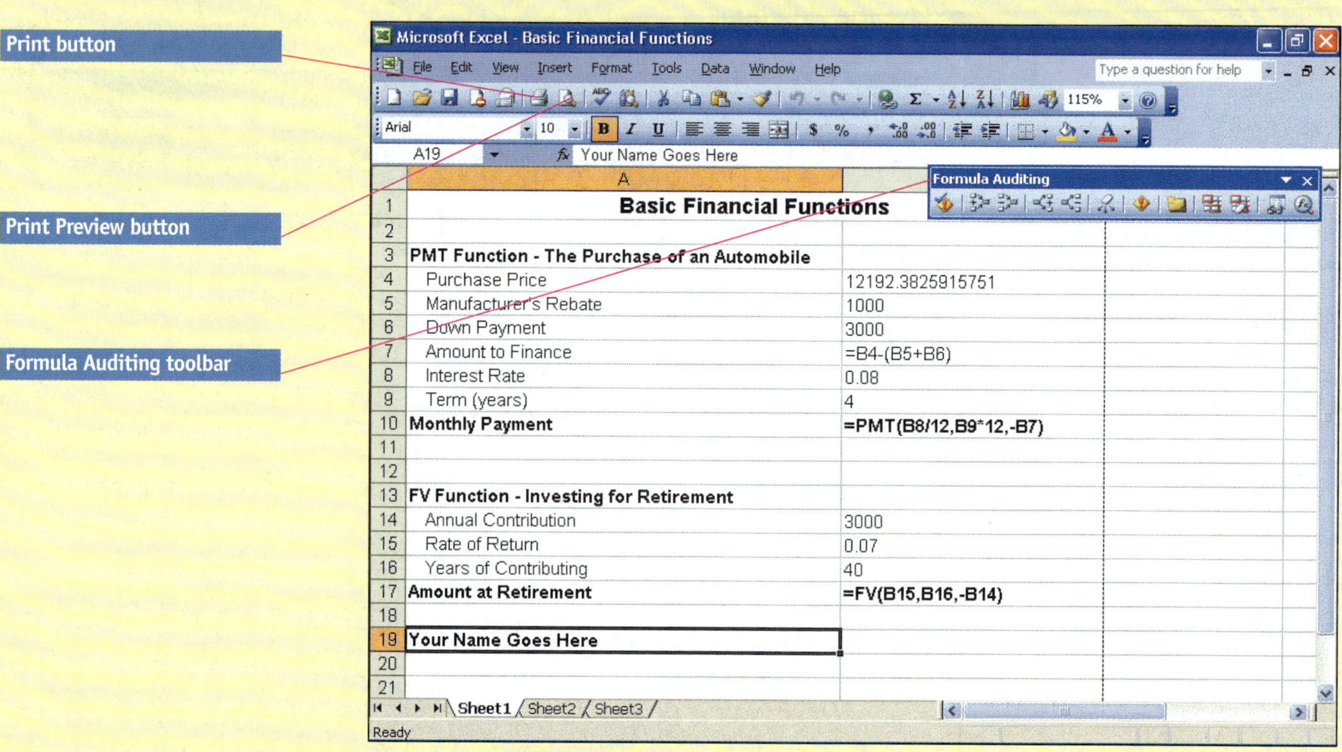

(f) Print the Cell Formulas (step 6)

FIGURE 4.4 Hands-on Exercise 1 *(continued)*

ARE THE PAYMENTS MONTHLY OR ANNUAL?

The FV function in this example computes the future value of a series of annual payments, with the term and interest rate specified as annual values, and thus there is no need to multiply or divide these values by 12. The car payment in the previous example, however, was on a monthly basis. Thus the annual interest rate was divided by 12 (to obtain the monthly rate), while the term of the loan was multiplied by 12, in order to put the numbers on a monthly basis.

HOME MORTGAGES

The PMT function is used in our next example in conjunction with the purchase of a home. The example also reviews the concept of relative and absolute addresses from Chapter 2. In addition, it introduces several other techniques to make you more proficient in Excel.

The spreadsheets in Figure 4.5 illustrate a variable rate mortgage, which will be developed over the next several pages. The user enters the amount he or she wishes to borrow and a starting interest rate, and the spreadsheet displays the associated monthly payment. The spreadsheet in Figure 4.5a enables the user to see the monthly payment at varying interest rates, and to contrast the amount of the payment for a 15- and a 30-year mortgage.

Most first-time buyers opt for the longer term, but they would do well to consider a 15-year mortgage. Note, for example, that the difference in monthly payments for a $100,000 mortgage at 7.5% is only $227.80 (the difference between $927.01 for a 15-year mortgage versus $699.21 for the 30-year mortgage). This is a significant amount of money, but when viewed as a percentage of the total cost of a home (property taxes and maintenance), it becomes less important, especially when you consider the substantial saving in interest over the life of the mortgage.

Figure 4.5b expands the spreadsheet to show the total interest over the life of the loan for both the 15- and the 30-year mortgage. The total interest on a $100,000 loan at 7.5% is $151,717 for a 30-year mortgage, but only $66,862 for a 15-year mortgage. In other words, you will pay back the $100,000 in principal plus another $151,717 in interest if you select the longer term.

Difference in monthly payment between a 30-year and a 15-year mortgage at 7.5%

	A	B	C	D
1	Amount Borrowed		$100,000	
2	Starting Interest		7.50%	
3				
4		Monthly Payment		
5	Interest	30 Years	15 Years	Difference
6	7.50%	$699.21	$927.01	$227.80
7	8.50%	$768.91	$984.74	$215.83
8	9.50%	$840.85	$1,044.22	$203.37
9	10.50%	$914.74	$1,105.40	$190.66
10	11.50%	$990.29	$1,168.19	$177.90
11	12.50%	$1,067.26	$1,232.52	$165.26

(a) Difference in Monthly Payment

Less interest is paid on a 15-year loan ($66,862 vs $151,717 on a 30-year loan)

	A	B	C	D	E
1	Amount Borrowed			$100,000	
2	Starting Interest			7.50%	
3					
4		30 Years		15 Years	
5	Interest	Monthly Payment	Total Interest	Monthly Payment	Total Interest
6	7.50%	$699.21	$151,717	$927.01	$66,862
7	8.50%	$768.91	$176,809	$984.74	$77,253
8	9.50%	$840.85	$202,708	$1,044.22	$87,960
9	10.50%	$914.74	$229,306	$1,105.40	$98,972
10	11.50%	$990.29	$256,505	$1,168.19	$110,274
11	12.50%	$1,067.26	$284,213	$1,232.52	$121,854

(b) Total Interest

FIGURE 4.5 15- versus 30-Year Mortgage

Relative versus Absolute Addresses

Figure 4.6 displays the cell formulas for the mortgage analysis. All of the formulas are based on the amount borrowed and the starting interest, in cells C1 and C2, respectively. You can vary either or both of these parameters, and the worksheet will automatically recalculate the monthly payments.

The similarity in the formulas from one row to the next implies that the copy operation will be essential to the development of the worksheet. You must, however, remember the distinction between a ***relative*** and an ***absolute reference***—that is, a cell reference that changes during a copy operation (relative) versus one that does not (absolute). Consider the PMT function as it appears in cell B6:

=PMT(A6/12,30*12,–$C$1)

- The amount of the loan, –$C$1, is an absolute reference that remains constant
- Number of periods (30 years*12 months/year)
- The interest rate, A6/12, is a relative reference that changes

The entry A6/12 (which is the first argument in the formula in cell B6) is interpreted to mean "divide the contents of the cell one column to the left by 12." Thus, when the PMT function in cell B6 is copied to cell B7, it (the copied formula) is adjusted to maintain this relationship and will contain the entry A7/12. The Copy command does not duplicate a relative address exactly, but adjusts it from row to row (or column to column) to maintain the relative relationship. The cell reference for the amount of the loan should not change when the formula is copied, and hence it is specified as an absolute address. Absolute references use a dollar sign before the row and column reference—for example, $C$1.

Relative reference (adjusts during copy operation)

Absolute reference (doesn't adjust during copy operation)

	A	B	C	D
1	Amount Borrowed		$100,000	
2	Starting Interest		7.50%	
3				
4	Monthly Payment			
5	Interest	30 Years	15 Years	Difference
6	=C2	=PMT(A6/12,30*12,-$C$1)	=PMT(A6/12,15*12,-$C$1)	=C6-B6
7	=A6+0.01	=PMT(A7/12,30*12,-$C$1)	=PMT(A7/12,15*12,-$C$1)	=C7-B7
8	=A7+0.01	=PMT(A8/12,30*12,-$C$1)	=PMT(A8/12,15*12,-$C$1)	=C8-B8
9	=A8+0.01	=PMT(A9/12,30*12,-$C$1)	=PMT(A9/12,15*12,-$C$1)	=C9-B9
10	=A9+0.01	=PMT(A10/12,30*12,-$C$1)	=PMT(A10/12,15*12,-$C$1)	=C10-B10
11	=A10+0.01	=PMT(A11/12,30*12,-$C$1)	=PMT(A11/12,15*12,-$C$1)	=C11-B11

FIGURE 4.6 Cell Formulas

ISOLATE ASSUMPTIONS

The formulas in a worksheet should be based on cell references rather than specific values—for example, C1 or $C$1 rather than $100,000. The cells containing these values should be clearly labeled and set apart from the rest of the worksheet. You can then vary the inputs (assumptions) to the worksheet and immediately see the effect. The chance for error is also minimized because you are changing the contents of a single cell, rather than changing multiple formulas.

Mixed References

Figure 4.7 displays a new worksheet that uses the FV function to calculate the value of an ***IRA (Individual Retirement Account)*** under various combinations of interest rates and years for investing. The annual contribution is $3,000 in all instances (the maximum that is allowed under current law). The interest rates appear in row 5, while the years for investing are shown in column B. The intersection of a row and column contains the future value of a series of $3,000 investments for the specific interest rate and year combination. Cell E21, for example, shows that $3,000 a year, invested over 40 years at 7%, will compound to $598,905.

The key to the worksheet is to realize that the Future Value function requires ***mixed references*** for both the interest rate and number of years. The interest rate will always come from row 5, but the column will vary. In similar fashion, the number of years will always come from column B, but the row will vary. Using this information we can enter the appropriate formula into cell C6, then copy that formula to the remaining cells in row 6, and finally copy row 6 to the remaining rows in the worksheet. The key to the worksheet is the formula in cell C6. Consider:

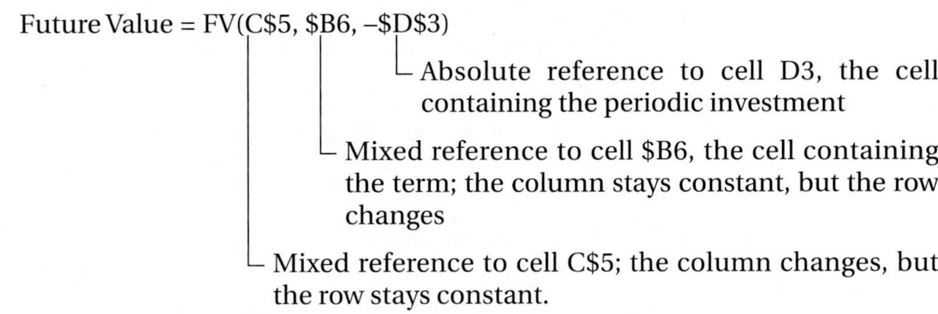

The majority of spreadsheets can be developed using a combination of relative and absolute references. Occasionally, however, you will need to incorporate mixed references as you will see in our next exercise.

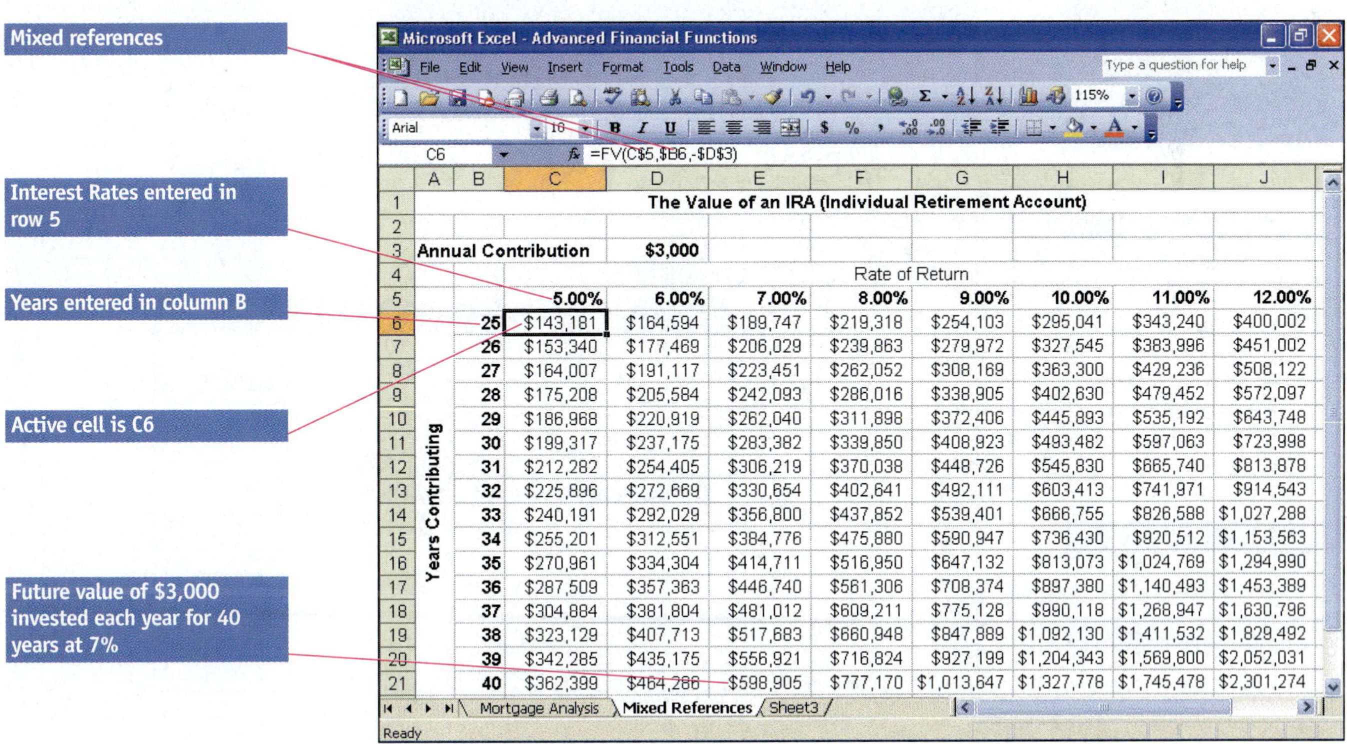

	A	B	C	D	E	F	G	H	I	J
1	The Value of an IRA (Individual Retirement Account)									
2										
3	Annual Contribution			$3,000						
4			Rate of Return							
5			5.00%	6.00%	7.00%	8.00%	9.00%	10.00%	11.00%	12.00%
6	Years Contributing	25	$143,181	$164,594	$189,747	$219,318	$254,103	$295,041	$343,240	$400,002
7		26	$153,340	$177,469	$206,029	$239,863	$279,972	$327,545	$383,996	$451,002
8		27	$164,007	$191,117	$223,451	$262,052	$308,169	$363,300	$429,236	$508,122
9		28	$175,208	$205,584	$242,093	$286,016	$338,905	$402,630	$479,452	$572,097
10		29	$186,968	$220,919	$262,040	$311,898	$372,406	$445,893	$535,192	$643,748
11		30	$199,317	$237,175	$283,382	$339,850	$408,923	$493,482	$597,063	$723,998
12		31	$212,282	$254,405	$306,219	$370,038	$448,726	$545,830	$665,740	$813,878
13		32	$225,896	$272,669	$330,654	$402,641	$492,111	$603,413	$741,971	$914,543
14		33	$240,191	$292,029	$356,800	$437,852	$539,401	$666,755	$826,588	$1,027,288
15		34	$255,201	$312,551	$384,776	$475,880	$590,947	$736,430	$920,512	$1,153,563
16		35	$270,961	$334,304	$414,711	$516,950	$647,132	$813,073	$1,024,769	$1,294,990
17		36	$287,509	$357,363	$446,740	$561,306	$708,374	$897,380	$1,140,493	$1,453,389
18		37	$304,884	$381,804	$481,012	$609,211	$775,128	$990,118	$1,268,947	$1,630,796
19		38	$323,129	$407,713	$517,683	$660,948	$847,889	$1,092,130	$1,411,532	$1,829,492
20		39	$342,285	$435,175	$556,921	$716,824	$927,199	$1,204,343	$1,569,800	$2,052,031
21		40	$362,399	$464,286	$598,905	$777,170	$1,013,647	$1,327,778	$1,745,478	$2,301,274

FIGURE 4.7 Mixed References

hands-on exercise

2 Advanced Financial Functions

Objective To use relative, absolute, and mixed references in conjunction with the PMT and FV functions; to practice various formatting commands. Use Figure 4.8 as a guide in the exercise.

Step 1: The Spell Check

- Start Excel and begin a new workbook. Click in **cell A1**. Type **Amount Borrowed**. Do not be concerned that the text is longer than the cell width, as cell B1 is empty and thus the text will be displayed in its entirety. Press the **Enter key** or **down arrow** to complete the entry.
- Type **Starting Interest** in **cell A2**. Click in **cell A4**. Type **Monthly Payment**. Enter the remaining labels in **cells A5** through **D5**, as shown in Figure 4.8a without concern for the column width.
- We suggest that you deliberately misspell one or more words in order to try the spell check. Click in **cell A1** to begin the spell check at the beginning of the worksheet.
- Click the **Spelling button** on the Standard toolbar to initiate the spell check as shown in Figure 4.8a. Make corrections, as necessary, just as you would in Microsoft Word.
- Click in **cell C1**. Type **$100,000** (include the dollar sign). Press the **Enter key** or **down arrow** to complete the entry and move to **cell C2**. Type **7.5%** (include the percent sign). Press **Enter**.
- Save the workbook as **Advanced Financial Functions** in the **Exploring Excel folder** on the appropriate drive.

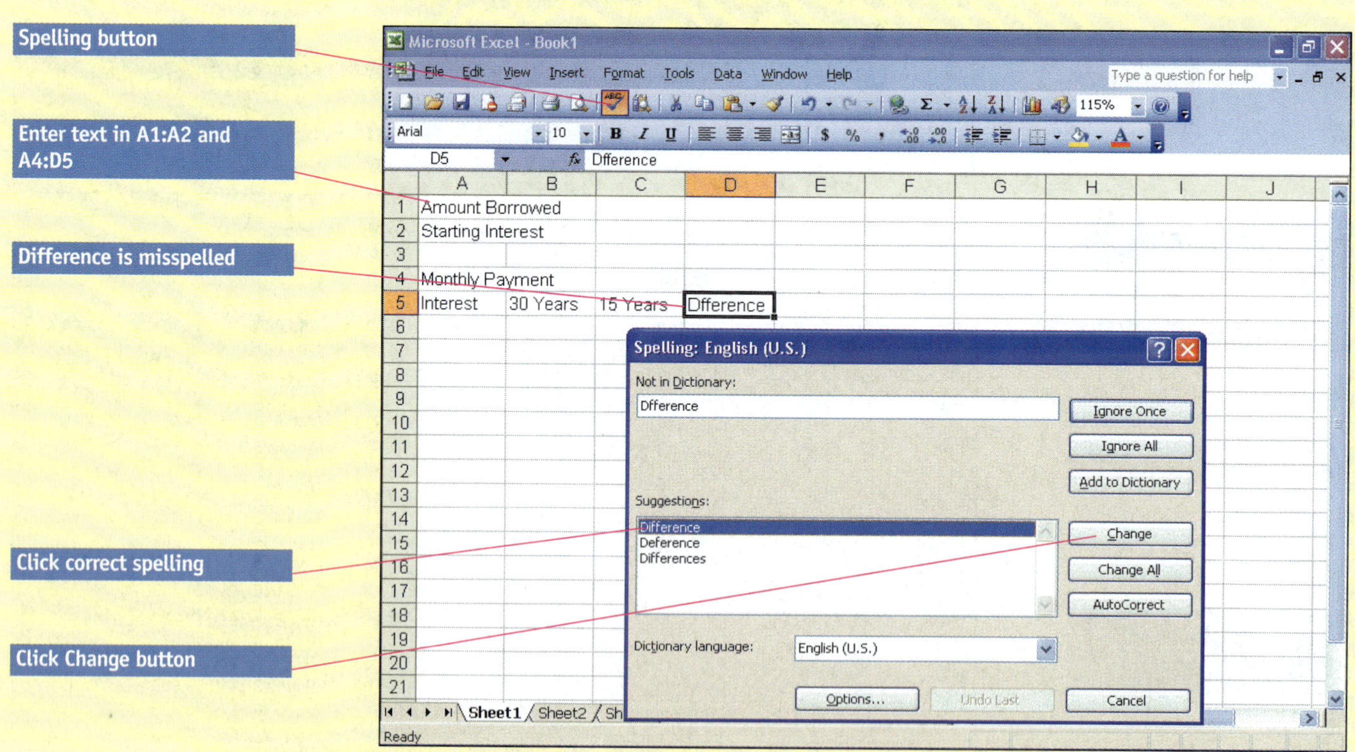

(a) The Spell Check (step 1)

FIGURE 4.8 Hands-on Exercise 2

Step 2: The Fill Handle

- Click in **cell A6**. Use pointing to enter the formula **=C2** to reference the starting interest rate in cell C2.
- Click in **cell A7**. Use pointing to enter the formula **=A6+.01** to compute the interest rate in this cell, which is one percent more than the interest rate in row 6. Press **Enter**.
- Click in **cell A7**. Point to the **fill handle** in the lower-right corner of cell A7. The mouse pointer changes to a thin crosshair.
- Drag the **fill handle** over **cells A8** through **A11**. A border appears to indicate the destination range as in Figure 4.8b. Release the mouse to complete the copy operation. The formula and associated percentage format in cell A7 have been copied to cells A8 through A11.
- Click in **cell C2**. Type **5%**. The entries in cells A6 through A11 change automatically. Click the **Undo button** on the Standard toolbar to return to the 7.5% interest rate.
- Save the workbook.

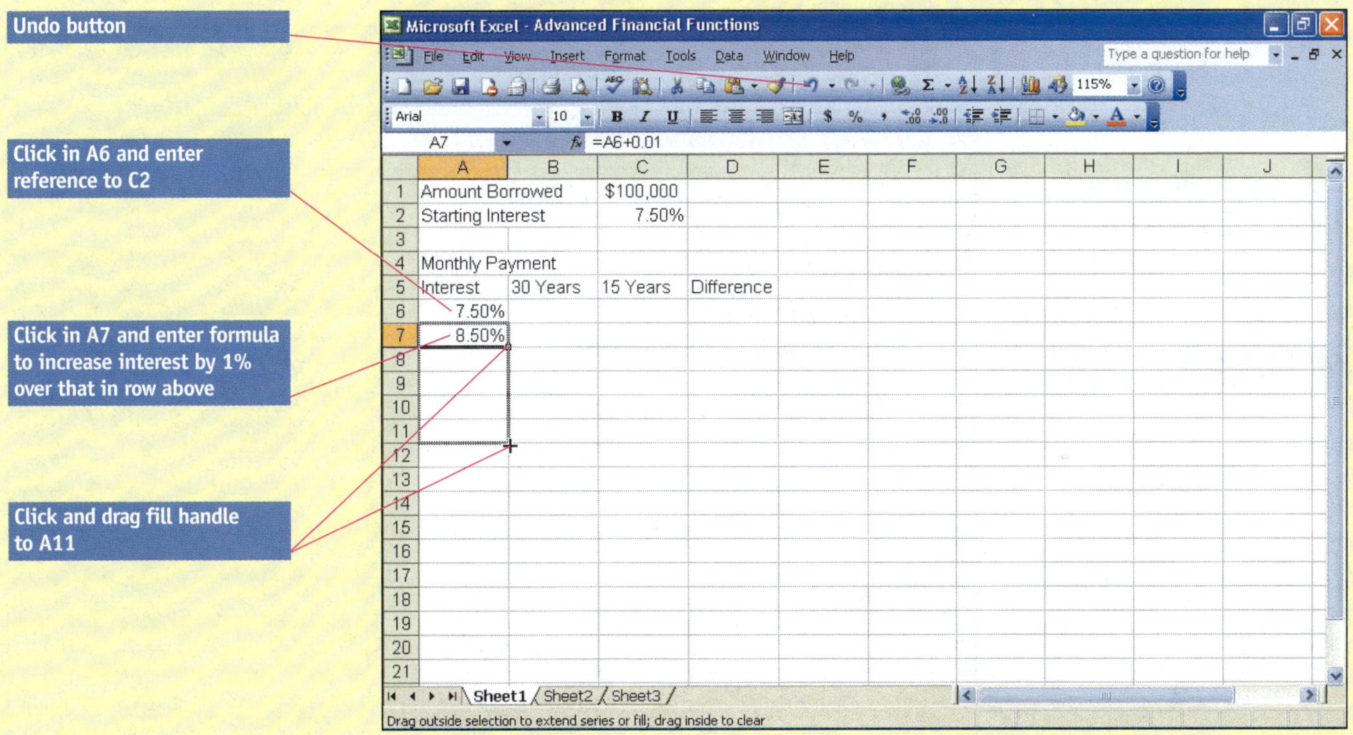

(b) The Fill Handle (step 2)

FIGURE 4.8 Hands-on Exercise 2 (*continued*)

FIND AND REPLACE

Anyone familiar with a word processor takes the Find and Replace commands for granted, but did you know the same capabilities exist in Excel? Pull down the Edit menu and choose either command. You have the same options as in the parallel command in Word, such as a case-sensitive (or insensitive) search. Use the command in the current worksheet to change "Interest" to "Interest Rate".

Step 3: Determine the 30-year Payments

- Click in **cell B6** and enter the formula **=PMT(A6/12,30*12,–$C$1)** as shown in Figure 4.8c. Note the ScreenTip that appears as you enter the function to indicate the order of the arguments. Note, too, that you can enter the references directly or you can use pointing (click the **F4 key** as necessary to change from relative to absolute addresses).
- Click in **cell B6**, which should display the value $699.21, as shown in Figure 4.8c. Click and drag the **fill handle** in the bottom-right corner of cell B6 over cells B7 through B11. Release the mouse to complete the copy operation.
- The PMT function in cell B6 has been copied to cells B7 through B11. The payment amounts are visible in cells B7 through B10, but cell B11 may display a series of number signs, meaning that the cell (column) is too narrow to display the computed results in the selected format.
- Check that cells B6:B11 are still selected. Pull down the **Format menu**, click **Column**, then click **AutoFit Selection** from the cascaded menu. Cell B11 should display $1,067.26.
- Save the workbook.

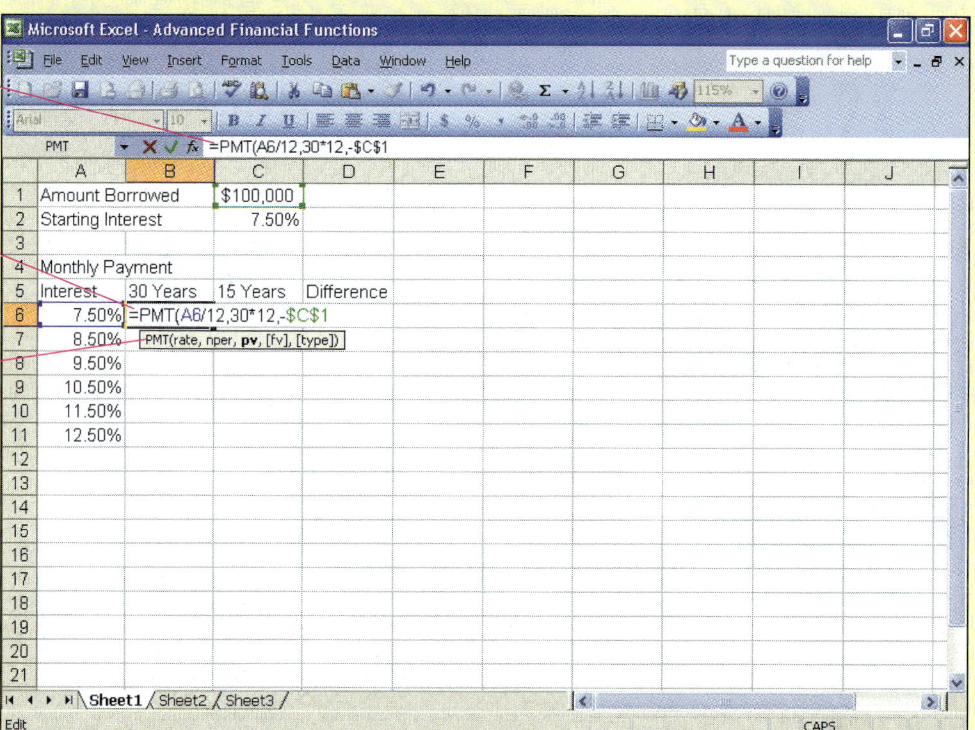

(c) Determine the 30-year Payments (step 3)

FIGURE 4.8 Hands-on Exercise 2 (*continued*)

POUND SIGNS AND COLUMN WIDTH

The appearance of pound signs within a cell indicates that the cell width (column width) is insufficient to display the computed results in the selected format. Double click the right border of the column heading to change the column width to accommodate the widest entry in that column. For example, to increase the width of column B, double click the border between the column headings for columns B and C.

Step 4: **Determine the 15-year Payments**

- Click in **cell C6** and enter the formula **=PMT(A6/12,15*12,–$C$1)** as shown in Figure 4.8d. Note the ScreenTip that appears as you enter the function to indicate the order of the arguments. You can enter the references directly, or you can use pointing (click the **F4 key** as necessary to change from relative to absolute addresses).
- Press **Enter** to complete the formula. Check that cell C6 displays the value $927.01. Make corrections as necessary.
- Use the **fill handle** to copy the contents of **cell C6** to **cells C7** through **C11**.
- If necessary, increase the width of column C. Cell C11 should display $1,232.52 if you have done this step correctly.
- Click in **cell D6** and enter the formula **=C6–B6**, then copy this formula to the remaining cells in this column. Cell D11 should display $165.26.
- Save the workbook.

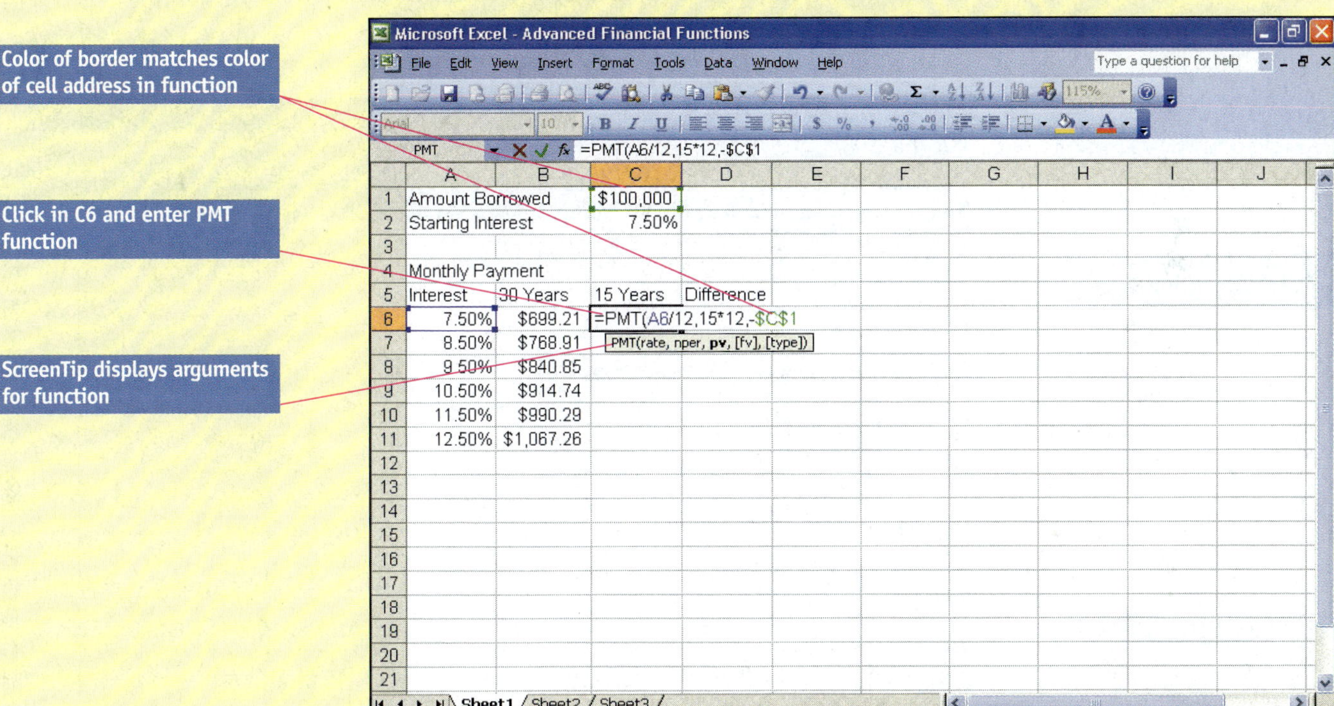

(d) Determine the 15-year Payments (step 4)

FIGURE 4.8 Hands-on Exercise 2 (*continued*)

KEYBOARD SHORTCUTS—CUT, COPY, AND PASTE

Ctrl+X (the X is supposed to remind you of a pair of scissors), Ctrl+C, and Ctrl+V are keyboard shortcuts to cut, copy, and paste, respectively, and apply to Excel as well as to Windows applications in general. The keystrokes are easier to remember when you realize that the operative letters X, C, and V are next to each other at the bottom left side of the keyboard. There is no need to memorize the keyboard shortcuts, but as you gain proficiency, they will become second nature.

Step 5: Format the Worksheet

- Click in **cell A13** and enter the label **Financial Consultant**. Enter **your name** in **cell A14**. Add formatting as necessary using Figure 4.8e as a guide.
- Click **cell A4**. Drag the mouse over cells **A4** through **D4**. Click the **Merge and Center button** on the Formatting toolbar to center the entry.
- Center the column headings in row 5. Add boldface and/or italics to the text and/or numbers as you see fit. Widen columns as necessary.
- Pull down the **File menu** and click the **Page Setup command** to display the Page Setup dialog box.
- Click the **Margins tab**. Check the box to center the worksheet horizontally. Click the **Sheet tab**. Check the boxes to include row and column headings and gridlines. Click **OK** to exit the Page Setup dialog box.
- Save the workbook. Pull down the **File menu**, click the **Print command** to display the Print dialog box, then click **OK** to print the worksheet. Press **Ctrl+~** to display the cell formulas. Widen the columns as necessary, then print.
- Press **Ctrl+~** to return to displayed values.

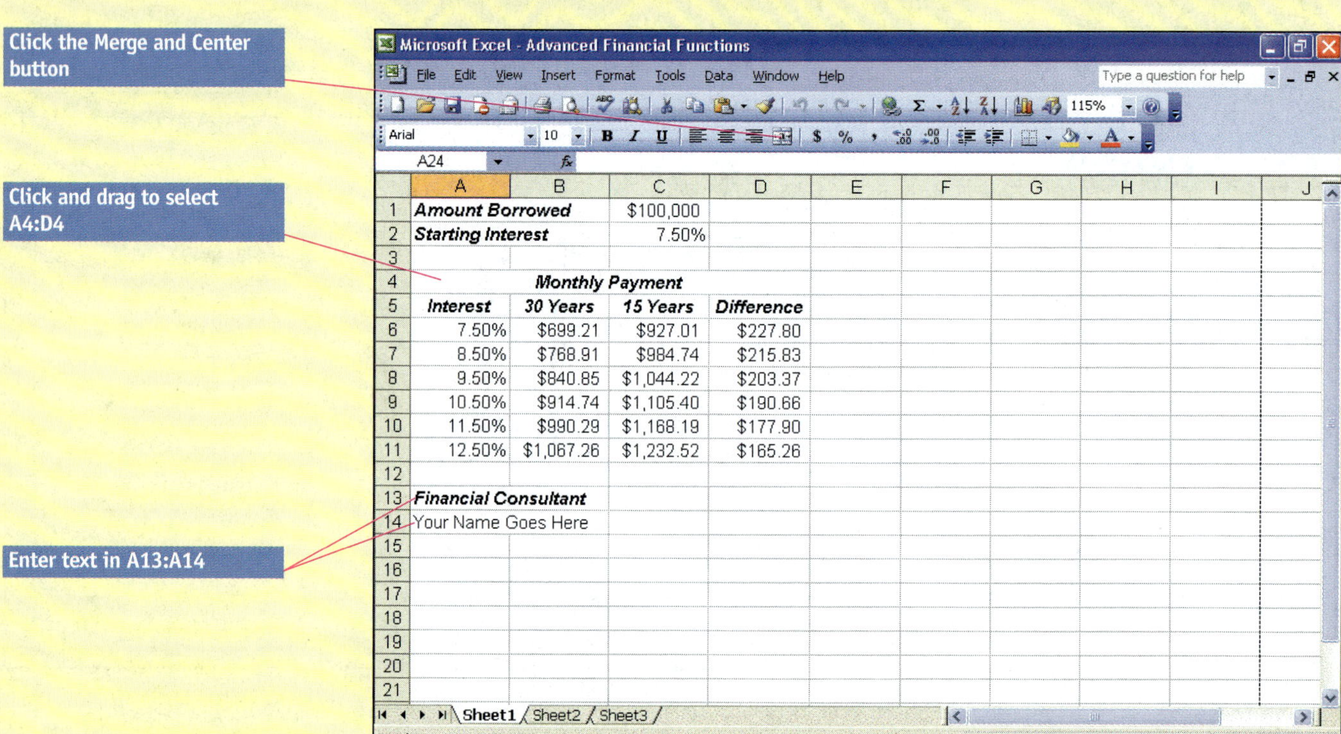

(e) Format the Worksheet (step 5)

FIGURE 4.8 Hands-on Exercise 2 (*continued*)

THE PPMT AND IPMT FUNCTIONS

The PMT function determines the periodic payment for a loan, which in turn is composed of two components, interest and principal. The amount of the payment that goes toward interest decreases each period, and conversely, the amount for the principle increases. These values can be computed through the IPMT and PPMT functions, respectively, which are used to compute the amortization (payoff) schedule for the loan.

Step 6: Merge and Center Text

- Click the **Sheet2 tab** to change to this worksheet. Click in **cell A1** and enter the title of the worksheet, **The Value of an IRA (Individual Retirement Account)**.
- Enter the indicated labels in **cells A3** and **C4** as shown in Figure 4.8f. Click in **cell A6** and type the label **Years Contributing**.
- Click and drag to select **cells A6** through **A21**, then click the **Merge and Center button** on the Standard toolbar to merge the cells. Right click within the merged cell, then click the **Format Cells command** to display the Format cells dialog box. Click the **Alignment tab**.
- Enter **90** in the Degrees list box to change to 90 degrees. Click the **down arrow** on the Vertical list box and choose **Center**. Click **OK**. Click the **Undo button** if the results are different from what you intended.
- Click and drag to select **cells A1** through **J1**, then click the **Merge and Center button** to center the title. Merge and center cells **C4** through **J4** in similar fashion.
- Click and drag the border between columns A and B to make the column narrower, as appropriate. Save the workbook.

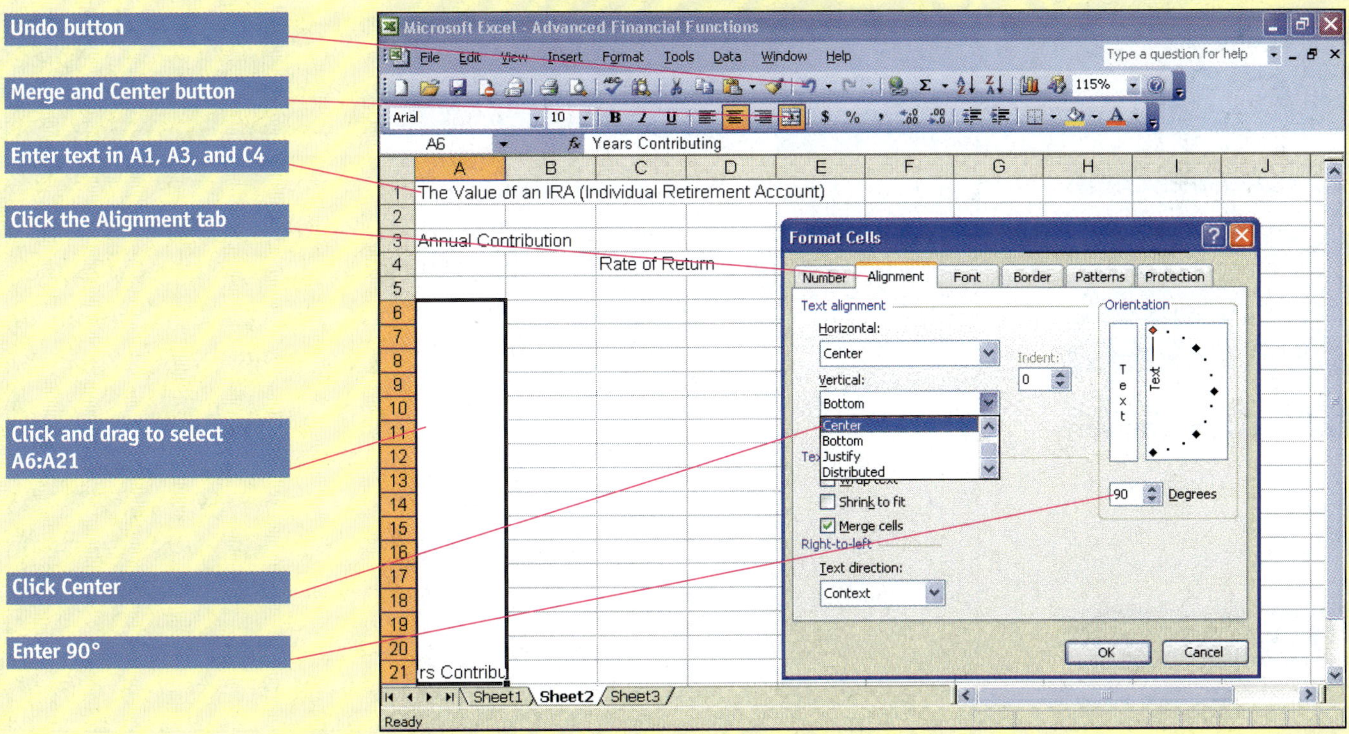

(f) Merge and Center Text (step 6)

FIGURE 4.8 Hands-on Exercise 2 (*continued*)

THE MERGE AND CENTER COMMAND

The Merge and Center command combines multiple cells into a single cell and is best used in conjunction with the headings in a worksheet. Cells can be merged horizontally or vertically, then the text in the merged cells can be aligned in a variety of styles. Text can also be rotated to provide interest in the worksheet. If necessary, you can restore the individual cells and remove the associated formatting using the Edit Clear command. Click in the merged cell, pull down the Edit menu, and click the Clear command. Click Formats to restore the individual cells to the default format.

Step 7: Enter the Row and Column Headings

- Check that the labels in your worksheet match those in Figure 4.8g. Click in **cell D3** and enter **$3,000**. Click in **cell C5** and type **5.00%**. Be sure to include the decimal point, zeros, and percent sign.
- Click in **cell D5** and enter the formula **=C5+.01**, then click and drag the **fill handle** to copy this formula to cells **E5** through **J5**.
- Click in **cell B6** and type the number **25**. Click in **cell B7** and enter the formula **=B6+1**, then click and drag the **fill handle** to copy this formula to **cells B8** through **B21**.
- Double click the **Sheet2 tab** to select the worksheet name, then type **Mixed References** as the name of this worksheet. Double click the **Sheet1 tab** to select the worksheet name, then type **Mortgage Analysis** as the name of this worksheet.
- Click the newly named **Mixed References worksheet tab** to return to this worksheet and continue working.
- Save the workbook.

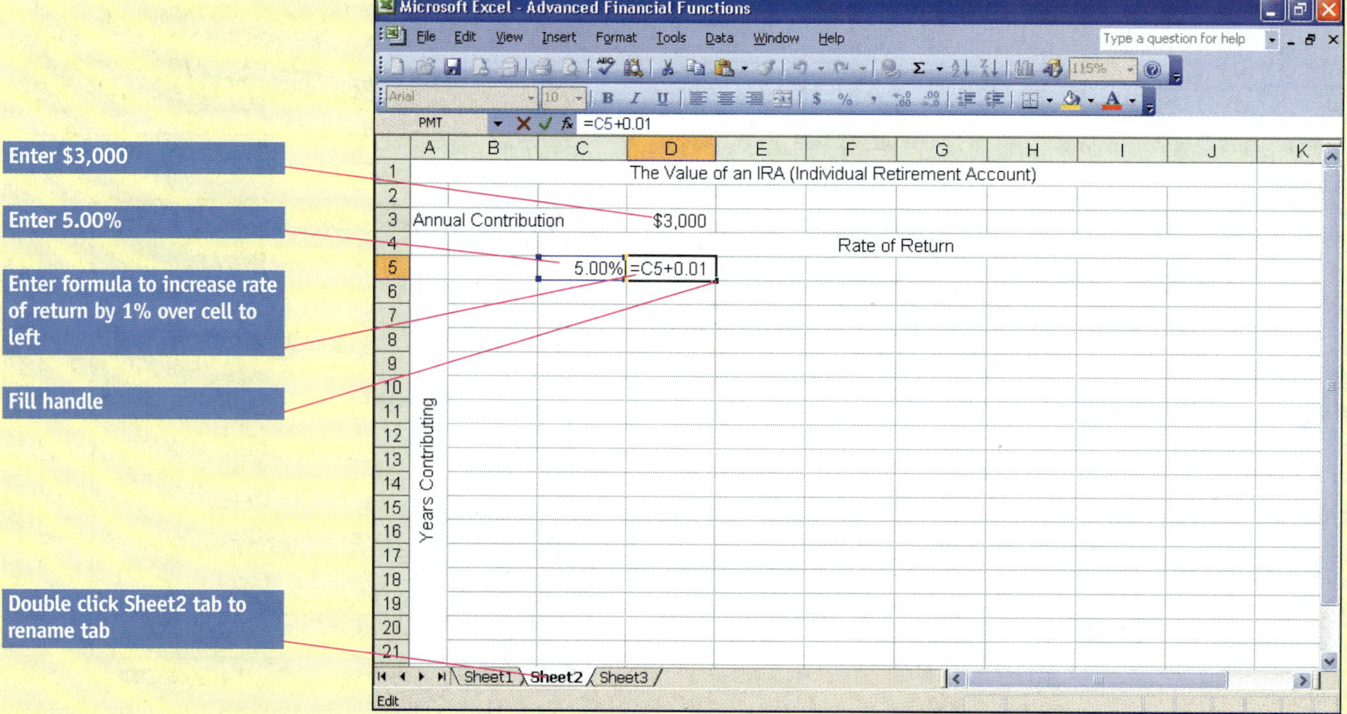

(g) Enter the Row and Column Headings (step 7)

FIGURE 4.8 Hands-on Exercise 2 (*continued*)

AUTOMATIC FORMATTING

Excel converts any number entered with a beginning dollar sign to currency format, and any number entered with an ending percent sign to percentage format. The automatic formatting enables you to save a step by typing $100,000 or 7.5% directly into a cell, rather than entering 100000 or .075 and having to format the number. The formatting is applied to the cell and affects any subsequent numbers in that cell. (Use the Clear command in the Edit menu to remove the formatting.)

Step 8: Create the Mixed References

- Click in **cell C6**. Pull down the **Insert menu** and click **Function** (or click the **Insert Function button** on the formula bar) to display the Insert Function dialog box.
- Click the **drop-down arrow**, then click **Financial** in the Select a Category list box. Click **FV** in the Select a Function list box. Click **OK**.
- Click and drag the Function Arguments dialog box so that you can see the underlying cells as shown in Figure 4.8h.
- Click the text box for rate, click in **cell C5**, then press the **F4 key** until you see **C$5** within the dialog box.
- Press **Tab** to move to (or click in) the **Nper text box**, click in **cell B6**, then press the **F4 key** until you see $B6 within the dialog box.
- Press **Tab** to move to (or click in) the **Pmt text box**, type a **minus sign**, click in **cell D3**, then press the **F4 key** until you see **–$D$3** in the dialog box.
- Check that the entries on your screen match those in Figure 4.8h, then click **OK**. Cell C6 should display the value $143,181.
- Save the workbook.

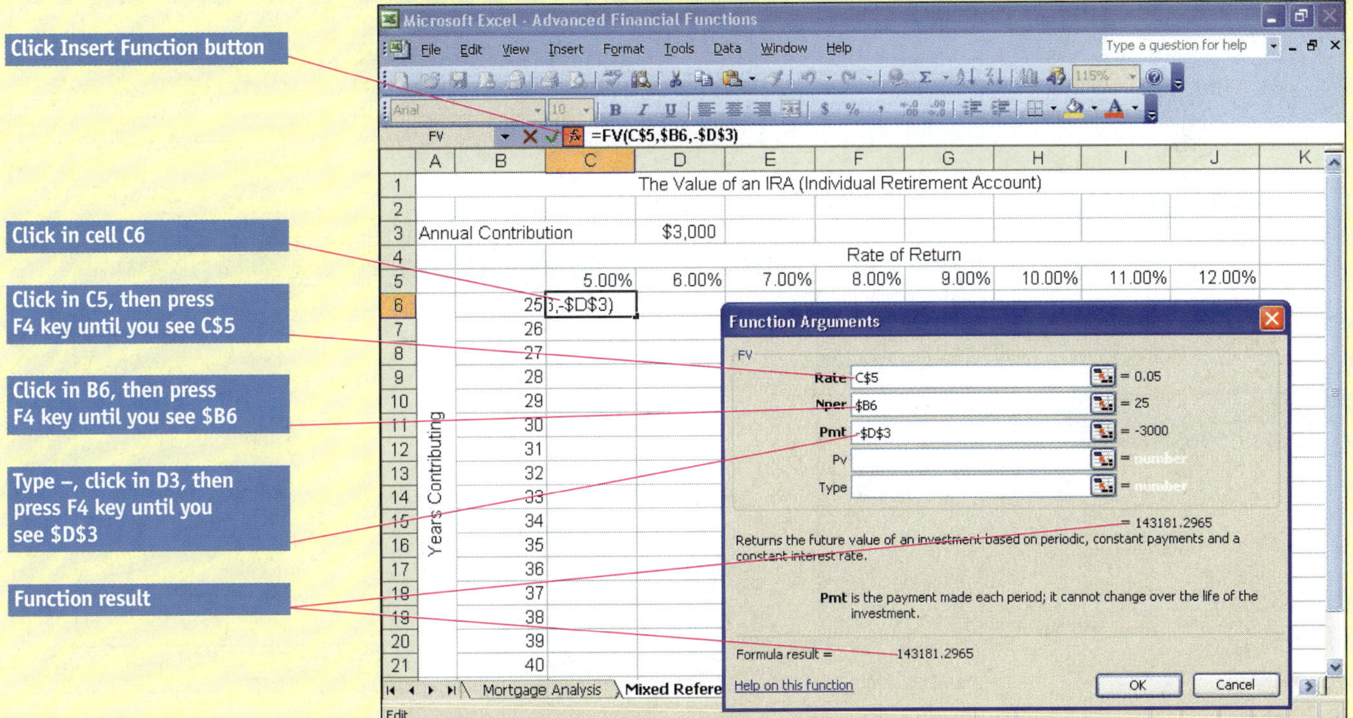

(h) Create the Mixed References (step 8)

FIGURE 4.8 Hands-on Exercise 2 *(continued)*

MIXED REFERENCES ARE NOT DIFFICULT

Mixed references are not difficult, provided you think clearly about what is required. In our example the interest rate should always come from row 5, but the column should change. Hence you enter C$5 for this parameter within the FV function. In similar fashion, the term of the investment should always come from column B, but the row should change. Thus you enter $B6 for this parameter. It's easy and it's powerful.

Step 9: Copy the Formula

- If necessary, click in **cell C6**, the cell that contains the formula you just created. Click and drag the **fill handle** in **cell C6** to **cells D6** through **J6**.
- Change the formatting to **zero decimal places**, then change column widths as necessary. Cell J6 should display the value $400,002.
- If necessary, select **cells C6** through **J6** as shown in Figure 4.8i. Click and drag the fill handle in **cell J6** to **cell J21** to copy the entire row to the remaining rows in the worksheet.
- Release the mouse. Cell J21 should display the value $2,301,274, corresponding to the future value of a $3,000 investment for 40 years at 12 percent. Change column widths as necessary.
- Click in **cell C6**, then press the **right arrow** to move from one cell to the next in this row to see how the cell formulas change to reflect the mixed references. Return to cell C6, then press the **down arrow** to view the cell formulas for the other cells in this column.
- Save the workbook.

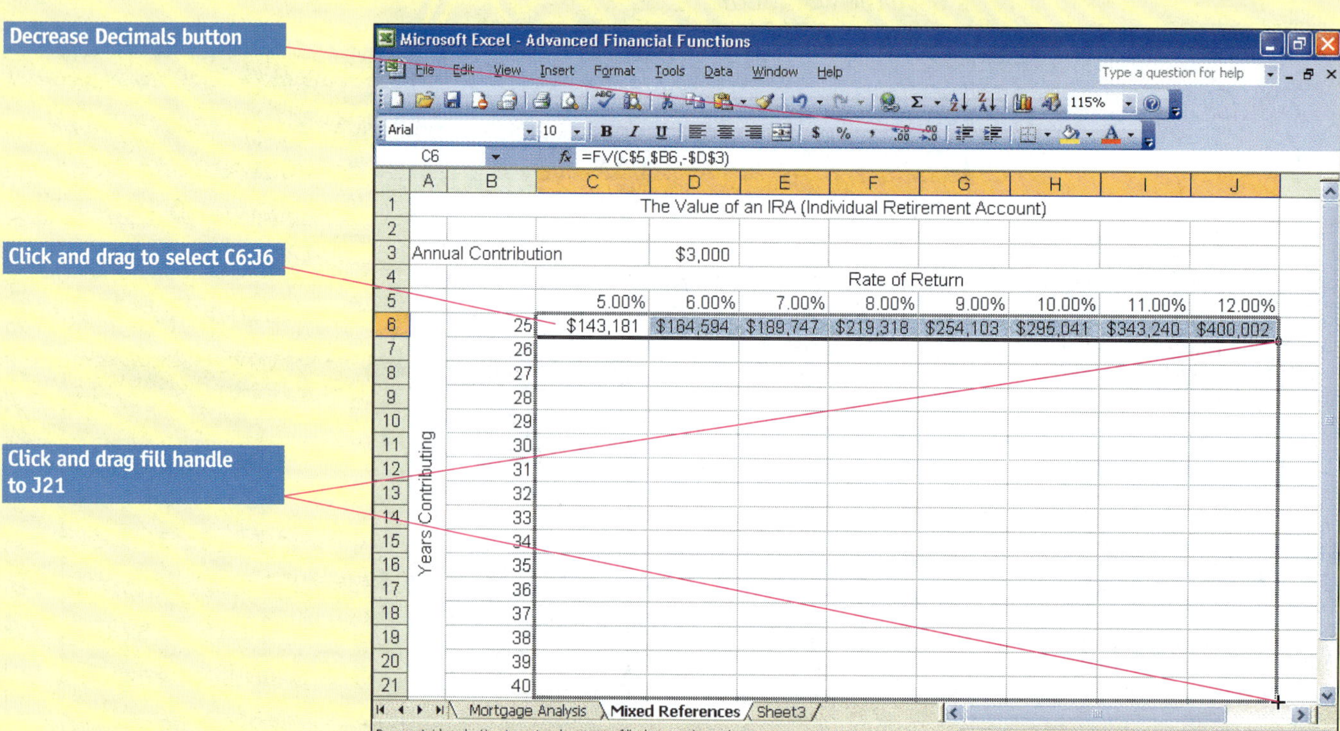

(i) Copy the Formula (step 9)

FIGURE 4.8 Hands-on Exercise 2 (*continued*)

THE ARRANGE WINDOWS COMMAND

It can be advantageous to view multiple worksheets within a workbook at the same time, with each worksheet in its own window. Pull down the Window menu and click the New Window command to open another window. Pull down the Window menu a second time, click the Arrange command, then click the option button that indicates how you want to display the windows; e.g., horizontal to display the windows one on top of another. Each window provides a different view of the workbook. Click in either window, then click the worksheet tab you want to display.

Step 10: The Finishing Touches

- Check that the numbers in your worksheet match those in Figure 4.8j. Make corrections as necessary.
- Use the **Page Setup command** to include gridlines and row and column headings. Use landscape formatting if necessary.
- Print the worksheet two ways, once with the displayed values and once with the cell contents.
- Add a cover sheet, then submit all five pages (the cover sheet, the displayed values and cell formulas for the mortgage analysis from step 5, and the displayed values and cell formulas from this step) to your instructor as proof that you completed this exercise.
- Exit Excel if you do not want to continue with the next exercise at this time.

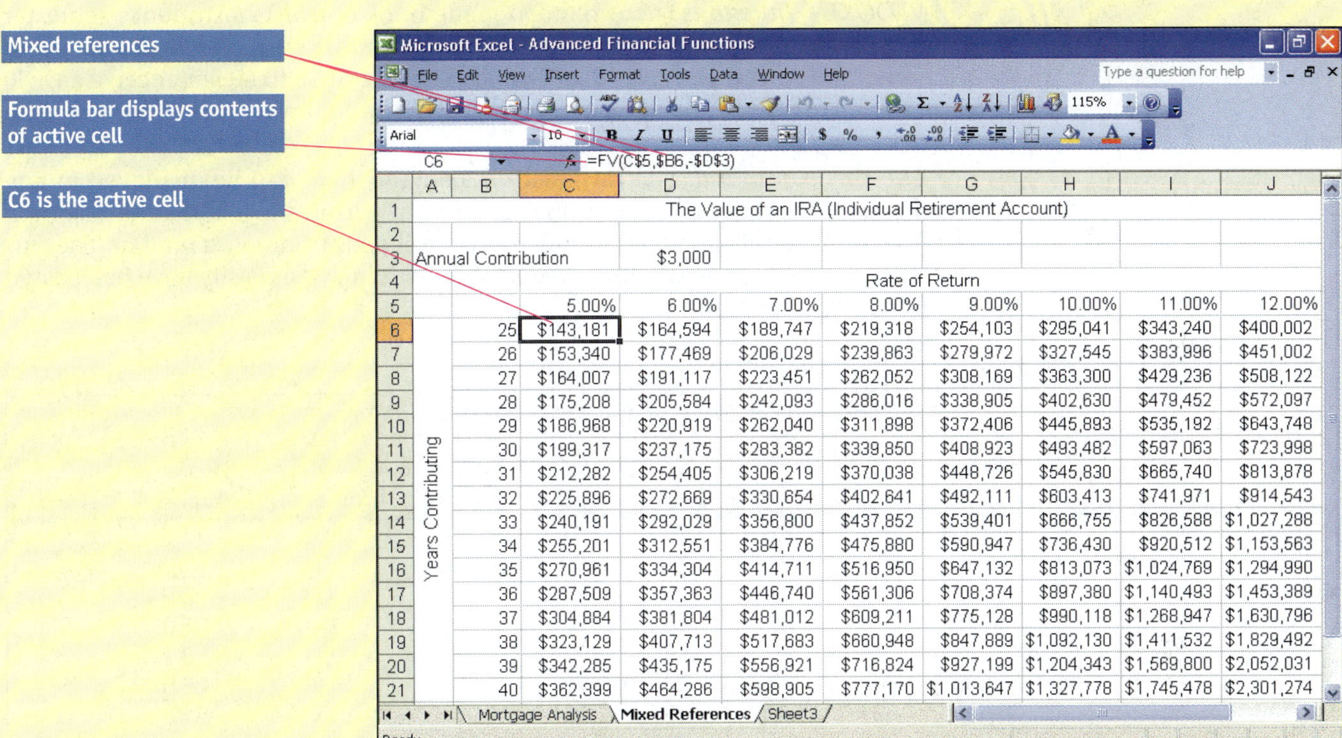

	A	B	C	D	E	F	G	H	I	J
1				The Value of an IRA (Individual Retirement Account)						
2										
3	Annual Contribution			$3,000						
4						Rate of Return				
5			5.00%	6.00%	7.00%	8.00%	9.00%	10.00%	11.00%	12.00%
6	Years Contributing	25	$143,181	$164,594	$189,747	$219,318	$254,103	$295,041	$343,240	$400,002
7		26	$153,340	$177,469	$206,029	$239,863	$279,972	$327,545	$383,996	$451,002
8		27	$164,007	$191,117	$223,451	$262,052	$308,169	$363,300	$429,236	$508,122
9		28	$175,208	$205,584	$242,093	$286,016	$338,905	$402,630	$479,452	$572,097
10		29	$186,968	$220,919	$262,040	$311,898	$372,406	$445,893	$535,192	$643,748
11		30	$199,317	$237,175	$283,382	$339,850	$408,923	$493,482	$597,063	$723,998
12		31	$212,282	$254,405	$306,219	$370,038	$448,726	$545,830	$665,740	$813,878
13		32	$225,896	$272,669	$330,654	$402,641	$492,111	$603,413	$741,971	$914,543
14		33	$240,191	$292,029	$356,800	$437,852	$539,401	$666,755	$826,588	$1,027,288
15		34	$255,201	$312,551	$384,776	$475,880	$590,947	$736,430	$920,512	$1,153,563
16		35	$270,961	$334,304	$414,711	$516,950	$647,132	$813,073	$1,024,769	$1,294,990
17		36	$287,509	$357,363	$446,740	$561,306	$708,374	$897,380	$1,140,493	$1,453,389
18		37	$304,884	$381,804	$481,012	$609,211	$775,128	$990,118	$1,268,947	$1,630,796
19		38	$323,129	$407,713	$517,683	$660,948	$847,889	$1,092,130	$1,411,532	$1,829,492
20		39	$342,285	$435,175	$556,921	$716,824	$927,199	$1,204,343	$1,569,800	$2,052,031
21		40	$362,399	$464,286	$598,905	$777,170	$1,013,647	$1,327,778	$1,745,478	$2,301,274

(j) The Finishing Touches (step 10)

FIGURE 4.8 Hands-on Exercise 2 (*continued*)

START SAVING EARLY

The longer you invest, the more time that compound interest has to work its magic. Investing $3,000 for 40 years at 7%, for example, yields a future value of $598,905. Delay for five years—that is, invest for 35 years rather than 40—and the amount goes down to $414,711. Put another way—Start your IRA at age 25, and 40 years later you will have accumulated more than half a million dollars. Wait until age 30, and you wind up with significantly less. The out-of-pocket difference is only $15,000 ($3,000 a year for five years), but the end result at retirement is more than $180,000. Too many people try to time the stock market, which is impossible. It is the time *in* the market that matters.

THE GRADE BOOK REVISITED

Financial functions are only one of several categories of functions that are included in Excel. Our next example presents an expanded version of the professor's grade book. It introduces several new functions and shows how those functions can aid in the professor's determination of a student's grade. The expanded grade book is shown in Figure 4.9. Consider:

Statistical functions: The AVERAGE, MAX, and MIN functions are used to compute the statistics on each test for the class as a whole. The range on each test is computed by subtracting the minimum value from the maximum value.

IF function: The IF function conditionally adds a homework bonus of three points to the semester average, prior to determining the letter grade. The bonus is awarded to those students whose homework is "OK." Students whose homework is not "OK" do not receive the bonus.

VLOOKUP function: The expanded grade book converts a student's semester average to a letter grade, in accordance with the table shown in the lower-right portion of the worksheet. A student with an average of 60 to 69 will receive a D, 70 to 79 a C, 80 to 89 a B, and 90 or higher an A. Any student with an average less than 60 receives an F.

The Sort command: The rows within a spreadsheet can be displayed in any sequence by clicking on the appropriate column within the list of students, then clicking the Ascending or Descending sort button on the Standard toolbar. The students in Figure 4.9 are listed alphabetically, but could just as easily have been listed by Social Security number.

	A	B	C	D	E	F	G	H	I	J
1	**Professor's Grade Book - Final Semester Averages**									
2										
3	**Name**	**Soc Sec Num**	**Test 1**	**Test 2**	**Test 3**	**Test 4**	**Test Average**	**Homework**	**Semester Average**	**Grade**
4	Adams, John	111-22-3333	80	71	70	84	77.8	Poor	77.8	C
5	Barber, Maryann	444-55-6666	96	98	97	90	94.2	OK	97.2	A
6	Boone, Dan	777-88-9999	78	81	70	78	77.0	OK	80.0	B
7	Borow, Jeff	123-45-6789	65	65	65	60	63.0	OK	66.0	D
8	Brown, James	999-99-9999	92	95	79	80	85.2	OK	88.2	B
9	Carson, Kit	888-88-8888	90	90	90	70	82.0	OK	85.0	B
10	Coulter, Sara	100-00-0000	60	50	40	79	61.6	OK	64.6	D
11	Fegin, Richard	222-22-2222	75	70	65	95	80.0	OK	83.0	B
12	Ford, Judd	200-00-0000	90	90	80	90	88.0	Poor	88.0	B
13	Glassman, Kris	444-44-4444	82	78	62	77	75.2	OK	78.2	C
14	Goodman, Neil	555-55-5555	92	88	65	78	80.2	OK	83.2	B
15	Milgrom, Marion	666-66-6666	94	92	86	84	88.0	OK	91.0	A
16	Moldof, Adam	300-00-0000	92	78	65	82	79.8	Poor	79.8	C
17	Smith, Adam	777-77-7777	60	50	65	80	67.0	Poor	67.0	D
18										
19	**Average**		81.9	78.3	71.4	80.5	**HW Bonus**	3	**Grading Criteria**	
20	**Highest Grade**		96.0	98.0	97.0	95.0			0	F
21	**Lowest Grade**		60.0	50.0	40.0	60.0			60	D
22	**Range**		36.0	48.0	57.0	35.0			70	C
23									80	B
24	**Exam Weights**		**20%**	**20%**	**20%**	**40%**			90	A

Statistical functions determine average, highest, and lowest grades on tests

IF function determines Semester Average

VLOOKUP Function determines Grade

FIGURE 4.9 The Expanded Grade Book

Statistical Functions

The ***MAX***, ***MIN***, and ***AVERAGE functions*** return the highest, lowest, and average values, respectively, from an argument list. The list may include individual cell references, ranges, numeric values, functions, or mathematical expressions (formulas). The ***statistical functions*** are illustrated in the worksheet of Figure 4.10.

The first example, =AVERAGE(A1:A3), computes the average for cells A1 through A3 by adding the values in the indicated range (70, 80, and 90), then dividing the result by three, to obtain an average of 80. Additional arguments in the form of values and/or cell addresses can be specified within the parentheses; for example, the function =AVERAGE(A1:A3,200), computes the average of cells A1, A2, and A3, and the number 200.

Cells that are empty or cells that contain text values are *not* included in the computation. Thus since cell A4 is empty, the function =AVERAGE(A1:A4) will also return an average value of 80 (240/3). In similar fashion, the function =AVERAGE(A1:A3,A5) includes only three values in its computation (cells A1, A2, and A3) because the text entry in cell A5 is excluded. The results of the MIN and MAX functions are obtained in a comparable way, as indicated in Figure 4.10. Empty cells and text entries are not included in the computation.

The COUNT and COUNTA functions each tally the number of entries in the argument list and are subtly different. The ***COUNT function*** returns the number of cells containing a numeric entry, including formulas that evaluate to numeric results. The ***COUNTA function*** includes cells with text as well as numeric values. The functions =COUNT(A1:A3) and =COUNTA(A1:A3) both return a value of 3 as do the two functions =COUNT(A1:A4) and =COUNTA(A1:A4). (Cell A4 is empty and is excluded from the latter computations.) The function =COUNT(A1:A3,A5) also returns a value of 3 because it does not include the text entry in cell A5. However, the function =COUNTA(A1:A3,A5) returns a value of 4 because it includes the text entry in cell A5.

Empty and/or text values are not included in the computation (AVERAGE)

Empty and/or text values are not included in the computation (COUNT)

Empty cells are not included in the computation (COUNTA)

Text values are included in the computation (COUNTA)

Function	Value
=AVERAGE(A1:A3)	80
=AVERAGE(A1:A3,200)	110
=AVERAGE(A1:A4)	80
=AVERAGE(A1:A3,A5)	80
=MAX(A1:A3)	90
=MAX(A1:A3,200)	200
=MAX(A1:A4)	90
=MAX(A1:A3,A5)	90
=MIN(A1:A3)	70
=MIN(A1:A3,200)	70
=MIN(A1:A4)	70
=MIN(A1:A3,A5)	70
=COUNT(A1:A3)	3
=COUNT(A1:A3,200)	4
=COUNT(A1:A4)	3
=COUNT(A1:A3,A5)	3
=COUNTA(A1:A3)	3
=COUNTA(A1:A3,200)	4
=COUNTA(A1:A4)	3
=COUNTA(A1:A3,A5)	4

(a) Illustrative Functions

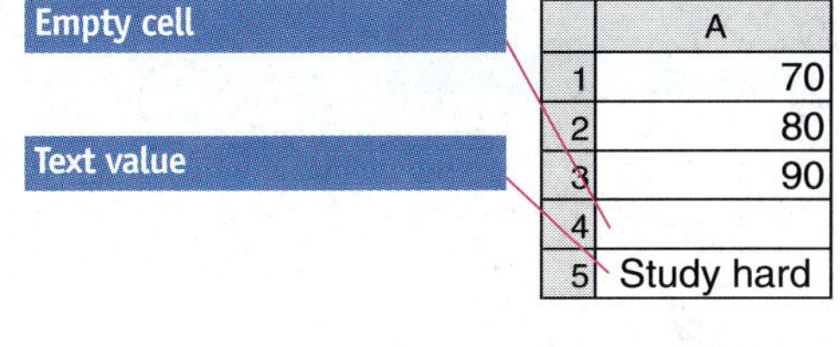

(b) The Spreadsheet

FIGURE 4.10 Statistical Functions with a Text Entry

Arithmetic Expressions versus Functions

Many worksheet calculations, such as an average or a sum, can be performed in two ways. You can enter a formula such as =(A1+A2+A3)/3, or you can use the equivalent function =AVERAGE(A1:A3). *The use of functions is generally preferable* as shown in Figure 4.11.

The two worksheets in Figure 4.11a may appear equivalent, but the ***SUM function*** is superior to the arithmetic expression. This is true despite the fact that the entries in cell A5 of both worksheets return a value of 100.

Consider what happens if a new row is inserted between existing rows 2 and 3, with the entry in the new cell equal to 25 as shown in Figure 4.11b. The SUM function adjusts automatically to include the new value (returning a sum of 125) because the SUM function was defined originally for the cell range *A1 through A4*. The new row is inserted within these cells, moving the entry in cell A4 to cell A5, and changing the range to include cell A5.

No such accommodation is made in the arithmetic expression, which was defined to include four *specific* cells rather than a range of cells. The addition of the new row modifies the cell references (since the values in cells A3 and A4 have been moved to cells A4 and A5), and does not include the new row in the adjusted expression.

Similar reasoning holds for deleting a row. Figure 4.11c deletes row 2 from the *original* worksheets, which moves the entry in cell A4 to cell A3. The SUM function adjusts automatically to =SUM(A1:A3) and returns the value 80. The formula, however, returns an error (to indicate an illegal cell reference) because it is still attempting to add the entries in four cells, one of which no longer exists. In summary, a function expands and contracts to adjust for insertions or deletions, and should be used wherever possible.

Function

	A
1	10
2	20
3	30
4	40
5	=SUM(A1:A4)

Formula

	A
1	10
2	20
3	30
4	40
5	=A1+A2+A3+A4

(a) Spreadsheets as Initially Entered

Range is automatically adjusted for inserted row

	A
1	10
2	20
3	25
4	30
5	40
6	=SUM(A1:A5)

Cell references adjust to follow moved entries but new row is not included

	A
1	10
2	20
3	25
4	30
5	40
6	=A1+A2+A4+A5

(b) Spreadsheets after the Addition of a New Row

Range is automatically adjusted for deleted row

	A
1	10
2	30
3	40
4	=SUM(A1:A3)

#REF! indicates that a referenced cell has been deleted

	A
1	10
2	30
3	40
4	=A1+#REF!+A2+A3

(c) Spreadsheets after the Deletion of a Row

FIGURE 4.11 Arithmetic Expressions versus Functions

IF Function

The ***IF function*** enables decision making to be implemented within a worksheet. It has three arguments: a condition that is either true or false, the value if the condition is true, and the value if the condition is false. Consider:

=IF(condition,value-if-true,value-if-false)

- Value returned for a false condition
- Value returned for a true condition
- Condition is either true or false

The IF function returns either the second or third argument, depending on the result of the condition; that is, if the condition is true, the function returns the second argument. If the condition is false, the function returns the third argument.

The condition includes one of the six ***relational operators*** in Figure 4.12a. The IF function is illustrated in the worksheet in Figure 4.12b, which is used to create the examples in Figure 4.12c. The arguments may be numeric (1000 or 2000), a cell reference to display the contents of the specific cell (B1 or B2), a formula (=B1+10 or =B1–10), a function (MAX(B1:B2) or MIN(B1:B2)), or a text entry enclosed in quotation marks ("Go" or "Hold").

Operator	Description
=	Equal to
<>	Not equal to
<	Less than
>	Greater than
<=	Less than or equal to
>=	Greater than or equal to

(a) Relational Operators

	A	B	C
1	10	15	April
2	10	30	May

(b) The Spreadsheet

IF Function	Evaluation	Result
=IF(A1=A2,1000,2000)	10 is equal to 10: TRUE	1000
=IF(A1<>A2,1000,2000)	10 is not equal to 10: FALSE	2000
=IF(A1<>A2,B1,B2)	10 is not equal to 10:FALSE	30
=IF(A1<B2,MAX(B1:B2),MIN(B1:B2)	10 is less than 30: TRUE	30
=IF(A1<A2,B1+10,B1-10)	10 is less than 10:FALSE	5
=IF(A1=A2,C1,C2)	10 is equal to 10: TRUE	April
=IF(SUM(A1:A2)>20,"Go","Hold")	10+10 is greater than 20:FALSE	Hold

(c) Examples

FIGURE 4.12 The IF Function

The IF function is used in the grade book of Figure 4.9 to award a bonus for homework. Students whose homework is "OK" receive the bonus, whereas other students do not. The IF function to implement this logic for the first student is:

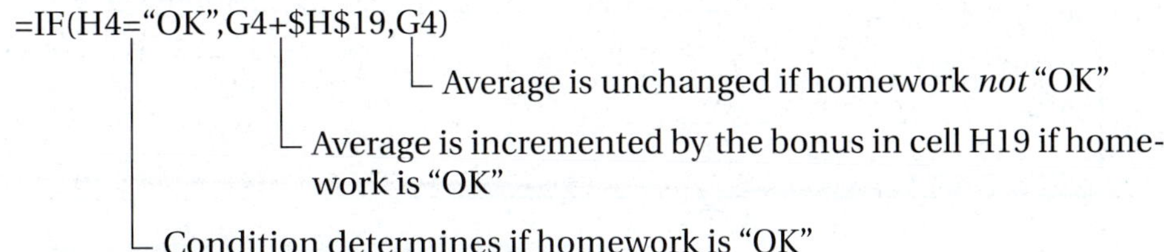

The IF function compares the value in cell H4 (the homework grade) to the literal "OK." If the condition is true (the homework is "OK"), the bonus in cell H19 is added to the student's test average in cell G4. If, however, the condition is false (the homework is not "OK"), the average is unchanged.

VLOOKUP Function

Consider, for a moment, how the professor assigns letter grades to students at the end of the semester. He or she computes a test average for each student and conditionally awards the bonus for homework. The professor then determines a letter grade according to a predetermined scale; for example, 90 or above is an A, 80 to 89 is a B, and so on.

The ***VLOOKUP*** (vertical lookup) ***function*** duplicates this process within a worksheet by assigning an entry to a cell based on a numeric value contained in another cell. The ***HLOOKUP*** (horizontal lookup) ***function*** is similar in concept except that the table is arranged horizontally. In other words, just as the professor knows where on the grading scale a student's numerical average will fall, the VLOOKUP function determines where within a specified table (the grading criteria) a numeric value (a student's average) is found, and retrieves the corresponding entry (the letter grade).

The VLOOKUP function requires three arguments: the value to look up, the range of cells containing the table in which the value is to be looked up, and the column number within the table that contains the result. These concepts are illustrated in Figure 4.13, which was taken from the expanded grade book in Figure 4.9. The table in Figure 4.13 extends over two columns (I and J), and five rows (20 through 24); that is, the table is located in the range I20:J24. The ***breakpoints*** or matching values (the lowest numeric value for each grade) are contained in column **I** (the first column in the table) and are in ascending order. The corresponding letter grades are found in column **J**.

The VLOOKUP function in cell J4 determines the letter grade (for John Adams) based on the computed average in cell I4. Consider:

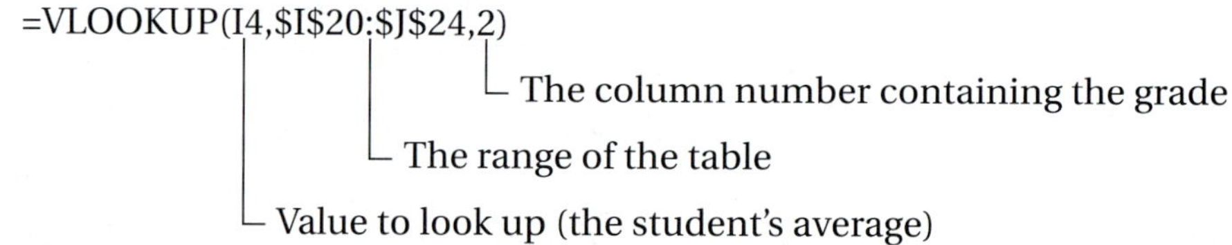

The first argument is the value to look up, which in this example is Adams's computed average, found in cell I4. A relative reference is used so that the address will adjust when the formula is copied to the other rows in the worksheet.

	A	. . .	G	H	I	J
1	Professor's Grade Book - Final Semester Averages					
2						
3	**Name**		**Test Average**	**Homework**	**Semester Average**	**Grade**
4	Adams, John		77.8	Poor		
.	.	.	.	.	.	.
19	**Average**		**HW Bonus**	3	**Grading Criteria**	
20	**Highest Grade**				0	F
21	**Lowest Grade**				60	D
22	**Range**				70	C
23					80	B
24	**Exam Weights**				90	A

=VLOOKUP(I4,$I$20:$J$24,2)

Breakpoints (in ascending order)

Grades are in column 2 of table

FIGURE 4.13 Table Lookup Function

WORKING WITH LARGE SPREADSHEETS

A large worksheet, such as the extended grade book, can seldom be seen on the monitor in its entirety. It's necessary, therefore, to learn how to view the distant parts of a worksheet, to keep certain parts of the worksheet in constant view, and/or to hide selected rows and columns. These concepts are illustrated in Figure 4.14. Figure 4.14a displays the initial worksheet, with cell A1 selected as the active cell, so that you see the upper-left portion of the worksheet, rows 1 through 20 inclusive, and columns A through I inclusive. You cannot see the semester grades in column J, nor can you see the class averages and other statistics that begin in row 21.

Clicking the right arrow on the horizontal scroll bar (or pressing the right arrow key when the active cell is already in the rightmost column of the screen) causes the entire screen to move one column to the right. In similar fashion, clicking the down arrow in the vertical scroll bar (or pressing the down arrow key when the active cell is in the bottom row of the screen) causes the entire screen to move down one row. This is known as ***scrolling*** and it comes about automatically as the active cell is changed as you work with the worksheet.

Freezing Panes

Scrolling brings the distant portions of a worksheet into view, but it also moves the headings for existing rows and/or columns off the screen. You can, however, retain the headings by freezing panes as shown in Figure 4.14b. The letter grades and the grading criteria are visible as in the previous figure, but so too are the names at the left of the worksheet and the column headings at the top of the worksheet.

Look closely at Figure 4.14b and you will see column B (containing the Social Security numbers) is missing, as are rows 4 through 7 (the first four students). You will also notice a horizontal line under row 3 and a vertical line after column A, to indicate that these rows and columns have been frozen. This is accomplished through the ***Freeze Panes command*** that always displays the desired row or column headings (column A and rows 1, 2, and 3 in this example) regardless of the scrolling in effect. The rows and/or columns that are frozen are the ones above and to the left of the active cell when the command is issued. The ***Unfreeze Panes command*** returns to normal scrolling.

Hiding Rows and Columns

Figure 4.14c illustrates the ability to hide rows and/or columns in a worksheet. We have hidden columns C through F (inclusive) that contain the results of the individual tests, and rows 19 through 24 that contain the summary statistics. The "missing" rows and columns remain in the workbook but are hidden from view. The cells are not visible in the monitor, nor do they appear when the worksheet is printed. To hide a row or column, click the row or column heading to select the entire row or column, then execute the Hide command from within the Format menu. ***Unhiding cells*** is trickier because you need to select the adjacent rows or columns prior to executing the Unhide command.

Printing a Large Worksheet

The ***Page Break Preview command*** (in the View menu) lets you see and/or modify the page breaks that will occur when the worksheet is printed as shown in Figure 4.14d. The dashed blue line between columns H and I indicates that the worksheet will print on two pages, with columns A to H on page 1 and columns I and J on page 2. The dialog box shows that you adjust (eliminate) the page break by dragging the dashed line to the right.

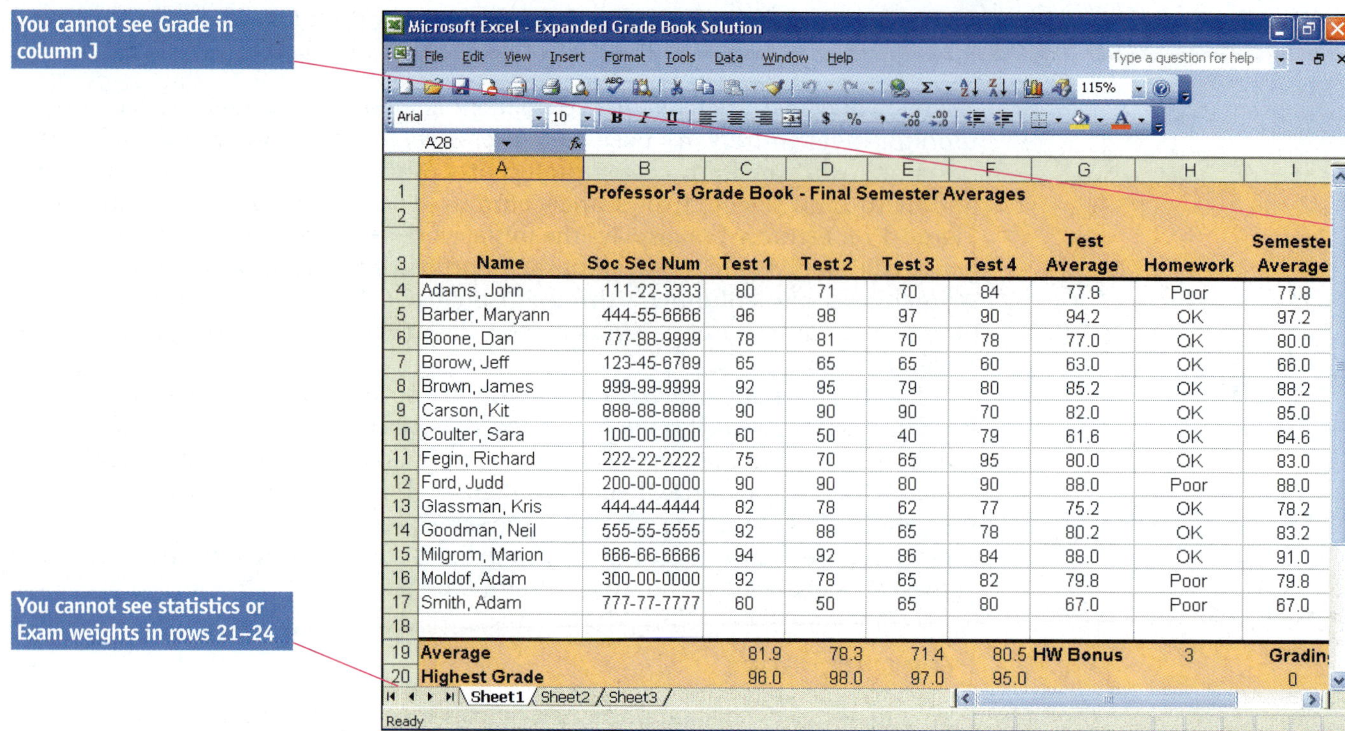

(a) The Grade Book

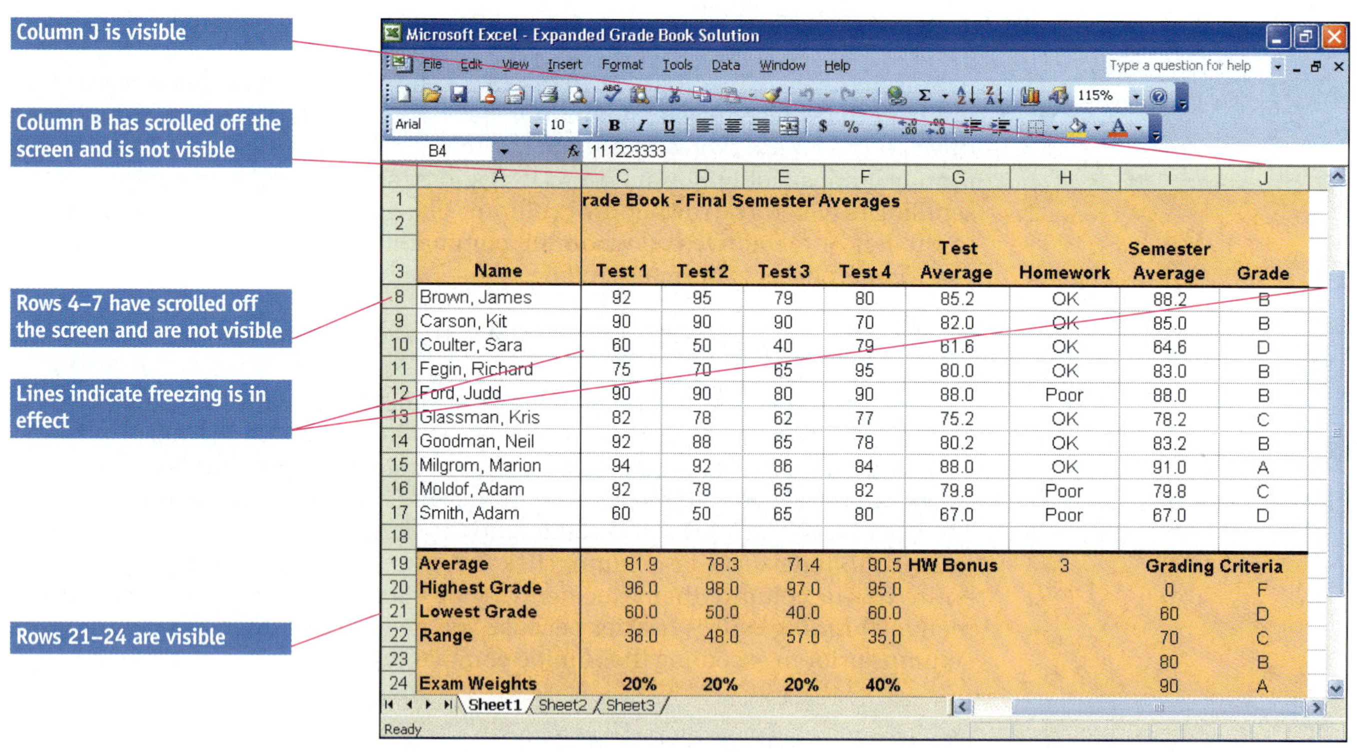

(b) Freezing Panes

FIGURE 4.14 Working with Large Spreadsheets

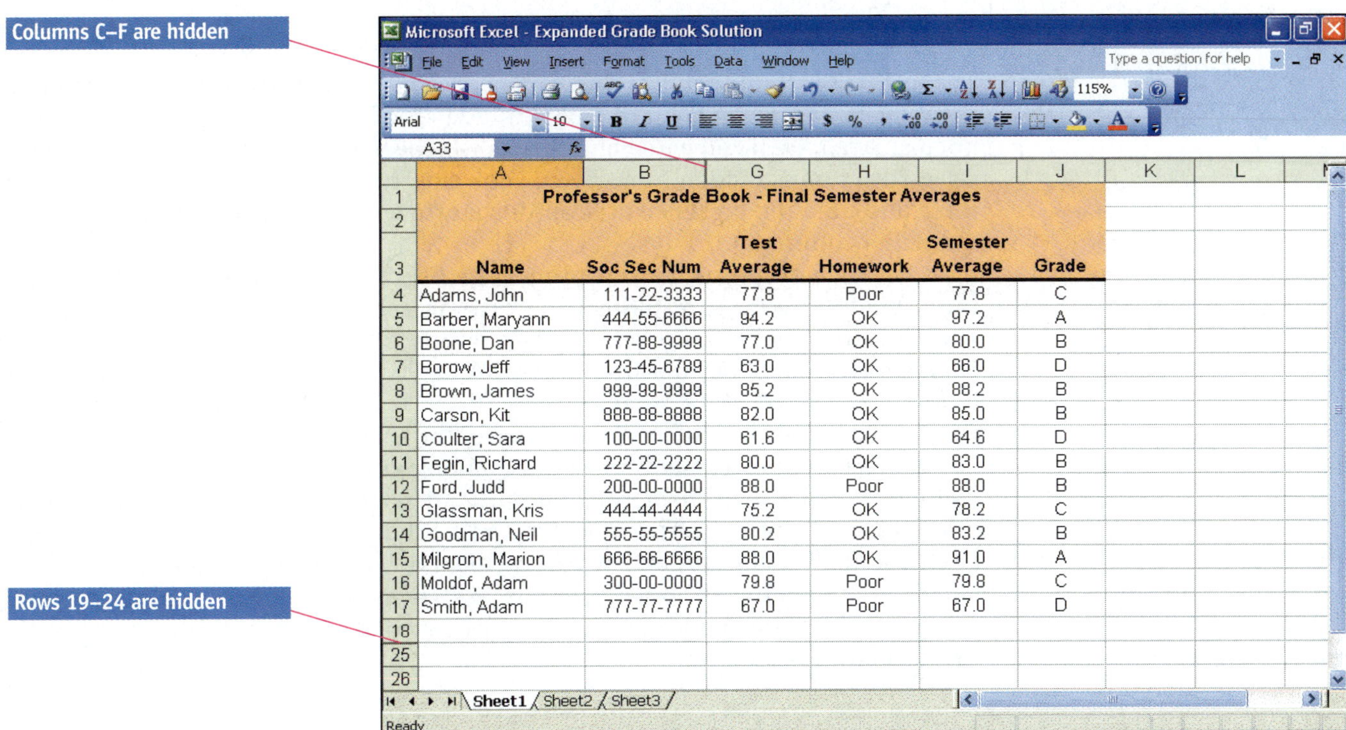

	A	B	G	H	I	J
1	Professor's Grade Book - Final Semester Averages					
2						
3	Name	Soc Sec Num	Test Average	Homework	Semester Average	Grade
4	Adams, John	111-22-3333	77.8	Poor	77.8	C
5	Barber, Maryann	444-55-6666	94.2	OK	97.2	A
6	Boone, Dan	777-88-9999	77.0	OK	80.0	B
7	Borow, Jeff	123-45-6789	63.0	OK	66.0	D
8	Brown, James	999-99-9999	85.2	OK	88.2	B
9	Carson, Kit	888-88-8888	82.0	OK	85.0	B
10	Coulter, Sara	100-00-0000	61.6	OK	64.6	D
11	Fegin, Richard	222-22-2222	80.0	OK	83.0	B
12	Ford, Judd	200-00-0000	88.0	Poor	88.0	B
13	Glassman, Kris	444-44-4444	75.2	OK	78.2	C
14	Goodman, Neil	555-55-5555	80.2	OK	83.2	B
15	Milgrom, Marion	666-66-6666	88.0	OK	91.0	A
16	Moldof, Adam	300-00-0000	79.8	Poor	79.8	C
17	Smith, Adam	777-77-7777	67.0	Poor	67.0	D
18						
25						
26						

(c) Hiding Rows and Columns

Dashed blue line indicates position of page break; click and drag line to change location of page break

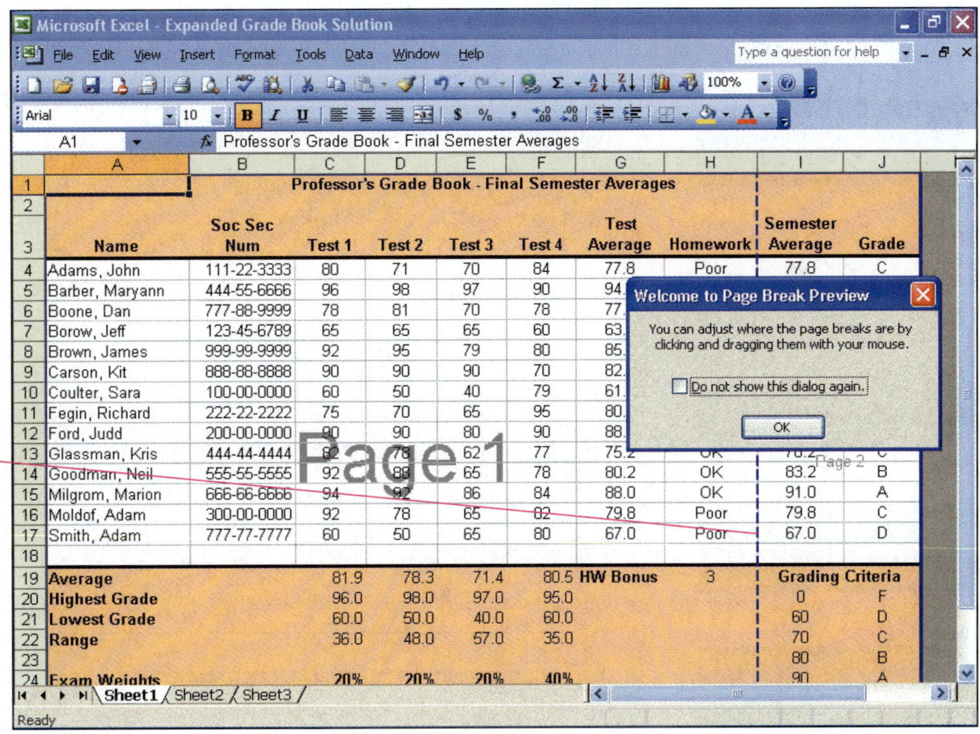

	A	B	C	D	E	F	G	H	I	J
1	Professor's Grade Book - Final Semester Averages									
2										
3	Name	Soc Sec Num	Test 1	Test 2	Test 3	Test 4	Test Average	Homework	Semester Average	Grade
4	Adams, John	111-22-3333	80	71	70	84	77.8	Poor	77.8	C
5	Barber, Maryann	444-55-6666	96	98	97	90	94.			
6	Boone, Dan	777-88-9999	78	81	70	78	77.			
7	Borow, Jeff	123-45-6789	65	65	65	60	63.			
8	Brown, James	999-99-9999	92	95	79	80	85.			
9	Carson, Kit	888-88-8888	90	90	90	70	82.			
10	Coulter, Sara	100-00-0000	60	50	40	79	61.			
11	Fegin, Richard	222-22-2222	75	70	65	95	80.			
12	Ford, Judd	200-00-0000	80	90	80	90	88.			
13	Glassman, Kris	444-44-4444	82	78	62	77	75.2			
14	Goodman, Neil	555-55-5555	92	88	65	78	80.2	OK	83.2	B
15	Milgrom, Marion	666-66-6666	94	92	86	84	88.0	OK	91.0	A
16	Moldof, Adam	300-00-0000	92	78	65	82	79.8	Poor	79.8	C
17	Smith, Adam	777-77-7777	60	50	65	80	67.0	Poor	67.0	D
18										
19	Average		81.9	78.3	71.4	80.5	HW Bonus	3	Grading Criteria	
20	Highest Grade		96.0	98.0	97.0	95.0			0	F
21	Lowest Grade		60.0	50.0	40.0	60.0			60	D
22	Range		36.0	48.0	57.0	35.0			70	C
23									80	B
24	Exam Weights		20%	20%	20%	40%			90	A

(d) Page Break Preview

FIGURE 4.14 Working with Large Spreadsheets (*continued*)

AutoFilter Command

The ***AutoFilter command*** lets you display a selected set of students (rows) within a worksheet as shown in Figure 4.15. The hidden rows are *not* deleted, but are simply not displayed. We begin with Figure 4.15a, which shows the list of all students (with selected columns hidden from view). Look closely at the column headings in row three and note the presence of drop-down arrows that appear in response to the AutoFilter command.

Clicking a drop-down arrow produces a list of the unique values for that column, enabling you to establish the criteria-selected records. To display the students with poor homework, for example, click the drop-down arrow for Homework, then click Poor from the resulting list. Figure 4.15b shows three students in rows 4, 12, and 17 that satisfy the filter. The remaining students are still in the worksheet but are not shown because of the selection criterion.

A filter condition can be imposed on multiple columns as shown in Figure 4.15c. As indicated, the worksheet in Figure 4.15b displays only the students with poor homework. Clicking the arrow next to Grade, then clicking "B", will filter the list further to display the students who received a "B" *and* who have poor homework. Only one student meets both conditions, as shown in Figure 4.15c. The drop-down arrows next to Homework and Grade are displayed in blue to indicate that a filter is in effect for these columns.

Drop-down arrows indicate AutoFilter is on

Click Poor to display only those students with Poor homework grades

	A	G	H	I	J	K
3	Name	Test Average	Homework	Semester Averag	Grade	
4	Adams, John	77.8		77.8	C	
5	Barber, Maryann	94.2		97.2	A	
6	Boone, Dan	77.0		80.0	B	
7	Borow, Jeff	63.0		66.0	D	
8	Brown, James	85.2		88.2	B	
9	Carson, Kit	82.0		85.0	B	
10	Coulter, Sara	61.6	OK	64.6	D	
11	Fegin, Richard	80.0	OK	83.0	B	
12	Ford, Judd	88.0	Poor	88.0	B	
13	Glassman, Kris	75.2	OK	78.2	C	
14	Goodman, Neil	80.2	OK	83.2	B	
15	Milgrom, Marion	88.0	OK	91.0	A	
16	Moldof, Adam	79.8	Poor	79.8	C	
17	Smith, Adam	67.0	Poor	67.0	D	

Sort Ascending
Sort Descending
(All)
(Top 10...)
(Custom...)
OK
Poor

(a) Unfiltered List

Blue arrow indicates filter is in effect for column H

Click B to further limit display to those who have a B Grade and Poor homework

	A	G	H	I	J	K
3	Name	Test Average	Homework	Semester Averag	Grade	
4	Adams, John	77.8	Poor	77.8		
12	Ford, Judd	88.0	Poor	88.0		
16	Moldof, Adam	79.8	Poor	79.8		
17	Smith, Adam	67.0	Poor	67.0		
18						
34						
35						

Sort Ascending
Sort Descending
(All)
(Top 10...)
(Custom...)
B
C
D

(b) Filtered List (students with poor homework)

Blue arrows indicate filter is in effect for 2 columns, H and J

Only 1 student has both a B and Poor homework

	A	G	H	I	J	K
3	Name	Test Average	Homework	Semester Averag	Grade	
12	Ford, Judd	88.0	Poor	88.0	B	

(c) Imposing a Second Condition

FIGURE 4.15 The AutoFilter Command

3 The Expanded Grade Book

Objective To develop the expanded grade book; to use statistical (AVERAGE, MAX, and MIN) and logical (IF and VLOOKUP) functions; to demonstrate scrolling and the Freeze Panes command. Use Figure 4.16 as a guide.

Step 1: The Fill Handle

- Open the **Expanded Grade Book** in the **Exploring Excel folder**. Click in **cell C3**, the cell containing the label Test 1 as shown in Figure 4.16a.
- Click and drag the **fill handle** over **cells D3, E3,** and **F3** (a ScreenTip shows the projected result in cell F3), then release the mouse. Cells D3, E3, and F3 contain the labels Test 2, Test 3, and Test 4, respectively.
- Save the workbook as **Expanded Grade Book Solution** so that you can always return to the original workbook if necessary.

Click in C3

Click and drag fill handle to F3

ScreenTip shows projected result in F4

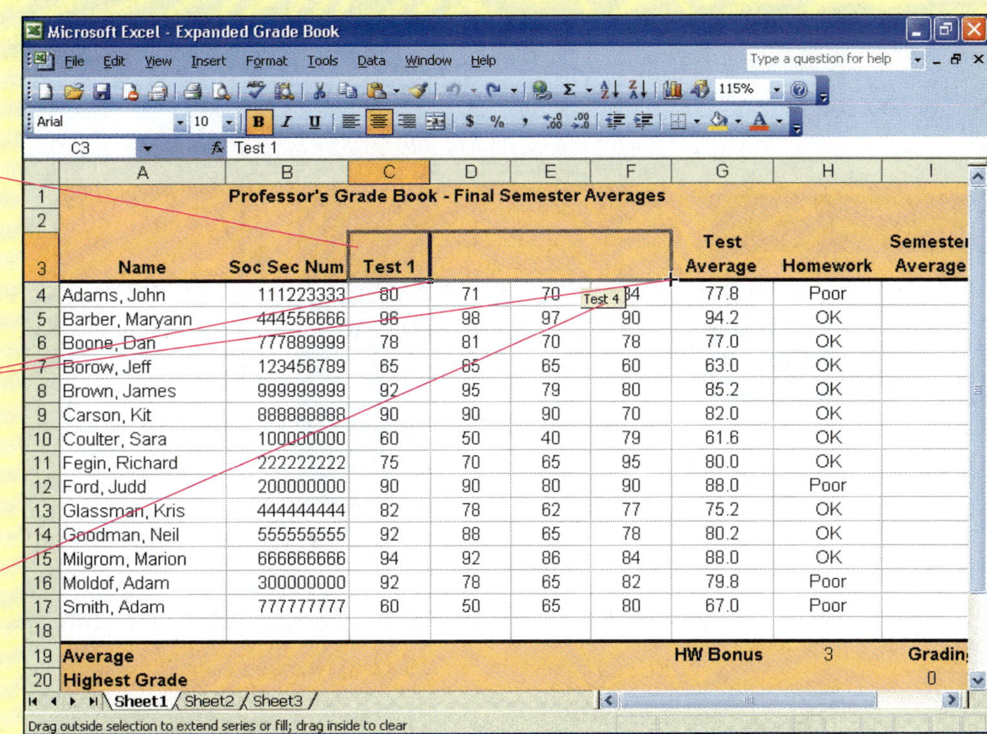

	A	B	C	D	E	F	G	H	I
1	Professor's Grade Book - Final Semester Averages								
2									
3	Name	Soc Sec Num	Test 1				Test Average	Homework	Semester Average
4	Adams, John	111223333	80	71	70	84	77.8	Poor	
5	Barber, Maryann	444556666	96	98	97	90	94.2	OK	
6	Boone, Dan	777889999	78	81	70	78	77.0	OK	
7	Borow, Jeff	123456789	65	65	65	60	63.0	OK	
8	Brown, James	999999999	92	95	79	80	85.2	OK	
9	Carson, Kit	888888888	90	90	90	70	82.0	OK	
10	Coulter, Sara	100000000	60	50	40	79	61.6	OK	
11	Fegin, Richard	222222222	75	70	65	95	80.0	OK	
12	Ford, Judd	200000000	90	90	80	90	88.0	Poor	
13	Glassman, Kris	444444444	82	78	62	77	75.2	OK	
14	Goodman, Neil	555555555	92	88	65	78	80.2	OK	
15	Milgrom, Marion	666666666	94	92	86	84	88.0	OK	
16	Moldof, Adam	300000000	92	78	65	82	79.8	Poor	
17	Smith, Adam	777777777	60	50	65	80	67.0	Poor	
18									
19	Average						HW Bonus	3	Gradin
20	Highest Grade								0

(a) The Fill Handle (step 1)

FIGURE 4.16 Hands-on Exercise 3

THE AUTOFILL CAPABILITY

The AutoFill capability is the fastest way to enter certain series into contiguous cells. Enter the starting value(s) in a series, then drag the fill handle to the adjacent cells. Excel completes the series based on the initial value. Type January (or Jan) or Monday (or Mon) then drag the fill handle in the direction you want to fill. Excel will enter the appropriate months or days of the week, respectively. You can also type text followed by a number, such as Product 1 or Quarter 1, then use the fill handle to extend the series.

Step 2: Format the Social Security Numbers

- Click and drag to select **cells B4** through **B17**, the cells containing the unformatted Social Security numbers.
- Point to the selected cells and click the **right mouse button** to display a shortcut (context-sensitive) menu.
- Click the **Format Cells command**, click the **Number tab**, then click **Special** in the Category list box as shown in Figure 4.16b.
- Click **Social Security Number** in the Type box, then click **OK** to accept the formatting and close the Format Cells dialog box. The Social Security numbers are displayed with hyphens.
- Save the workbook.

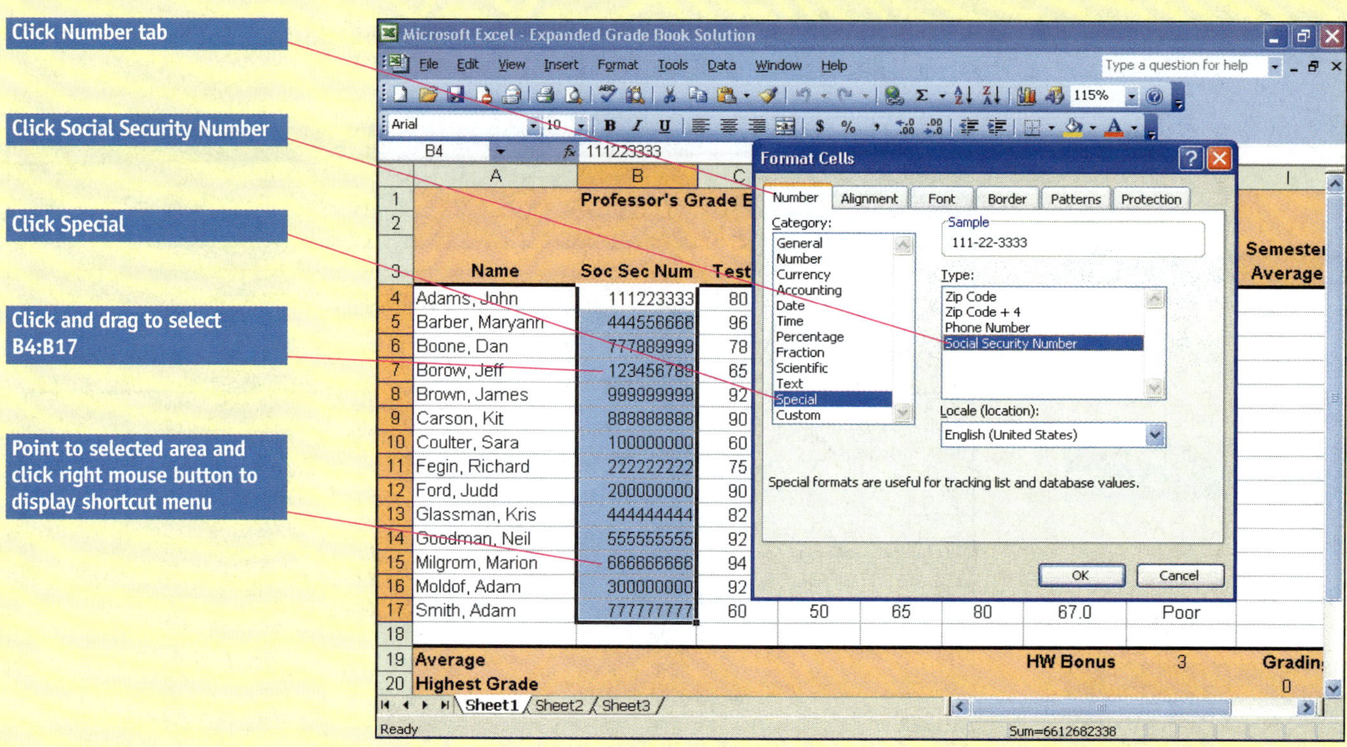

(b) Format the Social Security Numbers (step 2)

FIGURE 4.16 Hands-on Exercise 3 (*continued*)

THE LEFT AND RIGHT FUNCTIONS

A professor may want to post grades, but cannot do so by student name or Social Security number. One can, however, create an "ID number" consisting of the left- or rightmost digits in the Social Security number. Insert a new column into the worksheet, then go to the cell for the first student in this column (e.g., cell C4 if you insert a new column C). Enter the function =LEFT(B4,4) to display the first four digits from cell B4, corresponding to the first four (leftmost) digits in Adams's Social Security Number. You could also enter the function =RIGHT(B4,4) to display the last four (rightmost) digits. Hide the columns containing the names and Social Security numbers, then post the grades. See practice exercise 9 at the end of the chapter.

Step 3: The Freeze Panes Command

- Press **Ctrl+Home** to move to **cell A1**. Click the **right arrow** on the horizontal scroll bar until column A scrolls off the screen. Cell A1 is still the active cell, because scrolling with the mouse does not change the active cell.
- Press **Ctrl+Home**. Press the **right arrow key** until column A scrolls off the screen. The active cell changes as you scroll with the keyboard.
- Press **Ctrl+Home** again, then click in **cell B4**. Pull down the **Window menu**. Click **Freeze Panes** as shown in Figure 4.16c. You will see a line to the right of column A and below row 3.
- Click the **right arrow** on the horizontal scroll bar (or press the **right arrow key**) repeatedly until column J is visible. Note that column A is visible (frozen), but that one or more columns are not shown.
- Click the **down arrow** on the vertical scroll bar (or press the **down arrow key**) repeatedly until row 25 is visible. Note that rows 1 through 3 are visible (frozen), but that one or more rows are not shown.
- Press **Ctrl+Home** to go to **B4**.

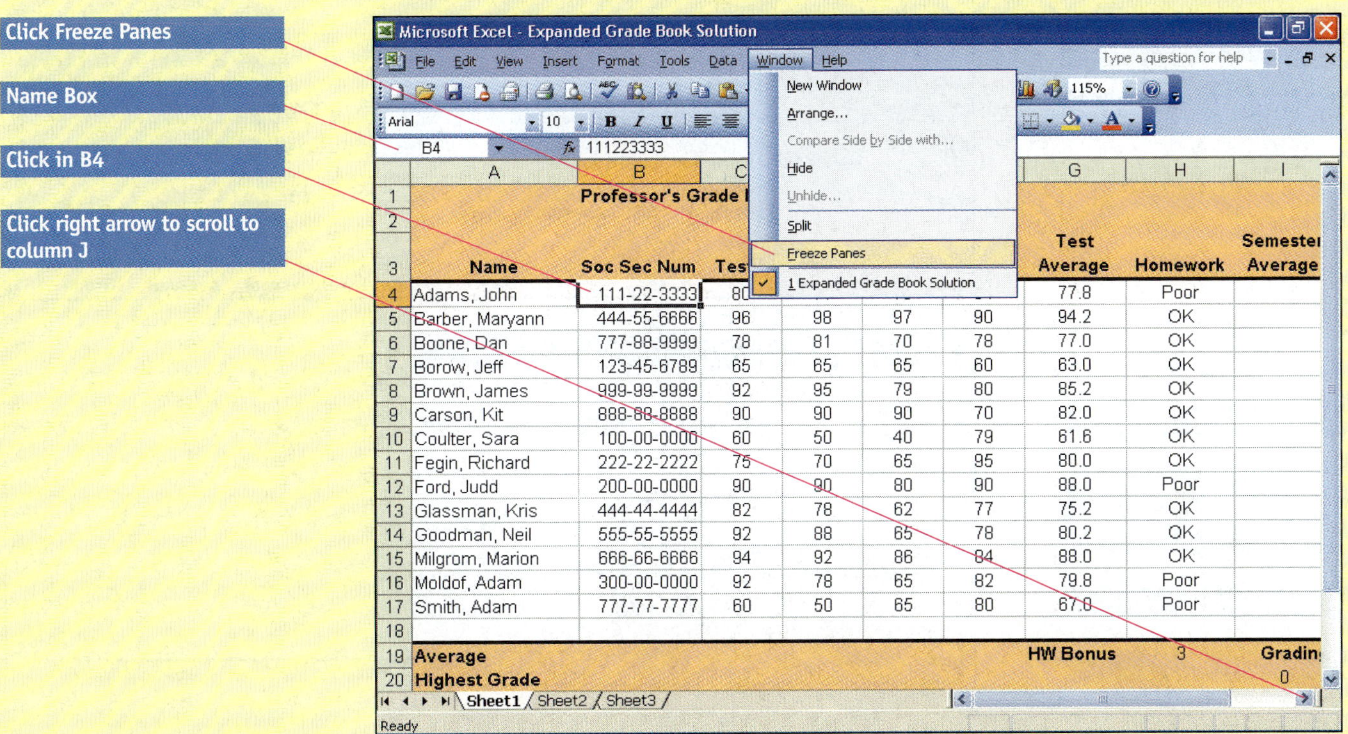

(c) The Freeze Panes Command (step 3)

FIGURE 4.16 Hands-on Exercise 3 (*continued*)

GO TO A SPECIFIC CELL

Ctrl+Home and Ctrl+End will take you to the upper-left and bottom-right cells within a worksheet, but how do you get to a specific cell? One way is to click in the Name box (to the left of the formula bar), enter the cell reference (e.g., K250), and press the Enter key. You can also pull down the Edit menu and click the Go To command (or press the F5 key) to display the Go To dialog box, enter the address of the cell in the Reference text box, then press Enter to go directly to the cell.

Step 4: The IF Function

- Scroll until Column I is visible on the screen. Click in **cell I4**.
- Click the **Insert Function button** on the formula bar. Click the **down arrow** on the Select a Category list box and click **Logical**. Click **IF** in the Select a Function list box, then click **OK** to display the Function Arguments dialog box in Figure 4.16d.
- You can enter the arguments directly, or you can use pointing as follows:
  - Click the **Logical_test** text box. Click **cell H4** in the worksheet. (You may need to click and drag the top border of the dialog box to move it out of the way.) Type **="OK"** to complete the logical test.
  - Click the **Value_if_true** text box. Click **cell G4** in the worksheet, type a **plus sign**, click **cell H19** in the worksheet (scrolling if necessary), and finally press the **F4 key** (see boxed tip) to convert the reference to cell H19 to an absolute reference ($H$19).
  - Click the **Value_if_false** text box. Click **cell G4** in the worksheet.
- Check that the dialog box on your worksheet matches the one in Figure 4.16d. Click **OK** to insert the function into your worksheet.
- Save the workbook.

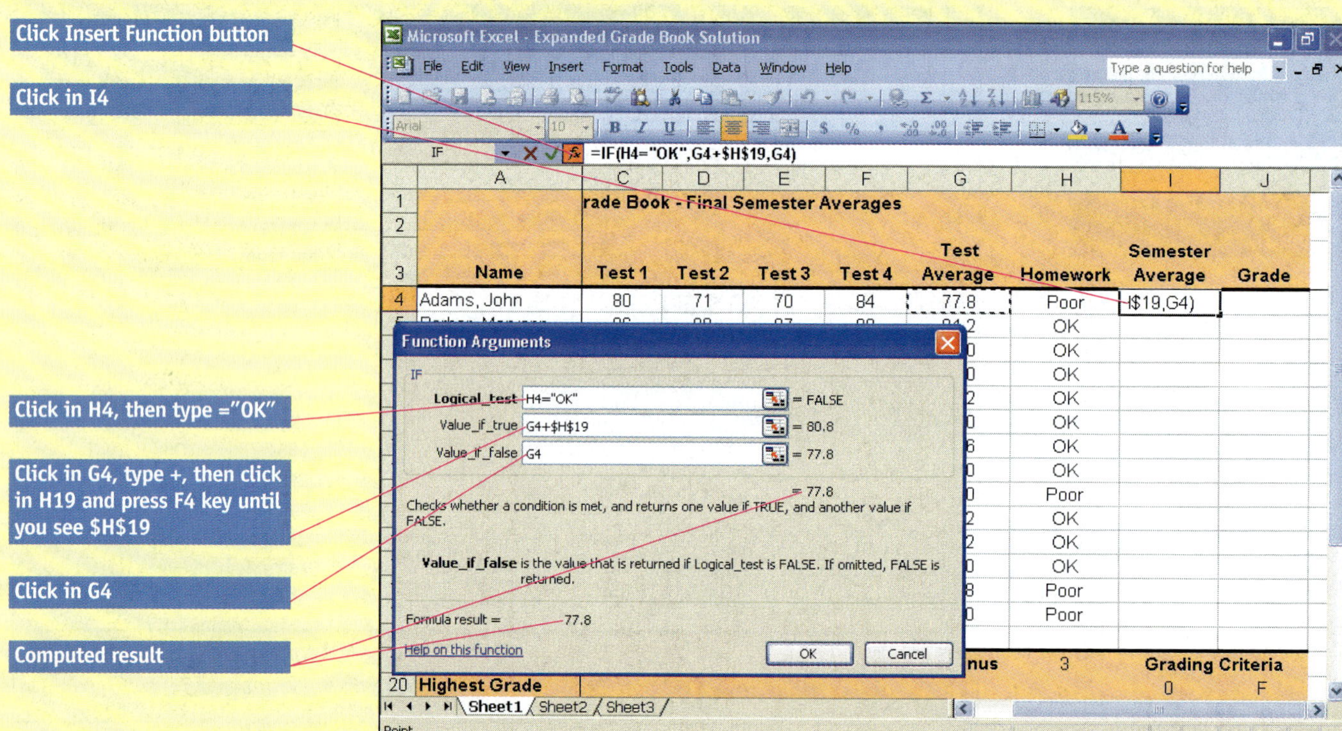

(d) The IF Function (step 4)

FIGURE 4.16 Hands-on Exercise 3 (*continued*)

THE F4 KEY

The F4 key cycles through relative, absolute, and mixed addresses. Click on any reference within the formula bar; for example, click on A1 in the formula =A1+A2. Press the F4 key once, and it changes to an absolute reference. Press the F4 key a second time, and it becomes a mixed reference, A$1; press it again, and it is a different mixed reference, $A1. Press the F4 key a fourth time, and return to the original relative address, A1.

Step 5: The VLOOKUP Function

- Click in **cell J4**. Click the **Insert Function button** on the formula bar. Click **Lookup & Reference** from the Select a Category list box. Scroll in the Function Name list box until you can select **VLOOKUP**. Click **OK** to display the Function Arguments dialog box in Figure 4.16e.
- Enter the arguments for the VLOOKUP function as shown in the figure. You can enter the arguments directly, or you can use pointing as follows:
  - Click the **Lookup_value** text box. Click **cell I4** in the worksheet.
  - Click the **Table_array** text box. Click **cell I20** and drag to **cell J24** (scrolling if necessary). Press the **F4 key** to convert to an absolute reference.
  - Click the **Col_index_num** text box. Type **2**.
- Check that the dialog box on your worksheet matches the one in Figure 4.16e. Make corrections as necessary.
- Click **OK** to insert the completed function into your worksheet.
- Save the workbook.

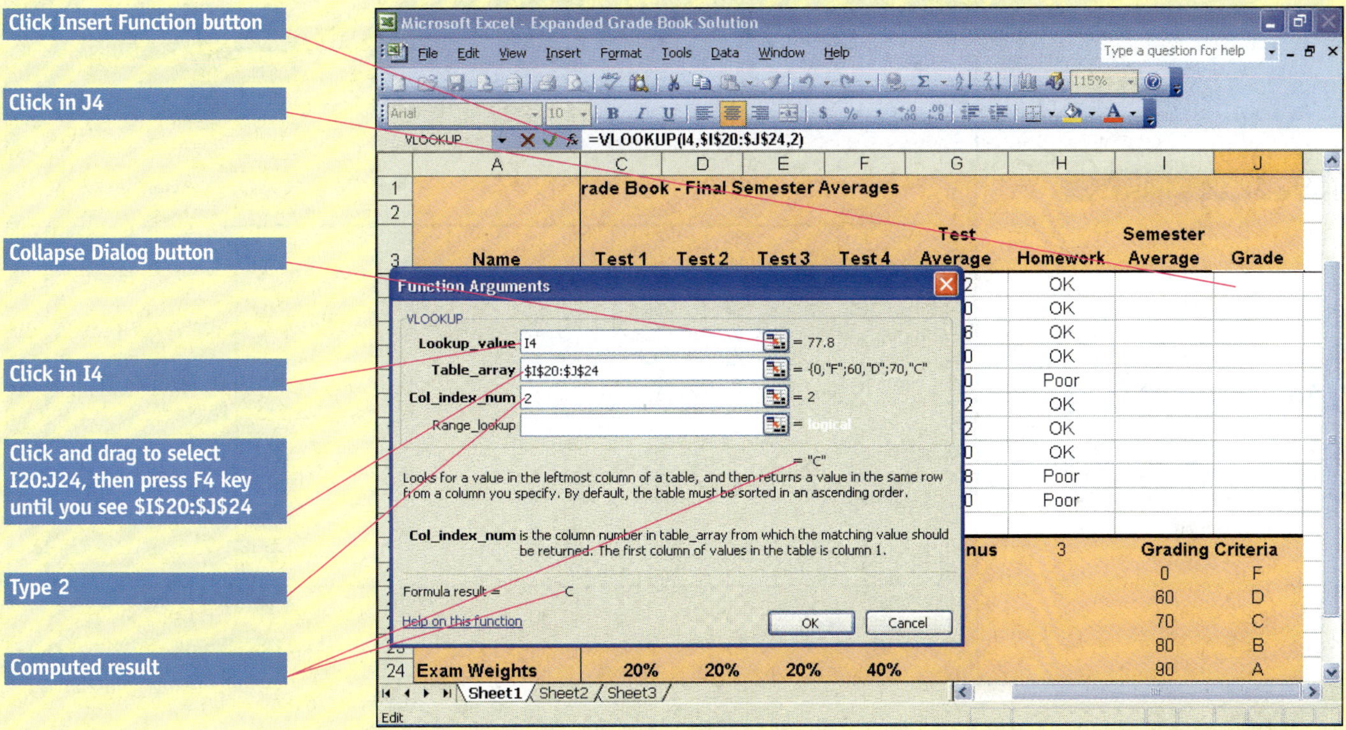

(e) The VLOOKUP Function (step 5)

FIGURE 4.16 Hands-on Exercise 3 (*continued*)

THE COLLAPSE DIALOG BUTTON

You can enter a cell reference in one of two ways: You can type it directly in the Function Arguments dialog box, or click the cell in the worksheet. The Function Arguments dialog box typically hides the necessary cell, however, in which case you can click the Collapse Dialog button (which appears to the right of any parameter within the dialog box). This collapses (hides) the Function Arguments dialog box so that you can click the underlying cell, which is now visible. Click the Collapse Dialog button a second time to display the entire dialog box.

Step 6: Copy the IF and VLOOKUP Functions

- If necessary, scroll to the top of the worksheet. Select **cells I4** and **J4** as in Figure 4.16f.
- Point to the **fill handle** in the lower-right corner of the selected range. The mouse pointer changes to a thin crosshair.
- Drag the **fill handle** over **cells I5** through **J17**. A border appears, indicating the destination range as shown in Figure 4.16f. Release the mouse to complete the copy operation.
- If you have done everything correctly, Adam Smith should have a grade of D based on a semester average of 67.
- Check that the semester averages in column I are formatted to one decimal place.
- Save the workbook.

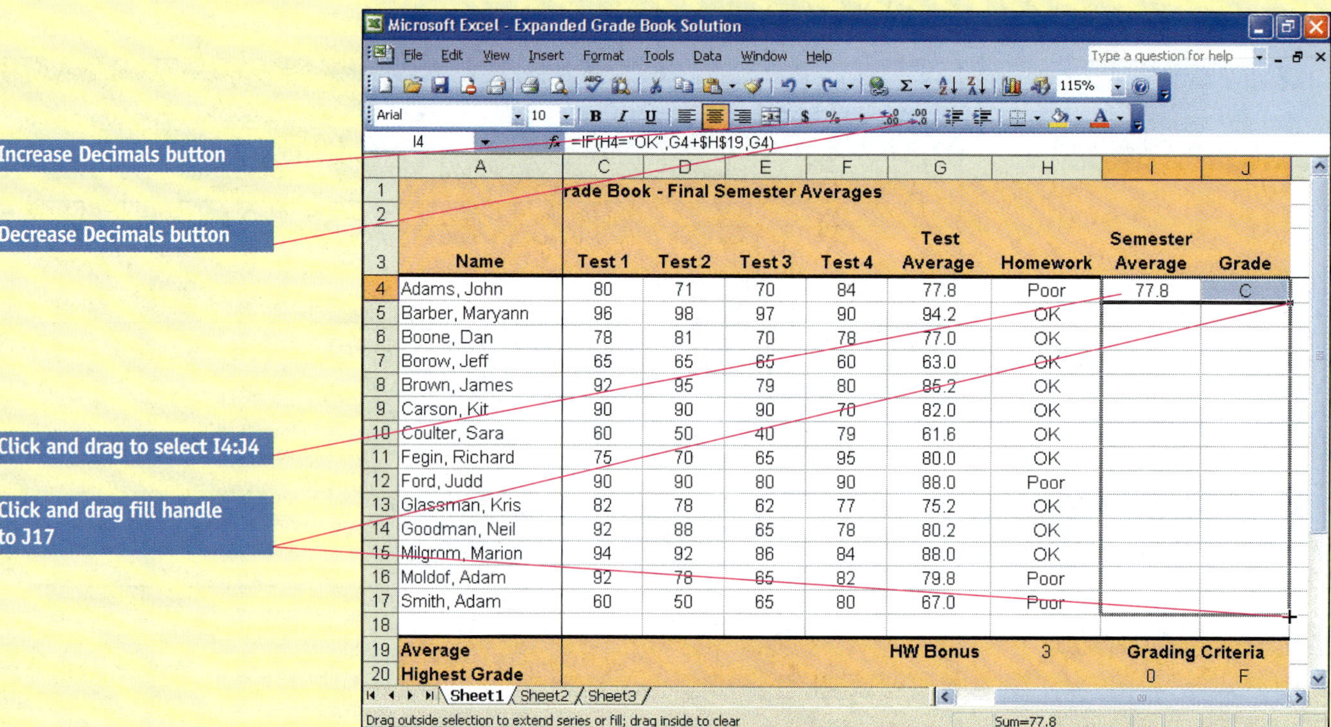

	A	C	D	E	F	G	H	I	J
1		rade Book - Final Semester Averages							
2									
3	Name	Test 1	Test 2	Test 3	Test 4	Test Average	Homework	Semester Average	Grade
4	Adams, John	80	71	70	84	77.8	Poor	77.8	C
5	Barber, Maryann	96	98	97	90	94.2	OK		
6	Boone, Dan	78	81	70	78	77.0	OK		
7	Borow, Jeff	65	65	65	60	63.0	OK		
8	Brown, James	92	95	79	80	85.2	OK		
9	Carson, Kit	90	90	90	70	82.0	OK		
10	Coulter, Sara	60	50	40	79	61.6	OK		
11	Fegin, Richard	75	70	65	95	80.0	OK		
12	Ford, Judd	90	90	80	90	88.0	Poor		
13	Glassman, Kris	82	78	62	77	75.2	OK		
14	Goodman, Neil	92	88	65	78	80.2	OK		
15	Milgrom, Marion	94	92	86	84	88.0	OK		
16	Moldof, Adam	92	78	65	82	79.8	Poor		
17	Smith, Adam	60	50	65	80	67.0	Poor		
18									
19	Average					HW Bonus	3	Grading Criteria	
20	Highest Grade							0	F

(f) Copy the IF and VLOOKUP Functions (step 6)

FIGURE 4.16 Hands-on Exercise 3 (*continued*)

THE ROUND FUNCTION

Adam Moldof has a semester average of 79.8, which returns a grade of C according to the strict interpretation of the VLOOKUP function. Your instructor might give Adam a break and round his average to 80, but the computer will not. Changing the format to display zero decimal places is not the answer, since formatting affects the display of a number, but not how the number is stored internally. The solution is to use the ROUND function in conjunction with the formula to compute the semester average. See exercise 9 at the end of the chapter.

Step 7: Create the Summary Statistics

- Scroll until you can click in **cell C19**. Type **=AVERAGE(C4:C17)**. Press **Enter**. Cell C19 should display 81.9 as shown in Figure 4.16g.
- Click in **cell C20** and enter the formula **=MAX(C4:C17)**. Click in **cell C21** and enter the formula **=MIN(C4:C17)**.
- Click in **cell C22** and enter the formula **=C20–C21**. Check that the displayed values match those in Figure 4.16g.
- Click and drag to select **cells C19** through **C22**, then click and drag the **fill handle** to **cell F22**. Release the mouse.
- Click outside the selection to deselect the cells. You will see the summary statistics for the other tests.
- Save the workbook.

Enter function to compute test Average in C19

Enter function to compute Highest Grade in C20

Enter function to compute Lowest Grade in C21

Enter formula to compute Range in C22

Click and drag fill handle to F22

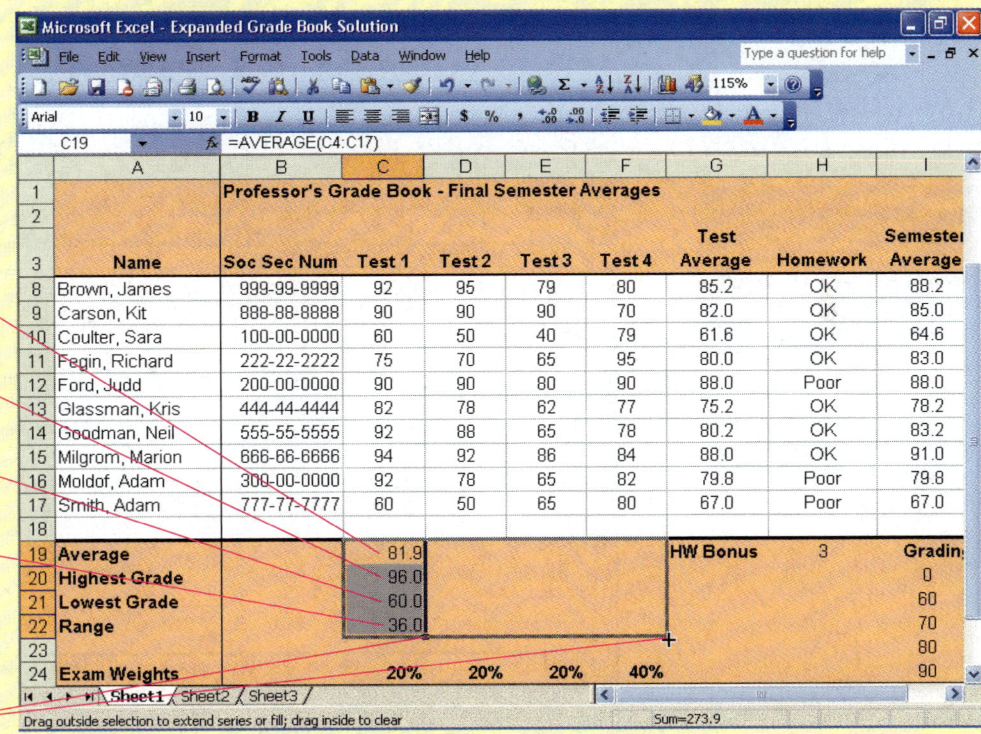

(g) Create the Summary Statistics (step 7)

FIGURE 4.16 Hands-on Exercise 3 (*continued*)

RANK IN CLASS

Use the Rank function to determine a student's rank in class. (Excel also has functions for quartiles and percentiles.) Add a new column to the worksheet, column K in this example, then click in the cell for the first student in the list (cell K4). Enter the function =RANK(I4,$I$4:$I$17), where I4 contains the value you want to look up (the individual student's semester average) and $I$4:$I$17 references the set of numbers on which to base the rank. The latter is entered as an absolute reference so that the cell formula may be copied to the remaining cells in column K. See practice exercise 9 at the end of the chapter.

Step 8: The Page Break Preview Command

- Pull down the **View menu** and click the **Page Break Preview command** to see the potential page breaks as shown in Figure 4.16h. Click **OK** if you see the welcome message.
- Click and drag the dashed blue line to the right to eliminate the page break. (You can also drag the solid blue line that appears on the right border to the left to create a page break.)
- Pull down the **View menu** and click **Normal** to return to the Normal view.
- Pull down the **File menu**. Click **Page Setup** to display the Page Setup dialog box. Click the **Margins tab**. Check the box to center the worksheet horizontally.
- Click the **Sheet tab**. Check the boxes to display the **Row and Column Headings** and the **Gridlines**.
- Click the **Print Preview button** to display the completed spreadsheet. Click the **Print button** and click **OK** to print the workbook.
- Print the worksheet with the cell formulas.

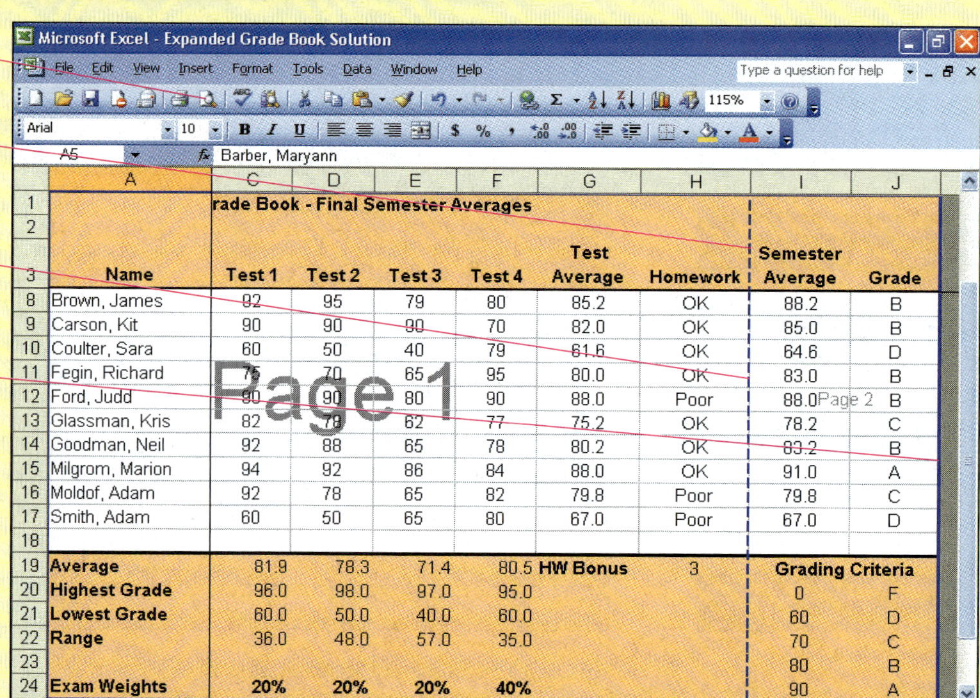

	A	C	D	E	F	G	H	I	J
1		rade Book - Final Semester Averages							
2									
3	Name	Test 1	Test 2	Test 3	Test 4	Test Average	Homework	Semester Average	Grade
8	Brown, James	92	95	79	80	85.2	OK	88.2	B
9	Carson, Kit	90	90	90	70	82.0	OK	85.0	B
10	Coulter, Sara	60	50	40	79	61.6	OK	64.6	D
11	Fegin, Richard	75	70	65	95	80.0	OK	83.0	B
12	Ford, Judd	90	90	80	90	88.0	Poor	88.0	B
13	Glassman, Kris	82	78	62	77	75.2	OK	78.2	C
14	Goodman, Neil	92	88	65	78	80.2	OK	83.2	B
15	Milgrom, Marion	94	92	86	84	88.0	OK	91.0	A
16	Moldof, Adam	92	78	65	82	79.8	Poor	79.8	C
17	Smith, Adam	60	50	65	80	67.0	Poor	67.0	D
18									
19	Average	81.9	78.3	71.4	80.5	HW Bonus	3	Grading Criteria	
20	Highest Grade	96.0	98.0	97.0	95.0			0	F
21	Lowest Grade	60.0	50.0	40.0	60.0			60	D
22	Range	36.0	48.0	57.0	35.0			70	C
23								80	B
24	Exam Weights	20%	20%	20%	40%			90	A

(h) The Page Break Preview Command (step 8)

FIGURE 4.16 Hands-on Exercise 3 (*continued*)

USE NESTED IFS FOR MORE COMPLEX DECISION MAKING

A "nested IF" (or "IF within an IF") is a common logic structure in every programming language. It could be used in the expanded grade book to implement more complicated logic such as a variable homework bonus (of –2, 3, and 5), depending on the grade (for poor, OK, and good, respectively). The IF function in Excel has three arguments—a condition, a value if the condition is true, and a value if the condition is false. A nested IF simply replaces the true and/or false value with another IF statement. See practice exercise 9 at the end of the chapter.

Step 9: Hide the Rows and Columns

- Click and drag the column headings for **columns C** through **F** to select these columns, point to the selected columns, then click the **right mouse button** to display the context-sensitive menu in Figure 4.16i. Click **Hide** to hide these columns.
- Click and drag the row headings for **rows 19** through **24** to select these rows, point to the selected rows, click the **right mouse button**, and click the **Hide command**. Print the worksheet.
- Now reverse the process and unhide the rows, but leave the columns hidden. Click and drag to select the row headings for **rows 18** and **25** (which are contiguous), right click to display a context-sensitive menu, then click the **Unhide command**.
- You should see all of the rows in the entire worksheet (within the limitations of scrolling). Save the workbook.

Click and drag to select column headings for columns C to F

Point to selected area and click right mouse button to display shortcut menu

Click Hide

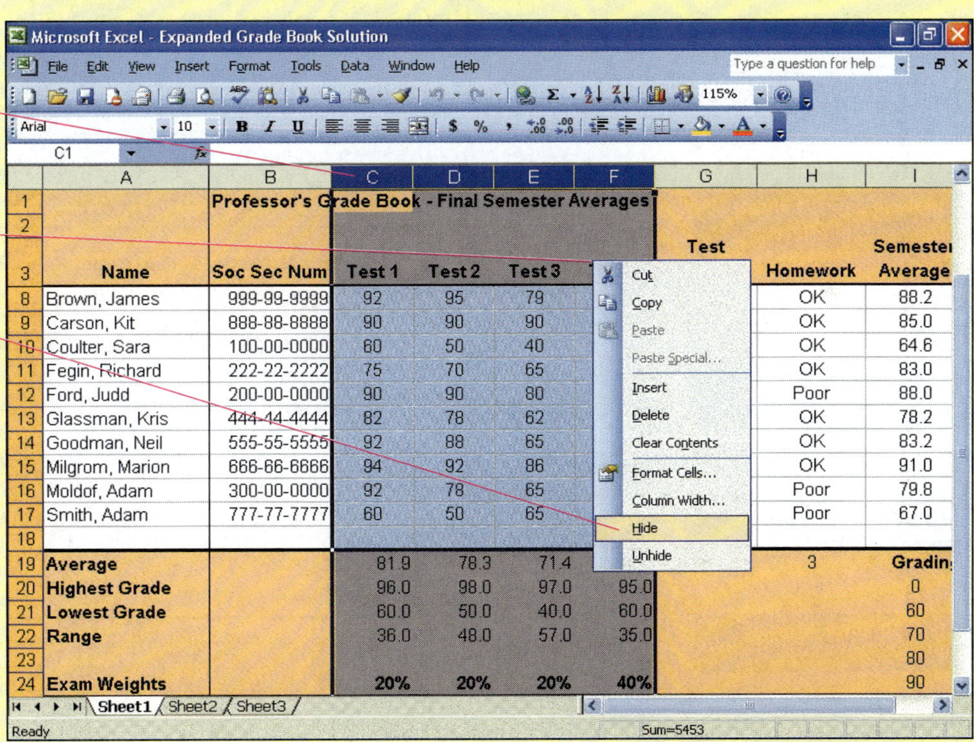

(i) Hide the Rows and Columns (step 9)

FIGURE 4.16 Hands-on Exercise 3 (*continued*)

UNHIDING ROWS AND COLUMNS

Hiding a row or column is easy: You just select the row or column(s) you want to hide, click the right mouse button, then select the Hide command from the shortcut menu. Unhiding a row or column is trickier because you cannot see the target cells. To unhide a column, for example, you need to select the columns on either side; for example, select columns A and C if you are trying to unhide column B. To unhide column A, however, click in the Name box and enter A1. Pull down the Format menu, click Column, then click the Unhide command.

Step 10: The AutoFilter Command

- Click anywhere within the list of students. Pull down the **Data menu**, click the **Filter command**, then click **AutoFilter**. The worksheet is essentially unchanged except that each column heading is followed by a drop-down arrow.
- Click the **drop-down arrow** in cell H3 (the column containing the students' homework grades). Click **Poor**. The list of students changes to show only those students who received this grade on their homework as shown in Figure 4.16j.
- Click the **drop-down arrow** in cell J3, then select **B** from the drop-down list of grade values. The list changes to show the one student who managed to receive a "B" despite having poor homework.
- Add your name and title (**Grading Assistant**) in cells G26 and G27. Save the workbook, then print it for your instructor.
- Pull down the **Data menu**, click **Filter**, and click the **AutoFilter command** to remove the filter and display all of the students.
- Exit Excel. Congratulations on a job well done.

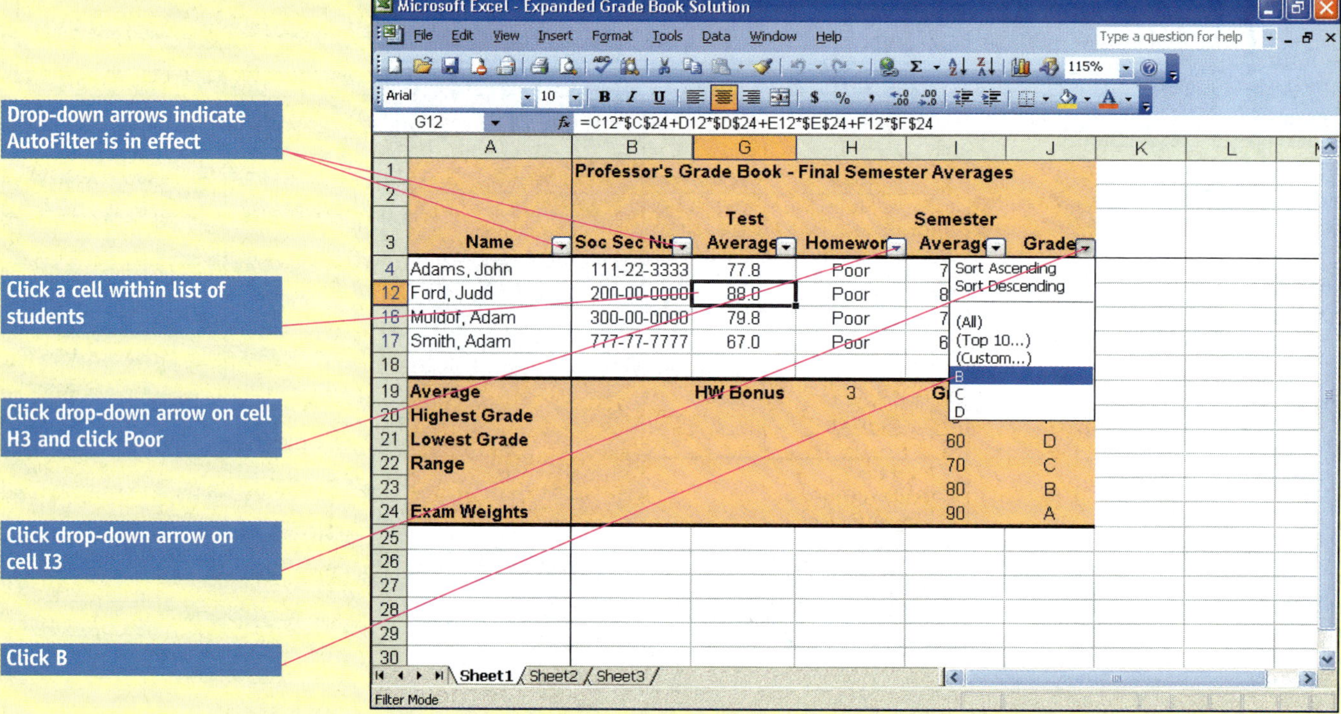

(j) The AutoFilter Command (step 10)

FIGURE 4.16 Hands-on Exercise 3 (*continued*)

SET PRINT AREAS

Press and hold the Ctrl key as you click and drag to select one or more areas in the worksheet, then pull down the File menu, select the Print Area command, and click Set Print Area. The print area is enclosed in dashed lines. The next time you execute the Print command, you will print just the print area(s), with each print area appearing on a separate page. Use the Print Area command in the File menu to clear the print area.

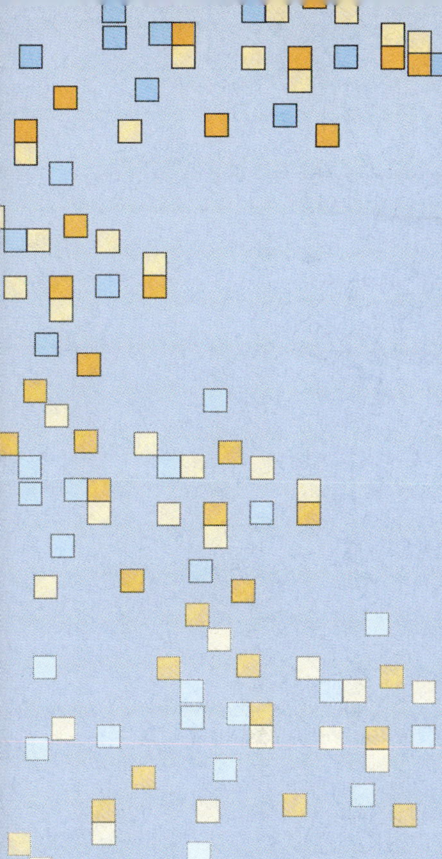

SUMMARY

Excel contains several categories of built-in functions. The PMT function computes the periodic payment for a loan based on three arguments (the interest rate per period, the number of periods, and the amount of the loan). The PMT function was used in worksheets to compute a car payment and a home mortgage. The IPMT and PPMT functions determine the amount of each periodic payment that goes toward interest and principal, respectively.

The FV function returns the future value of an investment based on constant periodic payments and a constant interest rate. The function is associated with Individual Retirement Accounts and 401K retirement plans. A spreadsheet was developed using mixed references to create a two-level table showing the future value of a retirement account at different interest rates and time periods.

Statistical functions were also discussed. The AVERAGE, MAX, and MIN functions return the average, highest, and lowest values in the argument list. The COUNT function returns the number of cells with numeric entries. The COUNTA function displays the number of cells with numeric and/or text entries.

The IF, VLOOKUP, and HLOOKUP functions implement decision making within a worksheet. The IF function has three arguments: a condition, which is evaluated as true or false; a value if the test is true; and a value if the test is false. The VLOOKUP and HLOOKUP functions also have three arguments: the value to look up, the range of cells containing the table, and the column or row number within the table that contains the result.

Several options were presented for working with large spreadsheets. Scrolling enables you to view any portion of a large worksheet but moves the labels for existing rows and/or columns off the screen. The Freeze Panes command keeps the row and/or column headings on the screen while scrolling within a large worksheet. The Page Break Preview command lets you see and/or modify the page breaks that will occur when a worksheet is printed. The AutoFilter command displays a selected set of rows within a worksheet according to a specified set of criteria. The hidden rows are not deleted but are simply not displayed.

A spreadsheet is first and foremost a tool for decision making, and thus Excel includes several commands to aid in that process. The Goal Seek command lets you enter the desired end result of a spreadsheet model (such as the monthly payment on a car loan) and determines the input (the price of the car) necessary to produce that result. The assumptions and initial conditions in a spreadsheet should be clearly labeled and set apart from the rest of the worksheet. This facilitates change and reduces the chance for error.

The hands-on exercises introduced several techniques to make you more proficient. The fill handle is used to copy a cell or group of cells to a range of adjacent cells. Pointing is a more accurate way to enter a cell reference into a formula as it uses the mouse or arrow keys to select the cell as you build the formula. The AutoFill capability creates a series based on the initial value(s) you supply.

KEY TERMS

MULTIPLE CHOICE

1. Which of the following options may be used to print a large worksheet?
   (a) Landscape orientation
   (b) Scaling
   (c) Reduced margins
   (d) All of the above

2. If the results of a formula contain more characters than can be displayed according to the present format and cell width,
   (a) The extra characters will be truncated under all circumstances
   (b) All of the characters will be displayed if the cell to the right is empty
   (c) A series of asterisks will be displayed
   (d) A series of pound signs will be displayed

3. Which cell—A1, A2, or A3—will contain the amount of the loan, given the function =PMT(A1,A2,A3)?
   (a) A1
   (b) A2
   (c) A3
   (d) Impossible to determine

4. Which of the following will compute the average of the values in cells D2, D3, and D4?
   (a) The function =AVERAGE(D2:D4)
   (b) The function =AVERAGE(D2,D4)
   (c) Both (a) and (b)
   (d) Neither (a) nor (b)

5. The function =IF(A1>A2,A1+A2,A1*A2) returns
   (a) The product of cells A1 and A2 if cell A1 is greater than A2
   (b) The sum of cells A1 and A2 if cell A1 is less than A2
   (c) Both (a) and (b)
   (d) Neither (a) nor (b)

6. Which of the following is the preferred way to sum the values contained in cells A1 to A4?
   (a) =SUM(A1:A4)
   (b) =A1+A2+A3+A4
   (c) Either (a) or (b) is equally good
   (d) Neither (a) nor (b) is correct

7. Which of the following will return the highest and lowest arguments from a list of arguments?
   (a) HIGH/LOW
   (b) LARGEST/SMALLEST
   (c) MAX/MIN
   (d) All of the above

8. Which of the following is a *required* technique to develop the worksheet for the mortgage analysis?
   (a) Pointing
   (b) Copying with the fill handle
   (c) Both (a) and (b)
   (d) Neither (a) nor (b)

9. Given that cells B6, C6, and D6 contain the numbers 10, 20, and 30, respectively, what value will be returned by the function =IF(B6>10,C6*2,D6*3)?
   (a) 10
   (b) 40
   (c) 60
   (d) 90

10. Which of the following is not an input parameter to the Goal Seek command?
    (a) The cell containing the end result
    (b) The desired value of the end result
    (c) The cell whose value will change to reach the end result
    (d) The value of the input cell that is required to reach the end result

... continued

multiple choice

11. What is the correct order of the arguments for the FV function?

(a) Interest Rate, Term, Principal
(b) Term, Interest Rate, Principal
(c) Interest Rate, Term, Annual Amount
(d) Term, Interest Rate, Annual Amount

12. Which function will return the number of nonempty cells in the range A2 through A6, including in the result cells that contain text as well as numeric entries?

(a) =COUNT(A2:A6)
(b) =COUNTA(A2:A6)
(c) =COUNT(A2,A6)
(d) =COUNTA(A2,A6)

13. The annual interest rate, term in years, and principal of a loan are stored in cells A1, A2, and A3, respectively. Which of the following is the correct PMT function, given monthly payments?

(a) =PMT(A1,A2,–A3)
(b) =PMT(A1/12,A2*12,–A3)
(c) =PMT(A1*12, A2/12,–A3)
(d) =PMT(A1,A2,A3)

14. The worksheet displayed in the monitor shows columns A and B, skips columns D, E, and F, then displays columns G, H, I, J, and K. What is the most likely explanation for the missing columns?

(a) The columns were previously deleted
(b) The columns are empty and thus are automatically hidden from view
(c) Either (a) or (b) is a satisfactory explanation
(d) Neither (a) nor (b) is a likely reason

15. Given the function =VLOOKUP(C6,D12:F18,3)

(a) The entries in cells D12 through D18 are in ascending order
(b) The entries in cells D12 through D18 are in descending order
(c) The entries in cells F12 through F18 are in ascending order
(d) The entries in cells F12 through F18 are in descending order

16. A formula containing the entry =$B3 is copied to a cell one column over and two rows down. How will the entry appear in its new location?

(a) =$B3
(b) =B3
(c) =$C5
(d) =$B5

17. You expect to contribute $2,000 a year for 10 years to a retirement plan and expect an annual return of 7%. Which of the following functions can you use to determine the expected future value?

(a) =FV(.07/12,10*12,–2000)
(b) =FV(.07,10,–2000)
(c) =FV(.07/12,10*12, 2000)
(d) =FV(.07,10, 2000)

18. Which of the following computes the monthly payment for a car loan of $10,000 that is amortized over 3 years at 5%?

(a) =PMT(.05/12,36,–10000)
(b) =PMT(.05,36,–10000)
(c) =PMT(.05,3,–10000)
(d) =PMT(.05,3,10000)

ANSWERS

1. d	**7.** c	**13.** b
2. d	**8.** d	**14.** d
3. c	**9.** d	**15.** a
4. a	**10.** d	**16.** d
5. d	**11.** c	**17.** b
6. a	**12.** b	**18.** a

PRACTICE WITH EXCEL

1. **Calculating Your Retirement:** Retirement is years away, but it is never too soon to start planning. The Future Value function enables you to calculate the amount of money you will have at retirement, based on a series of uniform contributions, made by you and/or your employer, during your working years. Once you reach retirement, however, you do not withdraw all of the money immediately, but withdraw it periodically as a monthly pension. Your assignment is to create a new worksheet similar to the one in Figure 4.17. Note the following:
   a. The accrual phase uses the FV value function to determine the amount of money you will accumulate. The total contribution in cell B7 is a formula based on a percentage of your annual salary, plus a matching contribution from your employer. The 6.2% in our figure corresponds to the percentages that are currently in effect for Social Security. (In actuality, the government currently deducts 7.65% from your paycheck, and allocates 6.2% for Social Security and the remaining 1.45% for Medicare.)
   b. The future value of your contributions (i.e., the amount of your "nest egg") depends on the assumptions in the left side of the worksheet. The 6% interest rate is conservative and can be achieved by investing in bonds, as opposed to equities. The 45 years of contributions corresponds to an individual entering the work force at age 22 and retiring at 67 (the age at which today's worker will begin to collect Social Security).
   c. The pension phase uses the PMT function to determine the payments you will receive in retirement. The formula in cell E4 is a simple reference to the amount accumulated in cell B10. The formula in cell E7 uses the PMT function to compute your monthly pension based on your nest egg, the interest rate, and the years in retirement. Note that accrual phase uses an *annual* contribution in its calculations, whereas the pension phase determines a *monthly* pension.
   d. Add a hyperlink to the page that goes to the Social Security Administration (www.ssa.gov), and then compare your calculation to the benefits provided by the government. Is Social Security providing a good return on your investment?
   e. Add your name to the worksheet, print the worksheet both ways to show displayed values and cell formulas, add a cover sheet, and then submit the assignment to your instructor.

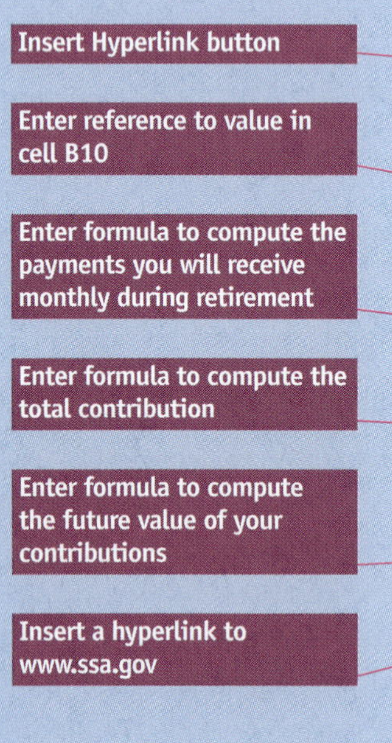

Microsoft Excel - Chapter 4 Practice 1 Solution - Calculating Your Retirement

	A	B	C	D	E
1	Calculating Your Retirement				
2					
3	**Accrual Phase**			**Pension Phase**	
4	Annual Salary	**$40,000**		The size of your "nest egg"	$1,055,208
5	Employee contribution	6.20%		Interest rate	6%
6	Employer contribution	6.20%		Years in retirement	25
7	Total contribution	$4,960		**Monthly Pension**	**$6,799**
8	Interest Rate	6%			
9	Years contributing	45			
10	**Future Value**	**$1,055,208**		**Your Name Goes Here**	
11					
12	Click here to compare to Social Security Projection				

Sheet1 / Social Security Comparison

FIGURE 4.17 Calculating Your Retirement (exercise 1)

2. **Alternate Grade Book:** Figure 4.18 displays an alternate version of the grade book that was used in the third hands-on exercise. The student names have changed as has the professor's grading scheme. Open the partially completed version of this worksheet in the *Chapter 4 Practice 2* workbook in the Exploring Excel folder, then complete the workbook as follows:
   a. The test average is computed by dropping the student's lowest grade, then giving equal weight to the three remaining tests. Steve Weinstein's test average, for example, is computed by dropping the 70 on test 1, then taking the average of 80, 90, and 100, his grades for tests 2, 3, and 4. You will need to use the SUM, MIN, and COUNT functions to implement this requirement.
   b. Students are required to complete a designated number of homework assignments (12 in Figure 4.18), then receive a bonus or penalty for every additional or missing homework assignment. Andrea Carrion completed 9 homework assignments, rather than 12, and thus has a 6-point penalty (2 points per each missing assignment). The bonus or penalty is added to the test average to determine the semester average.
   c. The grade for the course is based on the semester average and table of grading criteria according to an HLOOKUP function within the worksheet.
   d. Format the worksheet in an attractive manner. You do not have to duplicate our formatting exactly, but you are to use conditional formatting to display all failing grades and homework penalties in red.
   e. Add your name to the worksheet. Print the worksheet twice, once with displayed values and once with cell formulas. Use the Page Setup command to display grid lines and row and column headings. Add a custom header with your name, the course you are taking and your instructor's name. Create a custom footer with today's date and the current time.
   f. Print the worksheet a second time to reflect Maryann's comment. Add a cover sheet, and then submit both copies of the worksheet together with the cell formulas to your instructor.

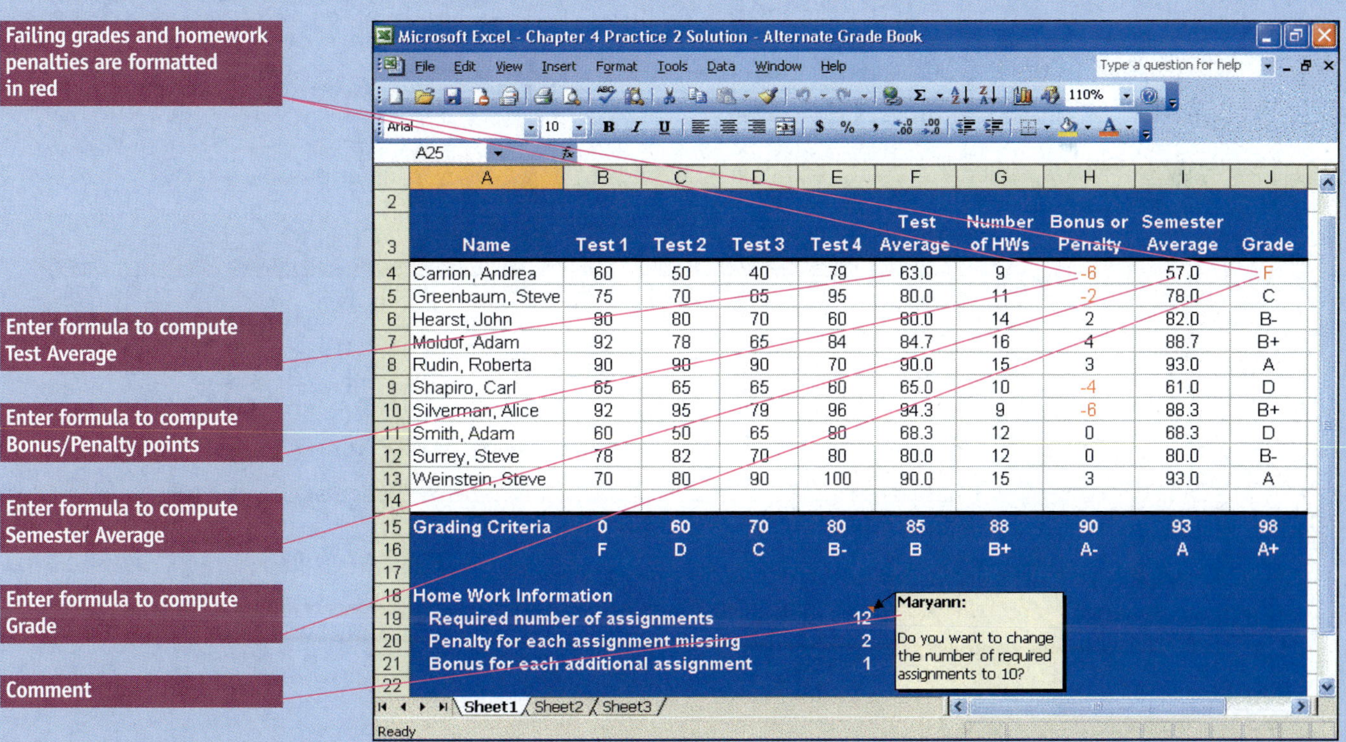

Name	Test 1	Test 2	Test 3	Test 4	Test Average	Number of HWs	Bonus or Penalty	Semester Average	Grade
Carrion, Andrea	60	50	40	79	63.0	9	-6	57.0	F
Greenbaum, Steve	75	70	65	95	80.0	11	-2	78.0	C
Hearst, John	90	80	70	60	80.0	14	2	82.0	B-
Moldof, Adam	92	78	65	84	84.7	16	4	88.7	B+
Rudin, Roberta	90	90	90	70	90.0	15	3	93.0	A
Shapiro, Carl	65	65	65	60	65.0	10	-4	61.0	D
Silverman, Alice	92	95	79	96	94.3	9	-6	88.3	B+
Smith, Adam	60	50	65	80	68.3	12	0	68.3	D
Surrey, Steve	78	82	70	80	80.0	12	0	80.0	B-
Weinstein, Steve	70	80	90	100	90.0	15	3	93.0	A
Grading Criteria	0	60	70	80	85	88	90	93	98
	F	D	C	B-	B	B+	A-	A	A+

Home Work Information	
Required number of assignments	12
Penalty for each assignment missing	2
Bonus for each additional assignment	1

FIGURE 4.18 Alternate Grade Book (exercise 2)

3. **Expanded Payroll:** Figure 4.19 displays an expanded version of the payroll example that was used earlier in the text. The assumptions used to determine an individual's net pay are listed in the worksheet and repeated below. Open the partially completed *Chapter 4 Practice 3* workbook in the Exploring Excel folder. Be sure to use the appropriate combination of relative and absolute addresses so that the formulas in row 2 may be copied to the remaining rows in the worksheet and, further, so that you can easily modify any of the underlying assumptions.
   a. Click in cell E2 to compute the employee's regular pay (regular hours worked times the hourly wage). The number of regular hours worked does not appear explicitly in the worksheet, but is calculated from the total hours worked and the overtime threshold (which is entered in the assumption area). Barber, for example, works a total of 48 hours, 40 regular, and 8 (every hour over the threshold) of overtime.
   b. Click in cell F2 and compute the overtime pay, which is the pay for all hours above the overtime threshold (40 hours in Figure 4.19). The employee receives the overtime rate (1.5 in this worksheet) times the hourly wage for every hour over the threshold.
   c. The gross pay in cell G2 is the sum of the regular pay and the overtime pay. The taxable pay in cell H2 is computed by subtracting the deduction per dependent times the number of dependents.
   d. The withholding tax in cell I2 is based on the taxable pay and the tax table. Use a VLOOKUP function to determine the tax rate, then multiply by the taxable pay.
   e. The Social Security/Medicare tax in cell J2 is a fixed percentage of gross pay.
   f. The Net Pay in cell K2 is equal to the gross pay minus the withholding and Social Security tax.
   g. Copy the formulas in row 2 to the remaining rows in the worksheet.
   h. Add your name to the worksheet, then print the worksheet to show both displayed values and cell formulas.
   i. Change the overtime threshold in cell D13 to 35 and the overtime rate in cell D14 to 2. Print the worksheet a second time to show the resulting displayed values.
   j. Add a cover sheet and submit all of the printouts to your instructor.

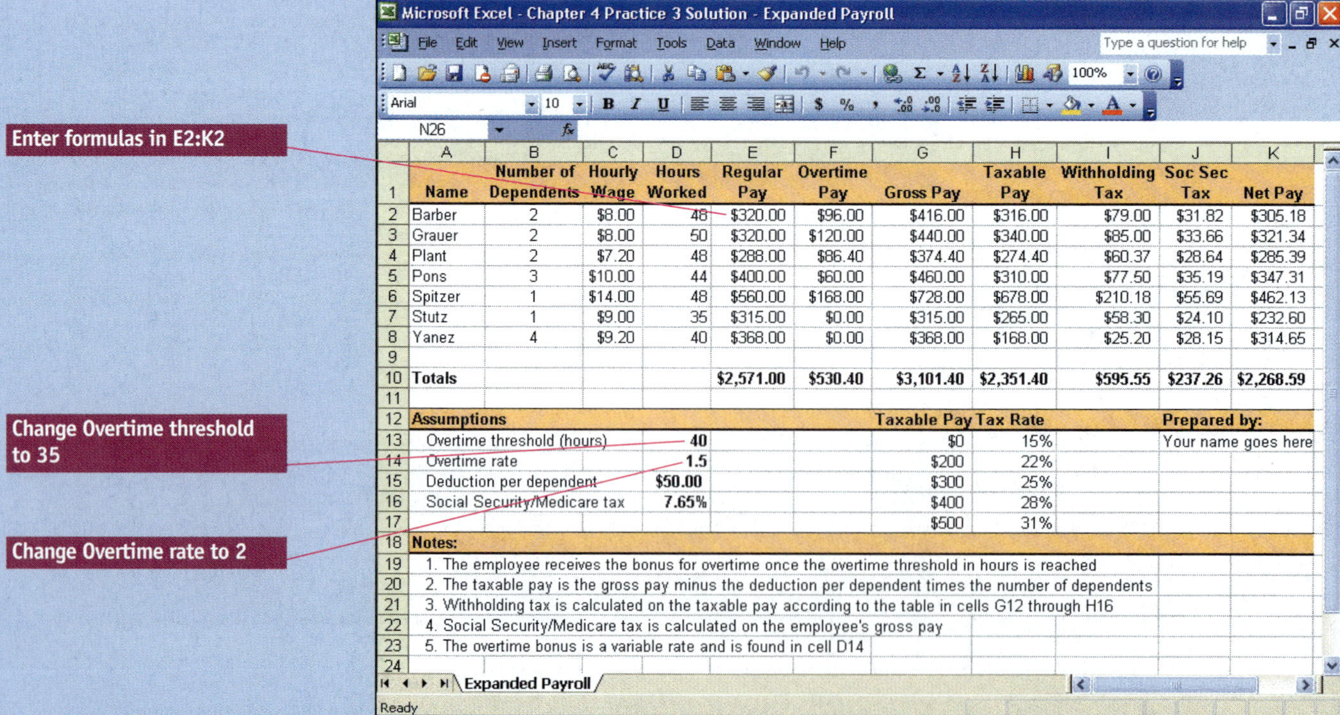

	A	B	C	D	E	F	G	H	I	J	K
1	Name	Number of Dependents	Hourly Wage	Hours Worked	Regular Pay	Overtime Pay	Gross Pay	Taxable Pay	Withholding Tax	Soc Sec Tax	Net Pay
2	Barber	2	$8.00	48	$320.00	$96.00	$416.00	$316.00	$79.00	$31.82	$305.18
3	Grauer	2	$8.00	50	$320.00	$120.00	$440.00	$340.00	$85.00	$33.66	$321.34
4	Plant	2	$7.20	48	$288.00	$86.40	$374.40	$274.40	$60.37	$28.64	$285.39
5	Pons	3	$10.00	44	$400.00	$60.00	$460.00	$310.00	$77.50	$35.19	$347.31
6	Spitzer	1	$14.00	48	$560.00	$168.00	$728.00	$678.00	$210.18	$55.69	$462.13
7	Stutz	1	$9.00	35	$315.00	$0.00	$315.00	$265.00	$58.30	$24.10	$232.60
8	Yanez	4	$9.20	40	$368.00	$0.00	$368.00	$168.00	$25.20	$28.15	$314.65
9											
10	**Totals**				**$2,571.00**	**$530.40**	**$3,101.40**	**$2,351.40**	**$595.55**	**$237.26**	**$2,268.59**
11											
12	**Assumptions**						**Taxable Pay**	**Tax Rate**		**Prepared by:**	
13	Overtime threshold (hours)			**40**			$0	15%		Your name goes here	
14	Overtime rate			**1.5**			$200	22%			
15	Deduction per dependent			**$50.00**			$300	25%			
16	Social Security/Medicare tax			**7.65%**			$400	28%			
17							$500	31%			
18	**Notes:**										
19	1. The employee receives the bonus for overtime once the overtime threshold in hours is reached										
20	2. The taxable pay is the gross pay minus the deduction per dependent times the number of dependents										
21	3. Withholding tax is calculated on the taxable pay according to the table in cells G12 through H16										
22	4. Social Security/Medicare tax is calculated on the employee's gross pay										
23	5. The overtime bonus is a variable rate and is found in cell D14										
24											

FIGURE 4.19 Expanded Payroll (exercise 3)

4. **Fuel Estimates:** Figure 4.20 displays a worksheet an airline uses to calculate the fuel requirements and associated cost for available flights. Open the partially completed worksheet in the *Chapter 4 Practice 4* workbook, and then complete the workbook to match our figure. Note the following:
   a. The fuel required for each flight is dependent on the type of aircraft and the number of flying hours. Use a VLOOKUP function in the formula to determine gallons per hour based on the type of plane, then multiply the result by the number of flying hours to compute the amount of fuel for each flight. (The table for the VLOOKUP function extends over three columns.)
   b. Use the fuel required from part (a) to compute the additional requirements for reserve fuel and holding fuel, which must then be added to the initial fuel requirements to get the total fuel needed for a trip. These parameters are shown at the bottom of the worksheet and are susceptible to change. Use the appropriate combination of relative and absolute references so that the formula for the first flight can be copied to the remaining rows in the worksheet.
   c. The estimated fuel cost for each flight is the number of gallons times the price per gallon. There is a price break, however, if the fuel required reaches or exceeds a threshold number of gallons. The Boeing-727 flight from Miami to Los Angeles, for example, requires 6,050 gallons, which exceeds the threshold, and therefore qualifies for the reduced price of fuel.
   d. Your worksheet should be completely flexible and amenable to change; that is, the hourly fuel requirements, price per gallon, price threshold, and holding and reserve percentages are all subject to change.
   e. Print the worksheet to show both displayed values and cell formulas. Use the Page Setup command to create a custom header and a custom footer that includes your name, your instructor's name, the name of your course, today's date, and the current time.
   f. Change the threshold for the price break to 3,500 gallons. Change the price per gallon to $1.50 and $1.75 if the threshold is met or not met, respectively. Print the spreadsheet to reflect these new values. Add a cover sheet and submit all of your printouts to your instructor.

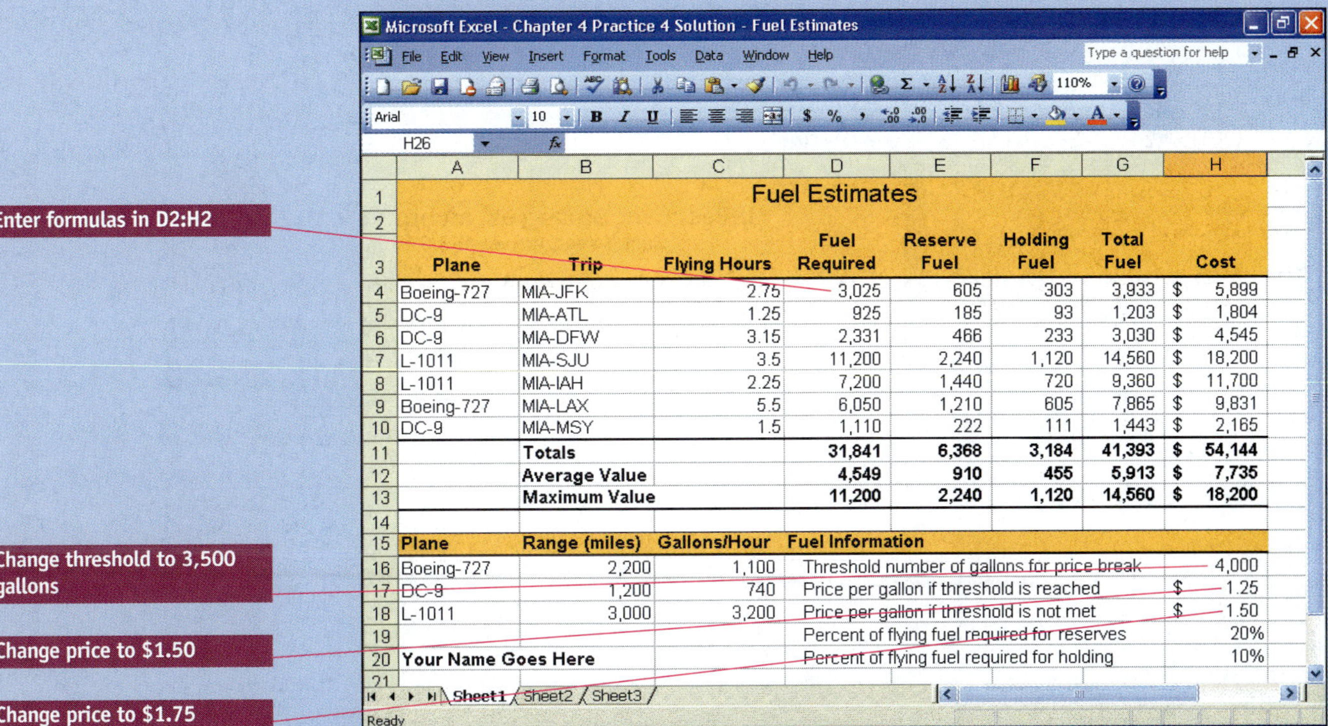

Fuel Estimates

Plane	Trip	Flying Hours	Fuel Required	Reserve Fuel	Holding Fuel	Total Fuel	Cost
Boeing-727	MIA-JFK	2.75	3,025	605	303	3,933	$ 5,899
DC-9	MIA-ATL	1.25	925	185	93	1,203	$ 1,804
DC-9	MIA-DFW	3.15	2,331	466	233	3,030	$ 4,545
L-1011	MIA-SJU	3.5	11,200	2,240	1,120	14,560	$ 18,200
L-1011	MIA-IAH	2.25	7,200	1,440	720	9,360	$ 11,700
Boeing-727	MIA-LAX	5.5	6,050	1,210	605	7,865	$ 9,831
DC-9	MIA-MSY	1.5	1,110	222	111	1,443	$ 2,165
	Totals		**31,841**	**6,368**	**3,184**	**41,393**	**$ 54,144**
	Average Value		**4,549**	**910**	**455**	**5,913**	**$ 7,735**
	Maximum Value		**11,200**	**2,240**	**1,120**	**14,560**	**$ 18,200**

Plane	Range (miles)	Gallons/Hour	Fuel Information	
Boeing-727	2,200	1,100	Threshold number of gallons for price break	4,000
DC-9	1,200	740	Price per gallon if threshold is reached	$ 1.25
L-1011	3,000	3,200	Price per gallon if threshold is not met	$ 1.50
			Percent of flying fuel required for reserves	20%
Your Name Goes Here			Percent of flying fuel required for holding	10%

FIGURE 4.20 Fuel Estimates (exercise 4)

5. **The Roth IRA:** Figure 4.21 displays a Word document with an Excel worksheet and associated chart that displays the value of an IRA for various combinations of interest rates and years invested. (The chart is not visible in Figure 4.21.) A partially completed version of that worksheet is found in the Exploring Excel folder, as is the associated Word document. Your assignment is to complete the worksheet, create the associated line chart, and then link the Excel objects to the Word document.
   a. Open the partially completed *Chapter 4 Practice 5* workbook. Click in cell C5 and enter the appropriate FV function using mixed references. Mixed references are not difficult if you ask yourself the right questions. The interest rate for the calculation in cell C5 will come from cell B5. Will the interest rate for other cells always come from column B? (Yes, so the reference to the column is absolute.) Will the interest rate always come from row 5? (No, so the reference to the column is relative.) Use similar reasoning to determine that the reference to the number of years in cell C4 should be expressed as C$4. Copy the formula in cell C5 to the remaining rows and columns in the worksheet. You should see the same dollar amounts as in Figure 4.21.
   b. The worksheet is designed so that the user can change the starting interest rate and associated increment, 4.50% and .5%, respectively in the figure, then have those values reflected in the body of the spreadsheet. The user can also change the number of years for the investment and the associated increment, as well as the annual contribution. Change the values in the assumption area of the worksheet to see how the worksheet changes.
   c. Create a line chart in its own chart sheet that shows the value of a Roth IRA at different interest rates for different time periods.
   d. Open the associated *Chapter 4 Practice 5* Word document in the Exploring Excel folder and link the portion of the worksheet shown in Figure 4.21 to the Word document. Return to Excel and link the line chart to a second page in the Word document. Save the workbook. Exit Excel.
   e. Add your name to the memo after the salutation, "To the New Graduate", then print the completed memo and submit it to your instructor. Compound interest has been called the eighth wonder of the world. Use it to your advantage!

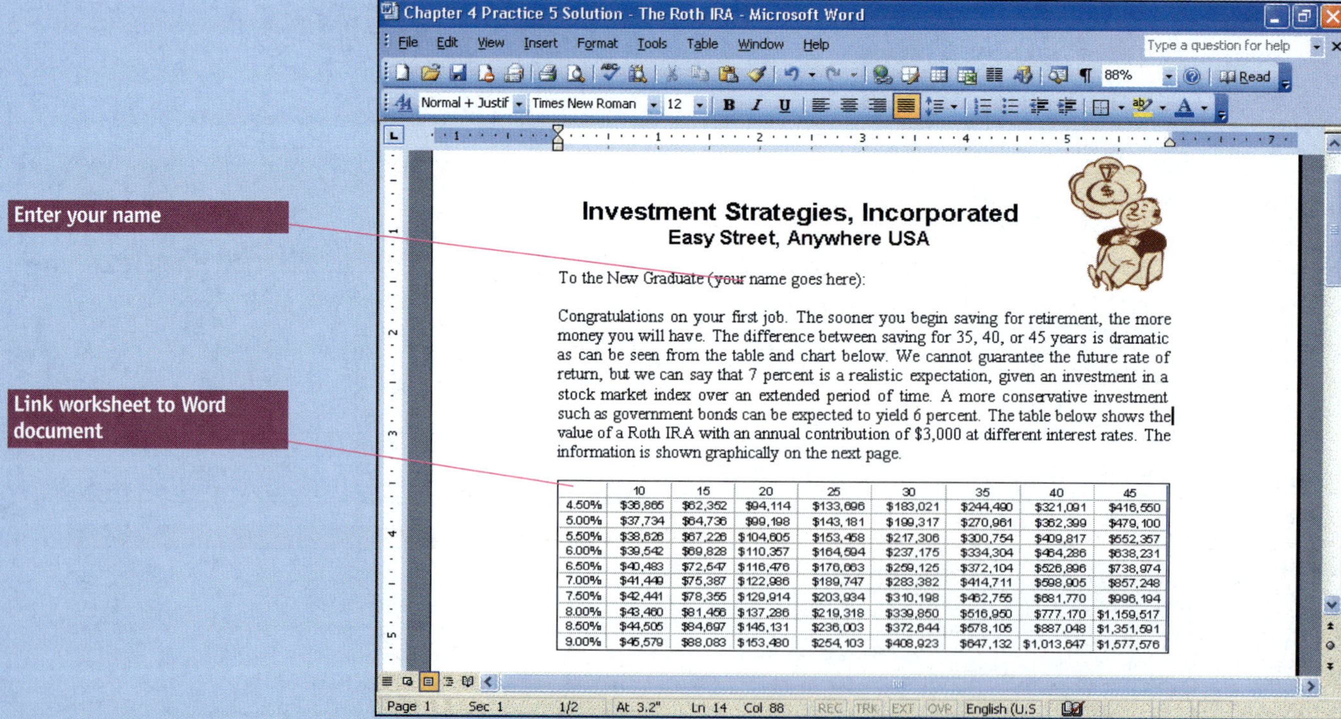

Investment Strategies, Incorporated
Easy Street, Anywhere USA

To the New Graduate (your name goes here):

Congratulations on your first job. The sooner you begin saving for retirement, the more money you will have. The difference between saving for 35, 40, or 45 years is dramatic as can be seen from the table and chart below. We cannot guarantee the future rate of return, but we can say that 7 percent is a realistic expectation, given an investment in a stock market index over an extended period of time. A more conservative investment such as government bonds can be expected to yield 6 percent. The table below shows the value of a Roth IRA with an annual contribution of $3,000 at different interest rates. The information is shown graphically on the next page.

	10	15	20	25	30	35	40	45
4.50%	$36,865	$62,352	$94,114	$133,696	$183,021	$244,490	$321,091	$416,550
5.00%	$37,734	$64,736	$99,198	$143,181	$199,317	$270,961	$362,399	$479,100
5.50%	$38,626	$67,226	$104,605	$153,458	$217,306	$300,754	$409,817	$552,357
6.00%	$39,542	$69,828	$110,357	$164,594	$237,175	$334,304	$464,286	$638,231
6.50%	$40,483	$72,547	$116,476	$176,663	$259,125	$372,104	$526,896	$738,974
7.00%	$41,449	$75,387	$122,986	$189,747	$283,382	$414,711	$598,905	$857,248
7.50%	$42,441	$78,355	$129,914	$203,934	$310,198	$462,755	$681,770	$996,194
8.00%	$43,460	$81,466	$137,286	$219,318	$339,850	$516,950	$777,170	$1,159,517
8.50%	$44,505	$84,697	$145,131	$236,003	$372,644	$578,105	$887,048	$1,351,591
9.00%	$45,579	$88,083	$153,480	$254,103	$408,923	$647,132	$1,013,647	$1,577,576

FIGURE 4.21 The Roth IRA (exercise 5)

6. **Celebrity Birthdays:** The spreadsheet in Figure 4.22 compares the age of its developer to that of several celebrities. It is a sophisticated spreadsheet that uses a nested IF function, the absolute value function, and conditional formatting. Open the partially completed version of this spreadsheet in *Chapter 4 Practice 6* and proceed as follows:
   a. Enter your name and birth date in cells B4 and B5, respectively. Enter the function to display today's date in cell E4. Enter the formula to compute your age in cell E5.
   b. Click in cell C8 and enter a nested IF function to indicate whether you are older, younger, or the same age as the celebrity in this row. Start the IF function as follows: =IF($B$5<B8,"older by",IF($B$5>B8, ...)). The absolute reference is to your birth date in cell B5; that is, if your birth date is less than the celebrity's birth date, you are older. If this condition is not true, the second IF function should tell whether you are younger or you are the same age.
   c. Apply conditional formatting to the formula in cell C8 to display the result in red, blue, or green, depending on whether you are older, younger, or the same age.
   d. Click in cell D8 and enter the formula to compute the difference in age, which is to appear as a positive number, regardless of whether you are older or younger than the celebrity. The easiest way to ensure positive numbers is to use the ABS (absolute value) function. (A zero age difference should not appear in the worksheet, however. Pull down the Tools menu, click the Options command, click the View tab, and then clear the box to display zero values.)
   e. Click in cell E8 and enter the appropriate IF function to display the word "years" if you are either older or younger than the celebrity. The cell should be blank if you are the same age. Center the entry.
   f. Copy the formulas in row 8 to the remaining rows of the worksheet. Be sure to test the worksheet completely; that is, change your birth date temporarily to match the birthday of a celebrity to see if you display the same age in column D.
   g. Click the link to find celebrity birthdays and add a person who is not in the original workbook. (We added Mia Hamm.) Boldface and highlight the row you added.
   h. Print the spreadsheet to show the displayed values in alphabetical order by the celebrities' last name. Print the cell formulas.

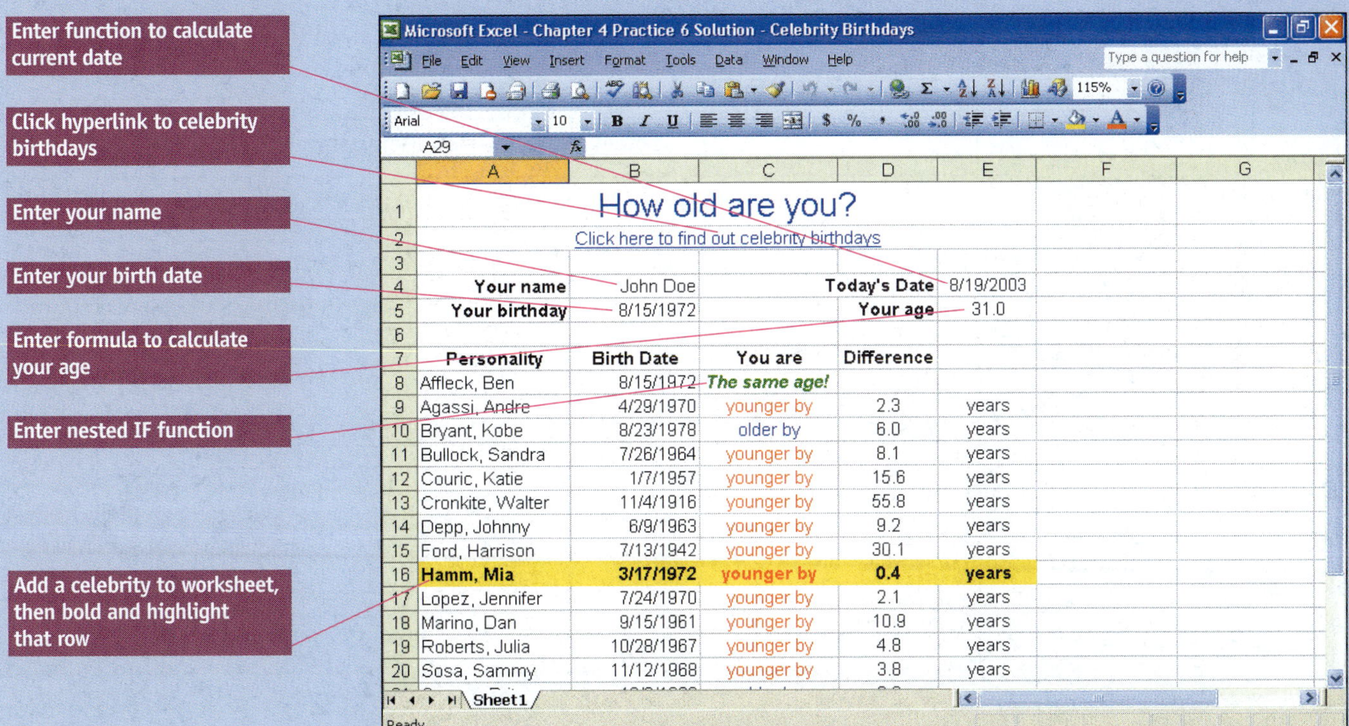

FIGURE 4.22 Celebrity Birthdays (exercise 6)

7. **The Health Club:** The worksheet in Figure 4.23 displays a list of new members in the Totally Fit Gym. Your assignment is to open the partially completed workbook in *Chapter 4 Practice 7,* in order to complete the workbook so that it matches our figure. You do not have to match our formatting exactly, but you are required to duplicate the functionality. Proceed as follows:
   a. Click in Cell C4 and enter the appropriate VLOOKUP function to determine the cost of the individual's membership. Your formula should contain an absolute reference to the table of membership costs that is contained in cells A17 through C19.
   b. Click in cell E4 and use an IF function to determine the annual total, which consists of the cost of membership plus an optional locker fee. Now click in cell G4 to compute the total amount due, which is the annual total times the number of years the individual has chosen.
   c. The down payment in cell H4 depends on the type of membership and is not dependent on the number of years. Thus Allen, George, and Grauer all have a required down payment of $250 for the deluxe membership, even though they selected a different number of years.
   d. Compute the balance (which is the total due minus the down payment) in cell I4. Use the PMT function to determine the monthly payment in cell J4.
   e. Copy the formulas in row 4 to the remaining rows in the worksheet.
   f. Enter your last name in cell A8 in place of "Grauer". Sort the client list in alphabetical order, then select the row containing your name and shade it.
   g. Enter the appropriate statistical functions in column H to determine summary statistics. Your values should match ours.
   h. Format the completed worksheet as you see fit. Insert clip art somewhere in the worksheet to serve as a logo.
   i. Print the displayed values and cell formulas for your instructor. Use landscape printing so that the worksheet fits on one page. Be sure that the grid lines and the row and column headings appear.

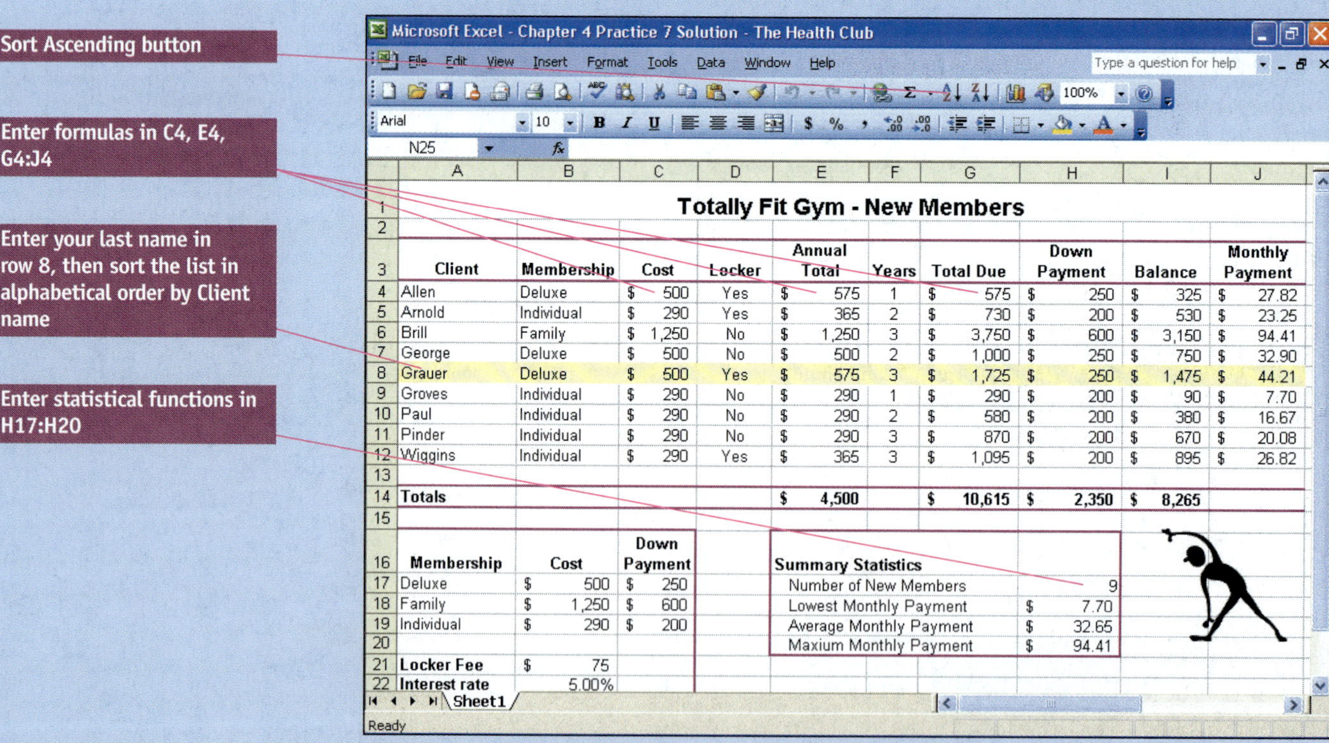

Totally Fit Gym - New Members

Client	Membership	Cost	Locker	Annual Total	Years	Total Due	Down Payment	Balance	Monthly Payment
Allen	Deluxe	$ 500	Yes	$ 575	1	$ 575	$ 250	$ 325	$ 27.82
Arnold	Individual	$ 290	Yes	$ 365	2	$ 730	$ 200	$ 530	$ 23.25
Brill	Family	$ 1,250	No	$ 1,250	3	$ 3,750	$ 600	$ 3,150	$ 94.41
George	Deluxe	$ 500	No	$ 500	2	$ 1,000	$ 250	$ 750	$ 32.90
Grauer	Deluxe	$ 500	Yes	$ 575	3	$ 1,725	$ 250	$ 1,475	$ 44.21
Groves	Individual	$ 290	No	$ 290	1	$ 290	$ 200	$ 90	$ 7.70
Paul	Individual	$ 290	No	$ 290	2	$ 580	$ 200	$ 380	$ 16.67
Pinder	Individual	$ 290	No	$ 290	3	$ 870	$ 200	$ 670	$ 20.08
Wiggins	Individual	$ 290	Yes	$ 365	3	$ 1,095	$ 200	$ 895	$ 26.82
Totals				**$ 4,500**		**$ 10,615**	**$ 2,350**	**$ 8,265**	

Membership	Cost	Down Payment
Deluxe	$ 500	$ 250
Family	$ 1,250	$ 600
Individual	$ 290	$ 200
Locker Fee	$ 75	
Interest rate	5.00%	

Summary Statistics	
Number of New Members	9
Lowest Monthly Payment	$ 7.70
Average Monthly Payment	$ 32.65
Maxium Monthly Payment	$ 94.41

FIGURE 4.23 The Health Club (exercise 7)

8. **File Formats and Folders:** One of the most common tasks in the workplace involves the exchange of data between different applications. You might use Excel to compute student grades for the semester, and then find it necessary to export that data to a mainframe computer. Proceed as follows.
   a. Open the Expanded Grade Book Solution from Hands-on Exercise 3. Click the rectangle in the upper left corner of the worksheet to select the entire worksheet. Pull down the Format menu, click Column, then click the Unhide command.
   b. Click the Copy button. Pull down the Edit menu, click Paste Special, click the option button for Values (in the Paste area), and click OK. This converts the Excel formulas to their numeric and literal equivalents.
   c. Delete the first two rows in the worksheet (which contain the title information) and all rows below the last student. Delete every column except the student's name, Social Security number, and letter grade. Delete the Sheet2 and Sheet3 worksheets.
   d. Pull down the File menu, Click the Save As command to display the Save As dialog box. Enter Semester Grades as the file name. Click the down arrow in the Save As type list box and choose CSV (Comma delimited). Click Yes if you see a message indicating that the workbook may contain features that are incompatible with the CSV format.
   e. Pull down the File menu and click the Save As command to display the Save As dialog box. Click the Create New Folder button and enter "Original Name" as the name. Click OK.
   f. Click the up arrow on the Save As toolbar to return to the Exploring Excel folder as shown in Figure 4.24. Select the new folder, click the down arrow on the Tools button, click the Rename command, and enter Data for Export as the name of the folder. Close the dialog box. Close the workbook.
   g. Click the Open button on the Standard toolbar and change to the Exploring Excel folder. Select the Semester Grades document and drag it to the Data for Export folder. (You can also move the document using "cut and paste".)
   h. Start the Notepad accessory and open the Semester Grades document in the Data Export folder. Use Notepad to print the Semester Grades document.

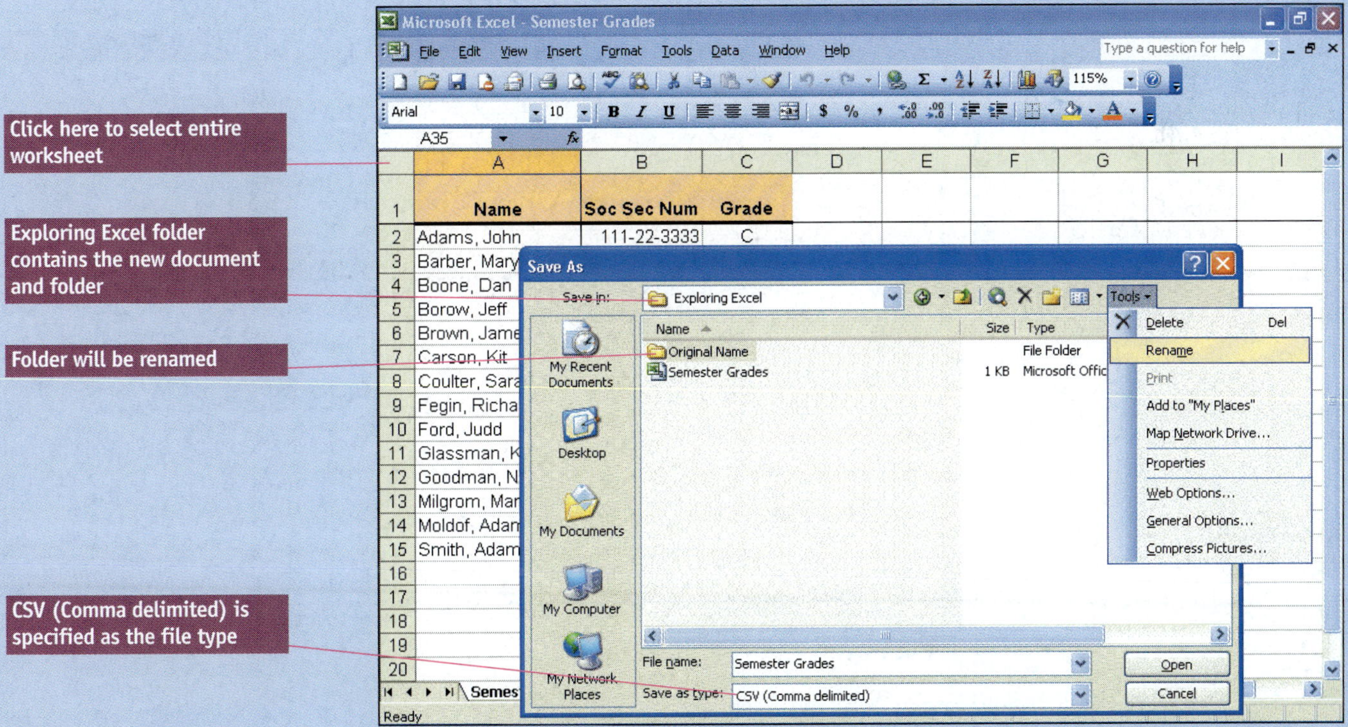

FIGURE 4.24 File Formats and Folders (exercise 8)

9. **Nested IFs and Other Functions:** Figure 4.25 displays a modified version of the expanded grade book. A Student ID has been inserted in column C, the explicit bonus or penalty for homework is displayed in column J, and the rank in class has been inserted in column M. Open the partially completed workbook in *Chapter 4 Practice 9,* then proceed as follows:
   a. Click in cell C4 and use the LEFT function to display the first four digits of the student's Social Security number in cell B4. Copy the formula to the remaining rows in the worksheet. Be sure that your results correspond to our figure. Hide columns A and B since the professor will post the worksheet by Student ID.
   b. Enter the formula to compute the student's test average in cell H4, which is based on the exam weights in row 24. Copy this formula to the remaining rows. Enter the appropriate statistical functions at the bottom of the worksheet for test 1. Copy these formulas to the appropriate cells for the other exams.
   c. Students are penalized two points for poor homework, and are rewarded two and four points, for satisfactory (OK) and good homework, respectively. Use a nested IF function in cell J4 to compute the homework bonus or penalty. Write the IF function in such a way that it will flag an invalid homework grade. Copy this formula to the remaining rows in the spreadsheet.
   d. Click in cell K4 and enter the formula for the semester average. Use a VLOOKUP function in cell L4 to determine the grade for the semester. Copy these formulas to the remaining rows in the worksheet.
   e. The VLOOKUP function does not give students a break; for example, the student with a 79.6 average (student ID is 4444) is assigned a C. (You can change the format in column K to omit decimals, but the assigned grade will not change because formatting does not change the actual value in a cell.) Thus you have to change the formula in cell K4 to round the student's grade to the nearest integer. Copy this formula to the remaining rows to be sure it works correctly.
   f. Use the Rank function to determine each student's rank in class according to the computed value of his or her semester average. (Use the Help menu if necessary.)
   g. Add your name to the worksheet as the grading assistant. Format the worksheet, then print it twice, to show both displayed values and cell formulas.

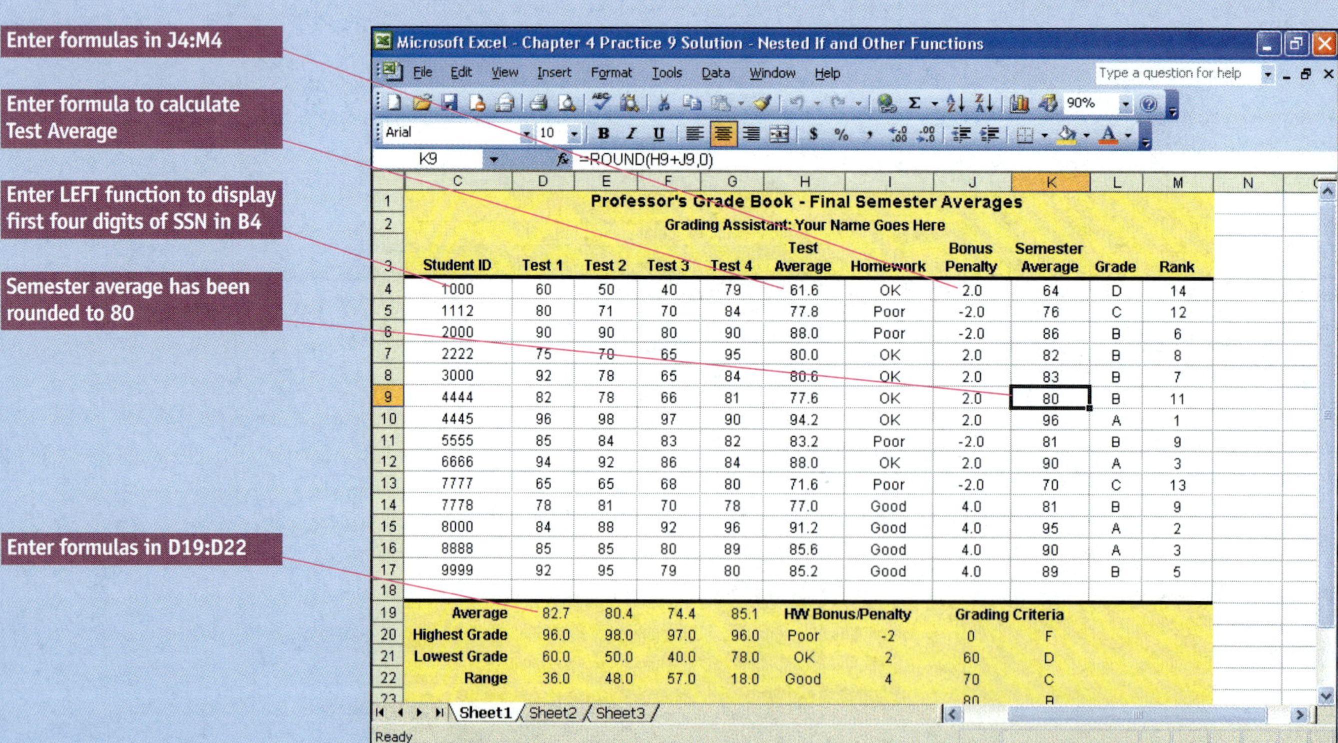

	C	D	E	F	G	H	I	J	K	L	M
1	Professor's Grade Book - Final Semester Averages										
2	Grading Assistant: Your Name Goes Here										
3	Student ID	Test 1	Test 2	Test 3	Test 4	Test Average	Homework	Bonus Penalty	Semester Average	Grade	Rank
4	1000	60	50	40	79	61.6	OK	2.0	64	D	14
5	1112	80	71	70	84	77.8	Poor	-2.0	76	C	12
6	2000	90	90	80	90	88.0	Poor	-2.0	86	B	6
7	2222	75	70	65	95	80.0	OK	2.0	82	B	8
8	3000	92	78	65	84	80.6	OK	2.0	83	B	7
9	4444	82	78	66	81	77.6	OK	2.0	80	B	11
10	4445	96	98	97	90	94.2	OK	2.0	96	A	1
11	5555	85	84	83	82	83.2	Poor	-2.0	81	B	9
12	6666	94	92	86	84	88.0	OK	2.0	90	A	3
13	7777	65	65	68	80	71.6	Poor	-2.0	70	C	13
14	7778	78	81	70	78	77.0	Good	4.0	81	B	9
15	8000	84	88	92	96	91.2	Good	4.0	95	A	2
16	8888	85	85	80	89	85.6	Good	4.0	90	A	3
17	9999	92	95	79	80	85.2	Good	4.0	89	B	5
18											
19	Average	82.7	80.4	74.4	85.1	HW Bonus/Penalty		Grading Criteria			
20	Highest Grade	96.0	98.0	97.0	96.0	Poor	-2	0	F		
21	Lowest Grade	60.0	50.0	40.0	78.0	OK	2	60	D		
22	Range	36.0	48.0	57.0	18.0	Good	4	70	C		
23								80	B		

FIGURE 4.25 Nested IFs and Other Functions (exercise 9)

10. **Election 2000:** Election 2000 has come and gone, but it will always be remembered as the closest election in our history. You will find a partially completed version of Figure 4.26 in the file, *Chapter 4 Practice 10*. Open the workbook and proceed as follows:
    a. Enter an appropriate IF function in cells D9 and F9 to determine the electoral votes for each candidate. The electoral votes are awarded on the all-or-nothing basis; that is, the candidate with the larger popular vote wins all of that states electoral votes. The other candidate gets zero votes. (Pull down the Tools menu, click the Options command, click the General tab, and then clear the box to display zero values.)
    b. Copy the entries in cells D9 and F9 to the remaining rows in the respective columns. Format these columns to display red and blue values, for Mr. Bush and Mr. Gore, respectively.
    c. Enter a formula in cell G9 to determine the difference in the popular vote between the two candidates. The result should always appear as a positive number. You can do this in one of two ways; by using either an absolute value function or an appropriate IF function. Copy this formula to the remaining rows in the column.
    d. Click in cell H9 and determine the percentage differential in the popular vote. This is the difference in the number of votes divided by the total number of votes.
    e. Enter the appropriate SUM functions in cells B4, B5, C4, and C5 to determine the electoral and popular vote totals for each candidate.
    f. Add your name and your instructor's name as indicated. Reduce the top and bottom margins to three quarters of an inch, then use the appropriate option in the Page Setup command to be sure your worksheet fits on one page. Adjust the column widths as necessary. Print the worksheet a second time to show the cell formulas.
    g. Use the Sort command to display the states in a different sequence, such as the smallest (or largest) vote differential. Print the worksheet in this sequence.
    h. Add a cover sheet. Submit all of your printouts to your instructor.

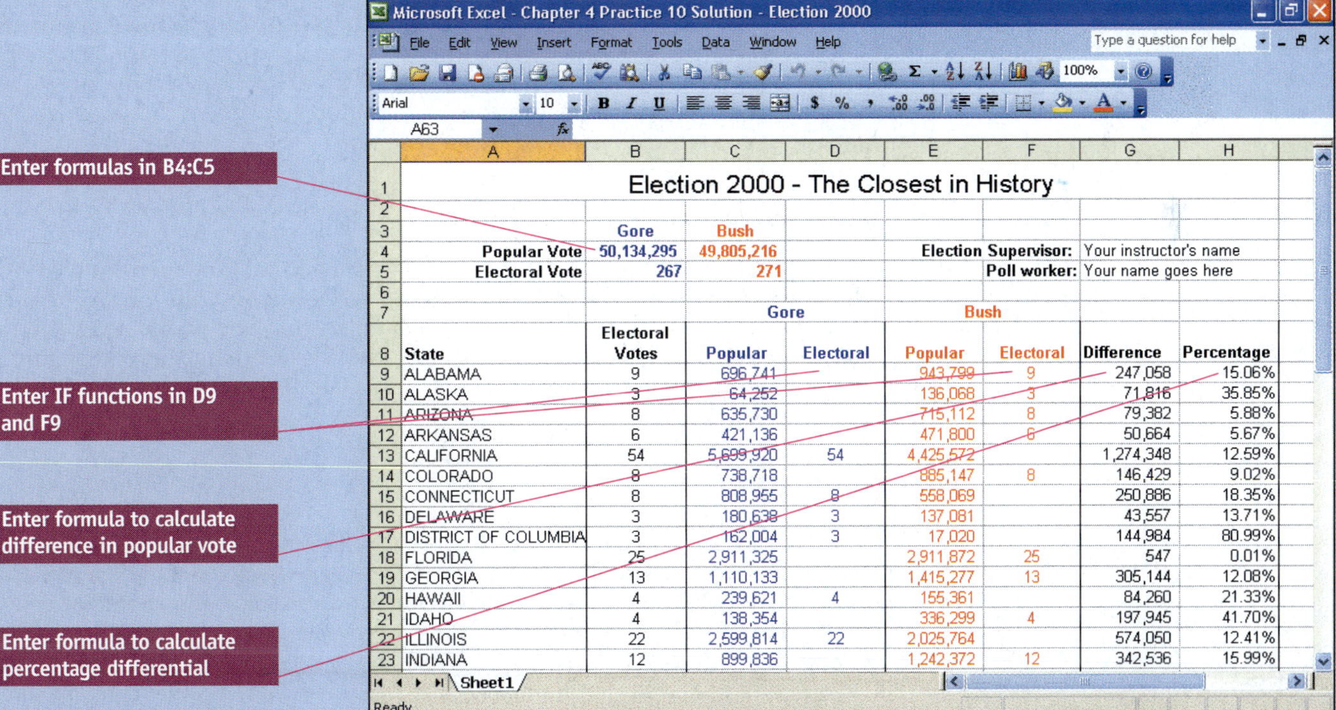

	A	B	C	D	E	F	G	H
1	Election 2000 - The Closest in History							
2								
3		Gore	Bush					
4	Popular Vote	50,134,295	49,805,216			Election Supervisor:	Your instructor's name	
5	Electoral Vote	267	271			Poll worker:	Your name goes here	
6								
7			Gore		Bush			
8	State	Electoral Votes	Popular	Electoral	Popular	Electoral	Difference	Percentage
9	ALABAMA	9	696,741		943,799	9	247,058	15.06%
10	ALASKA	3	64,252		136,068	3	71,816	35.85%
11	ARIZONA	8	635,730		715,112	8	79,382	5.88%
12	ARKANSAS	6	421,136		471,800	6	50,664	5.67%
13	CALIFORNIA	54	5,699,920	54	4,425,572		1,274,348	12.59%
14	COLORADO	8	738,718		885,147	8	146,429	9.02%
15	CONNECTICUT	8	808,955	8	558,069		250,886	18.35%
16	DELAWARE	3	180,638	3	137,081		43,557	13.71%
17	DISTRICT OF COLUMBIA	3	162,004	3	17,020		144,984	80.99%
18	FLORIDA	25	2,911,325		2,911,872	25	547	0.01%
19	GEORGIA	13	1,110,133		1,415,277	13	305,144	12.08%
20	HAWAII	4	239,621	4	155,361		84,260	21.33%
21	IDAHO	4	138,354		336,299	4	197,945	41.70%
22	ILLINOIS	22	2,599,814	22	2,025,764		574,050	12.41%
23	INDIANA	12	899,836		1,242,372	12	342,536	15.99%

FIGURE 4.26 Election 2000 (exercise 10)

MINI CASES

The Financial Consultant

A friend of yours is in the process of buying a home and has asked you to compare the payments and total interest on a 15- and 30-year loan at varying interest rates. You have decided to analyze the loans in Excel, and then incorporate the results into a memo written in Microsoft Word. As of now, the principal is $150,000, but it is very likely that your friend will change his mind several times, and so you want to use the linking and embedding capability within Windows to dynamically link the worksheet to the word processing document. Your memo should include a letterhead that takes advantage of the formatting capabilities within Word; a graphic logo would be a nice touch.

Fun with the If Statement

Open the *Chapter 4 Mini Case—Fun with the If Statement* workbook in the Exploring Excel folder, then follow the directions in the worksheet to view a hidden message. The message is displayed by various If statements scattered throughout the worksheet, but the worksheet is protected so that you cannot see these formulas. (Use help to see how to protect a worksheet.) We made it easy for you, however, because you can unprotect the worksheet since a password is not required. Once the worksheet is unprotected, pull down the Format menu, click the Cells command, click the Protection tab, and clear the Hidden check box. Prove to your professor that you have done this successfully, by changing the text of our message. Print the completed worksheet to show both displayed values and cell formulas.

The Lottery

Many states raise money through lotteries that advertise prizes of several million dollars. In reality, however, the actual value of the prize is considerably less than the advertised value, although the winners almost certainly do not care. One state, for example, recently offered a twenty million dollar prize that was to be distributed in twenty annual payments of one million dollars each. How much was the prize actually worth, assuming a long-term interest rate of five percent? Use the PV (Present Value) function to determine the answer. What is the effect on the answer if payments to the recipient are made at the beginning of each year, rather than at the end of each year?

A Penny a Day

What if you had a rich uncle who offered to pay you "a penny a day," and then double your salary each day for the next month? It does not sound very generous, but you will be surprised at how quickly the amount grows. Create a simple worksheet that enables you to use the Goal Seek command to answer the following questions. On what day of the month (if any) will your uncle pay you more than one million dollars? How much money will your uncle pay you on the 31st day?

The Rule of 72

Delaying your IRA for one year can cost you as much as $64,000 at retirement, depending on when you begin. That may be hard to believe, but you can check the numbers without a calculator, using the "Rule of 72." This financial rule of thumb states that to find out how long it takes money to double, divide the number 72 by the interest rate; for example, money earning 8% annually will double in approximately 9 years (72 divided by 8). The money doubles again in 18 years, again in 27 years, and so on. Now assume that you start your IRA at age 21, rather than 20, effectively losing 45 years of compound interest for the initial contribution. Use the rule of 72 to determine approximately how much you will lose, assuming an 8% rate of return. Check your calculation by creating a worksheet to determine the exact amount.

CHAPTER

5

Consolidating Data: Worksheet References and File Linking

OBJECTIVES

After reading this chapter you will:

1. Describe two ways to consolidate data from multiple workbooks.
2. Distinguish between a cell reference and a worksheet reference.
3. Select multiple worksheets to enter common formulas and formatting.
4. Use the AutoFormat command.
5. Explain the advantage of using a function rather than a formula to consolidate data.
6. Create a documentation worksheet.
7. Use a workbook reference to link one workbook to another.

hands-on exercises

1. COPYING WORKSHEETS
   Input: Atlanta, Boston, and Chicago (three workbooks)
   Output: Corporate Sales
2. WORKSHEET REFERENCES
   Input: Corporate Sales workbook (from exercise 1)
   Output: Corporate Sales (with additional modifications)
3. THE DOCUMENTATION WORKSHEET
   Input: Corporate Sales workbook (from exercise 2)
   Output: Corporate Sales (with additional modifications)
4. LINKING WORKBOOKS
   Input: Atlanta, Boston, and Chicago (three workbooks)
   Output: Corporate Links

CASE STUDY

BANDIT'S PIZZA

Bandit's Pizza offers a tasty pizza at a "steal" of a price, with a strong appeal to the college and family crowds. Their pizzas are generously proportioned, made with a homemade spicy pizza sauce to create a unique zesty flavor, and their list of toppings includes some of the most off-the-wall selections around. This tried and true proven product offering, combined with great customer service, keep their pizzas flying out the door! Bandit's Pizza has expanded from its initial restaurant downtown to two additional sites elsewhere in the city.

The owner, Andreas Marquis, wants to evaluate the overall performance of the chain before expanding further. He is especially interested in the comparative results of three dining categories: dine-in, pick-up, and delivery. Andreas knows you are studying Excel at the local college and asked for your help in return for a small stipend and all the pizza you can eat. You have already prepared a template and distributed it to each restaurant manager, who has entered the sales data for last year. Your next task is to consolidate the data into a single workbook that shows the total sales for each quarter and each dining category. The information should be shown in tabular as well as graphical form. ■

Your assignment is to read the chapter, paying special attention to the two different ways in which to consolidate data. You can use either technique for the solution; that is, you can create a summary workbook with multiple worksheets, or you can create a summary workbook that links to the individual workbooks. In any event, start with the partially completed *Case Study Chapter 5—Bandit's Summary* workbook in the Exploring Excel folder. Data for the individual stores (Eastside, Westside, and Downtown) are found in three additional workbooks in the same folder. Print the completed summary workbook for your instructor to show both displayed values and cell formulas. Print the associated chart as well.

CONSOLIDATING DATA

Assume that you are the marketing manager for a national corporation with offices in several cities. Each branch manager reports to you on a quarterly basis, providing information about each product sold in his or her office. Your job is to consolidate the data into a single report. The situation is depicted graphically in Figure 5.1. Figures 5.1a, 5.1b, and 5.1c show reports for the Atlanta, Boston, and Chicago offices, respectively. Figure 5.1d shows the summary report for the corporation.

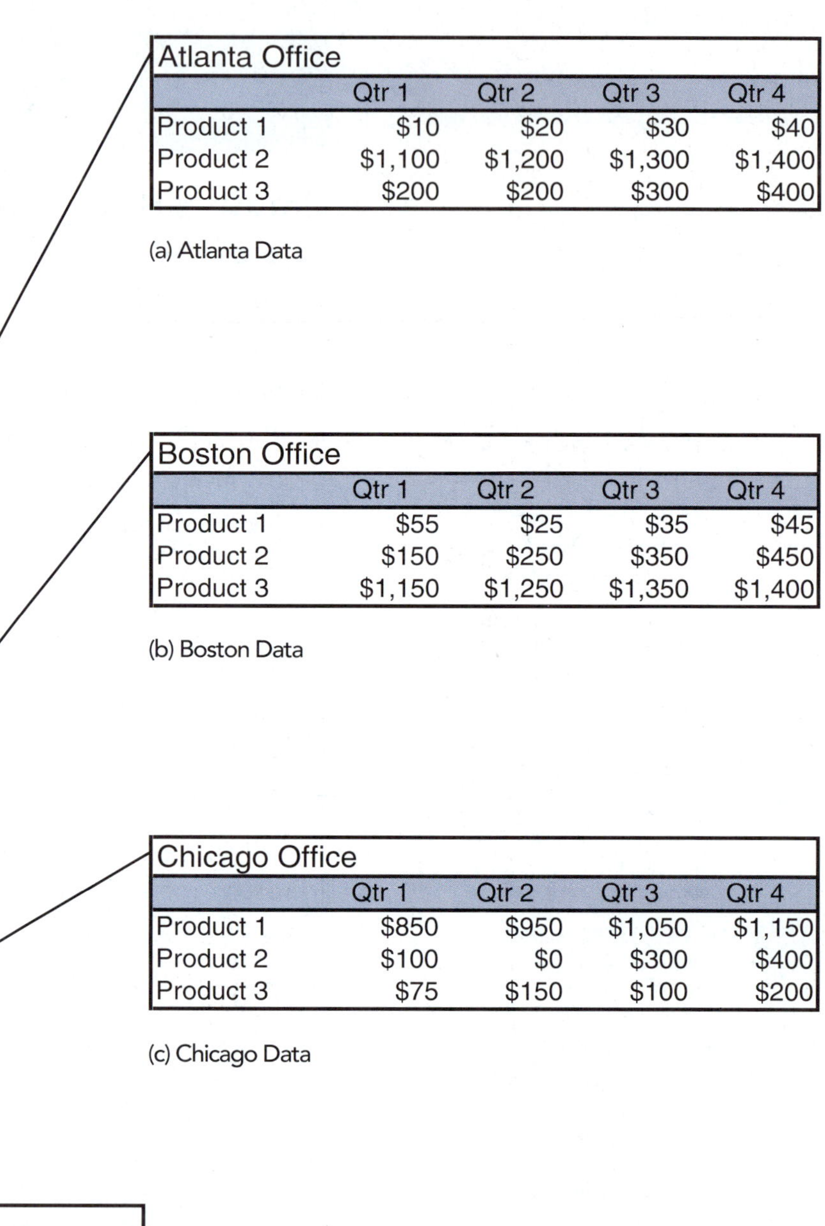

Atlanta Office

	Qtr 1	Qtr 2	Qtr 3	Qtr 4
Product 1	$10	$20	$30	$40
Product 2	$1,100	$1,200	$1,300	$1,400
Product 3	$200	$200	$300	$400

(a) Atlanta Data

Boston Office

	Qtr 1	Qtr 2	Qtr 3	Qtr 4
Product 1	$55	$25	$35	$45
Product 2	$150	$250	$350	$450
Product 3	$1,150	$1,250	$1,350	$1,400

(b) Boston Data

Chicago Office

	Qtr 1	Qtr 2	Qtr 3	Qtr 4
Product 1	$850	$950	$1,050	$1,150
Product 2	$100	$0	$300	$400
Product 3	$75	$150	$100	$200

(c) Chicago Data

Corporate Totals

	Qtr 1	Qtr 2	Qtr 3	Qtr 4
Product 1	$915	$995	$1,115	$1,235
Product 2	$1,350	$1,450	$1,950	$2,250
Product 3	$1,425	$1,600	$1,750	$2,000

(d) Corporate Summary

FIGURE 5.1 Consolidating Data

You should be able to reconcile the corporate totals for each product in each quarter with the detail amounts in the individual offices. Consider, for example, the sales of Product 1 in the first quarter. The Atlanta office has sold $10, the Boston office $55, and the Chicago office $850; thus, the corporation as a whole has sold $915 ($10+$55+$850). In similar fashion, the Atlanta, Boston, and Chicago offices have sold $1,100, $150, and $100, respectively, of Product 2 in the first quarter, for a corporate total of $1,350.

The chapter presents two approaches to computing the corporate totals in Figure 5.1. One approach is to use the three-dimensional capability within Excel, in which one workbook contains multiple worksheets. The workbook contains a separate worksheet for each of the three branch offices, and a fourth worksheet to hold the corporate data. An alternate technique is to keep the data for each branch office in its own workbook, then create a summary workbook that uses file linking to reference cells in the other workbooks.

There are advantages and disadvantages to each technique, as will be discussed in the chapter. As always, the hands-on exercises are essential to mastering the conceptual material.

THE THREE-DIMENSIONAL WORKBOOK

An Excel workbook is the electronic equivalent of the three-ring loose-leaf binder. It contains one or more worksheets, each of which is identified by a worksheet tab at the bottom of the document window. The workbook in Figure 5.2, for example, contains four worksheets. The title bar displays the name of the workbook (Corporate Sales). The tabs at the bottom of the workbook window display the names of the individual worksheets (Summary, Atlanta, Boston, and Chicago). The highlighted tab indicates the name of the active worksheet (Summary). To display a different worksheet, click on a different tab; for example, click the Atlanta tab to display the Atlanta worksheet.

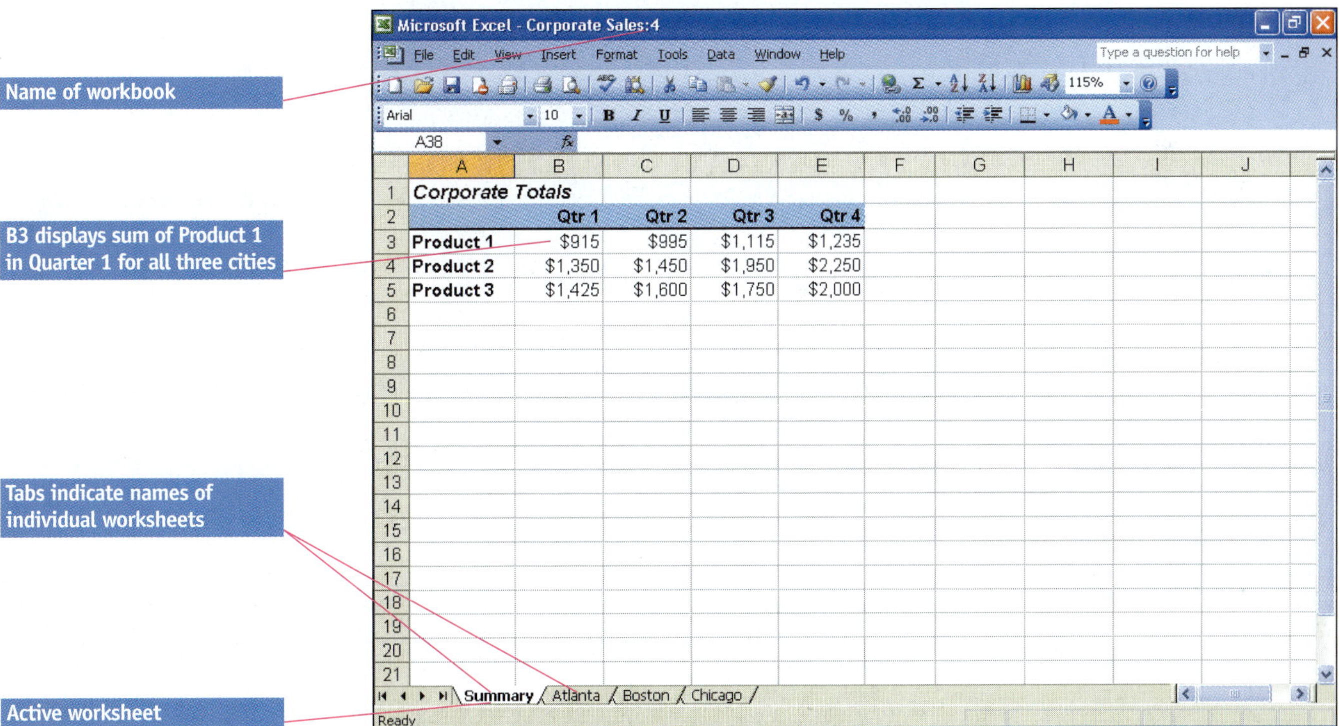

FIGURE 5.2 A Three-dimensional Workbook

The Summary worksheet shows the total amount for each product in each quarter. The data in the worksheet reflects the amounts shown earlier in Figure 5.1; that is, each entry in the Summary worksheet represents the sum of the corresponding entries in the worksheets for the individual cities. The amounts in the individual cities, however, are not visible in Figure 5.2. It is convenient, therefore, to open multiple windows to view the individual city worksheets at the same time you view the summary sheet.

Figure 5.3 displays the four worksheets in the Corporate Sales workbook, with a different sheet displayed in each window. The individual windows are smaller than the single view in Figure 5.2, but you can see at a glance how the Summary worksheet consolidates the data from the individual worksheets. The ***New Window command*** (in the Window menu) is used to open each additional window. Once the windows have been opened, the ***Arrange command*** (in the Window menu) is used to tile or cascade the open windows.

Only one window can be active at a time, and all commands apply to just the active window. In Figure 5.3, for example, the window in the upper left is active, as can be seen by the highlighted title bar. (To activate a different window, just click in that window.)

Copying Worksheets

The workbook in Figure 5.3 summarizes the data in the individual worksheets, but how was the data placed into the workbook? You could, of course, manually type in the entries, but there is an easier way, given that each branch manager sends you a workbook with the data for his or her office. All you have to do is copy the data from the individual workbooks into the appropriate worksheets in a new corporate workbook. (The specifics for how this is done are explained in detail in a hands-on exercise.)

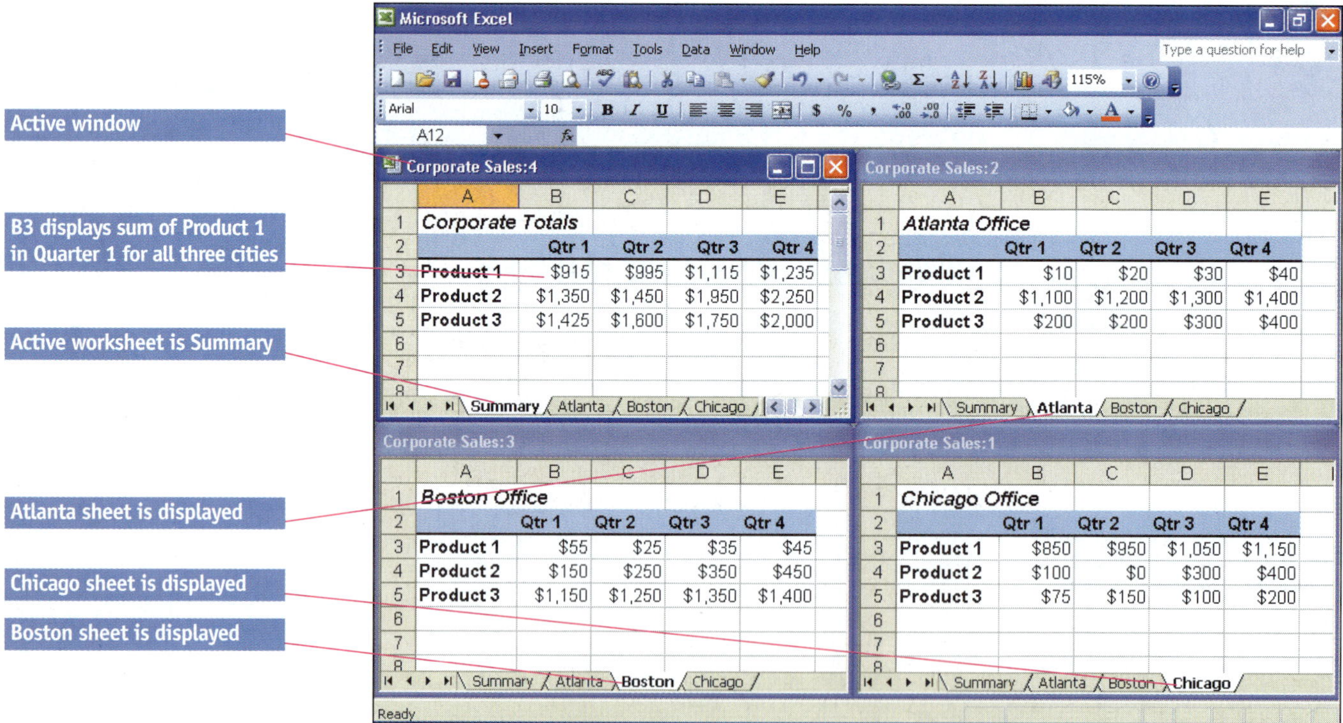

FIGURE 5.3 Multiple Worksheets

Multiple Workbooks

Consider now Figure 5.4, which at first glance appears to be almost identical to Figure 5.3. The two figures are very different, however. Figure 5.3 displayed four different worksheets from the same workbook. Figure 5.4, on the other hand, displays four different workbooks. There is one workbook for each city (Atlanta, Boston, and Chicago) and each of these workbooks contains only a single worksheet. The fourth workbook, Corporate Sales, contains four worksheets (Atlanta, Boston, Chicago, and Summary) and is the workbook displayed in Figure 5.3.

There are advantages and disadvantages to each technique. The single workbook in Figure 5.3 is easier for the manager in that he or she has all of the data in one file. The disadvantage is that the worksheets have to be maintained by multiple people (the manager in each city), and this can lead to confusion in that several individuals require access to the same workbook. The multiple workbooks of Figure 5.4 facilitate the maintenance of the data, but four separate files are required to produce the summary information. Both approaches are explored in detail within the chapter. The choice is up to you.

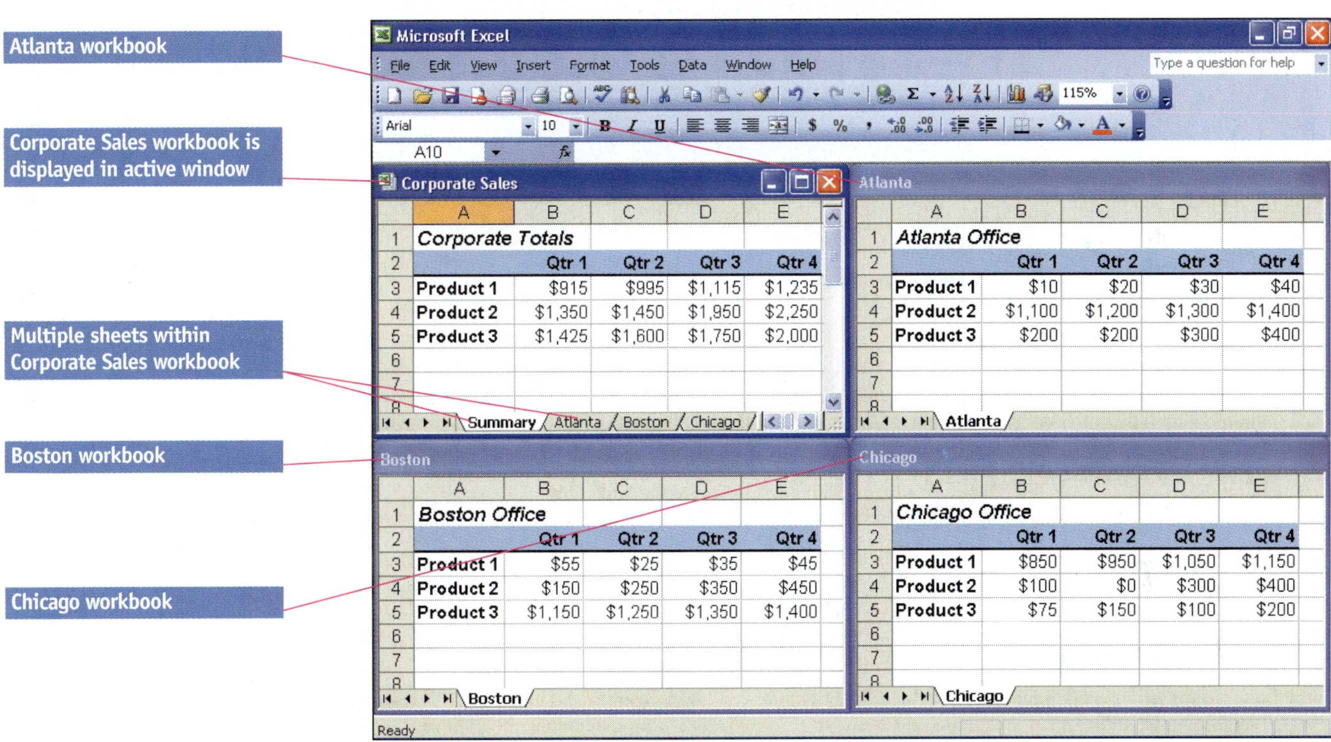

FIGURE 5.4 Multiple Workbooks

THE HORIZONTAL SCROLL BAR

The horizontal scroll bar contains four scrolling buttons to scroll through the worksheet tabs in a workbook. (The default workbook has three worksheets.) Click ◀ or ▶ to scroll one tab to the left or right. Click |◀ or ▶| to scroll to the first or last tab in the workbook. Once the desired tab is visible, click the tab to select it. The number of tabs that are visible simultaneously depends on the setting of the horizontal scroll bar; that is, you can drag the tab split bar to change the number of tabs that can be seen at one time.

hands-on exercise 1

Copying Worksheets

Objective To open multiple workbooks; to use the Windows Arrange command to tile the open workbooks; to copy a worksheet from one workbook to another. Use Figure 5.5 as a guide in the exercise.

Step 1: Open a New Workbook

- Start Excel. Close the task pane if it is open. If necessary, click the **New button** on the Standard toolbar to open a new workbook as shown in Figure 5.5a.
- Delete all worksheets except for Sheet1:
  - Click the tab for **Sheet2**. Press the **Shift key** as you click the tab for **Sheet3**.
  - Point to the tab for **Sheet3** and click the **right mouse button** to display a shortcut menu. Click **Delete**.
- The workbook should contain only Sheet1 as shown in Figure 5.5a. Save the workbook as **Corporate Sales** in the **Exploring Excel folder**.

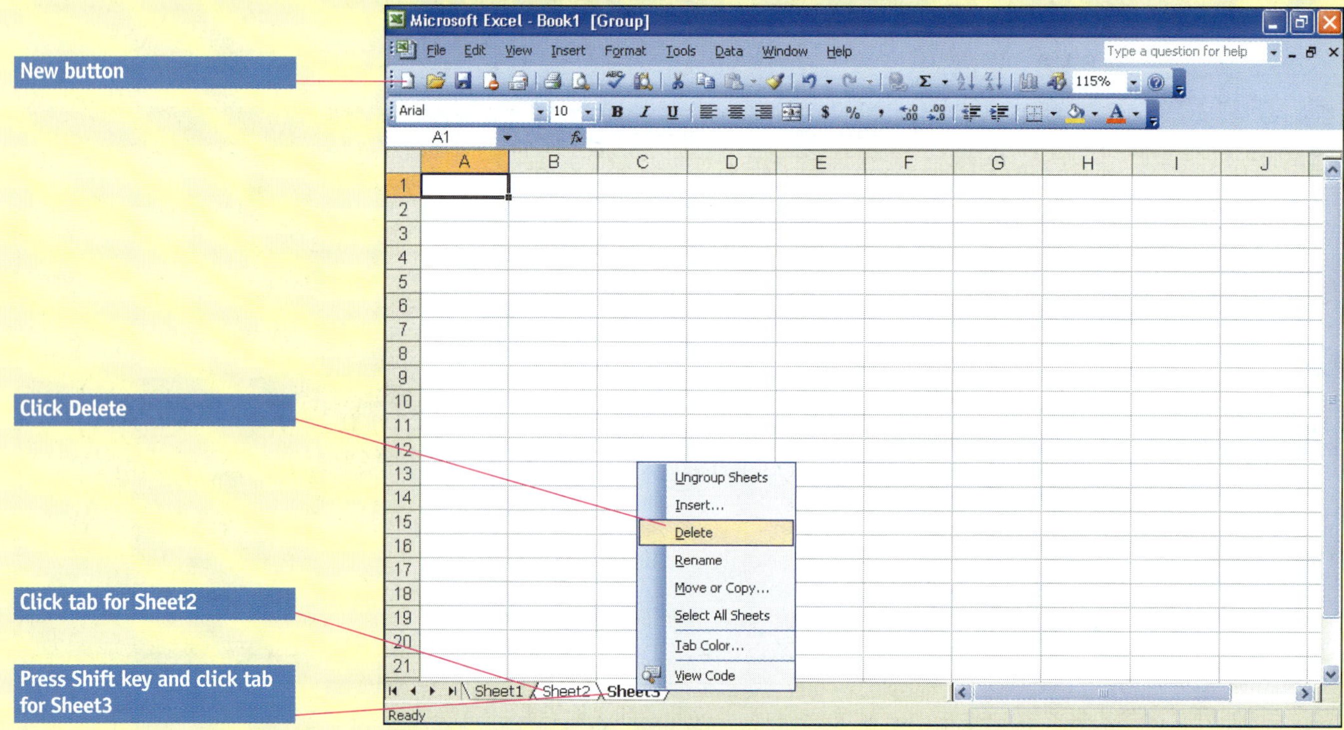

(a) Open a New Workbook (step 1)

FIGURE 5.5 Hands-on Exercise 1

THE RIGHT MOUSE BUTTON

Point to any object, then click the right mouse button to display a context-sensitive menu with commands appropriate to the item you are pointing to. Right clicking a cell, for example, displays a menu with selected commands from the Edit, Insert, and Format menus. Right clicking a toolbar displays a menu that lets you display (hide) additional toolbars. Right clicking a worksheet tab enables you to rename, move, copy, or delete a worksheet.

Step 2: Open the Individual Workbooks

- Pull down the **File menu**. Click **Open** to display the Open dialog box. (If necessary, open the Exploring Excel folder.)
- Click the **Atlanta workbook**, then press and hold the **Ctrl key** as you click the **Boston** and **Chicago workbooks** to select all three workbooks at the same time.
- Click **Open** to open the selected workbooks. The workbooks will be opened one after another with a brief message appearing on the status bar as each workbook is opened.
- Pull down the **Window menu**, which should indicate the four open workbooks at the bottom of the menu. Only one of the workbooks is visible at this time.
- Click **Arrange** to display the Arrange Windows dialog box. If necessary, select the **Tiled option**, then click **OK**. You should see four open workbooks as shown in Figure 5.5b. (Do not be concerned if your workbooks are arranged differently from ours.)

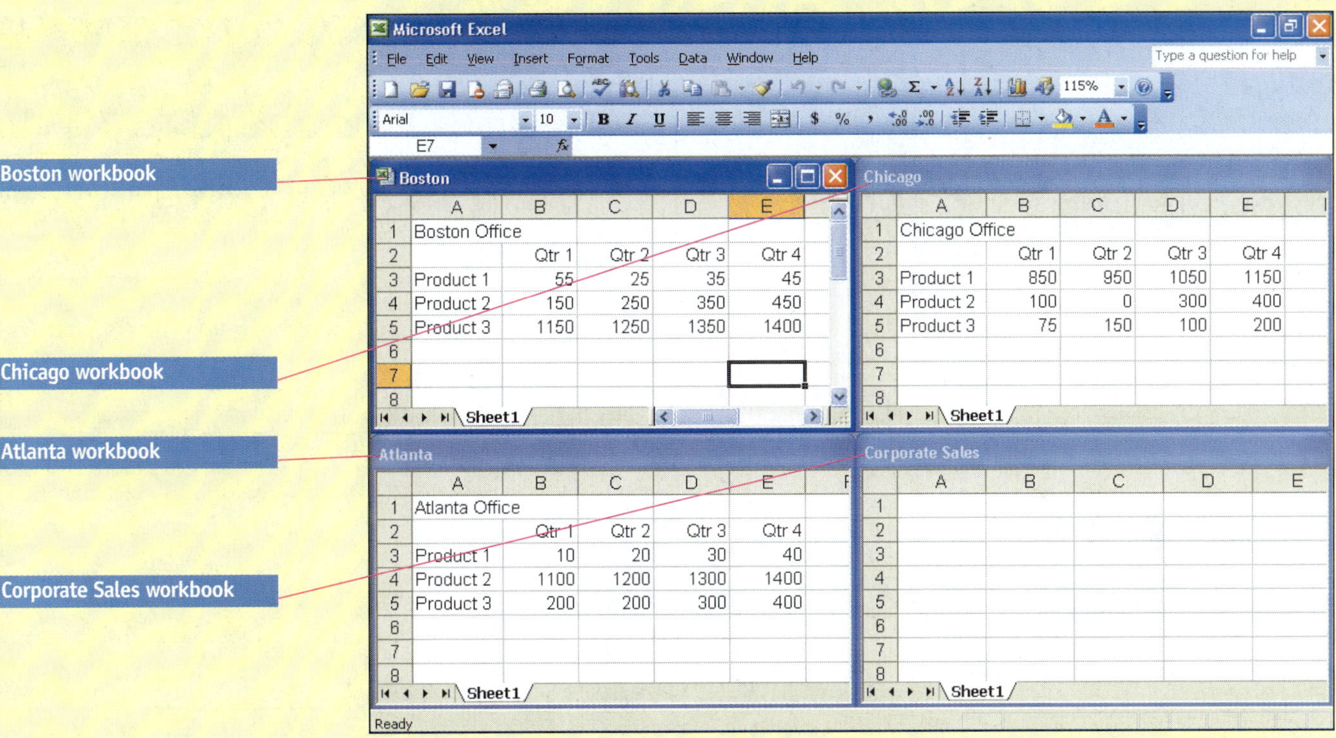

(b) Open the Individual Workbooks (step 2)

FIGURE 5.5 Hands-on Exercise 1 (*continued*)

DOWNLOAD THE PRACTICE FILES (DATA DISK)

The hands-on exercises in the text reference a series of practice files that are downloaded from our Web site. Go to www.prenhall.com/grauer, click the book icon for the series you want, and click the Student Download tab near the top of the window. Select the file you need according to the book you are using. Save the file to your desktop, then double click and follow the onscreen instructions. The installation procedure creates an Exploring Excel folder, which contains the files you need—for example, the Atlanta, Boston, and Chicago workbooks that are required for this exercise.

Step 3: Copy the Atlanta Data

- Click in the **Atlanta workbook** to make it the active workbook. Reduce the column widths (if necessary) so that you can see the entire worksheet.
- Click and drag to select **cells A1 through E5** as shown in Figure 5.5c. Pull down the **Edit menu** and click **Copy** (or click the **Copy button**).
- Click in **cell A1** of the **Corporate Sales workbook**.
- Click the **Paste button** on the Standard toolbar to copy the Atlanta data into this workbook. Press **Esc** to remove the moving border from the copy range.
- Point to the **Sheet1 tab** at the bottom of the Corporate Sales worksheet window, then click the **right mouse button** to produce a shortcut menu. Click **Rename**, which selects the worksheet name.
- Type **Atlanta** to replace the existing name and press **Enter**. The worksheet tab has been changed from Sheet1 to Atlanta. Reduce column widths as necessary.
- Click the **Save button** to save the active workbook (Corporate Sales).

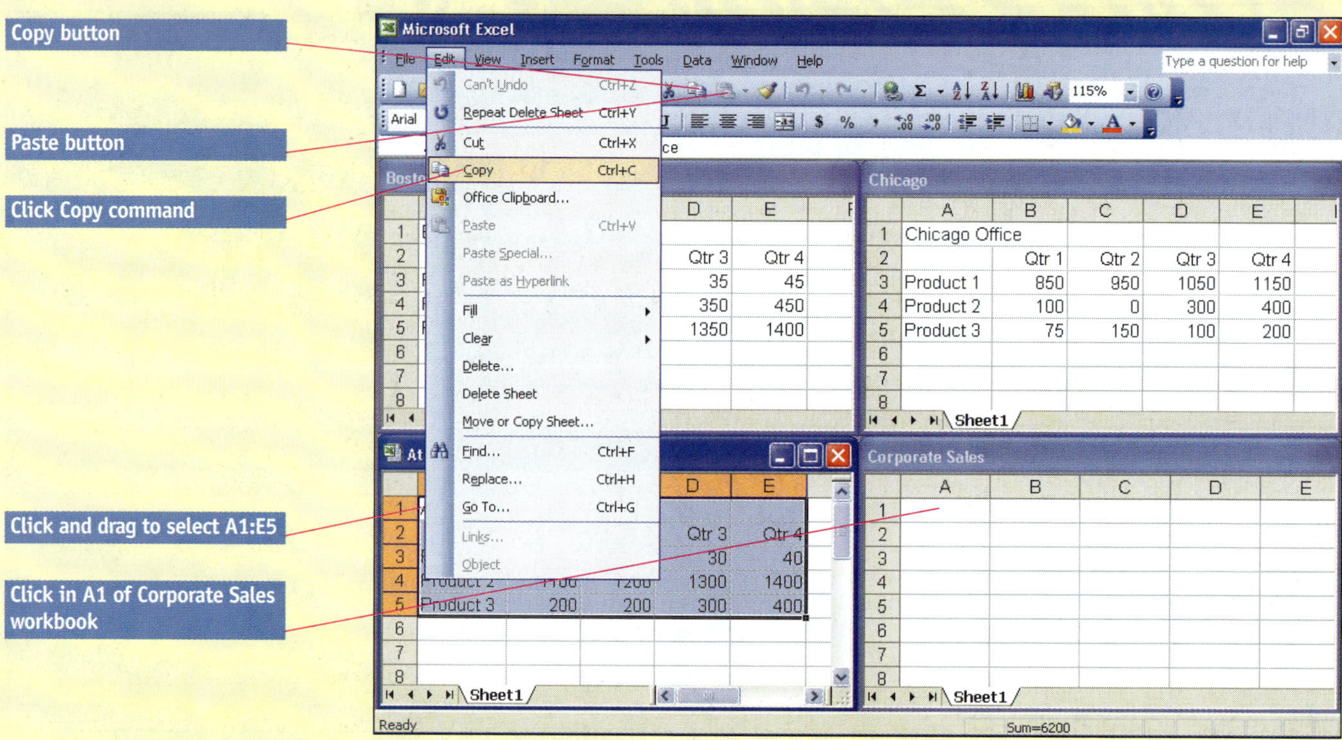

(c) Copy the Atlanta Data (step 3)

FIGURE 5.5 Hands-on Exercise 1 (*continued*)

CHANGE THE ZOOM SETTING

You can increase or decrease the size of a worksheet as it appears on the monitor by clicking the down arrow on the Zoom box and selecting an appropriate percentage. If you are working with a large spreadsheet and cannot see it at one time on the screen, choose a number less than 100%. Conversely, if you find yourself squinting because the numbers are too small, select a percentage larger than 100%. Changing the magnification on the screen does not affect printing; that is, worksheets are printed at 100% unless you change the scaling within the Page Setup command.

Step 4: Copy the Boston and Chicago Data

- Click in the **Boston workbook** to make it the active workbook as shown in Figure 5.5d.
- Click the **Sheet1 tab**, then press and hold the **Ctrl key** as you drag the tab to the right of the Atlanta tab in the Corporate Sales workbook. You will see a tiny spreadsheet with a plus sign as you drag the tab. The plus sign indicates that the worksheet is being copied; the ▼ symbol indicates where the worksheet will be placed.
- Release the mouse, then release the Ctrl key. The worksheet from the Boston workbook should have been copied to the Corporate Sales workbook and appears as Sheet1 in that workbook.
- The Boston workbook should still be open; if it isn't, it means that you did not press the Ctrl key as you were dragging the tab to copy the worksheet. If this is the case, pull down the **File menu**, reopen the Boston workbook, and if necessary, tile the open windows.
- Double click the **Sheet1 tab** in the Corporate Sales workbook to rename the tab. Type **Boston** as the new name, then press the **Enter key**.
- The Boston worksheet should appear to the right of the Atlanta worksheet; if the worksheet appears to the left of Atlanta, click and drag the tab to its desired position. (The ▼ symbol indicates where the worksheet will be placed.)
- Repeat the previous steps to copy the Chicago data to the Corporate Sales workbook, placing the new sheet to the right of the Boston sheet. Rename the copied worksheet **Chicago**.
- Save the Corporate Sales workbook. (The Summary worksheet will be built in the next exercise.)

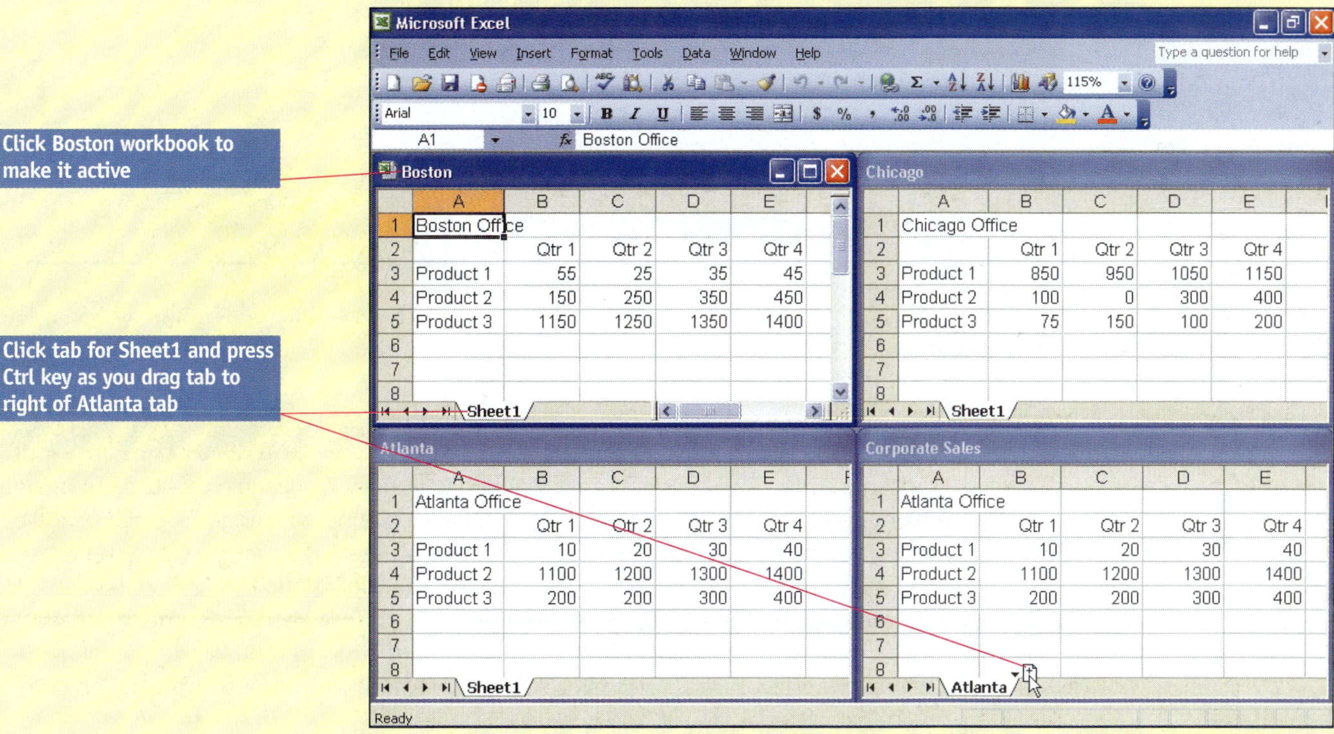

(d) Copy the Boston and Chicago Data (step 4)

FIGURE 5.5 Hands-on Exercise 1 (*continued*)

Step 5: The Corporate Sales Workbook

- Check that the Corporate Sales workbook is the active workbook. Click the **Maximize button** so that this workbook takes the entire screen.
- The Corporate Sales workbook contains three worksheets, one for each city, as can be seen in Figure 5.5e.
- Click the **Atlanta tab** to display the worksheet for Atlanta.
- Click the **Boston tab** to display the worksheet for Boston.
- Click the **Chicago tab** to display the worksheet for Chicago.
- Close all of the open workbooks, saving changes if requested to do so.
- Exit Excel if you do not want to continue with the next hands-on exercise at this time.

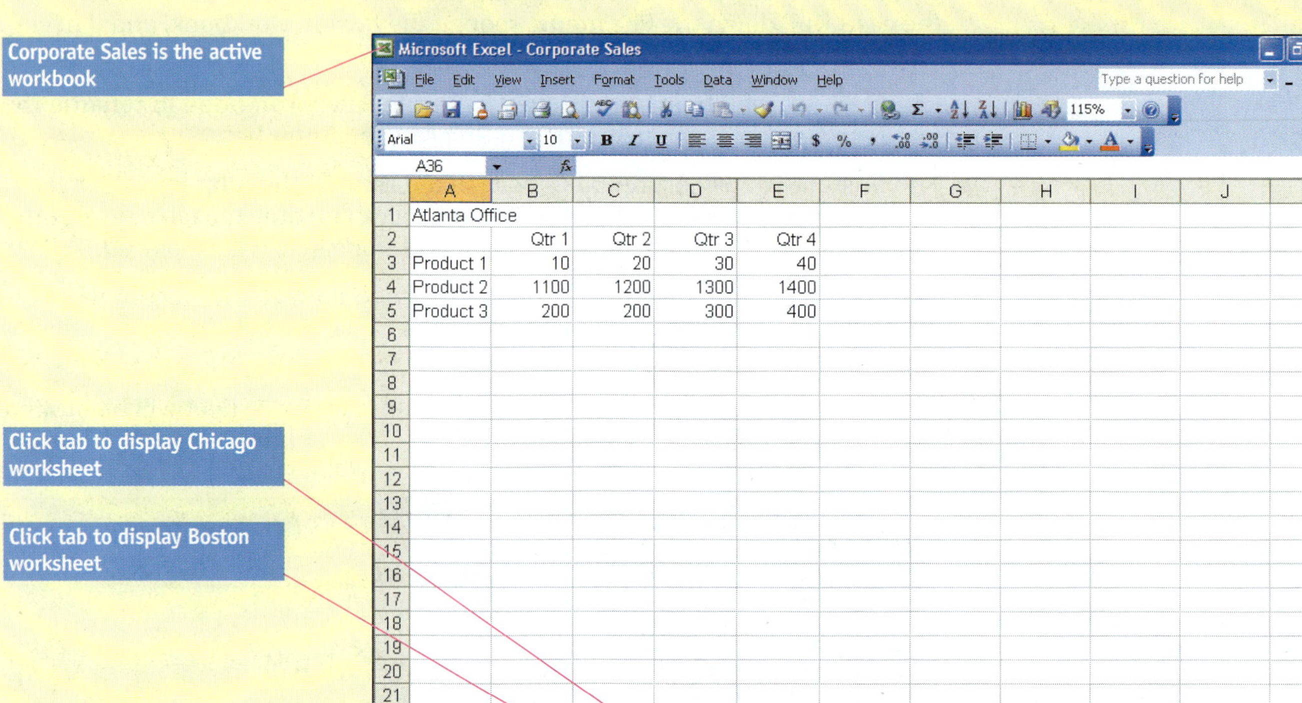

(e) The Corporate Sales Workbook (step 5)

FIGURE 5.5 Hands-on Exercise 1 (*continued*)

MOVING AND COPYING WORKSHEETS

You can move or copy a worksheet within a workbook by dragging its tab. To move a worksheet, click its tab, then drag the tab to the new location (a black triangle shows where the new sheet will go). To copy a worksheet, click its tab, then press and hold the Ctrl key as you drag the tab to its new location. The copied worksheet will have the same name as the original worksheet, followed by a number in parentheses indicating the copy number. Add color to your workbook by changing the color of a worksheet tab. Right click the worksheet tab, click the Tab Color command, select a new color, and click OK.

WORKSHEET REFERENCES

The presence of multiple worksheets in a workbook creates an additional requirement for cell references. You continue to use the same row and column convention when you reference a cell on the current worksheet; that is, cell A1 is still A1. What if, however, you want to reference a cell on another worksheet within the same workbook? It is no longer sufficient to refer to cell A1 because every worksheet has its own cell A1.

To reference a cell (or cell range) in a worksheet other than the current (active) worksheet, you need to preface the cell address with a ***worksheet reference***; for example, Atlanta!A1 references cell A1 in the Atlanta worksheet. A worksheet reference may also be used in conjunction with a cell range—for example, Summary!B2:E5 to reference cells B2 through E5 on the Summary worksheet. Omission of the worksheet reference in either example defaults to the cell reference in the active worksheet.

An exclamation point separates the worksheet reference from the cell reference. The worksheet reference is always an absolute reference. The cell reference can be either relative (e.g., Atlanta!A1 or Summary!B2:E5) or absolute (e.g., Atlanta!$A$1 or Summary!$B$2:$E$5).

Consider how worksheet references are used in the Summary worksheet in Figure 5.6. Each entry in the Summary worksheet computes the sum of the corresponding cells in the Atlanta, Boston, and Chicago worksheets. The cell formula in cell B3, for example, would be entered as follows:

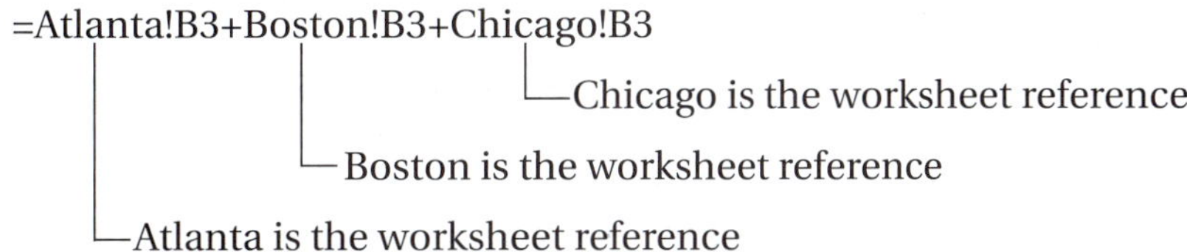

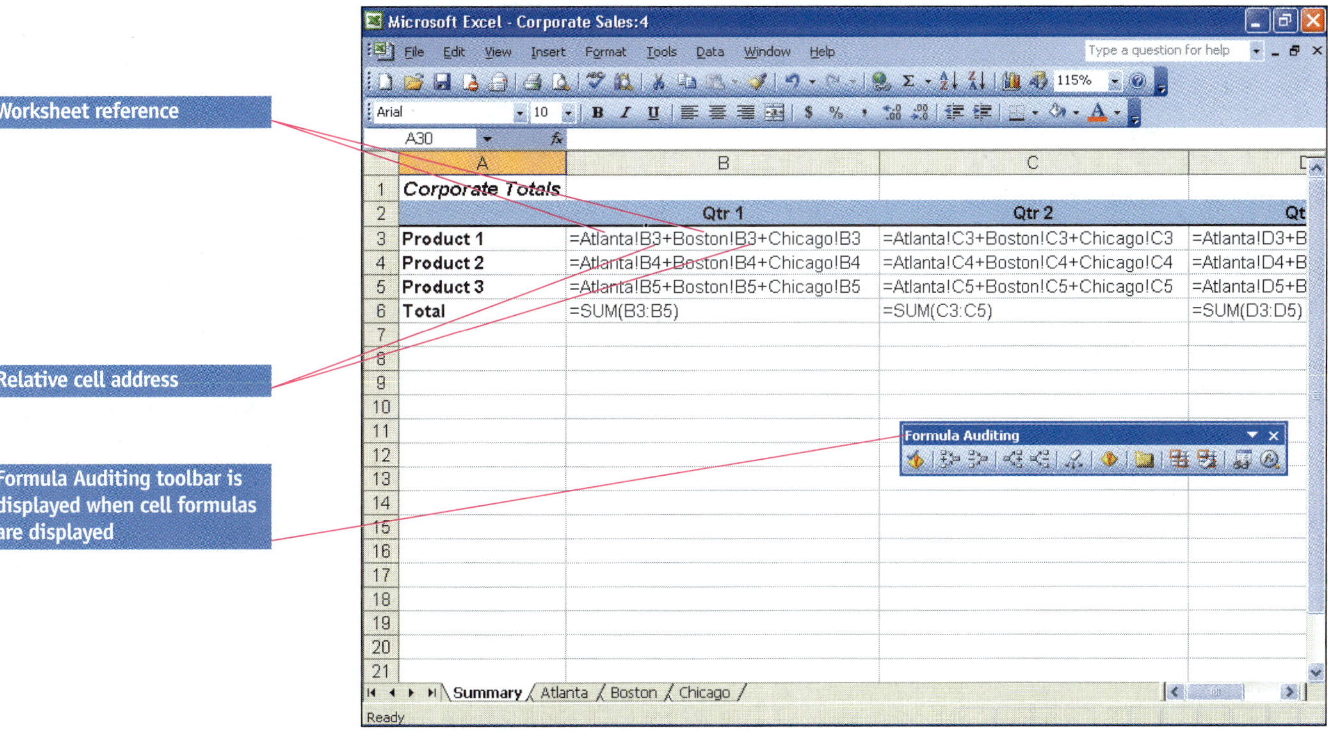

FIGURE 5.6 Worksheet References

The combination of relative cell references and constant worksheet references enables you to enter the formula once (into cell B3), then copy it to the remaining cells in the worksheet. In other words, you enter the formula into cell B3 to compute the total sales for Product 1 in Quarter 1, then you copy that formula to the other cells in row 3 (C3 through E3) to obtain the totals for Product 1 in Quarters 2, 3, and 4. You then copy the entire row (B3 through E3) to rows 4 and 5 (cells B4 through E5) to obtain the totals for Products 2 and 3 in all four quarters.

The proper use of relative and absolute references in the original formula in cell B3 is what makes it possible to copy the cell formulas. Consider, for example, the formula in cell C3 (which was copied from cell B3):

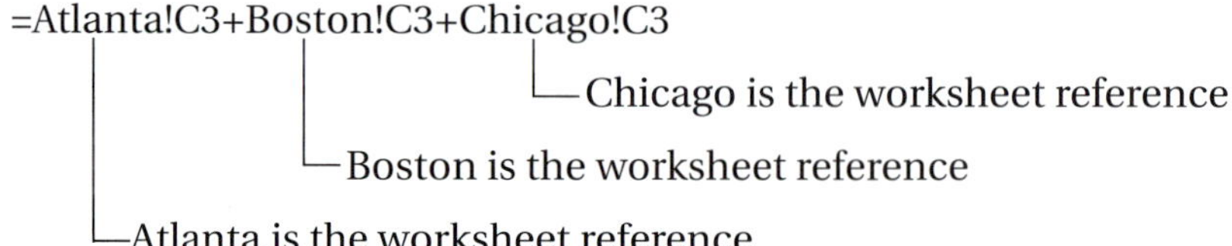

The worksheet references remain absolute (e.g., Atlanta!) while the cell references adjust for the new location of the formula (cell C3). Similar adjustments are made in all of the other copied formulas.

3-D Reference

A ***3-D reference*** is a range that spans two or more worksheets in a workbook—for example, =SUM(Atlanta:Chicago!B3) to sum cell B3 in the Atlanta, Boston, and Chicago worksheets. The sheet range is specified with a colon between the beginning and ending sheets. An exclamation point follows the ending sheet, followed by the cell reference. The worksheet references are constant and will not change if the formula is copied. The cell reference may be relative or absolute.

Three-dimensional references can be used in the Summary worksheet as an alternative way to compute the corporate total for each product–quarter combination. To compute the corporate sales for Product 1 in Quarter 1 (which appears in cell B3 of the Summary worksheet), you would use the following function:

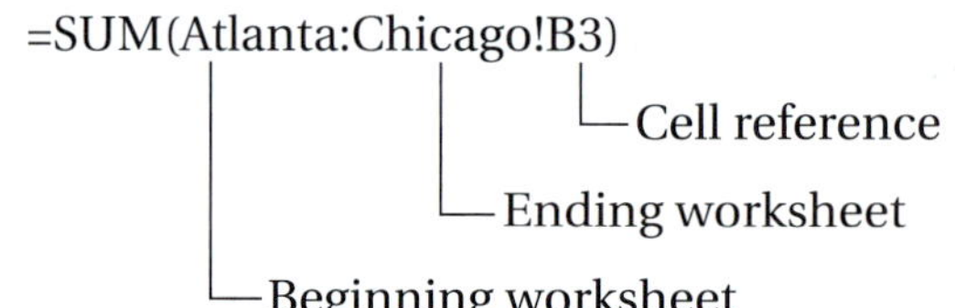

The 3-D reference includes all worksheets between the Atlanta and Chicago worksheets. (Only one additional worksheet, Boston, is present in the example, but the reference would automatically include any additional worksheets that were inserted between Atlanta and Chicago. In similar fashion, it would also adjust for the deletion of worksheets between Atlanta and Chicago.) Note, too, that the cell reference is relative and thus the formula can be copied from cell B3 in the Summary worksheet to the remaining cells in row 3 (C3 through E3). Those formulas can then be copied to the appropriate cells in rows 4 and 5.

A 3-D reference can be typed directly into a cell formula, but it is easier to enter the reference by pointing. Click in the cell that is to contain the 3-D reference, then enter an equal sign to begin the formula. To reference a cell in another worksheet, click the tab for the worksheet you want to reference, then click the cell or cell range you want to include in the formula. To reference a range from multiple worksheets, click in the cell in the first worksheet, press the Shift key as you click the tab for the last worksheet in the range, then click in the cell in the last worksheet.

Grouping Worksheets

The worksheets in a workbook are often similar to one another in terms of content and/or formatting. In Figure 5.3, for example, the formatting is identical in all four worksheets of the workbook. You can format the worksheets individually or more easily through grouping.

Excel provides the capability for ***grouping worksheets*** to enter or format data in multiple worksheets at the same time. Once the worksheets are grouped, anything you do in one of the worksheets is automatically done to the other sheets in the group. You could, for example, group all of the worksheets together when you enter row and column labels, when you format data, or when you enter formulas to compute row and column totals. You must, however, ungroup the worksheets when you enter data into a specific worksheet. Grouping and ungrouping is illustrated in the following hands-on exercise.

The AutoFormat Command

The formatting commands within Excel can be applied individually (as you have done throughout the text), or automatically and collectively by choosing a predefined set of formatting specifications. Excel provides several such designs as shown in Figure 5.7. You can apply any of these designs to your worksheet by selecting the range to be formatted, then executing the ***AutoFormat command*** from within the Format menu.

The AutoFormat command does not do anything that could not be done through the individual commands, but it does provide inspiration by suggesting several attractive designs. You can enter additional formatting commands after the AutoFormat command has been executed, as you will see in our next exercise.

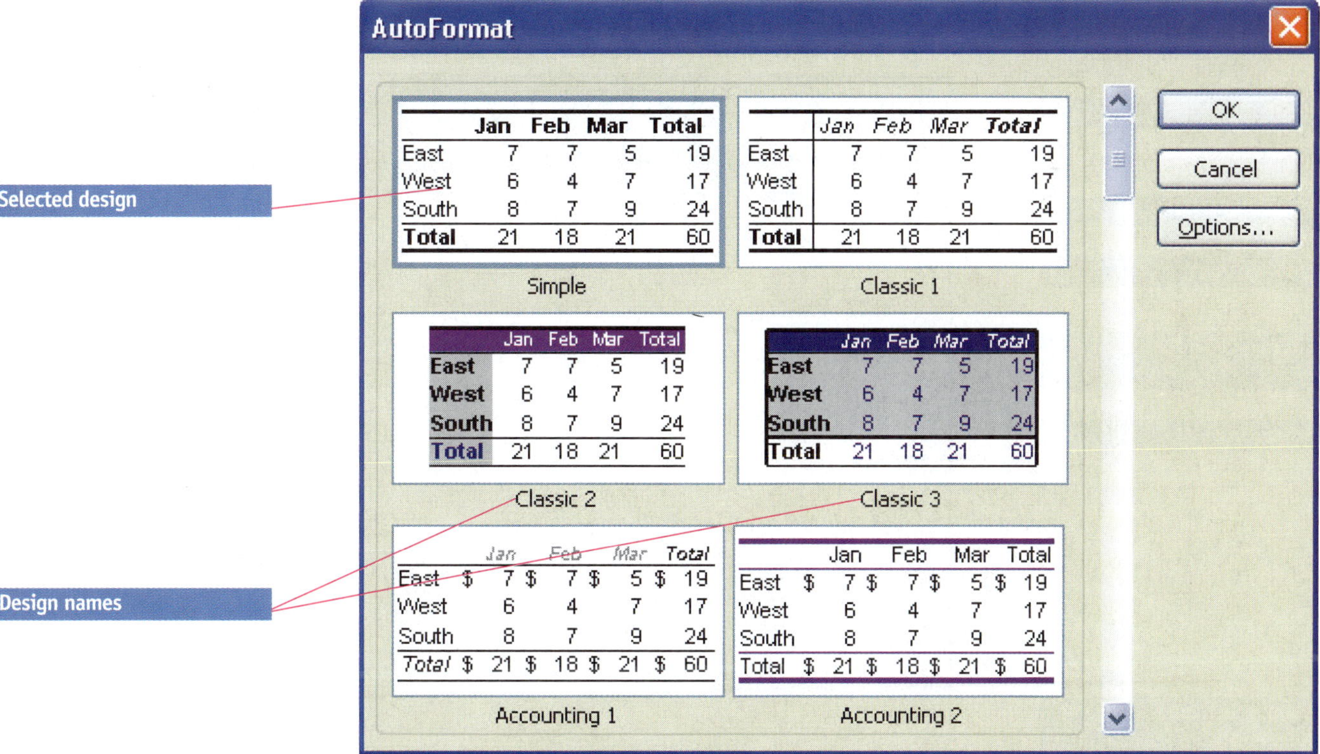

FIGURE 5.7 The AutoFormat Command

hands-on exercise

2 Worksheet References

Objective To use 3-D references to summarize data from multiple worksheets within a workbook; to group worksheets to enter common formatting and formulas; to open multiple windows to view several worksheets at the same time. Use Figure 5.8 as a guide in the exercise.

Step 1: Insert a Worksheet

- Start Excel. Open the **Corporate Sales workbook** created in the previous exercise. The workbook contains three worksheets.
- If necessary, click the ⏮ to display all three tabs. Click the **Atlanta tab** to select this worksheet. Pull down the **Insert menu**, and click the **Worksheet command**. You should see a new worksheet, Sheet1.
- Double click the **tab** of the newly inserted worksheet to select the name. Type **Summary** and press **Enter**. The name of the new worksheet has been changed.
- Click in **cell A1** of the Summary worksheet. Type **Corporate Totals** as shown in Figure 5.8a.
- Click in **cell B2**. Enter **Qtr 1**. Click in **cell B2**, then point to the fill handle in cell B2. The mouse pointer changes to a thin crosshair.
- Click and drag the fill handle over **cells C2**, **D2**, and **E2**. A border appears to indicate the destination range. Release the mouse. Cells C2 through E2 contain the labels Qtr 2, Qtr 3, and Qtr 4, respectively. Right align the column labels.
- Click in **cell A3**. Enter **Product 1**. Use the AutoFill capability to enter the labels **Product 2** and **Product 3** in cells A4 and A5.

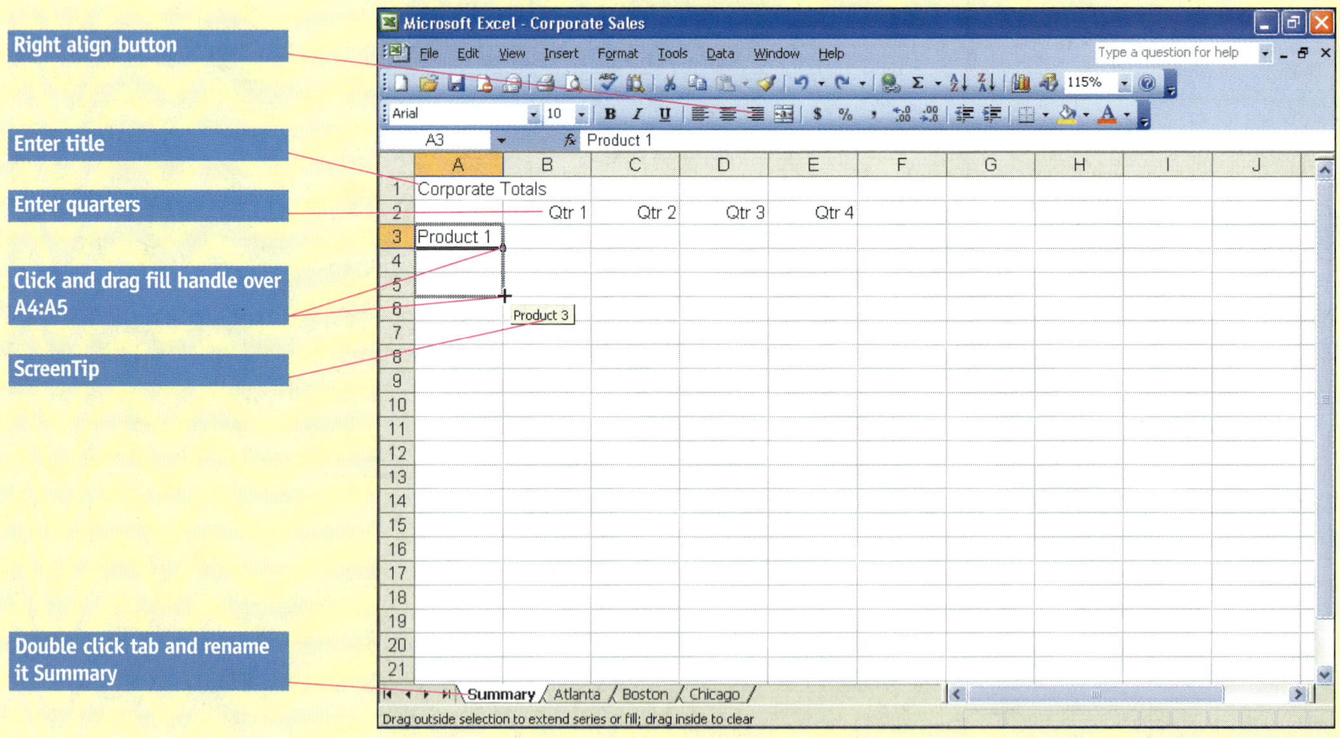

(a) Insert a Worksheet (step 1)

FIGURE 5.8 Hands-on Exercise 2

Step 2: Sum the Worksheets

- Click in **cell B3** of the Summary worksheet as shown in Figure 5.8b. Enter **=SUM(Atlanta:Chicago!B3)**, then press the **Enter key**. You should see 915 as the sum of the sales for Product 1 in Quarter 1 for the three cities (Atlanta, Boston, and Chicago).
- Click the **Undo button** on the Standard toolbar to erase the function so that you can reenter the function by using pointing.
- Check that you are in cell B3 of the Summary worksheet. Enter **=SUM(**.
  - Click the **Atlanta tab** to begin the pointing operation.
  - Press and hold the **Shift key**, click the **Chicago tab** (scrolling if necessary), then release the Shift key and click **cell B3**. The formula bar should now contain =SUM(Atlanta:Chicago!B3.
  - Press the **Enter key** to complete the function (which automatically enters the closing right parenthesis) and return to the Summary worksheet.
- You should see once again the displayed value of 915 in cell B3 of the Summary worksheet.
- If necessary, click in **cell B3**, then drag the fill handle over **cells C3 through E3** to copy this formula and obtain the total sales for Product 1 in all four quarters.
- Be sure that cells B3 through E3 are still selected, then drag the fill handle to **cell E5**. You should see the total sales for all products in all quarters.
- Click **cell E5** to examine the formula in this cell and note that the worksheet references are constant (i.e., they remained the same), whereas the cell references are relative (they were adjusted). Click in other cells to review their formulas in similar fashion.
- Save the workbook.

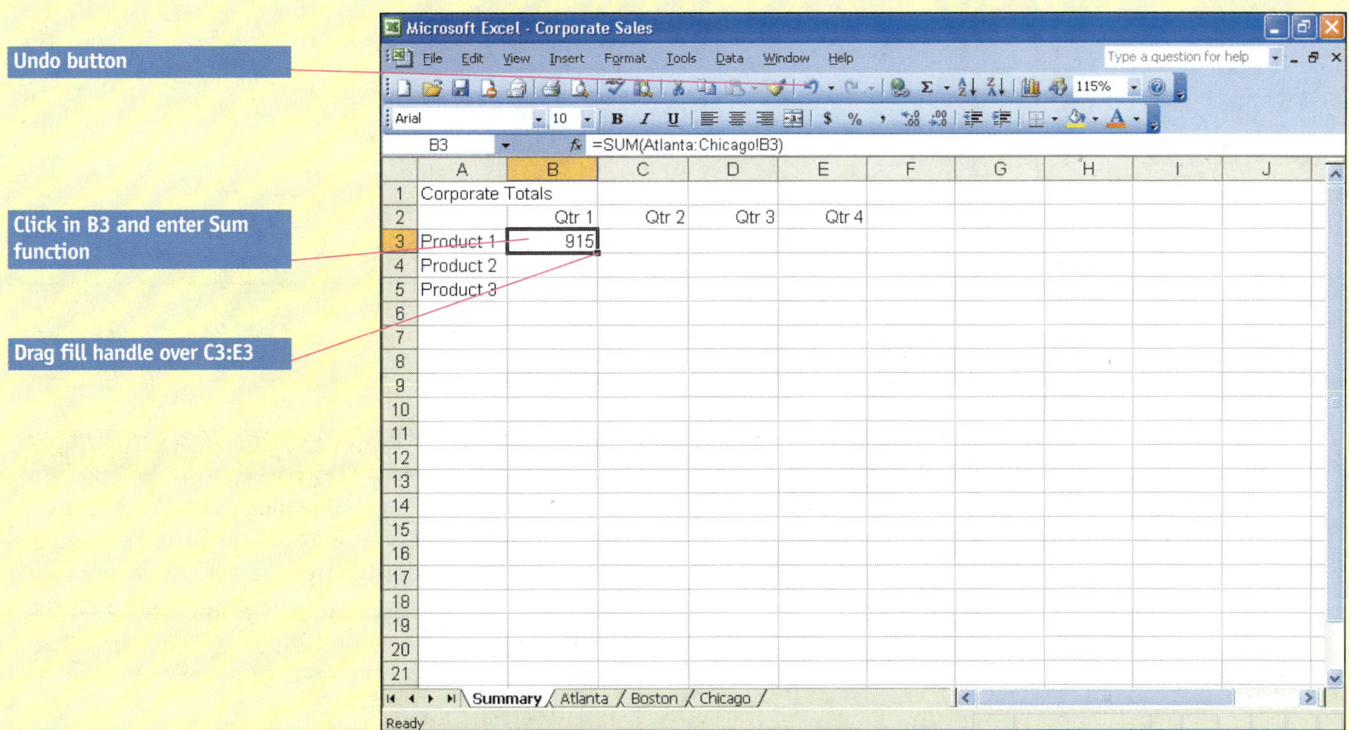

(b) Sum the Worksheets (step 2)

FIGURE 5.8 Hands-on Exercise 2 (*continued*)

Step 3: The Arrange Windows Command

- Pull down the **Window menu**, which displays the names of the open windows.
- The Corporate Sales workbook should be the only open workbook. Close any other open workbooks, including Book1.
- Pull down the **Window menu** a second time. Click **New Window** to open a second window. Note, however, that your display will not change at this time.
- Pull down the **Window menu** a third time. Click **New Window** to open a third window. Open a fourth window in similar fashion.
- Pull down the **Window menu** once again. You should see the names of the four open windows as shown in Figure 5.8c.
- Click **Arrange** to display the Arrange Windows dialog box. If necessary, select the **Tiled option**, then click **OK**. You should see four tiled windows.

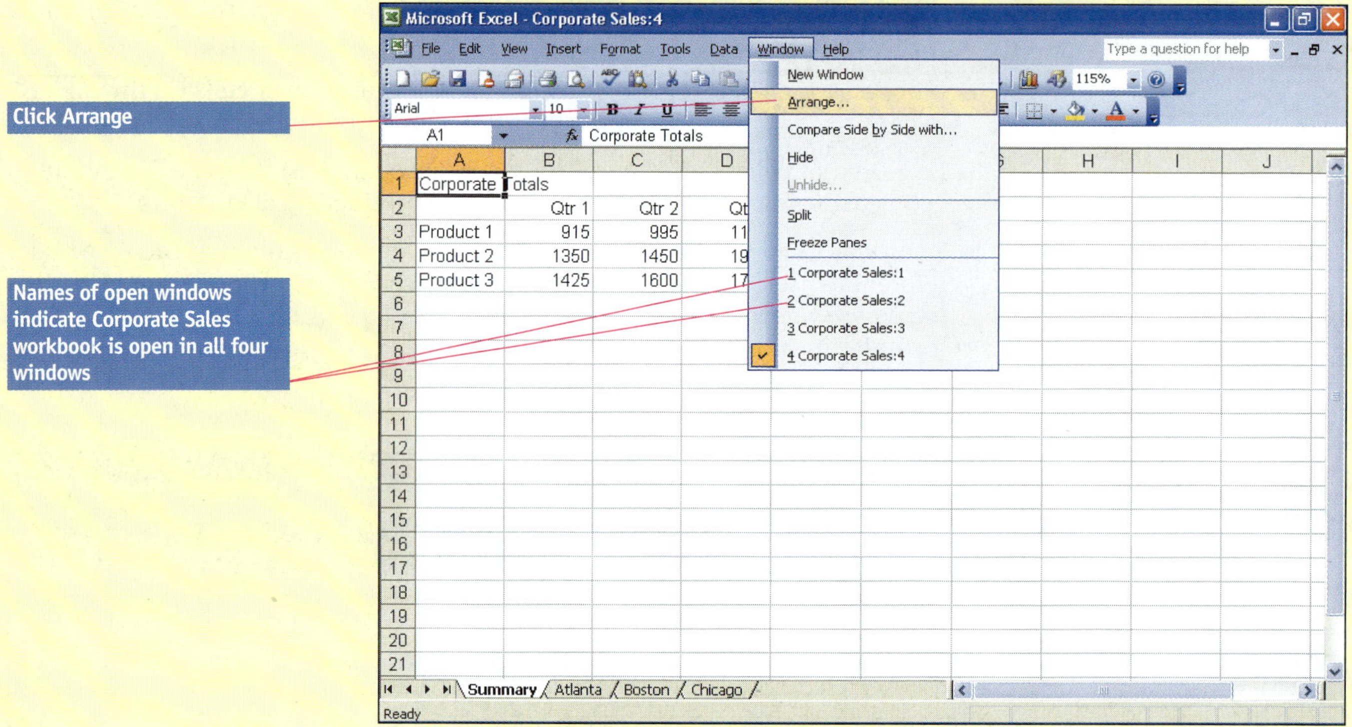

(c) The Arrange Windows Command (step 3)

FIGURE 5.8 Hands-on Exercise 2 (*continued*)

POINTING TO CELLS IN OTHER WORKSHEETS

A worksheet reference can be typed directly into a cell formula, but it is easier to enter the reference by pointing. Click in the cell that is to contain the reference, then enter an equal sign to begin the formula. To reference a cell in another worksheet, click the tab for the worksheet you want to reference, then click the cell or cell range you want to include in the formula. Complete the formula as usual, continuing to first click the tab whenever you want to reference a cell in another worksheet.

Step 4: Changing Data

- Click in the **upper-right window** in Figure 5.8d. Click the **Atlanta tab** to display the Atlanta worksheet in this window.
- Click the **lower-left window**. Click the **Boston tab** to display the Boston worksheet in this window.
- Click in the **lower-right window**. Click the **Tab scrolling button** until you can see the Chicago tab, then click the **Chicago tab**.
- Note that cell B3 in the Summary worksheet displays the value 915, which reflects the total sales for Product 1 in Quarter 1 for Atlanta, Boston, and Chicago (10, 55, and 850, respectively).
- Click in **cell B3** of the Chicago worksheet. Enter **250**. Press **Enter**. The value of cell B3 in the Summary worksheet changes to 315 to reflect the decreased sales in Chicago.
- Click the **Undo button** on the Standard toolbar. The sales for Chicago revert to 850 and the Corporate total is again 915.
- Save the workbook.

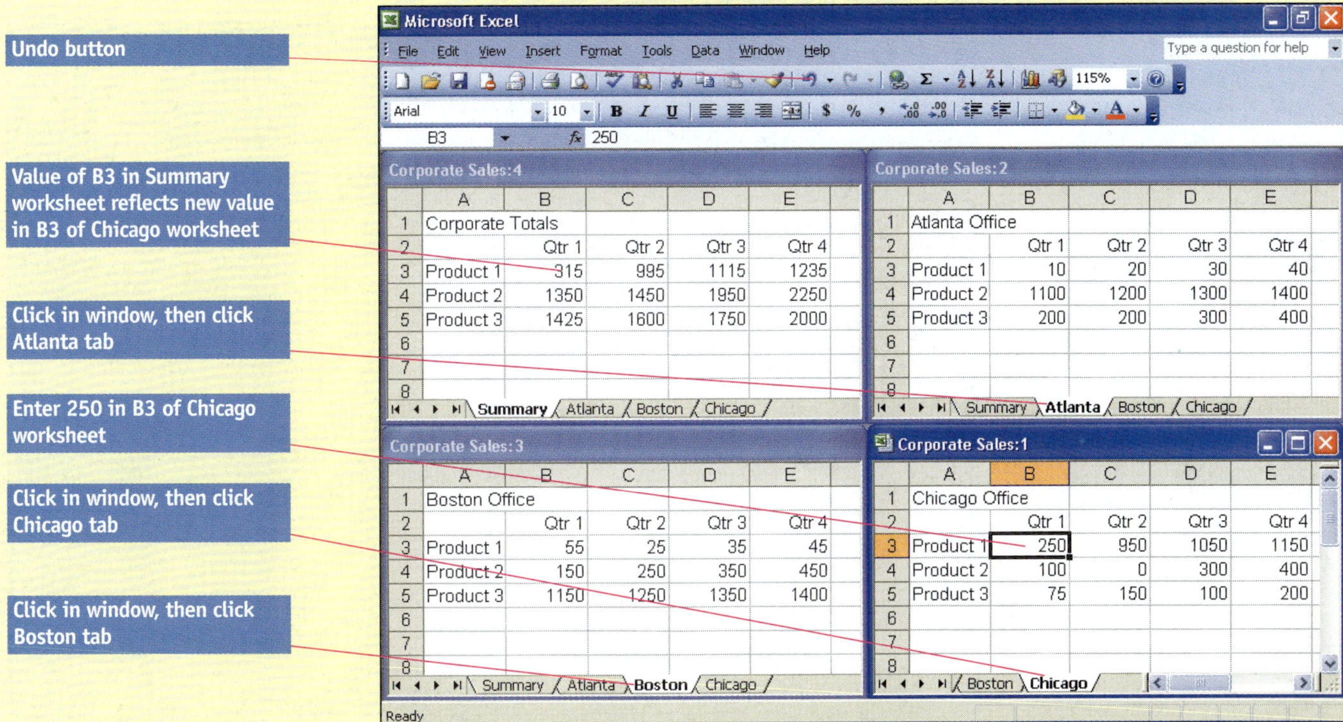

(d) Changing Data (step 4)

FIGURE 5.8 Hands-on Exercise 2 (*continued*)

CONTEXT-SENSITIVE MENUS

A context-sensitive menu provides an alternate (and generally faster) way to execute common commands. Point to a tab, then click the right mouse button to display a menu with commands to insert, delete, rename, move, copy, change color, or select all worksheets. Point to the desired command, then click the left mouse button to execute the command from the shortcut menu. Press the Esc key or click outside the menu to close the menu.

Step 5: Group Editing

- Click in the window where the Summary worksheet is active. Point to the split box separating the tab scrolling buttons from the horizontal scroll bar. (The pointer becomes a two-headed arrow.) Click and drag to the right until you can see all four tabs at the same time.
- If necessary, click the **Summary tab**. Press and hold the **Shift key** as you click the tab for the **Chicago worksheet**. All four tabs should be selected (and thus displayed in white) as shown in Figure 5.8e. You should also see [Group] in the title bar.
- Enter **Total** in **cell A6**. The text is centered in cell A6 of all four worksheets.
- Click in cell **B6** and enter the function **=SUM(B3:B5)**. Note that the formula is entered in all four sheets simultaneously because of group editing. Copy this formula to **cells C6 through E6**.
- Stay in the Summary worksheet and scroll until you can see column F. Enter **Total** in **cell F2**. Click in **cell F3** and enter the function **=SUM(B3:E3)**. Copy this formula to **cells F4 through F6**.
- Save the workbook.

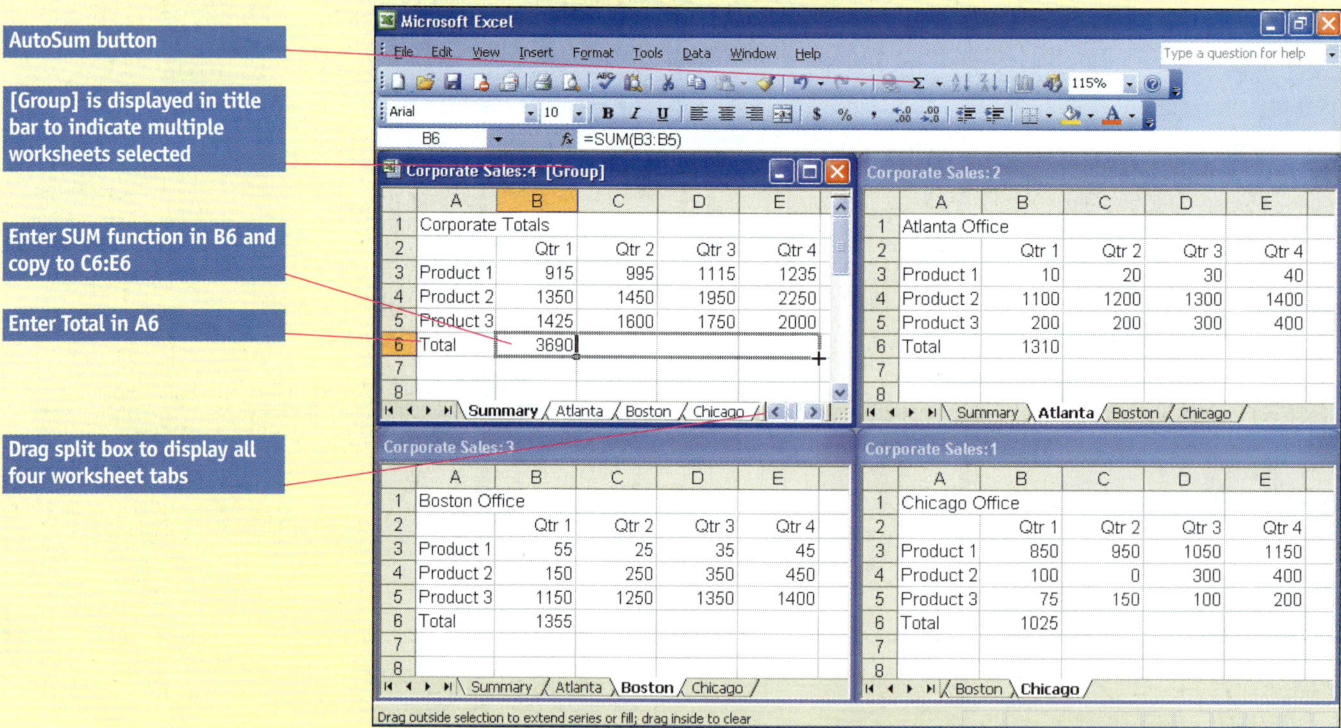

(e) Group Editing (step 5)

FIGURE 5.8 Hands-on Exercise 2 (*continued*)

THE AUTOSUM BUTTON

The AutoSum button on the Standard toolbar invokes the Sum function over a range of cells. To sum a single row or column, click in the blank cell at the end of the row or column, click the AutoSum button to see the suggested function, then click the button a second time to enter the function into the worksheet. To enter a sum function for multiple rows or columns, select the cell range prior to clicking the AutoSum button.

Step 6: The AutoFormat Command

- Be sure that all four tabs are still selected so that group editing is still in effect. Click and drag to select **cells A1 through F6** as shown in Figure 5.8f. (You may need to scroll in the worksheet to select all of the cells.)
- Pull down the **Format menu** and click the **AutoFormat command** to display the AutoFormat dialog box. Choose a format that appeals to you, then click the **Options button** to determine which parts of the format you want to apply.
- Experiment freely by selecting different designs and/or checking and unchecking the various check boxes within a design. Set a time limit, then make a decision. We chose the **Colorful 2** format and left all of the boxes checked. Click **OK**.
- The format is applied to all four selected sheets. You cannot see the effects in the summary worksheet, however, until you click elsewhere in the worksheet to deselect the cells.
- Save the workbook.

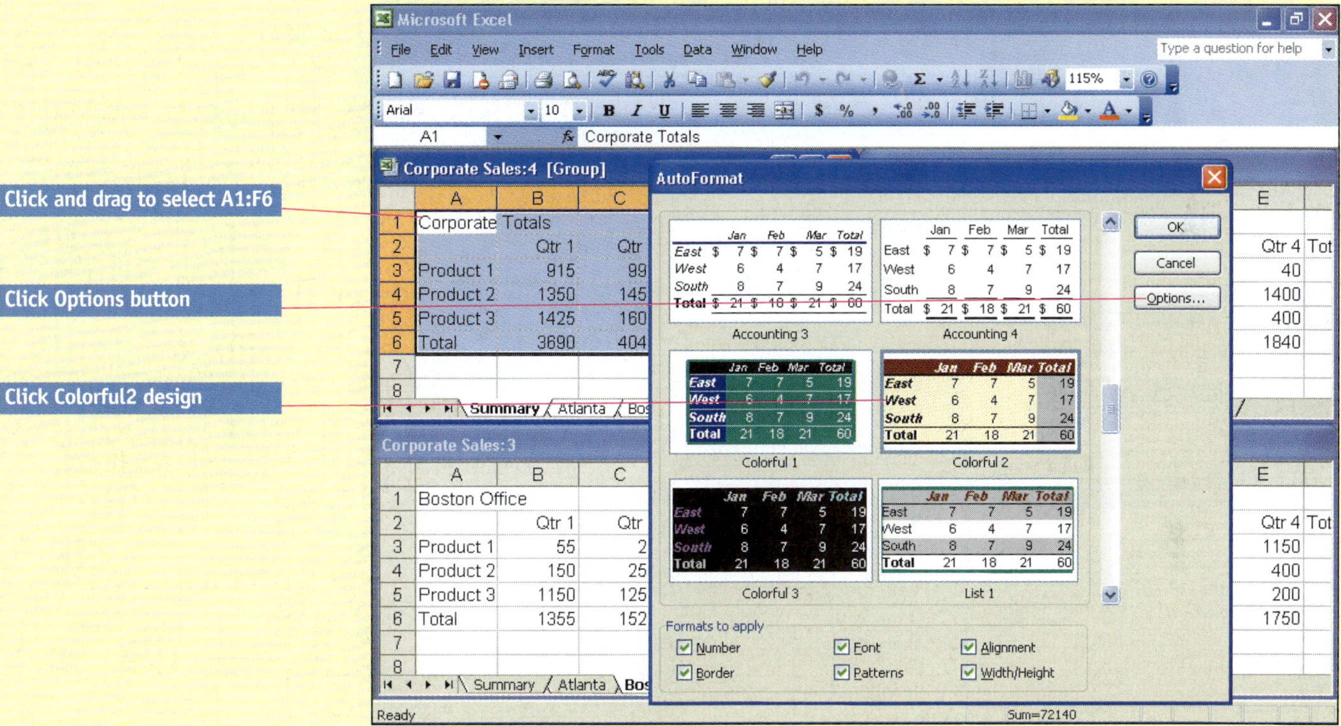

(f) The AutoFormat Command (step 6)

FIGURE 5.8 Hands-on Exercise 2 (*continued*)

SELECT MULTIPLE WORKSHEETS

You can group multiple worksheets simultaneously, then perform the same operation on the selected sheets at one time. To select adjacent worksheets, click the first sheet in the group, then press and hold the Shift key as you click the last sheet in the group. If the worksheets are not adjacent to one another, click the first tab, then press and hold the Ctrl key as you click the tab of each additional sheet. Excel indicates that grouping is in effect by appending [Group] to the workbook name in the title bar. Click any tab (other than the active sheet) to deselect the group.

Step 7: The Finishing Touches

- Click and drag to select **cells B3 through F6**, then pull down the **Format menu** and click the **Cells command** to display the Format Cells dialog box in Figure 5.8g. (You can also right click the selected cells, then select the **Format Cells command** from the context-sensitive menu.)
- Click the **Number tab**, click **Currency**, and set the number of decimal places to **zero**. Click **OK**.
- Change the width of columns B through F as necessary to accommodate the additional formatting. It's easiest to select all of the columns at the same time, then click and drag the border between any two of the selected columns to change the width of all selected columns.
- Click the **Atlanta tab** to ungroup the worksheets. Save the workbook. Close all four windows. Exit Excel if you do not want to continue with the next exercise at this time.

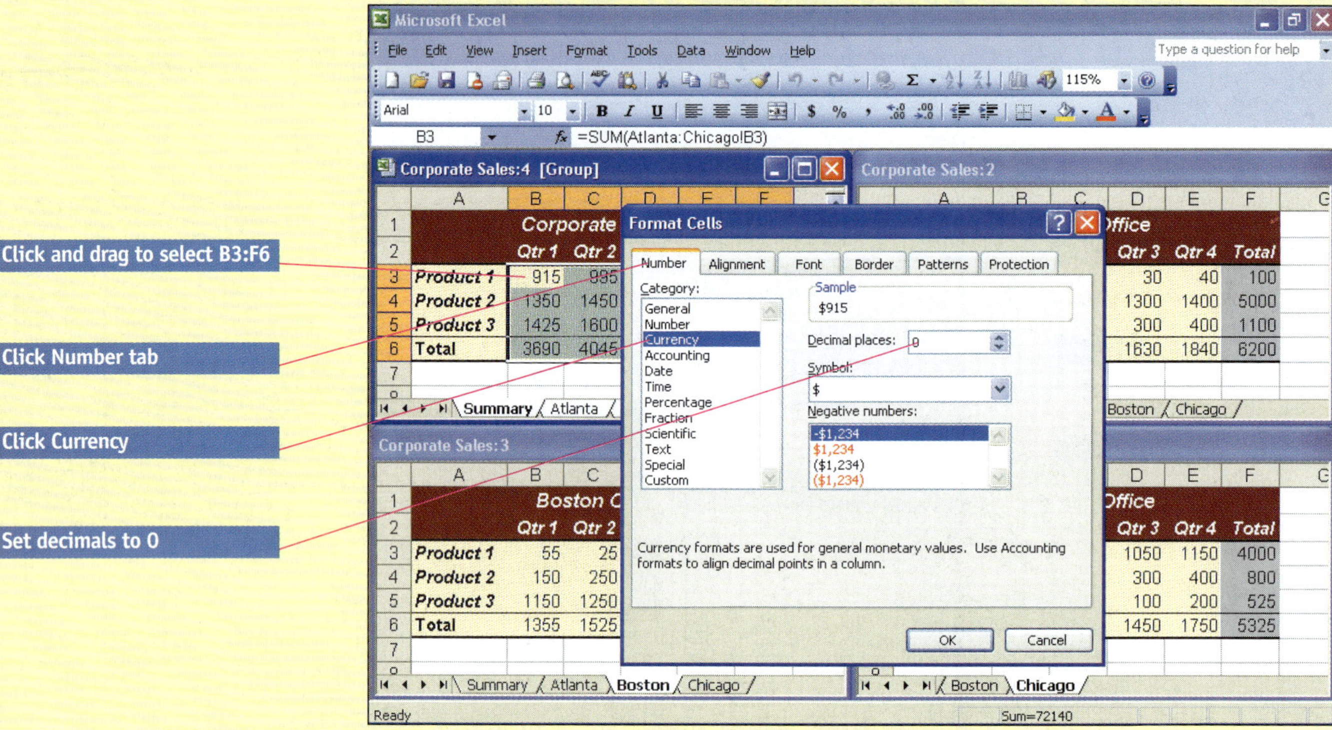

(g) The Finishing Touches (step 7)

FIGURE 5.8 Hands-on Exercise 2 (*continued*)

THE OPTIMAL (AUTOFIT) COLUMN WIDTH

The appearance of pound signs within a cell indicates that the cell width (column width) is insufficient to display the computed results in the selected format. Double click the right border of the column heading to change the column width to accommodate the widest entry in that column. For example, to increase the width of column B, double click the border between the column headings for columns B and C.

THE DOCUMENTATION WORKSHEET

Throughout the text we have emphasized the importance of properly designing a worksheet and of isolating the assumptions and initial conditions on which the worksheet is based. A workbook can contain up to 255 worksheets, and it, too, should be well designed so that the purpose of every worksheet is evident. Documenting a workbook, and the various worksheets within it, is important because spreadsheets are frequently used by individuals other than the author. You are familiar with every aspect of your workbook because you created it. Your colleague down the hall (or across the country) is not, however, and that person needs to know at a glance the purpose of the workbook and its underlying structure. Even if you don't share your worksheet with others, you will appreciate the documentation six months from now, when you have forgotten some of the nuances you once knew so well.

One way of documenting a workbook is through the creation of a ***documentation worksheet*** that describes the contents of each worksheet within the workbook as shown in Figure 5.9. The worksheet in Figure 5.9 has been added to the Corporate Sales workbook that was created in the first two exercises. (The Insert menu contains the command to add a worksheet.)

The documentation worksheet shows the author and date the spreadsheet was last modified. It contains a description of the overall workbook, a list of all the sheets within the workbook, and the contents of each. The information in the documentation worksheet may seem obvious to you, but it will be greatly appreciated by someone seeing the workbook for the first time.

The documentation worksheet is attractively formatted and takes advantage of the ability to wrap text within a cell. The description in cell B6, for example, wraps over several lines (just as in a word processor). The worksheet also takes advantage of color and larger fonts to call attention to the title of the worksheet. The grid lines have been suppressed through the View tab in the Options command of the Tools menu. The documentation worksheet is an important addition to any workbook.

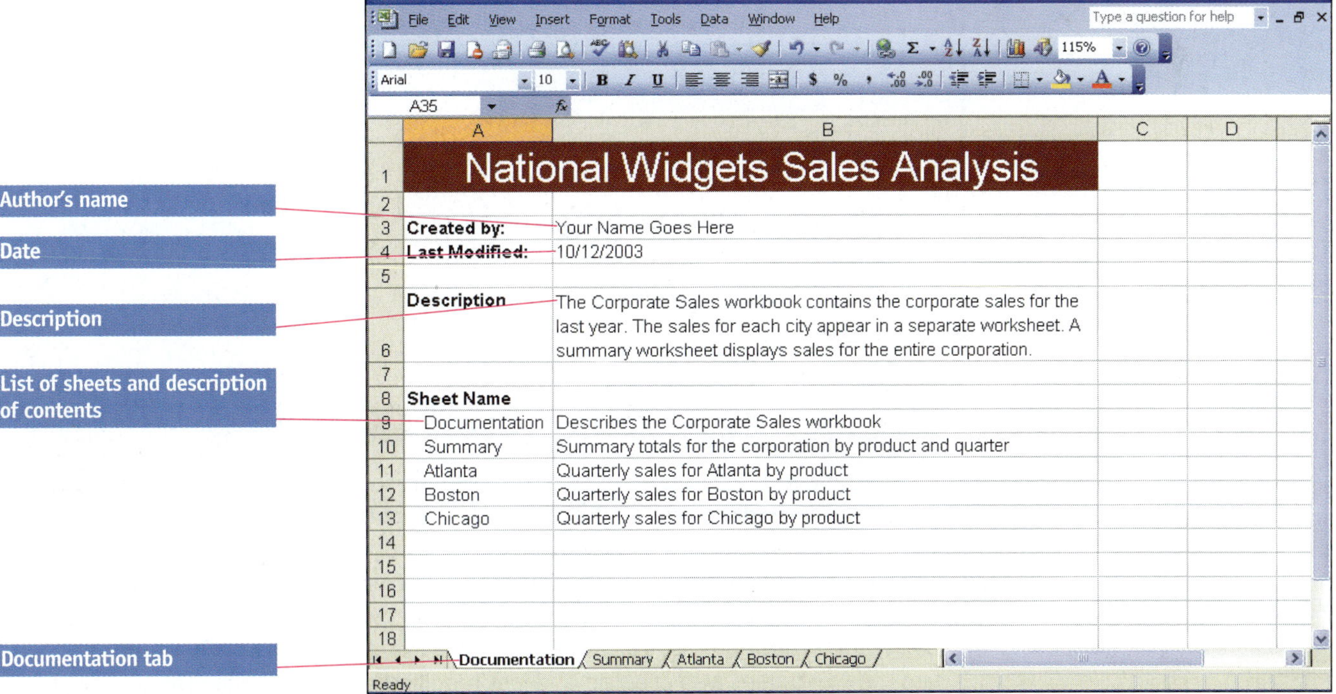

FIGURE 5.9 The Documentation Worksheet

hands-on exercise

3 The Documentation Worksheet

Objective To improve the design of a workbook through the inclusion of a documentation worksheet; to illustrate sophisticated formatting.

Step 1: Add the Documentation Worksheet

- Open the **Corporate Sales workbook** that was created in the previous exercise. Maximize the window. If necessary, click the **Atlanta tab** to turn off the group-editing feature. Click the **Summary tab** to select this worksheet.
- Pull down the **Insert menu** and click the **Worksheet command** to insert a new worksheet to the left of the Summary worksheet. Double click the **tab** of the new worksheet. Enter **Documentation** as the new name and press **Enter**.
- Enter the descriptive entries in column A as shown in Figure 5.10a. Enter your name in **cell B3**. Enter **=Today( )** in cell B4. Press **Enter**. Click the **Left Align button** to align the date as shown in the figure. Save the workbook.

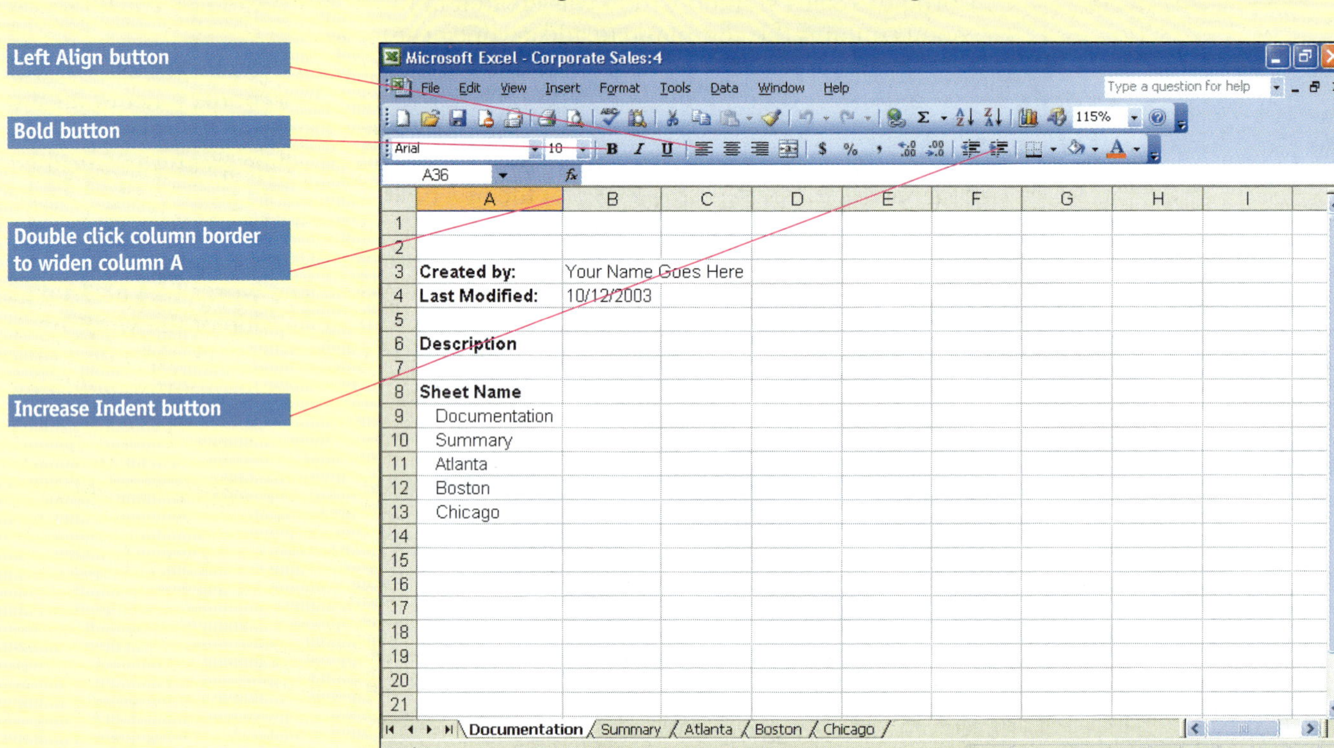

(a) Add the Documentation Worksheet (step 1)

FIGURE 5.10 Hands-on Exercise 3

WORKBOOK PROPERTIES

A documentation worksheet is one way to describe the author and other properties of a workbook. Excel also documents various properties automatically, but gives you the opportunity to modify that information. Pull down the File menu and click the Properties command to display the associated dialog box and explore the various tabs within the dialog box. Some properties are entered for you, such as the author in the Summary tab, the worksheet names in the Contents tab, and the date the worksheet was created and last modified in the Statistics tab. Other properties can be modified as necessary, especially in the Custom tab.

Step 2: The Wrap Text Command

- Increase the width of column B as shown in Figure 5.10b, then click in **cell B6** and enter the descriptive entry shown in the formula bar.
- Do not press the Enter key until you have completed the entire entry. Do not be concerned if the text in cell B6 appears to spill into the other cells in row six. Press the **Enter key** when you have completed the entry.
- Click in **cell B6**, then pull down the **Format menu** and click **Cells** (or right click **cell B6** and click the **Format Cells command**) to display the dialog box in Figure 5.10b.
- Click the **Alignment tab**, click the box to **Wrap Text** as shown in the figure, then click **OK**. The text in cell B6 wraps to the width of column B.
- Point to **cell A6**, then click the **right mouse button** to display a shortcut menu. Click **Format Cells** to display the Format Cells dialog box. If necessary, click the **Alignment tab**, click the **drop-down arrow** in the Vertical list box, and select **Top**. Click **OK**. Save the workbook.

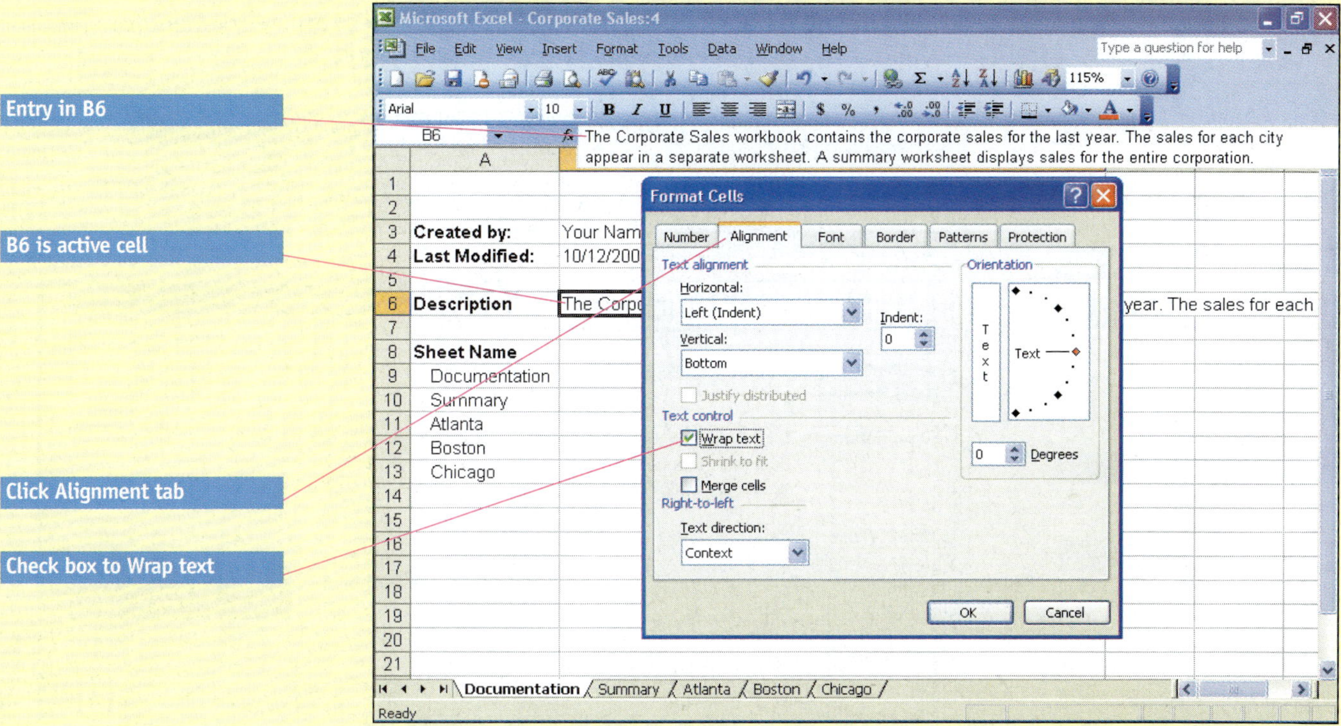

(b) The Wrap Text Command (step 2)

FIGURE 5.10 Hands-on Exercise 3 (*continued*)

EDIT WITHIN A CELL

Double click in the cell whose contents you want to change, then make the changes directly in the cell itself rather than on the formula bar. Use the mouse or arrow keys to position the insertion point at the point of correction. Press the Ins key to toggle between the insertion and overtype modes and/or use the Del key to delete a character. Press the Home and End keys to move to the first and last characters, respectively. If this feature does not work, pull down the Tools menu, click the Options command, click the Edit tab, then check the box to edit directly in a cell.

Step 3: Add the Worksheet Title

- Click in **cell A1**. Enter **National Widgets Sales Analysis**. Change the font size to **22**.
- Click and drag to select **cells A1 and B1**. Click the **Merge and Center button** to center the title across cells A1 and B1.
- Check that cells A1 and B1 are still selected. Pull down the **Format menu**. Click **Cells** to display the Format Cells dialog box as shown in Figure 5.10c.
  - Click the **Patterns tab**. Click the **Dark Red** color (to match the color used in the Colorful 2 AutoFormat that was applied in the previous exercise).
  - Click the **Font tab**. Click the drop-down arrow in the **Color list box**. Click the **White** color.
  - Click **OK** to accept the settings and close the Format Cells dialog box.
- Click outside the selected cells to see the effects of the formatting change. You should see white letters on a dark red background.
- Complete the text entries in **cells B9 through B13**. (Refer to Figure 5.9.) Add any additional documentation and formatting that you think is appropriate.
- Click in **cell A1**. Click the **Spelling button** to check the worksheet for spelling. Make corrections as necessary. Save the workbook.

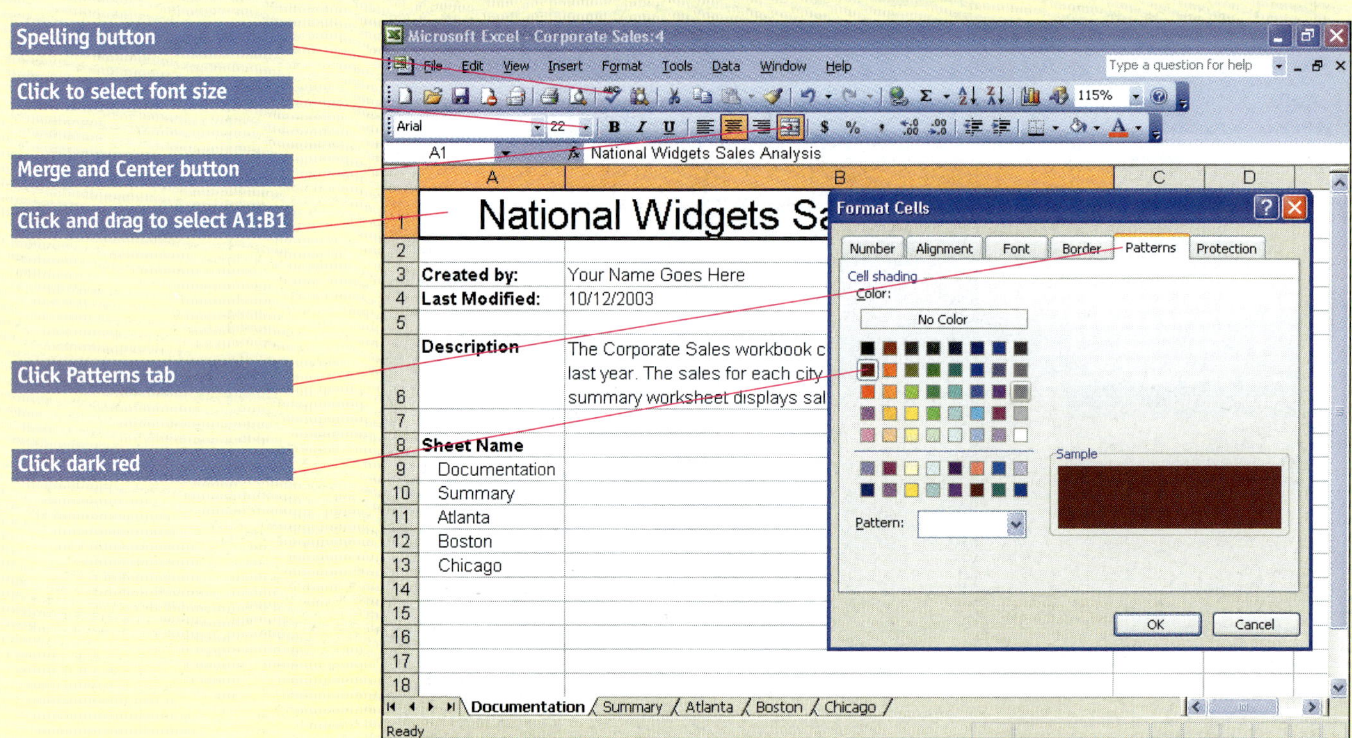

(c) Add the Worksheet Title (step 3)

FIGURE 5.10 Hands-on Exercise 3 (*continued*)

THE SPELL CHECK

Anyone familiar with a word processor takes the spell check for granted, but did you know the same capability exists within Excel? Click the Spelling button on the Standard toolbar to initiate the spell check, then implement corrections just as you do in Microsoft Word.

Step 4: The Page Setup Command

- If necessary, click the **Documentation tab** at the bottom of the window, then press and hold the **Shift key** as you click the tab for the **Chicago worksheet**. All five worksheet tabs should be selected, as shown in Figure 5.10d.
- Pull down the **File menu** and click the **Page Setup command** to display the Page Setup dialog box.
  - Click the **Header/Footer tab**. Click the **down arrow** on the Header list box and choose **Documentation** (the name of the worksheet). Click the **down arrow** on the Footer list box and choose **Corporate Sales** (the name of the workbook).
  - Click the **Margins tab**, then click the check box to center the worksheet horizontally. Change the top margin to **2 inches**.
  - Click the **Sheet tab**. Check the boxes to include row and column headings and gridlines. Click **OK** to exit the Page Setup dialog box.
- Save the workbook. Pull down the **File menu**. Click **Print** to display the Print dialog box. Click the option button to print the **Entire Workbook**. (Use the Preview command as necessary to ensure that the individual worksheets fit on a single page.) Click **OK**.

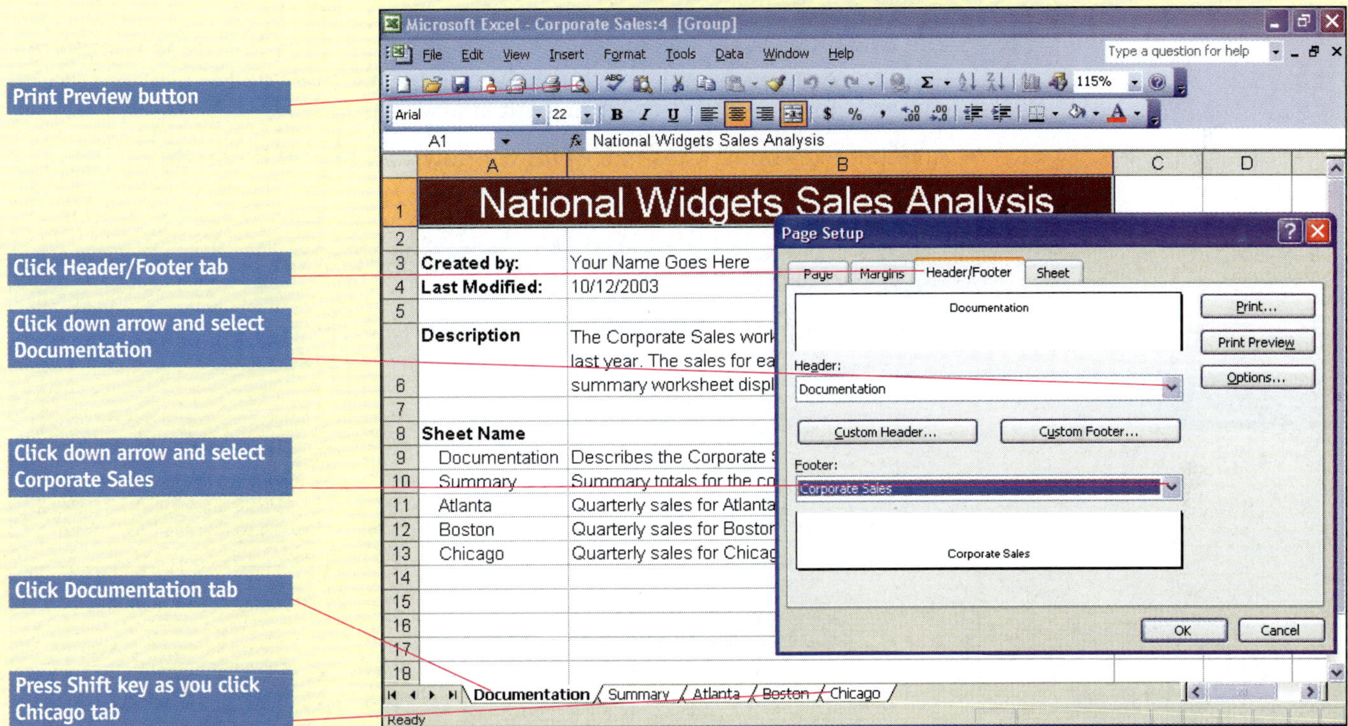

(d) The Page Setup Command (step 4)

FIGURE 5.10 Hands-on Exercise 3 (*continued*)

THE PRINT PREVIEW COMMAND

Use the Print Preview command to check the appearance of a worksheet to save time as well as paper. (Legend has it that the command was created by an unknown Microsoft programmer who tired of walking down the hall to pick up the printout.) You can execute the command by clicking the Print Preview button on the Standard toolbar or from the Print Preview command button within the Page Setup dialog box.

Step 5: Print the Cell Formulas

- Right click the **Summary tab** to display a context-sensitive menu, then click the **Ungroup Sheets command** to remove the group editing.
- Pull down the **View menu**, click **Custom Views** to display the Custom Views dialog box. Click the **Add button** to display the Add View dialog box.
- Enter **Displayed Values** as the name of the view (this is different from Figure 5.10e). Be sure that the Print Settings box is checked, and click **OK**.
- Press **Ctrl+`** to display the cell formulas. Double click the column borders between adjacent columns to increase the width of each column so that the cell formulas are completely visible.
- Pull down the **File menu** and click the **Page Setup command**. Click the **Page tab** and change to **Landscape orientation**. Click the option button to **Fit to 1 page**. Click **OK** to accept these settings and close the Page Setup dialog box. Click the **Print button** to print the summary worksheet.
- Pull down the **View menu**, click **Custom Views** to display the Custom View dialog box, then click the **Add button** to display the Add View dialog box. Enter **Cell Formulas** as shown in Figure 5.10f, verify that the Print Settings box is checked, and click **OK**.
- Pull down the **View menu**, click **Custom Views** to display the Custom View dialog box, then double click the **Displayed Values** view that was created earlier. You can switch back and forth at any time.
- Save the workbook. Close all open windows. Exit Excel if you do not want to continue with the next exercise at this time.

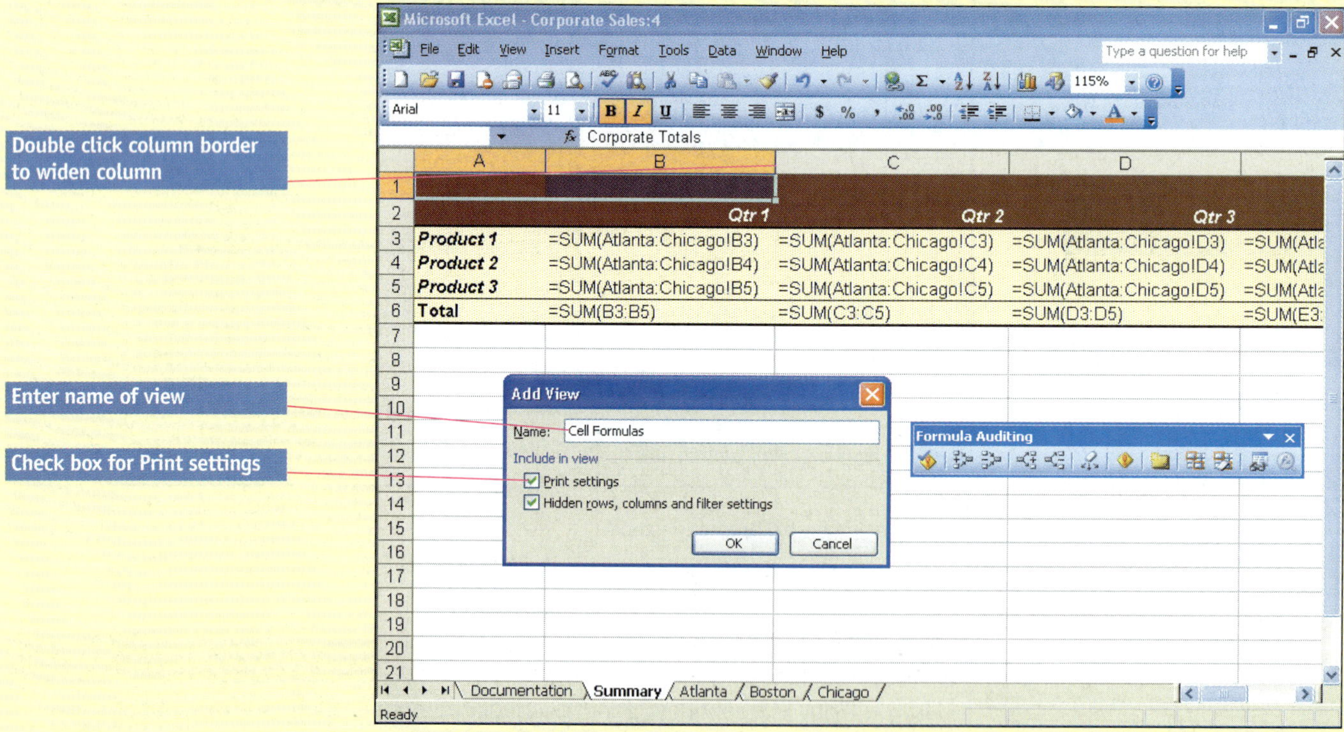

(e) Print the Cell Formulas (step 5)

FIGURE 5.10 Hands-on Exercise 3 (*continued*)

LINKING WORKBOOKS

There are two approaches to combining data from multiple sources. You can store all of the data on separate sheets in a single workbook, then create a summary worksheet within that workbook that references values in the other worksheets. Alternatively, you can retain the source data in separate workbooks, and create a summary workbook that references (links to) those workbooks.

Linking is established through the creation of ***external references*** that specify a cell (or range of cells) in another workbook. The ***dependent workbook*** (the Corporate Links workbook in our next example) contains the external references and thus reflects (is dependent on) data in the source workbook(s). The ***source workbooks*** (the Atlanta, Boston, and Chicago workbooks in our example) contain the data referenced by the dependent workbook.

Figure 5.11 illustrates the use of linking within the context of the example we have been using. Four different workbooks are open, each with one worksheet. The Corporate Links workbook is the dependent workbook and contains external references to obtain the summary totals. The Atlanta, Boston, and Chicago workbooks are the source workbooks.

Cell B3 is the active cell, and its contents are displayed in the formula bar. The corporate sales for Product 1 in the first quarter are calculated by summing the corresponding values in the source workbooks. Note how the workbook names are enclosed in square brackets to indicate the external references to the Atlanta, Boston, and Chicago workbooks.

The formulas to compute the corporate totals for Product 1 in the second, third, and fourth quarters contain external references similar to those shown in the formula bar. The ***workbook references*** and sheet references are absolute, whereas the cell reference may be relative (as in this example) or absolute. Once the formula has been entered into cell B3, it may be copied to the remaining cells in this row to compute the totals for Product 1 in the remaining quarters.

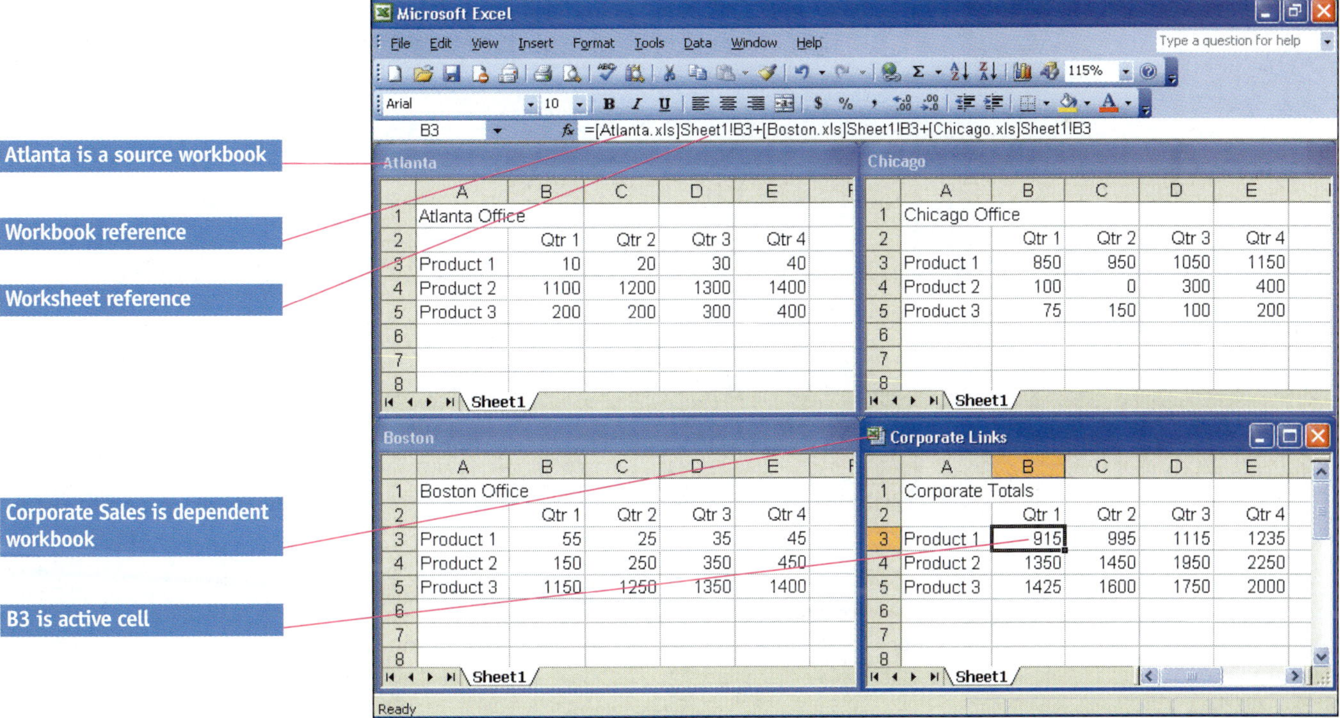

FIGURE 5.11 File Linking

hands-on exercise

4 Linking Workbooks

Objective To create a dependent workbook with external references to multiple source workbooks; to use pointing to create the external reference rather than entering the formula explicitly. Use Figure 5.12 as a guide in doing the exercise.

Step 1: Open the Workbooks

- Start Excel. If necessary, click the **New Workbook button** on the Standard toolbar to open a new workbook.
- Delete all worksheets except for Sheet1. Save the workbook as **Corporate Links** in the **Exploring Excel folder**.
- Pull down the **File menu**. Click **Open** to display the Open dialog box. Click the **Atlanta workbook**. Press and hold the **Ctrl key** as you click the **Boston** and **Chicago workbooks** to select all three workbooks at the same time as shown in Figure 5.12a.
- Click **Open** to open the selected workbooks. The workbooks will be opened one after another, with a brief message appearing on the status bar as each workbook is opened.
- Pull down the **Window menu**, which should indicate four open workbooks at the bottom of the menu. Click **Arrange** to display the Arrange Windows dialog box. If necessary, select the **Tiled option**, then click **OK**.

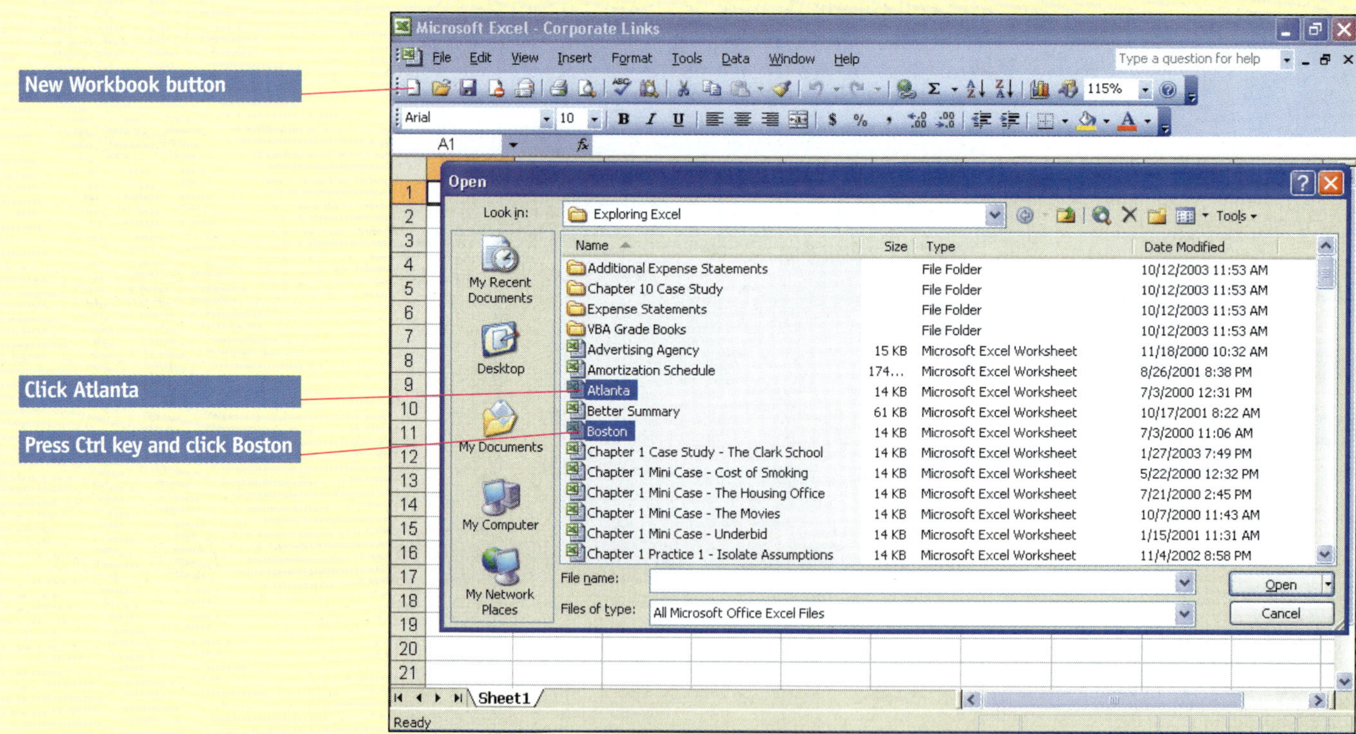

(a) Open the Workbooks (step 1)

FIGURE 5.12 Hands-on Exercise 4

Step 2: The AutoFill Command

- You should see four open workbooks as shown in Figure 5.12b, although the row and column labels have not yet been entered in the Corporate Links workbook. (Do not be concerned if your workbooks are arranged differently.)
- Click in **cell A1** in the **Corporate Links workbook** to make this the active cell in the active workbook. Enter **Corporate Totals**.
- Click **cell B2**. Enter **Qtr 1**. Click in **cell B2**, then point to the fill handle in the lower-right corner. The mouse pointer changes to a thin crosshair.
- Drag the fill handle over **cells C2, D2, and E2**. A border appears, to indicate the destination range. Release the mouse. Cells C2 through E2 contain the labels Qtr 2, Qtr 3, and Qtr 4, respectively.
- Right-align the entries in **cells B2 through E2**, then reduce the column widths so that you can see the entire worksheet in the window.
- Click **cell A3**. Enter **Product 1**. Use the AutoFill capability to enter the labels **Product 2** and **Product 3** in cells A4 and A5.

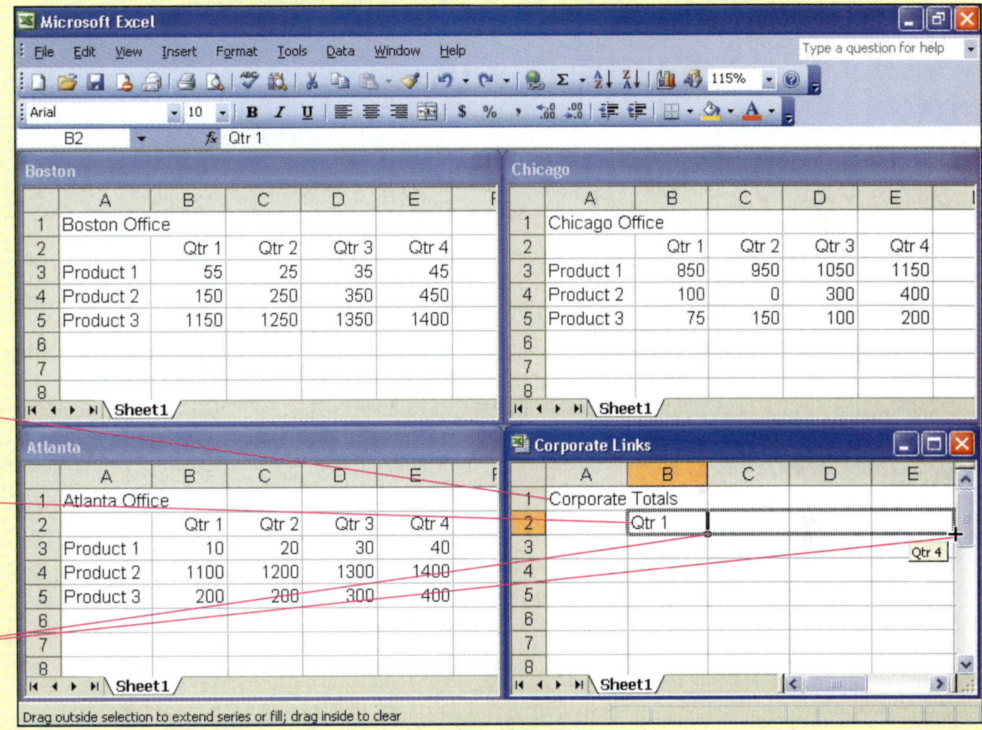

(b) The AutoFill Command (step 2)

FIGURE 5.12 Hands-on Exercise 4 (*continued*)

CREATE A CUSTOM SERIES

The AutoFill command is the fastest way to enter a series into adjacent cells. Type the first entry in the series (such as January, Monday, or Quarter 1), then click and drag the fill handle to adjacent cells to complete the series. You can also create your own series. Pull down the Tools menu, click Options, click the Custom Lists tab, and select New List. Enter the items in your series separated by commas (e.g., Tom, Dick, and Harry), click Add, and click OK. The next time you type Tom, Dick, or Harry in a cell you can use the fill handle to complete the series.

Step 3: File Linking

- Click **cell B3** of the **Corporate Links workbook**. Enter an **equal sign** so that you can create the formula by pointing.
- Click in the window for the **Atlanta workbook**. Click **cell B3**. The formula bar should display =[ATLANTA.XLS]Sheet1!$B$3. Press the **F4 key** continually until the cell reference changes to B3.
- Enter a **plus sign**. Click in the window for the **Boston workbook**. Click **cell B3**. The formula expands to include +[BOSTON.XLS]Sheet1!$B$3. Press the **F4 key** continually until the cell reference changes to B3.
- Enter a **plus sign**. Click in the window for the **Chicago workbook**. Click **cell B3**. The formula expands to include +[CHICAGO.XLS]Sheet1!$B$3. Press the **F4 key** continually until the cell reference changes to B3.
- Press **Enter**. The formula is complete, and you should see 915 in cell B3 of the Corporate Links workbook. Click in **cell B3**. The entry on the formula bar should match the entry in Figure 5.12c.
- Save the workbook.

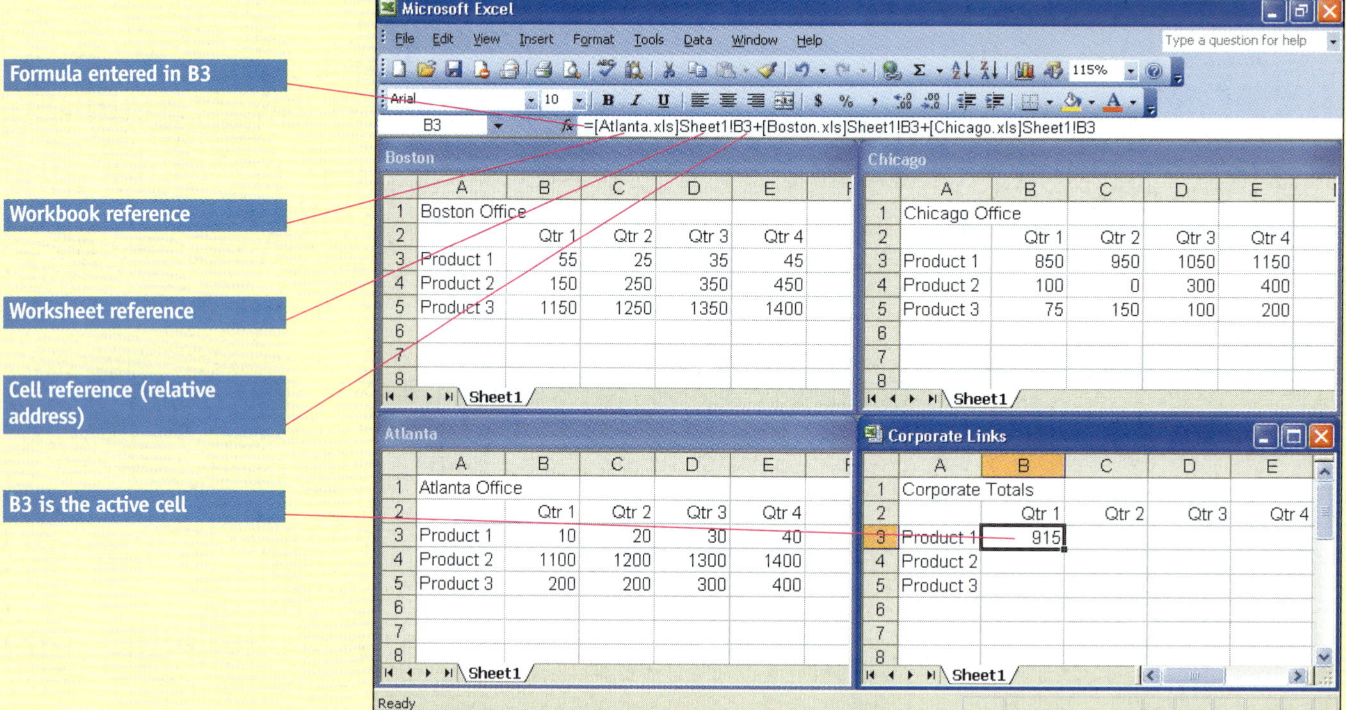

(c) File Linking (step 3)

FIGURE 5.12 Hands-on Exercise 4 (*continued*)

THE F4 KEY

The F4 key cycles through relative, absolute, and mixed addresses. Click on any reference within the formula bar; for example, click on A1 in the formula =A1+A2. Press the F4 key once, and it changes to an absolute reference, $A$1. Press the F4 key a second time, and it becomes a mixed reference, A$1; press it again, and it is a different mixed reference, $A1. Press the F4 key a fourth time, and it returns to the original relative address, A1.

Step 4: Copy the Cell Formulas

- If necessary, click **cell B3** in the **Corporate Links workbook**, then drag the fill handle over **cells C3 through E3** to copy this formula to the remaining cells in row 3.
- Be sure that cells B3 through E3 are still selected, then drag the fill handle to **cell E5**. You should see the total sales for all products in all quarters as shown in Figure 5.12d.
- Click **cell E5** to view the copied formula as shown in the figure. Note that the workbook and sheet references are the same but that the cell references have adjusted.
- Save the workbook.

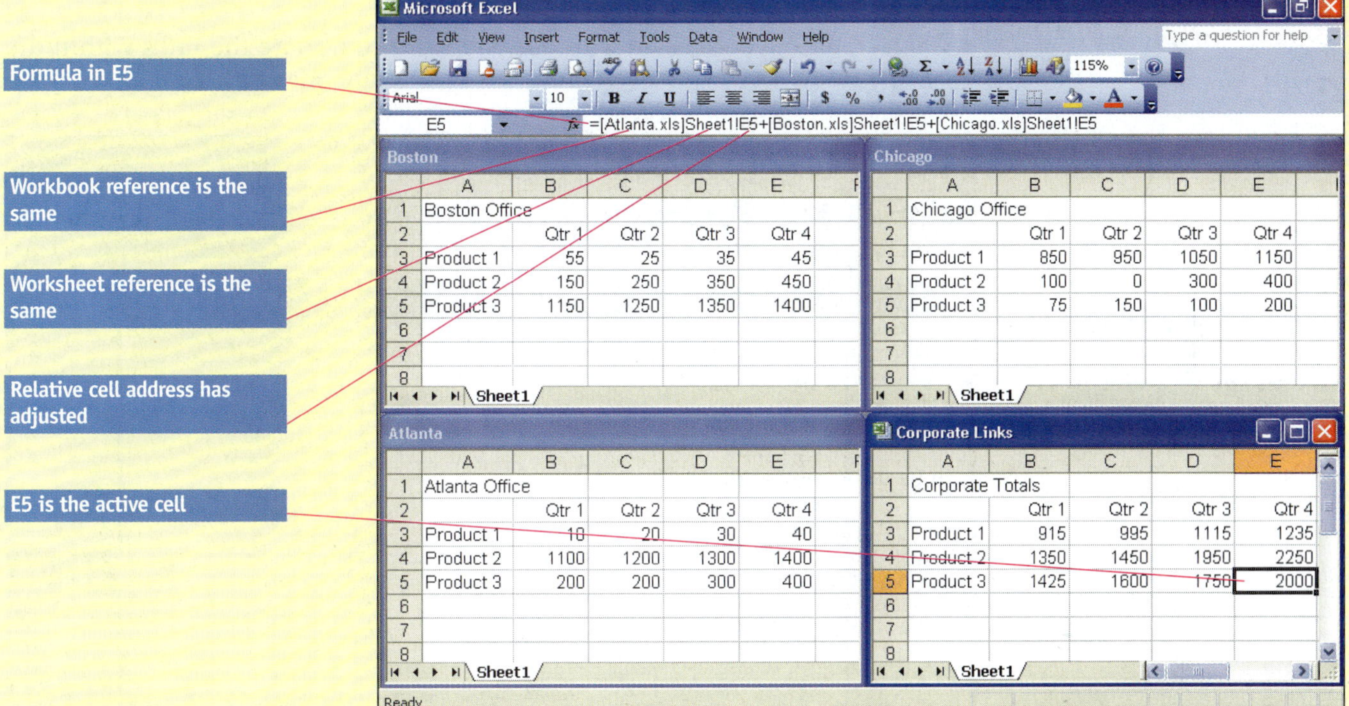

(d) Copy the Cell Formulas (step 4)

FIGURE 5.12 Hands-on Exercise 4 (*continued*)

DRIVE AND FOLDER REFERENCE

An external reference is updated regardless of whether or not the source workbook is open. The reference is displayed differently, depending on whether or not the source workbook is open. The references include the path (the drive and folder) if the source workbook is closed; the path is not shown if the source workbook is open. The external workbooks must be available to update the summary workbook. If the location of the workbooks changes (as may happen if you copy the workbooks to a different folder), pull down the Edit menu and click the Links command, then change the source of the external data.

Step 5: Create a Workspace

- Pull down the **File menu** and click the **Save Workspace command** to display the Save Workspace dialog box in Figure 5.12e.
- If necessary, click the **down arrow** in the Save in list box to select the **Exploring Excel folder**. Enter **Linked Workbooks** as the file name. Click the **Save button** in the dialog box to save the workspace. Click **Yes** if asked whether to save the changes to the Corporate Links workbook.
- The workspace is saved and you can continue to work as usual. The advantage of the workspace is that you can open all four workbooks with a single command.
- Click the **Close button** in each window to close all four workbooks. Pull down the **File menu**, click the **Open command**, then open the **Linked Workbooks** workspace that you just created.
- Click **Update** when asked whether you want to update the links within the Corporate Links workbook. All four workbooks are open as before.

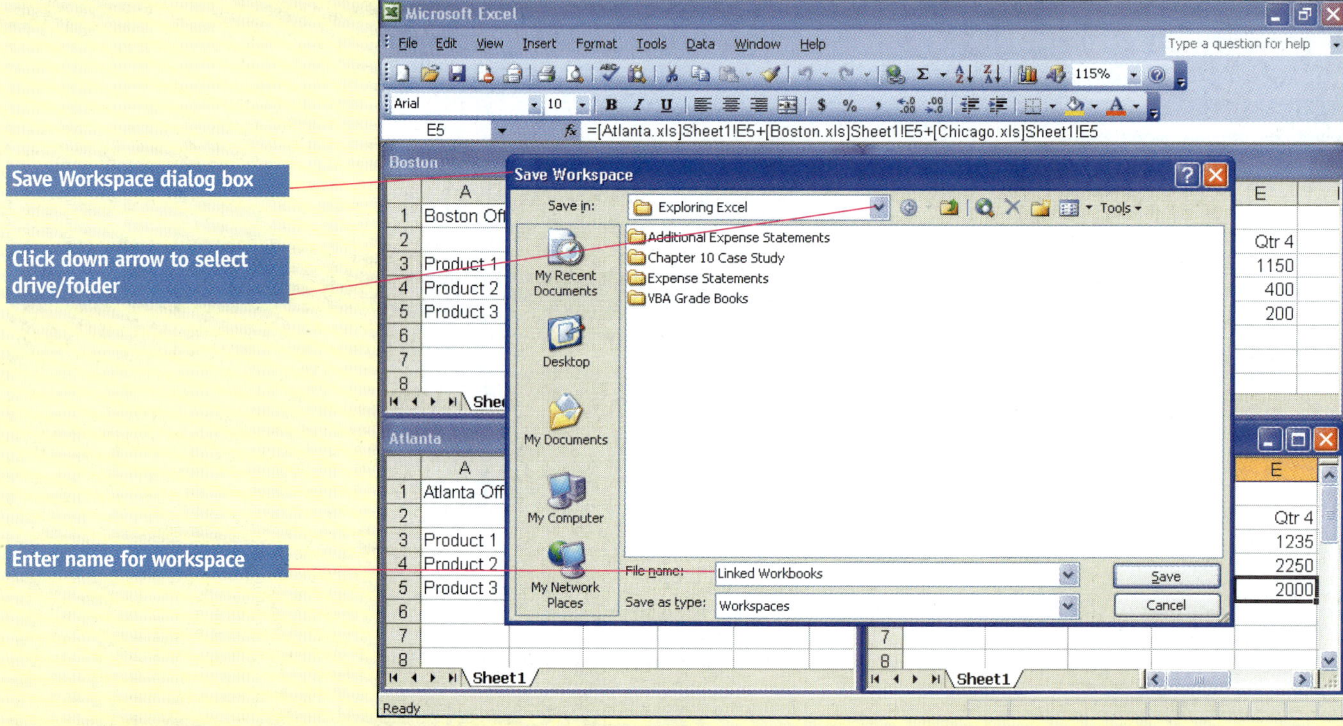

(e) Create a Workspace (step 5)

FIGURE 5.12 Hands-on Exercise 4 (*continued*)

THE WORKSPACE

A workspace enables you to open multiple workbooks in a single step, and further, will retain the arrangement of those workbooks within the Excel window. The workspace file does not contain the workbooks themselves, however, and thus you must continue to save changes you make to the individual workbooks.

Step 6: Change the Data

- Click **cell B3** in the **Corporate Links workbook** to make it the active cell. Note that the value displayed in the cell is 915.
- Pull down the **File menu**. Click **Close**. Answer **Yes** if asked whether to save the changes.
- Click in the window containing the **Chicago workbook**, click **cell B3**, enter **250**, and press **Enter**. Pull down the **File menu**. Click **Close**. Answer **Yes** if asked whether to save the changes. Only two workbooks, Atlanta and Boston, are now open.
- Pull down the **File menu** and open the **Corporate Links workbook**. You should see the dialog box in Figure 5.12f, asking whether to update the links. (Note that cell B3 still displays 915). Click **Update** to update the links.
- The value in cell B3 of the Corporate Links workbook changes to 315 to reflect the change in the Chicago workbook, even though the latter is closed.
- If necessary, click in **cell B3**. The formula bar displays the contents of this cell, which include the drive and folder reference for the Chicago workbook, because the workbook is closed.
- Close the Atlanta and Boston workbooks. Close the Corporate Links workbook. Click **Yes** if asked whether to save the changes.
- Saving the source workbook(s) before the dependent workbook ensures that the formulas in the source workbooks are calculated, and that all external references in the dependent workbook reflect current values.
- Exit Excel. Congratulations on a job well done.

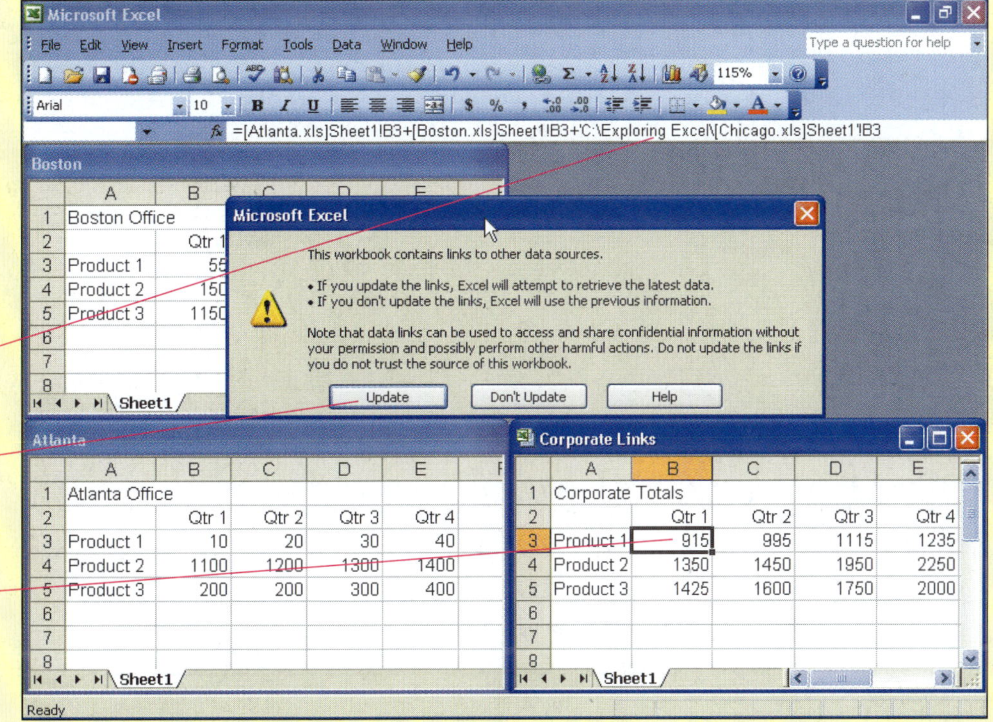

(f) Change the Data (step 6)

FIGURE 5.12 Hands-on Exercise 4 (*continued*)

SUMMARY

The chapter showed how to combine data from different sources into a summary report. The example is quite common and applicable to any business scenario requiring both detail and summary reports. One approach is to store all of the data in separate sheets of a single workbook, then summarize the data in a summary worksheet within that workbook. Alternatively, the source data can be kept in separate workbooks and consolidated through linking to a summary workbook. Both approaches are equally valid, and the choice depends on where you want to keep the source data.

An Excel workbook may contain up to 255 worksheets, each of which is identified by a tab at the bottom of the window. Worksheets may be added, deleted, moved, copied, or renamed through a shortcut menu. The color of the worksheet tab may also be changed. The highlighted tab indicates the active worksheet.

A worksheet reference is required to indicate a cell in another worksheet of the same workbook. An exclamation point separates the worksheet reference from the cell reference; e.g., =Atlanta!C3 references cell C3 in the Atlanta worksheet. The worksheet reference is absolute and remains the same when the formula is copied. The cell reference may be relative or absolute. A 3-D reference refers to a cell or range in another worksheet.

The best way to enter a reference to a cell in a different worksheet (or in a different workbook) is by pointing. Click in the cell that is to contain the formula, type an equal sign, click the worksheet tab that contains the external reference, then click in the appropriate cell. Use the F4 key as you select the cell to switch between relative, absolute, and mixed cell references.

Multiple worksheets may be selected (grouped) to execute the same commands on all of the selected worksheets simultaneously. You can, for example, insert formulas to sum a row or column and/or format the selected worksheets. The AutoFormat command provides access to a predefined set of formats that includes font size, color, boldface, alignment, and other attributes that can be applied automatically to a selected range.

A workbook should be clearly organized so that the purpose of every worksheet is evident. One way of documenting a workbook is through the creation of a documentation worksheet that describes the purpose of each worksheet within the workbook. Multiple worksheets (workbooks) can be displayed at one time, with each worksheet contained in its own window within the Excel application window. The Arrange command in the Window menu is used to tile or cascade the individual worksheets (workbooks).

A workbook may also be linked to cells in other workbooks through an external reference that specifies a cell (or range of cells) in a source workbook. The dependent workbook contains the external references and uses (is dependent on) the data in the source workbook(s). The external workbooks must be available to update the summary workbook. If the location of the workbooks changes (as may happen if you copy the workbooks to a different folder), pull down the Edit menu and click the Links command, then change the source of the external data.

KEY TERMS

3-D reference 228
Arrange command 220
AutoFormat command 229
AutoSum 234
Custom view 242
Dependent workbook 243
Documentation worksheet 237
External reference 243
Grouping worksheets 229
Linking 243
New Window command 220
Source workbook 243
Workbook properties 238
Workbook reference 243
Worksheet reference 227

MULTIPLE CHOICE

1. Which of the following is true regarding workbooks and worksheets?
   (a) A workbook contains one or more worksheets
   (b) Only one worksheet can be selected at a time within a workbook
   (c) Every workbook contains the same number of worksheets
   (d) All of the above

2. Assume that a workbook contains three worksheets. How many cells are included in the function =SUM(Sheet1:Sheet3!A1)?
   (a) Three
   (b) Four
   (c) Twelve
   (d) Twenty-four

3. Assume that a workbook contains three worksheets. How many cells are included in the function =SUM(Sheet1:Sheet3!A1:B4)?
   (a) Three
   (b) Four
   (c) Twelve
   (d) Twenty-four

4. Which of the following is the preferred way to sum the value of cell A1 from three different worksheets?
   (a) =Sheet1!A1+Sheet2!A1+Sheet3!A1
   (b) =SUM(Sheet1:Sheet3!A1)
   (c) Both (a) and (b) are equally good
   (d) Neither (a) nor (b)

5. The reference CIS120!$A$2:
   (a) Is an absolute reference to cell A2 in the CIS120 workbook
   (b) Is a relative reference to cell A2 in the CIS120 workbook
   (c) Is an absolute reference to cell A2 in the CIS120 worksheet
   (d) Is a relative reference to cell A2 in the CIS120 worksheet

6. What does City! refer to in the reference City!A1:F9?
   (a) A cell range
   (b) An error in a formula
   (c) A workbook
   (d) A worksheet

7. Which of the following is true about the reference Sheet1:Sheet3!A1:B2?
   (a) The worksheet reference is relative, the cell reference is absolute
   (b) The worksheet reference is absolute, the cell reference is relative
   (c) The worksheet and cell references are absolute
   (d) The worksheet and cell references are relative

8. You are in the Ready mode and are positioned in cell B2 of Sheet1. You enter an equal sign, click the worksheet tab for Sheet2, click cell B1, and press Enter.
   (a) The content of cell B2 in Sheet1 is =Sheet2!B1
   (b) The content of cell B1 in Sheet2 is = Sheet1!B2
   (c) Both (a) and (b)
   (d) Neither (a) nor (b)

9. You are positioned in cell A10 of Sheet1. You enter an equal sign, click the worksheet tab for the worksheet called This Year, and click cell C10. You then enter a minus sign, click the worksheet tab for the worksheet called LastYear, click cell C10, and press Enter. What are the contents of cell A10?
   (a) =ThisYear:LastYear!C10
   (b) =(ThisYear–LastYear)!C10
   (c) =ThisYear!C10-LastYear!C10
   (d) =ThisYear:C10-LastYear:C10

10. Which of the following can be accessed from a shortcut menu?
    (a) Inserting or deleting a worksheet
    (b) Moving or copying a worksheet
    (c) Renaming a worksheet
    (d) All of the above

... continued

multiple choice

11. You are positioned in cell A1 of Sheet1 of Book1. You enter an equal sign, click in the open window for Book2, click the tab for Sheet1, click cell A1, then press the F4 key continually until you have a relative cell reference. What reference appears in the formula bar?

(a) =[BOOK1.XLS]Sheet1!$A$1
(b) =[BOOK1.XLS]Sheet1!A1
(c) =[BOOK2.XLS]Sheet1!$A$1
(d) =[BOOK2.XLS]Sheet1!A1

12. The Arrange Windows command can display:

(a) Multiple worksheets from one workbook
(b) One worksheet from multiple workbooks
(c) Both (a) and (b)
(d) Neither (a) nor (b)

13. Pointing can be used to reference a cell in:

(a) A different worksheet
(b) A different workbook
(c) Both (a) and (b)
(d) Neither (a) nor (b)

14. The appearance of [Group] within the title bar indicates that:

(a) Multiple workbooks are open and are all active
(b) Multiple worksheets are selected within the same workbook
(c) Both (a) and (b)
(d) Neither (a) nor (b)

15. Which of the following is true regarding the example on file linking that was developed in the chapter?

(a) The Atlanta, Boston, and Chicago workbooks were dependent workbooks
(b) The Linked workbook was a source workbook
(c) Both (a) and (b)
(d) Neither (a) nor (b)

16. The formula =Office1!A3+Office2!A3+Office3!A3

(a) References the same cell in three different workbooks
(b) References the same cell on three different worksheets in the same workbook
(c) References the same cell on three different worksheets in three different workbooks
(d) Impossible to determine

17. The formula =City1!$B$1+City2!$B$1+City3!$B$1 specifies that

(a) The worksheet references are absolute and the cell references are relative
(b) The worksheet references are relative and the cell references are absolute
(c) Both the worksheet and the cell references are absolute
(d) Both the worksheet and cell references are relative

18. Which of the following is a valid reference to an external workbook?

(a) =Boston!B3
(b) =Boston!Sheet2!B3
(c) Both (a) and (b)
(d) Neither (a) nor (b)

ANSWERS

1. a	**7.** b	**13.** c
2. a	**8.** a	**14.** b
3. d	**9.** c	**15.** d
4. b	**10.** d	**16.** b
5. c	**11.** d	**17.** c
6. d	**12.** c	**18.** d

PRACTICE WITH EXCEL

1. **Linking Worksheets:** The workbook in Figure 5.13 features a summary worksheet that displays exam results for multiple sections of an introductory computer course. It also contains an individual worksheet for each section of the course. Your assignment is to open the partially completed *Chapter 5 Practice 1* workbook in the Exploring Excel folder, compute the test averages for each section, and then create the summary worksheet.
   a. Select the worksheet for Section N. Press and hold the Shift key as you click the worksheet tab for Section S to group all of the worksheets. Click in cell B10 and enter the formula, =AVERAGE(B3:B8) to compute the average on the first test for the students in Section N. Copy this formula to cells C10 and D10. (The sections have different numbers of students, but the last student in every section appears in row 8 or before. The Average function ignores empty cells within the designated range and thus you can use the same function for all four worksheets.)
   b. Check that the worksheets are still grouped, and then apply the same formatting to each worksheet. You do not have to duplicate our formatting exactly, but you are to merge and center the name of the section in the first row, and use bold text and a colored background. Change the color of the worksheet tab to match the formatting in the worksheet. You will not see the color change until you ungroup the worksheets.
   c. Ungroup the worksheets, then insert a blank worksheet for the summary as shown in Figure 5.13. Enter the title and column headings as shown in rows 1 and 2. Click in cell A3 of the summary worksheet. Type an equal sign, click the Worksheet tab for Section N, click in cell A1 of this worksheet, then press Enter to display the section name in the summary worksheet. Enter the names of the other sections.
   d. Click in cell B3 of the summary worksheet. Type an equal sign, click the Worksheet tab for Section N, click in cell B10, then press Enter to obtain the class average for section N on test 1. Copy the formula in cell B1 to cells C1 and D1 of the summary worksheet. Enter the test grades for the other sections in similar fashion.
   e. Format the summary worksheet in a similar style to the detailed worksheets.
   f. Use the Page Setup command to create a custom footer for all worksheets that includes your name, the name on the worksheet tab, and today's date. Print the worksheet for section N and the summary worksheet for your instructor. Print both worksheets a second time to show the cell formulas rather than the displayed values.

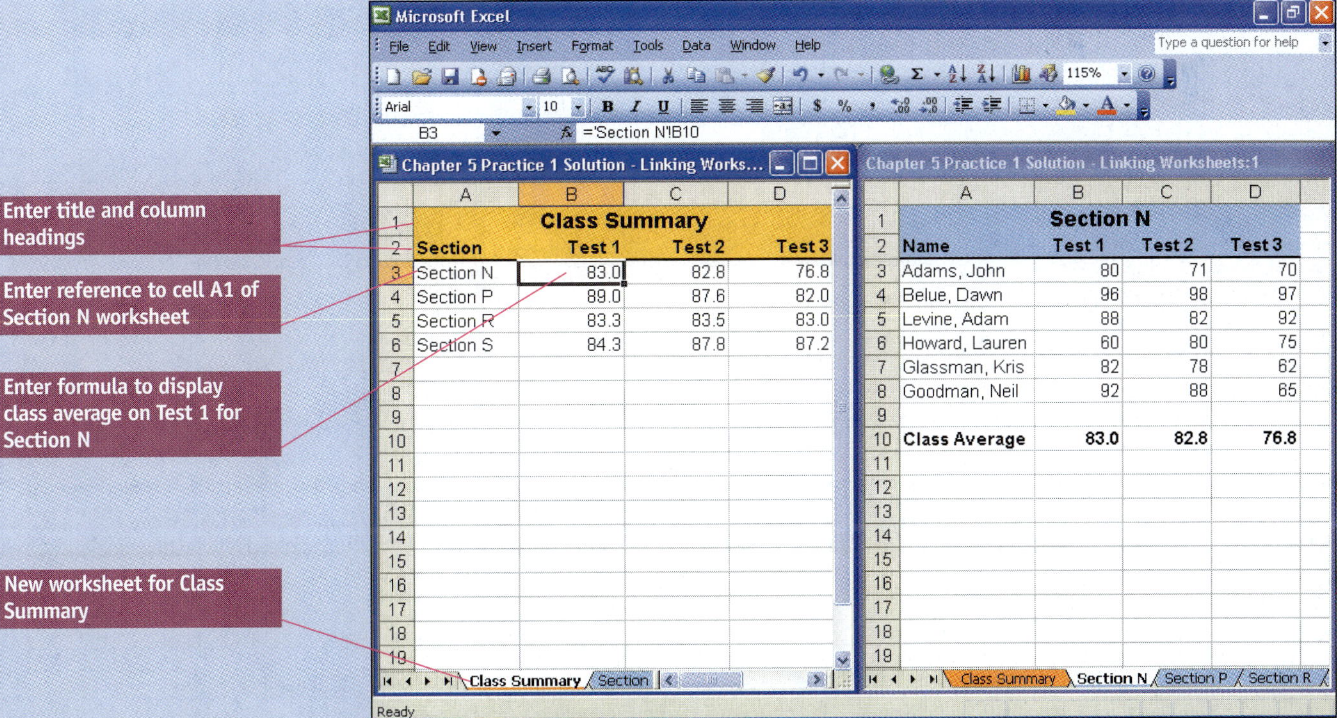

FIGURE 5.13 Linking Worksheets (exercise 1)

2. **Group Editing:** The workbook in Figure 5.14 contains a separate worksheet for each month of the year as well a summary worksheet for the entire year. Each monthly worksheet tallies the expenses for five divisions in each of four categories to compute a monthly total for each division. The summary worksheet is to display the total expense for each division. Thus far, however, only the months of January, February, and March are complete. Your assignment is to open the partially completed *Chapter 5 Practice 2* workbook in the Exploring Excel folder and proceed as follows:
   a. Insert a new worksheet for April to the right of the March worksheet and then enter the appropriate row and column headings. Assume that Division 1 spends $100 in each category, Division 2 spends $200 in each category, Division 3 spends $300 in each category, and so on. Change the worksheet tab to reflect April.
   b. Select the worksheet for January and then press and hold the Shift key as you click the worksheet tab for April. The title bar should reflect group editing. Click in cell F3 to compute the monthly total for Division 1, and then copy this formula to the remaining rows in this column. Compute the totals for each expense category in row eight.
   c. Format the worksheet in an attractive fashion. You do not have to match our formatting exactly, but you should include bold text, borders, and shaded cells as appropriate. Change the color of the worksheet tab. Right click any worksheet tab, click the Ungroup Worksheets command, then view the various monthly worksheets to verify that the formulas and formatting appear in each worksheet.
   d. Click the worksheet tab for the Summary worksheet. Insert a column for April to the right of the column for March. Click in cell B3, type an equal sign, click in the January worksheet, click in cell F3 (the cell that contains the January total for Division 1), and press Enter. Enter the formulas for the remaining months for Division 1 in similar fashion. Click in cell F3 and compute the year-to-date expenses for Division 1, then copy the formulas in cells B3 through F3 to the remaining rows in the Summary worksheet. Format the summary worksheet.
   e. Use the Page Setup command to create a custom footer for all worksheets that includes your name, the name on the worksheet tab, and today's date. Print the worksheet for April and the summary worksheet for your instructor. Print both worksheets a second time to show the cell formulas rather than the displayed values.

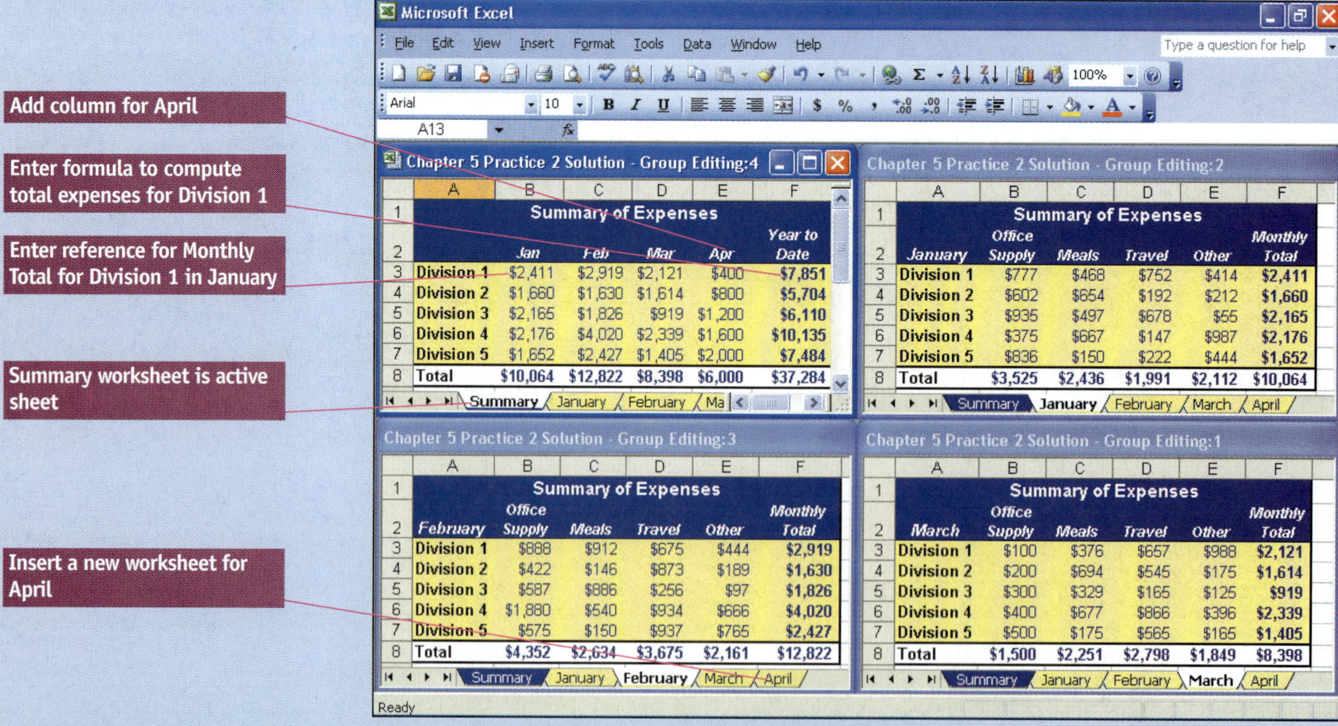

FIGURE 5.14 Group Editing (exercise 2)

3. **Object Linking and Embedding:** This exercise builds on the hands-on exercises within the chapter by creating a Word document that contains an Excel worksheet and associated chart. The chart is to be created in its own chart sheet within the Corporate Sales workbook and then incorporated into the memo. Proceed as follows:
   a. Start Word. Create a simple document that describes the corporate performance as shown in Figure 5.15. You do not have to match our document exactly, but you are required to create a letterhead and include your instructor's name and your name as indicated.
   b. Open the *Corporate Sales* workbook from the third hands-on exercise. Click the worksheet tab that contains the summary data, click and drag to select the completed worksheet, and then click the Copy button. Return to the Word document and click below the first paragraph. Pull down the Edit menu and click the Paste Special command to display the Paste Special dialog box. Select Microsoft Excel Worksheet Object in the displayed list, click the Paste Link button, and then click OK to insert the worksheet. Do not worry about the size or position at this time. Move the cursor so that it is below the worksheet. Add two or three blank lines.
   c. Return to the Excel workbook. Create a side-by-side column chart (in its own chart sheet) that plots the data in rows; that is, the X axis should display the four quarters, and the legend should display the product names. Use the same technique as in part (b) to link the side-by-side column chart to the Word document. Move and size the chart within the memo as necessary. You may find it convenient to change the zoom specification to "Whole Page" so that you can position the chart more easily.
   d. Save the completed document. Print the completed document for your instructor.
   e. Prove to yourself that Object Linking and Embedding really works by returning to the Atlanta worksheet *after* you have created the document in Figure 5.15. Change the sales for product 1 in Quarter 4 to $3,000. Switch back to the Word memo, and the chart should reflect the increase in the sales for product 1. Add a postscript to the memo indicating that the corrected chart reflects the last-minute sale of product 1 in Atlanta, and that you no longer want to discontinue the product. Print the revised memo and submit it to your instructor with the earlier version.

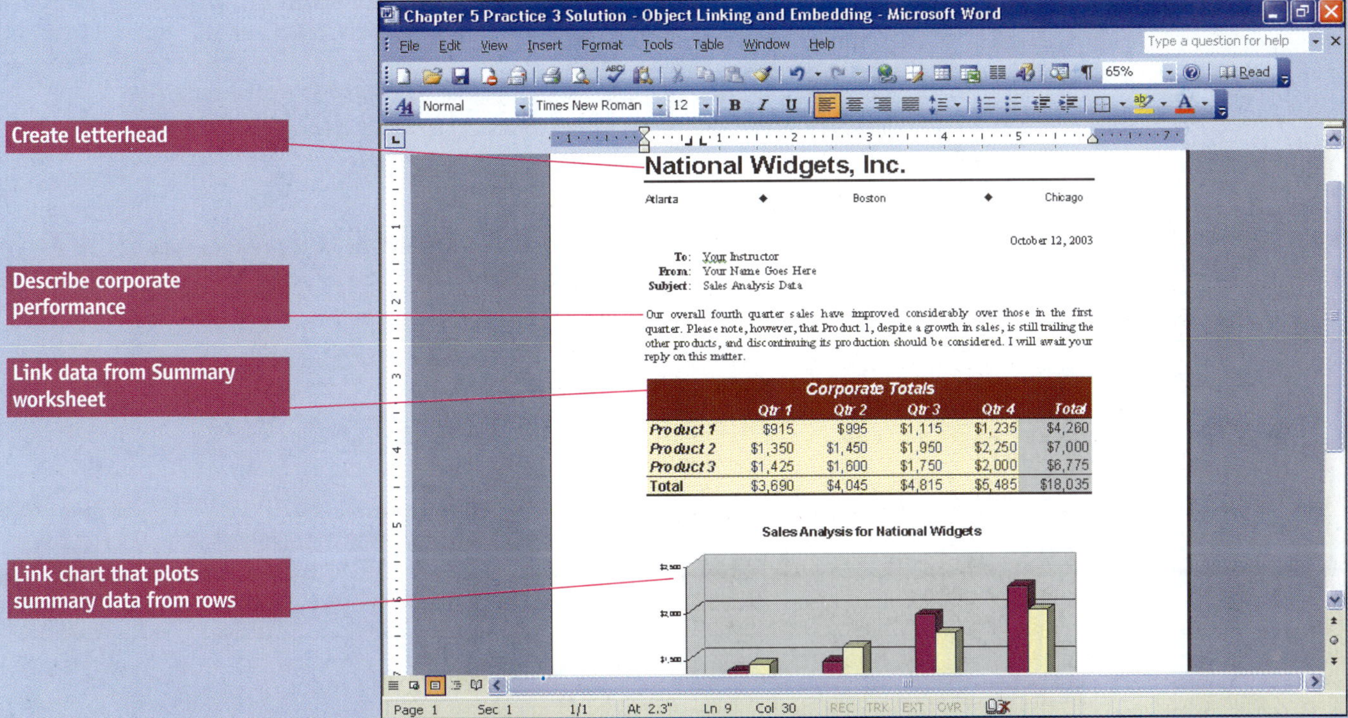

FIGURE 5.15 Object Linking and Embedding (exercise 3)

4. **National Computers:** You will find a partially completed version of the workbook in Figure 5.16 in the *Chapter 5 Practice 4* workbook in the Exploring Excel folder. That workbook has four partially completed worksheets, one for each city. Your assignment is to complete the workbook so that it parallels the Corporate Sales workbook that was used in the first three hands-on exercises in this chapter. Proceed as follows:
   a. Complete the individual worksheets by adding the appropriate formulas to compute the necessary row and column totals, then format these worksheets in attractive fashion. You can apply your own formatting, or you can use the AutoFormat command. You will find it easier, however, to use the group editing feature as you add the totals and apply the formatting, since all of the worksheets contain parallel data. Be sure to ungroup the worksheets after you have applied the formatting.
   b. Add a summary worksheet that provides corporate totals by product line. Apply the formatting from the individual worksheets to the summary worksheet.
   c. Create two side-by-side column charts, each in its own chart sheet, which display the summary information in graphical fashion. One chart should compare the sales revenue for each city by product, the other should compare the revenue for each product by city.
   d. Add a documentation worksheet similar to the worksheet in Figure 5.16. Change the color of the worksheet tabs as appropriate.
   e. Select the first worksheet, then press and hold the Shift key as you click the last worksheet tab to turn on the group editing feature. Use the Page Setup command to create a custom footer that includes your name, the name on the worksheet tab and today's date. Ungroup the worksheets, then change the orientation for the chart sheets to landscape.
   f. Print the entire workbook for your instructor. Print the Corporate (summary) worksheet a second time to show the cell formulas. (Change to landscape printing if necessary.)

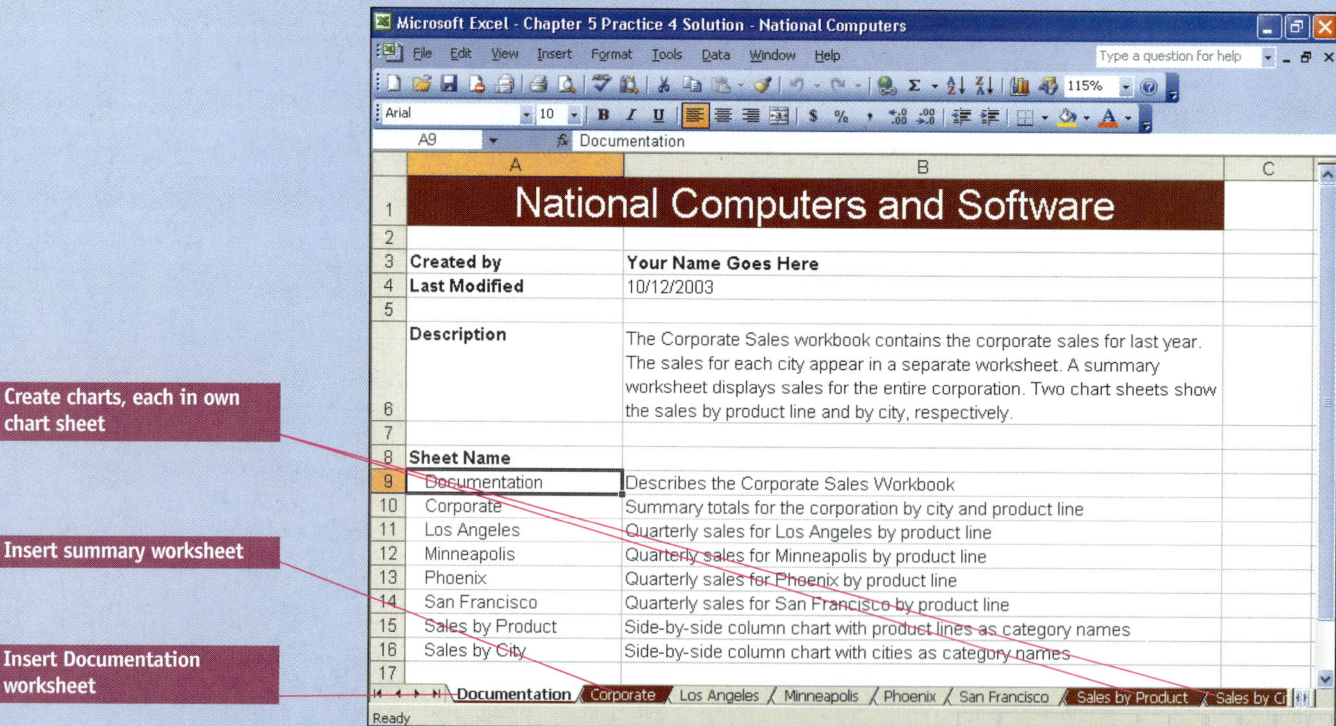

FIGURE 5.16 National Computers (exercise 4)

5. **The Stock Portfolio:** The workbook in Figure 5.17 uses Web queries (discussed in Chapter 2) to obtain current stock quotations from the Web, then uses those prices within an Excel workbook. The workbook contains five worksheets in all—a worksheet for each of three clients, Tom, Dick, and Harry; a worksheet containing stock prices as retrieved by the Web query; and a summary worksheet that shows the gain or loss for each client. Your assignment is to open the partially completed workbook in *Chapter 5 Practice 5*, and complete the workbook as follows.
   a. Complete the individual worksheets for Tom, Dick, and Harry by entering the appropriate formulas to obtain the current price of each company in the client's portfolio, then determining the value of that investment by multiplying the price times the number of shares. Tom, for example, has AOL in his portfolio, the current price of which is found in cell D11 of the Stock Prices worksheet. Compute the gain or loss for each investment, based on the difference between today's price and the purchase price.
   b. Update the current price of each client's portfolio by right clicking anywhere within the table of prices in the Stock Prices worksheet, then clicking the Refresh Data command. (The stock symbols that appear at the top of the Stock Prices worksheet were entered manually from the investments in the individual worksheets and are the basis of the Web query.)
   c. Enter the summary data for each client in the Summary worksheet using appropriate worksheet references. The total cost of Tom's portfolio, for example, is $9,260 and is found in cell E7 of Tom's worksheet. Thus, the corresponding entry in the summary worksheet would be =Tom!E7, indicating that the number is to come from this cell in Tom's worksheet.
   d. Add your name in row 9 of the summary worksheet as the investment adviser. Print the entire workbook for your instructor.
   e. Print the cell formulas for the summary worksheet. Add a cover sheet and submit the entire assignment to your instructor.

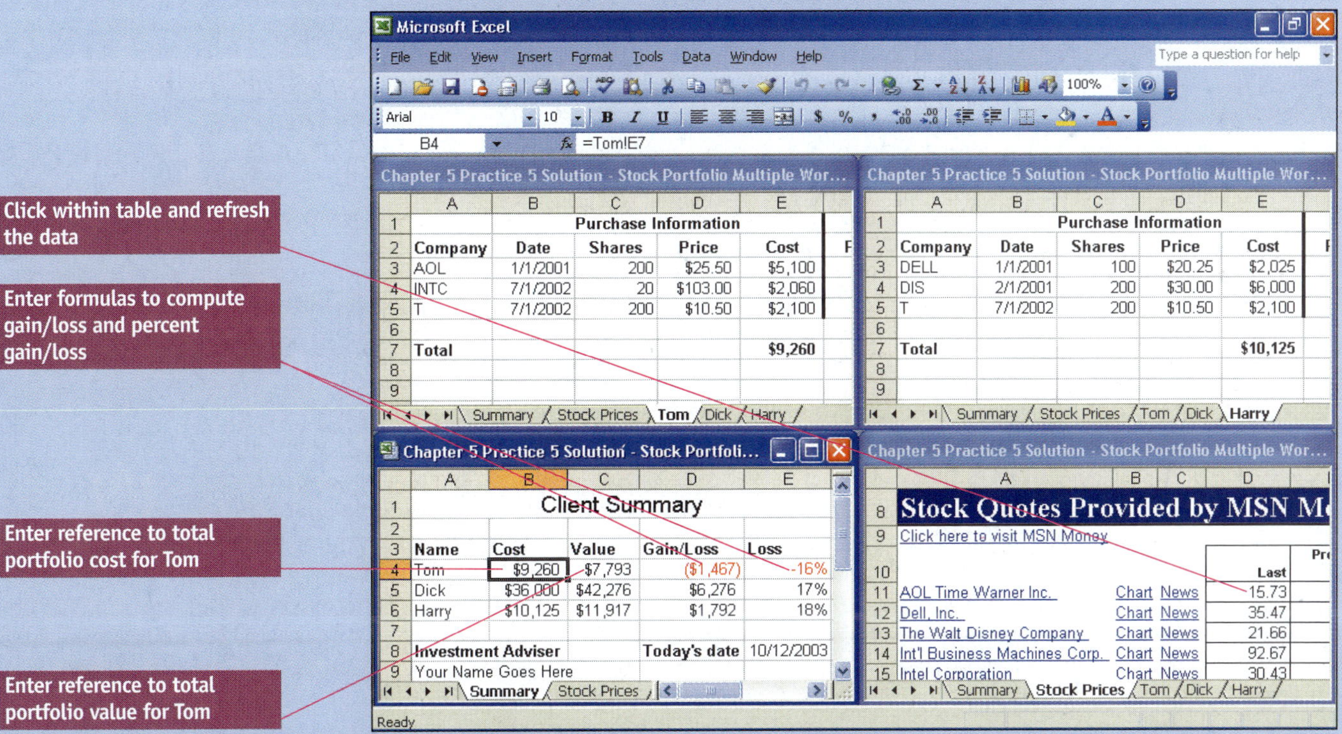

FIGURE 5.17 The Stock Portfolio (exercise 5)

6. **Weekly Sales:** The workbook in Figure 5.18 contains seven worksheets that provide detailed information on last week's sales for the Definitely Needlepoint boutique. The daily worksheets contain sales data for the indicated day of the week and are identical to one another except for the specific data. The summary worksheet displays the information for each day and computes the weekly total of all receipts in cell H13. In similar fashion, the total sales (across all categories of merchandise) are computed in cell H21, and the value should equal the value in cell H13. Open the *Chapter 5 Practice 6* workbook and complete the summary worksheet.
   a. Select the Monday worksheet. Press and hold the Shift key as you click the worksheet tab for Saturday, so that all six worksheets are selected and the Group editing formula is turned on. Enter the appropriate formulas and/or functions in the Monday worksheet to compute the totals in cells B6, B12, B13, and B21.
   b. Click the Weekly Summary worksheet tab (which also turns off the Group editing feature). Click in cell B4. Type an equal sign, click the worksheet tab for Monday, click in cell B4 of this worksheet, then press the Enter key. Enter the appropriate worksheet references for the remaining days of the week in similar fashion. Click in cell H4, then click the Sum button on the Standard toolbar to obtain the weekly total.
   c. Click and drag to select cells B4 through H4. Click the Copy button. Click and drag to select cells B5 through H21. Pull down the Edit menu, click the Paste Special command, then click the option button to paste the formulas. Delete the entries in cells B14 through H15 because these cells should not contain any formulas.
   d. Enter an IF function in cell A22 that compares the total payments in cell H13 to the total in cell H21. The numbers should be equal; if not, there is a potential accounting error somewhere in the worksheet. Use conditional formatting to display the text in blue or red, depending on whether the numbers check or are in error. (A similar IF function has been entered for you on the daily worksheets in cell A22.)
   e. Use the Page Setup command to create a custom footer for all worksheets that includes your name, the name on the worksheet tab, and today's date. Print the summary worksheet. (Use landscape orientation.) Print the summary worksheet a second time to show the cell formulas.

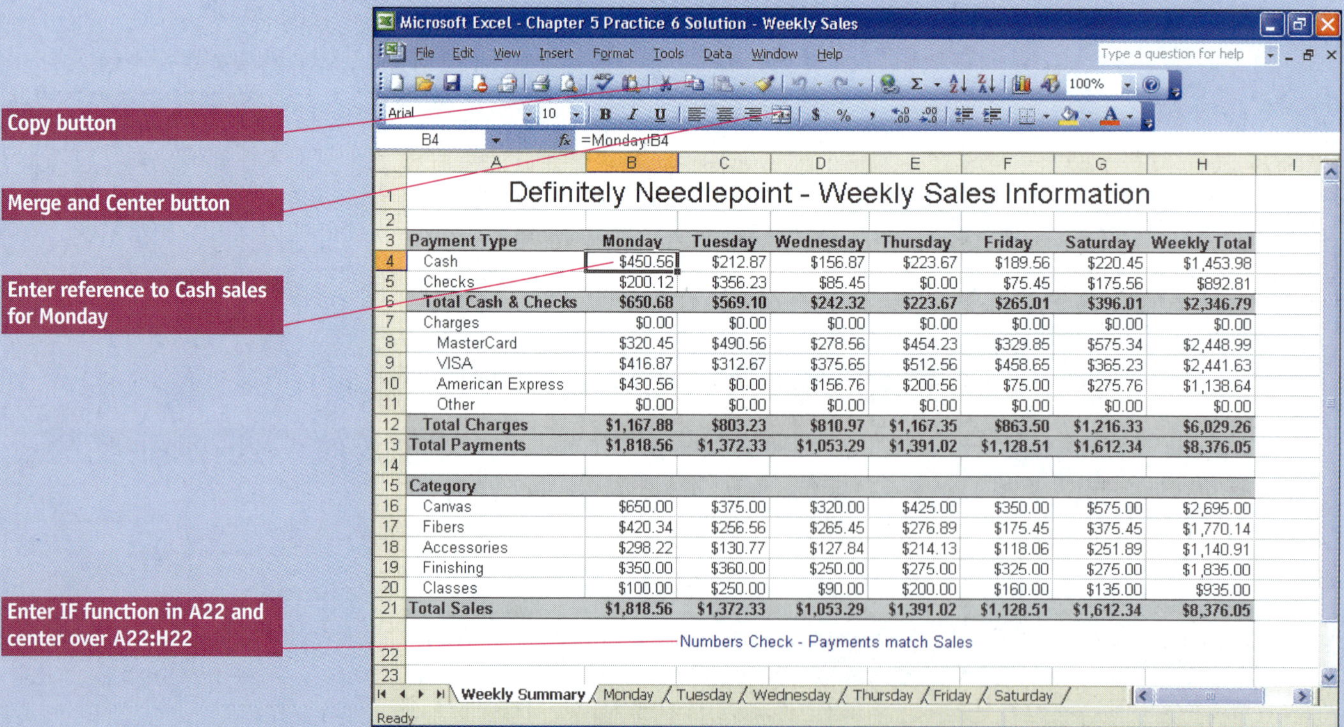

	A	B	C	D	E	F	G	H
1	Definitely Needlepoint - Weekly Sales Information							
2								
3	**Payment Type**	**Monday**	**Tuesday**	**Wednesday**	**Thursday**	**Friday**	**Saturday**	**Weekly Total**
4	Cash	$450.56	$212.87	$156.87	$223.67	$189.56	$220.45	$1,453.98
5	Checks	$200.12	$356.23	$85.45	$0.00	$75.45	$175.56	$892.81
6	**Total Cash & Checks**	**$650.68**	**$569.10**	**$242.32**	**$223.67**	**$265.01**	**$396.01**	**$2,346.79**
7	Charges	$0.00	$0.00	$0.00	$0.00	$0.00	$0.00	$0.00
8	MasterCard	$320.45	$490.56	$278.56	$454.23	$329.85	$575.34	$2,448.99
9	VISA	$416.87	$312.67	$375.65	$512.56	$458.65	$365.23	$2,441.63
10	American Express	$430.56	$0.00	$156.76	$200.56	$75.00	$275.76	$1,138.64
11	Other	$0.00	$0.00	$0.00	$0.00	$0.00	$0.00	$0.00
12	**Total Charges**	**$1,167.88**	**$803.23**	**$810.97**	**$1,167.35**	**$863.50**	**$1,216.33**	**$6,029.26**
13	**Total Payments**	**$1,818.56**	**$1,372.33**	**$1,053.29**	**$1,391.02**	**$1,128.51**	**$1,612.34**	**$8,376.05**
14								
15	**Category**							
16	Canvas	$650.00	$375.00	$320.00	$425.00	$350.00	$575.00	$2,695.00
17	Fibers	$420.34	$256.56	$265.45	$276.89	$175.45	$375.45	$1,770.14
18	Accessories	$298.22	$130.77	$127.84	$214.13	$118.06	$251.89	$1,140.91
19	Finishing	$350.00	$360.00	$250.00	$275.00	$325.00	$275.00	$1,835.00
20	Classes	$100.00	$250.00	$90.00	$200.00	$160.00	$135.00	$935.00
21	**Total Sales**	**$1,818.56**	**$1,372.33**	**$1,053.29**	**$1,391.02**	**$1,128.51**	**$1,612.34**	**$8,376.05**

FIGURE 5.18 Weekly Sales (exercise 6)

7. **Pivot Tables:** A pivot table is an extremely flexible tool that enables you to manipulate the data in multiple worksheets to produce new reports as shown in Figure 5.19. (Pivot tables are covered in more detail in Chapter 7.) Complete the first three hands-on exercises, then follow the instructions below:
    a. Open the Corporate Sales workbook that was completed at the end of the third hands-on exercise. Pull down the Data menu and click the Pivot Table and PivotChart Report command. Click the option buttons to select Multiple Consolidation Ranges and to specify Pivot Table. Click Next.
    b. Click the option button that says I will create the page fields. Click Next.
    c. Specify the range in step 2b of the PivotTable Wizard through pointing. Click the Sheet tab for Atlanta, select cells A2 through E5, then click the Add command button. You should see Atlanta!A$2:$E$5 in the All Ranges list box. Repeat this step for the other two cities.
    d. Remain in step 2b of the PivotTable Wizard. Click the option button for 1 page field. Select (click) the Atlanta range within the All Ranges list box, then click in the Field One list box and type Atlanta. Do not press the Enter key. Select (click) the Boston range within the All ranges list box, then click in the Field One list box and type Boston. Repeat this step for Chicago.
    e. Click Next. Click the option button to create the pivot table on a New Worksheet. Click Finish.
    f. You have a pivot table, but it does not match our figure. Click in cell B3 (the entry in the cell is Column), then click the formula bar and type Quarter, replacing the previous entry. Change the entry in cell A4 from Row to Product. Change the entry in cell A1 from Page1 to City.
    g. Pivot the table to match the figure. Drag Quarter to the row position (cell A4), Product to the column position (cell C3), and City to the row position below Quarter (cell A5). Release the mouse, and the Quarter and City labels will move to the positions shown in the figure.
    h. Format the pivot table so that it matches Figure 5.19. Modify the description on the Documentation worksheet to include the pivot table, then print the pivot table (or the entire workbook if you haven't done so previously).

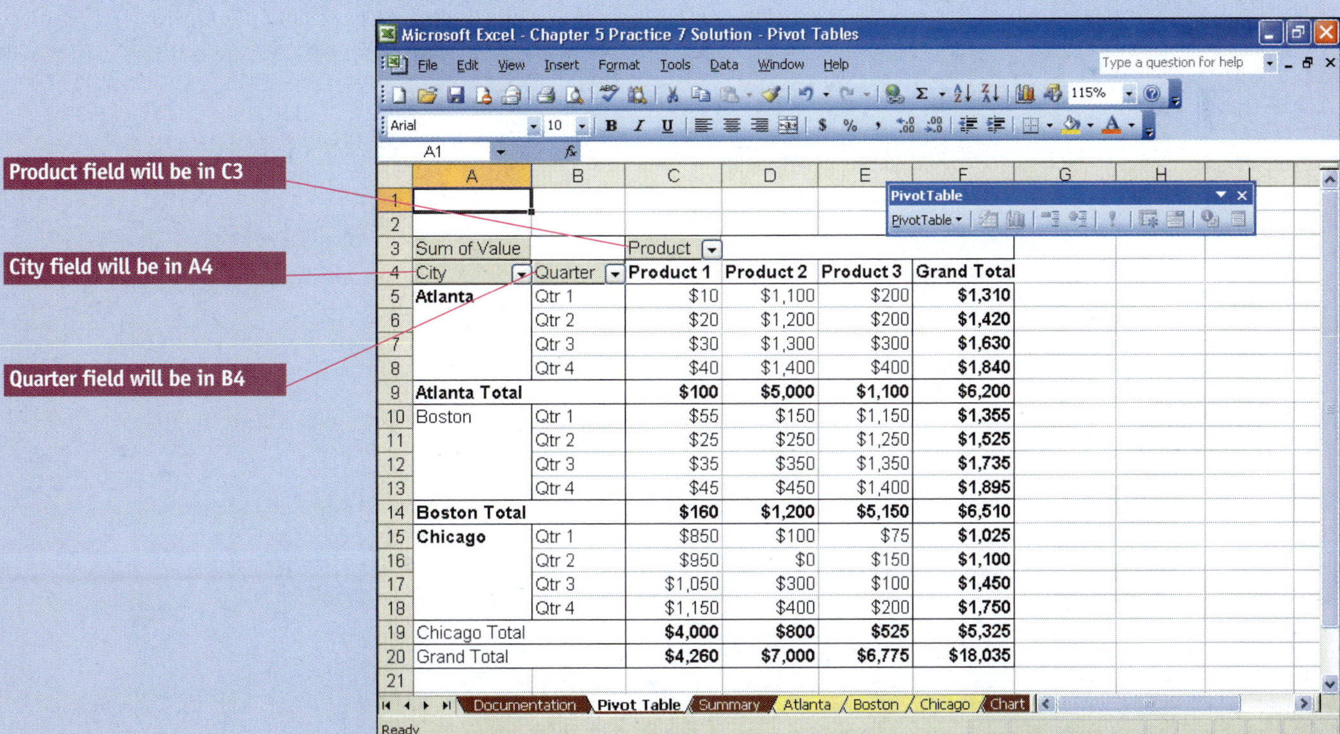

Sum of Value		Product			
City	Quarter	Product 1	Product 2	Product 3	Grand Total
Atlanta	Qtr 1	$10	$1,100	$200	**$1,310**
	Qtr 2	$20	$1,200	$200	**$1,420**
	Qtr 3	$30	$1,300	$300	**$1,630**
	Qtr 4	$40	$1,400	$400	**$1,840**
Atlanta Total		**$100**	**$5,000**	**$1,100**	**$6,200**
Boston	Qtr 1	$55	$150	$1,150	**$1,355**
	Qtr 2	$25	$250	$1,250	**$1,525**
	Qtr 3	$35	$350	$1,350	**$1,735**
	Qtr 4	$45	$450	$1,400	**$1,895**
Boston Total		**$160**	**$1,200**	**$5,150**	**$6,510**
Chicago	Qtr 1	$850	$100	$75	**$1,025**
	Qtr 2	$950	$0	$150	**$1,100**
	Qtr 3	$1,050	$300	$100	**$1,450**
	Qtr 4	$1,150	$400	$200	**$1,750**
Chicago Total		**$4,000**	**$800**	**$525**	**$5,325**
Grand Total		**$4,260**	**$7,000**	**$6,775**	**$18,035**

FIGURE 5.19 Pivot Tables (exercise 7)

MINI CASES

Babyland

The Babyland Toy Store has three branches, each of which operates independently. Your job is to consolidate the data in the *Chapter 5 Mini Case—Maplewood*, *Oakwood*, and *Ramblewood* workbooks, each of which is found in the Exploring Excel folder. You are to create a new workbook that contains a worksheet for each store, a summary worksheet that shows the corporate totals for each product in each quarter, and an appropriate chart reflecting the summary data. You are also asked to create a documentation worksheet with your name, date, and a list of all worksheets in the workbook. Print the completed workbook, along with the cell formulas from the summary worksheet, then submit the printout to your instructor as proof you did this exercise. Use the Page Setup command to display your name, today's date, and the name of the worksheet on the output.

Designs by Jessica

The *Chapter 5 Mini Case—Designs by Jessica* workbook in the Exploring Excel folder is only partially complete as it contains worksheets for individual stores, but does not as yet have a summary worksheet. Your job is to retrieve the workbook and create a summary worksheet that shows the corporate totals for each product in each quarter, and then use the summary worksheet as the basis of a three-dimensional column chart reflecting the sales for the past year. Add a documentation worksheet containing your name as financial analyst, then print the entire workbook and submit it to your instructor. Use the Page Setup command to display your name, today's date, and the name of the worksheet on the output.

External References

Each branch manager of Technology Associates creates an identically formatted workbook with the sales information for his or her branch office. Your job as marketing manager is to consolidate the information into a single workbook, and then graph the results appropriately. The branch data is to remain in the individual workbooks; that is, the formulas in your workbook are to contain external references to the *Chapter 5 Mini Case—Eastern*, *Western*, and *Foreign* workbooks in the Exploring Excel folder. Begin by opening the individual workbooks and entering the appropriate formulas to total the data for each product and each quarter. You can then create a summary workbook that reflects the quarterly totals for each branch through external references to the individual workbooks; that is, any change in the individual workbooks should be automatically reflected in the consolidated workbook.

CHAPTER 6

A Financial Forecast: Auditing, Protection, and Templates

OBJECTIVES

After reading this chapter you will:

1. Develop a spreadsheet model for a financial forecast.
2. Use the Scenario Manager to facilitate decision making.
3. Differentiate between precedent and dependent cells.
4. Use the Formula Auditing toolbar.
5. Track the editing changes that are made to a spreadsheet.
6. Resolve editing conflicts among different users in a work group.
7. Use conditional formatting.
8. Create a template based on an existing workbook.

hands-on exercises

1. A FINANCIAL FORECAST
   Input: Financial Forecast
   Output: Financial Forecast Solution
2. AUDITING AND WORKGROUPS
   Input: Erroneous Financial Forecast
   Output: Erroneous Financial Forecast Solution
3. CREATING A TEMPLATE
   Input: Erroneous Financial Forecast Solution (from exercise 2)
   Output: Get Rich Quick (Excel template rather than a workbook)

CASE STUDY

TIMELY SIGNS

Gary and Tonya Smith are the sole proprietors of Timely Signs, a business that specializes in creating custom signs. The business lost $5,000 last year, and the Smiths are concerned about the future. They currently produce two types of signs—ink-jet signs and vinyl signs—and believe they need to continue to offer both types going forward. Greg Hubit, a family friend and successful entrepreneur, suggested that they create a simple spreadsheet to analyze income and expenses for the year just ended, and then project these numbers for a three- or four-year period.

The Smiths realize that they need to increase sales and/or to reduce costs if their business is to survive. Gary is in favor of focusing on the ink-jet signs. He wants to increase the marketing budget by 20% a year and reduce the selling price of the ink-jet signs by 10% a year. He believes that the aggressive advertising and reduced price will increase demand by 25% a year, and further that the higher volume will reduce the manufacturing cost for the ink-jet signs by 5% a year.

Tonya is in favor of moving their business to a smaller plant where the rent and utilities will decrease 20% a year for the next three years. She proposes to use the savings to increase the marketing budget by 20% a year, and projects a 5% increase in the number of units for each sign. Greg suggests that they focus on reducing costs and urges that they reduce the manufacturing unit cost of both types of signs by 10% a year. Greg would use the savings to increase the marketing budget by 15% a year, which in turn will boost the number of signs in each category by 10% a year. ■

Your assignment is to read the chapter, open the partially completed *Chapter 6 Case Study—Timely Signs* workbook, and complete the forecast by supplying the missing formulas. If you do the work correctly, you will see that the business should earn just under $3,000 in the fourth year according to the Status Quo scenario that exists within the worksheet. You will then create three new scenarios, one each for Gary (ink-jet focus), Tonya (move location), and Greg (control costs), then combine the results in a scenario summary which you will print for your instructor. Print the completed workbook showing the values for the best scenario.

A FINANCIAL FORECAST

Financial planning and budgeting are two of the most common business applications of a spreadsheet. We thought it appropriate, therefore, to use a financial forecast as the vehicle with which to illustrate several additional capabilities in Excel. We begin by developing the forecast itself, with emphasis on the importance of isolating the assumptions on which the spreadsheet is based. We introduce the Scenario Manager, which enables you to specify multiple sets of assumptions and input conditions (scenarios), then see the results at a glance. We also introduce the Formula Auditing toolbar and explain how its tools can help ensure the accuracy of a worksheet.

Figure 6.1 displays a financial forecast for Get Rich Quick Enterprises, which contains the projected income and expenses for the company over a five-year period. The spreadsheet enables management to vary any of the ***assumptions*** at the bottom of the spreadsheet to see the effects on the projected earnings. You don't have to be a business major to follow our forecast. All you have to realize is that the profit for any given year is determined by subtracting expenses from income.

The income is equal to the number of units sold times the unit price. The projected revenue in 2003, for example, is $300,000, based on selling 100,000 units at a price of $3.00 per unit. The variable costs for the same year are estimated at $150,000 (100,000 units times $1.50 per unit). The production facility costs $50,000, and administrative expenses add another $25,000. Subtracting the total expenses from the estimated income yields a net income before taxes of $75,000.

The income and expenses for each succeeding year are based on estimated percentage increases over the previous year, as shown at the bottom of the worksheet. It is absolutely critical to isolate the initial values and assumed rates of increase in this manner, and further, that all entries in the body of the spreadsheet are developed as formulas that reference these cells. The entry in cell C4, for example, is *not* the constant 100,000, but rather a reference to cell C18, which contains the value 100,000.

The distinction may seem trivial, but most assuredly it is not, as two important objectives are achieved. The user sees at a glance which factors affect the results of the spreadsheet (i.e., the cost and earnings projections) and, further, the user can easily change any of those values to see their effect on the overall forecast. Assume, for example, that the first-year forecast changes to 80,000 units sold and that this number will increase at 8% a year (rather than 10%). The only changes in the worksheet are to the entries in cells C18 and E18, because the projected gross revenue is calculated using the values in these cells.

Once you appreciate the necessity of isolating the assumptions and ***initial conditions***, you can design the actual spreadsheet. Ask yourself why you are building the spreadsheet in the first place and what you hope to accomplish. (The financial forecast in this example is intended to answer questions regarding projected rates of growth, and more importantly, how changes in the assumptions and initial conditions will affect the income, expenses, and earnings in later years.) This facilitates the creation of the spreadsheet, which is done in five general stages:

1. Enter the row and column headings, and the values for the initial conditions and the assumed rates of change.
2. Develop the formulas for the first year of the forecast based on the initial conditions at the bottom of the spreadsheet.
3. Develop the formulas for the second year based on the values in year one and the assumed rates of change.
4. Copy the formulas for year two to the remaining years of the forecast.
5. Format the spreadsheet, then print the completed forecast.

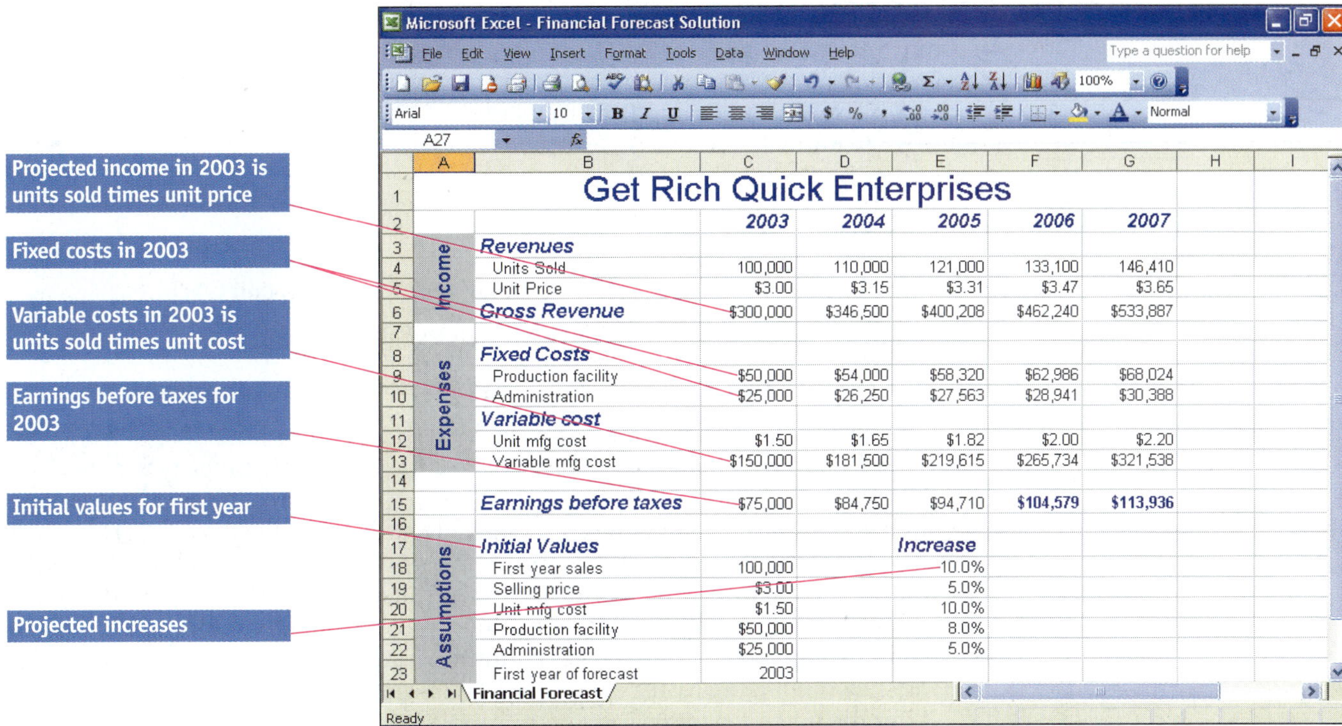

	A	B	C	D	E	F	G
1		Get Rich Quick Enterprises					
2			2003	2004	2005	2006	2007
3	Income	Revenues					
4		Units Sold	100,000	110,000	121,000	133,100	146,410
5		Unit Price	$3.00	$3.15	$3.31	$3.47	$3.65
6		Gross Revenue	$300,000	$346,500	$400,208	$462,240	$533,887
7							
8	Expenses	Fixed Costs					
9		Production facility	$50,000	$54,000	$58,320	$62,986	$68,024
10		Administration	$25,000	$26,250	$27,563	$28,941	$30,388
11		Variable cost					
12		Unit mfg cost	$1.50	$1.65	$1.82	$2.00	$2.20
13		Variable mfg cost	$150,000	$181,500	$219,615	$265,734	$321,538
14							
15		Earnings before taxes	$75,000	$84,750	$94,710	$104,579	$113,936
16							
17	Assumptions	Initial Values			Increase		
18		First year sales	100,000		10.0%		
19		Selling price	$3.00		5.0%		
20		Unit mfg cost	$1.50		10.0%		
21		Production facility	$50,000		8.0%		
22		Administration	$25,000		5.0%		
23		First year of forecast	2003				

(a) Displayed Values

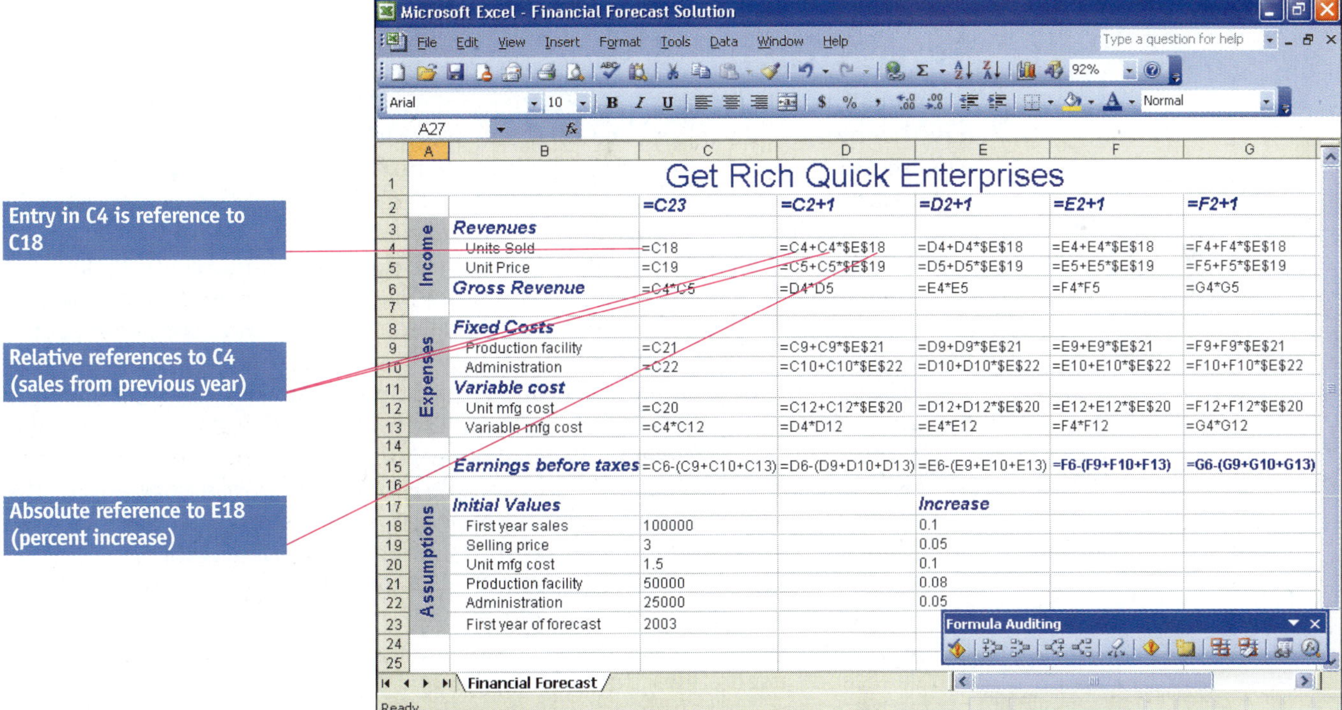

	A	B	C	D	E	F	G
1		Get Rich Quick Enterprises					
2			=C23	=C2+1	=D2+1	=E2+1	=F2+1
3	Income	Revenues					
4		Units Sold	=C18	=C4+C4*$E$18	=D4+D4*$E$18	=E4+E4*$E$18	=F4+F4*$E$18
5		Unit Price	=C19	=C5+C5*$E$19	=D5+D5*$E$19	=E5+E5*$E$19	=F5+F5*$E$19
6		Gross Revenue	=C4*C5	=D4*D5	=E4*E5	=F4*F5	=G4*G5
7							
8	Expenses	Fixed Costs					
9		Production facility	=C21	=C9+C9*$E$21	=D9+D9*$E$21	=E9+E9*$E$21	=F9+F9*$E$21
10		Administration	=C22	=C10+C10*$E$22	=D10+D10*$E$22	=E10+E10*$E$22	=F10+F10*$E$22
11		Variable cost					
12		Unit mfg cost	=C20	=C12+C12*$E$20	=D12+D12*$E$20	=E12+E12*$E$20	=F12+F12*$E$20
13		Variable mfg cost	=C4*C12	=D4*D12	=E4*E12	=F4*F12	=G4*G12
14							
15		Earnings before taxes	=C6-(C9+C10+C13)	=D6-(D9+D10+D13)	=E6-(E9+E10+E13)	=F6-(F9+F10+F13)	=G6-(G9+G10+G13)
16							
17	Assumptions	Initial Values			Increase		
18		First year sales	100000		0.1		
19		Selling price	3		0.05		
20		Unit mfg cost	1.5		0.1		
21		Production facility	50000		0.08		
22		Administration	25000		0.05		
23		First year of forecast	2003				

(b) Cell Formulas

FIGURE 6.1 Financial Forecast

Perhaps the most critical step is the development of the formulas for the second year (2004 in Figure 6.1), which are based on the results for 2003 and the assumption about how these results will change for the next year. The units sold in 2004, for example, are equal to the sales in 2003 (cell C4) plus the estimated increase in unit sales (C4*$E$18); that is,

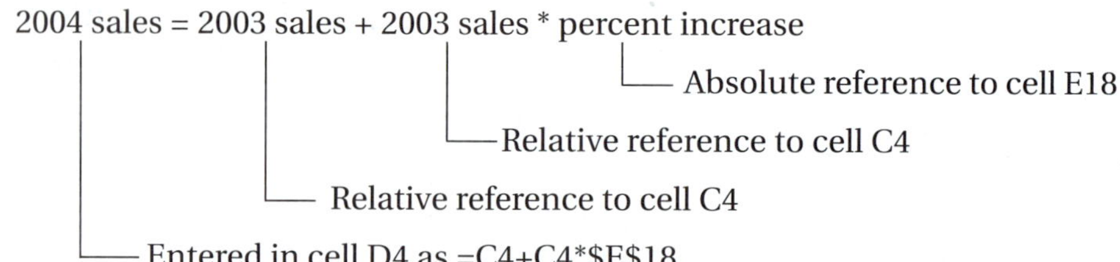

The formula to compute the sales for the year 2004 uses both absolute and relative references, which ensures that it will be copied properly to the other columns for the remaining years in the forecast. An absolute reference ($E$18) is necessary for the cell containing the percent increase in unit sales, because this reference should remain the same when the formula is copied. A relative reference (C4) is used for the sales from the previous year, because this reference should change when the formula is copied. Many of the other formulas in column D are also based on percentage increases from column C, and are developed in similar fashion, as shown in Figure 6.1b.

After the formulas for year two are completed in column D, the entire column is copied to columns E, F, and G to develop the remainder of the forecast. The worksheet is formatted and then printed to complete the exercise. It is now a simple matter to vary any of the assumptions or initial conditions at the bottom of the worksheet and see the result of those changes in the completed forecast.

Advanced Formatting

The spreadsheet in Figure 6.1 incorporates many of the formatting commands that have been used throughout the text. The spreadsheet also illustrates additional capabilities that will be implemented in the hands-on exercise that follows shortly. Some of these features are obvious, such as the ability to ***rotate text*** as seen in column A or the ability to ***indent text*** as was done in column B.

Other capabilities, such as ***conditional formatting***, are more subtle. Look at the projected earnings, for example, and note that amounts over $100,000 are displayed in blue, whereas values under $100,000 are not. One could simply select the two cells and change the font color to blue, but as the earnings change, the cells would have to be reformatted. Accordingly, we implemented the color by selecting the entire row of projected earnings and specifying a conditional format to display the value in blue if it exceeds $100,000, display it in red if it is negative, and default to black otherwise. The use of conditional formatting lets you vary any of the assumptions or initial conditions, which in turn change the projected earnings, yet automatically display the projected earnings in the appropriate color.

The last formatting feature in Figure 6.1 is the imposition of a user-defined style (Main Heading) for various cells in the spreadsheet. A ***style*** (or ***custom format***) is a set of formatting characteristics that is stored under a specific name. You've already used styles throughout the text that were predefined by Excel. Clicking the Comma, Currency, or Percent button on the Formatting toolbar, for example, automatically applies these styles to the selected cells. You can also define your own styles (e.g., Main Heading), as will be done in the hands-on exercise. The advantage of storing the formatting characteristics within a style, as opposed to applying the commands individually, is that you can change the definition of the style, which automatically changes the appearance of all cells defined by that style.

SCENARIO MANAGER

The ***Scenario Manager*** enables you to specify multiple sets of assumptions (***scenarios***), then see at a glance the results of any given scenario. Each scenario represents a different set of what-if conditions that you want to consider in assessing the outcome of a spreadsheet model. You could, for example, look at optimistic, pessimistic, and most likely (consensus) assumptions, as shown in Figure 6.2. The scenarios are saved with the workbook and are available whenever the workbook is opened.

Figure 6.2a displays the Scenario Manager dialog box that contains the various scenarios that have been created. Each scenario is stored under its own name and is composed of a set of cells whose values vary from scenario to scenario. Figure 6.2b, for example, shows the value of the ***changing cells*** for the consensus scenario. Figure 6.2c shows the values for the optimistic scenario. (The cells in the dialog box are identified by name, rather than cell reference through the ***Define Name command*** as will be shown in the next hands-on exercise. First_Year_Sales, for example, refers to cell C18 in the financial forecast. The use of a mnemonic name, as opposed to a cell reference, makes it much easier to understand precisely which values change from one scenario to the next.)

The ***scenario summary*** in Figure 6.2d compares the effects of the different scenarios to one another by showing the value of one or more ***result cells***. We see, for example, that the consensus scenario yields earnings of $113,936 in the fifth year (the same value shown earlier), compared to significantly higher or lower values for the other two scenarios.

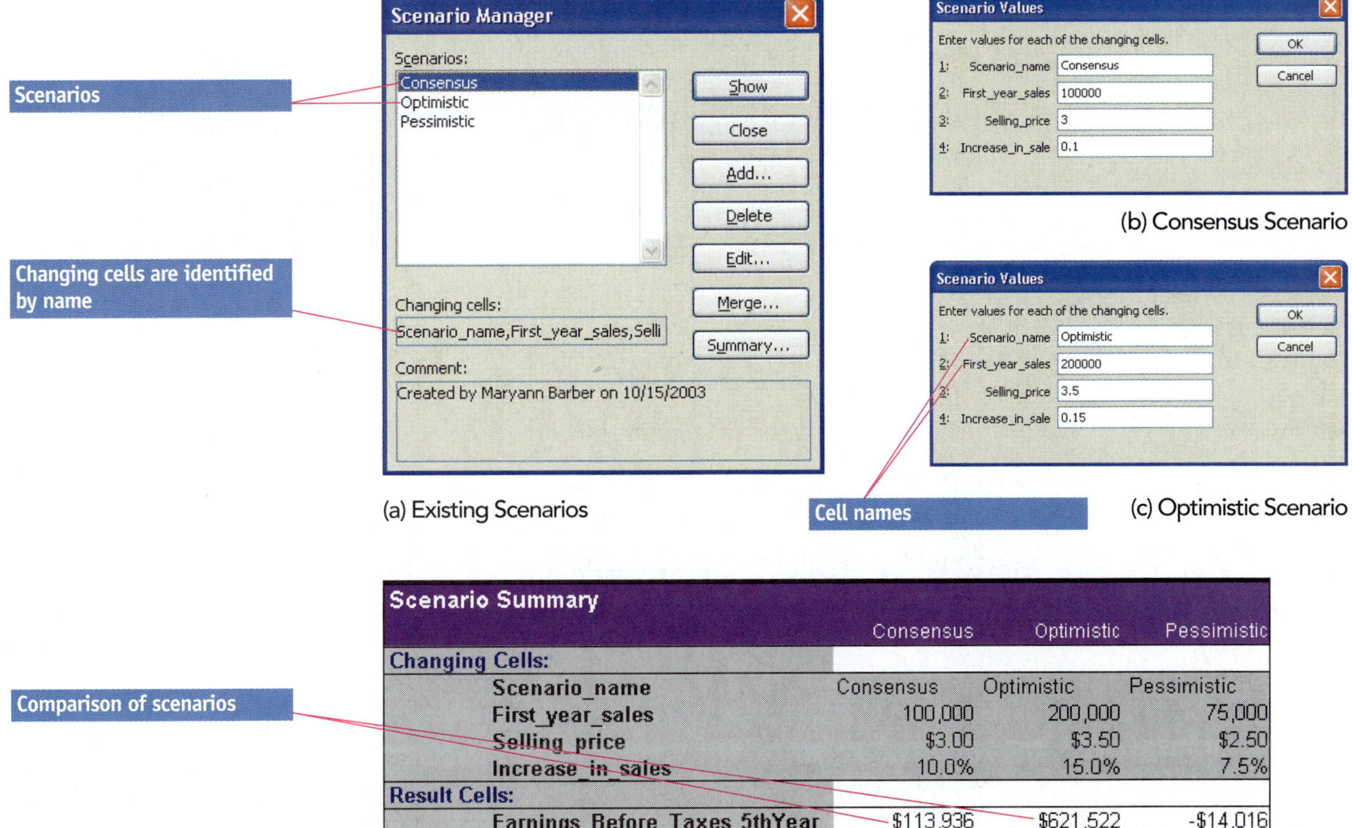

Scenario Summary	Consensus	Optimistic	Pessimistic
Changing Cells:			
Scenario_name	Consensus	Optimistic	Pessimistic
First_year_sales	100,000	200,000	75,000
Selling_price	$3.00	$3.50	$2.50
Increase_in_sales	10.0%	15.0%	7.5%
Result Cells:			
Earnings_Before_Taxes_5thYear	$113,936	$621,522	-$14,016

(d) Scenario Summary

FIGURE 6.2 Scenario Manager

hands-on exercise

1 A Financial Forecast

Objective To develop a spreadsheet for a financial forecast that isolates the assumptions and initial values; to use conditional formatting, styles, indentation, and rotated text to format the spreadsheet. Use Figure 6.3 as a guide in the exercise.

Step 1: Enter the Formulas for Year One

- Start Excel. Open the **Financial Forecast** workbook in the **Exploring Excel folder** to display the worksheet in Figure 6.3a. (Cells C4 through C15 are currently empty.)
- Click in **cell C2**. Type **=C23** and press **Enter**. Note that you are not entering the year explicitly, but rather a reference to the cell that contains the year, which is located in the assumptions area of the worksheet.
- Enter the remaining formulas for year one of the forecast:
  - Click in **cell C4**. Type **=C18**. Click in **cell C5**. Type **=C19**.
  - Click in **cell C6**. Type **=C4*C5**. Click in **cell C9**. Type **=C21**.
  - Click in **cell C10**. Type **=C22**. Click in **cell C12**. Type **=C20**.
  - Click in **cell C13**. Type **=C4*C12**.
  - Click in **cell C15**. Type **=C6-(C9+C10+C13)**.
- The cell contents for year one (2003 in this example) are complete. The displayed values in this column should match the numbers shown in Figure 6.3a.
- Save the workbook as **Financial Forecast Solution** in the **Exploring Excel Folder** you have used throughout the text.

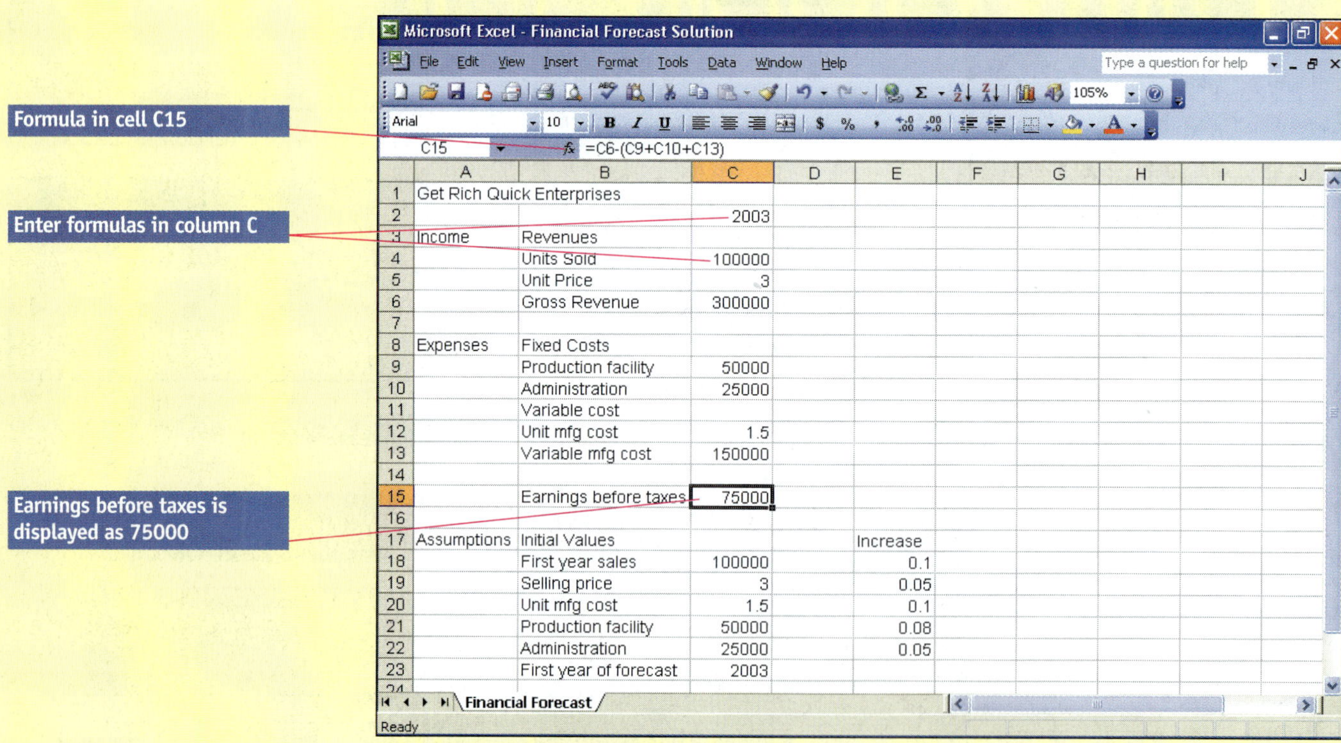

(a) Enter the Formulas for Year One (step 1)

FIGURE 6.3 Hands-on Exercise 1

Step 2: Enter the Formulas for Year Two

- Click in **cell D2**. Type **=C2+1** to determine the second year of the forecast.
- Click in **cell D4**. Type **=C4+C4*$E$18**. This formula computes the sales for year two as a function of the sales in year one and the rate of increase.
- Enter the remaining formulas for year two:
  - Click in **cell D5**. Type **=C5+C5*$E$19**. Copy the formula in cell C6 to D6.
  - Click in **cell D9**. Type **=C9+C9*$E$21**.
  - Click in **cell D10**. Type **=C10+C10*$E$22**.
  - Click in **cell D12**. Type **=C12+C12*$E$20**.
  - Copy the formulas in cells C13 and C15 to cells D13 and D15.
- The cell contents for the second year (2004) are complete. The displayed values should match the numbers shown in Figure 6.3b.
- Save the workbook.

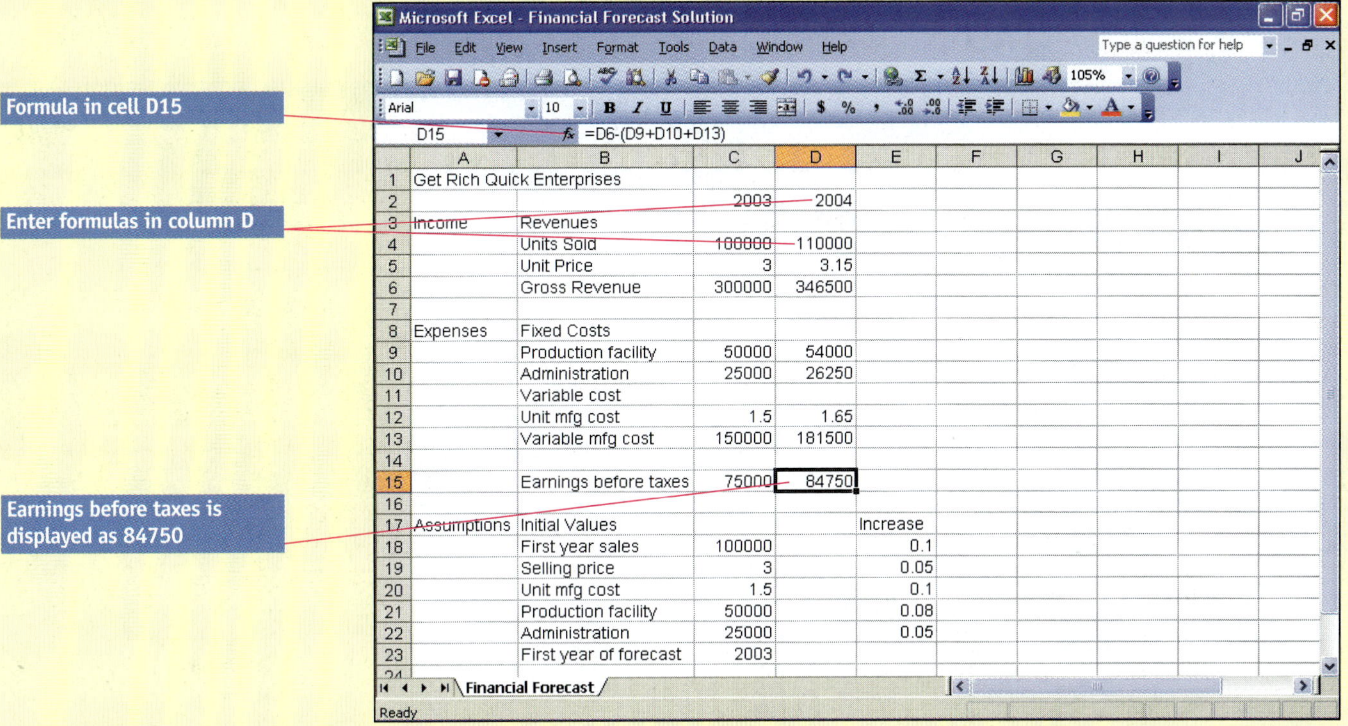

(b) Enter the Formulas for Year Two (step 2)

FIGURE 6.3 Hands-on Exercise 1 (*continued*)

USE POINTING TO ENTER CELL FORMULAS

A cell reference can be typed directly into a formula, or it can be entered more easily through pointing. The latter is also more accurate as you use the mouse or arrow keys to reference cells directly. To use pointing, select (click) the cell to contain the formula, type an equal sign to begin entering the formula, click (or move to) the cell containing the reference, then press the F4 key as necessary to change from relative to absolute references. Type any arithmetic operator to place the cell reference in the formula, then continue pointing to additional cells. Press the Enter key to complete the formula.

Step 3: Copy the Formulas to the Remaining Years

- Click and drag to select **cells D2 through D15** (the cells containing the formulas for year two). Click the **Copy button** on the Standard toolbar (or use the **Ctrl+C** keyboard shortcut).
- A moving border will surround these cells to indicate that their contents have been copied to the clipboard.
- Click and drag to select **cells E2 through G15** (the cells that will contain the formulas for years three to five). Point to the selection and click the **right mouse button** to display the context-sensitive menu in Figure 6.3c.
- Click **Paste** to paste the contents of the clipboard into the selected cells. The displayed values for the last three years of the forecast should be visible in the worksheet.
- You should see earnings before taxes of 113936 for the last year in the forecast. Press **Esc** to remove the moving border.
- Save the workbook.

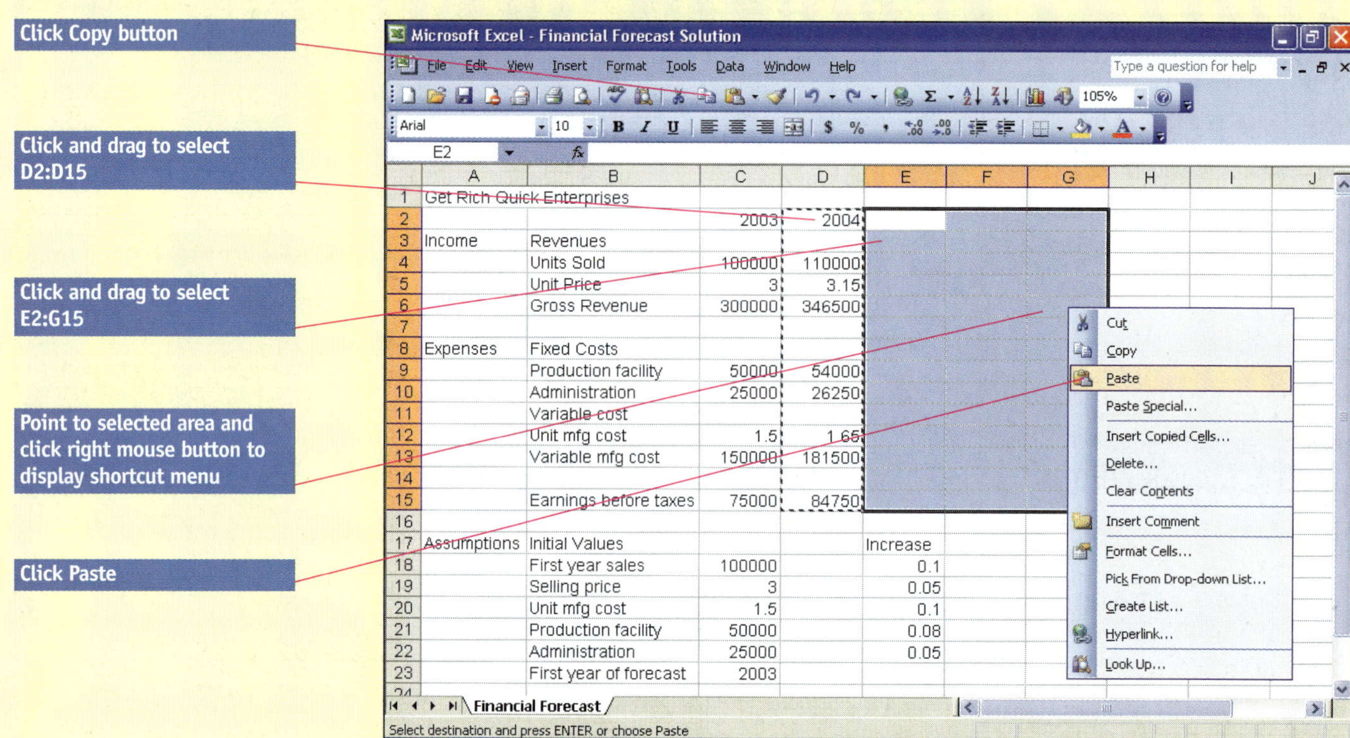

(c) Copy the Formulas to the Remaining Years (step 3)

FIGURE 6.3 Hands-on Exercise 1 (*continued*)

THE FILL HANDLE

There are several ways to copy a formula to cells in adjacent rows or columns. The easiest is the fill handle (the tiny black square) that appears in the lower-right corner of the selected cells. Select the cell (cells) to be copied, then click and drag the fill handle over the destination range. Release the mouse to complete the operation.

Step 4: Create a Style

- Point to any toolbar, click the **right mouse button** to display a context-sensitive menu, then click the **Customize command** to display the Customize dialog box. Click the **Commands tab**, then select (click) the **Format category**.
- Click and drag the **Style List box** from within the command section to the right of the font color button on the Formatting toolbar. (You must drag the tool inside the toolbar and will see a large I-beam as you do so.)
- Release the mouse when you position the tool where you want. Click **Close** to close the Custom dialog box.
- The Style list box now appears on the Formatting toolbar as shown in Figure 6.3d. (The Style dialog box is not yet visible.) Click in **cell C2** and note that the Style list box indicates the Normal style (the default style for all cells in a worksheet).
- Change the font in cell C2 to **12 point Arial bold italic**. Click the **down arrow** on the Font Color tool and click **blue**. Pull down the **Format menu** and click the **Style command** to display the Style dialog box.
- The Normal style is already selected. Type **Main Heading** to define a new style according to the characteristics of the selected cell. Click **OK** to create the style and close the dialog box.
- Click and drag to select **cells D2 through G2**. Click the down arrow on the Style list box and select the **Main Heading style** you just created to apply this style to the selected cells.
- Select **cell B3**. Press and hold the **Ctrl key** as you select **cells B6, B8, B11, B15, B17, and E17**, then apply the **Main Heading style** to these cells as well.
- Increase the width of column B so that you can see the text in cell B15. Save the workbook.

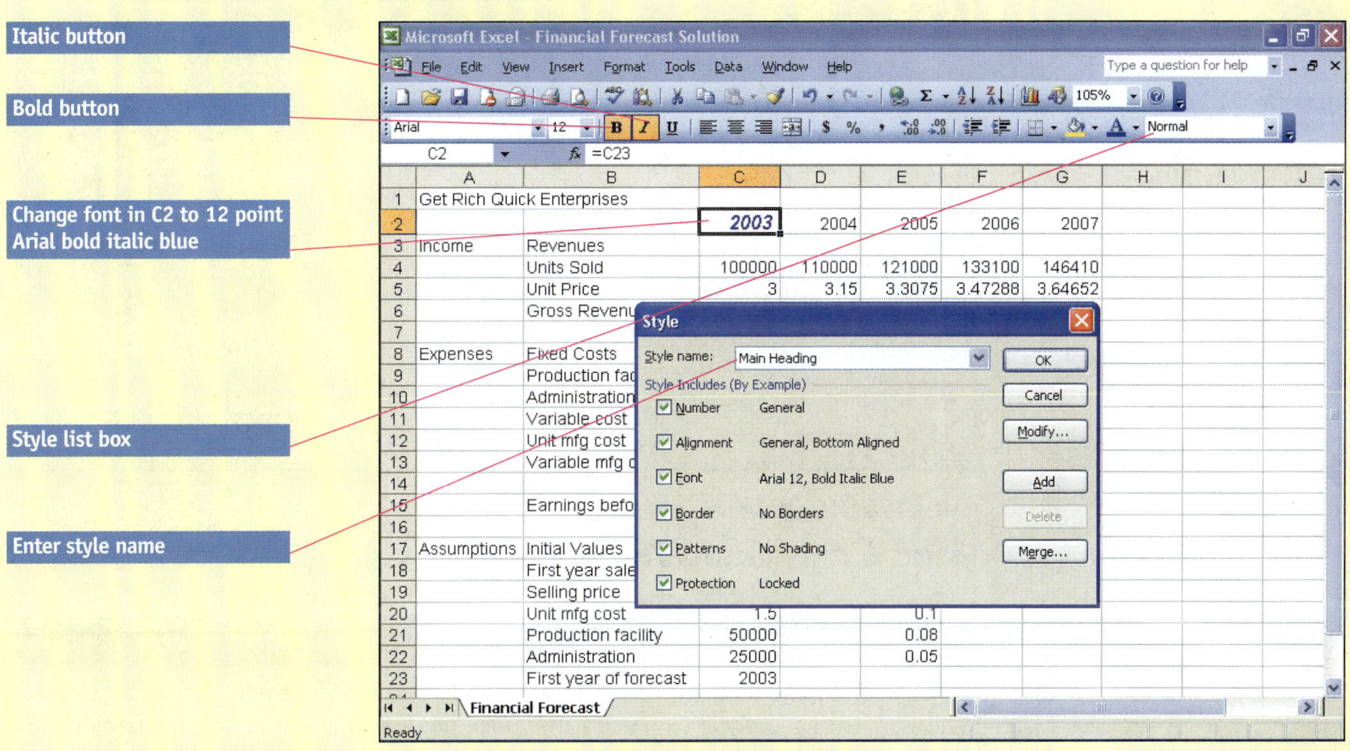

(d) Create a Style (step 4)

FIGURE 6.3 Hands-on Exercise 1 (*continued*)

Step 5: Rotate and Indent Text

- Click and drag to select **cell ranges A3:A6, A8:A13, and A17:A23** as shown in Figure 6.3e. Pull down the **Format menu** and click the **Cells command** to display the Format Cells dialog box shown in the figure.
- Click the **Alignment tab** and specify **center alignment** in both the horizontal and vertical list boxes. Check the box to **Merge cells**. Click in the **Degrees text box** and enter **90**.
- Click the **Font tab**, then change the font to **12 point Arial bold**. Change the font color to **blue**.
- Click the **Patterns tab** and choose **gray shading**.
- Click **OK** to accept these changes and close the Format Cells dialog box.
- Click and drag to select the labels in **cells B4 and B5**. Click the **Increase Indent button** on the Formatting toolbar to indent these labels.
- Press and hold the **Ctrl key** as you select **cells B9 and B10, B12 and B13**, and **B18 through B23**. Click the **Increase Indent button** to indent the labels that appear in these cells.
- Save the workbook.

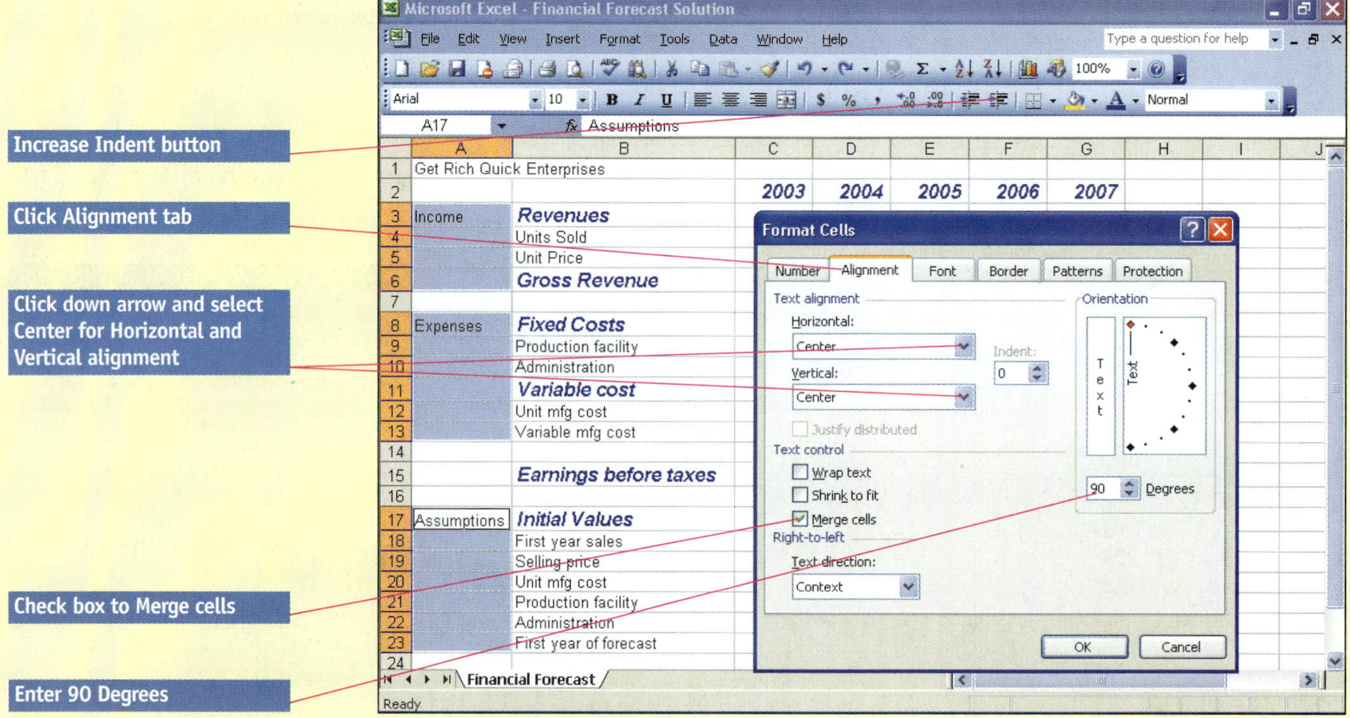

(e) Rotate and Indent Text (step 5)

FIGURE 6.3 Hands-on Exercise 1 (*continued*)

TOGGLE MERGE CELLS ON AND OFF

Click and drag to select multiple cells, then click the Merge and Center button on the Formatting toolbar to merge the cells into a single cell. Click in the merged cell, then click the Merge and Center button a second time and the cell is split. (This is different from Office 2000, where the only way to split cells was to clear the Merge cells check box within the Format Cells dialog box.)

Step 6: Conditional Formatting

- Click and drag to select **cells C15 through G15**. Pull down the **Format menu** and click the **Conditional Formatting command** to display the Conditional Formatting dialog box in Figure 6.3f.
- Set the relationships for condition 1 as shown in Figure 6.3f. Click the **Format button** to display the Format Cells dialog box and click the **Font tab**. Change the font style to **bold** and the font color to **blue**. Click **OK**.
- Click the **Add button** and enter the parameters for condition 2 as shown in Figure 6.3f. Click the **Format button**. Change the Font style to **bold** and the color to **red**. Click **OK**.
- Click **OK** to close the Conditional Formatting dialog box. Click any cell to deselect cells C15 to G15. The earnings before taxes for the last two years of the forecast are displayed in bold and in blue, since they exceed $100,000.
- Click in **cell C19**, change the selling price to **2.00**, and press the **Enter key**. The earnings before taxes are displayed in red since they are negative for every year. Click the **Undo button** to return the initial sales price to 3.00.
- Save the workbook.

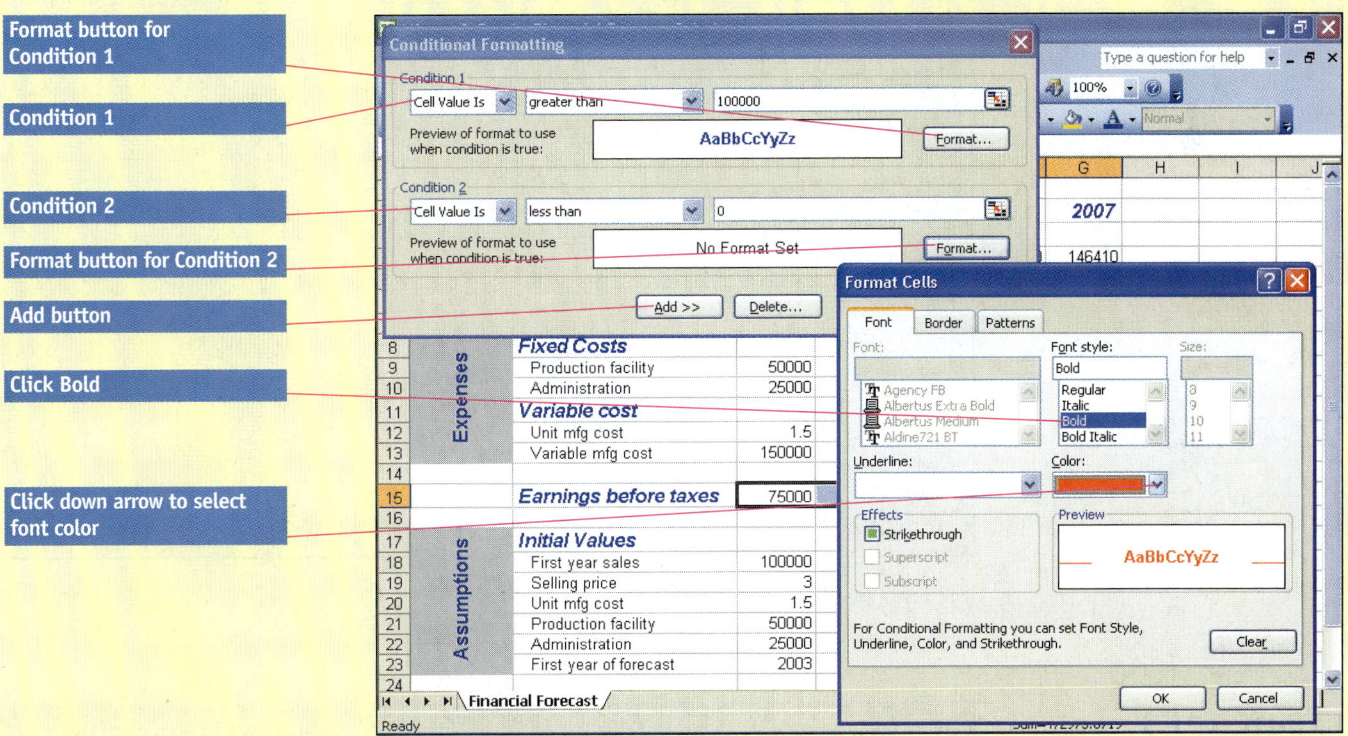

(f) Conditional Formatting (step 6)

FIGURE 6.3 Hands-on Exercise 1 (*continued*)

THE RIGHT MOUSE BUTTON

Point to a cell (or cell range), a worksheet tab, or a toolbar, then click the right mouse button to display a context-sensitive menu. Right clicking a cell, for example, displays a menu with selected commands from the Edit, Insert, and Format menus. Right clicking a toolbar displays a menu that lets you display or hide additional toolbars. Right clicking a worksheet tab enables you to rename, move, copy, or delete the worksheet.

Step 7: Complete the Formatting

- Click in **cell A1**. Change the font color to **blue**, and the font size to **22 points**. Click and drag to select **cells A1 through G1**, then click the **Merge and Center button** to center the entry.
- Use Figure 6.3g as a guide to implement the appropriate formatting for the remaining entries in the worksheet. Remember to press and hold the **Ctrl key** if you want to select noncontiguous cells prior to executing a command.
- Add your name in **cell A2**. Save the workbook.
- Print the spreadsheet twice, once to show the displayed values and once to show the cell formulas. Press **Ctrl+~** to toggle between cell formulas and displayed values.
- Submit both printouts to your instructor.

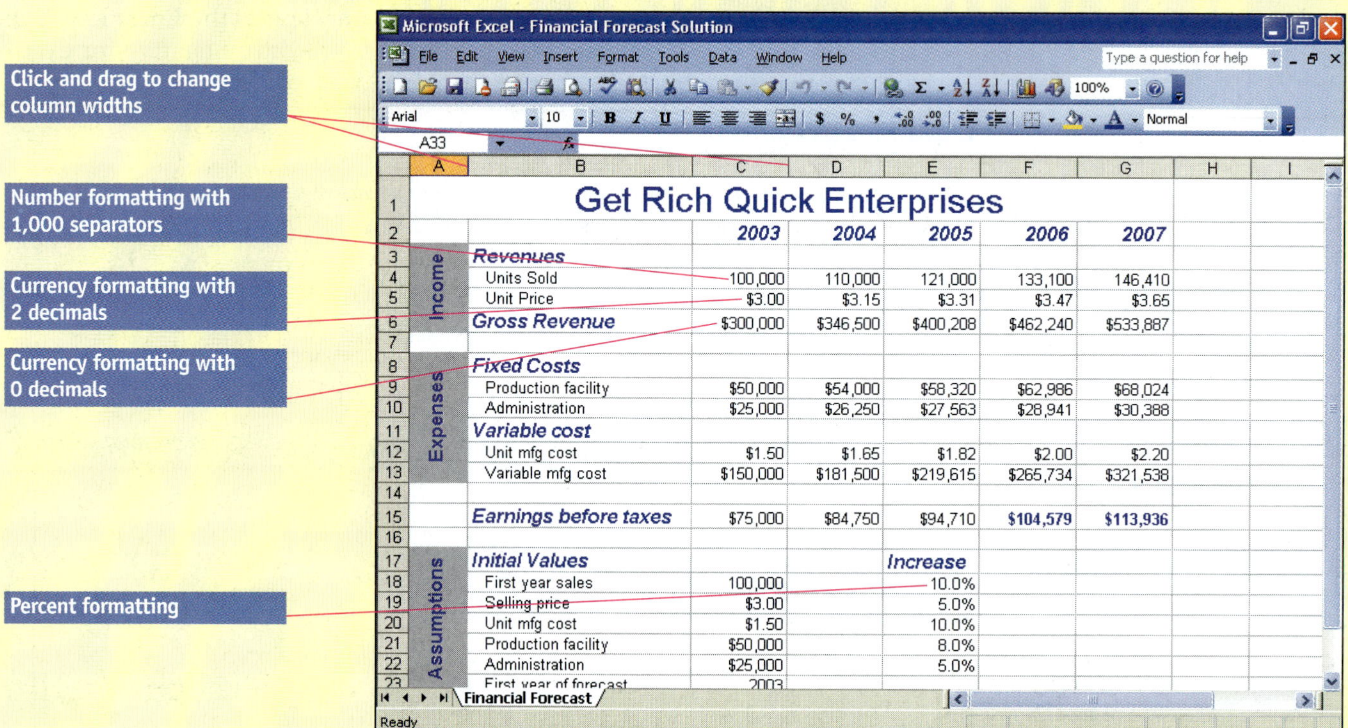

	A	B	C	D	E	F	G
1	Get Rich Quick Enterprises						
2			2003	2004	2005	2006	2007
3	Income	Revenues					
4		Units Sold	100,000	110,000	121,000	133,100	146,410
5		Unit Price	$3.00	$3.15	$3.31	$3.47	$3.65
6		Gross Revenue	$300,000	$346,500	$400,208	$462,240	$533,887
7							
8	Expenses	Fixed Costs					
9		Production facility	$50,000	$54,000	$58,320	$62,986	$68,024
10		Administration	$25,000	$26,250	$27,563	$28,941	$30,388
11		Variable cost					
12		Unit mfg cost	$1.50	$1.65	$1.82	$2.00	$2.20
13		Variable mfg cost	$150,000	$181,500	$219,615	$265,734	$321,538
14							
15		Earnings before taxes	$75,000	$84,750	$94,710	$104,579	$113,936
16							
17	Assumptions	Initial Values			Increase		
18		First year sales	100,000		10.0%		
19		Selling price	$3.00		5.0%		
20		Unit mfg cost	$1.50		10.0%		
21		Production facility	$50,000		8.0%		
22		Administration	$25,000		5.0%		
23		First year of forecast	2003				

(g) Complete the Formatting (step 7)

FIGURE 6.3 Hands-on Exercise 1 (*continued*)

CREATE A CUSTOM VIEW

Format the spreadsheet to print the displayed values, then pull down the View menu and click Custom Views to display the Custom Views dialog box. Click the button to Add a view, enter the name (e.g., Displayed Values), and click OK. Press Ctrl+` to display the cell formulas, adjust the column widths as necessary, then pull down the View menu a second time to create a second custom view (e.g., Cell Formulas). You can switch to either view at any time by selecting the Custom Views command and selecting the appropriate view.

Step 8: The Insert Name Command

- Click in **cell C18**, pull down the **Insert menu**, select the **Name command**, then click **Define** to display the Define Name dialog box in Figure 6.3h.
- **First_year_sales** is already entered as the default name (because this text appears as a label in the cell immediately to the left of the active cell. Underscores were added between the words, however, because blanks are not permitted in a cell name.) Click **OK** to accept this name.
- Name the other cells that will be used in the various scenarios. Use **Selling_price** as the name for **cell C19**. Enter names of **Increase_in_sales** for **cell E18**, and **Scenario_name** for **cell E23**. (Do not be concerned that cell E23 is currently empty.)
- Save the workbook.

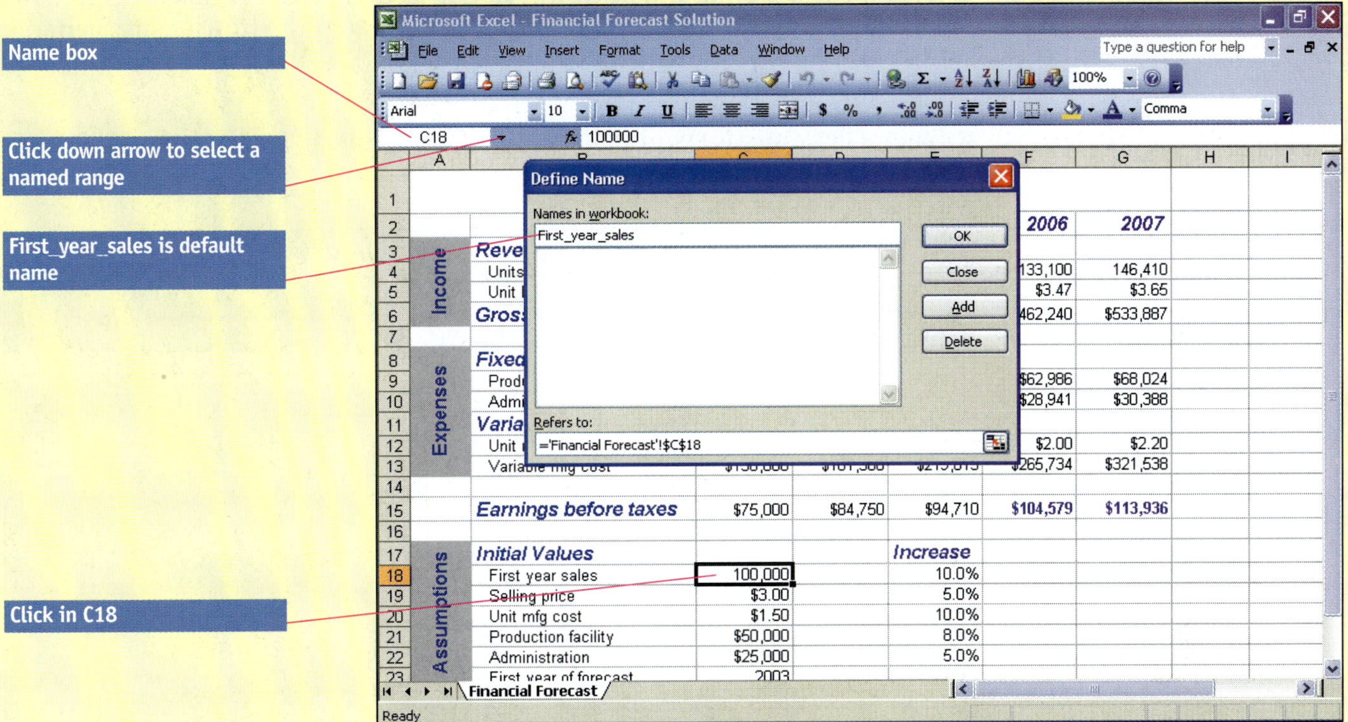

(h) The Insert Name Command (step 8)

FIGURE 6.3 Hands-on Exercise 1 (*continued*)

THE NAME BOX

Use the Name box on the formula bar to define a named range, by first selecting the cell in the worksheet to which the name is to apply, clicking in the Name box to enter the range name, and then pressing the Enter key. Once the name has been defined, you can use the Name box to select a named range by clicking in the box and then typing the appropriate cell reference or name or simply by clicking the drop-down arrow next to the Name box to select the name from a drop-down list. Named ranges make a scenario easier to read since we see mnemonic names as opposed to cell references such as C18.

Step 9: Create the Scenarios

- Click in **cell E23** and type the word **Consensus**. Click in **cell E17**, click the **Format Painter button** on the Formatting toolbar, then click in **cell E23** to copy the format from cell E17.
- Pull down the **Tools menu**. Click **Scenarios** to display the Scenario Manager dialog box. Click the **Add command button** to display the Add Scenario dialog box in Figure 6.3i. Type **Consensus** in the Scenario Name text box.
- Click in the **Changing Cells text box**. Cell E23 (the active cell) is already entered as the first cell in the scenario. Type a comma, then enter **C18, C19, and E18** as the remaining cells in the scenario. Click **OK**.
- You should see the Scenario Values dialog box with the values of this scenario already entered from the corresponding cells in the worksheet.
- Click the **Add command button** to add a second scenario called **Optimistic**. The changing cells are already entered and match the Consensus scenario. Click **OK**. Enter **Optimistic, 200000, 3.5**, and **.15**, as the values for the changing cells. Click **Add**.
- Enter a **Pessimistic scenario** in similar fashion, using **Pessimistic, 75000, 2.5**, and **.075**, for the changing cells. Click **OK**.

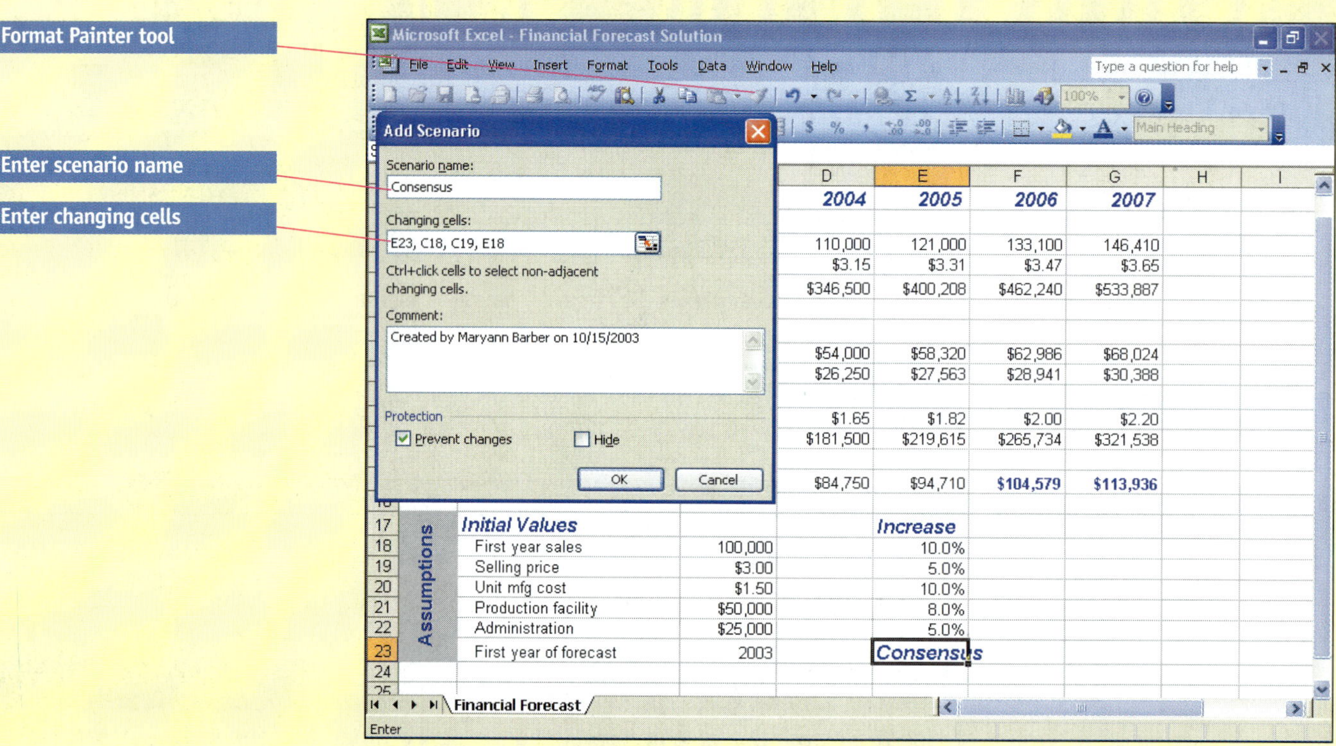

(i) Create the Scenarios (step 9)

FIGURE 6.3 Hands-on Exercise 1 (*continued*)

ISOLATE THE ASSUMPTIONS

The formulas in a worksheet should always be based on cell references that are clearly labeled, set apart from the rest of the worksheet. You can then vary the inputs (or assumptions) on which the worksheet is based to see the effect within the worksheet. You can change the values manually, or store sets of values within a specific scenario.

Step 10: View the Scenarios

- The Scenario Manager dialog box should still be open as shown in Figure 6.3j. If necessary, pull down the **Tools menu** and click the **Scenarios command** to reopen the Scenario Manager.
- There should be three scenarios listed—Consensus, Optimistic, and Pessimistic—corresponding to the scenarios that were just created.
- Select the **Optimistic scenario**, then click the **Show button** (or simply double click the scenario name) to display the financial forecast under the assumptions of this scenario.
- Double click the **Pessimistic scenario**, which changes the worksheet to show the forecast under these assumptions.
- Double click the **Consensus scenario** to return to this scenario. Do you see how easy it is to change multiple assumptions at one time by storing the values in a scenario?

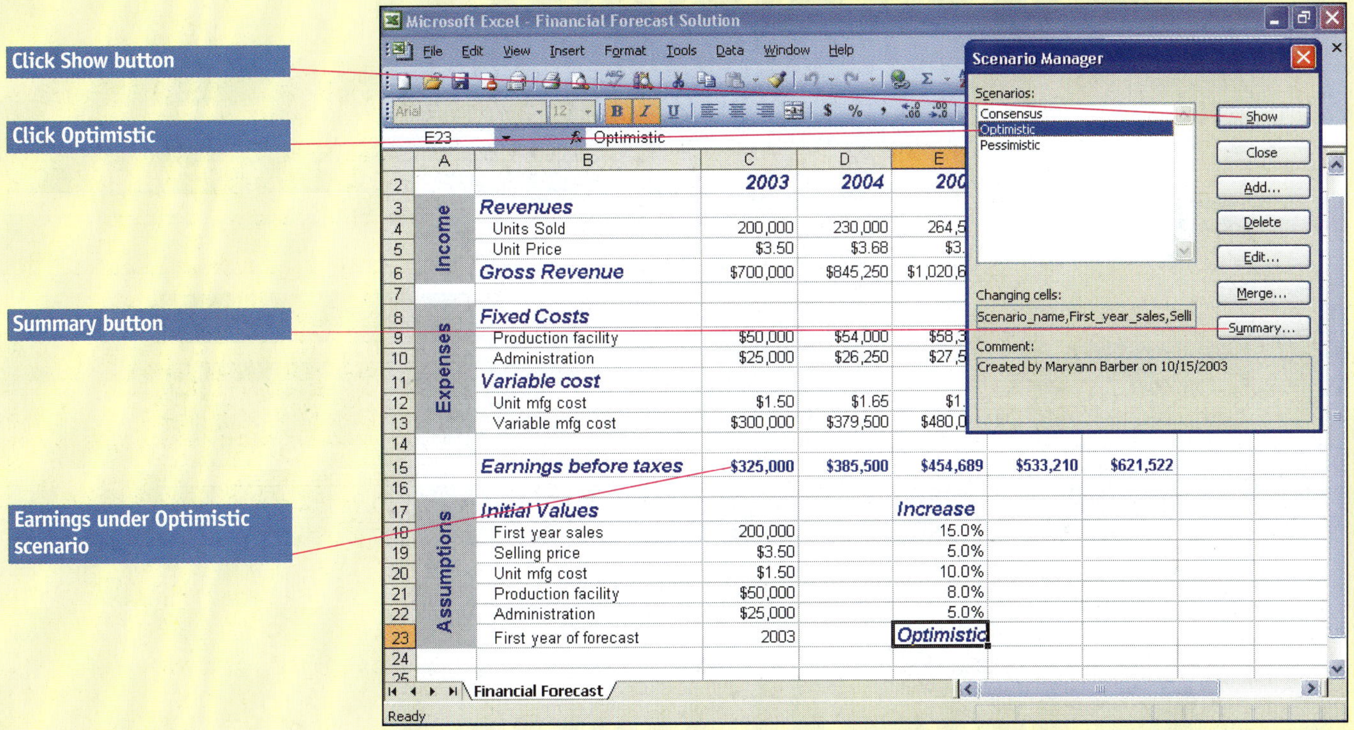

(j) View the Scenarios (step 10)

FIGURE 6.3 Hands-on Exercise 1 (*continued*)

THE SCENARIO MANAGER LIST BOX

The Scenario Manager list box lets you select a scenario directly from a toolbar. Point to any toolbar, click the right mouse button to display a shortcut menu, then click Customize to display the Customize dialog box. Click the Commands tab, select Tools in the Categories list box, then click and drag the Scenario list box to an empty space on the toolbar. Click Close to close the dialog box and return to the workbook. Click the down arrow on the Scenario list box, which now appears on the toolbar, to choose from the scenarios that have been defined within the current workbook. See exercise 6 at the end of the chapter.

Step 11: The Scenario Summary

- The Scenario Manager dialog box should still be open. Click the **Summary button** to display the Scenario Summary dialog box.
- If necessary, click the **Scenario Summary option button**. Click in the **Result Cells text box**, then click in **cell G15** (the cell that contains the earnings before taxes in the fifth year of the forecast). Click **OK**.
- You should see a Scenario Summary worksheet as shown in Figure 6.3k. Each scenario has its own column in the worksheet. The changing cells, identified by name rather than cell reference, are listed in column C.
- The Scenario Summary worksheet is an ordinary worksheet to the extent that it can be modified like any other worksheet. Click the header for **row 6**, then press and hold the **Ctrl key** as you click and drag **rows 12 to 14**. Right click the selected cells, then click the **Delete command** from the context-sensitive menu.
- Delete Column D in similar fashion. Add your name to the worksheet. Save the workbook, then print the summary worksheet for your instructor. Close the workbook.

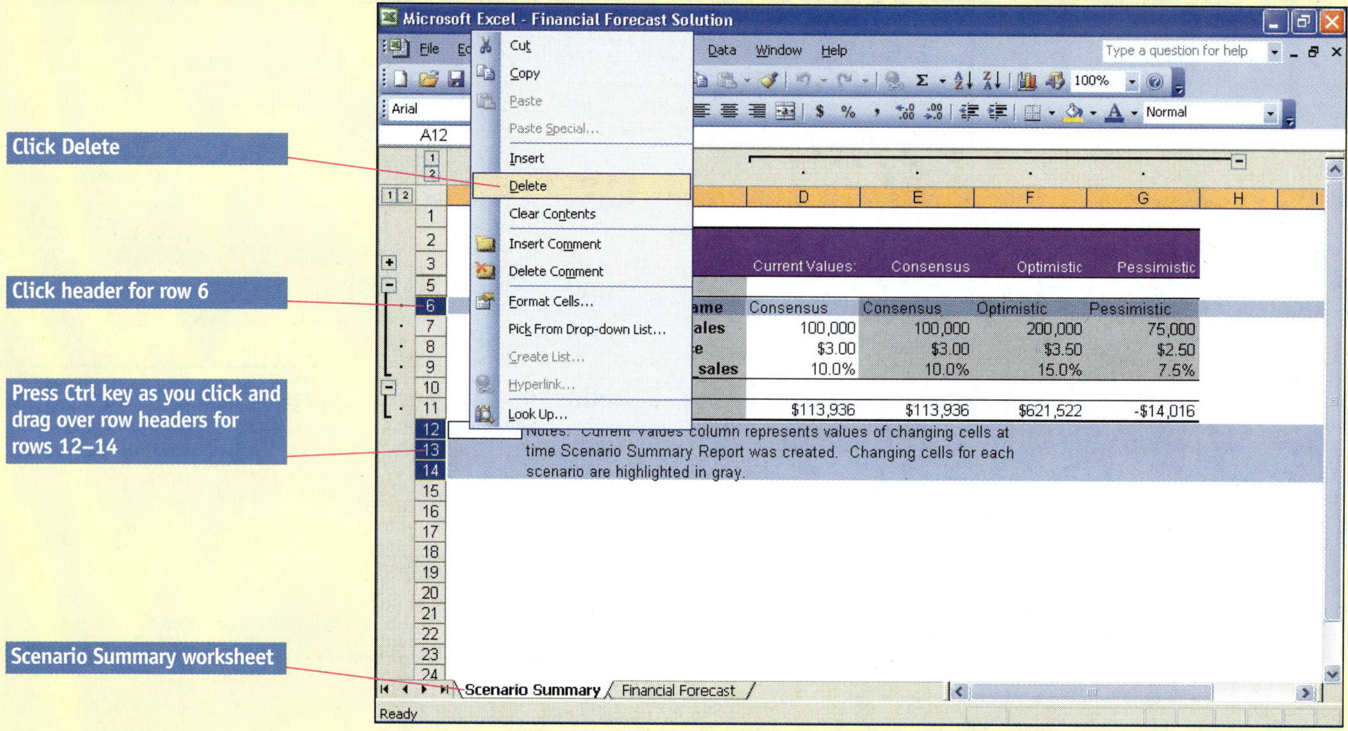

(k) The Scenario Summary (step 11)

FIGURE 6.3 Hands-on Exercise 1 (*continued*)

THE SCENARIO SUMMARY WORKSHEET

You can return to the Scenario Manager to add or modify an individual scenario, after which you can create a new scenario summary. You must, however, execute the command when the original worksheet is displayed on the screen. Note, too, that each time you click the Summary button within the Scenario Manager, you will create another summary worksheet called Scenario Summary 2, Scenario Summary 3, and so on. You can delete the extraneous worksheets by right clicking the worksheet tab, then clicking the Delete command.

WORKGROUPS AND AUDITING

The spreadsheet containing the financial forecast is a tool that will be used by management as the basis for decision making. Executives in the company will vary the assumptions on which the spreadsheet is based to see the effects on profitability, then implement changes in policy based on the results of the spreadsheet. But what if the spreadsheet is in error? Think, for a moment, how business has become totally dependent on the spreadsheet, and what the consequences might be of basing corporate policy on an erroneous spreadsheet.

It's one thing if the assumptions about the expected increases turn out to be wrong because the very nature of a forecast requires us to deal with uncertainty. It's inexcusable, however, if the formulas that use those assumptions are invalid. Thus, it's common for several people to collaborate on the same spreadsheet to minimize the chance for error. One person creates the initial version, then distributes copies to the ***work group*** (the persons working on a project). Each person enters his or her comments and/or proposed changes, then the various workbooks can be merged into a single workbook. It's also possible to create a ***shared workbook*** and place it on a network drive to give all reviewers access to a common file.

Consider, for example, Figure 6.4, which displays an *erroneous* version of the financial forecast. One of the first things you notice about Figure 6.4 is the comments by different people, Marion, Jodi, and Ben, who have reviewed the spreadsheet and suggested changes. Anyone with access to the shared workbook can change it using the tools on the ***Reviewing toolbar*** or through the ***Track Changes command***. The changes made by different people to cell formulas are even displayed in different colors. You, as the developer, can then review the collective changes and resolve any conflicts that might occur.

How can you, or any of the reviewers, know when a spreadsheet displays invalid results? One way is to "eyeball" the spreadsheet and try to approximate its results. Look for any calculations that are obviously incorrect. Look at the financial forecast, for example, and see whether all the values are growing at the projected rates

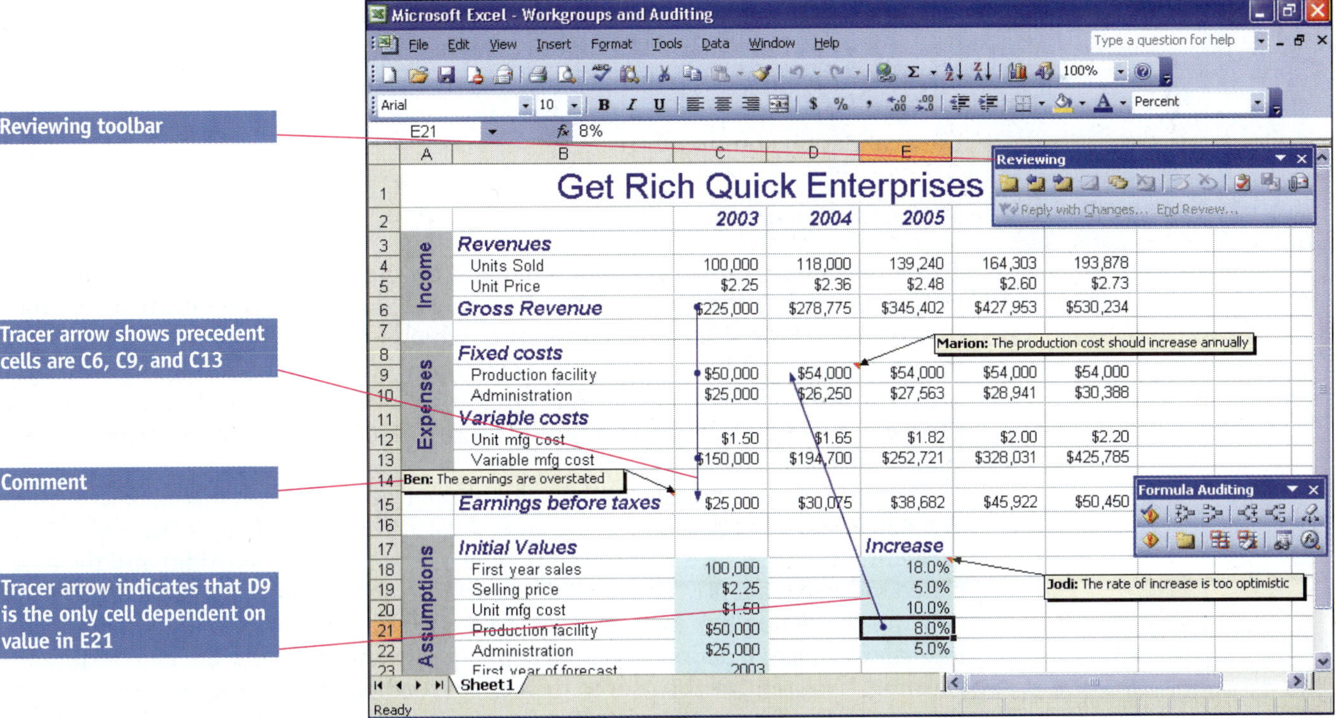

FIGURE 6.4 Workgroups and Auditing

of change. The number of units sold and the unit price increase every year as expected, but the cost of the production facility remains constant after 2004 (Marion's comment). This is an obvious error, because the production facility is supposed to increase at 8% annually, according to the assumptions at the bottom of the spreadsheet. The consequence of this error is that the production costs are too low and hence the projected earnings are too high. The error was easy to find, even without the use of a calculator.

A more subtle error occurs in the computation of the earnings before taxes. Look at the numbers for 2003. The gross revenue is $225,000. The total cost is also $225,000 ($50,000 for the production facility, $25,000 for administration, and $150,000 for the manufacturing cost). The projected earnings should be zero, but are shown incorrectly as $25,000 (Ben's comment), because the administration cost was not subtracted from the gross revenue in determining the profit.

You may be good enough to spot either of these errors just by looking at the spreadsheet. You can also use the ***Formula Auditing toolbar*** to display the relationships between the various cells in a worksheet. It enables you to trace the ***precedents*** for a formula and identify the cells in the worksheet that are referenced by that formula. It also enables you to trace the ***dependents*** of a cell and identify the formulas in the worksheet that reference that cell.

The identification of precedent and/or dependent cells is done graphically by displaying ***tracers*** on the worksheet. You simply click in the cell for which you want the information, then you click the appropriate button on the Formula Auditing toolbar. The blue lines (tracers) appear on the worksheet, and will remain on the worksheet until you click the appropriate removal button. The tracers always point forward, from the precedent cells to the dependent formula.

Look again at Figure 6.4 to see how the tracers are used. Cell C15 contains the formula to compute the earnings for the first year. There is a tracer (blue line) pointing to this cell, and it indicates the precedents for the cell. In other words, we can see that cells C6, C9, and C13 are used to compute the value of cell C15. Cell C10 is not a precedent, however, and therein lies the error.

The analysis of the cost of the production facility is equally telling. There is a single tracer pointing away from cell E21, indicating that there is only one other cell (cell D9) in the worksheet that depends on the value of cell E21. In actuality, however, cells E9, F9, and G9 should also depend on the value of cell E21. Hence the cost of the production facility does not increase as it is supposed to. Jodi's comment about the unrealistic rate of the sales increase is best addressed through the Data Validation command.

Data Validation

The results of the financial forecast depend on the accuracy of the spreadsheet as well as the underlying assumptions. One way to stop such errors from occurring is through the ***Data Validation command***, which enables the developer to restrict the values that can be entered into a cell. If the cell is to contain a text entry, you can limit the values to those that appear in a list such as Atlanta, Boston, or Chicago. In similar fashion, you can specify a quantitative relationship for numeric values such as > 0 or < 100.

Figure 6.5a displays the Settings tab in the Data Validation dialog box in which the developer prevents the value in cell E18 (the annual sales increase) from exceeding 15%. Figure 6.5b shows the type of error alert (a Warning) and the associated message that is to appear if the user does not enter a valid value. Figure 6.5c displays the dialog box the user sees if the criteria are violated, together with the indicated choice of actions. "Yes" accepts the invalid data into the cell despite the warning, "No" returns the user to the cell for further editing, and "Cancel" restores the previous value to the cell. The Formula Auditing toolbar contains a tool to ***circle invalid data*** if the warning is disregarded. (See practice exercise 2 at the end of the chapter.)

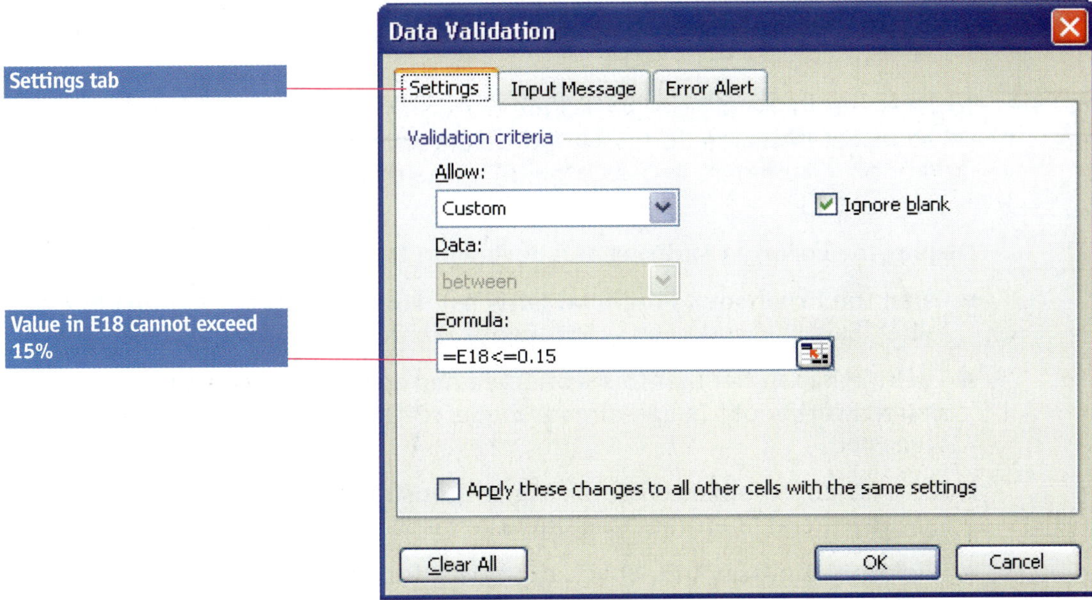

(a) Settings Tab

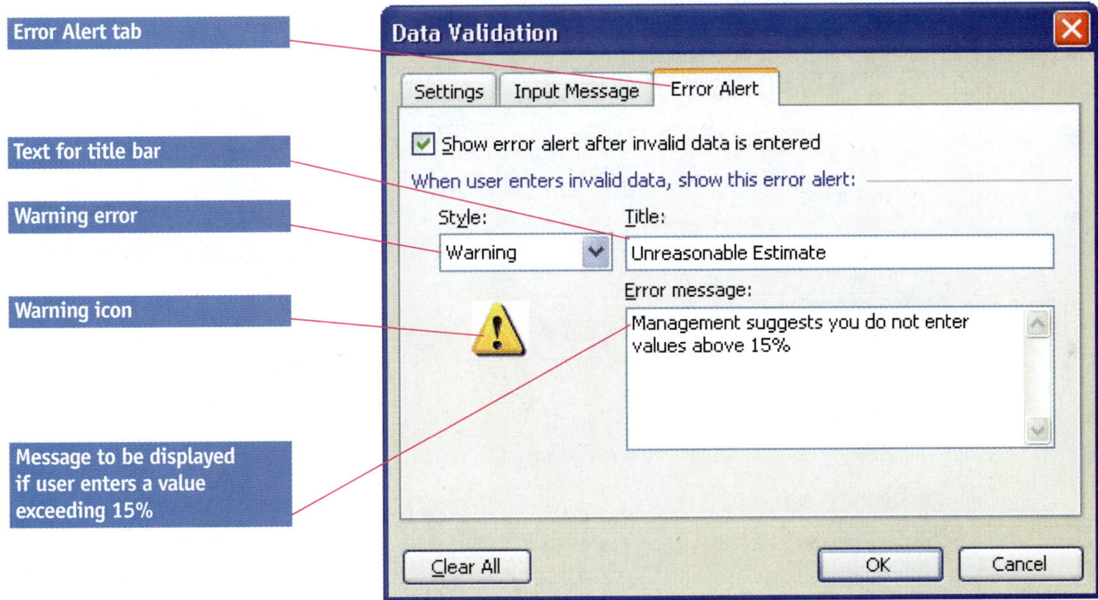

(b) Error Alert Tab

(c) Displayed Error Message

FIGURE 6.5 The Data Validation Command

hands-on exercise

2 Auditing and Workgroups

Objective To illustrate the tools on the Formula Auditing toolbar; to trace errors in spreadsheet formulas; to insert and delete comments; to track changes in a workbook. Use Figure 6.6 as a guide in the exercise.

Step 1: Display the Formula Auditing and Reviewing Toolbars

- Open the **Erroneous Financial Forecast workbook** in the **Exploring Excel folder**. Save the workbook as **Erroneous Financial Forecast Solution.**
- The title bar shows that this workbook has been previously established as a shared workbook. It has already been reviewed and changes have been suggested.
- Point to any toolbar, click the **right mouse button** to display a context-sensitive menu, then click **Customize** to display the Customize dialog box.
- Click the **Toolbars tab**, check the boxes for the **Reviewing** and **Formula Auditing toolbars**, then close the dialog box to display the toolbars as in Figure 6.6a.

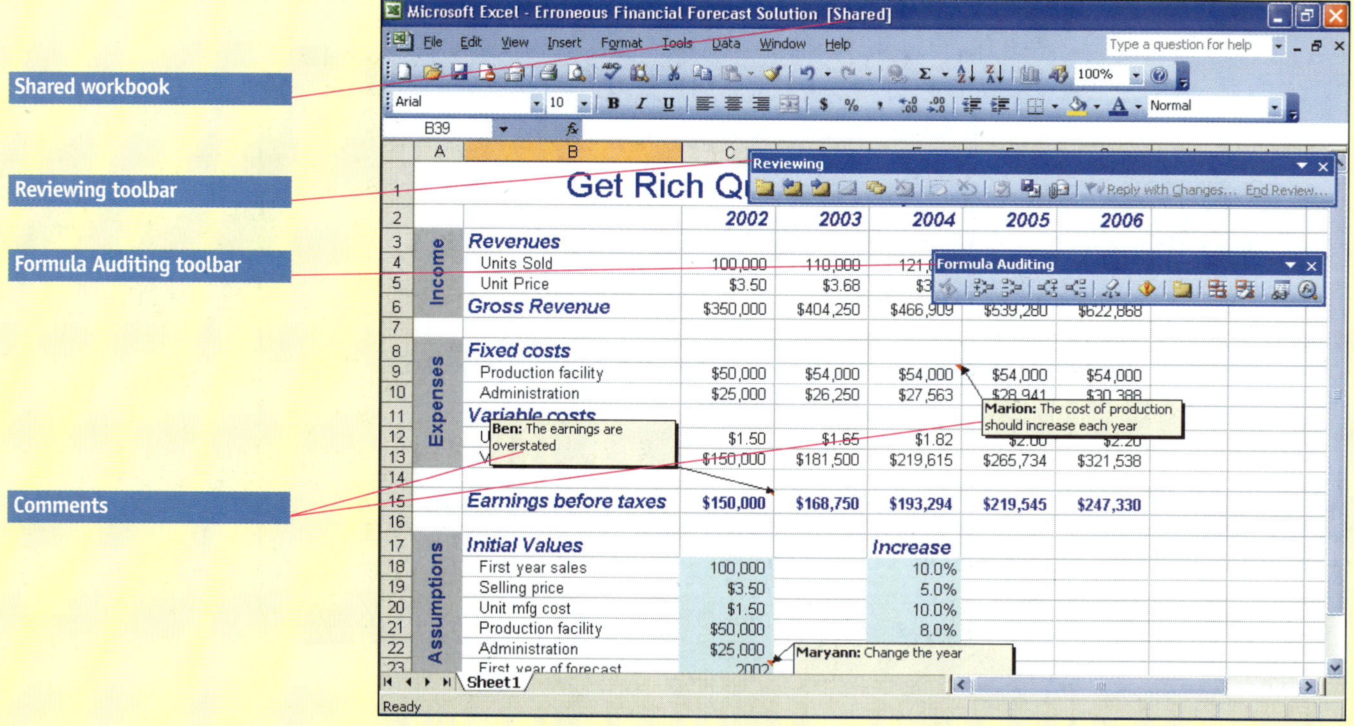

(a) Display the Formula Auditing and Reviewing Toolbars (step 1)

FIGURE 6.6 Hands-on Exercise 2

COMMENTS VERSUS CHANGES

A reviewer can suggest comments through the Insert Comment command and/or enter changes directly through the Track Changes command. Comments are visible immediately when you point to the cell, whereas changes are not visible until Track Changes is turned on. Comments display only the reviewer's name. Changes show the name, date, and time of the change.

Step 2: Highlight Changes

- Pull down the **Tools menu**, click (or point to) the **Track Changes command**, then click **Highlight Changes** to display the Highlight Changes dialog box. Set the various options to match our selections in Figure 6.6b. Click **OK**.
- You should see a border around cell C19 to indicate that a change has been made to the contents of that cell. Point to the cell and you will see a ScreenTip indicating that Robert Grauer changed the contents from $2.25 to $3.50.
- Click in **cell C23**. Type **2003** to modify the year (as suggested by Maryann) and press **Enter**. The years change automatically at the top of the forecast.
- Maryann's comment is now obsolete. Thus, right click in **cell C23** to display the context-sensitive menu, then click the **Delete Comment command**.
- The comment is removed from the cell and the red triangle disappears. The cell is still enclosed in a blue border and has a blue triangle to indicate that its value has changed. Point to **cell C23** to see the modification.
- Click the **Hide All Comments button** on the Reviewing toolbar. The comments are still in the worksheet, but are no longer visible.

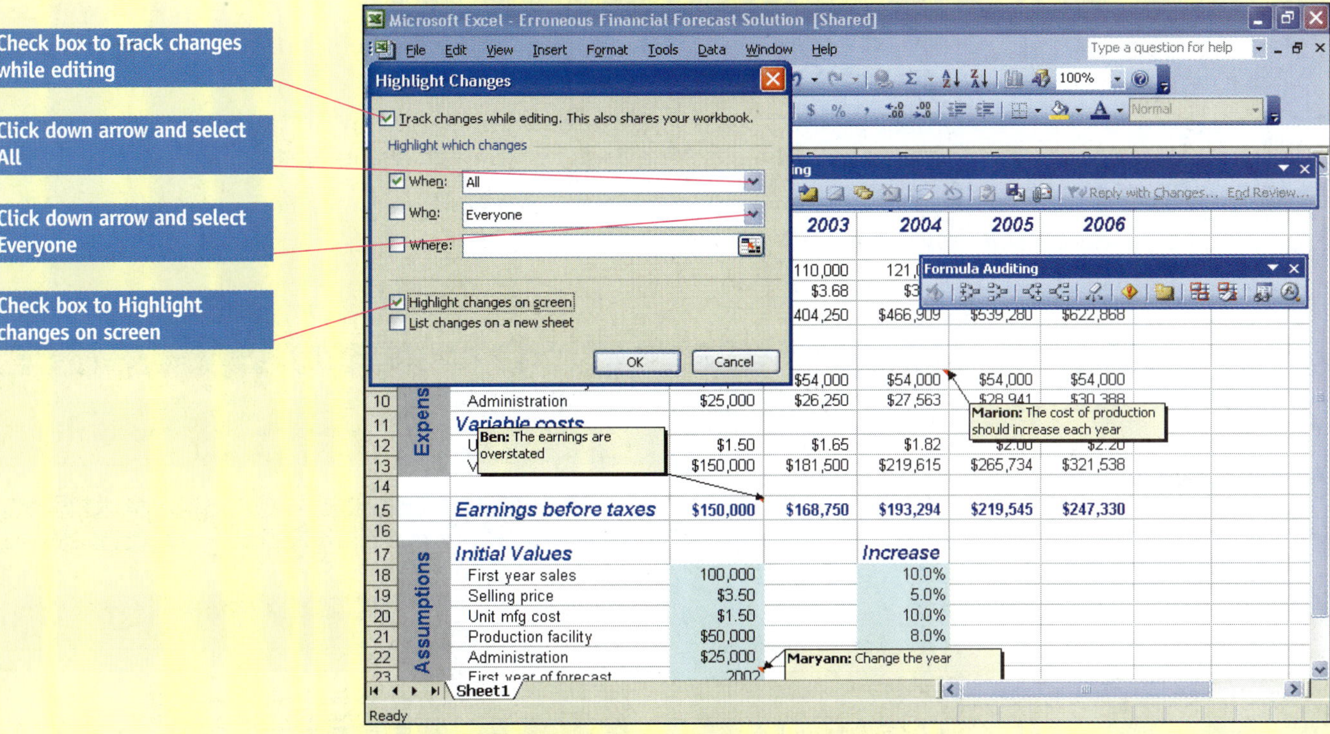

(b) Highlight Changes (step 2)

FIGURE 6.6 Hands-on Exercise 2 (*continued*)

CHANGE THE YEAR

A well-designed spreadsheet facilitates change by isolating the assumptions and initial conditions. 2002 has come and gone, but all you have to do to update the forecast is to click in cell C23, and enter 2003 as the initial year. The entries in cells C2 through G2 (containing years of the forecast) are changed automatically as they contain formulas (rather than specific values) that reference the value in cell C23.

Step 3: Trace Dependents

- Point to **cell E9** to display the comment, which indicates that the production costs do not increase after the second year. Click in **cell E21** (the cell containing the projected increase in the cost of the production facility).
- Click the **Trace Dependents button** on the Formula Auditing toolbar to display the dependent cells as shown in Figure 6.6c. Only one dependent cell (cell D9) is shown. This is clearly an error because cells E9 through G9 should also depend on cell E21.
- Click in **cell D9** to examine its formula. The production costs for the second year are based on the first-year costs (cell C9) and the rate of increase (cell E21). The latter, however, was entered as a relative rather than an absolute address.
- Change the formula in **cell D9** to include an absolute reference to cell E21 (i.e., the correct formula is =C9+C9*$E$21). The tracer arrow disappears due to the correction.
- Drag the fill handle in **cell D9** to copy the corrected formula to cells E9, F9, and G9. The displayed value for cell G9 should be $68,024. Delete Marion's comment in cell E9, which is no longer applicable.
- Cells D9 through G9 have a blue border and a blue triangle to indicate that changes were made to these cells.
- Click in **cell E21**. Click the **Trace Dependents button**, and this time it points to the production costs for years two through five in the forecast.
- Click the **Remove Dependent Arrows button** on the Formula Auditing toolbar to remove the arrows.
- Save the workbook.

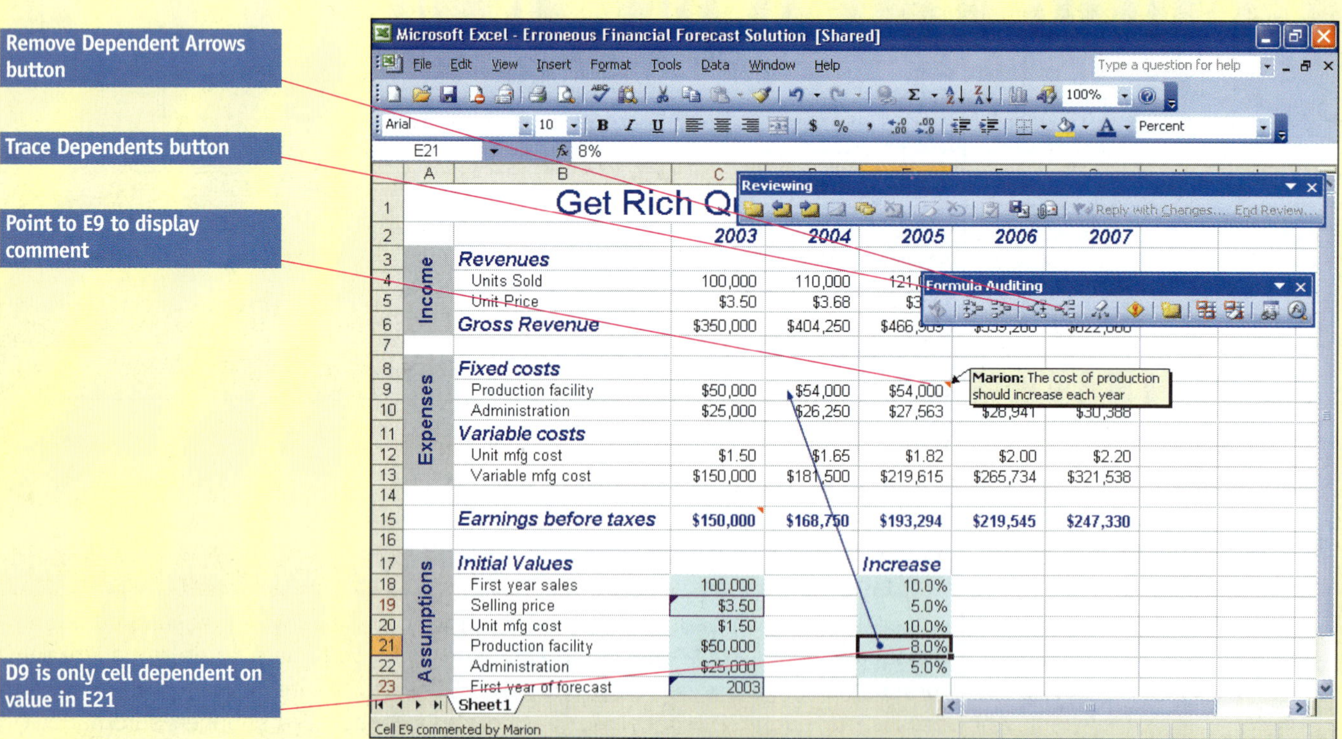

(c) Trace Dependents (step 3)

FIGURE 6.6 Hands-on Exercise 2 (*continued*)

Step 4: Trace Precedents

- Point to **cell C15** to display Ben's comment that questions the earnings before taxes. Now click in **cell C15** and click the **Trace Precedents button** to display the precedent cells as shown in Figure 6.6d.
- There is an error in the formula because the earnings do not account for the administration expense (cell C10).
- Change the formula in cell C15 to **=C6-(C9+C10+C13)**. The earnings change to $125,000 after the correction.
- Drag the fill handle in **cell C15** to copy the corrected formula to cells D15 through G15. (The latter displays a value of $202,918 after the correction.)
- Point to cell C15. You see both the change and the comment. Now right click in cell C15 and delete the comment, which is no longer applicable. Only the comment is deleted, not the ScreenTip associated with the change.
- Save the workbook.

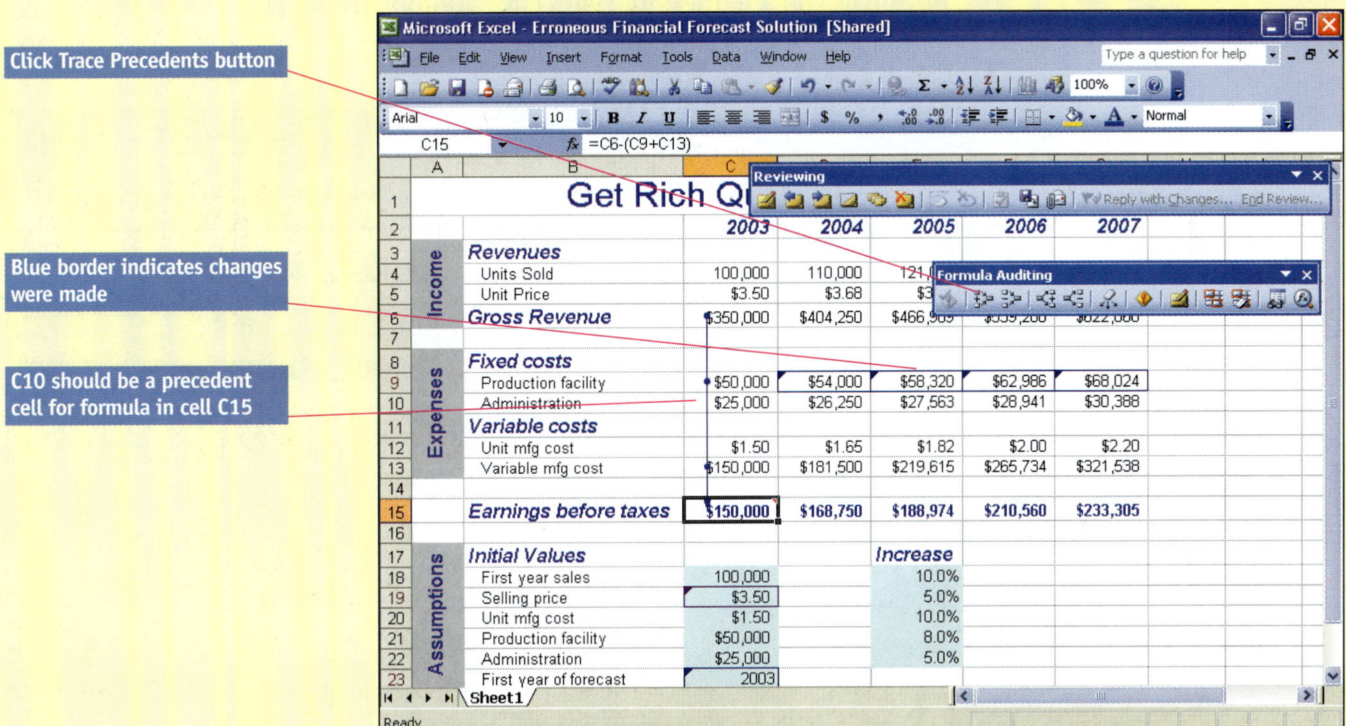

(d) Trace Precedents (step 4)

FIGURE 6.6 Hands-on Exercise 2 (*continued*)

THE FORMULAS ARE COLOR-CODED

The fastest way to change the contents of a cell is to double click in the cell, then make the changes directly in the cell rather than to change the entries on the formula bar. Note, too, that if the cell contains a formula (as opposed to a literal entry), Excel will display each cell reference in the formula in a different color, which corresponds to the border color of the referenced cells elsewhere in the worksheet. This makes it easy to see which cell or cell range is referenced by the formula. You can also click and drag the colored border to a different cell to change the cell formula.

Step 5: Accept or Reject Changes (resolve conflicts)

- Pull down the **Tools menu**, click the **Share Workbook command** to display the Share Workbook dialog box, then click the **Advanced tab**.
- Look for the Conflicting Changes Between Users section (toward the bottom of the dialog box), then if necessary, click the option button that says "Ask me which changes win". Click **OK**.
- Pull down the **Tools menu**, click (or point to) the **Track Changes command**, then click **Accept or Reject Changes**. You can accept the default selections in the Selection Changes dialog box. Click **OK**.
- You should see the Accept or Reject Changes dialog box in Figure 6.6e. You see Robert Grauer's change from $2.25 to $3.50. Click the **Reject button**. (The contents of cell C19 change in the worksheet to $2.25, which in turn affects several other values throughout the spreadsheet.)
- Click **Accept** (or press **Ctrl+A**) to accept the next change, which was the change you made earlier in the first year of the forecast. Press the **Accept button** as you are presented with each additional change.
- Save the workbook.

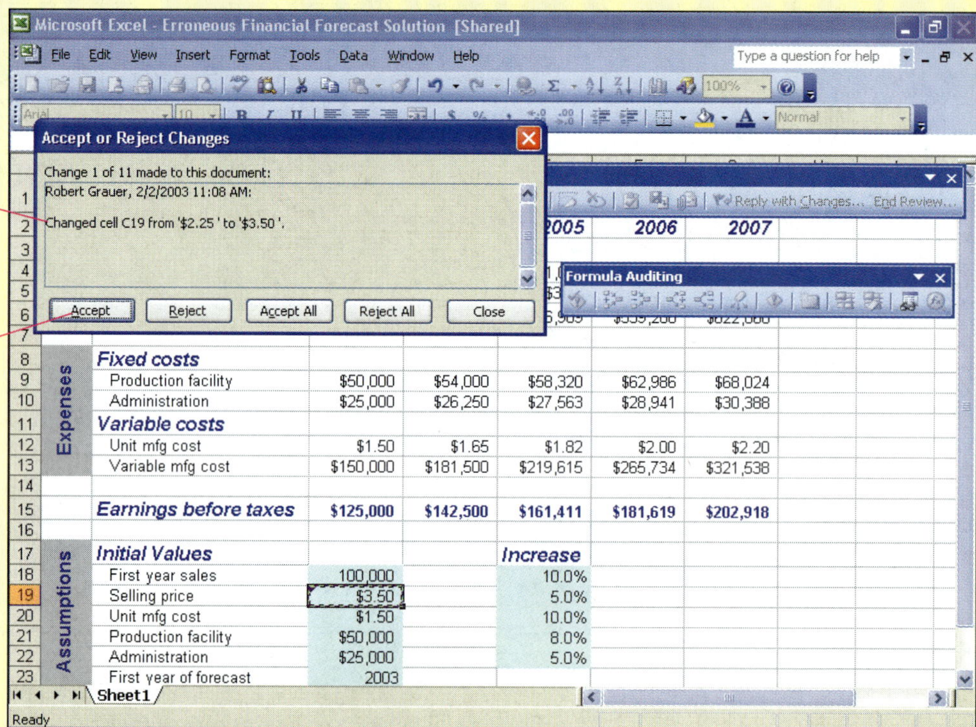

(e) Accept or Reject Changes (step 5)

FIGURE 6.6 Hands-on Exercise 2 (*continued*)

CIRCULAR REFERENCES

A circular reference occurs when a cell formula references itself, either directly or indirectly. Excel indicates the problem automatically and displays a circular reference toolbar which shows the interdependencies of the affected cells. Excel also gives you the option to remove the reference and/or to override the error and calculate the spreadsheet manually using multiple iterations to arrive at a steady state value. See practice exercise 8 at the end of the chapter.

Step 6: Insert a Comment

- Click in **cell C19** (the cell containing the selling price for the first year). Pull down the **Insert menu** and click the **Comment command** (or click the **New Comment button** on the Reviewing toolbar).
- A comment box opens, as shown in Figure 6.6f. Enter the text of your comment as shown in the figure, then click outside the comment when you are finished.
- The comment box closes, but a tiny red triangle appears in the upper-right corner of cell C19. (If you do not see the triangle, pull down the **Tools menu**, click **Options**, click the **View tab**, then click the option button in the Comments area to show **Comment Indicator only**.)
- Point to **cell C19** and the text of your comment appears. Point to a different cell and the comment disappears.
- Save the workbook.

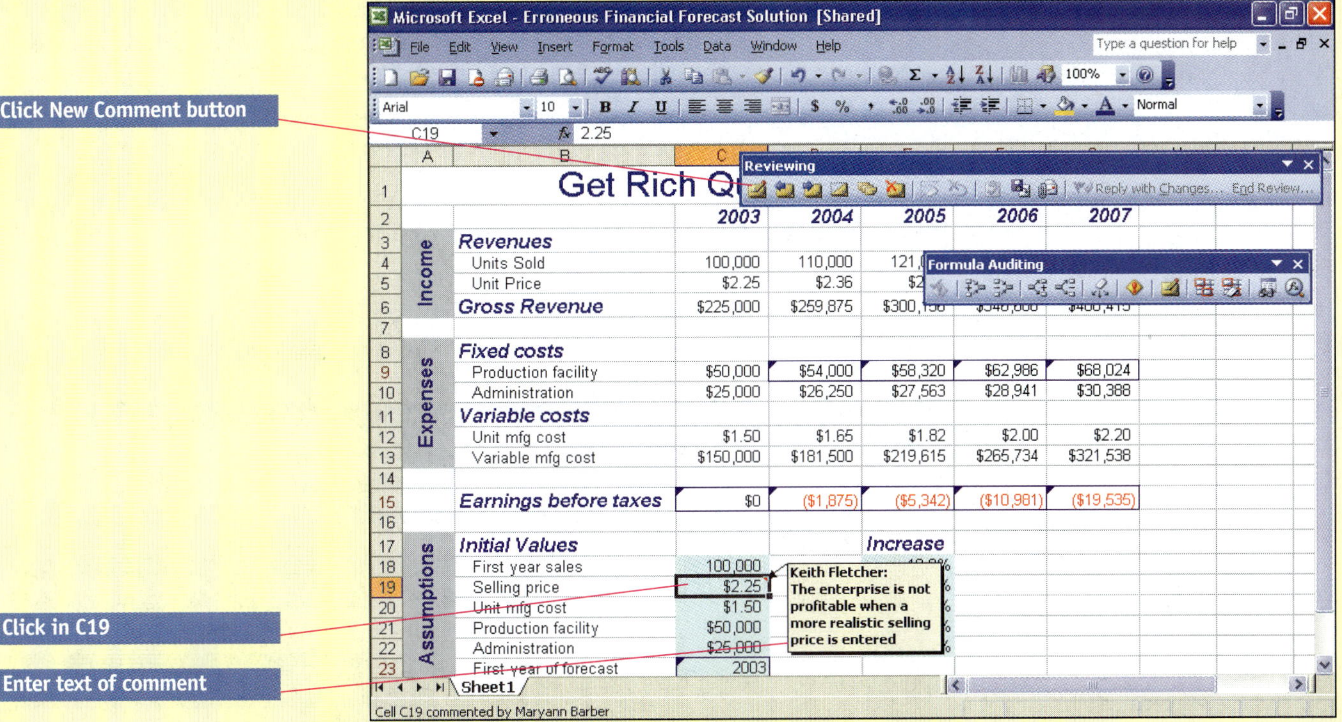

(f) Insert a Comment (step 6)

FIGURE 6.6 Hands-on Exercise 2 (*continued*)

EDITING OR DELETING COMMENTS

The easiest way to edit or delete an existing comment is to point to the cell containing the comment, then click the right mouse button to display a context-sensitive menu, in which you select the appropriate command. You can use the right mouse button to insert a comment by right clicking in the cell, then choosing the Insert Comment command. You can also insert or delete a comment by using the appropriate tool on the Reviewing toolbar.

Step 7: Data Validation

- Click in **cell E18**. Type **.18**. Excel displays the error message shown in Figure 6.6g. Press **Esc** to cancel and try another entry above 15%. No matter how many times you try, you will not be able to enter a value above .15 in cell E18 because the error type we previously defined was specified as "Stop" rather than a warning.
- Pull down the **Data menu**. The Validation command is dim and not currently accessible because the workbook is currently a shared workbook.
- Pull down the **Tools menu**, click (or point to) the **Track Changes command**, then click **Highlight Changes** to display the Highlight Changes dialog box. Clear the box to track changes while editing. Click **OK**.
- Click in **cell E18**. Pull down the **Data menu**. Click the **Validation command** (which is now accessible) to display the Data Validation dialog box, and if necessary, click the **Error Alert tab**.
- Click the **drop-down arrow** on the Style list box and click **Warning**. Change the text of the message to **Management frowns on values above 15%**. Click **OK** to accept the new settings and close the dialog box.
- Reenter **.18** in **cell E18**. This time you see a Warning message, rather than a Stop message. Click **Yes** to accept the new value.
- Add your name somewhere in the workbook. Save the workbook, then print the completed workbook for your professor as proof that you completed the exercise.
- Close the Reviewing and Formula Auditing toolbars. Close the workbook. Exit Excel if you do not want to continue with the next exercise at this time.

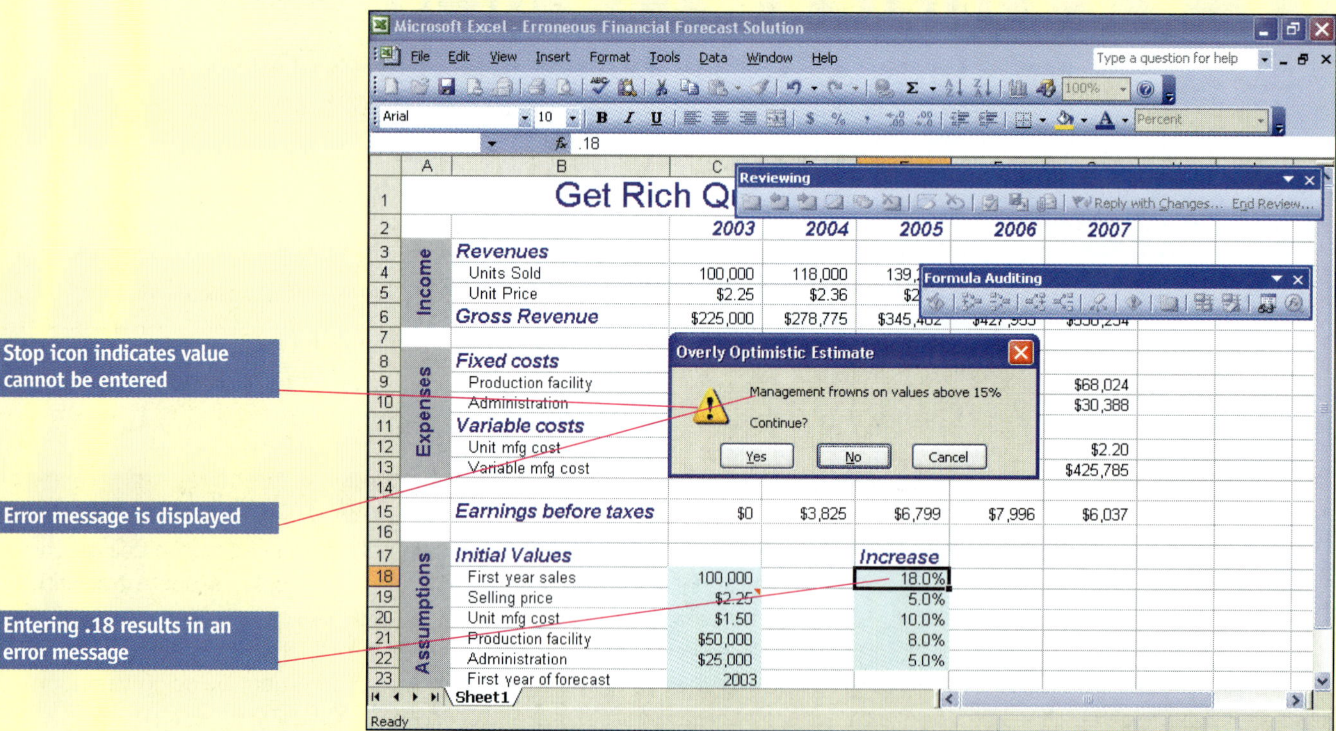

(g) Data Validation (step 7)

FIGURE 6.6 Hands-on Exercise 2 (*continued*)

TEMPLATES

The spreadsheet just completed is tailored to the needs of financial forecasting for Get Rich Quick Enterprises. It could also serve as the basis of a financial forecast for any organization, which leads in turn to the creation of a template. A ***template*** is a special type of workbook (it has its own file format) that is used as the basis for other workbooks. It contains text, formatting, formulas, and/or macros, but it does not contain data; the latter is entered by the end user as he or she uses the template to create a workbook.

Figure 6.7a contains the template you will create in the next hands-on exercise. It resembles the completed forecast from earlier in the chapter, except that the assumption area has been cleared of all values except the initial year of the forecast. Even the name of the company in cell A1 has been erased. Look at the active cell (cell C15), however, and note that its contents are visible in the Formula bar. Thus, you can see that the template contains the formulas from the worksheet, but without any data. (The results of the calculations within the body of the spreadsheet are uniformly zero, but the zeros are suppressed through an option set through the Tools menu.)

The template in Figure 6.7a is used to create specific forecasts such as the one in Figure 6.7b. Look closely at the entry in the title bar for that forecast, noting that it appears as Get Rich Quick1; that is, the number 1 has been appended to the name of the template. This is done automatically by Excel, which will add the next sequential number to the name of each additional forecast during a session. To create a specific forecast, just enter the desired values in the assumption area; then as each value is entered, the formulas in the body of the spreadsheet will automatically calculate the results.

Most templates are based on ***protected worksheets*** that enable the user to modify only a limited number of cells within the worksheet. The template for financial forecast, for example, enables the user to change the contents of any cell in the assumption area, but precludes changes elsewhere in the worksheet. This is very important, especially when templates are used throughout an organization. The protection prevents an individual who is not familiar with Excel from accidentally (or otherwise) changing a cell formula. Any attempt to do so produces a protected-cell message on the screen.

To create a template, you start with a finished workbook and check it for accuracy. Then you clear the assumption area and protect the worksheet. The latter is a two-step process. First, you ***unlock*** all of the cells that are subject to change, then you protect the worksheet. Once this is done, the user will be able to change the value of any cell that was unlocked, but will be unable to change the contents of any other cell. Finally, you save the template under its own name, but as a template rather than an ordinary workbook. Ideally, the template should be saved in a special ***Templates folder*** within the Microsoft Office folder so that it can be accessed automatically from the task pane. This is possible only if you have your own computer and/or if the network administrator puts the template in the folder for you. (You can, however, change the default folder when you save the template.)

Once created, a template can be accessed three different ways—through the File Open command, from the task pane, or by double clicking its icon from within Windows Explorer or My Computer. The File Open command opens the actual template, enabling you to modify the template if and when that becomes necessary. The task pane provides a link to General Templates that combines the function of the File Open command with that of the Save As command. It opens a template and automatically saves it as a workbook, assigning a name to the workbook by appending a number to the name of the template (e.g., Get Rich Quick1). Double clicking a file from within My Computer or Windows Explorer has the same effect as accessing the template from the task pane.

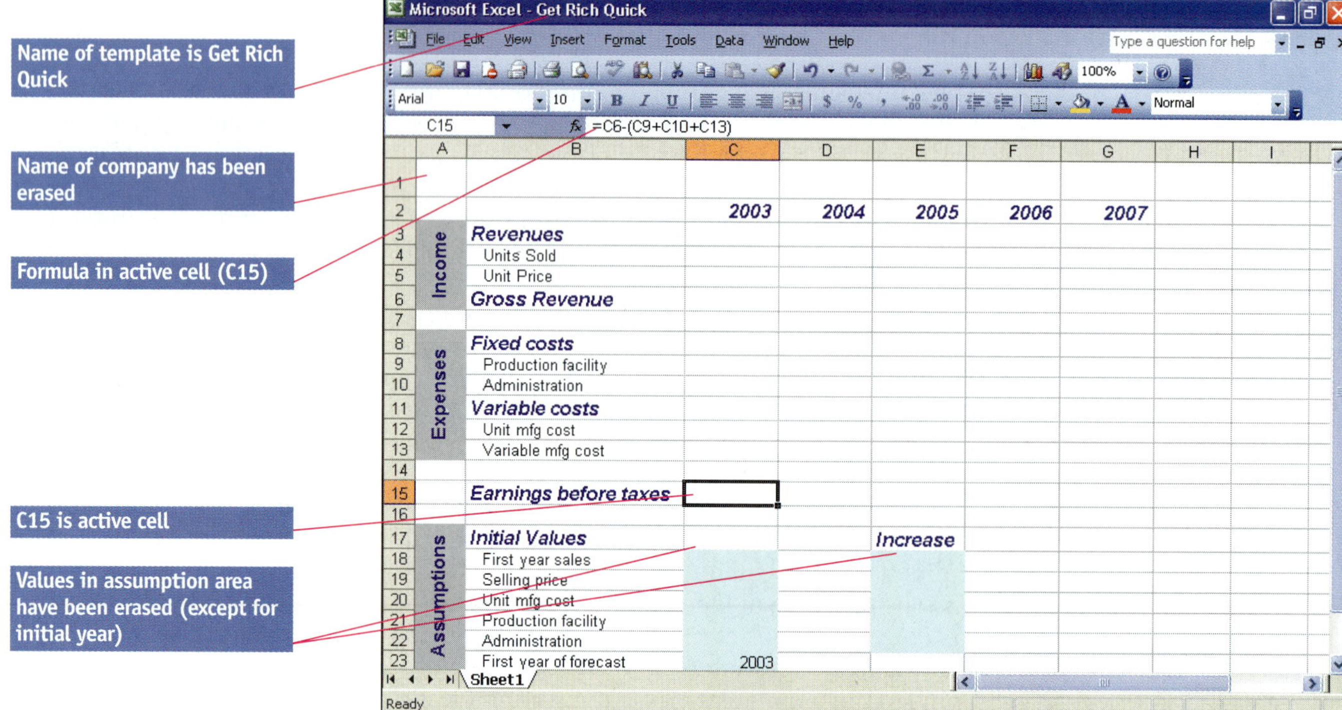

(a) Template

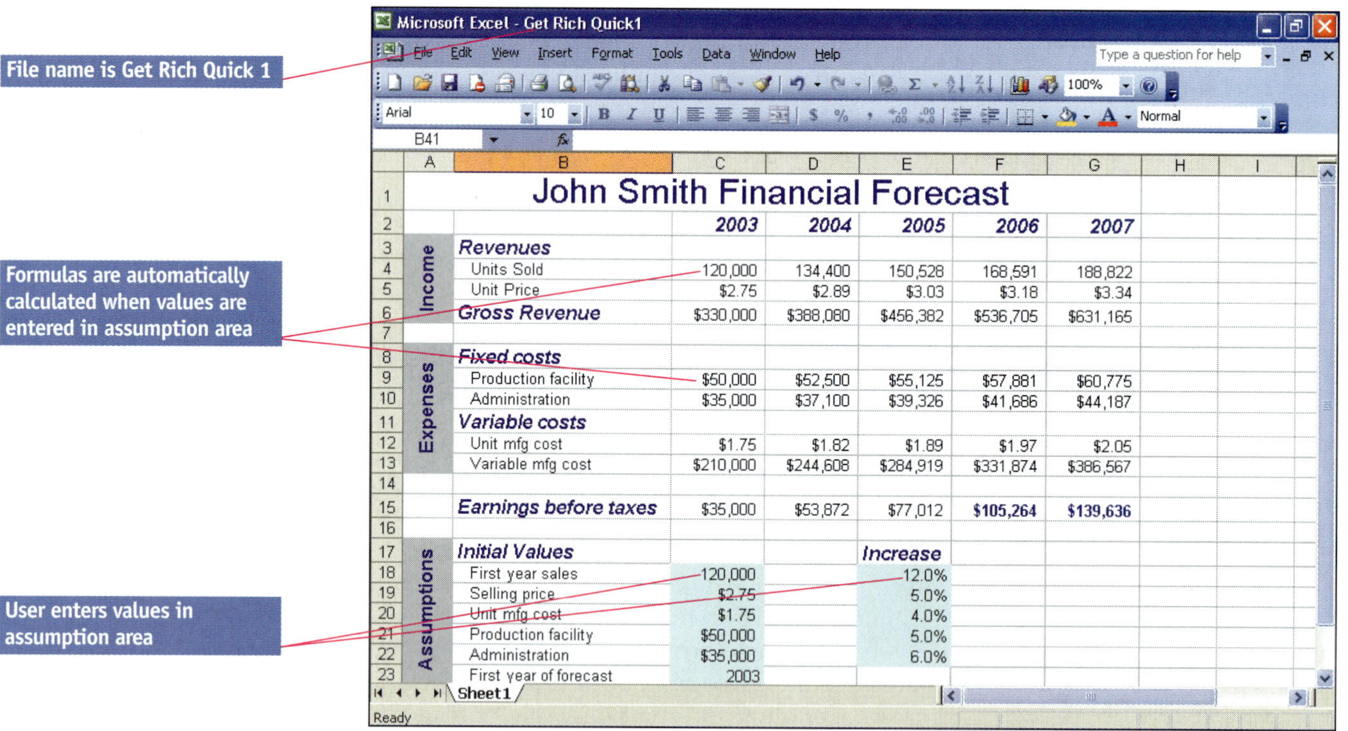

(b) Completed Worksheet

FIGURE 6.7 The Get Rich Quick Template

hands-on exercise 3

Creating a Template

Objective To unlock cells in a worksheet, then protect the worksheet; to create a template and then create a workbook from that template. Use Figure 6.8 as a guide in the exercise.

Step 1: Clear the Assumption Area

- Open the **Erroneous Financial Forecast Solution** from the previous exercise. Click in **cell A1**, then press and hold the **Ctrl key** as you click and drag to select **cells C18 through E23**.
- Pull down the **Edit menu**, click (or point to) the **Clear command**, then click **Contents** to delete the contents from the selected cells as shown in Figure 6.8a. The values in the body of the spreadsheet are all zero.
- Pull down the **Edit menu** a second time, click the **Clear command**, then click **Comments** to delete the comments from these cells as well.

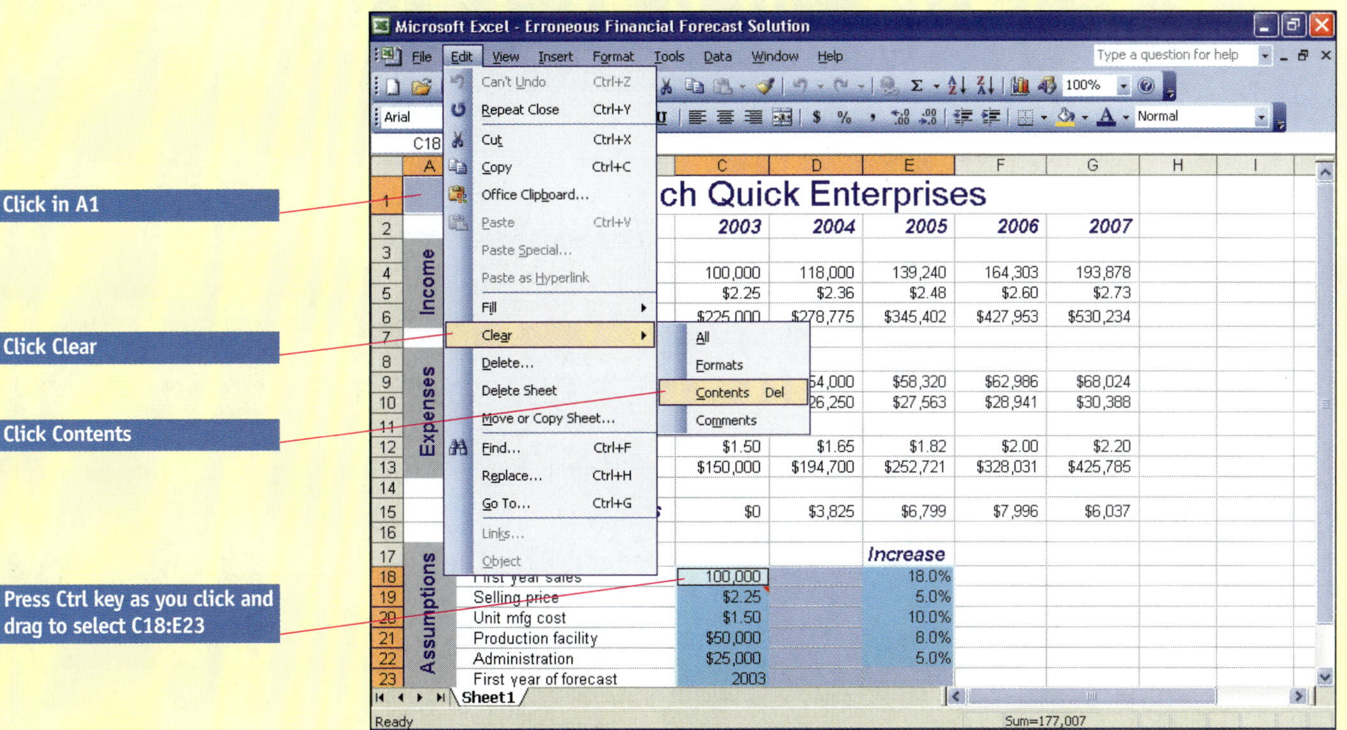

(a) Clear the Assumption Area (step 1)

FIGURE 6.8 Hands-on Exercise 3

WORKBOOK PROPERTIES

Do you know the original author of the workbook or other Office document that is currently open? When was the file created, modified, and last accessed? This and other information are stored within the workbook and can be viewed (or changed) by pulling down the File menu, clicking the Properties command, and clicking the Statistics tab.

Step 2: Protect the Worksheet

- Protecting a worksheet is a two-step process. First, you unlock the cells that you want to be able to change after the worksheet has been protected, then you protect the worksheet.
- Click in **cell A1**, then press and hold the **Ctrl key** as you click and drag to select **cells C18 through E23**. Pull down the **Format menu**, click the **Cells command** to display the Format Cells dialog box. Click the **Protection tab**, then clear the **Locked check box**. Click **OK**.
- Pull down the **Tools menu**, click **Protection**, then click the **Protect Sheet command** to display the Protect Sheet dialog box in Figure 6.8b. Be sure that your settings match those in the figure, then click **OK**. (A password is optional. If you do enter a password, be sure you remember it, or else you will not be able to modify the workbook.)
- Pull down the **Tools menu**, click the **Options command**, click the **View tab**, and clear the box to show zero values. Click **OK**. The zeros disappear.

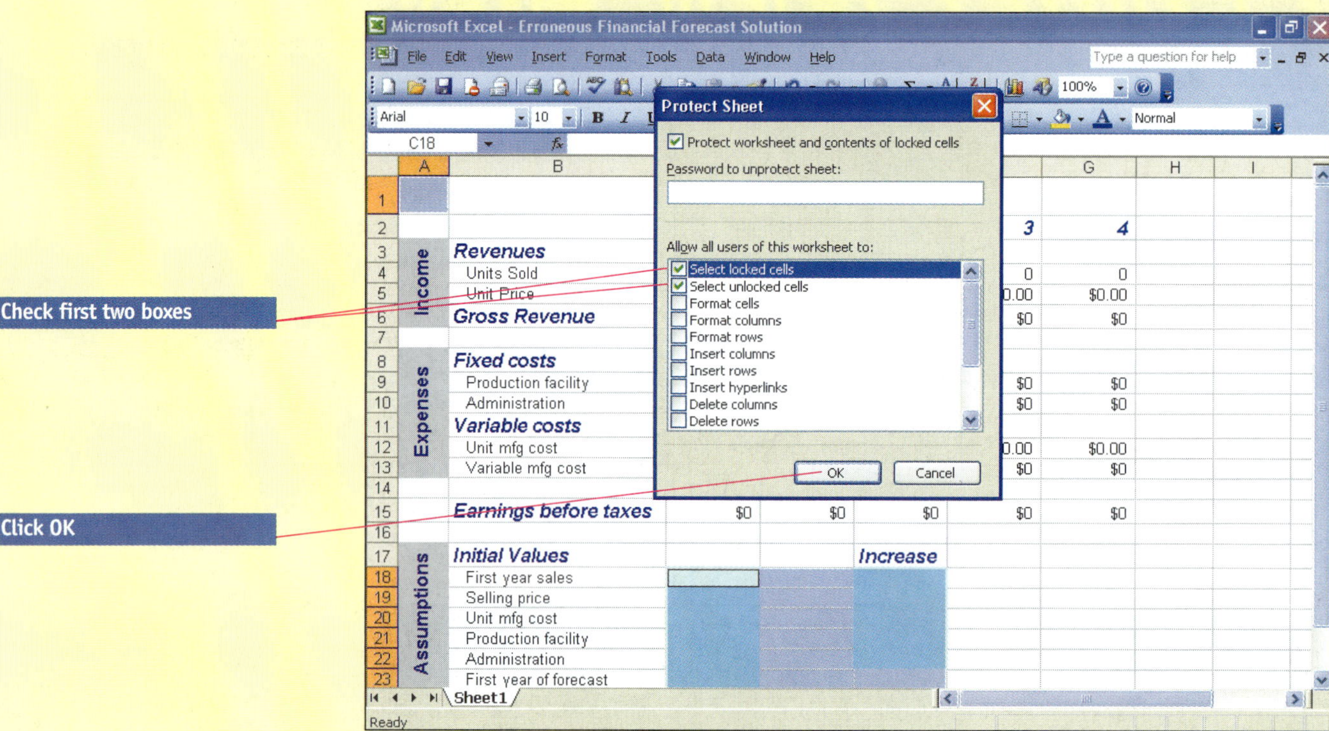

(b) Protect the Worksheet (step 2)

FIGURE 6.8 Hands-on Exercise 3 (*continued*)

THE OPTIONS MENU

Pull down the Tools menu and click the Options command to display the Options dialog box from where you can customize virtually every aspect of Excel. The General tab is especially useful as it enables you to change the default file location, the number of worksheets in a new workbook, the default font in a workbook, and/or the number of recently opened files that appear on the File menu. There is no need to memorize anything, just spend a few minutes exploring the options on the various tabs, then think of the Options command the next time you want to change an Excel feature.

Step 3: Test the Template

- Test the assumption area to be sure that you can change the contents of these cells. Click in **cell A1** and enter your name followed by the words **Financial Forecast**. The text will be centered automatically across the top of the worksheet.
- Click in **cell C23**, type **2003**, and press the **Enter key**. Excel should accept this value, and in addition, it should change the years as shown in Figure 6.8c. Enter the values **100000** and **.10** in **cells C18 and E18**, respectively. Excel should accept these values and build the spreadsheet accordingly.
- If you are prevented from entering a value in the assumption area, you need to unprotect the worksheet and unlock the cells.
  - Pull down the **Tools menu**, click **Protection**, then click the **Unprotect Sheet command**.
  - Select the cells in the assumption area, pull down the **Format menu**, click the **Cells command**, click the **Protection tab**, and clear the Locked box.
  - Repeat the steps to protect the worksheet.
- Test the protection feature by clicking in any cell in the body of the worksheet (e.g., cell C5) and entering a value. You should see the dialog box in Figure 6.8c indicating that the cell is protected. Click **OK**. If you do not see this message, undo the entry and then repeat the commands to protect the worksheet.
- Clear the contents from **cells A1, C18, E18, and C23**. You're ready to save the template.

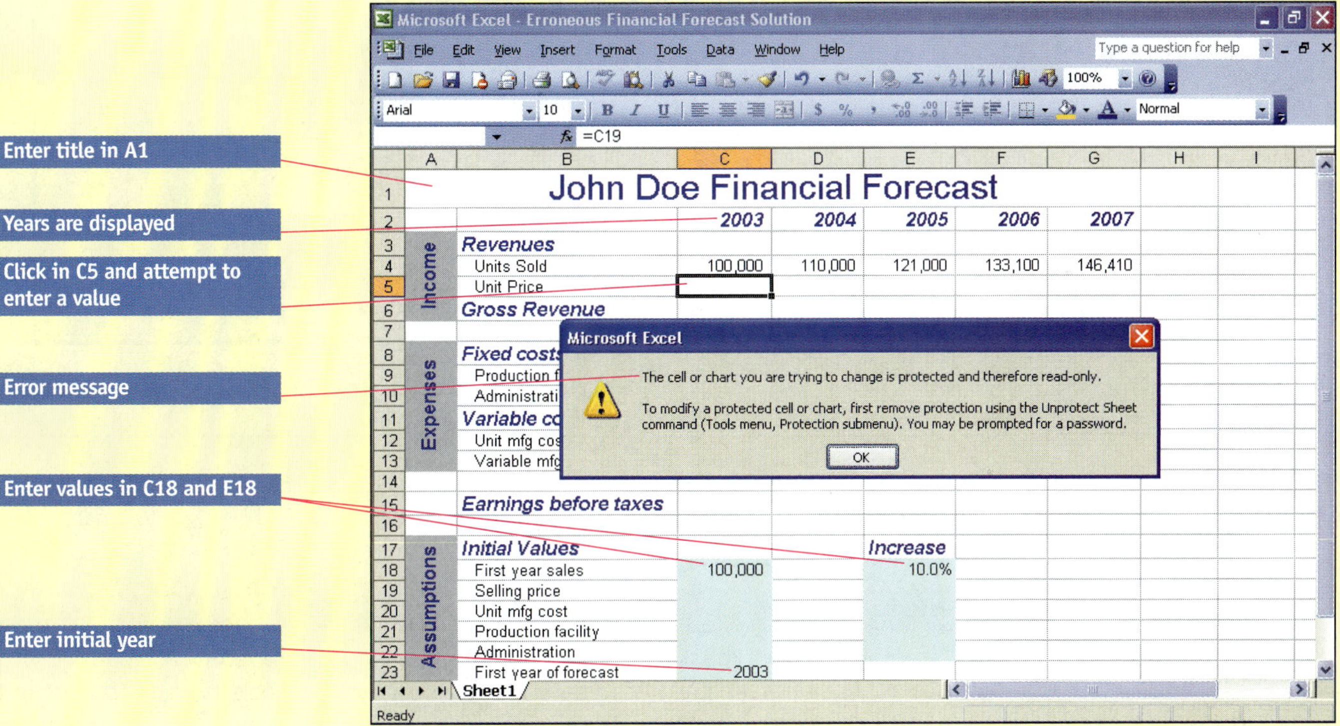

(c) Test the Template (step 3)

FIGURE 6.8 Hands-on Exercise 3 (*continued*)

Step 4: Save the Template

- Pull down the **File menu**, click the **Save As command** to display the Save As dialog box in Figure 6.8d. Enter **Get Rich Quick** as the name of the template.
- Click the **down arrow** in the Save as Type list box and choose **Template**. The folder where you will save the template depends on whether you have your own machine.
    - If you are working on your own computer and have access to all of its folders, save the template in the **Templates folder** (the default folder that is displayed automatically).
    - If you are working at school or otherwise sharing a computer, you should **change the default folder**. Click the down arrow in the Save in list box and save the template in the **Exploring Excel folder** that you have used throughout the text.
- Click the **Save button** to save the template.

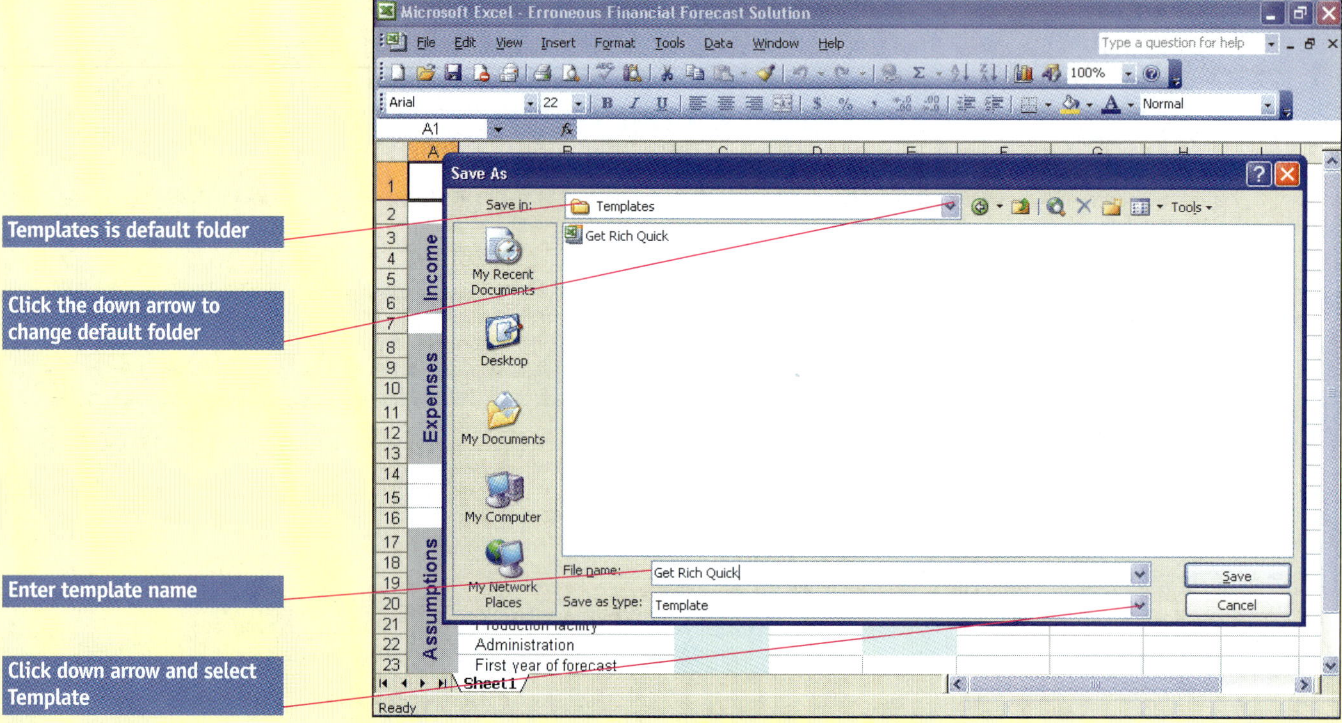

(d) Save the Template (step 4)

FIGURE 6.8 Hands-on Exercise 3 (*continued*)

PROTECT THE WORKBOOK

A template or workbook is not truly protected unless it is saved with a password, because a knowledgeable user can always pull down the Tools menu and access the Protect command to unprotect a worksheet. You can, however, use password protection to prevent this from happening. Pull down the File menu, click the Save As command to reveal the Save As dialog box, then click the Tools button and click General Options to display the Save Options dialog box. You can enter one or two passwords, one to open the file, and one to modify it. Be careful, however, because once you save a workbook or template with a password, you cannot open it if you forget the password.

Step 5: Open the Template

- Close Excel, then restart the program. The way in which you open the template depends on where you saved it in the previous step.
  - If you are working on your own computer, open the task pane, click the **down arrow** at the top of the task pane, and select **New workbook**. Click **On my computer** in the Templates section to display the dialog box in Figure 6.8e.
  - The Get Rich Quick template appears automatically because it was saved in the Templates folder. Double click the **Get Rich Quick template** to open it.
  - If you are working at school or otherwise sharing a computer, start Windows Explorer, change to the **Exploring Excel folder**, then double click the **Get Rich Quick template** to open it.
- You should see a blank workbook, named Get Rich Quick1. Excel automatically saves a copy of the template as a workbook and assigns it a name consisting of the template's name followed by a number.
- Complete and save the financial forecast. Print the completed workbook with displayed values and with the cell formulas. Exit Excel.

Double click Get Rich Quick

Click down arrow and select New Workbook

Click On my computer

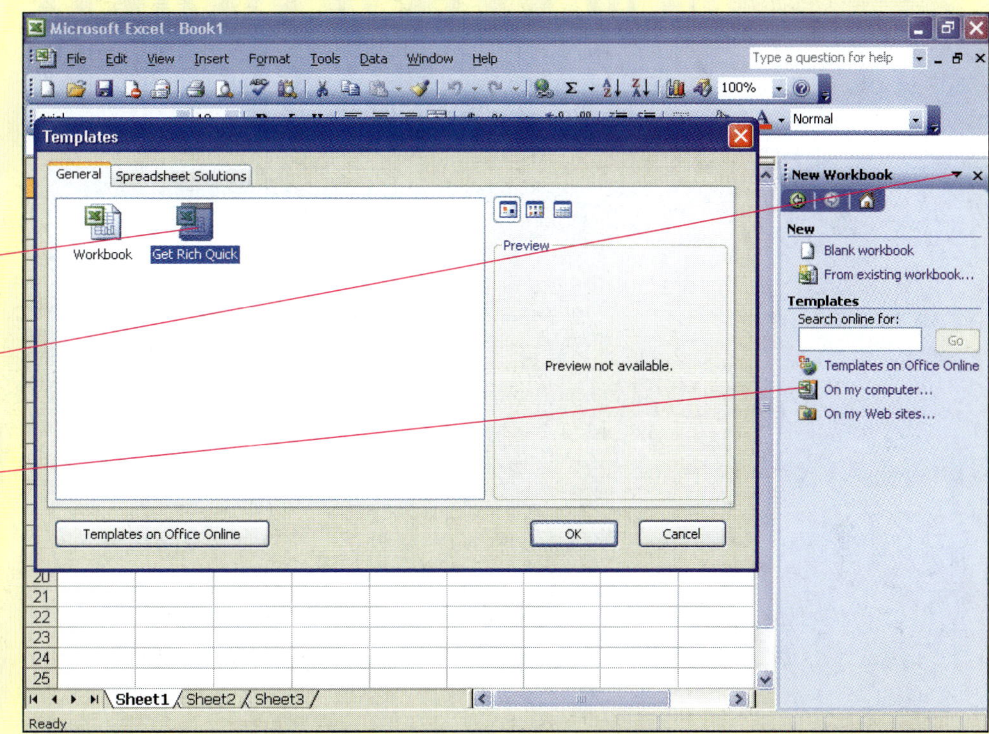

(e) Open the Template (step 5)

FIGURE 6.8 Hands-on Exercise 3 (*continued*)

CREATE A CHART AND ASSOCIATED TREND LINE

A chart adds impact to any type of numerical analysis. Use the template to create a financial forecast, and then plot the earnings before taxes against the associated year. A simple column chart is best. There is only one data series (the earnings before taxes) in cells C15 through G15. The category labels are in cells C2 through G2. Pull down the Chart menu after the chart has been created, then click the Add Trendline command to display the associated dialog box. Click the Type tab and choose a linear (straight-line) trend. Click OK to accept the setting and close the dialog box.

SUMMARY

A spreadsheet is used frequently as a tool in decision making, and as such, is the subject of continual what-if speculation. Thus, the initial conditions and assumptions on which the spreadsheet is based should be clearly visible so that they can be easily varied. In addition, the formulas in the body of the spreadsheet should be dependent on these cells.

A style is a set of formatting instructions that has been saved under a distinct name. Styles provide a consistent appearance to similar elements throughout a workbook. Existing styles can be modified to change the formatting of all cells that are defined by that style.

The Scenario Manager lets you specify multiple sets of assumptions (scenarios), then see the results at a glance within the associated worksheet. The scenario summary compares the effects of the different scenarios to one another by showing the value of one or more result cells in a summary table.

Conditional formatting may be implemented to change the appearance of a cell, based on its calculated value. The text in a cell may be rotated vertically to give the cell greater emphasis.

The Formula Auditing toolbar provides a graphical display for the relationships among the various cells in a worksheet. It enables you to trace the precedents for a formula and identify the cells in the worksheet that are referenced by that formula. It also enables you to trace the dependents of a cell and identify the formulas in the worksheet that reference that cell.

A shared workbook may be viewed and/or edited by multiple individuals simultaneously. The changes made by each user can be stored within the workbook, then subsequently reviewed by the developer, who has the ultimate authority to resolve any conflicts that might occur.

The Data Validation command enables you to restrict the values that will be accepted into a cell. You can limit the values to a list for cells containing text entries (e.g., Atlanta, Boston, or Chicago), or you can specify a quantitative relationship for cells that hold numeric values.

A template is a workbook that is used to create other workbooks. It contains text, formatting, formulas, and/or macros, but no specific data. A template that has been saved to the Templates or Spreadsheet Solutions folder is accessed automatically from the link to General Templates in the task pane.

A worksheet may be protected so that its contents cannot be altered or deleted. A protected worksheet may also contain various cells that are unlocked, enabling a user to vary the contents of these cells.

KEY TERMS

Assumptions 262
Changing cells 265
Circle invalid data 278
Circular reference 284
Conditional formatting 264
Custom format 264
Custom view 272
Data Validation command 278
Define Name command 265
Dependent cells 278
Formula Auditing toolbar 278
Indent text 264
Initial conditions 262
Insert Comment command 285
Insert Name command 273
Precedent cells 278
Protected worksheet 287
Result cells 265
Reviewing toolbar 277
Rotate text 264
Scenario 265
Scenario Manager 265
Scenario summary 265
Shared workbook 277
Style 264
Template 287
Templates folder 287
Tracers 278
Track Changes command 277
Unlock cells 287
Work group 277

MULTIPLE CHOICE

1. Which of the following best describes the formula to compute the sales in the second year of the financial forecast?
   (a) It contains a relative reference to the assumed rate of increase and an absolute reference to the sales from the previous year
   (b) It contains an absolute reference to the assumed rate of increase and a relative reference to the sales from the previous year
   (c) It contains absolute references to both the assumed rate of increase and the sales from the previous year
   (d) It contains relative references to both the assumed rate of increase and the sales from the previous year

2. The estimated sales for the first year of a financial forecast are contained in cell B3. The sales for year two are assumed to be 10% higher than the first year, with the rate of increase (10%) stored in cell C23 at the bottom of the spreadsheet. Which of the following is the best way to enter the projected sales for year two, assuming that this formula is to be copied to the remaining years of the forecast?
   (a) =B3+B3*.10
   (b) =B3+B3*C23
   (c) =B3+B3*$C$23
   (d) All of the above are equivalent entries

3. Which of the following describes the placement of assumptions in a worksheet as required by Microsoft Excel?
   (a) The assumptions must appear in contiguous cells but can be placed anywhere within the worksheet
   (b) The assumptions must appear in contiguous cells and, further, must be placed below the main body of the worksheet
   (c) The assumptions are not required to appear in contiguous cells and, further, can be placed anywhere within the worksheet
   (d) None of the above

4. Given that cell D4 contains the formula =D1+D2:
   (a) Cells D1 and D2 are precedent cells for cell D4
   (b) Cell D4 is a dependent cell of cells D1 and D2
   (c) Both (a) and (b)
   (d) Neither (a) nor (b)

5. Which of the following is true, given that cell C23 is displayed with three blue tracers that point to cells E4, F4, and G4, respectively?
   (a) Cells E4, F4, and G4 are dependent cells for cell C23
   (b) Cell C23 is a precedent cell for cells E4, F4, and G4
   (c) Both (a) and (b)
   (d) Neither (a) nor (b)

6. How can you enter a comment into a cell?
   (a) Click the New Comment command on the Formula Auditing toolbar
   (b) Click the New Comment command on the Reviewing toolbar
   (c) Right click in the cell, then select the Insert Comment command
   (d) All of the above

7. Which of the following best describes how to protect a worksheet, but still enable the user to change the value of various cells within the worksheet?
   (a) Protect the entire worksheet, then unlock the cells that are to change
   (b) Protect the entire worksheet, then unprotect the cells that are to change
   (c) Lock the cells that are to change, then protect the entire worksheet
   (d) Unlock the cells that are to change, then protect the entire worksheet

8. Which of the following describes the protection associated with the financial forecast that was developed in the chapter?
   (a) The worksheet is protected and all cells are locked
   (b) The worksheet is protected and all cells are unlocked
   (c) The worksheet is protected and the assumption area is locked
   (d) The worksheet is protected and the assumption area is unlocked

9. Which of the following may be stored within a style?
   (a) The font, point size, and color
   (b) Borders and shading
   (c) Alignment and protection
   (d) All of the above

... continued

multiple choice

10. What is the easiest way to change the formatting of five cells that are scattered throughout a worksheet, each of which has the same style?

(a) Select the cells individually, then click the appropriate buttons on the Formatting toolbar
(b) Select the cells at the same time, then click the appropriate buttons on the Formatting toolbar
(c) Change the format of the existing style
(d) Reenter the data in each cell according to the new specifications

11. Each scenario in the Scenario Manager:

(a) Is stored in a separate worksheet
(b) Contains the value of a single assumption or input condition
(c) Both (a) and (b)
(d) Neither (a) nor (b)

12. The Formula Auditing and Reviewing toolbars are floating toolbars by default. Which of the following is (are) true about fixed (docked) and floating toolbars?

(a) Floating toolbars can be changed to fixed toolbars, but the reverse is not true
(b) Fixed toolbars can be changed into floating toolbars, but the reverse is not true
(c) Fixed toolbars can be changed into floating toolbars and vice versa
(d) Fixed toolbars can be displayed only at the top of the screen

13. You open a template called Expense Account but see Expense Account1 displayed on the title bar. What is the most likely explanation?

(a) You are the first person to use this template
(b) Some type of error must have occurred
(c) All is in order since Excel has appended the number to differentiate the workbook from the template on which it is based
(d) The situation is impossible

14. Two adjacent cells are enclosed in hairline borders of different colors. Each of these cells also contains a tiny shaded triangle in the upper-left part of the cell. Which of the following is the most likely explanation?

(a) Conditional formatting is in effect
(b) Data validation is in effect for the cells in question
(c) A comment has been entered into each of the cells
(d) The cells have been changed by different members of a workgroup

15. The value in cell A7 is to be displayed in blue if the computed value exceeds $100,000. To which cell(s) would you apply conditional formatting so that the color changes as requested? (Cell A7 contains the formula =A5*A6).

(a) A5
(b) A6
(c) A7
(d) A5, A6, and A7

16. Which command would you use to restrict the value that can be entered into a specific cell?

(a) Protect Worksheet command
(b) Lock Worksheet command
(c) Data Validation command
(d) Conditional Formatting command

17. What is the most common reason to protect selected cells in a worksheet?

(a) To prevent the initial conditions and assumptions from ever being changed
(b) To prevent formulas in the worksheet from being changed
(c) To prevent additional scenarios from being added
(d) To prevent the worksheet from review by outsiders

ANSWERS

1. b	**7.** d	**13.** c
2. c	**8.** d	**14.** d
3. c	**9.** d	**15.** c
4. c	**10.** c	**16.** c
5. c	**11.** d	**17.** b
6. d	**12.** c	

PRACTICE WITH EXCEL

1. **Erroneous Payroll:** The worksheet in Figure 6.9 displays an *erroneous* version of a worksheet that computes the payroll for a fictitious company. The worksheet is nicely formatted, but several calculations are in error. Your assignment is to open the *Chapter 6 Practice 1* workbook in the Exploring Excel folder, find the errors, and correct the worksheet. Print the workbook as it exists initially, and then print the corrected workbook at the end of the exercise.

   You can "eyeball" the worksheet to find the mistakes, and/or you can use the Formula Auditing toolbar as shown in Figure 6.9. Note, too, that when you identify an error, such as the incorrect formula for gross pay in cell F4, you must first correct the error, then copy the corrected formula to the remaining cells in that column. The correct specifications are given below:

   a. The gross pay is the regular pay (hourly wage times regular hours) plus the overtime pay (hourly wage times the overtime hours times the overtime rate). The overtime rate is entered as an assumption within the worksheet; making it possible to change the overtime rate in a single place should that become necessary.
   b. The net pay is the gross pay minus the deductions (the withholding tax and the Social Security tax).
   c. The taxable income is the gross pay minus the deduction per dependent multiplied by the number of dependents.
   d. The withholding tax is based on the individual's taxable income. The Social Security tax is based on the individual's gross pay.
   e. Use the Page Setup command to include a custom footer with your name and today's date. Print the corrected worksheet with both displayed values and cell formulas. Add a cover sheet and submit the assignment to your instructor. Do you see the importance of checking a worksheet for accuracy?
   f. Describe the purpose of each tool on the Formula Auditing toolbar. Which tools were used in conjunction with the workbook displayed in Figure 6.9? Was the information useful in finding the errors within the worksheet?

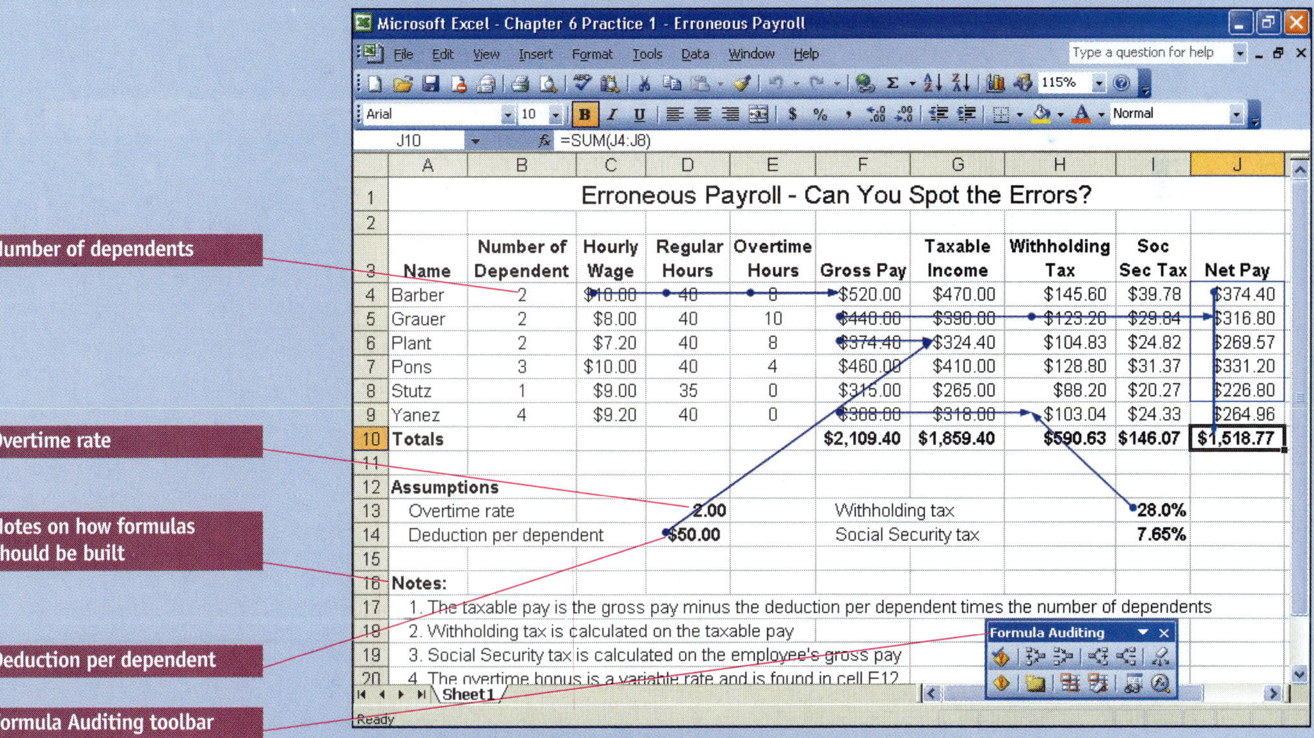

Name	Number of Dependent	Hourly Wage	Regular Hours	Overtime Hours	Gross Pay	Taxable Income	Withholding Tax	Soc Sec Tax	Net Pay
Barber	2	$10.00	40	8	$520.00	$470.00	$145.60	$39.78	$374.40
Grauer	2	$8.00	40	10	$440.00	$390.00	$123.20	$29.84	$316.80
Plant	2	$7.20	40	8	$374.40	$324.40	$104.83	$24.82	$269.57
Pons	3	$10.00	40	4	$460.00	$410.00	$128.80	$31.37	$331.20
Stutz	1	$9.00	35	0	$315.00	$265.00	$88.20	$20.27	$226.80
Yanez	4	$9.20	40	0	$368.00	$318.00	$103.04	$24.33	$264.96
Totals					$2,109.40	$1,859.40	$590.63	$146.07	$1,518.77

FIGURE 6.9 Erroneous Payroll (exercise 1)

2. **Protection and Validation:** The worksheet in Figure 6.10 will calculate the value of your retirement, based on a set of uniform annual contributions to a retirement account. In essence, you contribute a fixed amount of money each year ($3,000 in Figure 6.10), and the money accumulates at an estimated rate of return (7% in Figure 6.10). You indicate the age when you start to contribute, your projected retirement age, the number of years in retirement, and the rate of return you expect to earn on your money when you retire.
   a. The worksheet determines the total amount you will have contributed, the amount of money you will have accumulated, and the value of your monthly pension. The numbers are impressive, and the sooner you begin to save, the better. The calculations use the Future Value (FV) and Payment (Pmt) functions, respectively.
   b. You will find the completed worksheet in the *Chapter 6 Practice 2* workbook in the Exploring Excel folder. Your assignment is to implement data validation and password protection to ensure that the user does not enter unrealistic numbers nor alter the formulas within the worksheet.
   c. Three validity checks are required as indicated in the assumption area of the worksheet. The retirement age must be 59.5 or greater (as required by current law), the rate of return during the period you are investing money cannot exceed 8%, and the rate of return during retirement cannot exceed 7%. You are to display a warning message if the user violates any of these conditions. The warning will allow the user to override the assumptions.
   d. Enter the parameters that are displayed in Figure 6.10, including the *invalid* entry of .08 in cell B8 by overriding the warning message. Display the Formula Auditing toolbar, then click the button to circle invalid data to display the red circle.
   e. Unlock cells B2 through B8, where the user enters his or her name and assumptions. Protect the remainder of the worksheet. Use "password" as the password.
   f. Enter your name and your assumptions in the completed worksheet, then print the worksheet twice to show both displayed values and cell formulas for your instructor.
   g. A Roth IRA (Individual Retirement Account) is one of the best ways to save for retirement. The money that you contribute is taxed at the time you make your contribution, but the future withdrawals are tax free! In this example, the individual contributed a total of $135,000, which grew to more than $850,000.

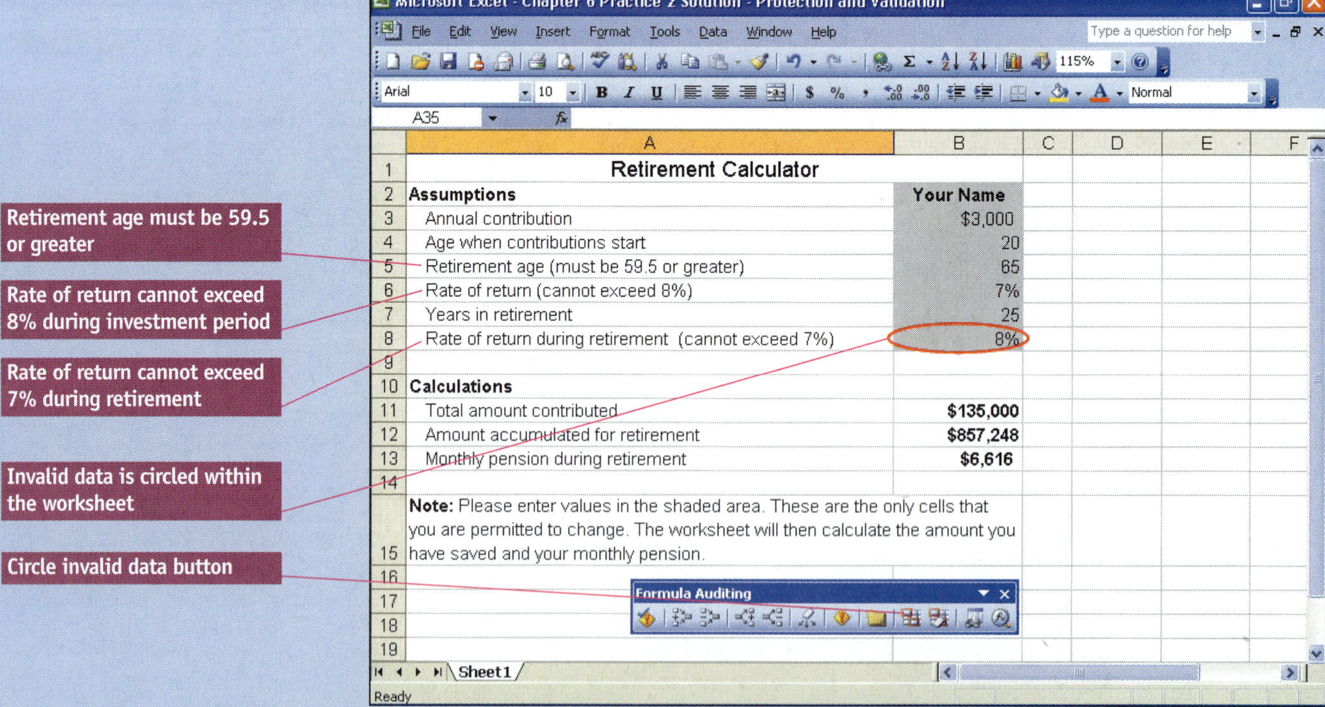

FIGURE 6.10 Protection and Validation (exercise 2)

3. **Retirement Scenarios:** The Social Security System has been in effect since 1935. An individual contributes a specified percentage of his or her pay check, which is matched by the employer. When the individual retires, he or she is paid a fixed amount as determined by law, with relatively little relation to the amount actually contributed. What if, however, Social Security were allowed to function as a private retirement plan, where the money was allowed to grow, and the monthly pension was a function of how much money had accumulated? This hypothetical plan is shown in Figure 6.11. Your assignment is to open the *Chapter 6 Practice 3* workbook in the Exploring Excel folder, create several scenarios, and then combine those scenarios in a scenario summary.
   a. The left side of the worksheet focuses on the accrual phase when money accumulates. The return on investment of 5% is conservative. The 45 years contributing to the plan matches the Social Security requirement, since a 22-year old entering the work force must reach age 67 before qualifying for the normal retirement benefit. The calculation is in constant dollars; that is, we did not build in an annual salary increase.
   b. The right side of the worksheet displays your monthly pension, which depends on a variety of factors, which include salary and the rates of return during both the accrual phase and the retirement phase. Note, however, that your income in retirement (approximately $6,500 per *month*) is almost 50% more than your income during your working life.
   c. Your assignment is to create several scenarios that vary these assumptions. Use the Define Name command prior to creating the scenarios so that the scenario summary is easily understood.
   d. It is interesting to compare the projected monthly pension in the worksheet of Figure 6.11 to the actual amounts provided by Social Security. Go to the Social Security Web site; locate the retirement calculator, then use the calculator to compute the projected benefit. (Choose a current salary of $35,000, $50,000, or $75,000 to match an existing scenario.) Press the Print Screen key to capture the Web page, and then paste the page into a new worksheet.
   e. Print the completed workbook for your instructor.

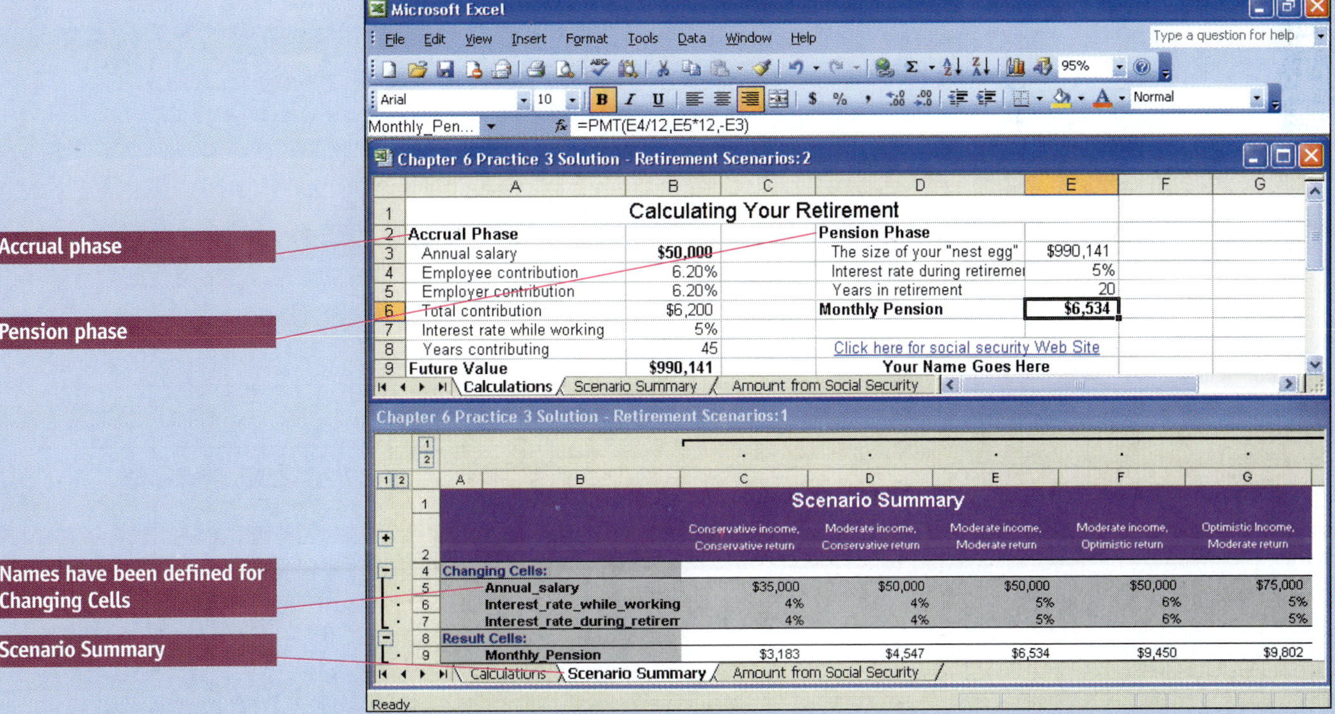

FIGURE 6.11 Retirement Scenarios (exercise 3)

4. **The Vacation Specialist:** The worksheet in Figure 6.12 computes the amount of vacation an employee has earned according to his or her years of service. An employee must complete the entire year to qualify for the next level; for example, an employee with 364 days of service has not worked a full year, and thus is not entitled to any vacation. Your assignment is to open the partially completed *Chapter 6 Practice 4* workbook, find and correct the errors that exist, and then complete the additional processing requirements. Note the following:
   a. Greg Hubit has reached five years of employment (January 31, 2002 has long since come and gone) and is now entitled to three weeks of vacation. Make the necessary correction, which will also change the amount of vacation for every employee.
   b. Click the Undo button to temporarily remove the correction from part (a) in order to address the next error. Note that Natalie Anderson, who was hired on February 4, 2001, has not yet earned any vacation (the date of the original spreadsheet was 1/31/02), yet she appears to have one year of service. Fix this error using the integer (Int) function to modify the appropriate formula, then copy the corrected formula to the remaining rows in the worksheet. Now restore the correction from part (a), which will increase everyone's vacation since today's date has been updated.
   c. Cathi Profitko has more than 25 years' service, but receives only four weeks of vacation. (The Show Precedents tool in the Auditing toolbar will help you to identify this error.) Fix the formula for Cathi, then copy the corrected formula to the other rows in the spreadsheet.
   d. Enter the appropriate formulas in cells F4 to F12 to compute the remaining days of vacation for each employee. (There are five days of vacation for every week of accrued vacation.) Enter the appropriate statistical functions in cells B15 through B18.
   e. Management is contemplating a new vacation plan, which will require less service than previously to earn the same amount of vacation; that is, an employee will need 1, 3, 5, 10, and 15 years of service to earn 2, 3, 4, 5, and 6 weeks of vacation, respectively. Create two scenarios that will allow management to quickly shift between existing and proposed plans.
   f. Print the completed worksheet to show the displayed values for each scenario. Print the worksheet again to show the cell formulas for the new plan.

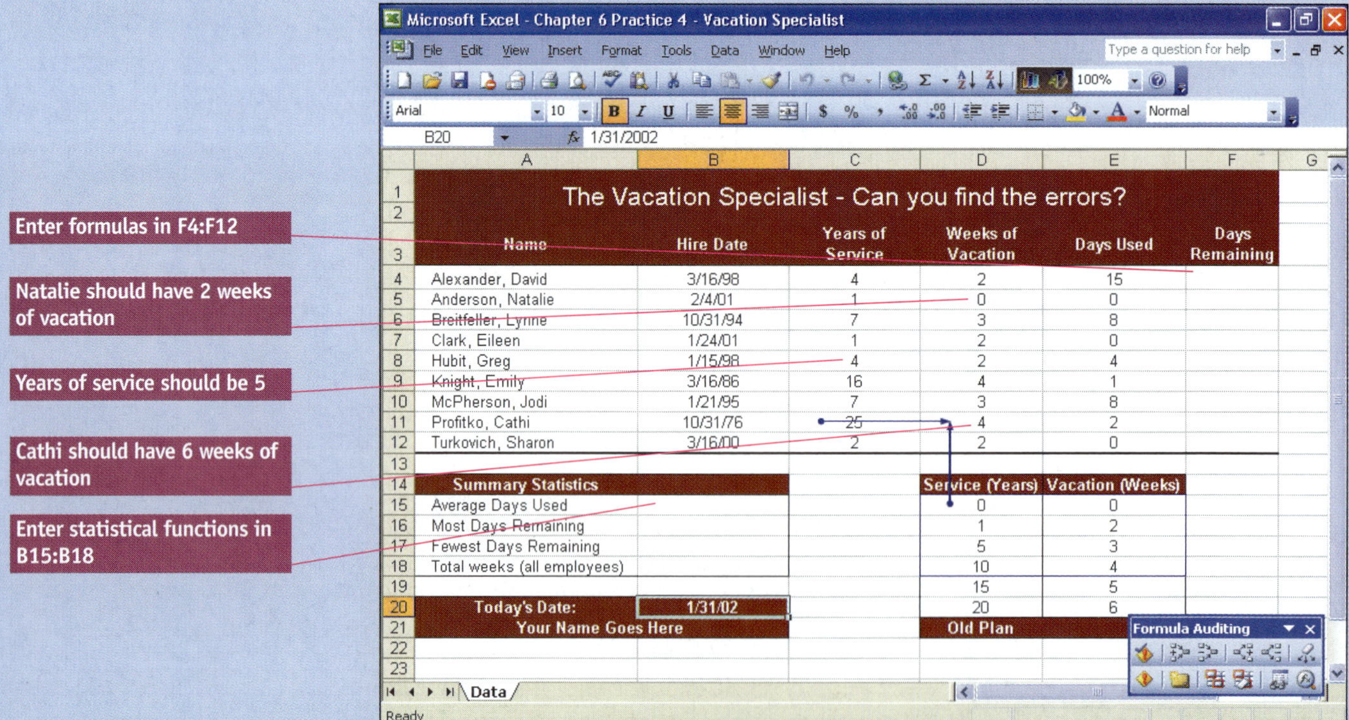

FIGURE 6.12 The Vacation Specialist (exercise 4)

5. **Erroneous Grade Book:** The worksheet in Figure 6.13 is intended to compute class grades. The worksheet is nicely formatted, but it contains some fundamental errors. Your assignment is to retrieve the *Chapter 6 Practice 5* workbook, correct the errors, and complete any additional processing requirements. Proceed as follows:
    a. Enter the appropriate VLOOKUP function in cell L3 to determine Alan's grade for the semester, based on the semester average in cell K3 and the table of numerical averages and associated grades at the bottom of the spreadsheet (cells G15 through H19). Copy the formula to the remaining cells in this column.
    b. Use the Formula Auditing toolbar to display the precedent cells for cell K3. Is the displayed value of 79.2 correct according to the indicated weights at the bottom of the spreadsheet? If not, fix the formula in this cell and then copy the corrected formula to the remaining rows in the column.
    c. Look closely at Charles' grades for the semester, especially the number of completed homework assignments. Did he really deserve a B, or should he have gotten an A? Display the precedent cells for cell J5, then correct the formula as necessary. Copy the corrected formula to all of the remaining students.
    d. What is the meaning of the green triangle that appears in cell H7 (the cell that contains the Quiz Average for Goodman)? How should the formula be corrected? Why does the green triangle remain after the formula has been corrected?
    e. Implement the necessary conditional formatting to display all grades of A and F (in column L) in blue and red, respectively.
    f. The professor has asked you to create two scenarios, with and without a curve. The changing cells are the same for each scenario, and consist of the name of the scenario (cell A14), the homework bonus (cell E15), and the minimum required semester average for each grade (cells G15 through G19). The values currently displayed in Figure 6.13 constitute one scenario. The new scenario includes a 3-point bonus for homework and breakpoints of 55, 67, 78, and 88, for grades of D, C, B, and A, respectively.
    g. Use the Page Setup command to create a custom footer with your name and today's date. Print the corrected worksheet to show the displayed values for each of the scenarios in part (f). Print the worksheet a third time to show the cell formulas for the new scenario.

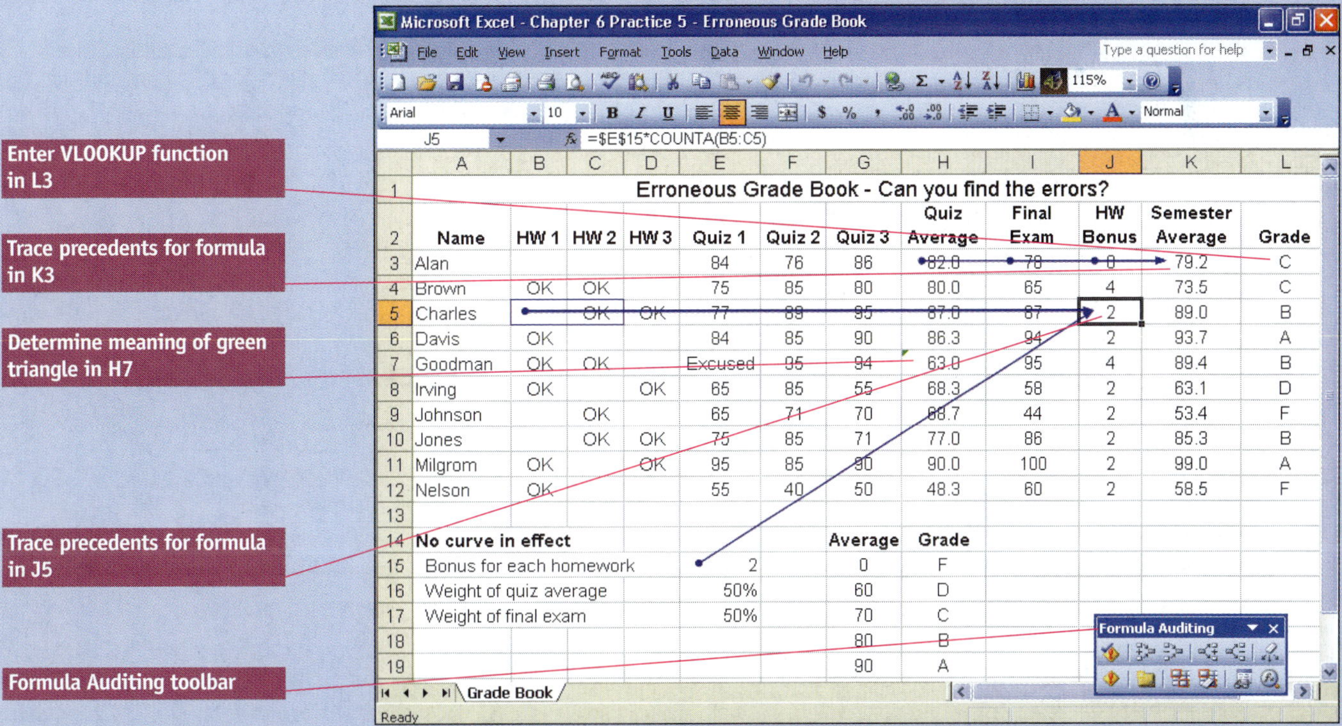

	A	B	C	D	E	F	G	H	I	J	K	L
1	Erroneous Grade Book - Can you find the errors?											
2	Name	HW 1	HW 2	HW 3	Quiz 1	Quiz 2	Quiz 3	Quiz Average	Final Exam	HW Bonus	Semester Average	Grade
3	Alan				84	76	86	82.0	78	0	79.2	C
4	Brown	OK	OK		75	85	80	80.0	65	4	73.5	C
5	Charles		OK	OK	77	89	85	87.0	87	2	89.0	B
6	Davis	OK			84	85	90	86.3	94	2	93.7	A
7	Goodman	OK	OK		Excused	85	94	63.0	95	4	89.4	B
8	Irving	OK		OK	65	85	55	68.3	58	2	63.1	D
9	Johnson		OK		65	71	70	68.7	44	2	53.4	F
10	Jones		OK	OK	75	85	71	77.0	86	2	85.3	B
11	Milgrom	OK		OK	95	85	90	90.0	100	2	99.0	A
12	Nelson	OK			55	40	50	48.3	60	2	58.5	F
13												
14	No curve in effect						Average	Grade				
15	Bonus for each homework				2		0	F				
16	Weight of quiz average				50%		60	D				
17	Weight of final exam				50%		70	C				
18							80	B				
19							90	A				

FIGURE 6.13 Erroneous Grade Book (exercise 5)

6. **The Scenario List Box:** Figure 6.14 displays a Word document that includes a screen capture of an Excel workbook. Look closely and note the presence of a scenario list box on the Formatting toolbar. This helpful list box lets you display a scenario (without going to the Tools menu) by clicking the down arrow and choosing the scenario from the displayed list. Proceed as follows:
   a. Choose any workbook that contains one or more scenarios (we used the Financial Forecast Solution workbook at the end of the first hands-on exercise). To display the list box, point to any toolbar, click the right mouse button to display a shortcut menu, then click Customize to display the Customize dialog box. Click the Commands tab, select Tools in the Categories list box, then click and drag the Scenario list box to an empty space on any toolbar. Click Close to close the dialog box and return to the workbook.
   b. The Scenario list box should appear on the toolbar. Click on the Financial Forecast tab and use the list box to view the various scenarios.
   c. Prove to your instructor that you have added the list box to your toolbar by capturing the Excel screen, then pasting it into a Word document. All you have to do is press the Print Screen key within Excel (after you display the scenario list box) to copy the screen to the Windows clipboard. Start Word, then click the Paste button to add the contents of the clipboard to the Word document. Word will ask if you want to compress the picture. Click Yes.
   d. You may find it useful to modify the position of the screen within the Word document. Thus, right click the figure from within Word to display a shortcut menu, click the Format Picture command to display the Format Picture dialog box, click the Layout tab, select Square wrapping, and click OK. You can now click and drag the picture anywhere within the document. You can also click and drag a sizing handle just as you can with any other Windows object.
   e. Complete the note in Figure 6.14, add your name somewhere in the document, then print the finished document for your instructor. Add a cover sheet to complete the assignment.

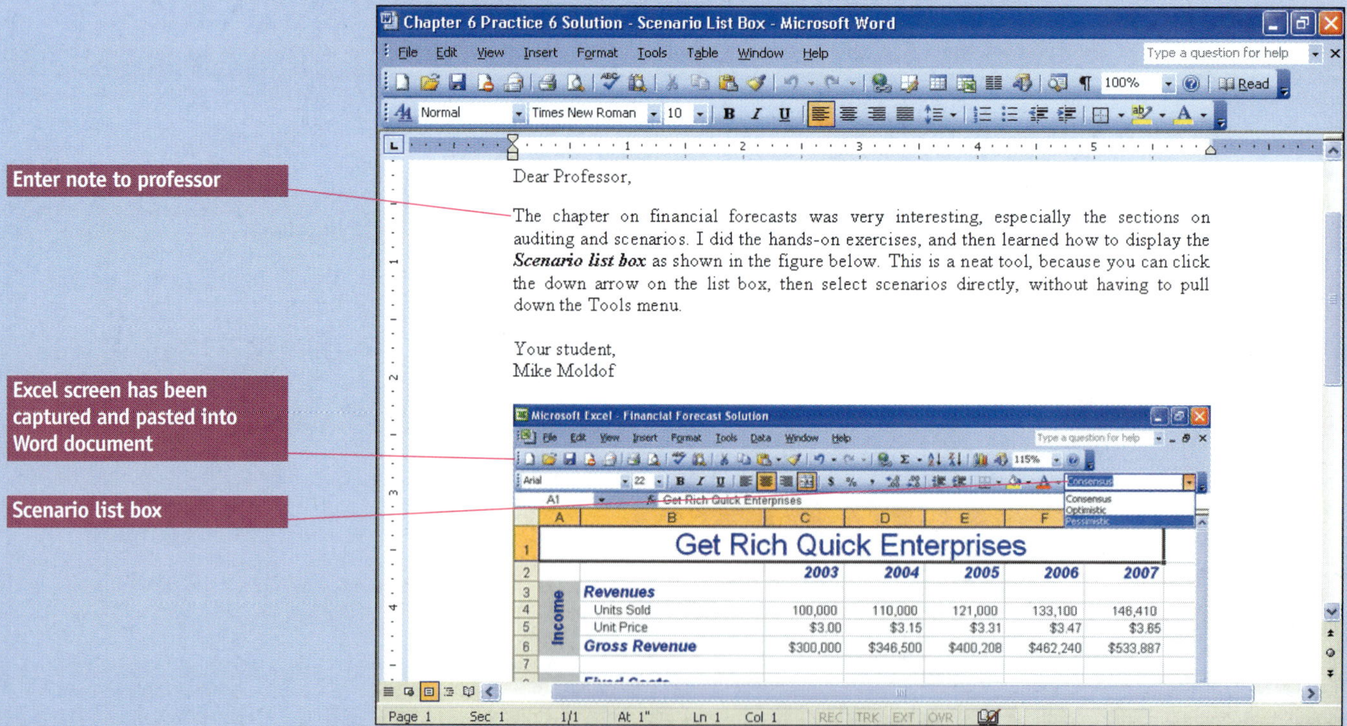

FIGURE 6.14 The Scenario List Box (exercise 6)

7. **The Mortgage Calculator:** The worksheet in Figure 6.15 is completely flexible in that it accepts the user's input in the shaded cells and then it computes the associated monthly payments in the body of the worksheet. It also introduces the Evaluate Formula tool on the Formula Auditing toolbar that lets you step through the calculation of any formula within a worksheet. Your assignment is to create the worksheet as shown in Figure 6.15. (You may want to review material on the PMT function and mixed references from Chapter 4.) Open the partially completed *Chapter 6 Practice 7* workbook, then proceed as follows:
   a. Click in cell B8 and enter the formula =E4; that is, the initial interest rate in the body of the spreadsheet is taken from the user's input in cell E4. Click in cell C8 and enter the formula, =B8+$E$5, then copy this formula to the remaining cells in this row. Enter parallel formulas in cells A9 to A19 to compute the various values for the principal amounts that will appear in the table. Check that your formulas are correct by changing the input parameters in rows 4 and 5. Any changes to the input parameters should be reflected in row 8 and/or column A.
   b. The "trick" to this assignment (if any) is to develop the PMT function with the correct mixed references in cell B9. The correct formula is =PMT(B$8/12,$B$6*12,-$A9) as can be seen by looking at the title bar in Figure 6.15. Enter this formula in cell B9 and copy it to the remaining rows and columns in the worksheet.
   c. Display the Formula Auditing toolbar. Click in Cell B9, then click the Evaluate Formula button to display the associated dialog box. You should see the complete formula for cell B9. Now click the Evaluate button, and the numeric value (.045) is substituted for the first argument, B$8. Continue to click the Evaluate button to see the numeric value of each cell reference until the computed value is shown. Do you see how this tool can help you to understand how a formula works?
   d. Enter your name in cell A1 and format the completed worksheet. You do not have to match our formatting exactly, but you are to shade the input parameters.
   e. Unlock cells B4 through B6 and cells E4 and E5, then protect the completed worksheet. Use "password" in lowercase letters as the password.
   f. Print the worksheet two ways, once with displayed values, and once with the cell formulas. Use landscape orientation.

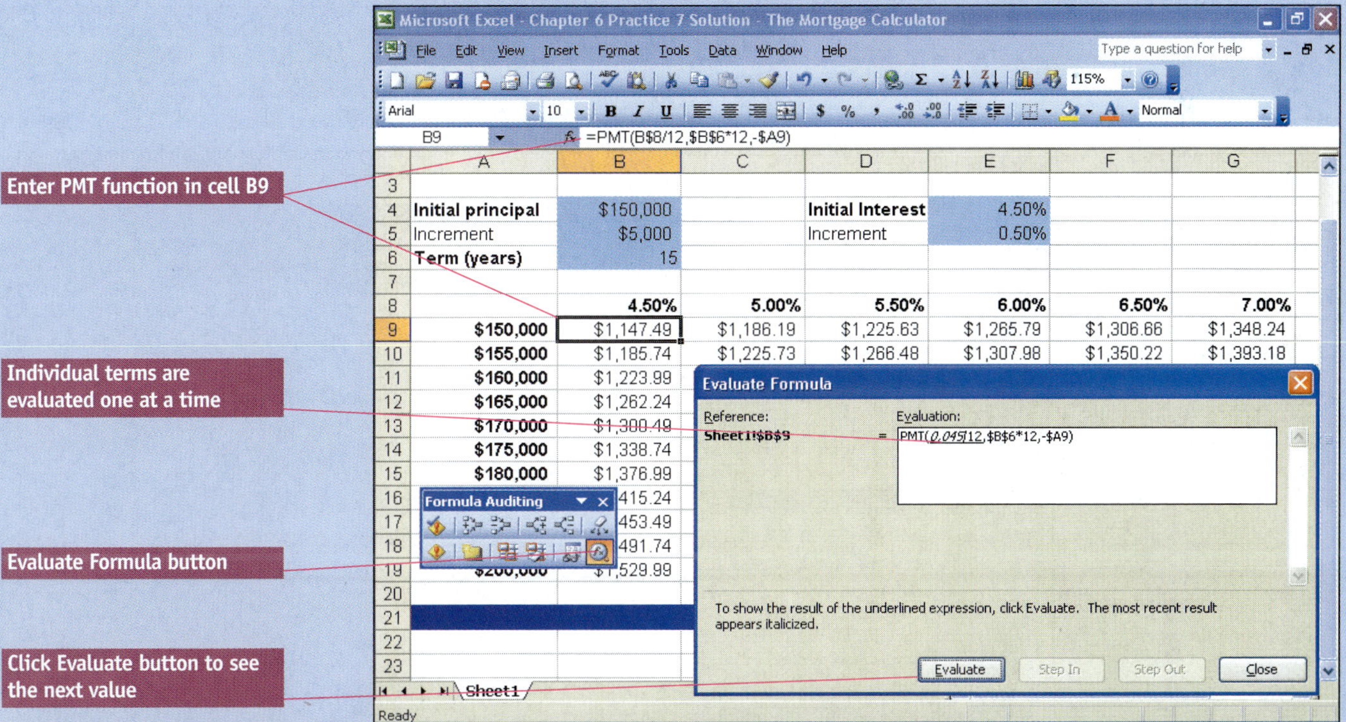

FIGURE 6.15 The Mortgage Calculator (exercise 7)

8. **Circular References:** A circular reference usually indicates a logic error, but there are instances when it can be valid. Figure 6.16 displays a hypothetical worksheet for an employee profit sharing plan, in which the company contributes 25% of its net income *after profit sharing is taken into account*, to profit sharing. The net income is determined by subtracting expenses from revenue, but one of those expenses is profit sharing, which in turn creates the circular reference. In other words, the formula in cell B7 depends on the formula in cell B6, which depends on the formula in cell B7. Open the partially completed spreadsheet in *Chapter 6 Practice 8* and proceed as follows:
   a. Click in cell B7 and enter the formula to compute the net income after profit sharing, =B4-B5-B6. Excel indicates that there is a circular reference. Click OK. Close the Help screen if it appears.
   b. The Circular Reference toolbar is displayed automatically, and the status bar shows a circular reference in cell B6. Pull down the View menu, click Toolbars, then click the Formula Auditing toolbar to display this toolbar as well. Click the Show Watch Window button and add cells B6 and B7.
   c. You can now recalculate the spreadsheet manually to see the effects of the circular reference. Pull down the Tools menu, click the Options command, then click the Calculation tab. Check the Iteration box and change the maximum number of iterations to one. Click the Manual option button in the Calculation area. Click OK to accept these settings and close the dialog box.
   d. Press the F9 (recalculate) key continually to see the spreadsheet go through multiple iterations, eventually settling on steady state values of $400,000 and $1,600,000 for the profit sharing and net income, respectively. Note that the profit sharing value of $400,000 is indeed 25% of the net income value of $1,600,000.
   e. Add your name to the worksheet, then print the completed worksheet for your professor. Close the Formula Auditing toolbar and Watch Window. Close the workbook.
   f. Open a blank workbook. Pull down the Tools menu, click the Options command, then click Calculation tab to restore the default settings. Click the option button for Automatic calculation and reset the maximum iterations to 100. Clear the iteration check box.

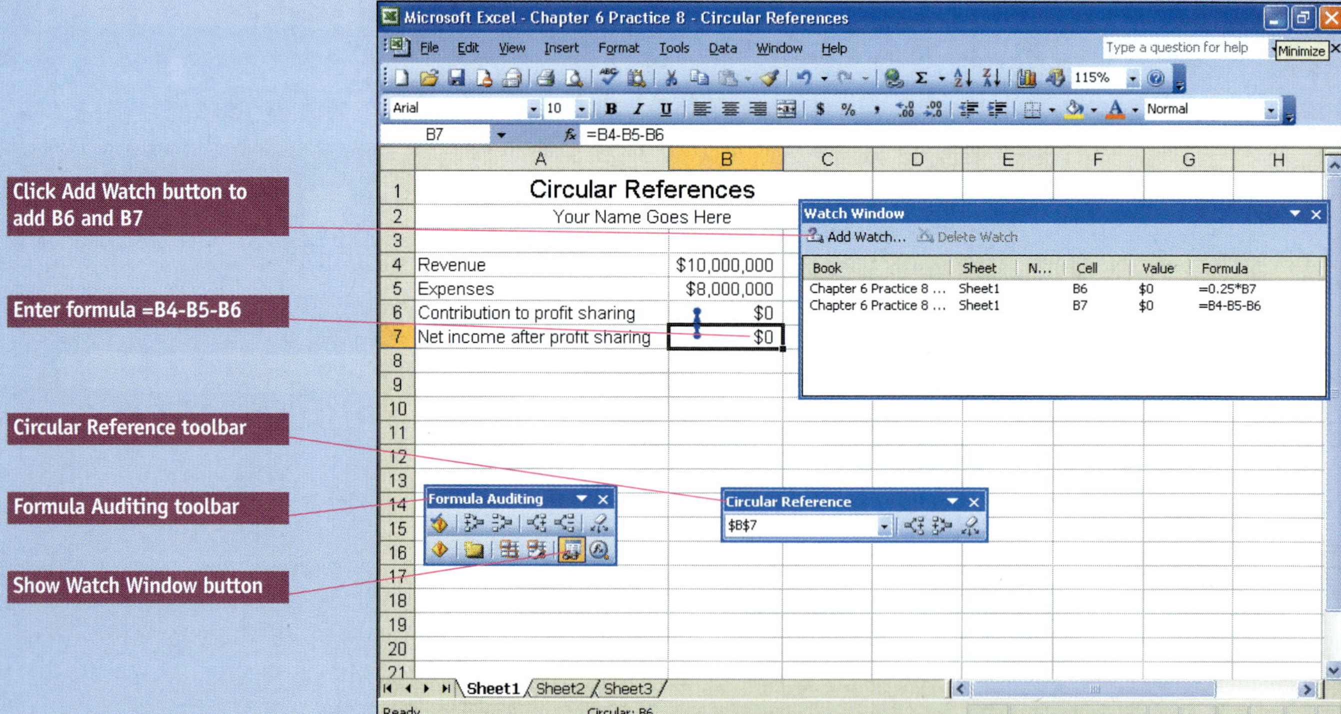

FIGURE 6.16 Circular References (exercise 8)

9. **Compare and Merge Workbooks:** The consensus workbook in Figure 6.17 is the result of merging three individual workbooks, provided by Tom, Dick, and Harry, each of whom added their comments to a shared workbook. Proceed as follows:
   a. Open the *Chapter 6 Practice 9* workbook that contains the original workbook sent out to each of the three reviewers.
   b. Pull down the Tools menu, click the Compare and Merge Workbooks command to display the associated dialog box, select the individual workbooks for Tom's Forecast, Dick's Forecast, and Harry's Forecast, then click OK. The workbooks will be opened individually, and any changes will be automatically merged into the consensus workbook. If there are conflicting changes (e.g., two individuals make different changes to the same cell), the changes are entered in the order that the workbooks are opened.
   c. Pull down the Tools menu, click Track Changes, and click the Highlight Changes command to display the Highlight Changes dialog box. Clear the Who, When, and Where check boxes so that you will see all of the changes made to the workbook. Check the box to list the changes on a new sheet. Click OK.
   d. A History worksheet is created automatically that shows all of the changes made to the shared workbook. Pull down the Window menu, click New window, then pull down the Window menu a second time, click Arrange, and tile the worksheets horizontally to match Figure 6.17. Click the Sales Data tab in one window and the History tab in the other.
   e. Look closely at the History worksheet and note that Harry and Tom changed the value of cell E4 to $90,000 and $125,000, respectively. The value that is shown in the consensus workbook ($125,000 in our figure) depends on the order in which the workbooks were merged. Tom was last in our example, so his change dominates. You can, however, use the Accept or Reject Changes command to go through all of the changes individually and accept (reject) the changes individually. If necessary, use this command to accept Tom's change ($125,000) rather than Harry's.
   f. Print the completed workbook, with both worksheets, for your instructor. Use the Page Setup command to include an appropriate footer that contains today's date and the name of the worksheet.

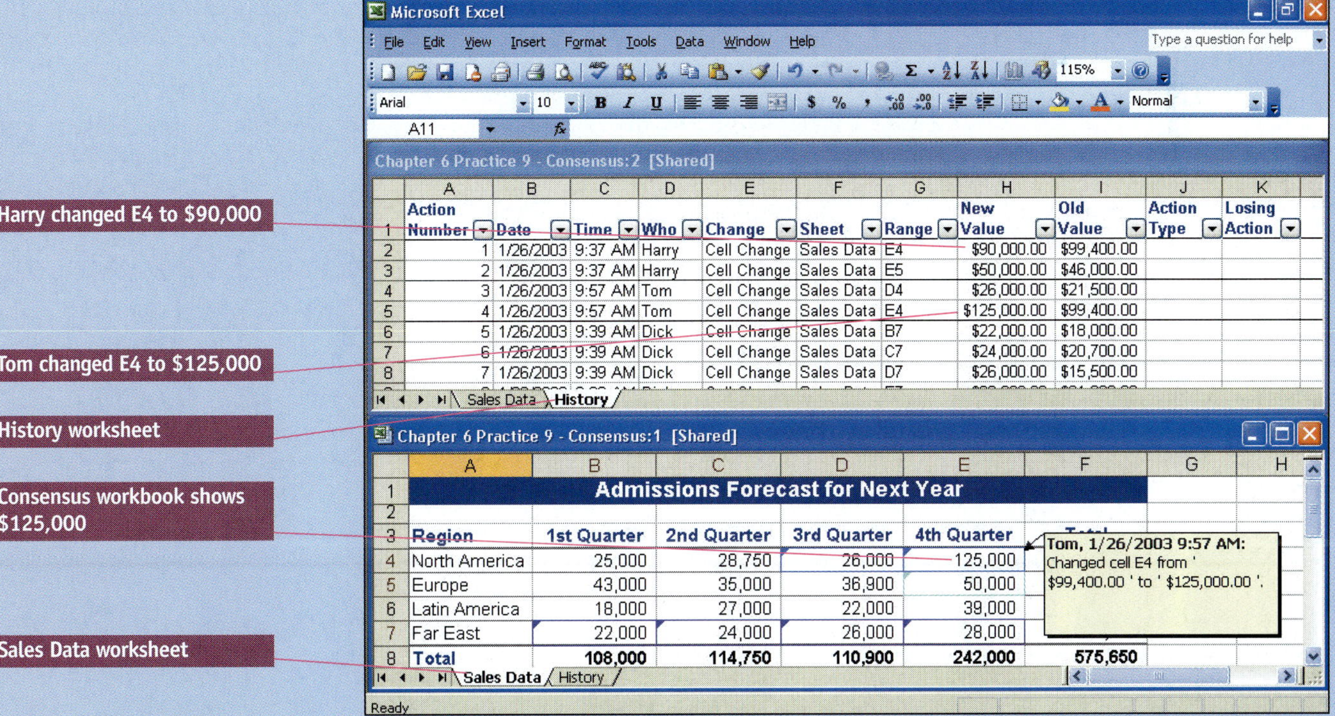

FIGURE 6.17 Compare and Merge Workbooks (exercise 9)

MINI CASES

The Entrepreneur

You have developed the perfect product and are seeking venture capital to go into immediate production. Your investors are asking for a projected income statement for the first four years of operation. The sales of your product are estimated at $350,000 the first year and are projected to grow at 10% annually. The cost of goods sold is 60% of the sales amount, and this percentage is expected to remain constant. You also have to pay a 10% sales commission, which is expected to remain constant.

Develop a financial forecast that will show the projected profits before and after taxes (assuming a tax rate of 36%). Your worksheet should be completely flexible and capable of accommodating a change in any of the initial conditions or projected rates of increase, *without* having to edit or recopy any of the formulas.

The worksheet should also be protected to the extent that users can make any changes they like in the assumption area, but are prevented from making changes in the body of the worksheet. Use "password" (in lowercase) as the password.

Error Checking—Good News and Bad

Microsoft Excel checks for certain errors automatically. If, for example, you are adding a column of numbers and you omit the top or bottom number, Excel will flag the formula to indicate a potential error. It will also flag an inconsistent formula within a row or column, and/or flag an unprotected cell if the cell contains a formula rather than a value. Potential errors are flagged with a green triangle, and the user is given the option to ignore or correct the error. Excel will even make the correction automatically for you.

This is a compelling feature, especially if you use Excel for financial calculations. Unfortunately, however, it falls short in one critical way. Your assignment is to open the *Chapter 6 Mini Case—Error Checking* workbook and correct all of the errors in the worksheet. Insert comments into the corrected cells to indicate which errors were detected by Excel, and which errors (if any) you had to correct manually.

Spreadsheet Solutions

Excel provides several templates locally with additional templates available on the Microsoft Web site. Start Excel, display the task pane, click the down arrow in the task pane to view the New Workbook task pane, then click the link to Other Templates on My Computer to open the Templates dialog box. Click the Spreadsheet Solutions tab, and then create at least one workbook based on the templates provided by Excel. Did the template contain formulas and/or protected cells? Was the formatting attractive? Was the template helpful, or would it have been just as easy to create the workbook from scratch? What additional templates are available on the Microsoft Web site?

CHAPTER 7

List and Data Management: Converting Data to Information

OBJECTIVES

After reading this chapter you will:

1. Add, edit, and/or delete records in a list within an Excel worksheet;
2. Use the Text Import Wizard to import data in character format.
3. Define XML; import XML data into an Excel workbook.
4. Describe the Today() function and its use in date arithmetic.
5. Use the Sort command; distinguish between an ascending and a descending sort
6. Use DSUM, DAVERAGE, DMAX, DMIN, and DCOUNT functions.
7. Use the AutoFilter and Advanced Filter commands.
8. Use the Subtotals command.
9. Create a pivot table and corresponding pivot chart.
10. Save a pivot table as a Web page.

hands-on exercises

1. IMPORTING, CREATING, AND MAINTAINING A LIST
   Input: Employee List (text file)
   Output: Employee List Solution
2. DATA VERSUS INFORMATION
   Input: Employee List Solution (from exercise 1)
   Output: Employee List Solution (additional changes)
3. PIVOT TABLES AND PIVOT CHARTS
   Input: Advertising Agency
   Output: Advertising Agency Solution (Excel workbook and Web Page)

CASE STUDY
THE SPA EXPERTS

Dan and Tim like to relax. The two fraternity brothers went into business shortly after graduation selling spas and hot tubs. Business has been good, and their expansive showroom and wide selection appeal to a variety of customers. The partners maintain a large inventory to attract the impulse buyer and currently have agreements with three manufacturers: Serenity Spas, The Original Hot Tub, and Port-a-Spa. Each manufacturer offers spas and hot tubs that appeal to different segments of the market with prices ranging from affordable to exorbitant.

The business has grown rapidly, and there is a need to analyze the sales data in order to increase future profits—for example, which vendor generates the most sales? Who is the leading salesperson? Do most customers purchase their spa or finance it? Are sales promotions necessary to promote business, or will customers pay the full price? Dan has created a simple workbook that has sales data for the current month. Each transaction appears on a separate row and contains the name of the salesperson, the manufacturer, and the amount of the sale. There is also an indication of whether the spa was purchased or financed, and whether a promotion was in effect. ■

Your assignment is to read the chapter, open the *Chapter 7 Case Study—The Spa Experts* workbook, and complete the workbook. A criteria range has been established at the top of the worksheet that displays the sales performance for any combination of salesperson, manufacturer, and/or other fields within the sales list. The summary statistics appear immediately below the criteria range, but you will have to enter the appropriate data management functions to compute the indicated statistics.

Use the Edit command to substitute your name for Jessica Benjamin throughout the worksheet. You can then enter your name in cell B5 (within the criteria range) to view your sales statistics for the month. Create a pivot table and associated pivot chart (each in its own worksheet) that displays summary information by vendor and salesperson.

LIST AND DATA MANAGEMENT

All businesses maintain data in the form of lists. Companies have lists of their employees. Magazines and newspapers keep lists of their subscribers. Political candidates monitor voter lists, and so on. This chapter presents the fundamentals of list management as it is implemented in Excel. It begins with the definition of basic terms, such as field and record, then covers the commands to create a list, to add a new record, and to modify or delete an existing record.

The second half of the chapter distinguishes between data and information and describes how one is converted to the other. We introduce the AutoFilter and Advanced Filter commands that display selected records in a list. We use the Sort command to rearrange the list. We discuss database functions and the associated criteria range. We also review date functions and date arithmetic. The chapter ends with a discussion of subtotals, pivot tables, and pivot charts—three powerful capabilities associated with lists.

Imagine that you are the personnel director of a medium-sized company with offices in several cities, and that you manually maintain employee data for the company. Accordingly, you have recorded the specifics of every individual's employment (name, salary, location, title, and so on) in a manila folder, and you have stored the entire set of folders in a file cabinet. You have written the name of each employee on the label of his or her folder and have arranged the folders alphabetically in the filing cabinet.

The manual system just described illustrates the basics of data management terminology. The set of manila folders corresponds to a ***file***. Each individual folder is known as a ***record.*** Each data item (fact) within a folder is called a ***field***. The folders are arranged alphabetically in the file cabinet (according to the employee name on the label) to simplify the retrieval of any given folder. Likewise, the records in a computer-based system are also in sequence according to a specific field known as a ***key***.

Excel maintains data in the form of a list. A ***list*** is an area in the worksheet that contains rows of similar data. A list can be used as a simple ***database***, where the rows in a worksheet correspond to records and the columns correspond to fields. The first row contains the column labels or ***field names***, which identify the data that will be entered in that column (field). Each additional row in the list contains a record. Each column represents a field. Each cell in the list area (other than the field names) contains a value for a specific field in a specific record. Every record (row) contains the same fields (columns) in the same order as every other record.

Figure 7.1 contains an employee list with 13 records. There are four fields in every record—name, location, title, and salary. The field names should be meaningful and must be unique. (A field name may contain up to 255 characters, but you should keep them as short as possible so that a column does not become too wide and thus difficult to work with.) The arrangement of the fields within a record is consistent from record to record. The employee name was chosen as the key, and thus the records are in alphabetical order.

Normal business operations require that you make repeated trips to the filing cabinet to maintain the accuracy of the data. You will have to add a folder whenever a new employee is hired. In similar fashion, you will have to remove the folder of any employee who leaves the company, or modify the data in the folder of any employee who receives a raise, changes location, and so on.

Changes of this nature (additions, deletions, and modifications) are known as file maintenance and constitute a critical activity within any system. Indeed, without adequate file maintenance, the data in a system quickly becomes obsolete and the information useless. Imagine the consequences of producing a payroll based on data that is six months old.

Row 1 contains the field names

Each row represents a record

Chicago is misspelled

Account Rep is misspelled

	A	B	C	D
1	Name	Location	Title	Salary
2	Adams	Atlanta	Trainee	$29,500
3	Adamson	Chicago	Manager	$52,000
4	Brown	Atlanta	Trainee	$28,500
5	Charles	Boston	Account Rep	$40,000
6	Coulter	Atlanta	Manager	$100,000
7	Frank	Miami	Manager	$75,000
8	James	Chicago	Account Rep	$42,500
9	Johnson	Chicag	Account Rep	$47,500
10	Manin	Boston	Accout Rep	$49,500
11	Marder	Chicago	Account Rep	$38,500
12	Milgrom	Boston	Manager	$57,500
13	Rubin	Boston	Account Rep	$45,000
14	Smith	Atlanta	Account Rep	$65,000

FIGURE 7.1 The Employee List

Nor is it sufficient simply to add (edit or delete) a record without adequate checks on the validity of the data. Look carefully at the entries in Figure 7.1 and ask yourself whether a computer-generated report that is intended to show the employees in the Chicago office will include Johnson. Will a report listing account reps include Manin? The answer to both questions is *no* because the data for these employees was entered incorrectly.

Chicago is misspelled in Johnson's record (the "o" was omitted). Account rep is misspelled in Manin's title. *You* know that Johnson works in Chicago, but the computer does not, because it searches for the correct spelling. It also will omit Manin from a listing of account reps because of the misspelled title. Remember, a computer does what you tell it to do, not necessarily what you want it to do. There is a significant difference.

GARBAGE IN, GARBAGE OUT (GIGO)

The information produced by a system is only as good as the data on which it is based. It is absolutely critical, therefore, that you validate the data that goes into a system, or else the associated information will not be correct. No system, no matter how sophisticated, can produce valid output from invalid input. In other words, garbage in—garbage out.

IMPLEMENTATION IN EXCEL

Creating a list is easy because there is little to do other than enter the data. You choose the area in the worksheet that will contain the list, then you enter the field names in the first row of the designated area. Each field name should be a unique text entry. The data for the individual records should be entered in the rows immediately below the row of field names.

Once a list has been created, you can edit any field, in any record, just as you would change the entries in an ordinary worksheet. The ***Insert Rows command*** lets you add new rows (records) to the list. The ***Insert Columns command*** lets you add additional columns (fields). The ***Delete command*** in the Edit menu enables you to delete a row or column. You can also use shortcut menus to execute commands more quickly. And finally, you can also format the entries within a list, just as you format the entries in any other worksheet.

Data Form Command

A ***data form*** provides an easy way to add, edit, and delete records in a list. The ***Form command*** in the Data menu displays a dialog box based on the fields in the list and contains the command buttons shown in Figure 7.2. Every record in the list contains the same fields in the same order (e.g., Name, Location, Title, and Salary in Figure 7.2), and the fields are displayed in this order within the dialog box. You do not have to enter a value for every field; that is, you may leave a field blank if the data is unknown.

Next to each field name is a text box into which data can be entered for a new record, or edited for an existing record. The scroll bar to the right of the data is used to scroll through the records in the list. As indicated, the Data Form command provides an easy way to add, edit, and delete records in a list. It is not required, however, and you can use the Insert and Delete commands within the Edit menu as an alternate means of data entry.

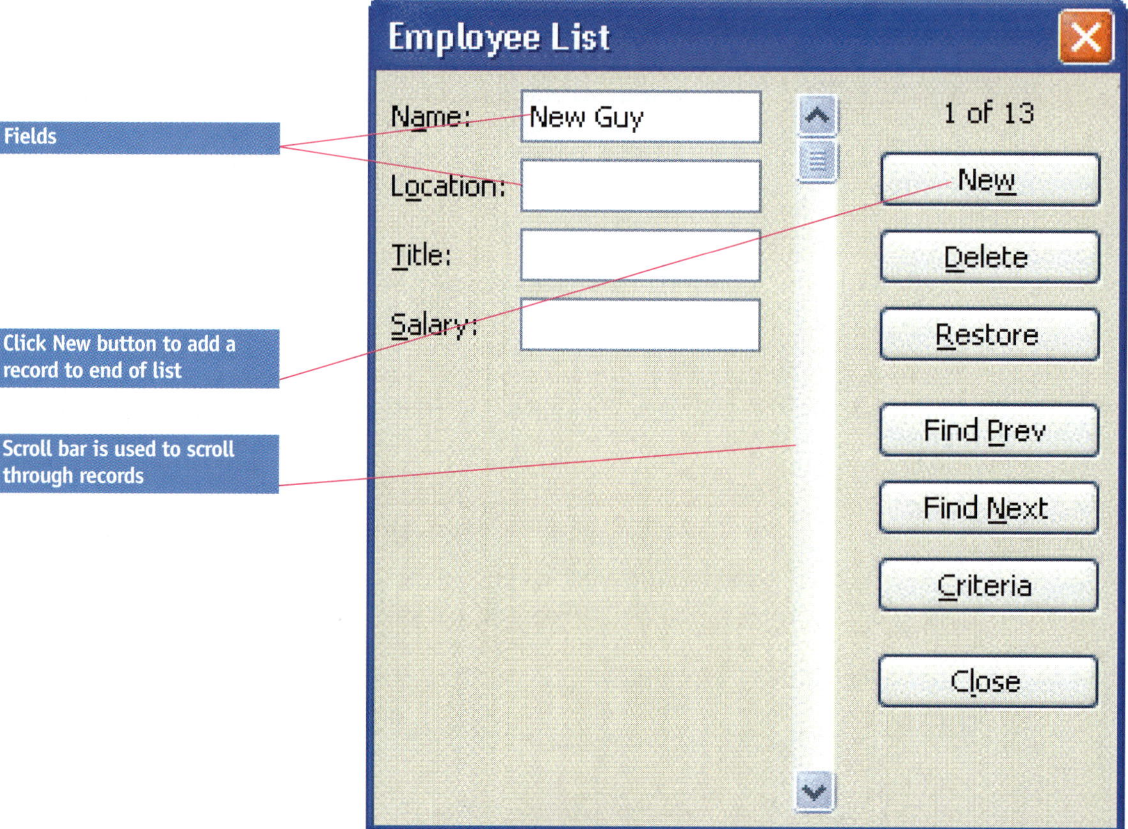

FIGURE 7.2 The Data Form Command

LIST SIZE AND LOCATION

A list can appear anywhere within a worksheet and can theoretically be as large as an entire worksheet (65,536 rows by 256 columns). Practically, the list will be much smaller, giving rise to the following guideline for its placement: Leave at least one blank column and one blank row between the list and the other entries in the worksheet. Excel will then be able to find the boundaries of the list automatically whenever a cell within the list is selected. It simply searches for the first blank row above and below the selected cell, and for the first blank column to the left and right of the selected cell.

The functions of the various command buttons are explained briefly:

New—Adds a record to the end of a list, then lets you enter data into that record. The formulas for computed fields, if any, are automatically copied to the new record.

Delete—Permanently removes the currently displayed record. The remaining records move up one row.

Restore—Cancels any changes made to the current record. (You must press the Restore button before pressing the Enter key or scrolling to a new record.)

Find Prev—Displays the previous record (or the previous record that matches the existing criteria when criteria are defined).

Find Next—Displays the next record (or the next record that matches the existing criteria when criteria are defined).

Criteria—Displays a dialog box in which you specify the criteria for the Find Prev and/or Find Next command buttons to limit the displayed records to those that match the criteria.

Close—Closes the data form and returns to the worksheet.

Sort Command

Data is easier to understand if it is displayed in a meaningful sequence. The ***Sort command*** arranges the records in a list according to the value of one or more fields within that list. You can sort the list in ***ascending*** (low-to-high) or ***descending*** (high-to-low) ***sequence***. (Putting a list in alphabetical order is considered an ascending sort.) You can also sort on more than one field at a time—for example, by location and then alphabetically by last name within each location. The field(s) on which you sort the list is (are) known as the key(s).

Each worksheet in Figure 7.3 displays the same set of employee records, but in a different order. The records in Figure 7.3a are listed alphabetically (in ascending sequence) according to the employees' last names. Adams comes before Adamson, who comes before Brown, and so on. Figure 7.3b displays the identical records but in descending sequence by employee salary. The employee with the highest salary is listed first, and the employee with the lowest salary is last.

Figure 7.3c sorts the employees on two keys—by location, and by descending salary within location. Location is the more important, or primary key. Salary is the less important, or secondary key. The Sort command groups employees according to like values of the primary key (location) in ascending (alphabetical) sequence, then within the like values of the primary key arranges them in descending sequence (ascending could have been chosen just as easily) according to the secondary key (salary). Excel provides a maximum of three keys—primary, secondary, and tertiary.

CHOOSE A CUSTOM SORT SEQUENCE

Alphabetic fields are normally arranged in strict alphabetical order. You can, however, choose a custom sort sequence such as the days of the week or the months of the year. Pull down the Data menu, click Sort, click the Options command button, then click the arrow on the drop-down list box to choose a sequence other than the alphabetic. You can also create your own sequence. Pull down the Tools menu, click Options, click the Custom Lists tab, select NewList, then enter the items in desired sequence in the List Entries Box. Click Add to create the sequence, then close the dialog box.

Records are in ascending sequence by employee name

	A	B	C	D
1	**Name**	**Location**	**Title**	**Salary**
2	Adams	Atlanta	Trainee	$29,500
3	Adamson	Chicago	Manager	$52,000
4	Brown	Atlanta	Trainee	$28,500
5	Charles	Boston	Account Rep	$40,000
6	Coulter	Atlanta	Manager	$100,000
7	Frank	Miami	Manager	$75,000
8	James	Chicago	Account Rep	$42,500
9	Johnson	Chicago	Account Rep	$47,500
10	Manin	Boston	Account Rep	$49,500
11	Marder	Chicago	Account Rep	$38,500
12	Milgrom	Boston	Manager	$57,500
13	Rubin	Boston	Account Rep	$45,000
14	Smith	Atlanta	Account Rep	$65,000

(a) Ascending Sequence (by name)

Records are in descending sequence by salary

	A	B	C	D
1	**Name**	**Location**	**Title**	**Salary**
2	Coulter	Atlanta	Manager	$100,000
3	Frank	Miami	Manager	$75,000
4	Smith	Atlanta	Account Rep	$65,000
5	Milgrom	Boston	Manager	$57,500
6	Adamson	Chicago	Manager	$52,000
7	Manin	Boston	Account Rep	$49,500
8	Johnson	Chicago	Account Rep	$47,500
9	Rubin	Boston	Account Rep	$45,000
10	James	Chicago	Account Rep	$42,500
11	Charles	Boston	Account Rep	$40,000
12	Marder	Chicago	Account Rep	$38,500
13	Adams	Atlanta	Trainee	$29,500
14	Brown	Atlanta	Trainee	$28,500

(b) Descending Sequence (by salary)

Location is the primary key (in ascending sequence)

Salary is the secondary key (in descending sequence)

	A	B	C	D
1	**Name**	**Location**	**Title**	**Salary**
2	Coulter	Atlanta	Manager	$100,000
3	Smith	Atlanta	Account Rep	$65,000
4	Adams	Atlanta	Trainee	$29,500
5	Brown	Atlanta	Trainee	$28,500
6	Milgrom	Boston	Manager	$57,500
7	Manin	Boston	Account Rep	$49,500
8	Rubin	Boston	Account Rep	$45,000
9	Charles	Boston	Account Rep	$40,000
10	Adamson	Chicago	Manager	$52,000
11	Johnson	Chicago	Account Rep	$47,500
12	James	Chicago	Account Rep	$42,500
13	Marder	Chicago	Account Rep	$38,500
14	Frank	Miami	Manager	$75,000

(c) Multiple Keys

FIGURE 7.3 The Sort Command

THE TEXT IMPORT WIZARD

It's easy to create a list in Excel and/or to modify data in that list. What if, however, the data already exists, but it is not in the form of a workbook? This is very common, especially in organizations that collect data on a mainframe, but analyze it on a PC. It can also occur when data is collected by one application, then analyzed in another. Excel provides a convenient solution in the form of the ***Text Import Wizard*** that converts a text (ASCII) file to an Excel workbook as shown in Figure 7.4. (Conversely, you can export an Excel workbook to another application by using the Save As command and specifying a text file.)

Figures 7.4a and 7.4b each contain the 13 records from the employee list shown, but in different formats. Both figures contain text files. The data in Figure 7.4a is in ***fixed width format***, where each field requires the same number of positions in an input record. The data in Figure 7.4b is in ***delimited format***, where the fields are separated from one another by a specific character.

You can access either file via the Open command in Excel, which in turn displays step 1 of the Text Import Wizard in Figure 7.4c. The Wizard prompts you for information about the external data, then it converts that data into an Excel workbook as shown in Figure 7.4d.

```
Name       Location    Title          Salary
Adams      Atlanta     Trainee        29500
Adamson    Chicago     Manager        52000
Brown      Atlanta     Trainee        28500
Charles    Boston      Account Rep    40000
Coulter    Atlanta     Manager        100000
Frank      Miami       Manager        75000
James      Chicago     Account Rep    42500
Johnson    Chicago     Account Rep    47500
Manin      Boston      Account Rep    49500
Marder     Chicago     Account Rep    38500
Milgrom    Boston      Manager        57500
Rubin      Boston      Account Rep    45000
Smith      Atlanta     Account Rep    65000
```

(a) Fixed Width

```
Name,Location,Title,Salary
Adams,Atlanta,Trainee,29500
Adamson,Chicago,Manager,52000
Brown,Atlanta,Trainee,28500
Charles,Boston,Account Rep,40000
Coulter,Atlanta,Manager,100000
Frank,Miami,Manager,75000
James,Chicago,Account Rep,42500
Johnson,Chicago,Account Rep,47500
Manin,Boston,Account Rep,49500
Marder,Chicago,Account Rep,38500
Milgrom,Boston,Manager,57500
Rubin,Boston,Account Rep,45000
Smith,Atlanta,Account Rep,65000
```

(b) Delimited

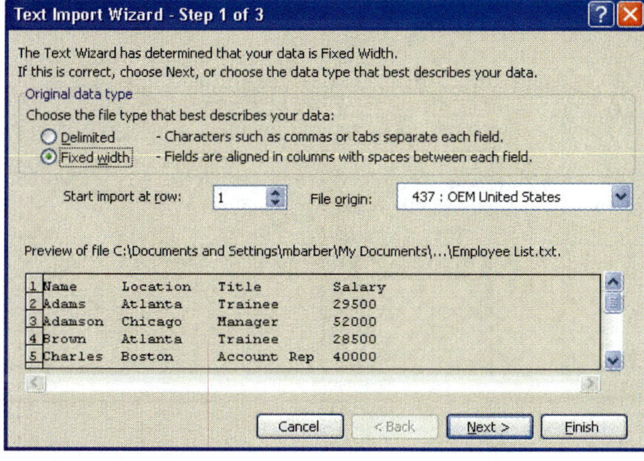

(c) Text Import Wizard

	A	B	C	D
1	Name	Location	Title	Salary
2	Adams	Atlanta	Trainee	$29,500
3	Adamson	Chicago	Manager	$52,000
4	Brown	Atlanta	Trainee	$28,500
5	Charles	Boston	Account Rep	$40,000
6	Coulter	Atlanta	Manager	$100,000
7	Frank	Miami	Manager	$75,000
8	James	Chicago	Account Rep	$42,500
9	Johnson	Chicag	Account Rep	$47,500
10	Manin	Boston	Account Rep	$49,500
11	Marder	Chicago	Accout Rep	$38,500
12	Milgrom	Boston	Manager	$57,500
13	Rubin	Boston	Account Rep	$45,000
14	Smith	Atlanta	Account Rep	$65,000

(d) Workbook

FIGURE 7.4 Importing Data from Other Applications

Excel and XML

A text file is a universal file format, in that it can be read by virtually any application. ***XML (Extensible Markup Language)*** goes one step further by enabling a developer to create customized tags to define and interpret the data within the file. (XML is an industry standard for structuring data and not a Microsoft product.) XML is not to be confused with ***HTML (Hypertext Markup Language)***, nor is it intended as a replacement for HTML.

HTML is intended to display data and it has only a finite set of tags; e.g., <B> or <UL>, for bold and underlining, respectively. XML, however, describes the data and it has an infinite number of tags. XML tags are not defined in any XML standard, however, but are created by the author of the XML document. Consider:

HTML:

```
<B>John Doe</B>
```

XML:

```
<name>
    <first>John</first>
    <last>Doe</last>
</name>
```

The HTML code tells us that "John Doe" will appear in boldface, but it does not tell us anything more. We don't know that "John" is the first name or that "Doe" is the last name. XML, on the other hand, is "data about data". You can see at a glance that it is conveying information about a name, and that there is a first name and a last name, within the name. The real advantage of XML, however, is that it is easily expanded (extensible) to include additional information about a person's name such as a prefix or middle initial. We just extend the definition of the elements within the name to include the additional data, and then we mark up the data accordingly by including additional tags.

Microsoft Excel 2003 provides full XML support that enables you to exchange information between an XML source document and an Excel workbook. You attach the XML definition or ***schema*** to the workbook and then you map the XML elements in the schema to the cells in your workbook. Once this is accomplished you can import and/or export XML data into or out of the individual cells. Figure 7.5a displays the first three employee records in an XML document, Figure 7.5b shows the XML source task pane in which the mapping takes place, and Figure 7.5c displays the associated list within a worksheet.

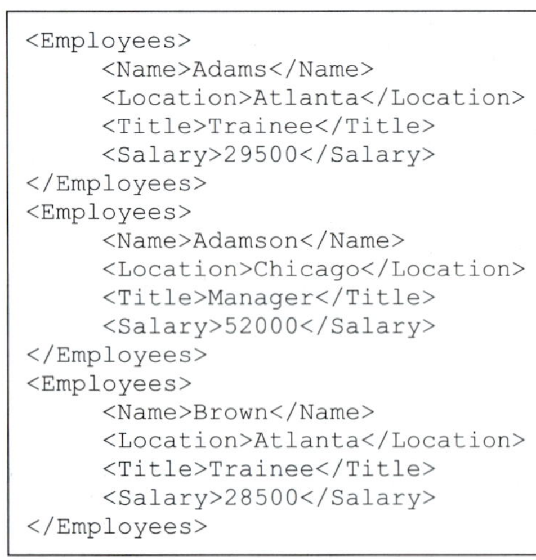

```
<Employees>
     <Name>Adams</Name>
     <Location>Atlanta</Location>
     <Title>Trainee</Title>
     <Salary>29500</Salary>
</Employees>
<Employees>
     <Name>Adamson</Name>
     <Location>Chicago</Location>
     <Title>Manager</Title>
     <Salary>52000</Salary>
</Employees>
<Employees>
     <Name>Brown</Name>
     <Location>Atlanta</Location>
     <Title>Trainee</Title>
     <Salary>28500</Salary>
</Employees>
```

(a) XML Document

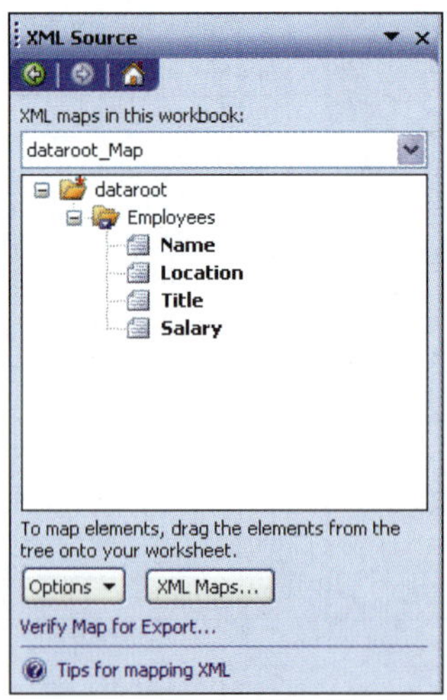

(b) XML Source Task Pane

	A	B	C	D
1	Name	Location	Title	Salary
2	Adams	Atlanta	Trainee	29500
3	Adamson	Chicago	Manager	52000
4	Brown	Atlanta	Trainee	28500
5	Charles	Boston	Account Rep	40000
6	Coulter	Atlanta	Manager	100000
7	Frank	Miami	Manager	75000
8	James	Chicago	Account Rep	42500
9	Johnson	Chicago	Account Rep	47500
10	Manin	Boston	Account Rep	49500
11	Marder	Chicago	Account Rep	38500
12	Milgrom	Boston	Manager	57500
13	Rubin	Boston	Account Rep	45000
14	Smith	Atlanta	Account Rep	65000
15	*			

(c) Excel Spreadsheet

FIGURE 7.5 Excel and XML

hands-on exercise

1 Importing, Creating, and Maintaining a List

Objective To use the Text Import Wizard; to add, edit, and delete records in an employee list. Use Figure 7.6 as a guide in the exercise.

Step 1: The Text Import Wizard

- Start Excel. Pull down the **File menu** and click the **Open command** (or click the **Open button** on the Standard toolbar) to display the Open dialog box.
- Open the **Exploring Excel folder** that you have used throughout the text. Click the **drop-down arrow** on the Files of Type list box and specify **All Files**, then double click the **Employee List** text document.
- The Text Import Wizard opens automatically as shown in Figure 7.6a. The Wizard recognizes that the file is in Delimited format. Click **Next**.
- Clear the **Tab Delimiter** check box. Check the **Comma Delimiter** check box. Each field is now shown in a separate column. Click **Next**.
- There is no need to change the default format (general) of any of the fields. Click **Finish**. You see the Employee List within an Excel workbook.
- Click and drag to select **cells A1 through D1**, then click the **Bold** and **Center buttons** to distinguish the field names from the data records. Click the **down arrow** for the **Fill Color button** and select **Light Yellow**. Adjust the column widths. Format the Salary field as Currency with zero decimals.
- Save the workbook as **Employee List Solution.** Click the **down arrow** in the Save as type list box and select **Microsoft Excel workbook**. Click **Save**.

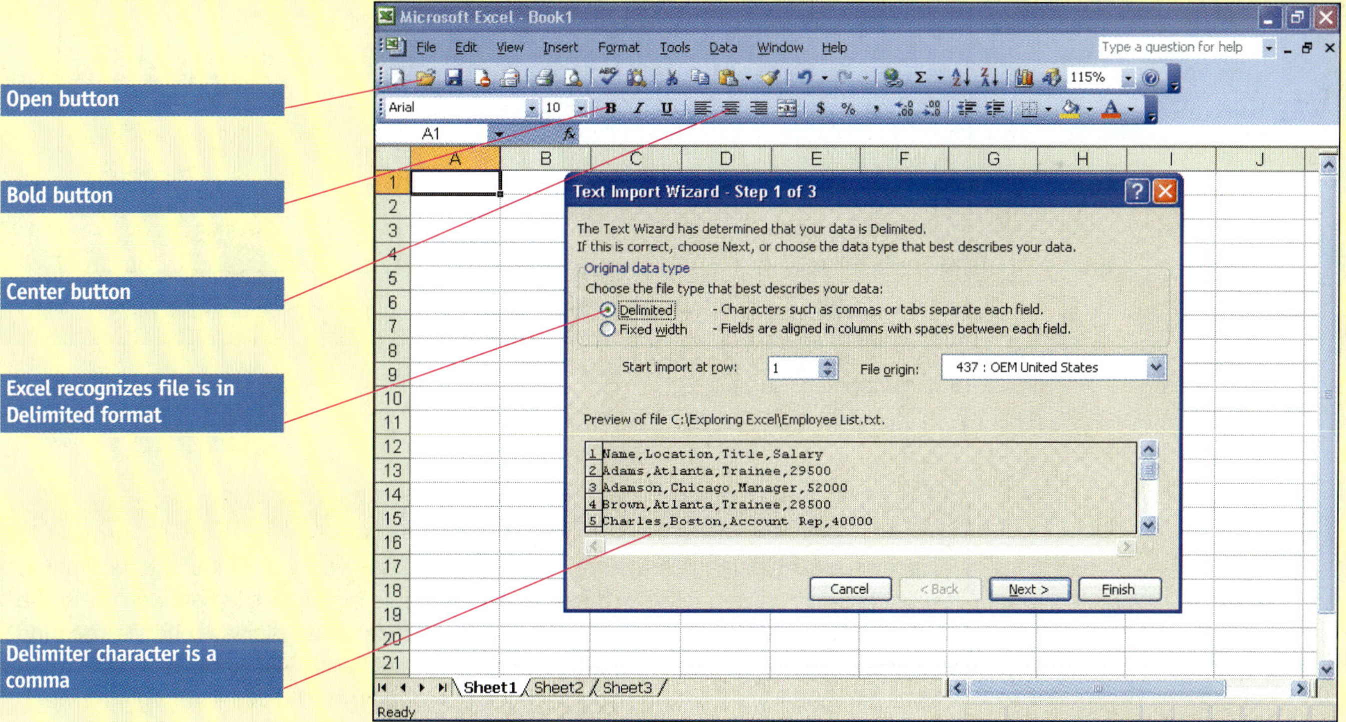

(a) The Text Import Wizard (step 1)

FIGURE 7.6 Hands-on Exercise 1

Step 2: Add New Records

- Click a single cell anywhere within the employee list **(cells A1 through D14)**. Pull down the **Data menu**. Click **Form** to display a dialog box with data for the first record in the list (Adams).
- Click the **New command button** at the right of the dialog box to clear the text boxes and begin entering a new record.
- Enter the data for **Elofson** as shown in Figure 7.6b, using the **Tab key** to move from field to field within the data form.
- Click the **Close command button** after entering the salary. Elofson has been added to the list and appears in row 15.
- Add a second record for **Gillenson**, who works in **Miami** as an **Account Rep** with a salary of **$55,000**.
- Save the workbook.

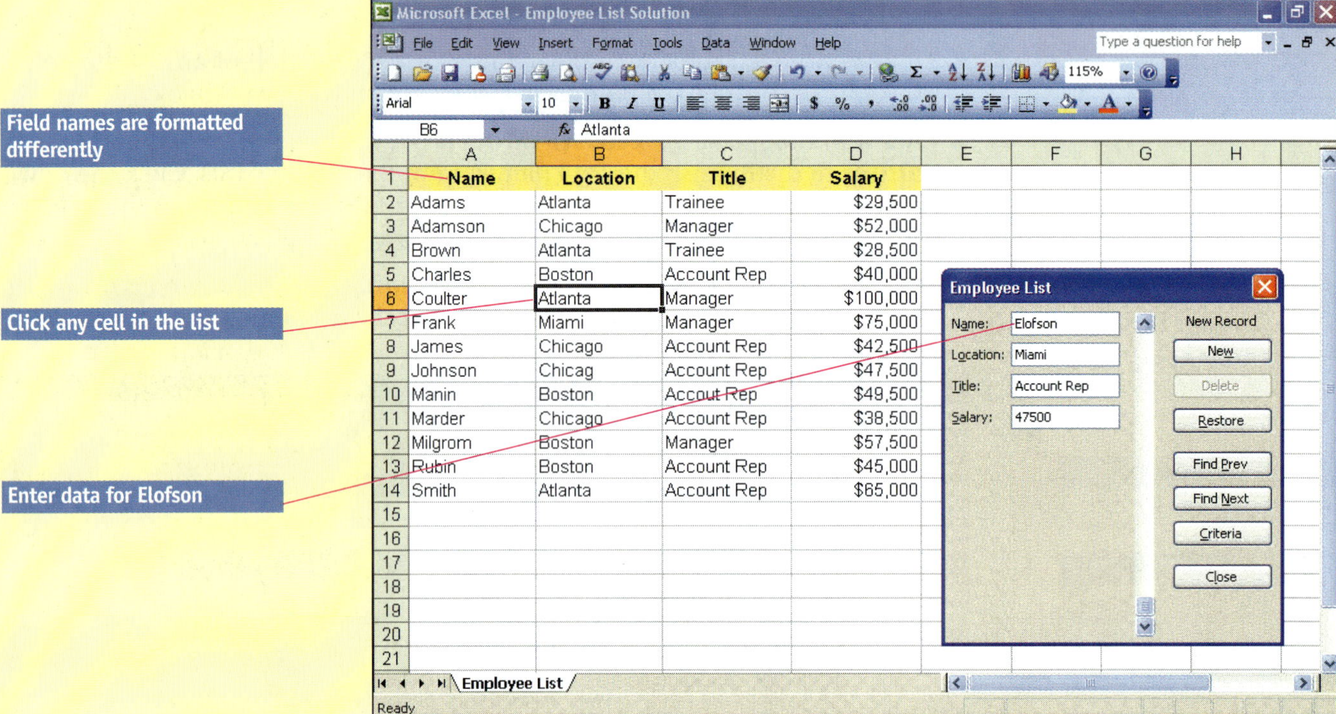

(b) Add New Records (step 2)

FIGURE 7.6 Hands-on Exercise 1 (*continued*)

THE CREATE LIST COMMAND

All previous versions of Excel enabled you to work with a list or area in a worksheet that contained rows of similar data. The user would highlight the field names in the first row, turn the AutoFilter command on and off, and/or display a border around the entire list. Microsoft Excel 2003 introduces a Create List command that does this automatically. Click and drag to select the entire list (include the field names), pull down the Data menu, click the List command, and then click the Create List command. Click anywhere in the list and you will see an asterisk in the last row; enter data in this row and the new record is added to the list automatically.

Step 3: The Spell Check

- Select **cells B2:C16** as in Figure 7.6c. Pull down the **Tools menu** and click **Spelling** (or click the **Spelling button** on the Standard toolbar).
- Chicago is misspelled in cell B9 and flagged accordingly. Click the **Change command button** to accept the suggested correction and continue checking the document.
- Account is misspelled in cell C10 and flagged accordingly. Click **Account** in the Suggestions list box, then click the **Change command button** to correct the misspelling.
- Excel will indicate that it has finished checking the selected cells. Click **OK** to return to the worksheet.
- Save the workbook.

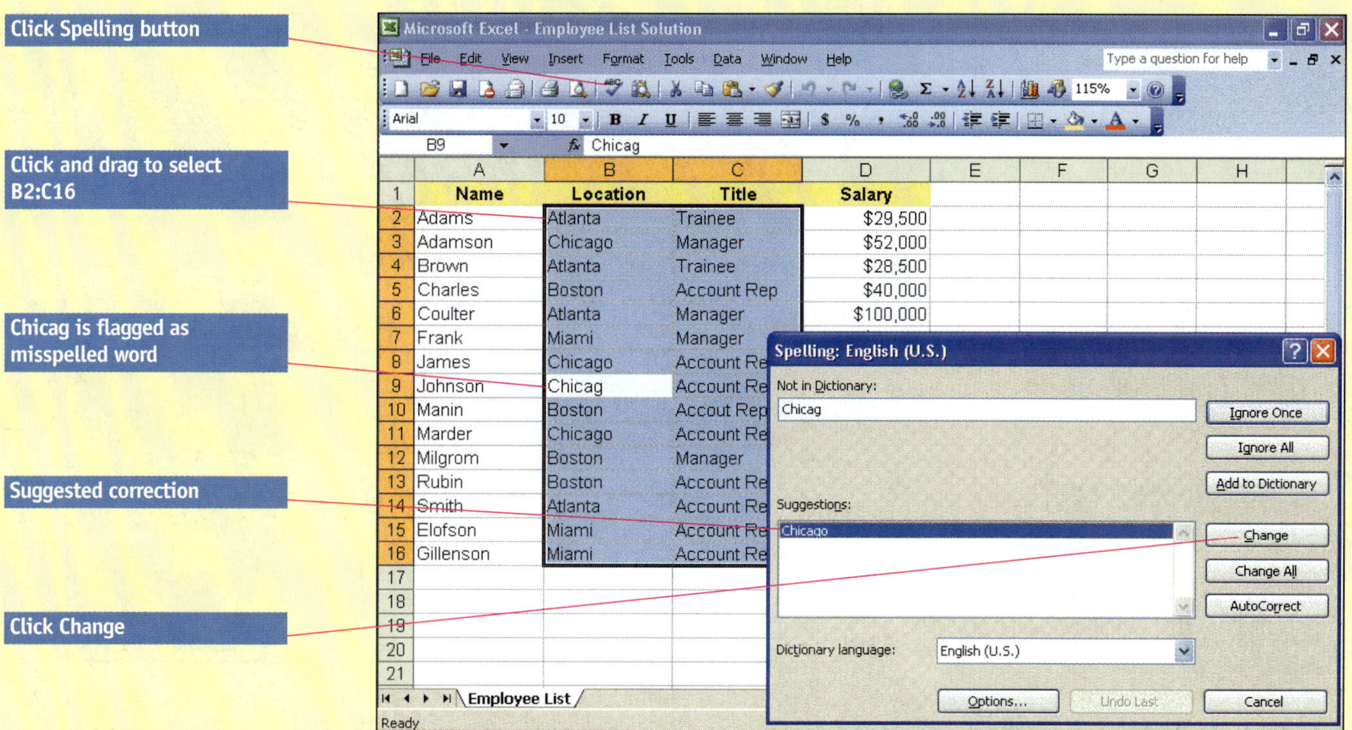

(c) The Spell Check (step 3)

FIGURE 7.6 Hands-on Exercise 1 (*continued*)

CREATE YOUR OWN SHORTHAND

Use the AutoCorrect capability within Microsoft Office to create your own shorthand by having it expand abbreviations such as *cis* for *Computer Information Systems.* Pull down the Tools menu, click AutoCorrect Options to display the associated dialog box, then click the AutoCorrect tab. Type the abbreviation in the Replace text box and the expanded entry in the With text box. Click the Add command button, then click OK to exit the dialog box. The next time you type *cis* in a spreadsheet, it will automatically be expanded to *Computer Information Systems.*

Step 4: Sort the Employee List

- Click a single cell anywhere in the employee list (**cells A1 through D16**). Pull down the **Data menu.** Click **Sort** to display the dialog box in Figure 7.6d.
- Click the **drop-down arrow** in the Sort By list box. Select **Location.**
- Click the **drop-down arrow** in the first Then By list box. Select **Name.**
- Be sure the **Header Row option button** is selected (so that the field names are not sorted with the records in the list).
- Check that the **Ascending option button** is selected for both the primary and secondary keys. Click **OK.**
- The employees are listed by location and alphabetically within location.
- Save the workbook.

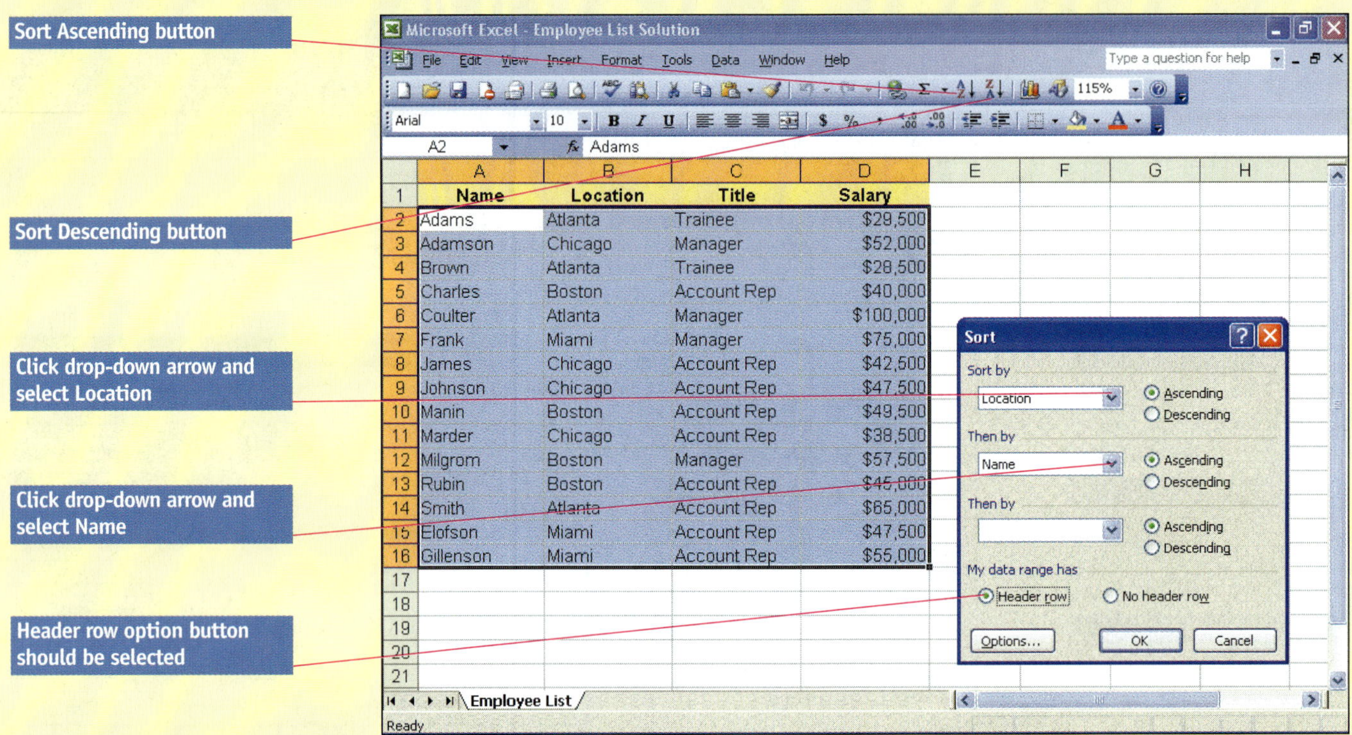

(d) Sort the Employee List (step 4)

FIGURE 7.6 Hands-on Exercise 1 (*continued*)

USE THE SORT BUTTONS

Use the Sort Ascending or Sort Descending button on the Standard toolbar to sort on one or more keys. To sort on a single key, click any cell in the column containing the key, then click the appropriate button, depending on whether you want an ascending or a descending sort. You can also sort on multiple keys, by clicking either button multiple times, but the trick is to do it in the right sequence. Sort on the least significant field first, then work your way up to the most significant. For example, to sort a list by location, and name within location, sort by name first (the secondary key), then sort by location (the primary key).

Step 5: Delete a Record

- A record may be deleted by using the Edit Delete command or the Data Form command. To delete a record by using the Edit Delete command:
  - Click the **row heading** in **row 15** (containing the record for Frank, which is slated for deletion).
  - Pull down the **Edit menu**. Click **Delete**. Frank has been deleted.
- Click the **Undo button** on the Standard toolbar. The record for Frank has been restored.
- To delete a record by using the Data Form command:
  - Click a single cell within the employee list. Pull down the **Data menu**. Click **Form** to display the data form. Click the **Criteria button**. Enter **Frank** in the Name text box, then click the **Find Next button** to locate Frank's record.
  - Click the **Delete command button**. Click **OK** in response to the warning message shown in Figure 7.6e. (The record cannot be undeleted as it could with the Edit Delete command.) Click **Close** to close the Data Form.
- Save the workbook.

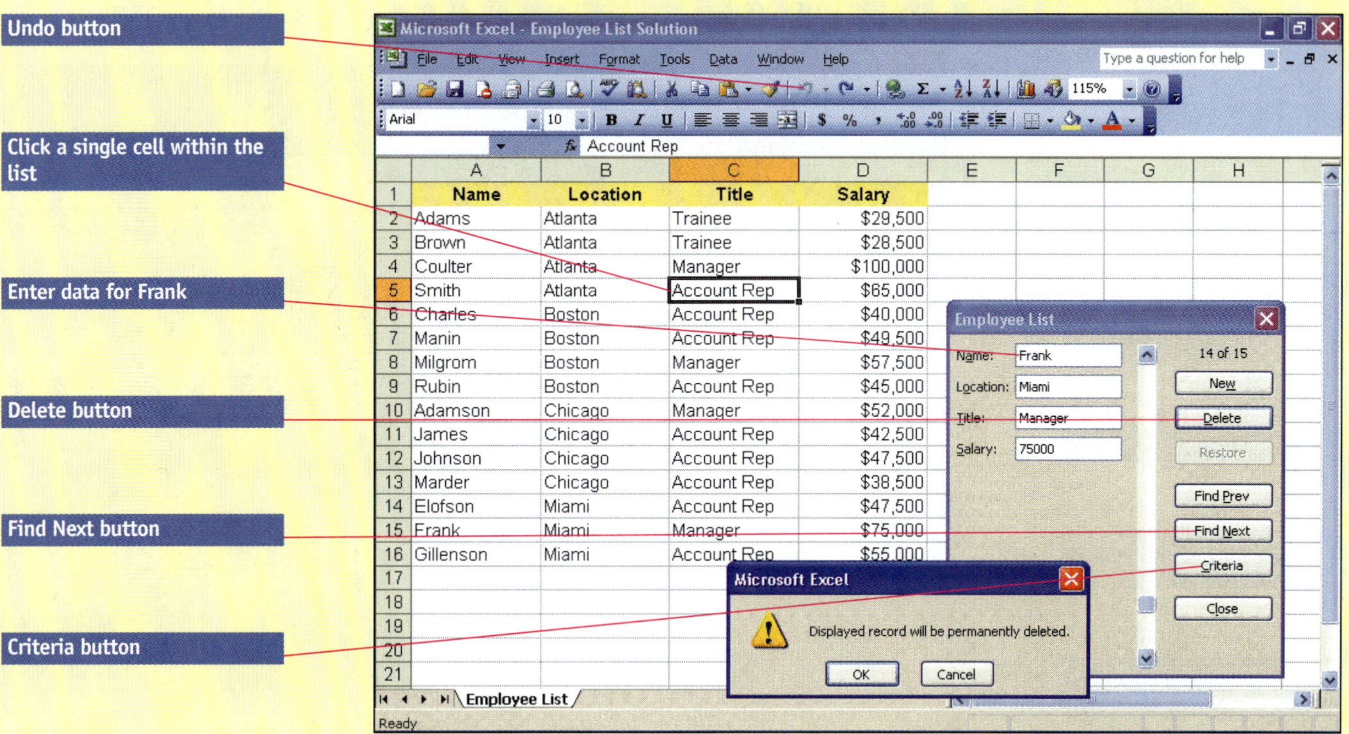

(e) Delete a Record (step 5)

FIGURE 7.6 Hands-on Exercise 1 (*continued*)

EDIT CLEAR VERSUS EDIT DELETE

The Edit Delete command deletes the selected cell, row, or column from the worksheet, and thus its execution will adjust cell references throughout the worksheet. It is very different from the Edit Clear command, which erases the contents (and/or formatting) of the selected cells, but does not delete the cells from the worksheet and hence has no effect on the cell references in formulas that reference those cells. Pressing the Del key erases the contents of a cell and thus corresponds to the Edit Clear command.

Step 6: Enter the Hire Date

- Click the **column heading** in column D. Point to the selection, then click the **right mouse button** to display a shortcut menu. Click **Insert**. The employee salaries have been moved to column E, as shown in Figure 7.6f.
- Click **cell D1**. Type **Hire Date** and press **Enter**. Adjust the column width if necessary. Dates may be entered in several different formats.
  - Type **11/24/98** in cell D2. Press the **down arrow key**.
  - Type **11/24/1998** in cell D3. Press the **down arrow key**.
  - Type **Nov 24, 1998** in cell D4. Type a **comma** after the day but do not type a period after the month. Press the **down arrow key** to move to cell D5.
  - Type **11-24-98** in cell D5. Press **Enter**.
- For ease of data entry, assume that the next several employees were hired on the same day, 3/16/99. Click in **cell D6**. Type **3/16/99**. Press **enter**. Click in **cell D6**. Click the **Copy button** on the Standard toolbar.
- Drag the mouse over cells **D7 through D10**. Click the **Paste button**. Press **Esc** to remove the moving border around cell D6.
- Save the workbook.

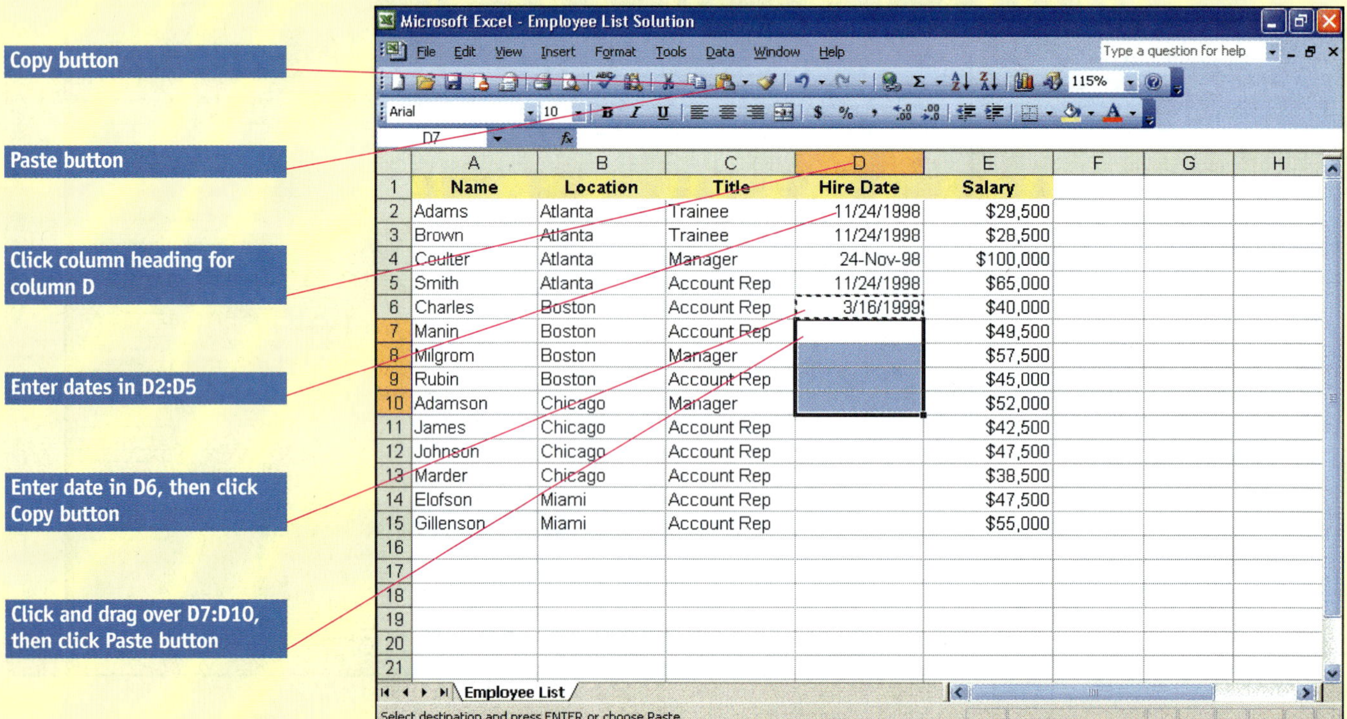

(f) Enter the Hire Date (step 6)

FIGURE 7.6 Hands-on Exercise 1 (*continued*)

TWO-DIGIT DATES AND THE YEAR 2000

Excel assumes that any two-digit year up to and including 29 is in the 21st century; that is, 12/31/29 will be stored as December 31, 2029. (The year 2029 is arbitrary.) Any year after 29, however, is assumed to be in the 20th century; for example, 1/1/30 will be stored as January 1, 1930. When in doubt, however, enter a four-digit year to be sure.

Step 7: Format the Hire Dates

- The next five employees were hired one year apart beginning October 31, 1998.
  - ❑ Click in cell **D11** and type **10/31/98**. Click in cell **D12** and type **10/31/99**.
  - ❑ Select cells **D11 and D12**.
  - ❑ Drag the **fill handle** at the bottom of cell D12 over cells **D13**, **D14**, and **D15**. Release the mouse to complete the AutoFill operation.
- Click in the column heading for **column D** to select the column of dates.
- Point to the selected cells and click the **right mouse button** to display a shortcut menu. Click **Format Cells**.
- Click the **Number tab** in the Format Cells dialog box. Click **Date** in the Category list box. Select (click) the date format shown in Figure 7.6g. Click **OK**.
- Click elsewhere in the workbook to deselect the dates. Reduce the width of column D as appropriate. Save the workbook.
- Exit Excel if you do not want to complete the next exercise at this time.

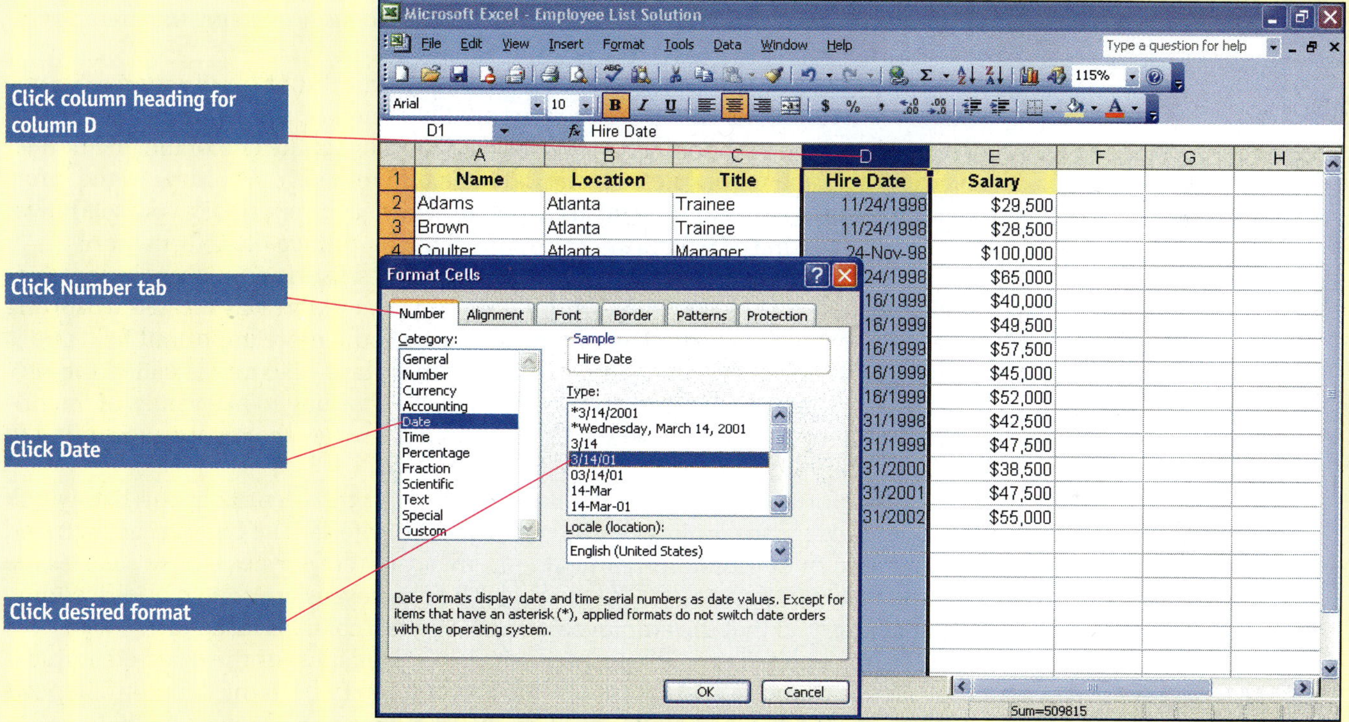

(g) Format the Hire Dates (step 7)

FIGURE 7.6 Hands-on Exercise 1 (*continued*)

EXPORTING DATA FROM EXCEL

We began the exercise by importing data from a text file into an Excel workbook. You can also go in the opposite direction; i.e., you can export the data in an Excel worksheet into a CSV (comma-separated value) or text file, an XML document, or an Access database. Pull down the File menu, click the Save As command, then specify the file type; e.g., a text file. Exporting an Excel worksheet to an Access table is done differently, however, in that you have to import the Excel table from within Access. See the Excel and Access mini case at the end of the chapter.

DATA VERSUS INFORMATION

Data and information are not synonymous. ***Data*** refers to a fact or facts about a specific record, such as an employee's name, title, or salary. ***Information***, on the other hand, is data that has been rearranged into a form perceived as useful by the recipient. A list of employees earning more than $35,000 or a total of all employee salaries are examples of information produced from data about individual employees. Put another way, data is the raw material, and information is the finished product.

Decisions in an organization are based on information rather than raw data; for example, in assessing the effects of a proposed across-the-board salary increase, management needs to know the total payroll rather than individual salary amounts. In similar fashion, decisions about next year's hiring will be influenced, at least in part, by knowing how many individuals are currently employed in each job category.

Organizations maintain data to produce information. Data maintenance entails three basic operations—adding new records, modifying (editing or updating) existing records, and deleting existing records. The exercise just completed showed you how to maintain the data. This section focuses on using that data to create information.

Data is converted to information through a combination of database commands and functions whose capabilities are illustrated by the reports in Figure 7.7. The reports are based on the employee list as it existed at the end of the first hands-on exercise. Each report presents the data in a different way, according to the information requirements of the end-user. As you view each report, ask yourself how it was produced; that is, what was done to the data to produce the information?

Figure 7.7a contains a master list of all employees, listing employees by location, and alphabetically by last name within location. The report was created by sorting the list on two keys, location and name. Location is the more important field and is known as the primary key. Name is the less important field and is called the secondary key. The sorted report groups employees according to like values of the primary key (location), then within the primary key groups the records according to the secondary key (name).

The report in Figure 7.7b displays a subset of the records in the list, which includes only those employees who meet specific criteria. The criteria can be based on any field or combination of fields—in this case, employees whose salaries are between $40,000 and $60,000 (inclusive). The employees are shown in descending order of salary so that the employee with the highest salary is listed first.

The report in Figure 7.7c displays summary statistics for the selected employees—in this example, the salaries for the account reps within the company. Reports of this nature omit the salaries of individual employees (known as detail lines), to present an aggregate view of the organization. Remember, too, that the information produced by any system is only as good as the data on which it is based. Thus, it is very important that organizations take steps to ensure the validity of the data as it is entered into a system.

BIRTH DATE VERSUS AGE

An individual's age and birth date provide equivalent information, as one is calculated from the other. It might seem easier, therefore, to enter the age directly into the list and avoid the calculation, but this would be a mistake. A person's age changes continually, whereas the birth date remains constant. Thus, the date, not the age, should be stored, so that the data in the list remains current. Similar reasoning applies to an employee's hire date and length of service.

Location Report

Name	Location	Title	Service	Hire Date	Salary
Adams	Atlanta	Trainee	4.6	11/24/98	$29,500
Brown	Atlanta	Trainee	4.6	11/24/98	$28,500
Coulter	Atlanta	Manager	4.6	11/24/98	$100,000
Smith	Atlanta	Account Rep	4.6	11/24/98	$65,000
Charles	Boston	Account Rep	4.3	3/16/99	$40,000
Manin	Boston	Account Rep	4.3	3/16/99	$49,500
Milgrom	Boston	Manager	4.3	3/16/99	$57,500
Rubin	Boston	Account Rep	4.3	3/16/99	$45,000
Adamson	Chicago	Manager	4.3	3/16/99	$52,000
James	Chicago	Account Rep	4.7	10/31/98	$42,500
Johnson	Chicago	Account Rep	3.7	10/31/99	$47,500
Marder	Chicago	Account Rep	2.7	10/31/00	$38,500
Elofson	Miami	Account Rep	1.7	10/31/01	$47,500
Gillenson	Miami	Account Rep	0.7	10/31/02	$55,000

(a) Employees by Location and Name within Location

Earnings Between $40,000 and $60,000

Name	Location	Title	Service	Hire Date	Salary
Milgrom	Boston	Manager	4.3	3/16/99	$57,500
Gillenson	Miami	Account Rep	0.7	10/31/02	$55,000
Adamson	Chicago	Manager	4.3	3/16/99	$52,000
Manin	Boston	Account Rep	4.3	3/16/99	$49,500
Johnson	Chicago	Account Rep	3.7	10/31/99	$47,500
Elofson	Miami	Account Rep	1.7	10/31/01	$47,500
Rubin	Boston	Account Rep	4.3	3/16/99	$45,000
James	Chicago	Account Rep	4.7	10/31/98	$42,500
Charles	Boston	Account Rep	4.3	3/16/99	$40,000

(b) Employees Earning Between $40,000 and $60,000, Inclusive

Summary Statistics	
Total Salary for Account Reps	$430,500
Average Salary for Account Reps	$47,833
Maximum Salary for Account Reps	$65,000
Minimum Salary for Account Reps	$38,500
Number of Account Reps	9

(c) Account Rep Summary Data

FIGURE 7.7 Data versus Information

AutoFilter Command

A ***filtered list*** displays a subset of records that meet a specific criterion or set of criteria. It is created by the ***AutoFilter command*** (or the Advanced Filter command discussed in the next section). Both commands temporarily hide those records (rows) that do not meet the criteria. The hidden records are *not* deleted; they are simply not displayed.

Figure 7.8a displays the employee list in alphabetical order. Figure 7.8b displays a filtered version of the list in which only the Atlanta employees (in rows 2, 4, 6, and 15) are visible. The remaining employees are still in the worksheet but are not shown as their rows are hidden.

AutoFilter command places drop-down arrow next to field name

Click to display Atlanta employees only

	A	B	C	D	E
1	Name	Location	Title	Hire Date	Salary
2	Adams		Trainee	11/24/98	$29,500
3	Adamson		Manager	3/16/99	$52,000
4	Brown		Trainee	11/24/98	$28,500
5	Charles		Account Rep	3/16/99	$40,000
6	Coulter		Manager	11/24/98	$100,000
7	Elofson		Account Rep	10/31/01	$47,500
8	Gillenson		Account Rep	10/31/02	$55,000
9	James	Chicago	Account Rep	10/31/98	$42,500
10	Johnson	Chicago	Account Rep	10/31/99	$47,500
11	Manin	Boston	Account Rep	3/16/99	$49,500
12	Marder	Chicago	Account Rep	10/31/00	$38,500
13	Milgrom	Boston	Manager	3/16/99	$57,500
14	Rubin	Boston	Account Rep	3/16/99	$45,000
15	Smith	Atlanta	Account Rep	11/24/98	$65,000

Sort Ascending
Sort Descending
(All)
(Top 10...)
(Custom...)
Atlanta
Boston
Chicago
Miami

(a) Unfiltered List

Only rows 2, 4, 6, and 15 are visible

Only Atlanta employees are displayed

	A	B	C	D	E
1	Name	Location	Title	Hire Date	Salary
2	Adams	Atlanta	Trainee	11/24/98	$29,500
4	Brown	Atlanta	Trainee	11/24/98	$28,500
6	Coulter	Atlanta	Manager	11/24/98	$100,000
15	Smith	Atlanta	Account Rep	11/24/98	$65,000

(b) Filtered List (Atlanta employees)

Click drop-down arrow to further filter list by Title

	A	B	C	D	E
1	Name	Location	Title	Hire Date	Salary
2	Adams	Atlanta		11/24/98	$29,500
4	Brown	Atlanta		11/24/98	$28,500
6	Coulter	Atlanta		11/24/98	$100,000
15	Smith	Atlanta		11/24/98	$65,000
16					
17					
18					

Sort Ascending
Sort Descending
(All)
(Top 10...)
(Custom...)
Account Rep
Manager
Trainee

(c) Imposing a Second Condition

Blue drop-down arrows indicate filter condition is in effect for those fields

	A	B	C	D	E
1	Name	Location	Title	Hire Date	Salary
6	Coulter	Atlanta	Manager	11/24/98	$100,000

(d) Filtered List (Atlanta managers)

FIGURE 7.8 Filter Command

Execution of the AutoFilter command places drop-down arrows next to each column label (field name). Clicking a drop-down arrow produces a list of the unique values for that field, enabling you to establish the criteria for the filtered list. Thus, to display the Atlanta employees, click the drop-down arrow for Location, then click Atlanta.

A filter condition can be imposed on multiple columns as shown in Figure 7.8c. The filtered list in Figure 7.8c contains just the Atlanta employees. Clicking the arrow next to Title, then clicking Manager, will filter the list further to display the employees who both work in Atlanta *and* have Manager as a title. Only one employee meets both conditions, as shown in Figure 7.8d. The drop-down arrows next to Location and Title are displayed in blue to indicate that a filter is in effect for these columns.

The AutoFilter command has additional options as can be seen from the drop-down list box in Figure 7.8c. (All) removes existing criteria in that column. (Custom . . .) enables you to use the relational operators (=, >, <, >=, <=, or <>) within a criterion. (Top 10 . . .) displays the records with the top (or bottom) values in the field, and makes most sense if you sort the list to see the entries in sequence.

Advanced Filter Command

The ***Advanced Filter command*** extends the capabilities of the AutoFilter command in two important ways. It enables you to develop more complex criteria than are possible with the AutoFilter Command. It also enables you to filter the list in place and/or to copy (extract) the selected records to a separate area in the worksheet. The Advanced Filter command is illustrated in detail in the hands-on exercise that follows shortly.

Criteria Range

A ***criteria range*** is used with both the Advanced Filter command and the database functions that are discussed in the next section. It is defined independently of the list on which it operates and exists as a separate area in the worksheet. A criteria range must be at least two rows deep and one column wide as illustrated in Figure 7.9.

The simplest criteria range consists of two rows and as many columns as there are fields in the list. The first row contains the field names as they appear in the list. The second row holds the value(s) you are looking for. The criteria range in Figure 7.9a selects the employees who work in Atlanta; that is, it selects those records where the value of the Location Field is equal to Atlanta.

Multiple values in the same row are connected by an AND and require that the selected records meet *all* of the specified criteria. The criteria range in Figure 7.9b identifies the account reps in Atlanta; that is, it selects any record in which the Location field is Atlanta *and* the Title field is Account Rep. (Both fields must be spelled exactly; e.g., specifying Account Rep*s* instead of Account Rep will not return any employees.)

Values entered in multiple rows are connected by an OR in which the selected records satisfy *any* of the indicated criteria. The criteria range in Figure 7.9c will identify employees who work in Atlanta *or* whose title is Account Rep.

Relational operators may be used with date or numeric fields to return records within a designated range. The criteria range in Figure 7.9d selects the employees hired before January 1, 1993. The criteria range in Figure 7.9e returns employees whose salary is more than $40,000.

An upper and lower boundary may be established for the same field by repeating the field within the criteria range. This was done in Figure 7.9f, which returns all records in which the salary is more than $40,000 but less than $60,000.

First row contains field names

Second row contains filter condition

Name	Location	Title	Hire Date	Salary
	Atlanta			

(a) Employees Who Work in Atlanta

Multiple criteria in same row indicate both must be met

Name	Location	Title	Hire Date	Salary
	Atlanta	Account Rep		

(b) Account Reps Who Work in Atlanta (AND condition)

Multiple criteria in different rows indicate either may be met

Name	Location	Title	Hire Date	Salary
	Atlanta			
		Account Rep		

(c) Employees Who Work in Atlanta or Who Are Account Reps (OR condition)

Name	Location	Title	Hire Date	Salary
			<1/1/93	

(d) Employees Hired before January 1, 1993

Relational operators may be used with dates and numerical data

Name	Location	Title	Hire Date	Salary
				>$40,000

(e) Employees Who Earn More Than $40,000

Lower boundary

Upper boundary

Name	Location	Title	Hire Date	Salary	Salary
				>$40,000	<$60,000

(f) Employees Who Earn More Than $40,000 But Less Than $60,000

Selects records with no entry in Location field

Name	Location	Title	Hire Date	Salary
	=			

(g) Employees without a Location

Empty criteria row returns every record

Name	Location	Title	Hire Date	Salary

(h) All Employees (blank row)

FIGURE 7.9 The Criteria Range

The equal and unequal signs select records with empty and nonempty fields, respectively. An equal sign with nothing after it will return all records without an entry in the designated field; for example, the criteria range in Figure 7.9g selects any record that is missing a value for the Location field. An unequal sign (<>) with nothing after it will select all records with an entry in the field.

An empty row in the criteria range returns *every* record in the list, as shown in Figure 7.9h. All criteria are *case-insensitive* and return records with any combination of upper- and lowercase letters that match the entry. Remember, too, that all text entries must be spelled correctly in order to return the intended records.

THE IMPLIED WILD CARD

Any text entry within a criteria range is treated as though it were followed by the asterisk wild card; that is, *New* is the same as *New**. Both entries will return New York and New Jersey. To match a text entry exactly, begin with an equal sign, enter a quotation mark followed by another equal sign, the entry you are looking for, and the closing quotation mark—for example, = " =New" to return only the entries that say New.

Database Functions

The ***database functions*** DSUM, DAVERAGE, DMAX, DMIN, and DCOUNT operate on *selected* records in a list. These functions parallel the statistical functions (SUM, AVERAGE, MAX, MIN, and COUNT) except that they affect only records that satisfy the established criteria.

The summary statistics in Figure 7.10 are based on the salaries of the managers in the list, rather than the salaries of all employees. Each database function includes the criteria range in cells A17:E18 as one of its arguments, and thus limits the employees that are included to managers. The ***DAVERAGE function*** returns the average salary for just the managers. The ***DMAX*** and ***DMIN functions*** display the maximum and minimum salaries for the managers. The ***DSUM function*** computes the total salary for all the managers. The ***DCOUNT function*** indicates the number of managers.

Each database function has three arguments: the range for the list on which it is to operate, the field to be processed, and the criteria range. Consider, for example, the DAVERAGE function as shown below:

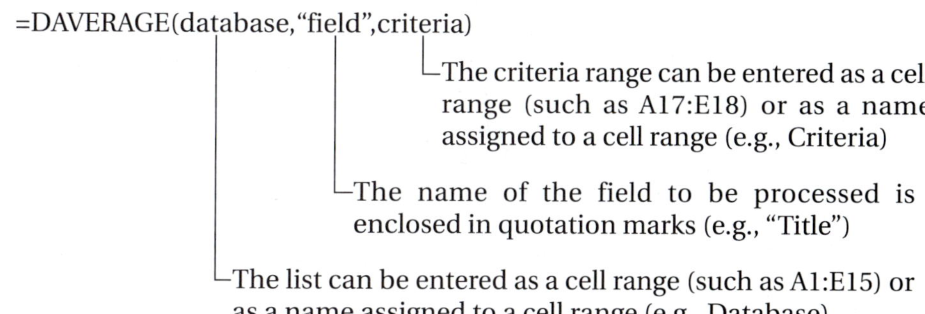

The entries in the criteria range may be changed at any time, in which case the values of the database functions are automatically recalculated. The other database functions have arguments identical to those used in the DAVERAGE function. The functions will adjust automatically if rows or columns are inserted or deleted within the specified range.

Criteria range is A17:E18

Criteria is Manager

Summary statistics for Managers

	A	B	C	D	E
1	Name	Location	Title	Hire Date	Salary
2	Adams	Atlanta	Trainee	11/24/98	$29,500
3	Adamson	Chicago	Manager	3/16/99	$52,000
4	Brown	Atlanta	Trainee	11/24/98	$28,500
5	Charles	Boston	Account Rep	3/16/99	$40,000
6	Coulter	Atlanta	Manager	11/24/98	$100,000
7	Elofson	Miami	Account Rep	10/31/01	$47,500
8	Gillenson	Miami	Account Rep	10/31/02	$55,000
9	James	Chicago	Account Rep	10/31/98	$42,500
10	Johnson	Chicago	Account Rep	10/31/99	$47,500
11	Manin	Boston	Account Rep	3/16/99	$49,500
12	Marder	Chicago	Account Rep	10/31/00	$38,500
13	Milgrom	Boston	Manager	3/16/99	$57,500
14	Rubin	Boston	Account Rep	3/16/99	$45,000
15	Smith	Atlanta	Account Rep	11/24/98	$65,000
16					
17	Name	Location	Title	Hire Date	Salary
18			Manager		
19					
20					
21			Summary Statistics		
22	Average Salary				$69,833
23	Maximum Salary				$100,000
24	Minimum Salary				$52,000
25	Total Salary				$209,500
26	Number of Employees				3

FIGURE 7.10 Database Functions

Insert Name Command

The ***Name command*** in the Insert menu equates a mnemonic name such as *EmployeeList* to a cell or cell range such as *A1:E15,* then enables you to use that name to reference the cell(s) in all subsequent commands. A name can be up to 255 characters in length, but must begin with a letter or an underscore. It can include upper- or lowercase letters, numbers, periods, and underscore characters but no blank spaces.

Once defined, range names will adjust automatically for insertions and/or deletions within the range. If, in the previous example, you were to delete row 4, the definition of *EmployeeList* would change to A1:E14. And, in similar fashion, if you were to insert a new column between columns B and C, the range would change to A1:F14.

A name can be used in any formula or function instead of a cell address; for example, =SALES–EXPENSES instead of =C1–C10, where Sales and Expenses have been defined as the names for cells C1 and C10, respectively. A name can also be entered into any dialog box where a cell range is required.

THE GO TO COMMAND

Names are frequently used in conjunction with the Go To command. Pull down the Edit menu and click Go To (or click the F5 key) to display a dialog box containing the names that have been defined within the workbook. Double click a name to move directly to the first cell in the associated range and simultaneously select the entire range.

SUBTOTALS

The ***Subtotals command*** uses a summary function (such as SUM, AVERAGE, or COUNT) to compute subtotals for groups of records within a list. The records are grouped according to the value in a specific field, such as location, as shown in Figure 7.11. The Subtotals command inserts a subtotal row into the list whenever the value of the designated field (location in this example) changes from one record to the next.

The subtotal for the Atlanta employees is inserted into the list as we go from the last employee in Atlanta to the first employee in Boston. In similar fashion, the subtotal for Boston is inserted into the list as we go from the last employee in Boston to the first employee in Chicago. A grand total is displayed after the last record. The list must be in sequence, according to the field on which the subtotals will be grouped, prior to executing the Subtotals command.

The summary information can be displayed with different levels of detail. Figure 7.11a displays the salary data for each employee (known as the detail lines), the subtotals for each location, and the grand total. Figure 7.11b suppresses the detail lines but shows both the subtotals and grand total. Figure 7.11c shows only the grand total. The worksheet in all three figures is said to be in outline format, as seen by the ***outline symbols*** at the extreme left of the application window.

The records within the list are grouped to compute the summary information. A plus sign indicates that the group has been collapsed, and that the detail information is suppressed. A minus sign indicates the opposite, namely that the group has been expanded and that the detail information is visible. You can click any plus or minus sign to expand or collapse that portion of the outline. You can also click the symbols (1, 2, or 3) above the plus or minus signs to collapse or expand the rows within the worksheet. Level one shows the least amount of detail and displays only the grand total. Level two includes the subtotals as well as the grand total. Level three includes the detail records, the subtotals, and the grand total.

Level buttons

Subtotal rows

	A	B	C	D
1	Name	Location	Title	Salary
2	Adams	Atlanta	Trainee	$29,500
3	Brown	Atlanta	Trainee	$28,500
4	Coulter	Atlanta	Manager	$100,000
5	Smith	Atlanta	Account Rep	$65,000
6		**Atlanta Total**		$223,000
7	Charles	Boston	Account Rep	$40,000
8	Manin	Boston	Account Rep	$49,500
9	Milgrom	Boston	Manager	$57,500
10	Rubin	Boston	Account Rep	$45,000
11		**Boston Total**		$192,000
12	Adamson	Chicago	Manager	$52,000
13	James	Chicago	Account Rep	$42,500
14	Johnson	Chicago	Account Rep	$47,500
15	Marder	Chicago	Account Rep	$38,500
16		**Chicago Total**		$180,500
17	Elofson	Miami	Account Rep	$47,500
18	Gillenson	Miami	Account Rep	$55,000
19		**Miami Total**		$102,500
20		**Grand Total**		$698,000

Minus sign indicates group has been expanded

(a) Detail Lines (level 3)

Plus sign indicates group has been collapsed

	A	B	C	D
1	Name	Location	Title	Salary
6		**Atlanta Total**		$223,000
11		**Boston Total**		$192,000
16		**Chicago Total**		$180,500
19		**Miami Total**		$102,500
20		**Grand Total**		$698,000

(b) Location Totals (level 2)

Only Grand Total is displayed

	A	B	C	D
1	Name	Location	Title	Salary
20		**Grand Total**		$698,000

(c) Grand Total (level 1)

FIGURE 7.11 Subtotals and Outlining

hands-on exercise

2 Data versus Information

Objective To sort a list on multiple keys; to use the AutoFilter and Advanced Filter commands; to define a named range; to use date arithmetic; to use the DSUM, DAVERAGE, DMAX, DMIN, and DCOUNT functions.

Step 1: Calculate the Years of Service

- Open the **Employee List Solution workbook** created in the previous exercise.
- Right click the **column heading** in **column D** to display a shortcut menu. Click **Insert.** The column of hire dates has been moved to column E. Click in **cell D1**. Type **Service** and press **Enter.**
- Click in **cell D2** and enter **=(Today()-E2)/365** as shown in Figure 7.12a. Press **Enter**; the years of service for the first employee are displayed in cell D2.
- Click in **cell D2**, then click the **Decrease Decimal button** on the Formatting toolbar several times to display the length of service with only one decimal.
- Drag the **fill handle** in cell D2 to the remaining cells in that column **(cells D3 through D15)** to compute the length of service for the remaining employees.

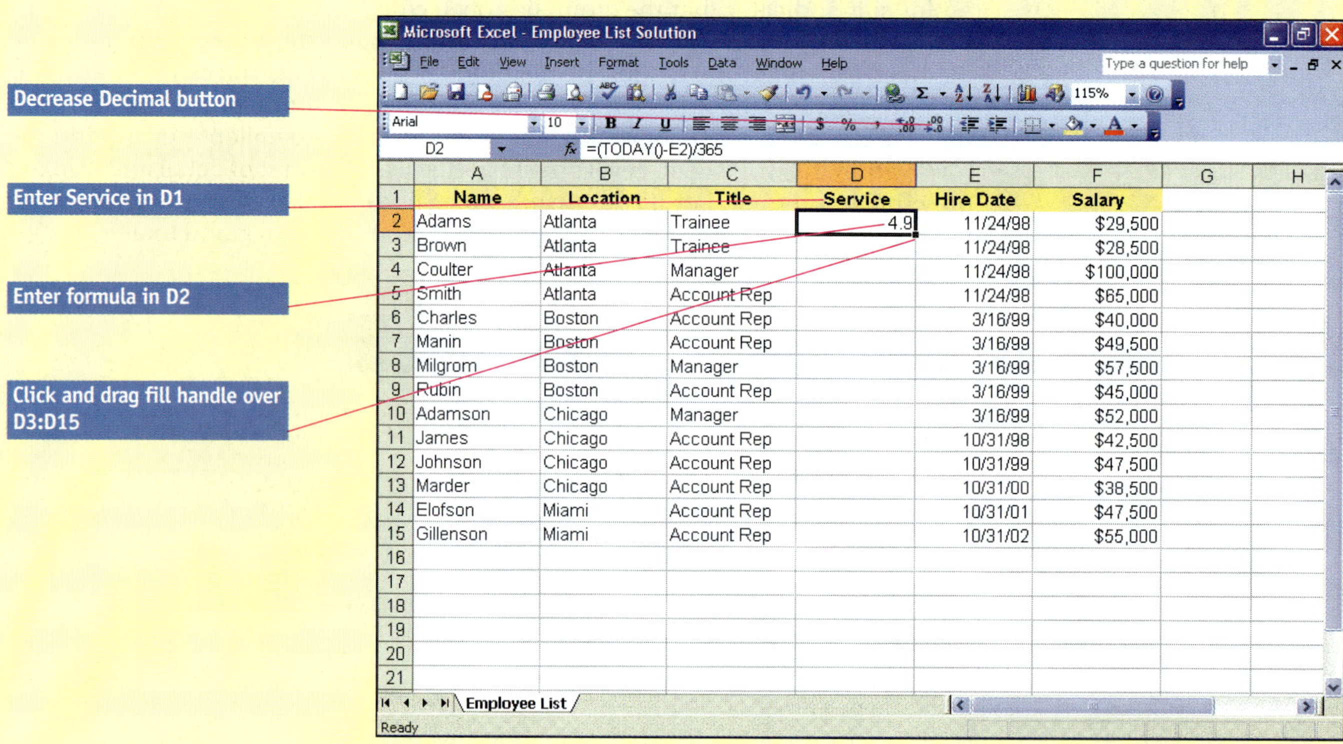

	A	B	C	D	E	F
1	Name	Location	Title	Service	Hire Date	Salary
2	Adams	Atlanta	Trainee	4.9	11/24/98	$29,500
3	Brown	Atlanta	Trainee		11/24/98	$28,500
4	Coulter	Atlanta	Manager		11/24/98	$100,000
5	Smith	Atlanta	Account Rep		11/24/98	$65,000
6	Charles	Boston	Account Rep		3/16/99	$40,000
7	Manin	Boston	Account Rep		3/16/99	$49,500
8	Milgrom	Boston	Manager		3/16/99	$57,500
9	Rubin	Boston	Account Rep		3/16/99	$45,000
10	Adamson	Chicago	Manager		3/16/99	$52,000
11	James	Chicago	Account Rep		10/31/98	$42,500
12	Johnson	Chicago	Account Rep		10/31/99	$47,500
13	Marder	Chicago	Account Rep		10/31/00	$38,500
14	Elofson	Miami	Account Rep		10/31/01	$47,500
15	Gillenson	Miami	Account Rep		10/31/02	$55,000

(a) Calculate the Years of Service (step 1)

FIGURE 7.12 Hands-on Exercise 2

DATE ARITHMETIC

Microsoft Excel stores a date as an integer (serial number) equivalent to the elapsed number of days since December 31, 1899; e.g., January 1, 1900 is stored as the number 1, January 2, 1900 as the number 2, and so on. This enables you to use dates in an arithmetic computation. An employee's service, for example, is computed by subtracting the hire date from the Today() function and dividing the result by 365.

Step 2: The AutoFilter Command

- Click a single cell anywhere within the list. Pull down the **Data menu**. Click the **Filter command**.
- Click **AutoFilter** from the resulting cascade menu to display the drop-down arrows to the right of each field name.
- Click the **drop-down arrow** next to **Title** to display the list of titles in Figure 7.12b. Click **Account Rep**.
- The display changes to show only those employees who meet the filter. The row numbers for the visible records are blue. The drop-down arrow for Title is also blue, indicating that it is part of the filter condition.
- Click the **drop-down arrow** next to **Location**. Click **Boston** to display only the employees in this city. The combination of the two filter conditions shows only the account reps in Boston.
- Click the **drop-down arrow** next to **Location** a second time. Click **(All)** to remove the filter condition on location. Only the account reps are displayed since the filter on Title is still in effect.
- Save the workbook.

Click a cell in the list

Click down arrow on Title field

Click Account Rep

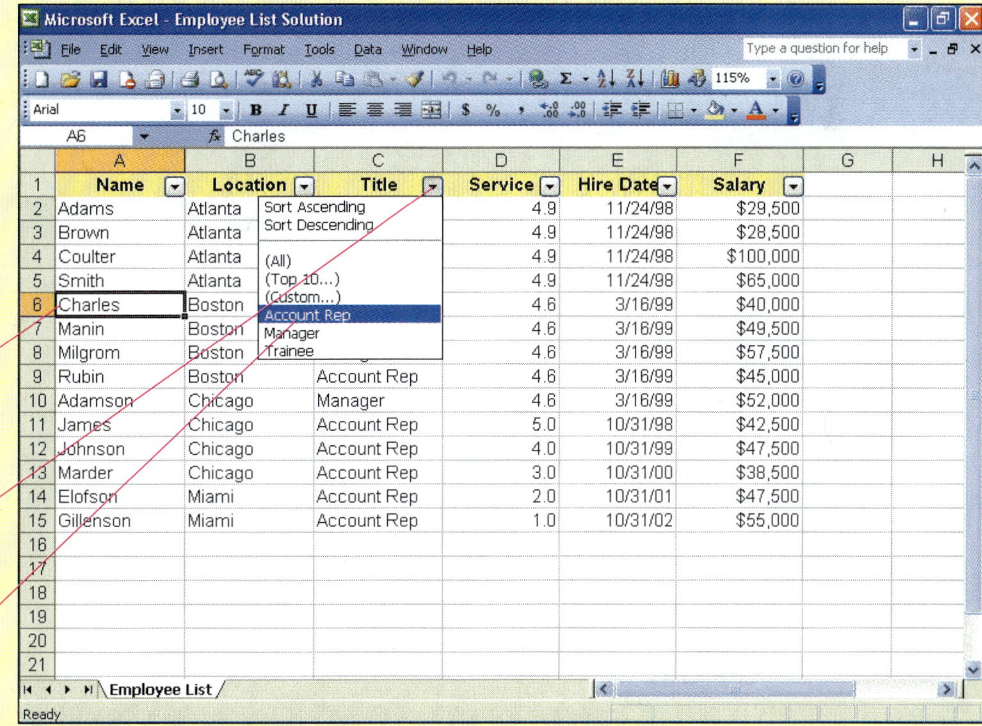

(b) The AutoFilter Command (step 2)

FIGURE 7.12 Hands-on Exercise 2 (*continued*)

THE TOP 10 AUTOFILTER

Use the Top 10 AutoFilter option to see the top (or bottom) 10, or for that matter any number of records in a list. Just turn the AutoFilter condition on, click the down arrow in the designated field, then click Top 10 to display the associated dialog box, where you specify the records you want to view. You can also specify a percentage, as opposed to a number—for example, the top 10% of the records in a list. See exercise 7 at the end of the chapter.

Step 3: The Custom AutoFilter Command

- Click the **drop-down arrow** next to **Salary** to display the list of salaries. Click **Custom** to display the dialog box in Figure 7.12c.
- Click the **arrow** in the leftmost drop-down list box for **Salary**, then click the **is greater than** as the relational operator.
- Click in the text box for the salary amount. Type **45000**. Click **OK**.
- The list changes to display only those employees whose title is account rep *and* who earn more than $45,000.
- Pull down the **Data menu**. Click **Filter**. Click **AutoFilter** to toggle the AutoFilter command off, which removes the arrows next to the field names and cancels all filter conditions. All of the records in the list are visible.
- Save the workbook.

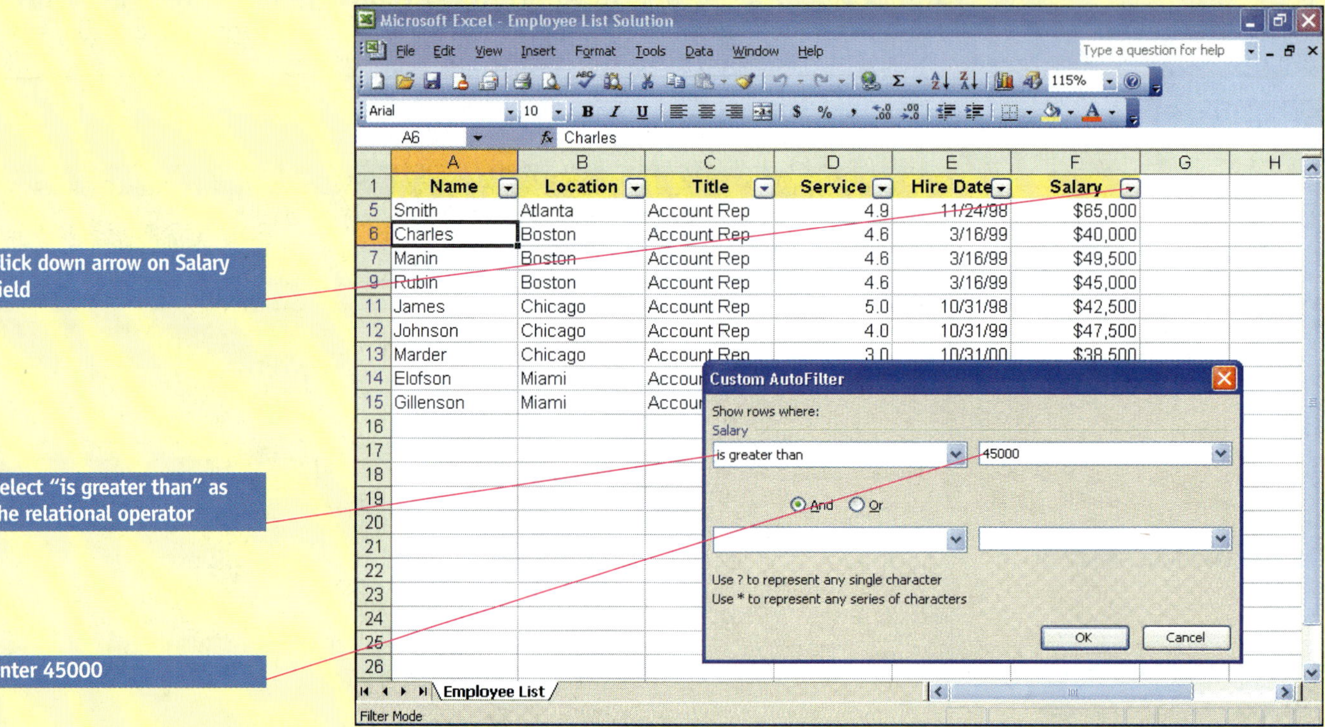

(c) The Custom AutoFilter Command (step 3)

FIGURE 7.12 Hands-on Exercise 2 (*continued*)

THE ANALYSIS TOOLPAK

Do you need to perform a statistical analysis on data within a worksheet? If so, you will want to use the Analysis ToolPak, one of several supplemental programs (or add-ins) that is included with Microsoft Excel. Pull down the Tools menu, click the Add-Ins command to display the associated dialog box, check the box for the Analysis ToolPak, then click OK to load the program. Pull down the Tools menu a second time, and then click the newly added Data Analysis command to access the tool pack, which provides access to a set of statistical functions to provide sophisticated analyses. See practice exercise 9 at the end of the chapter.

Step 4: The Advanced Filter Command

- The field names in the criteria range must be spelled exactly the same way as in the associated list. The best way to ensure that the names are identical is to copy the entries from the list to the criteria range.
- Click and drag to select **cells A1 through F1**. Click the **Copy button** on the Standard toolbar. A moving border appears around the selected cells. Click in **cell A17**. Click the **Paste button** on the Standard toolbar to complete the copy operation. Press **Esc** to cancel the moving border.
- Click in **cell C18**. Enter **Manager**. (Be sure you spell it correctly.)
- Click a single cell anywhere within the employee list. Pull down the **Data menu**. Click **Filter**. Click **Advanced Filter** from the resulting cascade menu to display the dialog box in Figure 7.12d. (The list range is already entered because you had selected a cell in the list prior to executing the command.)
- Click in the **Criteria Range** text box. Click in **cell A17** in the worksheet and drag the mouse to cell F18. Release the mouse. A moving border appears around these cells in the worksheet, and the corresponding cell reference is entered in the dialog box.
- Check that the **option button** to Filter the list, in-place is selected. Click **OK**. The display changes to show just the managers; that is, only rows 4, 8, and 10 are visible.
- Click in **cell B18**. Type **Atlanta**. Press **Enter**.
- Pull down the **Data menu**. Click **Filter**. Click **Advanced Filter**. The Advanced Filter dialog box already has the cell references for the list and criteria ranges.
- Click **OK**. The display changes to show just the manager in Atlanta; that is, only row 4 is visible.
- Pull down the **Data menu**. Click **Filter**. Click **Show All** to remove the filter condition. The entire list is visible.

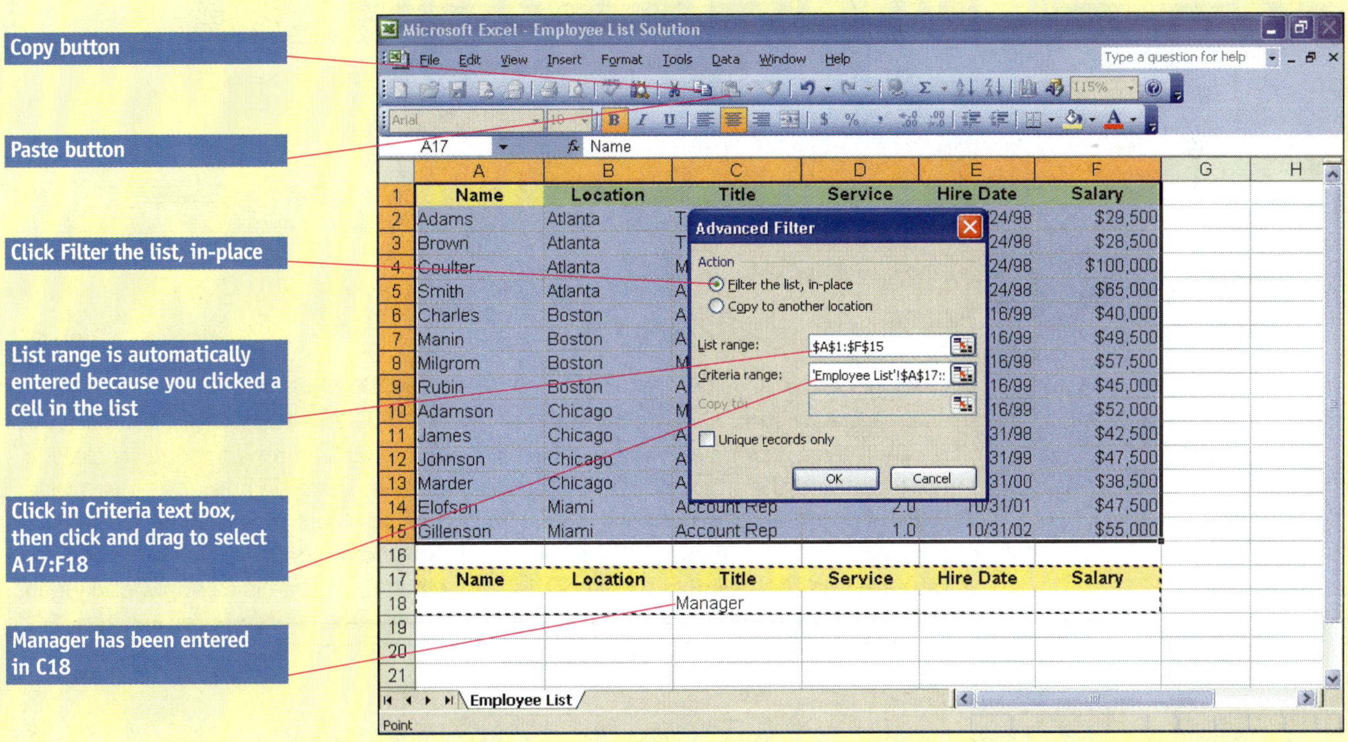

(d) The Advanced Filter Command (step 4)

FIGURE 7.12 Hands-on Exercise 2 (*continued*)

Step 5: The Insert Name Command

- Click and drag to select **cells A1 through F15** as shown in Figure 7.12e.
- Pull down the **Insert menu**. Click **Name**. Click **Define**. Type **Database** in the Names in workbook text box. Click **OK**.
- Pull down the **Edit menu** and click **Go To** (or press the **F5 key**) to display the Go To dialog box. There are two names in the box: **Database**, which you just defined, and **Criteria**, which was defined automatically when you specified the criteria range in step 4.
- Double click **Criteria** to select the criteria range **(cells A17 through F18)**. Click elsewhere in the worksheet to deselect the cells.
- Save the workbook.

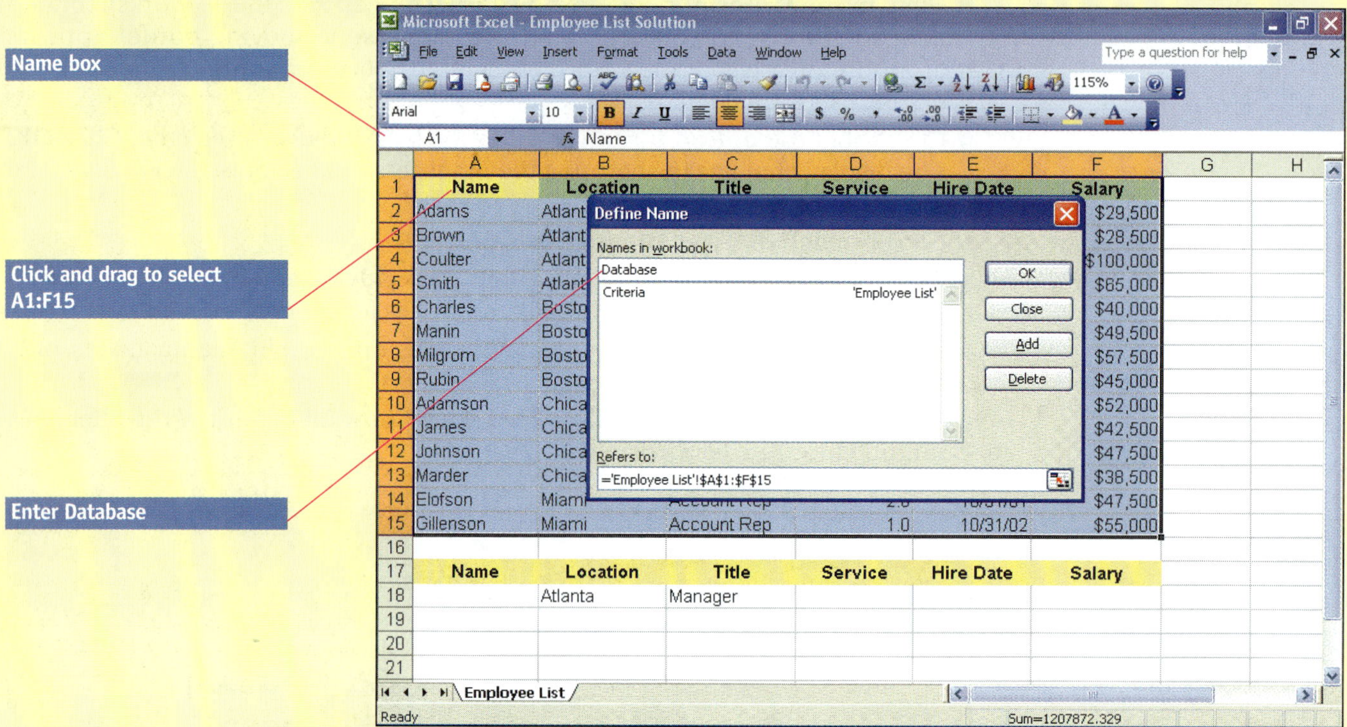

(e) The Insert Name Command (step 5)

FIGURE 7.12 Hands-on Exercise 2 (*continued*)

THE NAME BOX

Use the Name box on the formula bar to select a cell or named range by clicking in the box and then typing the appropriate cell reference or name. You can also click the drop-down arrow next to the Name box to select a named range from a drop-down list. And, finally, you can use the Name box to define a named range, by first selecting the cell(s) in the worksheet to which the name is to apply, clicking in the Name box to enter the range name, and then pressing the Enter key.

Step 6: Database Functions

- Click in **cell A21**, type **Summary Statistics**, press the **Enter key**, then click and drag to select cells **A21 through F21**.
- Pull down the **Format menu**, click **Cells**, click the **Alignment tab**, then select **Center Across Selection** as the horizontal alignment. Click **OK**. Change the fill color for this range to **light yellow**.
- Enter the labels for **cells A22 through A26** as shown in Figure 7.12f.
- Click in **cell B18**. Press the **Del key**. The criteria range is now set to select only managers.
- Click in **cell F22**. Click the **Insert Function button** on the formula bar to display the dialog box in Figure 7.12f.
- Select **Database** from the Category list box, select **DAVERAGE** as the function name, then click **OK**.

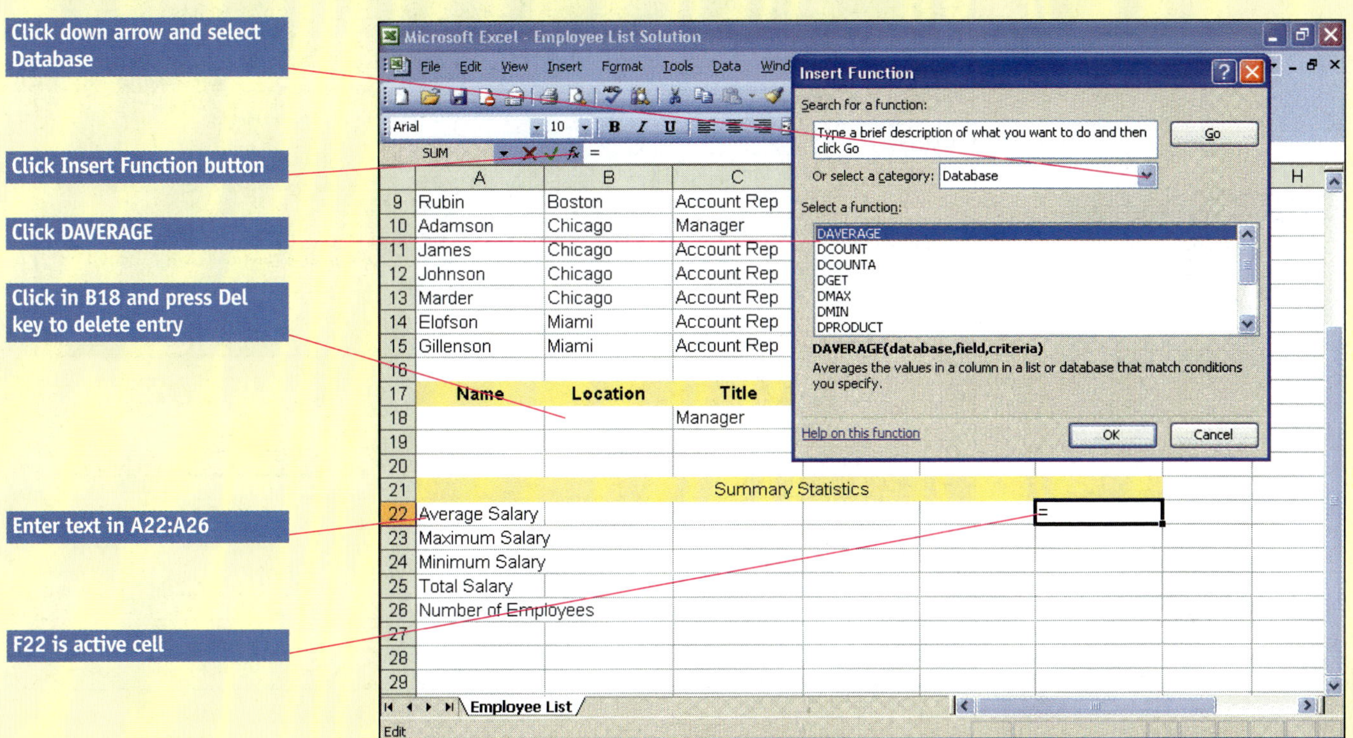

(f) Database Functions (step 6)

FIGURE 7.12 Hands-on Exercise 2 (*continued*)

HIDE A COLUMN

An individual's hire date and length of service convey essentially the same information, and thus there is no need to display both columns. Point to the column heading of the field you wish to hide, then click the right mouse button to select the column and display a shortcut menu. Click the Hide command, and the column is no longer visible (although it remains in the worksheet). To display (unhide) a column, click and drag the adjacent column headings on both sides, click the right mouse button to display a shortcut menu, then click the Unhide command.

Step 7: The DAVERAGE Function

- Click the **Database** text box in the dialog box as shown in Figure 7.12g. Type **Database** (the range name defined in step 5), which references the employee list.
- Click the **Field** text box. Type **"Salary"** (you must include the quotation marks), which is the name of the field (column name) within the list that you want to average.
- Click the **Criteria** text box. Type **Criteria** (the range name automatically assigned to the criteria range during the Advanced Filter operation). The dialog box displays the computed value of 69833.33333.
- Click **OK** to enter the DAVERAGE function into the worksheet.
- Save the workbook.

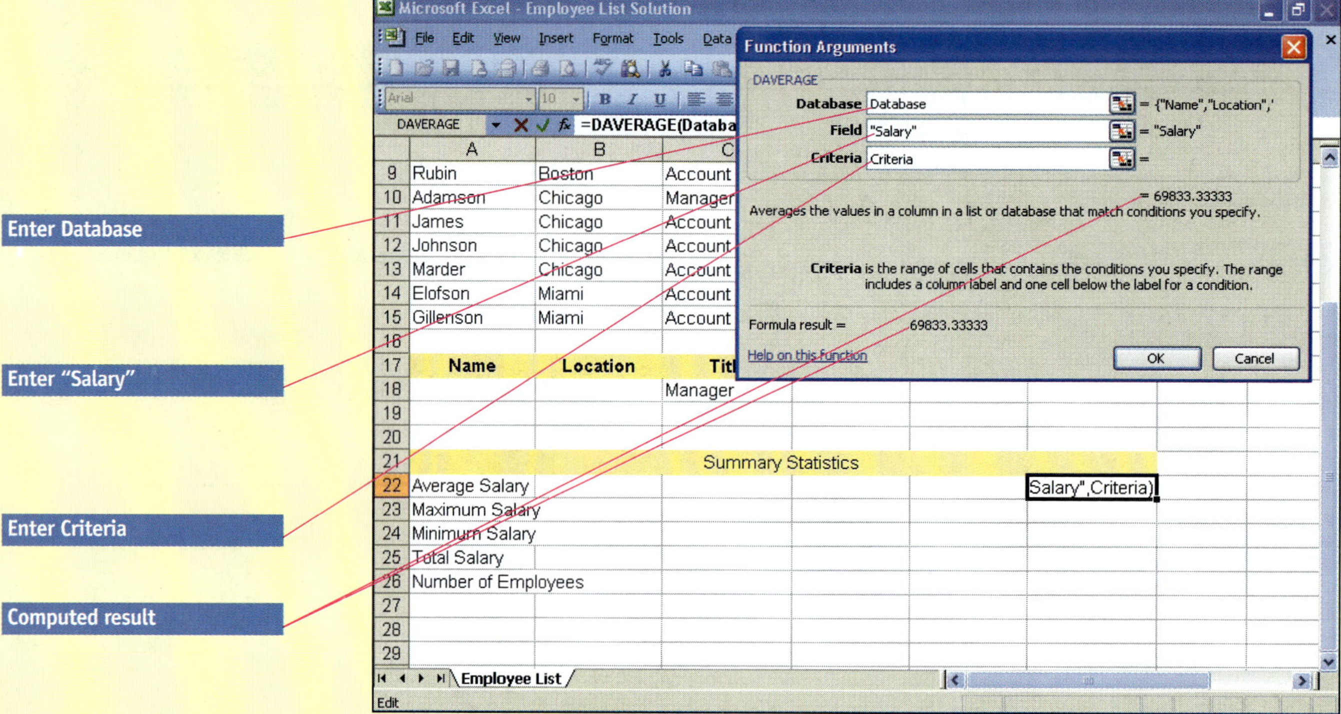

(g) The DAVERAGE Function (step 7)

FIGURE 7.12 Hands-on Exercise 2 (*continued*)

DIVISION BY ZERO—#DIV/0—AND HOW TO AVOID IT

The DAVERAGE function displays a division by zero error message if there are no records that meet the specified criteria. You can hide the error message, however, by using conditional formatting to display the message in white, which renders it invisible. Click in the cell containing the DAVERAGE function, pull down the Format menu, click Conditional formatting, and then click the drop-down arrow in the left list box to select Formula Is. Click in the box to the right and type = ISERROR(F22), where F22 is the cell containing the DAVERAGE function. Click the Format button, click Font, and change the color to white. The message is in the cell but you cannot see it.

Step 8: The DMAX, DMIN, DSUM, and DCOUNT Functions

- Enter the DMAX, DMIN, DSUM, and DCOUNT functions in cells F23 through F26, respectively. You can use the **Insert Function button** to enter each function individually, *or* you can copy the DAVERAGE function and edit appropriately:
  - Click in **cell F22**. Drag the **fill handle** to **cells F23 through F26** to copy the DAVERAGE function to these cells.
  - Double click in **cell F23** to edit the contents of this cell, then click within the displayed formula to substitute **DMAX** for DAVERAGE. Press **Enter**.
  - Double click in the remaining cells and edit them appropriately.
- The computed values (except for the DCOUNT function, which has a computed value of 3) are shown in Figure 7.12h.
- Format **cells F22 through F25**, to currency with no decimals.
- Click and drag the border between columns F and G to widen column F as necessary. Save the workbook.

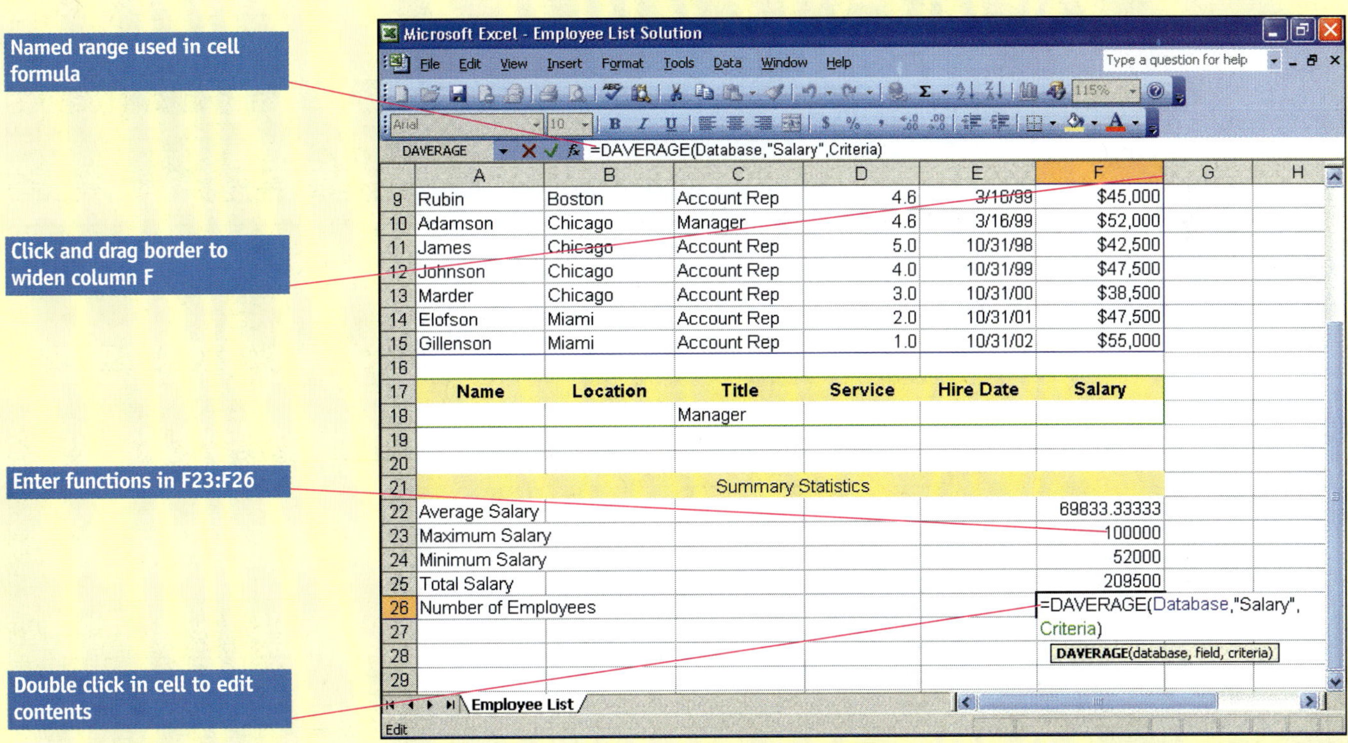

(h) The DMAX, DMIN, DSUM, DCOUNT Functions (step 8)

FIGURE 7.12 Hands-on Exercise 2 (*continued*)

IMPORT DATA FROM ACCESS

The data in a worksheet can be imported from an Access database. Pull down the Data menu, click the Import External Data command, then click Import Data to display the Select Data Source dialog box. Use the Look In list box to locate the folder containing the database and choose Access Databases as the file type. Select the database, then click the Open command to bring the Access table(s) into an Excel workbook. (See Excel and Access mini case at the end of the chapter.)

Step 9: Change the Criteria

- Click in the **Name box**. Type **B18** and press **Enter** to make cell B18 the active cell. Type **Chicago** to change the criteria to Chicago managers. Press **Enter**.
- The values displayed by the DAVERAGE, DMIN, DMAX, and DSUM functions change to $52,000, reflecting the one employee (Adamson) who meets the current criteria (a manager in Chicago). The value displayed by the DCOUNT function changes to 1 to indicate one employee as shown in Figure 7.12i.
- Click in **cell C18**. Press the **Del key**.
- The average salary changes to $45,125, reflecting all employees in Chicago.
- Click in **cell B18**. Press the **Del key**.
- The criteria range is now empty. The DAVERAGE function displays $49,857, which is the average salary of all employees in the database.
- Click in **cell C18**. Type **Manager** and press the **Enter key**. The average salary is $69,833, the average salary for all managers.
- Save the workbook.

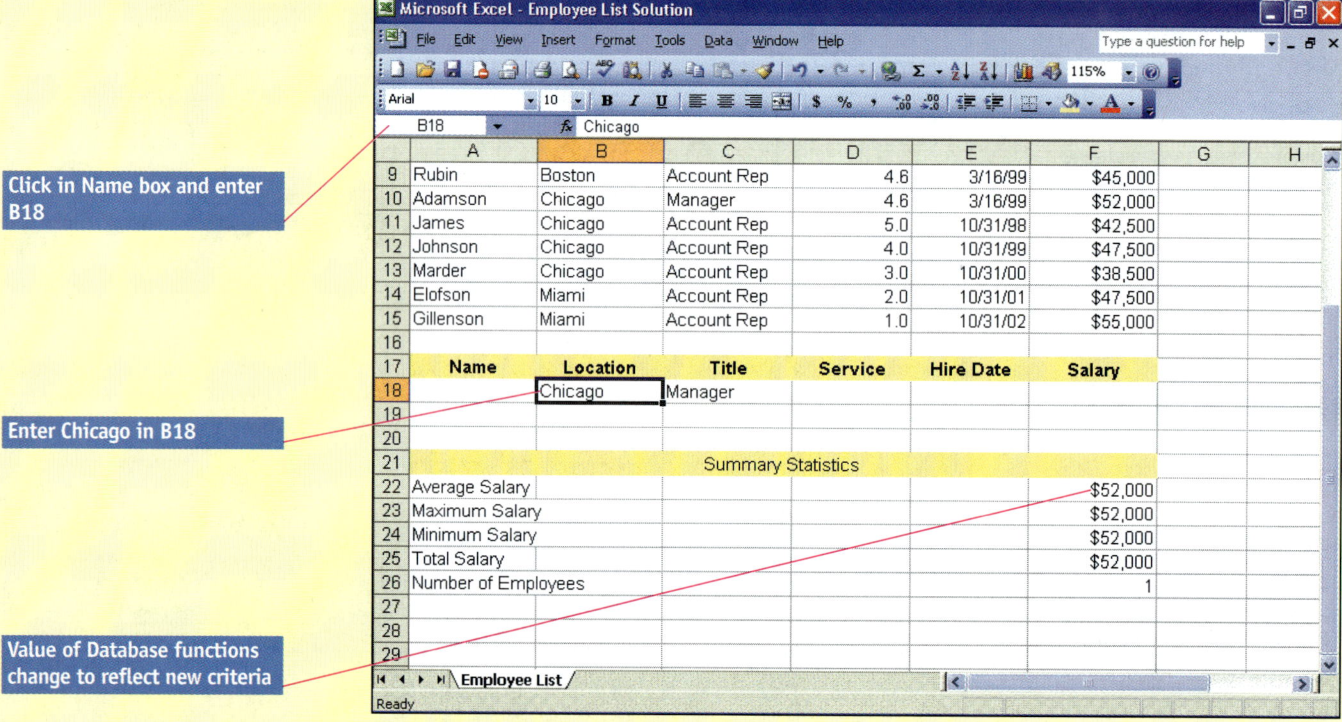

(i) Change the Criteria (step 9)

FIGURE 7.12 Hands-on Exercise 2 (*continued*)

FILTER THE LIST IN PLACE

Use the Advanced Filter command to filter the list in place and display the records that meet the current criteria. Click anywhere in the list, pull down the Data menu, click the Filter command, then choose Advanced Filter to display the Advanced Filter dialog box. Click the option button to filter the list in place, then click OK to display the selected records. You have to execute this command each time the criteria change.

Step 10: Create the Subtotals

- A list must be in sequence prior to computing the subtotals. Click any cell in the list in **Column C**, the column containing the employee titles, then click the **Sort Ascending button** on the Standard toolbar. The employees should be sequenced according to title as shown in Figure 7.12j.
- Click in any cell in column F, the column containing the field for which you want subtotals. Pull down the **Data menu** and click the **Subtotals command**. Click the **drop-down arrow** in the **At each change in** list box. Click **Title** to create a subtotal whenever there is a change in title. Set the other options to match the dialog box in Figure 7.12j. Click **OK** to create the subtotals.
- You should see the three subtotals, one for each title, followed by the grand total for the company. The total for the Account Reps should appear first, and it is equal to $430,500.
- The total for managers is $209,500 and matches the value obtained by the DSUM command.
- Save the workbook.

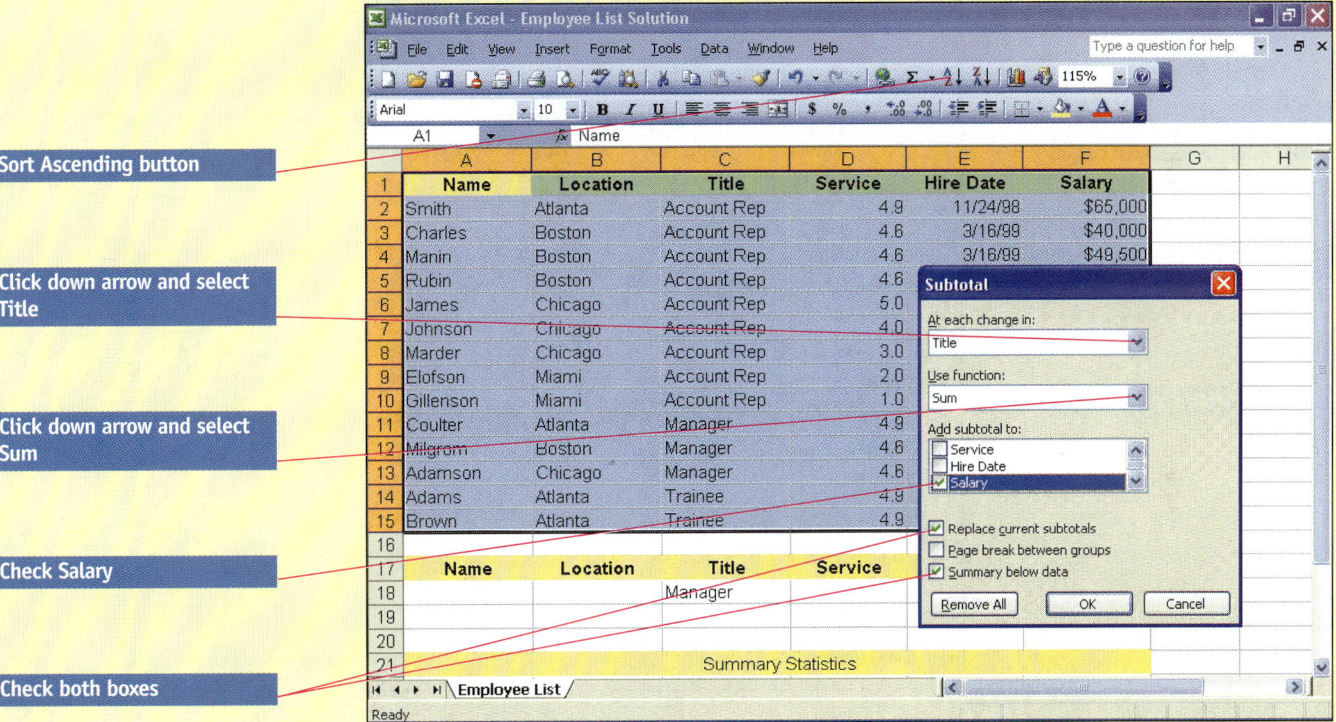

(j) Create the Subtotals (step 10)

FIGURE 7.12 Hands-on Exercise 2 (*continued*)

TWO SETS OF SUBTOTALS

You can obtain multiple sets of subtotals in the same list, provided you do the operations in the correct sequence. First, sort the list according to the sequence you want, for example, by title within location. Click in the list, and compute the subtotals based on the primary key (location in this example). Click on the list a second time and compute the subtotals based on the secondary key (title in this example), but clear the check box to replace the current subtotals. You will see the subtotal for each title in the first location, followed by the subtotal for that location, and so on.

Step 11: Collapse and Expand the Subtotals

- The vertical lines at the left of the worksheet indicate how the data is aggregated within the list. Click the **minus sign** corresponding to the total for the Account Reps.
- The minus sign changes to a plus sign, and the detail lines (the names of the Account Reps) disappear from the worksheet as shown in Figure 7.12k. Click the **plus sign** next to the Account Rep total, and you see the detailed information for each Account Rep.
- Click the **level 2 button** (under the Name box) to suppress the detail lines for all employees. The list collapses to display the subtotals and grand total.
- Click the **level 1 button** to suppress the subtotals. The list collapses further to display only the grand total. Click the **level 3 button** to restore the detail lines and subtotals.
- Click the **Print button** to print the list with the subtotals. Close the workbook. Exit Excel if you do not want to continue with the next exercise at this time.

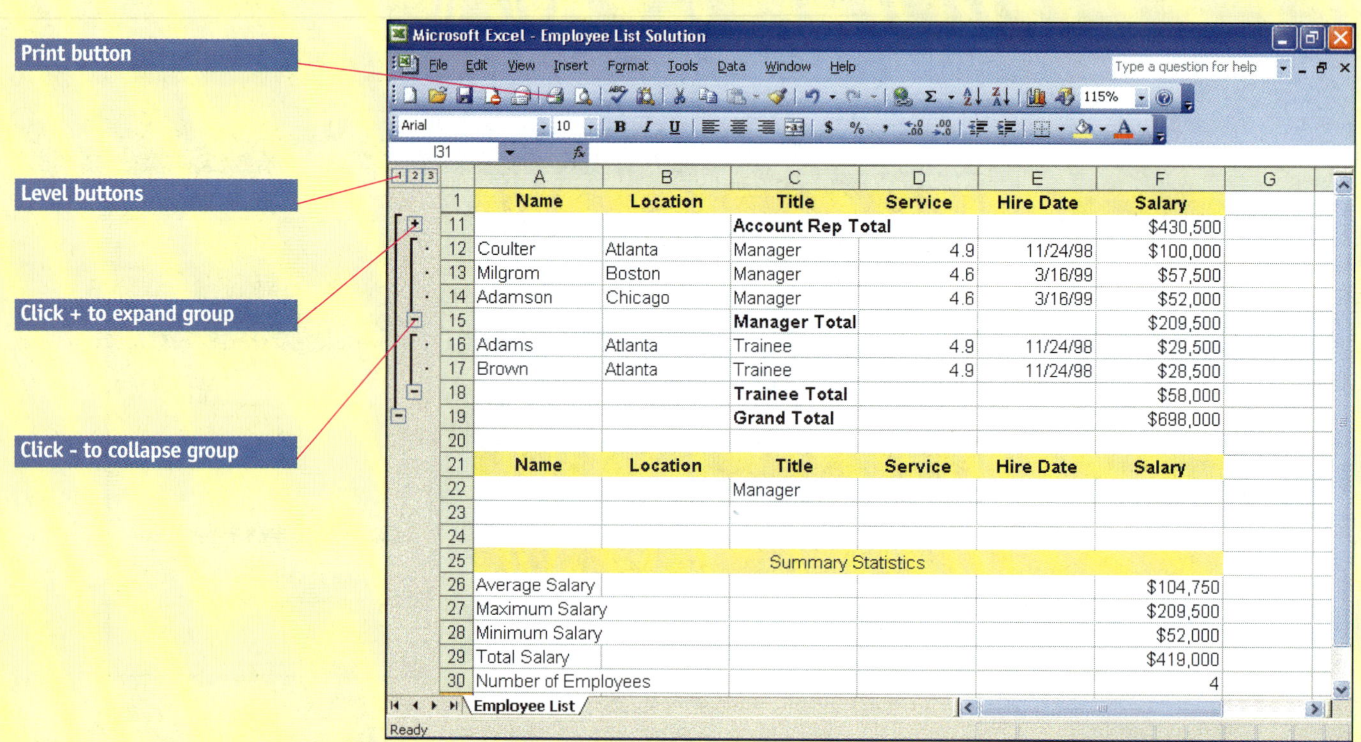

(k) Collapse and Expand the Subtotals (step 11)

FIGURE 7.12 Hands-on Exercise 2 (*continued*)

INCOMPATIBLE FUNCTIONS AND SUBTOTALS

The Subtotals command introduces additional rows within a list, which are then double counted in the computations of the database functions. In this example the total salary for all managers (as computed by the DSUM function in cell F29) is $419,000, when it should be $209,500. This is due to the insertion of row 15, which contains 'Manager Total' in cell C15, which falsely counts this row as a Manager. One way to 'correct' the problem is to move the text entries in cells C11, C15, C18, and C19 to the corresponding cells in column D.

PIVOT TABLES AND PIVOT CHARTS

A ***pivot table*** provides the ultimate flexibility in data analysis. It divides the records in a list into categories, then computes summary statistics for those categories. Pivot tables are illustrated in conjunction with the data in Figure 7.13 that displays sales information for a hypothetical advertising agency. Each record in the list in Figure 7.13a displays the name of the sales representative, the quarter in which the sale was recorded, the type of media, and the amount of the sale.

The pivot table in Figure 7.13b shows the total sales for each Media–Sales Rep combination. Look closely and you will see four shaded buttons, each of which corresponds to a different area in the table. The Media and Sales Rep buttons are in the row and column areas, respectively. Thus, each row in the pivot table displays the data for a different media type (magazine, radio, or TV), whereas each column displays data for a different sales representative. The Quarter button in the page area provides a third dimension. The value in the drop-down list box indicates that all of the records in the underlying worksheet are used to compute the totals in the body of the table. You can, however, display different pages corresponding to the totals in the first, second, third, or fourth quarters. You can also click the arrows next to the other buttons to suppress selected values for the media type or sales representative.

The best feature about a pivot table is its flexibility because you can change the orientation to provide a different analysis of the associated data. Figure 7.13c, for example, displays an alternate version of the pivot table in which the fields have been rearranged to show the total for each combination of quarter and sales representative. You go from one pivot table to another simply by clicking and dragging the buttons corresponding to the field names to different positions.

You can also change the means of computation within the data area. Both of the pivot tables in Figure 7.13 use the Sum function, but you can choose other functions such as Average, Minimum, Maximum, or Count. You can also change the formatting of any element in the table. More importantly, pivot tables are dynamic in that they reflect changes to the underlying worksheet. Thus, you can add, edit, or delete records in the associated list and see the results in the pivot table, provided you execute the ***Refresh command*** to update the pivot table.

The ***Pivot Table Wizard*** is used to create the initial pivot table in conjunction with an optional pivot chart. The ***pivot chart*** in Figure 7.14, for example, corresponds to the pivot table in Figure 7.13b, and at first glance, it resembles any other Excel chart. Look closely, however, and you will see shaded buttons similar to those in the pivot table, enabling you to change the chart by dragging the buttons to different areas. Reverse the position of the Media and Sales Rep buttons, for example, and you have a completely different chart. Any changes to the chart are reflected in the underlying pivot table and vice versa.

Drop-down arrows next to each button on the pivot chart let you display selected values. Click either arrow to display a drop-down list in which you select the values you want to appear in the chart. You could, for example, click the drop-down arrow next to the Sales Rep field and clear the name of any sales rep to remove his/her data from the chart.

Pivot tables may also be saved as Web pages with full interactivity as shown in Figure 7.15. The Address bar indicates that you are viewing a Web document (note the mht extension), as opposed to an Excel workbook. As with an ordinary pivot table, you can pivot the table within the Web page by repositioning the buttons for the row, column, and page fields. The plus and minus next to the various categories enable you to show or hide the detailed information. (The interactivity extends to Netscape as well as Internet Explorer, provided that you install the Office Web components.)

Pivot tables are one of the best-kept secrets in Excel, even though they have been available in the last several releases of Excel. (Pivot charts were introduced in Excel 2000.) Be sure to share this capability with your friends and colleagues.

	A	B	C	D
1	**Sales Rep**	**Quarter**	**Media**	**Amount**
2	Alice	1st quarter	TV	$15,000
3	Alice	1st quarter	Radio	$4,000
4	Alice	2nd quarter	Magazine	$2,000
5	Alice	2nd quarter	Radio	$4,000
6	Alice	3rd quarter	Radio	$2,000
7	Alice	4th quarter	Radio	$4,000
8	Alice	4th quarter	Radio	$1,000
9	Bob	1st quarter	Magazine	$2,000
10	Bob	1st quarter	Radio	$1,000
11	Bob	2nd quarter	Radio	$4,000
12	Bob	3rd quarter	TV	$10,000
13	Bob	4th quarter	Magazine	$10,000
14	Bob	4th quarter	Magazine	$12,000
15	Bob	4th quarter	Radio	$1,000
16	Bob	4th quarter	Magazine	$7,000

	A	B	C	D
17	Carol	1st quarter	Radio	$4,000
18	Carol	2nd quarter	Magazine	$2,000
19	Carol	2nd quarter	Magazine	$7,000
20	Carol	2nd quarter	TV	$10,000
21	Carol	3rd quarter	TV	$8,000
22	Carol	3rd quarter	TV	$18,000
23	Carol	4th quarter	TV	$13,000
24	Ted	1st quarter	Radio	$2,000
25	Ted	2nd quarter	TV	$6,000
26	Ted	2nd quarter	TV	$6,000
27	Ted	3rd quarter	TV	$20,000
28	Ted	3rd quarter	Magazine	$15,000
29	Ted	3rd quarter	Magazine	$2,000
30	Ted	4th quarter	TV	$13,000
31	Ted	4th quarter	TV	$15,000

(a) Sales Data (Excel list)

Quarter is in page area

Computation is Sum of Amount

Media is in row area

Click down arrow to show data for all quarters or to select a specific quarter

Sales Rep is in column area

	A	B	C	D	E	F
1						
2	Quarter	(All)				
3						
4	Sum of Amount	Sales Rep				
5	Media	Alice	Bob	Carol	Ted	Grand Total
6	Magazine	$2,000	$31,000	$9,000	$17,000	$59,000
7	Radio	$15,000	$6,000	$4,000	$2,000	$27,000
8	TV	$15,000	$10,000	$49,000	$60,000	$134,000
9	Grand Total	$32,000	$47,000	$62,000	$79,000	$220,000

(b) Analysis by Media Type and Sales Representative

Media is in page area

Sales Rep is in row area

Quarter is in column area

	A	B	C	D	E	F
1						
2	Media	(All)				
3						
4	Sum of Amount	Quarter				
5	Sales Rep	1st quarter	2nd quarter	3rd quarter	4th quarter	Grand Total
6	Alice	$19,000	$6,000	$2,000	$5,000	$32,000
7	Bob	$3,000	$4,000	$10,000	$30,000	$47,000
8	Carol	$4,000	$19,000	$26,000	$13,000	$62,000
9	Ted	$2,000	$12,000	$37,000	$28,000	$79,000
10	Grand Total	$28,000	$41,000	$75,000	$76,000	$220,000

(c) Analysis by Sales Representative and Quarter

FIGURE 7.13 Pivot Tables

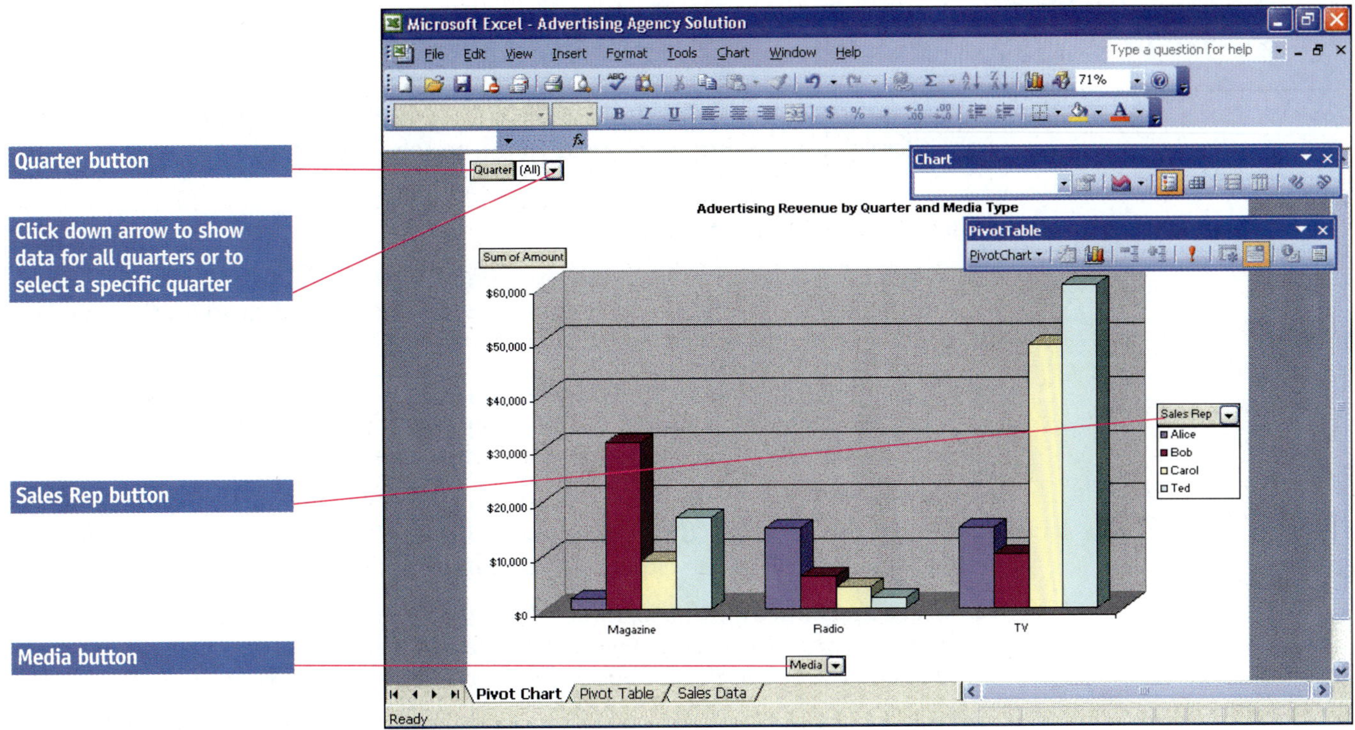

FIGURE 7.14 A Pivot Chart

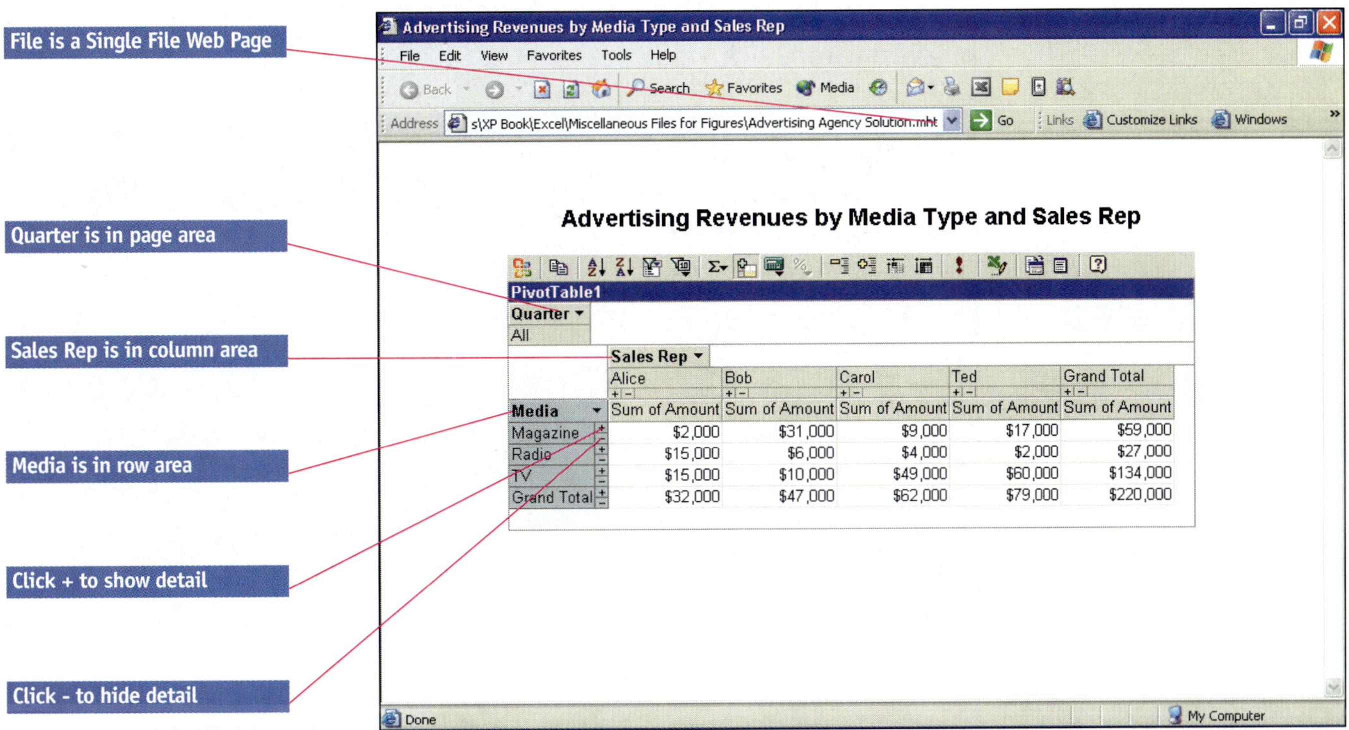

	Sales Rep				
	Alice	Bob	Carol	Ted	Grand Total
Media	Sum of Amount	Sum of Amount	Sum of Amount	Sum of Amount	Sum of Amount
Magazine	$2,000	$31,000	$9,000	$17,000	$59,000
Radio	$15,000	$6,000	$4,000	$2,000	$27,000
TV	$15,000	$10,000	$49,000	$60,000	$134,000
Grand Total	$32,000	$47,000	$62,000	$79,000	$220,000

FIGURE 7.15 Pivot Tables on the Web

hands-on exercise

3 Pivot Tables and Pivot Charts

Objective To create a pivot table and pivot chart; to create a Web page based on the pivot table. Use Figure 7.16 as a guide in the exercise.

Step 1: Start the Pivot Table Wizard

- Start Excel. Open the **Advertising Agency workbook** in the **Exploring Excel folder**. Save the workbook as **Advertising Agency Solution** so that you will be able to return to the original workbook.
- The workbook contains a list of sales records for the advertising agency. Each record displays the name of the sales representative, the quarter in which the sale was recorded, the media type, and the amount of the sale.
- Click anywhere in the list of sales data. Pull down the **Data menu**. Click **PivotTable and PivotChart Report** to start the Pivot Table Wizard as shown in Figure 7.16a. Close the Office Assistant if necessary.
- Select the same options as in our figure. The pivot table will be created from data in a Microsoft Excel List or Database. In addition, you want to create a Pivot Chart report (that includes the Pivot Table). Click **Next**.
- Cells A1 through D31 have been selected automatically as the basis of the pivot table. Click **Next**.
- The option button to put the pivot table into a new worksheet is already selected. Click **Finish**. Two additional sheets have been added to the workbook, but the pivot table and chart area are not yet complete.
- Save the workbook.

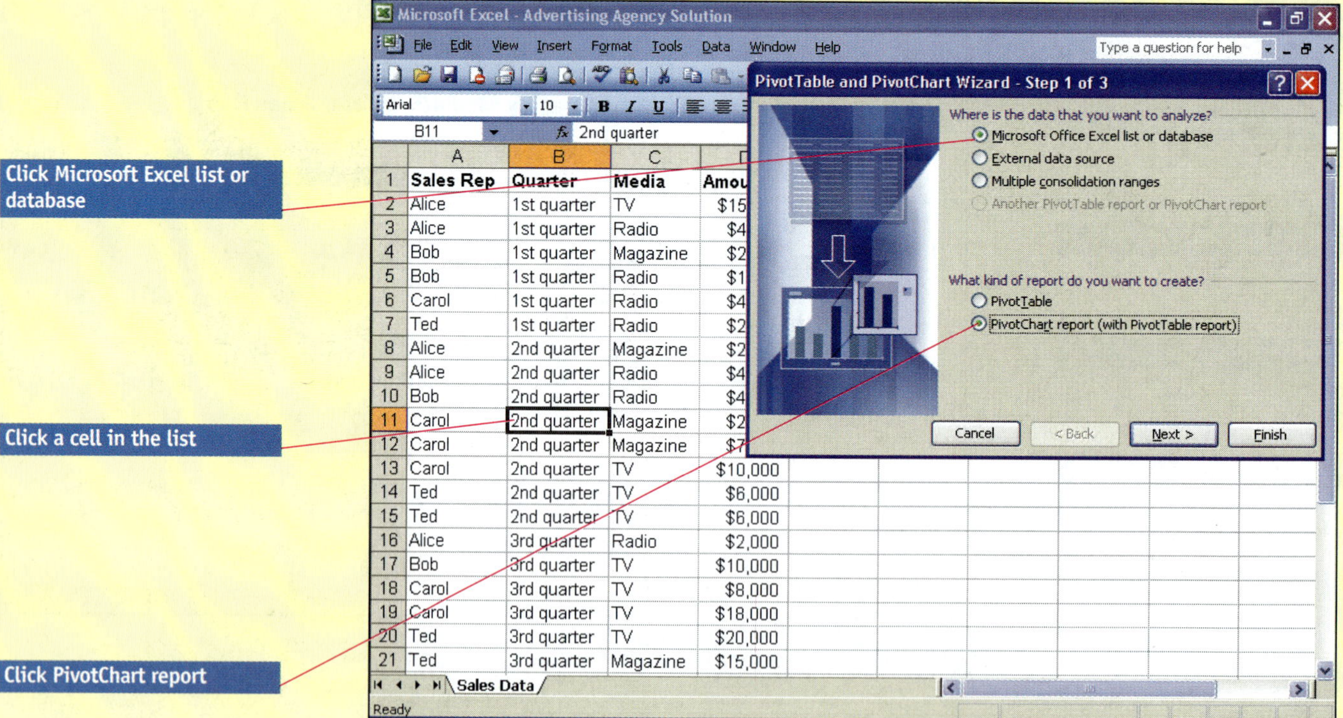

(a) Start the Pivot Table Wizard (step 1)

FIGURE 7.16 Hands-on Exercise 3

Step 2: Complete the Pivot Table

- Click the tab that takes you to the new worksheet (Sheet1 in our workbook). Your screen should be similar to Figure 7.16b. Complete the pivot table as follows:
  - Click the **Media field button** and drag it to the row area.
  - Click the **Sales Rep button** and drag it to the column area.
  - Click the **Quarter field button** and drag it to the page area.
  - Click the **Amount field button** and drag it to the data area.
- You should see the total sales for each sales representative for each type of media within a pivot table.
- Rename the worksheets so that they are more descriptive of their contents. Double click the **Sheet1 tab** (the worksheet that contains the pivot table) to select the name of the sheet. Type **Pivot Table** as the new name, and press **enter**.
- Double click the tab for the **Chart1** worksheet and change its name to **Pivot Chart** in similar fashion.
- Save the workbook.

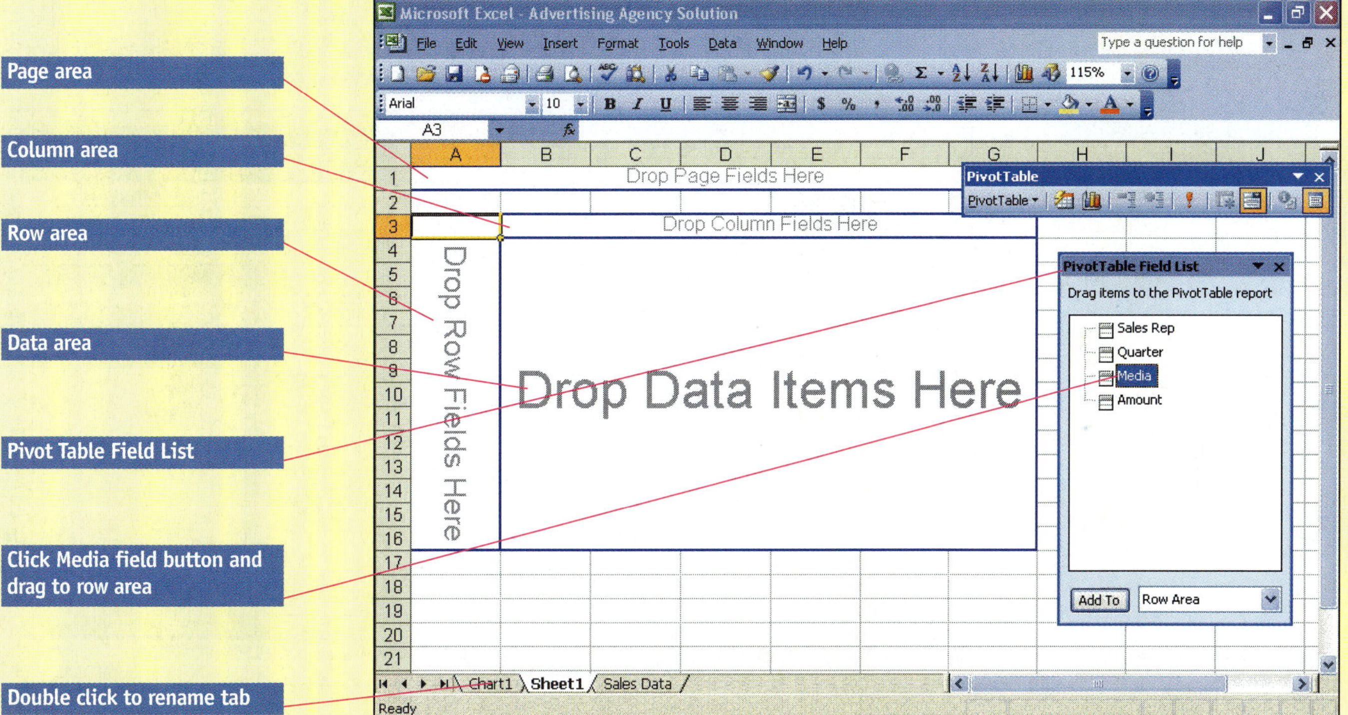

(b) Complete the Pivot Table (step 2)

FIGURE 7.16 Hands-on Exercise 3 (*continued*)

THE PAGE FIELD

A page field adds a third dimension to a pivot table. Unlike items in the row and column fields, however, the items in a page field are displayed one at a time. Creating a page field on Quarter, for example, lets you view the data for each quarter separately, by clicking the drop-down arrow on the page field list box, then clicking the appropriate quarter.

Step 3: Modify the Sales Data

- You will replace Bob's name within the list of transactions with your own name. Click the **Sales Data tab** to return to the underlying worksheet. Pull down the **Edit menu** and click the **Replace command** to display the Find and Replace dialog box.
- Enter **Bob** in the Find What dialog box, type **Your Name** (first and last) in the Replace With dialog box, then click the **Replace All button**. Click **OK** after the replacements have been made. Close the Find and Replace dialog box.
- Click the **Pivot Table tab** to return to the pivot table as shown in Figure 7.16c. The name change is not yet reflected in the pivot table because the table must be manually refreshed whenever the underlying data changes.
- Click anywhere in the pivot table, then click the **Refresh Data button** on the Pivot Table toolbar to update the pivot table. (You must click the Refresh button to update the pivot table whenever the underlying data changes.) You should see your name as one of the sales representatives.
- Save the workbook.

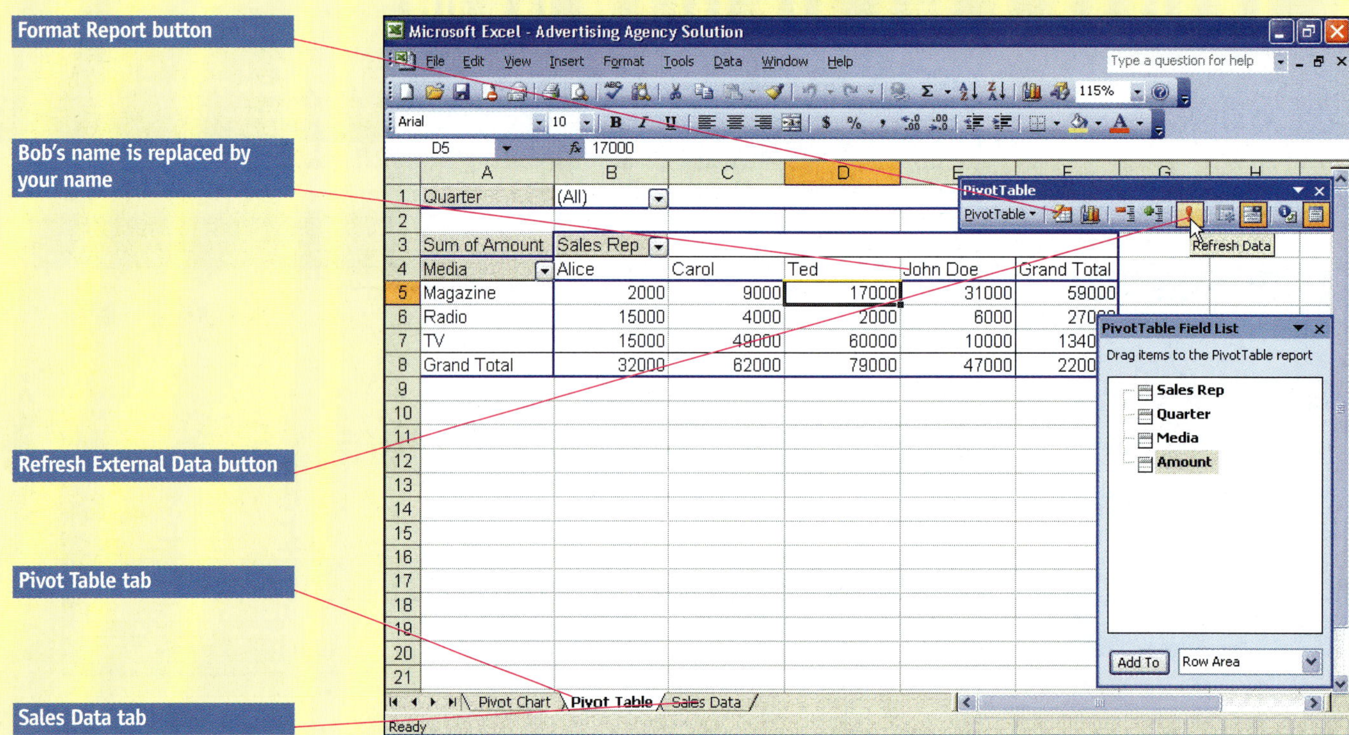

(c) Modify the Sales Data (step 3)

FIGURE 7.16 Hands-on Exercise 3 (*continued*)

THE FORMAT REPORT BUTTON

Why settle for a traditional report in black and white or shades of gray when you can choose from preformatted reports in a variety of styles and colors? Click the Format Report button on the Pivot Table toolbar to display the AutoFormat dialog box, where you select the style of your report. (To return to the default formatting, scroll to the end of the AutoFormat dialog box and select PivotTable Classic.) Use the Undo command if the result is not what you intended.

Step 4: Pivot the Table

- You can change the arrangement of a pivot table simply by dragging fields from one area to another. Click and drag the **Quarter field** to the row area. The page field is now empty, and you can see the breakdown of sales by quarter and media type.
- Click and drag the **Media field** to the column area, then drag the **Sales Rep field** to the page area. Your pivot table should match the one in Figure 7.16d.
- Click anywhere in the pivot table, then click the **Field Settings button** on the Pivot Table toolbar to display the PivotTable Field dialog box.
- Click the **Number button**, choose **Currency format** (with zero decimals). Click **OK** to close the Format Cells dialog box. Click **OK** a second time to close the Pivot Table Field dialog box.
- Save the workbook.

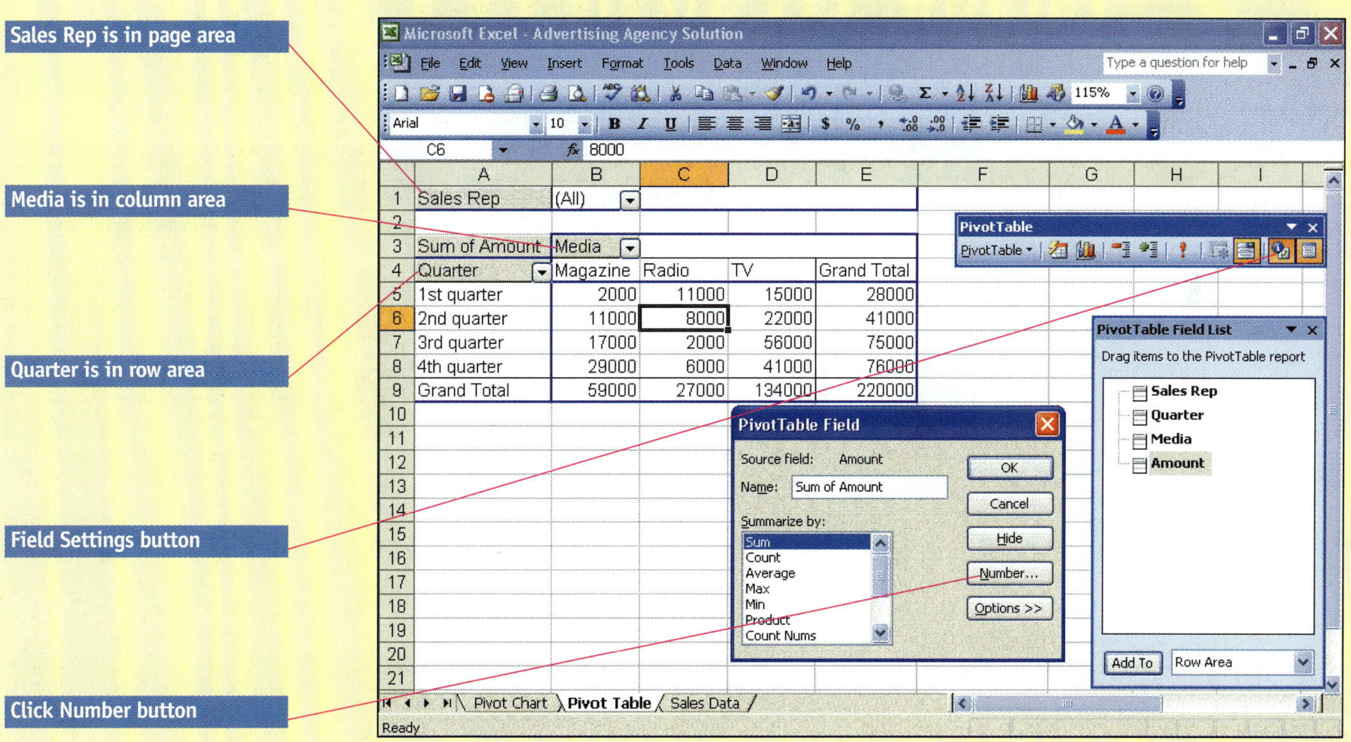

(d) Pivot the Table (step 4)

FIGURE 7.16 Hands-on Exercise 3 (*continued*)

CUSTOMIZE THE PIVOT TABLE

Right click anywhere within a pivot table to display a context-sensitive menu, then click the Table Options command to display the PivotTable Options dialog box. The default settings work well for most tables, but you can customize the table in a variety of ways. You can, for example, suppress the row or column totals or display a specific value in a blank cell. You can also change the formatting for any field within the table by right clicking the field and selecting the Format Cells button from the resulting menu.

Step 5: Change the Chart Type

- Click the **Pivot Chart tab** to view the default pivot chart as shown in Figure 7.16e. If necessary, close the field list to give yourself more room in which to work.
- Pull down the **Chart menu** and click the **Chart Type command** to display the dialog box in Figure 7.16e.
- Select the **Clustered column with a 3-D visual effect**. (Take a minute to appreciate the different types of charts that are available.)
- Check the box for **Default formatting**. This is a very important option, because without it, the chart is rotated in an awkward fashion. Click **OK**.
- The chart changes to display a three-dimensional column for each of the media in each quarter.
- Save the workbook.

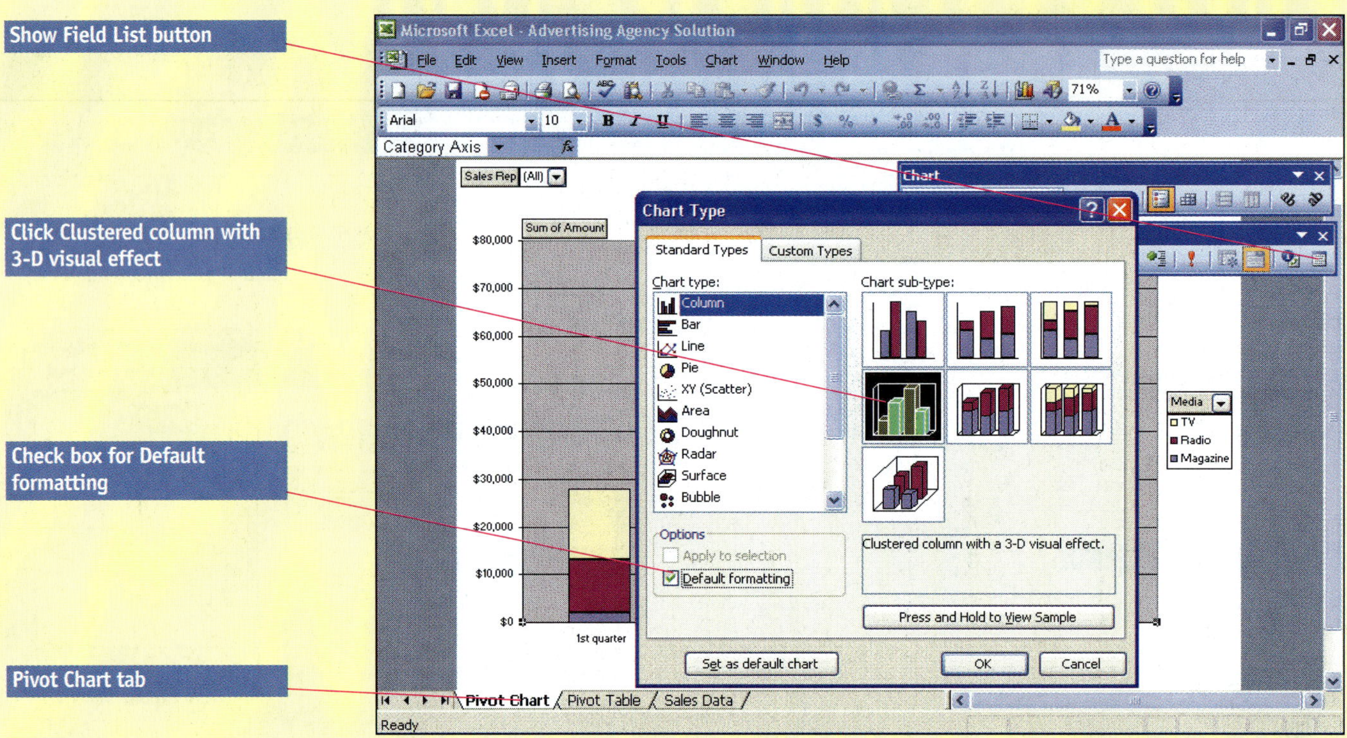

(e) Change the Chart Type (step 5)

FIGURE 7.16 Hands-on Exercise 3 (*continued*)

IT'S A PIVOT CHART

The shaded buttons for Sales Rep, Quarter, and Media that appear on the chart are similar in appearance and function to their counterparts in the underlying pivot table. Thus you can click and drag any of the buttons to a different position on the chart to change the underlying structure. You can also click and drag a field button from the PivotTable Field List to a new position on the chart. (Click the Show Field List button on the Pivot Table toolbar to show or hide the field list.) Any changes to the pivot chart affect the pivot table and vice versa.

Step 6: Complete the Chart

- Pull down the **Chart menu**, click **Chart Options** to display the Chart Options dialog box, then click the **Titles tab**. Enter **Advertising Revenue by Quarter and Media Type** as the chart title. Click **OK** to complete the chart as shown in Figure 7.16f.
- Click the **Sales Data tab** to select this worksheet. Press and hold the **Ctrl key** as you select the **Pivot Table tab** to select the worksheet containing the pivot table. Both worksheets are selected and hence both will be affected by the next command.
- Pull down the **File menu**, click the **Page Setup command**, and click the **Sheet tab**. Check the boxes to print **Gridlines** and **Row and Column headings**.
- Click the **Margins tab** and check the box to center the worksheet **horizontally**. Click **OK.**
- Pull down the **File menu** and click the **Print command** to display the Print dialog box. Click the option button to print the entire workbook. Click **OK**.
- Save the workbook.

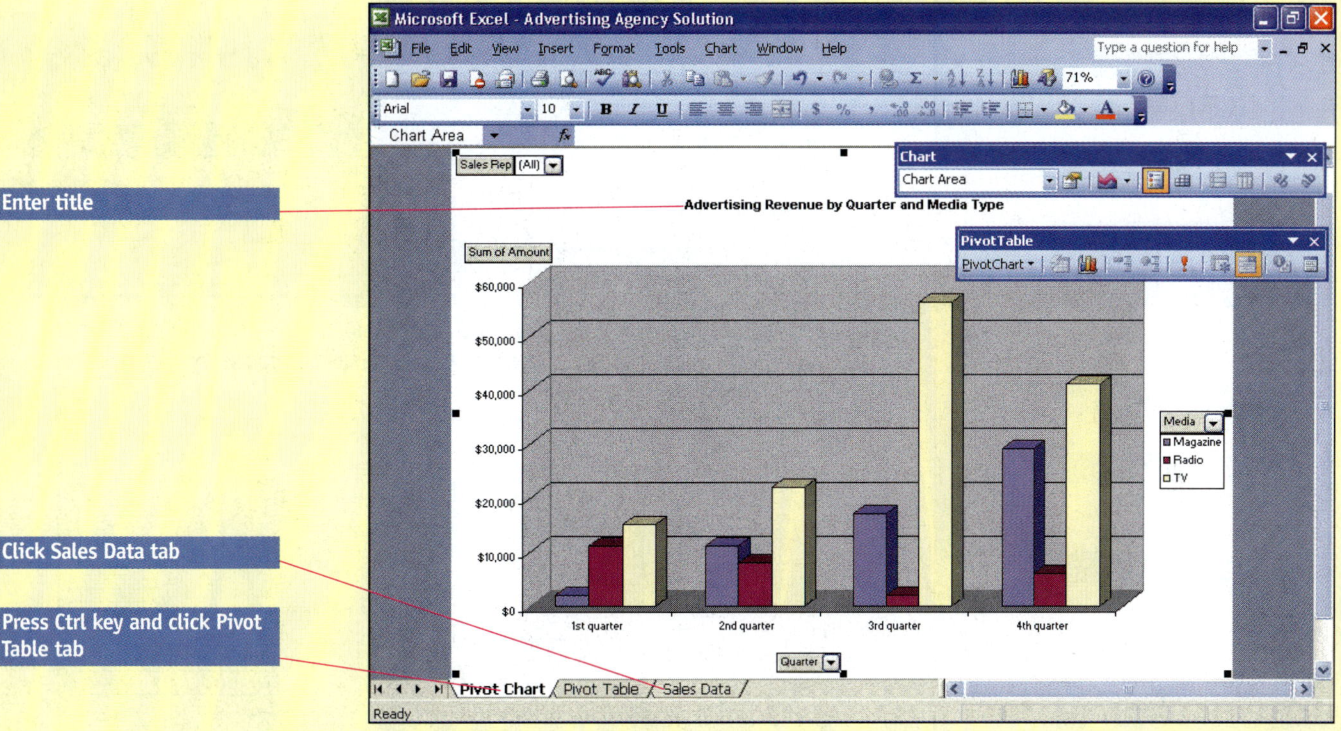

(f) Complete the Chart (step 6)

FIGURE 7.16 Hands-on Exercise 3 (*continued*)

FORMAT THE DATA SERIES

Why settle for a traditional bar chart when you can change the color, pattern, or shape of its components? Right click any column to select a data series to display a shortcut menu, then choose the Format Data Series command to display a dialog box in which you can customize the appearance of the vertical columns. We warn you that it is addictive, and that you can spend much more time than you intended initially. Set a time limit, and stop when you reach it.

Step 7: Save the Pivot Table as a Web Page

- Click the **Pivot Chart tab** to deselect the two tabs, then click the **Pivot Table tab**. Click and drag to select the entire pivot table. (If you have difficulty selecting the table, click and drag from the bottom-right cell to the top-left cell.)
- Pull down the **File menu**, click the **Save As Web Page command** to display the Save As dialog box, then click the **Publish button** (within the Save As dialog box) to display the Publish as Web Page dialog box in Figure 7.16g. Click **No** if the Office Assistant offers help.
- Change the name of the web page to **Advertising Agency Solution**. Save it in the **Exploring Excel folder**.
- Check the box to **Add interactivity** and select **Pivot Table functionality**. Check the boxes to **AutoRepublish every time this workbook is saved** and to **Open published web page in browser**.
- Click the **Change button** and enter an appropriate title that includes your name. Click **OK** to close the Set Title dialog box.
- Check that your settings match those in Figure 7.16g. Click the **Publish button** to publish the pivot table.

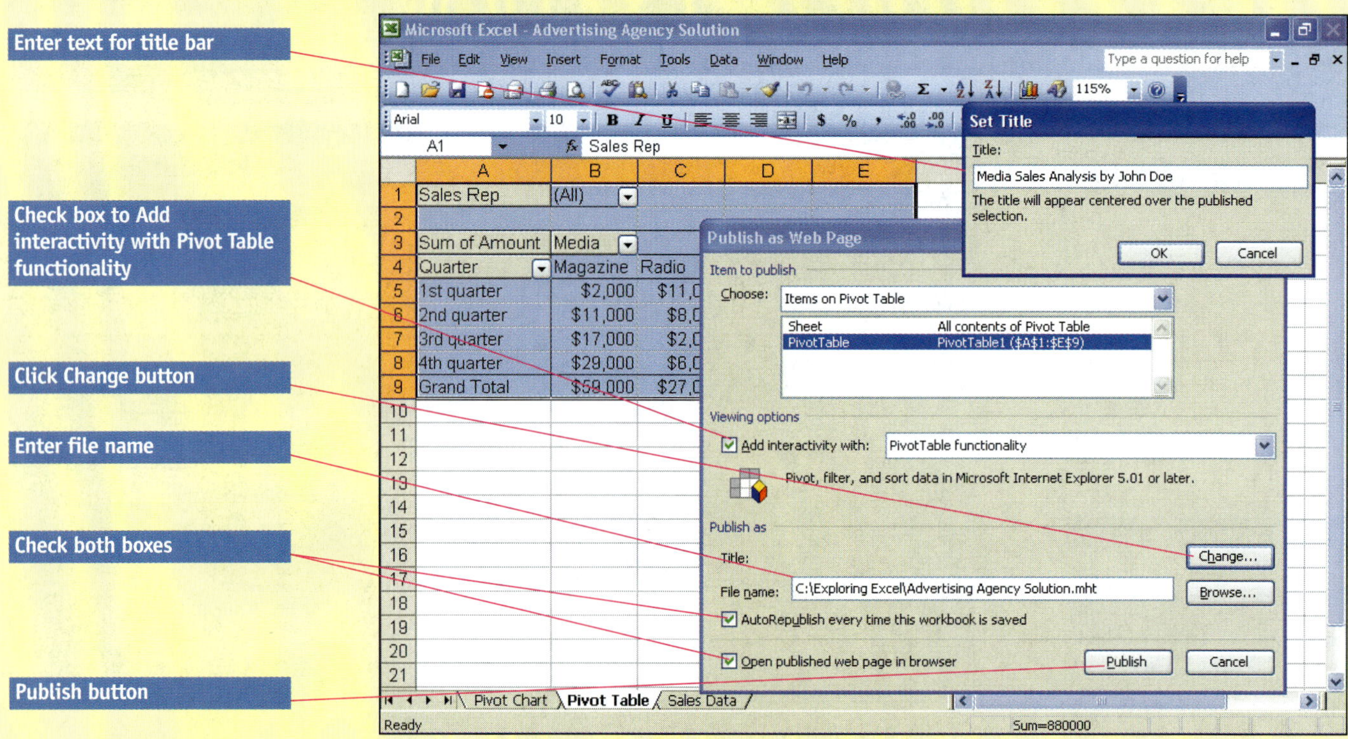

(g) Save the Pivot Table as a Web Page (step 7)

FIGURE 7.16 Hands-on Exercise 3 (*continued*)

SINGLE FILE WEB PAGE

Microsoft Office 2003 introduces the Single File Web Page (MHTML) format that saves all of the elements of a Web page, including text and graphics, in a single file. (A supporting folder to hold the extra elements was created previously.) The new format enables you to upload a single file to a Web server, as opposed to sending multiple files and folders. It also lets you send the entire page as a single e-mail attachment. The new file format is supported by Internet Explorer 4.0 and higher.

Step 8: Pivot the Web Page

- The pivot table will open automatically in your browser because of the option you selected in the previous step. If Internet Explorer is your default browser, you will see the pivot table in Figure 7.16h.
- If Netscape Navigator is your default browser, you will be prompted to install the Microsoft Web components, after which you should see the pivot table.
- Pivot the table so that its appearance matches Figure 7.16h. Thus, you need to drag the **Sales Rep button** to the column area and the **Media button** to the row area to the right of the Quarter field. (You can click the **Fields List button** on the Pivot Table toolbar to display/hide the fields in the table, should you lose a field button.)
- Click the **Plus sign** next to each quarter to display the detailed information. Click the **Print button** on the Internet Explorer toolbar to print the pivot table for your instructor.

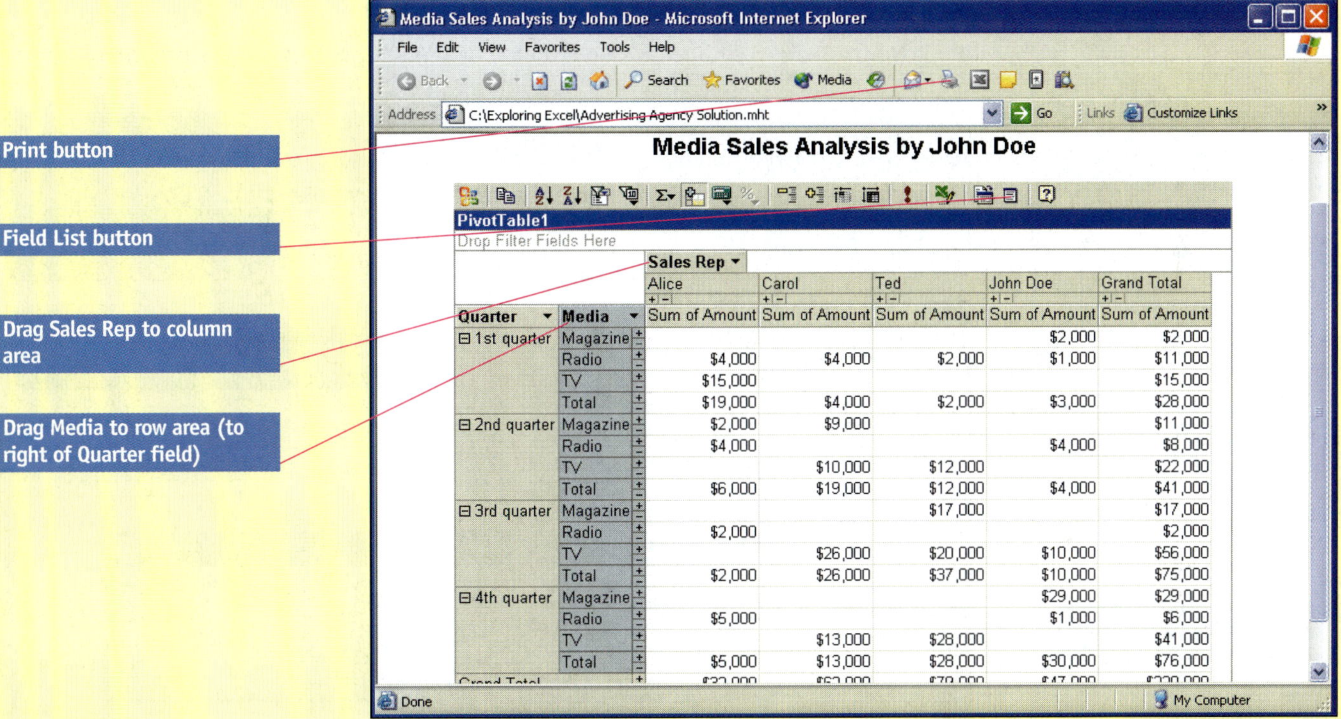

Quarter	Media	Alice Sum of Amount	Carol Sum of Amount	Ted Sum of Amount	John Doe Sum of Amount	Grand Total Sum of Amount
1st quarter	Magazine				$2,000	$2,000
	Radio	$4,000	$4,000	$2,000	$1,000	$11,000
	TV	$15,000				$15,000
	Total	$19,000	$4,000	$2,000	$3,000	$28,000
2nd quarter	Magazine	$2,000	$9,000			$11,000
	Radio	$4,000			$4,000	$8,000
	TV		$10,000	$12,000		$22,000
	Total	$6,000	$19,000	$12,000	$4,000	$41,000
3rd quarter	Magazine			$17,000		$17,000
	Radio	$2,000				$2,000
	TV		$26,000	$20,000	$10,000	$56,000
	Total	$2,000	$26,000	$37,000	$10,000	$75,000
4th quarter	Magazine				$29,000	$29,000
	Radio	$5,000			$1,000	$6,000
	TV		$13,000	$28,000		$41,000
	Total	$5,000	$13,000	$28,000	$30,000	$76,000
Grand Total		[illegible]	[illegible]	[illegible]	[illegible]	[illegible]

(h) Pivot the Web Page (step 8)

FIGURE 7.16 Hands-on Exercise 3 (*continued*)

XML IS NOT HTML

Extensible Markup Language, or XML for short, is an industry standard for structuring data. It is very different from HTML and it is not intended as a replacement. HTML describes how a document should look; e.g., <B>John Doe</B> indicates that John Doe should appear in boldface, but it does not tell us anything more. You don't know that "John" is the first name or that "Doe" is the last name. XML, on the other hand, is data about data, and it lets you define your own tags; e.g., <name><first>John</first><last>Doe</last></name>. The XML codes can be read by any XML-compliant application and processed accordingly. Formatting can also be implemented in XML through style sheets.

Step 9: Change the Underlying Data

- Click the **Excel button** on the Windows taskbar to return to Excel. Click the **Sales Data worksheet** and change the data for John Doe's (your name) magazine sales in the first quarter from $2000 to $22000.
- Click the **Worksheet tab** for the pivot table. Click anywhere in the pivot table and click the **Refresh External Data button** on the Pivot Table toolbar. The magazine sales in the 1st quarter increase to $22,000 and the grand total changes to $240,000.
- Click the **Save button** to save the changes to the worksheet. You will see the dialog box in Figure 7.16i. Click the option button to **Enable the Autopublish feature**. Click **OK**.
- Return to Internet Explorer. Click the **Refresh button** on the Pivot Table toolbar to update the Web page. The numbers within the Web pivot table change to reflect the change in magazine sales. If the numbers do not refresh, close Internet Explorer, reopen it, and then reopen the Web page from the Exploring Excel folder.
- Close Internet Explorer. Close Excel. Click **Yes** if prompted to save the changes.

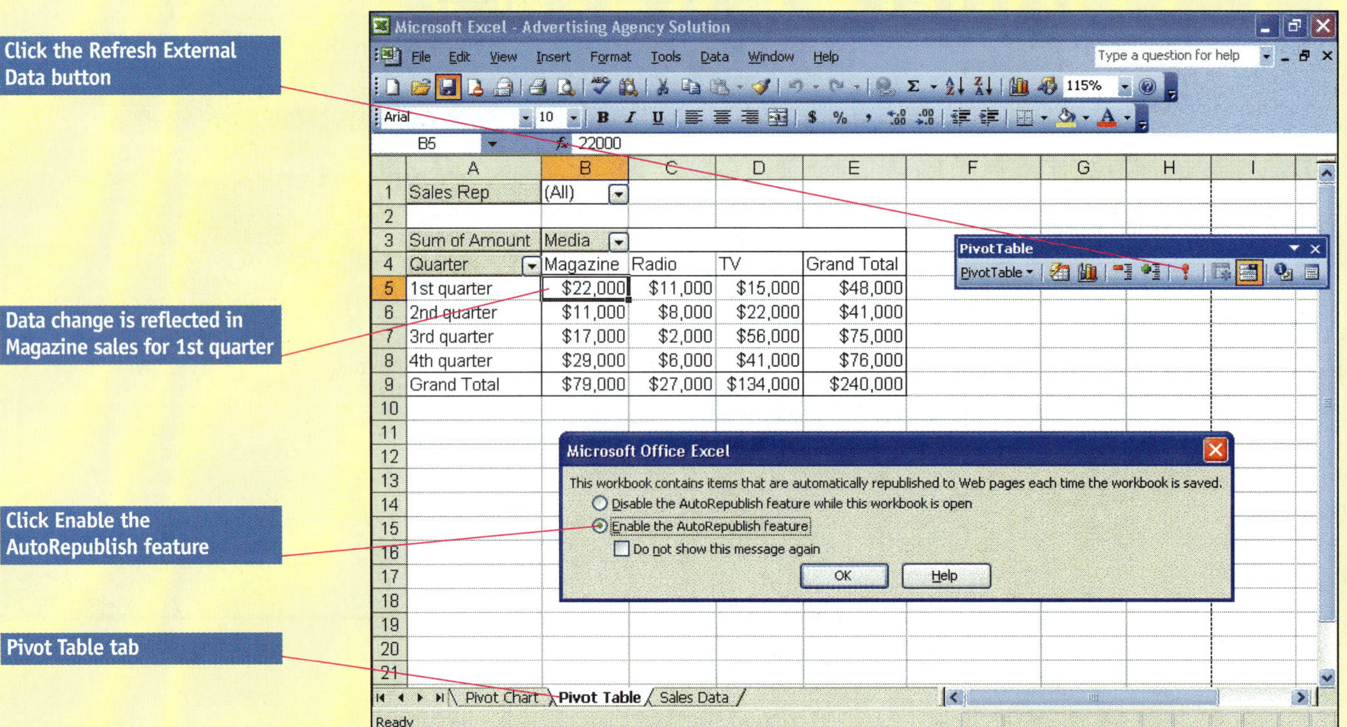

(i) Change the Underlying Data (step 9)

FIGURE 7.16 Hands-on Exercise 3 (*continued*)

THE NEED TO REFRESH

A pivot table and/or a Web page based on a pivot table do not automatically reflect changes in the underlying data. You must first refresh the pivot table as it exists within the workbook, by clicking in the pivot table, then clicking the refresh button on the Pivot Table toolbar. Next, you must save the workbook and enable the AutoPublish feature. And finally, the Single File Web page format requires you to close Internet Explorer, reopen it, and then reopen the Web page.

SUMMARY

A list is an area in a worksheet that contains rows of similar data. The first row in the list contains the column labels (field names). Each additional row contains data for a specific record. A data form provides an easy way to add, edit, and delete records in a list.

The Text Import Wizard converts data in either fixed width or delimited format to an Excel workbook. The Wizard is displayed automatically if you attempt to open a text file. Data can also be imported into an Excel workbook from other applications such as Microsoft Access.

XML (Extensible Markup Language) enables a developer to create customized tags to define data within a file. It is an industry standard for structuring data and not a Microsoft product. XML is not to be confused with HTML (Hypertext Markup Language), nor is it intended as a replacement for HTML. Microsoft Excel 2003 provides full XML support to exchange information between an XML source document and an Excel workbook. You attach the XML definition or schema to the workbook and then you map the XML elements in the schema to the cells in your workbook.

A date is stored internally as an integer number corresponding to the number of days since 1900. (January 1, 1900 is stored as the number 1.) The number of elapsed days between two dates can be determined by simple subtraction. The TODAY function always returns the current date (the date on which a worksheet is created or retrieved).

A filtered list displays only those records that meet specific criteria. Filtering is implemented through AutoFilter or the Advanced Filter command. The latter enables you to specify a criteria range and to copy the selected records elsewhere in the worksheet.

The Sort command arranges a list according to the value of one or more keys (known as the primary, secondary, and tertiary keys). Each key may be in ascending or descending sequence.

The database functions (DSUM, DAVERAGE, DMAX, DMIN, and DCOUNT) have three arguments: the associated list, the field name, and the criteria range. The simplest criteria range consists of two rows and as many fields as there are in the list.

The Subtotals command uses a summary function (such as SUM, AVERAGE, or COUNT) to compute subtotals for data groups within a list. The data is displayed in outline view, where outline symbols can be used to suppress or expand the detail records.

A pivot table extends the capability of individual database functions by presenting the data in summary form. It divides the records in a list into categories, then computes summary statistics for those categories. Pivot tables provide the utmost flexibility in that you can vary the row or column categories and/or the way that the statistics are computed. A pivot chart extends the capability of a pivot table to a chart.

KEY TERMS

Advanced Filter command 325
Analysis ToolPak 332
Ascending sequence 311
AutoFilter command 324
Criteria range 325
Data 322
Data form 310
Database 308
Database functions 327
Date arithmetic 330
DAVERAGE function 327
DCOUNT function 327
Delete command 309
Delimited format 313
Descending sequence 311
Division by zero 336
DMAX function 327
DMIN function 327
DSUM function 327
Extensible Markup Language (XML) 314
Field 308
Field name 308
File 308
Filtered list 324
Fixed width format 313
Form command 310
Hypertext Markup Language (HTML) 314
Information 322
Insert Columns command 309
Insert Name command 328
Insert Rows command 309
ISERROR function 336
Key 308
List 308
Outline symbols 329
Pivot chart 341
Pivot table 341
Pivot Table Wizard 341
Record 308
Refresh command 341
Schema 314
Single File Web Page 350
Sort command 311
Subtotals command 329
Text Import Wizard 313
TODAY () function 330

MULTIPLE CHOICE

1. Which of the following best describes data management in Excel?
   (a) The rows in a list correspond to records in a file
   (b) The columns in a list correspond to fields in a record
   (c) Both (a) and (b)
   (d) Neither (a) nor (b)

2. How should a list be placed within a worksheet?
   (a) There should be at least one blank row between the list and the other entries in the worksheet
   (b) There should be at least one blank column between the list and the other entries in the worksheet
   (c) Both (a) and (b)
   (d) Neither (a) nor (b)

3. Which of the following is suggested for the placement of database functions within a worksheet?
   (a) Above or below the list with at least one blank row separating the database functions from the list to which they refer
   (b) To the left or right of the list with at least one blank column separating the database functions from the list to which they refer
   (c) Both (a) and (b)
   (d) Neither (a) nor (b)

4. Cells A21:B22 have been defined as the criteria range, cells A21 and B21 contain the field names City and Title, respectively, and cells A22 and B22 contain New York and Manager. The selected records will consist of:
   (a) All employees in New York, regardless of title
   (b) All managers, regardless of the city
   (c) Only the managers in New York
   (d) All employees in New York (regardless of title) or all managers

5. Cells A21:B23 have been defined as the criteria range, cells A21 and B21 contain the field names City and Title, respectively, and cells A22 and B23 contain New York and Manager, respectively. The selected records will consist of:
   (a) All employees in New York regardless of title
   (b) All managers regardless of the city
   (c) Only the managers in New York
   (d) All employees in New York and all managers

6. If employees are to be listed so that all employees in the same city appear together in alphabetical order by the employee's last name:
   (a) City and last name are both considered to be the primary key
   (b) City and last name are both considered to be the secondary key
   (c) City is the primary key and last name is the secondary key
   (d) Last name is the primary key and city is the secondary key

7. Which of the following can be used to delete a record from a database?
   (a) The Edit Delete command
   (b) The Data Form command
   (c) Both (a) and (b)
   (d) Neither (a) nor (b)

8. Which of the following is true about the DAVERAGE function?
   (a) It has a single argument
   (b) It can be entered into a worksheet using the Function Wizard
   (c) Both (a) and (b)
   (d) Neither (a) nor (b)

9. Which of the following can be converted to an Excel workbook?
   (a) A text file in delimited format
   (b) A text file in fixed width format
   (c) Both (a) and (b)
   (d) Neither (a) nor (b)

10. Which of the following is recommended to distinguish the first row in a list (the field names) from the remaining entries (the data)?
    (a) Insert a blank row between the first row and the remaining rows
    (b) Insert a row of dashes between the first row and the remaining rows
    (c) Either (a) or (b)
    (d) Neither (a) nor (b)

... continued

multiple choice

11. The AutoFilter command:

(a) Permanently deletes records from the associated list
(b) Requires the specification of a criteria range elsewhere in the worksheet
(c) Either (a) or (b)
(d) Neither (a) nor (b)

12. Which of the following is true of the Sort command?

(a) The primary key must be in ascending sequence
(b) The secondary key must be in descending sequence
(c) Both (a) and (b)
(d) Neither (a) nor (b)

13. What is the best way to enter January 21, 2004 into a worksheet, given that you create the worksheet on that date, and further, that you always want to display that specific date?

(a) =TODAY()
(b) 1/21/2004
(c) Both (a) and (b) are equally acceptable
(d) Neither (a) nor (b)

14. Which of the following best describes the relationship between the Sort and Subtotals commands?

(a) The Sort command should be executed before the Subtotals command
(b) The Subtotals command should be executed before the Sort command
(c) The commands can be executed in either sequence
(d) There is no relationship because the commands have nothing to do with one another

15. Which of the following may be implemented in an existing pivot table?

(a) A row field may be added or deleted
(b) A column field may be added or deleted
(c) Both (a) and (b)
(d) Neither (a) nor (b)

16. How many rows (including the header row) are necessary in a criteria range that selects employees in the New York Office who earn more than $100,000 annually?

(a) 1
(b) 2
(c) 3
(d) 4

17. You have applied the Advanced Filter command to filter a customer list in place, expecting to see a subset of the entire customer list. All of the customers were displayed, however. What is the most likely reason?

(a) There is a blank row in the criteria range
(b) There is a blank row in the list (database)
(c) Both (a) and (b)
(d) Neither (a) nor (b)

18. You want to use the Subtotals command to show total salaries for each location with the locations appearing in alphabetical order. What should you do before executing the Subtotals command?

(a) Sort the list by salary in ascending order
(b) Sort the list by salary in descending order
(c) Sort the list by location in ascending order
(d) Sort the list by location in descending order

ANSWERS

1. c	**7.** c	**13.** b
2. c	**8.** b	**14.** a
3. a	**9.** c	**15.** c
4. c	**10.** d	**16.** b
5. d	**11.** d	**17.** a
6. c	**12.** d	**18.** c

PRACTICE WITH EXCEL

1. **Election 2000:** Election 2000 has been decided, but it will always be remembered for its closeness and controversy. Your assignment is to open a partially completed version of the workbook in *Chapter 7 Practice 1,* then complete the workbook so that it matches Figure 7.17. Proceed as follows:
   a. Enter the appropriate IF function in cell C8 to determine the winner of the state's electoral votes. Use conditional formatting to display the indicated colors for Bush and Gore. Develop the formula in such a way that it can be copied to the remaining rows in this column.
   b. Enter the appropriate formulas in cells F8 and G8 to compute the difference in the number of votes and the associated percentages. (Use the absolute value function for the formula in cell F8 so that the difference in the number of votes is always shown as a positive number.) Copy the formulas to the remaining rows in the worksheet.
   c. Use an ordinary SUM function to determine the popular vote for each candidate as shown in cells B4 and C4. Use the DSUM function to determine the number of electoral votes for each candidate. (You will need to establish separate criteria ranges for each candidate.)
   d. Add your name somewhere in the worksheet, then print the completed worksheet to show both displayed values and cell formulas. Be sure the worksheet fits on a single page.
   e. Print the worksheet in at least one other sequence—for example, in order by the vote differential.
   f. What do you remember about the 2000 election? Was the election settled immediately? Do you understand how the Electoral College works? Explain how a candidate can lose the popular vote, yet still win an election. Has this happened prior to the 2000 election?
   g. Add a cover sheet, then submit the completed assignment to your instructor. Be sure to vote in the next election. Your vote makes a difference!

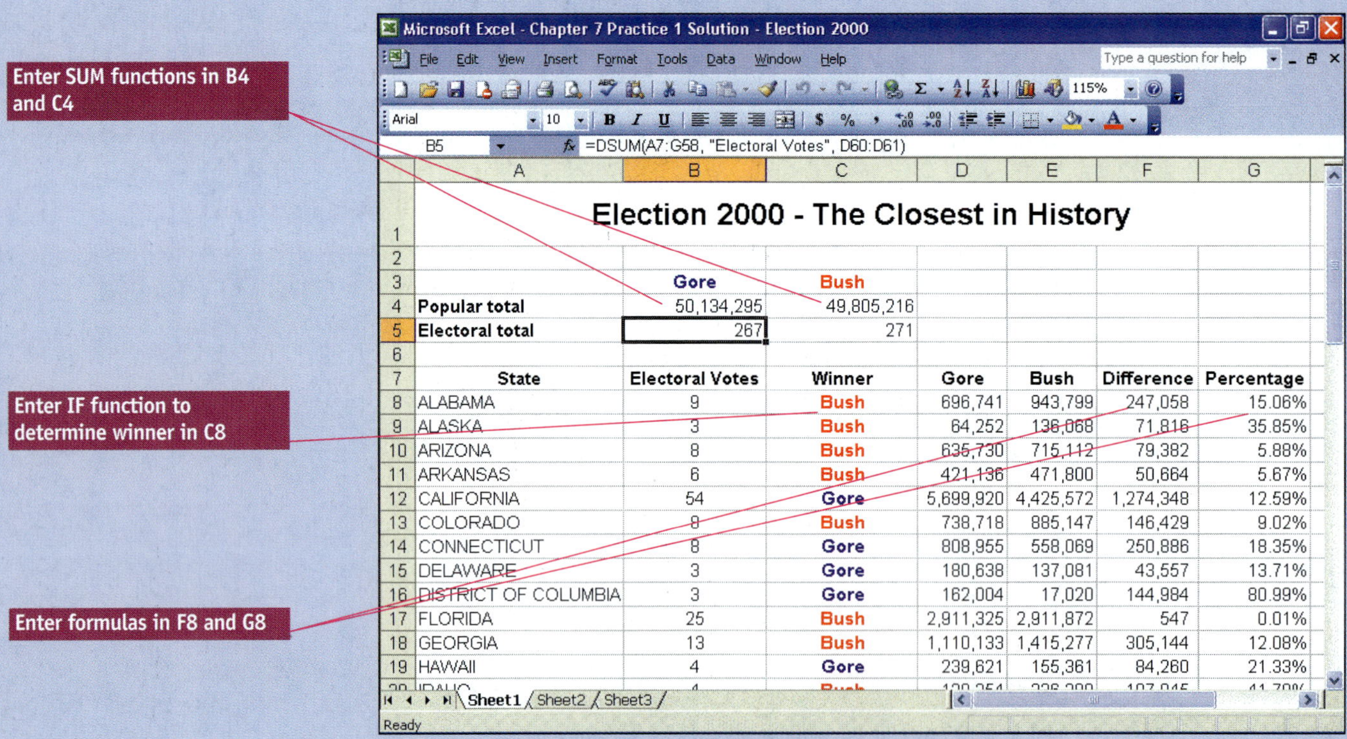

	A	B	C	D	E	F	G
3		Gore	Bush				
4	Popular total	50,134,295	49,805,216				
5	Electoral total	267	271				
7	State	Electoral Votes	Winner	Gore	Bush	Difference	Percentage
8	ALABAMA	9	Bush	696,741	943,799	247,058	15.06%
9	ALASKA	3	Bush	64,252	136,068	71,816	35.85%
10	ARIZONA	8	Bush	635,730	715,112	79,382	5.88%
11	ARKANSAS	6	Bush	421,136	471,800	50,664	5.67%
12	CALIFORNIA	54	Gore	5,699,920	4,425,572	1,274,348	12.59%
13	COLORADO	8	Bush	738,718	885,147	146,429	9.02%
14	CONNECTICUT	8	Gore	808,955	558,069	250,886	18.35%
15	DELAWARE	3	Gore	180,638	137,081	43,557	13.71%
16	DISTRICT OF COLUMBIA	3	Gore	162,004	17,020	144,984	80.99%
17	FLORIDA	25	Bush	2,911,325	2,911,872	547	0.01%
18	GEORGIA	13	Bush	1,110,133	1,415,277	305,144	12.08%
19	HAWAII	4	Gore	239,621	155,361	84,260	21.33%

FIGURE 7.17 Election 2000 (exercise 1)

2. **The Dean's List:** The *Chapter 7 Practice 2* workbook contains a partially completed version of the workbook in Figure 7.18. Your assignment is to open the workbook, then implement the following changes:
   a. Add a transfer student, Jeff Borow, majoring in Engineering. Jeff has completed 14 credits and has 45 quality points. (Jeff's record can be seen in Figure 7.18, but it is not in the workbook that you will retrieve from the Exploring Excel folder.) Do not, however, enter Jeff's GPA or year in school, as both will be computed from formulas in the next two steps.
   b. Enter the appropriate formula in F4 to compute the GPA for the first student (the quality points divided by the number of credits). Copy the formula to the other cells in this column.
   c. Enter the appropriate formula in cell G4 to determine the year in school for the first student. (Use the HLOOKUP function based on the table in cells B24 through E25. The entries in cells A24 and A25 contain labels and are not part of the table per se.) Copy the formula to the other cells in this column.
   d. Format the worksheet attractively. You can use our formatting or develop your own. Sort the list so that the students are listed alphabetically.
   e. Use the Advanced Filter command to filter the list in place so that the only visible students are those on the Dean's List (with a GPA greater than 3.2) as shown in Figure 7.18.
   f. Add your name as the academic advisor in cell A28. Print the worksheet two ways, with displayed values and cell formulas. Use the Page Setup command to specify landscape printing and display gridlines and row and column headings. Be sure that each printout fits on a single sheet of paper.
   g. Remove the filter condition, then print the worksheet in a different sequence—for example, by ascending or descending GPA.
   h. Add a cover sheet, then submit the complete assignment to your instructor.

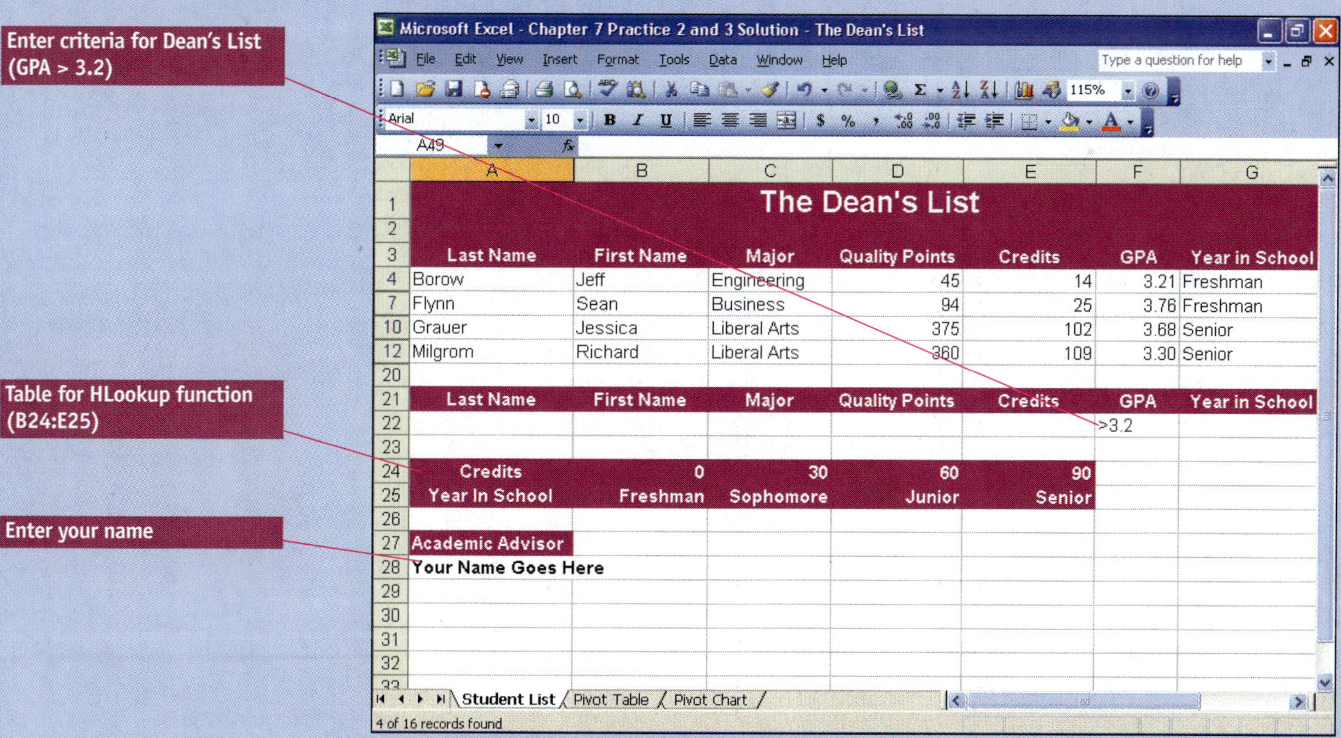

FIGURE 7.18 The Dean's List (exercise 2)

3. **The Pivot Chart:** Complete the previous exercise, then add a pivot table and pivot chart as shown in Figure 7.19. Start the Pivot Table Wizard. In step 1, select the option to create a PivotChart report (with PivotTable report). Specify the range of the pivot table in step 2, then in step 3 select the option to put the pivot table on a new worksheet. Rename the resulting worksheets, Sheet1 and Chart1, to Pivot Table and Pivot Chart as shown in Figure 7.19.
   a. Modify the pivot table so that major and year in school are the row and column fields, respectively. Use GPA as the data field, but be sure to specify the average GPA rather than the sum. Format the GPA to two decimal places.
   b. Change the format of the pivot chart to a 3-D clustered column chart with default formatting. Right click any column within the chart, select the Format Data Series command, then select the Series Order tab. Change the order of the columns to Freshman, Sophomore, Junior, and Senior, as opposed to the default alphabetical order.
   c. Pull down the Chart menu, click the Chart Options command to display the associated dialog box, then select the Data Table tab. Check the box to display the data table. Save the workbook.
   d. Use the Page Setup command to create a custom footer containing your name, the name of the worksheet, and today's date. Check the boxes to include gridlines and row and column headings.
   e. Print the pivot chart as shown in Figure 7.19. You do not need to print the pivot table since the equivalent information is shown in the data table that appears below the pivot chart.
   f. Pivot tables are one of the best-kept secrets in Excel, even though they have been available in the last several releases of Excel. (Pivot charts, however, were first introduced in Excel 2000.) Write a short note to a fellow student that describes how this feature facilitates data analysis.
   g. Add a cover sheet, then submit the complete assignment to your instructor.

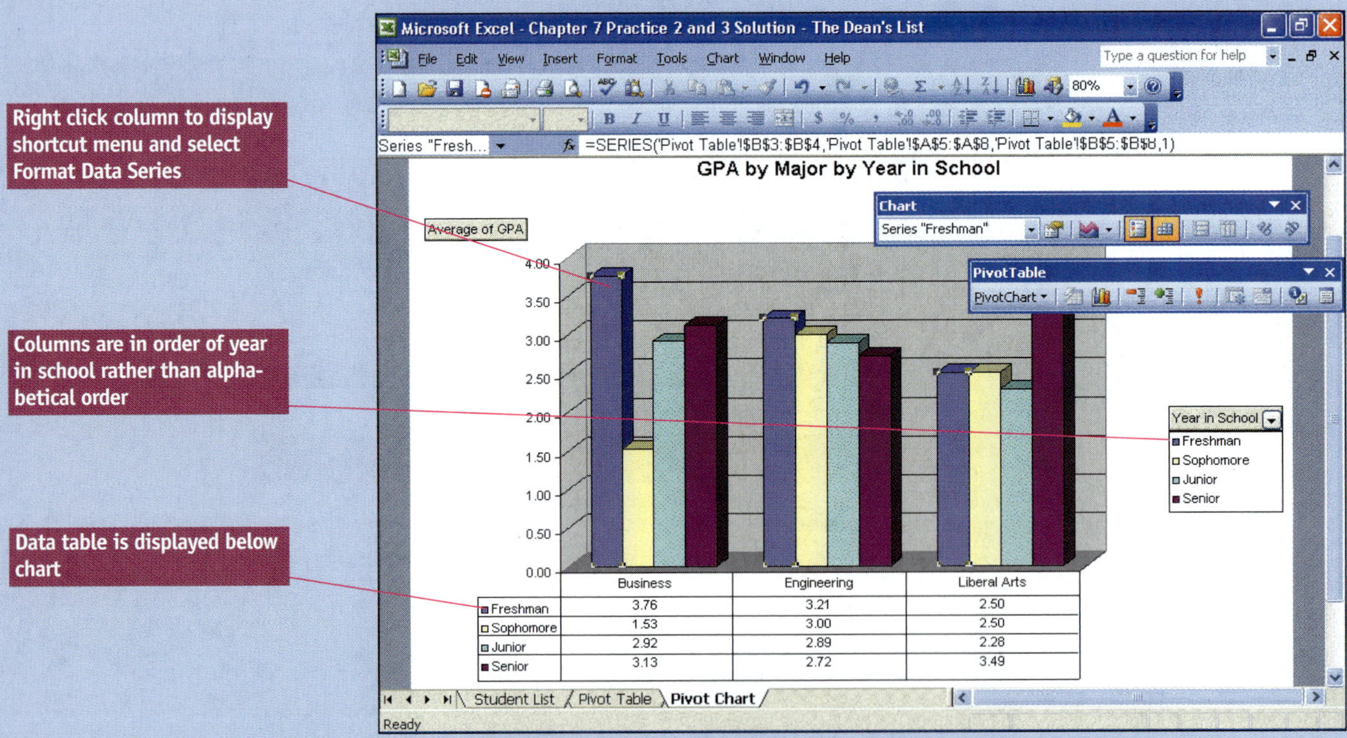

FIGURE 7.19 The Pivot Chart (exercise 3)

4. **Compensation Analysis:** The workbook in Figure 7.20 is used to analyze employee compensation with respect to the dollar amount and percentage of their latest salary increase. Your assignment is to open the partially completed workbook in *Chapter 7 Practice 4* and complete the workbook to match our figure.
   a. Open the workbook, then enter the formula to compute the dollar increase for the first employee in cell G4. Note, however, that not every employee has a previous salary, and thus the formula requires an IF function. Copy this formula to the remaining rows in column G.
   b. Enter the formula to compute the percentage increase for the first employee in cell H4. The percentage increase is found by dividing the amount of the increase by the previous salary. Again, not every employee has a previous salary, and hence the formula requires an IF function to avoid dividing by zero when there is no previous salary. Copy this formula to the remaining rows in column H.
   c. Enter the indicated database functions in rows 21 and 22 to reflect only those employees who have received a raise. Thus, be sure to include the greater than zero entry under Previous Salary in the criteria row.
   d. Format the worksheet in attractive fashion. You can copy our formatting or use your own design. Note, too, that you should suppress the display of zero values. (If necessary, pull down the Tools menu, click the Options command, then click the View tab and clear the box to display zero values.)
   e. Add your name as a financial analyst, then print the worksheet with both displayed values and cell formulas. Use landscape printing as necessary to be sure that the worksheet fits on a single sheet of paper.
   f. Print the worksheet in at least one other sequence—for example, by the smallest (or largest) percentage increase.
   g. Add a cover sheet, then submit the complete assignment to your instructor.

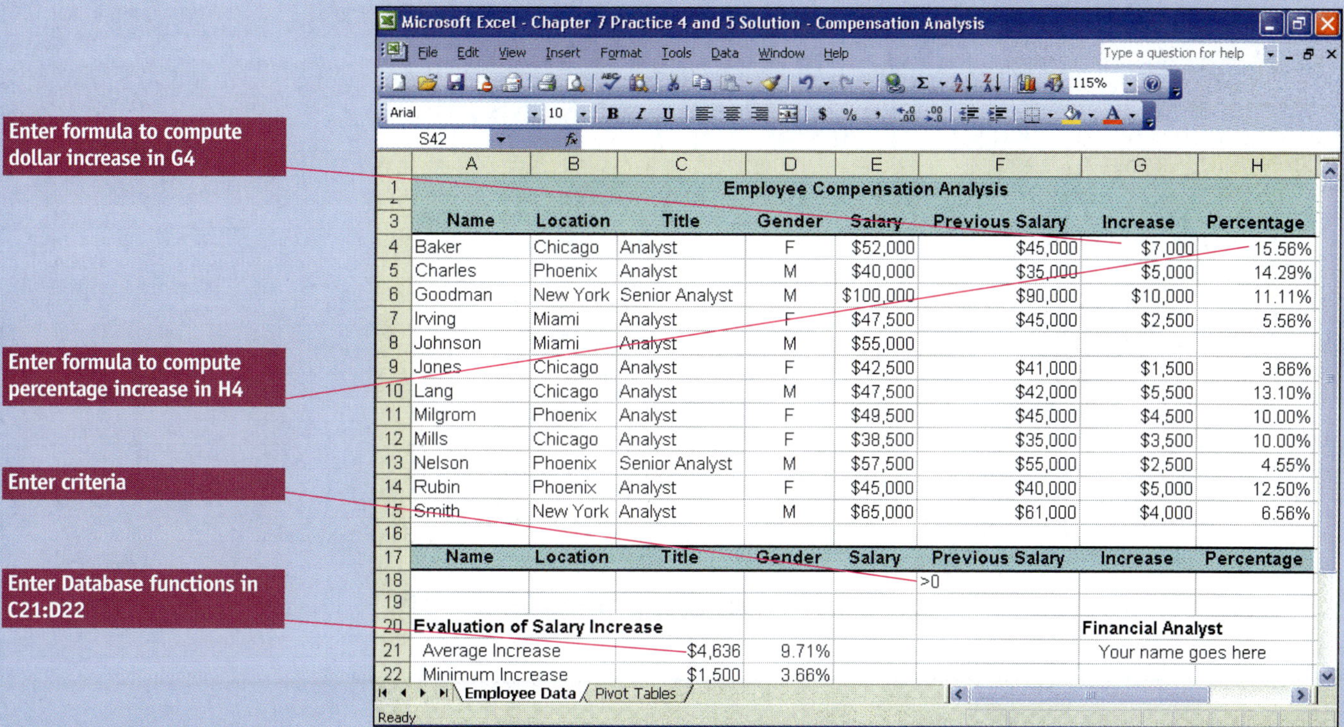

	A	B	C	D	E	F	G	H
1	Employee Compensation Analysis							
3	Name	Location	Title	Gender	Salary	Previous Salary	Increase	Percentage
4	Baker	Chicago	Analyst	F	$52,000	$45,000	$7,000	15.56%
5	Charles	Phoenix	Analyst	M	$40,000	$35,000	$5,000	14.29%
6	Goodman	New York	Senior Analyst	M	$100,000	$90,000	$10,000	11.11%
7	Irving	Miami	Analyst	F	$47,500	$45,000	$2,500	5.56%
8	Johnson	Miami	Analyst	M	$55,000			
9	Jones	Chicago	Analyst	F	$42,500	$41,000	$1,500	3.66%
10	Lang	Chicago	Analyst	M	$47,500	$42,000	$5,500	13.10%
11	Milgrom	Phoenix	Analyst	F	$49,500	$45,000	$4,500	10.00%
12	Mills	Chicago	Analyst	F	$38,500	$35,000	$3,500	10.00%
13	Nelson	Phoenix	Senior Analyst	M	$57,500	$55,000	$2,500	4.55%
14	Rubin	Phoenix	Analyst	F	$45,000	$40,000	$5,000	12.50%
15	Smith	New York	Analyst	M	$65,000	$61,000	$4,000	6.56%
16								
17	Name	Location	Title	Gender	Salary	Previous Salary	Increase	Percentage
18						>0		
19								
20	Evaluation of Salary Increase						Financial Analyst	
21	Average Increase		$4,636	9.71%			Your name goes here	
22	Minimum Increase		$1,500	3.66%				

FIGURE 7.20 Compensation Analysis (exercise 4)

5. **Pivot Tables:** The pivot table in Figure 7.21 is based on the compensation analysis in the worksheet from the previous exercise. Open the completed *Chapter 7 Practice 4* workbook (or complete the exercise at this time), then create the associated pivot table. Proceed as follows:
   a. Click anywhere within the Employee table, pull down the Data menu, and create the pivot chart in Figure 7.21. You will need to specify two data fields (the salary increase and the percent of salary increase), and choose the average function for each.
   b. Format the pivot table in an attractive fashion. You do not have to duplicate our formatting exactly, but you are to use the currency and percent symbols as appropriate, as well as a reasonable number of decimal places.
   c. Use the same style of formatting for the text (e.g., 10 point Arial) in your pivot table as in the previous exercise, so that your workbook has a uniform look. Use the Options command as described in the previous exercise to suppress the display of zero values.
   d. Use the Page Setup command to create a custom footer containing your name, the name of the worksheet, and today's date. Check the boxes to print the gridlines and row and column headings.
   e. Print the completed workbook for your instructor to show the displayed values for each worksheet. Print the Employee Data worksheet a second time to show the cell formulas.
   f. Save the worksheet, then experiment with pivoting the table by changing the row, column, and/or page fields and/or the function associated with the data fields. Pivot tables are one of the best-kept secrets in Excel even though they have been available in the last several releases of Excel. Write a short note to your instructor that describes how this feature facilitates data analysis.
   g. Add a cover sheet, then submit the complete assignment to your instructor.

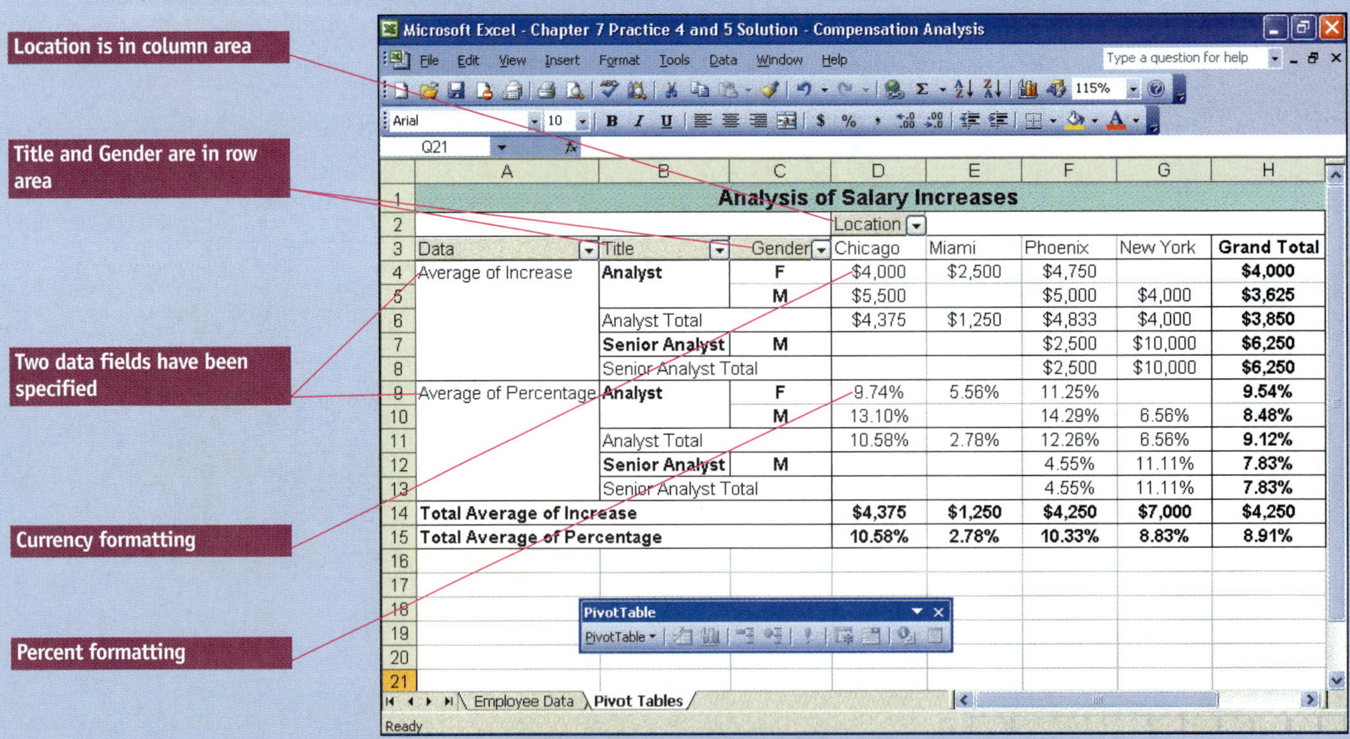

Analysis of Salary Increases

Data	Title	Gender	Chicago	Miami	Phoenix	New York	Grand Total
Average of Increase	Analyst	F	$4,000	$2,500	$4,750		$4,000
		M	$5,500		$5,000	$4,000	$3,625
	Analyst Total		$4,375	$1,250	$4,833	$4,000	$3,850
	Senior Analyst	M			$2,500	$10,000	$6,250
	Senior Analyst Total				$2,500	$10,000	$6,250
Average of Percentage	Analyst	F	9.74%	5.56%	11.25%		9.54%
		M	13.10%		14.29%	6.56%	8.48%
	Analyst Total		10.58%	2.78%	12.26%	6.56%	9.12%
	Senior Analyst	M			4.55%	11.11%	7.83%
	Senior Analyst Total				4.55%	11.11%	7.83%
Total Average of Increase			$4,375	$1,250	$4,250	$7,000	$4,250
Total Average of Percentage			10.58%	2.78%	10.33%	8.83%	8.91%

FIGURE 7.21 Pivot Tables (exercise 5)

6. **Consumer Loans:** The worksheet in Figure 7.22 displays selected loans (those with a loan type of "A") from a comprehensive set of loan records. Your assignment is to open the partially completed *Chapter 7 Practice 6* workbook in the Exploring Excel folder to create the worksheet in our figure.
   a. Open the workbook, then go to cell H4, the cell containing the ending date for the first loan. Enter the formula to compute the ending date, based on the starting date and the term of the loan. For the sake of simplicity, you do not have to account for leap year. Thus, to compute the ending date, multiply the term of the loan by 365 and add that result to the starting date. Be sure to format the starting and ending dates to show a date format.
   b. Go to cell I4 and enter the PMT function to compute the monthly payment for the first loan. Copy the formulas in cells H4 and I4 to the remaining rows in the worksheet.
   c. Enter the indicated criteria in cell D29, then enter the indicated database functions toward the bottom of the worksheet.
   d. Use the Advanced Filter command to filter the list in place to display only those loans that satisfy the indicated criteria as shown in Figure 7.22.
   e. Format the list in attractive fashion. Add your name as the loan officer.
   f. Look closely at the bottom of Figure 7.22 and note the presence of a Pivot Table worksheet. You are to create a pivot table that has the loan type and branch location in the row and column fields, respectively. Your pivot table is to contain two data fields, the total amount of the loans, and the average interest rate.
   g. Print the entire workbook for your instructor. Print both the displayed values and cell formulas for the loans worksheet, but only the displayed values for the pivot table. Use the Page Setup command to create a custom footer containing your name, the name of the worksheet, and today's date. Be sure to print the gridlines and row and column headings.
   h. Add a cover sheet, then submit the complete assignment to your instructor.

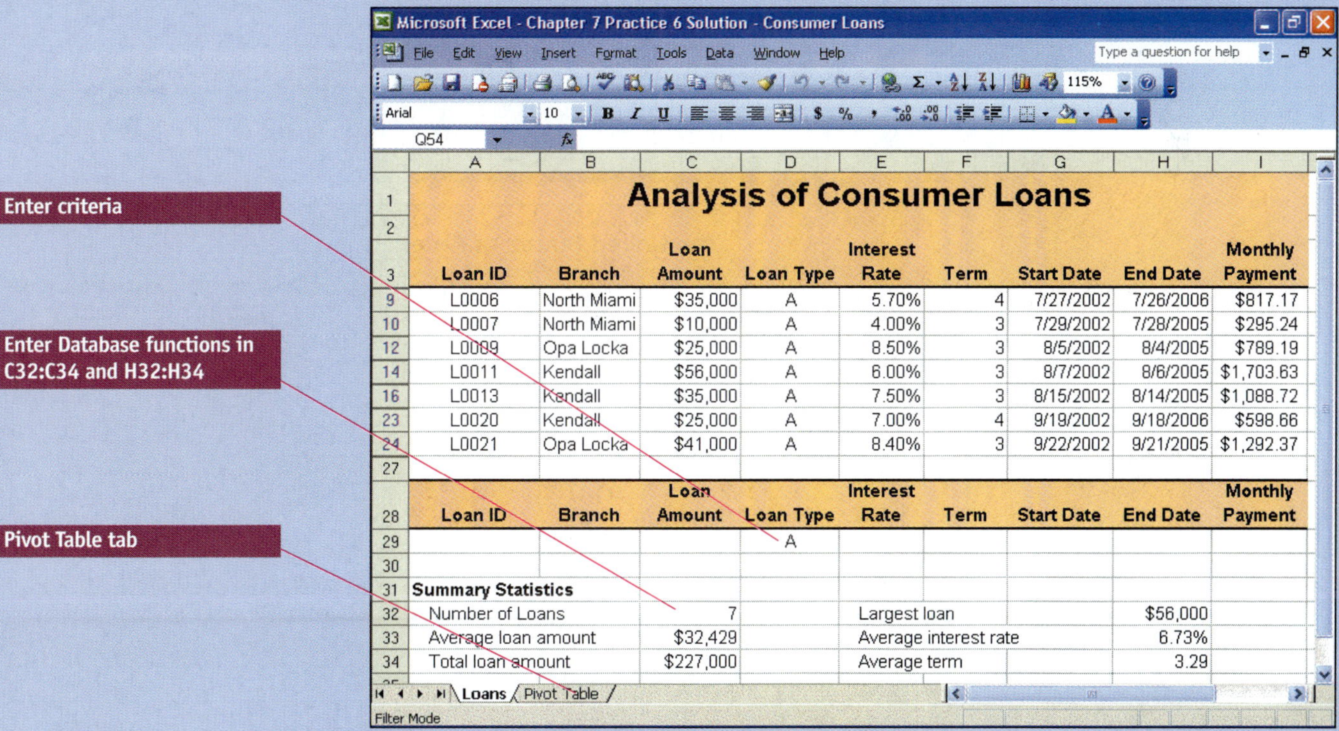

	A	B	C	D	E	F	G	H	I
1	Analysis of Consumer Loans								
2									
3	Loan ID	Branch	Loan Amount	Loan Type	Interest Rate	Term	Start Date	End Date	Monthly Payment
9	L0006	North Miami	$35,000	A	5.70%	4	7/27/2002	7/26/2006	$817.17
10	L0007	North Miami	$10,000	A	4.00%	3	7/29/2002	7/28/2005	$295.24
12	L0009	Opa Locka	$25,000	A	8.50%	3	8/5/2002	8/4/2005	$789.19
14	L0011	Kendall	$56,000	A	6.00%	3	8/7/2002	8/6/2005	$1,703.63
16	L0013	Kendall	$35,000	A	7.50%	3	8/15/2002	8/14/2005	$1,088.72
23	L0020	Kendall	$25,000	A	7.00%	4	9/19/2002	9/18/2006	$598.66
24	L0021	Opa Locka	$41,000	A	8.40%	3	9/22/2002	9/21/2005	$1,292.37
27									
28	Loan ID	Branch	Loan Amount	Loan Type	Interest Rate	Term	Start Date	End Date	Monthly Payment
29				A					
30									
31	Summary Statistics								
32	Number of Loans		7		Largest loan			$56,000	
33	Average loan amount		$32,429		Average interest rate			6.73%	
34	Total loan amount		$227,000		Average term			3.29	

FIGURE 7.22 Consumer Loans (exercise 6)

7. **The Top Ten Filter:** Figure 7.23 displays a workbook containing three worksheets, each with a different view of the same data about the United States. Open the *Chapter 7 Practice 7* workbook in the Exploring Excel folder, which contains just the original data worksheet. Proceed as follows:
   a. Click in cell F5 and enter the formula to compute the population density for the first state in the list. Format the cell to display the value to zero decimal places. Copy the formula to the remaining rows in the list.
   b. Format the worksheet appropriately. You do not have to match our formatting exactly.
   c. Right click the worksheet tab, select the command to Move or Copy the worksheet, check the box to create a copy, click OK, and then rename the copied worksheet to Population Density. Copy the worksheet a second time, renaming this worksheet to 13 Original States as shown in our figure. You will now apply the AutoFilter command to each of the new worksheets.
   d. Click the tab for the Population Density worksheet. Turn on the AutoFilter command. Click the down arrow next to the Population Density field, click Top 10 to display the Top 10 AutoFilter dialog box. Be sure that you have the appropriate entries in each of the three list boxes—that is, Top rather than Bottom, 10 for the number of entries, and items rather than percentages. Click OK to display the filtered list, which displays the filtered records in the same order as in the original list. Click in column F, then click the Sort Descending button on the Standard toolbar to display the population densities in descending sequence. Add the appropriate subtitle to this worksheet.
   e. Click the tab for the 13 Original States worksheet and create a filtered list to display the first 13 states admitted to the Union. Sort the list in ascending sequence by year admitted.
   f. Press and hold the Ctrl key as you select all three worksheets to enter the group mode for editing. Create a custom footer that contains your name, the worksheet tab, and today's date. Check the boxes to show gridlines and row and column headings. Force each worksheet to fit on one page.
   g. Print the entire workbook for your instructor. Add a cover sheet to complete the assignment.

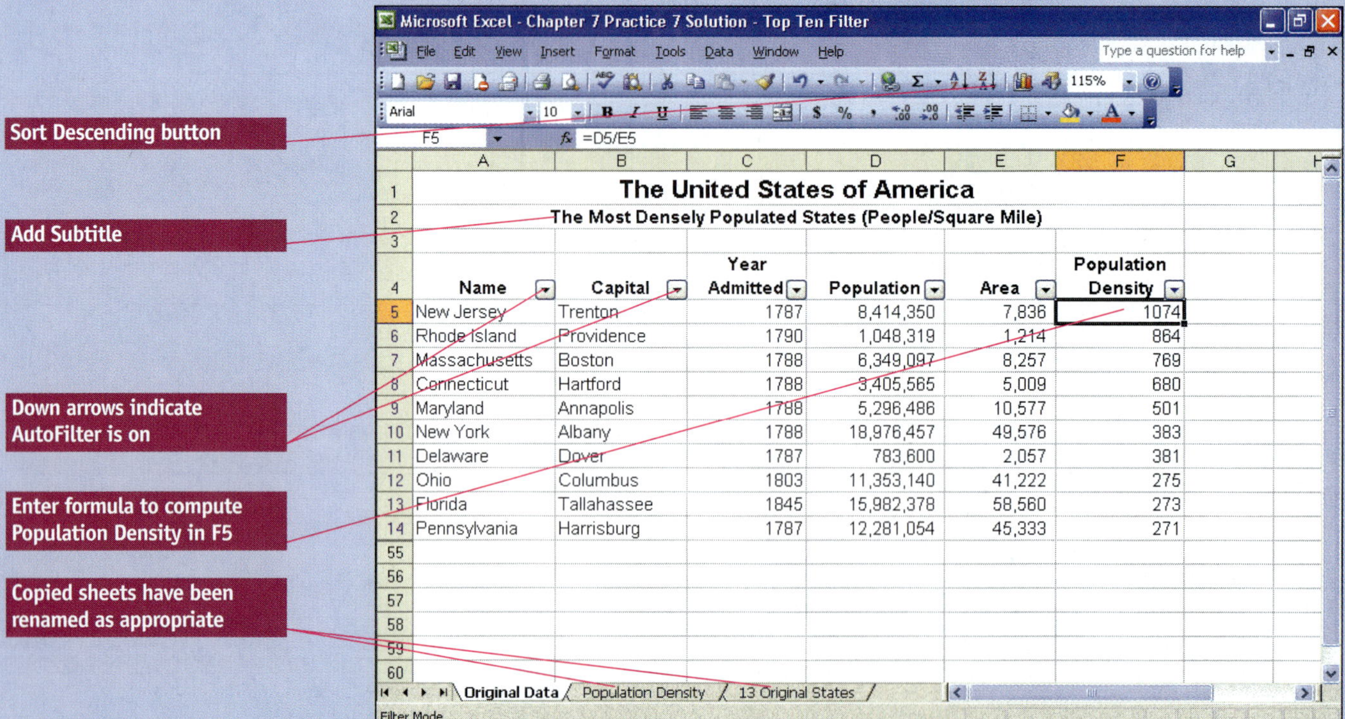

FIGURE 7.23 The Top Ten Filter (exercise 7)

8. **Compensation Report:** The document in Figure 7.24 consists of a memo created in Microsoft Word that is linked to a pivot table from exercise 5. The document was created in such a way that any change in the pivot table within the Excel workbook will be automatically reflected in the memo.
   a. Complete practice exercises 4 and 5 in this chapter to create the pivot table that will be used in the memo.
   b. Start Word, create a simple letterhead (we used the Drop Cap command in the Format menu to create our letterhead), then enter the text of the memo in Figure 7.24. You can use our text, or modify the wording as you see fit. Be sure to include your name in the signature area.
   c. Use the Windows taskbar to switch to Excel, copy either pivot table to the clipboard, then use the Paste Link command within Word to bring the pivot table into the Word document as a worksheet object.
   d. Move and/or size the table as necessary. Note, too, that you may have to insert or delete hard returns within the memo to space it properly. *Print this version of the memo for your instructor.*
   e. Prove to yourself that the linking really works by returning to Excel to modify the pivot table to show the total (as opposed to average) salary increase. Change the title of the pivot table as well.
   f. Use the Windows taskbar to return to the Word memo, which should show an updated copy of the pivot table. If you did the exercise correctly, you should see $51,000 as the total amount for all salary increases. Modify the text of the memo to say "revised" salary analysis, as opposed to "preliminary," then print this version of the memo for your instructor.
   g. Add a cover sheet, then submit the complete assignment, consisting of both versions of the memo, to your instructor.
   h. Save the Word document. Exit Word. Save the workbook. Exit Excel.

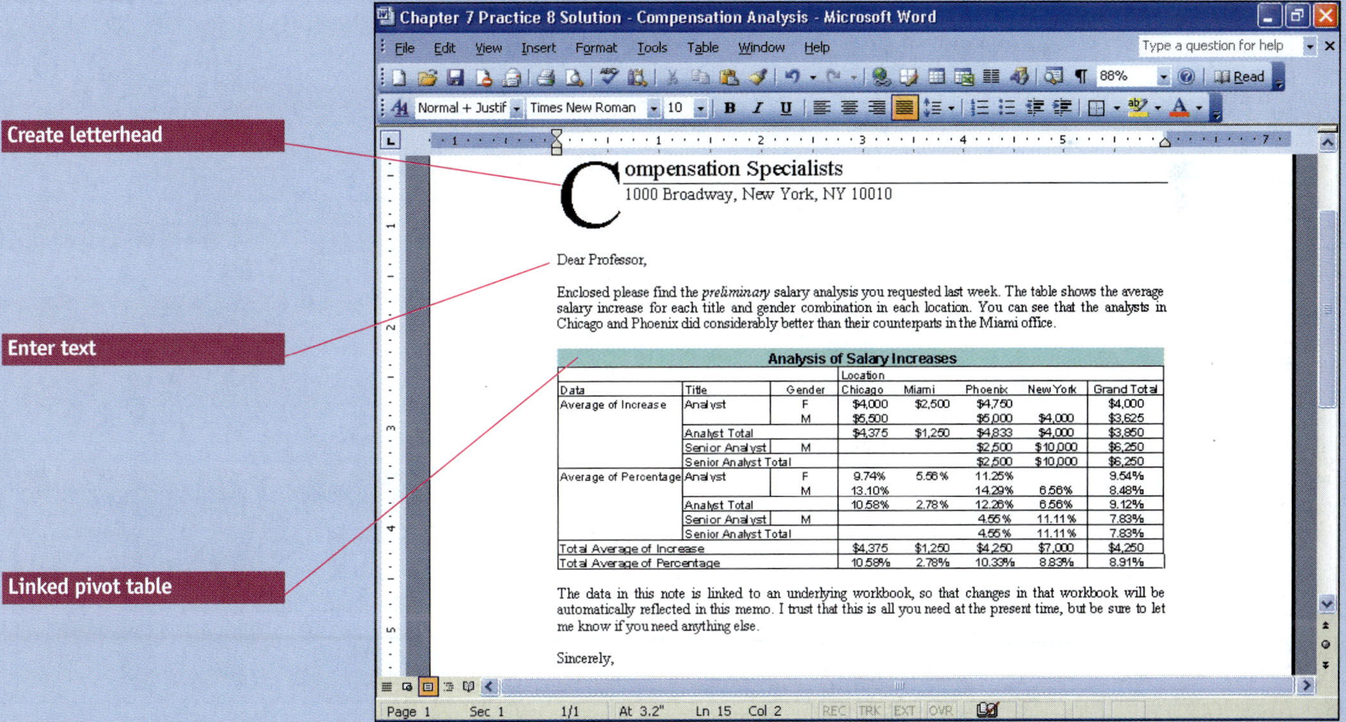

Compensation Specialists
1000 Broadway, New York, NY 10010

Dear Professor,

Enclosed please find the *preliminary* salary analysis you requested last week. The table shows the average salary increase for each title and gender combination in each location. You can see that the analysts in Chicago and Phoenix did considerably better than their counterparts in the Miami office.

Analysis of Salary Increases

			Location				
Data	Title	Gender	Chicago	Miami	Phoenix	New York	Grand Total
Average of Increase	Analyst	F	$4,000	$2,500	$4,750		$4,000
		M	$5,500		$5,000	$4,000	$3,625
	Analyst Total		$4,375	$1,250	$4,833	$4,000	$3,850
	Senior Analyst	M			$2,500	$10,000	$6,250
	Senior Analyst Total				$2,500	$10,000	$6,250
Average of Percentage	Analyst	F	9.74%	5.56%	11.25%		9.54%
		M	13.10%		14.29%	6.56%	8.48%
	Analyst Total		10.58%	2.78%	12.26%	6.56%	9.12%
	Senior Analyst	M			4.55%	11.11%	7.83%
	Senior Analyst Total				4.55%	11.11%	7.83%
Total Average of Increase			$4,375	$1,250	$4,250	$7,000	$4,250
Total Average of Percentage			10.58%	2.78%	10.33%	8.83%	8.91%

The data in this note is linked to an underlying workbook, so that changes in that workbook will be automatically reflected in this memo. I trust that this is all you need at the present time, but be sure to let me know if you need anything else.

Sincerely,

FIGURE 7.24 Compensation Report (exercise 8)

9. **The Analysis ToolPak:** The degree to which you will benefit from the analysis tools in Excel depends in part on your proficiency in statistics. Even if you are not a statistician, however, you can use a few basic techniques as shown in Figure 7.25. This worksheet uses three tools to perform some basic analysis. Start Excel, open a new workbook, and proceed as follows:
   a. Pull down the Tools menu and click the Add-Ins command to display the associated dialog box. Check the box for the Analysis TookPak. Click OK.
   b. Pull down the Tools menu a second time and click the Data Analysis command that has been added to the Tools menu. Scroll down the list of analysis tools until you can select random number generation. Click OK to display the Random Number Generation dialog box where you specify the type of random numbers that you want to generate.
   c. Enter 1 as the number of variables and 200 as the number of random numbers. Choose Normal as the distribution and enter 0 and 1 as the mean and standard deviation, respectively. Specify cell A2 as the output range and click OK. You should see 200 random numbers in cells A2 through A201. (Your values will be different from ours.) Click in cell A1 and enter Random Number as the column heading.
   d. Pull down the Tools menu, click the Data Analysis command, and then scroll down the list of analysis tools until you can select Descriptive Statistics. Enter A1:A201 as the input range, check the box that indicates there are labels in the first row, specify C1 as the output range, and check the box for summary statistics. Click OK. The descriptive statistics for the 200 random numbers will appear in columns C and D. The mean and standard deviation will differ from the theoretical values of 0 and 1, but they should be close.
   e. Enter the lower bounds for the histogram you are about to create in cells F1 through F13 as shown in Figure 7.25. Execute the Data Analysis command one final time and specify Histogram as the analysis tool. Enter A2:A201 as the input range and F2:F12 as the Bin range. Specify C17 as the output range. Click OK to create the histogram. Note how the values are clustered around the middle, which is what you'd expect from a normal distribution.
   f. Format the worksheet as appropriate and then print the completed worksheet for your instructor. Are you less intimated by statistics than previously?

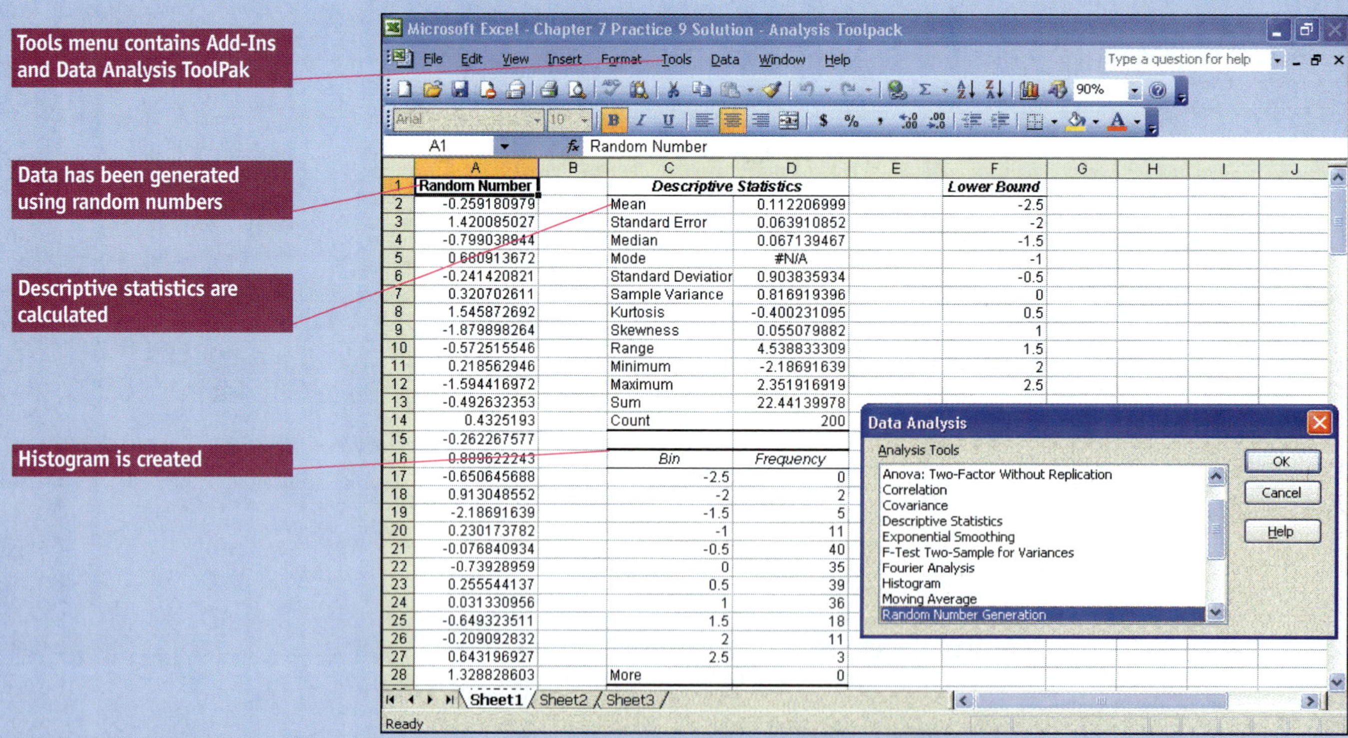

FIGURE 7.25 The Analysis ToolPak (exercise 9)

10. **XML and the Super Bowl:** The workbook in Figure 7.26 was created by importing data from an XML document into an Excel workbook, adding two new fields within the data (Winner and Victory Margin), and inserting two database functions to determine the number of times that each conference has won the big game. Proceed as follows:
    a. Start Excel. Pull down the Data menu, click the Import External Data command, and then click Import Data to display the Select Data Source dialog box. Change to the Exploring Excel folder and specify the file type as XML files. Select the *Chapter 7 Practice 10* XML document and click the Open button. Click OK when you see the message indicating that Excel will create a schema based on the XML source data.
    b. You should see the Import Data dialog box. The option button to put the data as an XML list in an existing worksheet is already selected, with cell A1 specified by default. Change the location of the list to cell A5. Click OK. The XML data is imported into the workbook.
    c. Pull down the View menu and open the XML Source task pane as shown in Figure 7.26. Click the Options button within the task pane to see the available options for an XML list. Press Esc to suppress the option list. Click the XML Maps button to explore a dialog box that allows you to add, delete, or rename an XML map. Close the XML Maps dialog box.
    d. Click in cell F5, type Winner, press the right arrow key to move to cell G5, type Victory Margin, and press enter. These fields have been added to the list (they appear within the blue border), but they do not appear within the XML map in the task pane.
    e. Click in cell F6 and enter an If function to determine the winner for that year. Click in cell G6. Enter the appropriate formula to display the victory margin. (Use the absolute value function to display the result as a positive number.) Copy both formulas to remaining rows in the worksheet.
    f. Complete the worksheet by developing the appropriate database functions to determine the number of times each conference has won the Super Bowl. You will need to create two criteria ranges elsewhere in the worksheet.
    g. Format the worksheet in an attractive fashion. Print the complete workbook for your instructor to show both displayed values and cell formulas.

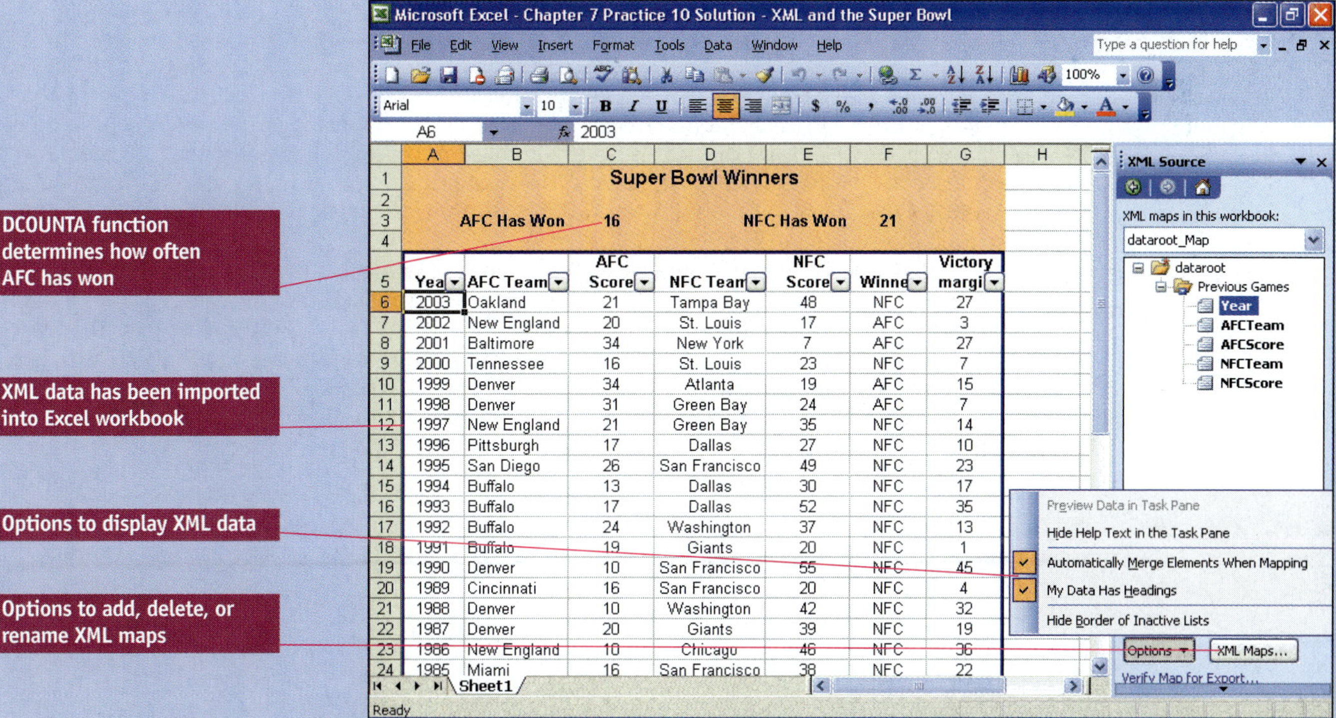

FIGURE 7.26 XML and the Super Bowl (exercise 10)

MINI CASES

Excel and Access

You can import data into Excel from Access. You can also export data from Excel to Access, except there is no Export wizard. Instead, you start Access as a separate application, open an existing database, then import the data from Excel; i.e., exporting data from Excel is equivalent to importing the data within Access.

Start Access and open the *Chapter 7 Mini Case—Excel and Access* database in the Exploring Excel folder. The Tables button should be selected within the Database window. Pull down the File menu, click the Get External Data command, and click Import to display the associated dialog box. Use the Look In box to change to the Exploring Excel folder, specify Microsoft Excel as the file type, and import the *Chapter 7 Mini Case—Excel and Access* workbook, which contains statistical data on countries around the world. You will be taken through the Import Spreadsheet wizard. Import the data into a new table and specify the Country field as the primary key (a unique field in every record). The wizard will end by indicating that it has imported the data. Click the Reports button in the Database window and print one or more of the existing reports that are based on the data that you just imported.

Asset Allocation

It's several years in the future and you find yourself happily married and financially prosperous. You and your spouse have accumulated substantial assets in a variety of accounts. Some of the money is in a regular account for use today, whereas other funds are in retirement accounts for later use. Much of the money, both regular and retirement, is invested in equities (i.e., the stock market), but a portion of your funds is also in nonequity funds such as money-market checking accounts and bank certificates of deposit. Your accounts are also in different places such as banks and brokerage houses. A summary of your accounts can be found in the *Asset Allocation* workbook. Your assignment is to open the workbook and develop a pivot table that will enable you and your spouse to keep track of your investments.

Fly by Night Airways

Fly by Night Airways is an independent airline offering charters and special tours. The airline has several independent agents, each of whom books trips for the airline. The data for all trips is maintained in the *Chapter 7 Mini Case—Fly by Night Airlines* Access database that is stored in the Exploring Excel folder. Your assignment is to start a new Excel workbook and import the data from the Access database into the Excel workbook to create a pivot table for data analysis. (Pull down the File menu, click the Open command, specify an Access database in the File Type list box, select the database in the Exploring Excel folder, and then click the Open button.)

Your pivot table should show the amount of contracts by marketing representative and contract status (whether the trip is still in the proposal stage or whether it has already been signed). The table should also have the flexibility to show all trips or trips that do or do not require passage through customs. Use the Page Setup command to create a custom footer that contains your name and the name of the worksheet. Print the completed workbook for your instructor.

CHAPTER 8

Automating Repetitive Tasks: Macros and Visual Basic for Applications

OBJECTIVES

After reading this chapter you will:

1. Define a macro; describe the relationship between Excel macros and VBA procedures.
2. Record a macro; use the Visual Basic Editor to modify a macro.
3. Use the VBA MsgBox and InputBox statements to enhance a macro.
4. Execute a macro via a keyboard shortcut or button.
5. Describe the Personal Macro workbook.
6. Use the Step Into command to debug a macro.
7. Use the VBA If and Do statements to implement decision making.

hands-on exercises

1. INTRODUCTION TO MACROS
   Input: None
   Output: My Macros
2. THE PERSONAL MACRO WORKBOOK
   Input: None
   Output: Personal Macro workbook
3. DATA MANAGEMENT MACROS
   Input: Employee List Solution (from Chapter 7)
   Output: Employee List Solution (additional changes)
4. ADDITIONAL MACROS
   Input: Employee List Solution (from exercise 3)
   Output: Employee List Solution (additional changes)
5. LOOPS AND DECISION MAKING
   Input: Loops and Decision Making
   Output: Loops and Decision Making Solution

CASE STUDY

THE SLEEPY SHOWROOM

Simon Key opened the Sleepy Showroom 30 years ago with a limited selection of twin and full-sized mattresses from one vendor. Today he offers a complete product line (twin, full, queen, and king-sized mattresses) in a variety of styles and prices from four different vendors. Simon prides himself on his huge selection; for example, he offers 20 different mattresses from just the Heavenly Sleep Company. The business is very profitable, yet Simon believes he has too many vendors and too many choices from each vendor. He has come to you for advice.

Simon has given you complete access to the financial information for his business in the form of an Excel workbook, which contains detailed information for every item in the showroom. The workbook also contains a criteria range and two database functions that display the units sold and corresponding profit for indicated criteria. The Sleep Wonderfully product line, for example, accounted for only 38% of the units sold, yet it generated 69% of the total profit. You can change the criteria to see similar statistics for other vendors and/or other parameters (e.g., mattress size). ■

Your assignment is to read the chapter, open the *Chapter 8 Case Study—The Sleepy Showroom* workbook, and create a series of four macros that will enable Simon to change the criteria to see the results for any vendor and/or any size mattress. The first macro should prompt Simon for the vendor and mattress, enter these values within the criteria range, and then filter the list to display only those items that match the indicated criteria. The second macro should clear the criteria range and display the entire list. The third and fourth macros should display the top ten items according to the percent of the total profit and the number of units sold, respectively. All of your macros should use range names, as opposed to specific cell references. (The range names are already defined in the workbook.) Simon has promised you the king-sized bed of your choice and a sizeable bonus if you can improve his bottom line.

INTRODUCTION TO MACROS

Have you ever pulled down the same menus and clicked the same sequence of commands over and over? Easy as the commands may be to execute, it is still burdensome to have to continually repeat the same mouse clicks or keystrokes. If you can think of any task that you do repeatedly, whether in one workbook or in a series of workbooks, you are a perfect candidate to use macros.

A ***macro*** is a set of instructions that tells Excel which commands to execute. It is in essence a program, and its instructions are written in Visual Basic, a programming language. Fortunately, however, you don't have to be a programmer to write macros. Instead, you use the macro recorder within Excel to record your commands, and let Excel write the macros for you.

The ***macro recorder*** stores Excel commands, in the form of ***Visual Basic*** instructions, within a workbook. (***Visual Basic for Applications***, or ***VBA***, is a subset of Visual Basic that is built into Microsoft Office.) To use the recorder, you pull down the Tools menu and click the Record New Macro command. From that point on (until you stop recording), every command you execute will be stored by the recorder. It doesn't matter whether you execute commands from pull-down menus via the mouse, or whether you use the toolbar or ***keyboard shortcuts***. The macro recorder captures every action you take and stores the equivalent Visual Basic statements as a macro within the workbook.

Figure 8.1 illustrates a simple macro to enter your name and class in cells A1 and A2 of the active worksheet. The macro is displayed in the ***Visual Basic Editor (VBE)***, which is used to create, edit, execute, and debug Excel macros. The Visual Basic Editor is a separate application (as can be determined from its button on the taskbar in Figure 8.1), and it is accessible from any application in Microsoft Office.

The left side of the VBE window in Figure 8.1 contains the ***Project Explorer***, which is similar in concept and appearance to the Windows Explorer, except that it displays only open workbooks and/or other Visual Basic projects. The Visual Basic statements for the selected module (Module1 in Figure 8.1) appear in the ***Code window*** in the right pane. As you shall see, a Visual Basic module consists of one or more procedures, each of which corresponds to an Excel macro. Thus, in this example, Module1 contains the NameAndCourse procedure corresponding to the Excel macro of the same name. Module1 itself is stored in the My Macros.XLS workbook.

As indicated, a macro consists of Visual Basic statements that were created through the macro recorder. We don't expect you to be able to write the Visual Basic procedure yourself, and you don't have to. You just invoke the recorder and let it capture the Excel commands for you. We do think it is important, however, to understand the macro, and so we proceed to explain its statements. As you read our discussion, do not be concerned with the precise syntax of every statement, but try to get an overall appreciation for what the statements do.

A macro always begins and ends with the Sub and End Sub statements, respectively. The ***Sub statement*** contains the name of the macro—for example, NameAndCourse in Figure 8.1. (Spaces are not allowed in a macro name.) The ***End Sub statement*** is physically the last statement and indicates the end of the macro. Sub and End Sub are Visual Basic keywords and appear in blue.

The next several statements begin with an apostrophe, appear in green, and are known as ***comments***. They provide information about the macro, but do not affect its execution. In other words, the results of a macro are the same, whether or not the comments are included. Comments are inserted automatically by the recorder to document the macro name, its author, and ***shortcut key*** (if any). You can add comments (a comment line must begin with an apostrophe), or delete or modify existing comments, as you see fit. Comments may also be added at the end of a statement by typing an apostrophe, then adding the explanatory text; i.e., anything after the apostrophe is considered a comment.

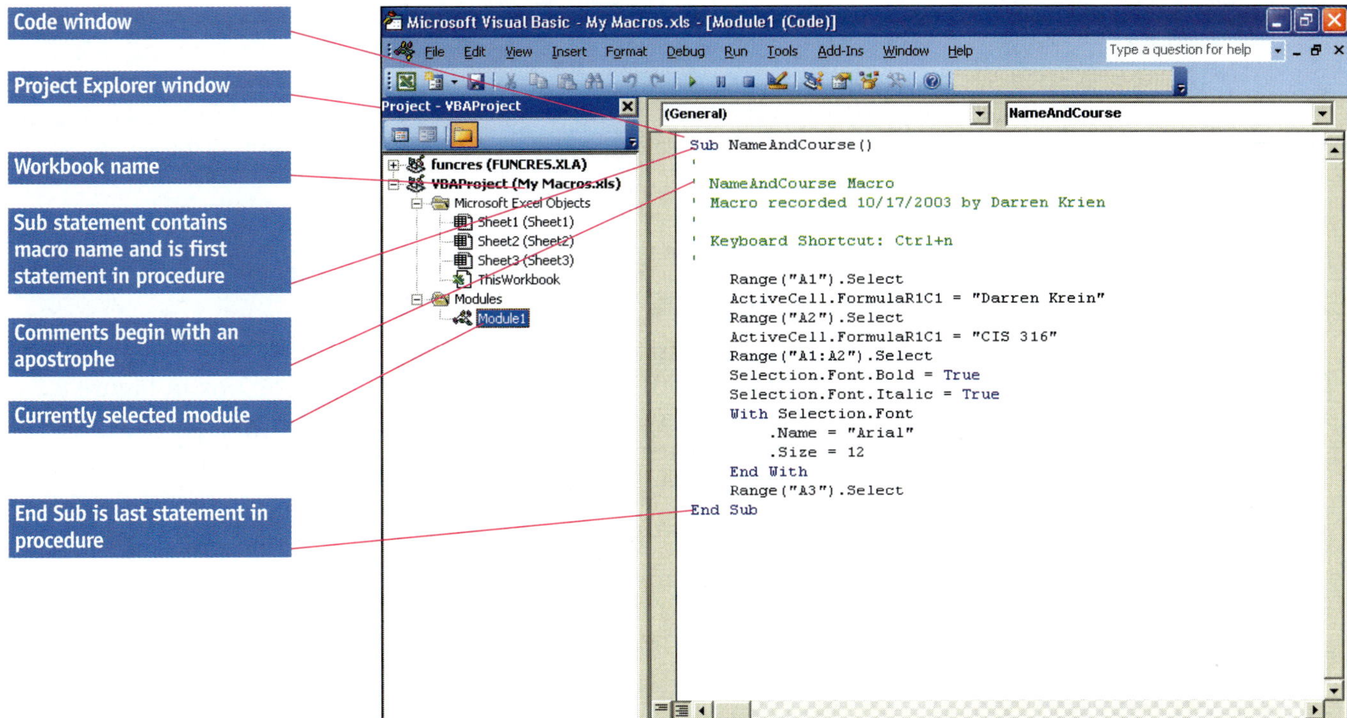

FIGURE 8.1 A Simple Macro

Every other statement is a Visual Basic instruction that was created as a result of an action taken in Excel. For example, the statements

Range ("A1").Select
and ActiveCell.FormulaR1C1 = "Darren Krein"

select cell A1 as the active cell, then enter the text "Darren Krein" into the active cell. These statements are equivalent to clicking in cell A1 of a worksheet, typing the indicated entry into the active cell, then pressing the Enter key (or an arrow key) to complete the entry. In similar fashion, the statements

Range ("A2").Select
and ActiveCell.FormulaR1C1 = "CIS 316"

select cell A2 as the active cell, then enter the text entry "CIS 316" into that cell. The concept of select-then-do applies equally well to statements within a macro. Thus, the statements

```
Range ("A1:A2").Select
Selection.Font.Bold = True
Selection.Font.Italic = True
```

select cells A1 through A2, then change the font for the selected cells to bold italic. The ***With statement*** enables you to perform multiple actions on the same object. All commands between the With and corresponding ***End With statement*** are executed collectively; for example, the statements

```
With Selection.Font
    .Name = "Arial"
    .Size = 12
End With
```

change the formatting of the selected cells (A1:A2) to 12 point Arial. The last statement in the macro, Range ("A3").Select, selects cell A3, thus deselecting all other cells, a practice we use throughout the chapter.

hands-on exercise

1 Introduction to Macros

Objective To record, run, view, and edit a simple macro; to establish a keyboard shortcut to run a macro. Use Figure 8.2 as a guide in doing the exercise.

Step 1: Create a Macro

- Start Excel. Open a new workbook if one is not already open. Save the workbook as **My Macros** in the **Exploring Excel folder**.
- Pull down the **Tools menu**, click (or point to) the **Macro command**, then click **Record New Macro** to display the Record Macro dialog box in Figure 8.2a. (If you don't see the Macro command, click the double arrow at the bottom of the menu to see more commands.)
- Enter **NameAndCourse** as the name of the macro. (Spaces are not allowed in the macro name.)
- The description is entered automatically and contains today's date and the name of the person in whose name this copy of Excel is registered. If necessary, change the description to include your name.
- Click in the **Shortcut Key** check box and enter a **lowercase n**. Ctrl+n should appear as the shortcut as shown in Figure 8.2a. (If you see Ctrl+Shift+N it means you typed an uppercase N rather than a lowercase letter. Correct the entry to a lowercase n.)
- Check that the option to Store macro in **This Workbook** is selected. Click **OK** to record the macro, which displays the Stop Recording toolbar.

Enter macro name

Enter lowercase n as shortcut key

Click down arrow and select This Workbook

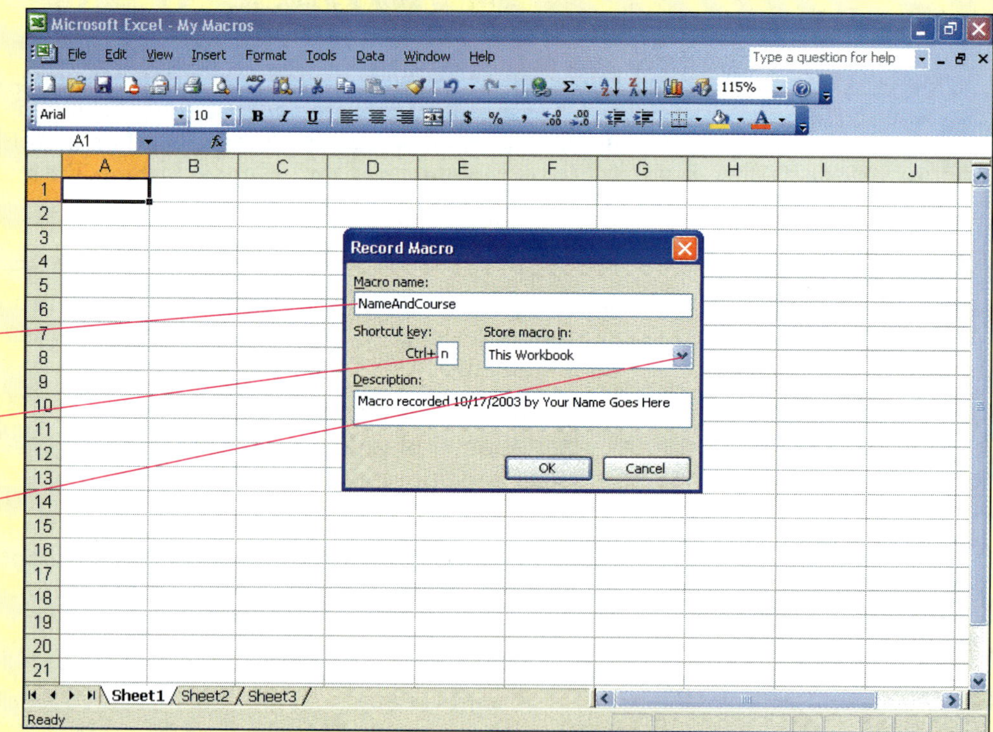

(a) Create a Macro (step 1)

FIGURE 8.2 Hands-on Exercise 1

Step 2: Record the Macro

- Look carefully at the Relative References button on the Stop Recording button to be sure it is flush with the other buttons; that is, the button should *not* be pushed in. (See boxed tip on "Is the Button In or Out?")
- You should be in Sheet1, ready to record the macro, as shown in Figure 8.2b. The status bar indicates that you are in the Recording mode:
  - Click in **cell A1** even if it is already selected. Enter your name.
  - Click in **cell A2**. Enter the course you are taking.
  - Click and drag to select **cells A1 through A2**.
  - Click the **Bold button**. Click the **Italic button**.
  - Click the arrow on the **Font Size list box**. Click **12** to change the point size.
  - Click in **cell A3** to deselect all other cells prior to ending the macro.
- Click the **Stop Recording button**. (If you do not see the Stop Recording toolbar, pull down the **Tools button**, click **Macro**, then click the **Stop Recording command**.)
- Save the workbook.

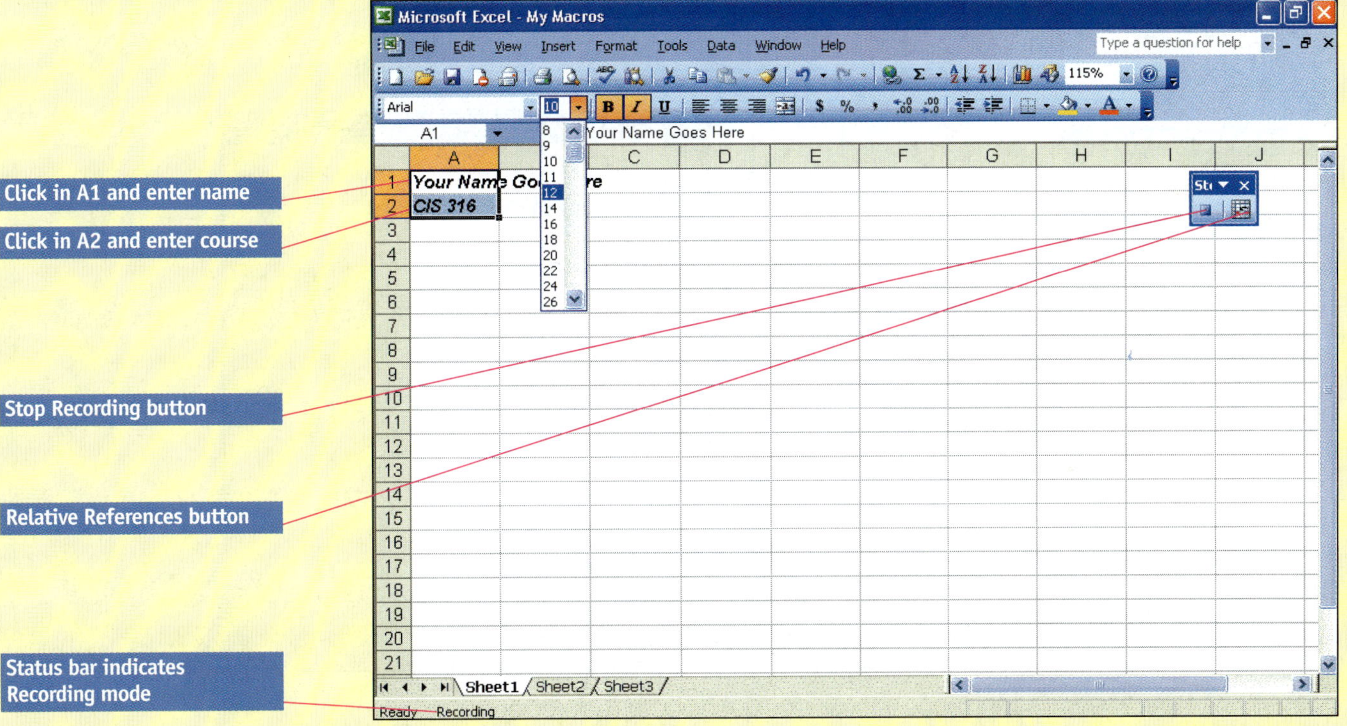

(b) Record the Macro (step 2)

FIGURE 8.2 Hands-on Exercise 1 (*continued*)

IS THE BUTTON IN OR OUT?

The distinction between relative and absolute references within a macro is critical and is described in detail at the end of this exercise. The Relative References button on the Stop Recording toolbar toggles between the two—absolute references when the button is out, relative references when the button is in. The ScreenTip, however, displays Relative References regardless of whether the button is in or out. We wish that Microsoft had made it easier to tell which type of reference you are recording, but they didn't.

Step 3: Test the Macro

- To run (test) the macro, you have to remove the contents and formatting from cells A1 and A2. Click and drag to select **cells A1 through A2**.
- Pull down the **Edit menu**. Click **Clear**. Click **All** from the cascaded menu to erase both the contents and formatting from the selected cells. Cells A1 through A2 are empty as shown in Figure 8.2c.
- Pull down the **Tools menu**. Click **Macro**, then click the **Macros . . . command** to display the dialog box in Figure 8.2c.
- Click **NameAndCourse**, which is the macro you just recorded. Click **Run**. Your name and class are entered in cells A1 and A2, then formatted according to the instructions in the macro.
- Clear the contents and formatting in cells A1 and A2. Press **Ctrl+n** (the keyboard shortcut) to rerun the NameAndCourse macro. Your name and class should reappear in cells A1 and A2.

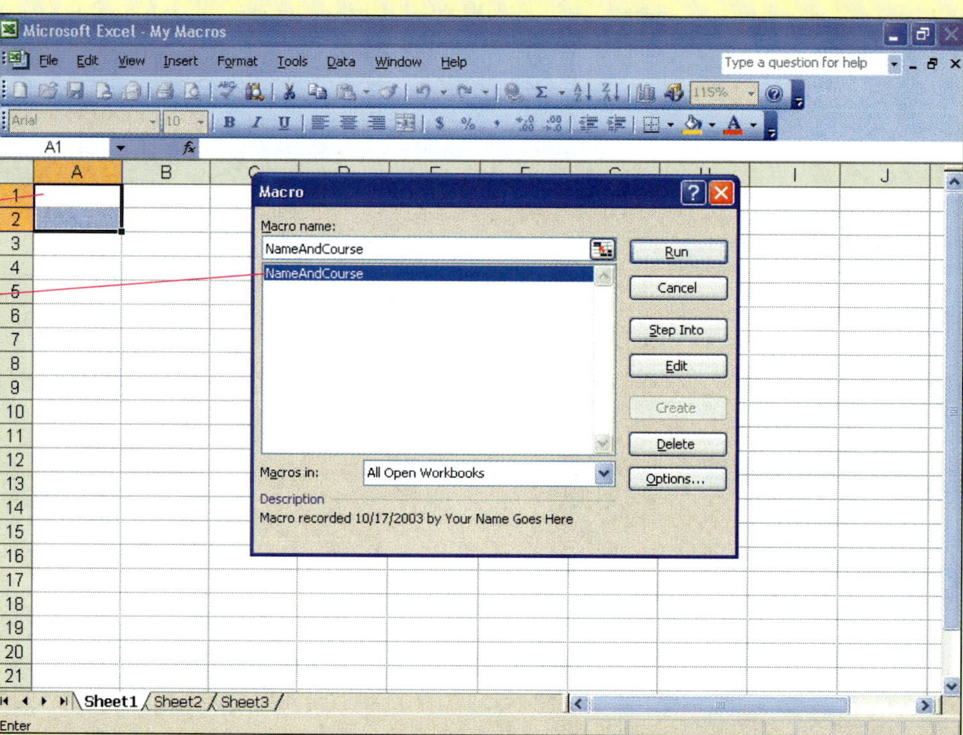

(c) Test the Macro (step 3)

FIGURE 8.2 Hands-on Exercise 1 (*continued*)

THE EDIT CLEAR COMMAND

The Edit Clear command erases the contents of a cell, its formatting, and/or its comments. Select the cell or cells to erase, pull down the Edit menu, click the Clear command, then click All, Formats, Contents, or Comments from the cascaded menu. Pressing the Del key is equivalent to executing the Edit Clear Contents command as it clears the contents of a cell, but retains the formatting and comments.

Step 4: Start the Visual Basic Editor

- Pull down the **Tools menu**, click the **Macro command**, then click **Visual Basic Editor** (or press **Alt+F11**) to open the Visual Basic Editor. Maximize the VBE window.
- If necessary, pull down the **View menu**. Click **Project Explorer** to open the Project Explorer window in the left pane. There is currently one open VBA project, My Macros.xls, which is the name of the open workbook in Excel.
- If necessary, click the **plus sign** next to the Modules folder to expand that folder, click (select) **Module1**, pull down the **View menu**, and click **Code** to open the Code window in the right pane. Click the **Maximize button** in the Code window.
- Your screen should match the one in Figure 8.2d. The first statement below the comments should be *Range("A1").Select*, which indicates that the macro was correctly recorded with absolute references.
- If you see a very different statement, *ActiveCell.FormulaR1C1*, it means that you incorrectly recorded the macro with relative references. Right click **Module1** in the Project Explorer window, select the **Remove Module1 command** (respond **No** when asked if you want to export it), then return to step 1 and rerecord the macro.

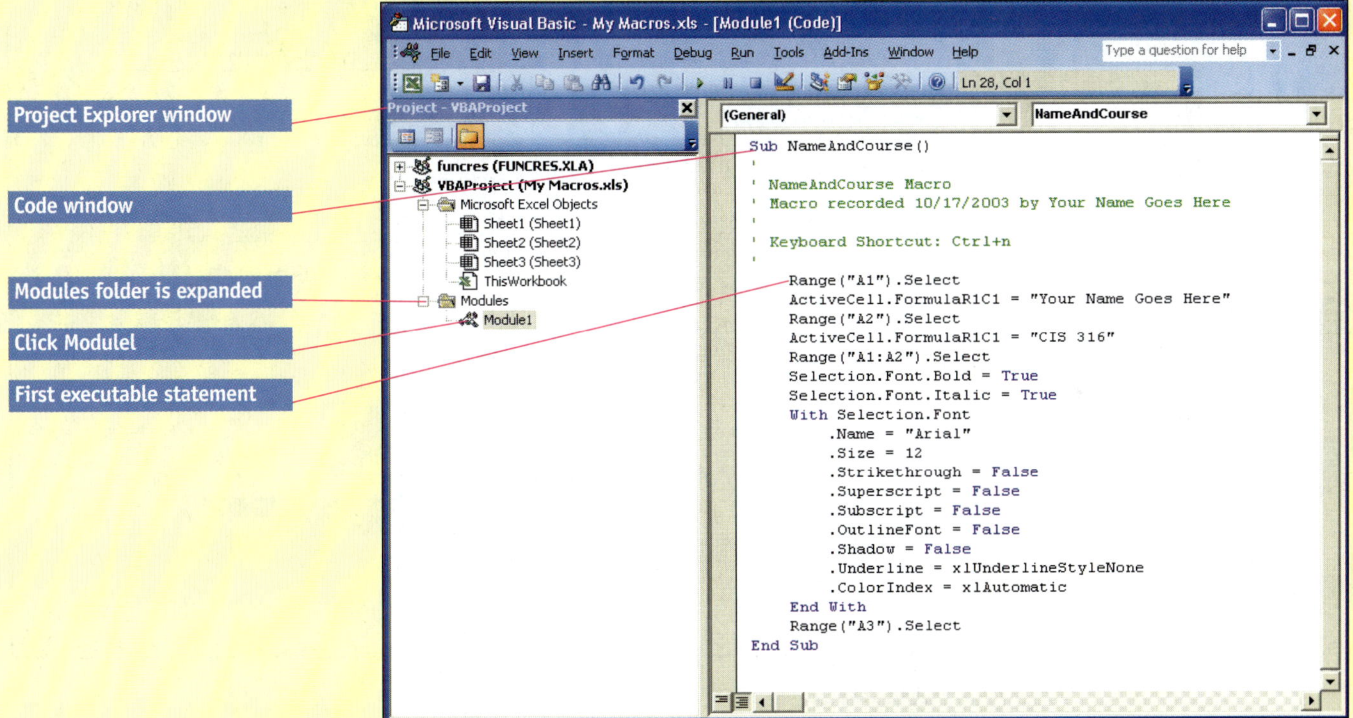

(d) Start the Visual Basic Editor (step 4)

FIGURE 8.2 Hands-on Exercise 1 (*continued*)

THE END RESULT

Excel provides multiple ways to accomplish the same task; for example, you can click the Bold button on the Formatting toolbar, or you can use the Ctrl+B shortcut. The macro recorder records only the end result, with no indication of which technique was used. Thus, you will see Selection.Font.Bold = True (or False) regardless of whether you used the toolbar or the mouse.

Step 5: Edit the Macro

- Edit the NameAndCourse macro by changing the font name and size to **"Times New Roman"** and **24**, respectively, as shown in Figure 8.2e.
- Click and drag to select the next seven statements as shown in Figure 8.2e.
- Press the **Del key** to delete these statements from the macro. (These statements contain default values and are unnecessary.) Delete any blank lines as well.
- Press **Alt+F11** to toggle back to the Excel workbook (or click the **Excel button** on the Windows taskbar).
- Clear the entries and formatting in cells A1 and A2 as you did earlier, then rerun the NameAndCourse macro.
- Your name and class should once again be entered in cells A1 and A2 but in a different and larger font. (If the macro does not execute correctly, press **Alt+F11** to toggle back to the Visual Basic Editor to correct your macro.)
- Save the workbook.

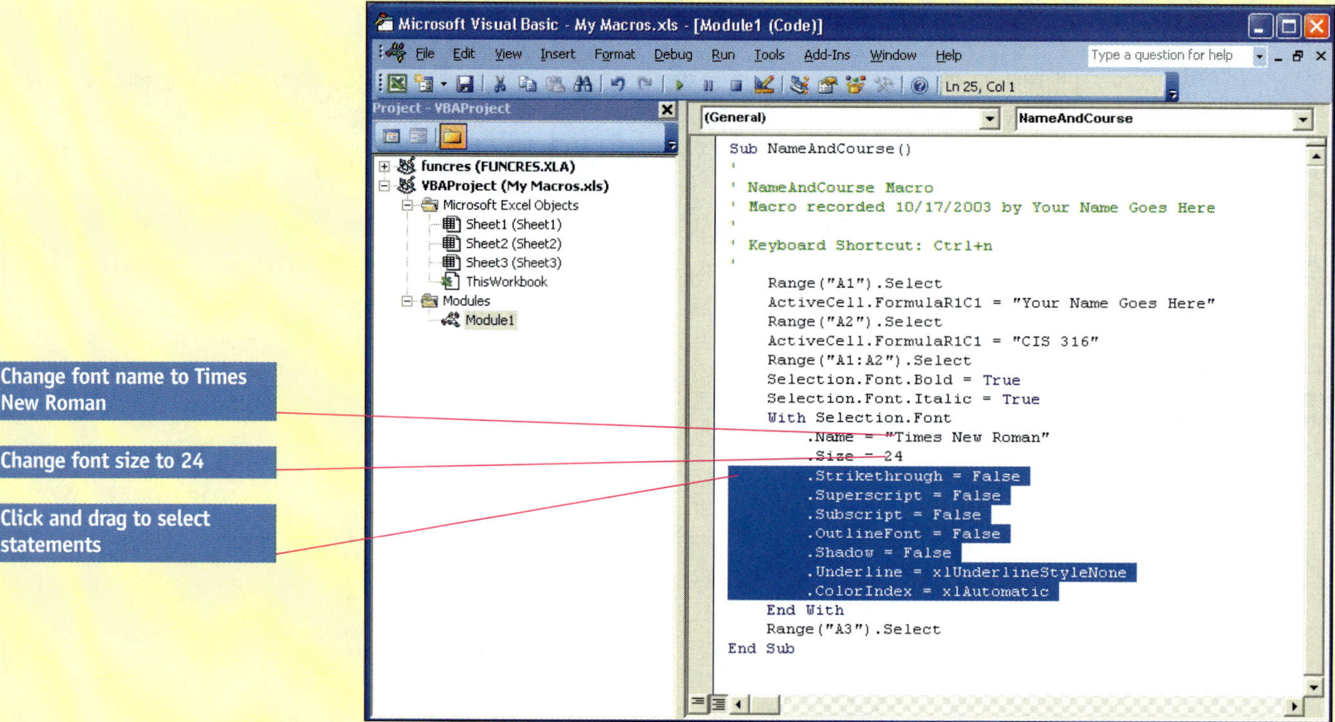

(e) Edit the Macro (step 5)

FIGURE 8.2 Hands-on Exercise 1 (*continued*)

SIMPLIFY THE MACRO

The macro recorder usually sets all possible options for an Excel command or dialog box even if you do not change those options. We suggest, therefore, that you make a macro easier to read by deleting the unnecessary statements. Take a minute, however, to review the statements prior to removing them, so that you can see the additional options. (You can click the Undo button to restore the deleted statements if you make a mistake.)

Step 6: Create the Erase Macro

- Pull down the **Tools menu**. Click the **Macro command**, then click **Record New Macro** from the cascaded menu. You will see the Record Macro dialog box.
- Enter **EraseNameAndCourse** as the name of the macro. Do not leave any spaces in the macro name. If necessary, change the description to include your name.
- Click in the **Shortcut Key** check box and enter a **lowercase e**. (Ctrl+e should appear as the shortcut.) Check that the option to Store macro in **This Workbook** is selected.
- Click **OK** to begin recording the macro, which displays the Stop Recording toolbar. Be sure you are recording absolute references (i.e., the Relative References button should be flush on the toolbar).
  - Click and drag to select **cells A1 through A2** as shown in Figure 8.2f, even if they are already selected.
  - Pull down the **Edit menu**. Click **Clear**. Click **All** from the cascaded menu. Cells A1 through A2 should now be empty.
  - Click in **cell A3** to deselect all other cells prior to ending the macro.
- Click the **Stop Recording button** to end the macro.

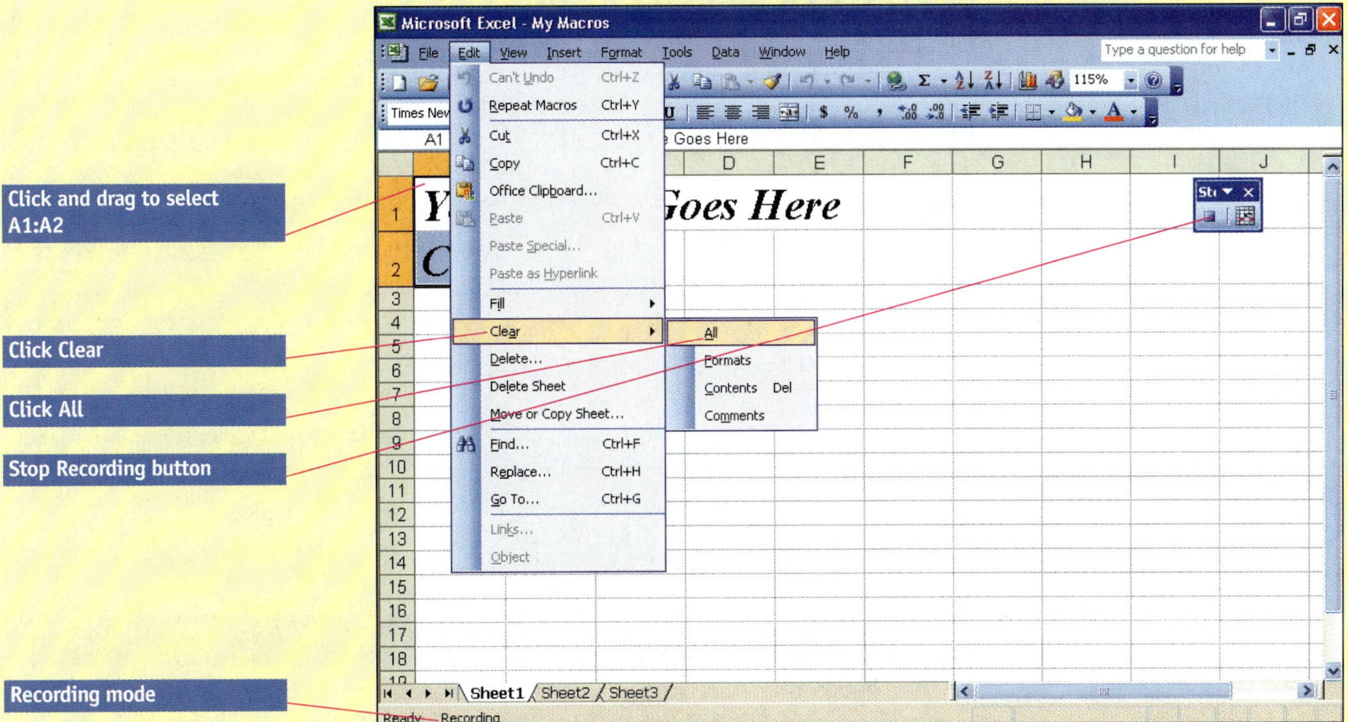

(f) Create the Erase Macro (step 6)

FIGURE 8.2 Hands-on Exercise 1 (*continued*)

TO SELECT OR NOT SELECT

If you start recording, then select a cell(s) within the macro, the selection becomes part of the macro, and the macro will always operate on the same cell. If, however, you select the cell(s) prior to recording, the macro is more general and operates on the selected cells, which may differ every time the macro is executed. Both techniques are valid, and the decision depends on what you want the macro to do.

Step 7: Shortcut Keys

- Press **Ctrl+n** to execute the NameAndCourse macro. (You need to reenter your name and course to test the newly created EraseNameAndCourse macro.)
- Your name and course should again appear in cells A1 and A2 as shown in Figure 8.2g.
- Press **Ctrl+e** to execute the EraseNameAndCourse macro. Cells A1 and A2 should again be empty.
- You can press **Ctrl+n** and **Ctrl+e** repeatedly, to enter and then erase your name and course. End this step after having erased the data.
- Save the workbook.

Press Ctrl+n to run the NameAndCourse macro

Press Ctrl+e to run the macro to erase your name and course

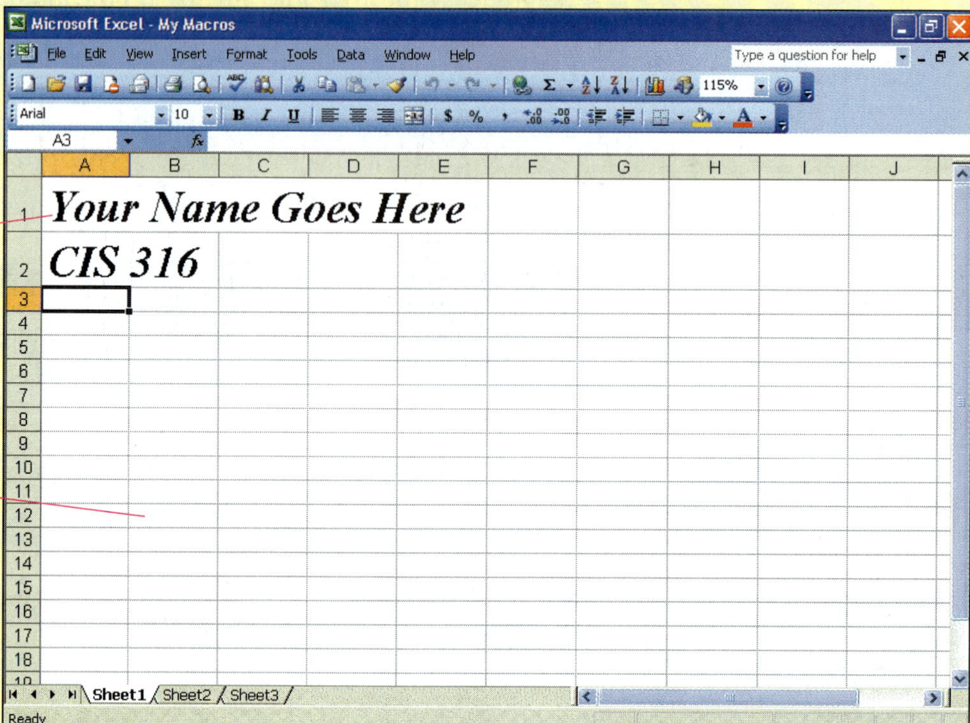

(g) Shortcut Keys (step 7)

FIGURE 8.2 Hands-on Exercise 1 (*continued*)

TROUBLESHOOTING

If the macro shortcut keys do not work, it is probably because they were not defined properly. Pull down the Tools menu, click Macro to display a cascaded menu, click the Macros . . . command, then select the desired macro in the Macro Name list box. Click the Options button, then check the entry in the Shortcut Key text box. A lowercase letter creates a shortcut with just the Ctrl key, whereas an uppercase letter uses Ctrl+Shift with the shortcut. Thus, "n" and "N" will establish shortcuts of Ctrl+n and Ctrl+Shift+N, respectively.

Step 8: Step through the Macro

- Press **Alt+F11** to switch back to the VBE window. Click the **Close button** to close the **Project window** within the Visual Basic Editor. The Code window expands to take the entire Visual Basic Editor window.
- Point to an empty area on the Windows taskbar, then click the **right mouse button** to display a shortcut menu. Click **Tile Windows Vertically**.
- Your desktop should be similar to Figure 8.2h. It doesn't matter if the workbook is in the left or right window.
- Click in the **Visual Basic Editor window**, then click anywhere within the NameAndCourse macro. Pull down the **Debug menu** and click the **Step Into command** (or press the **F8 key**). The Sub statement is highlighted.
- Press the **F8 key** to move to the first executable statement (the comments are skipped). The statement is highlighted, but it has not yet been executed.
- Press the **F8 key** again to execute this statement (which selects cell A1 and moves to the next statement). Continue to press the **F8 key** to execute the statements one at a time. You see the effect of each statement in the Excel window.

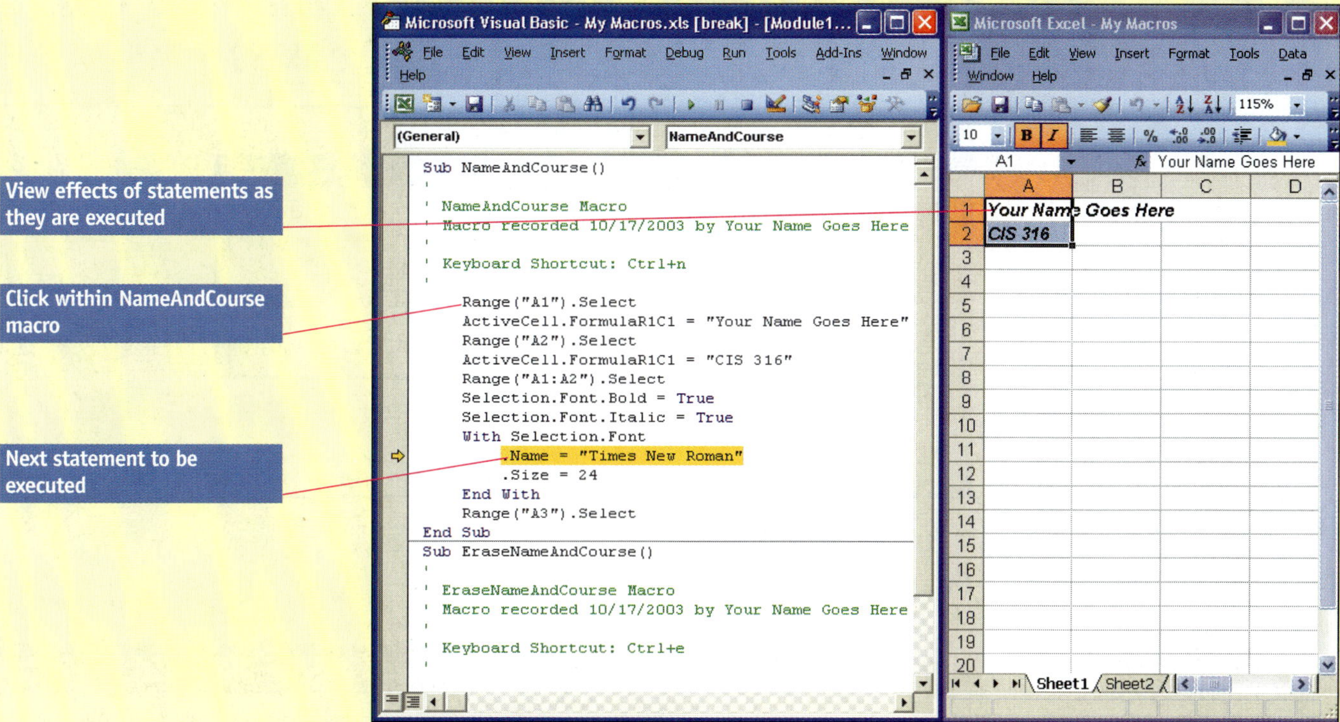

(h) Step through the Macro (step 8)

FIGURE 8.2 Hands-on Exercise 1 (*continued*)

THE STEP INTO COMMAND

The Step Into command is useful to slow down the execution of a macro in the event the macro does not perform as intended. In essence, you execute the macro one statement at a time, while viewing the results of each statement in the associated worksheet. If a statement does not do what you want it to do, just change the statement in the Visual Basic window, then continue to press the F8 key to step through the procedure.

Step 9: Print the Module

- Click in the **Visual Basic window**. Pull down the **File menu**. Click **Print** to display the Print - VBAProject dialog box in Figure 8.2i.
- Click the option button to print the current module. Click **OK**. Submit the listing of the current module, which contains the procedures for both macros, to your instructor as proof you did this exercise.
- Close the My Macros workbook. Click **Yes** if asked to save the workbook. The macros are stored within the workbook.
- Exit Excel if you do not wish to continue with the next hands-on exercise at this time.

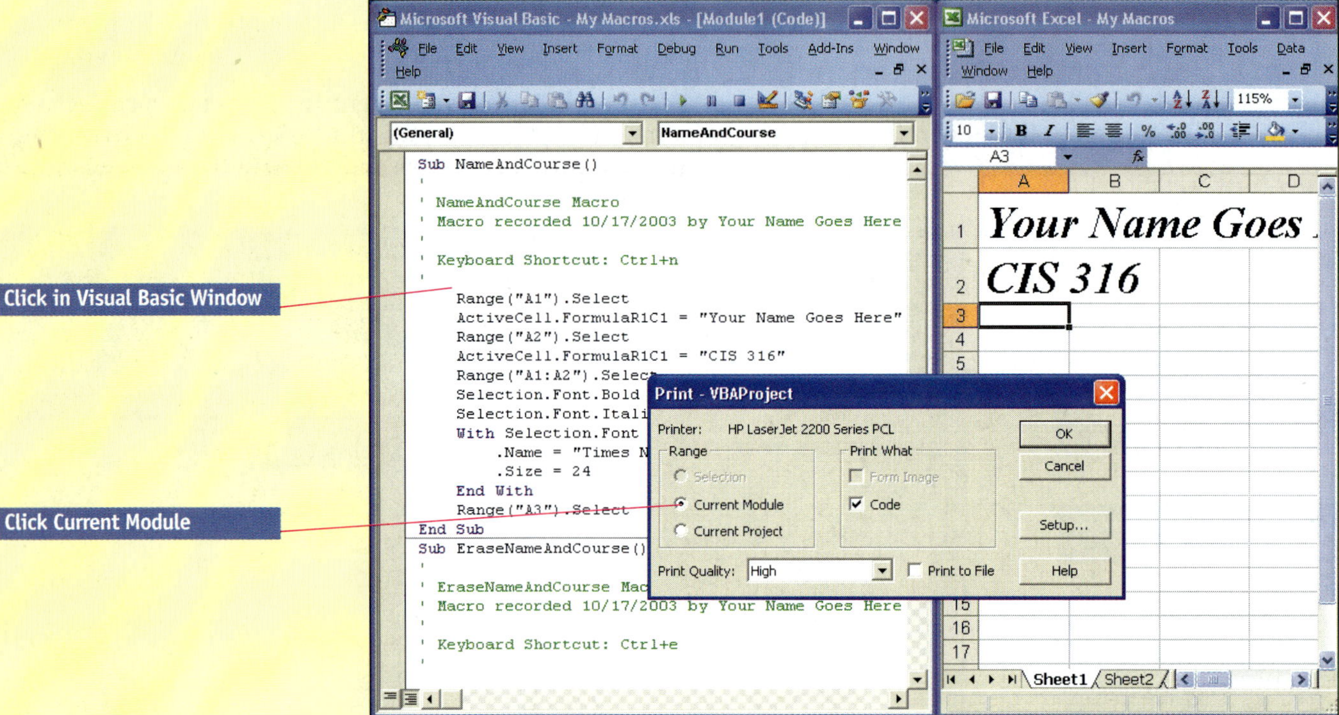

(i) Print the Module (step 9)

FIGURE 8.2 Hands-on Exercise 1 (*continued*)

PROCEDURE VIEW VERSUS FULL MODULE VIEW

The procedures within a module can be displayed individually, or alternatively, multiple procedures can be viewed simultaneously. To go from one view to the other, click the Procedure View button at the bottom of the window to display just the procedure you are working on, or click the Full Module View button to display multiple procedures. You can press Ctrl+PgDn and Ctrl+PgUp to move between procedures in either view. Use the vertical scroll bar to move up and down within the VBA window.

RELATIVE VERSUS ABSOLUTE REFERENCES

One of the most important options to specify when recording a macro is whether the references are to be relative or absolute. A reference is a cell address. An ***absolute reference*** is a constant address that always refers to the same cell. A ***relative reference*** is variable in that the reference will change from one execution of the macro to the next, depending on the location of the active cell when the macro is executed.

To appreciate the difference, consider Figure 8.3, which displays two versions of the NameAndCourse macro from the previous exercise, one with absolute and one with relative references. Figure 8.3a uses absolute references to place your name, course, and date in cells A1, A2, and A3. The data will always be entered in these cells regardless of which cell is selected when you execute the macro.

Figure 8.3b enters the same data, but with relative references, so that the cells in which the data are entered depend on which cell is selected when the macro is executed. If cell A1 is selected, your name, course, and date will be entered in cells A1, A2, and A3. If, however, cell E4 is the active cell when you execute the macro, then your name, course, and date will be entered in cells E4, E5, and E6.

A relative reference is specified by an ***offset*** that indicates the number of rows and columns from the active cell. An offset of (1,0) indicates a cell one row below the active cell. An offset of (0,1) indicates a cell one column to the right of the active cell. In similar fashion, an offset of (1,1) indicates a cell one row below and one column to the right of the active cell. Negative offsets are used for cells above or to the left of the current selection.

Absolute References to cells A1, A2, and A3

```
Range("A1").Select
ActiveCell.FormulaR1C1 = "Darren Krein"
Range("A2").Select
ActiveCell.FormulaR1C1 = "CIS 316"
Range("A3").Select
ActiveCell.FormulaR1C1 = "=TODAY()"
Range("A1:A3").Select
Selection.Font.Italic = True
With Selection.Font
    .Name = "Arial"
    .Size = 12
End With
Range("A4").Select
```

(a) Absolute References

Relative references to cell one row below the active cell

Indicates a column of 3 cells is to be selected

```
ActiveCell.FormulaR1C1 = "Darren Krein"
ActiveCell.Offset(1, 0).Range("A1").Select
ActiveCell.FormulaR1C1 = "CIS 316"
ActiveCell.Offset(1, 0).Range("A1").Select
ActiveCell.FormulaR1C1 = "=TODAY()"
ActiveCell.Offset(-2, 0).Range("A1:A3").Select
Selection.Font.Italic = True
With Selection.Font
    .Name = "Arial"
    .Size = 12
End With
ActiveCell.Offset(3, 0).Range("A1").Select
```

(b) Relative References

FIGURE 8.3 Absolute versus Relative References

Relative references may appear confusing at first, but they extend the power of a macro by making it more general. You will appreciate this capability as you learn more about macros. Let us begin by recognizing that the statement

ActiveCell.Offset (1,0).Range ("A1").Select

means select the cell one row below the active cell. It has nothing to do with cell A1, and you might wonder why the entry Range ("A1") is included. The answer is that the offset specifies the location of the new range (one row below the current cell), and the A1 indicates that the size of that range is a single cell (A1). In similar fashion, the statement

ActiveCell.Offset (–2,0).Range ("A1:A3").Select

selects a range, starting two rows above the current cell, that is one column by three rows in size. Again, it has nothing to do with cells A1 through A3. The offset specifies the location of a new range (two rows above the current cell) and the shape of that range (a column of three cells). If you are in cell D11 when the statement is executed, the selected range will be cells D9 through D11. The selection starts with the cell (cell D9) two rows above the active cell, then it continues from that point to select a range consisting of one column by three rows (cells D9:D11).

RELATIVE VERSUS ABSOLUTE REFERENCES

Relative references appear confusing at first, but they extend the power of a macro by making it more general. Macro statements that have been recorded with relative references include an offset to indicate the number of rows and columns the selection is to be from the active cell. An offset of (–1,0) indicates a cell one row above the active cell, whereas an offset of (0,–1) indicates a cell one column to the left of the active cell. Positive offsets are used for cells below or to the right of the current selection.

THE PERSONAL MACRO WORKBOOK

The hands-on exercise at the beginning of the chapter created the NameAndCourse macro in the My Macros workbook, where it is available to that workbook or to any other workbook that is in memory when the My Macros workbook is open. What if, however, you want the macro to be available at all times, not just when the My Macros workbook is open? This is easily accomplished by storing the macro in the Personal Macro workbook when it is first recorded.

The ***Personal Macro workbook*** opens automatically whenever Excel is loaded. This is because the Personal Macro workbook is stored in the XLStart folder, a folder that Excel checks each time it is loaded into memory. Once open, the macros in the Personal workbook are available to any other open workbook. The following hands-on exercise creates the NameAndCourse macro with relative references, then stores that macro in the Personal Macro workbook.

The exercise also expands the macro to enter the date of execution, and further generalizes the macro to accept the name of the course as input. The latter is accomplished through the Visual Basic ***InputBox function*** that prompts the user for a specific response, then stores that response within the macro. In other words, the Excel macro is enhanced through the inclusion of a VBA statement that adds functionality to the original macro. You start with the macro recorder to translate Excel commands into a VBA procedure, then you modify the procedure by adding the necessary VBA statements. (The InputBox function must be entered manually into the procedure since there is no corresponding Excel command, and hence the macro recorder would not work.)

hands-on exercise

2 The Personal Macro Workbook

Objective To create and store a macro in the Personal Macro workbook; to assign a toolbar button to a macro; to use the Visual Basic InputBox function. Use Figure 8.4 as a guide in the exercise.

Step 1: The Personal Macro Workbook

- Start Excel. Be sure to close the My Macros workbook from the previous exercise to avoid any conflict with an existing macro.
- Open a new workbook if one is not already open. Pull down the **Tools menu**, click (or point to) the **Macro command**, then click **Record New Macro** to display the Record Macro dialog box.
- Enter **NameAndCourse** as the name of the macro. Do not leave any spaces in the macro name. Click in the **Shortcut Key** check box and enter a **lowercase n**. Ctrl+n should appear as the shortcut.
- Click the **drop-down arrow** in the Store macro in list box and select the Personal Macro workbook as shown in Figure 8.4a. (If you are working on a network, as opposed to a standalone machine, you may not be able to access the **Personal Macro workbook**, in which case you can save the macro in This Workbook.)
- Click **OK** to begin recording the macro, which in turn displays the Stop Recording toolbar.

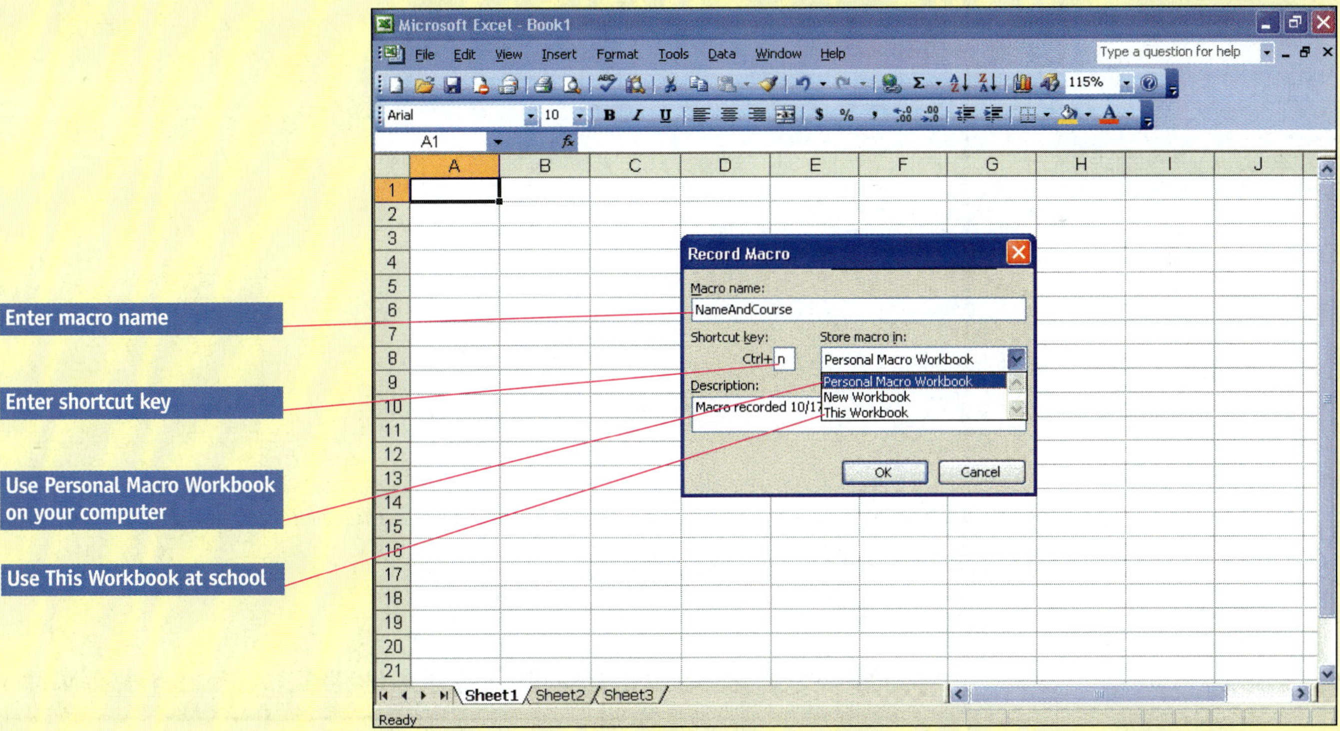

(a) The Personal Macro Workbook (step 1)

FIGURE 8.4 Hands-on Exercise 2

Step 2: Record with Relative References

- Click the **Relative References button** on the Stop Recording toolbar so that the button is pushed in as shown in Figure 8.4a.
- The Relative References button functions as a toggle switch—click it, and the button is pushed in to record relative references. Click it again, and you record absolute references. Be sure to record relative references.
- Enter your name in the active cell. Do *not* select the cell.
- Press the **down arrow key** to move to the cell immediately underneath the current cell. Enter the course you are taking.
- Press the **down arrow key** to move to the next cell. Enter **=TODAY()**.
- Click and drag to select the three cells containing the data values you just entered (cells A1 through A3 in Figure 8.4b).
  - Click the **Bold button**. Click the **Italic button**.
  - Click the arrow on the **Font Size list box**. Click **12** to change the point size.
  - Click in **cell A4** to deselect all other cells prior to ending the macro.
- Click the **Stop Recording button** to end the macro.

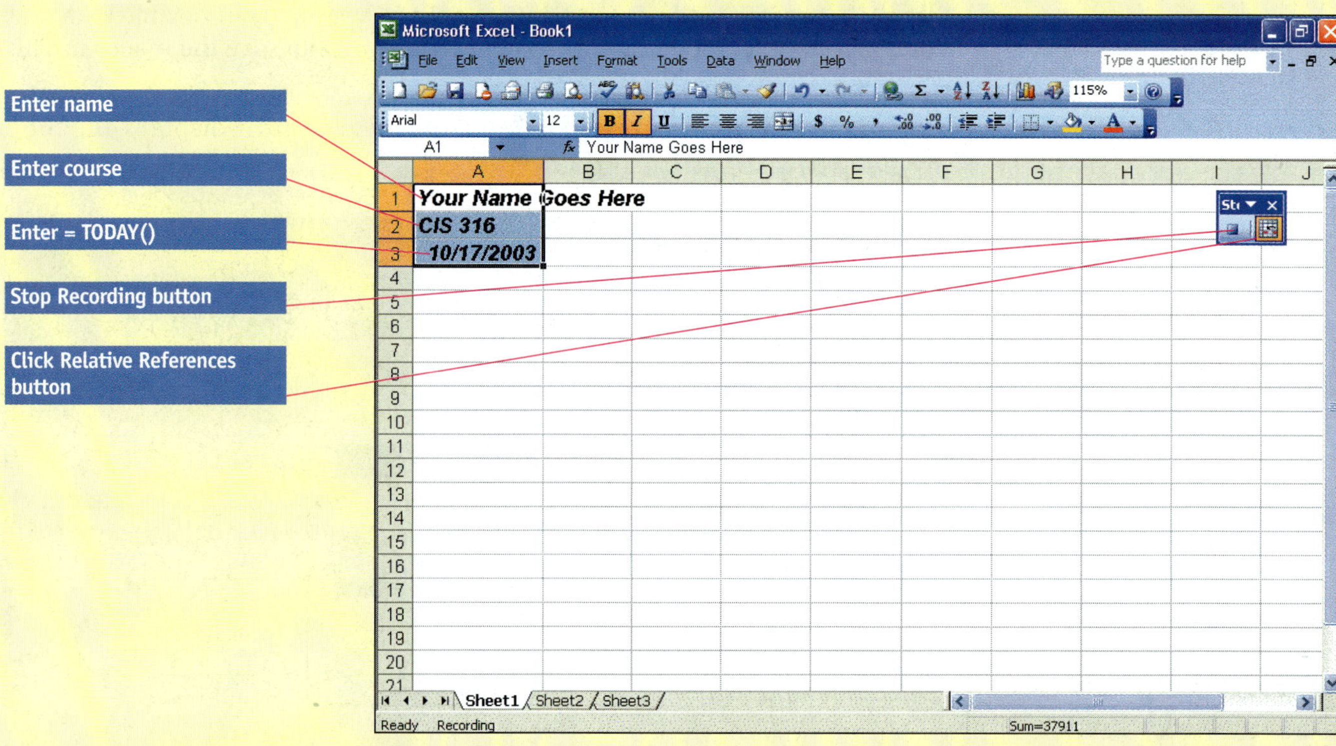

(b) Record with Relative References (step 2)

FIGURE 8.4 Hands-on Exercise 2 (*continued*)

PLAN AHEAD

The macro recorder records everything you do, including entries that are made by mistake or commands that are executed incorrectly. Plan the macro in advance, before you begin recording. Write down what you intend to do, then try out the commands with the recorder off. Be sure you go all the way through the intended sequence of operations prior to turning the macro recorder on.

Step 3: The Visual Basic Editor

- Pull down the **Tools menu**, click the **Macro command**, then click **Visual Basic Editor** (or press **Alt+F11**) to open the Visual Basic Editor in Figure 8.4c.
- If necessary, pull down the **View menu**. Click **Project Explorer** to open the Project Explorer window in the left pane.
- There are currently two open VBA projects (Book1, the name of the open workbook, and PERSONAL.XLS, the Personal Macro workbook).
- Click the **plus sign** to expand the Personal Workbook folder, then click the **plus sign** to expand the **Modules** folder within this project.
- Click (select) **Module1**, pull down the **View menu**, and click **Code** to open the Code window in the right pane. Maximize the Code window.
- Close any other open windows within the Visual Basic Editor. The first executable statement should begin with *ActiveCell.FormulaR1C1*.
- If you see a very different statement, *Range("A1").Select*, it means that you incorrectly recorded the macro with absolute references. Right click Module1 in the Project window, select the **Remove Module command** (respond **No** when asked if you want to export it), then return to step 1 and rerecord the macro.

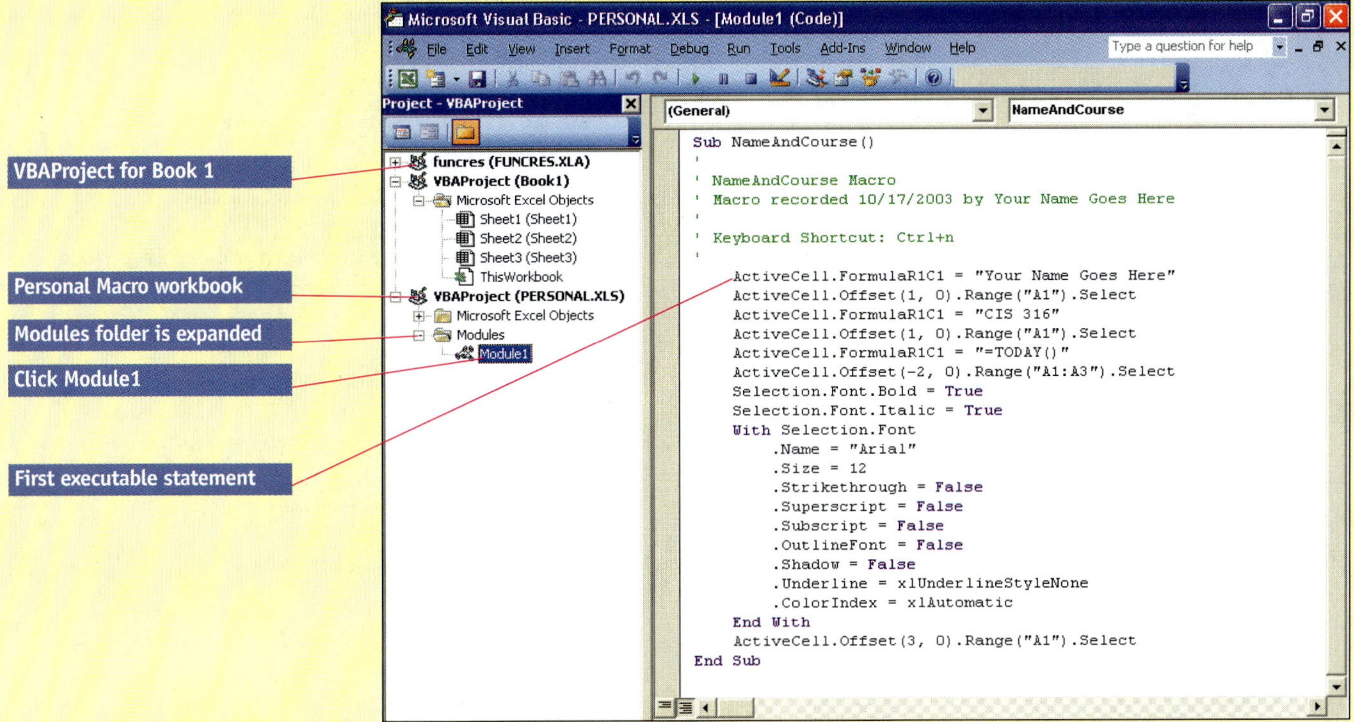

(c) The Visual Basic Editor (step 3)

FIGURE 8.4 Hands-on Exercise 2 (*continued*)

WHAT DOES RANGE ("A1:A3") REALLY MEAN?

The statement ActiveCell.Offset (–2,0).Range ("A1:A3").Select has nothing to do with cells A1 through A3, so why is the entry Range ("A1:A3") included? The effect of the statement is to select three cells (one cell under the other) starting with the cell two rows above the current cell. The offset (–2,0) specifies the starting point of the selected range (two rows above the current cell). The range ("A1:A3") indicates the size and shape of the selected range (a vertical column of three cells).

Step 4: Edit the Macro

- Click and drag to select the name of the course, which is found in the third executable statement of the macro. Be sure to include the quotation marks (e.g., "CIS316" in our example) in your selection.
- Enter **InputBox("Enter the Course You Are Taking")** to replace the selected text. Note that as you enter the Visual Basic keyword, *InputBox*, a prompt (containing the correct syntax for this statement) is displayed on the screen as shown in Figure 8.4d.
- Just ignore the prompt and keep typing to complete the entry. Press the **Home key** when you complete the entry to scroll back to the beginning of the line.
- Click immediately after the number **12**, then click and drag to select the next seven statements. Press the **Del key** to delete the highlighted statements from the macro.
- Delete the **Selection.Font.Bold=True** statement. Click the **Save button** to save the modified macro.

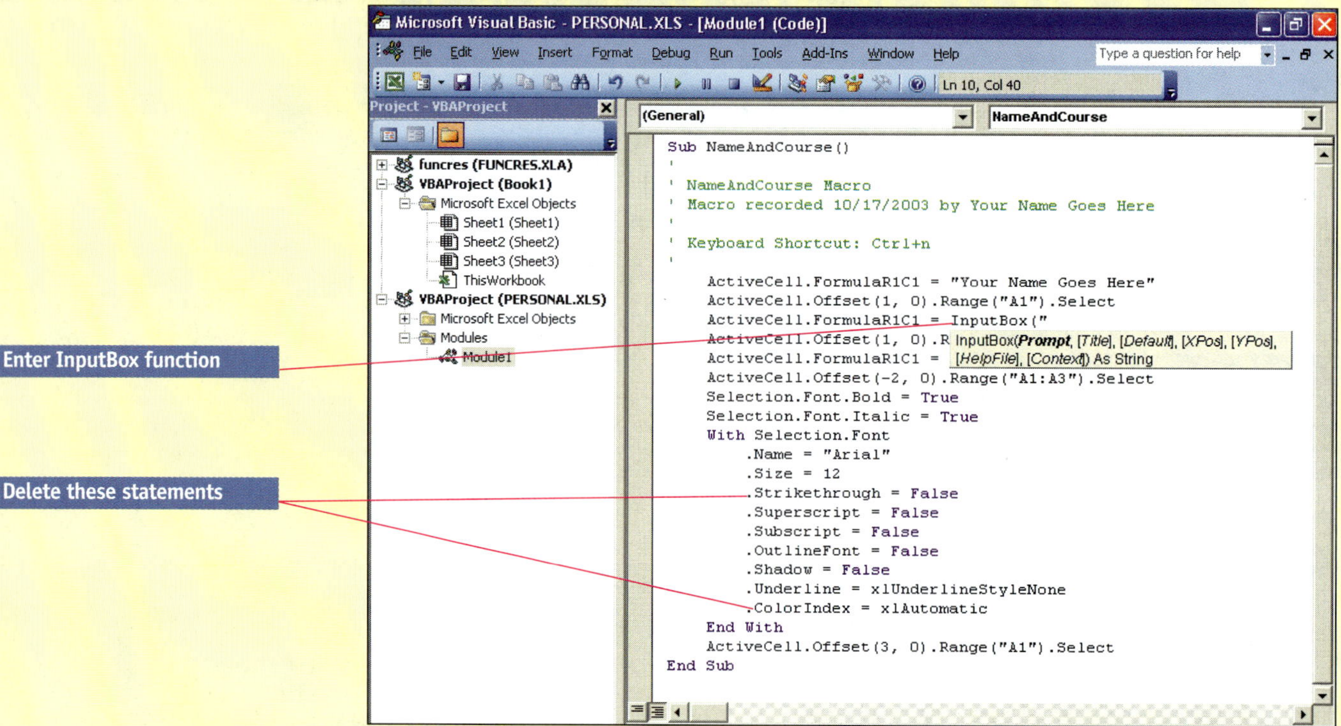

(d) Edit the Macro (step 4)

FIGURE 8.4 Hands-on Exercise 2 (*continued*)

THE INPUTBOX FUNCTION

The InputBox function adds flexibility to a macro by obtaining input from the user when the macro is executed. It is used in this example to generalize the NameAndCourse macro by asking the user for the name of the course, as opposed to storing the name within the macro. The InputBox function, coupled with storing the macro in the Personal Macro workbook, enables the user to personalize any workbook by executing the associated macro.

Step 5: Test the Revised Macro

- Press **Alt+F11** to view the Excel workbook. Click in any cell—for example, **cell C5** as shown in Figure 8.4e.
- Pull down the **Tools menu**. Click **Macro**, click the **Macros . . . command**, select **PERSONAL.XLS!NameAndCourse**, then click the **Run command button** to run the macro. (Alternatively you can use the **Ctrl+n** shortcut.)
- The macro enters your name in cell C5 (the active cell), selects the cell one row below, then displays the input dialog box shown in Figure 8.4e.
- Enter any appropriate course and press the **Enter key**. You should see the course you entered followed by the date. All three entries will be formatted according to the commands you specified in the macro.
- Click in a different cell, then press **Ctrl+n** to rerun the macro. The macro will enter your name, the course you specify, and the date in the selected location because it was recorded with relative references.

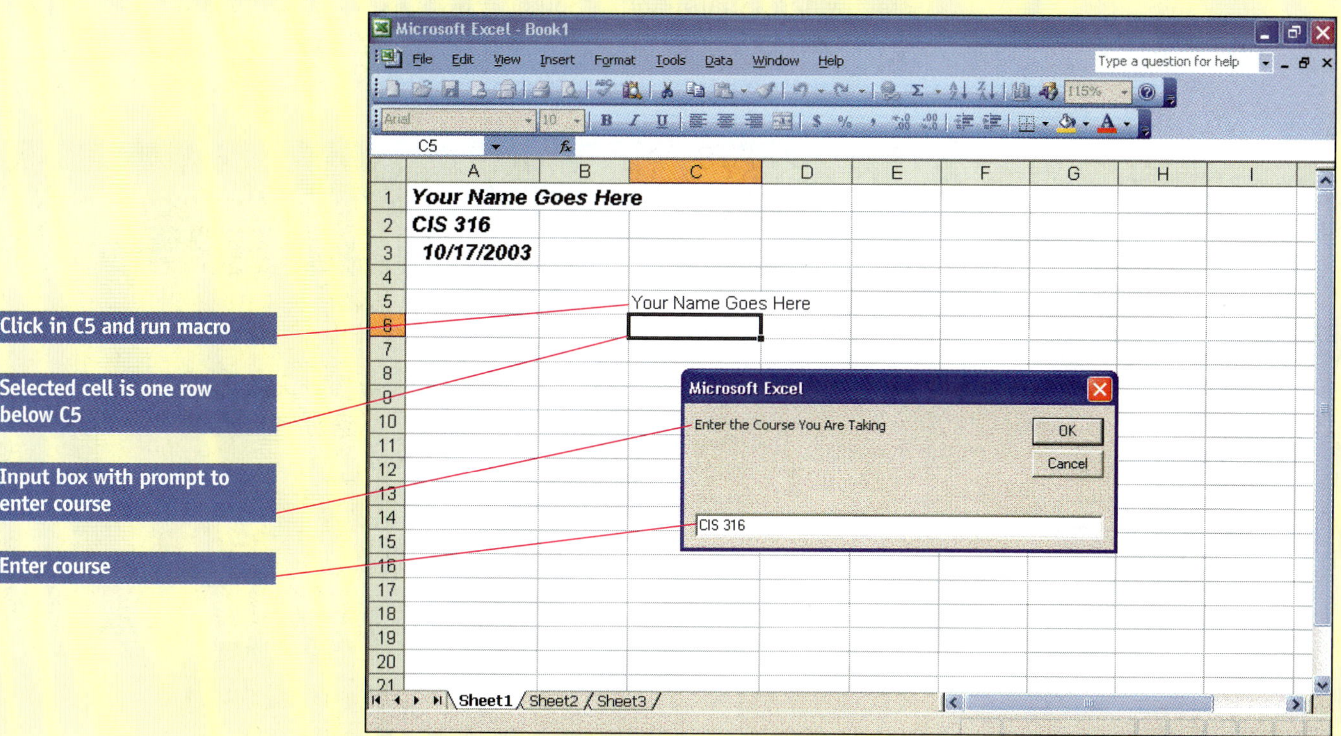

(e) Test the Revised Macro (step 5)

FIGURE 8.4 Hands-on Exercise 2 (*continued*)

RED, GREEN, AND BLUE

Visual Basic automatically assigns different colors to different types of statements (or a portion of those statements). Any statement containing a syntax error appears in red. Comments appear in green. Keywords—such as Sub and End Sub, With and End With, and True and False—appear in blue. The different colors are intended to make the code easier to read. Indentation and/or blank lines can also improve readability.

Step 6: Add a Custom Button

- Point to any toolbar, then click the **right mouse button** to display a shortcut menu. Click **Customize** to display the Customize dialog box in Figure 8.4f.
- Click the **Commands tab**. Click the **down arrow** to scroll through the Categories list box until you can select the **Macros category**.
- Click and drag the **Custom (Happy Face) button** to an available space at the right of the Standard toolbar. Release the mouse. (You must drag the button *within* the toolbar.)
- Click the **Modify Selection button** within the Customize dialog box to display the cascaded menu in Figure 8.4f.
- Click and drag to select the name of the button (&Custom Button) and replace it with **NameAndCourse**, to create a ScreenTip for that button. Do not press the Enter key.
- Click the **Assign Macro command** at the bottom of the menu to display the Assign Macro dialog box. Select **PERSONAL.XLS!NameAndCourse** and click **OK**.
- Click **Close** to exit the Custom dialog box.

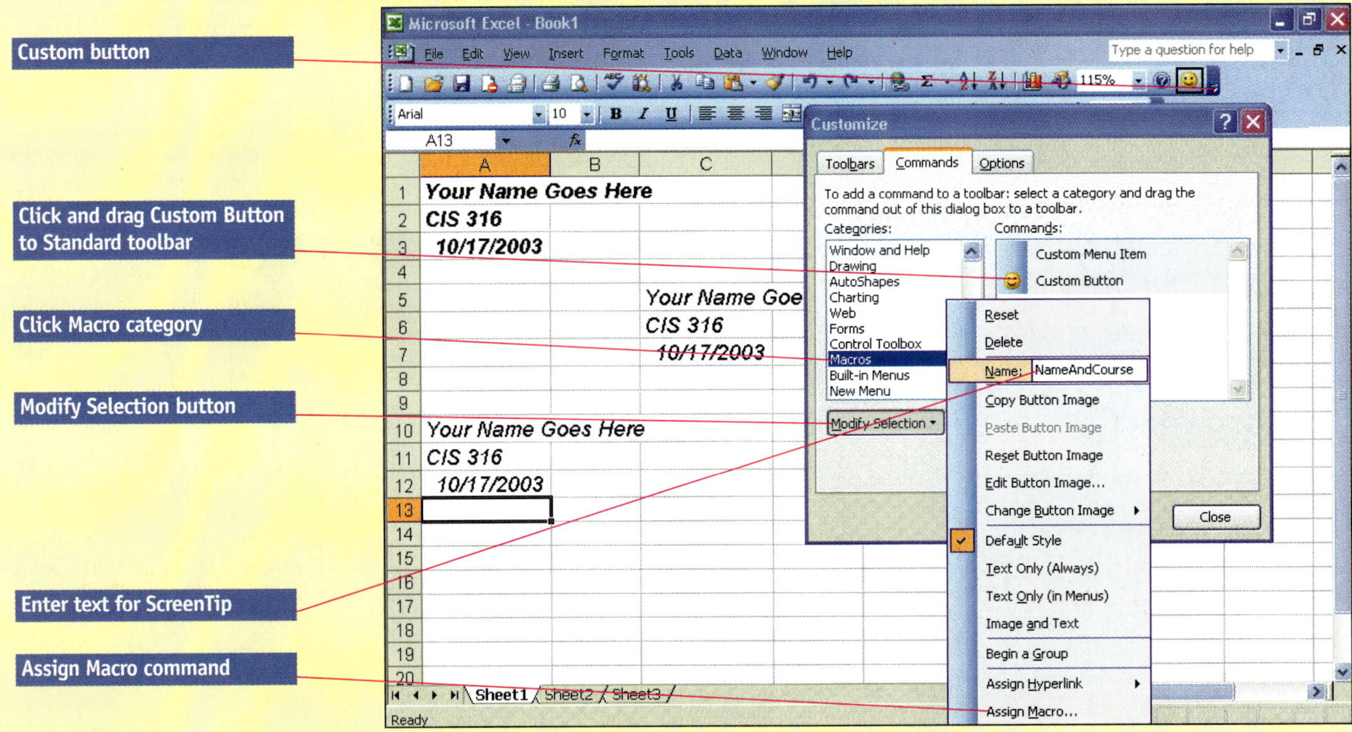

(f) Add a Custom Button (step 6)

FIGURE 8.4 Hands-on Exercise 2 (*continued*)

CUSTOMIZE THE TOOLBAR OR A MENU

You can customize any toolbar or menu to display additional buttons or commands as appropriate. Pull down the View menu, click Toolbars, click Customize to display the Customize dialog box, then click the Commands tab. Choose the category containing the button or command you want, then click and drag that object to an existing toolbar or menu.

Step 7: Test the Custom Button

- Click the **New button** on the Standard toolbar to open a new workbook (Book2 in Figure 8.4g; the book number is not important). Click **cell B2** as the active cell from which to execute the macro.
- Point to the **Happy Face button** to display the ScreenTip you just created. The ScreenTip will be useful in future sessions should you forget the function of this button.
- Click the **Happy Face button** to execute the NameAndCourse macro. Enter the name of a course you are taking. The macro inserts your name, course, and today's date in cells B2 through B4.
- Pull down the **File menu** and click the **Exit command** to exit the program.
- Click **No** when prompted to save the changes to Book1 and/or Book2, the workbooks you created in this exercise. Click **Yes** if asked to save the changes to the Personal Workbook.

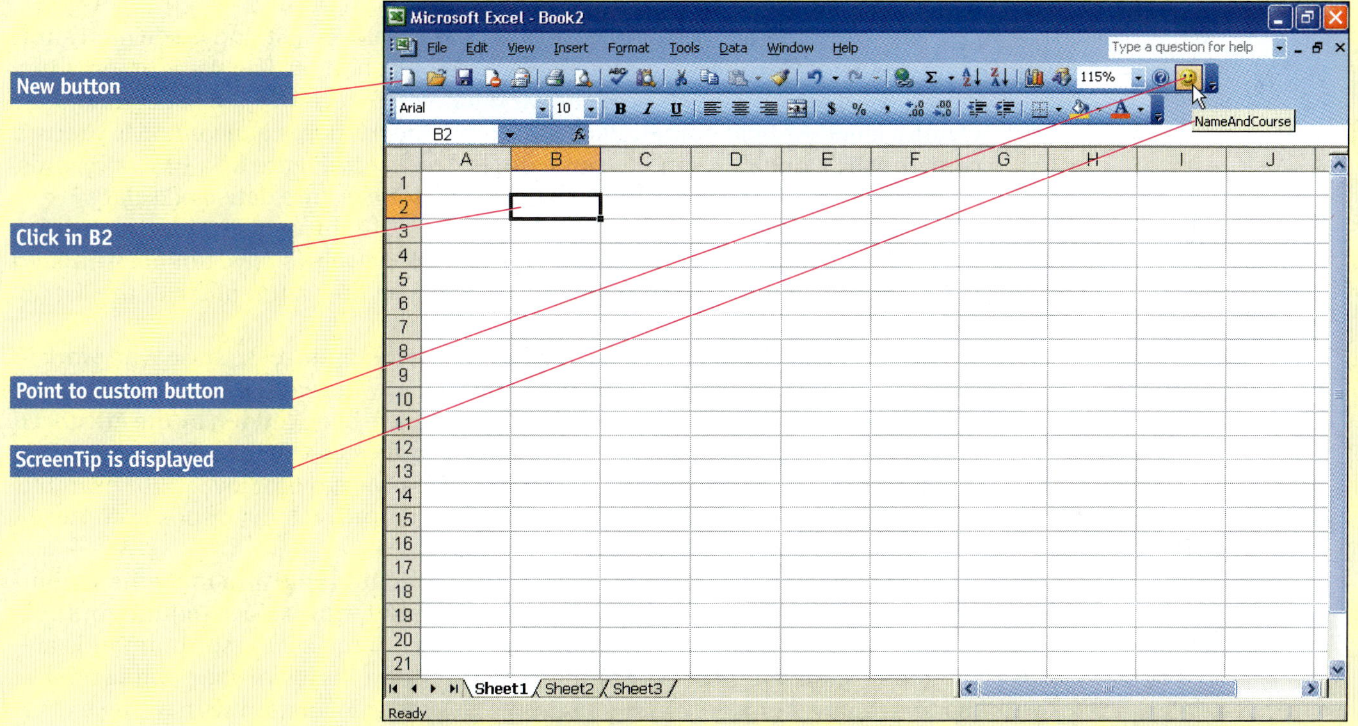

(g) Test the Custom Button (step 7)

FIGURE 8.4 Hands-on Exercise 2 (*continued*)

CHANGE THE CUSTOM BUTTON ICON

The Happy Face icon is automatically associated with the Custom Macro button. You can, however, change the image after the button has been added to a toolbar. Right click the button and click Customize to display the Customize dialog box, which must remain open to change the image. Right click the button a second time to display a different shortcut menu with commands pertaining to the specific button. Click the command to Change Button Image, select a new image, then close the Customize dialog box.

DATA MANAGEMENT MACROS

Thus far we have covered the basics of macros in the context of entering your name, course, and today's date into a worksheet. As you might expect, macros are capable of much more and can be used to automate any repetitive task. The next several pages illustrate the use of macros in conjunction with the list (data) management examples that were presented in an earlier chapter.

Data and information are not synonymous. Data is typically a fact (or facts) about a specific record (or set of records), such as an employee's name or title, or a list of all employees and their titles. Information is something more and refers to data that has been summarized, or otherwise rearranged, into a form perceived as useful by the recipient. A list of all the employees is considered raw data, whereas a subset of that list—such as the employees who worked in Chicago—could be thought of as information derived from that list. Information is also obtained by summarizing the data. Individual salaries are important to the employees who receive those salaries, whereas a manager is more interested in knowing the total of all salaries in order to make decisions. Macros can help in the conversion of data to information.

The worksheet in Figure 8.5a displays the employee list and associated summary statistics from the example in the previous chapter. The list is an area in a worksheet that contains rows of similar data. The first row in the list contains the column labels or field names. Each additional row contains a record. Every record contains the same fields in the same order. The list in Figure 8.5a has 14 records. Each record has six fields: name, location, title, service, hire date, and salary.

A criteria range has been established in cells A17 through F18 for use with the database functions in cells F22 through F26. Criteria values have not been entered in Figure 8.5a, and so the database functions reflect the values of the entire list (all 14 employees).

The worksheet in Figure 8.5b displays selected employees, those who work in Chicago. Look carefully at the worksheet and you will see that only rows 3, 9, 10, and 12 are visible. The other rows within the list have been hidden by the Advanced Filter command, which displays only those employees who satisfy the specified criteria. The summary statistics reflect only the Chicago employees; for example, the DCOUNT function in cell F26 shows four employees (as opposed to the 14 employees in Figure 8.5a).

The previous chapter described how to execute the list management commands to filter the list. The process is not difficult, but it does require multiple commands and keystrokes. Our purpose here is to review those commands and then automate the process through creation of a series of data management macros that will enable you to obtain the desired information with a single click. We begin by reviewing the commands that would be necessary to modify the worksheet in Figure 8.5b to show managers rather than the Chicago employees.

The first step is to clear the existing criterion (Chicago) in cell B18, then enter the new criterion (Manager) in cell C18. You would then execute the Advanced Filter command, which requires the specification of the list (cells A1 through F15), the location of the criteria range (cells A17 through F18), and the option to filter the list in place.

And what if you wanted to see the Chicago employees after you executed the commands to display the managers? You would have to repeat all of the previous commands to change the criterion back to what it was, then filter the list accordingly. Suffice it to say that the entire process can be simplified through creation of the appropriate macros.

The following exercise develops the macro to select the Chicago employees from the worksheet in Figure 8.5a. A subsequent exercise develops two additional macros, one to select the managers and another to select the managers who work in Chicago.

All of the macros use the concept of a ***named range*** to establish a mnemonic name (e.g., database) for a cell range (e.g., A1:F15). The advantage of using a named range in a macro over the associated cell reference is twofold. First, the macro is easier to read. Second, and perhaps more important, a named range adjusts automatically for insertions and/or deletions within the worksheet, whereas a cell reference remains constant. Thus, the use of a named range makes the macro immune to changes in the worksheet in that the macro references a flexible "database," as opposed to a fixed cell range. You can add or delete employee records within the list, and the macro will still work.

Field names are in first row of list

Criteria range (A17:F18)

Database functions (F22:F26)

	A	B	C	D	E	F
1	**Name**	**Location**	**Title**	**Service**	**Hire Date**	**Salary**
2	Adams	Atlanta	Trainee	4.6	11/24/98	$29,500
3	Adamson	Chicago	Manager	4.3	3/16/99	$52,000
4	Brown	Atlanta	Trainee	4.6	11/24/98	$28,500
5	Charles	Boston	Account Rep	4.3	3/16/99	$40,000
6	Coulter	Atlanta	Manager	4.6	11/24/98	$100,000
7	Elofson	Miami	Account Rep	1.7	10/31/01	$47,500
8	Gillenson	Miami	Account Rep	0.7	10/31/02	$55,000
9	James	Chicago	Account Rep	4.7	10/31/98	$42,500
10	Johnson	Chicago	Account Rep	3.7	10/31/99	$47,500
11	Manin	Boston	Account Rep	4.3	3/16/99	$49,500
12	Marder	Chicago	Account Rep	2.7	10/31/00	$38,500
13	Milgrom	Boston	Manager	4.3	3/16/99	$57,500
14	Rubin	Boston	Account Rep	4.3	3/16/99	$45,000
15	Smith	Atlanta	Account Rep	4.6	11/24/98	$65,000
16						
17	**Name**	**Location**	**Title**	**Service**	**Hire Date**	**Salary**
18						
19						
20						
21	Summary Statistics					
22	Average Salary					$49,857
23	Maximum Salary					$100,000
24	Minimum Salary					$28,500
25	Total Salary					$698,000
26	Number of Employees					14

(a) All Employees

Filtered list (Chicago employees)

Criterion is Chicago

Database functions reflect data for Chicago employees only

	A	B	C	D	E	F
1	**Name**	**Location**	**Title**	**Service**	**Hire Date**	**Salary**
3	Adamson	Chicago	Manager	4.3	3/16/99	$52,000
9	James	Chicago	Account Rep	4.7	10/31/98	$42,500
10	Johnson	Chicago	Account Rep	3.7	10/31/99	$47,500
12	Marder	Chicago	Account Rep	2.7	10/31/00	$38,500
16						
17	**Name**	**Location**	**Title**	**Service**	**Hire Date**	**Salary**
18		Chicago				
19						
20						
21	Summary Statistics					
22	Average Salary					$45,125
23	Maximum Salary					$52,000
24	Minimum Salary					$38,500
25	Total Salary					$180,500
26	Number of Employees					4

(b) Chicago Employees

FIGURE 8.5 Data Management Macros

hands-on exercise

3 Data Management Macros

Objective To create a data management macro in conjunction with an employee list; to create a custom button to execute a macro. Use Figure 8.6 as a guide in completing the exercise.

Step 1: Data Management Functions

- Start Excel. Open the **Employee List Solution workbook** that was created in the previous chapter on data management.
- Click anywhere within the employee list. Pull down the **Data Menu**, click **Subtotals**, and click the **Remove All button**.
- Click any cell between A2 and A15, then click the **Sort Ascending button** on the Standard toolbar. The employees should be listed in alphabetical order as shown in Figure 8.6a.
- Clear all entries in the range **A18 through F18**.
- Click in **cell F22**, which contains the DAVERAGE function, to compute the average salary of all employees who satisfy the specified criteria. No criteria have been entered, however, so the displayed value of $49,857 represents the average salary of all 14 employees.
- Click **cell B18**. Enter **Chicago**. Press **Enter**. The average salary changes to $45,125 to indicate the average salary of the four Chicago employees.
- Click **cell C18**. Enter **Manager**. Press **Enter**. The average salary changes to $52,000 to indicate the average salary of the one Chicago manager.
- Save the workbook.

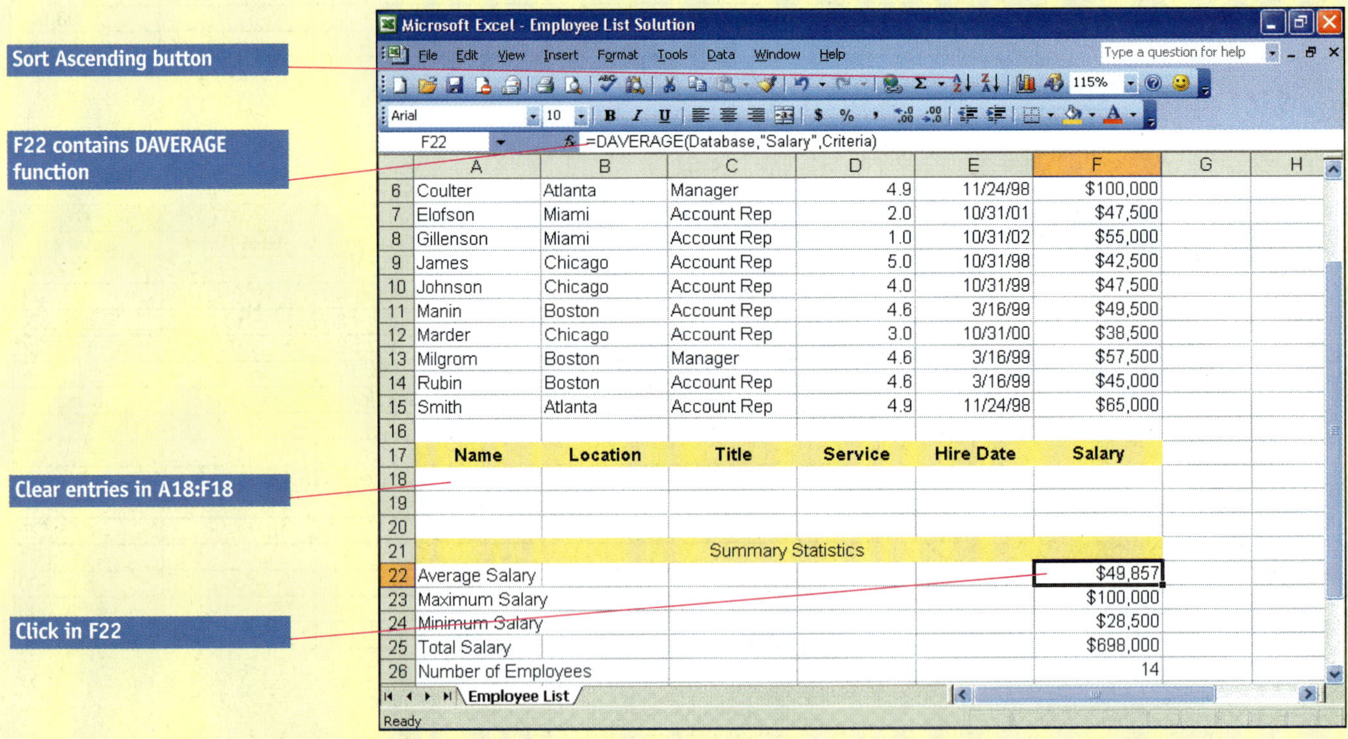

(a) Data Management Functions (step 1)

FIGURE 8.6 Hands-on Exercise 3

Step 2: The Create Name Command

- Click and drag to select **cells A17 through F18** as shown in Figure 8.6b. Pull down the **Insert menu**, click **Name**, then click **Create** to display the Create Names dialog box.
- The box to **Create Names in Top Row is already checked. Click OK**. This command assigns the text in each cell in row 17 to the corresponding cell in row 18; for example, cells B18 and C18 will be assigned the names Location and Title, respectively.
- Click and drag to select only **cells A18 through F18**. (You need to assign a name to these seven cells collectively, as you will have to clear the criteria values in row 18 later in the chapter.)
- Pull down the **Insert menu**. Click **Name**. Click **Define**. Enter **CriteriaValues** in the Define Name dialog box. Click **OK**.
- Save the workbook.

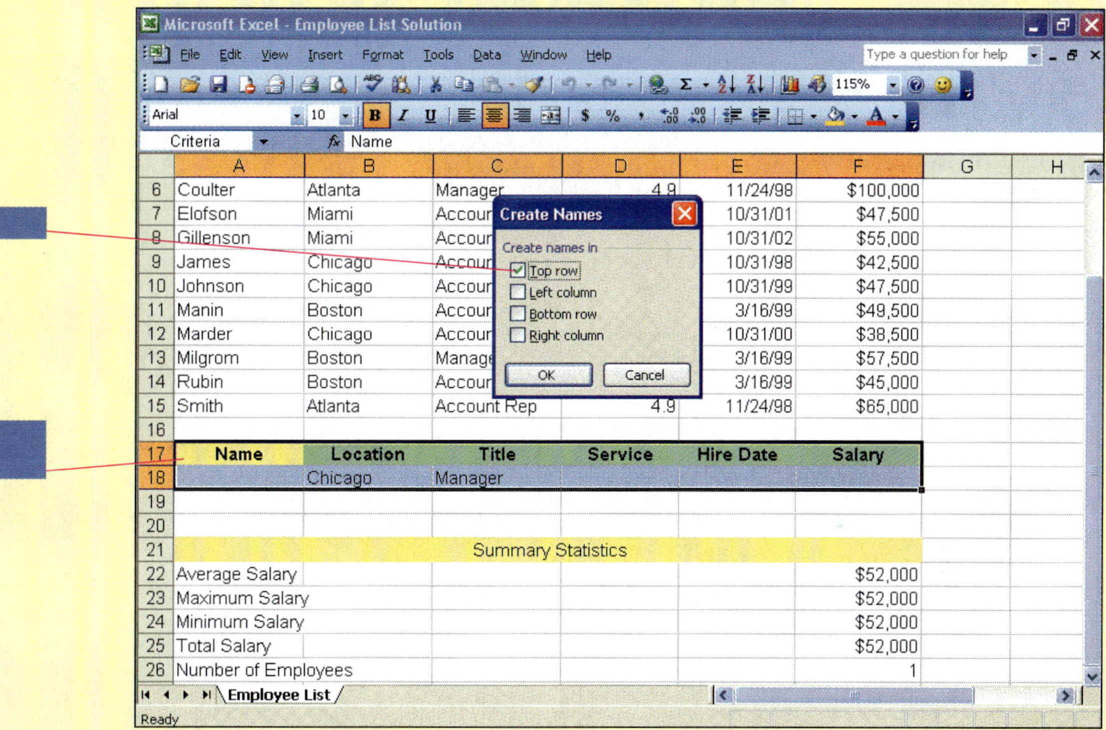

(b) The Create Name Command (step 2)

FIGURE 8.6 Hands-on Exercise 3 (*continued*)

CREATE SEVERAL NAMES AT ONCE

The Insert menu contains two different commands to create named ranges. The Insert Name Define command affects only one cell or range at a time, then has you enter the name into a dialog box. The Insert Name Create command requires you to select adjacent rows or columns, then assigns multiple names from the adjacent row or column in one command. The latter command is very useful in assigning range names within a criteria range.

Step 3: The Go To Command

- Pull down the **Edit menu**. Click **Go To** to produce the Go To dialog box in Figure 8.6c. If you do not see the command, click the double arrow to display more commands.
- You should see the names you defined (CriteriaValues, Hire_Date, Location, Name, Salary, Service, and Title) as well as the two names defined previously by the authors (Criteria and Database).
- Click **Database**. Click **OK**. Cells A1 through F15 should be selected, corresponding to cells assigned to the name *Database*.
- Press the **F5 key** (a shortcut for the Edit Go To command), which again produces the Go To dialog box. Click **Criteria**. Click **OK**. Cells A17 through F18 should be selected.
- Click the **drop-down arrow** next to the Name box. Click **Location**. Cell B18 should be selected.
- You are now ready to record the macro.

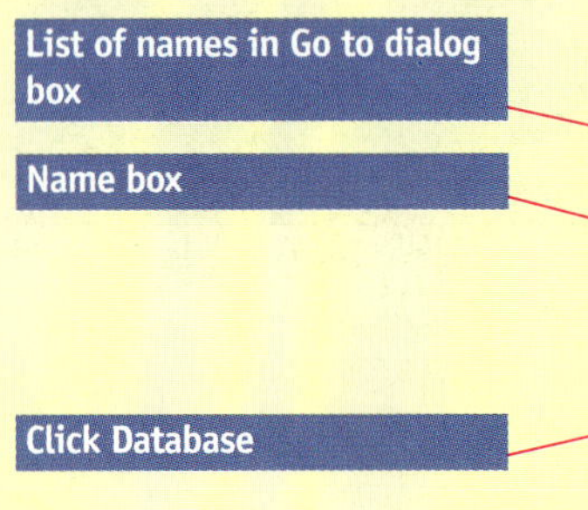

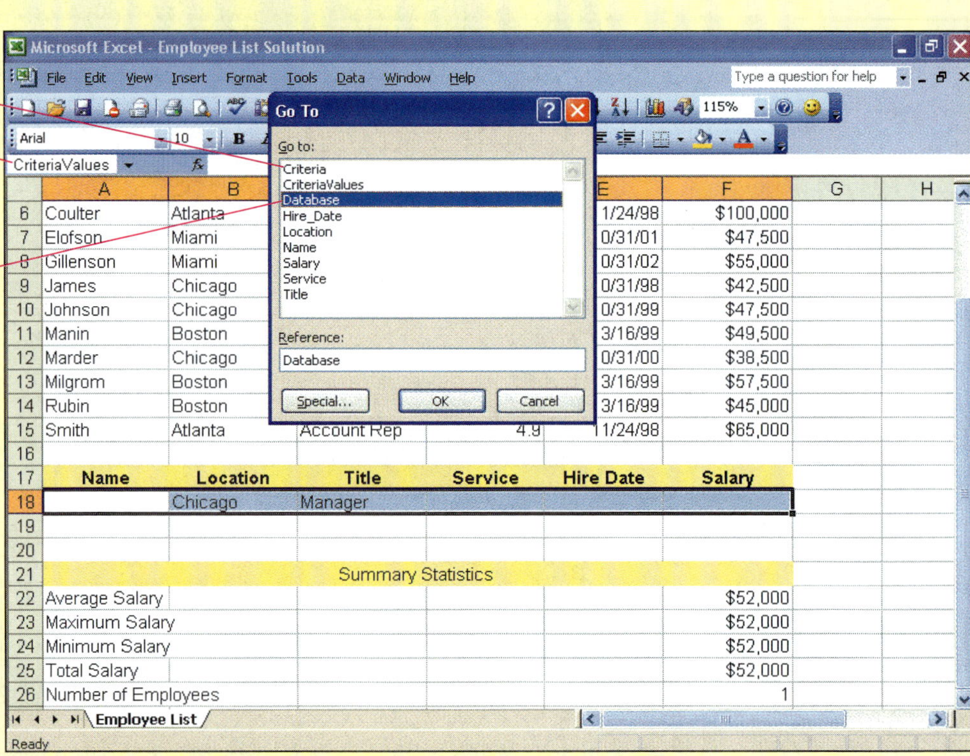

(c) The Go To Command (step 3)

FIGURE 8.6 Hands-on Exercise 3 (*continued*)

THE NAME BOX

Use the Name box (at the left of the Formula bar) to define a range name by selecting the cell(s) in the worksheet to which the name is to apply, clicking the Name box, then entering the name. For example, to assign the name CriteriaValues to cells A18:F18, select the range, click in the Name box, type CriteriaValues, and press Enter. The Name box can also be used to select a previously defined range by clicking the drop-down arrow next to the box and choosing the desired name from the drop-down list.

Step 4: Record the Macro (Edit Clear command)

- Pull down the **Tools menu**, click the **Macro command**, then click **Record New Macro** to display the Record Macro dialog box.
- Enter **Chicago** in the Macro Name text box. Verify that the macro will be stored in **This Workbook** and then make sure that the shortcut key text box is empty.
- Click **OK** to begin recording the macro. If necessary, click the **Relative References button** on the Stop Recording toolbar to record Absolute references (the button should be out).
- Pull down the **Edit menu**, click **Go To**, select **CriteriaValues** from the Go To dialog box, and click **OK**. Cells A18 through F18 should be selected as shown in Figure 8.6d. (Alternatively, you can also use the **F5 key** or the **Name box** to select CriteriaValues.)
- Pull down the **Edit menu**. Click **Clear**, then click **All** from the cascaded menu as shown in Figure 8.6d. Cells A18 through F18 (the criteria range) should be empty, and a new criterion can be entered through the macro.

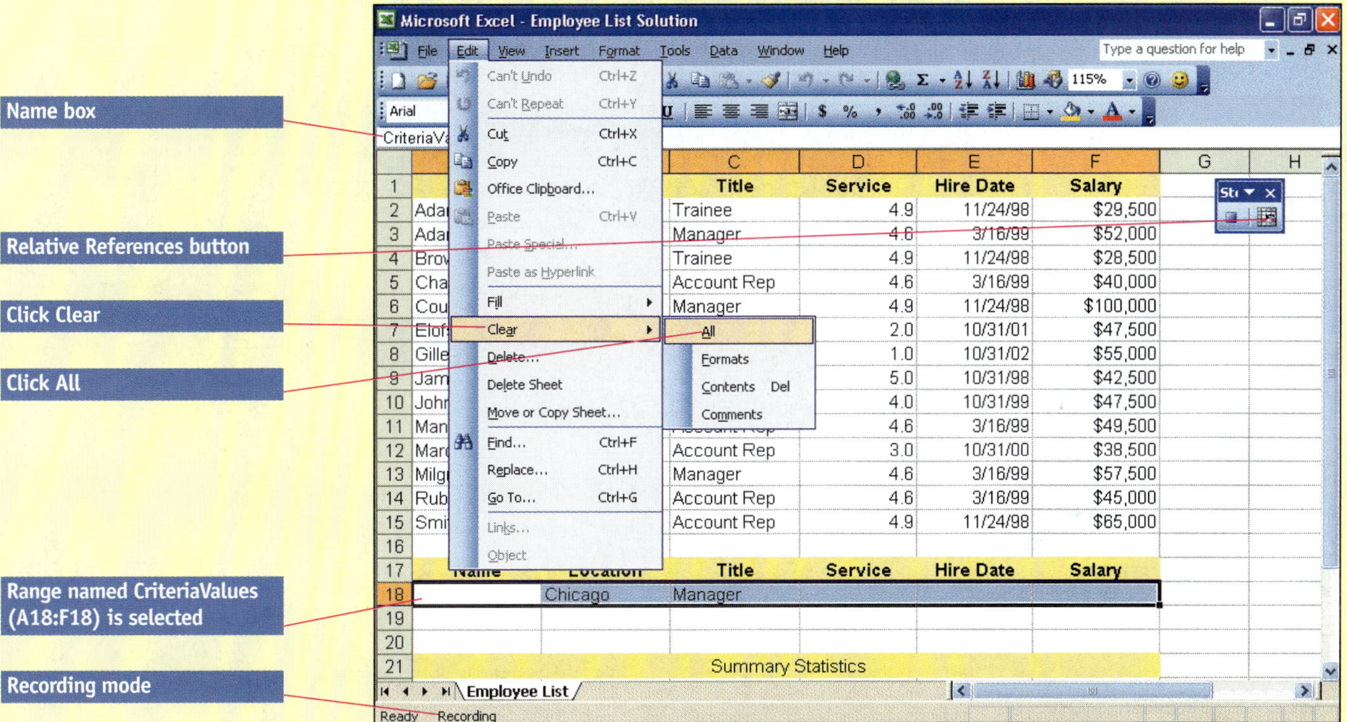

(d) Record the Macro (Edit Clear command) (step 4)

FIGURE 8.6 Hands-on Exercise 3 (*continued*)

GOOD MACROS ARE FLEXIBLE MACROS

The macro to select Chicago employees has to be completely general and work under all circumstances, regardless of what may appear initially in the criteria row. Thus, you have to clear the entire criteria range prior to entering "Chicago" in the Location column. Note, too, the use of range names (e.g., CriteriaValues), as opposed to specific cells (e.g., A18:F18 in this example) to accommodate potential additions or deletions to the employee list. (A macro does not update cell references within its statements to accommodate insertions and/or deletions of rows and columns in the associated worksheet. It is good practice, therefore, to always use range names, as opposed to cell references, within a macro.)

Step 5: Record the Macro (Advanced Filter command)

- Pull down the **Edit menu**, click **Go To**, select **Location** from the Go to dialog box, and click **OK**.
- Cell B18 should be selected. Enter **Chicago** to establish the criterion for both the database functions and the Advanced Filter command.
- Click in **cell B2** to position the active cell within the employee list. Pull down the **Data menu**. Click **Filter**, then click **Advanced Filter** from the cascaded menu to display the dialog box in Figure 8.6e.
- Enter **Database** as the List Range. Press the **tab key**. Enter **Criteria** as the Criteria Range.
- Check that the option to **Filter the list, in-place** is checked.
- Click **OK**. You should see only those employees who satisfy the current criteria (i.e., Adamson, James, Johnson, and Marder, who are the employees who work in Chicago).
- Click the **Stop Recording button** to stop recording.
- Click the **Save button** to save the workbook with the macro.

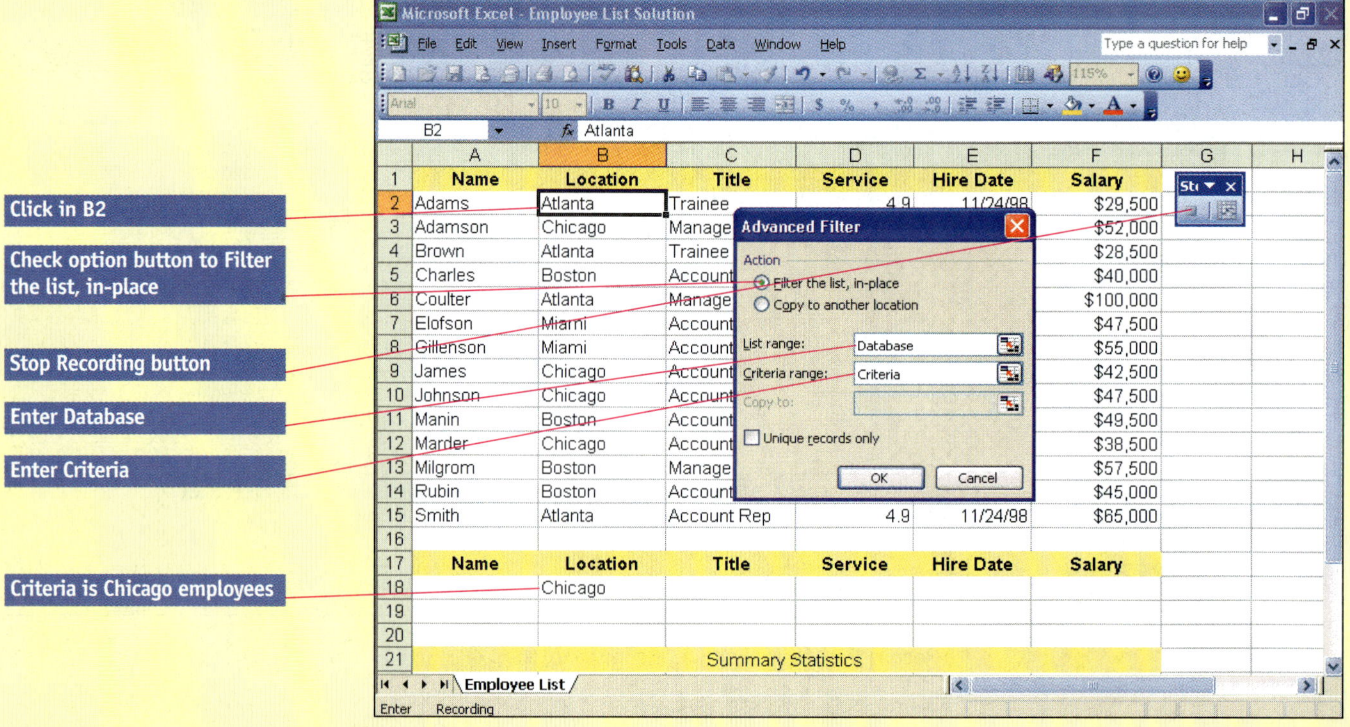

(e) Record the Macro (Advanced Filter command) (step 5)

FIGURE 8.6 Hands-on Exercise 3 (*continued*)

THE FILTER VERSUS THE DATABASE FUNCTIONS

Change the criteria—for example, from Chicago to Chicago Managers—and the values displayed by the database functions (DAVERAGE, DSUM, and so on) change automatically. The filtered records do not change, however, until you reexecute the command to filter the records in place. The advantage of a macro becomes immediately apparent, because the macro is built to change the criteria and filter the records with a single click of the mouse.

Step 6: View the Macro

- Press **Alt+F11** to open the Visual Basic editor as shown in Figure 8.6f. If necessary, pull down the **View menu**. Click **Project Explorer** to open the Project window in the left pane.
- If necessary, expand the **Modules folder**, under the VBA project for Employee List Solution. Click (select) **Module1**, pull down the **View menu**, and click **Code** to display the code for the Chicago macro in the right pane. Maximize the Code window.
- Close any other open windows within the Visual Basic Editor. Your screen should match the one in Figure 8.6f. If necessary, correct your macro so that it matches ours.
- If the correction is minor, it is easiest to edit the macro directly; otherwise delete the macro, then return to step 4 and rerecord the macro from the beginning. (To delete a macro, pull down the Tools menu, click **Macro**, click **Macros...**, select the macro you wish to delete, then click the **Delete button**.)
- Click the **View Microsoft Excel button** at the left of the toolbar or press **Alt+F11** to return to the Employee worksheet.

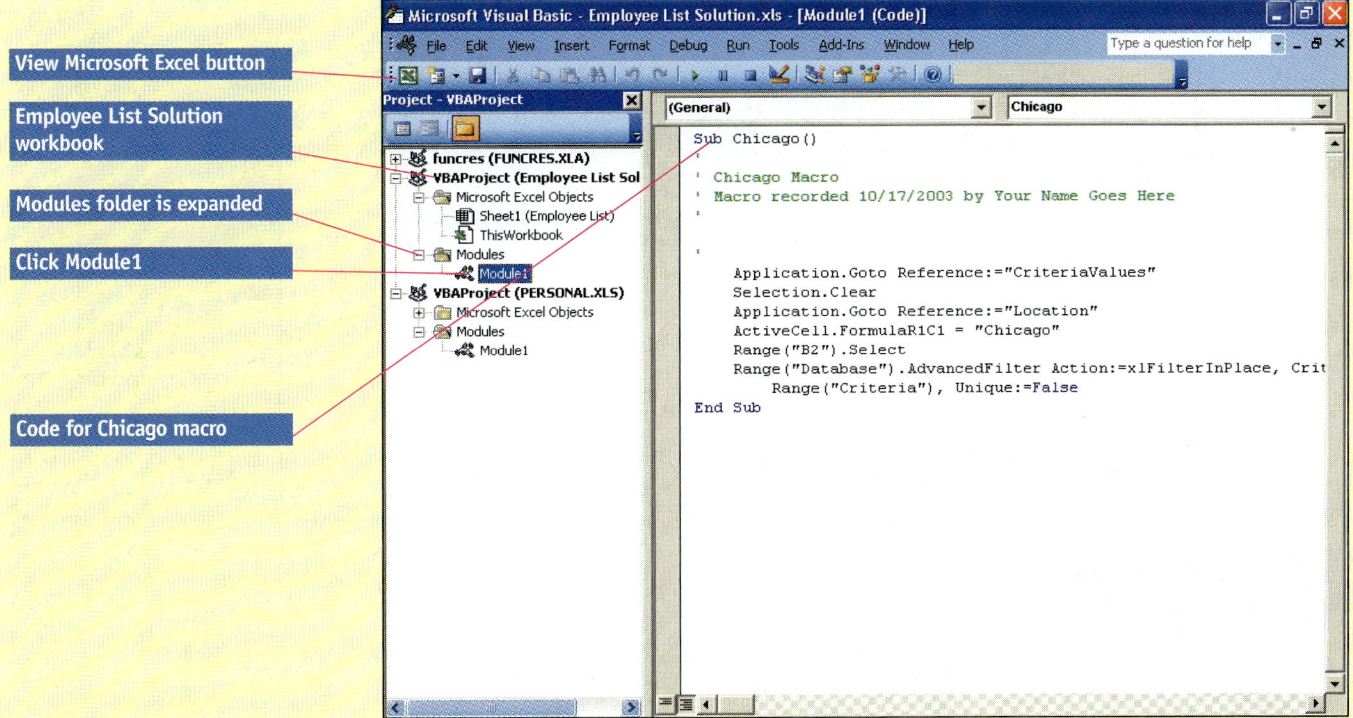

(f) View the Macro (step 6)

FIGURE 8.6 Hands-on Exercise 3 (*continued*)

THE VISUAL BASIC TOOLBAR

The Visual Basic Toolbar consists of seven buttons associated with macros and Visual Basic. You will find a button to run an existing macro, to record (or stop recording) a new macro, and to open (toggle to) the Visual Basic Editor. The toolbar can be displayed (or hidden) by right clicking any visible toolbar, then checking (or clearing) Visual Basic from the list of toolbars.

Step 7: Assign the Macro

- Pull down the **View menu**, click **Toolbars**, then click **Forms** to display the Forms toolbar as shown in Figure 8.6g.
- Click the **Button tool** (the mouse pointer changes to a tiny crosshair). Click and drag in the worksheet as shown in Figure 8.6g to draw a command button on the worksheet.
- Be sure to draw the button *below* the employee list, or the button may be hidden when a subsequent Data Filter command is executed.
- Release the mouse, and the Assign Macro dialog box will appear. Choose **Chicago** (the macro you just created) from the list of macro names. Click **OK**.
- The button should still be selected. Click and drag to select the name of the button, **Button 1**.
- Type **Chicago** as the new name. Do *not* press the Enter key. Click outside the button to deselect it.
- Save the workbook.

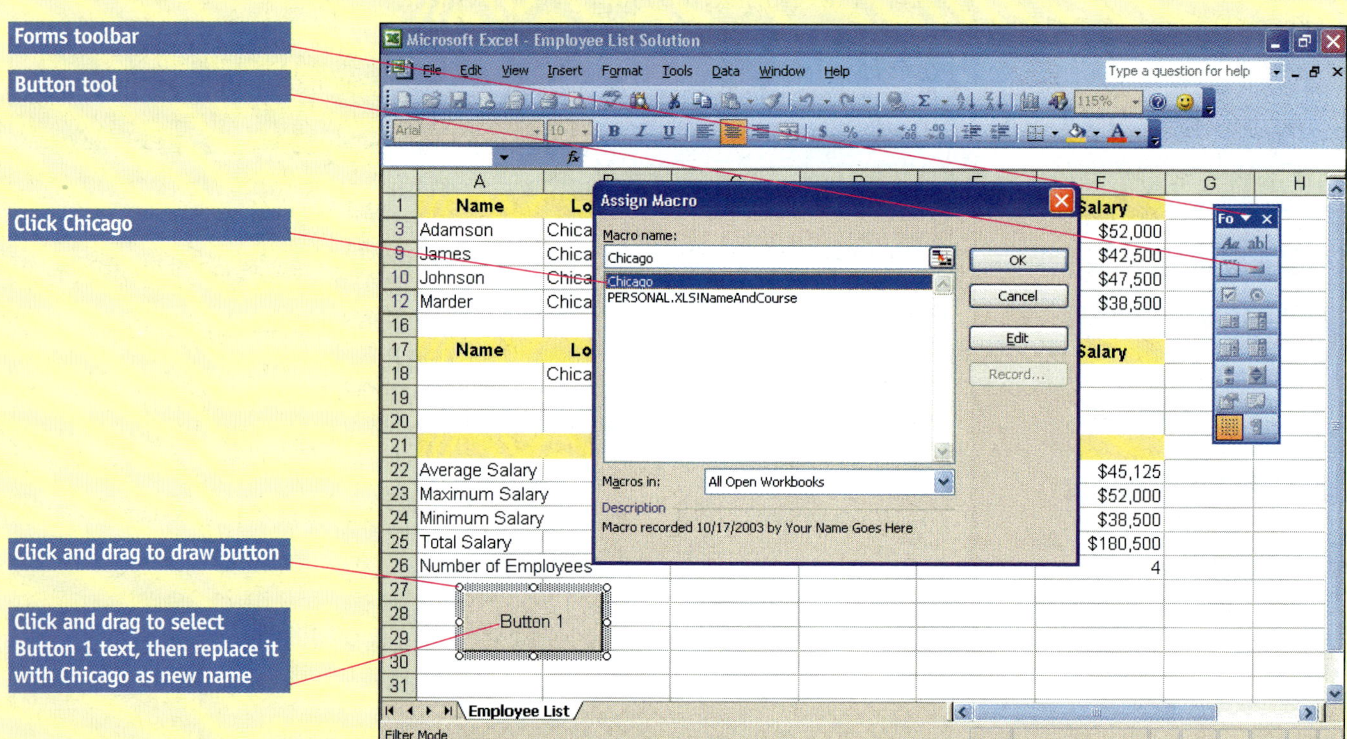

(g) Assign the Macro (step 7)

FIGURE 8.6 Hands-on Exercise 3 (*continued*)

SELECTING A BUTTON

You cannot select a Macro button by clicking it, because that executes the associated macro. Thus, to select a macro button, you must press and hold the Ctrl key as you click the mouse. (You can also select a button by clicking the right mouse button to produce a shortcut menu.) Once the button has been selected, you can edit its name, and/or move or size the button just as you can any other Windows object.

Step 8: Test the Macro

- Pull down the **Data menu**, click **Filter**, then click **Show All**.
- Click **cell B12**. Enter **Miami** to change the location for Marder. Press **Enter**. The number of employees in the summary statistics area changes, as do the results of the other summary statistics.
- Click the **Chicago button** as shown in Figure 8.6h to execute the macro. Marder is *not* listed this time because she is no longer in Chicago.
- Pull down the **Data menu**. Click **Filter**. Click **Show All** to display the entire employee list.
- Click **cell B12**. Enter **Chicago** to change the location for this employee back to Chicago. Press **Enter**. Click the **Chicago button** to execute the macro a second time. Marder is once again displayed with the Chicago employees.
- Pull down the **Data menu**. Click **Filter**. Click **Show All**.
- You do not have to print the workbook at this time, since we will print the entire workbook at the end of the next exercise.
- Save the workbook. Exit Excel if you do not want to continue with the next exercise at this time.

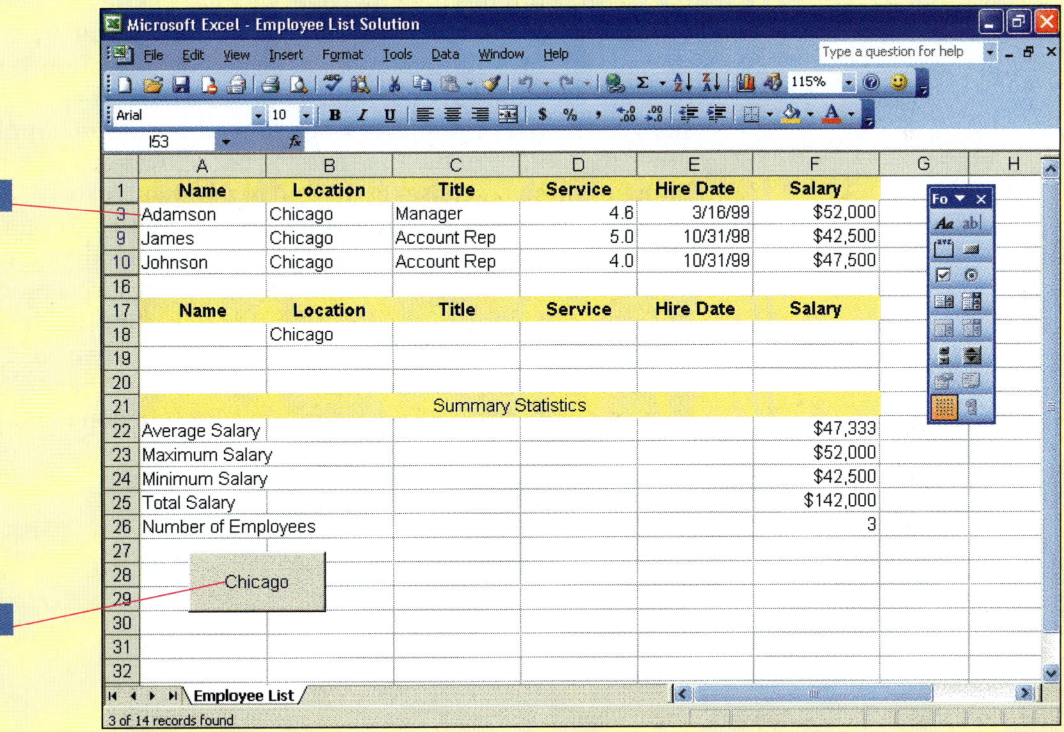

(h) Test the Macro (step 8)

FIGURE 8.6 Hands-on Exercise 3 (*continued*)

EXECUTING A MACRO

There are several different ways to execute a macro. The most basic way is to pull down the Tools menu, click Macro, click Macros . . . to display the Macros dialog box, then double click the desired macro to run it. You can assign a macro to a button within a worksheet or to a custom button on a toolbar, then click the button to run the macro. The fastest way is to use a keyboard shortcut, provided that a shortcut has been defined.

Excel macros were originally nothing more than recorded keystrokes. Earlier versions of Excel had you turn on the macro recorder to capture the associated keystrokes, then "play back" those keystrokes when you ran the macro. Starting with Office 95, however, the recorded keystrokes were translated into Visual Basic commands, which made the macros potentially much more powerful because you could execute Visual Basic programs (known as procedures) from within Excel. (In actuality, Microsoft Office uses a subset of Visual Basic known as *Visual Basic for Applications (VBA)*, and we will use this terminology from now on.)

You can think of the macro recorder as a shortcut to generate the VBA code. Once you have that code, however, you can modify the various statements using techniques common to any programming language. You can move and/or copy statements within a procedure, search for one character string and replace it with another, and so on. And finally, you can insert additional VBA statements that are beyond the scope of ordinary Excel commands. You can, for example, display information to the user in the form of a message box any time during the execution of the macro. You can also accept information from the user into a dialog box for subsequent use in the macro.

Figure 8.7 illustrates the way that these tasks are accomplished in VBA. Figure 8.7a contains the VBA code, whereas Figures 8.7b and 8.7c show the resulting dialog boxes, as they would appear during execution of the associated VBA procedure. The ***MsgBox statement*** displays information to the user. The text of the message is entered in quotation marks, and the text appears within a dialog box as shown. The user clicks the OK command button to continue. (The MsgBox has other optional parameters that are not shown at this time, but are illustrated through various exercises at the end of the chapter.)

The InputBox function accepts input from the user for subsequent use in the procedure. Note the subtle change in terminology, in that we refer to the InputBox function, but the MsgBox statement. That is because a function returns a value, in this case the name of the location that was supplied by the user. That value is stored in the active cell within the worksheet, where it will be used later in the procedure. There is also a difference in syntax in that the MsgBox statement does not contain parentheses, whereas the InputBox function requires parentheses.

```
MsgBox "The MsgBox statement displays information"
ActiveCell.FormulaR1C1 = InputBox("Enter employee location")
```

(a) Visual Basic Statements

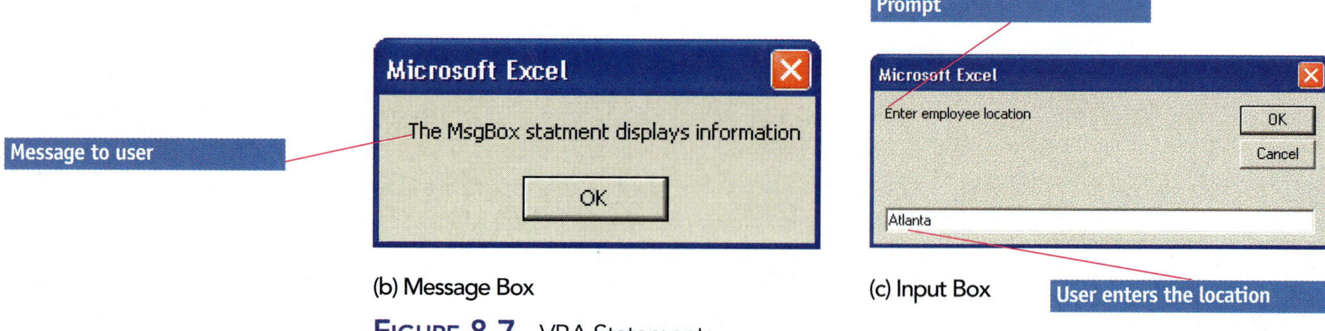

(b) Message Box

(c) Input Box

FIGURE 8.7 VBA Statements

hands-on exercise

4 Creating Additional Macros

Objective To duplicate an existing macro, then modify the copied macro to create an entirely new macro. Use Figure 8.8 as a guide.

Step 1: Enable Macros

- Start Excel. Open the **Employee List Solution workbook** from the previous exercise. You should see the warning in Figure 8.8a.
- Click the **More Info button** to display the Help window to learn more about macro virus prevention. (Pull down the **Tools menu**, click **Options**, click the **Security tab**, and click the **Macro Security button** if you do not see the warning message.)
- Click the **Close button** when you are finished reading the information.
- Click the **Enable Macros button** to open the Employee List Solution workbook.

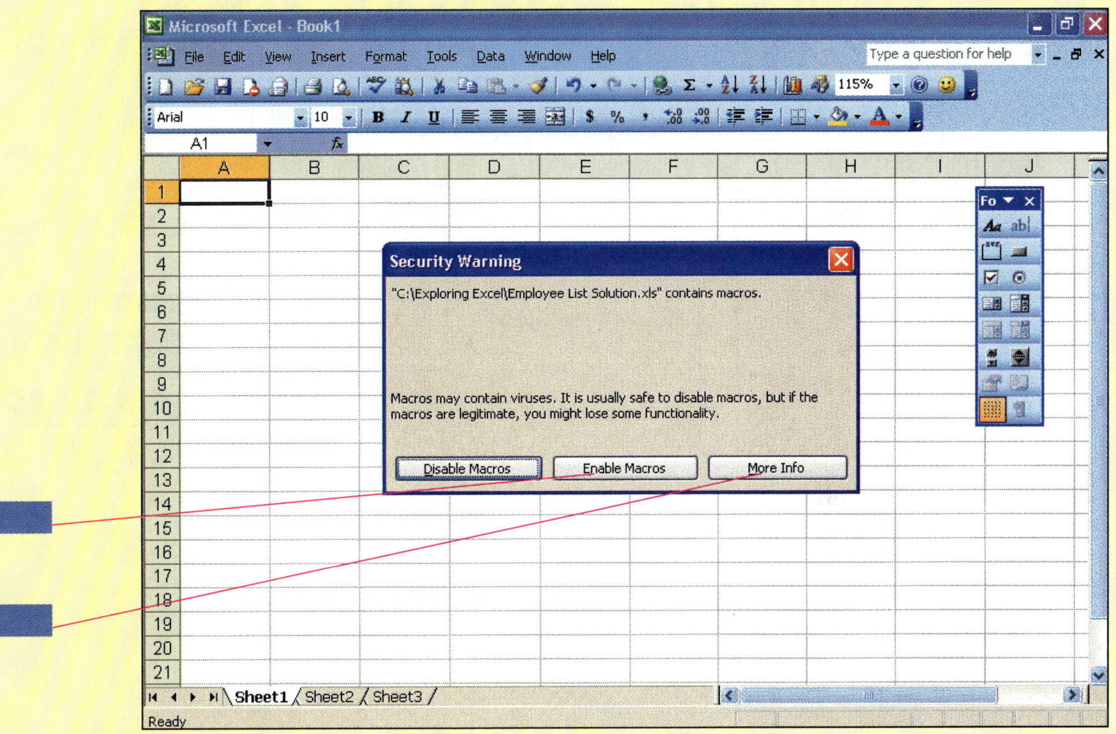

(a) Enable Macros (step 1)

FIGURE 8.8 Hands-on Exercise 4

MACRO SECURITY

A computer virus could take the form of an Excel macro in which case Excel will warn you that a workbook contains a macro, provided the security option is set appropriately. Pull down the Tools menu, click the Options command, click the Security tab, and then set the Macro Security to either High or Medium. High security disables all macros except those from a trusted source. Medium security gives you the option to enable macros. Click the button only if you are sure the macro is from a trusted source.

Step 2: Copy the Chicago Macro

- Pull down the **Tools menu**, click the **Macro command**, then click **Visual Basic Editor** (or press **Alt+F11**) to open the Visual Basic Editor.
- Click the **plus sign** on the Modules folder for the Employee List Solution project, select **Module1**, pull down the **View menu**, and click **Code**.
- Click and drag to select the entire Chicago macro as shown in Figure 8.8b.
- Pull down the **Edit menu** and click **Copy**, or press **Ctrl+C**, or click the **Copy button** on the Standard toolbar.
- Click below the End Sub statement to deselect the macro and simultaneously establish the position of the insertion point.
- Pull down the **Edit menu** and click **Paste**, or press **Ctrl+V**, or click the **Paste button** on the Standard toolbar.
- The Chicago macro has been copied and now appears twice in Module1.
- Save the module.

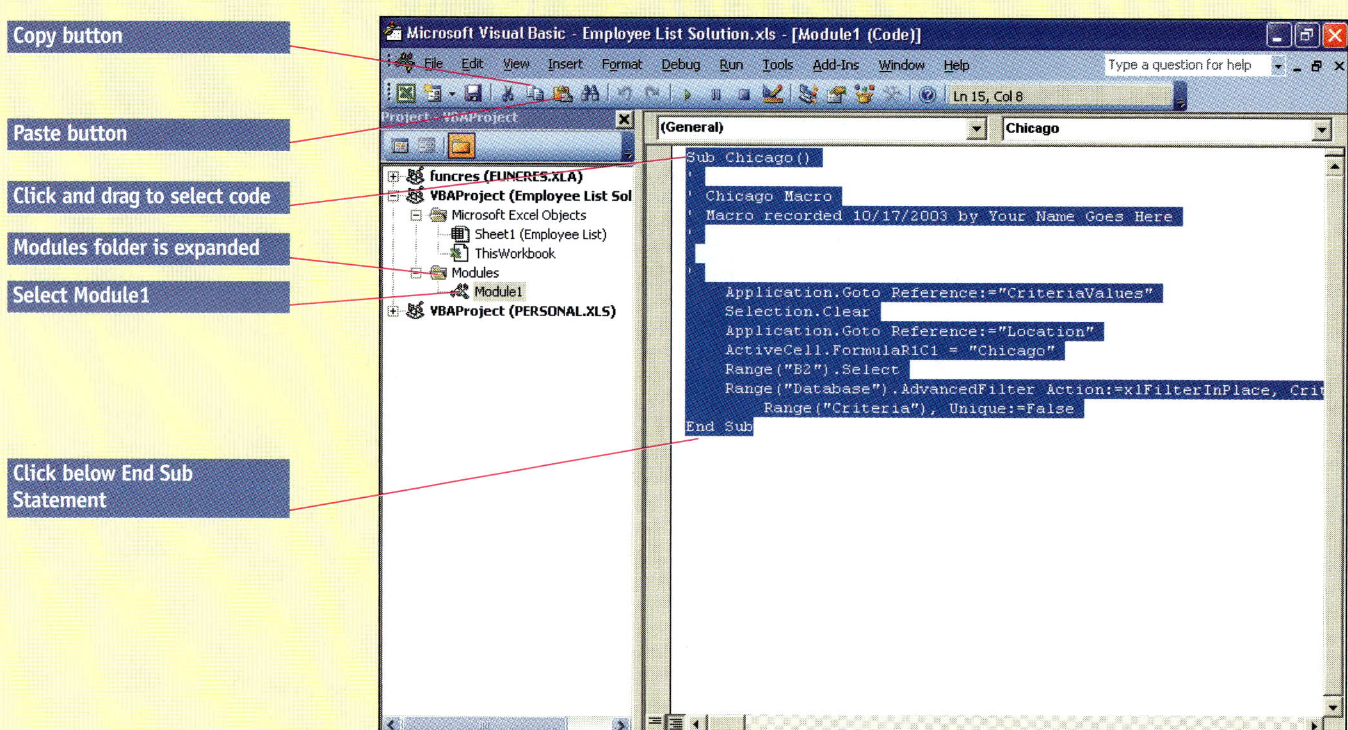

(b) Copy the Chicago Macro (step 2)

FIGURE 8.8 Hands-on Exercise 4 (*continued*)

THE SHIFT KEY

You can select text for editing (or replacement) with the mouse, or alternatively, you can select by using the cursor keys on the keyboard. Set the insertion point where you want the selection to begin, then press and hold the Shift key as you use the cursor keys to move the insertion point to the end of the selection. The selected statements are affected by the next command(s).

Step 3: Create the Manager Macro

- Click in front of the second (i.e., the copied) Chicago macro to set the insertion point. Pull down the **Edit menu**. Click **Replace** to display the Replace dialog box as shown in Figure 8.8c.
- Enter **Chicago** in the Find What text box. Press the **tab key**. Enter **Manager** in the Replace With text box. Select the option button to search in the *Current Procedure*. Click the **Find Next command button**.
- Excel searches for the first occurrence of Chicago, which should be in the Sub statement of the copied macro. (If this is not the case, click the **Find Next command button** until your screen matches Figure 8.8c.)
- Click the **Replace command button**. Excel substitutes Manager for Chicago, then looks for the next occurrence of Chicago. Click **Replace**. Click **Replace** a third time to make another substitution. Click **OK** in response to the message that the specified region has been searched. Close the Replace dialog box.
- Click and drag to select **Location** within the Application.Goto.Reference statement in the Manager macro. Enter **Title**. (The criteria within the macro have been changed to employees whose title is Manager.)
- Save the module.

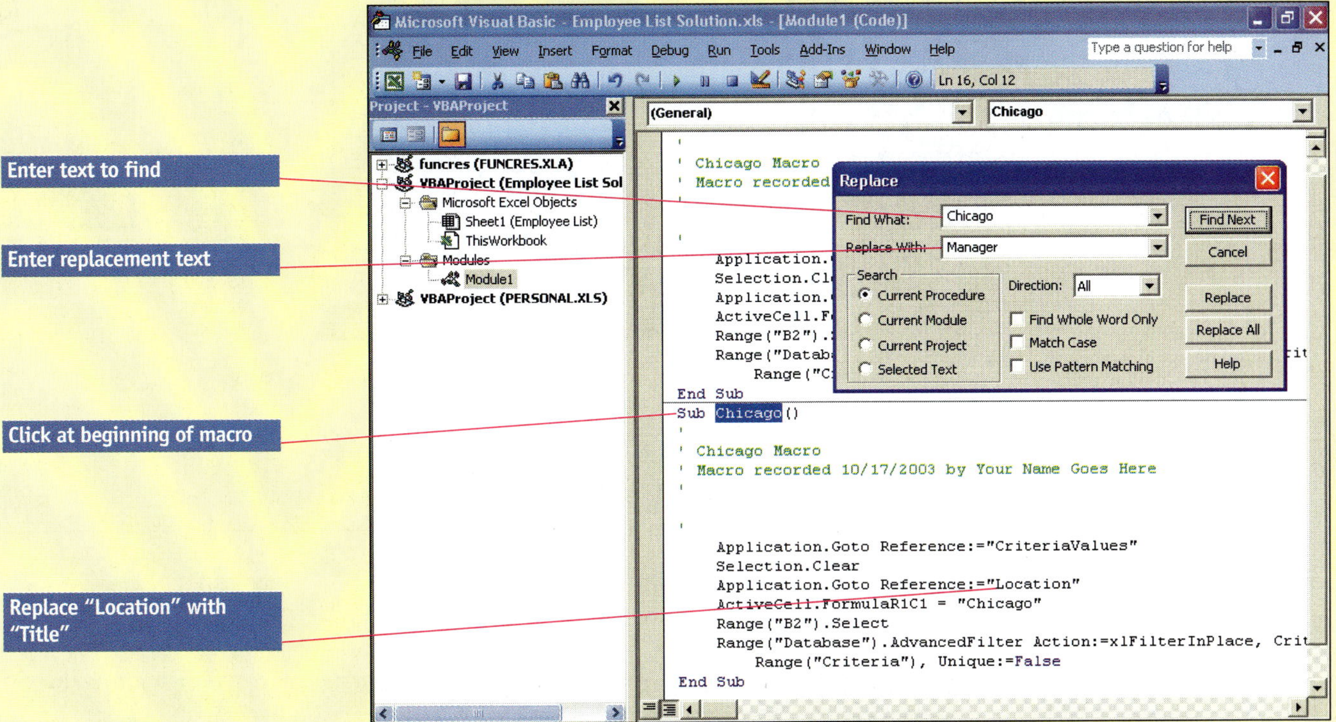

(c) Create the Manager Macro (step 3)

FIGURE 8.8 Hands-on Exercise 4 (*continued*)

THE FIND AND REPLACE COMMANDS

Anyone familiar with a word processor takes the Find and Replace commands for granted, but did you know the same capabilities exist in Excel as well as in the Visual Basic Editor? Pull down the Edit menu and choose either command. You have the same options as in the parallel command in Word, such as a case-sensitive (or insensitive) search or a limitation to a whole-word search.

Step 4: Run the Manager Macro

- Click the **Excel button** on the Windows taskbar or press **Alt+F11** to return to the Employee List Solution worksheet.
- Pull down the **Tools menu**. Click **Macro**, then click the **Macros . . . command** to display the Macro dialog box as shown in Figure 8.8d.
- You should see two macros: Chicago, which was created in the previous exercise, and Manager, which you just created. (If the Manager macro does not appear, return to the Visual Basic Editor and correct the appropriate Sub statement to include Manager() as the name of the macro.)
- Select the **Manager macro**, then click **Run** to run the macro, after which you should see three employees (Adamson, Coulter, and Milgrom). If the macro does not execute correctly, return to the Visual Basic Editor to make the necessary corrections, then rerun the macro.

List of macros

Click Manager

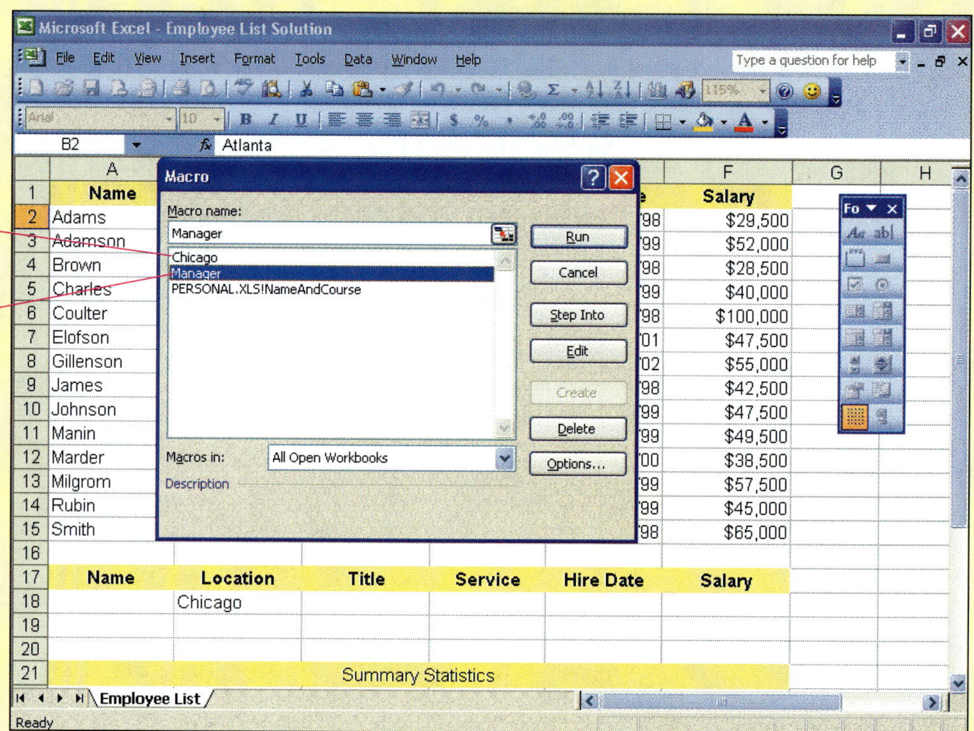

(d) Run the Manager Macro (step 4)

FIGURE 8.8 Hands-on Exercise 4 (*continued*)

THE STEP INTO COMMAND

The Step Into command helps to debug a macro, as it executes the statements one at a time. Pull down the Tools menu, click Macro, click Macros, select the macro to debug, then click the Step Into command button. Move and/or size the Visual Basic Editor window so that you can see both the worksheet and the macro. Pull down the Debug menu and click the Step Into command (or press the F8 function key) to execute the first statement in the macro and view its results. Continue to press the F8 function key to execute the statements one at a time until the macro has completed execution.

Step 5: Assign a Button

- Click the **Button tool** on the Forms toolbar (the mouse pointer changes to a tiny crosshair), then click and drag in the worksheet to draw a button on the worksheet. Release the mouse.
- Choose **Manager** (the macro you just created) from the list of macro names as shown in Figure 8.8e. Click **OK** to close the Assign Macro dialog box.
- The button should still be selected. Click and drag to select the name of the button, **Button 2**, then type **Manager** as the new name. Do *not* press the Enter key. Click outside the button to deselect it.
- There should be two buttons on your worksheet, one each for the Chicago and Manager macros.
- Click the **Chicago button** to execute the Chicago macro. You should see four employees with an average salary of $45,125.
- Click the **Manager button** to execute the Manager macro. You should see three employees with an average salary of $69,833.

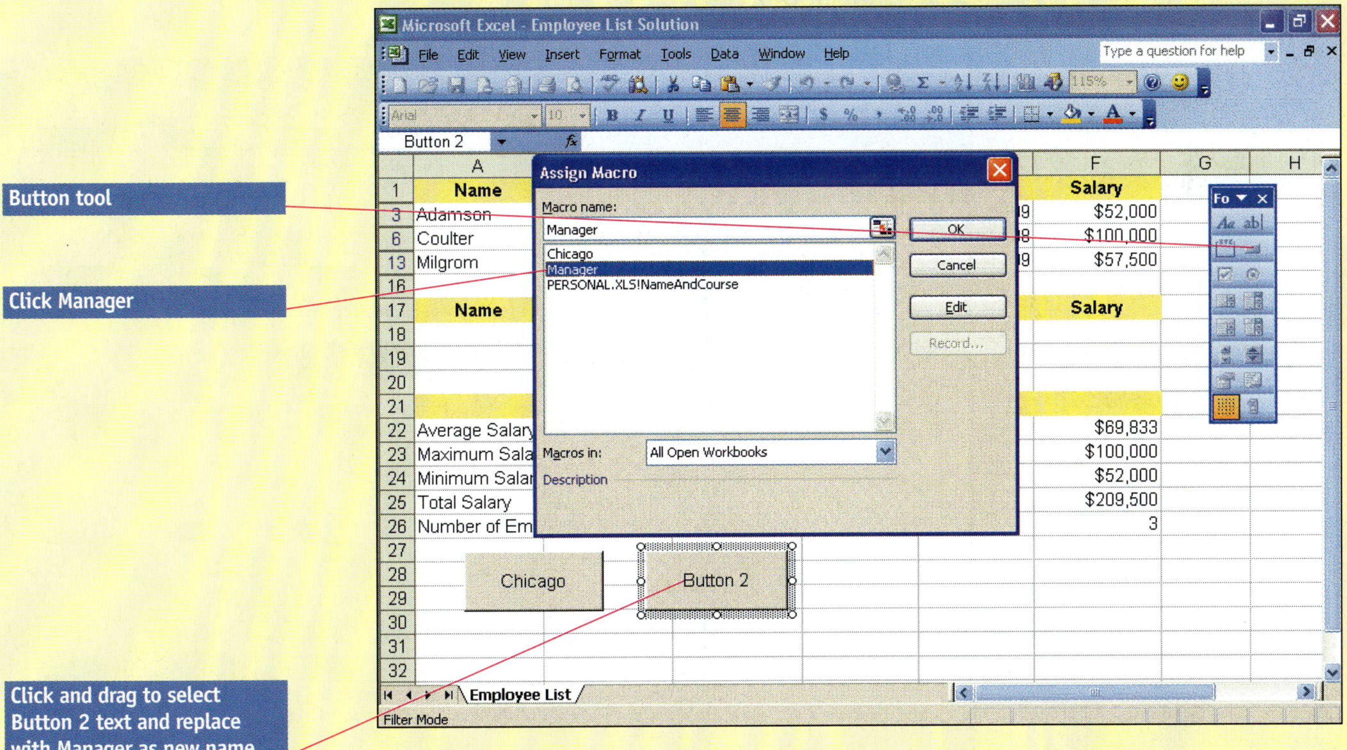

(e) Assign a Button (step 5)

FIGURE 8.8 Hands-on Exercise 4 (*continued*)

CREATE UNIFORM BUTTONS

One way to create buttons of a uniform size is to create the first button, then copy that button to create the others. To copy a button, press the Ctrl key as you select (click) the button, then click the Copy button on the Standard toolbar. Click in the worksheet where you want the new button to appear, then click the Paste button. Click and drag over the name of the button and enter a new name. Right click the border of the new button, then click Assign Macro from the shortcut menu. Select the name of the new macro, then click OK.

Step 6: Create the ChicagoManager Macro

- Return to the Visual Basic Editor. Press **Ctrl+Home** to move to the beginning of Module1. Click and drag to select the entire Chicago macro. Be sure to include the End Sub statement in your selection.
- Click the **Copy button** on the Standard toolbar to copy the Chicago macro to the clipboard. Press **Ctrl+End** to move to the end of the module sheet. Click the **Paste button** on the Standard toolbar to complete the copy operation.
- Change **Chicago** to **ChicagoManager** in both the comment statement and the Sub statement as shown in Figure 8.8f.
- Click and drag to select the two statements in the **Manager macro** as shown in Figure 8.8f. Click the **Copy button**.
- Scroll, if necessary, until you can click in the **ChicagoManager macro** at the end of the line, ActiveCell. FormulaR1C1 = "Chicago". Press **Enter** to begin a new line. Click the **Paste button** to complete the copy operation.
- Delete any unnecessary blank lines or spaces that may remain.
- Save the module.

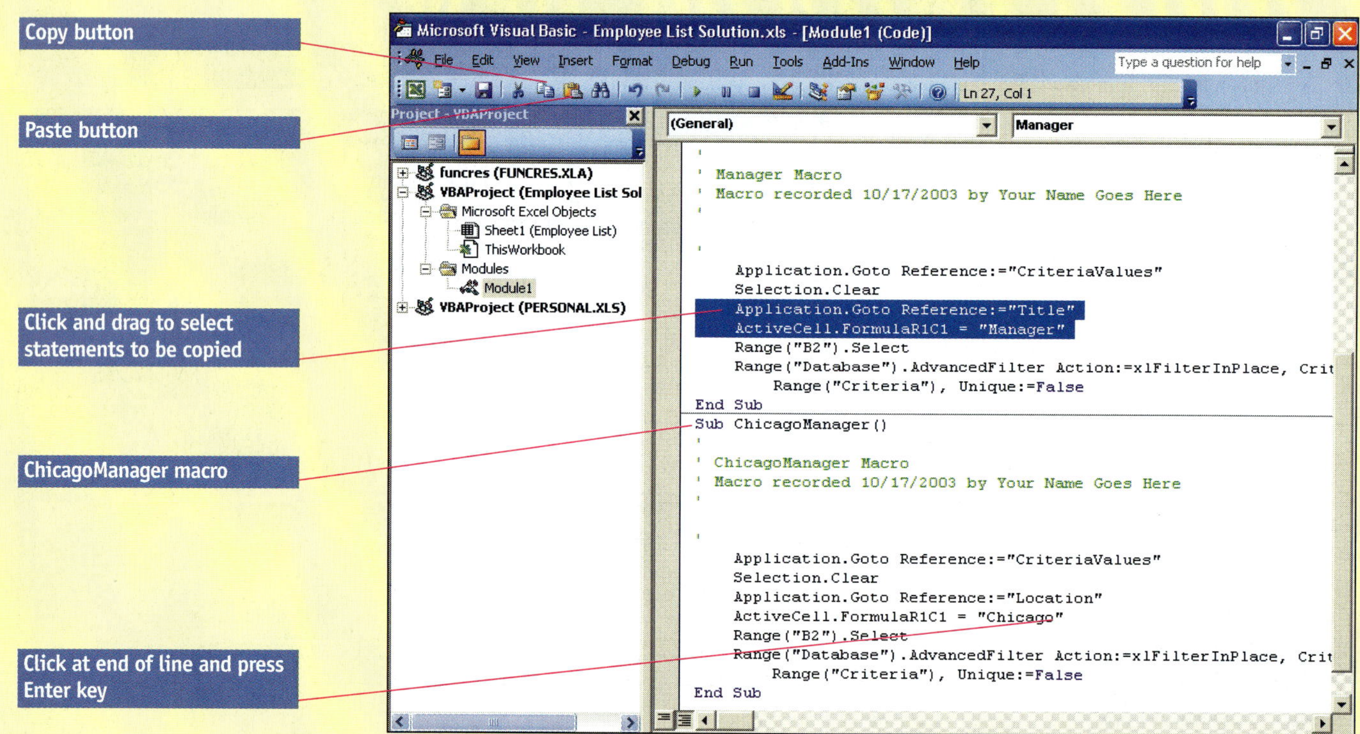

(f) Create the ChicagoManager Macro (step 6)

FIGURE 8.8 Hands-on Exercise 4 (*continued*)

ADD A SHORTCUT

You can add and/or modify the shortcut key associated with a macro at any time. Pull down the Tools menu, click the Macro command, then click Macros to display the Macro dialog box. Select the desired macro and click the Options button to display the Macro Options dialog box, where you assign a shortcut. Type a lowercase letter to create a shortcut with just the Ctrl key, such as Ctrl+m. Enter an uppercase letter to create a shortcut using the Ctrl and Shift keys, such as Ctrl+Shift+M.

Step 7: The MsgBox Statement

- Check that the statements in your ChicagoManager macro match those in Figure 8.8g. (The MsgBox statement has not yet been added.)
- Click immediately before the End Sub statement. Press **Enter** to begin a new line, press the **up arrow** to move up one line, then press **Tab** to indent. (Indentation is not a VBA requirement; it is done to enhance the readability of the code.)
- Type the word **MsgBox**, then press the **Space bar**. VBA responds with a Quick Info box that displays the complete syntax of the statement. You can ignore this information at the present time, since we are not entering any additional parameters.
- Enter the rest of the MsgBox statement exactly as it appears in Figure 8.8g. Be sure to include a blank space and the **underscore** at the end of the first line, which indicates that the statement is continued to the next line.
- Save the module, then return to the Excel workbook.

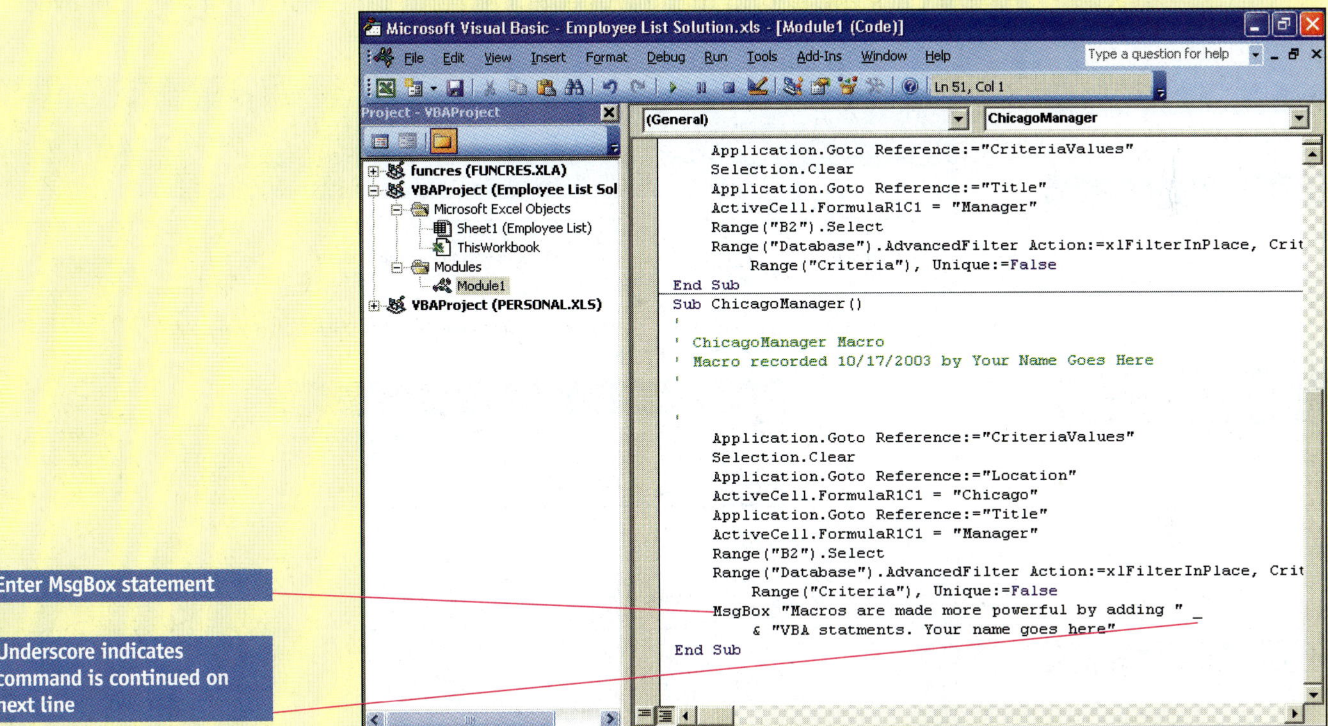

(g) The MsgBox Statement (step 7)

FIGURE 8.8 Hands-on Exercise 4 (*continued*)

THE UNDERSCORE AND AMPERSAND

A VBA statement is continued from one line to the next by typing a blank space followed by an underscore at the end of the line to be continued. You may not, however, break a line in the middle of a literal. Hence, the first line ends with a closing quotation mark, followed by a space and the underscore. The next line starts with an ampersand to indicate continuation of the previous literal, followed by the remainder of the literal in quotation marks.

Step 8: Test the ChicagoManager Macro

- You can assign a macro to a command button by copying an existing command button, then changing the name of the button and the associated macro. Right click either of the existing command buttons, click the **Copy command** from the shortcut menu, then click the **Paste button** on the Standard toolbar.
- Click and drag the copied button to the right of the two existing buttons. Click and drag the text of the copied button (which should still be selected) to select the text, then type **Chicago Manager** as the name of the button.
- Click anywhere in the worksheet to deselect the button, then **Right click** the new button, click the **Assign Macro command**, choose the newly created ChicagoManager macro, and click **OK**.
- Click anywhere in the workbook to deselect the button. Save the workbook.
- Click the **Chicago Manager button** to execute the macro. You should see the matching employees as shown in Figure 8.8h, followed by the message box.
- Click **OK**. Return to the VBA editor to correct the macro if it does not execute as intended.

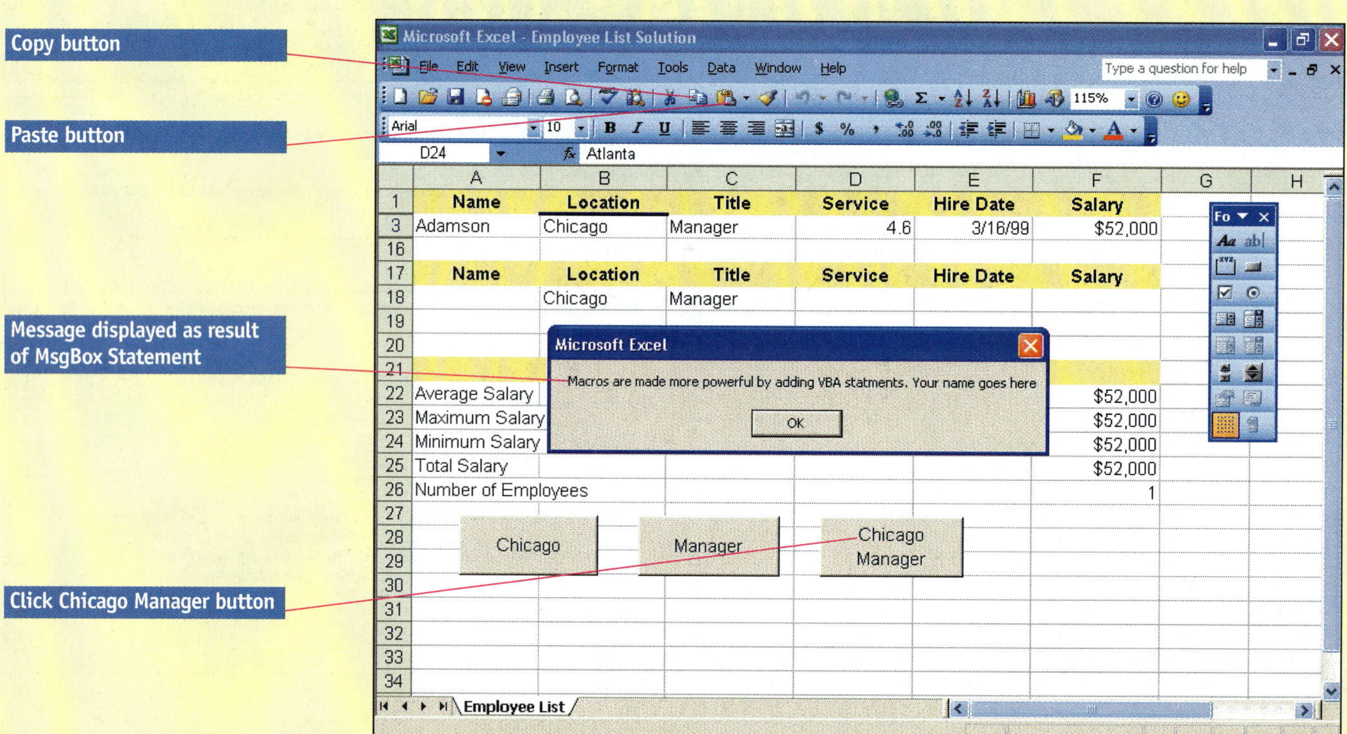

(h) Test the ChicagoManager Macro (step 8)

FIGURE 8.8 Hands-on Exercise 4 (*continued*)

CUSTOMIZE THE MESSAGE BOX

You can add a personal touch to the output of the MsgBox statement by including optional parameters to change the text of the title bar and/or include an icon within the message box. The statement, MsgBox "Hello World", vbinformation, "Your Name on Title Bar" uses both parameters. Be sure to use quotation marks for both the first and last parameter.

Step 9: Create the AnyCityAnyTitle Macro

- Press **Alt+F11** to return to the Visual Basic editor. Click and drag to select the entire ChicagoManager macro. Click the **Copy button**, click the blank line below the End Sub statement, then click the **Paste button** to duplicate the module.
- Click and drag the name of the copied macro. Type **AnyCityAnyTitle()** to change the name of the macro. Do not leave any spaces in the macro name. Delete or modify the comments as you see fit.
- Click and drag to select **"Chicago"** as shown in Figure 8.8i. You must include the quotation marks in your selection.
- Type **InputBox("Enter the location")** to replace the specific location with the InputBox function. Be sure to use left and right parentheses and to enclose the literal in quotation marks.
- Click and drag to select **"Manager"**. Type **InputBox("Enter the title")** to replace the specific title with the InputBox function.
- Save the module and return to the Excel workbook.

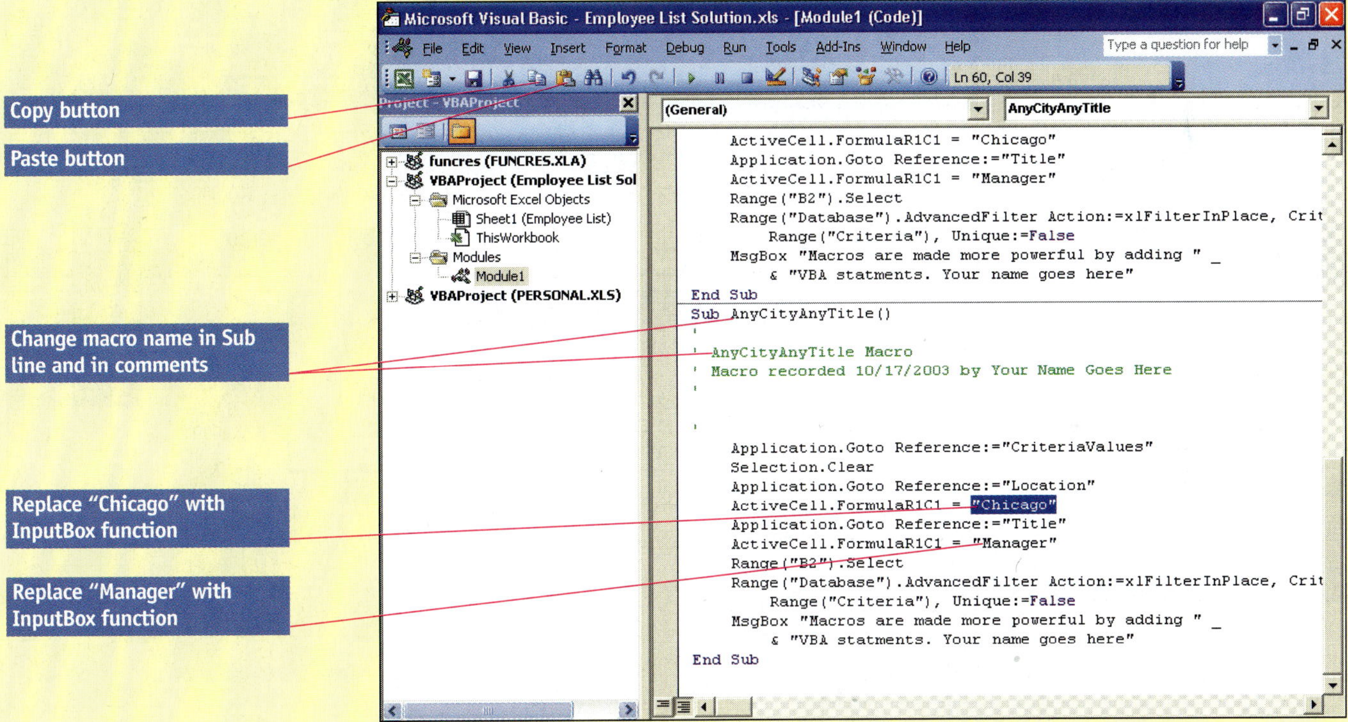

(i) Create the AnyCityAnyTitle Macro (step 9)

FIGURE 8.8 Hands-on Exercise 4 (*continued*)

USE WHAT YOU KNOW

Use the techniques acquired from other applications such as Microsoft Word to facilitate editing within the VBA window. Press the Ins key to toggle between the insert and overtype modes as you modify the statements within a procedure. You can also cut, copy, and paste statements (or parts of statements) within a procedure and from one procedure to another. The Find and Replace commands are also useful.

Step 10: Test the AnyCityAnyTitle Macro

- Copy any of the existing command buttons to create a new button for the **AnyCityAnyTitle** macro as shown in Figure 8.8j. Be sure to assign the correct macro to this button.
- Click the **Any City Any Title command button** to run the macro. You will be prompted for the location. Type **Atlanta** and click **OK**. (A second input box will appear in which you will enter the title.)
- At this time Atlanta has been entered into the criteria area, and the summary statistics reflect the Atlanta employees. The filtered list will not change, however, until you have entered the title and completed the Advanced Filter command.
- Enter **Trainee** as the employee title as shown in Figure 8.8j. Click **OK**. The workbook changes to reflect the Atlanta trainees. Click **OK** in response to the message box.
- Return to the VBA editor if the macro does not execute as intended. Save the workbook.

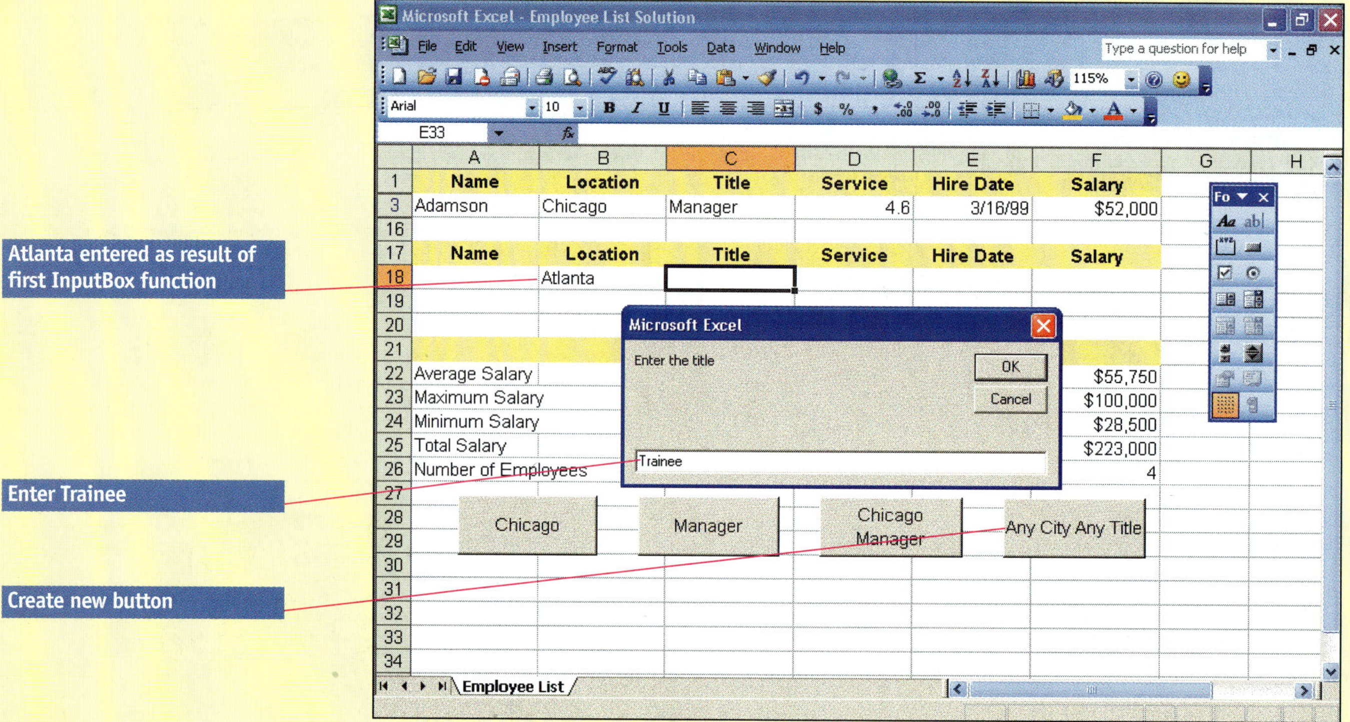

(j) Test the AnyCityAnyTitle Macro (step 10)

FIGURE 8.8 Hands-on Exercise 4 (*continued*)

ONE MACRO DOES IT ALL

The AnyCityAnyTitle macro is the equivalent of the more specific macros that were created earlier; that is, you would enter "Chicago" and "Manager" to replace the Chicago Manager macro. You can also enter "Chicago" as the city and leave the title field blank to select all Chicago employees, or alternatively, leave the city blank and enter "Manager" as the title to select all managers. And finally, you could omit both city and title to select all employees.

Step 11: Change the Button Properties

- Press and hold the **Shift** and **Ctrl keys**, then click each of the command buttons to select all four buttons as shown in Figure 8.8k.
- Pull down the **Format menu** and click the **Control command** to display the Format Control dialog box. Click the **Properties tab**, then check the box to **Print object** so that the command buttons will appear on the printed worksheet.
- Click the **Move but don't size with cells option button**. Click **OK** to exit the dialog box and return to the worksheet. Click anywhere in the worksheet to deselect the buttons.
- Click the **Print button** on the Standard toolbar to print the worksheet. Return to the Visual Basic Editor. Pull down the **File menu**, click the **Print command**, select **Current Module**, then click **OK**.
- Save the workbook a final time. Close the workbook. Exit Excel if you don't want to continue with the next exercise at this time.

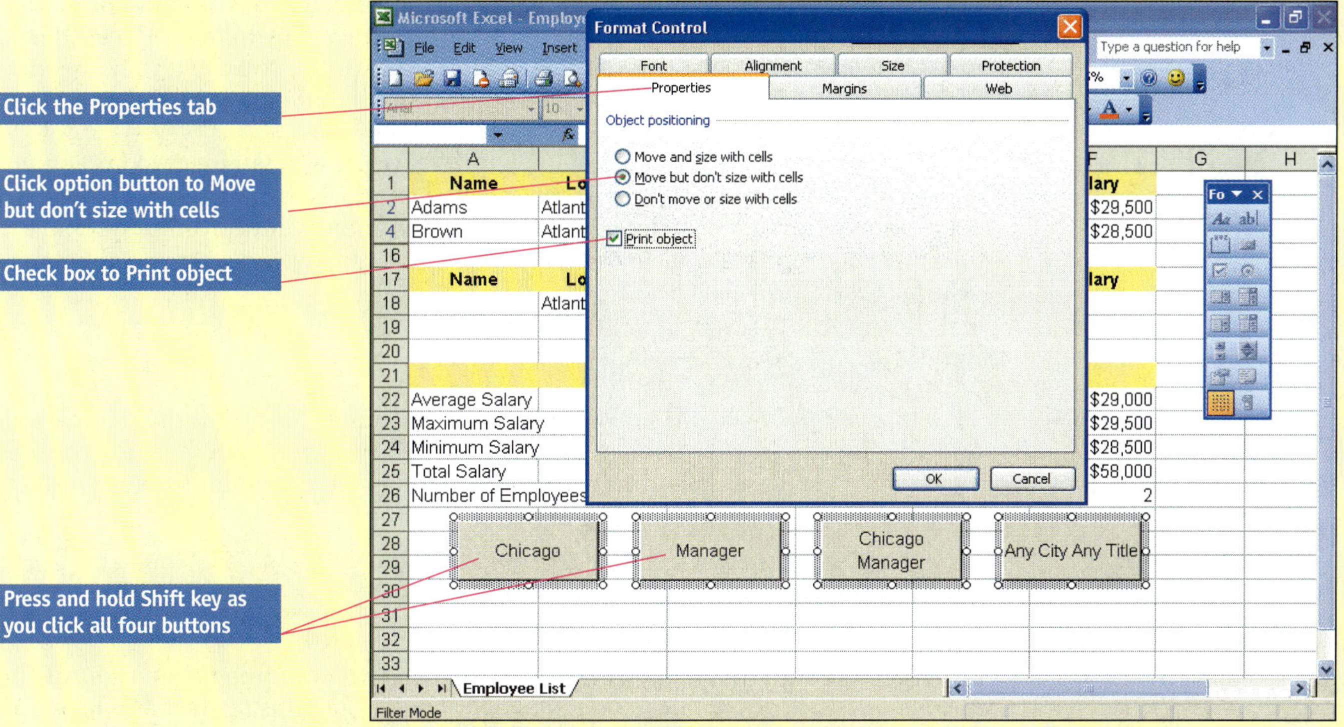

(k) Change the Button Properties (step 11)

FIGURE 8.8 Hands-on Exercise 4 (*continued*)

THE SIZE PROPERTY

Use the Size property to obtain a consistent look for your command buttons. Press and hold the Shift and Ctrl keys as you select the individual buttons. Pull down the Format menu and click the Control command to display the Format Control dialog box. Click the Size tab, enter the width and height for the selected buttons, then click OK. The buttons will be a uniform size, but they may overlap. Click anywhere in the worksheet to deselect the buttons, then right click and drag to reposition a button.

LOOPS AND DECISION MAKING

Excel macros can be made significantly more powerful by incorporating additional Visual Basic statements that enable true programming. These include the If statement for decision making, and the Do statement to implement a ***loop*** (one or more commands that are executed repeatedly until a condition is met).

Consider, for example, the worksheet and associated macro in Figure 8.9. The worksheet is similar to those used in the preceding exercises, except that the font color of the data for managers is red. Think for a minute how you would do this manually. You would look at the first employee in the list, examine the employee's title to determine if that employee is a manager, and if so, change the font color for that employee. You would then repeat these steps for all of the other employees on the list. It sounds tedious, but that is exactly what you would do if asked to change the font color for the managers.

Now ask yourself whether you could implement the entire process with the macro recorder. You could use the recorder to capture the commands to select a specific row within the list and change the font color. You could not, however, use the recorder to determine whether or not to select a particular row (i.e., whether the employee is a manager) because you have to make that decision by comparing the cell contents to a specific criterion. Nor is there a way to tell the recorder to repeat the process for every employee. In other words, you need to go beyond merely capturing Excel commands. You need to include additional Visual Basic statements within the macro.

The HighlightManager macro in Figure 8.9 uses the If statement to implement a decision (to determine whether the selected employee is a manager) and the Do statement to implement a loop (to repeat the commands until all employees in the list have been processed). To understand how the macro works, you need to know the basic syntax of each statement.

If Statement

The ***If statement*** conditionally executes a statement (or group of statements), depending on the value of an expression (condition). The If statement determines whether an expression is true, and if so, executes the commands between the If and the ***End If statement***. For example:

```
If ActiveCell.Offset(0, 2) = "Manager" Then
    Selection.Font.ColorIndex = 3
End If
```

This If statement determines whether the cell two columns to the right of the active cell (the offset indicates a relative reference) contains the text *Manager,* and if so, changes the font color of the (previously) selected text. The number three corresponds to the color red. No action is taken if the condition is false. Either way, execution continues with the command below the End If.

IF-THEN-ELSE

The If statement includes an optional Else clause whose statements are executed if the condition is false. Consider:

If condition **Then** statements [**Else** statements] **End If**

The condition is evaluated as either true or false. If the condition is true, the statements following Then are executed; otherwise the statements following Else are executed. Either way, execution continues with the statement following End If. Use the Help command for additional information and examples.

Do Statement

The ***Do statement*** repeats a block of statements until a condition becomes true. For example:

```
Do Until ActiveCell = ""
    ActiveCell.Range("A1:F1").Select
    If ActiveCell.Offset(0, 2) = "Manager" Then
        Selection.Font.ColorIndex = 3
    End If
    ActiveCell.Offset(1, 0).Select
Loop
```

The statements within the loop are executed repeatedly until the active cell is empty (i.e., ActiveCell = ""). The first statement in the loop selects the cells in columns A through F of the current row. Relative references are used, and you may want to refer to the earlier discussion that indicated that A1:F1 specifies the shape of a range rather than a specific cell address.

The If statement determines whether the current employee is a manager and, if so, changes the font color for the selected cells. (The offset (0, 2) refers to the entry two columns to the right of the active cell.) The last statement selects the cell one row below the active cell to process the next employee. (Omission of this statement would process the same row indefinitely, creating what is known as an infinite loop.)

The macro in Figure 8.9 is a nontrivial example that illustrates the potential of Visual Basic to enhance a macro. Try to gain a conceptual understanding of how the macro works, but do not be concerned if you are confused initially. Do the hands-on exercise, and you'll be pleased at how much clearer it will be when you have created the macro yourself. The addition of loops and decision-making statements in a VBA procedure enables true programming within an Excel macro.

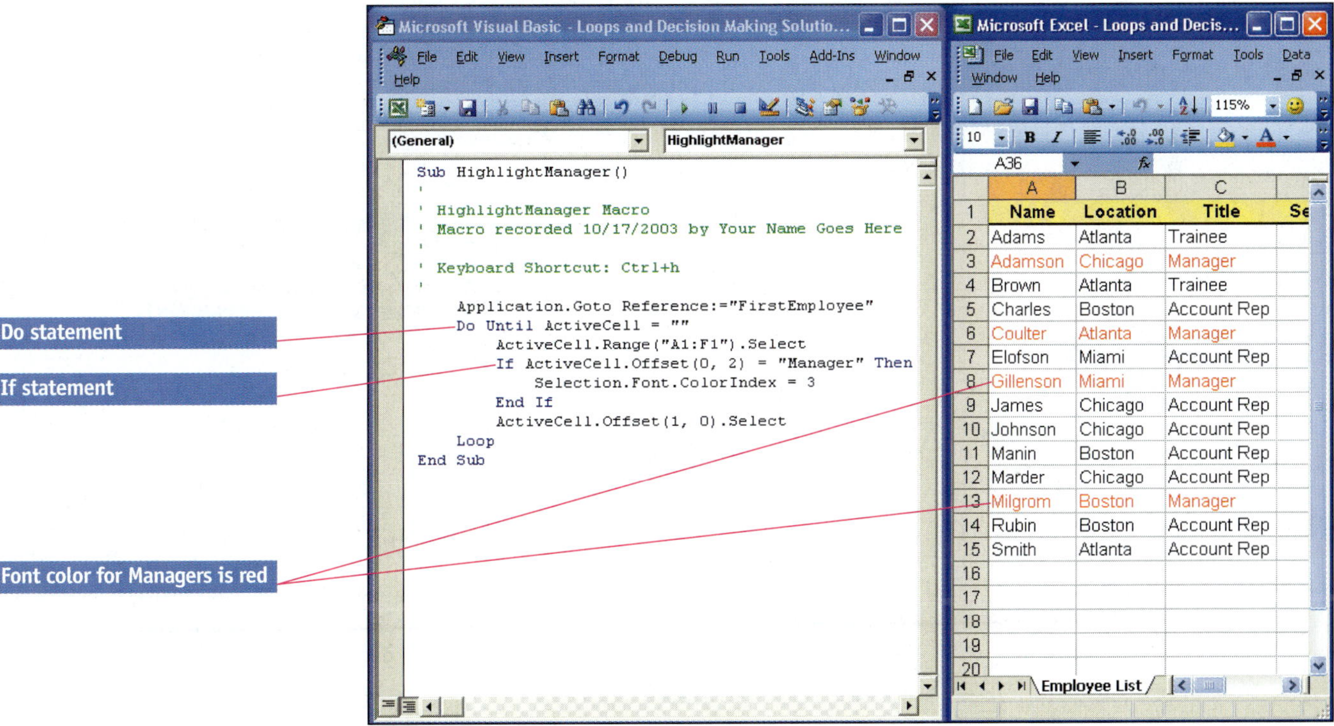

FIGURE 8.9 Loops and Decision Making

hands-on exercise

5 Loops and Decision Making

Objective To implement loops and decision making in a macro through relative references and the Visual Basic Do Until and If statements. Use Figure 8.10 as a guide in doing the exercise.

Step 1: The ClearColor Macro

- Open the **Loops and Decision Making workbook** in the **Exploring Excel folder**. Click the button to **Enable Macros** when prompted by the security warning. Close the Forms toolbar.
- Save the workbook as **Loops and Decision Making Solution workbook**. The data for the employees in rows 3, 6, 8, and 13 appears in red to indicate these employees are managers.
- Pull down the **Tools menu**. Click the **Macro command** and click **Macros** to display the dialog box in Figure 8.10a. (Do not be concerned if you do not see the NameAndCourse macro.)
- Select **ClearColor**, then click **Run** to execute this macro and clear the red color from the managerial employees.
- Use the **Font Color button** on the Standard toolbar to change the color of any entry within the list, then rerun the ClearColor macro. It is important to know that the ClearColor macro works, as you will use it throughout the exercise.
- Save the workbook.

Font color for Managers is red

Click ClearColor macro

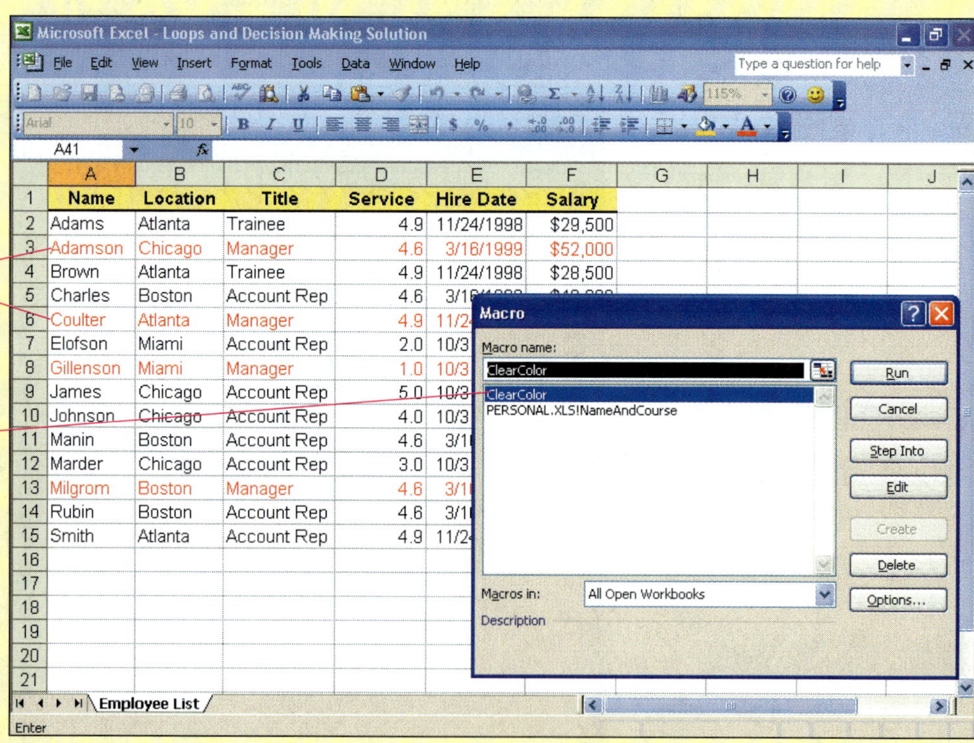

(a) The ClearColor Macro (step 1)

FIGURE 8.10 Hands-on Exercise 5

Step 2: Record the HighlightManager Macro

- You must choose the active cell before recording the macro. Click **cell A3**, the cell containing the name of the first manager.
- Pull down the **Tools menu**, click (or point to) the **Macro command**, then click **Record New Macro** (or click the **Record macro button** on the Visual Basic toolbar) to display the Record Macro dialog box.
- Enter **HighlightManager** as the name of the macro. Do not leave any spaces in the macro name. Click in the **Shortcut Key** check box and enter a **lowercase h**. Check that **This Workbook** is selected. Click **OK**.
- The Stop Recording toolbar appears, and the status bar indicates that you are recording the macro as shown in Figure 8.10b. Click the **Relative References button** so that the button is pushed in.
- Click and drag to select **cells A3 through F3** as shown in Figure 8.10b. Click the arrow in the **Font color list box**. Click **Red**. Click the **Stop Recording button**.
- Click anywhere in the worksheet to deselect cells A3 through F3 so you can see the effect of the macro; cells A3 through F3 should be displayed in red.
- Save the workbook.

Click and drag to select A3:F3

Click down arrow on Font Color box

Click Red

Recording mode

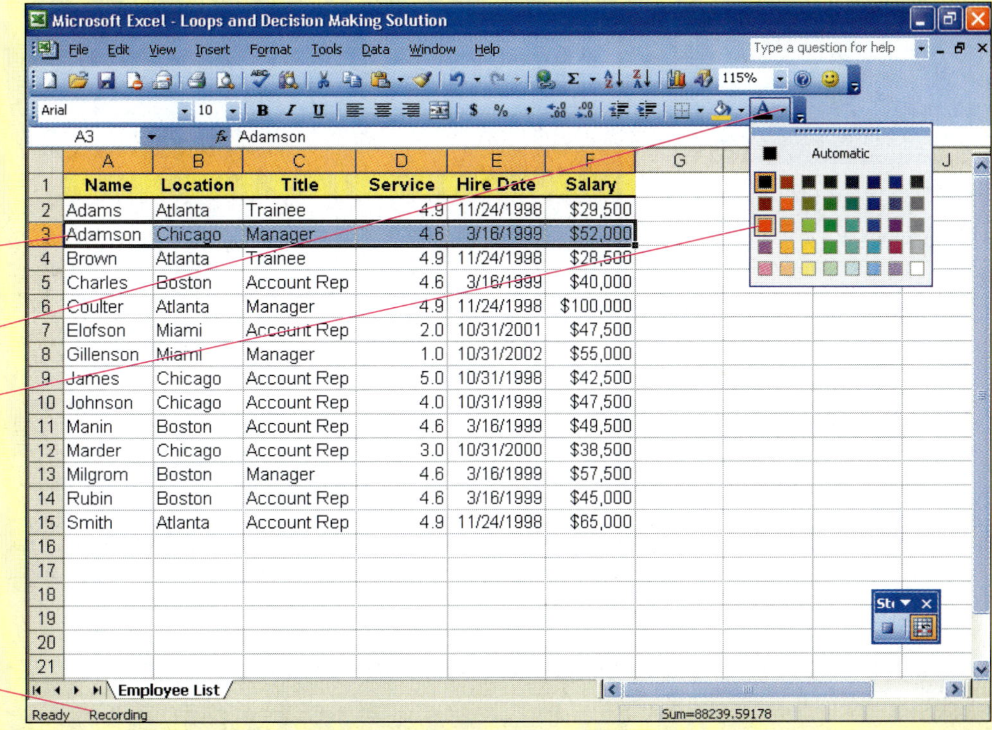

(b) Record the HighlightManager Macro (step 2)

FIGURE 8.10 Hands-on Exercise 5 (*continued*)

A SENSE OF FAMILIARITY

Visual Basic has the basic capabilities found in any other programming language. If you have programmed before, whether in Pascal, C, or even COBOL, you will find all of the familiar logic structures. These include the Do While and Do Until statements, the If-Then-Else statement for decision making, nested If statements, a Case statement, and/or calls to subprograms.

Step 3: View the Macro

- Press **Alt+F11** to open the Visual Basic Editor. If necessary, double click the **Modules folder** for the Loops and Decision Making Solution Project within the Project Explorer window to display the two modules within the workbook.
- Select (click) **Module2**. Pull down the **View menu** and click **Code** (or press the **F7 key**) to display the Visual Basic code for the HighlightManager macro you just created as shown in Figure 8.10c.
- Be sure that your code is identical to ours (except for the comments). If you see the absolute reference, Range("A3:F3"), rather than the relative reference in our figure, you need to correct your macro to match ours.
- Click the **close button** (the X on the Project Explorer title bar) to close the Project Explorer window. (You can reopen the Project Explorer at any time by pulling down the View menu.) The Code window expands to occupy the entire Visual Basic Editor window.

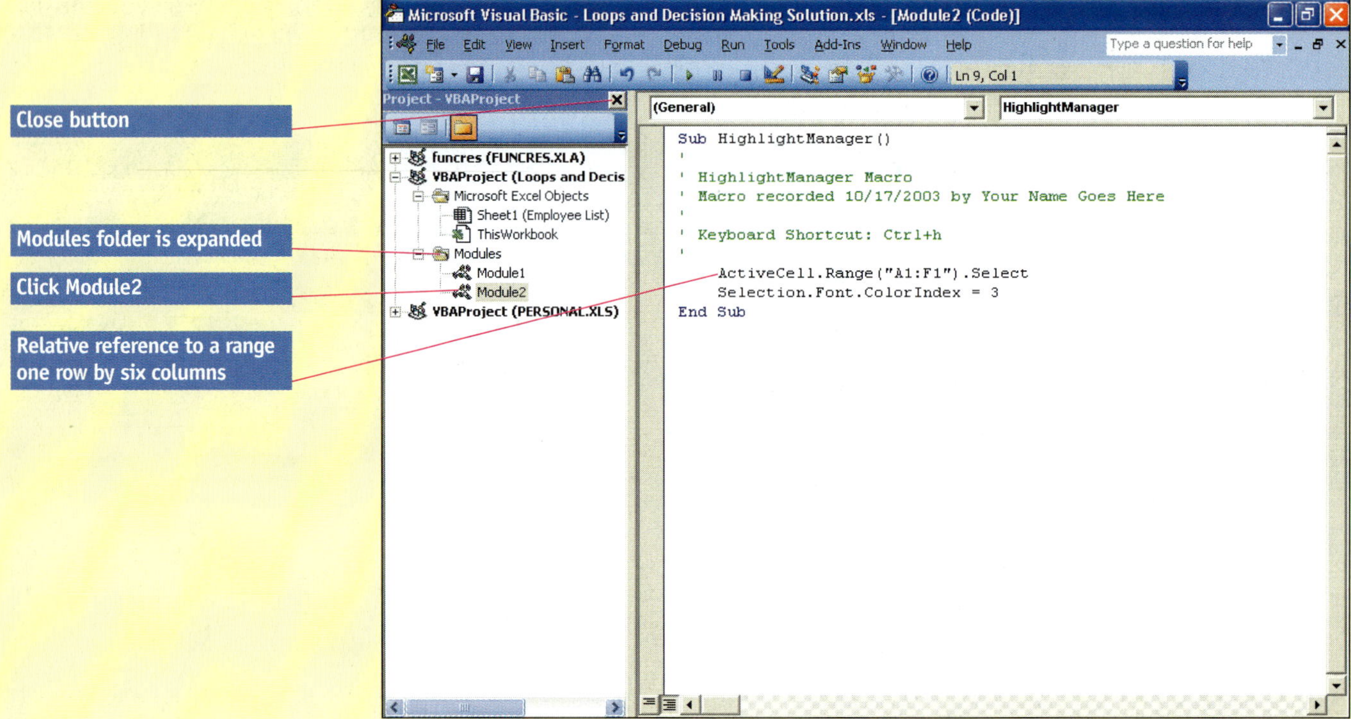

(c) View the Macro (step 3)

FIGURE 8.10 Hands-on Exercise 5 (*continued*)

WHY SO MANY MODULES?

Multiple macros that are recorded within the same Excel session are all stored in the same module. If you close the workbook, then subsequently reopen it, Excel will store subsequent macros in a new module. It really doesn't matter where (in which module) the macros are stored. You can, however, cut and paste macros from one module to another if you prefer to have all of the macros in a single module. Delete the additional (now superfluous) modules after you have copied the procedures.

Step 4: Test the Macro

- Point to an empty area on the Windows taskbar, then click the **right mouse button** to display a shortcut menu. Click **Tile Windows Vertically** to tile the open windows (Excel and the Visual Basic Editor).
- Your desktop should be similar to Figure 8.10d except that the additional employees will not yet appear in red. It doesn't matter if the workbook is in the same window as ours. (If additional windows are open on the desktop, minimize each window, then repeat the previous step to tile the open windows.)
- Click the **Excel window**. Click **cell A6** (the cell containing the name of the next manager). Press **Ctrl+h** to execute the HighlightManager macro. The font in cells A6 to F6 changes to red.
- Click **cell A7**. Press **Ctrl+h** to execute the HighlightManager macro. The font for this employee is also in red, although the employee is not a manager.
- Save the workbook.

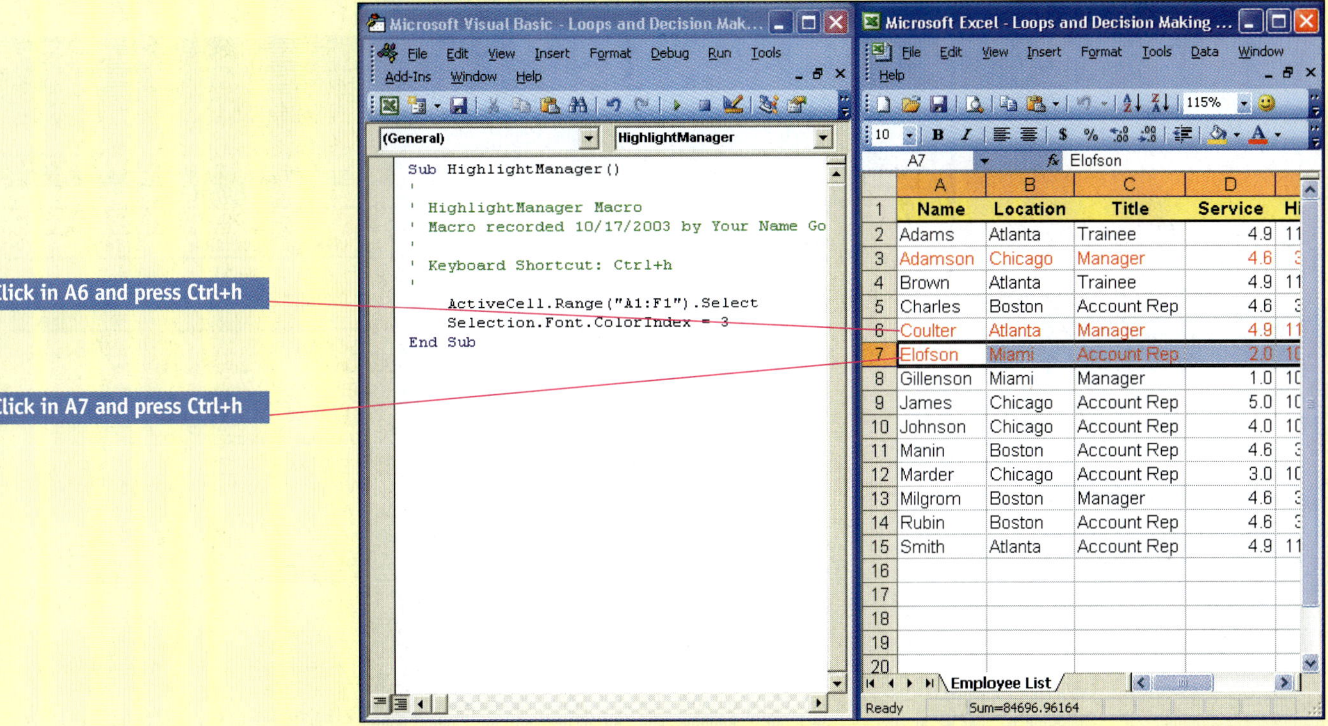

(d) Test the Macro (step 4)

FIGURE 8.10 Hands-on Exercise 5 (*continued*)

THE FIRST BUG

A bug is a mistake in a computer program; hence debugging refers to the process of correcting program errors. According to legend, the first bug was an unlucky moth crushed to death on one of the relays of the electromechanical Mark II computer, bringing the machine's operation to a halt. The cause of the failure was discovered by Grace Hopper, who promptly taped the moth to her logbook, noting, *"First actual case of bug being found."*

Step 5: Add the If Statement

- Press **Ctrl+c** to execute the ClearColor macro. The data for all employees is again displayed in black.
- Click in the window containing the **HighlightManager macro**. Add the **If** and **End If** statements exactly as they are shown in Figure 8.10e. Use the **Tab key** (or press the **space bar**) to indent the Selection statement within the If and End If statements.
- Click in the window containing the worksheet, then click **cell A3**. Press **Ctrl+h** to execute the modified HighlightManager macro. The text in cells A3 through F3 is red since this employee is a manager.
- Click **cell A4**. Press **Ctrl+h.** The row is selected, but the color of the font remains unchanged. The If statement prevents these cells from being highlighted because the employee is not a manager. Press **Ctrl+c** to remove all highlighting.
- Save the workbook.

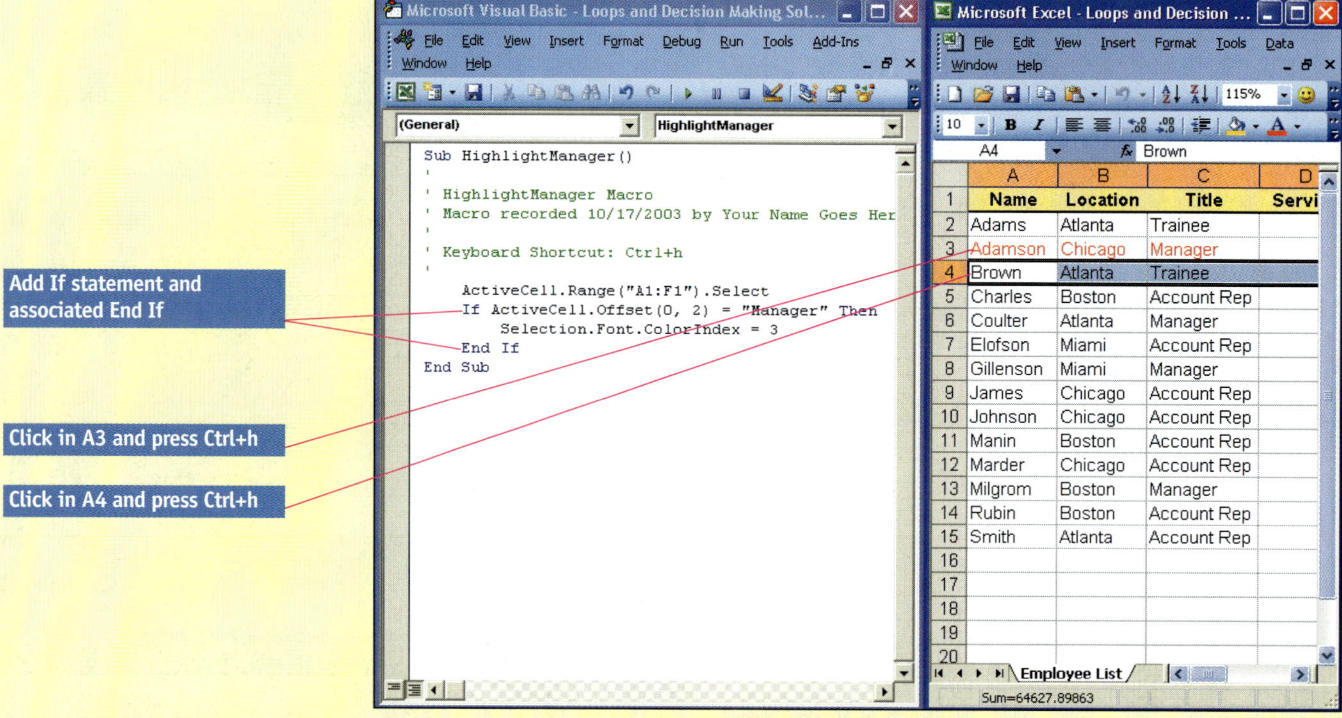

(e) Add the If Statement (step 5)

FIGURE 8.10 Hands-on Exercise 5 (*continued*)

INDENT

Indentation does not affect the execution of a macro. It, does, however, make the macro easier to read, and we suggest you follow common conventions in developing your macros. Indent the conditional statements associated with an If statement by a consistent amount. Place the End If statement on a line by itself, directly under the associated If.

Step 6: An Endless Loop

- Click in the window containing the **HighlightManager macro**. Add the **Do Until** and **Loop** statements exactly as they appear in Figure 8.10f. Indent the other statements as shown in the figure.
- Click **cell A3** of the worksheet. Press **Ctrl+h** to execute the macro. Cells A3 through F3 will be displayed in red, but the macro continues to execute indefinitely as it applies color to the same record over and over.
- Press **Ctrl+Break** to cease execution of the macro. You will see the dialog box in Figure 8.10f, indicating that code execution has been interrupted. Click the **End button**.
- Click within the macro code, pull down the **Debug menu**, and click the **Step Into command** (or press the **F8 key**) to enter the macro. The first statement is highlighted in yellow.
- Press the **F8 key** repeatedly to execute the next several steps over and over again. You will see that the macro is stuck in a loop as the If statement is executed indefinitely.
- Click the **Reset button** in the Visual Basic window to end the debugging.

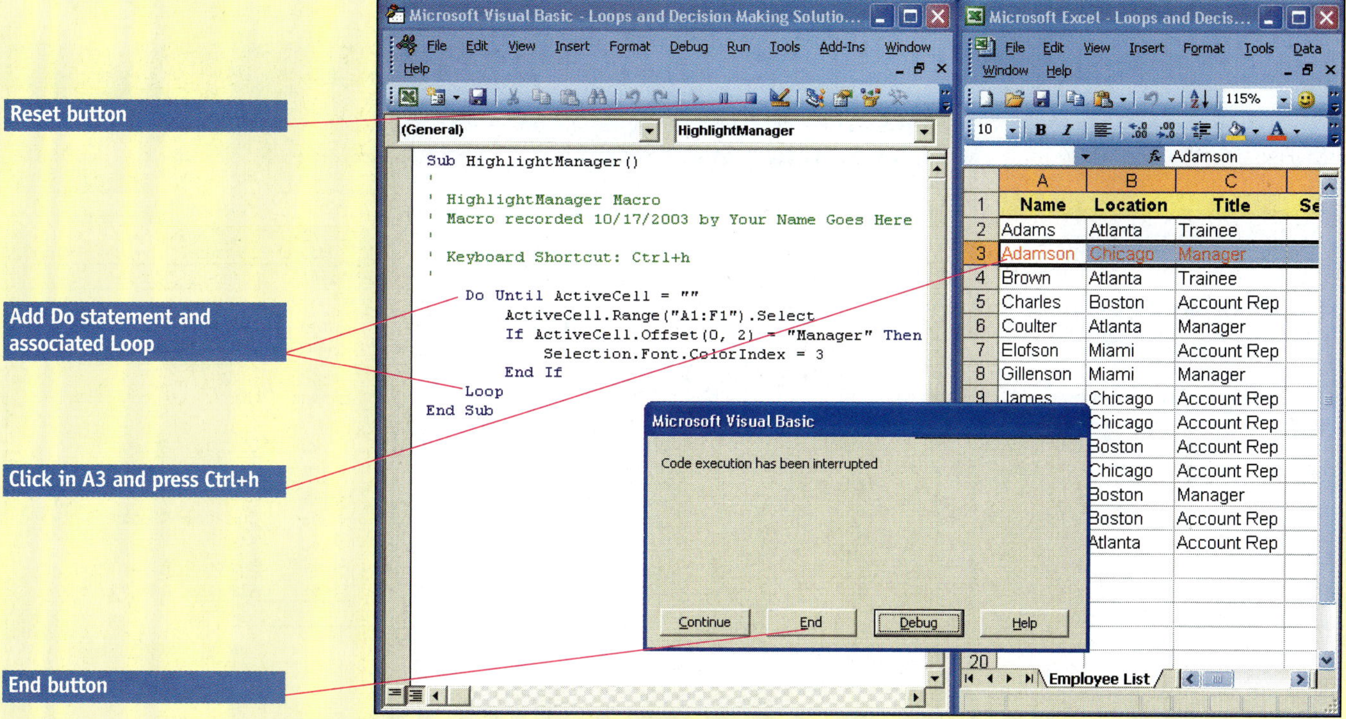

(f) An Endless Loop (step 6)

FIGURE 8.10 Hands-on Exercise 5 (*continued*)

AN ENDLESS LOOP

The glossary in the Programmer's Guide for a popular database contains the following definitions "Endless loop"—See loop, endless and "Loop, endless"—See endless loop.

We don't know whether these entries were deliberate or not, but the point is made either way. Endless loops are a common and frustrating bug. Press Ctrl+Break to halt execution, then click the Debug command button to step through the macro and locate the source of the error.

Step 7: The Completed Macro

- Click in **cell A2** of the worksheet. Click in the **Name Box**. Enter **FirstEmployee** to name this cell. Press **Enter**.
- Click in the window containing the macro. Click after the last comment line and press **Enter** to insert a blank line.
- Add the statement to select the cell named FirstEmployee as shown in Figure 8.10g. This ensures that the macro always begins in row two by selecting the cell named FirstEmployee.
- Click immediately after the End If statement. Press **Enter**. Add the statement containing the offset (1,0) as shown in Figure 8.10g, which selects the cell one row below the current row.
- Click anywhere in the worksheet. Press **Ctrl+c** to clear the color. Press **Ctrl+h** to execute the HighlightManager macro.
- The macro begins by selecting cell A2, then proceeds to highlight all managers in red. Save the workbook a final time.
- Print the workbook and its macro for your instructor. Exit Excel. Congratulations on a job well done.

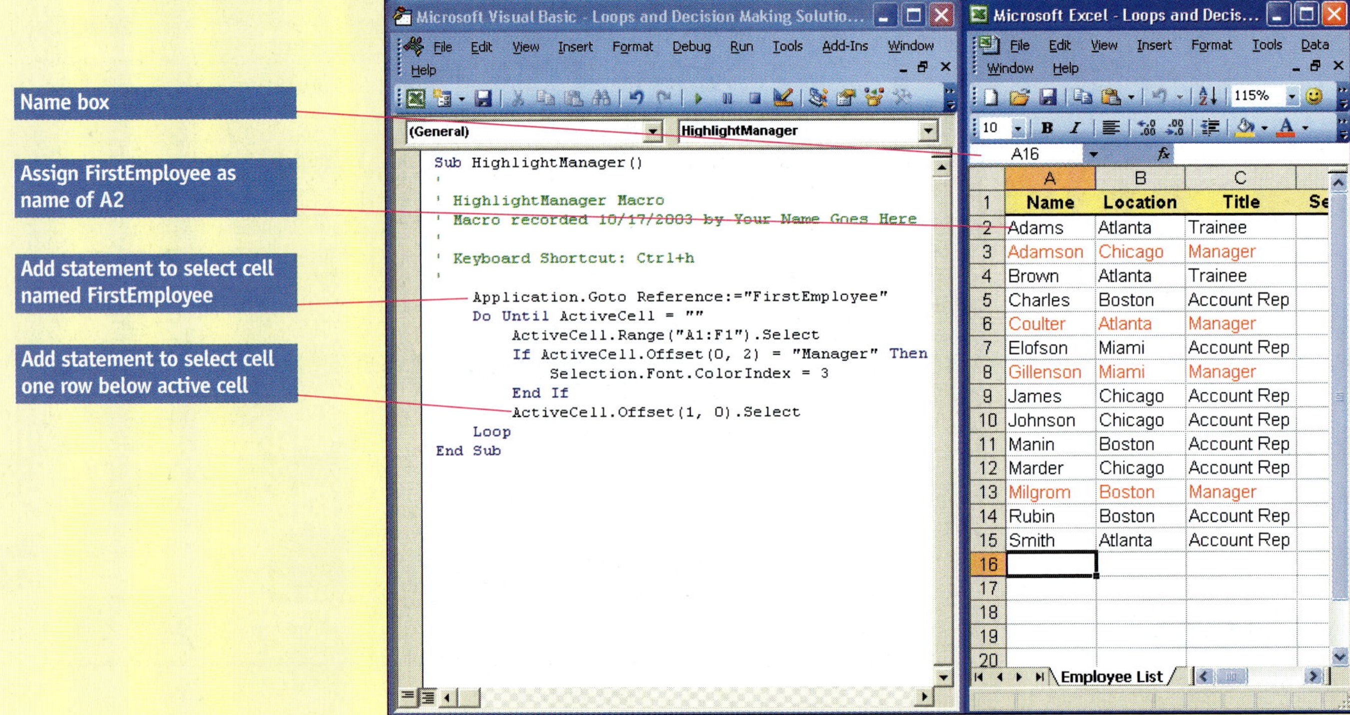

(g) The Completed Macro (step 7)

FIGURE 8.10 Hands-on Exercise 5 (*continued*)

HELP FOR VISUAL BASIC

Click within any Visual Basic keyword, then press the F1 key for context-sensitive help. You will see a help screen containing a description of the statement, its syntax, key elements, and several examples. You can print the help screen by clicking the Printer icon. (If you do not see the help screens, ask your instructor to install Visual Basic Help.)

SUMMARY

A macro is a set of instructions that automates a repetitive task. It is, in essence, a program, and its instructions are written in Visual Basic, a programming language. The macro recorder in Excel records your commands and writes the macro for you. Once a macro has been created, it can be modified in the Visual Basic Editor by manually inserting, deleting, or changing its statements.

Macros are stored in one of two places, either in the current workbook or in a Personal Macro workbook. Macros that are specific to a particular workbook should be stored in that workbook. Generic macros that can be used with any workbook should be stored in the Personal Macro workbook.

A computer virus may be contained in an Excel macro. Thus, Excel will warn you if a workbook you are about to open contains a macro, provided the security option is set appropriately. High security disables all macros except from a previously designated trusted source. Medium security gives you the option to enable macros.

A macro is run (executed) by pulling down the Tools menu and selecting the Run Macro command. A macro can also be executed through a keyboard shortcut, by placing a command button on the worksheet, or by customizing a toolbar to include an additional button to run the macro.

A comment is a nonexecutable statement that begins with an apostrophe. Comments are inserted automatically at the beginning of a macro by the macro recorder to remind you of what the macro does. Comments may be added, deleted, or modified, just as any other statement. A VBA statement is continued from one line to the next by typing a blank space followed by an underscore at the end of the line to be continued. An ampersand concatenates (joins together) two adjacent text strings if a literal has to be continued to a second line.

A macro begins and ends with the Sub and End Sub statements, respectively. The Sub statement contains the name of the macro or VBA procedure. The With statement enables you to perform multiple actions on the same object. All commands between the With and corresponding End With statements are executed collectively.

A macro contains either absolute or relative references. An absolute reference is constant; that is, Excel keeps track of the exact cell address and selects that specific cell. A relative reference depends on the previously selected cell, and is entered as an offset, or number of rows and columns from the current cell. The Relative Reference button on the Stop Recording toolbar toggles between the two.

A good macro is completely general and immune to changes in the underlying workbook. VBA does not, however, update cell references to accommodate insertions or deletions of rows and columns in the associated worksheet. It is good practice, therefore, to always use range names, as opposed to absolute cell references, within a macro.

An Excel macro can be made more powerful through inclusion of Visual Basic statements that enable true programming. These include the MsgBox statement to display information, the InputBox function to obtain user input, the If statement to implement decision making, and the Do statement to implement a loop. The macro recorder creates the initial macro by translating Excel commands to Visual Basic statements. The additional VBA statements are added to the resulting code using the Visual Basic Editor.

A bug is a mistake in a computer program and debugging is the process of finding and correcting program errors. The Step Into command is useful in debugging as it executes a macro (VBA procedure) one statement at a time to see the effects of each statement.

KEY TERMS

MULTIPLE CHOICE

1. Which of the following best describes recording and executing a macro?
   (a) A macro is recorded once and executed once
   (b) A macro is recorded once and executed many times
   (c) A macro is recorded many times and executed once
   (d) A macro is recorded many times and executed many times

2. Which of the following can be used to execute a macro?
   (a) A keyboard shortcut
   (b) A customized toolbar button
   (c) A button on the worksheet
   (d) All of the above

3. A macro can be stored:
   (a) In any Excel workbook
   (b) In the Personal Macro workbook
   (c) Both (a) and (b)
   (d) Neither (a) nor (b)

4. Which of the following is true regarding comments in Visual Basic?
   (a) A comment is executable; that is, its inclusion or omission affects the outcome of a macro
   (b) A comment begins with an apostrophe
   (c) Both (a) and (b)
   (d) Neither (a) nor (b)

5. Which statement must contain the name of the macro?
   (a) The Sub statement at the beginning of the macro
   (b) The first comment statement
   (c) Both (a) and (b)
   (d) Neither (a) nor (b)

6. Which of the following indicates an absolute reference within a macro?
   (a) ActiveCell.Offset(1,1).Range("A1")
   (b) $A$1
   (c) Range("A1")
   (d) All of the above

7. Selection.Offset (1,0).Range ("A1").Select will select the cell that is:
   (a) In the same column as the active cell but one row below
   (b) In the same row as the active cell but one column to the right
   (c) In the same column as the active cell but one row above
   (d) In the same row as the active cell but one column to the left

8. Selection.Offset (1,1).Range ("A1").Select will select the cell that is:
   (a) One cell below and one cell to the left of the active cell
   (b) One cell below and one cell to the right of the active cell
   (c) One cell above and one cell to the right of the active cell
   (d) One cell above and one cell to the left of the active cell

9. Selection.Offset (1,1).Range ("A1:A2").Select will select:
   (a) Cell A1
   (b) Cell A2
   (c) Both (a) and (b)
   (d) Neither (a) nor (b)

10. Which commands are used to duplicate an existing macro so that it can become the basis of a new macro?
    (a) Copy command
    (b) Paste command
    (c) Both (a) and (b)
    (d) Neither (a) nor (b)

11. Which of the following is used to protect a macro from the subsequent insertion or deletion of rows or columns in the associated worksheet?
    (a) Range names
    (b) Absolute references
    (c) Both (a) and (b)
    (d) Neither (a) nor (b)

... continued

multiple choice

12. Which of the following is true regarding a customized button that has been inserted as an object onto a worksheet and assigned to an Excel macro?

(a) Point to the customized button, then click the left mouse button to execute the associated macro
(b) Point to the customized button, then click the right mouse button to select the macro button and simultaneously display a shortcut menu
(c) Point to the customized button, then press and hold the Ctrl key as you click the left mouse to select the button
(d) All of the above

13. The InputBox function:

(a) Displays a message (prompt) requesting input from the user
(b) Stores the user's response in a designated cell
(c) Both (a) and (b)
(d) Neither (a) nor (b)

14. You want to create a macro to enter your name into a specific cell. The best way to do this is to:

(a) Select the cell for your name, turn on the macro recorder with absolute references, then type your name
(b) Turn on the macro recorder with absolute references, select the cell for your name, then type your name
(c) Either (a) or (b)
(d) Neither (a) nor (b)

15. Which of the following is true about indented text in a VBA procedure?

(a) The indented text is always executed first
(b) The indented text is always executed last
(c) The indented text is rendered a comment and is never executed
(d) None of the above

16. You want to create a macro to enter your name in the active cell (which will vary whenever the macro is used) and the course you are taking in the cell immediately below. The best way to do this is to:

(a) Select the cell for your name, turn on the macro recorder with absolute references, type your name, press the down arrow, and type the course
(b) Turn on the macro recorder with absolute references, select the cell for your name, type your name, press the down arrow, and type the course
(c) Select the cell for your name, turn on the macro recorder with relative references, type your name, press the down arrow, and type the course
(d) Turn on the macro recorder with relative references, select the cell for your name, type your name, press the down arrow, and type the course

17. A VBA statement contains the reference, ActiveCell.Offset(1,0).Range("A1:A3"). Which cells are selected if cell B3 is the active cell when the command is executed?

(a) The range B1:B3
(b) The range B4:B6
(c) The range A1:A3
(d) The range A2:A4

18. You have created a named range called AllEmployees which is assigned to cells A2:H100 in the worksheet. Which of the following actions will change the cells that are included in the named range?

(a) Inserting or deleting an employee in the middle of the list
(b) Inserting or deleting a field in the middle of the list
(c) Both (a) and (b)
(d) Neither (a) nor (b)

ANSWERS

1. b	**7.** a	**13.** c
2. d	**8.** b	**14.** b
3. c	**9.** d	**15.** d
4. b	**10.** c	**16.** c
5. a	**11.** a	**17.** b
6. c	**12.** d	**18.** c

PRACTICE WITH EXCEL

1. **Data Management Macros:** Figure 8.11 displays an alternate version of the Employee List Solution workbook that was used in the third and fourth hands-on exercises. The existing macros have been deleted and replaced by the five macros represented by the command buttons in the figure. Your assignment is to create the indicated macros and assign the macros to the command buttons. The purpose of each macro should be apparent from the name of the command button.
   a. You can "cut and paste" macros from the Employee List Solution workbook as it existed at the end of the fourth hands-on exercise, or you can create the macros from scratch using the *Chapter 8 Practice 1* workbook (which contains the equivalent workbook used in Hands-on Exercise 3). Choose whichever technique you think is easier. You will need to use the Insert Name Create command to assign names to various cells in the worksheet for use in your macros.
   b. The AllEmployees macro should clear the criteria row, then display all employees within the list (the summary statistics will reflect all employees as well). The other four macros prompt the user for the specific criteria. Note that the user can include relational operators for service or salary, such as >60000 to display employees with salaries greater than $60,000. All of the macros should include a MsgBox statement that displays the indicated message in Figure 8.11.
   c. Run the AnySalary macro, then print the workbook as it appears in Figure 8.11. Print the worksheet with row and column headings and be sure that it fits on a single sheet of paper. Be sure to change the properties of the command buttons so that the buttons appear on the printed worksheet.
   d. Run the All Employees macro and then print the worksheet after the macro is complete. Print the worksheet a second time to show the cell formulas.
   e. Change to the Visual Basic Editor, pull down the File menu, click the Print command, then print the current project to print all of the modules (macros) within your workbook.
   f. Add a cover sheet and submit the entire assignment to your instructor.

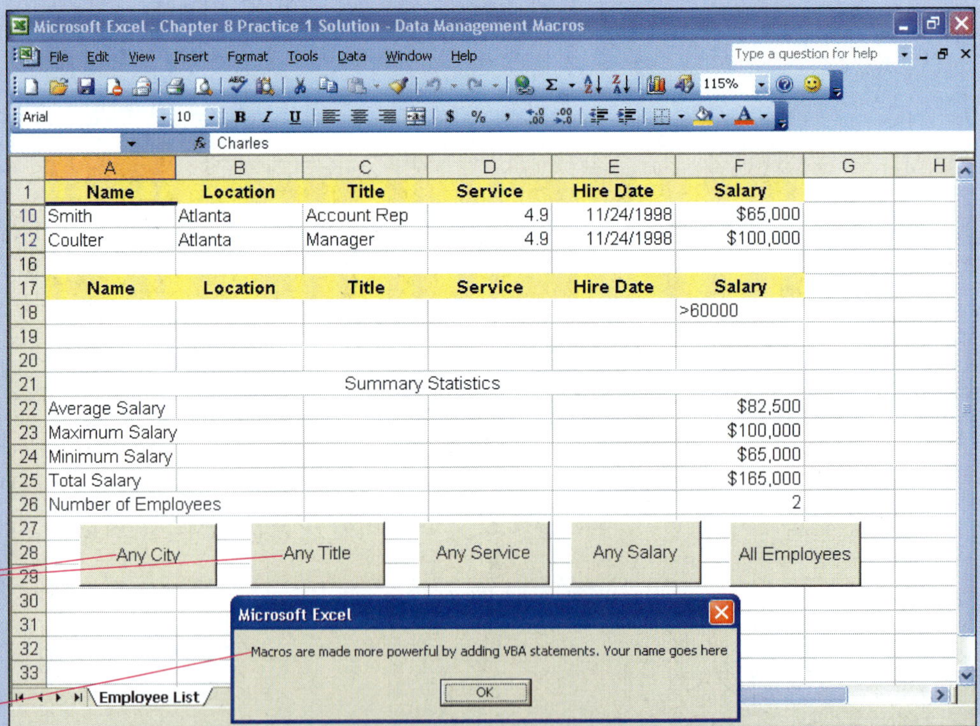

FIGURE 8.11 Data Management Macros (exercise 1)

2. **Employee Selection:** Figure 8.12 extends the previous problem to include one additional macro that prompts the user for city, title, service, and salary. The user enters all four parameters, then the macro displays the selected records within the list together with the summary statistics. It is quite possible, however, that no employee will meet all the criteria, in which case the macro should display a message to that effect as shown.
   a. Your assignment is to complete the previous problem, then add the additional macro to prompt for the multiple criteria. The macro will always ask the user for all four parameters, but you need not enter every parameter. If, for example, you do not specify a city, the macro will return matching employees regardless of the city.
   b. You can include relational operators in the service and/or salary fields as shown in Figure 8.12. The figure is searching for Chicago Account reps with less than eight years of service, earning more than $60,000.
   c. The DAVERAGE function displays a division by zero error message if there is no record that meets the specified criteria. You can hide the error message, however, by using conditional formatting to display the message in white, which renders it invisible. Click in the cell containing the DAVERAGE function. Pull down the Format menu, click Conditional formatting, and then click the drop-down arrow in the left list box to select Formula Is. Click in the box to the right and type =ISERROR(F22) where F22 is the cell containing the function that caused the error. Now click the Format button, click Font, and change the color to white. The message is in the cell, but you cannot see it.
   d. You need to include an If statement in your macro that tests whether the number of qualified employees is equal to zero, and if so, it should display the associated message box. It's easy to do. Use the Insert Name command within the Excel workbook to assign the name "QualifiedEmployees" to cell F26. Then insert a statement in the macro to go to this cell, which makes it the active cell. The If statement can then compare the value of the active cell to zero, and if it is zero, use the MsgBox statement to display the indicated message.
   e. Print the worksheet in Figure 8.12 for your instructor. (The dialog box will not appear on your printout.) Print the module containing the macro.

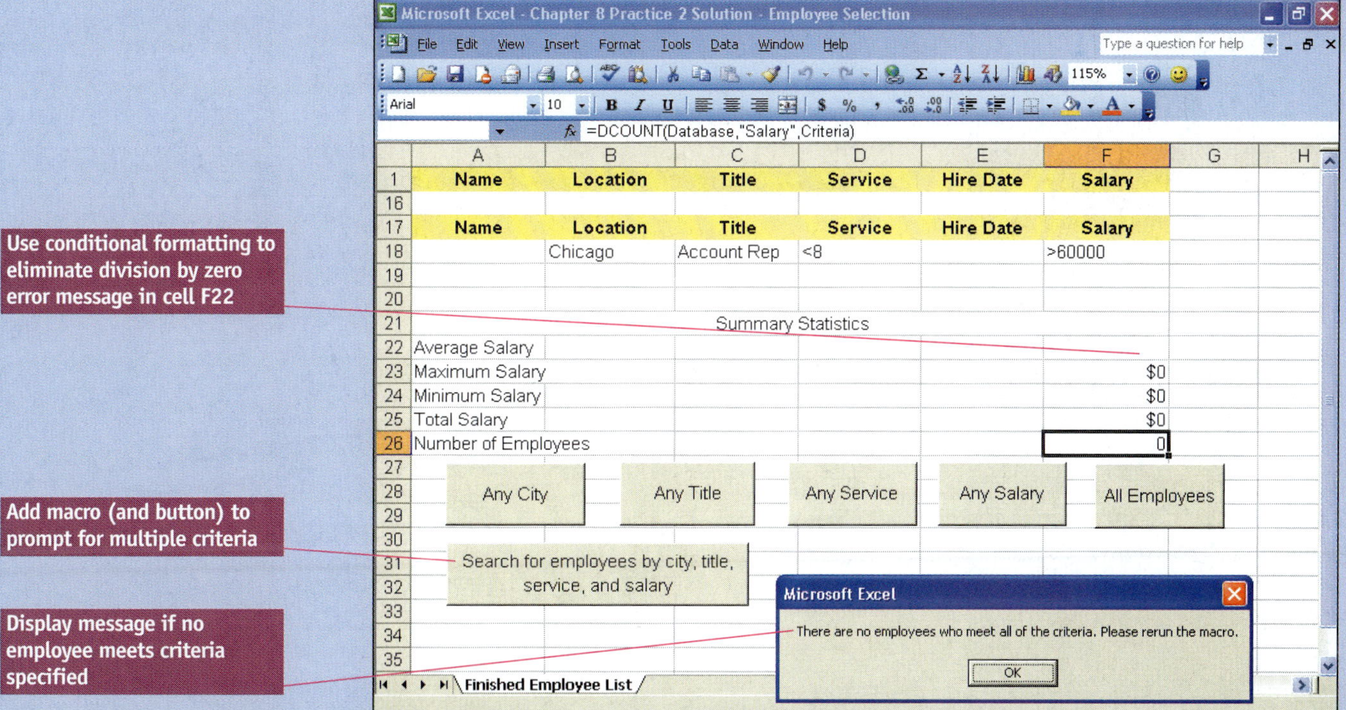

FIGURE 8.12 Employee Selection (exercise 2)

3. **Highlighting Employees:** Figure 8.13 extends the Loops and Decision Making workbook from the fifth hands-on exercise to include command buttons and an additional macro. The new macro highlights the Atlanta and Chicago employees in red and blue, respectively.
   a. Open the Loops and Decision Making Solution workbook from the fifth hands-on exercise. Start the Visual Basic Editor, then copy the existing HighlightManager macro so that you can use it as the basis of the new macro, which will highlight the employees in two locations. Change the name of the copied macro. Then change the offset in the If statement to (0, 1) to reference the location column within the list, and further to compare that value to "Atlanta," as opposed to "Manager."
   b. Switch to the Excel workbook, pull down the Tools menu, select the Macro command, click Macros, select the new macro, click Options, then assign a keyboard shortcut. (We used Ctrl+a). Press Ctrl+c to execute the ClearColor macro, then press Ctrl+a to test the newly created macro. The Atlanta employees should be highlighted in red.
   c. Return to the VBA editor and insert the ElseIf clause immediately above the existing End If clause. The ElseIf should compare the value of the cell with the appropriate offset to "Chicago," and if that condition is true, highlight the selection in blue (color 5). Test the modified macro.
   d. Add command buttons to the worksheet as shown in Figure 8.13, then test the buttons to be sure that they work properly. You will discover that the macros require one subtle adjustment; that is, if you run the Chicago and Atlanta macro, followed immediately by the Manager macro (or vice versa), employees from both macros will be highlighted. In other words, you need to clear any existing highlighting prior to running either of the other two. *You can make this happen automatically by including ClearColor (the name of the macro you want to run) as the first statement in the other two macros.*
   e. Print the completed worksheet for your instructor. Be sure to change the properties of the command buttons so that they print with the worksheet.
   f. Print the module containing the code for all three macros. Add a cover sheet to complete the assignment.

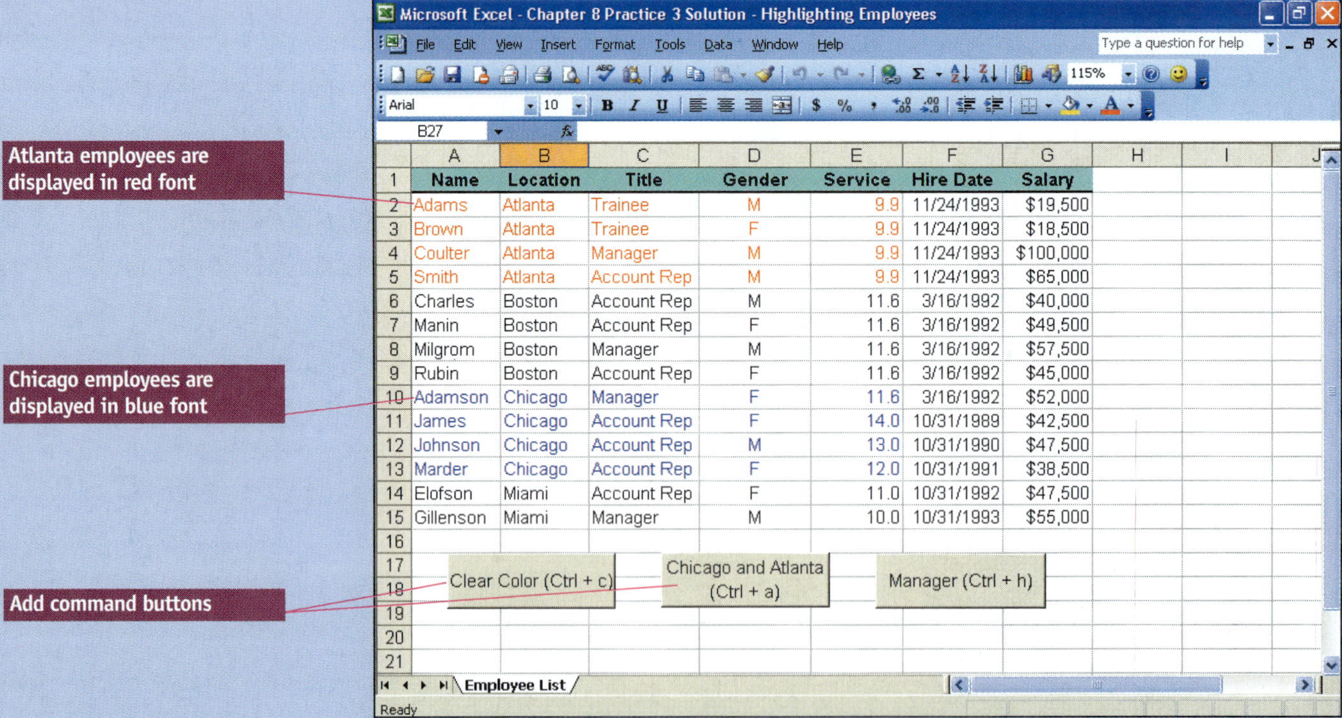

Name	Location	Title	Gender	Service	Hire Date	Salary
Adams	Atlanta	Trainee	M	9.9	11/24/1993	$19,500
Brown	Atlanta	Trainee	F	9.9	11/24/1993	$18,500
Coulter	Atlanta	Manager	M	9.9	11/24/1993	$100,000
Smith	Atlanta	Account Rep	M	9.9	11/24/1993	$65,000
Charles	Boston	Account Rep	M	11.6	3/16/1992	$40,000
Manin	Boston	Account Rep	F	11.6	3/16/1992	$49,500
Milgrom	Boston	Manager	M	11.6	3/16/1992	$57,500
Rubin	Boston	Account Rep	F	11.6	3/16/1992	$45,000
Adamson	Chicago	Manager	F	11.6	3/16/1992	$52,000
James	Chicago	Account Rep	F	14.0	10/31/1989	$42,500
Johnson	Chicago	Account Rep	M	13.0	10/31/1990	$47,500
Marder	Chicago	Account Rep	F	12.0	10/31/1991	$38,500
Elofson	Miami	Account Rep	F	11.0	10/31/1992	$47,500
Gillenson	Miami	Manager	M	10.0	10/31/1993	$55,000

FIGURE 8.13 Highlighting Employees (exercise 3)

4. **Student List:** The worksheet in Figure 8.14 is shown after execution of the macro, Any Year Any Major, which prompts the user for these values, then displays the selected students and summary statistics. All of the macros in the worksheet are flexible and use range names, as opposed to specific cell references. We have created three range names for you: Criteria (A19:G20), CriteriaValues (A20:G20), and StudentList (A1:G17), but you will have to create the remaining names as necessary. Proceed as follows:
   a. Open the *Chapter 8 Practice 4* workbook. Click and drag to select cells A19 through G20, then use the Insert Name Create command (using the entries in the top row) to create the additional range names.
   b. Create the macro to show all students. This requires you to clear the range name CriteriaValues, then use the Advanced Filter command (with the range names StudentList and Criteria) to display all of the students.
   c. Display the Forms toolbar. Click the Button tool, draw a button on the worksheet, and assign the AllStudents macro that you just created to the button. Right click the button, click Format Control, click the Properties tab, then check the box to print the object.
   d. Use the macro recorder to create a macro for a specific major, and then edit the macro to substitute the InputBox function for the name of the major. The macro should begin by clearing the criteria area and end by displaying the message box in Figure 8.14.
   e. Return to the Excel workbook. Right click the All Students command button, click the Copy button, click the Paste button, and drag the duplicate button to the right. Right click the new button and assign the AnyMajor macro to the new button. Change the text of the button as well. Test both buttons to be sure that the associated macros work correctly.
   f. The easiest way to create the remaining macros is to duplicate the AnyMajor macro and then make changes in the VBA editor. Copy an existing macro button, and then assign each new macro to a new button.
   g. Execute the macro to display students in any year and any major (use any values you like). Print the completed worksheet and the module(s) containing the macros for your instructor.

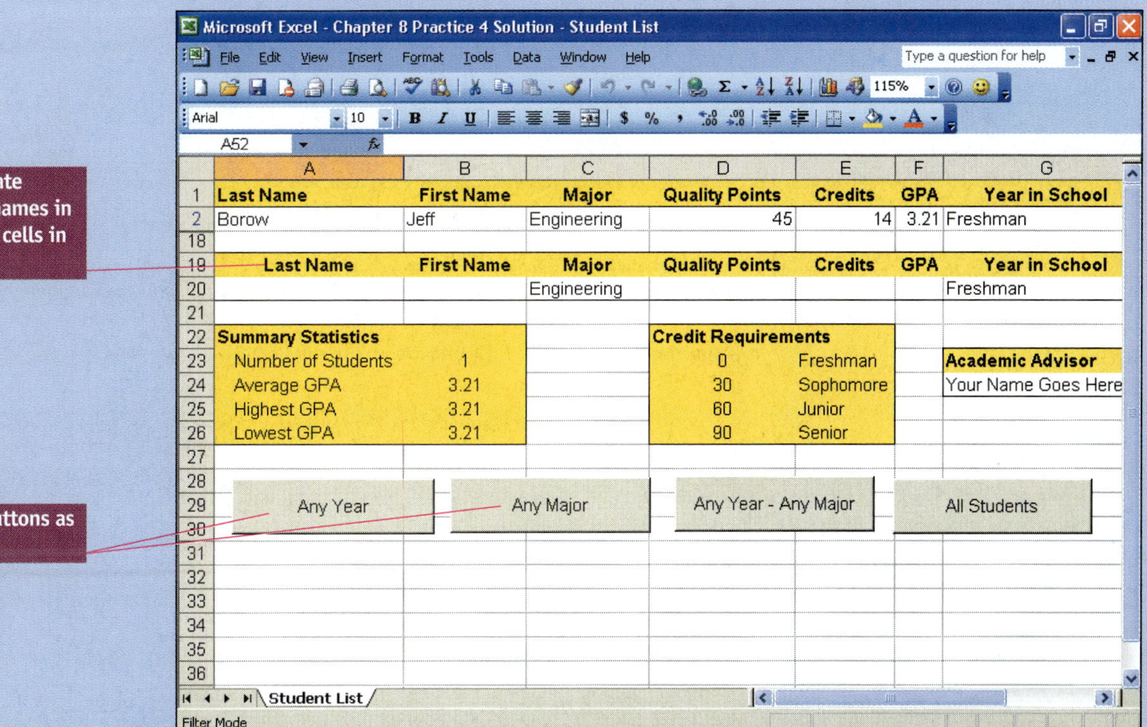

FIGURE 8.14 Student List (exercise 4)

5. **Election Macros:** Open the completed *Chapter 7 Practice 1* workbook from the previous chapter and then add the macros shown in Figure 8.15. The easiest way to complete this exercise is to create the first macro, copy it, make the necessary changes within the VBA editor to create the next macro, and so on. Proceed as follows:
   a. All macros should use range names, as opposed to specific cell references so that they are immune to subsequent insertions or deletions of rows or columns in a worksheet. Assign the range names "State", "Difference", and "Percentage", to cells A7, F7, and G7, respectively.
   b. Start the macro recorder. Specify Alphabetical as the macro name. Click the down arrow in the Name box and select "State" (to go to cell A7), then click the Ascending Sort button. Click the Stop Recording button.
   c. Display the Forms toolbar. Click the Button tool, draw a button on the worksheet, and assign the Alphabetical macro that you just created to the button. Right click the button, click Format Control, click the Properties tab, then check the box to print the object.
   d. Press Alt+F11 to display the Visual Basic editor. Click and drag to select the complete Alphabetical macro (including the Sub and End Sub statements). Press Ctrl+C then Ctrl+V to duplicate the macro. Change the name of the duplicate macro to SmallestPercentage (spaces are not allowed in the name). Change *all* occurrences of the reference to "State" to "Percentage", effectively changing the sort from column A to column F.
   e. Return to Excel. Right click the Alphabetical command button, click the Copy command, click the Paste button, and drag the duplicate button to the right. Right click the new button and assign the SmallestPercentage macro to the new button. Change the text of the button as well.
   f. Create the remaining macros and associated command buttons in similar fashion. Note, however, that you will also have to change the sort order in the macros that specify a descending sequence.
   g. Print the completed worksheet in at least two different sequences. Use the Page Setup command to be sure the entire worksheet fits on one page.
   h. Print the VBA module that contains all five procedures.

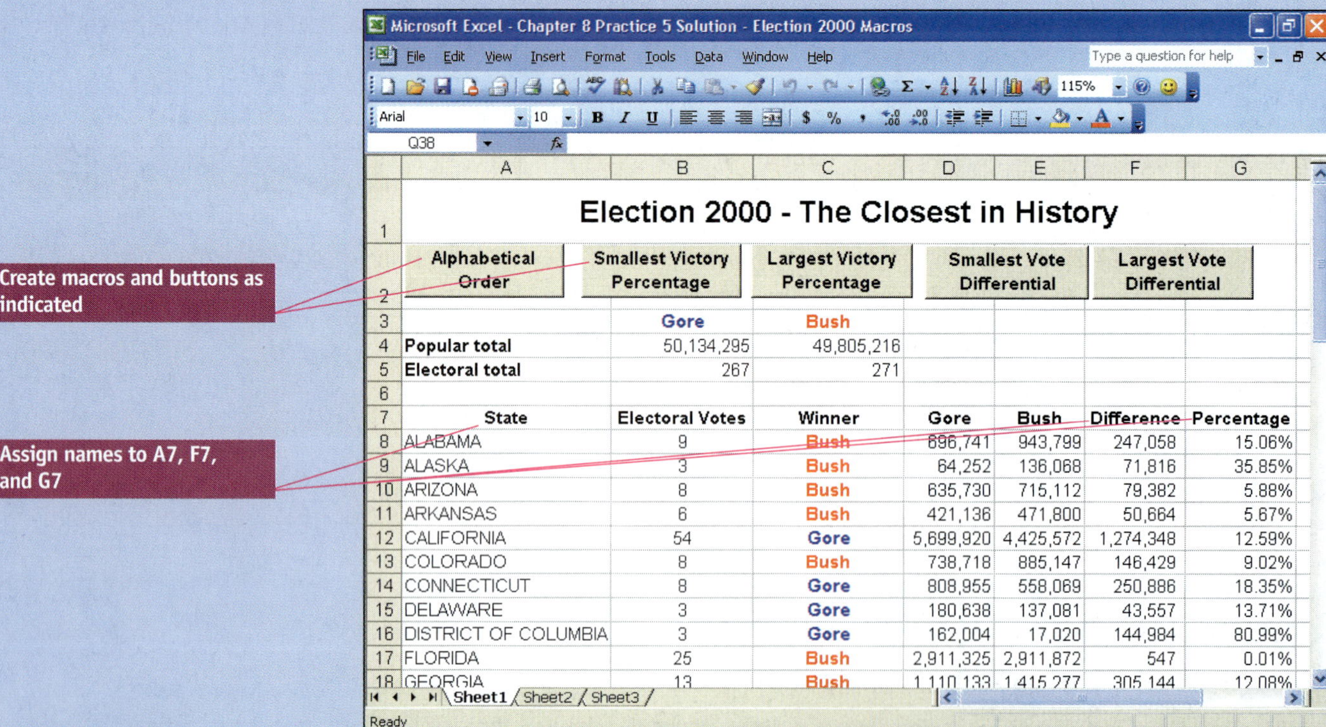

FIGURE 8.15 Election Macros (exercise 5)

6. **Stock Portfolio:** Figure 8.16 displays a worksheet that uses macros in conjunction with Web queries to update a stock portfolio. You have seen this worksheet before, most recently in Chapter 5 when we studied worksheet references within a workbook. Now we complete the example through the introduction of macros.

   a. Open the partially completed *Chapter 8 Practice 6* workbook and click the worksheet tab that contains your portfolio. The macros are already in the worksheet, and all you have to do is click the appropriate command buttons. The macro to enter your investments will prompt you for three investments for which you need to enter the company symbol, number of shares, and purchase price. This macro will also copy the stock symbols you have entered to the end of the stock symbol table in the Stock Prices worksheet.

   b. Click the command button to Update Your Portfolio, which in turn will execute the Web query to retrieve the current price of your investments and automatically calculate the value of your portfolio. The worksheet is password protected to prevent you from accidentally changing any of the formulas that have been entered. (The password is "password", in lowercase letters so you can remove the protection if you like using the Tools menu.)

   c. After you have updated your portfolio, click the button to View Summary to take you to the summary worksheet. The macros for that worksheet have not been created, however, so it is up to you to create the macros and assign them to the indicated command buttons as shown in Figure 8.16. The UpdatePrices macro refreshes the Web query in the Stock Prices worksheet. (It is the same as the UpdateYourPortfolio macro except that it returns to the Summary worksheet.) The Best Investors and Worst Investors list the portfolios in descending and ascending order according to the percentage gain or loss.

   d. Print the Summary worksheet for your instructor as well as the worksheet that contains your portfolio. Print the module(s) containing all of the macros within the worksheet. Add a short note explaining the purpose of the various modules that were originally in the workbook.

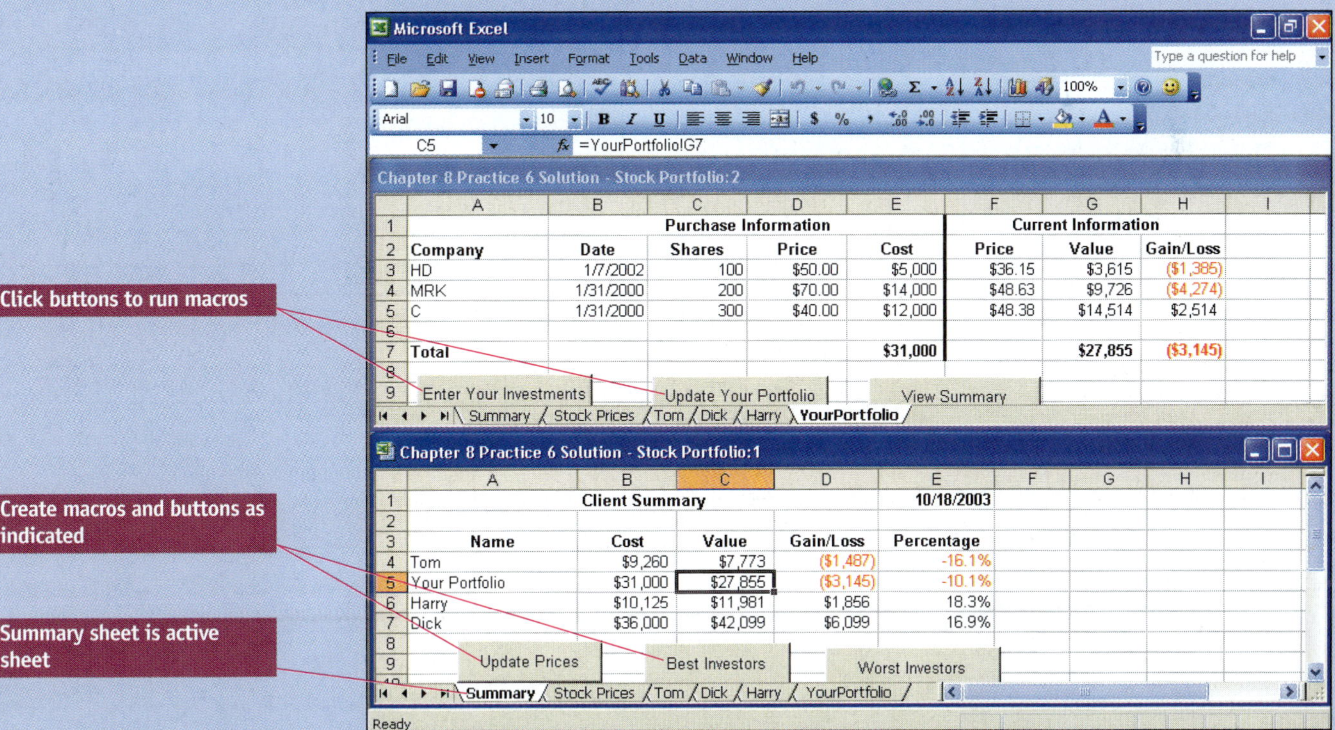

FIGURE 8.16 Stock Portfolio (exercise 6)

7. **Consumer Loans:** Figure 8.17 displays a worksheet containing hypothetical data for a series of consumer loans. The associated workbook also contains four macros: to select loans by type, date, and amount; to clear the associated criteria range and display all loans; to highlight the mortgages in red within the complete list of loans and show the summary statistics for mortgages only; and finally to remove the highlighting and reset the summary statistics to include all records. We have already created the ShowAllLoans and ClearColor macros for you. Your assignment is to create the remaining two macros. Proceed as follows:

   a. Open the *Chapter 8 Practice 7* workbook in the Exploring Excel folder. Use the concepts from the third and fourth hands-on exercises to create the macro to display loans by type, date, and amount. The user is to be prompted for each parameter. The macro should be written to use the range names that have been defined within the workbook rather than specific cell references. End the macro by selecting cell A1 and displaying the message in Figure 8.17. Assign the macro to a command button.

   b. Use the concepts from the fifth hands-on exercise to create the macro to highlight the mortgages within the complete list of loans, and further to set the criteria range so that the summary statistics for only the mortgages are displayed. (*Hint:* The first statement of this macro should be ShowAllLoans, which will execute the existing macro of that name.) Assign the macro to a command button.

   c. Click the button to run the HighlightMortgages macro. You should see all of the mortgage loans in red. Now click the button to run the LoansByTypeDateandAmount macro. Do not enter a loan type in response to the first prompt (to display loans of all types). Specify a start date after 9/20/2002 and a loan amount less than $100,000. You should see the loans in Figure 8.17.

   d. Print the completed worksheet for your instructor. Use the Page Setup command to be sure the entire worksheet fits on one page. Print the worksheet a second time to show the cell formulas.

   e. Print the VBA module that contains all four procedures. Add a cover sheet to complete the assignment.

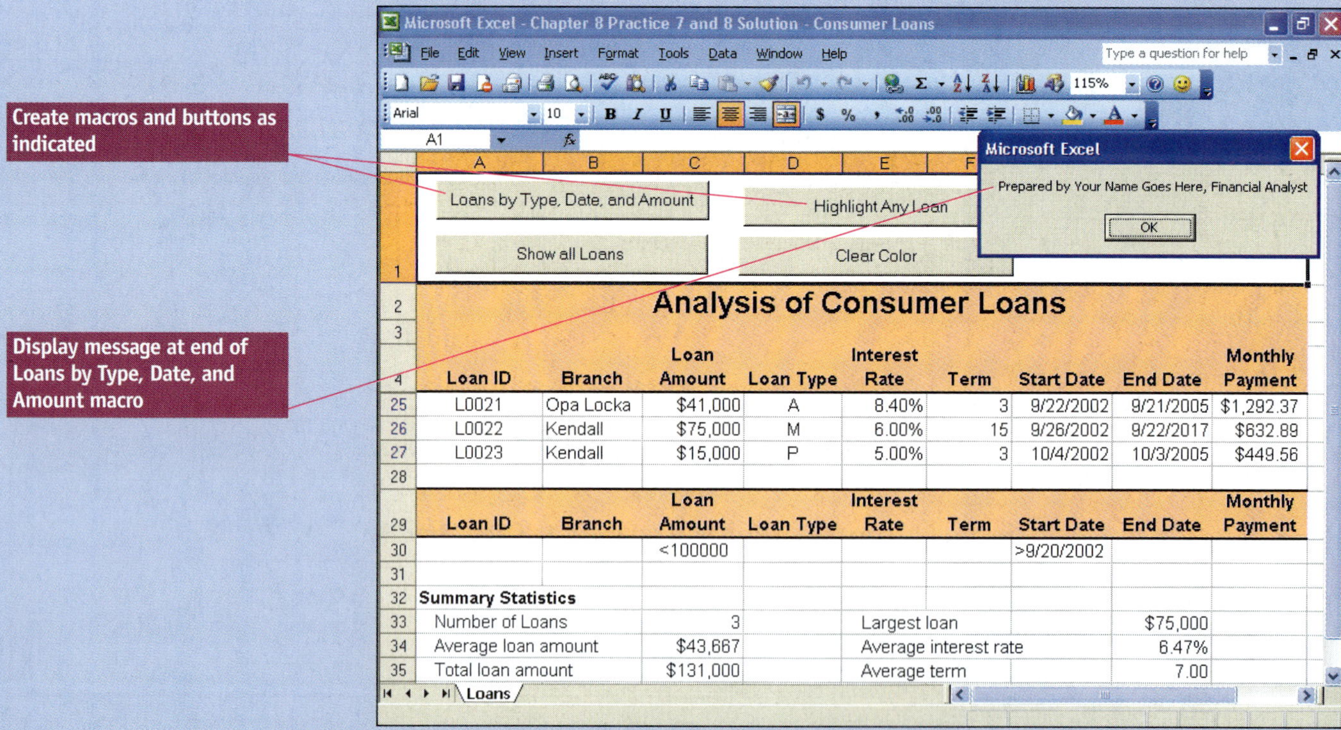

FIGURE 8.17 Consumer Loans (exercise 7)

8. **A Look Ahead:** Figure 8.18 extends the previous exercise to include a procedure to highlight any loan, as opposed to highlighting only mortgages. The VBA code for that procedure is shown in the figure. Your job is to complete the previous hands-on exercise, delete the macro (and associated command button) for the HighlightMortgages macro, then substitute the new macro in its place. The VBA statements within the new procedure parallel those of its predecessor, but introduce some new material in Visual Basic. There are several comments within the macro to explain these statements, with additional explanation added below. Use the VBA primer that appears at the end of the Excel chapters in this text as a reference.

   a. The most important concept is that of a variable to store information received from the user. The Dim statement near the beginning of the procedure assigns a name to the variable (strLoanType) and indicates that it will hold text (i.e., the variable is declared to be a character string). The subsequent Input Box statement prompts the user for the loan type, then stores that value in the strLoanType variable. The procedure will highlight all loans of that type.

   b. The If statement within the loop to highlight the selected records compares the loan type to the uppercase value of the strLoanType variable. This is important because if the user inadvertently enters a lowercase letter, the comparison would fail.

   c. The MsgBox statement at the end of the procedure includes two additional parameters. The vbInformation variable indicates the type of icon that is supposed to appear within the message box. The underscore is there to show that the statement is continued to the next line, which in turn contains the text that will appear in the title bar of the message box.

   d. Enter the procedure as it appears in Figure 8.18. Assign a command button to the macro within the worksheet, then test the macro. Run the procedure two times to show two different loan types. Print each worksheet for your instructor.

   e. Print the VBA module containing all of the procedures. Add a cover sheet to complete the assignment.

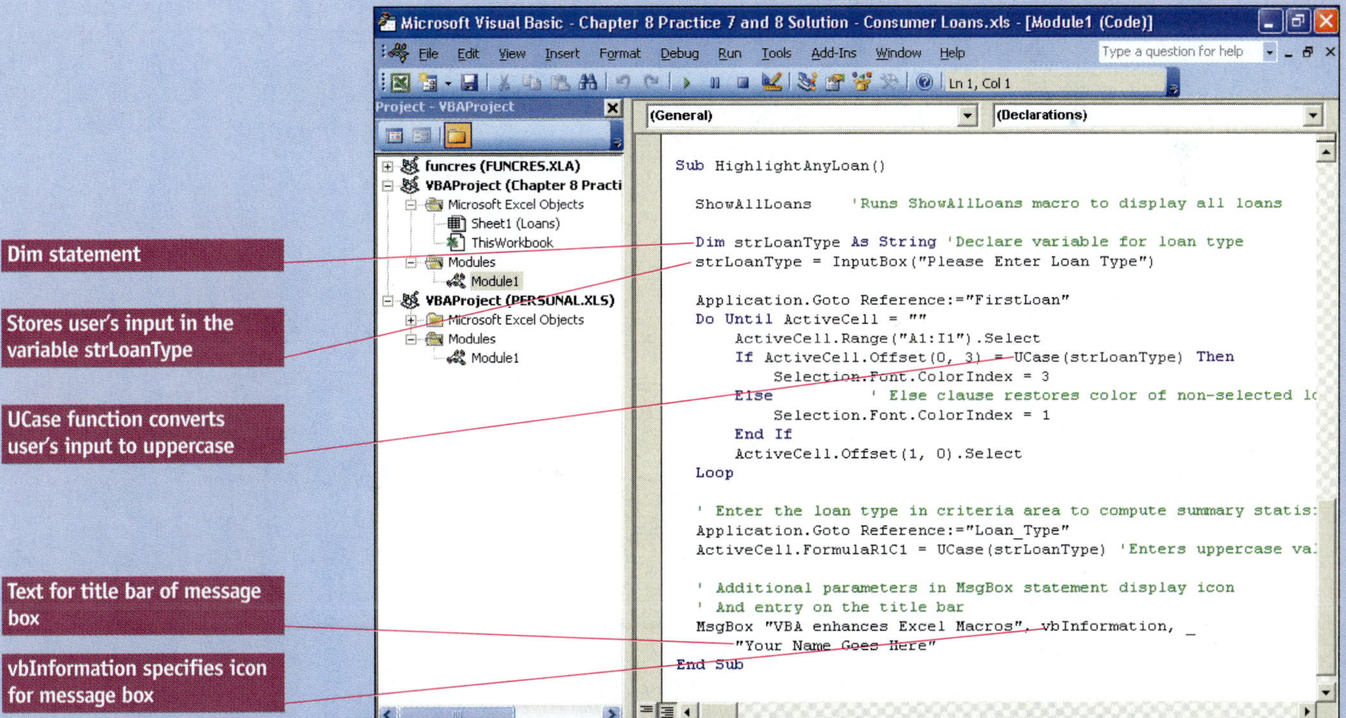

FIGURE 8.18 A Look Ahead (exercise 8)

MINI CASES

Microsoft Word

Do you use Microsoft Word on a regular basis? Are there certain tasks that you do repeatedly, whether in the same document or in a series of different documents? If so, you would do well to explore the macro capabilities within Microsoft Word. How are these capabilities similar to Excel's? How do they differ?

Starting Up

Your instructor is very impressed with the various Excel workbooks and associated macros that you have created. He would like you to take the automation process one step further and simplify the way in which Excel is started and the workbook is loaded. The problem is open ended, and there are many different approaches. You might, for example, create a shortcut on the desktop to open the workbook. You might also explore the use of the Startup folder in Microsoft Excel.

Antivirus Programs

What is an antivirus program and how do you get one? How do these programs supplement the macro virus protection that is built into Microsoft Excel? Use your favorite search engine to find two such programs, then summarize their capability and cost in a short note to your instructor. You can also visit the National Computer Security Association (www.ncsa.com) and the Computer Emergency Response Team (www.cert.org) to learn more about computer security.

Extending Excel Macros through VBA

You do not have to know VBA to create Excel macros, but knowledge of VBA will help you to create better macros. VBA is accessible from all major applications in Microsoft Office, so that anything you learn in one application is also applicable to other applications. The VBA syntax is identical. Locate the VBA primer that appears at the end of this text, study the basic statements it contains, and complete the associated hands-on exercises. Write a short note to your instructor that describes similarities and differences from one Office application to the next.

CHAPTER

9 A Professional Application: VBA and Date Functions

OBJECTIVES

After reading this chapter you will:

1. Explain the importance of data validation in a spreadsheet.
2. Describe the YEAR, MONTH, DAY, and DATE FUNCTIONS.
3. Describe the PMT, IPMT, and PPMT functions.
4. Describe the logical functions AND and OR.
5. Describe the Excel object model.
6. Use the macro recorder to "jump-start" a VBA procedure.
7. Distinguish between event and general procedures.
8. Develop a custom toolbar and attach it to a workbook.
9. Set the print area in a worksheet.
10. Create a user form.
11. Explain how pseudocode is used to develop procedures.

hands-on exercises

1. AMORTIZATION WORKBOOK
   Input: Amortization Schedule
   Output: Amortization Schedule Solution
2. EXPLORING VBA SYNTAX
   Input: Amortization Schedule Solution (from exercise 1)
   Output: Amortization Schedule Solution (additional modifications)
3. EVENT PROCEDURES
   Input: Amortization Schedule Solution (from exercise 2)
   Output: Amortization Schedule Solution (additional modifications)
4. OPTIONAL PAYMENTS
   Input: Amortization Schedule Solution (from exercise 3)
   Output: Amortization Schedule Solution (additional modifications)

CASE STUDY
REFINANCE NOW

You purchased your first home three years ago. It's in a great neighborhood, your neighbors are friendly, you have a large yard for your dog, and you are truly at home. You took out a 30-year mortgage for $100,000 at 7.5%, which resulted in a monthly payment of just under $700. You have paid approximately $25,000 to the bank (principal and interest) during the three years you have lived in the house, but are shocked to learn that you still owe approximately $97,000 on the mortgage. In other words, you have paid approximately $22,000 in interest and only $3,000 in principal.

The good news is that interest rates are at or near their lowest level in 40 years. You have been approached by multiple mortgage brokers about the benefits of refinancing, yet you still have doubts about whether you should refinance. You know that your monthly payment will go down, but you will incur additional closing costs of 4% to obtain the new loan on the remaining principal of $97,000; thus, you plan to roll the closing costs into the new mortgage to avoid an out-of-pocket expense. You can obtain either a 15- or 30-year mortgage and you want to explore the advantages of each. Is it possible that the lower interest rates on a new 15-year loan could keep your payments at the same level as your existing 30-year mortgage? ■

Your assignment is to create a simple workbook that will compare your existing mortgage to a new 15-year mortgage at 5%. It should show the monthly payment, the savings per month, and the total interest over the life of each loan. It should also determine the number of months to break even on the new 30-year mortgage. This is a simple workbook that does not require macros or VBA.

You are then to read the chapter and create the loan amortization workbook that is described within the chapter. The end result is a sophisticated workbook that includes macros and a custom toolbar that allows you to make extra payments. Use the completed workbook to enter one additional payment a year; that is, how long will it take you to pay off a 30-year mortgage if you make 13 payments a year (one every month as scheduled, plus an extra payment once a year)?

APPLICATION DEVELOPMENT

Any application originates with the client or end user. He or she has a need and is willing to pay a developer to fulfill that need. The developer in turn goes through an iterative process that presents the client with multiple versions of the application, until the finished application is delivered. The key to a successful application is a systematic approach that includes continual testing and interaction between the client and the developer. We suggest these basic steps, which provide a broad outline of the chapter:

1. Determine what the application is to accomplish
2. Design the user interface (the worksheet)
3. Develop the spreadsheet
4. Test and debug the spreadsheet
5. Add automation (macros and VBA procedures) as necessary
6. Test and debug the completed application

The first (and perhaps most important) step is to determine precisely what the application is to accomplish. The client has an idea of his or her requirements, and the developer can make suggestions as to the additional functionality that can be included. The example in this chapter is that of a payment ***(amortization)*** schedule for a loan, based on parameters supplied by the end user. The client has further specified that he wants to see the scheduled date of each payment, how much of each payment goes toward interest, and how much goes toward principal. He also wants the ability to include optional (extra) payments of principal that will shorten the time required to pay off the loan.

Data validation is an implied requirement of any application, something the developer should bring to the attention of the client if the client does not request it independently. Every input parameter should be checked so that the end results will make sense. The end user should be prevented, for example, from entering a term (more than 30 years) that exceeds the maximum number of possible payments. The user might also be cautioned against (but not prevented from) entering an inappropriate (exorbitant) interest rate. A good worksheet will anticipate errors the user may make during data entry and prevent those errors from occurring.

The application should be flexible, visually appealing, easy to use, and bulletproof. A flexible worksheet enables the user to enter parameters in a clearly defined input area, then bases all of its formulas on those parameters, so that any change in the input automatically changes the body of the worksheet. A worksheet should also be visually appealing and include any logo or other formatting requirements of the client.

The completed application should be easy to use and enable the end user to accomplish tasks that he or she would not otherwise be able to do. The specifications may call for macros or VBA procedures to automate command sequences that are executed from custom toolbars or menus. A bulletproof application will work correctly with any set of input parameters and will prevent the display of zero values when they are not appropriate. The application should also insulate itself from the nontechnical user by protecting the formulas in the worksheet so that they cannot be accidentally (or otherwise) altered or deleted.

Continual testing and debugging is essential. The developer has to ensure that the formulas within the worksheet are correct, and further that any and all VBA procedures are also correct. This is an iterative process that occurs throughout the development cycle. All of these requirements should be clearly specified in advance, after which both client and developer should sign a written statement of the intended specifications and schedule. The end result is a polished application that is suitable for general distribution.

The Amortization Workbook

Figure 9.1a displays the application that will be developed throughout this chapter. The worksheet does not appear unduly complex, but it is more sophisticated than any worksheet we have studied thus far. One significant item is what you do *not* see—the payments in the body of the worksheet will not appear until all of the loan parameters have been entered, and further the worksheet will display and print only as many rows (payments) as are necessary. A 30-year loan, for example, requires 360 payments, whereas a 15-year loan takes only 180. Data validation is also built into the worksheet. For example, the worksheet will reject any loans greater than 30 years or any loans with artificially high interest rates.

Figure 9.1b displays the worksheet after the last required parameter has been entered. Only the first several payments are visible, but the information in these rows is indicative of the underlying function. The date of each payment, for example, occurs on the 16th of each month, which is consistent with the specified date of the first payment within the input area. This calculation is accomplished through various date functions and is discussed later in the chapter.

The worksheet also divides the monthly payment of $665.30 into two components, interest and principal. The outstanding balance on the loan is reduced each month by the amount of the payment that went toward principal. Thus, the amount of the next payment that goes toward interest decreases (if only by pennies initially), while the amount that goes toward principal increases.

The summary information in the upper-right portion of the worksheet indicates a total of 360 scheduled payments, which is what you would expect for a 30-year loan. The worksheet also displays the normal payoff date of 2/16/2033, which occurs after the 360th payment has been made. Note, too, that the total interest on the loan is more than $139,000, which is more than the amount of the actual loan.

The client also requested the ability to include additional payments toward principal, which is reflected in Figure 9.1c. Here we see that a constant (optional) payment of $100 a month will reduce the total interest over the life of the loan to just over $89,000 (a savings of more than $50,000). The loan is paid off after 247 payments on September 16, 2023, almost 10 years earlier than the original loan. The borrower has paid $24,700 (247 payments of $100 each) in early payments, but this is not truly "additional" money. It is principal that would have been paid eventually during the original 30-year schedule. The borrower has simply elected to make these payments earlier than necessary in order to reduce the total interest.

All of the calculations within the worksheet are accomplished through various functions, without macros of any kind. Figure 9.1d displays some of the underlying formulas and may appear unduly complicated. We prefer to say, however, that these formulas add functionality, as opposed to complexity. Consider, for example, the ***AND function***, =AND(C4>0,C5>0,C6>0,C7>0), that appears in cell D6.

The AND function returns one of two values, true or false. It is considered true if all of its arguments are true, and false otherwise. In this example the AND function is checking the values in cells C4 through C7, and it requires that each of these entries be greater than zero if the function is to be true. In other words, we can check the value in cell D6 (which has been assigned the name DataEntered) to determine if all of the required parameters have been supplied, and if so, we can display these values in the body of the worksheet. (The ***OR function*** is not used in this worksheet, but it is also very useful. The OR function requires only one argument to be true for the function to be true.)

Cell A14 contains the formula =IF(DataEntered, 1,0). Recall that the IF function has three arguments—a condition that is evaluated as true or false, the value if the condition is true, and the value if the condition is false. Thus, the number of the first payment will be 1 if all parameters have been entered and zero otherwise. (The Options command has been set to hide zero values in the spreadsheet.) All of the other formulas in the worksheet are based on the value in cell A14, which in turn allows us to display only as many rows (payments) as are necessary.

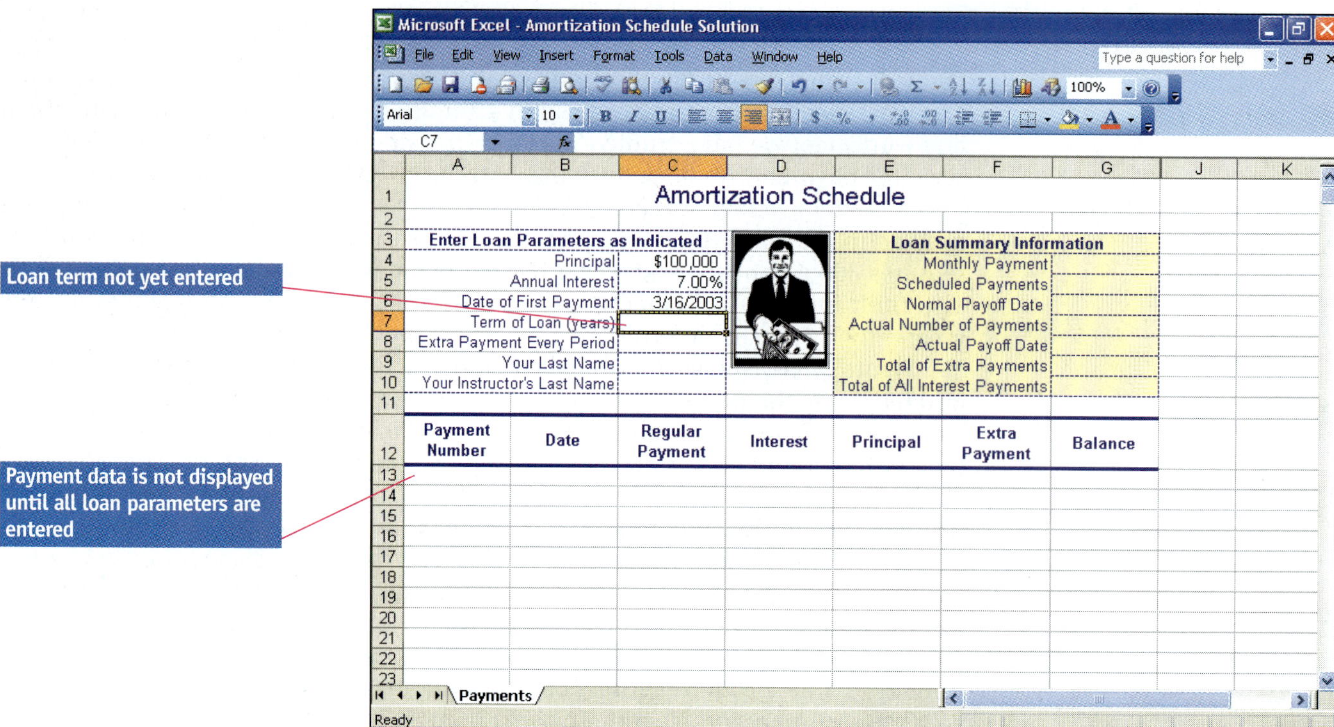

(a) Data Entry

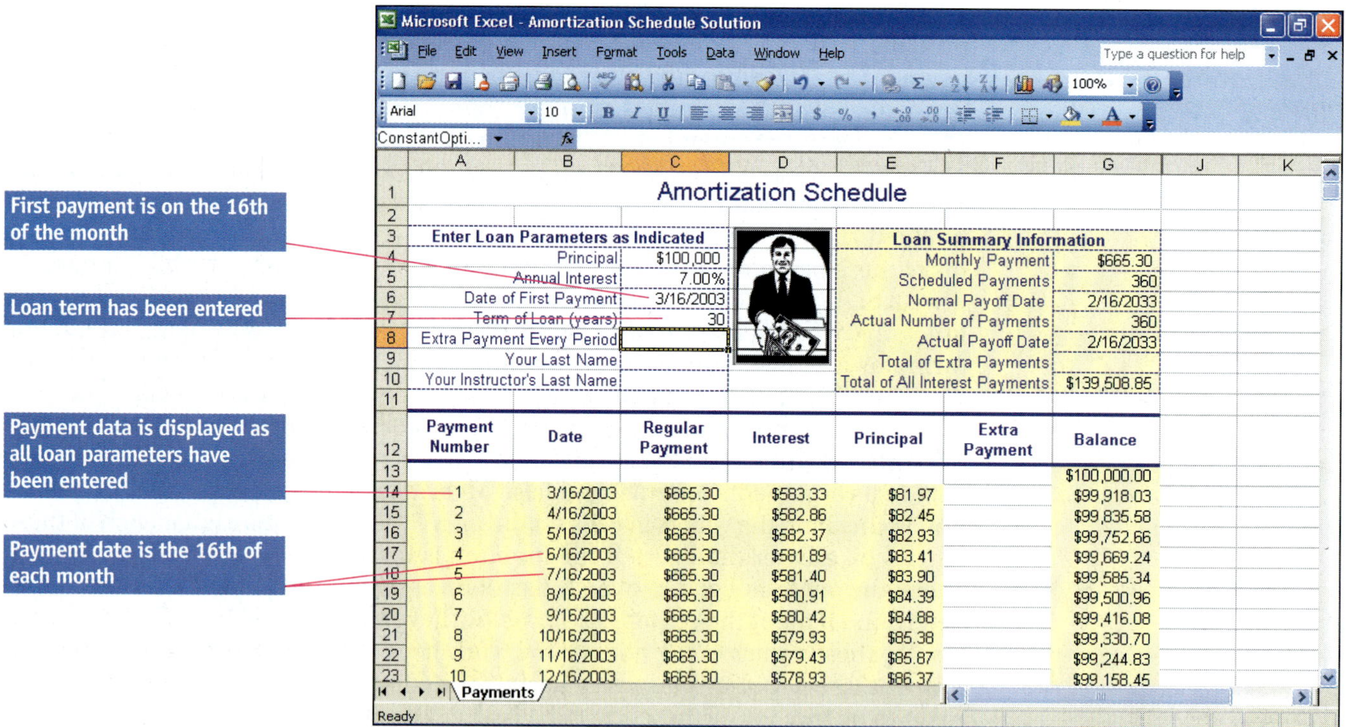

(b) 30-year Mortgage

FIGURE 9.1 The Amortization Schedule Workbook

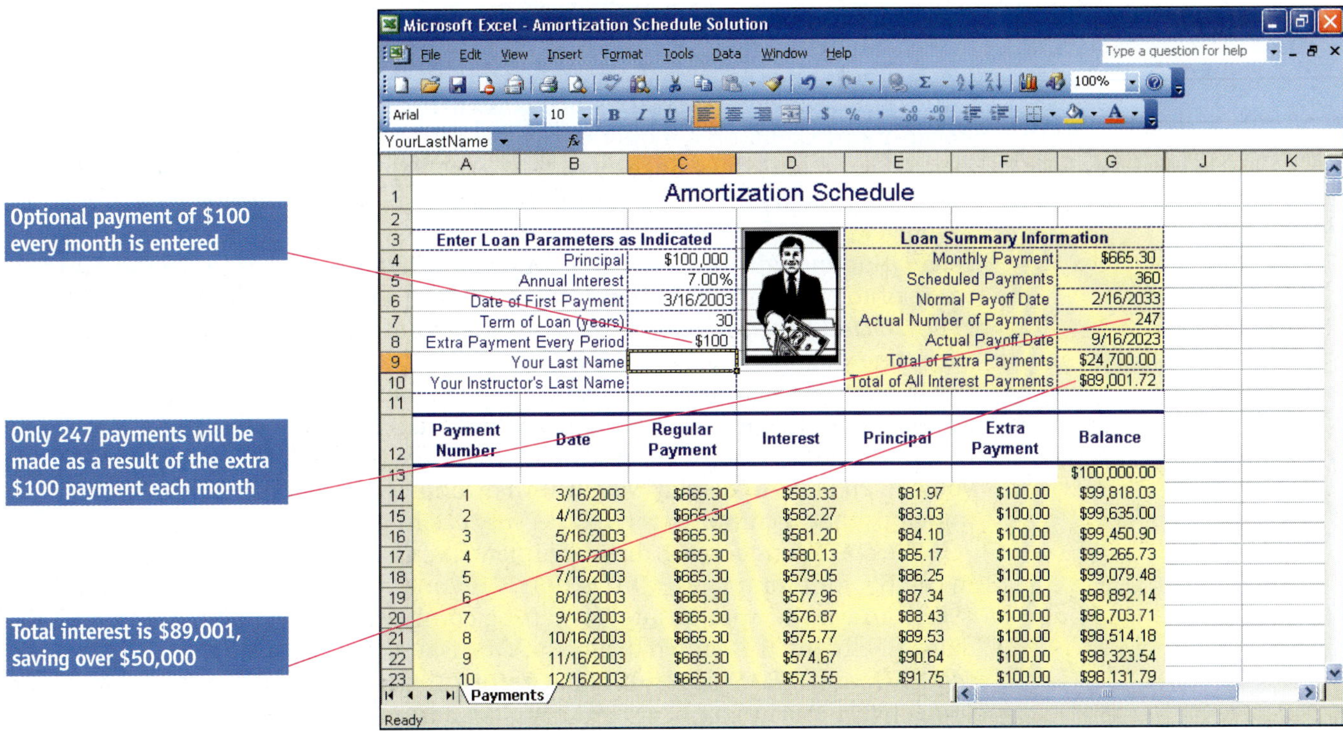

(c) Optional Extra Payment

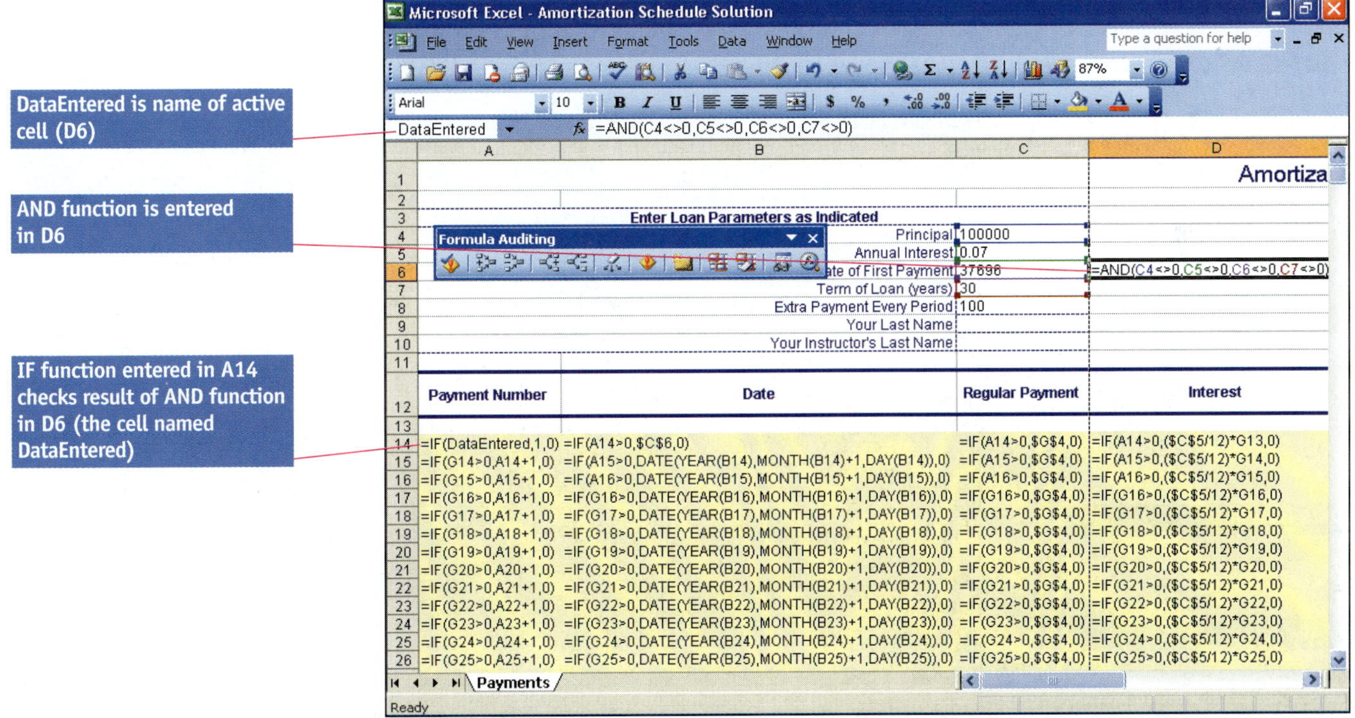

(d) Partial Cell Formulas

FIGURE 9.1 The Amortization Schedule Workbook (*continued*)

DATE FUNCTIONS

The use of dates within a worksheet has been discussed at various points in the text. Recall that Excel stores a date as an integer (serial number) equivalent to the elapsed number of days since January 1, 1900. Thus, January 1, 1900 is stored as the number 1, January 2, 1900 as the number 2, and so on. The fact that dates are stored as integer numbers enables you to perform date arithmetic as illustrated in the age calculation in Figure 9.2. To determine an individual's age, we take the (integer) value of today's date, subtract the birth date, and then divide the result by 365. (The ***TODAY function*** always returns today's date and is updated automatically each time you open the workbook.)

It's easy enough to determine tomorrow's date because all you have to do is add one to the integer value of today's date. What if, however, you want to determine next month's date? Do you add 30 or 31? And what if today's date is February 15? Do you add 28 or 29 to display March 15? Fortunately, Excel includes additional date functions that accomplish these tasks very easily.

The ***DATE function*** has three arguments: year, month, and day. The cell formula in cell B5, for example, is =DATE(1982,3,16) and it displays the date as March 16, 1982 through the appropriate formatting command. (We could have entered the date directly, but we wanted to illustrate the Date function.) Excel also has the ***DAY, MONTH***, and ***YEAR functions*** that return the numeric day, month, and year, respectively. The function, =MONTH(B3), for example, returns the numeric month of the date in cell B3. In similar fashion, =MONTH(B3)+1 adds one to the numeric month. Excel is smart enough to know that if today's date is sometime in December, next month will occur in January.

Look now at the cell formulas for cells B11 and B13 that display next month's date and next year's date, respectively. These formulas may have seemed complex initially, but on closer inspection are easy to understand. The various date functions are used in the following exercise to determine the payment schedule.

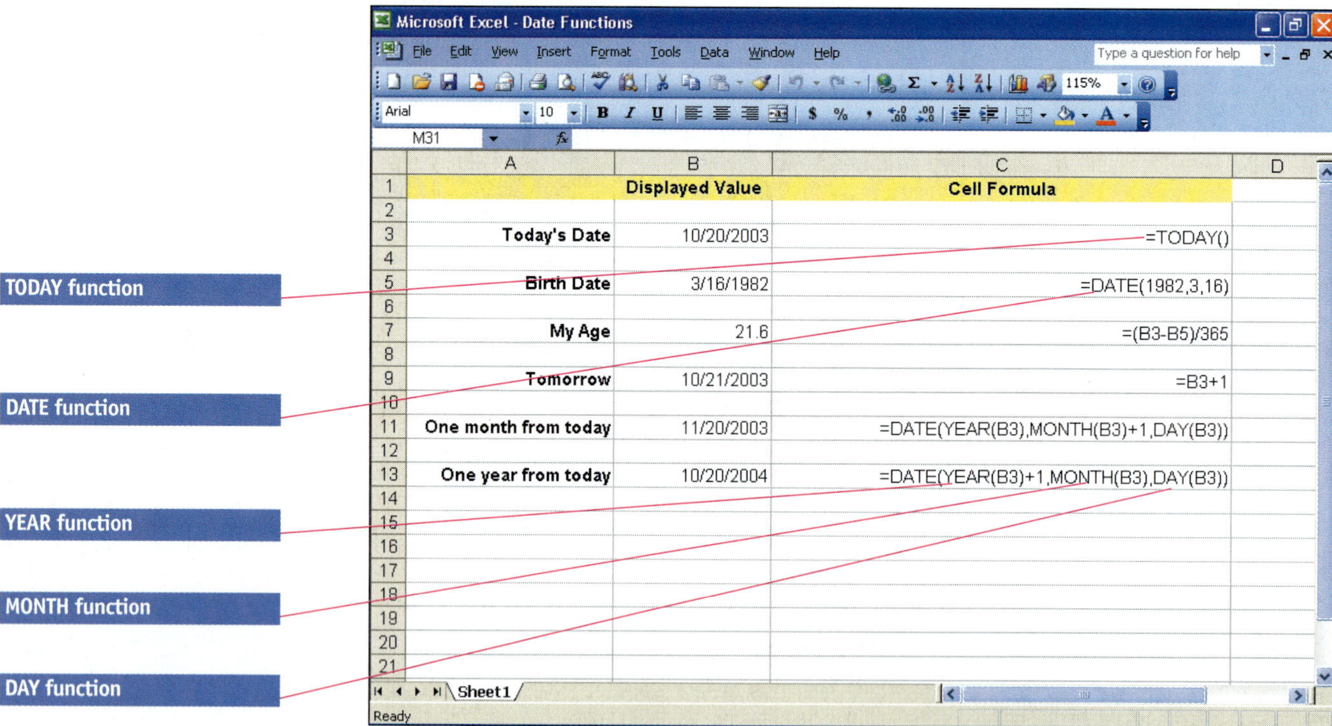

FIGURE 9.2 Date Functions

hands-on exercise

1 The Amortization Workbook

Objective Explore the amortization workbook with respect to data validation, cell protection, optional extra payments, and a variable print area.

Step 1: Data Entry and Validation

- Start Excel. Open the **Amortization Schedule** workbook in the Exploring Excel folder. Click the button to **Enable macros**. (This exercise, however, accomplishes all of its tasks without the use of macros.)
- Save the workbook as **Amortization Schedule Solution** so that you can return to the original workbook if necessary. Click in **cell C4**. Enter **$100,000** and press **Enter**.
- Enter **.09** as the interest rate, which in turn displays the message box in Figure 9.3a. Click **No**, then enter **.07** as the interest rate. This time the value is accepted, and you see 7.00% in cell B5.

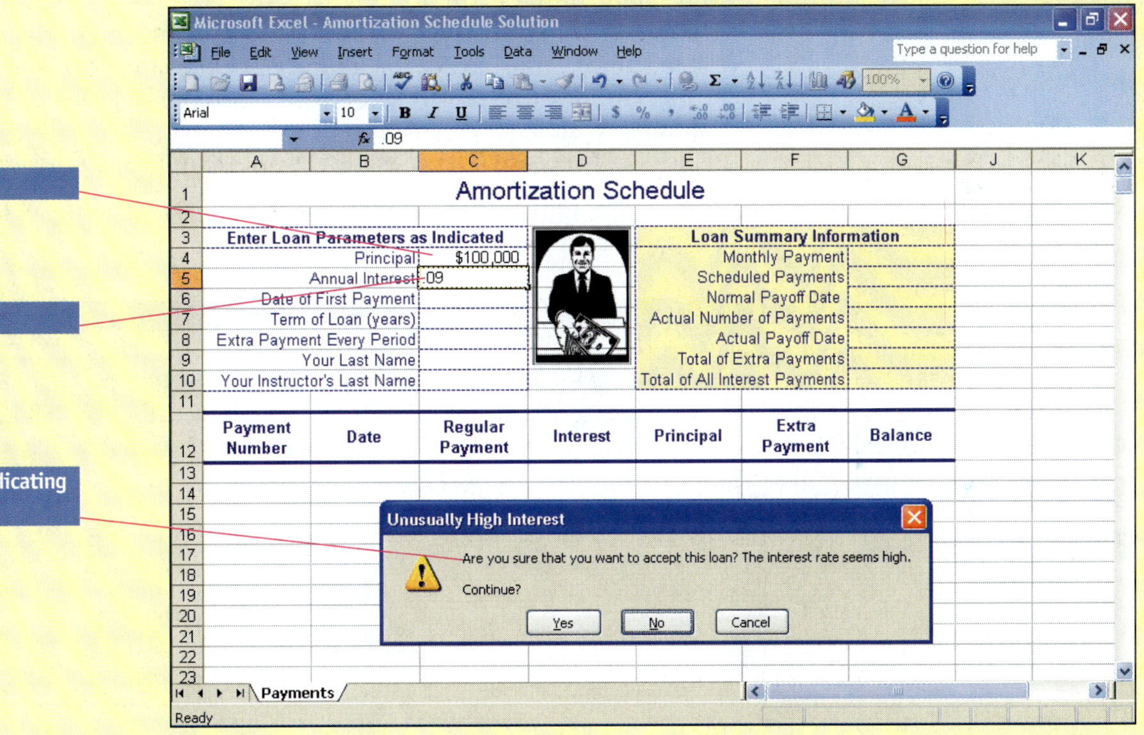

(a) Data Entry and Validation (step 1)

FIGURE 9.3 Hands-on Exercise 1

DATA VALIDATION

The Data Validation command enables you to restrict the values that can be entered into a specific cell. Click in the cell where you want to impose validation, then pull down the Data menu and click the Validation command to display the Data Validation dialog box. (The command is disabled if the worksheet is protected.)

Step 2: A Protected Worksheet

- Complete the entries in cells **C6 and C7** as shown in Figure 9.3b. Enter the date of the first payment so as to reflect the 15th of next month. The monthly payments and summary information appear as soon as you complete the last required entry (the term of the loan).
- Click in **cell A1** and attempt to enter a new title for the worksheet. You will see a message box indicating that the cell is protected and that you cannot change its value. Click **OK** after you have read the message.
- Pull down the **Tools menu**, click the **Protection command**, and click the **Unprotect Sheet command** to unprotect the worksheet. (You are not prompted for a password, because we protected the worksheet without a password.) The worksheet is now unprotected and you have full access to all of its cells.
- Click the clip art to select the image and display the sizing handles. Click and drag any of the four corners to increase (decrease) the size of the clip art.
- The Picture toolbar should be displayed automatically. If not, right click the clip art and click the command to **Show Picture toolbar** as shown in Figure 9.3b. Experiment with the different tools:
  - Click the **Crop tool**, then click and drag the bottom border of the figure up to delete (crop) this part of the figure. Click the Undo button.
  - Click the **Rotate tool** to rotate the figure 90 degrees to the left. Click the **Undo button** to reverse the command.
  - Click the **Increase (Decrease) Brightness tool** to see the effect (if any).
- Click off the figure to deselect it and continue working. The Picture toolbar closes automatically. Save the workbook.

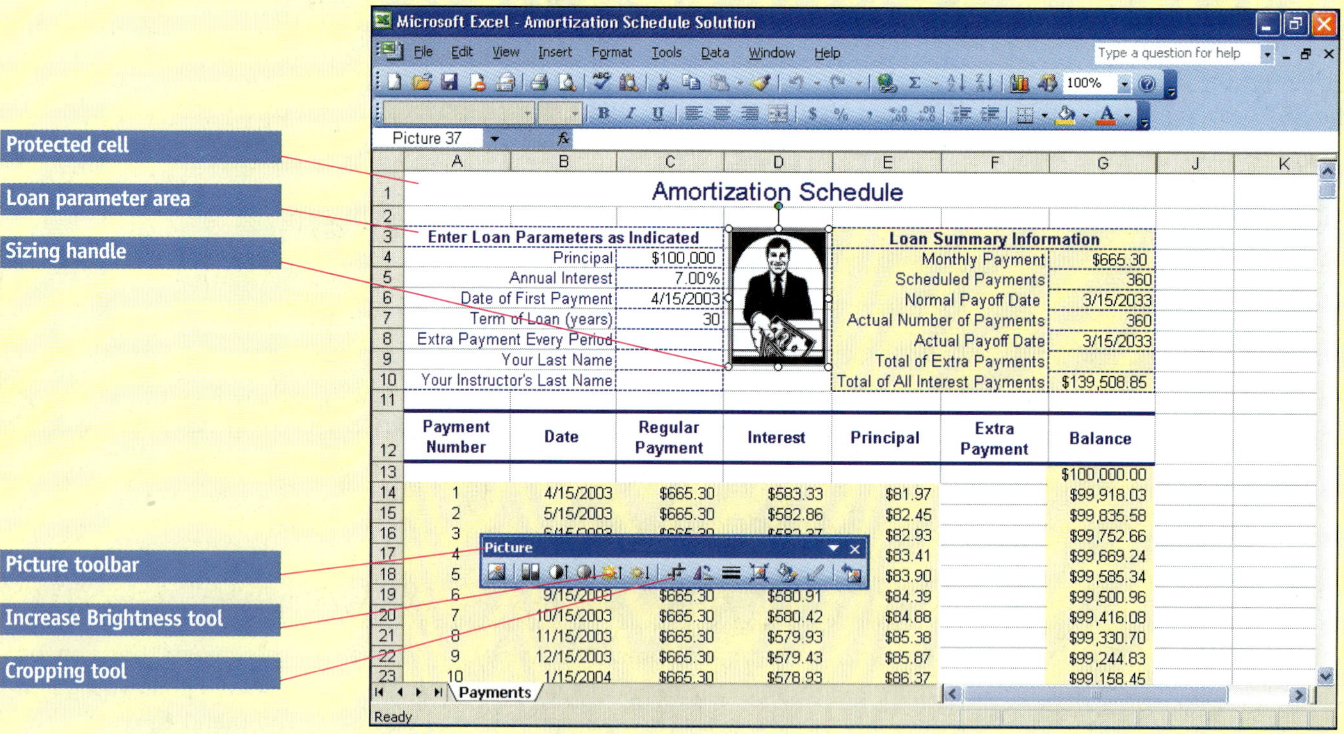

(b) A Protected Worksheet (step 2)

FIGURE 9.3 Hands-on Exercise 1 (*continued*)

Step 3: The Logical AND Function

- Click and drag the clip art image to the right as shown in Figure 9.3c. The displayed value in cell D6 is "TRUE", and the monthly payments and summary information are displayed in G4:G10.
- Click in **cell C7** and delete the term of the loan. The value in cell D6 changes to "FALSE", and the payments and summary information are no longer visible.
- Click the **Undo button** to restore the 30 in cell C7. The loan parameters are now complete and the value of cell D6 returns to "TRUE".
- Click in **cell D6** and note the following:
  - The formula bar contains a logical AND function with four arguments, all of which have to be true for the function to be true. In other words, data has to be entered in cells C4, C5, C6, and C7 for the value in cell D6 to be true.
  - The Name box displays "DataEntered" to indicate that cell D6 is associated with this range name, which can be used in any worksheet formula.
- Click in **cell A14**, the cell containing the formula for the first payment. The IF function checks the value of the range name "DataEntered", and if that value is true, enters the number 1 for the payment number. If the value is false, however, zero is entered for the payment number. (Zero values are not displayed.)
- Click and drag the clip art image back to its original place in the worksheet.

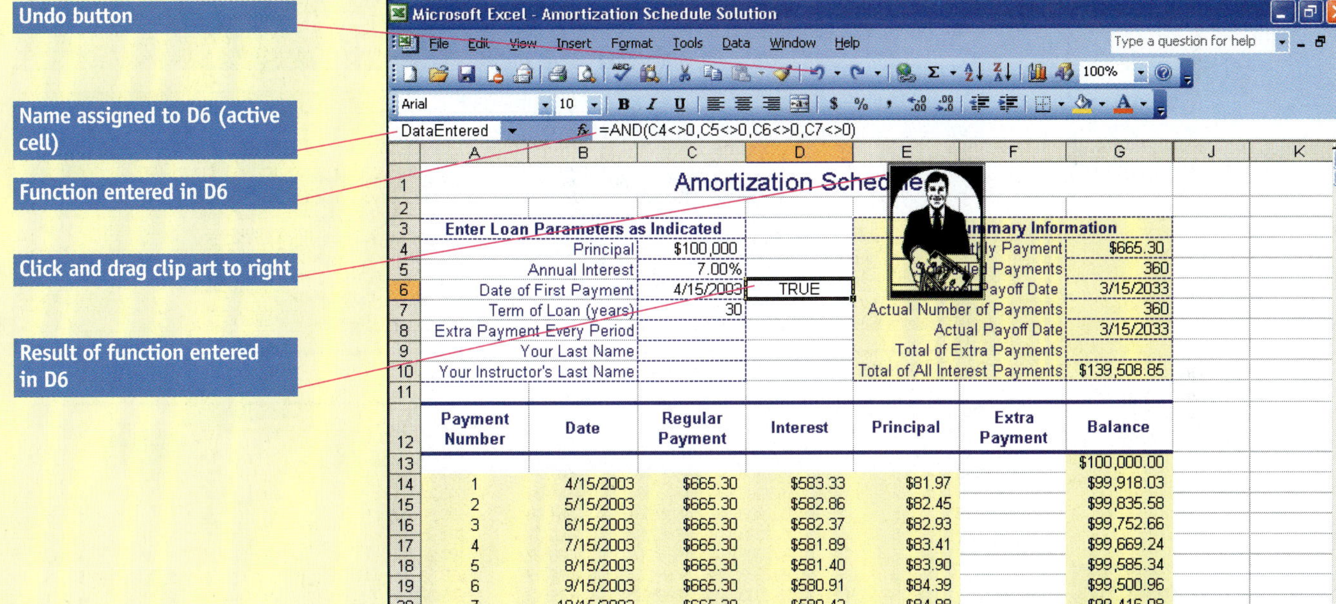

(c) The Logical AND Function (step 3)

FIGURE 9.3 Hands-on Exercise 1 (*continued*)

SUPPRESS ZERO VALUES

Many spreadsheets are visually enhanced by suppressing the display of zero values. The amortization worksheet, for example, contains formulas to compute 360 monthly loan payments, but it displays the entries for only those cells with nonzero values. Pull down the Tools menu, click the Options command, click the View tab, and clear the box for Zero values. Click OK.

Step 4: Check the Calculations

- The formulas in columns D and E to compute the portion of each payment towards interest and principal, respectively, are not trivial. It is important, therefore, to verify the results through alternate calculations.
- Click and drag to select **columns G and J**. (Columns H and I are not visible because they are currently hidden.) Pull down the **Format menu**, click the **Column command**, then click **Unhide** to display columns H and I, as shown in Figure 9.3d.
- Click in **cell H14** to examine the amount of the first payment that goes toward interest. The displayed value of $583.33 is obtained through the IPMT function and matches the amount in cell D14.
- Click in **cell I14** to examine the amount of the first payment that goes toward principal. The displayed value of $81.97 is obtained through the PPMT function and matches the amount in cell E14.
- Click and drag the column headings to select **columns H and I**. Pull down the **Format menu**, click the **Column command**, then click **Hide** to suppress these columns. Save the workbook.

IPMT function is within the If function

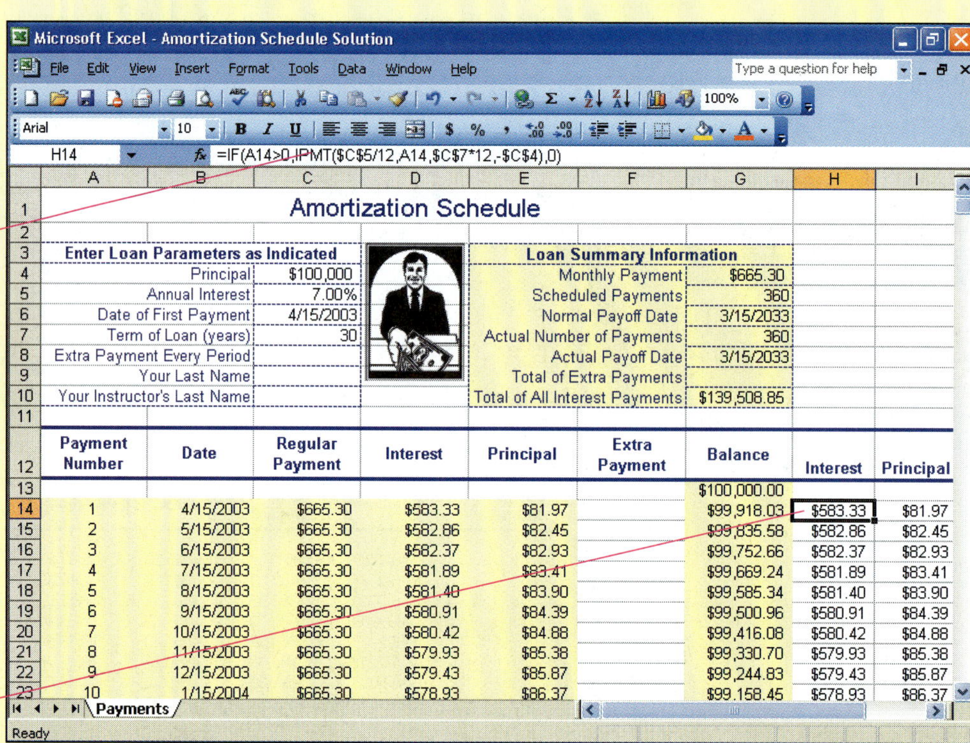

Click in H14 and note that amount matches result in D14

(d) Check the Calculations (step 4)

FIGURE 9.3 Hands-on Exercise 1 (*continued*)

THE IPMT AND PPMT FUNCTIONS

The IPMT and PPMT functions compute the portion of a monthly payment that goes toward interest and principal, respectively. These functions refer to the original principal and cannot accommodate extra payments toward principal. Hence, they could not be used in the body of the worksheet, but serve only to validate that the formulas in columns D and E are correct. These formulas are for the developer to check his or her work, not the user.

Step 5: What If?

- Examine the information in the summary area of the worksheet. The total interest for the 30-year loan is found in cell G10 and is equal to $139,508.
- Change the term of the loan to **15 years**, and the interest decreases to $61,789, a savings of almost $80,000. Note, too, that the payoff date is now 15 years (less one month, but 180 payments) from the initial payment.
- Change the starting date of the loan to the first of next month as shown in Figure 9.3e. The payoff date changes, as do the dates for the individual payments.
- Click in **cell C8** and enter **$100** as an optional extra payment you hope to make each month toward principal. The payoff date, actual number of payments, and total interest decrease further.
- Enter **your last name** and **your instructor's last name** in **cells C9 and C10**.
- Pull down the **Tools menu**, click the **Protection command**, and click the **Protect Sheet command** to protect the worksheet. Leave the password blank. Click **OK**.
- Save the workbook.

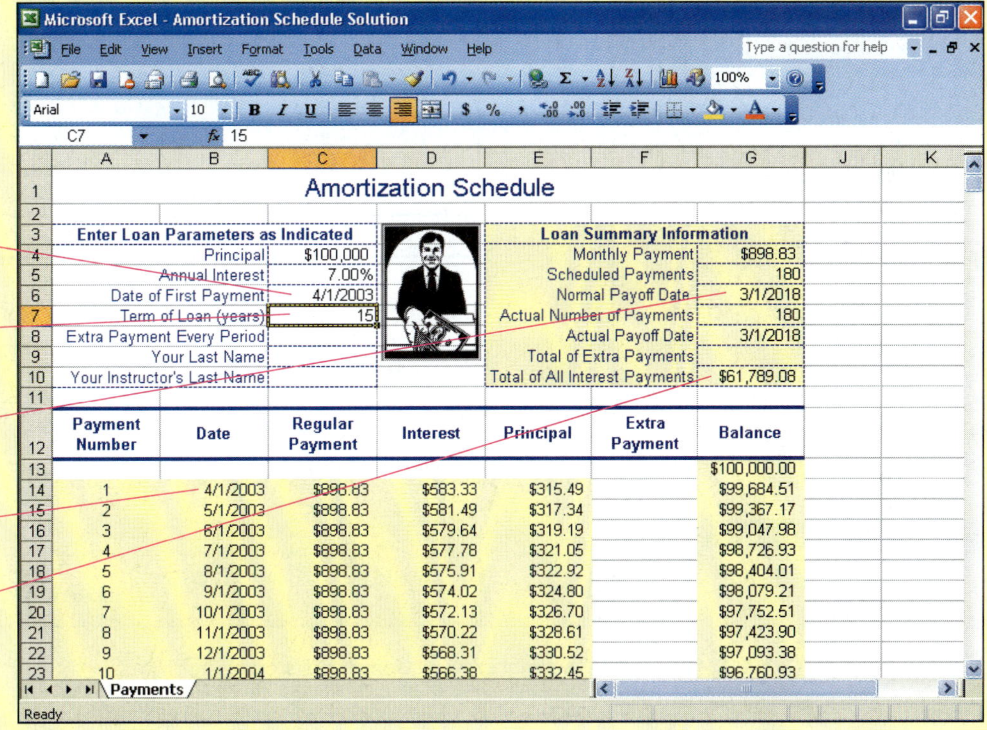

Payment Number	Date	Regular Payment	Interest	Principal	Extra Payment	Balance
						$100,000.00
1	4/1/2003	$898.83	$583.33	$315.49		$99,684.51
2	5/1/2003	$898.83	$581.49	$317.34		$99,367.17
3	6/1/2003	$898.83	$579.64	$319.19		$99,047.98
4	7/1/2003	$898.83	$577.78	$321.05		$98,726.93
5	8/1/2003	$898.83	$575.91	$322.92		$98,404.01
6	9/1/2003	$898.83	$574.02	$324.80		$98,079.21
7	10/1/2003	$898.83	$572.13	$326.70		$97,752.51
8	11/1/2003	$898.83	$570.22	$328.61		$97,423.90
9	12/1/2003	$898.83	$568.31	$330.52		$97,093.38
10	1/1/2004	$898.83	$566.38	$332.45		$96,760.93

(e) What If? (step 5)

FIGURE 9.3 Hands-on Exercise 1 (*continued*)

PROTECTING A WORKSHEET

Protecting a worksheet is a two-step process. First, you unlock all of the cells that are subject to change, then you protect the worksheet. Select the cell(s) you want to unlock, pull down the Format menu, click the Cells command, then select the Protection tab in the Format Cells dialog box. Clear the Locked check box. To protect the worksheet, pull down the Tools menu, click Protection, then click the Protect Sheet command to display the Protect Sheet dialog box where you can enter a password. *Be careful, because once you password-protect a worksheet, you cannot unprotect it without the password.*

Step 6: The Print Preview Command

- Click the **Print Preview button** to see how your worksheet will appear when it is printed, as shown in Figure 9.3f. Click the **Zoom button**, if necessary, so that you see the worksheet more easily.
- Look at the status bar and note that the entire worksheet requires three pages. Click the **Next button** on the Print Preview toolbar to view page two of the printout, which repeats the column headings, then begins with payment number 46. (You may see a different payment number, depending on your printer.)
- Click the **Next button** to move to page 3, which again repeats the payment headings and starts with payment 103 and continues to the last payment.
- Click the **Print button** to print the worksheet for your instructor. Click **OK** when you see the Print dialog box.

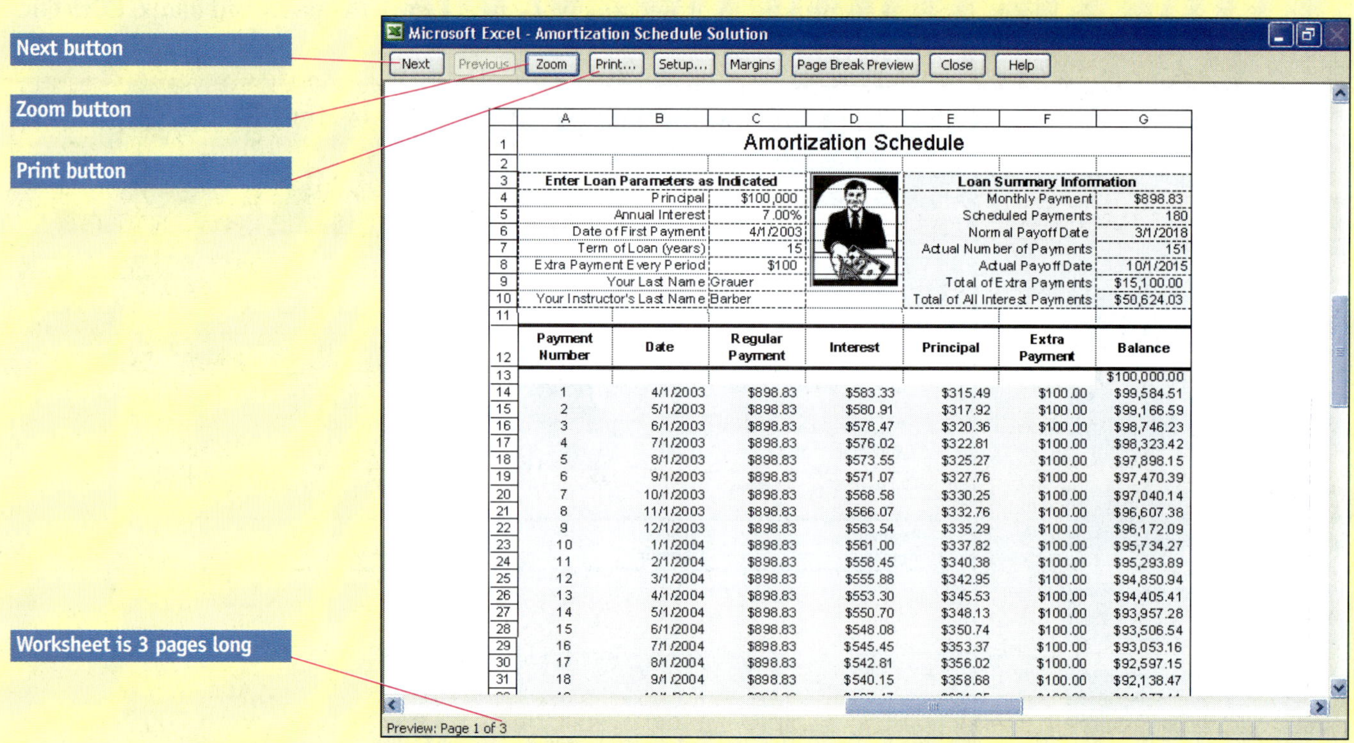

(f) The Print Preview Command (step 6)

FIGURE 9.3 Hands-on Exercise 1 (*continued*)

THE MULTIPLE-PAGE PRINTOUT—REPEATING ROWS AND COLUMNS

It is very helpful to repeat one or more rows and/or columns of a worksheet if the worksheet extends to several printed pages. Pull down the File menu and click the Page Setup command to display the Page Setup dialog box. Click the Sheet tab. Click in the Rows to repeat at top text box, then click and drag in the worksheet to select the row(s) you want to repeat. Click in the Columns to repeat at left text box, click and drag in the worksheet to select the columns, then click OK to accept the settings and close the dialog box. Use the Print Preview command to see the effect of these changes.

Step 7: Print the Cell Formulas

- We want you to print the cell formulas so that you will be able to study the worksheet in detail. We are going to change the term of the loan, however, so that the worksheet will take fewer pages.
- Click in **cell C7** and change the term of the loan to **1 year**. The displayed values will change, but the formulas remain constant. Press **Ctrl+~** (the ~ character appears immediately below the Esc key) to display cell formulas.
- Unprotect the worksheet. Click and drag the column borders to see the entire formula within a cell as shown in Figure 9.3g.
- Click the **Print Preview button**. The worksheet should require three pages. All of the rows fit on one page, but the wider columns spill over to pages two and three. Click **Print**. Click **OK**.
- Close the workbook. Click **No** if asked whether to save the changes. Exit Excel if you do not want to continue with the next exercise at this time.

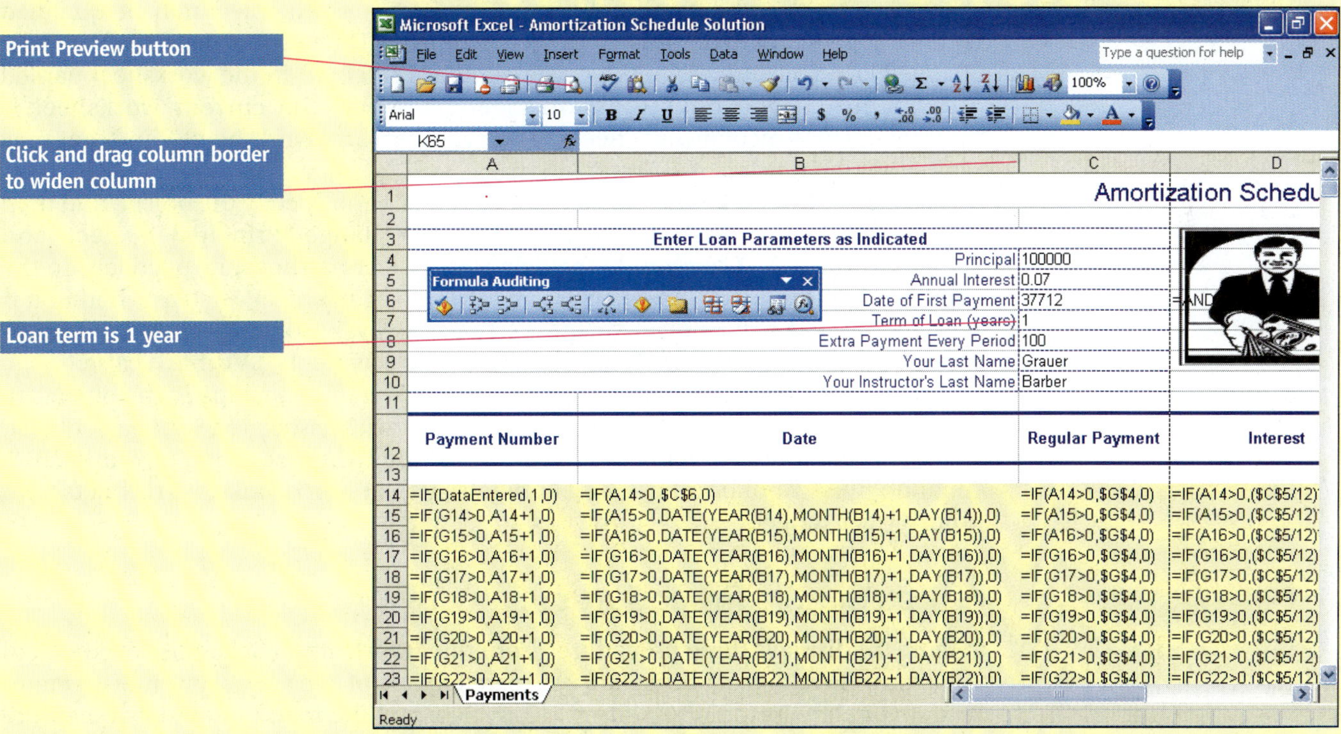

(g) Print the Cell Formulas (step 7)

FIGURE 9.3 Hands-on Exercise 1 (*continued*)

CHANGING THE PRINT AREA

It's easy to set a print area manually. You select the range that is to print, pull down the File menu, click Print Area, and then click Set Print Area. (You can clear the print area by choosing the Clear Print Area command.) The problem with this technique is that the desired print area changes according to the number of required payments, each of which adds a row to the worksheet. We have, however, found a way to set the print area dynamically, according to the number of rows in a worksheet. If this does not happen in your worksheet, press Ctrl+r to execute a macro to reset the dynamic print area. See exercises 3 and 4 at the end of the chapter.

EXPLORING VBA SYNTAX

You could study VBA for weeks on end prior to coding a simple procedure. We prefer to plunge right in, use the ***macro recorder*** to capture Excel commands, and then learn about VBA through inference and observation. Nevertheless, you need a grasp of basic terminology as presented in this section.

VBA accomplishes its tasks by manipulating ***objects***. The objects within Excel include workbooks, worksheets, ranges, charts, pivot tables, and individual cells. The ***object model*** describes the hierarchical way in which different objects are related to one another. The workbook object, for example, contains the worksheet object, which in turn contains the range object, and so on.

A ***collection*** is a group of similar objects within the object model. The worksheet collection is a group of individual worksheets. A specific object within a collection is referenced by the collection name followed by the object name enclosed in quotation marks within parentheses. Worksheets("Documentation"), for example, refers to the worksheet named "Documentation" within the Worksheets collection. In similar fashion, Range("Principal") refers to the range object named "Principal" within the Range collection. A reference to an object may be qualified (joined together with periods) over several objects. Thus, Worksheets("Payments"). Range("Principal") refers to the range named "Principal" in the worksheet named "Payments". If you omit the worksheet reference, the current worksheet is assumed. (VBA recognizes "Sheets" as a synonym for "Worksheets", and you may see either reference in a VBA statement.)

A ***method*** is an action performed by an object. You specify the object, and then you indicate the method. The statements Range("Principal").Select and Range("Principal").Clear apply the Select and Clear methods, respectively, to the indicated range object. A ***property*** is an attribute of an object, such as whether it is visible. You specify the object, the property, and the value of the property; for example, Sheets("Payments").Visible = True or Sheets("Payments").Visible = False.

That's all there is. The object model defines the relationships of the objects to one another and defines the methods and properties associated with each object. The object model also provides a link between the user interface and VBA, enabling VBA to manipulate Excel objects such as workbooks, worksheets, and specific cell ranges.

Three Simple Procedures

Figure 9.4 displays three procedures from the Amortization Schedule workbook to illustrate VBA syntax. A procedure is created in one of two ways—by entering statements directly in the VBA editor and/or by using the macro recorder to capture Excel commands and convert them to their VBA equivalents. You can also combine the two techniques by starting with the recorder to capture basic statements, then view the resulting syntax and embellish those statements with additional VBA statements.

The procedure in Figure 9.4a is used by the developer to verify his or her calculations. The procedure displays two hidden columns that contain the ***IPMT*** and ***PPMT functions***, to compute the amount of each payment for interest and principal, respectively. (See step 4 in the previous hands-on exercise.) The procedure was created entirely through the macro recorder. The resulting VBA statements are easily understood within the context of our basic definitions. The Unprotect method is applied to the active worksheet object so that its contents may be modified. The named range called ValidationColumns is selected, and its hidden property is set to False. The Protect method is then applied to the worksheet so that it cannot be modified further. You might not be able to write the procedure from scratch, but you can understand its statements once they have been created for you. All of a sudden, VBA does not seem so intimidating.

VBA statements were generated by macro recorder

```
Sub DisplayValidationColumns()
    ActiveSheet.Unprotect
    Application.Goto Reference:="ValidationColumns"
    Selection.EntireColumn.Hidden = False
    ActiveSheet.Protect
End Sub
```

(a) Display Validation Columns (Macro Recorder)

If statement tests to see if data has been entered in cell named DataEntered

Else clause

MsgBox statement

```
Sub DisplayValidationColumns()
    ActiveSheet.Unprotect
    If Range("DataEntered").Value = True Then
        Application.Goto Reference:="ValidationColumns"
        Selection.EntireColumn.Hidden = False
        MsgBox "This macro displays additional columns for validation " _
            & "of the spreadsheet formulas using the IPMT and PPMT " _
            & "functions, respectively. The values should match the " _
            & "corresponding columns in the body of the spreadsheet " _
            & "provided that no extra payments are made.", _
                vbInformation, ApplicationTitle
    Else
        MsgBox "Validation meaningless - Loan parameters not entered", _
                vbInformation, ApplicationTitle
    End If
    ActiveSheet.Protect
End Sub
```

(b) Display Validation Columns (Additional VBA Statements)

User is prompted for a Yes or No response, and response is tested against vbYes

```
Public Sub EnableSinglePayments()
    If MsgBox("This procedure unprotects the extra payments " _
        & "columns enabling you to enter individual payments. " _
        & "Do you want to unprotect the spreadsheet?", _
        vbYesNo + vbQuestion, ApplicationTitle) = vbYes _
    Then
        ActiveSheet.Unprotect
    Else
        ActiveSheet.Protect
    End If
End Sub
```

(c) Enable Single Payments

FIGURE 9.4 VBA Procedures

The real power of VBA, however, lies in the ability to add VBA statements that do not have an Excel equivalent to procedures that were created by the macro recorder. The procedure in Figure 9.4b expands the procedure to display the hidden columns by first testing to see that data has been entered in the main body of the worksheet, because it does not make sense to display the validation columns if the data is incomplete. Thus, we took the procedure in Figure 9.4a and added the If . . . Else . . . End If construct to see if data has been entered.

Figure 9.4c displays a procedure that expands the functionality of the worksheet by enabling the user to enter individual payments within the optional payments column. The new procedure uses the ***MsgBox function***, as opposed to a simple ***MsgBox statement***. The MsgBox function displays a prompt to the user, then returns a value such as which button was clicked.

hands-on exercise

2 Exploring VBA Syntax

Objective To use the Excel macro recorder to jump-start the creation of VBA procedures; to add VBA statements to create more powerful procedures. Use Figure 9.5 as a guide in the exercise.

Step 1: Open the VBA Editor

- Start Excel. Open the **Amortization Schedule Solution** from the previous exercise. Click the button to **Enable macros**.
- Pull down the **Tools menu**, click the **Macro command**, then click the **Visual Basic Editor command** (or use the **Alt+F11** keyboard shortcut) to open the editor. You should see a window similar to Figure 9.5a.
- If necessary, pull down the **View menu**, and click **Project Explorer** to display the Project Explorer pane at the left of the window.
- Click the **plus sign** next to the Modules folder to list the existing modules, then double click **Module1** to display its contents in the code window.
- Click and drag to select the public constant, **Your Name Goes Here**. (Do not select the quotation marks.)
- Type your name, and it will replace the selected text. Click the **Save button** to save the changes to Module1.
- Click the **View Microsoft Excel button** to return to the workbook.

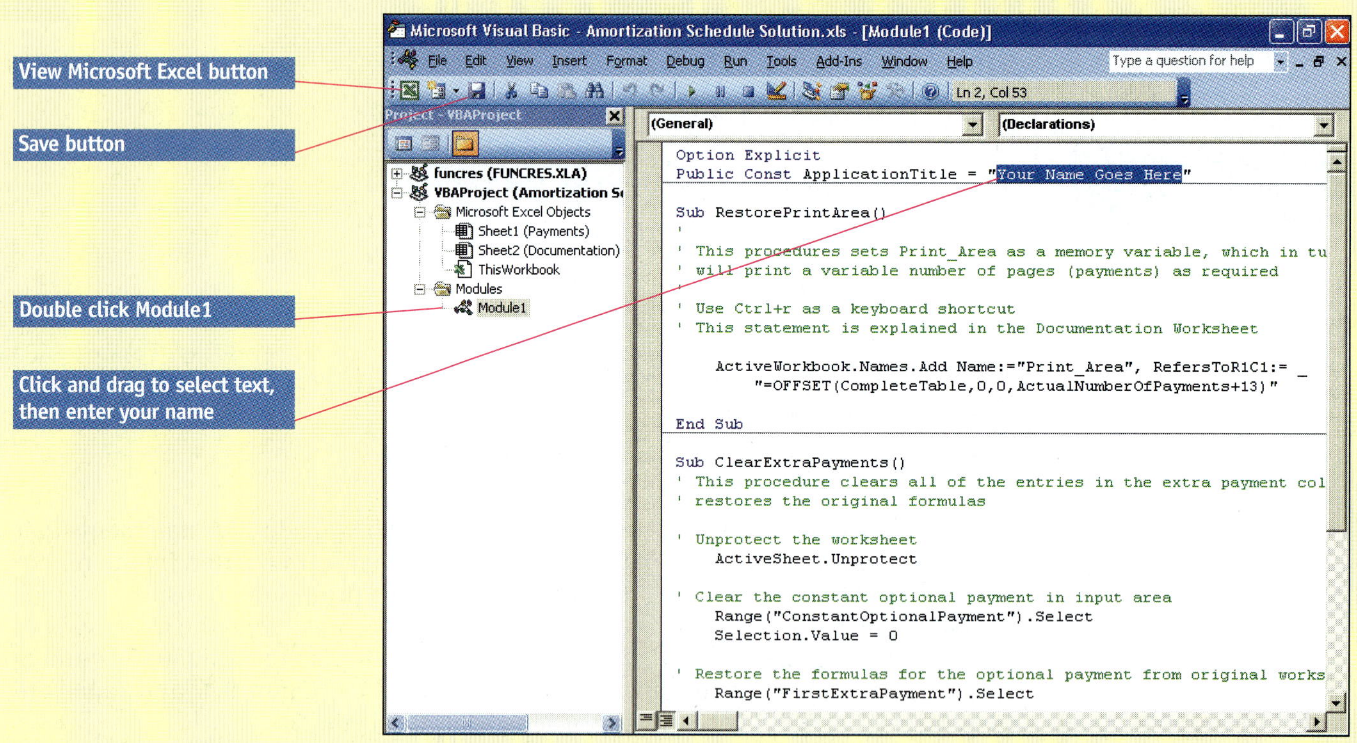

(a) Open the VBA Editor (step 1)

FIGURE 9.5 Hands-on Exercise 2

Step 2: Record the Display Validation Columns Macro

- Pull down the **Tools menu** and click the **Macro command**, then click **Record New Macro** to display the Record Macro dialog box. Enter **DisplayValidationColumns** (spaces are not allowed) as the name of the macro.
- Click in the **Shortcut Key** text box and enter a **lowercase d**. Ctrl+d should appear as the shortcut. Be sure that the macro is stored in This Workbook. Click **OK** to begin recording and display the Stop Recording toolbar in Figure 9.5b.
- Pull down the **Tools menu**, click **Protection**, and click the **Unprotect Sheet command**. (A password is not required.)
- Click the **down arrow** in the Name box and click **ValidationColumns** to select columns H and I. You see only a thick vertical line between columns G and J because the columns are still hidden.
- Pull down the **Format menu**, click the **Column command** and click **Unhide**. You should see the validation columns. Pull down the **Tools menu**, click **Protection**, and click the **Protect Sheet command**. Click **OK**. (A password is not required.)
- Click the **Stop Recording button**. (If you do not see the Stop Recording toolbar, pull down the **Tools menu**, click **Macro**, and then click **Stop Recording**.)

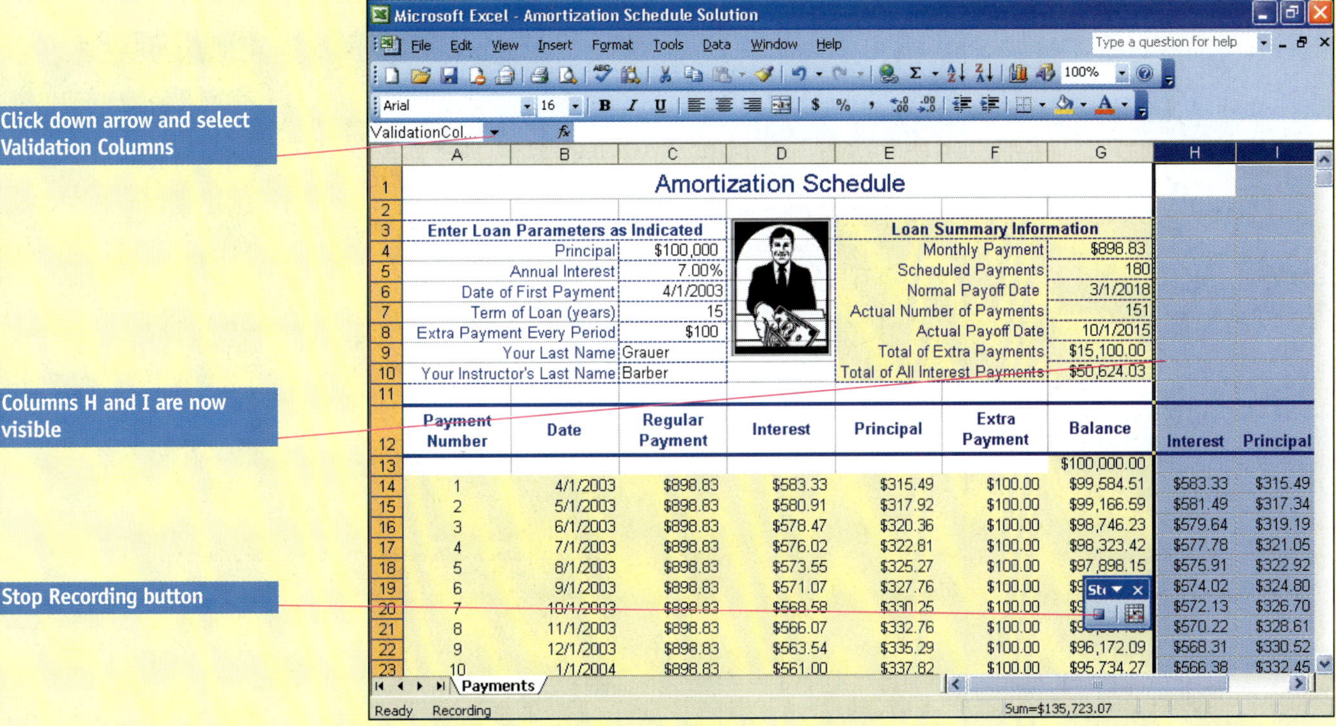

(b) Record the Display Validation Columns Macro (step 2)

FIGURE 9.5 Hands-on Exercise 2 (*continued*)

INSULATE YOUR MACROS AND PROCEDURES

Excel formulas adjust automatically for the insertion or deletion of rows and columns. This is not true of macros and VBA procedures; that is, if you record a macro to go to a specific column, such as column H, then you subsequently add or remove a column, the macro will no longer work. You can prevent this from happening by defining range names within the worksheet, and referring to those range names within a macro.

Step 3: Create the Hide Validation Columns Macro

- Press **Alt+F11** to open the VBA editor. Double click **Module2**.
- You should see the DisplayValidationColumns procedure in Figure 9.5c. Modify your procedure to match our code. (The second procedure is not yet there.)
- Return to Excel. Pull down the **Tools menu**, click the **Macro command**, then click **Record New Macro** to display the Record Macro dialog box.
- Enter **HideValidationColumns** as the name of the macro. Click in the **Shortcut Key** text box and enter a **lowercase h**. Click **OK** to begin recording.
- Pull down the **Tools menu**, click **Protection**, and click **Unprotect Sheet**. Click the **down arrow** in the Name box and click **ValidationColumns** to select columns H and I. Do this even if the columns are still selected.
- Pull down the **Format menu**, click the **Column command** and click the **Hide command**. The validation columns should no longer be visible.
- Pull down the **Tools menu**, click **Protection**, click **Protect Sheet**, then click **OK**. Click the **Stop Recording button** to complete the macro. Save the workbook.
- Now test the two macros by using the keyboard shortcuts. Press **Ctrl+d** to display the columns. Press **Ctrl+h** to hide the columns.

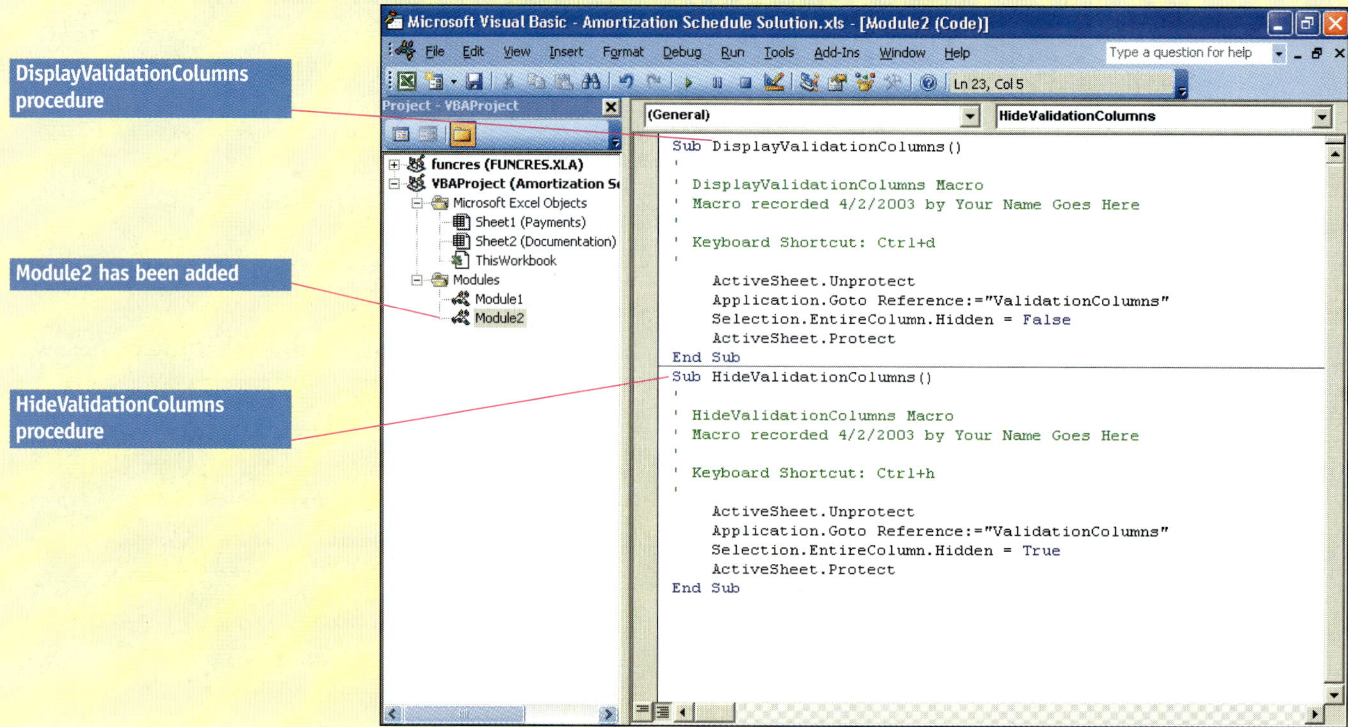

(c) Create the Hide Validation Columns Macro (step 3)

FIGURE 9.5 Hands-on Exercise 2 (*continued*)

WHICH MODULE IS IT IN?

All macros that are recorded within the same Excel session will be stored in the same module. If you close the workbook, however, then subsequently reopen it, Excel will store subsequent macros in a new module. It really doesn't matter where (in which module) the macros are stored. You can, however, move a macro from one module to another for organizational purposes.

Step 4: Complete the Display Validation Columns Procedure

- Press **Alt+F11** to return to the VBA editor as shown in Figure 9.5d.
- Think for a minute about what you are doing. You know that the basic macro works, but you want to enhance the macro to include error checking and meaningful messages to the user.
- Click at the end of the first statement, ActiveSheet.Unprotect, in the first procedure, and press the **Enter key**. Add the first line of the **If statement**, indent the next two existing lines, then click after the keyword False and press **Enter** twice.
- Enter the first **MsgBox statement**, continuing from one line to the next as shown in Figure 9.5d. Type **Else**, press **Enter**, then complete the second **MsgBox statement**. Complete the If statement by adding the **End If** delimiter.
- Check that your code matches Figure 9.5d. Click the **Save button**.
- Return to the Excel worksheet to test the procedure. Delete one input parameter, then press **Ctrl+d** to (attempt) to display the validation columns.
- You should see the message box indicating that the validation is meaningless because the loan parameters are not entered. If the procedure does not work as intended, press **Alt+F11** to return to the VBA editor and make corrections.

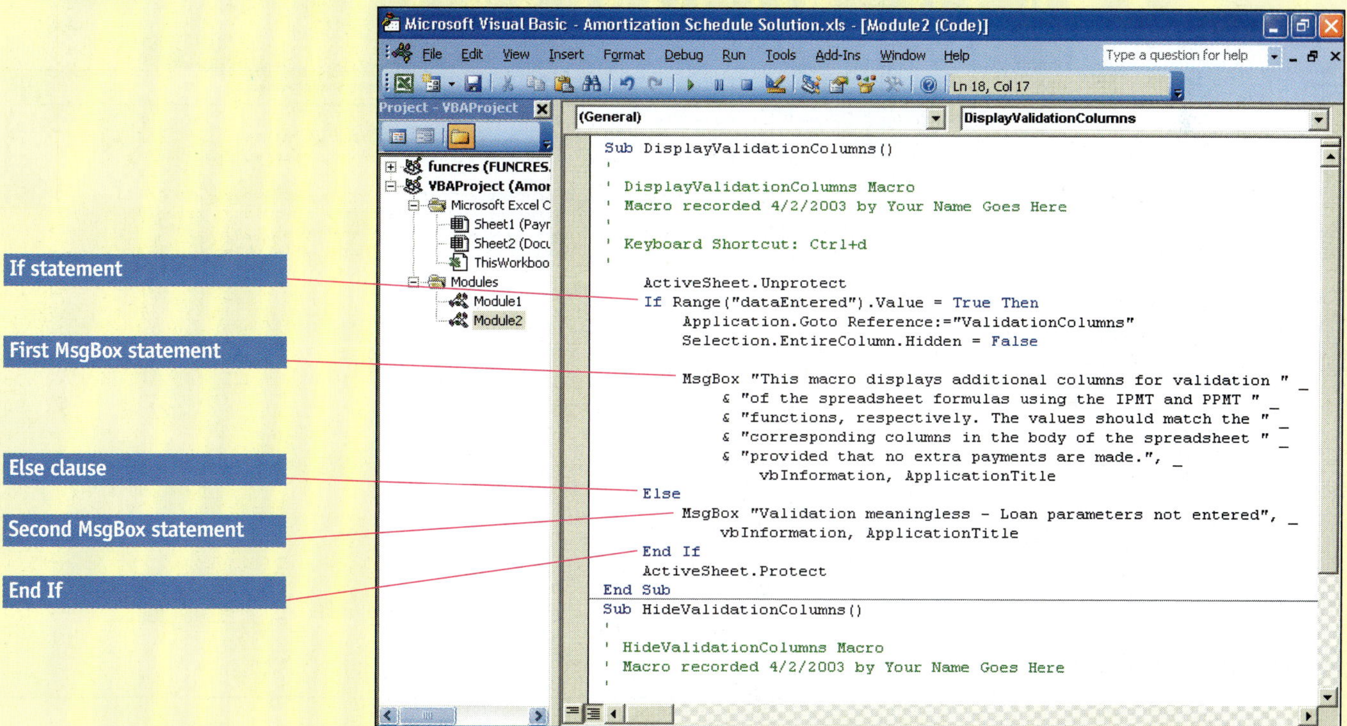

(d) Complete the Display Validation Columns Procedure (step 4)

FIGURE 9.5 Hands-on Exercise 2 (*continued*)

THE UNDERSCORE AND THE AMPERSAND

A VBA Statement is continued from one line to the next by typing an underscore at the end of the line to be continued. You may not, however, break a line in the middle of a literal. Hence, several lines within the MsgBox statement end with a closing quotation mark, followed by a space and the underscore. Each continued line starts with an ampersand to indicated continuation (concatenation) of the previous literal, followed by the remainder of the literal in quotation marks.

Step 5: Create the Enable Single Payments Procedure

- The procedure we are about to create enables the user to enter single payments within the extra payments columns. Return to the VBA editor. Press **Ctrl+End** to move to the end of the current module.
- Pull down the **Insert menu** and click the **Procedure command** to display the Add Procedure dialog box. Enter **EnableSinglePayments** (spaces are not allowed) as the procedure name. Select option buttons for **Sub** and **Public**. Click **OK**.
- The Sub and End Sub statements are created automatically. Click the **Procedure View button** to view only this procedure. Complete the procedure as shown in Figure 9.5e. You are using the **MsgBox function**, which means that:
  - The parameters of the MsgBox function are enclosed in parentheses. (Parentheses are not used when MsgBox is used as a statement.)
  - The MsgBox function returns a value, in this case an indication of which button the user clicked, Yes or No.
  - The value returned by the MsgBox function is compared to the VBA intrinsic constant vbYes.
- Click the **Save button**. Click the **Excel button** to test the procedure.

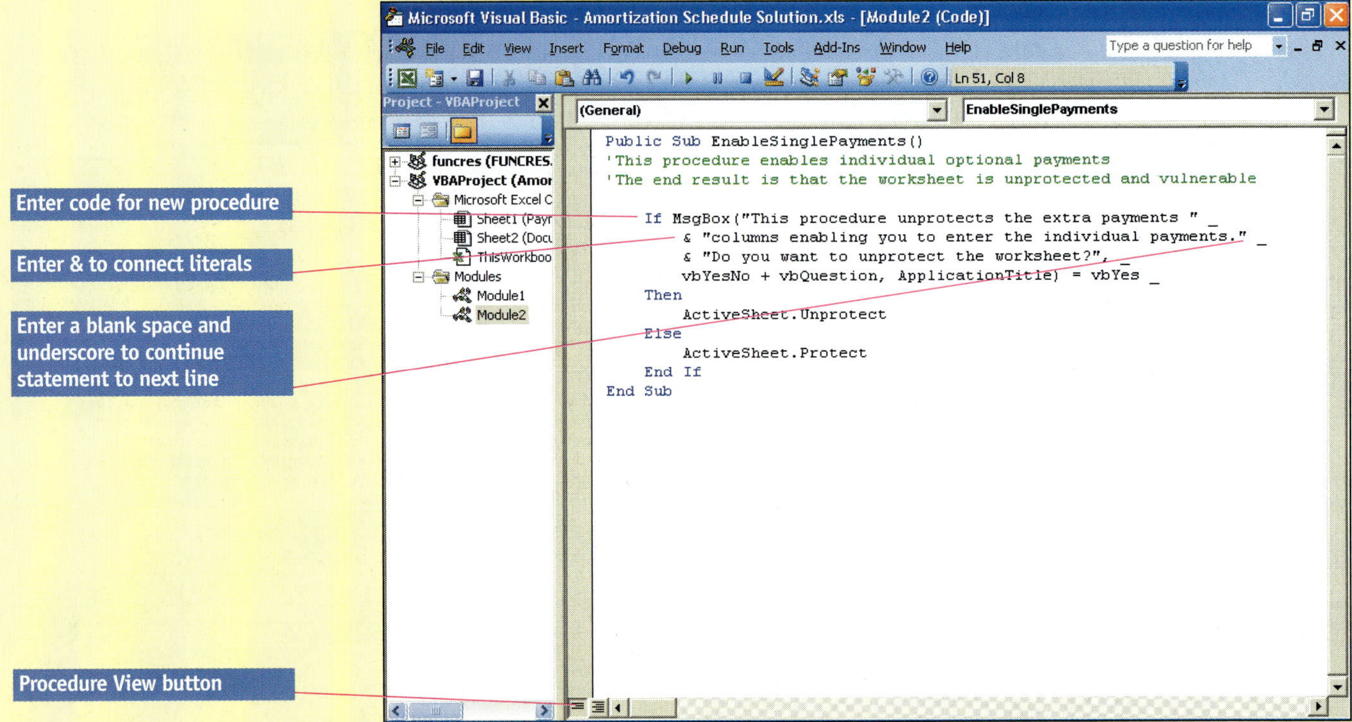

(e) Create the Enable Single Payments Procedure (step 5)

FIGURE 9.5 Hands-on Exercise 2 (*continued*)

USE WHAT YOU KNOW

Use the techniques acquired from other Office applications to facilitate editing within the VBA window. Press the Ins key to toggle between the insert and overtype modes as you modify the statements within a VBA procedure. You can also cut, copy, and paste statements (or parts of statements) within a procedure and from one procedure to another. You can access these commands via buttons on the Standard toolbar, as commands in the Edit menu, or by using the appropriate keyboard shortcuts.

Step 6: Test the Procedure

- You should be back in Excel. Delete the entry in **cell C8**. Pull down the **Tools menu**, click **Macro**, then click **Macros** to display the Macro dialog box.
- Double click the **EnableSinglePayments macro** that was just created. You should see the message box in Figure 9.5f. Click **No**.
- Click anywhere in **column F**, the column that contains the optional extra payments, and try to enter a value. You should see a message indicating that the cell is protected and that you cannot alter its contents. Click **OK** when you have read this message.
- Rerun the **EnableSinglePayments macro**, but this time click **Yes**, indicating that you want to enter extra payments. This will unprotect the worksheet.
- Return to any cell in column F and enter **$1000** as an optional payment for that month. This time Excel accepts the payment. Click the **Undo button** to cancel the extra payment.
- If the procedure does not function as intended, return to the Visual Basic editor and correct it. Save the workbook.

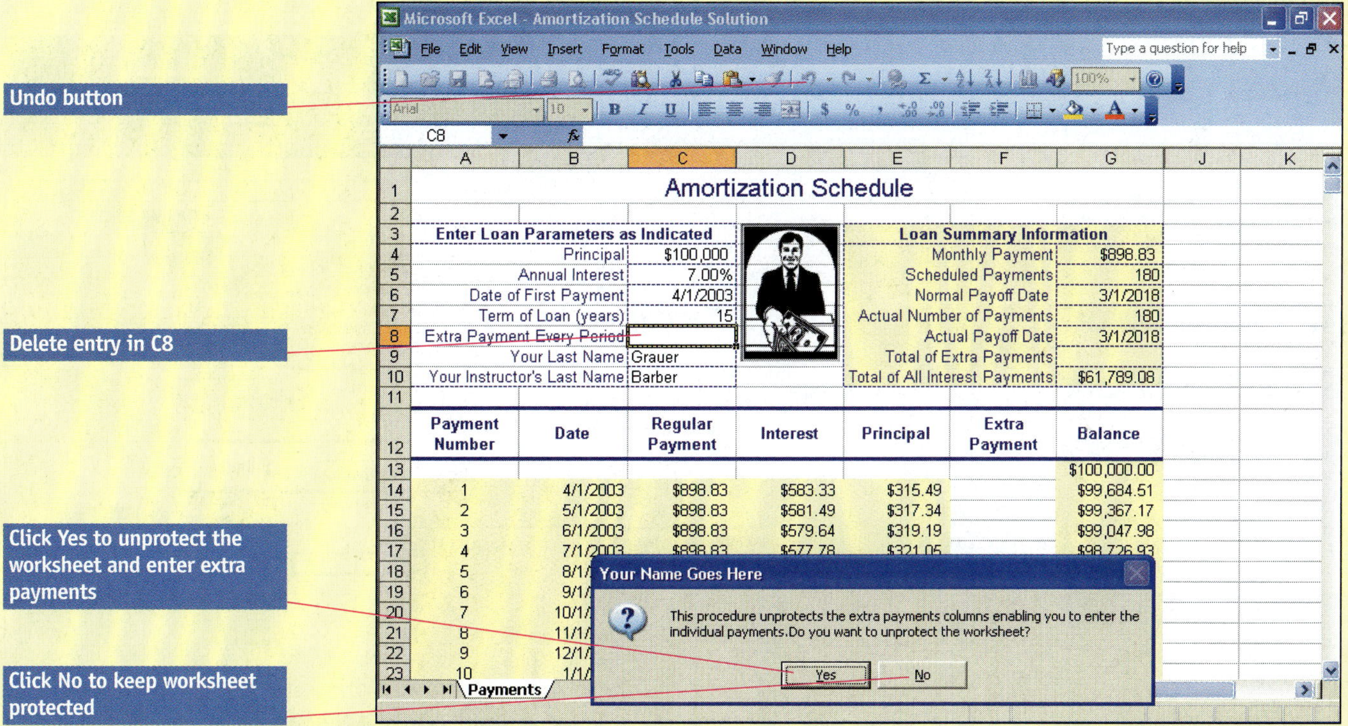

(f) Test the Procedure (step 6)

FIGURE 9.5 Hands-on Exercise 2 (*continued*)

ADD A MACRO SHORTCUT

You can add and/or modify the shortcut key associated with a macro at any time. Pull down the Tools menu, click the Macro command, then click Macros to display the Macro dialog box. Select the desired macro and click the Options button to display the Macro Options dialog box where you assign a shortcut. Type a lowercase letter to create a shortcut with just the Ctrl key such as Ctrl+e. Enter an uppercase letter to create a shortcut using the Ctrl and Shift keys such as Ctrl+Shift+E.

Step 7: Create a Custom Toolbar

- Pull down the **View menu**, click the **Toolbars command**, then click **Customize** to display the Customize dialog box. Click the **Toolbars tab**, then click the **New button** to create a new toolbar.
- Type **Amortization Schedule** as the toolbar name and click **OK**. You will see a floating toolbar as shown in Figure 9.5g. Click the **Commands tab** within the Custom dialog box, then scroll until you can select the **Macros category**.
- Click and drag the **Custom button** (with the smiley face image) to the newly created toolbar. Release the mouse. The smiley face appears on the toolbar. Click (select) the **smiley face button**, then click the **Modify Selection button** in the Customize dialog box.
- Click the **Name command** within the menu options, select the existing text, and type **Display Validation Columns** as the name of the button.
- Click the **Change Button Image command**. Choose an icon. We selected the **eye**.
- Click the **Modify Selection button**, click **Assign macro** and choose the **DisplayValidationColumns macro**. Click **OK**. Close the dialog box. Save the workbook.

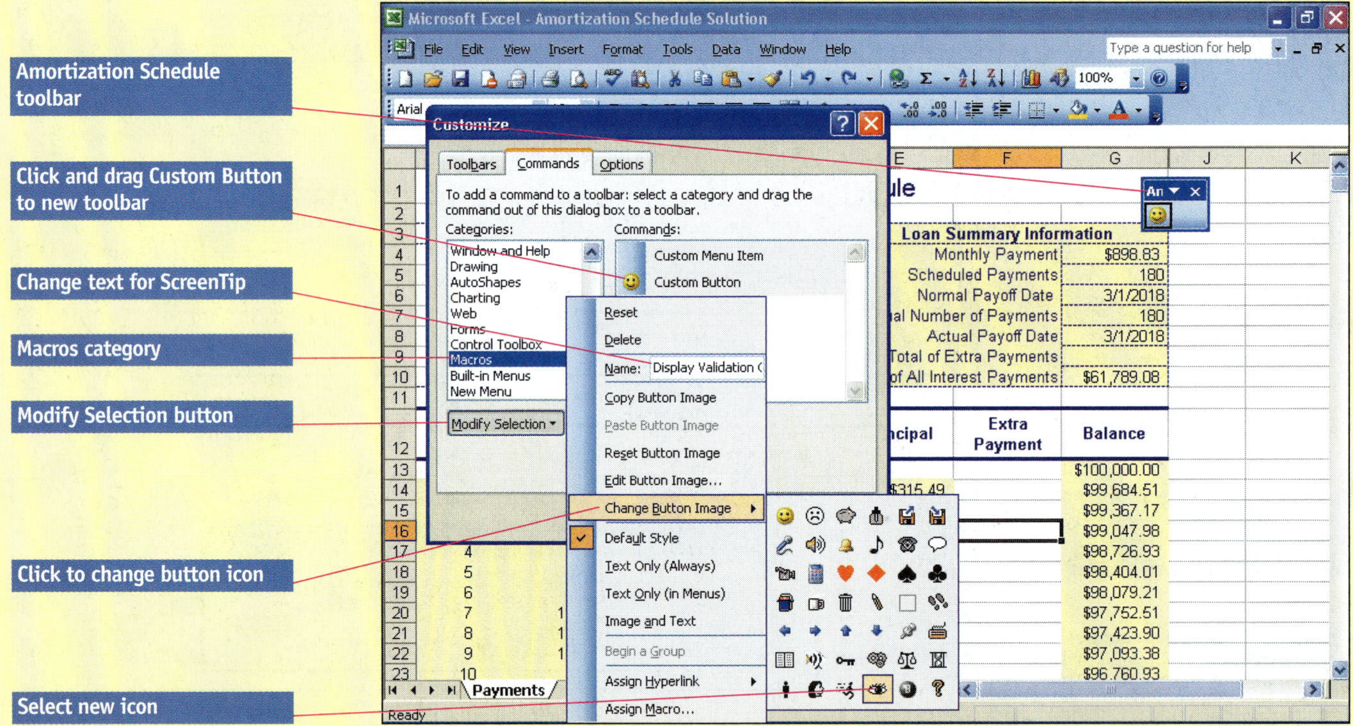

(g) Create a Custom Toolbar (step 7)

FIGURE 9.5 Hands-on Exercise 2 (*continued*)

MOVING AND/OR REMOVING A BUTTON

You can change the position of any button on a custom toolbar and/or remove the button altogether. Pull down the View menu, click Toolbars, then click the Customize command to display the Customize dialog box. To change the position of a button, select the button, then drag it to its new position. To remove the button, just drag the button off the toolbar. The same techniques apply to any standard toolbar within Microsoft Office.

Step 8: Test the Toolbar Button

- Point to the newly created toolbar button. You should see the name (ScreenTip) you entered, just as you would with any other toolbar button.
- Click the button to display the validation columns. Click **OK** after you have read the message.
- If necessary, pull down the **View menu**, click **Toolbars**, and click the **Customize command** to correct any element (the description, image, or macro) that did not work correctly.
- Add buttons for the **HideValidationColumns** and **EnableSinglePayments** macros. We used the runner and piggy bank icons, respectively.
- Test these buttons as shown in Figure 9.5h after they have been created. Make corrections as necessary.
- Save the workbook.

Add buttons for Hide Validation Columns and Enable Single Payments

Message box displayed when macro is tested (Display Validation Columns)

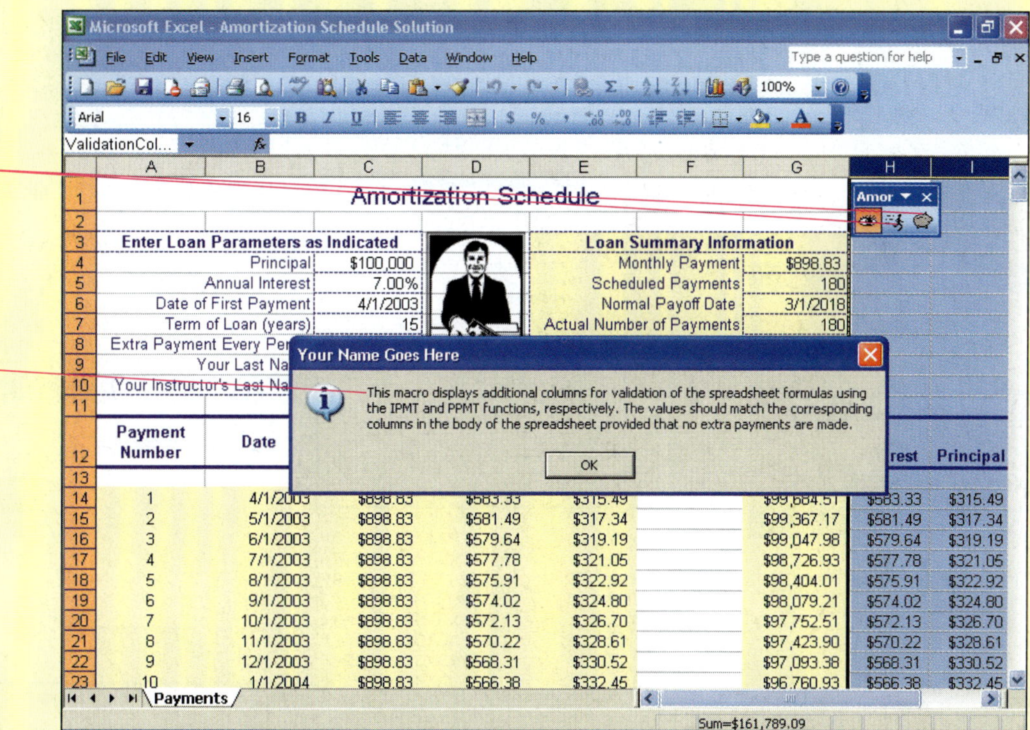

(h) Test the Toolbar Button (step 8)

FIGURE 9.5 Hands-on Exercise 2 (*continued*)

MODIFY THE BUTTON'S IMAGE

Excel provides only a limited number of images from which to choose, so it is convenient to be able to modify the images that are provided. Pull down the View menu, click Toolbars, click Customize to display the Customize dialog box, and click the Commands tab. Select the toolbar button, click Modify Selection, then click the Edit Button Image command to display the Button editor. Each button consists of 256 squares in a 16 by 16 grid. You can change the color of any square by selecting a new color, then clicking the appropriate square within the grid. You can also erase any square by double clicking the square. Click OK.

Step 9: Attach the Toolbar

- *This step is very important.* You must attach the custom toolbar to your workbook, so that it (the toolbar) will travel with the workbook if you copy the file and try to use it on a different computer.
- Pull down the **View menu**, click **Toolbars**, and click the **Customize command** to display the Customize dialog box. Click the **Toolbars tab**, then click the **Attach button** to display the Attach Toolbars dialog box in Figure 9.5i.
- Select the Amortization Schedule toolbar in the left pane, then click the **Copy button** to copy the custom toolbar to this workbook. (The custom toolbar resides in a special Excel folder that is stored on your computer and not in the workbook. Only after you attach the toolbar will it travel with the workbook.) Click **OK**. Click **Close**.
- Close the Amortization Schedule toolbar. Save the workbook. Exit Excel if you do not want to continue with the next exercise at this time.

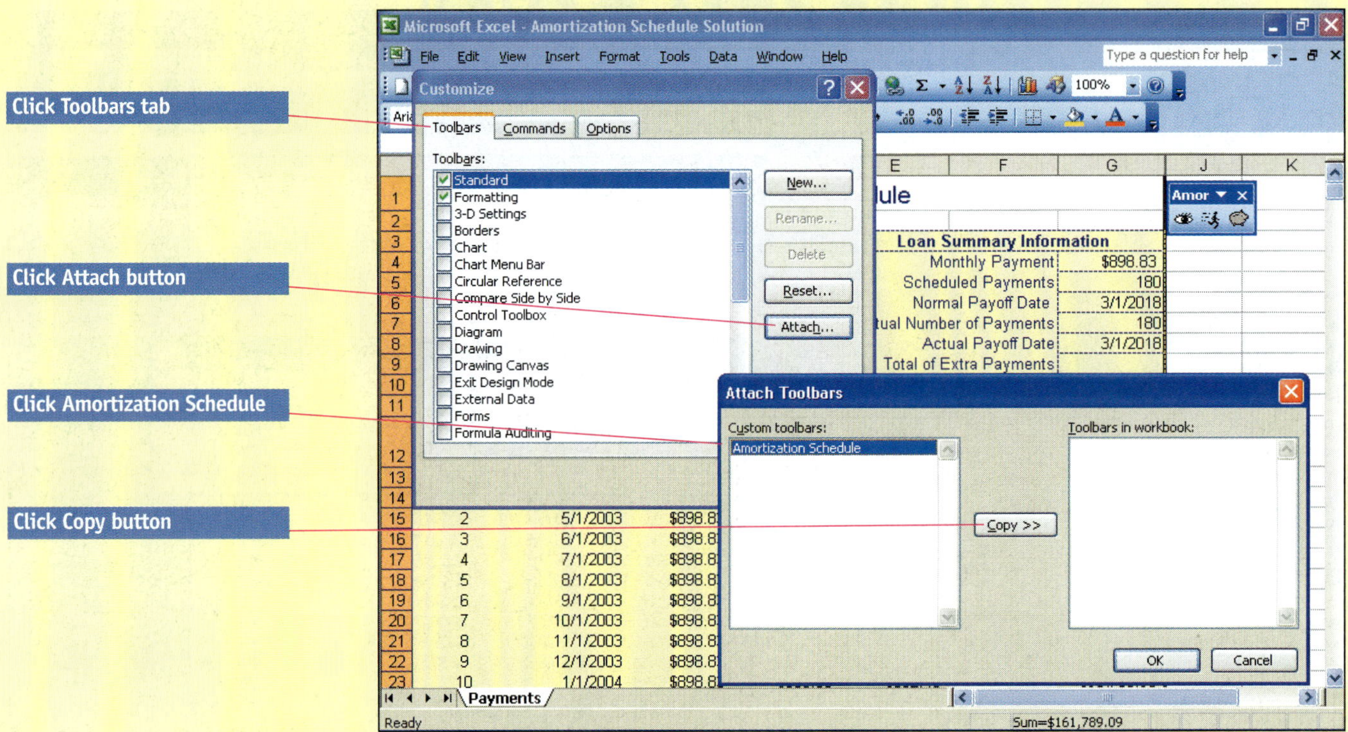

(i) Attach the Toolbar (step 9)

FIGURE 9.5 Hands-on Exercise 2 (*continued*)

ATTACHING TOOLBARS

The copy of the toolbar that is stored in a workbook reflects its contents at the time you attach the toolbar. Thus, if you subsequently modify a toolbar after attaching it, the changes are not automatically stored within the workbook. Pull down the View menu, click Toolbars, click Customize, click the Toolbars tab, then click the Attach button. Select the old toolbar in the Toolbars in workbook area at the right of the Attach Toolbar dialog box. Click the Delete button to delete the old toolbar. Select the new toolbar at the left of the dialog box, then click the Copy command to attach the new version. Click OK and save the workbook.

EVENT PROCEDURES

VBA has two types of procedures. There are ***general procedures*** such as those in the preceding exercise that are executed explicitly by the user whenever the user chooses. VBA also recognizes ***event procedures*** that are executed automatically when a specified event occurs. An ***event*** is defined as any action that is recognized by an application. Opening, closing, or printing a workbook is an event, as is clicking a button on a ***custom toolbar***. (The Excel object model describes the specific events that are recognized by VBA.)

You can enhance an Excel application by deciding which events are significant, and what is to happen when those events occur. Then you develop the appropriate event procedures to execute automatically in conjunction with those events. This is in contrast to a traditional program that is executed sequentially, beginning with the first line of code and continuing in order through the remainder of the program. It is the program, not the user, that determines the order in which the statements are executed. VBA, on the other hand, is event-driven, meaning that the order in which the procedures are executed depends on the events that occur. It is the user, rather than the program, that determines which events occur, and consequently which procedures are executed.

The ***Open workbook event procedure*** is common to many applications. It accomplishes a variety of tasks such as the display of a custom toolbar or splash screen, checking for special conditions to alert the user, and/or performing other tasks for the developer. The ***Before Close event procedure*** is also common and typically hides the custom toolbar and displays a closing message to the user, such as a reminder to back up the system. It may also check for special conditions and/or perform one or more tasks for the developer.

Figures 9.6a and 9.6b display the results of these two event procedures for the Amortization Schedule workbook. The Open workbook event procedure in Figure 9.6a displays the custom toolbar and a splash screen. A ***splash screen*** is a simple form that appears for a brief period of time to identify an application, and then it disappears from view. (The form itself is created in the VBA editor as described in the next section.) The Open workbook event procedure may also include additional code to accomplish other tasks, but you may not be aware of the additional actions by merely looking at the worksheet.

Figure 9.6b displays the results of the Before Close event procedure. The custom toolbar has been hidden from view and a message is displayed to the user. The message box is different from the splash screen and requires the user to click OK to close the dialog box. Again, there may be additional code within the Before Close event procedure, the effects of which are not visible from this figure.

Remember too that an event procedure is executed regardless of how the event is triggered. Think about the various ways in which you close a workbook. You may pull down the File menu and click the Close command, or you can click the Close button in the application window, or you can use the Ctrl+F4 keyboard shortcut. All of these commands close the active workbook and in turn will trigger the Before Close event procedure.

SIGN YOUR DOCUMENTS

Excel displays a security warning prior to opening any Excel workbook that contains a VBA procedure. You can, however, display a different dialog box that identifies the publisher of the workbook and that the workbook is to be trusted as a safe source. This is accomplished by applying a digital signature, an electronic, encryption-based stamp of authentication, which confirms the origin of a document, and further that the document has not been altered since it was last saved by the signer. (See step 9 in Hands-on Exercise 3.)

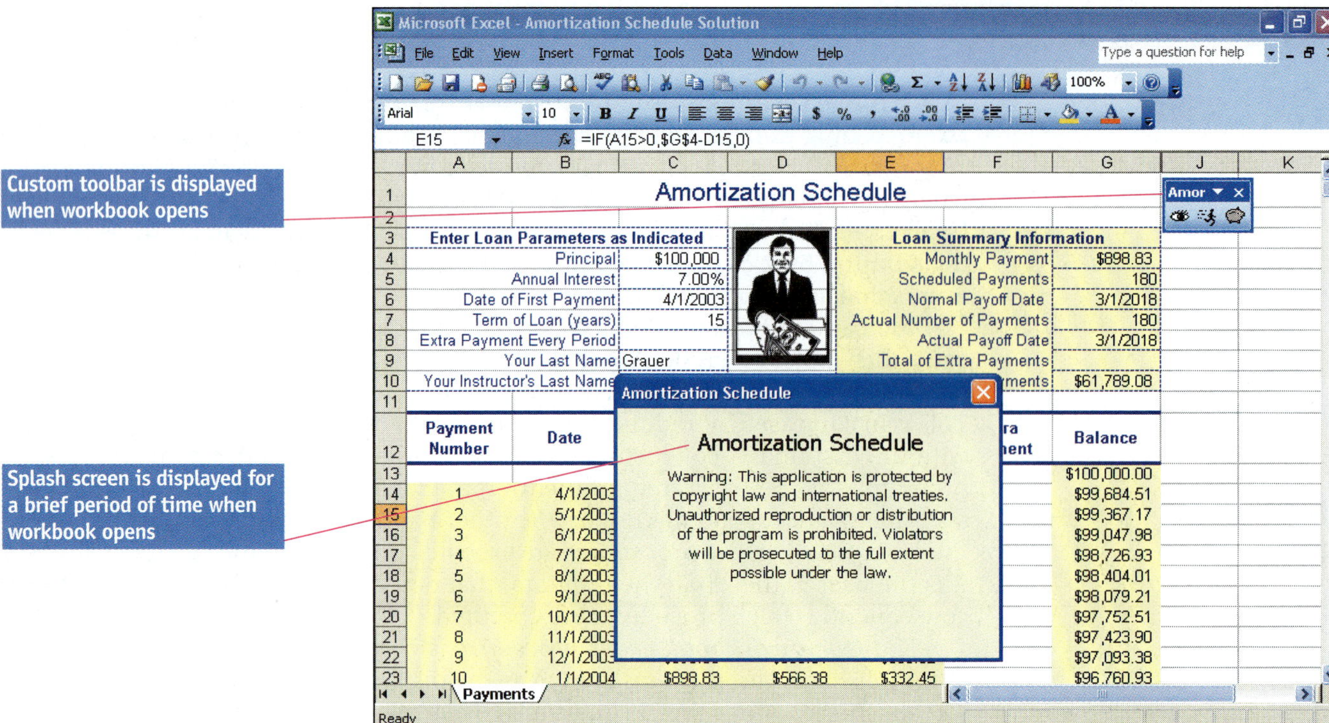

(a) The Open Workbook Event Procedure

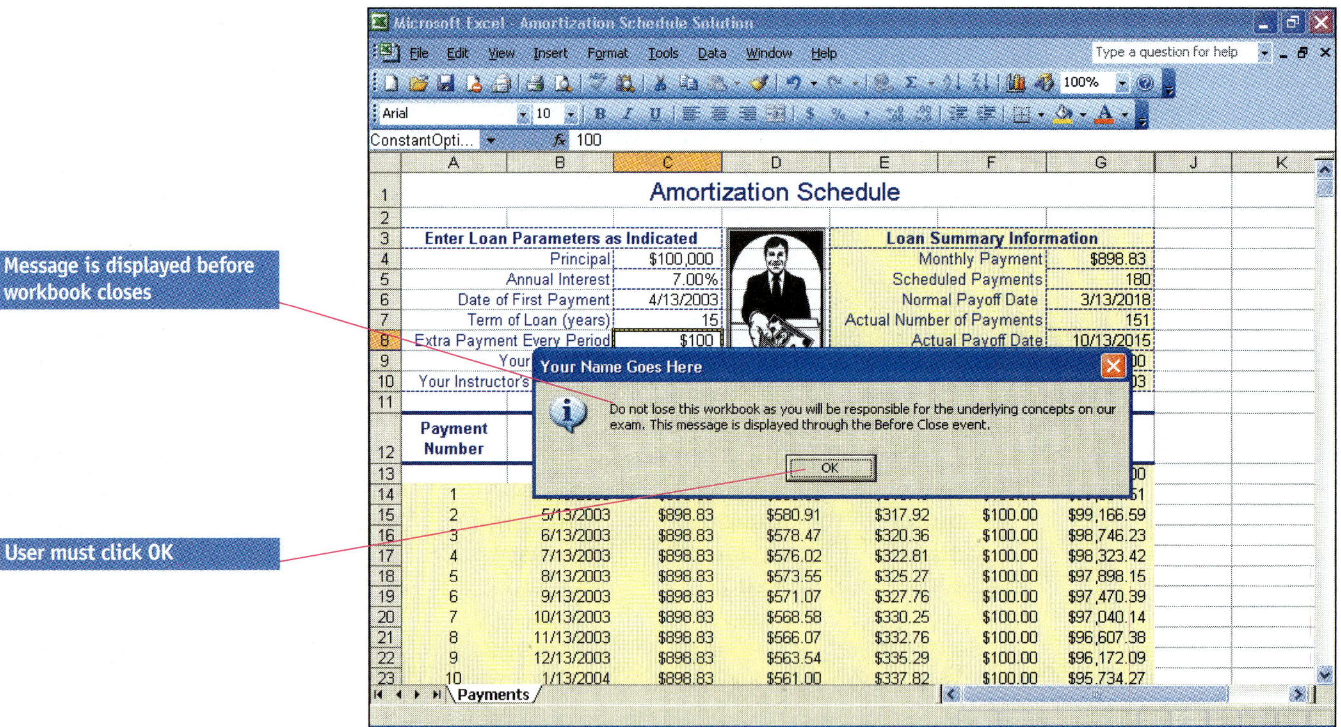

(b) The Before Close Event Procedure

FIGURE 9.6 Event Procedures

A ***user form*** is typically created to facilitate data entry and is most commonly associated with Microsoft Access. A user form can also be created in Excel to enter data in a worksheet and/or to display a splash screen, which in turn requires several steps. First, you create the user form. Next, you develop the procedure(s) to load (display) the form. And finally, you create the procedure to unload (hide) the form.

Figure 9.7 depicts the creation of a splash screen for the Amortization Schedule workbook. The Project Explorer window in the upper-left pane contains a Forms folder, which contains a single object, UserForm1. The form itself appears in Design view in the upper-right pane. You start with a blank form, then use the controls on the Toolbox to create the form. Click the appropriate tool (e.g., the "A" or label tool), then click and drag on the form to create the corresponding control. Once the label has been created, you click within the control and enter the desired text.

Every object (control) on a form as well as the form itself has a distinct set of properties (attributes) that are displayed and modified in the ***Properties window*** in the lower-left portion of the screen. You select the object on the form, and then you change the desired property, such as the font style, color, or size.

Once the form has been created, you have to develop the procedure to display the form, and another procedure to hide the form after it has been on the screen for the specified amount of time. The form is displayed by a single line of code, UserForm1.Show, which appears in the Open workbook event procedure. (The event procedure is not visible in Figure 9.7.)

The ***UserForm Activate event procedure*** in the lower-right portion of Figure 9.7 executes automatically when the form is opened. The ***OnTime method*** sets the amount of time the form is visible by adding five seconds to the Now function that contains the current time. The OnTime method then calls a third procedure, CloseScreen, which contains a single statement to unload (hide) the form. It's easier than it sounds as you will see in our next hands-on exercise.

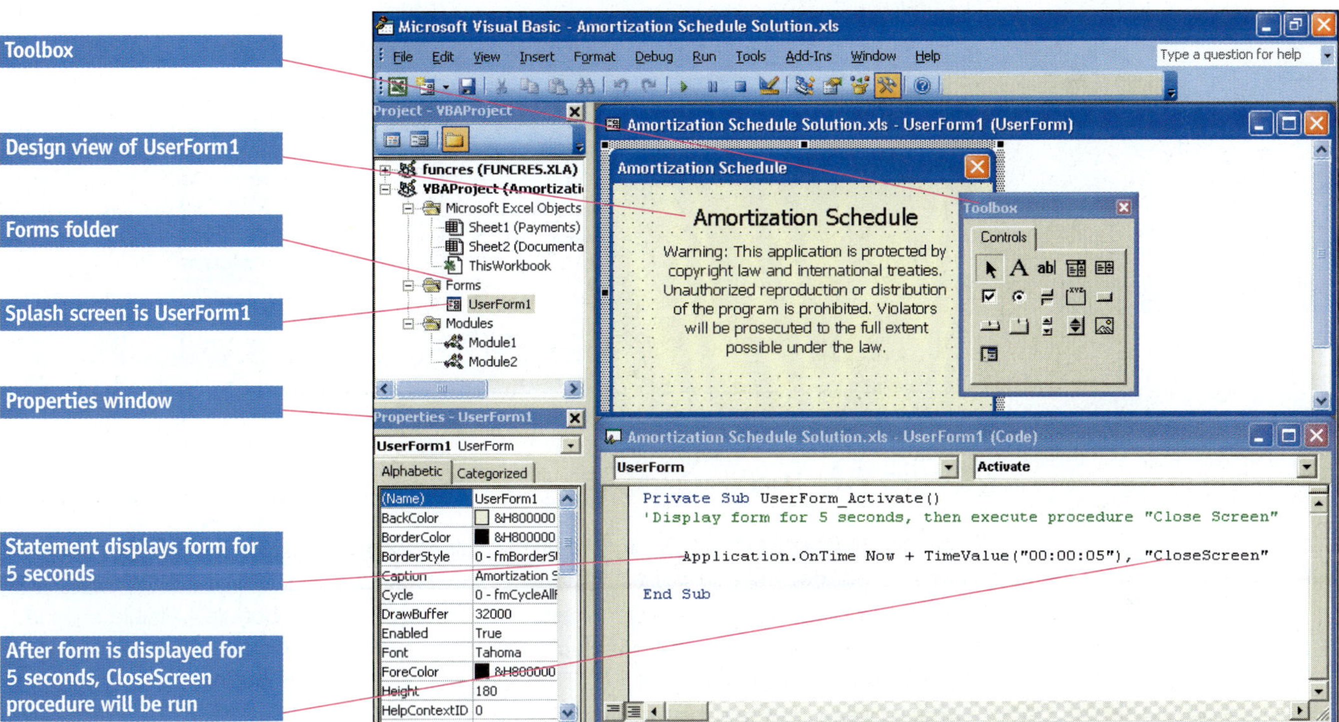

FIGURE 9.7 Creating a User Form

hands-on exercise

3 Event Procedures

Objective To create an Open workbook event procedure that displays a splash screen and custom toolbar; to create a Before Close event procedure to close the custom toolbar and display a message to the user. Use Figure 9.8 as a guide.

Step 1: Start the Macro Recorder

- Start Excel. Open the **Amortization Schedule Solution** workbook from the previous exercise. Click the button to **Enable macros.**
- Pull down the **Tools menu**, click the **Macro command**, then click **Record New Macro** to display the Record Macro dialog box. You can accept the default name (such as Macro1), since we are just using the recorder to obtain the correct VBA syntax. Click **OK** to begin recording the macro.
- Pull down the **View menu**, click the **Toolbars command**, then click the **Amortization Schedule toolbar** as shown in Figure 9.8a.
- Click the **Stop Recording button.** (If you do not see the button, pull down the **Tools menu**, click the **Macro command**, and then click **Stop Recording.**)

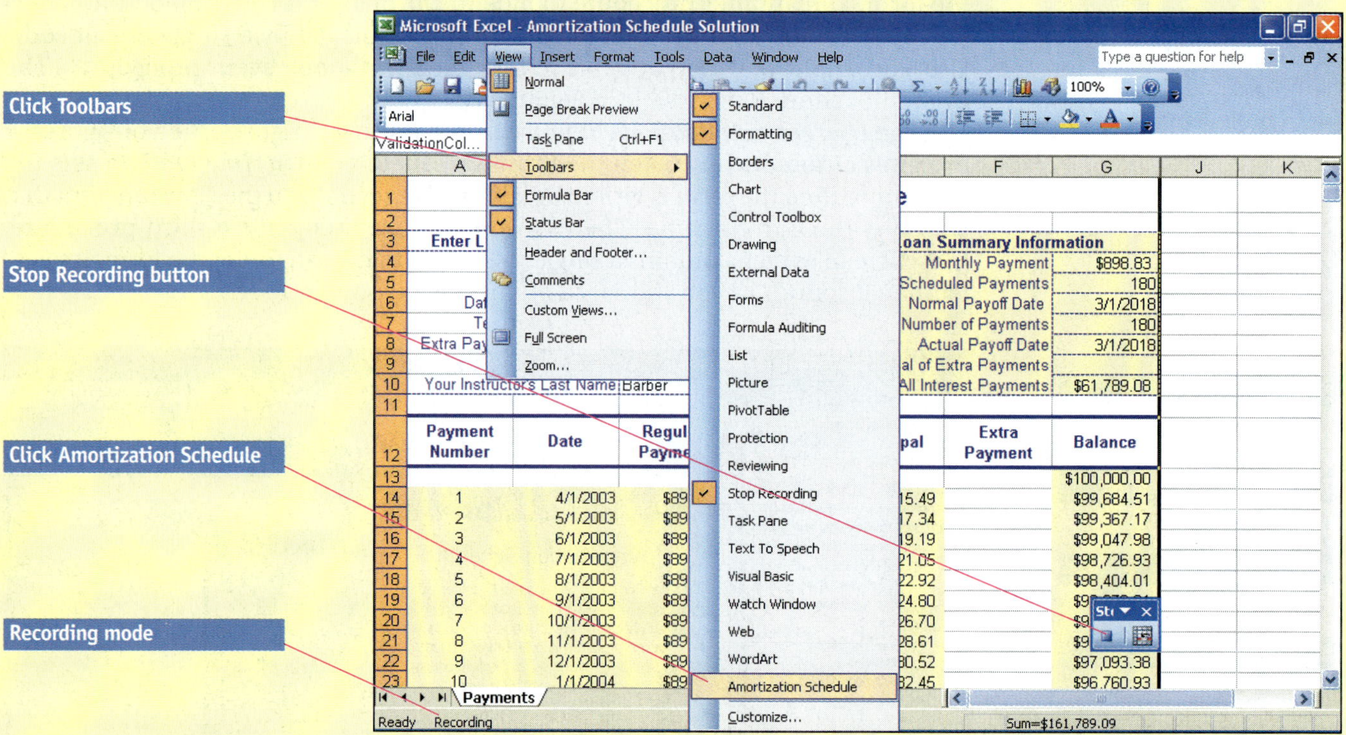

(a) Start the Macro Recorder (step 1)

FIGURE 9.8 Hands-on Exercise 3

WRITE VBA THE EASY WAY

The statement, Application.CommandBars("Amortization Schedule").Visible = True, displays the Amortization Schedule toolbar. It's easy to understand the statement, but it is not so easy to write it. The good news is you do not have to. Start the macro recorder and create a macro to display the toolbar. Stop the recorder, open the VBA editor, then use the generated code as the basis of a more sophisticated VBA procedure.

Step 2: Create the Open Workbook Event Procedure

- Press **Alt+F11** to open the VBA editor. Open the **Modules folder**, then select the newest module that contains the macro you just recorded.
- You should see a procedure called Macro1 that contains a single statement to display the Amortization Schedule toolbar. Select that statement, then click the **Copy button** on the Standard toolbar.
- Double click **ThisWorkbook** within the Project Explorer to display the code for the event procedures within the workbook. (There are none so far.)
- Click the **down arrow** in the Object list box (the leftmost list box) to select **Workbook**. The **Open workbook event procedure** is created automatically. The insertion point appears below the procedure header.
- Press the **Tab key** or **space bar** to indent the code, then click the **Paste button** (or use the **Ctrl+V** keyboard shortcut) to paste the VBA statement to display the Amortization schedule toolbar.
- Add the additional statements and comments as shown in Figure 9.8b. Click the **Save button** to save the event procedures within the workbook.

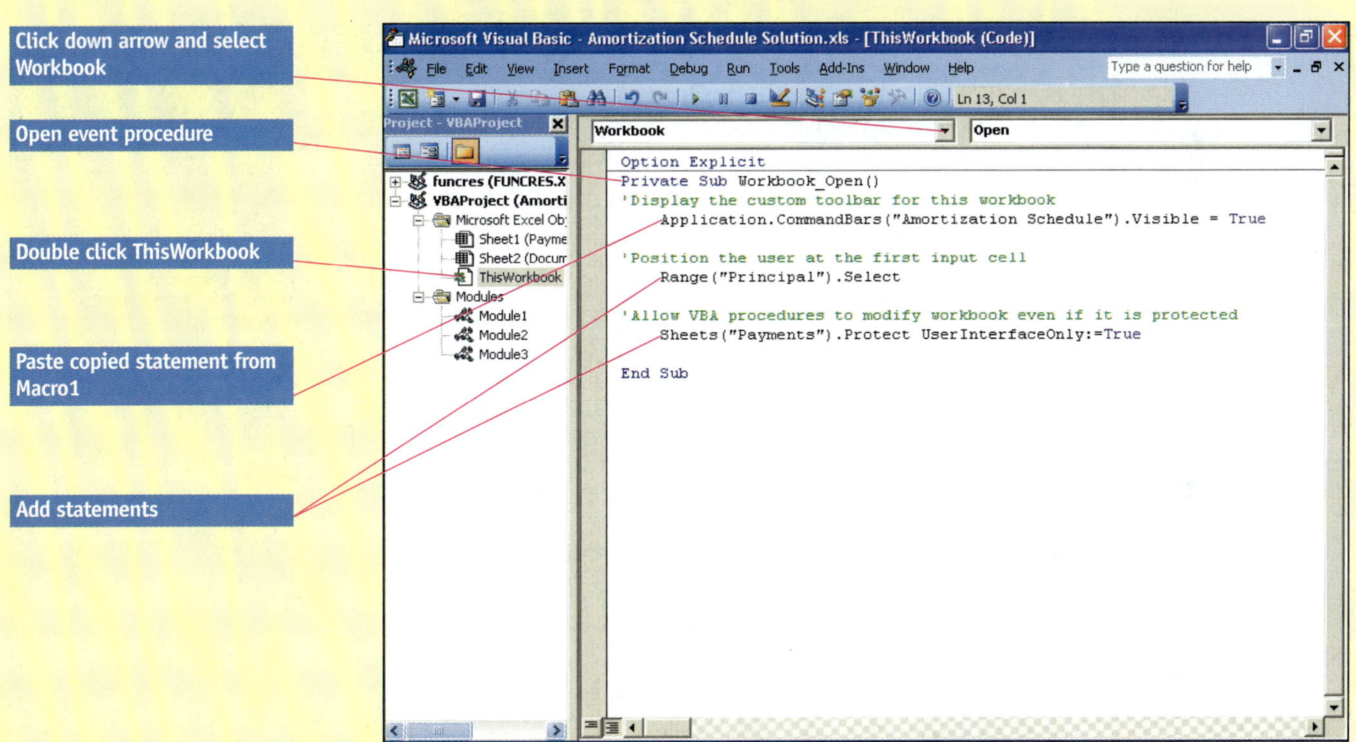

(b) Create the Open Workbook Event Procedure (step 2)

FIGURE 9.8 Hands-on Exercise 3 (*continued*)

PROTECT USER INTERFACE ONLY

A worksheet is protected to prevent the end user from accidentally (or otherwise) altering or deleting the formulas in the worksheet. The developer, however, should be able to modify the worksheet without having to protect and unprotect the worksheet within individual procedures. This is accomplished by setting the UserInterfaceOnly property. All VBA procedures will be able to modify the worksheet. The user, however, will be prevented from doing so when protection is in effect.

Step 3: Create the Before Close Event Procedure

- Click the **down arrow** in the Procedure list box (at the top of the right side of the Code window), then scroll until you can select the **Before Close event**. The Before Close event procedure is created automatically as shown in Figure 9.8c.
- Enter the statement and associated comment to hide the Amortization Schedule toolbar. You can type the statement directly, or you can copy the existing statement from the Open workbook event procedure and change the **Visible property** to **False**.
- Create the **MsgBox statement** that will be displayed prior to the workbook closing. The VBA syntax requires the underscore character when the MsgBox statement is continued from one line to the next. The ampersand is used to concatenate (join together) the various literals within the statement.
- Click the **Save button**. (You can remove the module that contains the Macro1 "dummy" procedure. Right click the module, click **Remove Module3**, then click **No** when asked to export the module. This macro was created only to obtain the basic VBA syntax for the event procedures and has no further purpose.)

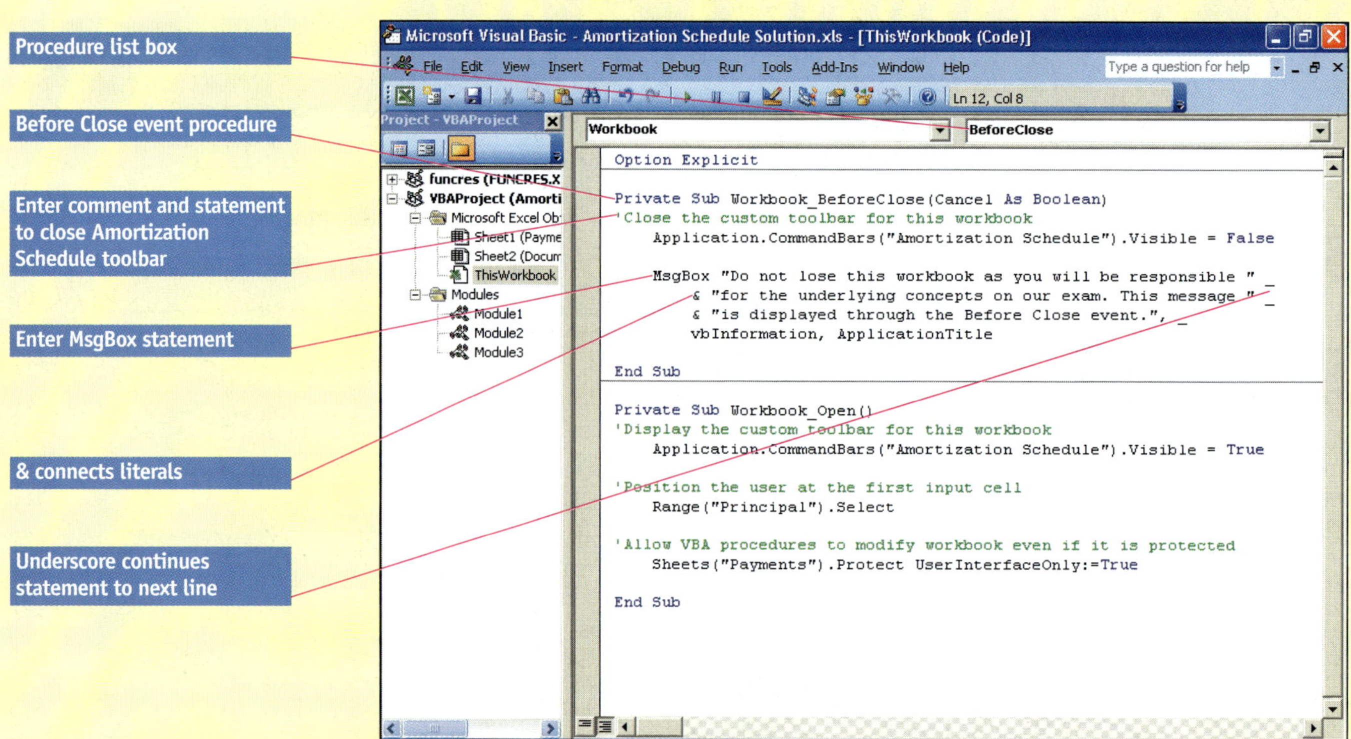

(c) Create the Before Close Event Procedure (step 3)

FIGURE 9.8 Hands-on Exercise 3 (*continued*)

EVENT PROCEDURES VERSUS GENERAL PROCEDURES

Event procedures such as opening and closing a workbook execute only when the designated event occurs. General procedures can be executed at any time. The macro recorder cannot be used with event procedures. Thus, we create a "dummy" macro to obtain the VBA statement to display a toolbar, we copy that statement to the event procedure, and then we delete the "dummy" procedure since it is no longer necessary.

Step 4: Test the Procedures

- Return to the Excel worksheet. The Amortization Schedule toolbar should still be visible on your screen (but not in our figure). If you do not see the toolbar, pull down the **View menu**, click **Toolbars** to display the list of available toolbars, then click the **Amortization Schedule toolbar**.
- Pull down the **File menu** and click the **Close command** to close the workbook but leave the Excel application open.
- The Amortization Schedule toolbar disappears, after which you should see the message box in Figure 9.8d, which is displayed by the Before Close event procedure that you just created.
- Read the statement carefully, and make a note of any potential corrections. Click **OK** after you have read the message. Click **Yes** if you are prompted to save the changes to the workbook.
- Excel should still be open. Pull down the **File menu**, click the **Open command**, then double click the **Amortization Schedule Solution** workbook.
- Click the button to **Enable macros**. The workbook opens and you should see the Amortization Schedule toolbar. Make corrections as necessary to the event procedures. Save the workbook.

Message box is displayed by Before Close event procedure

Click OK

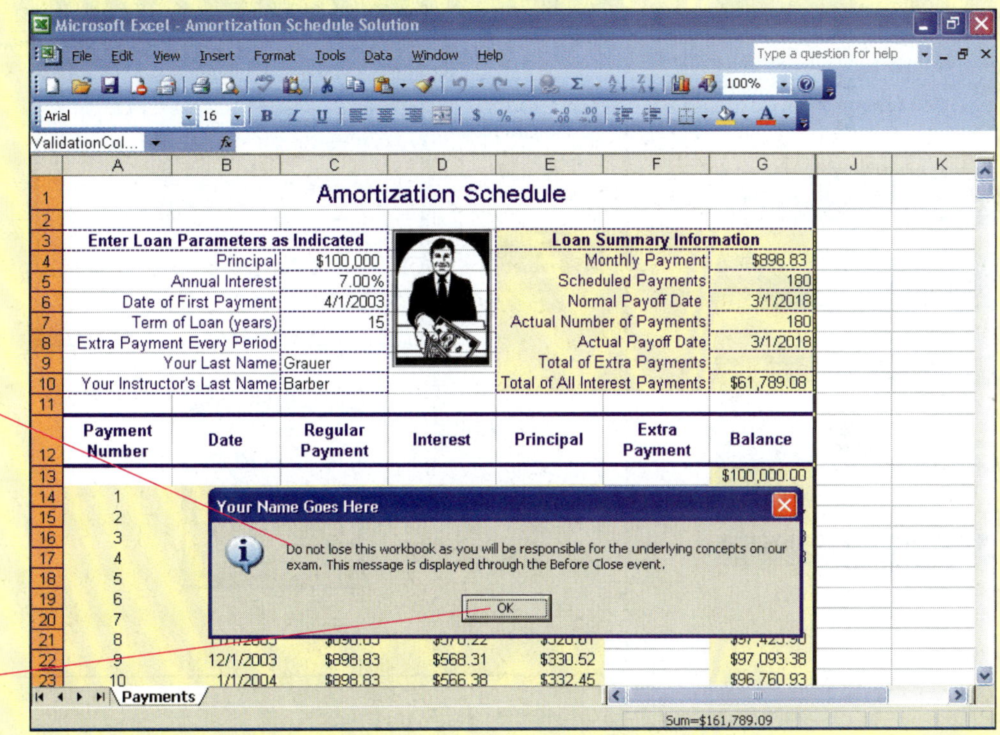

(d) Test the Procedures (step 4)

FIGURE 9.8 Hands-on Exercise 3 (*continued*)

THE WEEKDAY FUNCTION TEST FOR SPECIAL CONDITIONS

Use the WEEKDAY function within the Open and Before Close event procedures to test for special conditions. You can, for example, use the Open event to test for Monday, the first day of the business week, then display a message to check for new interest rates. In similar fashion, you can use the Before Close event to display a message on Friday, reminding the user to perform a weekly backup. See Exercise 5 at the end of the chapter.

Step 5: Create the User Form

- Press **Alt+F11** to return to the Visual Basic Editor. Pull down the **Insert menu** and click **UserForm** to create a new user form as shown in Figure 9.8e. The form is stored within the Forms folder that appears automatically within the Project Explorer.
- The toolbox should appear automatically. If not, you can click the **Toolbox button** on the Standard toolbar to toggle the toolbox on and off. Do not be concerned if the size and or position of the window for the form is different from ours.
- Click the **Label tool** (the large letter "A"), then click and drag in the form to create the first label, containing the title of the form. Click and drag within the newly created label to select the default text, **Label1**, then type **Amortization Schedule** to replace the existing text.
- Click the **Label tool** a second time. Click and drag in the form to create the second label, then enter the text shown in the figure.
- Click the **Save button** to save the form.

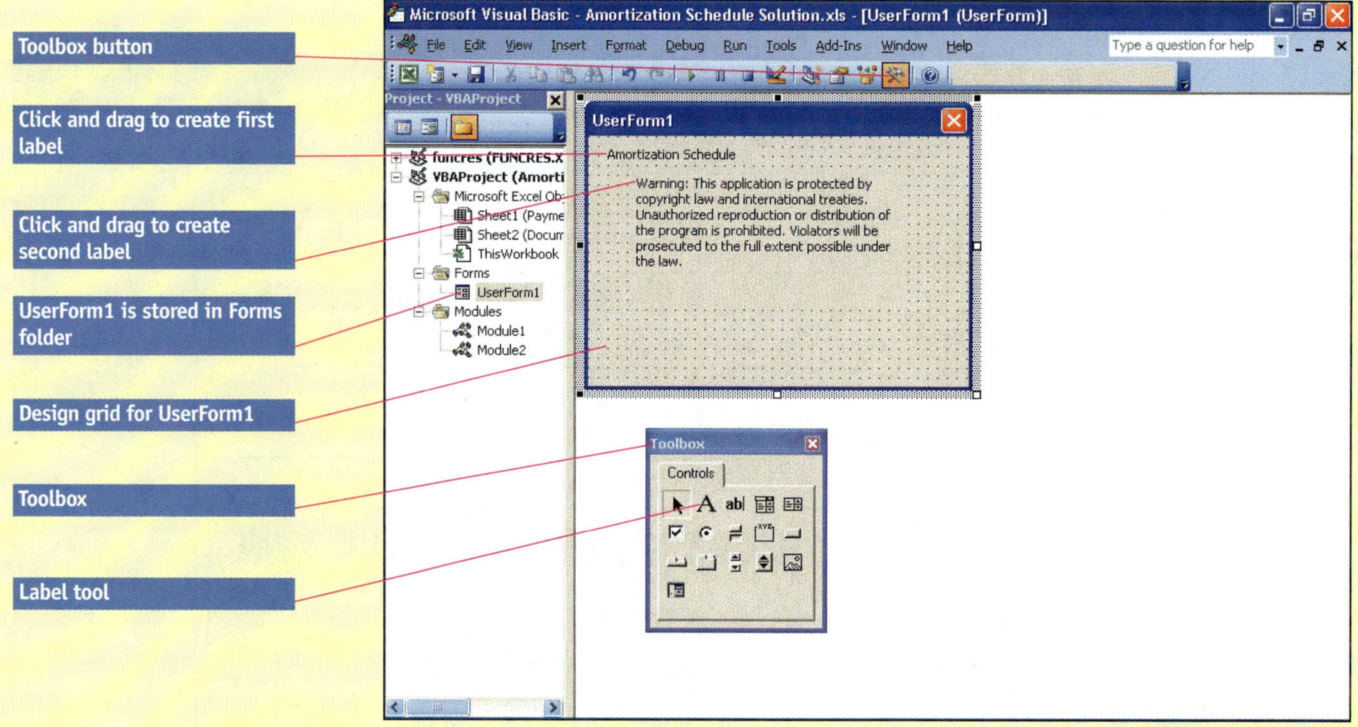

(e) Create the User Form (step 5)

FIGURE 9.8 Hands-on Exercise 3 (*continued*)

MANAGE THE OPEN WINDOWS

Multiple windows are open simultaneously within the VBA editor. Every module and form has its own window. The Project Explorer and Properties sheet are also open in separate windows. It may be helpful, therefore, to close the windows that you do not need. You can also move and size windows within the VBA editor. And finally, you can use the Window menu to tile or cascade the open windows.

Step 6: Modify the Form Properties

- Pull down the **View menu** and click the **Properties Window command** (or press the **F4 keyboard shortcut**) to open the Properties window in Figure 9.8f. Click the **Alphabetic tab** so that the properties are displayed alphabetically.
- Click the **second label** (the copyright notice), and you see its properties as shown in Figure 9.8f. Change the **Name property** to **CopyrightNotice**.
- Click in the **Back Color text box** to display a down arrow, then click the **down arrow** to display the available colors. Click the **System tab**, then choose the ToolTip color.
- Change the name and back color of the other label in similar fashion. Change the back color and caption property **(to Amortization Schedule)** of the form itself. Experiment further with the available properties (we changed the font size and alignment). Set a time limit. Five minutes is enough. Close the Properties window.
- Check that the user form is still selected in the Project Explorer. Click the background area on the form. Click the **View Code** and **View Object buttons** to switch between the code and the form, respectively. It doesn't matter if you see both windows simultaneously, or if one window overlays the other. The Code window contains only a Sub and End Sub. Save the form.

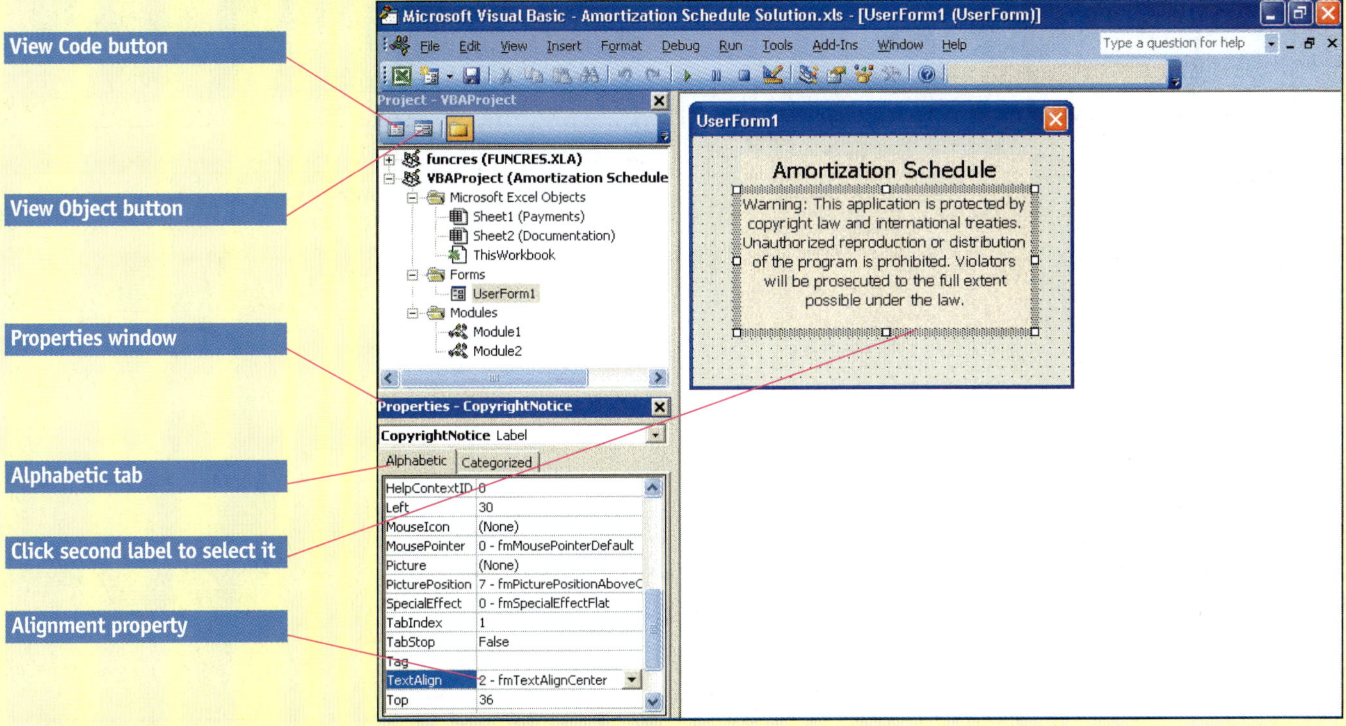

(f) Modify the Form Properties (step 6)

FIGURE 9.8 Hands-on Exercise 3 (*continued*)

THE SPLASH SCREEN

There are four distinct steps to creating a splash screen. First, you create the screen as a user form. Next, you create the Activate event procedure to display the form for a specified time. You then modify the Open workbook event procedure to load the user form when the workbook opens. And finally, you have to create a public procedure to unload the form after it has been displayed for the specified amount of time.

Step 7: Create the Code for the User Form

- Display the Code window for the user form. Click the **down arrow** in the Procedure list box (near the top of the VBA window) and select the **Activate event**. Delete the UserForm_Click procedure that is created by default.
- Enter the code for the **ActivateForm** event procedure as shown in Figure 9.8g. This procedure will display the form for five seconds once the form is activated, then it calls a second procedure to unload the form.
- It is still necessary to load the form initially within the Open workbook event procedure. Double click **ThisWorkbook** within the Project Explorer to return to the events associated with the workbook.
- Locate the **Open workbook procedure**. Add the statement **UserForm1.Show** on a separate line, after the statement to display the Amortization Schedule toolbar.
- You're almost finished but not quite. You still have to create the procedure to unload the form after the five seconds are up.
- Double click **Module1** within the Project Explorer window and create the **CloseScreen procedure**, which consists of three statements: **Public Sub CloseScreen()**, **Unload UserForm1**, and **End Sub**. Save the project.

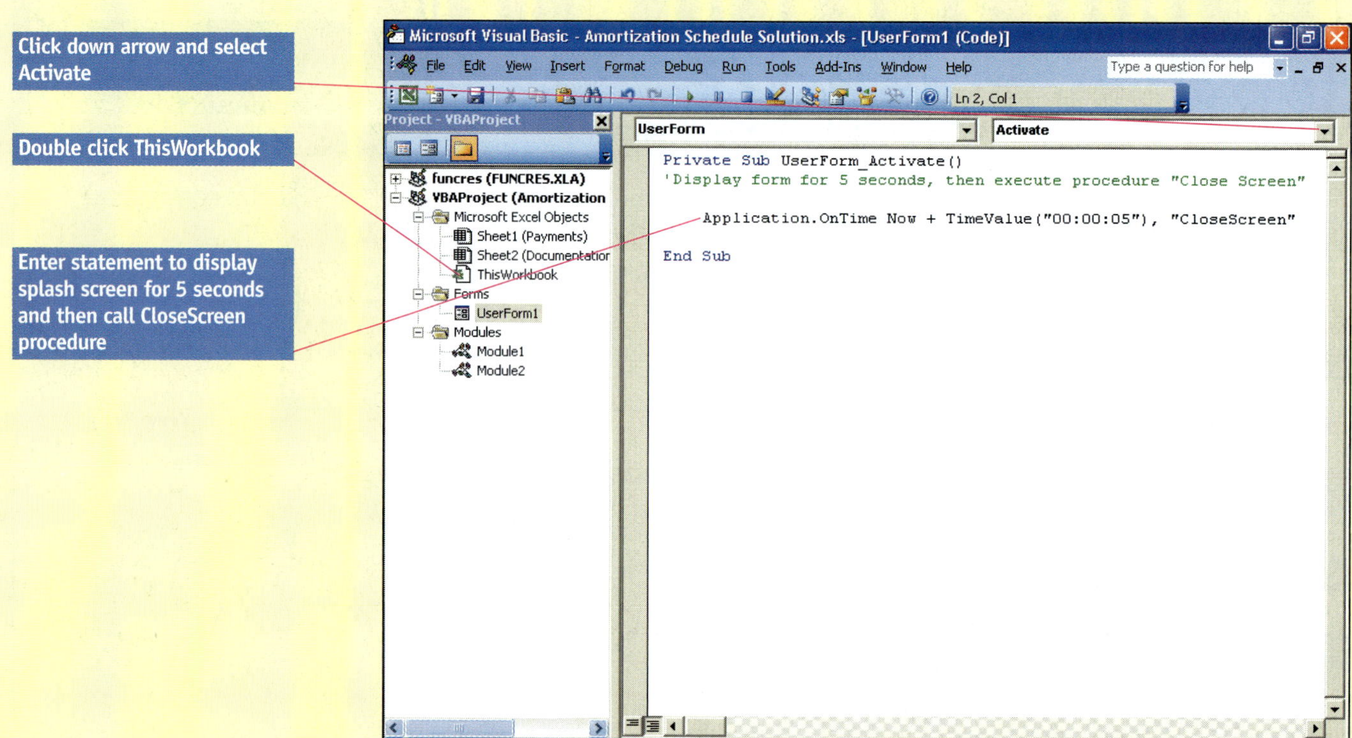

(g) Create the Code for the User Form (step 7)

FIGURE 9.8 Hands-on Exercise 3 (*continued*)

PUBLIC VERSUS PRIVATE PROCEDURES

The Amortization Schedule workbook is a VBA project. Each module in the project contains one or more procedures. Each procedure is either public or private. The scope of a procedure determines how the procedure can be accessed. A public procedure can be called from any module within the VBA project. A private procedure, however, can be accessed only from within the module in which it is stored.

Step 8: Test the Splash Screen

- Return to the Excel window. Close the workbook, but remain in Excel. Click **Yes** if asked whether to save the changes.
- Reopen the **Amortization Schedule Solution** workbook that appears at the top of the list of recently opened workbooks. Click the button to **Enable macros** when you see the security warning.
- The workbook opens and the Amortization Schedule toolbar is displayed, followed by the splash screen as shown in Figure 9.8h. The splash screen should remain for approximately five seconds, then it closes automatically.
- Enter any set of loan parameters, then test each of the toolbar buttons to be sure that they work properly. If the buttons do not function as intended, it could be because you forgot to attach the custom toolbar at the end of the previous exercise. Return to that exercise and repeat the steps correctly.
- Save the workbook. Exit Excel if you do not want to apply a digital signature to the workbook.

Custom toolbar is displayed

Splash screen is displayed

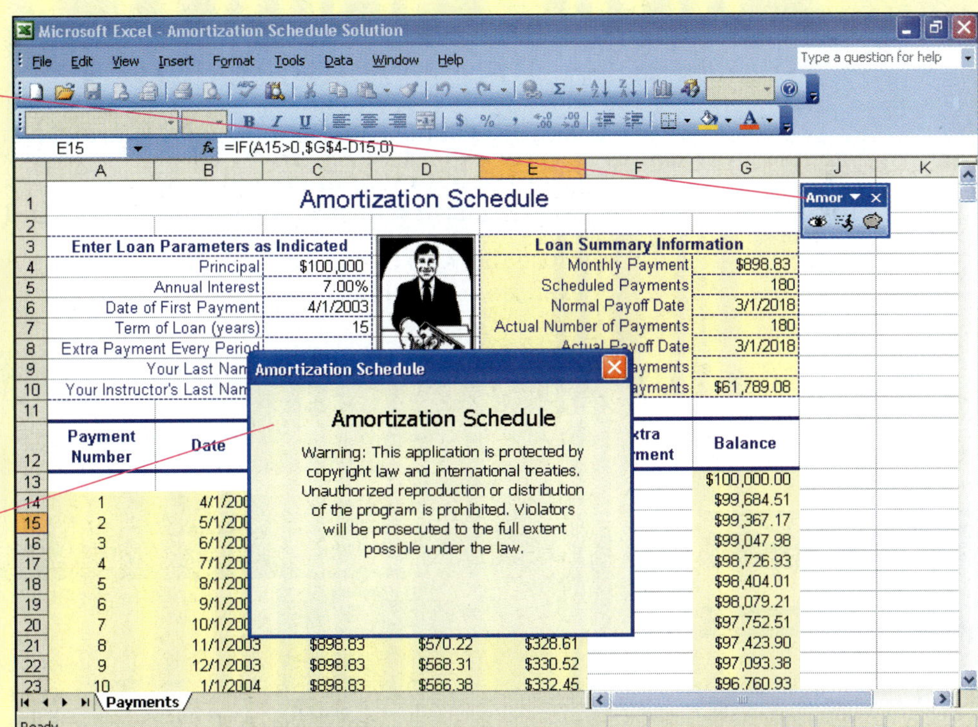

(h) Test the Splash Screen (step 8)

FIGURE 9.8 Hands-on Exercise 3 (*continued*)

SCREEN CAPTURE

The ability to capture a screen, then print the captured screen as part of a document, is very useful. The process is quite simple. Press the PrintScreen key any time you want to capture a screen to copy the screen to the Windows clipboard, an area of memory that is accessible to any Windows application. Next, start (or switch to) a Word document, and then execute the Paste command in the Edit menu to paste the contents of the clipboard into the current document. The screen is now part of the Word document, where it can be moved and sized like any other Windows object. See exercise 10 at the end of the chapter.

Step 9: Authenticate the Workbook

- You cannot digitally sign a workbook unless you have a digital signature. Click the **Start button**, click **All Programs**, click **Microsoft Office**, click **Microsoft Office Tools**, and then click **Digital Certificate for VBA Projects**.
- Type **Your Name** in the Create Digital Certificate dialog box. Click **OK** to create your signature and close the dialog box.
- The Amortization Schedule Solution workbook should still be open. Press **Alt+F11** to switch to the VBA editor. Pull down the **Tools menu** and click the **Digital Signature command** to display the associated dialog box.
- Click the **Choose button** to display the Select Certificate dialog box, click the signature you just created, click **OK** to close the Select Certificate dialog box, then click **OK** a second time to close the Digital Signature dialog box. Close the VBA editor.
- Save the workbook. Close the workbook, but leave Excel open. Pull down the **File menu** and click the **Amortization Schedule Solution workbook** that appears at the bottom of the File menu.
- You should see the Security Warning in Figure 9.8i. Your name should appear as the publisher of the workbook. Look closely, however, and note the message that indicates your credentials cannot be trusted. This is because your certificate has not been authenticated by a formal certification agency.
- Click the button to **Enable Macros** to return to the Excel workbook. You will see the splash screen, amortization toolbar, and so on.
- Close the workbook. Exit Excel if you do not want to continue with the next exercise at this time.

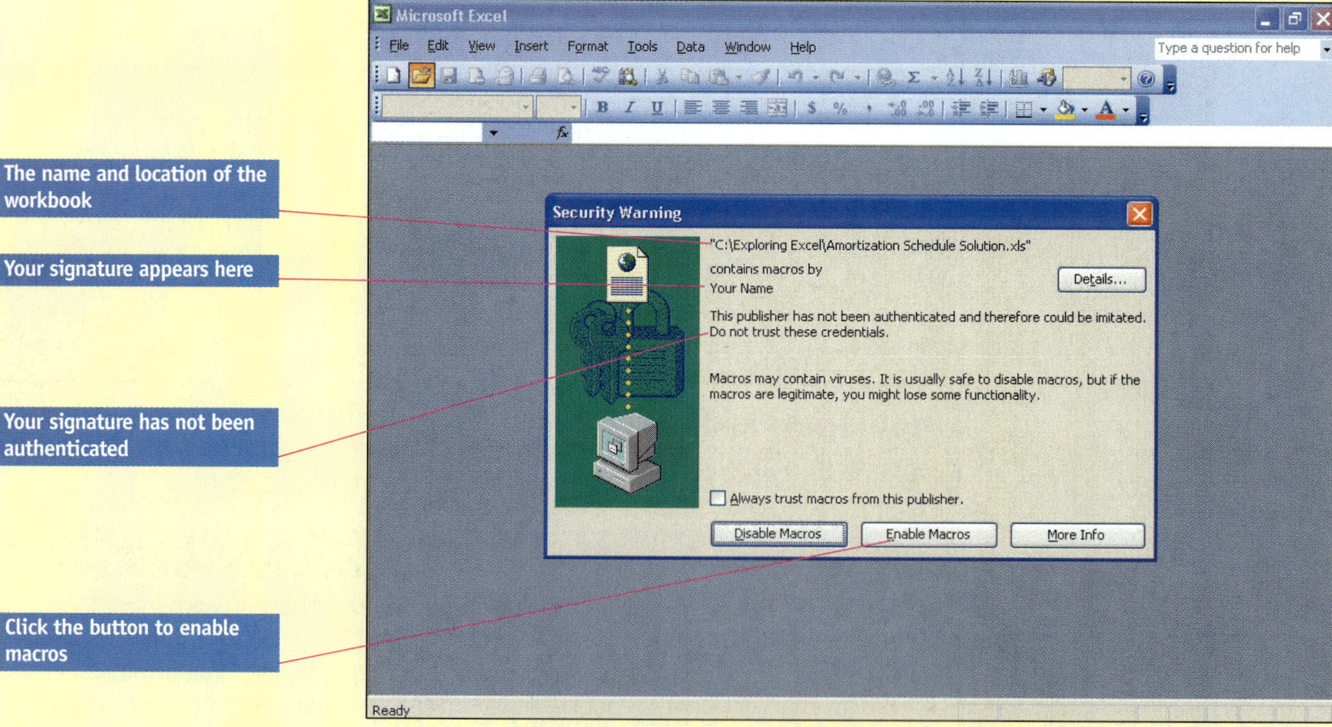

(i) Authenticate the Workbook (step 9)

FIGURE 9.8 Hands-on Exercise 3 (*continued*)

MORE COMPLEX PROCEDURES

A good application lets a user accomplish tasks that he or she could not (easily) do through ordinary Excel commands. The original amortization worksheet gave the user the capability to apply an optional extra payment *every month.* What if, however, the user wanted to see the effect of an *annual* optional payment (that is, an extra payment once a year)? This is best accomplished through a VBA procedure that prompts the user for the amount of the annual payment and the date it is to begin, after which the procedure applies that payment annually until the loan is paid off. Such a procedure entails more complex logic than what we have shown so far.

The difficulty (if any) is not the VBA per se, but rather the underlying logic. Think carefully about the implication of the preceding sentence. VBA is a powerful tool, and because it is powerful, developers use it to implement sophisticated procedures that entail nontrivial logic.

Pseudocode or "neat notes to oneself" is the most common way of expressing logic. Pseudocode does not have any precise syntax and is intended only to convey the logic within a program. One develops pseudocode by thinking in very general terms about the steps required to solve the problem. Our problem, simply stated, is to write a VBA procedure that will apply an annual extra payment to the existing payments table until the loan is paid off. This requires that we

1. Ask the user for the amount of the extra payment.
2. Ask the user when the extra payments are to begin.
3. Determine where in the table the payments are to begin.
4. Apply the extra payments annually until the loan is paid off.

This version of the pseudocode is almost trivial, but it does get you started thinking about the problem. You prompt the user for the amount and date of the periodic payment, go to the first date in the table where the payments are to begin, and then apply the periodic payment annually until the loan is paid off. The logic is accurate and complete, but it is not sufficiently detailed to provide a real help in writing the procedure.

It is necessary, therefore, to further develop the steps that determine when the payments are to begin, and how to apply the payments within the table. The expanded pseudocode is shown in Figure 9.9a and includes decision making and loops. To determine the first extra payment, you go to the first date within the payments table, then look at each successive date within the table until you reach a date greater than or equal to the date the payments are to begin. You then move the active cell to the payments column within this row.

Once you have the position of the first extra payment, you create a second loop in which you apply a payment once a year until the loan is paid off. This is accomplished through a ***switch***, a programming term for a variable that assumes one of two values. We set the switch (PayoffMade in this example) to "No" outside of the loop, then we go through the loop until the loan has been paid off. The first statement in the loop applies the extra payment to the active cell, after which the If statement compares the balance at the end of that year to zero. If the loan has been paid off, the switch is set to "Yes" and the loop is terminated. If the loan has not been paid, we move one year down in the table and return to the top of the loop.

Only when you are comfortable with this logic should you begin to write the VBA procedure, starting with the macro recorder to provide basic syntax. We used the macro recorder to capture the statement to select a specific cell (FirstTableDate in this example). We also used it to get the syntax for the relative references to various cells within the table. Once we had these basic statements, we added the additional VBA control structures to complete the procedure. The indentation within the procedure and the blank lines between statements are there only to enhance the readability.

User supplies amount and start date for extra payments

Determines where in table payments begin

Applies extra payments until loan is paid off

```
Input amount of extra payment and date payments are to begin

Set active date to first table date
Do Until active cell >= Date that payments are to begin
      Check next date
Loop
Move active cell to the extra payment column in this row

PayoffMade = "No"
Do Until PayoffMade = "Yes"
      Apply extra payment here
      If Ending Balance at end of year <=0
            PayoffMade = "Yes"
      Else
            Drop active cell 12 rows (1 year)
      End if
Loop

Display summary area
```

(a) Pseudocode

User supplies amount and start date for extra payment

Determines where in table payments begin

Applies extra payments until loan is paid off

```
Sub PeriodicExtraPayments()
    Dim DateExtraPaymentsBegin As Date
    Dim AmountofExtraPayment As Currency
    Dim PayoffMade As String
    AmountofExtraPayment = InputBox("Enter amount of extra payment")
    DateExtraPaymentsBegin = InputBox("Enter date when payments begin")

    Application.Goto Reference:="FirstTableDate"

    Do Until ActiveCell >= DateExtraPaymentsBegin
        ActiveCell.Offset(1, 0).Range("A1").Select
    Loop

    ActiveCell.Offset(0, 4).Range("A1").Select

    PayoffMade = "No"
    Do Until PayoffMade = "Yes"
        ActiveCell = AmountofExtraPayment
        If ActiveCell.Offset(11, 1) <= 0 Then 'Check one year later
            PayoffMade = "Yes"
        Else
            ActiveCell.Offset(12, 0).Select    'New Payment necessary
        End If
    Loop

    Range("TotalOfExtraPayments").Select

End Sub
```

(b) The VBA Procedure

FIGURE 9.9 Periodic Extra Payments

hands-on exercise

4 Periodic Optional Payments

Objective Develop a procedure to apply periodic extra payments to a loan until the loan is paid off. Use Figure 9.10 as a guide in the exercise.

Step 1: Start the Macro Recorder

- Open the **Amortization Schedule Solution** and click the button to **Enable macros**. Pull down the **Tools menu** to start recording a new macro. Enter **PeriodicExtraPayment** as the name of the macro. Click **OK** to begin recording.
- The Relative Reference button on the Stop Recording toolbar should be out, so that you are recording absolute references. Click the **down arrow** in the Name box at the upper left of the window, then select **FirstTableDate**, which positions you in cell B14.
- Click the **Relative Reference button** to record relative references from now on. Click in **cell B15** as shown in Figure 9.10a to move down one row.
- Click the **Stop Recording button**. Save the workbook.

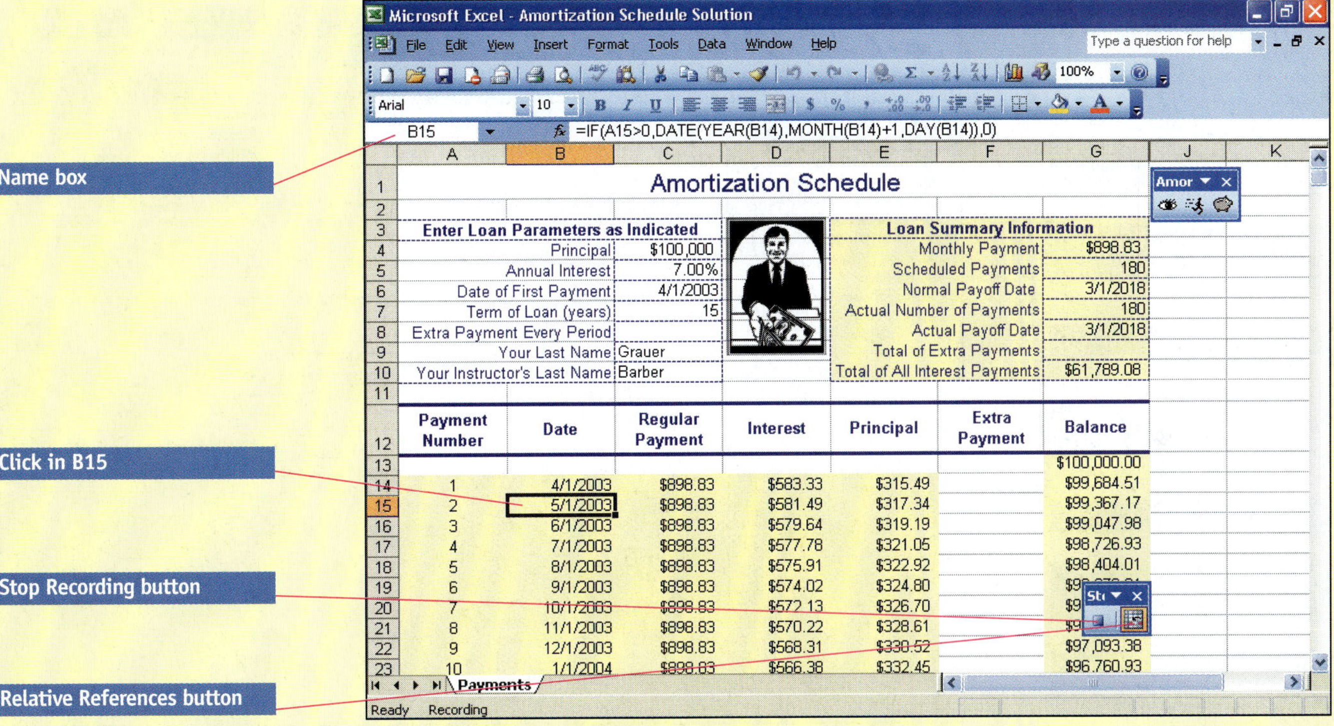

(a) Start the Macro Recorder (step 1)

FIGURE 9.10 Hands-on Exercise 4

IS THE BUTTON IN OR OUT?

The Relative Reference button on the Stop Recording toolbar toggles between relative (the button is in) and absolute (the button is out) references. The ScreenTip, however, displays "Relative References" regardless of whether the button is in or out. We wish that Microsoft had made it easier to tell which type of reference you are recording, but it didn't.

Step 2: View and Add Code

- Press **Alt+F11** to open the VBA editor. Open the **Modules folder**. Double click the module that contains the current macro (Module3 in our figure).
- You should see two statements within the procedure. The first statement, **Application.Goto Reference: ="FirstTableDate"** goes to the first date within the table (cell B14).
- The second statement, **ActiveCell.Offset(1,0).Range("A1").Select** moves the active cell down one row, but remains in column B. (The Range property can be deleted—see the boxed tip below.)
- Add the remaining statements as shown in Figure 9.10b.
  - The **Dim statement** defines a variable
  - The **InputBox function** prompts the user for the value of this variable.
  - The **Do** and **Loop statements** go down the column of dates until the starting date is reached.
  - The **Offset property** selects the cell four columns to the right of the active cell (the Extra Payment column).
- Save the procedure.

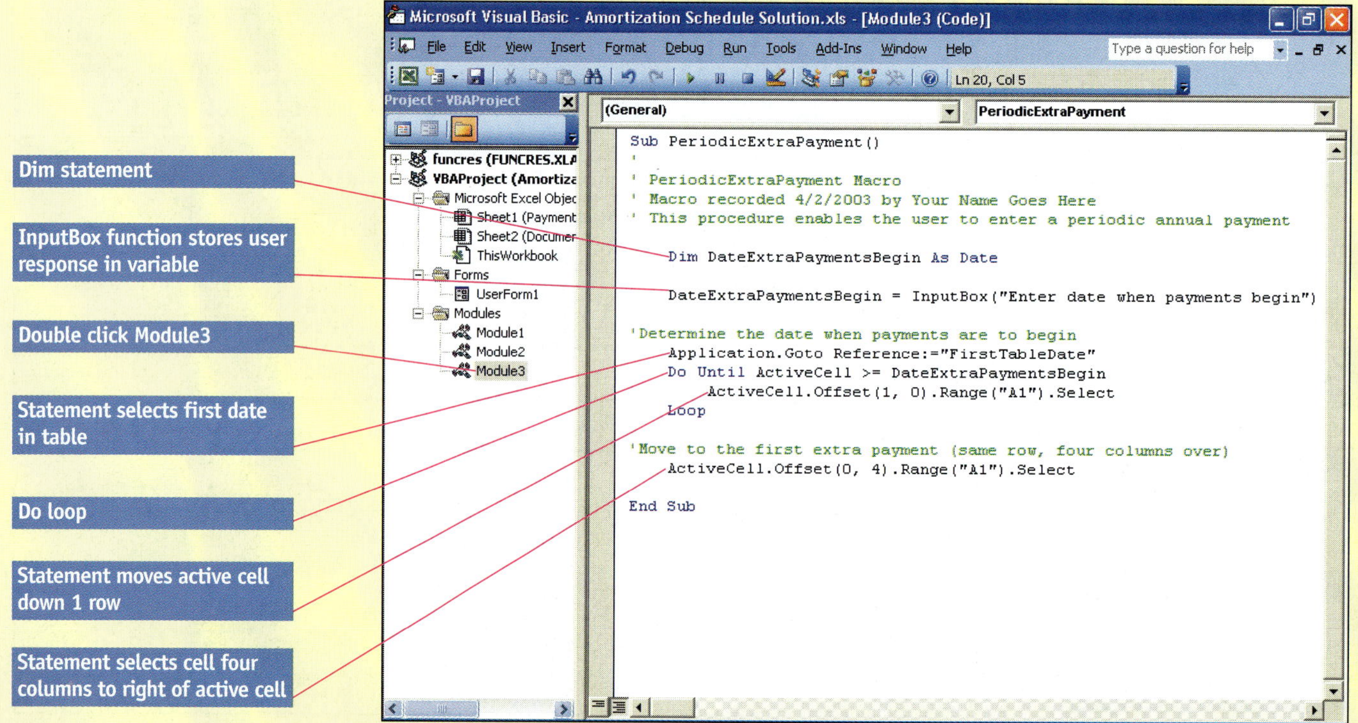

(b) View and Add Code (step 2)

FIGURE 9.10 Hands-on Exercise 4 (*continued*)

WHAT DOES RANGE("A1") REALLY MEAN?

The statement ActiveCell.Offset(1,0).Range("A1").Select has nothing to do with cell A1, so why is the entry (Range"A1") included? The Range property describes the number and shape of the selected cells—Range("A1") refers to a single cell. The default, however, is to select a single cell and so the Range property can be deleted, which results in the simpler statement ActiveCell.Offset(1,0).Select. If, however, you were selecting multiple cells, the Range property would be necessary.

Step 3: Step through the Procedure

- Point to a blank area at the right of the Windows taskbar, and then click the **right mouse button**. Click the command to **Show the Desktop**.
- Click the **VBA** and **Excel buttons** on the taskbar. Right click a blank area of the taskbar a second time, then click the command to **Tile Windows Vertically**.
- Your desktop should be similar to Figure 9.10c. It does not matter if the Excel window is on the left or right. Click in the Excel zoom box and lower the zoom percentage to **75%** to view more entries within the payments table.
- Click in the window containing the VBA editor. Close the Project Explorer. Click after the Sub statement within the PeriodicExtraPayment procedure.
- Press the **F8 key** or click the **Step Into button** on the Debug toolbar. The procedure header is highlighted. Press the **F8 key** a second time.
- The InputBox statement is highlighted, indicating that it will be executed next. Press the **F8 key** again to display the input box in the figure. Type any date that occurs two or three months after the first payment, then press **Enter.**
- Press the **F8 key** continually until you reach the date at which payments are to begin. At that point, the cell four columns to the right is selected.
- Press the **F8 key** one last time to move below the End Sub statement.

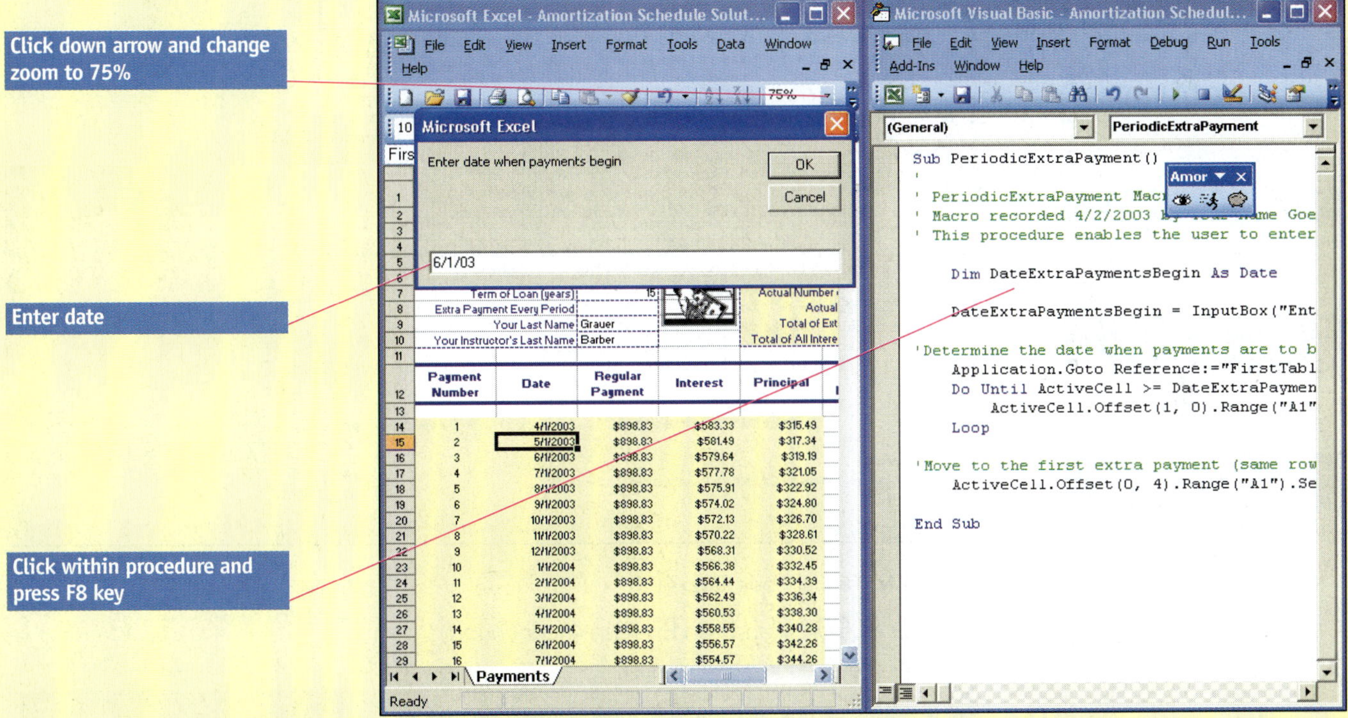

(c) Step through the Procedure (step 3)

FIGURE 9.10 Hands-on Exercise 4 (*continued*)

DIVIDE AND CONQUER

The logic to apply periodic payments is nontrivial and consists of three basic building blocks—obtain input from the user, determine the cell for the first extra payment, and apply periodic payments until the loan is paid off. The best way to develop the procedure is to code and test each block in sequence. Once you are sure of one step, move on to the next.

Step 4: Add Additional Code

- Maximize the VBA window. Add the additional statements to complete the procedure as shown in Figure 9.10d. Note the following:
  - The additional Dim statements define the amount of the extra payment and the switch to control the loop to apply the payments.
  - The additional InputBox function obtains the amount of the extra payment.
  - The additional loop applies the first extra payment, then continues to apply an annual payment until the loan is paid off.
  - The last statement selects a cell in the summary portion of the worksheet so that the user sees the relevant information about the loan in a single place.
- Add indentation, blank lines, and comments as you see fit to enhance the readability of the code. (These elements will make the procedure easier to follow and are not required by VBA.)
- Save the procedure.

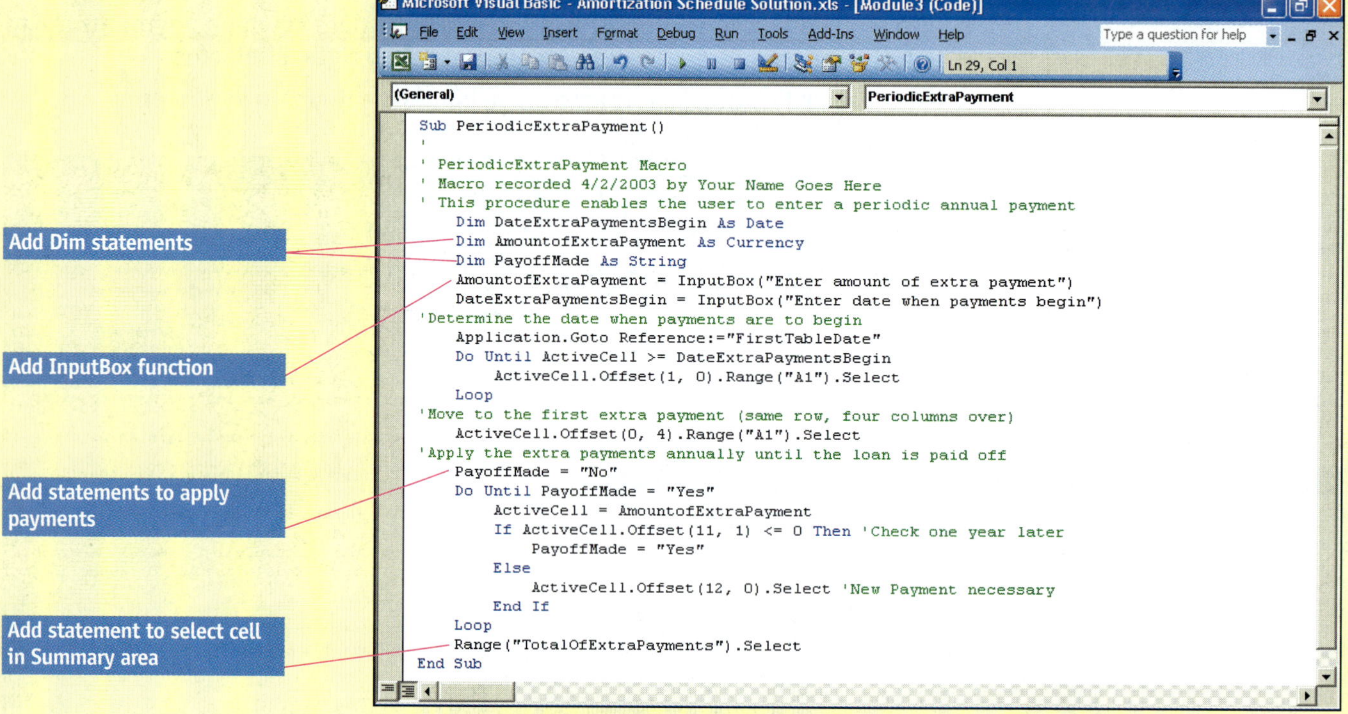

(d) Add Additional Code (step 4)

FIGURE 9.10 Hands-on Exercise 4 (*continued*)

SETTING A SWITCH

The use of a switch to control an action within a procedure is a common programming technique. The PayoffMade switch in this example is initially set to "no", prior to applying the first optional payment. The procedure then steps through the table to apply additional payments, testing after each optional payment to see if the loan is paid off, and if so, resetting the switch to "yes". At that point the loop is terminated and control passes to the next sequential statement.

Step 5: Test the Procedure

- Return to Excel. Maximize the Excel window and increase the magnification to **100%**. Check that your loan parameters match those in Figure 9.10e.
- Pull down the **Tools menu**, click **Macro**, click **Macros . . .**, then run the **PeriodicExtraPayment** procedure that you completed in the previous step. Enter **$1,500** and a date two months after the first payment as the amount of the extra payment and the date the payments are to begin.
- The macro executes, and if all goes well, you will see the summary information in our figure. The actual number of payments has been reduced to 145 (from 180). The total of the extra payments was $18,000.
- If you did not get these results, check that your loan parameters match ours and try again. If you still do not get these results, return to the previous step and check your code. If you cannot find an obvious error, tile the Excel and VBA windows as described in step 3 and step through the procedure.
- Pull down the **Tools menu**, click **Macro**, then click **Macros . . .** and run the **ClearExtraPayments** macro that we provided with the workbook. The extra payments disappear, and the loan requires the full 180 payments.
- Delete the term of the loan so that the loan parameters are incomplete. The individual payments disappear from the body of the worksheet. Rerun the **PeriodicExtraPayment** procedure.
- You are prompted for the amount of the extra payment and the starting date. This time the procedure is stuck in a loop because it cannot find the starting date. Press **Ctrl+Break** to stop the execution of the macro.
- Click the **Debug button** in the dialog box that appears. This takes you to the Visual Basic editor, where you can correct the code.

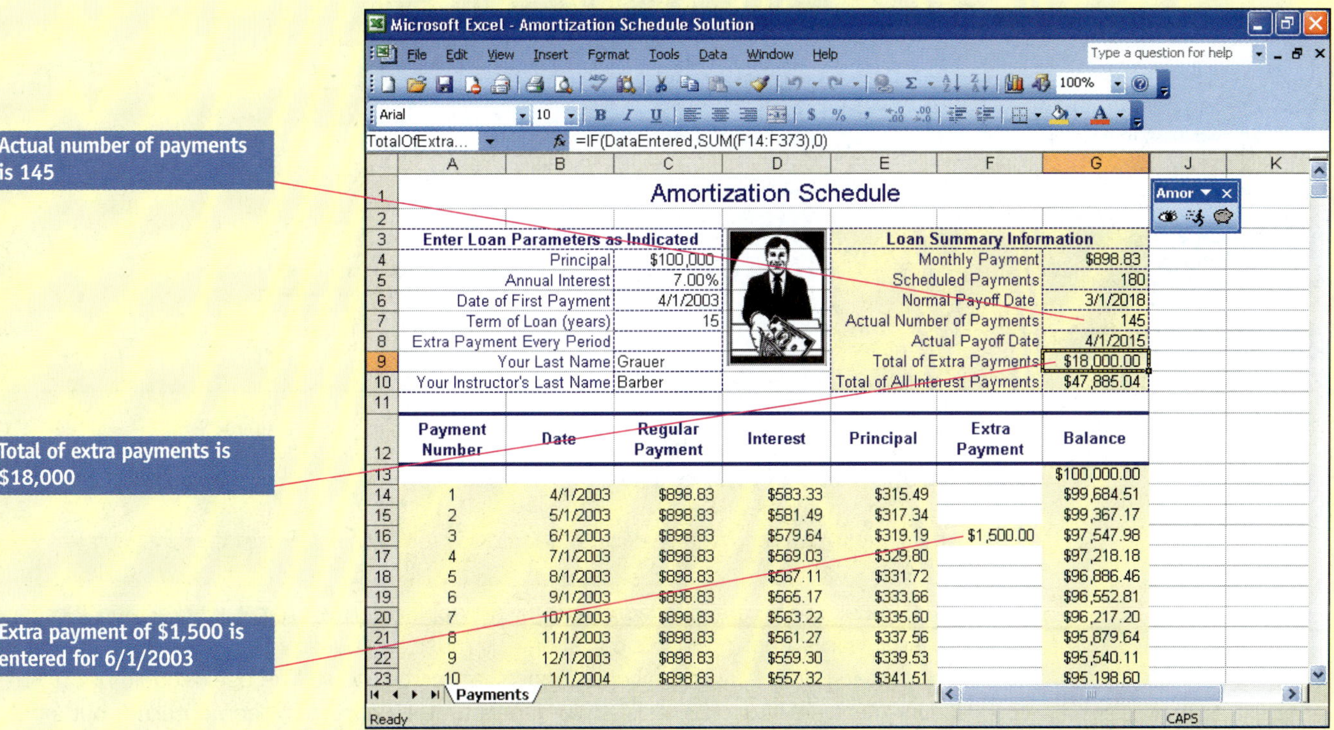

(e) Test the Procedure (step 5)

FIGURE 9.10 Hands-on Exercise 4 (*continued*)

Step 6: Revise the Procedure

- You are back in the Visual Basic editor within the PeriodicExtraPayment procedure. One line within the procedure is highlighted, indicating where the procedure stopped executing.
- Click the **Reset button** (the tiny square) on the Standard toolbar. The highlighting disappears. You can now add the additional VBA statements to complete the procedure.
- The procedure executes correctly as long as the loan parameters were entered. It does not work, however, if the information is missing. Hence you need to test for the parameters within an If statement.
- Modify the procedure as shown in Figure 9.10f to include the **If statement**, the associated **Else clause**, and the concluding **End If**.
  - The If statement toward the top of the procedure tests to see if the loan parameters are present in the worksheet.
  - The Else clause displays an error message if the loan parameters are missing.
- Save the revised procedure.

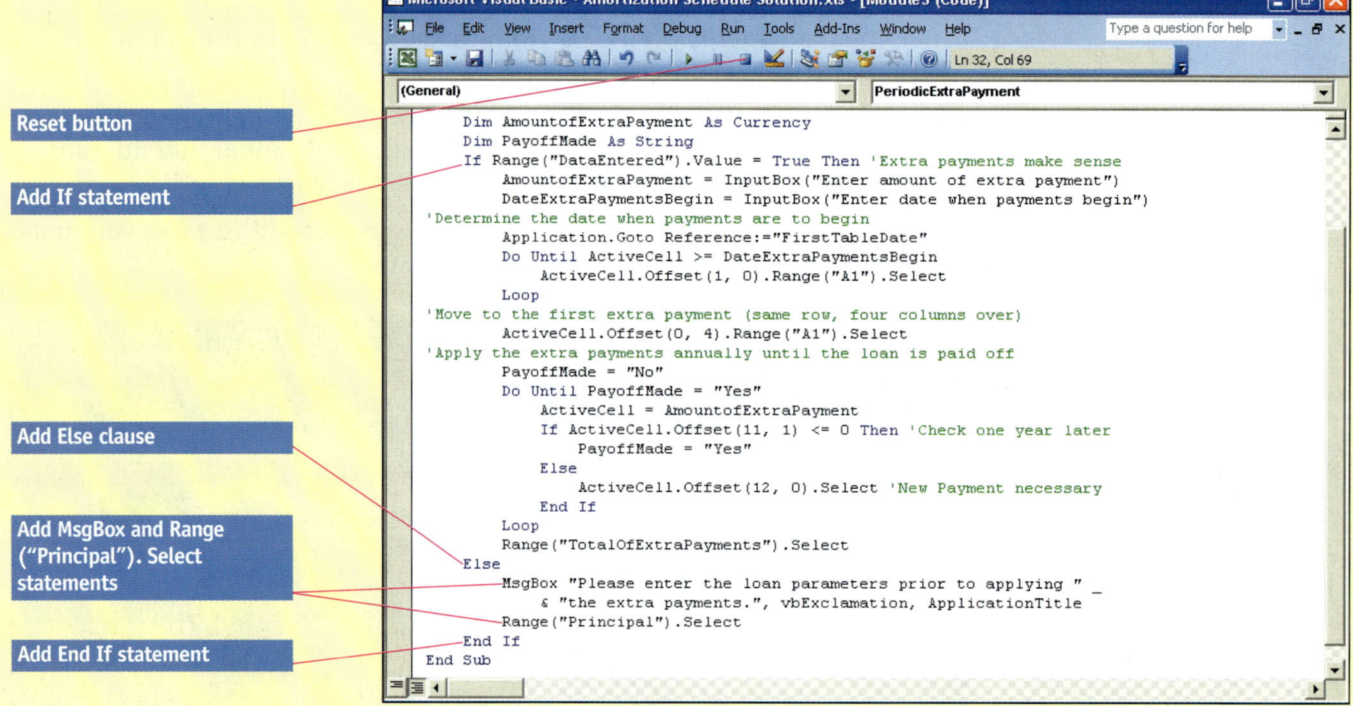

(f) Revise the Procedure (step 6)

FIGURE 9.10 Hands-on Exercise 4 (*continued*)

TEST UNDER ALL CONDITIONS

The most important characteristic of an application is that it works, and further that it works under all circumstances. It must be "bulletproof," and thus it should be tested under any and all conditions that might occur. The user should not try to apply periodic extra payments if loan parameters have not been entered, but what if that happens? The developer should have anticipated the possibility and built in the additional code to prevent the application from crashing.

Step 7: Retest the Procedure

- Click the **Excel button** on the Windows taskbar to return to Excel. Check that the loan information is still incomplete, then pull down the **Tools menu** and retest the **PeriodicExtraPayment procedure**.
- You should see the message box in Figure 9.10g that indicates the missing data. Click **OK** to close the dialog box.
- Pull down the **View menu**, click the **Toolbars command**, click **Customize**, and then modify the custom toolbar from the earlier exercise to include buttons for the additional procedures you developed. Use the **smiley face** and **sad face** for the **PeriodicExtraPayment** and **ClearExtraPayments procedures**, respectively.
- You must also attach the modified toolbar to your workbook. Pull down the **View menu**, click **Toolbars**, and click the **Customize command** to display the Customize dialog box. Click the **Toolbars tab**, then click the **Attach button** to display the Attach Toolbars dialog box.
- Select the Amortization Schedule toolbar in the right pane and click the **Delete button** to remove the old version. Select the **Amortization Schedule toolbar** in the left pane and click the **Copy button**. Click **OK**. Click **Close**.
- Save the workbook. The application is complete, but we provide additional practice through end-of-chapter exercises. Exit Excel.

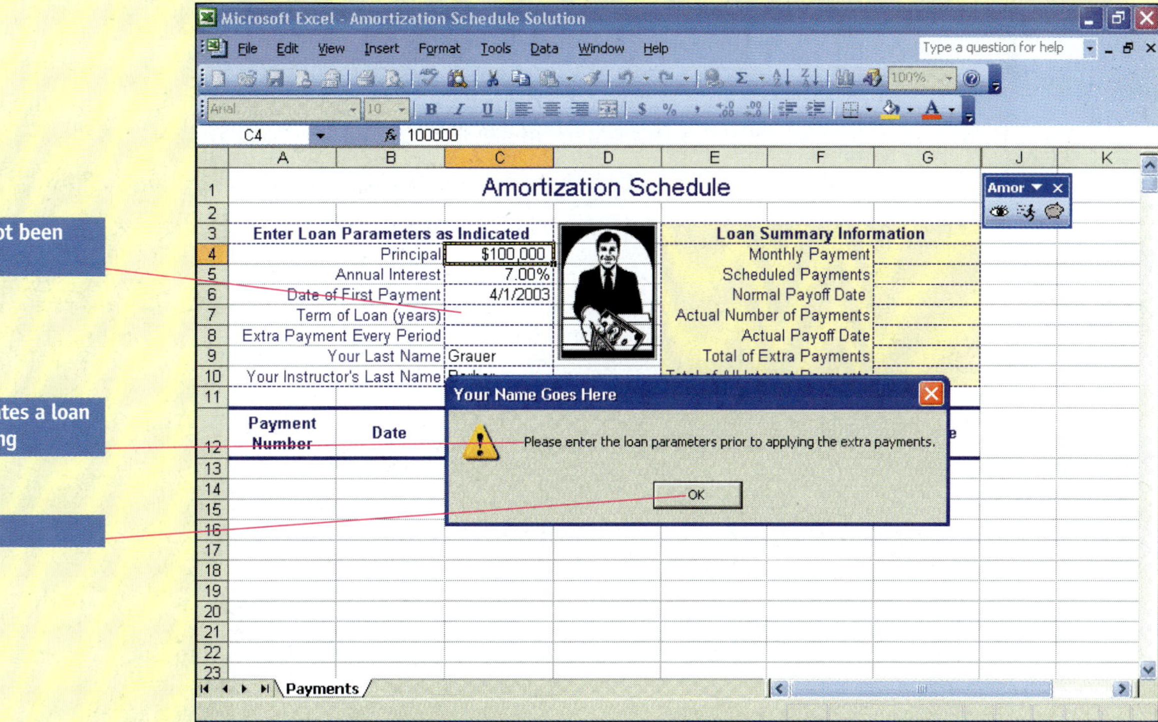

(g) Retest the Procedure (step 7)

FIGURE 9.10 Hands-on Exercise 4 (*continued*)

PRINT THE VBA CODE

It is good practice to obtain hard copy of the modules you have created for future study. Press Alt+F11 to return to the VBA editor. Select Module1. Pull down the File menu and click the Print command to display the Print dialog box. Select the option to print the current module, then click OK. Print any other modules in similar fashion.

SUMMARY

This chapter focused on the development of the Amortization Schedule workbook, a professional application that is suitable for distribution to individuals who need not be proficient in Excel. The workbook is visually appealing. It includes data validation to ensure sensible results and automation to facilitate ease of use. The workbook also enables the end user to do things that he or she could not do without benefit of VBA.

Excel contains various date functions to facilitate date arithmetic and/or to isolate the individual components of a date. The TODAY function returns the current date. The DATE function creates a date from three individual arguments (year, month, and day). The DAY, MONTH, and YEAR functions each have a single argument (a numeric date) and return the numeric day, month, and year, respectively.

VBA accomplishes its tasks by manipulating objects. Each object (such as a workbook, worksheet, a single cell, or chart) has a well-defined set of characteristics called properties, and each object can perform a set of actions called methods. The object model describes the hierarchical way the different objects are related to one another. Each application in Microsoft Office has its own object model. A collection is a group of similar objects within the object model.

An event is any action that is recognized by an application. An event procedure is a procedure that is activated in response to a specific event. To use VBA effectively, you decide which events are significant, and what is to happen when those events occur. Then you develop the appropriate event procedures. Event procedures are distinguished from general procedures that can be executed any time at the discretion of the user.

A custom toolbar can be created as a convenient way to run the procedures for any application. The toolbar must be attached to the workbook to distribute the toolbar with the workbook. The custom toolbar can be displayed and hidden automatically through the Open workbook and Before Close event procedures.

A user form is a convenient way to enter data within an application. A splash screen is a simple form that consists entirely of text. There are two essential tasks to display a splash screen. First, you have to create the form and then you develop the procedure(s) to display (and hide) the form.

Pseudocode or "neat notes to oneself" is the most common way of expressing logic. Pseudocode does not have any precise syntax and is intended only to convey the logic within a procedure.

A digital signature is an electronic, encryption-based stamp of authentication, which confirms the origin of a document, and further that the document has not been altered since it was last saved by the signer. You can create your own signature using a tool within Microsoft Office. Any certificate that you create yourself is unauthenticated, however, and generates a warning in the Security Warning box if the security level is set to High or Medium. You can also obtain an authenticated digital certificate from an internal security administrator and/or a variety of commercial sources.

KEY TERMS

Amortization 432
AND function 433
Before Close event procedure . . . 455
Collection 444
Custom toolbar 455
Data validation 432
DATE function 436
DAY function 436
Digital signature 455
Event 455
Event procedure 455
General procedure 455
IPMT function 444
Macro recorder 444
Method 444
MONTH function 436
MsgBox function 445
MsgBox statement 445
Object 444
Object model 444
OnTime method 457
Open workbook event procedure 455
OR function 433
PPMT function 444
Print area 443
Properties window 457
Property 444
Pseudocode 467
Splash screen 455
Switch 467
TODAY function 436
User form 457
UserForm Activate event procedure 457
WEEKDAY function 461
YEAR function 436
Zero suppression 439

MULTIPLE CHOICE

1. Which of the following will display the date November 16, 2002?
   (a) =DATE(11,16,2002)
   (b) =DATE(2002, 11, 16)
   (c) =DATE(2002, 16, 11)
   (d) =11/16/2002

2. Given that cell A4 contains the date 1/21/2002, what date will be displayed as a result of the function =DATE(YEAR(A4)+1,MONTH(A4)+2,DAY(A4)+3)?
   (a) 2/23/2005
   (b) 1/24/2005
   (c) 3/24/2003
   (d) 2/22/2003

3. What values will be returned by the logical functions =AND(10>5, 6<3) and =OR (10>5, 6<3)?
   (a) Both functions will return True
   (b) Both functions will return False
   (c) True and False, respectively
   (d) False and True, respectively

4. Which of the following is true about the PPMT function?
   (a) It determines the periodic payment for a loan
   (b) It determines the amount of a periodic payment that goes toward principal
   (c) It will adjust automatically if an additional payment toward principal was made during the preceding period
   (d) All of the above

5. What is a program switch?
   (a) A setting to start or stop the macro recorder
   (b) A variable that assumes one of two values, typically "yes" or "no"
   (c) An indication of whether the macro recorder is relative or absolute
   (d) All of the above

6. A single workbook, worksheet, chart, or range is called a(n):
   (a) Object
   (b) Property
   (c) Method
   (d) Collection

7. Which of the following is true, given the VBA statements Selection.Copy and Selection.Value=0?
   (a) Selection is a VBA object
   (b) Copy is a method of the Selection object
   (c) Value is a property of the Selection object
   (d) All of the above

8. Given the statement If MsgBox("Are you George?", vbyesno) = vbNo Then . .
   (a) MsgBox is used as a function rather than a statement
   (b) The question mark icon will be displayed within the message box
   (c) The Then portion of the If statement will address anyone named George
   (d) All of the above

9. Which of the following is typically *not* done in conjunction with adding a button to a custom toolbar?
   (a) An image is selected for the button
   (b) A description is written for the button
   (c) A macro is assigned to the button
   (d) A sound is assigned to the button

10. Which of the following is true regarding a VBA procedure that attempts to modify one or more cells in a protected worksheet?
    (a) The procedure *must* include an Unprotect worksheet statement at the beginning of the procedure
    (b) The procedure *must* include an Unprotect worksheet statement at the beginning and a Protect worksheet statement at the end
    (c) The procedure need not include Protect or Unprotect statements provided the Open workbook event procedure enables changes to the user interface
    (d) The procedure need not include Protect or Unprotect statements provided the Close workbook event procedure enables changes to the user interface

... continued

multiple choice

11. Which of the following is *not* necessary to create a splash screen?

(a) Create a user form as the basis of the splash screen, then modify the Open workbook event procedure to show the user form
(b) Create the Activate Form event procedure to set the timer
(c) Create an Open Form event procedure
(d) Create a public procedure to unload the form

12. Which of the following is least appropriate in the Open workbook event procedure?

(a) A statement to display a custom toolbar
(b) A message to the user to back up the system at the end of the session
(c) A statement to display a splash screen
(d) A statement to protect the user interface only

13. Which of the following will trigger the Before Close event procedure?

(a) Pulling down the File menu and clicking the Close command
(b) Pulling down the File menu and clicking the Exit command
(c) Clicking either Close button at the upper right of the Excel window
(d) All of the above

14. Which of the following best describes how to protect a worksheet but still enable the user to change the value of selected cells within the worksheet?

(a) Unprotect the cells that are to change, then protect the entire sheet
(b) Unlock the cells that are to change, then protect the entire worksheet
(c) Protect the entire worksheet, then unlock the cells that are to change
(d) Protect the entire worksheet, then unprotect the cells that are to change

15. Which of the following is a true statement about pseudocode?

(a) It is defined as neat notes to oneself
(b) It is required by the VBA editor for all procedures that include loops and decision making
(c) It has a precise set of syntactical rules
(d) It is displayed automatically within the VBA editor as the associated procedure is executing

16. A group of similar objects within the object model is called a(n):

(a) Module
(b) Procedure
(c) Attribute
(d) Collection

17. An action performed by an object is called a:

(a) Command
(b) Property
(c) Method
(d) Procedure

18. Worksheets("Forecast").Range("NextYear") refers to:

(a) The range "NextYear" in the current worksheet
(b) The range "NextYear" in the current worksheet in the current workbook
(c) The range "NextYear" in the worksheet named "Forecast" in the current workbook
(d) The range "NextYear" in the workbook named "Forecast"

ANSWERS

1. b	**7.** d	**13.** d
2. c	**8.** a	**14.** b
3. d	**9.** d	**15.** a
4. b	**10.** c	**16.** d
5. b	**11.** c	**17.** c
6. a	**12.** b	**18.** c

PRACTICE WITH EXCEL AND VBA

1. **Practice with Dates:** Open the partially completed version of the workbook in Figure 9.1 in *Chapter 9 Practice 1* in the Exploring Excel folder. (Click the button to Enable Macros.) The workbook will open, and you will see the message box that is displayed in the figure indicating that the dates in the workbook are reset automatically. Click OK after you have read the message.
   a. The invoice dates in your worksheet will differ from those in our figure, but the values in the Days Elapsed column should be identical to ours after you complete the worksheet. Enter the appropriate formula in cell B4 and change the formatting as necessary. Copy the formula in cell B4 to the remaining rows in the column.
   b. Enter the appropriate formulas for the first invoice to compute current amount due, as well as the amounts that are 30, 60, and 90 days late. Two of these formulas are simple If statements (the current amount due, and the amount over 90 days). The other two formulas require nested If statements (an If function within an If function). We suggest you do the 60-day formula first, since that is the easier one. Then once you have that formula, you will be able to extend it to the 30-day formula.
   c. Copy the formulas for the first invoice to the remaining rows in the column. Add the formulas to compute the totals in each category, then compare your values to ours. The dollar amounts in each column should match Figure 9.11 even though the individual invoice dates are different.
   d. Open the Visual Basic editor and look at the Open workbook event procedure. What is the significance of the "UpdateDates" statement that is found in this event procedure?
   e. Add your name and birth date in the indicated cells, then add the formula to compute your age as shown in the worksheet. Format the worksheet appropriately, then print it two ways, once to show the displayed values, and once to show the cell formulas.

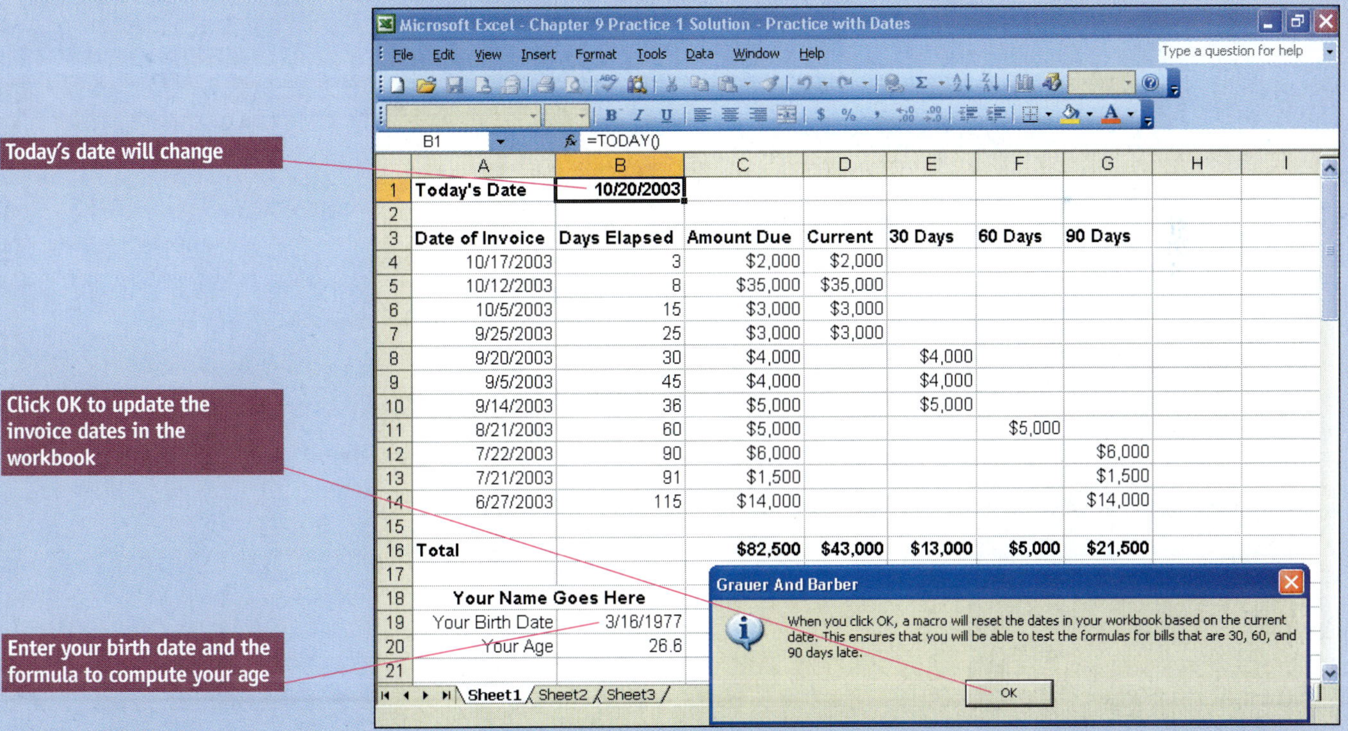

	A	B	C	D	E	F	G
1	Today's Date	10/20/2003					
2							
3	Date of Invoice	Days Elapsed	Amount Due	Current	30 Days	60 Days	90 Days
4	10/17/2003	3	$2,000	$2,000			
5	10/12/2003	8	$35,000	$35,000			
6	10/5/2003	15	$3,000	$3,000			
7	9/25/2003	25	$3,000	$3,000			
8	9/20/2003	30	$4,000		$4,000		
9	9/5/2003	45	$4,000		$4,000		
10	9/14/2003	36	$5,000		$5,000		
11	8/21/2003	60	$5,000			$5,000	
12	7/22/2003	90	$6,000				$6,000
13	7/21/2003	91	$1,500				$1,500
14	6/27/2003	115	$14,000				$14,000
15							
16	Total		$82,500	$43,000	$13,000	$5,000	$21,500
17							
18	Your Name Goes Here						
19	Your Birth Date	3/16/1977					
20	Your Age	26.6					

FIGURE 9.11 Practice with Dates (exercise 1)

2. **Change the Magnification:** The screen in Figure 9.12 displays a pair of procedures that increase and decrease the magnification percentage within the Excel window. These procedures do not do anything that the user could not accomplish manually. They are, however, more convenient ways to change the magnification incrementally and are truly useful in that regard. They also serve to illustrate how simple Excel macros are enhanced through the inclusion of VBA statements.
   a. Open the Amortization Schedule Solution workbook and start the macro recorder. Click in the Zoom box and change the magnification to 110. Stop the recorder. Press Alt+F11 to open the Visual Basic Editor.
   b. Locate the module that contains the macro you just created, which contains the single statement ActiveWindow.Zoom =110. That changes the zoom property of the active window to 110. The single statement, plus a little imagination, is all you need to create the procedures in Figure 9.12.
   c. Add a Dim statement to define the variable intMagnification as an integer. The second statement sets this variable 10% higher than the current magnification. It does not change the magnification, however, because you have to check that you do not exceed the maximum magnification (400%) that is permitted—hence the If statement prior to changing the actual magnification, which is controlled by the Zoom property of the ActiveWindow object.
   d. Use the completed procedure to increase the magnification as the basis for the procedure to decrease the magnification. (You can enter the entire procedure manually, or you can copy the existing procedure, then make the necessary modifications.)
   e. Add two additional buttons (an up and a down arrow, respectively) to the custom toolbar to execute these procedures. Be sure to attach the modified toolbar to the completed workbook. Save the workbook.

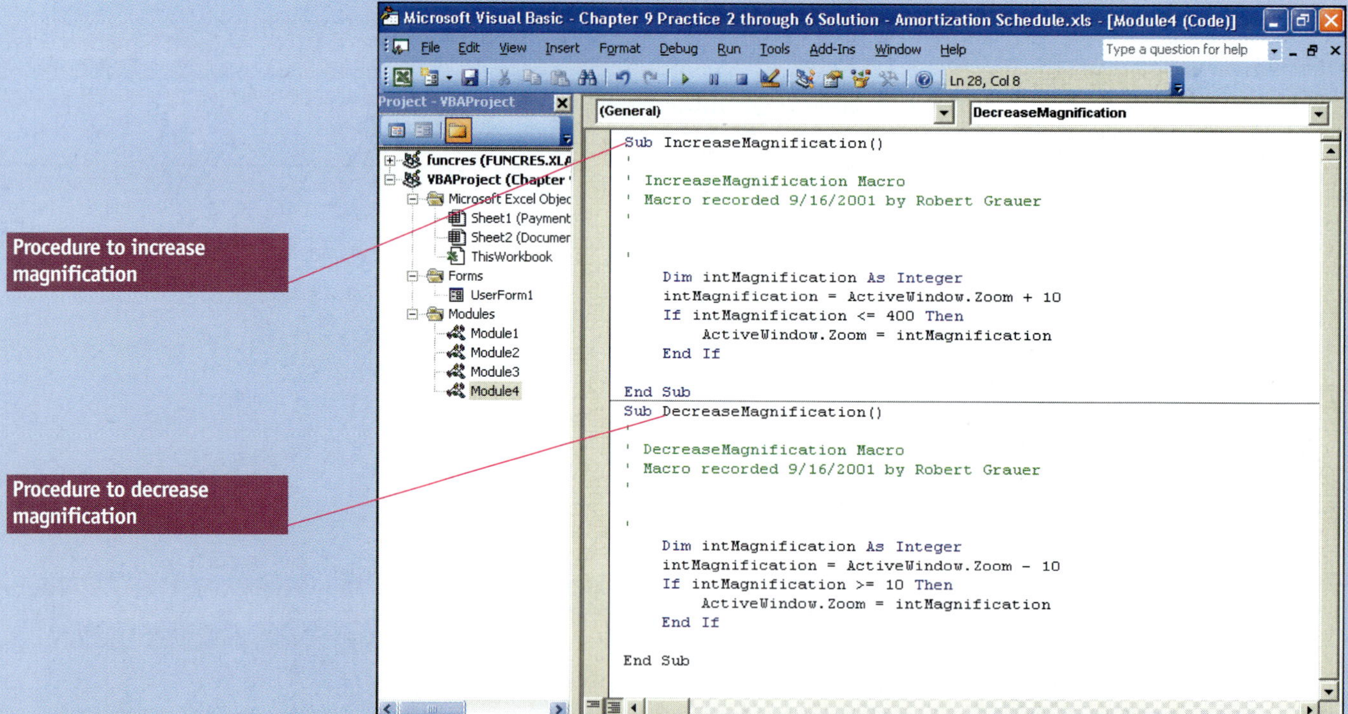

FIGURE 9.12 Change the Magnification (exercise 2)

3. **Toggle the Documentation Worksheet:** Figure 9.13 displays the Documentation worksheet that is included in the Amortization Schedule Solution workbook. This worksheet explains how the OFFSET function is used in conjunction with a memory variable to set a variable print area to print only as many rows as there are payments. This is not an easy concept, and so we include the complete explanation within the workbook so that you can apply this technique to other workbooks that you might create.

   The purpose of this exercise, however, is to create a VBA procedure that will toggle the Documentation worksheet on and off. Thus, if the worksheet is hidden, the procedure will display it; if the worksheet is visible, the procedure will hide it. The logic is simple, but you need to obtain the VBA statement to display or hide the worksheet. Proceed as follows:

   a. Open the Amortization Schedule Solution workbook that you have been working on throughout the chapter. Start the macro recorder. Pull down the Format menu, click Sheet, click the Unhide command, select the worksheet, then click OK. (The Documentation worksheet is hidden initially, and so the Unhide command is active. If the worksheet is already visible, however, click the Hide command instead of Unhide.) Stop the recorder.
   b. Start the Visual Basic editor to view the code in the macro you just created. You will see a single VBA statement that sets the Visible property for the Documentation worksheet to True. Use this statement as the basis of the procedure that will toggle the worksheet on or off. You have to add an If/Else statement that hides a visible worksheet and displays a hidden worksheet.
   c. Assign a button (use the book image) to add the procedure to the custom toolbar. Test the button to be sure that it works properly.
   d. Add your name to cell A2 in the documentation worksheet, then print the documentation worksheet for your instructor.

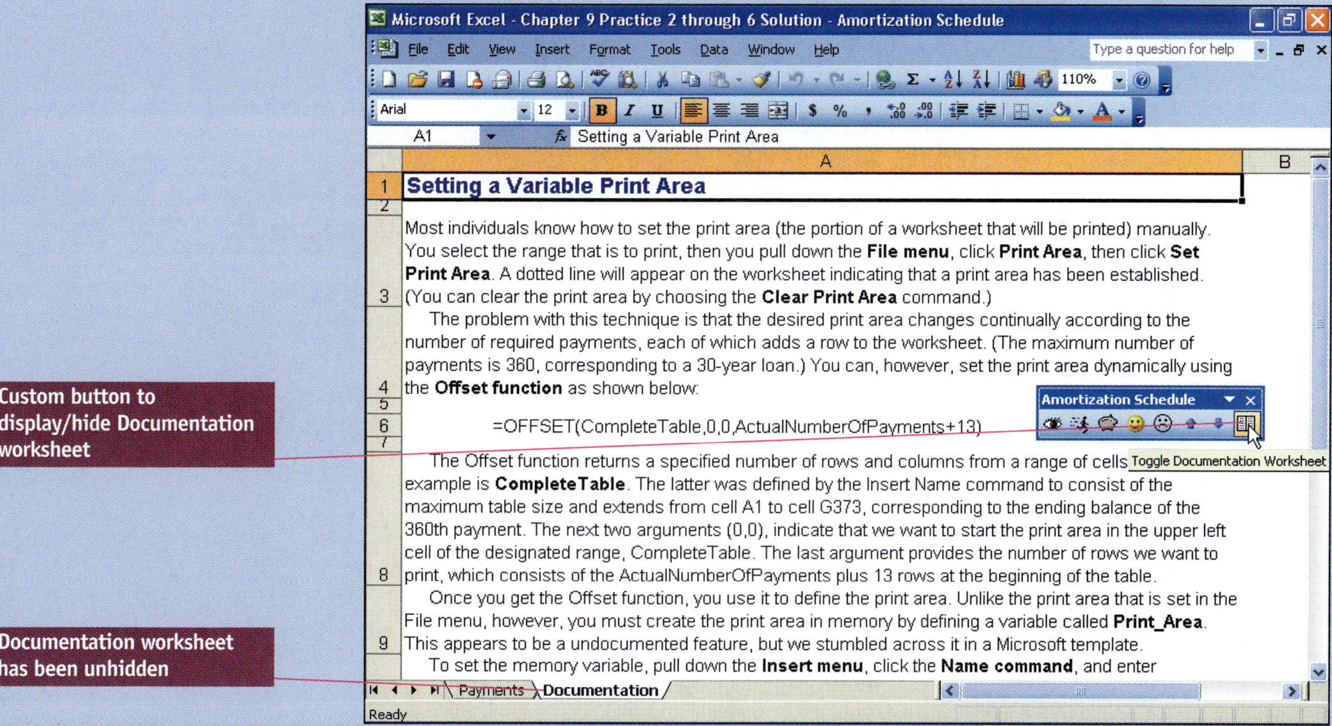

FIGURE 9.13 Toggle the Documentation Worksheet (exercise 3)

4. **Print the Summary Area:** Figure 9.14 displays two VBA procedures, one to print the summary area of the worksheet and a second to reset the print area. The PrintSummaryOnly procedure has not yet been created and is the subject of this exercise. The RestorePrintArea procedure was included in the original workbook; it incorporates the information that was contained in the Documentation worksheet from the previous exercise.
   a. Open the Amortization Schedule Solution workbook. Enter the parameters for any loan, but specify the term as two years. Click the Print Preview button and notice that the printout fits on one page. Change the term of the loan to 10 years, click Print Preview a second time, and the printout requires 3 pages.
   b. Pull down the File menu, click Print Area, then click the Clear Print Area command. Click the Print Preview button. The printout requires 7 pages even though many of the pages are blank. This is because the previous step had you clear the print area which had been set to print only as many rows as contained nonzero values. Close the Print Preview window, and press Ctrl+r, which is the keyboard shortcut for the RestorePrintArea procedure in the workbook. The printout once again takes three pages.
   c. You will set the print area to print just the summary portion of the worksheet. Start the macro recorder. Name the macro PrintSummaryOnly. Click the down arrow in the Name box, select the SummaryArea range name, then pull down the File menu, click Print Area, then click the command to Set the print area. Click the Print button. Stop the macro recorder.
   d. Open the VBA editor to examine the statements you just created. They are similar to, but different from, the code in Figure 9.14. Look closely at the recorded statements, however, and see how they can be simplified to create the code in Figure 9.14. The last statement runs the RestorePrintArea procedure, so that the print area will be automatically reset.
   e. Add a button (use the calculator button) to the custom toolbar to run the Print Summary Area procedure. Add a second button (the pencil) to restore the print area. Attach the toolbar to the workbook.

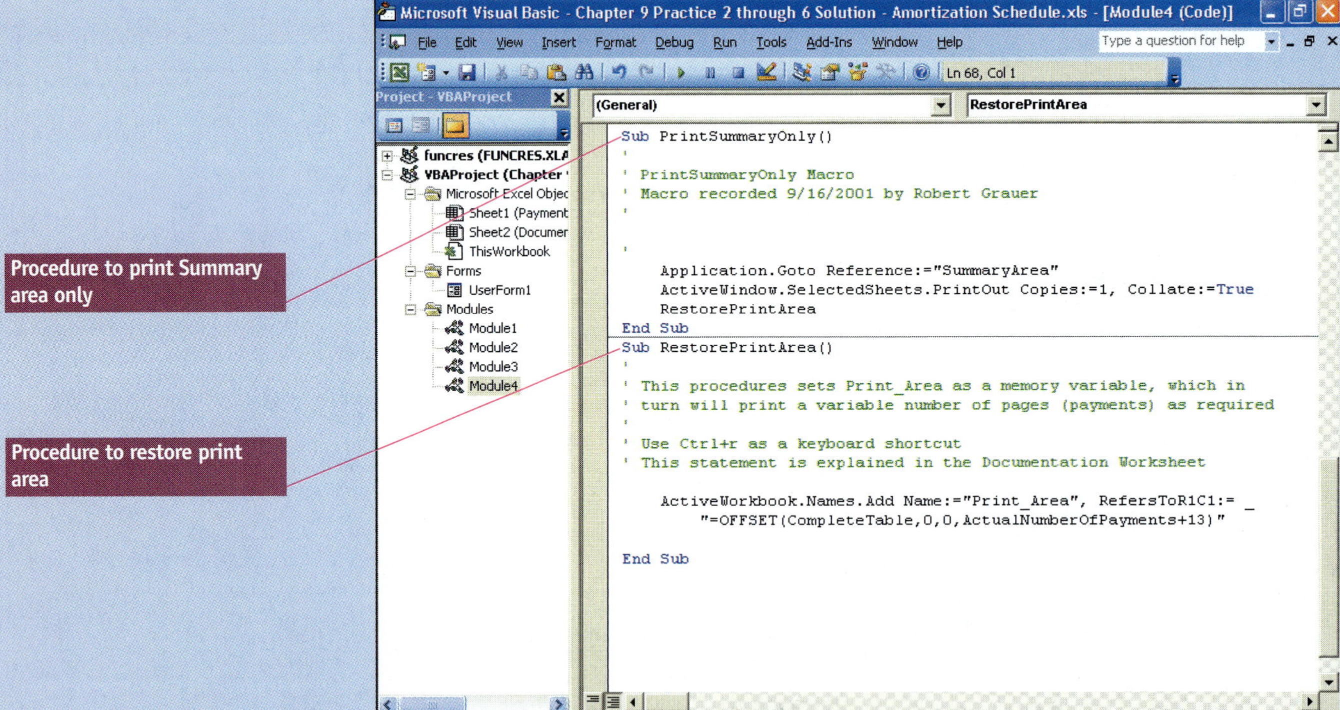

FIGURE 9.14 Print the Summary Area (exercise 4)

5. **Nested Ifs and Other Logic:** A nested If statement (or "an If within an If") is a common logic structure in every programming language. It tests an initial condition, then it tests a second condition if the first condition is true. Open the Amortization Schedule Solution workbook and expand the Before Close event procedure as shown in Figure 9.15. The original procedure has been modified to accomplish several additional tasks.
   a. The procedure checks to see whether your name or your instructor's last name has been omitted from the worksheet, and if so, it gives the user the option to cancel the Close command. First, the procedure sets the active cell to the range name "YourLastName". It then checks that cell and the cell one row below for null values. If either cell is blank, the second If statement is executed.
   b. The MsgBox function within the nested If displays a message to the user and displays Yes and No buttons within the resulting message box. The user's response is compared to the VBA intrinsic constant, vbNo. If the user clicked the No button, then the comparison is true, the close operation is canceled, and the switch to close the workbook is set to No.
   c. The second nested If statement tests to see if the workbook is to be closed, and if so, it hides the custom toolbar, and also displays a message to the user. The custom toolbar is then deleted from the collection of custom toolbars (but not from this workbook). This ensures that the toolbar will work correctly if the workbook is subsequently opened in a different folder.
   d. A second If statement tests for the day of the week (Friday in this example) and displays an appropriate message.
   e. There is a lot of logic here, and hence you might want to close the workbook two or three times (with different responses) to better appreciate the underlying logic. Print this procedure for your professor.

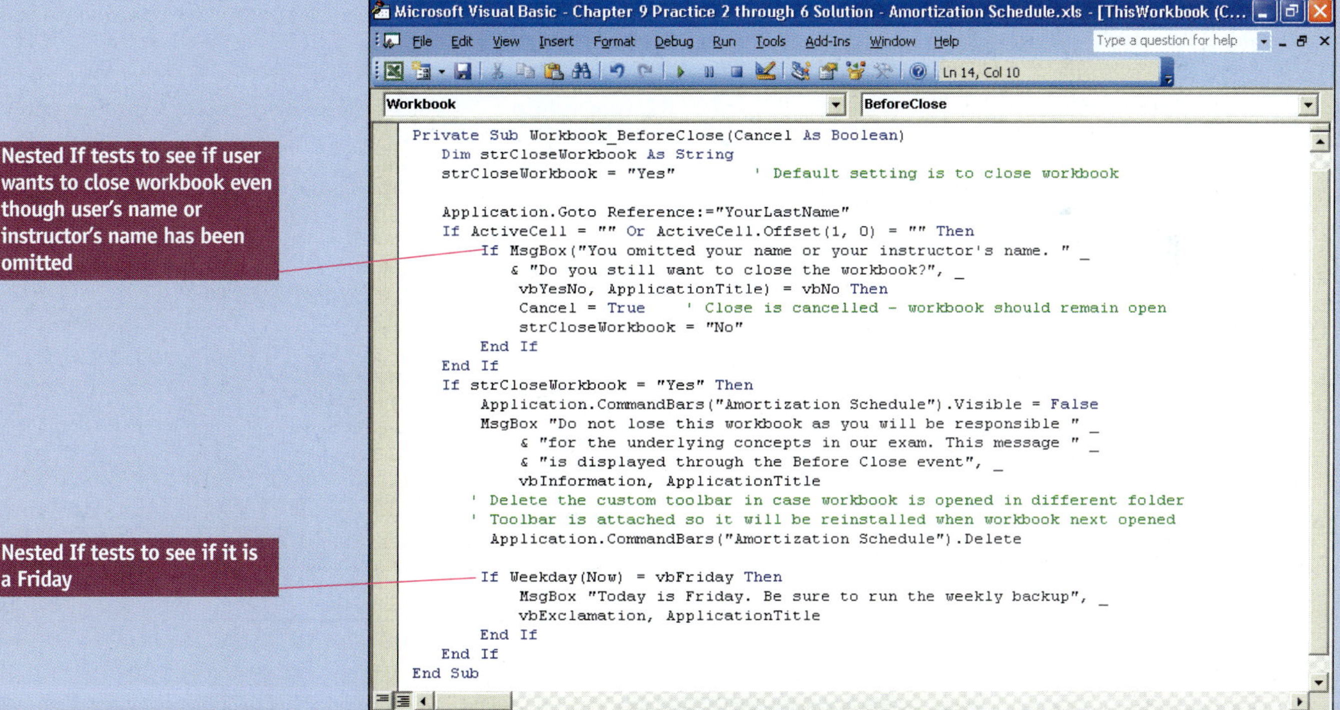

FIGURE 9.15 Nested Ifs and Other Logic (exercise 5)

6. **Custom Menus and Toolbars:** Figure 9.16 displays the completed Amortization Schedule Solution workbook immediately prior to closing the workbook. The custom toolbar (and corresponding menu) contains a total of 10 buttons that were created during the various hands-on exercises and end-of-chapter problems. Compare your toolbar to ours to be sure that you have completed the entire application.
   a. The eye and runner correspond to the procedures to display and hide the validation columns, respectively, and were developed in the second hands-on exercise.
   b. The piggy bank icon runs the procedure to enable individual optional payments of principal and was created in the second hands-on exercise.
   c. The smiley and sad faces contain the procedures to apply an optional payment and clear the optional payments column, respectively. The procedures were developed in the fourth hands-on exercise.
   d. The up and down arrows increase and decrease the magnification within the Excel window. These procedures were developed in problem 2 at the end of the chapter.
   e. The book toggles the documentation worksheet on or off and was developed in problem 3 at the end of the chapter.
   f. The calculator and pencil print the summary area and restore the print area, respectively. These procedures were created in problem 4 at the end of the chapter.
   g. You can also create a custom menu with the same commands. Pull down the View menu, click Tools, click Customize to display the Customize dialog box, then click the Commands tab and scroll until you can select New Menu. Click and drag the New Menu command to the right of the menu bar, then release the mouse to create a menu called "New Menu". Select the new menu on the menu bar, click the Modify Selection button in the Customize dialog box, then change the name of the menu to Amortization.
   h. You are now ready to add commands to the menu. Select the Macros category in the Category area, then drag a Custom button to the Amortization menu. Pull down the menu, select the Custom Button command and assign a macro. Repeat this process to add additional commands.
   i. Complete the Amortization menu. Press the Print Screen key to capture this screen, start Word, then paste the screen into a Word document to submit to your instructor.

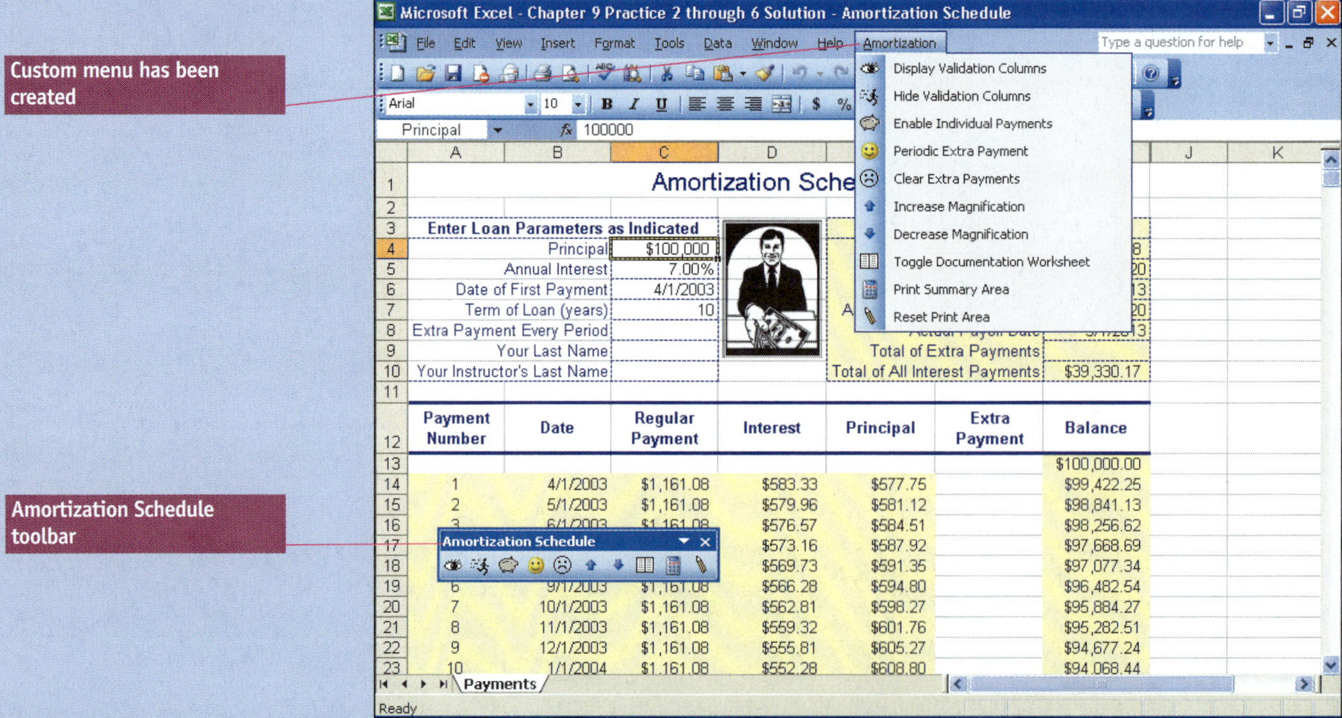

FIGURE 9.16 Custom Menus and Toolbars (exercise 6)

7. **The Get Out of Debt Worksheet:** The Get Out of Debt workbook in Figure 9.17 is similar to the Amortization Schedule Solution application that was developed in the chapter. The new workbook is designed to let you practice all of the skills in the chapter within the context of a different application. It is also intended as a gentle reminder to think twice about using your credit card, because once you acquire this type of debt, it is very difficult to get out from under.
   a. Open the partially completed version of this workbook in *Chapter 9 Practice 7* and complete the basic worksheet. Unprotect the worksheet (a password is not required) so that you can make the necessary modifications.
   b. Implement a validation requirement in cell C7, the cell that contains the projected monthly payment, to ensure that the payment is greater than the interest due in the first month. Use the Insert Name command to assign the range name FirstMonthInterest to cell D13, then use this name as needed throughout the worksheet.
   c. Enter the appropriate If functions in cells E8 and G8 to display the indicated error message and remaining balance (if, in fact, there is a remaining balance after 30 years). These functions check the value in the cell G372, which has been assigned the range name, BalanceAfter30Years. Display these values in red, bold, and italics. Test the functions by entering appropriate values in the spreadsheet; for example, if you make the minimum monthly payment (the amount the credit card company requires), you will still owe $4,800 after 30 years, after paying out more than $25,000 in interest. Press the Print Screen key to capture this screen, start Word, then paste the screen into a Word document to submit to your instructor.
   d. Click the Retry button and drop your monthly payment by $1.00. Not only are you still in debt, but the debt has almost quadrupled to more than $18,000. This is *not* a spreadsheet error, but rather an indication of the power of compound interest. It is wonderful when it works for you, as in a retirement account, but a disaster when it works against you with debt.
   e. Change the monthly payment to $100. You are finally out of debt, but it took more than seven years. Add your name and your instructor's name in the appropriate cells, then print this worksheet for your instructor.

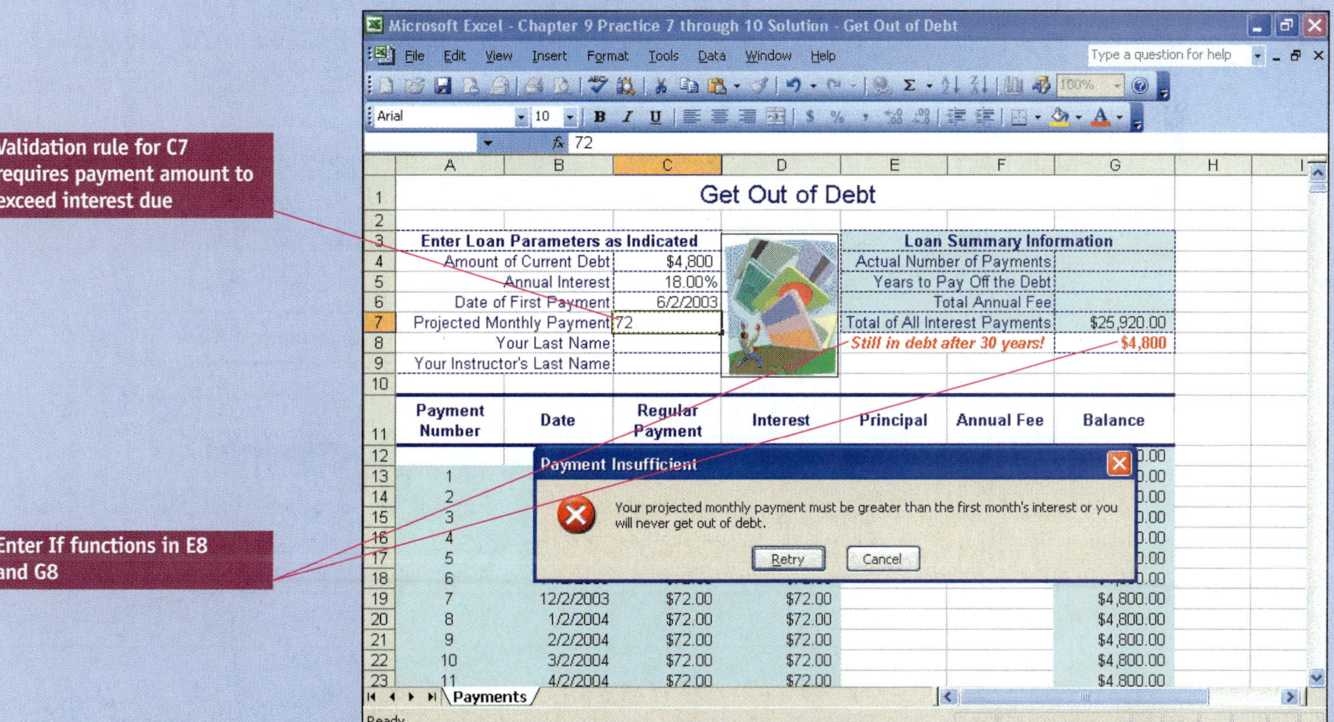

FIGURE 9.17 The Get Out of Debt Worksheet (exercise 7)

8. **Expand the Application:** Create a custom toolbar (and/or a custom menu) to execute the procedures that are already in the workbook to print the summary area and to reset the print area. Use the same icons (the calculator and the pencil) that were used in the Amortization Schedule Solution workbook. Include additional procedures as described below:
   a. Create a general procedure that imposes an annual fee once a year within the body of the worksheet. The procedure should prompt the user for the amount of the fee and the first date that it takes effect. The logic parallels that of the periodic extra payments module in the other workbook. Add a button for this procedure to the custom toolbar using the sad face image.
   b. Use the procedure you just created to enter an annual fee of $50 that takes effect the first month. Compare the results of this calculation with those of the previous exercise; that is, an annual fee of $50 extends the time required to pay off your loan by another seven months. Click the toolbar button to print the summary area for these parameters.
   c. Create a second general procedure to clear the annual fee. Add this procedure to the custom toolbar using the smiley face button.
   d. Create an Open workbook event procedure to display the custom toolbar and to enable VBA procedures to modify a protected worksheet. This logic parallels that in the Amortization workbook. You do not need a splash screen at this time.
   e. Create a Before Close event procedure to hide the custom toolbar and display a meaningful message (choose your own text) as shown in Figure 9.18. The procedure should also check for the presence of your name and your instructor's name prior to closing. You can copy the code from the Amortization Schedule Solution workbook as appropriate.
   f. Add your name and your instructor's name to the worksheet in the indicated cells. Print the summary portion of this worksheet for your instructor.

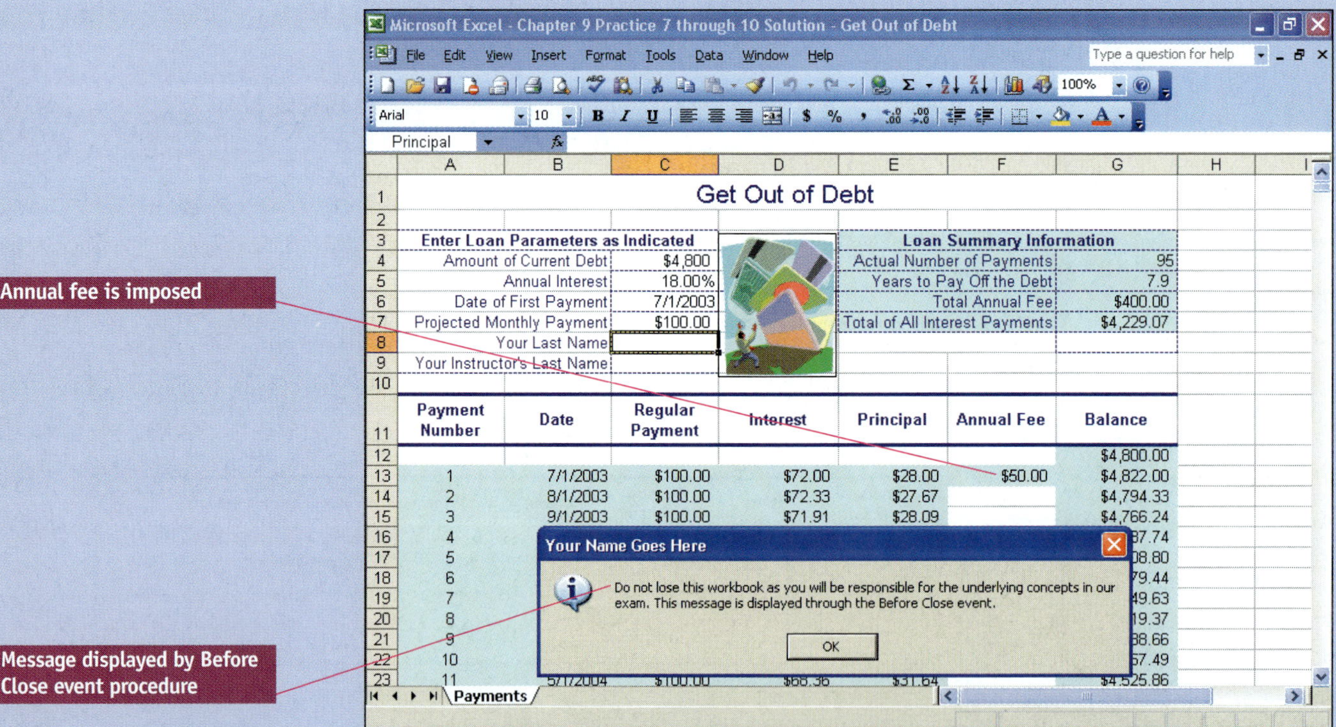

FIGURE 9.18 Expand the Application (exercise 8)

9. **The Get Out of Debt Procedure:** The procedure in Figure 9.19 uses the PMT function to calculate the required monthly payment to pay off the debt within a specified amount of time. The procedure uses existing values within the worksheet for the principal and annual interest rate. It displays an Input Box that prompts the user for the desired number of monthly payments, and then places the result of the calculation (vbPayment) into cell C7 (that has been associated with the range name ProjectedMonthlyPayment).
   a. Open the Get Out of Debt workbook and create the procedure in Figure 9.19. Our procedure includes the statement ClearAnnualFee, which runs the procedure we created in the previous exercise to erase any annual fee that may have been entered into the worksheet. Explain why this is necessary for the Get Out of Debt procedure to work correctly.
   b. Add the completed procedure to the custom toolbar using the image of a heart for the button image.
   c. Test the procedure using the existing loan parameters of $4,800 at 18% interest. Specify that you want to pay off the loan in 36 months. If you do the work correctly, the projected monthly payment should be $173.53. Be sure that your name and your instructor's name have both been entered into the worksheet, then print the payment schedule for your instructor.
   d. Look closely at your worksheet. The value in cell G4 (the cell that contains the actual number of payments) is also 36, which corresponds to the number of months you specified. This is significant because the computation associated with cell G4 is independent of the Get Out of Debt procedure, and thus serves to validate the calculations in the worksheet.
   e. What is the value in cell G48 of the worksheet? How does this serve to further validate the worksheet?

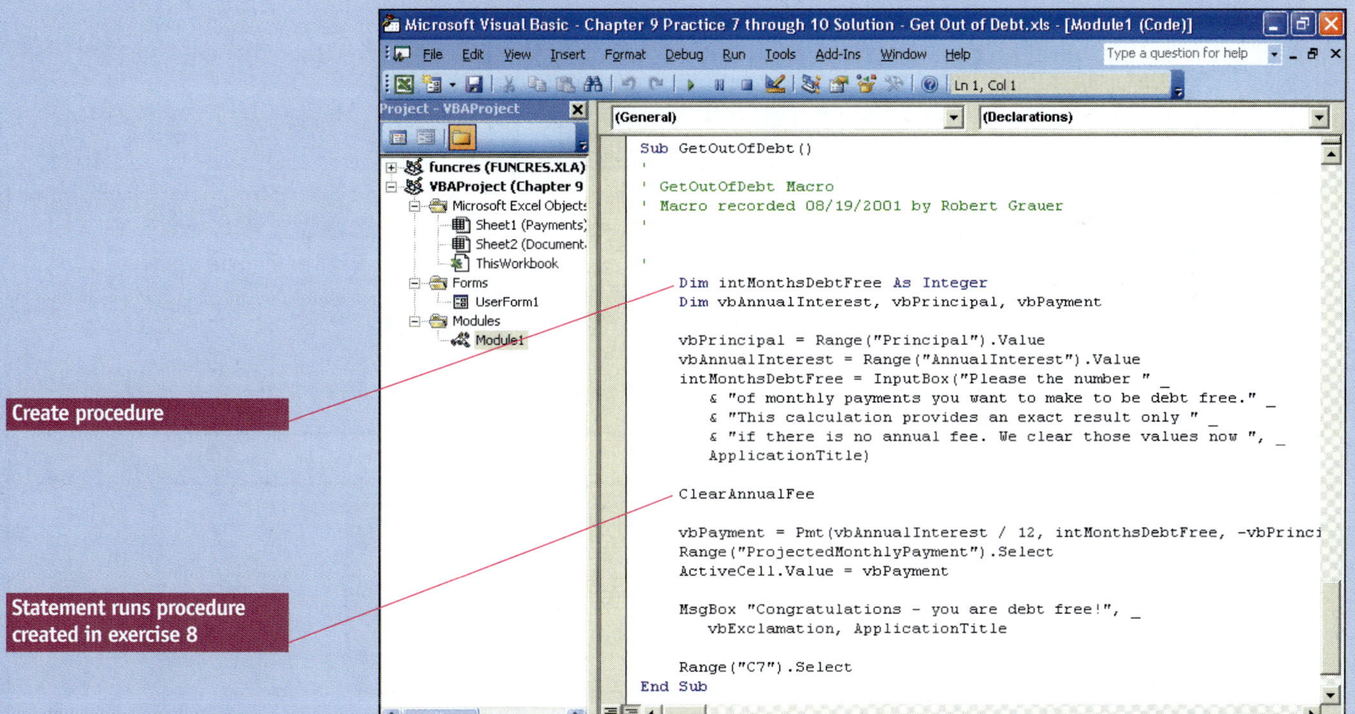


```
Sub GetOutOfDebt()
'
' GetOutOfDebt Macro
' Macro recorded 08/19/2001 by Robert Grauer
'

'
    Dim intMonthsDebtFree As Integer
    Dim vbAnnualInterest, vbPrincipal, vbPayment

    vbPrincipal = Range("Principal").Value
    vbAnnualInterest = Range("AnnualInterest").Value
    intMonthsDebtFree = InputBox("Please the number " _
       & "of monthly payments you want to make to be debt free." _
       & "This calculation provides an exact result only " _
       & "if there is no annual fee. We clear those values now ", _
       ApplicationTitle)

    ClearAnnualFee

    vbPayment = Pmt(vbAnnualInterest / 12, intMonthsDebtFree, -vbPrinci
    Range("ProjectedMonthlyPayment").Select
    ActiveCell.Value = vbPayment

    MsgBox "Congratulations - you are debt free!", _
       vbExclamation, ApplicationTitle

    Range("C7").Select
End Sub
```

FIGURE 9.19 The Get Out of Debt Procedure (exercise 9)

10. **The Completed Application:** Complete the Get Out of Debt application by adding all of the functionality implied by Figure 9.20. This step is actually quite easy in that you can copy code from the Amortization Schedule Solution workbook as necessary.
    a. Add the procedures and corresponding buttons to toggle the documentation worksheet on and off, and to increase or decrease the magnification in the Excel window.
    b. Add a splash screen that is displayed for 5 seconds when the workbook is opened initially. Press the PrintScreen key to capture the splash screen when it appears, then paste the screen into a Word document. Print the Word document for your instructor to show that you created the splash screen successfully.
    c. Print the procedures within the workbook for your instructor. You can print the VBA procedures from within the VBA editor, but the procedures are printed without any formatting. You get a better result by printing from within Microsoft Word. Open the VBA editor, select the procedures you want to print, then click the Copy button (or use the Ctrl+C keyboard shortcut) to copy these procedures to the Windows clipboard.
    d. Start Microsoft Word and open a new document. Click the Paste button (or use the Ctrl+V keyboard shortcut) to paste the contents of the clipboard (the VBA procedures) into the Word document.
    e. Return to the VBA editor to copy the contents of the other modules to the Word document in similar fashion.
    f. Format the procedures in the Word document as you see fit. We suggest you use a monospaced font such as Courier New so that the indentation and alignment are easier to see. We also suggest that you boldface the Sub and End Sub statements of each procedure, and that you insert a horizontal border to separate the procedures from one another.
    g. Add a title page, then submit the completed assignment to your instructor.

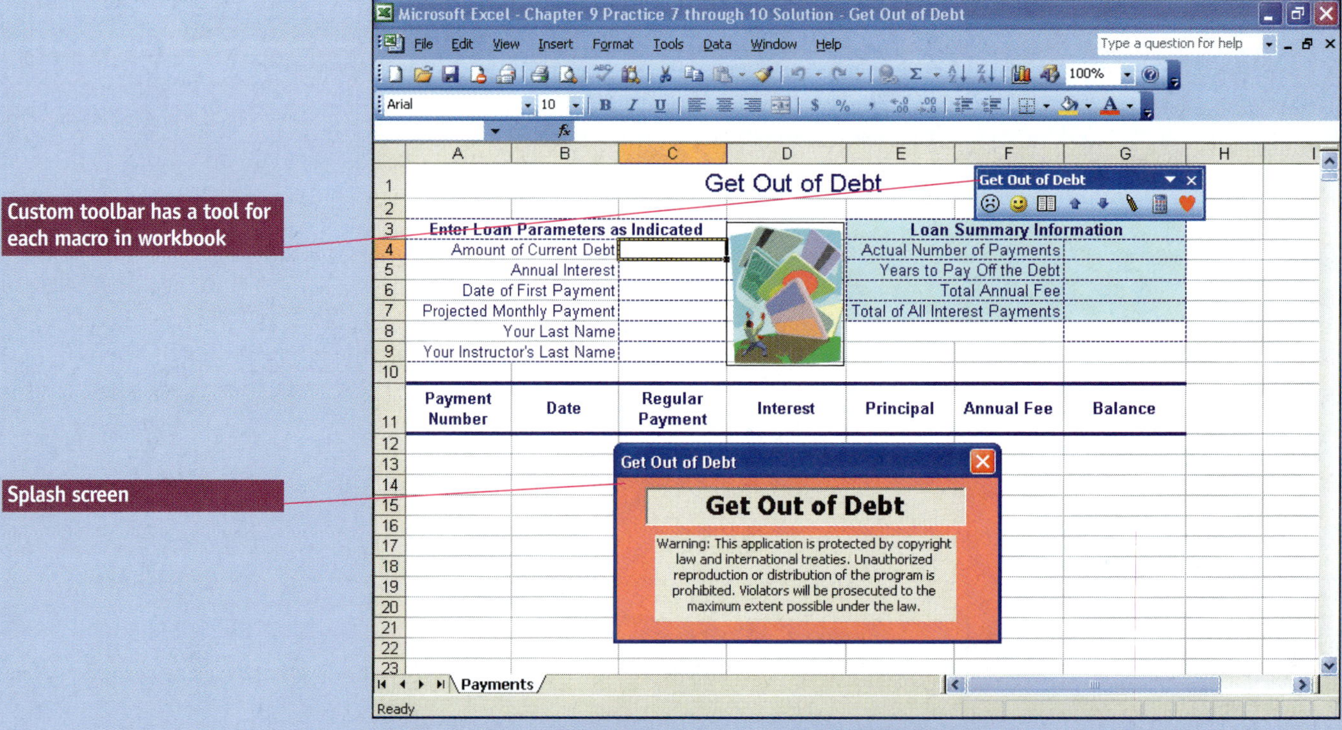

FIGURE 9.20 The Completed Application (exercise 10)

11. **The Mind Reader:** The puzzle in Figure 9.21 was created for the Web by Andy Naughton (www.cyberglass.co.uk) and converted to an Excel workbook by the authors. We thank Andy for permission to use his very clever puzzle. Open the *Chapter 9 Practice 11* workbook, enable the macros, and follow the directions. Choose any two-digit number; add the digits, then subtract the sum from the original number. If you choose 75, for example, the sum is 12, and you wind up with 63 (75 – 12). Look for the number in the table, notice the symbol next to the number, then click the Show Me button. The puzzle will read your mind and display the symbol that is next to your number.

    Click the button to play again. Choose a different number, do the math, and more than likely you will get a different symbol. But no matter how many times you play the game, the puzzle will always be able to guess the symbol. Are you intrigued? We were. Now let's see if we can determine how the puzzle works.

    a. Open the VBA editor and look at Module 1. There are four procedures. Run each procedure to determine what each procedure does. (You may want to tile the Excel and VBA windows to step through each procedure to see the effect of each statement.)
    b. You now know the function of each procedure, but that does not explain how the puzzle works. Return to the Excel window and click the button to Play Again to reset the puzzle. Pull down the Format menu, click the Sheet command, click Unhide, and then unhide the Symbols worksheet. Look at the formula in cell C2. What is the purpose of the RAND function? Press the F9 (Calculate) key. How does the worksheet change?
    c. Click in cell C3 of the Symbols worksheet and examine the formula. How does that formula relate to the value in cell C2 and the table of symbols in column A? Press the F9 key. What happens to the worksheet?
    d. Click the tab for the ReadYourMind worksheet. It would be very helpful to see the cell formulas in this worksheet except that we have protected the worksheet to hide the formulas. We'll give you one more hint. Pull down the Tools menu, click the Protection command, and click the Unprotect Sheet command. A password is not required. Now look at the formulas in the table of symbols to see if you can find the pattern.

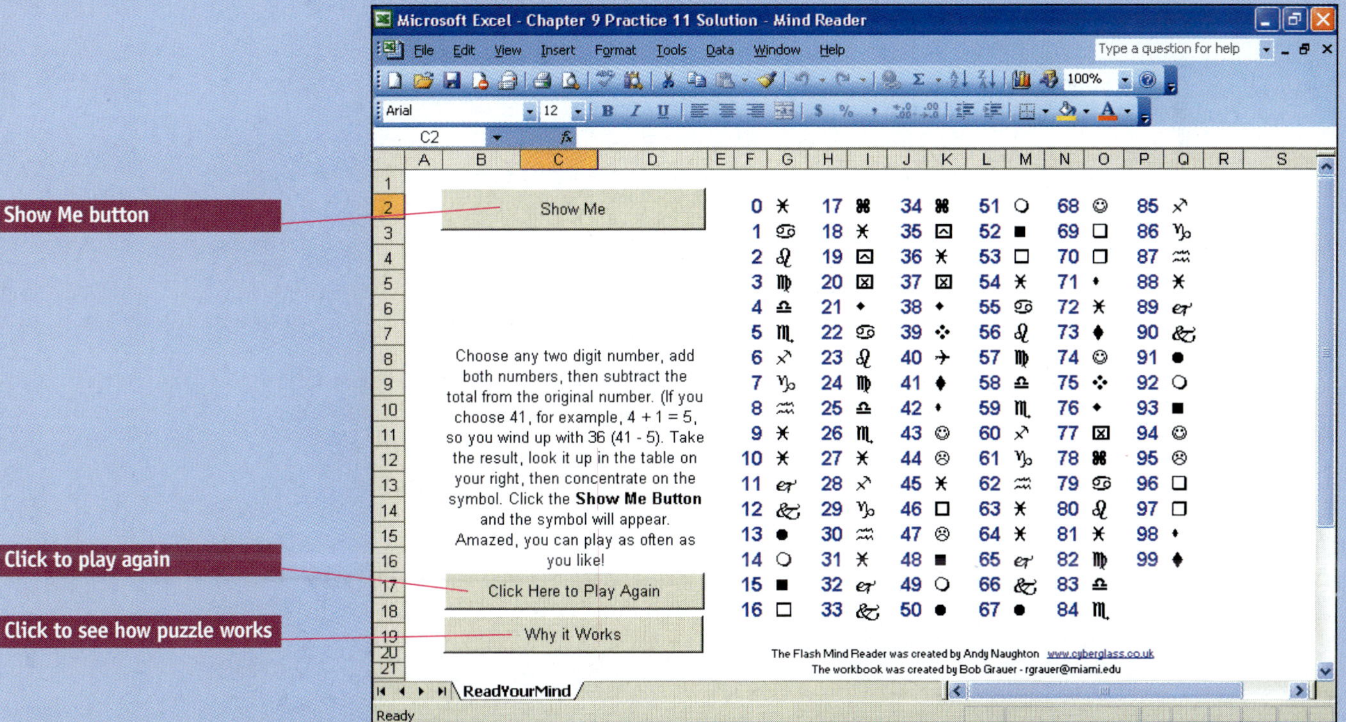

FIGURE 9.21 The Mind Reader (exercise 11)

MINI CASES

The Robot and the Wall

This problem is an exercise in logic and has nothing to do with VBA per se. A robot is sitting on a chair facing a wall a short distance away. Your assignment is to provide the necessary instructions to the robot to stand up, walk to the wall, then turn around, walk back, and sit down in the chair. The robot understands a set of very basic commands—Stand, Sit, Turn (90 degrees to the right), and Step.

The robot can also raise its arms and sense the wall with its fingertips. It cannot, however, sense the chair on its return trip, since the chair is below arm level. Accordingly, the robot must count the number of steps to the wall or chair by using another set of commands—Add (increment a counter by 1), Subtract (decrement the counter by 1), Initialize Counter to zero, Arms Up, and Arms Down. The wall is an integer number of steps away.

Open the partially completed PowerPoint presentation, *Chapter 9 Mini Case—The Robot and the Wall,* which describes this assignment. Enter the completed pseudocode on a new slide, and then present your solution to the class. Ask for a volunteer to play the part of the robot.

The Object Browser

The Object Browser is a useful tool to explore the objects within the Excel object model. Open any Excel workbook, start the VBA editor, pull down the View menu, and choose Object Browser. Specify the Excel object library and then scroll through the various classes that appear within the class list. A class is the formal definition of an object; it describes the properties, methods, and events that are available for that object.

The list is overwhelming at first. We suggest you focus initially on the Range object that was used in multiple procedures throughout the chapter. Once you choose the object (class) in the left pane, you will see the members of that class (its properties, methods, and events) in the right pane. Each type of member has a different symbol. Locate the Select method and Value property for the Range object and try to relate this information to the procedures in the chapter.

Experiment further with the worksheets collection and the worksheet object. (A collection is a group of similar objects.) Summarize your thoughts about the Object Browser in a short note to your instructor.

Your Own Application

Develop a VBA application of comparable function and complexity to the Amortization Schedule or Get Out of Debt applications from the chapter or end-of-chapter exercises. The application should be flexible, visually appealing, easy to use, and bulletproof. Choose any scenario that is of interest to you. The only restriction is that you *cannot* develop an application based on the PMT function.

The completed application should include event procedures for opening and closing the workbook, a splash screen, and a custom toolbar. It should also contain one or two nontrivial procedures that include loops and decision making. You can copy the generic macros to increase or decrease the zoom percentage or toggle a documentation worksheet on or off that were creatd in the chapter. Present the completed application to the class.

CHAPTER

10

Extending VBA: Processing Worksheets and Workbooks

OBJECTIVES

After reading this chapter you will:

1. Use the Dir function to open all workbooks in a specific folder.
2. Explain how the Len function indicates an "empty" folder.
3. Use the On Error and Exit Sub statements for error trapping.
4. Use the Forms toolbar to add a command button to a worksheet.
5. Use the For/Next statement to process all worksheets in a workbook.
6. Change the color of a worksheet tab based on a value in the worksheet.
7. Explain how to "divide and conquer" to create an application.
8. Call one VBA procedure from another procedure.

hands-on exercises

1. CREATE SUMMARY WORKBOOK
Input: Expense Statement; Expense Summary
Output: Expense Statement (modified to include your name); Expense Summary Solution
2. ERROR TRAPPING
Input: Expense Summary Solution
Output: Expense Summary Solution (additional modifications)
3. CREATE SUMMARY WORKSHEET
Input: Expense Summary Solution (from exercise 2)
Output: Expense Summary Solution (additional modifications)
4. BETTER SUMMARY WORKBOOK
Input: Better Summary
Output: Better Summary Solution

CASE STUDY

END OF THE MONTH

It happens at the end of every month—you want to leave the office at a reasonable hour, but are inundated with a set of employee expense statements, each in a separate workbook. You cannot leave until you have extracted the data from each individual workbook into a summary workbook, retaining each employee's data on a separate worksheet in the summary workbook. You then have to evaluate each employee's expenses individually to see whether the total is under the allocated amount.

It's time consuming, tedious, and rather boring. Were it not for this monthly "nuisance," your job would be much easier and you would be much happier. If only there were a way to make it happen with the push of a button or two, then you could be spending that extra time making plans for the weekend. Just when you were feeling down about your work, a colleague suggested that you automate the entire process using Excel macros and VBA. ■

Your assignment is to read the chapter and complete all four hands-on exercises, which have you create the Better Summary Solution workbook. The completed workbook will contain all of the macros to consolidate the expense statements as applied to a specific set of employee worksheets. Prove to yourself how easy the automation procedure is by using the completed workbook to process a different set of expense statements.

Open the *Better Summary Solution* workbook. Pull down the Tools menu, click Macro, run the macro to Reset the Summary Worksheet, then manually delete all of the existing employee worksheets from the Better Summary Solution workbook. Now click the button to Create Summary workbook and enter "*C:\Exploring Excel\Chapter 10 Case Study*" as the name of the folder containing the new set of employee expense statements. You will be prompted to save each workbook in this folder, after which you will be prompted for the maximum allowable expense. Enter $1,000, and then sit back as the new summary workbook is created for you. Print the new summary worksheet for your instructor.

THE EXPENSE SUMMARY APPLICATION

A good application enables an end user to accomplish tasks that he or she could not (easily) do through ordinary Excel commands. Consider, for example, the Expense Summary workbook that appears in Figure 10.1. Each employee submits an expense statement at the beginning of each month with his or her expenses for the previous month. The expense statements are submitted as separate Excel workbooks such as the one in Figure 10.1a. Your task is to consolidate the individual workbooks to create a summary workbook, as shown in Figure 10.1b.

Each individual workbook contains a single worksheet listing the expenses for that employee. The summary workbook, on the other hand, contains multiple worksheets with one worksheet for each employee. The summary workbook also contains a summary worksheet that lists the expenses for all employees, as well as an indication of whether the expenses are approved or require further review.

You could build the summary workbook manually using specific Excel commands to open each employee workbook, and copy the associated worksheet to the summary workbook. You then have to review the employee expenses on each worksheet and copy the relevant information to the summary worksheet. This is tedious, to say the least, and it is also prone to error. And what if there were 100 employees, as opposed to five? Clearly, you need to automate the process.

You should not, however, attempt to write a single VBA procedure to build the summary workbook because it is too complicated. It is better to divide the overall task into a series of smaller, more manageable tasks, each of which requires its own procedure. The procedures are developed and tested individually, then executed collectively to create the summary workbook. This is the methodology that we follow throughout the chapter. The end result will be an "empty" workbook that contains multiple procedures to obtain the individual employee data and produce the summary information. You will be able to click a single command button and build the entire workbook.

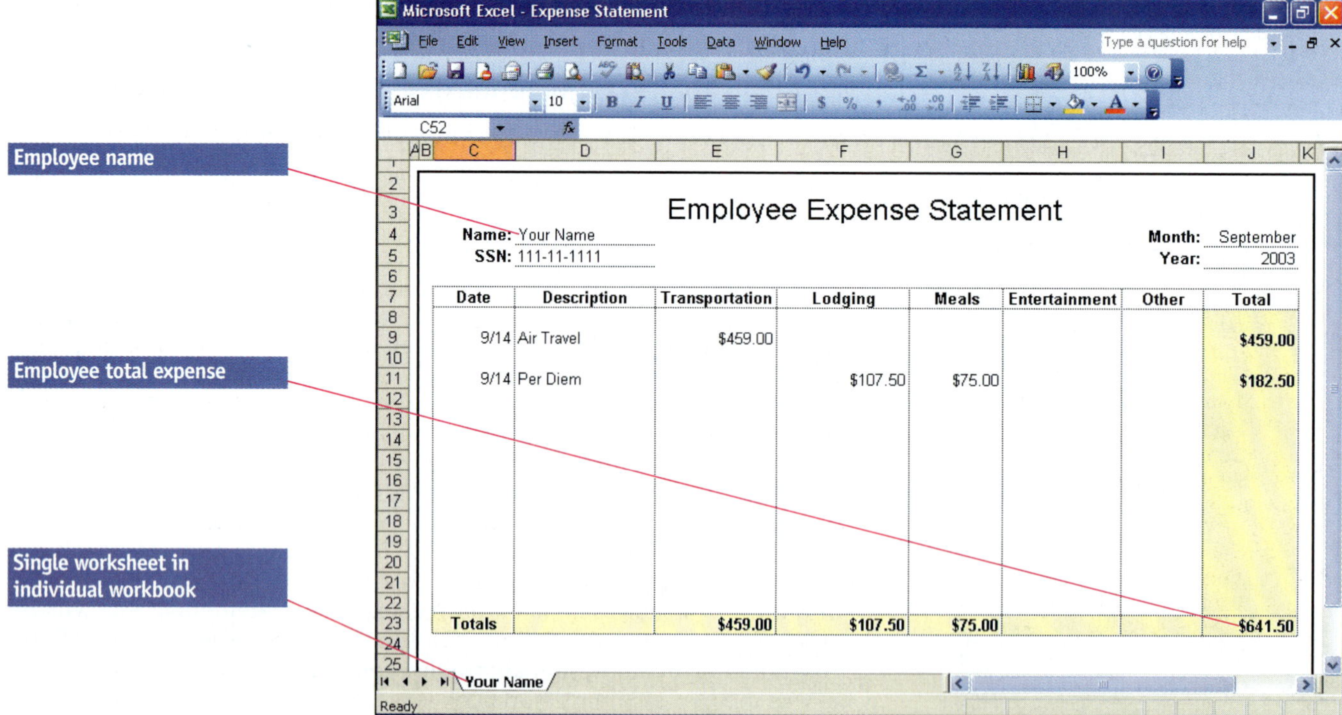

(a) Individual Expense Statement

FIGURE 10.1 The Expense Summary Application

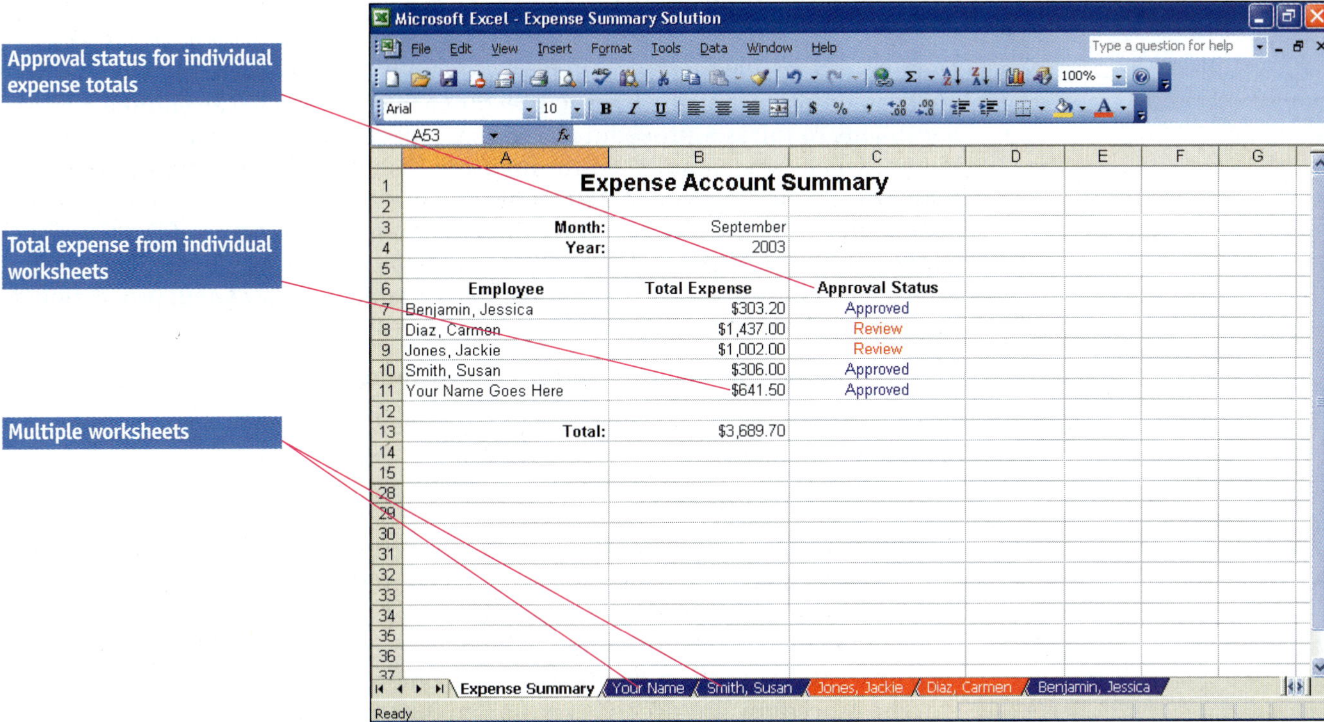

(b) Summary Workbook

FIGURE 10.1 The Expense Summary Application (*continued*)

A QUICK REVIEW

The VBA procedures to create the summary workbook use many VBA statements that do not have equivalent Excel commands. These statements are presented collectively in the VBA primer at the end of this text, and it is important that you are comfortable with their use and syntax. A quick summary is shown below.

The ***MsgBox statement*** displays information to the user. It has one required argument, which is the message (or prompt) that is displayed to the user. The other two arguments, the icon that is to be displayed in the message box, and the text of the title bar, are optional. The ***InputBox function*** displays a prompt for information, and then it stores that information for later use.

Every variable must be declared (defined) before it can be used. This is accomplished through the ***Dim*** (short for Dimension) ***statement*** that appears at the beginning of a procedure. The Dim statement indicates the name of the variable and its type (for example, whether it will hold a character string or an integer number), which in turn reserves the appropriate amount of memory for that variable.

The ability to make decisions within a procedure and then branch to alternative sets of statements is implemented through the ***If. . .Then. . .Else statement***. The Else clause is optional, but may be repeated multiple times within an If statement.

The ***For. . .Next statement*** (or For. . .Next loop as it is also called) executes all statements between the words For and Next a specified number of times, using a counter to keep track of the number of times the loop is executed. The ***Do Until*** and/or the ***Do While statements*** are used when the number of iterations is not known in advance.

Remember, too, that a VBA procedure is created in one of two ways—by entering statements directly into the VBA editor and/or by using the macro recorder to capture Excel commands and convert them to their VBA equivalents. You can also combine the two techniques by starting with the macro recorder to capture basic statements, view the resulting syntax, and then embellish the original statements.

The Dir Function

The first task in creating the summary workbook is to open the individual workbooks in order to copy the information for each employee to the summary workbook. This requires a procedure to process all of the workbooks in a specified folder, which is accomplished through the Visual Basic Dir function. The ***Dir function*** returns the name of the first file that matches a specified character string. For example, *Dir(C:\Expense Statements*.xls)* returns the name of the first Excel workbook in the Expense Statements folder on drive C. The file name of the workbook that was found can be stored in a variable for subsequent processing by the following statement:

strWorkbookName = Dir("C:\Expense Statements*.xls")

The next workbook in the folder is obtained by calling the Dir function without any arguments as shown below:

strWorkbookName = Dir

The two Dir statements are used in conjunction with one another to process all of the workbooks in a folder, as shown in Figure 10.2. The initial Dir statement is executed once to be sure that the specified folder exists, and further, to obtain the name of the first workbook in that folder. The second Dir statement is placed in a loop to access every other workbook in that folder.

The procedure also depends on the Len function to determine when all of the workbooks have been processed. The ***Len function*** returns the number of characters in the specified variable. (A length of zero indicates an empty character string, which implies that no more workbooks were found.) The Len function appears in an If statement immediately following the initial Dir statement to ensure that the folder contains at least one workbook. The function is also used to terminate the Do While loop after the last employee workbook has been processed; i.e., the loop ends when the length of the file name is zero to indicate there are no more workbooks in the folder.

The procedure in Figure 10.2 contains statements that were inserted by the macro recorder as well as VBA statements that were entered directly. The recorder was used to capture the keystrokes to open a specified workbook, to select a worksheet in the workbook, to copy the selected sheet to the Expense Summary workbook, and finally to close the workbook. The remaining statements were entered explicitly by the developer.

Initial Dir function

Len function

Dir Statement within loop

```
Public Sub OpenAllWorkbooks()
    Dim strWorkbookName

    strWorkbookName = Dir("C:\Exploring Excel\Expense Statements\*.xls")
    If Len(strWorkbookName) > 0 Then
        Do While Len(strWorkbookName) > 0
            Workbooks.Open Filename:= _
                "C:\Exploring Excel\Expense Statements\" & strWorkbookName
            Sheets(1).Select
            Sheets(1).Copy After:=Workbooks("Expense Summary Solution.xls").Sheets(1)
            Workbooks(strWorkbookName).Close
            strWorkbookName = Dir
        Loop
    Else
        MsgBox "Error - The folder C:\Exploring Excel\Expense Statements " _
            & "does not exist and/or there are no workbooks in the folder. " _
            & "Please check the folder name and then rerun the macro.", _
            vbCritical, ApplicationTitle
    End If
End Sub
```

FIGURE 10.2 The Open All Workbooks Procedure

hands-on exercise

1 Create the Summary Workbook

Objective Run a VBA procedure to combine worksheets from multiple workbooks into a single workbook. Use Figure 10.3 as a guide in the exercise.

Step 1: Open the Expense Statement Workbook

- Open the **Expense Statement workbook** in the Exploring Excel Folder. Click the button to **Enable Macros** to display the worksheet in Figure 10.3a.
- Enter your name into **cell D4** in the indicated format. Type your **last name, a comma and a space**, then **your first name**.
- Press the **Tab key** to move to **cell J4**, where you will enter the **previous month** (the month for which you are submitting expenses). You can type the month yourself, or you can select the month by clicking the **down arrow** in the list box.

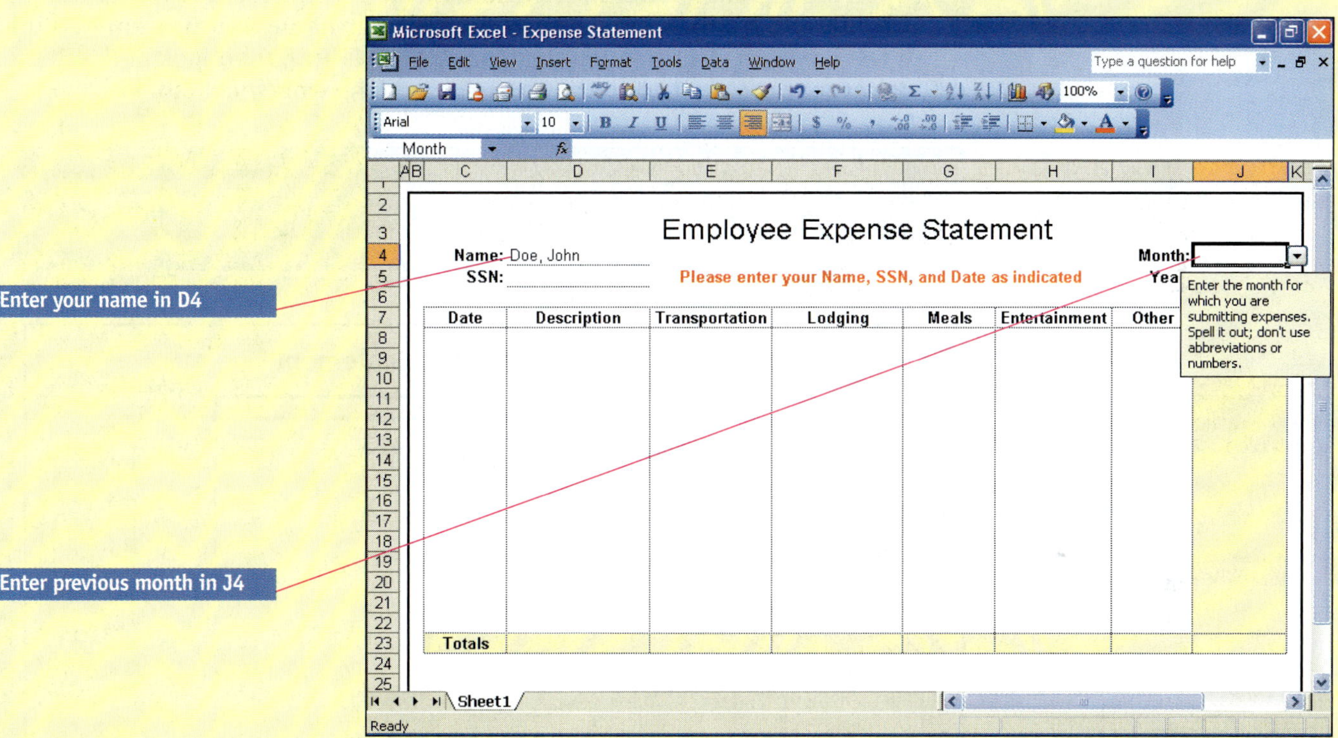

(a) Open the Expense Statement Workbook (step 1)

FIGURE 10.3 Hands-on Exercise 1

DATA VALIDATION

The Expense Statement worksheet uses the Data Validation command to ensure that the user enters a valid month. Pull down the Tools menu, click Protection, then click the Unprotect Sheet command. Scroll down in the worksheet until you can click and drag to select rows 27 to 40, pull down the Format menu, click Row, then click Unhide. Now click in cell J4, pull down the Data menu, and click the Validation command to see how the input for this cell is restricted to the list in cells C28 to C39. Click the Undo command twice to reverse the last commands and hide these rows. Reprotect the worksheet.

Step 2: Understanding the Workbook

- Click in **cell D5** and enter your **student ID number** in place of the Social Security number. The text in cell E5 is no longer visible. Delete your student ID number, and the text reappears.
- Click in **cell E5** as shown in Figure 10.3b. The formula in this cell uses the OR function within an IF function to determine if any of four cells is blank, and if so, it displays the text requesting you to enter the appropriate information.
- Click in **cell D5** and reenter your **Social Security number**.
- The year is entered automatically into the worksheet. Click in **cell J5** to see how this is accomplished. (The worksheet assumes that you are always entering expenses for the previous month.)
- The Expense Statement workbook contains a single worksheet that is named Sheet1. Close the workbook. Click **Yes** when prompted to save the changes.
- Reopen the **Expense Statement workbook**, enable macros, and notice that the worksheet tab has been renamed to match your name as it was entered into cell D4. Press **Alt+F11** to open the Visual Basic Editor, then look at the Before Close event procedure to see how we changed the worksheet tab.

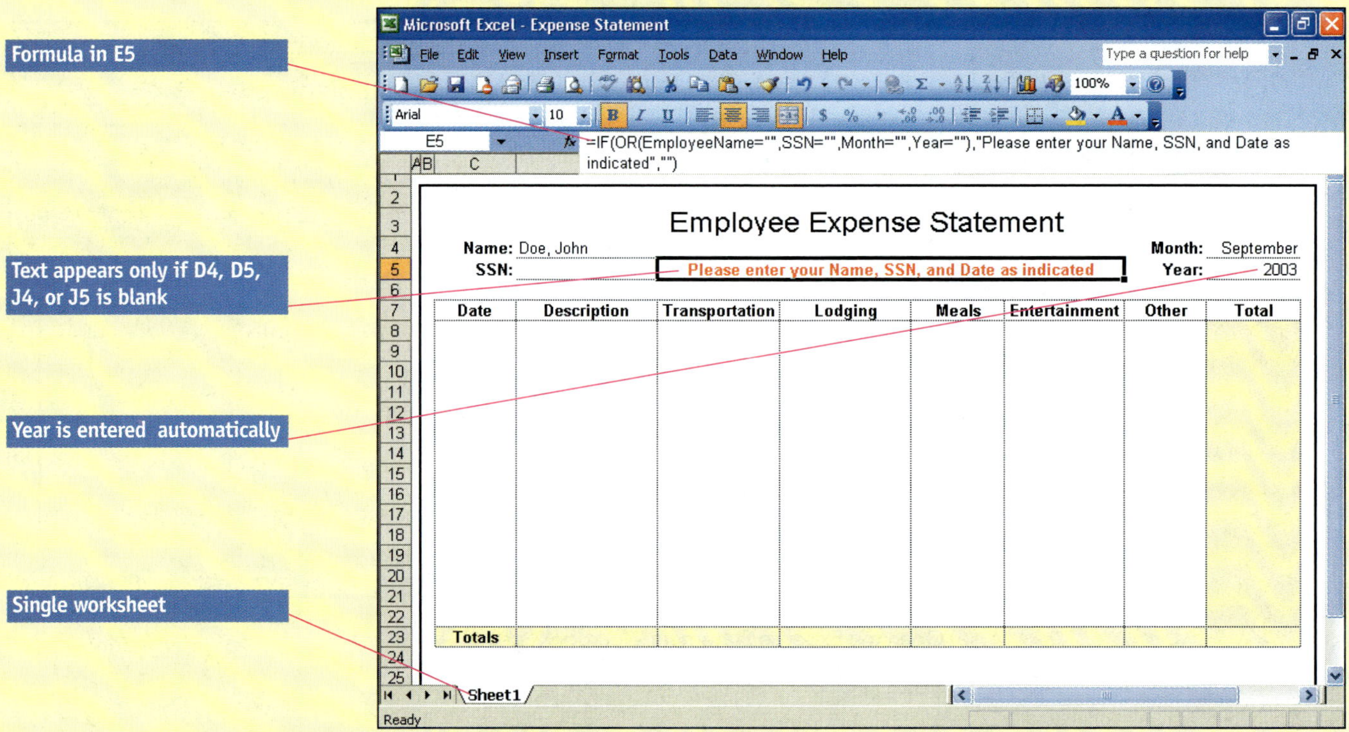

(b) Understanding the Workbook (step 2)

FIGURE 10.3 Hands-on Exercise 1 (*continued*)

EVENT-DRIVEN PROGRAMMING

The Open Workbook and Before Close event procedures may contain VBA code to accomplish certain "housekeeping" at the beginning and end of an application, respectively. The Before Close event procedure in this application confirms that the employee name has been entered, and if so, it changes the worksheet tab to reflect the employee name. This becomes important in subsequent steps, when the individual worksheets are combined into a summary workbook.

Step 3: The Expense Statements Folder

- Return to the Excel workbook. Click in **cell C9**. Enter an appropriate date—that is, a date in which the month matches the value in cell J4. You can enter the date with or without the year—for example, as 9/14 or as 9/14/03. (The year will not be displayed.)
- Enter the indicated description and expense for this date as shown in Figure 10.3c. Use the **Tab key** to move from one column to the next within the row. The total is computed automatically.
- Enter the second set of expenses into row 11. You can choose any date (within the month), but use the Description and the dollar amounts that are shown in the figure.
- Pull down the **File menu** and click the **Save As command** to display the Save As dialog box in Figure 10.3c. Double click the **Expense Statements folder** that exists within the Exploring Excel folder.
- Click in the **File name** text box and save the workbook in Expense Statements folder as **Your Last Name - Expense Statement**.
- Pull down the **File menu** and click the **Close command** (or click the **Close button** in the document window) to close your workbook. Click **Yes** if prompted to save the changes.

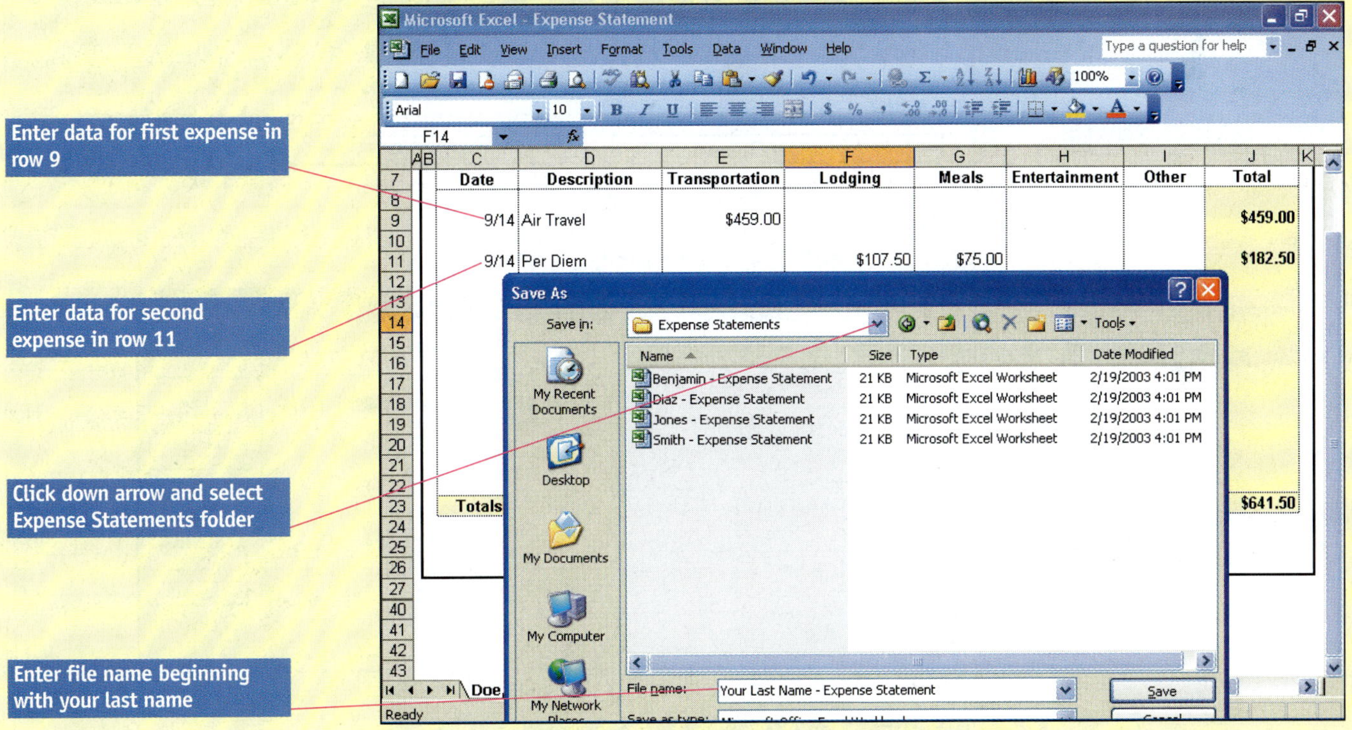

(c) The Expense Statements Folder (step 3)

FIGURE 10.3 Hands-on Exercise 1 (*continued*)

THE EXPENSE STATEMENTS FOLDER

The Expense Statements folder has been created for you. It contains four existing workbooks, each of which represents the expenses of a different employee. You have just added your workbook to this folder. The next step in this exercise will copy the expense worksheet from each of these workbooks into a summary workbook.

Step 4: Run the Open All Workbooks Procedure

- Open the **Expense Summary workbook** in the Exploring Excel folder. Click the button to **Enable macros**. Save the workbook as **Expense Summary Solution** so that you can return to the original workbook if necessary.
- The workbook consists of a single worksheet. The month and year are entered automatically and should reflect last month (the month for which the expenses are being submitted).
- Pull down the **Tools menu**, click **Macro**, then click **Macros...** to display the Macro dialog box as shown in Figure 10.3d. Select the **OpenAllWorkbooks macro**, then click the **Run button** to execute the VBA procedure.
- The procedure opens the first employee workbook in the Expense Statements folder, then it displays a message asking whether you want to save the changes to this workbook. Click **No**. (If this does not occur, skip the remainder of this step, and go to step 5.)
- The procedure continues to open each employee workbook in the folder, prompting you to save each workbook. Click **No** and continue in this fashion until all five workbooks have been opened.
- Save the Expense Summary Solution workbook.

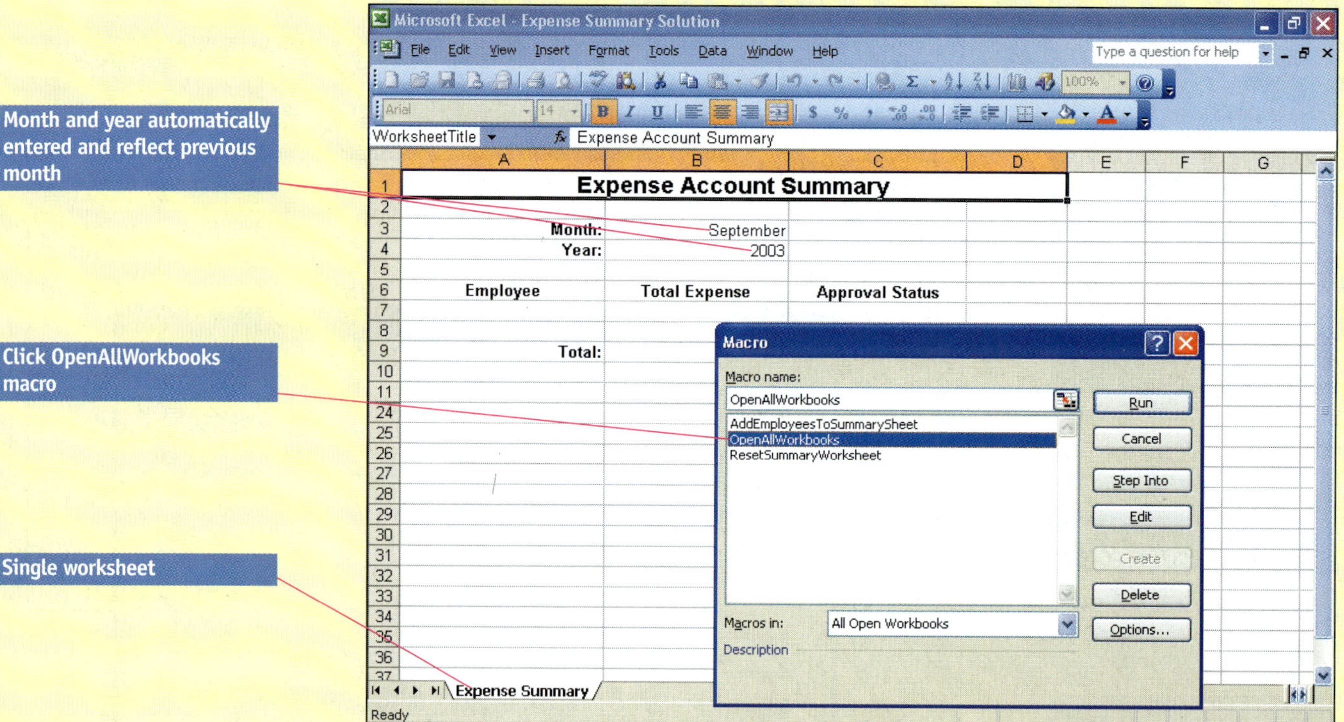

(d) Run the Open All Workbooks Procedure (step 4)

FIGURE 10.3 Hands-on Exercise 1 (*continued*)

SAVING THE INDIVIDUAL WORKBOOKS

Our application takes "poetic license" in that the individual employee workbooks are modified each time they are opened through date functions. This was done to keep the workbooks current; that is, the employee workbooks will reference the same month for which you are submitting your expense report. The contents (dates) in the workbooks change, however, and thus Excel prompts you to save the changes.

Step 5: Debugging

- Your actions in this step depend on the success of the previous step:
  - If the procedure executed successfully, press **Alt+F11** to open the editor.
  - If the procedure did not execute correctly, Click **OK** in response to the error message in Figure 10.3e, then press **Alt+F11** to open the VBA editor.
- Double click **Module1** within Project Explorer to display the procedures within this module. Locate the OpenAllWorkbooks procedure that was shown earlier in Figure 10.2. Note the following:
  - The Dir function obtains the names of the Excel workbooks in the **Expense Statements folder**, which is located in the Exploring Excel folder on drive C.
  - If your procedure did not execute correctly, it is most likely because the folder does not exist on your system and/or it is on a different drive. Make the necessary changes, either by changing the folder name and/or location using Windows Explorer or by modifying the procedure. Return to the previous step and reexecute the procedure.
- Close the VBA window to return to Excel.

Error message indicates that designated folder was not found

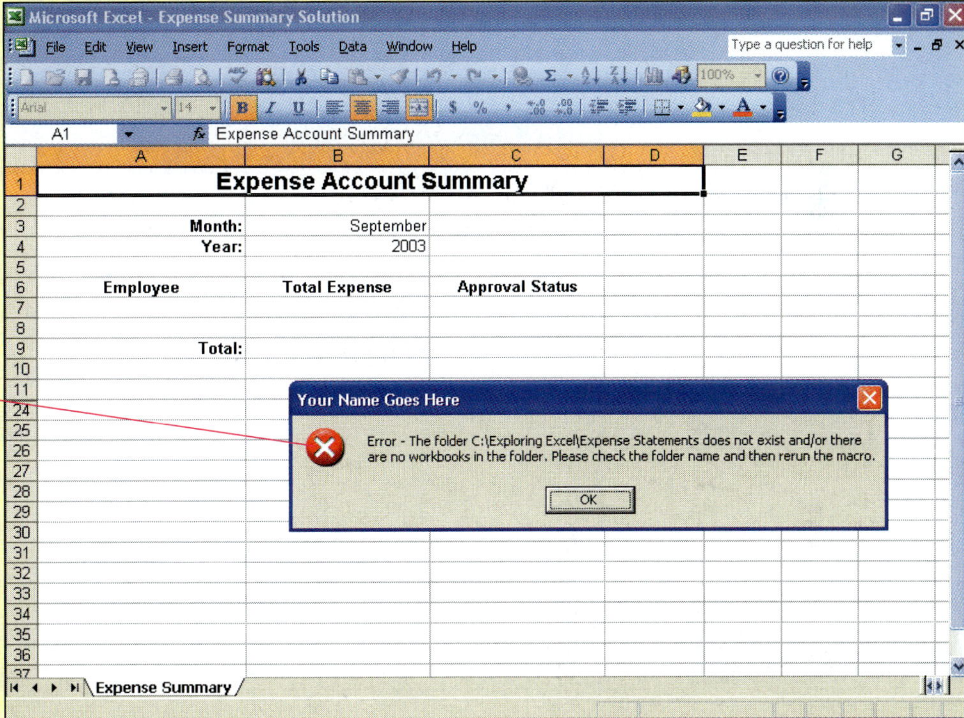

(e) Debugging (step 5)

FIGURE 10.3 Hands-on Exercise 1 (*continued*)

ANTICIPATE USER ERRORS

The developer will understand why a procedure fails to execute properly and/or the meaning of the associated error message. The end user will not, however, and thus a good application anticipates mistakes that a user may make and displays meaningful messages to correct the problem. The OpenAllWorkbooks procedure checks the value returned by the initial Dir function, then displays the appropriate message if the function does not locate an Excel workbook.

Step 6: The Expense Summary Workbook

- You should see the Expense Summary Solution workbook as shown in Figure 10.3f. There are a total of six worksheets:
  - The Expense Summary worksheet that existed at the start of the exercise. This worksheet does not yet contain any employee information.
  - A worksheet with your name that contains the expenses you entered earlier.
  - Four additional worksheets that contain the expenses of other employees.
- Select the worksheet containing your expenses. Recall that you entered the month manually into cell J4, and further that you were instructed to enter the previous month. (Expenses are submitted in the current month for the previous month.)
- Select any other employee worksheet. The month and year in this worksheet should match the values in your worksheet. This was accomplished through the use of Date functions and a VLOOKUP function to provide consistency among the worksheets. (See boxed tip.)
- Save the Expense Summary Solution workbook. Exit Excel if you do not want to continue with the next exercise at this time.

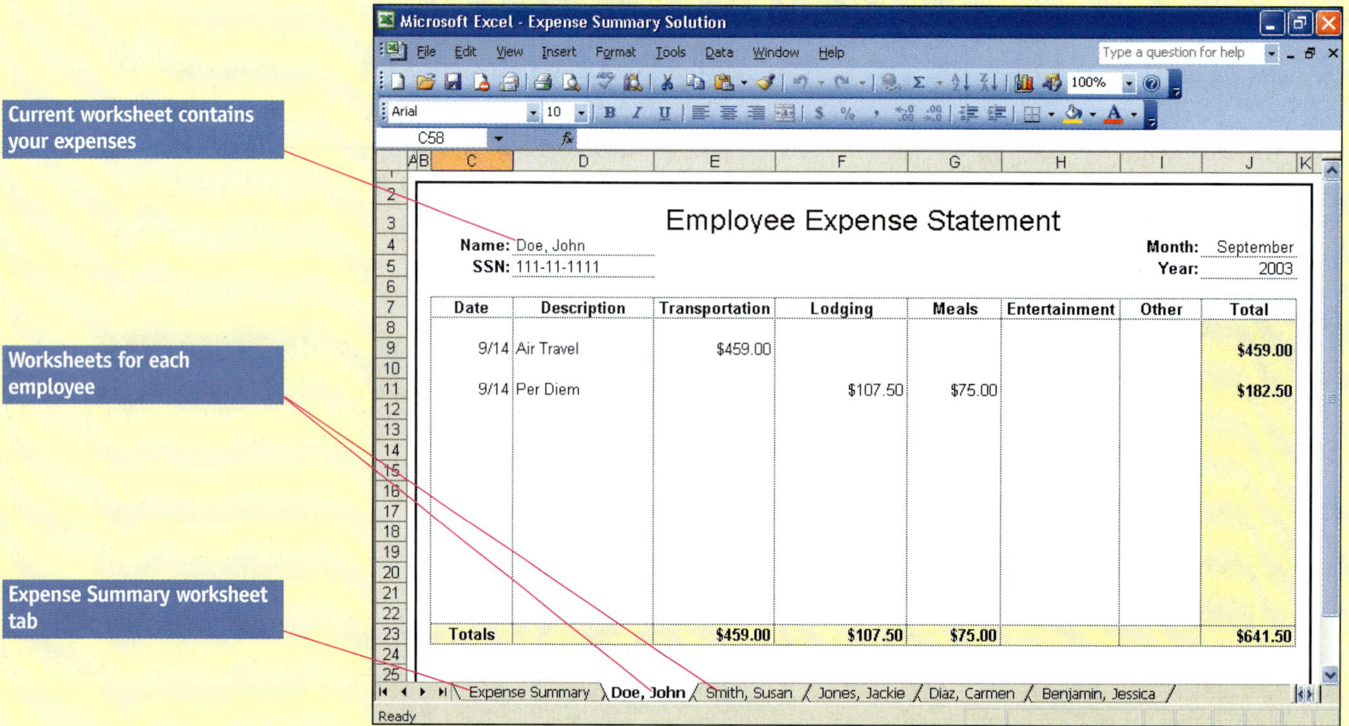

(f) The Expense Summary Workbook (step 6)

FIGURE 10.3 Hands-on Exercise 1 (*continued*)

THE VLOOKUP FUNCTION

Cell D28 in each employee worksheet contains the Excel formula =Month(Today())-1 to determine the previous month. This is a numeric value, however, and it is converted to text through a VLOOKUP function. Click in cell J4 of any employee worksheet to display the formula =VLOOKUP(D28,B28:C39,2). The VLOOKUP function takes the numeric month in cell D28 and applies it to a table of the month names in cells B28 through C39. Unprotect the worksheet, then unhide the indicated rows to see these functions.

DISPLAYING A SPECIFIC WORKSHEET

The summary workbook that has been created contains a worksheet for each employee who submitted an expense report. Our next task is to display the expenses for a specific employee on demand, perhaps when speaking to that employee to obtain additional documentation for his or her expenses. This could be done within the Excel interface, without benefit of a VBA procedure, simply by clicking the worksheet tab for that employee. It's easy to find the worksheet in a workbook with only a few employees, but much more tedious in a large workbook. Excel does not have a command to sort the worksheets within a workbook. Accordingly, we will develop a procedure to display a specific worksheet.

The user is prompted to enter the name of a specific employee as shown in Figure 10.4a, after which the procedure selects (displays) the associated worksheet. It sounds easy, and it is, provided the user enters the employee name *exactly* as it appears on a worksheet tab within the summary workbook. If the user makes a mistake, even one as insignificant as omitting the comma or space, an error results and the worksheet will not be displayed. You may know that "Smith John" and "Smith, John" are one and the same, but VBA does not. If it cannot find the worksheet, it will display a rather intimidating error message, "Run Time Error 9—Subscript Out of Range", and the user is left to decipher the meaning of this message.

Error Trapping

The preceding error is a ***run-time error*** that occurs during the execution of a procedure. (A ***syntax error*** occurs prior to execution and must be corrected to execute the procedure.) A run-time error terminates a procedure immediately, then it displays an explanation in a message box. The developer may know the meaning of the message, but the typical user does not. Thus, a good application will anticipate (trap) errors that are likely to occur and take appropriate action when they do occur. This is accomplished through the ***On Error statement*** that transfers control to a special error-handling section at the end of the procedure. The latter contains additional processing statements and/or simply displays a more meaningful error message.

Consider now the procedure in Figure 10.4b. The Dim statement at the beginning of the procedure defines the variable strEmployeeName. The user is asked to enter the employee's name, and the result is stored in strEmployeeName. The next statement selects the appropriate worksheet, which in turn displays the worksheet in the Excel window. Syntactically, the statement is specifying a ***worksheet object*** and applying the Select method to the object. The generic format for that statement is Sheets("SheetName").Select. Instead of the worksheet name, however, we use the variable strEmployeeName, which contains the name of the desired worksheet. (Quotation marks are not used, or else VBA would attempt to display a worksheet called "strEmployeeName".)

The ***Exit Sub statement*** follows, and it terminates the procedure. The Exit Statement is essential because, without it, the procedure would continue to execute and process the statements in the error-handling routine.

Now consider what happens in the event of an error. The On Error statement takes effect any time a run-time error occurs. The procedure ceases its normal processing and jumps to the section called ErrorHandler. (ErrorHandler is a user-defined name, as opposed to a VBA reserved word.) The ErrorHandler section (note the colon to indicate that ErrorHandler is a label and not an executable statement) appears at the end of the procedure. It consists of a single MsgBox statement to display a more helpful error message. Additional statements could be added to this section to take further action. The End Sub statement is reached, and the procedure terminates. The procedure in Figure 10.4b is a simple, but solid, example of ***error trapping***.

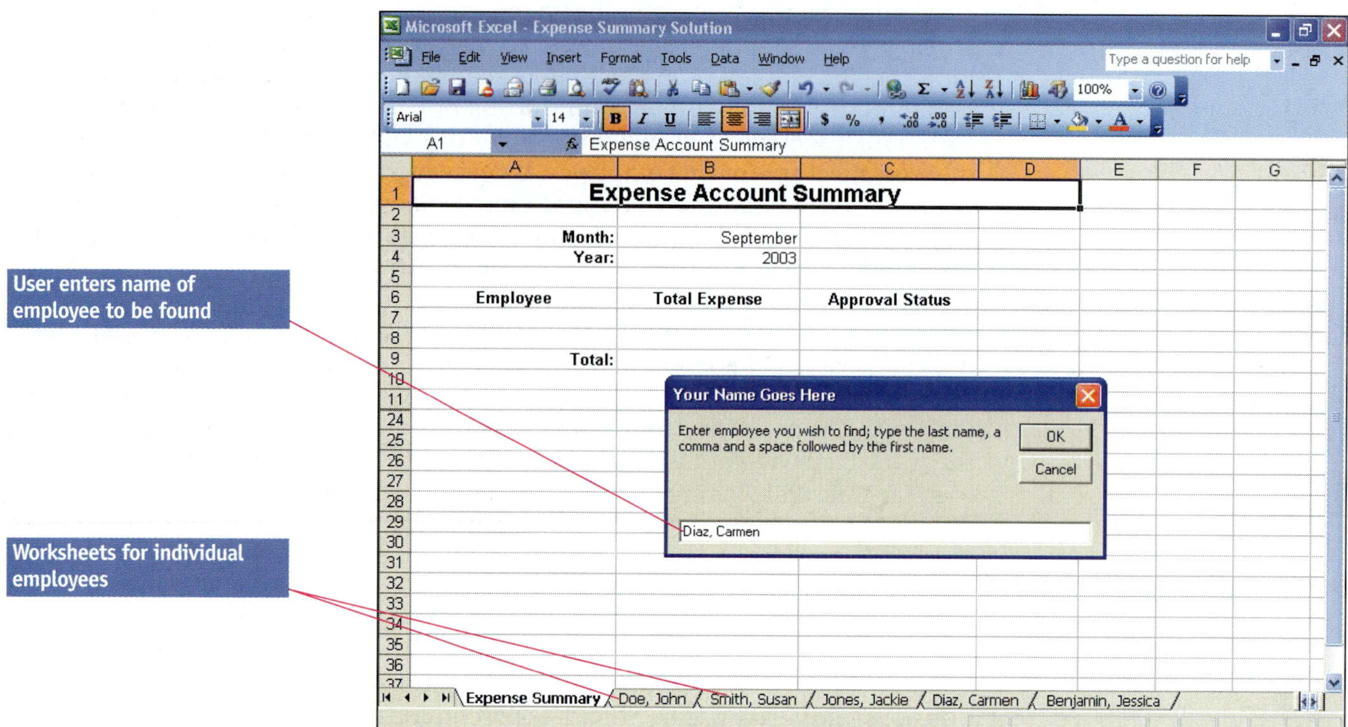

(a) Excel Workbook

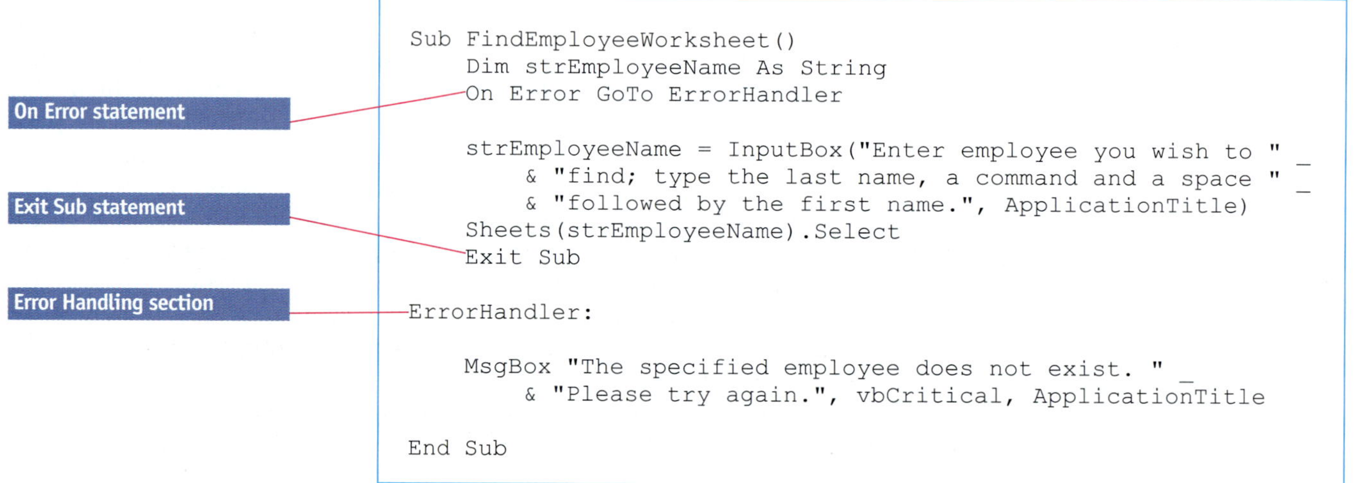


```
Sub FindEmployeeWorksheet()
    Dim strEmployeeName As String
    On Error GoTo ErrorHandler

    strEmployeeName = InputBox("Enter employee you wish to " _
        & "find; type the last name, a command and a space " _
        & "followed by the first name.", ApplicationTitle)
    Sheets(strEmployeeName).Select
    Exit Sub

ErrorHandler:

    MsgBox "The specified employee does not exist. " _
        & "Please try again.", vbCritical, ApplicationTitle

End Sub
```

(b) VBA Procedure

FIGURE 10.4 Finding an Employee Worksheet

hands-on exercise

2 Error Trapping

Objective Develop a VBA procedure to display a specific worksheet within a workbook; include the appropriate error-trapping statements.

Step 1: **Start the Macro Recorder**

- Open the **Expense Summary Solution workbook** from the last exercise. Click the button to **Enable Macros**. Click the **Expense Summary worksheet tab**.
- Pull down the **Tools menu**, click the **Macro command**, then click **Record New Macro** to display the Record Macro dialog box in Figure 10.5a.
- Enter **FindEmployeeWorksheet** as the name of the procedure. Click the **Shortcut Key** check box and enter a **lowercase f**. **Ctrl+f** should appear as the keyboard shortcut. Click **OK** to begin recording.
- Click the worksheet tab for **Susan Smith**. Click the **Stop Recording button**. (If you do not see the Stop Recording toolbar, pull down the **Tools menu**, click **Macro**, and click the **Stop Recording command**.)

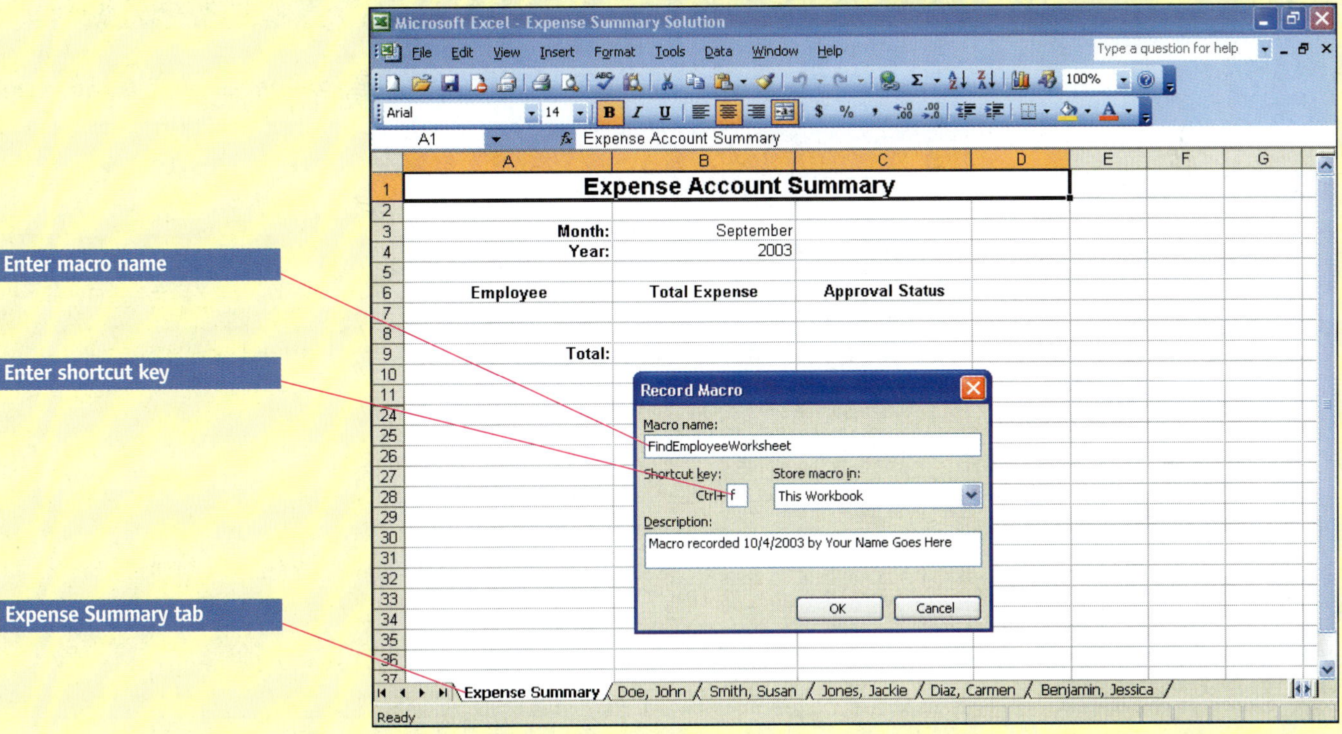

(a) Start the Macro Recorder (step 1)

FIGURE 10.5 Hands-on Exercise 2

KEYBOARD SHORTCUTS

You can add and/or modify the shortcut key associated with a macro at any time. Pull down the Tools menu, click the Macro command, then click Macros. . . to display the Macro dialog box. Select the desired macro and click the Options button to display the Macro Options dialog box, where you assign a shortcut.

Step 2: Modify the Procedure

- Press **Alt+F11** to display the VBA editor. Open Project Explorer if it is not visible. You will see that Module2 has been added to the Modules folder. Double click **Module2** to display its contents.
- The procedure at this point consists of a single executable statement, Sheets("Smith, Susan").Select. The other statements include the procedure header and End Sub statement and various comments. Enter the additional code as shown in Figure 10.5b:
  - Add the **Comment statements** as indicated.
  - The **Dim statement** defines the variable strEmployeeName that will contain the name of the employee whose worksheet you want to display.
  - The **InputBox function** prompts the user for the employee name, then stores the result in the strEmployeeName variable.
- Click and drag to select **"Smith, Susan"** (include the quotation marks) as shown in Figure 10.5b. Type **strEmployeeName**. The statement now reads **Sheets(strEmployeeName).Select**.
- Save the procedure.

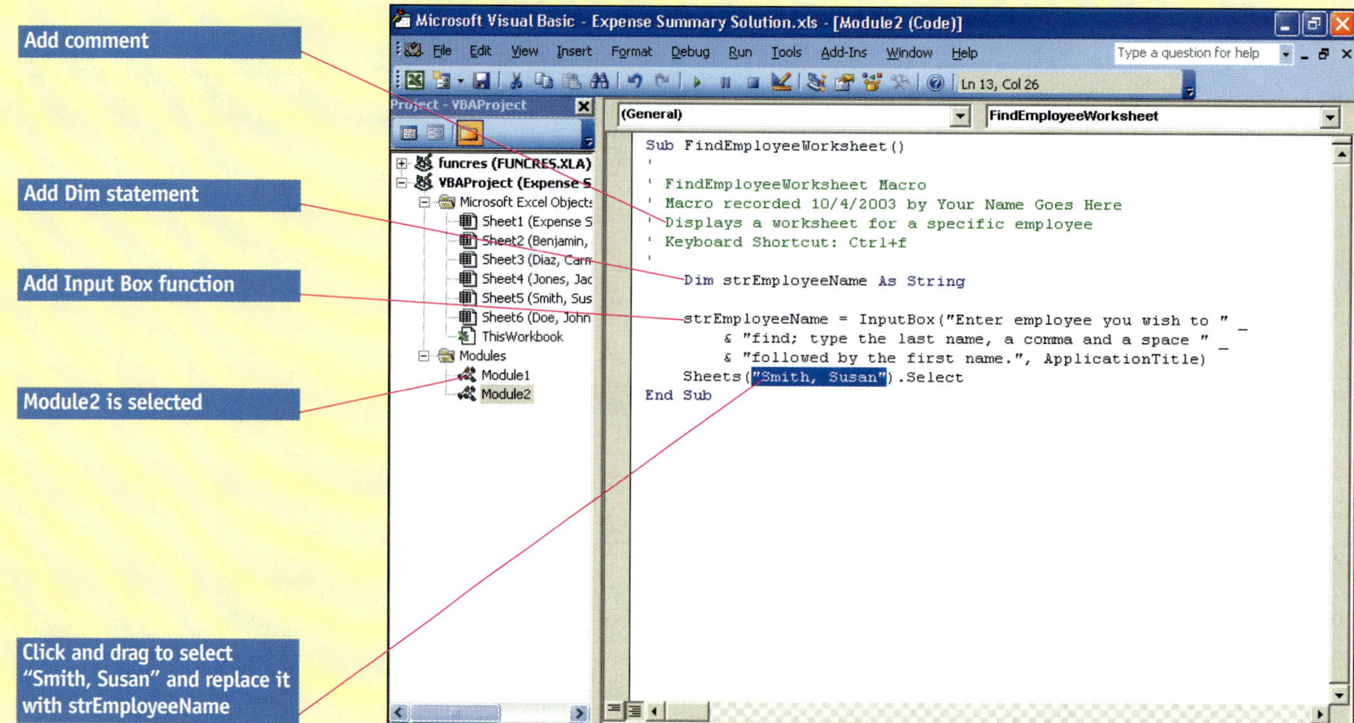

(b) Modify the Procedure (step 2)

FIGURE 10.5 Hands-on Exercise 2 (*continued*)

UNDERSTANDING THE VBA SYNTAX

The syntax of any VBA statement is easy to follow if you go back to the basics. VBA accomplishes its tasks by manipulating objects such as workbooks and worksheets. A collection is a group of similar objects. A method is an action that is performed on an object. Given this information, it is easy to understand the statement, *Sheets("Susan Smith").Select*. VBA is applying the Select method to a specific worksheet within the worksheets collection.

Step 3: Test the Procedure

- Return to the Excel window and select the **Expense Summary worksheet**. **Press Ctrl+f** to test the procedure you just created. You should see the message box in Figure 10.5c that asks you to enter an employee name.
- Enter the name that appears on any worksheet tab, but be sure to enter the name correctly. Click **OK** and you should see the worksheet for that employee.
- Press **Ctrl+f** to rerun the procedure, but this time, misspell the name of the employee you wish to find. You will see an error message, "Run-time error 9: Subscript out of range".
- Click the **Debug button**. You are back in the VBA editor, and the statement that caused the problem—Sheets(strEmployeeName).Select—is highlighted.
- Click the **Reset (square) button** on the Standard toolbar to reset the procedure to modify its code, as described in the next step.

Enter employee name as it exists on worksheet tab

Expense Summary is active worksheet

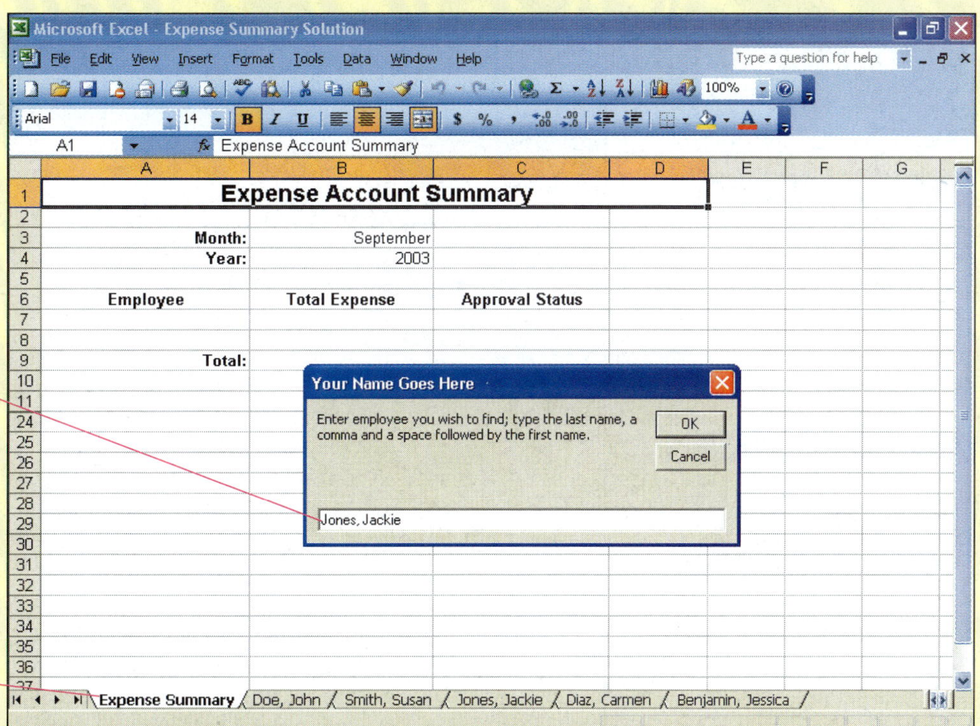

(c) Test the Procedure (step 3)

FIGURE 10.5 Hands-on Exercise 2 (*continued*)

RUN-TIME ERRORS

A run-time (execution) error results when VBA is unable to perform a specific task. VBA displays an explanation for the error, which typically does not make sense to the end user. The error in this example occurs because VBA was unable to reference a specific worksheet because it (the worksheet) does not exist. The internal subscript used by VBA to reference the worksheet within the workbook is out of range and hence the error message. A good application will anticipate (trap) the errors a user is apt to make and provide more meaningful explanations than the standard error messages.

Step 4: Add the Error Handling

- You can insulate a procedure against runtime errors by including the appropriate code. Add the additional statements as shown in Figure 10.5d:
  - The **On Error statement** suppresses the normal error message and transfers control to the user-defined location ErrorHandler, which appears elsewhere in the procedure. This statement is executed automatically whenever an error occurs during the procedure.
  - The **Exit Sub statement** exits the procedure immediately, effectively bypassing the statements within the ErrorHandler routine.
  - The **MsgBox statement** within the ErrorHandler routine displays a meaningful message to the user that describes the nature of the error.
- Save the procedure. Return to the Excel window, then press **Ctrl+f** to rerun the procedure to locate a specific employee. **Misspell the employee's name** to test the modified procedure. You should see the message box indicating that the employee worksheet cannot be found. Click **OK**.

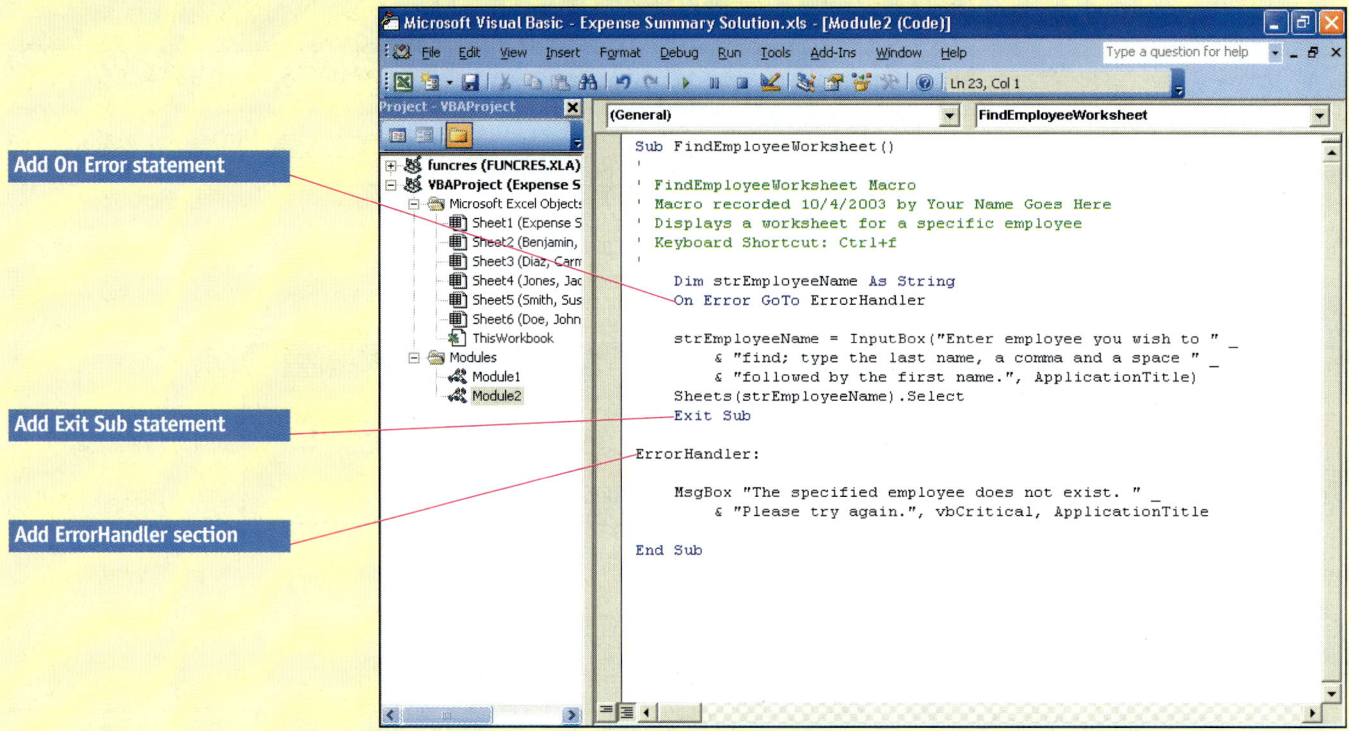

(d) Add the Error Handling (step 4)

FIGURE 10.5 Hands-on Exercise 2 (*continued*)

TOGGLE COMMENTS ON AND OFF

A comment is used primarily to explain the logic within a VBA procedure, but it can also render a statement nonexecutable (as opposed to deleting it altogether). Click at the beginning of the On Error statement within the procedure, type an apostrophe, and then press the down arrow. The statement turns green, indicating that it has been converted to a comment, and thus will not affect the outcome of the procedure. Now reexecute the procedure, misspell the employee name, and you once again see the VBA error message. Remove the apostrophe, try the procedure again, and you see the meaningful error message.

Step 5: Create a Command Button

- Select the **Expense Summary worksheet**. Pull down the **View menu**, click **Toolbars**, then click **Forms** to display the Forms toolbar. Click the **Button tool** (the mouse pointer changes to a tiny crosshair).
- Click and drag in the worksheet to draw a command button. Release the mouse. The Assign Macro dialog box will appear as shown in Figure 10.5e. Select **FindEmployeeWorksheet** (the procedure you just created). Click **OK**.
- The button should still be selected. Click and drag to select the name of the button, **Button 1**. Type **Find Employee Worksheet** as the new name. Do not press the Enter key.
- Click outside of the button to deselect it. Right click the button you just created to display a context-sensitive menu, click the **Format Control** to display the associated dialog box, then click the **Properties tab**. Click the Option button that says **Don't move or size with cells**. Click **OK**.
- Add a second command button to run the **OpenAllWorkbooks procedure**.
- Close the Forms toolbar. Save the workbook.

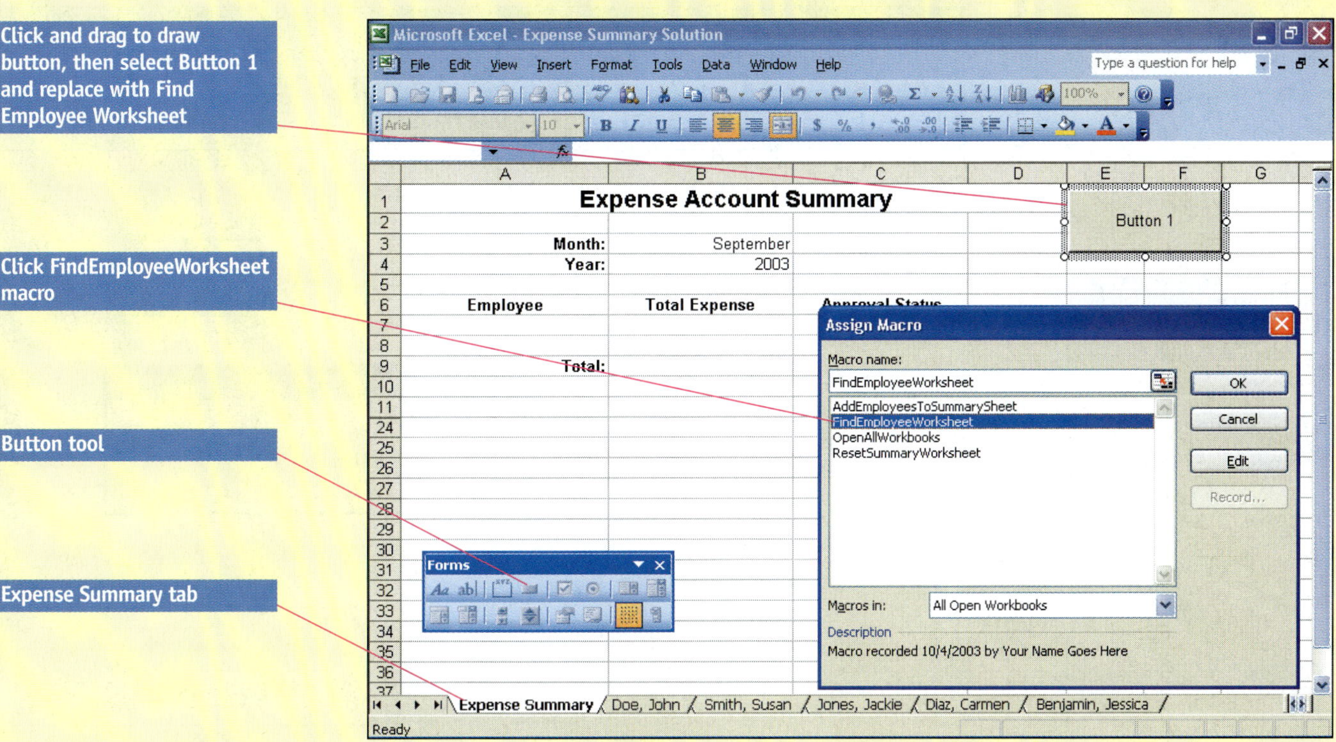

(e) Create a Command Button (step 5)

FIGURE 10.5 Hands-on Exercise 2 (*continued*)

COMMAND BUTTON PROPERTIES

A command button is not physically in a cell, but it will (by default) move and/or resize itself in conjunction with the cells on which it is placed. This is a potential problem if you insert and/or delete rows or columns within a worksheet. Hence we find it convenient to fix the button properties so that the button is unaffected by subsequent changes in the worksheet. Note, too, that you cannot select a command button by clicking it, because that would execute the associated VBA procedure. You can, however, right click the button to display a context-sensitive menu, which in turn selects the button.

Step 6: Test the Command Buttons

- You should see two command buttons as shown in Figure 10.5f. Select (click) the worksheet tab for the first employee.
- Press and hold the **Shift key** as you click the name of the last worksheet to select all of the employee worksheets.
- Point to any tab and click the **right mouse button**, then click the **Delete command**. Click the **Delete button** to confirm that you want to delete the employee worksheets.
- Click the command button to **Open All Workbooks**, which in turn runs the procedure from the first exercise. Click **No** when prompted to save the contents of each workbook.
- Select the **Expense Summary** worksheet. Click the button to **Find Employee Worksheet**. Misspell the employee name to test the error handing. Click **OK** when you see the message box in Figure 10.5f.
- Save the workbook. Exit Excel if you do not want to continue with the next exercise at this time.

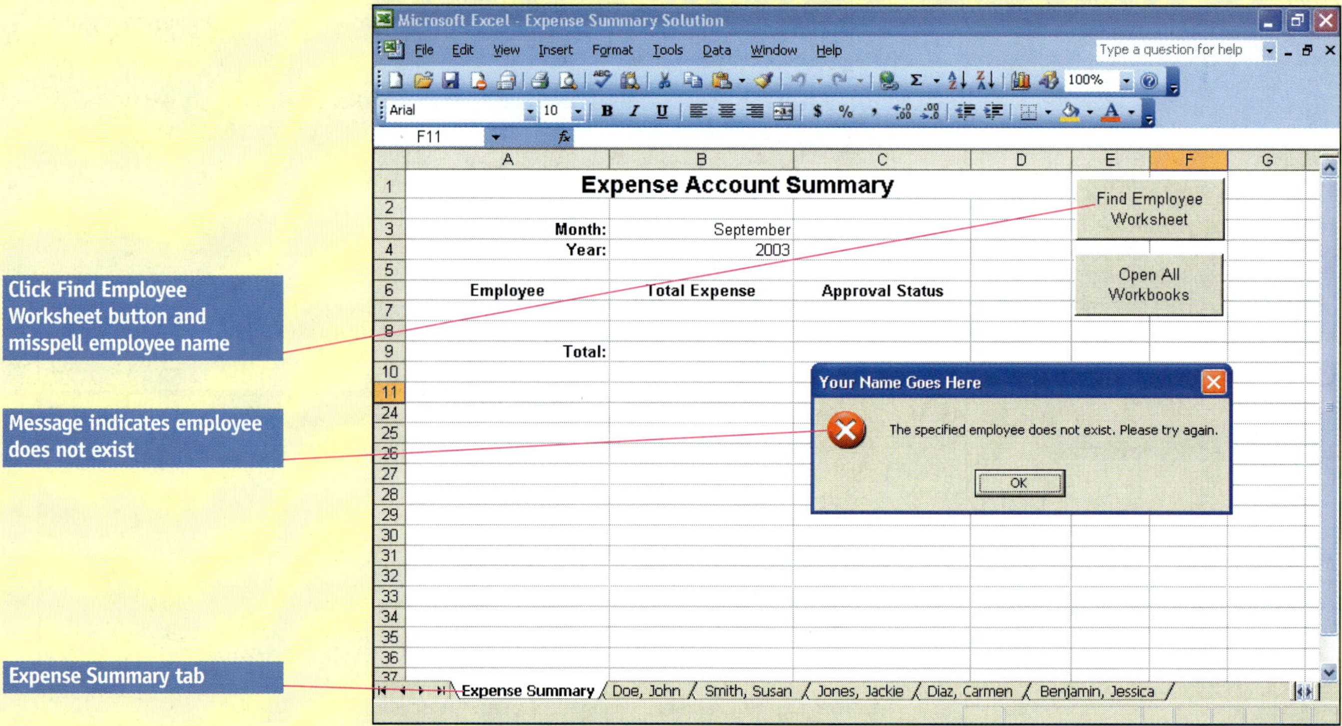

(f) Test the Command Buttons (step 6)

FIGURE 10.5 Hands-on Exercise 2 (*continued*)

DUPLICATE WORKSHEETS

Excel will not allow you to create multiple worksheets with the same name within a workbook. It is important, therefore, to delete the employee worksheets before running the procedure to add the employee information to the summary workbook. If you inadvertently run the procedure twice in a row, Excel will insert the second worksheet, but will append a subscript to its name within the worksheet tab, such as Your Name(2). Select the first sheet to be deleted, then press and hold the Ctrl key to select the remaining worksheets, click the right mouse button, then click the Delete command to remove the duplicate sheets.

PROCESSING WORKSHEETS IN A WORKBOOK

The Expense Summary workbook contains a single summary worksheet as well as a detailed worksheet for each employee who submitted an expense workbook. Our next task is to process all of the worksheets within the summary workbook. We will develop two separate procedures:

- A procedure to examine the individual worksheets in order to approve the indicated expenses or send the expense worksheet for further review. (The approval criterion is simple. The individual preparing the summary worksheet is asked to enter the threshold amount for the total expense for one employee, below which the expenses are approved automatically.)
- A second procedure to copy the total expense from each employee worksheet, as well as an indication of whether that amount was approved, to a row on the summary worksheet.

Figure 10.6a displays the detailed worksheet for one employee in conjunction with the first procedure. The individual preparing the summary workbook is prompted initially for the threshold amount ($1,000 in this example—the Input Box is not visible in this figure), that value is compared to the employee's total expense in cell J23 ($641.50 on this worksheet), and the approval status is entered into cell D25. Conditional formatting is used in the cell to display "Approved" or "Review" in blue or red, respectively. The procedure also modifies the worksheet tab so that you can see at a glance the status of individual employees. (The ability to change the color of a worksheet tab was introduced in Office XP.)

Figure 10.6b contains the associated VBA procedure, which includes a For . . . Next statement to process all of the worksheets within the workbook. (Technically speaking, it is processing each worksheet object within the worksheets collection.) The logic is not difficult, but it helps to examine the logic in pseudocode prior to looking at the actual VBA statements. Consider this:

Loop to process every worksheet

Determines whether expenses are approved

```
Input threshold amount for automatic approval
For each worksheet in the workbook
    If this is an employee worksheet
        Unprotect this worksheet
        If the expenses are less than or equal to threshold amount
            Approve these expenses and set worksheet tab to blue
        Else
            Review these expenses and set worksheet tab to red
        End if
        Protect this worksheet
    End If
Next worksheet
```

The For. . .Next loop automatically processes all of the worksheets within the workbook. Realize, however, that the first worksheet is a summary (rather than an employee) worksheet and thus the If statement to process only employee worksheets is required. The second If statement compares the total expense on the employee worksheet to the threshold amount and takes the appropriate action.

Figure 10.6b displays the associated VBA procedure. The Dim statement defines the variable mysheet as a worksheet object, which controls the For. . .Next statement that drives the procedure. The loop looks at every worksheet within the workbook, checks to see that each worksheet is an employee worksheet, and if so, compares the total expense on that worksheet to the threshold amount. (WorksheetTitle, TotalExpense, and ApprovedRejected are range names on the Excel worksheet.) The ColorIndex property is set to 5 (blue) or 3 (red), respectively, to indicate whether the expenses are approved or subject to further review.

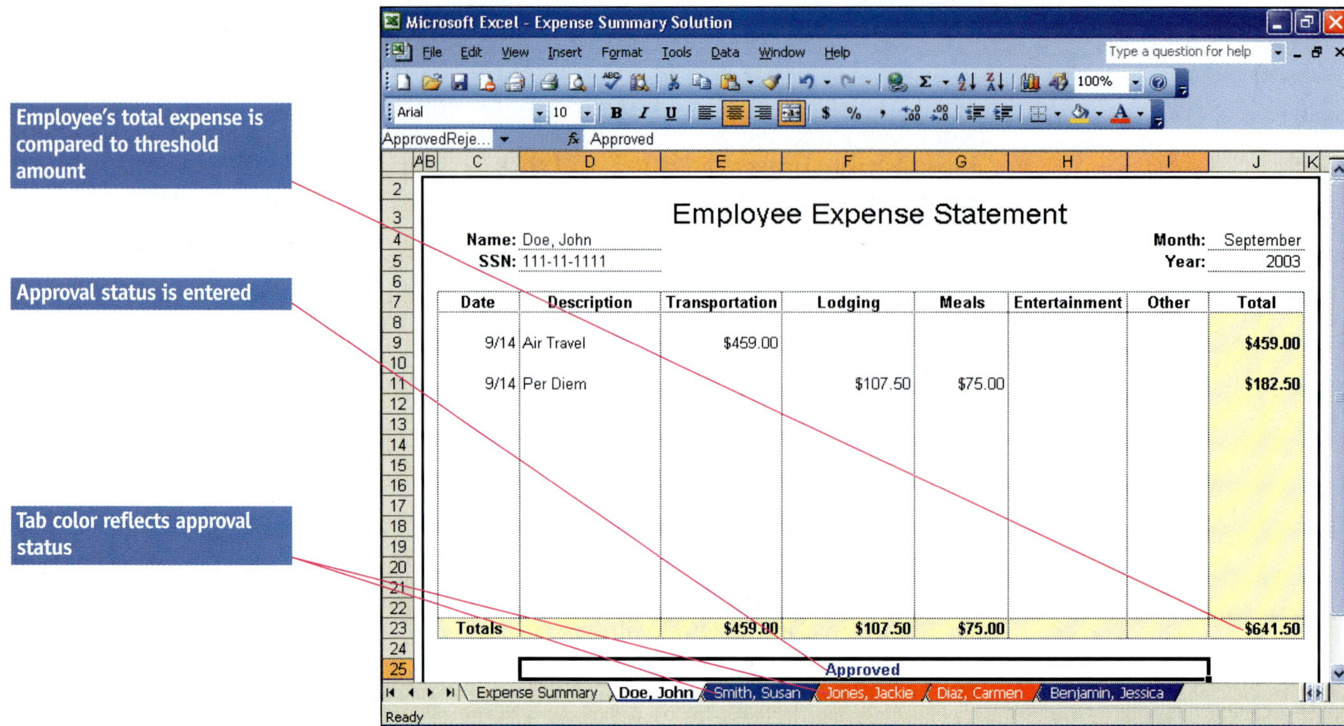

(a) Employee Worksheet

User is prompted for threshold amount

Worksheet tab color is set to blue

Worksheet tab color is set to red

Summary worksheet is selected when loop is exited

```
Sub ReviewEmployeeExpenses()
    Dim mysheet As Worksheet
    Dim curMaxApprovedExpense As Currency

    curMaxApprovedExpense = InputBox("Enter the maximum expense that " _
        & "will be approved without further review.", ApplicationTitle)

    For Each mysheet In Worksheets
        Sheets(mysheet.Name).Select
        If Range("WorksheetTitle") = "Employee Expense Statement" Then
            ActiveSheet.Unprotect
            If Range("TotalExpense") <= curMaxApprovedExpense Then
                Range("ApprovedRejected") = "Approved"
                ActiveSheet.Tab.ColorIndex = 5
            Else
                Range("ApprovedRejected") = "Review"
                ActiveSheet.Tab.ColorIndex = 3
            End If
            ActiveSheet.Protect
        End If

    Next mysheet
    Sheets("Expense Summary").Select

End Sub
```

(b) VBA Procedure

FIGURE 10.6 Review Employee Expenses

Adding Employees to the Summary Worksheet

Our next task is to copy the information from the individual employee worksheets (within the summary workbook) to a summary worksheet as shown in Figure 10.7. The summary worksheet contains a single line for each employee with his or her name, the total expense for that employee, and an indication of the approval status. (***Conditional Formatting*** is used to display the status in red or blue for "review" or "approved", respectively.) Row 7, for example, contains the data for Jessica Benjamin, and it reflects the data in the associated worksheet. The color of the worksheet tab also indicates the approval status.

Each of the entries in this row contains a formula that references the appropriate cell from Jessica's worksheet. Cell B7 displays Jessica's total expenses ($303.20) according to the formula ='Benjamin,Jessica'!TotalExpense. The name of the worksheet is enclosed in apostrophes and corresponds to a worksheet tab at the bottom of the window. The exclamation point indicates a worksheet reference. TotalExpense is a range name on that worksheet.

Figure 10.7b displays the procedure to process all of the employee worksheets in the summary workbook and build the appropriate formulas on the summary worksheet. The procedure is easier to understand if we look first at the underlying logic as expressed in pseudocode. Consider the following:

Sets insertion point on Summary worksheet

Tests for employee worksheet

Adjusts insertion point for next employee

Sorts Summary worksheet after all employees were added

```
Select the cell for the first employee on the summary worksheet

For each worksheet in the workbook
    If this is an employee worksheet
        Store the name of this worksheet for use in a cell formula
        Select the active cell in the summary worksheet
        Enter the formula to reference cell D4 in the employee worksheet
        Move one column to the right (on the summary worksheet)
        Enter the formula for the total expenses in the employee worksheet
        Move one column to the right (on the summary worksheet)
        Enter the formula for the approval status in the employee worksheet
        Move down one row and two columns to the left (for the next employee)
        Insert a blank row to update the Sum function for the new employee
    End If
Next worksheet

Delete extra blank row after all employees have been processed
Sort the employees in alphabetical order
```

The procedure begins by selecting the cell that will contain the first employee on the summary worksheet, then it enters a loop to process all of the worksheets in the workbook. The first statement within the loop is an If statement to check that the worksheet is an employee worksheet; we do not want to copy information from the summary worksheet itself. We then build three formulas on the current row of the summary worksheet. The offset property is used to create a relative reference to various cells on this row; for example, Offset (0,1) refers to the cell on the same row, but one column to the right.

Each formula begins with a reference to the current worksheet name, which is then concatenated (joined) to the other parts of the formula. The ampersand indicates concatenation in the formula and joins one character string to another. After the third formula has been created, we drop down one row and move two columns to the left for the next employee. A blank row is inserted to accommodate this employee, and the loop continues.

After all of the employee data has been copied to the summary worksheet, we exit the loop and delete a superfluous blank line after the last employee. The employees are then displayed in alphabetical order by last name. The summary worksheet is complete.

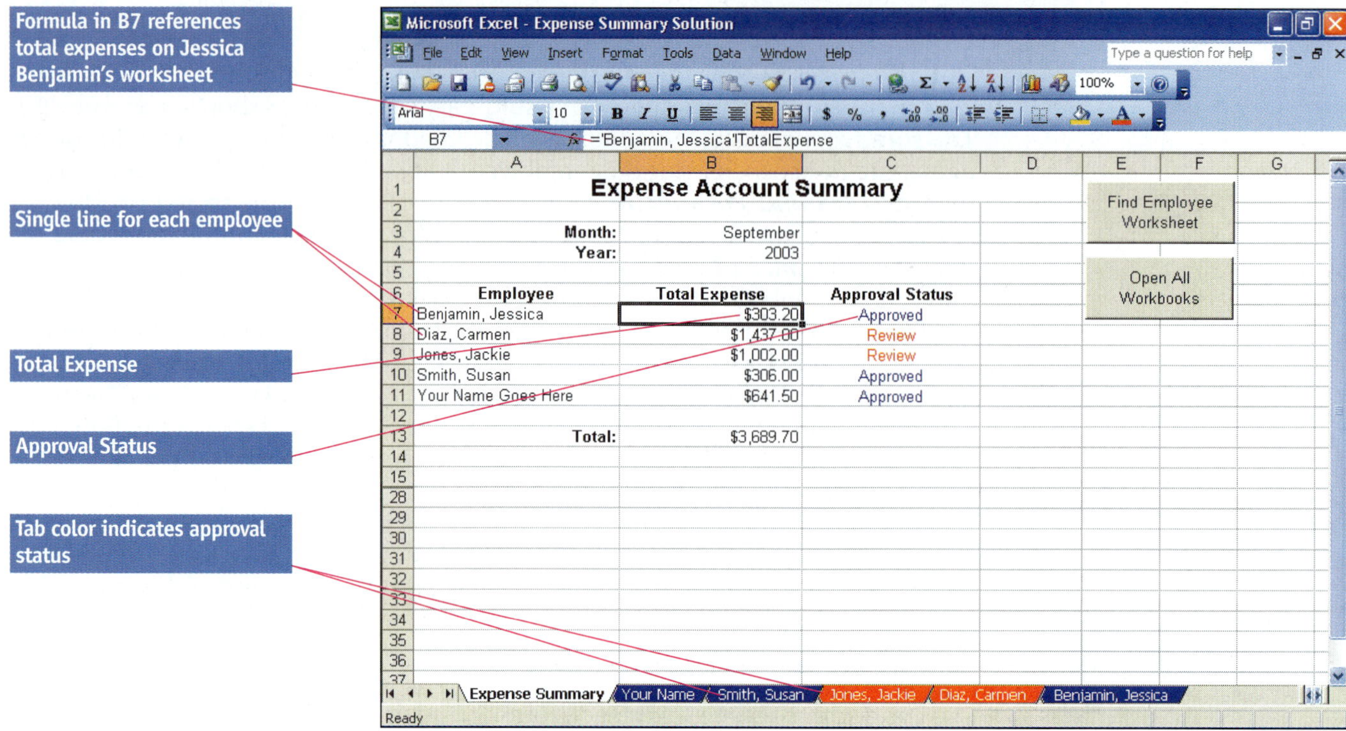

(a) The Summary Worksheet

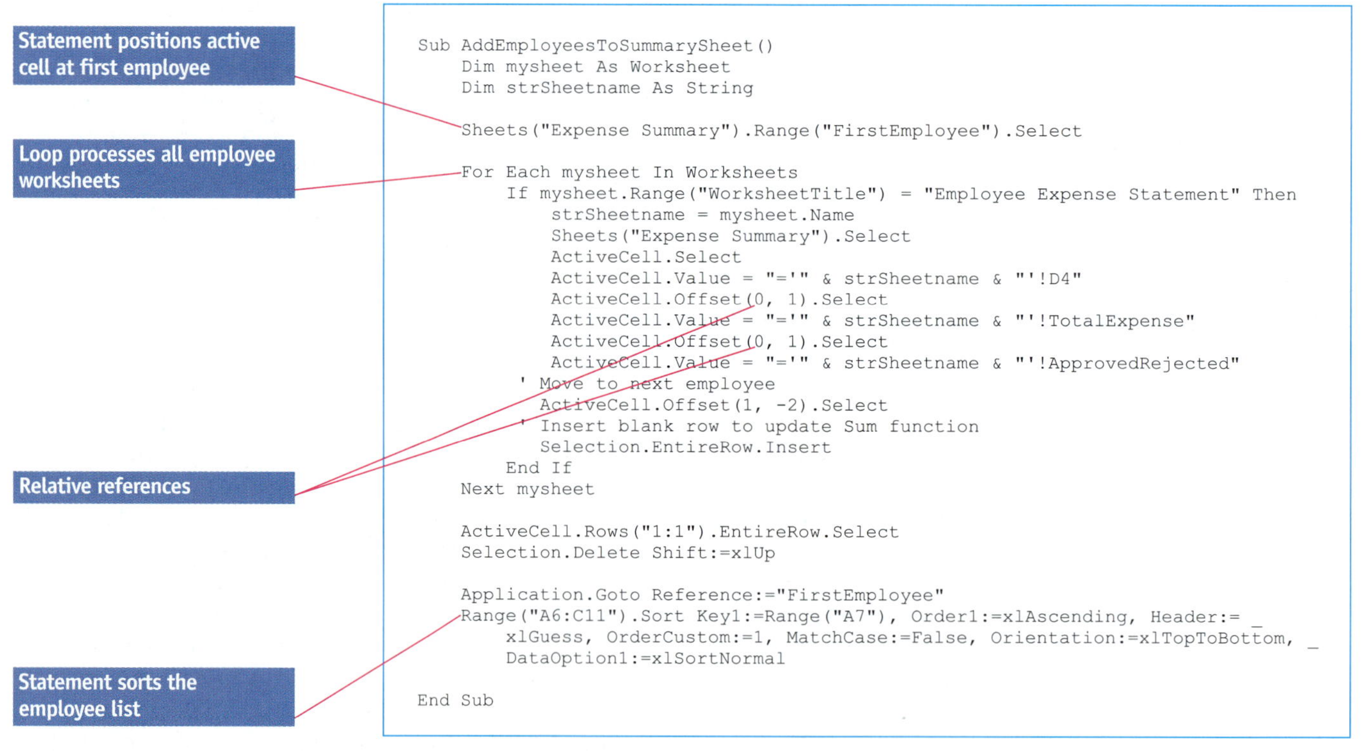


```
Sub AddEmployeesToSummarySheet()
    Dim mysheet As Worksheet
    Dim strSheetname As String

    Sheets("Expense Summary").Range("FirstEmployee").Select

    For Each mysheet In Worksheets
        If mysheet.Range("WorksheetTitle") = "Employee Expense Statement" Then
            strSheetname = mysheet.Name
            Sheets("Expense Summary").Select
            ActiveCell.Select
            ActiveCell.Value = "='" & strSheetname & "'!D4"
            ActiveCell.Offset(0, 1).Select
            ActiveCell.Value = "='" & strSheetname & "'!TotalExpense"
            ActiveCell.Offset(0, 1).Select
            ActiveCell.Value = "='" & strSheetname & "'!ApprovedRejected"
          ' Move to next employee
           ActiveCell.Offset(1, -2).Select
          ' Insert blank row to update Sum function
           Selection.EntireRow.Insert
        End If
    Next mysheet

    ActiveCell.Rows("1:1").EntireRow.Select
    Selection.Delete Shift:=xlUp

    Application.Goto Reference:="FirstEmployee"
    Range("A6:C11").Sort Key1:=Range("A7"), Order1:=xlAscending, Header:= _
        xlGuess, OrderCustom:=1, MatchCase:=False, Orientation:=xlTopToBottom, _
        DataOption1:=xlSortNormal

End Sub
```

(b) VBA Procedure

FIGURE 10.7 Create the Summary Worksheet

hands-on exercise

3 Create the Summary Worksheet

Objective Create two procedures to process the worksheets in a workbook. Use Figure 10.8 as a guide in the exercise.

Step 1: Start the Macro Recorder

- Open the **Expense Summary Solution workbook** from the previous exercise. Enable the macros. Click the worksheet tab that contains your expenses.
- Click the **down arrow** in the Name box to see the range names that have been previously defined in this worksheet. Note the following:
  - The range name WorksheetTitle refers to cell C3, which contains the title of this worksheet, "Employee Expense Statement".
  - The range name ApprovedRejected refers to cell D25. This cell is presently blank, but it will contain an indication of whether the expenses are approved.
  - The range name TotalExpense refers to cell J23, which contains the total expenses for this employee.
- Pull down the **Tools menu**, click the **Macro command**, then click **Record New Macro** to display the Record Macro dialog box in Figure 10.8a.
- Enter **ReviewEmployeeExpenses** as the name of the procedure, enter the description shown, and then click **OK** to begin recording.
- Pull down the **Tools menu**, click **Protection**, then click **Unprotect Sheet**.
- If you are using Excel 2002 or a later release, right click the worksheet tab to display a context-sensitive menu, click **Tab Color** to display the Format Tab Color dialog box, click a **Blue square** from the palette, then click **OK**.
- Click the **Expense Summary worksheet tab**. Click the **Stop Recording button**.

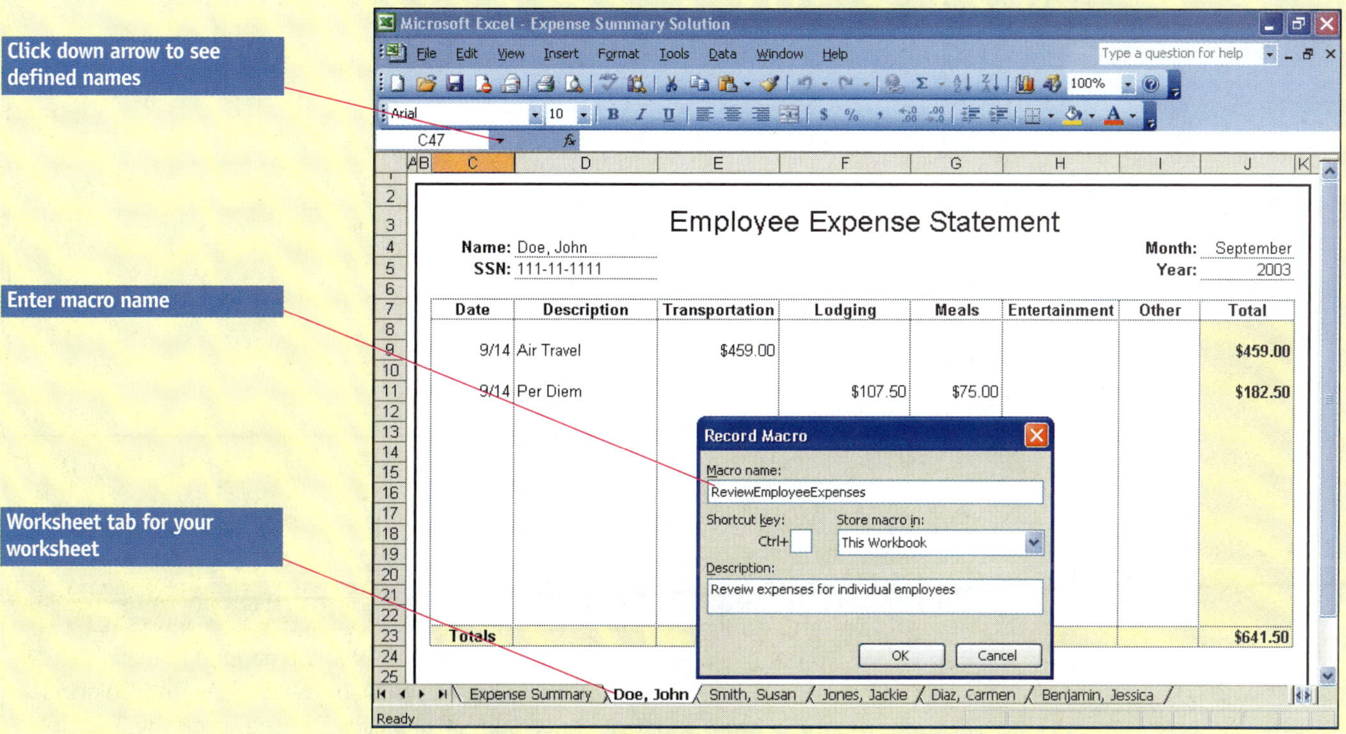

(a) Start the Macro Recorder (step 1)

FIGURE 10.8 Hands-on Exercise 3

Step 2: Loops and Decision Making

- Press **Alt+F11** to display the VBA editor. If necessary, pull down the **View menu** and click **Project Explorer** (or use the **Ctrl+r** keyboard shortcut) to display the Project Explorer window.
- Open the modules folder, then double click the last module that appears to display the procedures in that module. Locate the **ReviewEmployeeExpenses procedure** that you just created.
- Close Project Explorer. Your procedure contains only a few of the statements in Figure 10.8b. Proceed as follows:
  - Add the **Dim statement** at the beginning of the procedure to define the variable **mysheet**. Add the **For** and **Next statements** as shown in the figure.
  - Change Sheets("Your Name").Select, to **Sheets(mysheet.Name).Select**.
  - Add the **If** and **End If** statements to test for an employee worksheet.
  - Change the statement for tab color to **ActiveSheet.Tab.ColorIndex = 5**. (This statement will not appear in Office 2000.)
  - Add the statement to protect the worksheet. Check that your procedure matches Figure 10.8b. Save the procedure.
- Click in the procedure, then click the **RunSub button** to run the procedure, then click the **Excel button** to see the results. All of the worksheet tabs (except the summary tab) should be blue. Save the workbook.

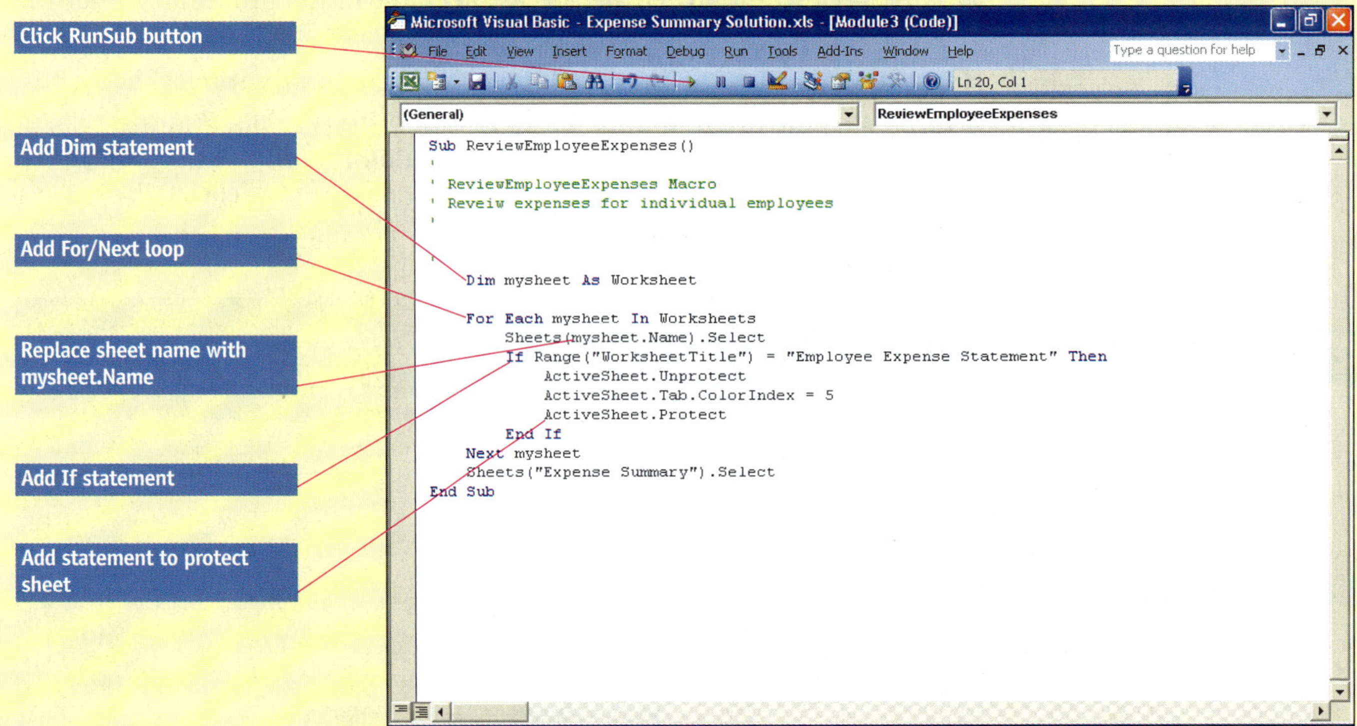

(b) Loops and Decision Making (step 2)

FIGURE 10.8 Hands-on Exercise 3 (*continued*)

CHANGE THE COLOR OF A WORKSHEET TAB

The ability to change the color of a worksheet tab was introduced in Excel 2002. The tab color can be changed in two ways—in VBA by setting the Tab.ColorIndex property and/or from the Excel interface. (Right click the tab, click the Tab Color command to display the associated dialog box, select a color, and click OK.) The feature does not exist in Excel 2000.

Step 3: Complete the Procedure

- Return to the VBA editor to complete the procedure as shown in Figure 10.8c. Add a second **Dim statement** to define the **curMaxApprovedExpense** variable. Add **the Input Box function** to prompt the user for the value of this variable.
- Add the second (nested) **If statement** to compare the value in the range named "TotalExpenses" to the maximum approved expense, then take the appropriate action. Enter **"Approved"** in the range named "ApprovedRejected" if the expenses are less than or equal to the maximum amount.
- Add the **Else clause**, which enters "Review" in the range named "ApprovedRejected" and changes the tab color to red if the expenses are greater than the threshold amount. (A color index of 3 changes the worksheet tab to red.)
- Add the **End If** delimiter to complete the statement. Save the procedure. Run the procedure. Enter **$1,000** when prompted for the maximum expense.
- Click the **View Microsoft Excel button** to view the workbook, which should contain a combination of red and blue worksheet tabs. Click any blue tab (e.g., Susan Smith) and you should see an approved message at the bottom of the worksheet. Click any red tab (e.g., Jackie Jones) and you should see the review message.

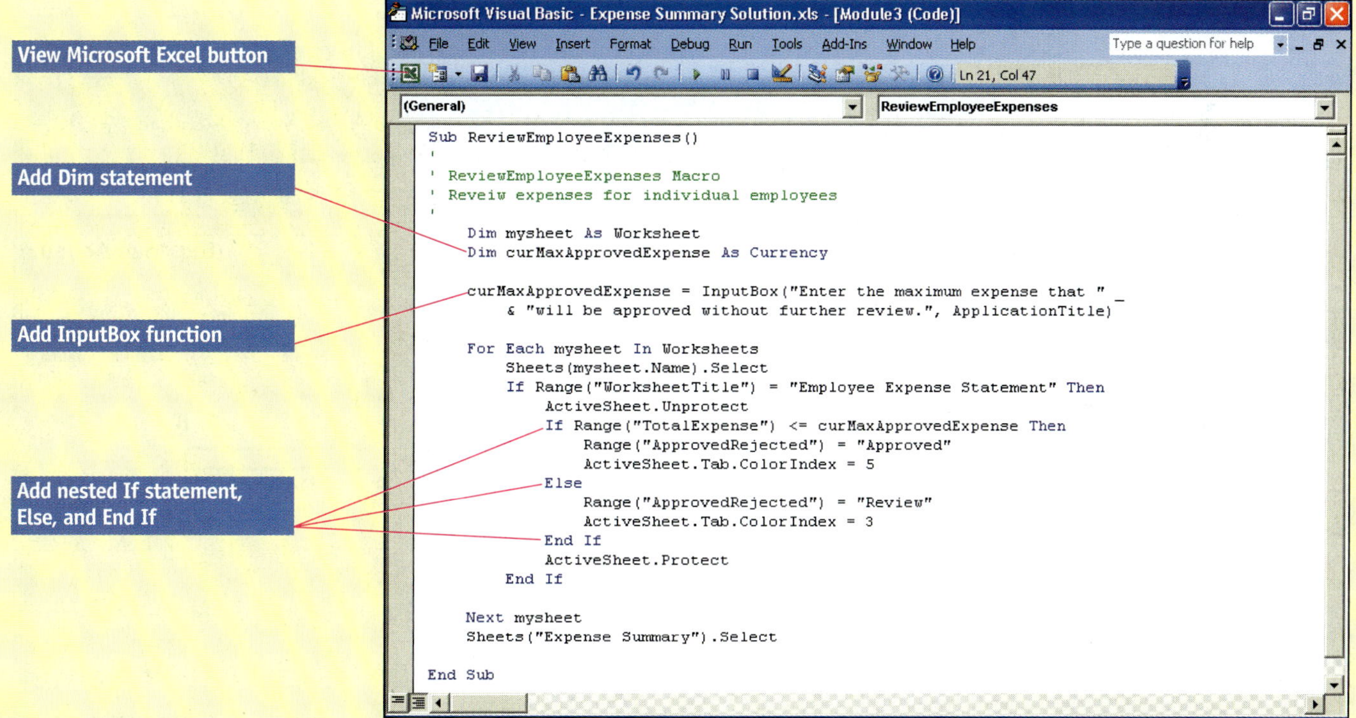

(c) Complete the Procedure (step 3)

FIGURE 10.8 Hands-on Exercise 3 (*continued*)

NESTED IF STATEMENTS

A nested If statement (or an If within an If) is easy to understand if you indent properly and follow basic syntax. Recall that an ordinary If statement tests a condition, then follows one of two paths, depending on whether the condition is true or false. The If statement must end with the End If delimiter, but the Else clause is optional. A nested If simply adds another If statement to either path. Each If (within the nested If) has its own End If delimiter. Indentation is used to make the statement easier to read.

Step 4: Step through a Procedure

- Return to the VBA editor. Pull down the **View menu** to display the Project Explorer window, then double click **Module1** to open its code window. Locate the **AddEmployeesToSummarySheet** procedure. Close Project Explorer.
- Point to a blank area at the right of the Windows taskbar and then click the **right mouse button**. Click the command to **Show the Desktop**.
- Click the **VBA** and **Excel buttons** on the taskbar to reopen these windows. Right click a blank area of the taskbar a second time, then click the command to **Tile Windows Vertically**.
- Your desktop should be similar to Figure 10.8d. Click in the Excel window, then click on the **Expense Summary tab** to select that worksheet. Click in the window containing the VBA editor. Click after the **Sub statement**.
- Press the **F8 key**. The procedure header is highlighted. Press the **F8 key** a second time. The Sheets("Expense Summary").Range("FirstEmployee").Select statement is highlighted.
- Continue to press the **F8 key** to view the progress of the procedure as it is executed one statement at a time. Each employee worksheet is selected in succession, and the appropriate information is moved to the summary worksheet.

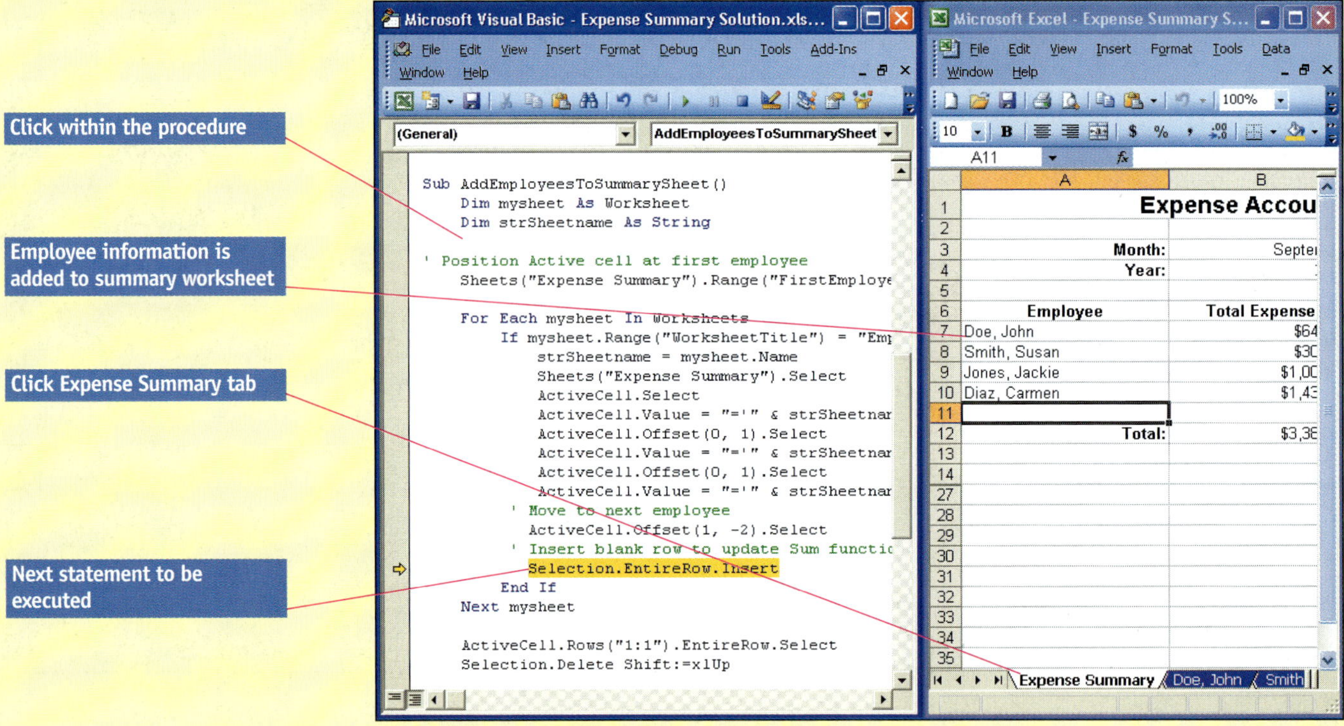

(d) Step through a Procedure (step 4)

FIGURE 10.8 Hands-on Exercise 3 (*continued*)

RELATIVE REFERENCES—THE OFFSET PROPERTY

The Offset property returns a range of cells that is offset (displaced) from the active cell by a designated number of rows and columns; for example, ActiveCell.Offset(0,1).Range("A1").Select selects the cell in the same row and one column to the right of the active cell. The Range object may be omitted if you are selecting only a single cell.

Step 5: Check Your Progress

- Maximize the Excel window to check your progress as shown in Figure 10.8e. The total expense for each employee as well as the approval status has been copied to the summary worksheet. The color of the worksheet tabs corresponds to the approval status for each employee.
- Click in any cell in the body of the worksheet—for example, **cell B8**, which contains the total expenses for Susan Smith on our worksheet. Look at the formula bar to see the contents of this cell, ='Smith, Susan'!TotalExpense.
- The employees are not yet in alphabetical order. We could sort the employees at this point, without modifying the existing procedure. We want the procedure to include this function, however, and so we will use the macro recorder to obtain these commands.
- Pull down the **Tools menu**, click the **Macro command**, then click **Record New Macro** to display the Record Macro dialog box. Enter **Dummy** as the name of the procedure. The keyboard shortcut and description are optional. Click **OK**.
- Click the **down arrow** in the Name box and select **FirstEmployee**. Click the **Sort Ascending button**. Click the **Stop Recording button**.

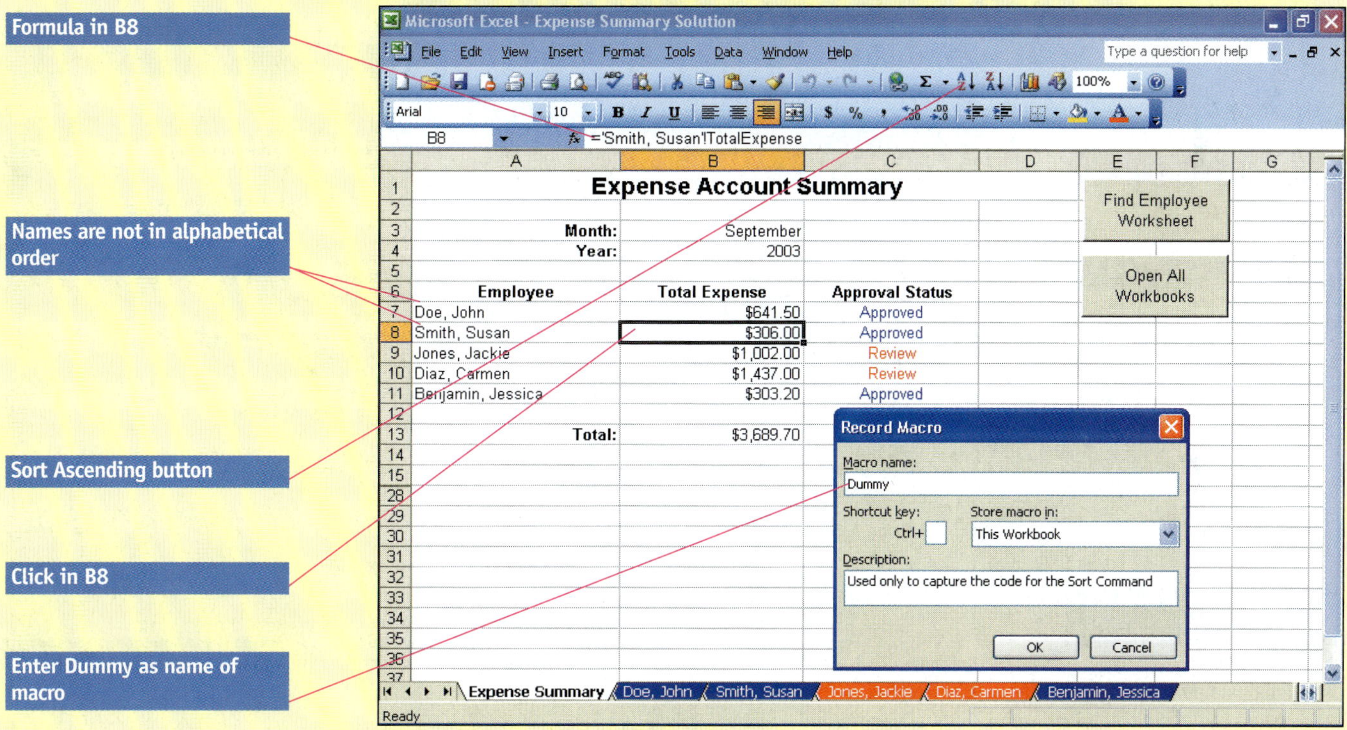

(e) Check Your Progress (step 5)

FIGURE 10.8 Hands-on Exercise 3 (*continued*)

WORKSHEET REFERENCES—THE EXCLAMATION MARK

An Excel formula may reference cells in other worksheets, in which case you need to include the name of the worksheet with the cell address; for example, =Sheet4!A1, references cell A1 in the worksheet called Sheet4. The name of the worksheet is always followed by an exclamation point. The cell reference, A1, may be replaced by a named range such as TotalExpense. The name of the worksheet is enclosed in apostrophes if it (the worksheet name) contains a space, as in 'Smith, Susan'!TotalExpense.

Step 6: Complete the Procedure

- Press **Alt+F11** to return to the VBA editor. Maximize the window. Open Project Explorer and double click the module that contains the newly recorded Dummy procedure.
- Click and drag to select the four lines of code in that procedure. You will see a statement to select the cell called "FirstEmployee", followed by a Sort statement that is continued over several lines. Select all four lines.
- Click the **Copy button** on the Standard toolbar or use the **Ctrl+C** keyboard shortcut to copy these statements to the clipboard.
- Switch to the **AddEmployeesToSummarySheet** procedure on Module1 that you were working on earlier. Click to the left of the **End Sub** statement and press the **Enter key** to insert a blank line, then click the **up arrow key** to move to the blank line.
- Click the **Paste button** or use the **Ctrl+V** keyboard shortcut. Close Project Explorer. The statements from the Dummy procedure should appear as shown in Figure 10.8f.
- Save the procedure.

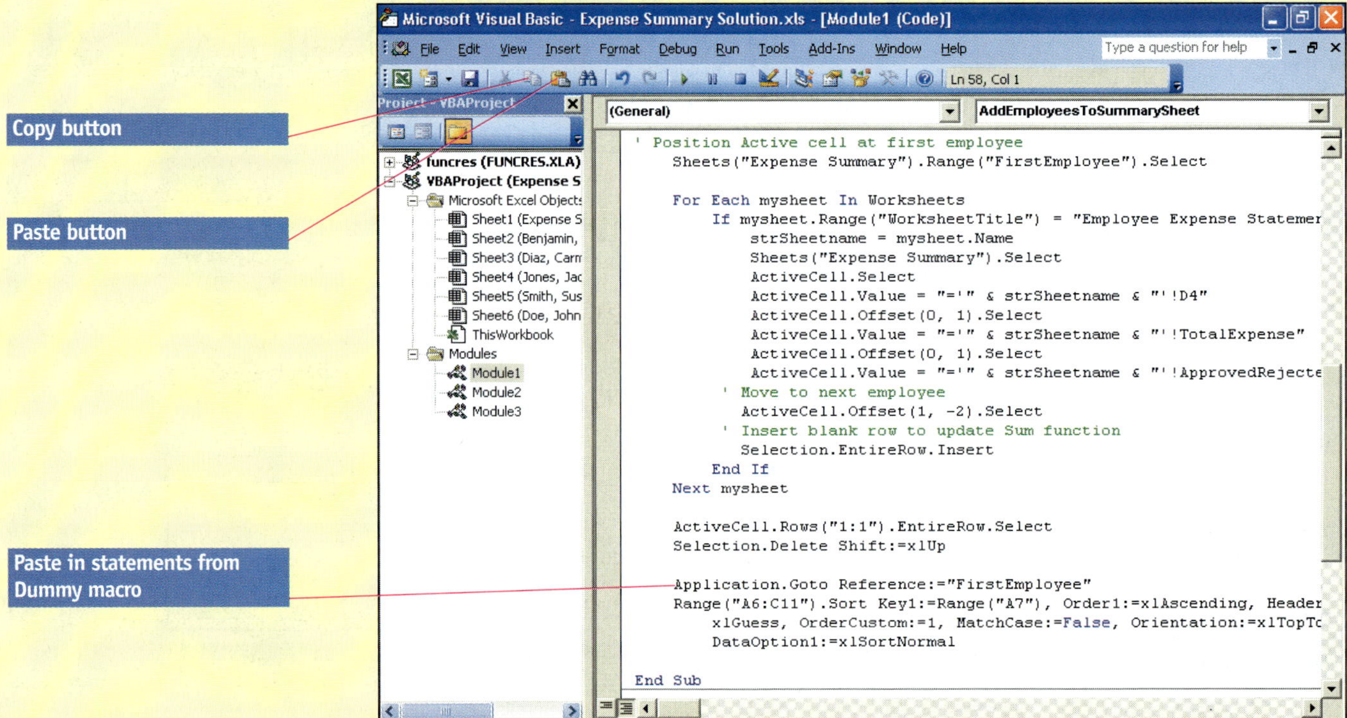

(f) Complete the Procedure (step 6)

FIGURE 10.8 Hands-on Exercise 3 (*continued*)

BE FLEXIBLE AND USE WHAT YOU KNOW

There is no single way to create a VBA procedure. You can use the Excel macro recorder to "jump-start" the process to obtain the syntax for lesser-known VBA statements. You can also create a procedure by entering code directly into the VBA editor. Once you have the procedure, you can return to the macro recorder to capture additional statements you may not have thought of initially. Be flexible and use the editing techniques that you learned in other applications.

Step 7: Test the Completed Procedure

- Click the **Excel button** to return to the Excel worksheet, where you can test the completed procedure. First, however, you need to delete and/or clear the rows containing the employee information. Thus:
  - Click and drag to select **rows 8 through 11** (do not select row 7) as shown in Figure 10.8g. Right click the selected rows to display the context-sensitive menu, then click the **Delete command** to remove these rows.
  - Click and drag to select the entries in **row 7**. Press the **Del key** to erase the contents of these cells—the cells, however, remain in the workbook.
  - Click in **cell A7**. Be sure that the Name box contains the reference FirstEmployee (since this reference is used in a VBA procedure).
  - Click in **cell B9**. Be sure that this cell contains the formula =Sum(B7:B8).
- Pull down the **Tools menu** and rerun the **AddEmployeesToSummarySheet** procedure. The employee data is added to the worksheet, but this time the employees should be in alphabetical order.
- Save the workbook.

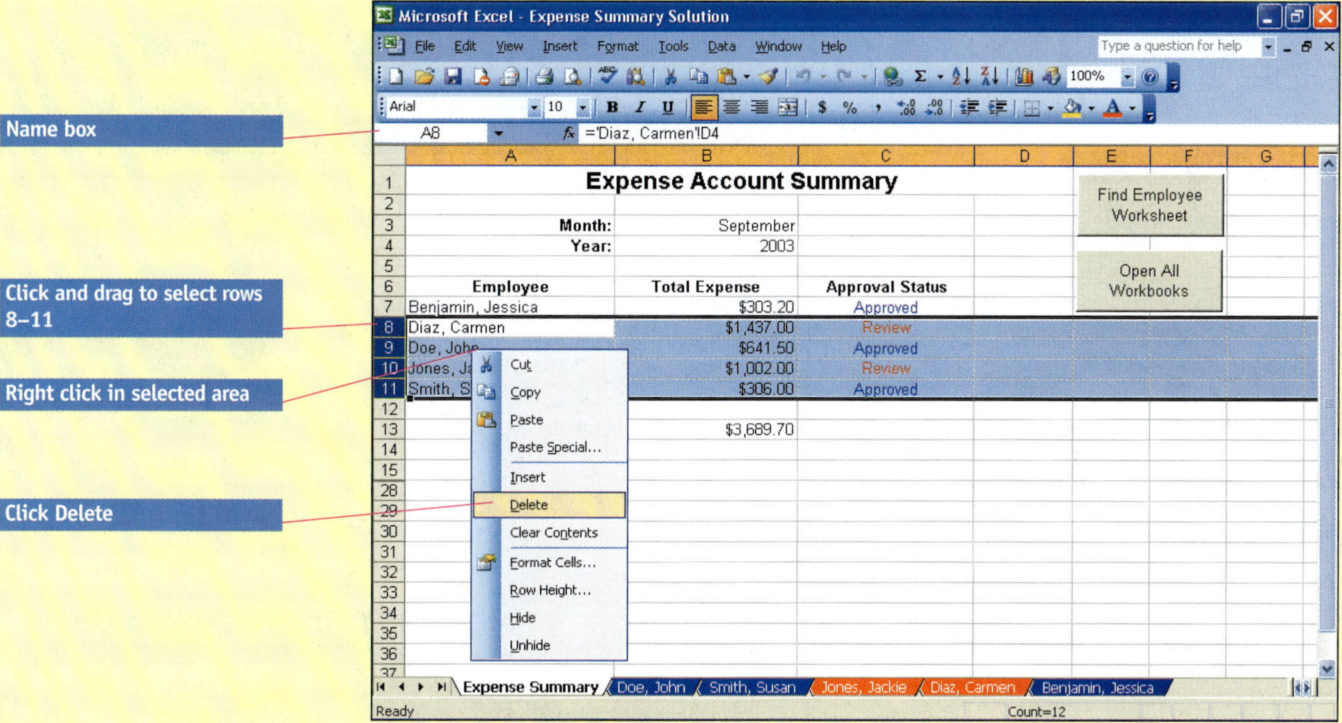

(g) Test the Completed Procedure (step 7)

FIGURE 10.8 Hands-on Exercise 3 (*continued*)

KEYBOARD SHORTCUTS

We have created a procedure to reset (clear) the Summary worksheet and have assigned the keyboard shortcut Ctrl+r to that procedure. You can test this procedure in conjunction with the procedure to add the employee data to the summary worksheet. Thus, press Ctrl+a to add the employee data, then press Ctrl+r to clear the summary data. You can execute the latter procedure several times in succession. The first procedure should be executed only once; that is, if you add the employee data twice in a row, you will wind up with duplicate rows for each employee.

Step 8: Print the Cell Formulas

- Press **Ctrl+~** to display the cell formulas as shown in Figure 10.8h. (Press **Ctrl+~** a second time to return to the displayed values.)
- Click and drag to select the row headers for **rows 15 through 28** (rows 16 through 27 are currently hidden). Right click the selected rows, then click the **Unhide command** to display these cells.
- Click in **cell B3**, the cell containing the month for which the expenses were submitted. Note how the VLOOKUP function uses the data in rows 16 to 27 to display the current month.
- Click and drag to adjust the column widths. Pull down the **File menu**, select the **Page Setup command** and switch to **Landscape printing**. Select the **scaling option** to force the output onto one page. Print the formulas for the summary worksheet.
- Close the workbook. Do not save the workbook when the cell formulas are displayed. Exit Excel if you do not want to continue with the next hands-on exercise at this time.

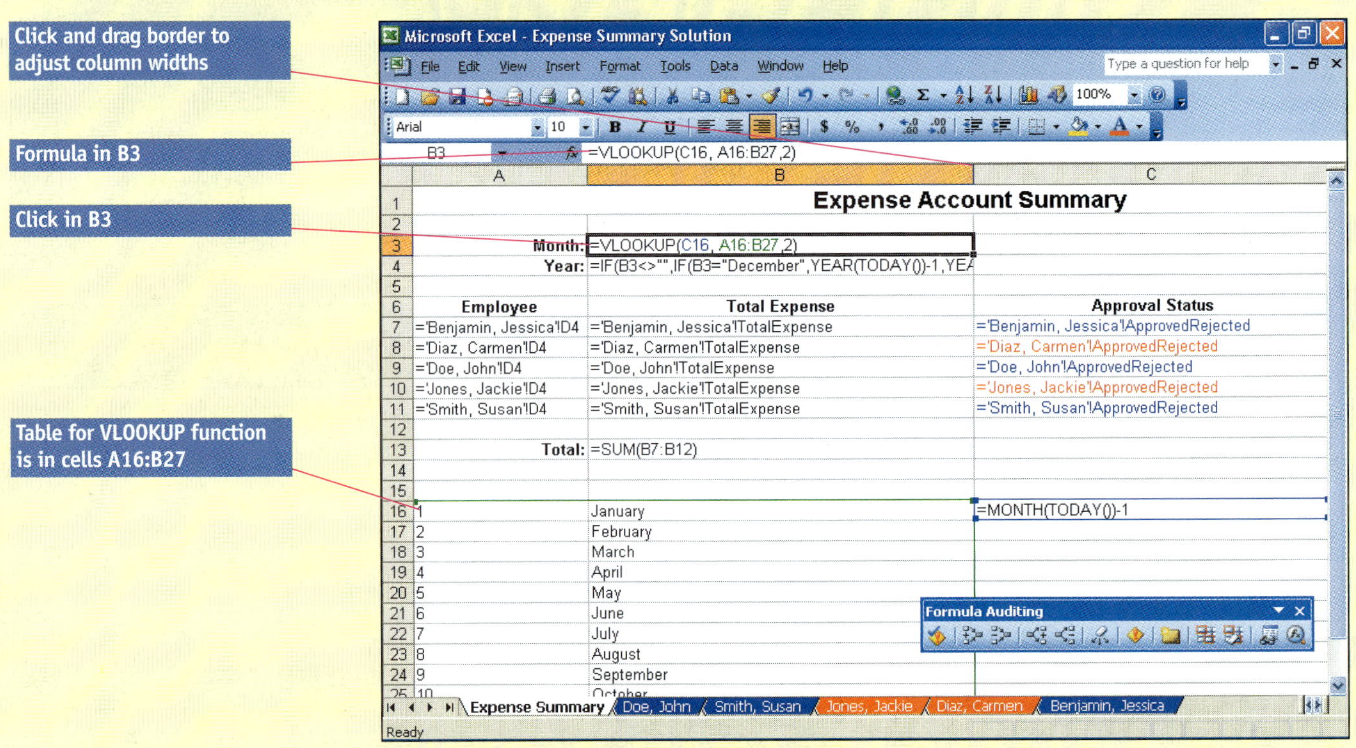

(h) Print the Cell Formulas (step 8)

FIGURE 10.8 Hands-on Exercise 3 (*continued*)

PRINT THE CELL FORMULAS—THE PAGE SETUP COMMAND

A worksheet should always be printed twice—once to show the displayed values and once to show the underlying cell formulas. Use the keyboard shortcut, Ctrl+~ to toggle between the two. Pull down the File menu and click the Page Setup command to change settings as necessary, when printing the cell formulas. You may want to change the orientation, column width, and/or margins.

A BETTER SUMMARY WORKBOOK

The summary workbook is finished, but you had to complete three hands-on exercises to accomplish that task. First, you had to open each individual workbook to copy the information for that employee to a new worksheet in the summary workbook. Next, you had to review the expenses on each worksheet within the summary workbook, and finally, you had to add the individual employee data to the summary worksheet. It would be much easier if you could execute a single procedure and with one click of the mouse, create the entire workbook. This is accomplished by creating a simple procedure that calls the three procedures (you ran individually) as shown below:

Three procedures are executed in succession

```
Public Sub CreateSummaryWorkbook()
  OpenAllWorkbooks
  ReviewEmployeeExpenses
  AddEmployeesToSummarySheet
End Sub
```

The CreateSummaryWorkbook procedure calls three procedures in succession, resulting in the completed summary workbook. The subordinate procedures may reside in the same module or in different modules provided that they have been defined as public procedures. The ***scope*** of a procedure refers to its availability or use by another procedure. ***Public procedures*** are available to any procedure in any module. ***Private procedures*** are available only to other procedures in the same module.

What if, however, the OpenAllWorkbooks procedure was unable to locate the folder containing the individual employee workbooks? It would be pointless to run the subsequent procedures because the summary worksheet would not contain any employee data. Accordingly, we modified the CreateSummaryWorkbook procedure to include an If statement to check that the number of worksheets in the summary workbook is greater than one (i.e., that the summary workbook contains the individual employee worksheets), and if so, it executes the next two procedures. (There is no need to include an error message since the OpenAllWorkbooks procedure contains its own error message if it is unsuccessful.) The modified procedure becomes:

These procedures are executed provided there is at least one employee worksheet

```
Public Sub CreateSummaryWorkbook()
  OpenAllWorkbooks
  If Worksheets.Count > 1
    ReviewEmployeeExpenses
    AddEmployeesToSummarySheet
  End If
End Sub
```

The workbook in Figure 10.9a displays the "empty" summary workbook prior to adding the employee information. The user clicks the Create Summary Workbook command button to execute the associated procedure, which runs the three individual procedures, one after the other.

Look closely at the input box in Figure 10.9a, which is displayed by a modified OpenAllWorkbooks procedure in Figure 10.9b. The user is prompted to enter the path of the folder that contains the employee workbooks. This is a more general approach than was used in the first hands-on exercise in which the name of the folder was coded directly into the macro. The user's response (the name of the folder) is stored in the variable strPathName, which becomes an argument in the subsequent Dir statements. The end result is a flexible procedure that lets the user specify where the individual expense statements are stored.

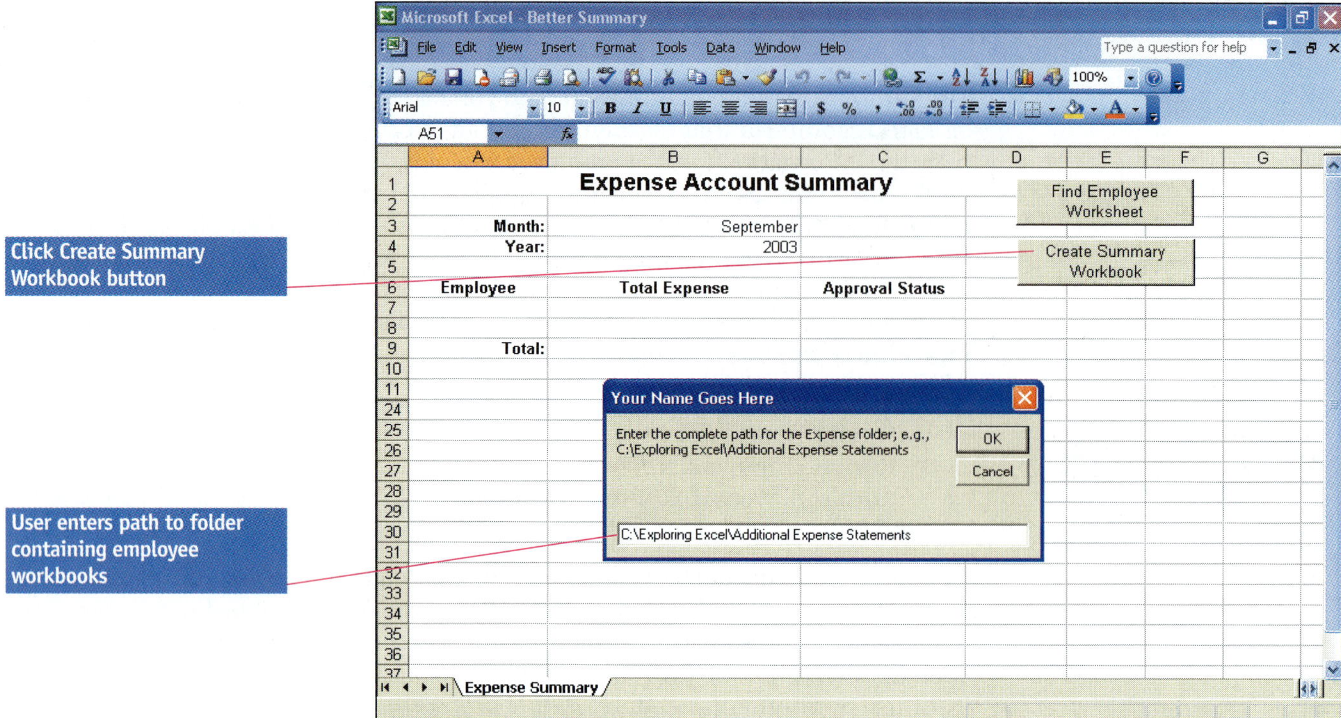

(a) Variable Input Folder

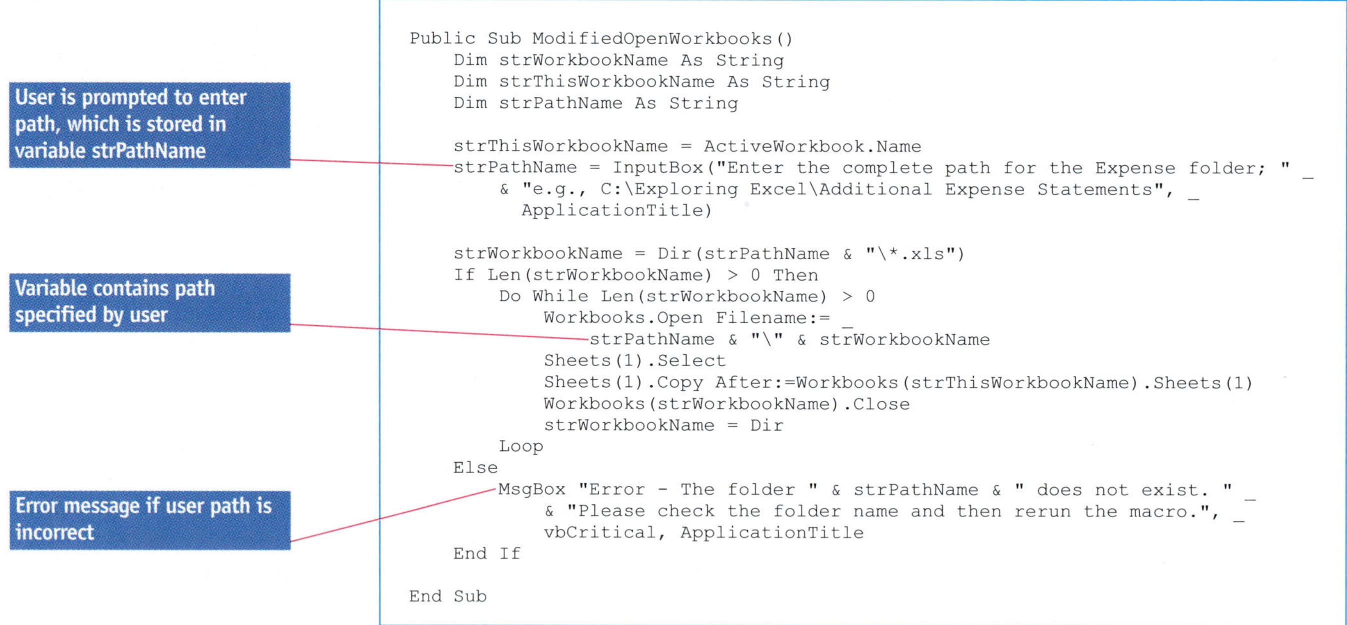


```
Public Sub ModifiedOpenWorkbooks()
    Dim strWorkbookName As String
    Dim strThisWorkbookName As String
    Dim strPathName As String

    strThisWorkbookName = ActiveWorkbook.Name
    strPathName = InputBox("Enter the complete path for the Expense folder; " _
        & "e.g., C:\Exploring Excel\Additional Expense Statements", _
          ApplicationTitle)

    strWorkbookName = Dir(strPathName & "\*.xls")
    If Len(strWorkbookName) > 0 Then
        Do While Len(strWorkbookName) > 0
            Workbooks.Open Filename:= _
                strPathName & "\" & strWorkbookName
            Sheets(1).Select
            Sheets(1).Copy After:=Workbooks(strThisWorkbookName).Sheets(1)
            Workbooks(strWorkbookName).Close
            strWorkbookName = Dir
        Loop
    Else
        MsgBox "Error - The folder " & strPathName & " does not exist. " _
            & "Please check the folder name and then rerun the macro.", _
            vbCritical, ApplicationTitle
    End If

End Sub
```

(b) The VBA Procedure

FIGURE 10.9 An Improved Summary Worksheet

hands-on exercise

4 A Better Summary Workbook

Objective Use a modified version of the Expense Summary workbook with additional flexibility and automation. Use Figure 10.10 as a guide in the exercise.

Step 1: Open the Better Workbook

- Open the **Better Summary workbook** in the Exploring Excel folder. Click the button to **Enable Macros** in response to the security warning.
- You will see the message box in Figure 10.10a. Click **No**. You will see a second message indicating that you can run the procedure at a later time. Click **OK**.
- Save the workbook as **Better Summary Solution** so that you can return to the original workbook if necessary.
- The Better Summary workbook contains a single (empty) summary worksheet and parallels the Expense Summary workbook you were using earlier. The command buttons correspond to the command buttons that you added in a previous hands-on exercise.
- The previous month (the month for which expenses are submitted) is determined automatically using Date functions. The year is also entered automatically.

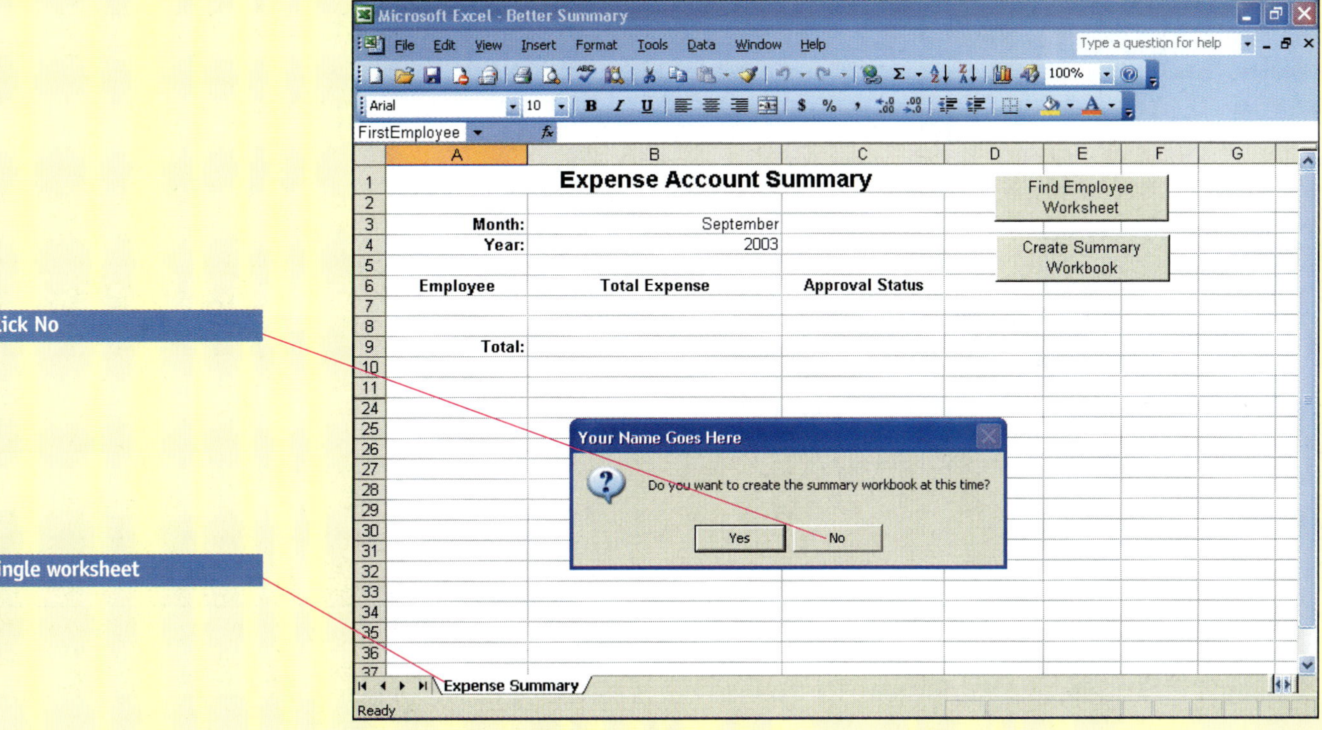

(a) Open the Better Workbook (step 1)

FIGURE 10.10 Hands-on Exercise 4

A BETTER SUMMARY WORKBOOK

The workbook in this exercise improves on its predecessor in two important ways. It is more general because it enables the user to enter the folder containing the employee workbooks, verifies that the folder exists, and displays an error message if it doesn't. It is also easier to use because the summary workbook is created with a single mouse click, as opposed to executing multiple procedures.

Step 2: Event Procedures

- Press **Alt+F11** to open the VBA Editor. Maximize this window. If necessary, pull down the **View menu** to display the Project Explorer window.
- Double click **ThisWorkbook** within the list of Excel objects to display the event procedures for this workbook as shown in Figure 10.10b. (The BeforeClose event procedure has not yet been created.) Close Project Explorer.
- Look at the Open Workbook event procedure. The MsgBox function asks the user whether to create the summary workbook, and if so, runs a general procedure called CreateSummaryWorkbook. (We examine this procedure in step 3.)
- If necessary, click the **down arrow** on the Object list box and select **Workbook**. Click the **down arrow** on the Procedure list box and select the **BeforeClose** event to create this event procedure.
- Enter the statements in the BeforeClose event procedure as shown in Figure 10.10b. Save the workbook. Click the **Close button** to close the window containing the event procedures.

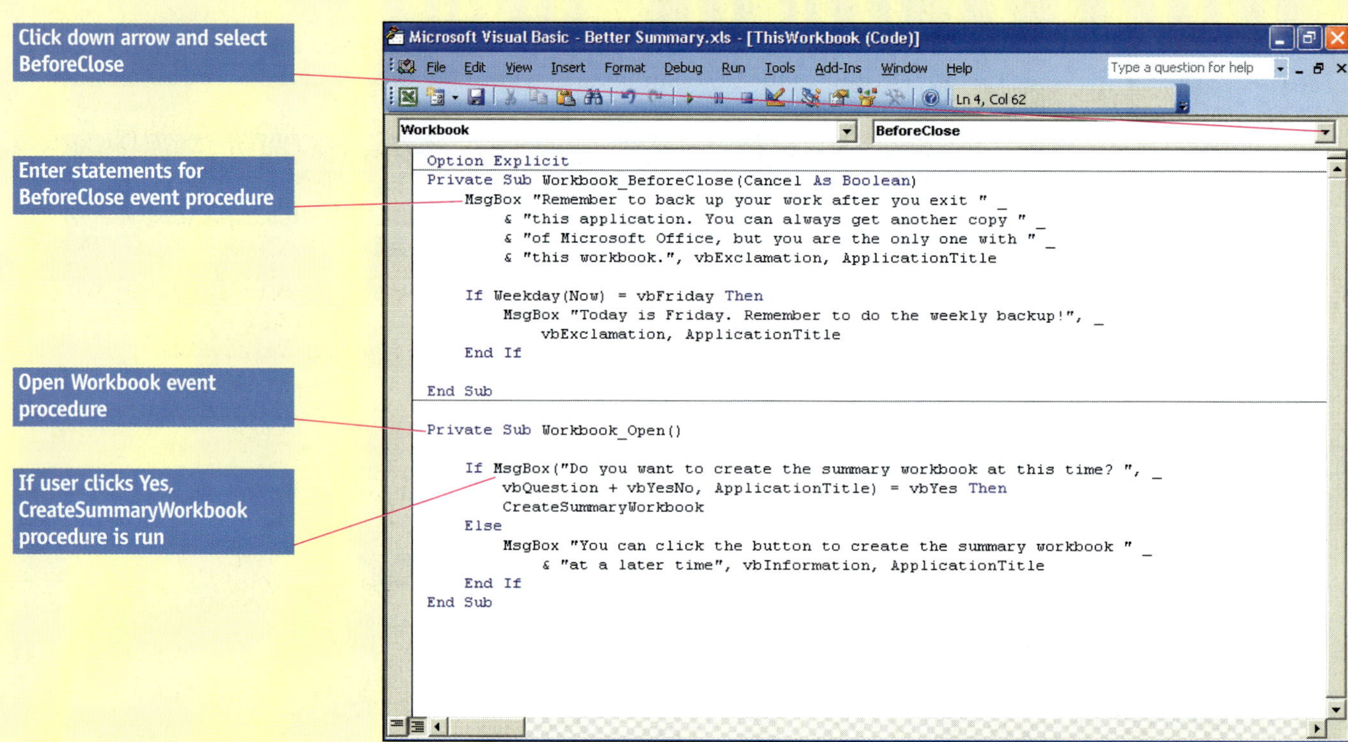

(b) Event Procedures (step 2)

FIGURE 10.10 Hands-on Exercise 4 (*continued*)

DAYS OF THE WEEK—INTRINSIC CONSTANTS

You can test for a specific day of the week using a combination of the Weekday and Now functions in conjunction with VBA intrinsic (predefined) constants. The Now function returns today's date. Thus, the expression Weekday(Now) returns today's day, which is then compared to a specific day of the week such as vbFriday. In other words, the condition in the If statement will be considered true if today is Friday. Use the Help function in VBA to search for other sets of intrinsic constants.

Step 3: **Test the CreateSummaryWorkbook Procedure**

- Open Project Explorer. Double click **Module1** to display the code for this module. Maximize the code window. Close Project Explorer.
- Click within the **CreateSummaryWorkbook procedure**, then click the **Procedure View button** at the bottom of the window to display one procedure at a time. (Use the **PgUp** and **PgDn keys** to move between procedures.)
- Right click an empty area of the taskbar, then click the **Show the Desktop command**. Click the Excel and VBA buttons to reopen these windows.
- Right click the taskbar a second time and click the **Tile Windows Vertically command** to display the windows as shown in Figure 10.10c. Close Project Explorer.
- Click the **Run button** on the VBA standard toolbar. Enter an **invalid folder** when prompted for the name of the folder that contains the expense statements. Click **OK**. You will see the error message in Figure 10.10c. Click **OK**.
- Rerun the **CreateSummaryWorkbook** procedure, but this time, enter the correct folder, **C:\Exploring Excel\Additional Expense Statements**. Click **Yes** when prompted to save each employee workbook.
- You will be asked for the maximum expense. Enter **$1,000**. Click **OK**. The summary workbook is created for you.

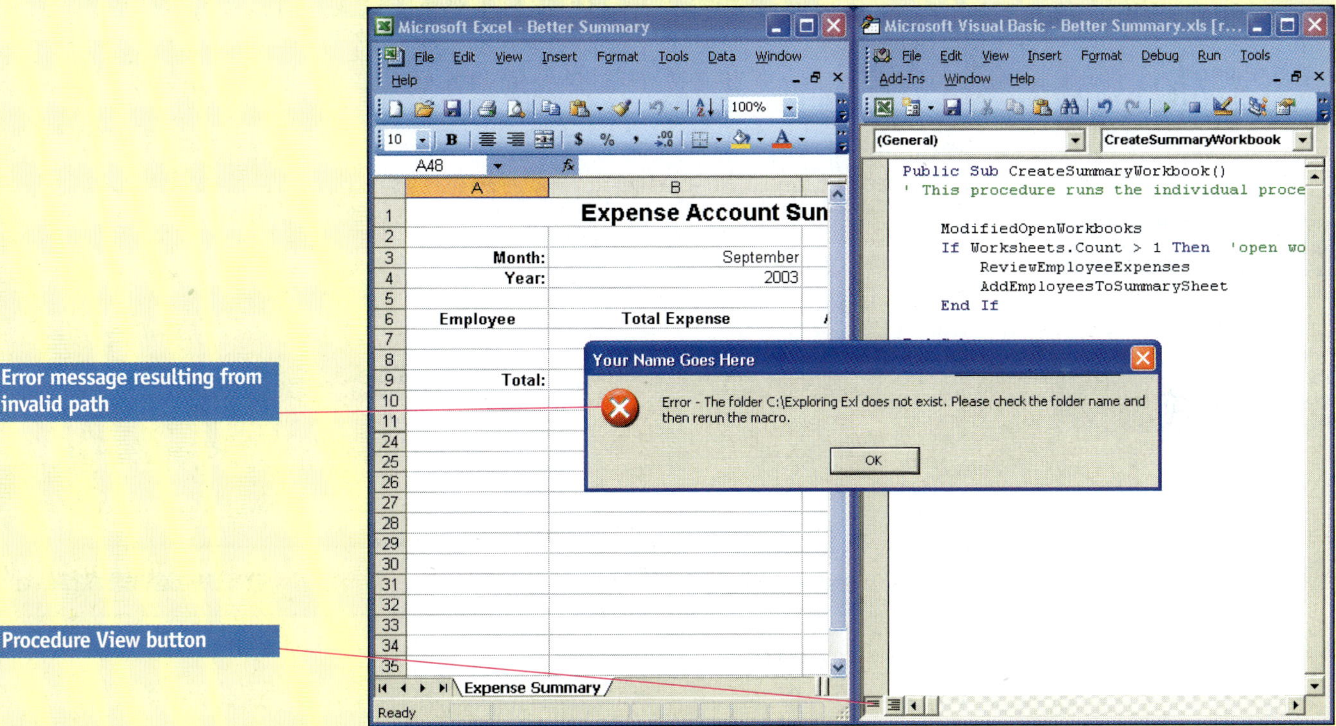

(c) Test the CreateSummaryWorkbook Procedure (step 3)

FIGURE 10.10 Hands-on Exercise 4 (*continued*)

OBJECTS, COLLECTIONS, AND PROPERTIES

A collection is a set of similar objects. For example, the worksheets collection is the set of worksheets in a workbook. Collections, like objects, have properties that can be tested. The statement If Worksheets.Count > 1 in our procedure is testing the Count property of the Worksheets collection to ensure that there are multiple worksheets within the workbook before executing the next two commands.

Step 4: Find an Employee's Worksheet

- Maximize the Excel window. You should see the summary worksheet with the employees listed in alphabetical order as shown in Figure 10.10d. (The input box is not yet visible.)
- The names in the worksheet are different from those in the earlier exercise because we used a different folder to obtain the employee workbooks.
- Save the workbook. Print the summary worksheet for your instructor as proof you completed the exercise.
- Click the button to **Find Employee Worksheet**. Disregard the message in the box and enter only the employee's last name; for example, enter **Beesaw**, then click **OK**. You will see an error message indicating that the specified employee does not exist.
- Click **OK** in response to the error message. Click the **Find Employee Worksheet button** a second time, and enter the name correctly as shown in Figure 10.10d. Click **OK**.

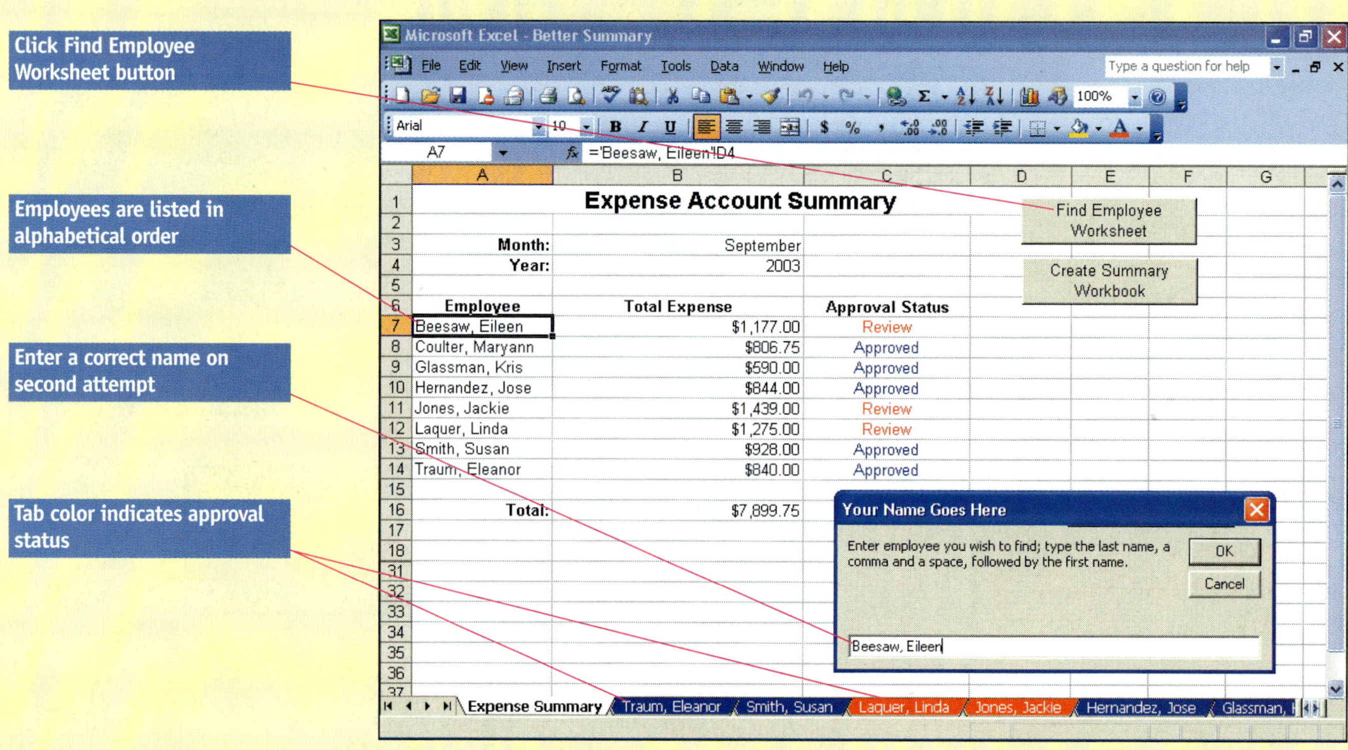

(d) Find an Employee's Worksheet (step 4)

FIGURE 10.10 Hands-on Exercise 4 (*continued*)

ENTER THE EMPLOYEE'S LAST NAME

The existing procedure requires you to enter the employee's complete name in a precise syntax. What if, however, you know only the last name? You can develop an alternate procedure to prompt the user for the employee's last name, then search through the workbook to see if any worksheet tab contains that name. The resulting procedure will be driven by a For. . .Next statement to process all of the worksheets within the workbook. It also requires elementary string processing to search for the last name within the combination of first and last name that appears on the worksheet tab. See exercise 3 at the end of the chapter.

Step 5: Exit the Application

- You should see the worksheet for Eileen Beesaw as shown in Figure 10.10e. Note the indication to review Eileen's expenses at the bottom of the worksheet is consistent with the red color of the worksheet tab.
- Take a minute to review all that was accomplished in this exercise.
  - You opened the Better Summary workbook and were asked if you wanted to create the summary workbook. If you answered yes, you were asked to enter the name of the folder that contained the employee workbooks.
  - Each employee workbook was opened automatically, the worksheets were copied to the summary workbook, the expenses on the individual worksheets were evaluated, and the associated information was copied to the summary worksheet.
  - You were able to display an employee worksheet that needed review.
  - The BeforeClose event procedure reminds the user to back up the workbook.
- Press **Alt+F11** to switch to the VBA editor. Print the event procedures as well as the procedures in Module1 for your instructor. Close the VBA window.
- Exit Excel. Congratulations on a job well done.

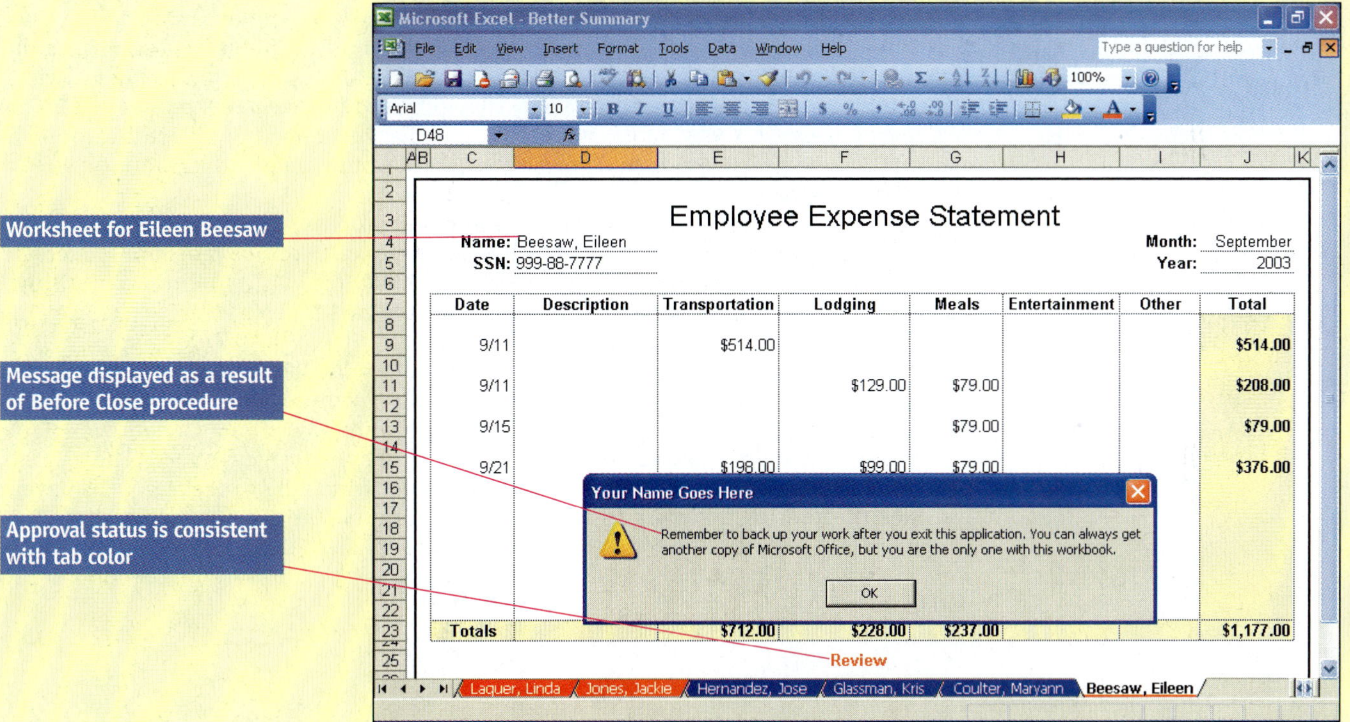

(e) Exit the Application (step 5)

FIGURE 10.10 Hands-on Exercise 4 (*continued*)

PRINT THE PROCEDURES FROM MICROSOFT WORD

The Print command within the VBA editor will print all of the procedures in the current module or in the entire project. The command is limited, however, in that it prints the procedures without formatting of any kind, and thus we find it helpful to print the final version of our procedures using Microsoft Word. The end result is a more polished document from which to study. See exercise 6 at the end of the chapter.

SUMMARY

The chapter developed an Excel application to process employee expenses that exist initially in individual workbooks. The overall objective is to automate the process of consolidating data from different sources. A "divide and conquer" approach is used to divide a complex task into smaller, more manageable tasks. The end result is an "empty" summary workbook that contains multiple VBA procedures to accomplish the objective. These procedures include several VBA statements that do not have equivalent Excel menu commands such as MsgBox, InputBox, If. . .Else, For. . .Next, Do Until, and Do While. (The VBA primer at the end of the text contains detailed information on these statements.)

The reader is presented with an expense statement workbook at the beginning of the chapter and asked to enter a set of hypothetical expenses to gain familiarity with the application. The completed workbook is then saved in an Expense Statement folder that contains additional workbooks from other employees, which in turn will be incorporated into the summary workbook.

The Visual Basic Dir function is used to process all of the workbooks in the Expense Statement folder. The first time this function is called, it returns the name of the first file in the folder, then each subsequent time the function is called, it returns the next file (if any) in the same folder. Eventually no additional files are found and the function returns a null value. The Dir function is incorporated into a loop that opens each individual workbook, then copies the information from that workbook onto a worksheet in the summary workbook.

Two additional procedures are developed to process the employee worksheets once they have been added to the summary workbook. The first procedure evaluates the expenses on each worksheet to indicate immediate approval or further review. Conditional formatting is used to display the approved or rejected expenses in blue or red, respectively. The color of the worksheet tab is also changed to reflect the approval status. A second procedure then copies information from the individual worksheets to a summary worksheet.

Both procedures use the For. . .Next statement to process all of the worksheets within the worksheets collection (i.e., with a specified workbook). The three procedures to create the summary workbook may be executed individually (as was done in the first three hands-on exercises). The procedures may also be executed collectively from a single procedure as illustrated in the fourth hands-on exercise.

The scope of a procedure or variable refers to its availability or use by another procedure. Public procedures are available to any procedure in any module. Private procedures are available only to other procedures in the same module.

A procedure was also developed to display a specific worksheet. The user is prompted for the employee's first and last name, after which the worksheet is displayed, provided the information was entered correctly. The procedure also introduces error processing in the event that the worksheet cannot be found. This is accomplished through the On Error statement that transfers control to a special error-handling section at the end of the procedure.

KEY TERMS

Conditional Formatting 511
Debugging 499
Dim statement 493
Dir function 494
Do Until statement 493
Do While statement 493
Error Trapping 501
Exit Sub statement 501
For. . .Next statement 493
If. . .Then. . .Else statement 493
InputBox function 493
Intrinsic constant 524
Len function 494
MsgBox statement 493
On Error statement 501
Private procedure 521
Public procedure 521
Run-time error 501
Scope 521
Syntax error 501
Worksheet object 501

MULTIPLE CHOICE

1. The statement strWorkbookName = Dir("C:\My Assignments"*.xls) will
   (a) Open the My Assignments workbook on drive C
   (b) Return the names of all workbooks in the My Assignments folder
   (c) Return the name of the first workbook in the My Assignments folder
   (d) Display the message "File Does Not Exist" if there are no workbooks in the My Assignments folder

2. What happens if the Dir function cannot find the specified file?
   (a) The function returns an empty (zero length) character string
   (b) The associated procedure displays an error message
   (c) The associated procedure ceases execution
   (d) All of the above

3. The statement strWorkbookName = Dir(strFolderName & "*.xls") will
   (a) Open the workbook called strFolderName
   (b) Return the name of the first workbook in the folder called strFolderName
   (c) Return the name of the first workbook in the folder where the folder name is stored in the variable strFolderName
   (d) Display the message "File Does Not Exist" if there are no workbooks in the strFolderName folder

4. Which of the following is a true statement?
   (a) A run-time error occurs because the user violated a syntactical requirement of VBA
   (b) The statement that produced a run-time error is indicated in red within the VBA procedure
   (c) A run-time error is accompanied by a standard VBA error message unless the procedure includes an error-handling procedure
   (d) All of the above

5. How do you implement an error-handling procedure?
   (a) Include an On Error statement that transfers control elsewhere in the procedure if a run-time error occurs
   (b) Develop an error-handling section that is referenced by the On Error statement
   (c) Include an Exit Sub statement to bypass the error-handling code if the error does not occur
   (d) All of the above

6. Which of the following statements is true regarding VBA syntax?
   (a) An underscore at the end of a line indicates continuation
   (b) An ampersand indicates concatenation of a character string
   (c) An apostrophe at the beginning of a line indicates a comment
   (d) All of the above

7. Where does the macro recorder store the macros (procedures) it creates?
   (a) In a hidden worksheet called Module1
   (b) In a hidden worksheet, but not necessarily Module1
   (c) In Module1 of the current project
   (d) In a module of the current project, but not necessarily Module1

8. The statement ActiveCell.Offset(1, -2).Select moves to the cell that is:
   (a) One row down and two columns to the left of the current cell
   (b) One row down and two columns to the right of the current cell
   (c) One row up and two columns to the left of the current cell
   (d) One row up and two columns to the right of the current cell

9. The Excel formula ='Smith'!TotalExpense is
   (a) Syntactically incorrect because a worksheet tab must include the employee's first and last name
   (b) Syntactically incorrect because a cell formula must contain a relative or absolute cell reference
   (c) Referencing the range name TotalExpense on the current worksheet
   (d) Referencing the range name TotalExpense on the worksheet called Smith

10. What value will be returned by the function Len(strName), given that the variable strName was previously initialized to "Your Name"?
    (a) Seven
    (b) Nine
    (c) Eleven
    (d) Impossible to determine

... continued

multiple choice

11. Which of the following statements is true, given the VBA statement ActiveWorkbook.Sheets("Jessica Benjamin").Tab.ColorIndex = 3?

(a) ActiveWorkbook is used as a qualifier to indicate the specific workbook that contains the indicated worksheets collection
(b) "JessicaBenjamin" is a worksheet within the worksheets collection of the active workbook
(c) ColorIndex is a property of the Tab object
(d) All of the above

12. Which of the following is a true statement?

(a) Every If statement must include an Else clause
(b) Every If statement must include an End If delimiter
(c) An If statement must be precisely indented if it is to compile correctly
(d) All of the above

13. Given that the variable strName contains the value "George", what will be displayed by the statement, msgbox "Hello", & strName & ". How are you?"?

(a) HelloGeorge. How are you?
(b) HelloGeorge.How are you?
(c) Hello George.How are you?
(d) Hello George. How are you?

14. The statement If Worksheets.Count > 1 is:

(a) Applying the Count method to a worksheet object
(b) Testing the Count property of a worksheet object
(c) Applying the Count method to the worksheets collection
(d) Testing the Count property of the worksheets collection

15. Given the partial statement MsgBox ("Do you want to continue?", vbYesNo), which of the following is true?

(a) The user will see the indicated prompt and Yes and No command buttons
(b) A question mark icon will appear in the resulting message box
(c) "Your Name Goes Here" will appear on the title bar of the message box
(d) All of the above

16. Which statement will prompt the user to enter his or her name and store the result in a variable called strUserName?

(a) InputBox.strUserName
(b) strUserName = MsgBox("Please enter your name.")
(c) strUserName = InputBox("Please enter your name.")
(d) InputBox("Please enter strUserName.")

17. Given the statement Sheets("Sheet1").Select

(a) Sheets is the collection, Select is the method
(b) Sheets is the object, Select is the method
(c) Sheets is the collection, Select is the property
(d) Sheets is the object, Select is the property

18. If the variable strName is set to "George", the expression "Good morning, strName" will return:

(a) Good morning, George
(b) Good morning, strName
(c) Good morning George
(d) Good morning strName

ANSWERS

1. c	**7.** d	**13.** a
2. a	**8.** a	**14.** d
3. c	**9.** d	**15.** a
4. c	**10.** b	**16.** c
5. d	**11.** d	**17.** a
6. d	**12.** b	**18.** b

PRACTICE WITH EXCEL AND VBA

1. **Finding the Month and Day:** The workbook in Figure 10.11 illustrates table lookup functions in conjunction with date functions. Proceed as follows:
   a. Create a new workbook. Enter the title of the worksheet into cell A1, then merge cells A1 through D1 to center the title at the top of the worksheet. Enter the indicated labels in cells A3, A4, and C4. Enter the tables for the day of the week and month of the year into cells A9 through B15 and C9 through D20, respectively. Widen columns as necessary.
   b. Enter any date into cell B3. Use the Weekday and Month functions in cells B8 and D8, respectively, to obtain the numerical value for the day of the week and month of the year, respectively. Cell B8, for example, will contain the function =Weekday(B3).
   c. Enter a VLOOKUP function into cell B4 to display the day of the week based on the numeric value in cell B8 and the associated table. Enter a second VLOOKUP function into cell D4 to display the month of the year based on the numeric value in cell D8 and the associated table.
   d. Modify the formulas in cells B4 and D4 to include an IF statement that displays a blank value if cell B3 is empty. Modify the formulas in cells B8 and D8 to include similar If statements. Delete the date in cell B3 to test the revised formulas.
   e. Create an Open Workbook event procedure to prompt the user for his or her birth date to enter the response into cell B3.
   f. Turn on the macro recorder to create a "dummy" macro to hide rows 8 through 20 in the worksheet. Modify the Open Workbook event procedure to prompt the user as shown in Figure 10.11. Use the VBA statements that were captured in part e to hide the indicated rows.
   g. Print the cell formulas for the completed worksheet. Print the Open Workbook event procedure. Capture the screen in Figure 10.11 and use that as a cover sheet when you submit the completed assignment.

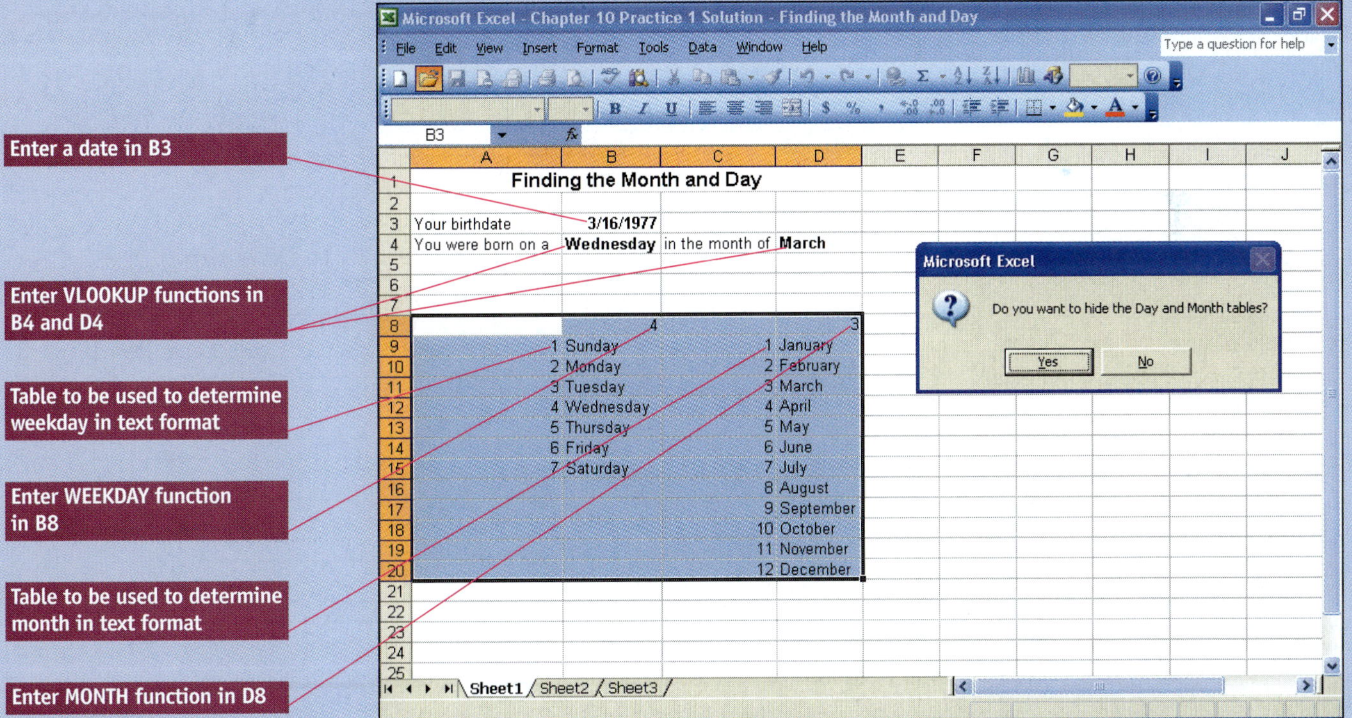

FIGURE 10.11 Finding the Month and Day (exercise 1)

2. **A Puzzle for You:** The workbook in Figure 10.12 contains a traditional puzzle that you may have seen before. Even so, you may not be able to solve every entry. We don't want you to be unduly frustrated, and so we have included the answers in the workbook, but you have to find the hidden password to see the solution. The intent of the exercise, however, is not to solve the puzzle per se, but to use your knowledge of Excel and VBA to display the password. Proceed as follows:
   a. Open the *Chapter 10 Practice 2* workbook in the Exploring Excel folder. Click the button to Enable Macros to see the worksheet in Figure 10.12. Try to solve as many of the entries as possible, without resorting to the answers. There are 26 questions. A good score is 20 or better.
   b. You can begin your quest for the solution without knowing the password. Use the appropriate Excel command to display the gridlines and the row and column headings.
   c. Look for a hidden worksheet. Does this worksheet contain any hints to help you find the password?
   d. Locate the VBA procedure that will display the cell formulas, provided you make the necessary change. Once you run the modified procedure, the password will become obvious to you.
   e. Use the password to unhide the columns containing the solution to complete the workbook.
   f. Print the workbook two ways, once to show the displayed values and once to show the cell formulas. (You will not be able to print the cell formulas until you complete part d correctly.) Print all of the VBA procedures within the workbook.
   g. Add a cover sheet, then submit the completed assignment to your instructor. Include a brief discussion of how you found the hidden password. Can you create an Excel workbook with another puzzle that contains the solution and a hidden password?

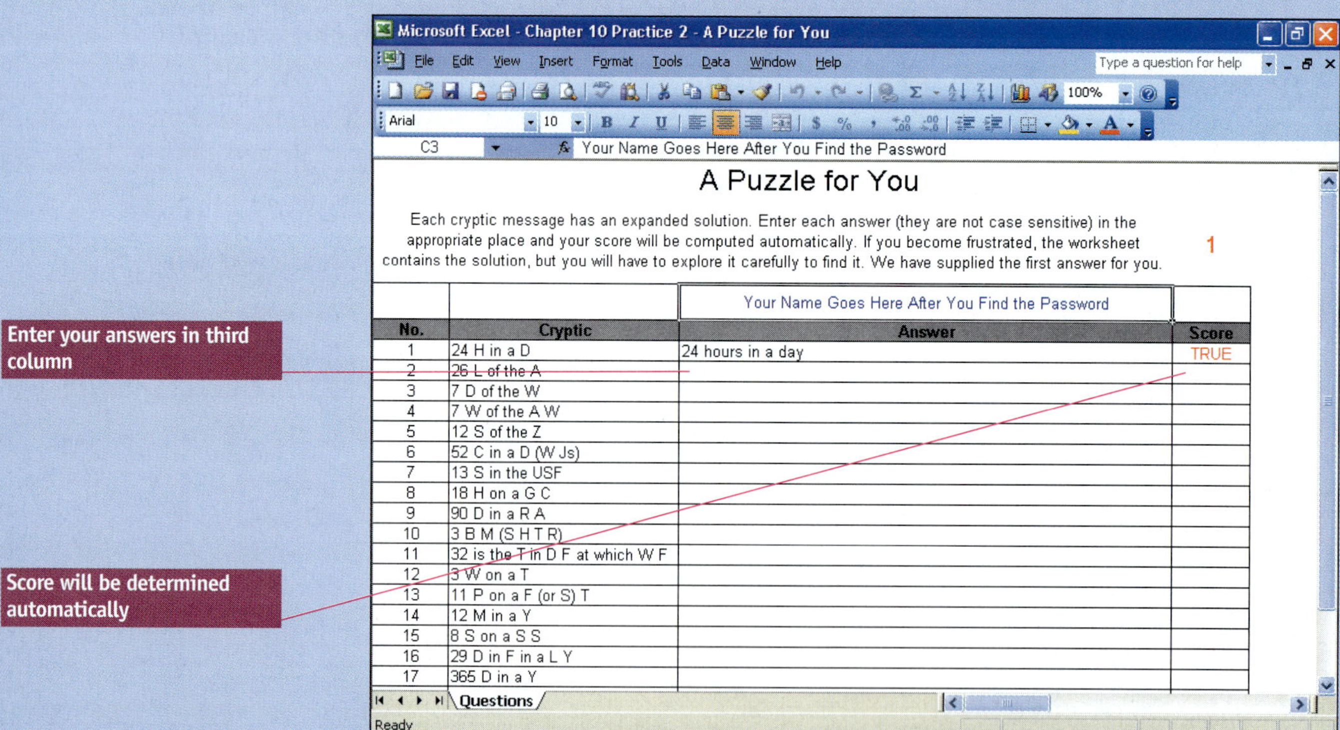

FIGURE 10.12 A Puzzle for You (exercise 2)

3. **Search for an Employee's Last Name:** Figure 10.13 displays a procedure to search for an employee's last name, and then to display the associated worksheet. It achieves the same result as the procedure in the second hands-on exercise, but it allows the user to enter only the last name, as opposed to the combination of last name and first name. It also introduces additional programming techniques. Open the *Chapter 10 Practice 3* workbook and click "Yes" when asked whether to create the summary workbook. (Use the expense statements in the Additional Expense Statements folder and specify $1,000 as the amount required for review.) You now have the same workbook as at the end of the fourth hands-on exercise. You will improve this workbook by adding additional procedures, beginning with the procedure in Figure 10.13, which can be added to any existing module.
   a. Use the VBA Help function to determine the meaning of the Visual Basic Like function. What is the statement Like strEmployeeName & "*" searching for?
   b. The variable strFoundWorksheet is an example of a programming switch. It is set to "No" prior to looking at the first worksheet, then set to "Yes" if the last name entered by the user matches the last name in any worksheet tab within the workbook. What action will the procedure take if the designated name cannot be found?
   c. What happens if the procedure locates a worksheet that contains the designated last name? Is it possible to locate more than one worksheet for the same last name?
   d. What is the significance of the intrinsic constant vbQuestion? How is it used in this procedure?
   e. Test the completed procedure to be sure that it works correctly. Print the completed procedure for your instructor.
   f. Modify the error-handling section in the FindEmployeeWorksheet procedure to execute this procedure if the combination of the employee's first and last name is not found. Is this a meaningful enhancement to the earlier procedure?
   g. Submit your answers to the various questions in this exercise to your instructor. Be sure to include the printed procedure with your submission. Add a cover sheet to complete the assignment.

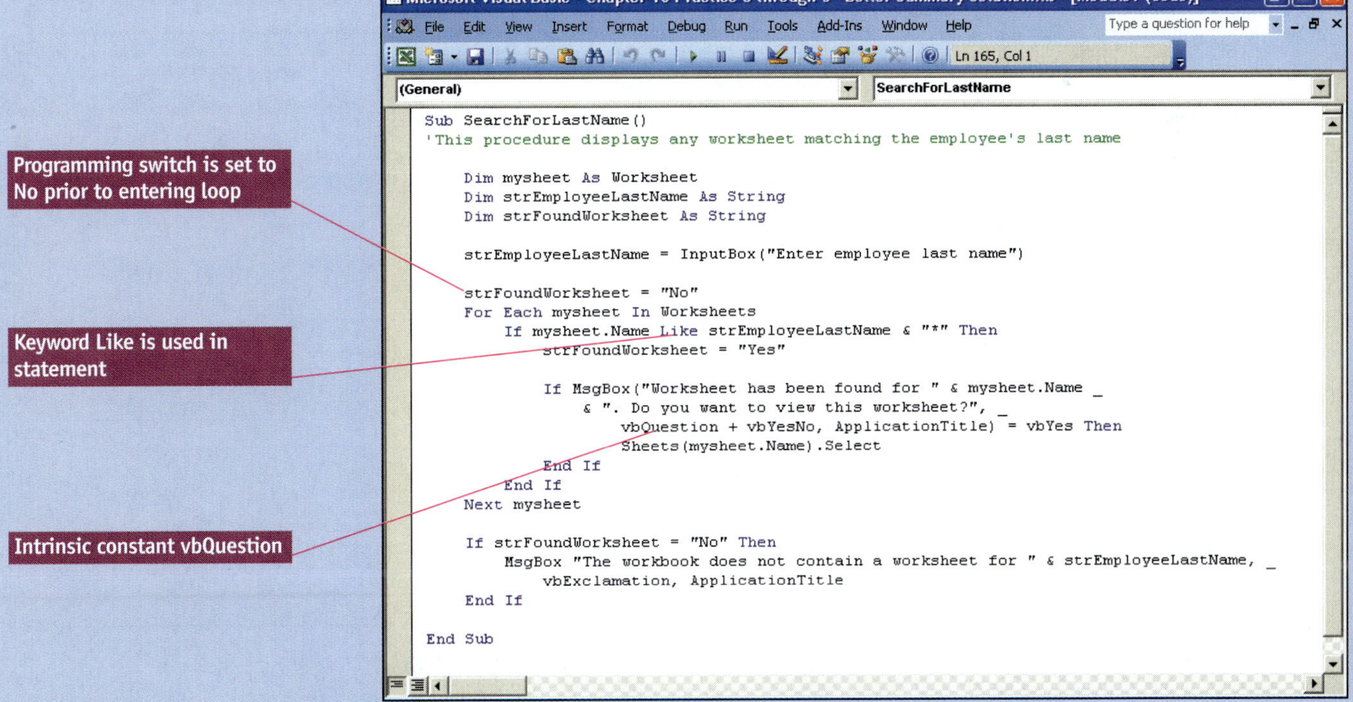

FIGURE 10.13 Search for an Employee's Last Name (exercise 3)

4. **Print Selected Worksheets:** The completed summary workbook has evaluated the expenses for each employee and colored the corresponding worksheet tabs to blue or red, respectively, indicating expenses that are approved or expenses subject to further review. Either (or both) sets of worksheets may be printed at different times by manually selecting the worksheets. It's better to do it automatically.

   The SelectSheetsForPrinting procedure in Figure 10.14 prompts the user to determine which set of worksheets to print, then it calls one of three other procedures to comply with the request. Your assignment is to complete the four required procedures using Figure 10.14 as a guide.

   a. Use the macro recorder to capture the Excel key strokes to print the selected worksheet. Once you have the Print statement, use it as the basis for three separate procedures—to print the approved expense worksheets, to print the worksheets for further review, and to print every employee worksheet. Look closely at Figure 10.14 to see the beginning of the PrintApprovedExpenses procedure.

   b. Create the SelectSheetsForPrinting procedure as shown in Figure 10.14. The Msgbox statement within this procedure inserts line feeds within the message box to force a break from one line to the next. (You can see this message box by looking at Figure 10.15 in the next exercise.) The procedure also uses a Case statement to test the user's response to ensure that it is valid. Note, too, the use of the Visual Basic UCase function to make the user's response case insensitive.

   c. Return to Excel and execute the SelectSheetsForPrinting procedure. Capture the screen that displays the input box asking for the user's response and use that image as the cover sheet for this assignment.

   d. Print all four procedures for your instructor as proof you completed this exercise. Include a short note describing how to call one procedure from another. Add a cover sheet with your name and date.

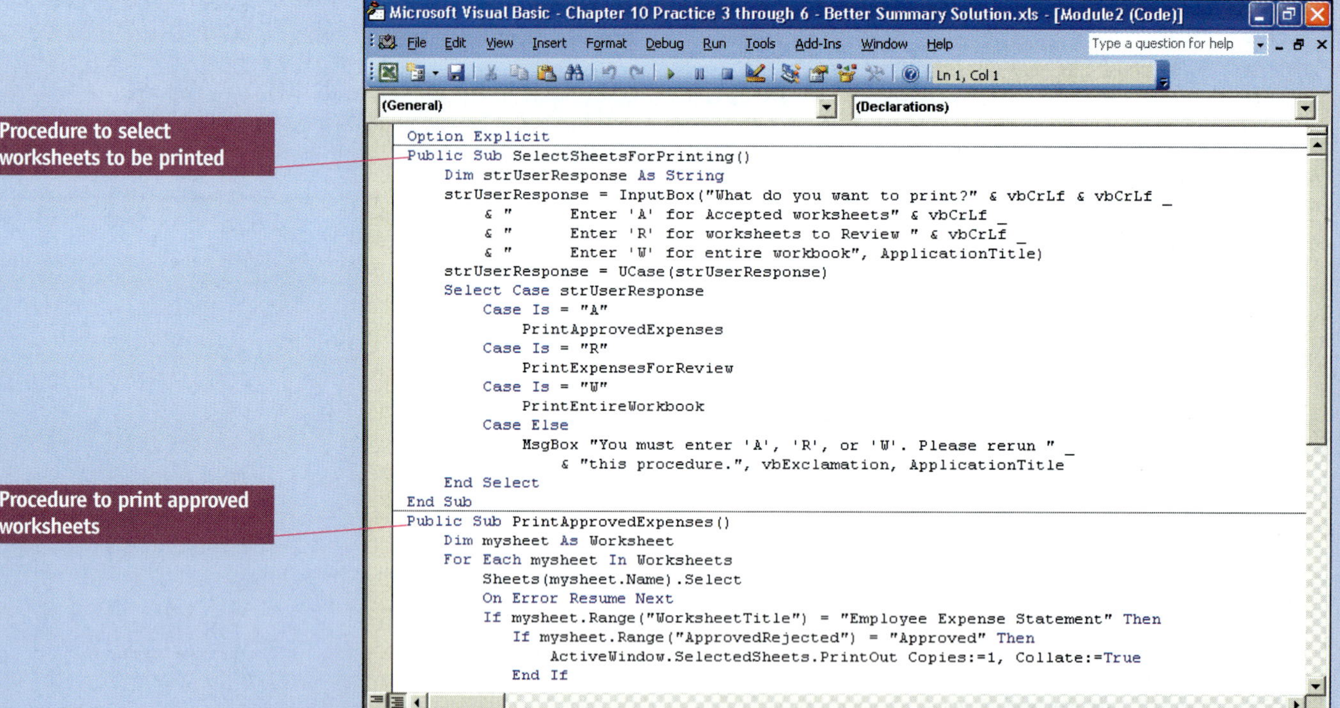

FIGURE 10.14 Print Selected Worksheets (exercise 4)

5. **Add Command Buttons:** The workbook in Figure 10.15 contains a total of five command buttons that collectively execute all of the procedures associated with the Better Summary workbook that has been developed throughout the chapter.
   a. Complete the fourth hands-on exercise in the chapter, which creates the basic version of the Better Summary Solution workbook. There are two command buttons on the summary worksheet at this point.
   b. Complete practice exercise 3 to develop the procedure to search for an employee using only the last name. Add the command button corresponding to this procedure to the worksheet.
   c. Add the fourth command button to change the approval criterion, which runs the ReviewEmployeeExpenses procedure from the third hands-on exercise. Click the button and change the approval criterion to $500 (rather than $1,000 used earlier).
   d. Complete the previous problem to print selected worksheets, then add the fifth command button to run this procedure. Enter "A" to print just the approved worksheet(s).
   e. You can improve the appearance of the worksheet by creating command buttons of uniform size. Choose any command button and size it appropriately. Now right click that button, click the Format Control command, and click the Size tab to see the size of your button. Click the Properties tab and check the box to Print Object. Change the properties of the other command buttons in similar fashion.
   f. Print the summary worksheet (with the command buttons) for your instructor as proof you did this exercise. Use landscape printing if necessary to print the worksheet on a single page.
   g. Create a custom menu that contains five commands that are equivalent to the command buttons in the worksheet. Which technique do you prefer—command buttons on the worksheet or a custom menu? Summarize your thoughts in a short note to your instructor.
   h. Capture the screen in Figure 10.15 (or a different screen that displays the custom menu) to use as a cover sheet for your completed assignment.

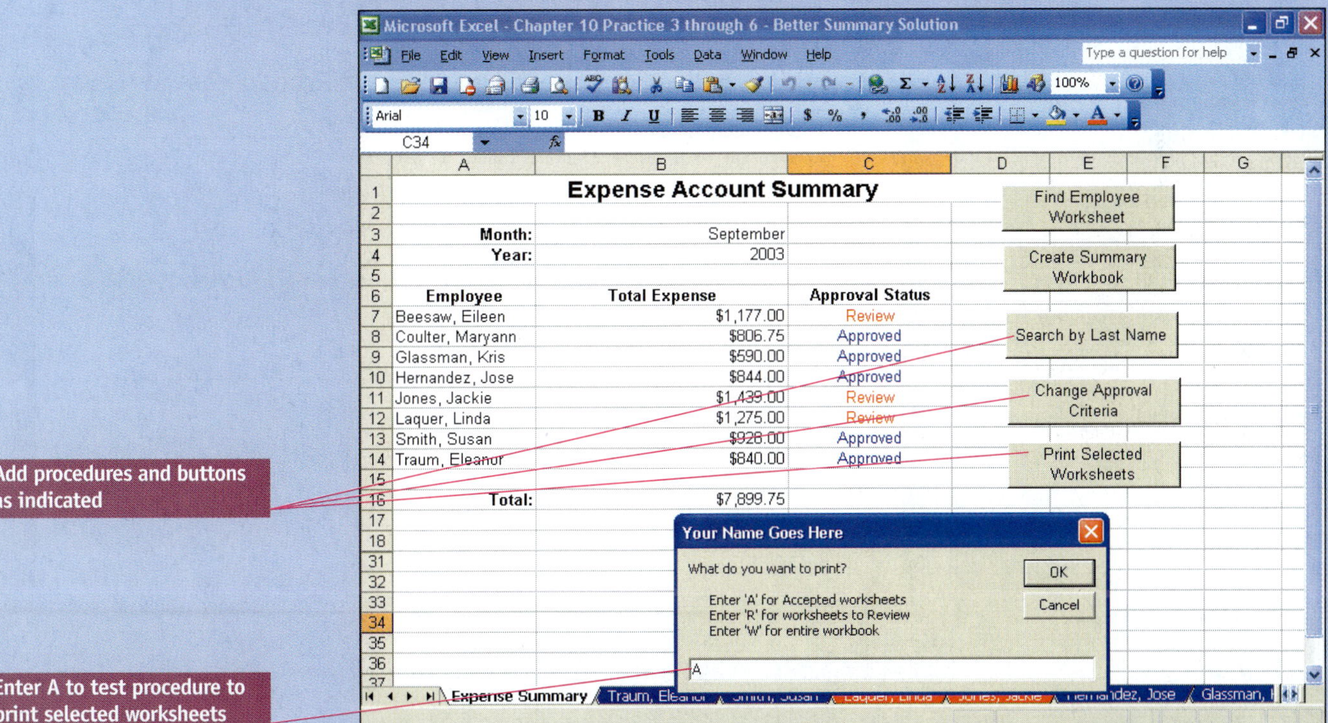

FIGURE 10.15 Add Command Buttons (exercise 5)

6. **Print the VBA Procedures in Microsoft Word:** You can print VBA procedures from within the VBA editor, but the procedures are printed without any formatting. You get a better result by printing from within Microsoft Word as shown in Figure 10.16. Complete the previous exercise to create all of the VBA procedures, and then print the procedures as described below.
   a. Open the VBA editor, select ThisWorkbook within Project Explorer, and click and drag to select all of the statements in both event procedures. Click the Copy button (or use the Ctrl+C keyboard shortcut) to copy these procedures to the Windows clipboard.
   b. Start Microsoft Word and open a new document. Click the Paste button (or use the Ctrl+V keyboard shortcut) to paste the contents of the clipboard (the VBA procedures) into the Word document.
   c. Use the Windows taskbar to return to the VBA editor to copy the contents of the other modules to the Word document in similar fashion. Be sure to copy all of the procedures in all of the modules.
   d. Format the procedures in the Word document as you see fit. We suggest you use a monospaced font such as Courier New so that the indentation and alignment are easier to see. We also suggest that you boldface the Sub and End Sub statements of each procedure, and that you insert a horizontal border to separate the procedures from one another.
   e. Experiment with styles and a table of contents. Format each procedure in a heading style, then use the Reference command in the Insert menu to create the table of contents automatically.
   f. Add a title page, then submit the completed assignment to your instructor. Do you think the additional formatting is worth the trouble? What happens if a procedure changes in the Excel workbook?

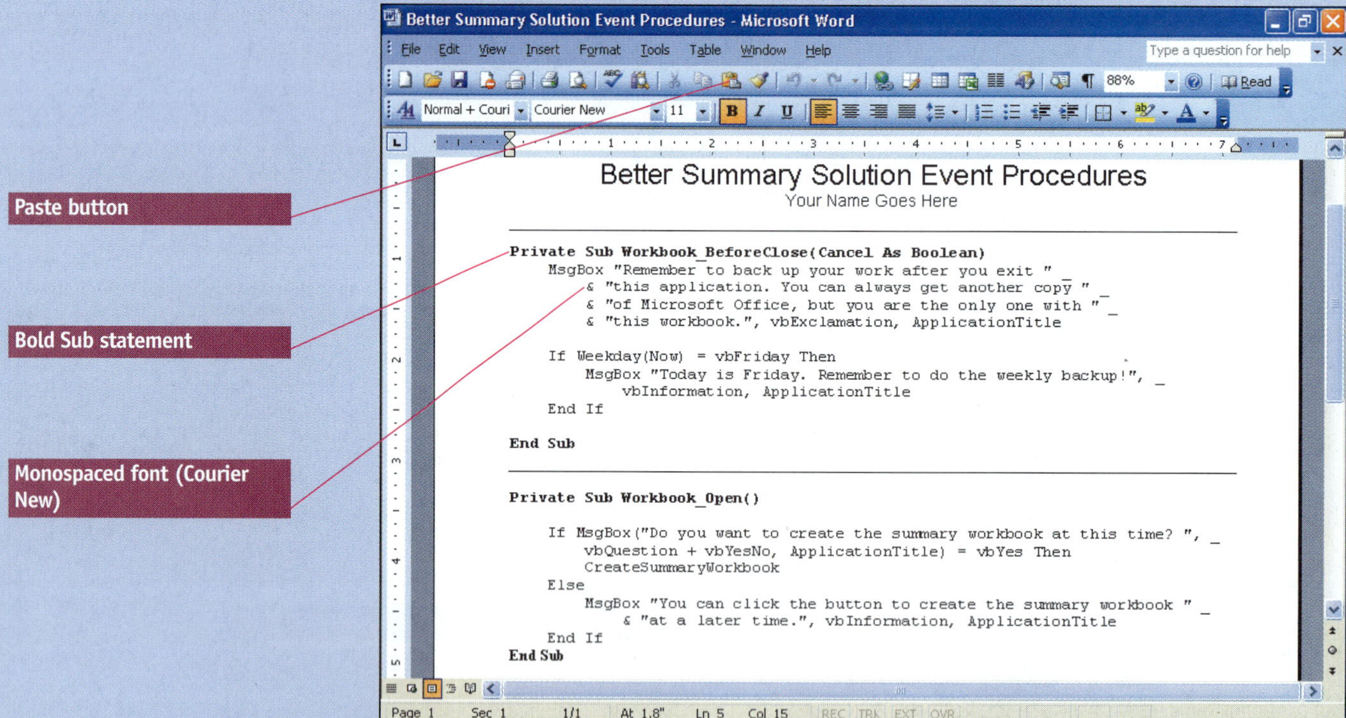

FIGURE 10.16 Print the VBA Procedures in Microsoft Word (exercise 6)

7. **Random Numbers as Test Data:** Open the partially completed version of the workbook in Figure 10.17, which can be found in the *Chapter 10 Practice 7* workbook in the Exploring Excel folder. You will not be able to duplicate the figure exactly, however, because the random number function is used to generate test data for the workbook. Proceed as follows:
   a. Click in cell C4 and note that the formula contains the expression 70+20*Rand( ). The random number function returns a value between 0 and 1, so that the expression returns a value between 70 and 90. (The Round function is used in the actual cell formula to eliminate the decimal portion.)
   b. Pull down the Tools menu, click the Options command, click the Calculation tab, then click the Calculate now button. The test grade changes. Press the F9 (shortcut) key. The value changes again. Click in Cell G1, enter your name, and press the Enter key. The random numbers change again because the spreadsheet is automatically recalculated each time you change the contents of a cell.
   c. Copy the formulas in cells C4 to G4 to rows 5 through 21 to generate the grades for the remaining students. Press the F9 key once or twice to see how the grades change.
   d. The worksheet you just created will be used in a subsequent problem where it will be combined with other grade books. Pull down the File menu and click the Save As command to display the Save As dialog box in Figure 10.17. Change the folder to VBA Grade Books (within the Exploring Excel folder). This folder was created automatically when you installed the practice files. Change the file name to Section R. Click the Save button.
   e. The last step is to convert the formulas (containing the random numbers) in the workbook to fixed values so that they remain constant. Click and drag to select cells C4 through G21. Click the Copy button. Pull down the Edit menu, click the Paste Special command to display the Paste Special dialog box, click the option button for Values, then click OK.
   f. Press the F9 key to recalculate the spreadsheet. The displayed values do not change because the formulas have been converted to a constant value.
   g. Save the spreadsheet a final time.

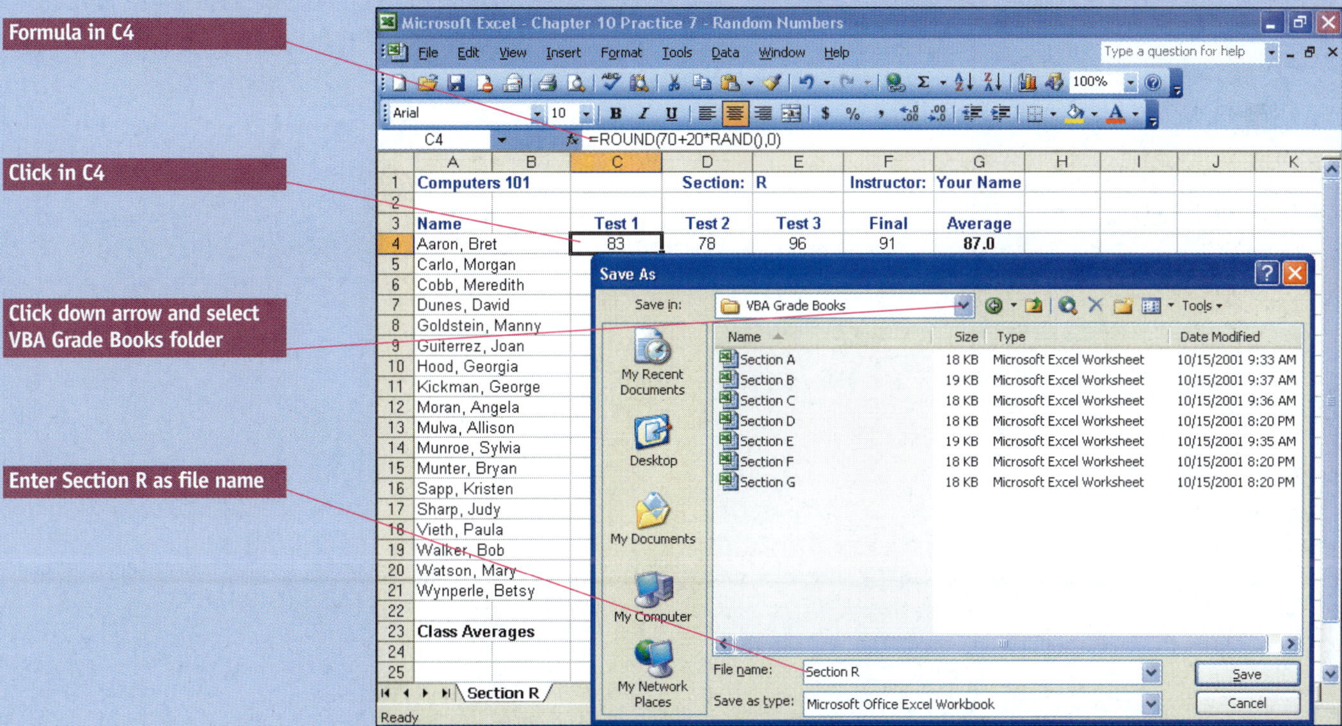

FIGURE 10.17 Random Numbers as Test Data (exercise 7)

8. **The Composite Grade Book:** The workbook in Figure 10.18 is similar in concept to the expense summary workbook that was developed in the chapter. We started with an empty summary workbook and developed the necessary procedures to create the composite grade book by inserting data from individual workbooks. Proceed as follows:
   a. Open the partially completed workbook in *Chapter 10 Practice 8* to display a partially completed workbook. Click Yes when asked whether to create the Summary Grade Book.
   b. You will be prompted for the path to the individual grade books. Type C:\Exploring Excel\VBA Grade Books (assuming that you used the default location when you installed the practice files).
   c. Sit back and relax. The individual grade books will be brought into the summary workbook, after which the summary worksheet will be created. You will not be prompted to save the changes to the individual workbooks because there are no calculations associated with opening and closing these workbooks.
   d. The appearance of Section R in the workbook and on the summary worksheet depends on whether you did the previous exercise, and further, whether you saved this workbook in the VBA Grade Books folder as instructed.
   e. Print the All Sections worksheet two ways—once to show the displayed values, and once to show the cell contents.
   f. Open the VBA editor and print the event procedures that exist within this workbook. What differences (if any) are there in the procedures in this workbook compared to those in the Better Summary that you developed earlier? What differences (if any) are there in the procedures in Module1 compared to the comparable procedures in the Better Summary workbook?
   g. Add a cover sheet and submit the assignment to your instructor.

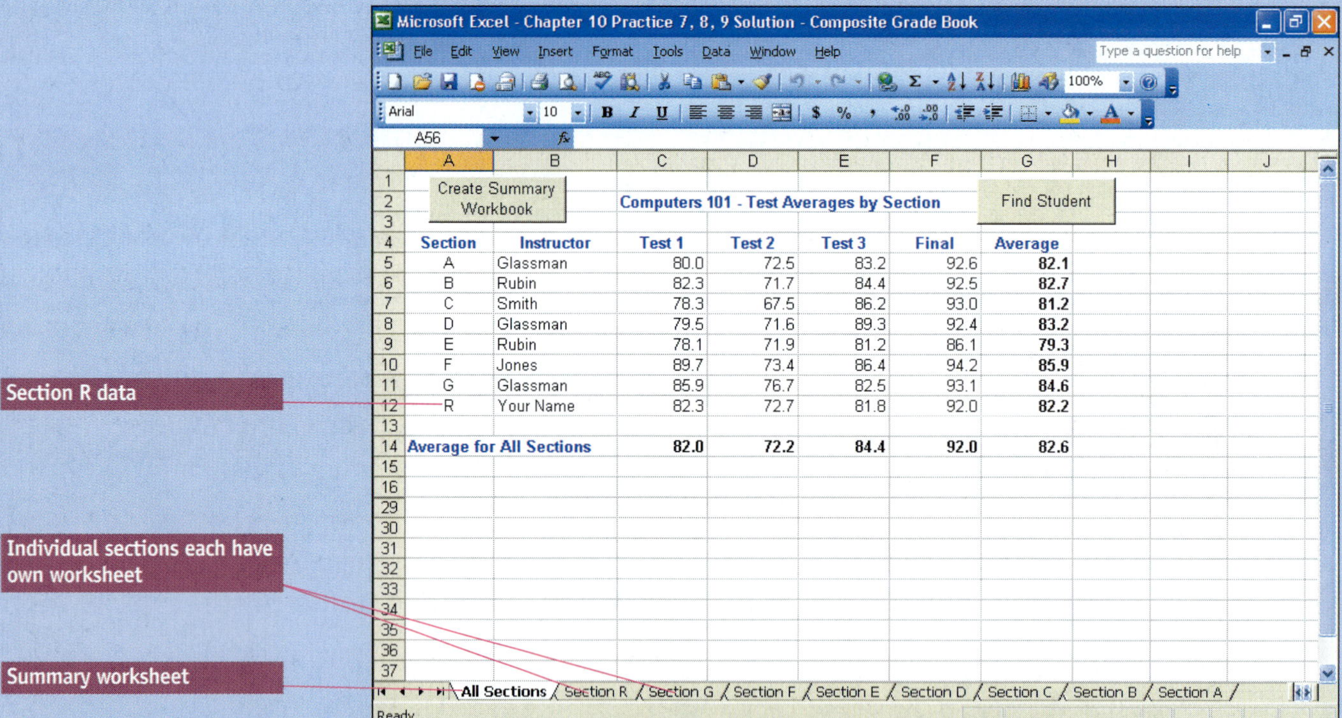

FIGURE 10.18 The Composite Grade Book (exercise 8)

9. **Locate a Student:** This exercise continues the development of the Composite Grade Book by developing a procedure to locate a specific student. It is similar to the Expense Summary workbook from the chapter, except that you are searching for student names within a worksheet, as opposed to an employee name on a worksheet tab.
   a. Open the *Chapter 10 Practice 8* workbook from the previous exercise. What happens if you click the Find Student command button? Is this a reasonable action for the original workbook?
   b. You will replace the original procedure with the VBA code in Figure 10.19, but first we want you to see how the procedure was created. Start the macro recorder. Pull down the Edit menu, click the Find command, then search for a student, "Smith, Doe". Click the Stop Recording button. Which part of the procedure in Figure 10.19 was adopted from the macro you just recorded?
   c. Replace the existing FindStudent procedure in the *Chapter 10 Practice 8* workbook with the VBA code in Figure 10.19. Test the procedure by looking for two students, one who is somewhere in the workbook, and one who is not in the workbook at all. Does the procedure work correctly in both instances?
   d. Place an apostrophe in front of the On Error statement to convert the statement to a comment. Rerun the procedure, specifying the name of a student who is not in the workbook. Does the procedure run successfully? What is the purpose of the On Error statement?
   e. Summarize your answers in a short note to your instructor. Add a cover sheet to complete the assignment.

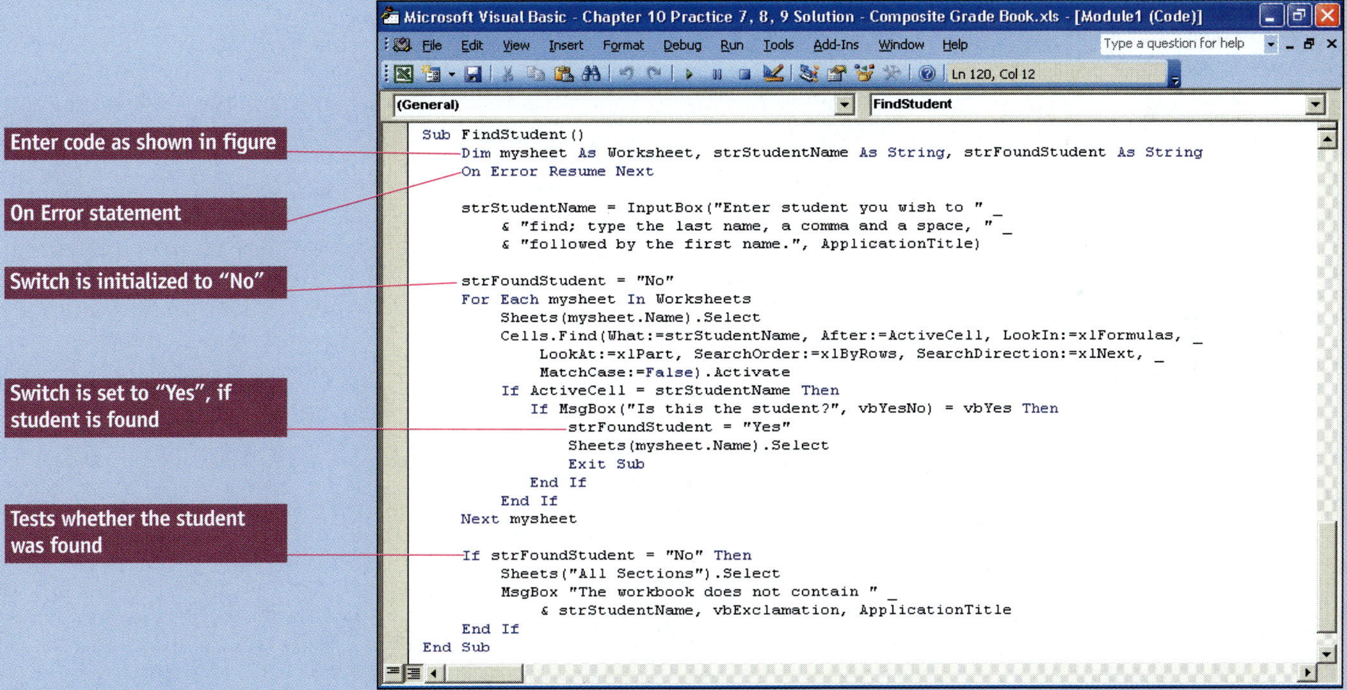

FIGURE 10.19 Locate a Student (exercise 9)

MINI CASES

VBA Review

You should be very familiar with the syntax of Visual Basic. You should also be comfortable with the definition of key terms such as object model, collection, method, and property. Nevertheless, we have created a Word document to review this material. Open the *Chapter 9 Mini Case—VBA Review* document in the Exploring Excel folder, fill in the blanks, add a cover page, and submit the completed document to your instructor.

Your Own Help Manual

Detailed help is available on any VBA topic if only you will take the trouble to look. Start the VBA editor, pull down the Help menu, and select Visual Basic Help (or press the F1 key) to display the Visual Basic Help window. You will see the same type of Help screen that is common to all Office applications. Click the Contents tab, select at least five topics of interest to you, and print the associated Help pages. Add a cover sheet and submit the information to your instructor.

Cleaning Up VBA Code

The macro recorder jump-starts the process of creating a VBA procedure by capturing Excel commands and converting them to their VBA equivalents. The result, however, can be cluttered (inefficient) code that can be simplified by going to the VBA editor and deleting the superfluous entries. For example, turn on the macro recorder, pull down the File menu, click the Page Setup command, and change to Landscape orientation. Turn off the recorder, then look at the resulting procedure.

You may be somewhat surprised at the number of statements because the recorder set every property associated with printing a worksheet. If your intention is just to change the orientation property, you can replace the entire procedure with the single statement, ActiveSheet.PageSetup.Orientation = xlLandscape. Not only is this easier to read, but it runs much more efficiently. You can find similar examples if you use the recorder to change the font or style. A different example is obtained by selecting a cell on a different worksheet.

Turn on the macro recorder, click the tab for Sheet2, select cell A5, then turn off the recorder. The macro recorder produces two statements, Sheets("Sheet2").Select and Range("A5").Select, but you can combine the statements using qualification to Sheets("Sheet2").Range("A5").Select. Study the procedures you created in this chapter and the previous chapter for other examples. Add a cover sheet and submit your assignment to your instructor.

Your Own Application

Develop a VBA application of comparable function to the Expense Summary workbook from the chapter or the Composite Grade Book from the end-of-chapter exercises. The application should be flexible, visually appealing, easy to use, and bulletproof. Choose any scenario that is of interest to you.

The completed application should include event procedures for opening and closing the workbook, for copying a worksheet from other workbooks into an "empty" summary workbook, and for copying information from worksheets within a workbook to a summary worksheet. Present the completed application to the class.

Toolbars for Microsoft® Office Excel 2003

TOOLBARS

3-D Settings
Borders
Chart
Circular Reference
Compare Side by Side
Control Toolbox
Diagram
Drawing
Drawing Canvas
Exit Design Mode
External Data
Formatting
Forms
Formula Auditing
Full Screen
List and XML
Organization Chart
Picture
Pivot Table
Protection
Reviewing
Shadow Settings
Standard
Stop Recording
Text to Speech
Visual Basic
Watch Window
Web
WordArt

OVERVIEW

Microsoft Excel has 29 predefined toolbars that provide access to commonly used commands. The toolbars are displayed in Figure A.1 and are listed here for convenience. They are: the Standard, Formatting, 3-D Settings, Borders, Chart, Circular Reference, Compare Side by Side, Control Toolbox, Diagram, Drawing, Drawing Canvas, Exit Design Mode, External Data, Forms, Formula Auditing, Full Screen, List, Organization Chart, Picture, Pivot Table, Protection, Reviewing, Shadow Settings, Stop Recording, Text to Speech, Visual Basic, Watch Window, Web, and WordArt. The Standard and Formatting toolbars are displayed by default and appear on the same row immediately below the menu bar. The other predefined toolbars are displayed (hidden) at the discretion of the user, and in some cases, are displayed automatically when their corresponding features are in use (e.g., the Chart toolbar and the Pivot Table toolbar).

The buttons on the toolbars are intended to be indicative of their function. Clicking the Printer button (the sixth button from the left on the Standard toolbar), for example, executes the Print command. If you are unsure of the purpose of any toolbar button, point to it, and a ScreenTip will appear that displays its name.

You can display multiple toolbars at one time, move them to new locations on the screen, customize their appearance, or suppress their display.

- To separate the Standard and Formatting toolbars and simultaneously display all of the buttons for each toolbar, pull down the Tools menu, click the Customize command, click the Options tab, then check the box to show the toolbars on two rows. Alternatively, the toolbars appear on the same row, so that only a limited number of buttons are visible on each toolbar; hence you may need to click the double arrow at the end of the toolbar to view additional buttons. Additional buttons will be added to either toolbar as you use the associated feature, and conversely, buttons will be removed from the toolbar if the feature is not used.
- To display or hide a toolbar, pull down the View menu and click the Toolbars command. Select (deselect) the toolbar that you want to display (hide). The selected toolbar will be displayed in the same position as when last displayed. You may also point to any toolbar and click with the right mouse button to bring up a shortcut menu, after which you can select the toolbar to be displayed (hidden). If the toolbar to be displayed is not listed, click the Customize command, click the Toolbars tab, check the box for the toolbar to be displayed, and then click the Close button.

- To change the size of the buttons, suppress the display of the ScreenTips, or display the associated shortcut key (if available), pull down the View menu, click Toolbars, and click Customize to display the Customize dialog box. If necessary, click the Options tab, then select (deselect) the appropriate check box. Alternatively, you can right click on any toolbar, click the Customize command from the context-sensitive menu, then select (deselect) the appropriate check box from within the Options tab in the Customize dialog box.

- Toolbars are either docked (along the edge of the window) or floating (in their own window). A toolbar moved to the edge of the window will dock along that edge. A toolbar moved anywhere else in the window will float in its own window. Docked toolbars are one tool wide (high), whereas floating toolbars can be resized by clicking and dragging a border or corner as you would with any window.
  - To move a docked toolbar, click anywhere in the background area and drag the toolbar to its new location. You can also click and drag the move handle (the single vertical line) at the left of the toolbar.
  - To move a floating toolbar, drag its title bar to its new location.

- To customize one or more toolbars, display the toolbar on the screen. Then pull down the View menu, click Toolbars, and click Customize to display the Customize dialog box. Alternatively, you can click on any toolbar with the right mouse button and select Customize from the shortcut menu.
  - To move a button, drag the button to its new location on that toolbar or any other displayed toolbar.
  - To copy a button, press the Ctrl key as you drag the button to its new location on that toolbar or any other displayed toolbar.
  - To delete a button, drag the button off the toolbar and release the mouse button.
  - To add a button, click the Commands tab in the Customize dialog box, select the category (from the Categories list box) that contains the button you want to add, then drag the button to the desired location on the toolbar.
  - To restore a predefined toolbar to its default appearance, pull down the View menu, click Toolbars, click Customize, click the Toolbars tab, select (highlight) the desired toolbar, and click the Reset command button.

- Buttons can also be moved, copied, or deleted without displaying the Customize dialog box.
  - To move a button, press the Alt key as you drag the button to the new location.
  - To copy a button, press the Alt and Ctrl keys as you drag the button to the new location.
  - To delete a button, press the Alt key as you drag the button off the toolbar.

- To create your own toolbar, pull down the View menu, click Toolbars, click Customize, click the Toolbars tab, then click the New command button. Alternatively, you can click on any toolbar with the right mouse button, select Customize from the shortcut menu, click the Toolbars tab, and then click the New command button.
  - Enter a name for the toolbar in the dialog box that follows. The name can be any length and can contain spaces.
  - The new toolbar will appear on the screen. Initially it will be big enough to hold only one button. Add, move, and delete buttons following the same procedures as outlined above. The toolbar will automatically size itself as new buttons are added and deleted.
  - To delete a custom toolbar, pull down the View menu, click Toolbars, click Customize, and click the Toolbars tab. *Verify that the custom toolbar to be deleted is the only one selected (highlighted).* Click the Delete command button. Click Yes to confirm the deletion. (Note that a predefined toolbar cannot be deleted.)

MICROSOFT OFFICE EXCEL 2003 TOOLBARS

Standard

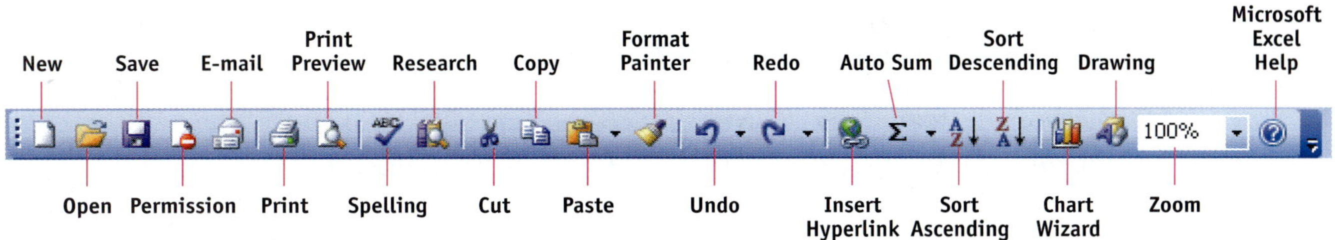

Formatting

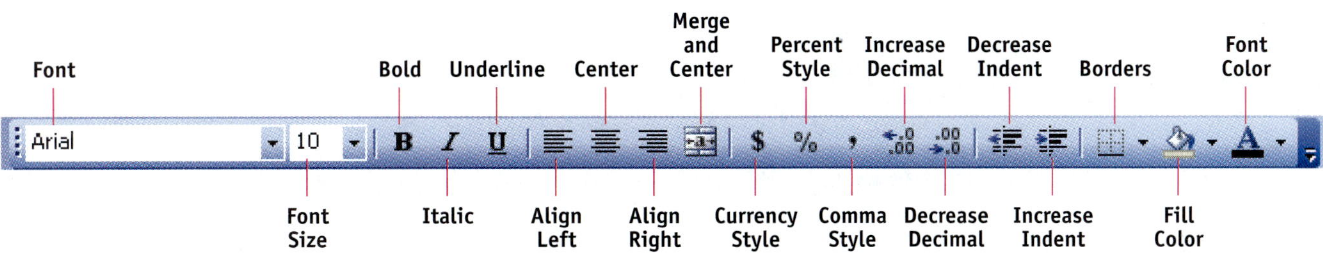

3-D Settings

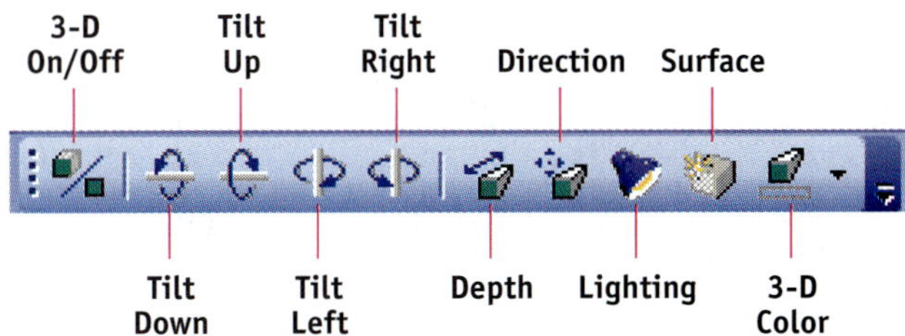

Borders

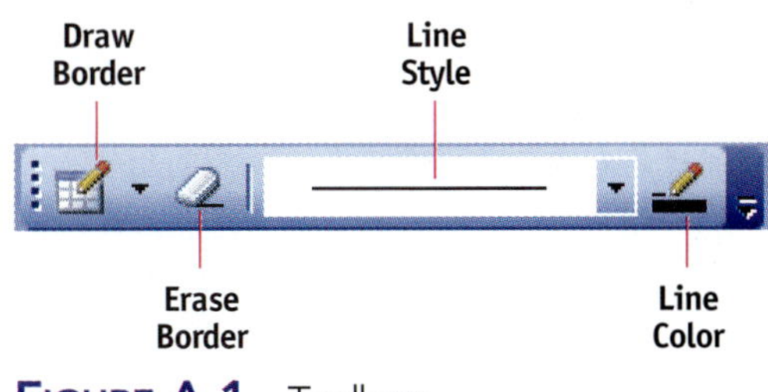

FIGURE A.1 Toolbars

Chart

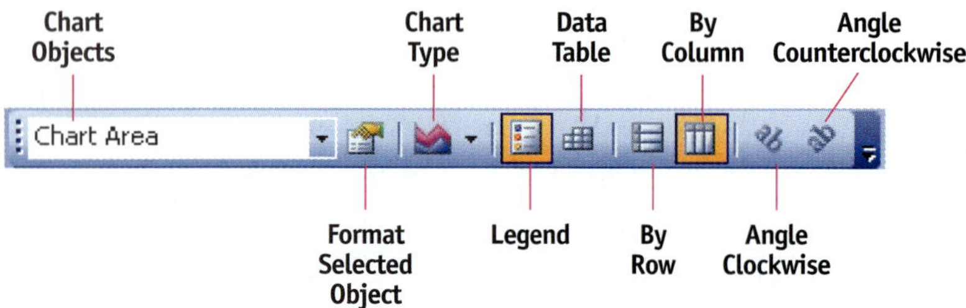

Circular Reference

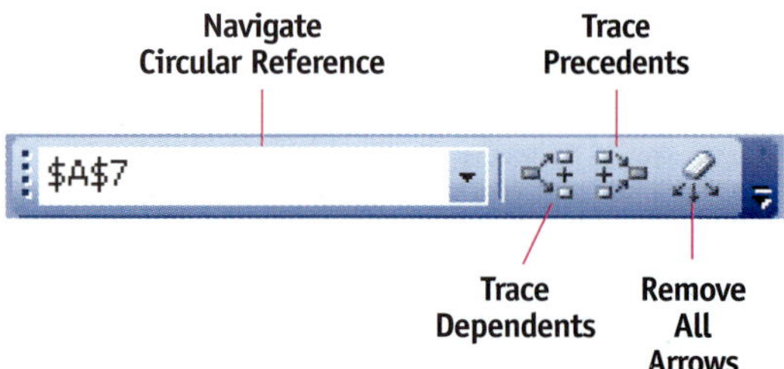

Compare Side by Side

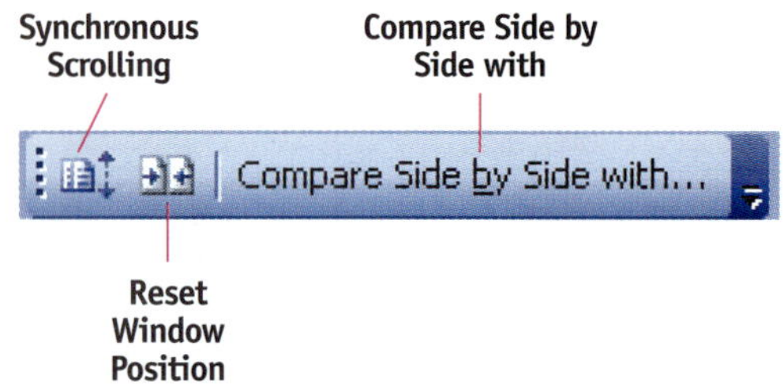

Control Toolbox

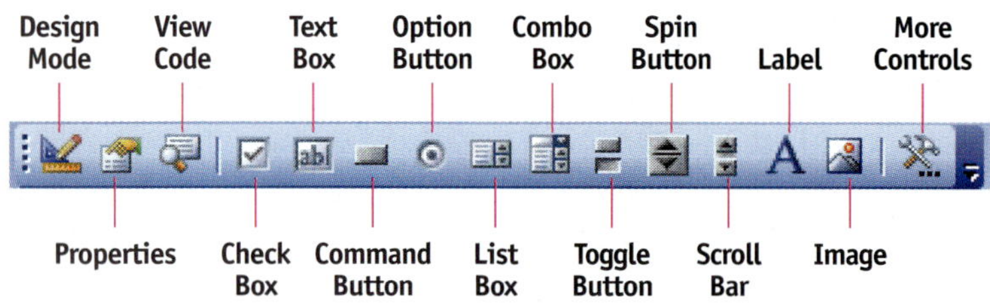

FIGURE A.1 Toolbars (*continued*)

Diagram

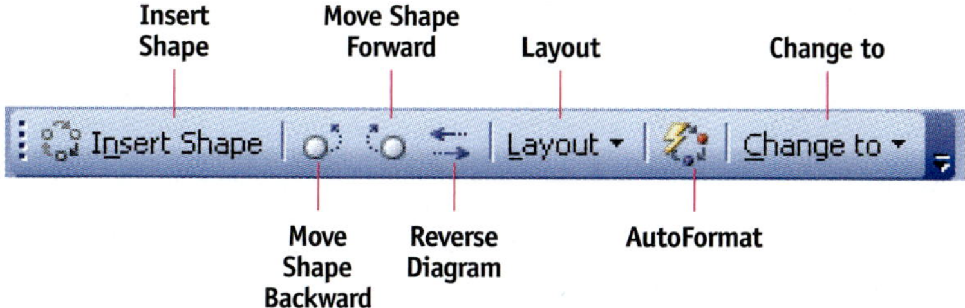

Drawing

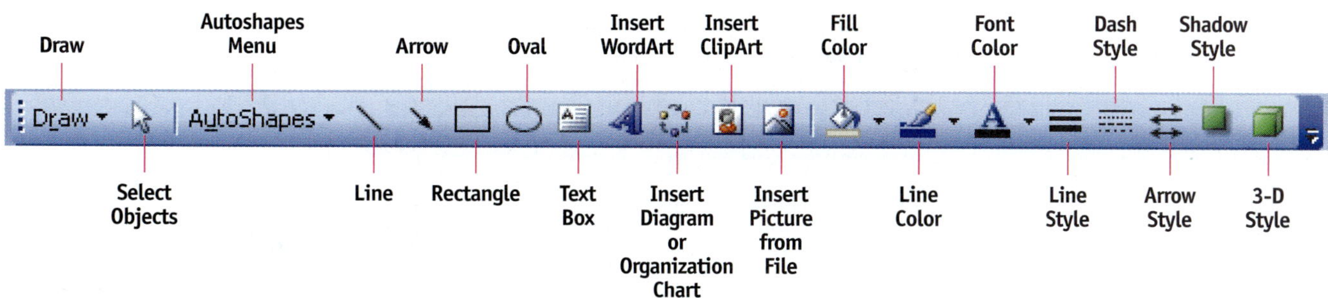

Drawing Canvas

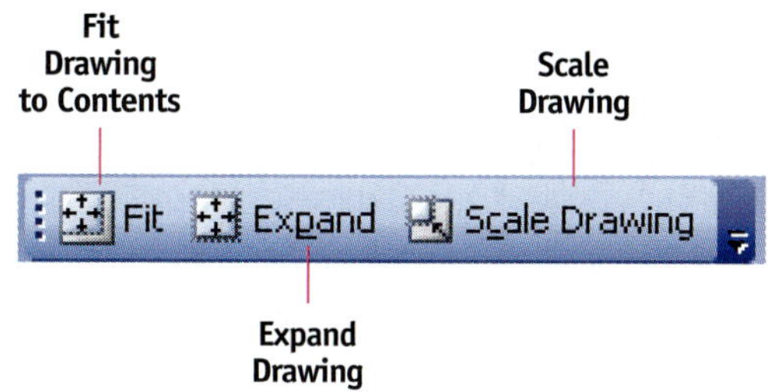

Exit Design Mode

FIGURE A.1 Toolbars *(continued)*

External Data

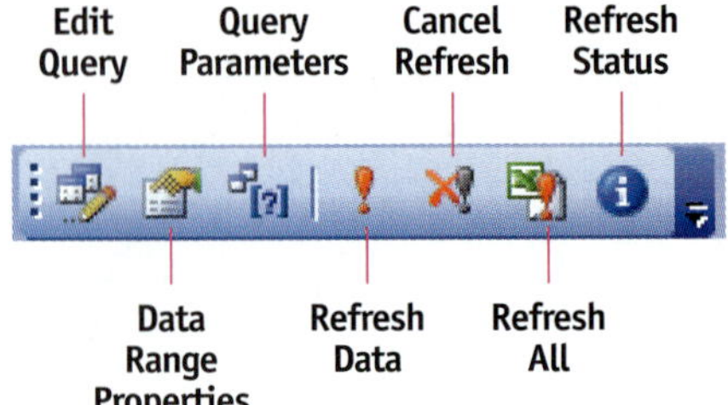

Forms

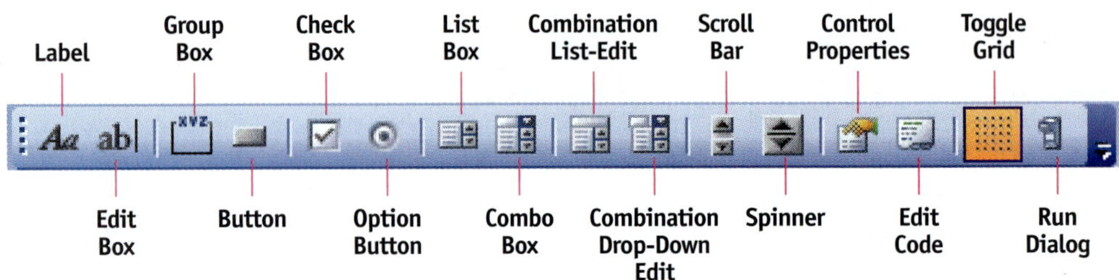

Formula Auditing

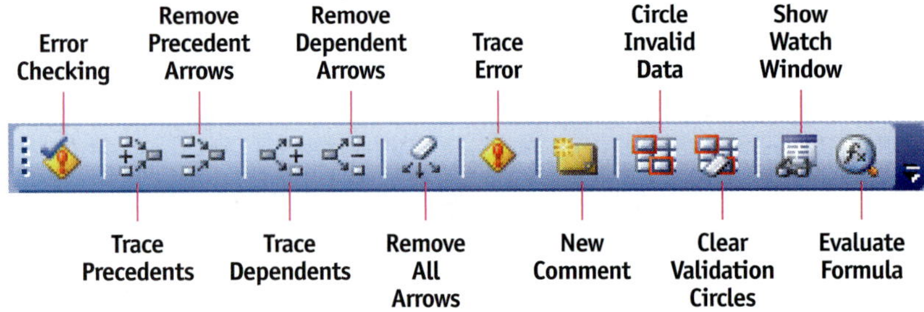

Full Screen

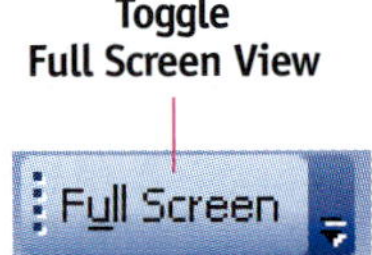

FIGURE A.1 Toolbars (*continued*)

List

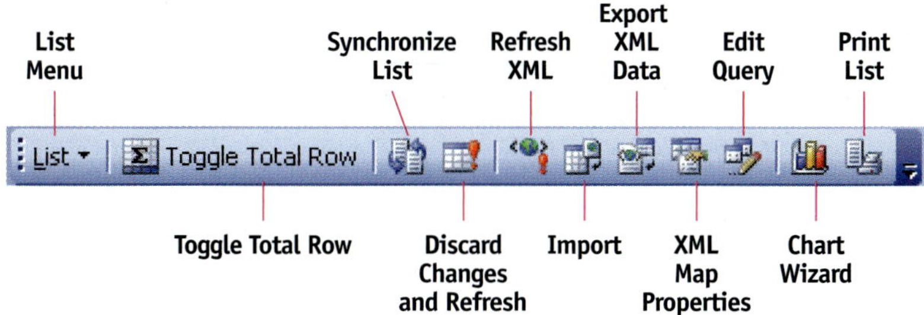

Organization Chart

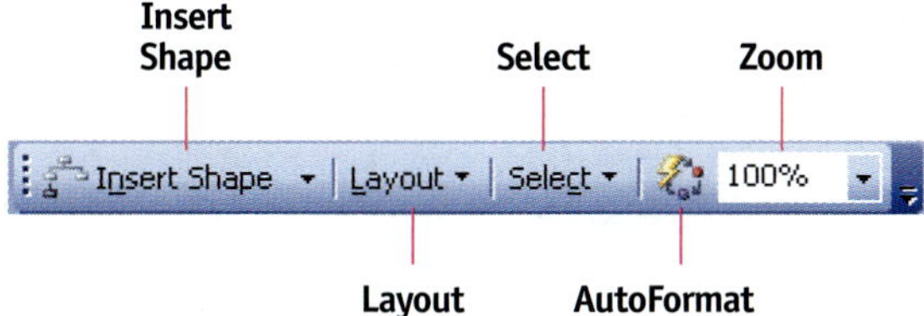

Picture

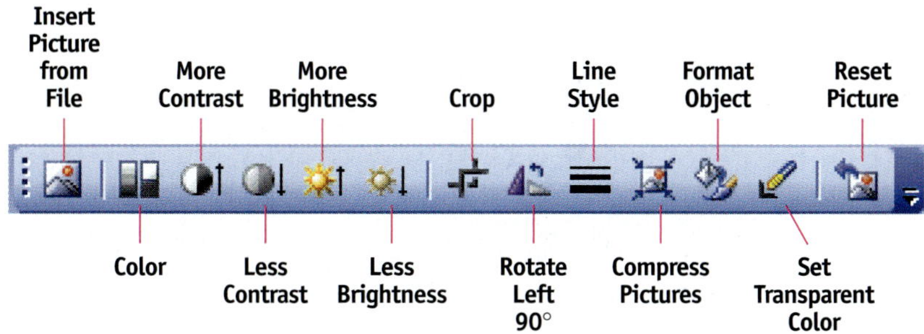

Pivot Table

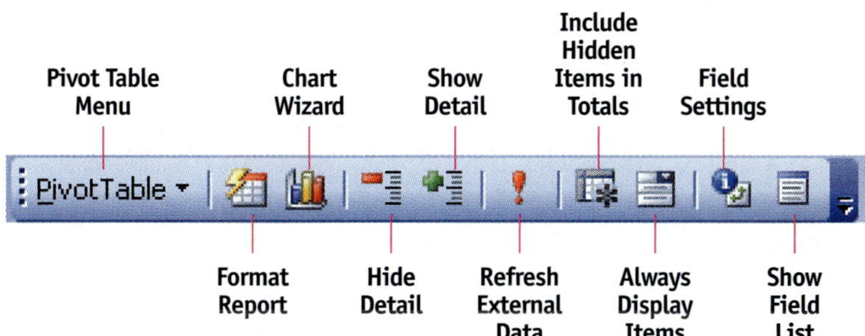

FIGURE A.1 Toolbars (*continued*)

Protection

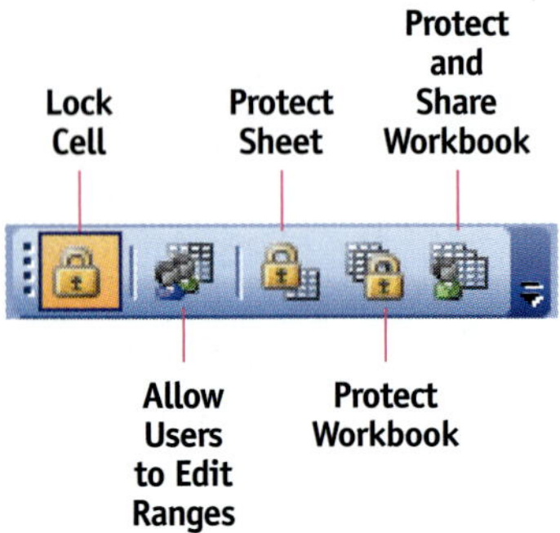

Reviewing

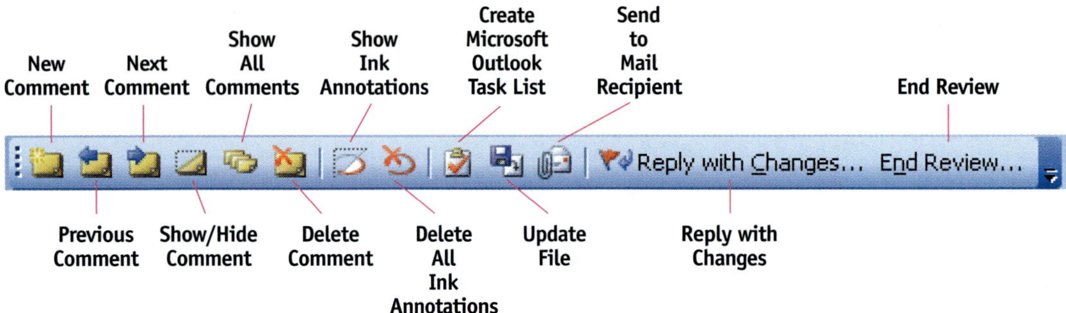

Shadow Settings

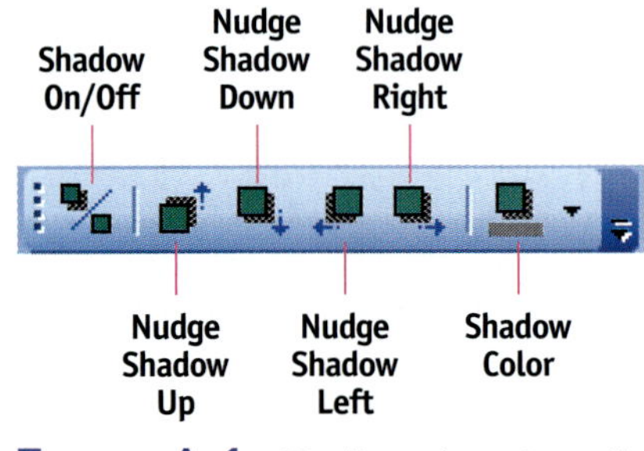

FIGURE A.1 Toolbars (*continued*)

Stop Recording

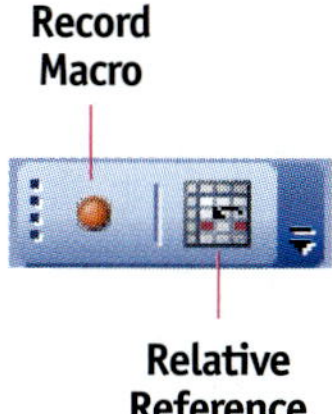

Text to Speech

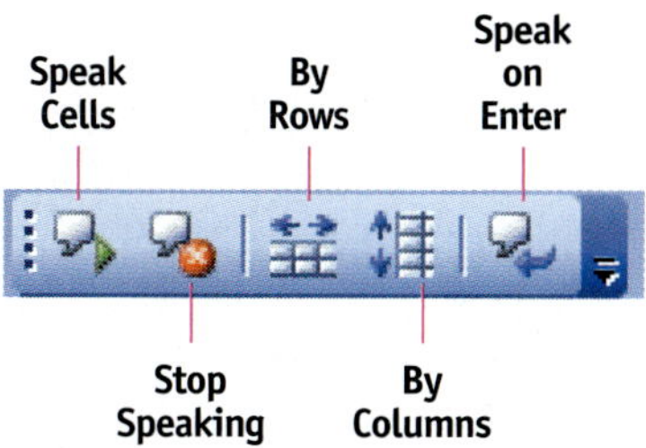

Visual Basic

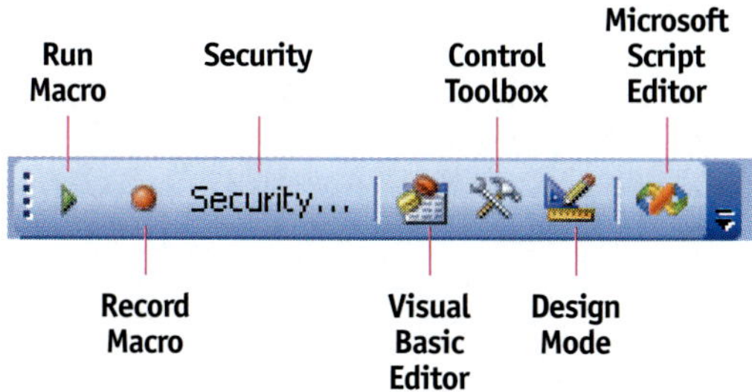

Watch Window

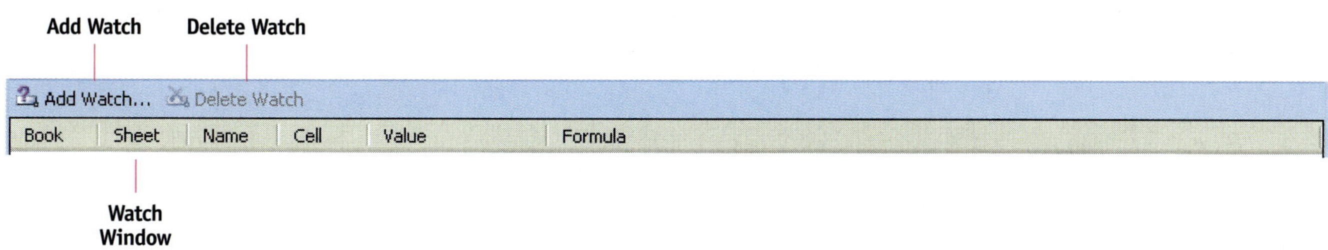

FIGURE A.1 Toolbars (*continued*)

Web

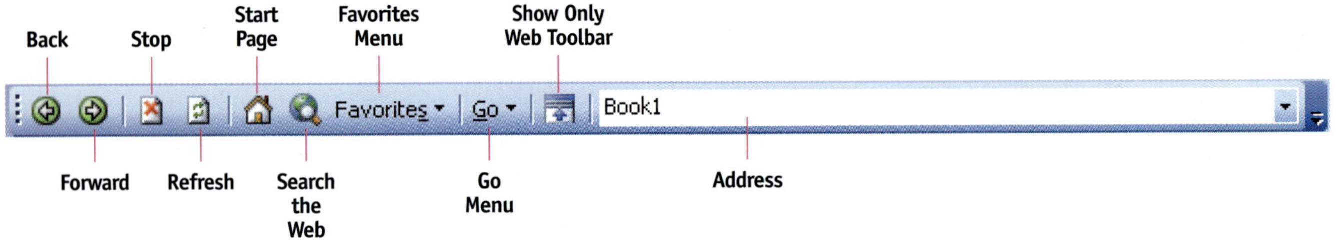

WordArt

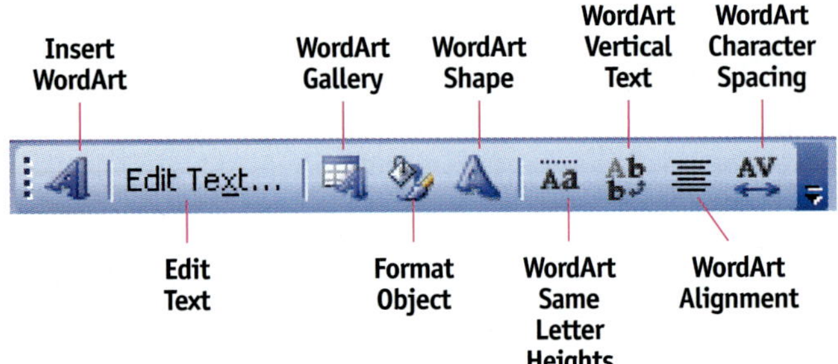

FIGURE A.1 Toolbars (*continued*)

APPENDIX

B Solver: A Tool for Optimization

CASE STUDY

MAXIMIZE PROFIT

Assume that you are the production manager for a company that manufactures computers. Your company divides its product line into two basic categories—desktop computers and laptops. Each product is sold under two labels, a discount line and a premium line. As production manager you are to determine how many computers of each type, and of each product line, to make each week.

Your decision is subject to various constraints that must be satisfied during the production process. Each computer requires a specified number of hours for assembly. Discount and premium-brand desktops require two and three hours, respectively. Discount and premium-brand laptops use three and five hours, respectively. The factory is working at full capacity, and you have only 4,500 hours of labor to allocate among the various products.

Your production decision is also constrained by demand. The marketing department has determined that you cannot sell more than 800 desktop units, nor more than 900 laptops, per week. The total demand for the discount and premium lines is 700 and 1,000 computers, respectively, per week.

Your goal (objective) is to maximize the total profit, which is based on a different profit margin for each type of computer. A desktop and a laptop computer from the discount line have unit profits of $600 and $800, respectively. The premium desktop and laptop computers have unit profits of $1,000 and $1,300, respectively. How many computers of each type do you manufacture each week to maximize the total profit?

This is a complex problem, but one that can be easily solved provided you can design a spreadsheet that is equivalent to Figure B.1. The top half of the spreadsheet contains the information about the individual products. There are three numbers associated with each product—the quantity that will be produced, the number of hours required, and the unit profit. The bottom half of the spreadsheet contains the information about the available resources, such as the total number of labor hours that are available. The spreadsheet also contains various formulas that relate the resources to the quantities that are produced. Cell E8, for example, will contain a formula that computes the total number of hours used, based on the quantity of each computer and the associated hourly requirements.

The problem is to determine the values of cells B2 through B5, which represent the quantity of each computer to produce. You might be able to solve the problem manually through trial and error, by substituting different values and seeing the impact on profit. That is exactly what Solver will do for you, only it will do it much more quickly. (Solver uses various optimization techniques that are beyond the scope of this discussion.)

Once Solver arrives at a solution, assuming that it can find one, it creates a report such as the one shown in Figure B.2. The solution shows the value of the target cell (the profit in this example), based on the values of the adjustable cells (the quantity of each type of computer). The solution that will maximize profit is to manufacture 700 discount laptops and 800 premium desktops for a profit of $1,270,000.

The report in Figure B.2 also examines each constraint and determines whether it is binding or not binding. A ***binding constraint*** is one in which the resource is fully utilized (i.e., the slack is zero). The number of available hours, for example, is a binding constraint because every available hour is used, and hence the value of the target cell (profit) is limited by the amount of this resource (the number of hours). Or stated another way, any increase in the number of available hours (above 4,500) will also increase the profit.

A ***nonbinding constraint*** is just the opposite. It has a nonzero slack (i.e., the resource is not fully utilized), and hence it does not limit the value of the target cell. The laptop demand, for example, is not binding because a total of only 700 laptops were produced, yet the allowable demand was 900 (the value in cell E13). In other words, there is a slack value of 200 for this constraint, and increasing the allowable demand will have no effect on the profit. (The demand could actually be decreased by up to 200 units with no effect on profit.)

Problem is to determine values of cells B2:B5, given the constraints

E8 will contain formula to compute total hours used

Formula to calculate total profit will be entered in E19

	A	B	C	D	E
1		Quantity	Hours	Unit Profit	
2	**Discount desktop**		2	$600	
3	**Discount laptop**		3	$800	
4	**Premium desktop**		3	$1,000	
5	**Premium laptop**		5	$1,300	
6					
7	**Constraints**				
8	Total number of hours used				
9	Labor hours available				4,500
10	Number of desktops produced				
11	Total demand for desktop computers				800
12	Number of laptops produced				
13	Total demand for laptop computers				900
14	Number of discount computers produced				
15	Total demand for discount computers				700
16	Number of premium computers produced				
17	Total demand for premium computers				1,000
18	Hourly cost of labor				$20
19	**Profit**				

FIGURE B.1 The Initial Worksheet

Value of target cell (E19)

Quantities to be produced (B2:B5)

Constraints

Status indicates whether constraint is binding or not binding

Target Cell (Max)

Cell	Name	Original Value	Final Value
$E$19	Profit	$0	$1,270,000

Adjustable Cells

Cell	Name	Original Value	Final Value
$B$2	Discount desktop Quantity	0	0
$B$3	Discount laptop Quantity	0	700
$B$4	Premium desktop Quantity	0	800
$B$5	Premium laptop Quantity	0	0

Constraints

Cell	Name	Cell Value	Formula	Status	Slack
$E$8	Total number of hours used	4500	$E$8<=$E$9	Binding	0
$E$10	Number of desktops produced	800	$E$10<=$E$11	Binding	0
$E$12	Number of laptops produced	700	$E$12<=$E$13	Not Binding	200
$E$14	Number of discount computers produced	700	$E$14<=$E$15	Binding	0
$E$16	Number of premium computers produced	800	$E$16<=$E$17	Not Binding	200
$B$2	Discount desktop Quantity	0	$B$2>=0	Binding	0
$B$3	Discount laptop Quantity	700	$B$3>=0	Not Binding	700
$B$4	Premium desktop Quantity	800	$B$4>=0	Not Binding	800
$B$5	Premium laptop Quantity	0	$B$5>=0	Binding	0

FIGURE B.2 The Solution

The information required by Solver is entered through the ***Solver Parameters dialog box*** as shown in Figure B.3. The dialog box is divided into three sections: the target cell, the adjustable cells, and the constraints. The dialog box in Figure B.3 corresponds to the spreadsheet shown earlier in Figure B.1.

The ***target cell*** identifies the goal (or objective function)—that is, the cell whose value you want to maximize, minimize, or set to a specific value. Our problem seeks to maximize profit, the formula for which is found in cell E19 (the target cell) of the underlying spreadsheet.

The ***adjustable cells*** (or decision variables) are the cells whose values are adjusted until the constraints are satisfied and the target cell reaches its optimum value. The changing cells in this example contain the quantity of each computer to be produced and are found in cells B2 through B5.

The ***constraints*** specify the restrictions. Each constraint consists of a cell or cell range on the left, a relational operator, and a numeric value or cell reference on the right. (The constraints can be entered in any order, but they always appear in alphabetical order.) The first constraint references a cell range, cells B2 through B5, and indicates that each of these cells must be greater than or equal to zero. The remaining constraints reference a single cell rather than a cell range.

The functions of the various command buttons are apparent from their names. The Add, Change, and Delete buttons are used to add, change, or delete a constraint. The Options button enables you to set various parameters that determine how Solver attempts to find a solution. The Reset All button clears all settings and resets all options to their defaults. The Solve button begins the search for a solution.

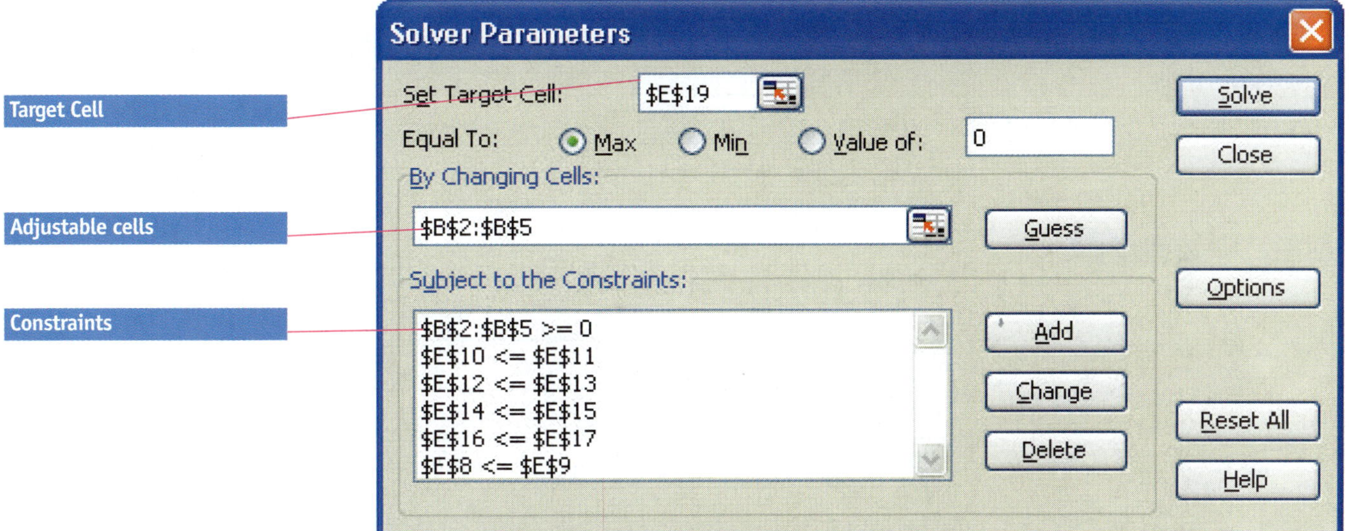

FIGURE B.3 Solver Parameters Dialog Box

THE GREATER-THAN-ZERO CONSTRAINT

One constraint that is often overlooked is the requirement that the value of each adjustable cell be greater than or equal to zero. Physically, it makes no sense to produce a negative number of computers in any category. Mathematically, however, a negative value in an adjustable cell may produce a higher value for the target cell. Hence the nonnegativity (greater than or equal to zero) constraint should always be included for the adjustable cells.

hands-on exercise

1 Maximize Profit

Objective To use Solver to maximize profit; to create a report containing binding and nonbinding constraints. Use Figure B.4 as a guide in the exercise.

Step 1: Enter the Cell Formulas

- Start Excel. Open the **Optimization workbook** in the Exploring Excel folder. Save the workbook as **Optimization Solution** so that you can return to the original workbook if necessary.
- If necessary, click the tab for the **Production Mix worksheet**, then click **cell E8** as shown in Figure B.4a.
- Enter the formula shown in Figure B.4a to compute the total number of hours used in production.
- Enter the remaining cell formulas as shown below:
  - Cell E10 (Number of desktops produced) **=B2+B4**
  - Cell E12 (Number of laptops produced) **=B3+B5**
  - Cell E14 (Number of discount computers produced) **=B2+B3**
  - Cell E16 (Number of premium computers produced) **=B4+B5**
  - Cell E19 (Profit) **=B2*D2+B3*D3+B4*D4+B5*D5–E18*E8**
- Save the workbook.

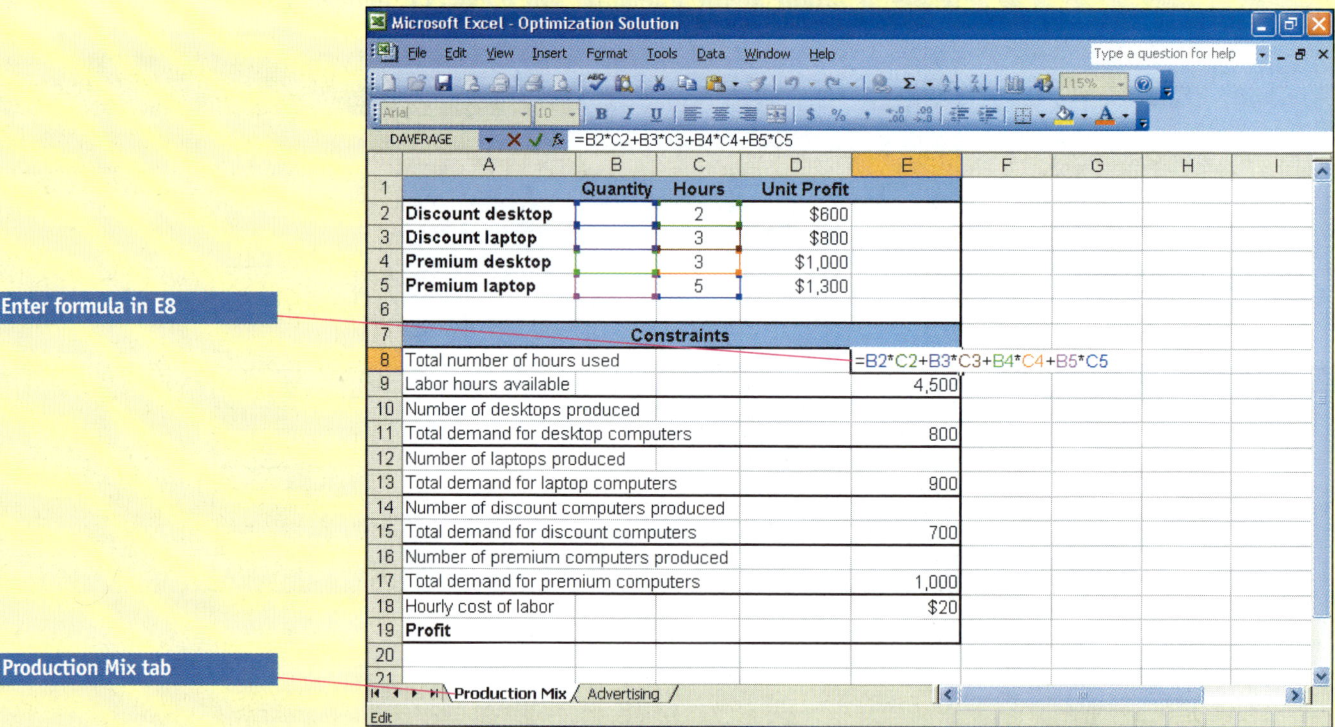

(a) Enter the Cell Formulas (step 1)

FIGURE B.4 Hands-on Exercise 1

Step 2: Set the Target and Adjustable Cells

- Check that the formula in cell E19 is entered correctly as shown in Figure B.4b. Pull down the **Tools menu**. Click **Solver** to display the Solver Parameters dialog box shown in Figure B.4b.
- If necessary, click in the text box for **Set Target Cell**. Click in **cell E19** to set the target cell. The Max option button is selected by default.
- Click in the **By Changing Cells** text box. Click and drag **cells B2 through B5** in the worksheet to select these cells.
- Click the **Add command button** to add the first constraint as described in step 3.

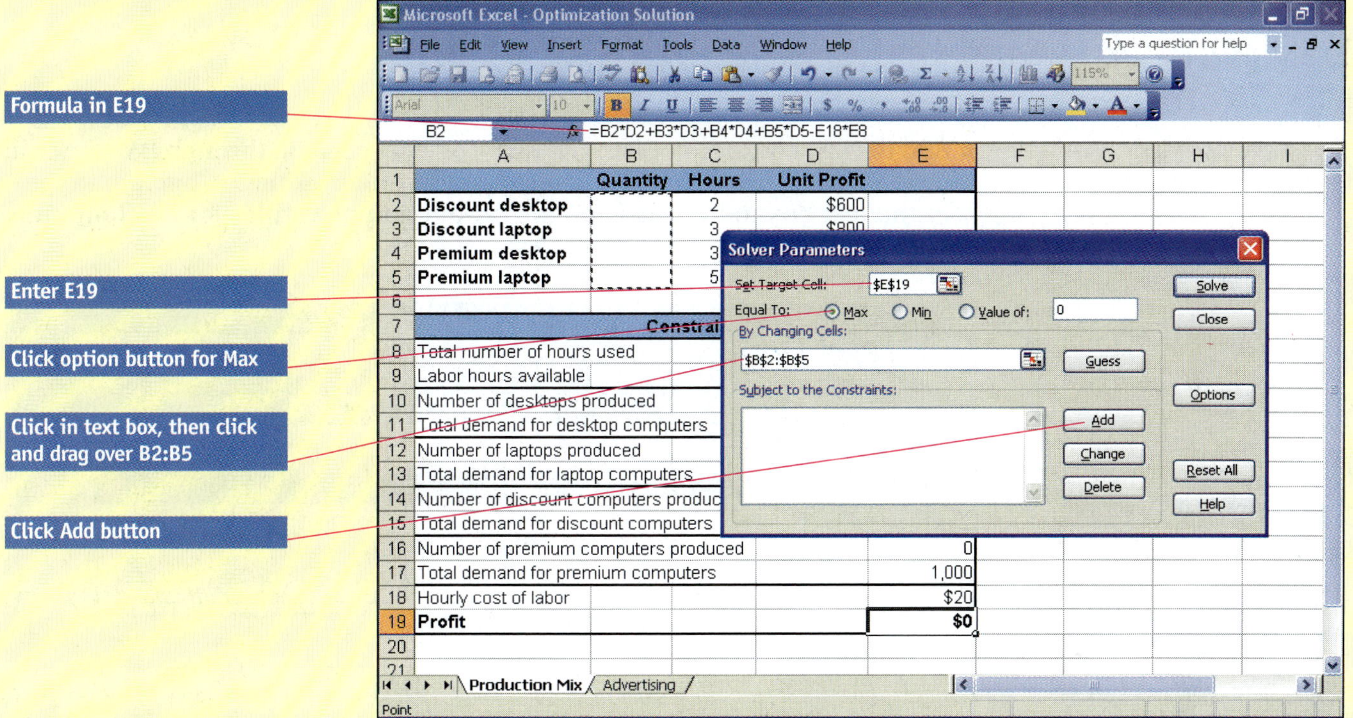

(b) Set the Target and Adjustable Cells (step 2)

FIGURE B.4 Hands-on Exercise 1 (*continued*)

MISSING SOLVER

Solver is an optional component of Microsoft Excel, and hence it may not be installed on your system. If you are working on a computer at school, your instructor should be able to notify the network administrator to correct the problem. If you are working on your own machine, pull down the Tools menu, click the Add-Ins command, check the box for Solver, then click OK to close the Add-Ins dialog box. Click Yes when asked to install Solver. You will need the Microsoft Office CD.

Step 3: Enter the Constraints

- You should see the Add Constraint dialog box in Figure B.4c with the insertion point (a flashing vertical line) in the Cell Reference text box.
  - Click in **cell E8** (the cell containing the formula to compute the total number of hours used). The <= constraint is selected by default.
  - Click in the **Constraint** text box, which will contain the value of the constraint, then click **cell E9** in the worksheet to enter the cell reference.
  - Click **Add** to complete this constraint and add another.
- You will see a new (empty) Add Constraint dialog box, which enables you to enter additional constraints. Use pointing to enter each of the constraints shown below. (Solver automatically enters each reference as an absolute reference.)
  - Enter the constraint **E10<=E11**. Click **Add**.
  - Enter the constraint **E12<=E13**. Click **Add**.
  - Enter the constraint **E14<=E15**. Click **Add**.
  - Enter the constraint **E16<=E17**. Click **Add**.
- Add the last constraint. Click and drag to select **cells B2 through B5**. Click the drop-down arrow for the relational operators and click the **>=** operator. Type **0** in the text box to indicate that the production quantities for all computers must be greater than or equal to zero. Click **OK**.

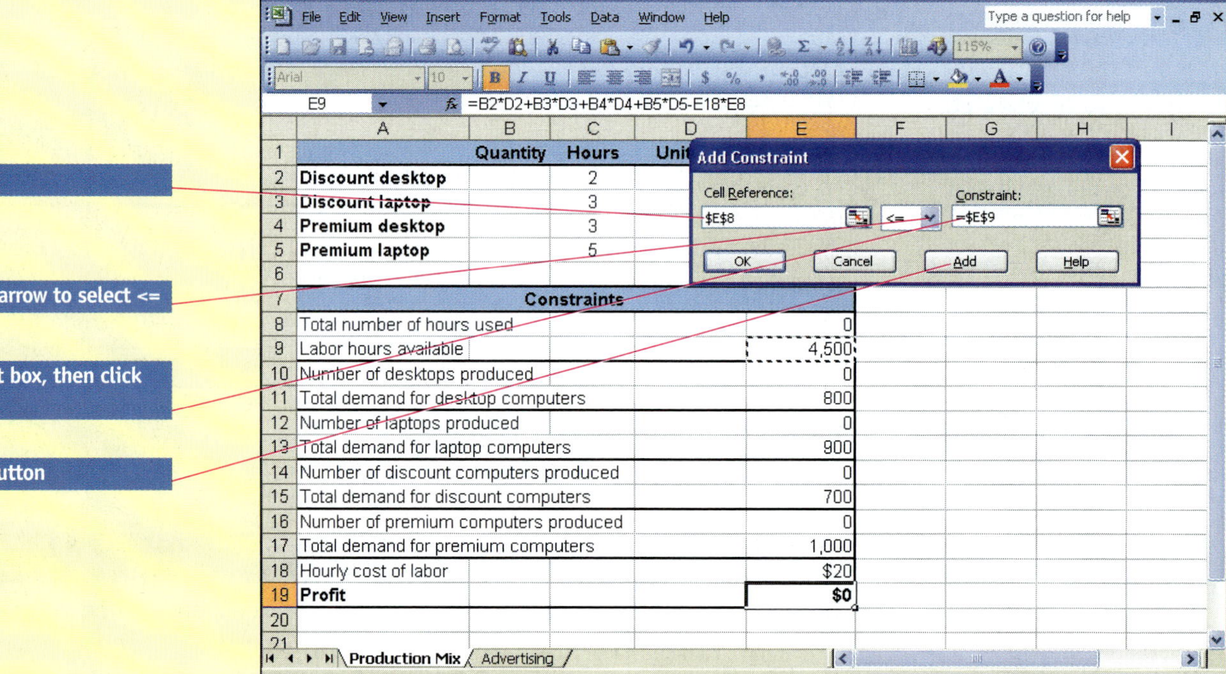

(c) Enter the Constraints (step 3)

FIGURE B.4 Hands-on Exercise 1 (*continued*)

ADD VERSUS OK

Click the Add button to complete the current constraint and display an empty dialog box to enter another constraint. Click OK only when you have completed the last constraint and want to return to the Solver Parameters dialog box to solve the problem.

Step 4: Solve the Problem

- Check that the contents of the Solver Parameters dialog box match those of Figure B.4d. (The constraints appear in alphabetical order rather than the order in which they were entered.)
  - To change the Target cell, click the **Set Target Cell** text box, then click the appropriate target cell in the worksheet.
  - To change (edit) a constraint, select the constraint, then click the **Change button**.
  - To delete a constraint, select the constraint and click the **Delete button**.
- Click the **Solve button** to solve the problem.
- You should see the Solver Results dialog box, indicating that Solver has found a solution. The maximum profit is $1,270,000. The option button to Keep Solver Solution is selected by default.
- Click **Answer** in the Reports list box, then click **OK** to generate the report. You will see the report being generated, after which the Solver Results dialog box closes automatically.
- Save the workbook.

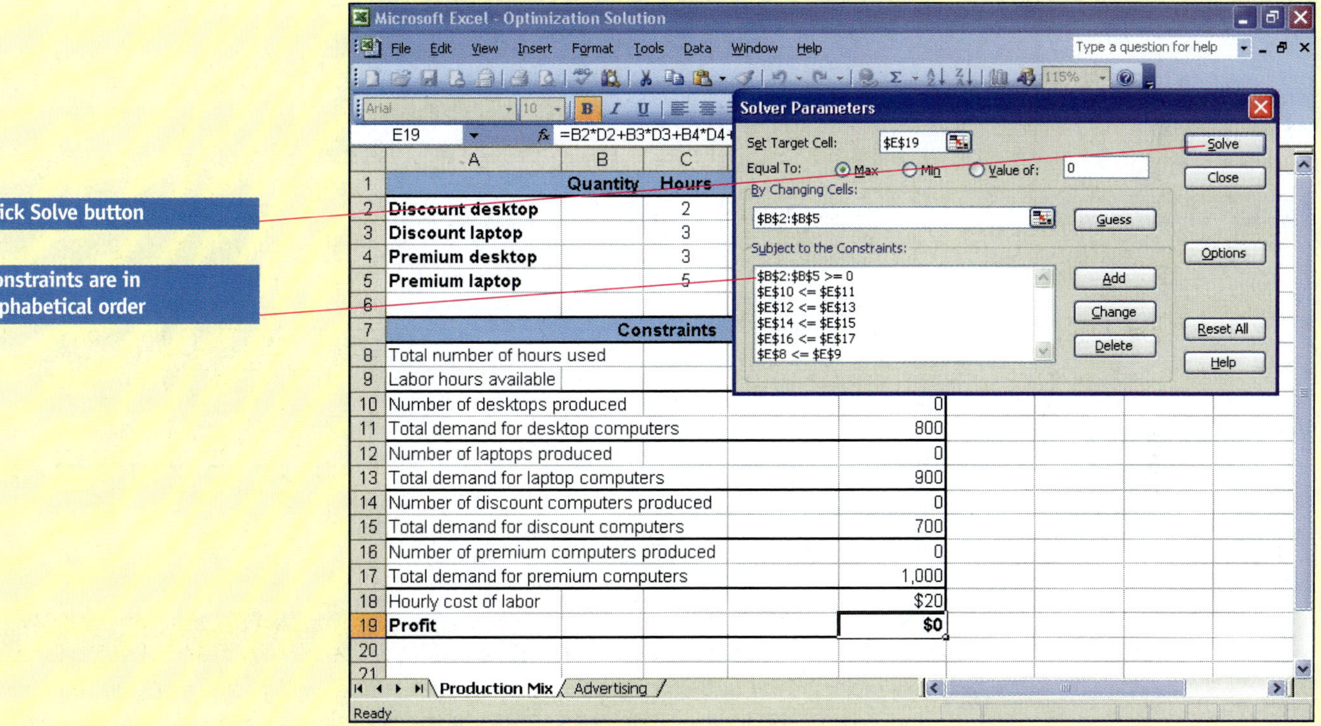

(d) Solve the Problem (step 4)

FIGURE B.4 Hands-on Exercise 1 (*continued*)

Step 5: View the Report

- Click the **Answer Report 1 worksheet tab** to view the report as shown in Figure B.4e. Click in **cell A4**, the cell immediately under the entry showing the date and time the report was created. (The gridlines and row and column headings are suppressed by default for this worksheet.)
- Enter your name in boldface as shown in the figure, then press **Enter** to complete the entry. Print the answer sheet and submit it to your instructor as proof you did the exercise.
- Save the workbook. Exit Excel if you do not wish to continue with the next exercise at this time.

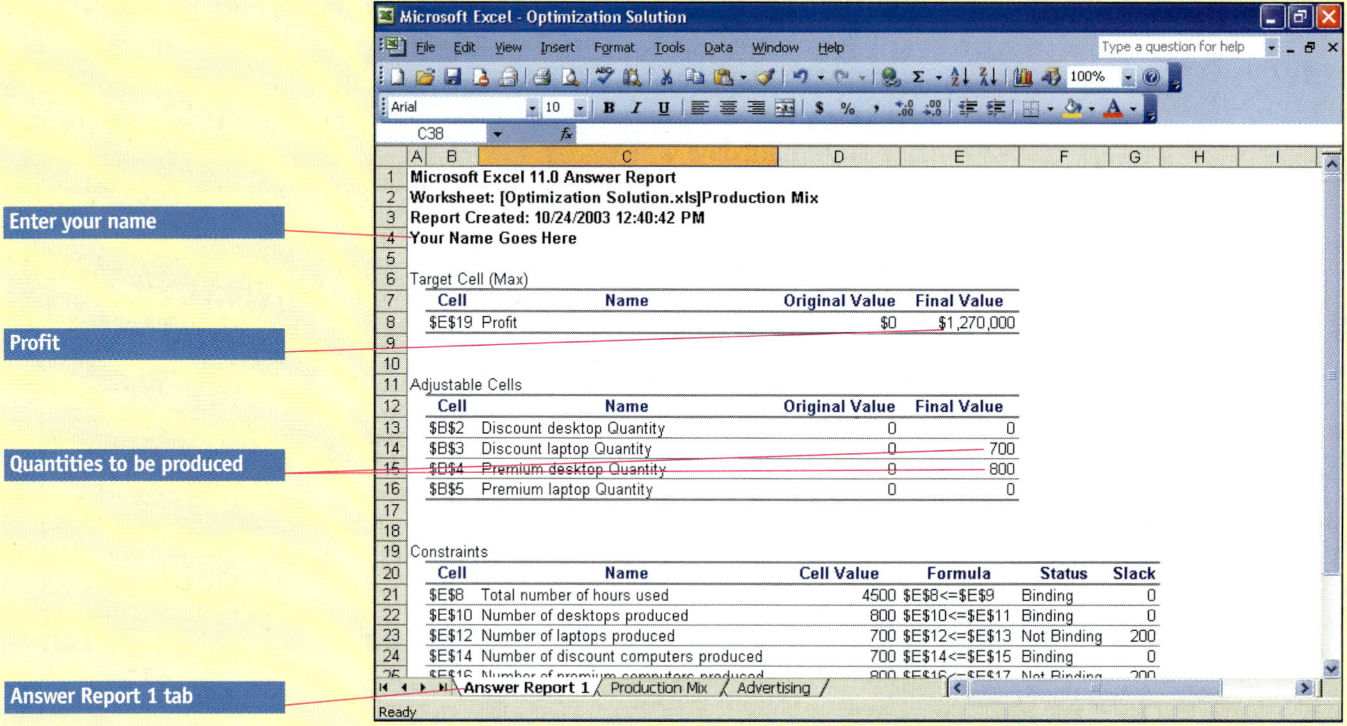

(e) View the Report (step 5)

FIGURE B.4 Hands-on Exercise 1 (*continued*)

VIEW OPTIONS

Any worksheet used to create a spreadsheet model will display gridlines and row and column headers by default. Worksheets containing reports, however, especially reports generated by Excel, often suppress these elements to make the reports easier and more appealing to read. To suppress (display) these elements, pull down the Tools menu, click Options, click the View tab, then clear (check) the appropriate check boxes under Window options.

EXAMPLE 2—MINIMIZE COST

The example just concluded introduced you to the basics of Solver. We continue now with a second hands-on exercise, to provide additional practice, and to discuss various subtleties that can occur. This time we present a minimization problem in which we seek to minimize cost subject to a series of constraints. The problem will focus on the advertising campaign that will be conducted to sell the computers you have produced.

The director of marketing has allocated a total of $125,000 in his weekly advertising budget. He wants to establish a presence in both magazines and radio, and requires a minimum of four magazine ads and ten radio ads each week. Each magazine ad costs $10,000 and is seen by one million readers. Each radio commercial costs $5,000 and is heard by 250,000 listeners. How many ads of each type should be placed to reach at least 10 million customers at minimum cost?

All of the necessary information is contained within the previous paragraph. You must, however, display that information in a worksheet before you can ask Solver to find a solution. Accordingly, reread the previous paragraph, then try to set up a worksheet from which you can call Solver. (Our worksheet appears in step 1 of the following hands-on exercise. Try, however, to set up your own worksheet before you look at ours.)

FINER POINTS OF SOLVER

Figure B.5 displays the ***Solver Options dialog box*** that enables you to specify how Solver will approach the solution. The Max Time and Iterations entries determine how long Solver will work on finding the solution. If either limit is reached before a solution is found, Solver will ask whether you want to continue. The default settings of 100 seconds and 100 ***iterations*** are sufficient for simpler problems, but may fall short for complex problems with multiple constraints.

The Precision setting determines how close the computed values in the constraint cells come to the specified value of the resource. The smaller the precision, the longer Solver will take in arriving at a solution. The default setting of .0000001 is adequate for most problems and should not be decreased. The remaining options are beyond the scope of our discussion.

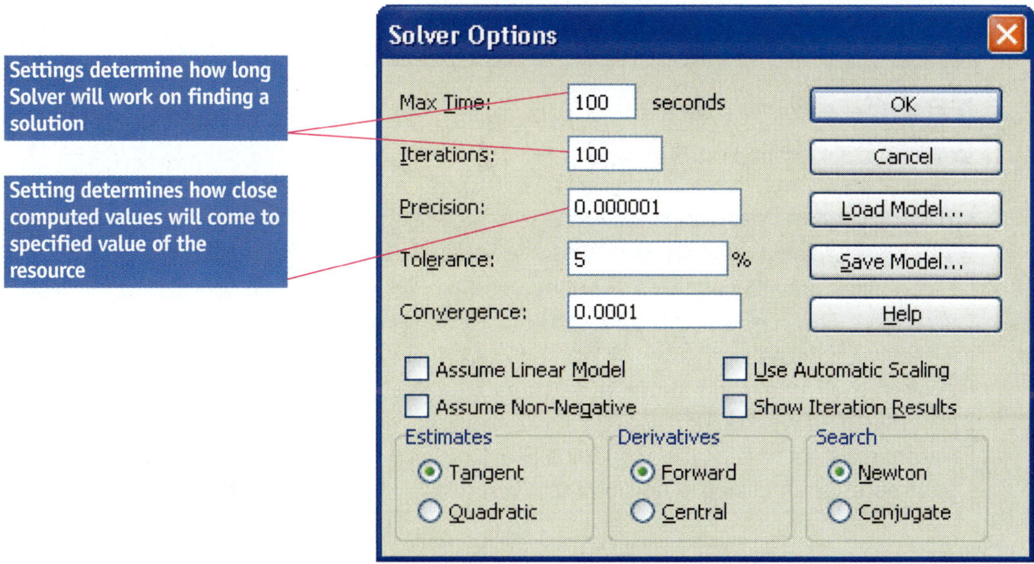

FIGURE B.5 Options Dialog Box

hands-on exercise

2 Minimize Cost

Objective To use Solver to minimize cost; to impose an integer constraint and examine its effect on the optimal solution; to relax a constraint in order to find a feasible solution. Use Figure B.6 as a guide in the exercise.

Step 1: Enter the Cell Formulas

- Open the **Optimization Solution workbook** from the previous exercise.
- Click the tab for the **Advertising worksheet**, then click in **cell E6**. Enter the formula **=B2*C2+B3*C3** as shown in Figure B.6a.
- Click in **cell E10**. Enter the formula **=B2*D2+B3*D3** to compute the size of the audience. Save the workbook.

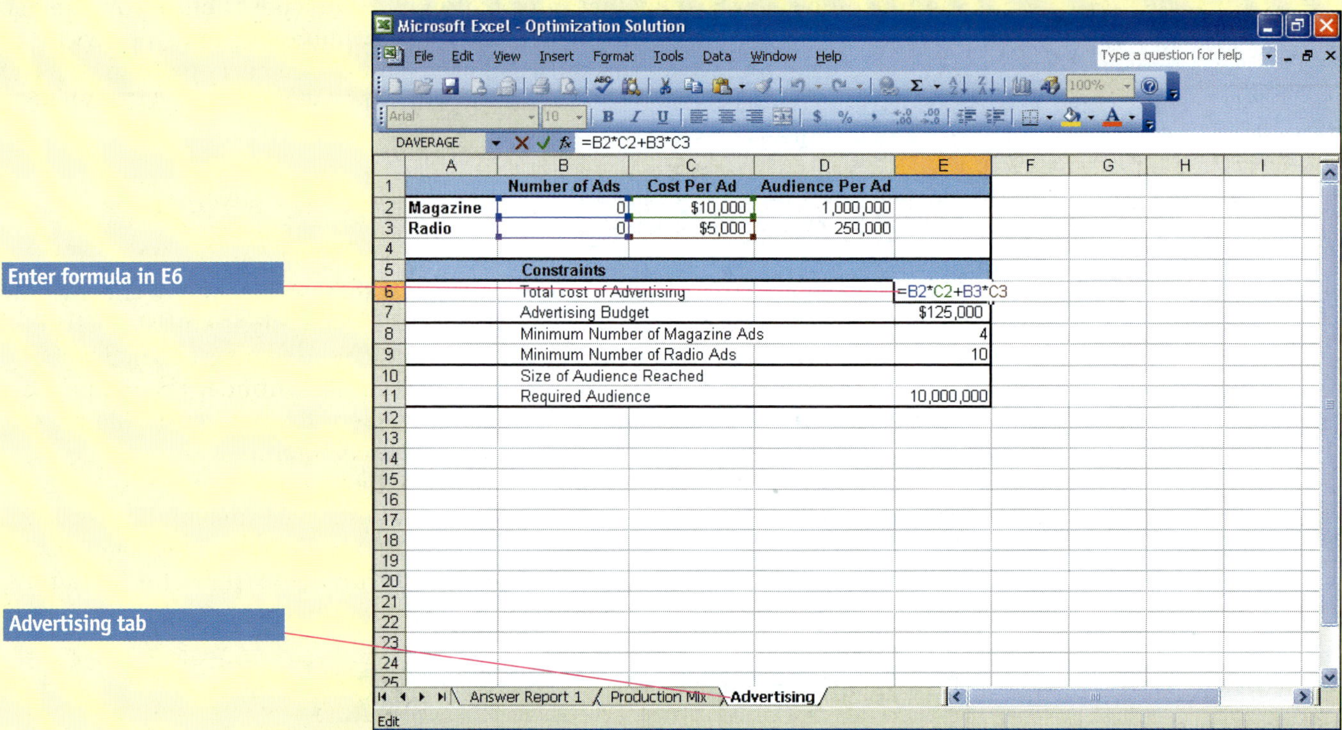

(a) Enter the Cell Formulas (step 1)

FIGURE B.6 Hands-on Exercise 2

USE THE TASK PANE

The easiest way to reopen a recently used workbook is to use the task pane. Pull down the View menu and toggle the Task Pane command on so that the task pane is displayed in the right side of the application window. Click the name of the workbook in the Open a workbook area to reopen the workbook. You can also open a recently used workbook from the list that appears at the bottom of the File menu. Another way is to click the Windows Start button, click the My Recent Documents command, then click the name of the workbook when it appears in the submenu.

Step 2: Set the Target and Adjustable Cells

- Pull down the **Tools menu**. Click **Solver** to display the Solver Parameters dialog box shown in Figure B.6b.
- Set the target cell to **cell E6**. Click the **Min (Minimize) option button**. Click in the **By Changing Cells** text box.
- Click and drag **cells B2 and B3** in the worksheet to select these cells as shown in Figure B.6b.
- Click the **Add command button** to add the first constraint as described in step 3.

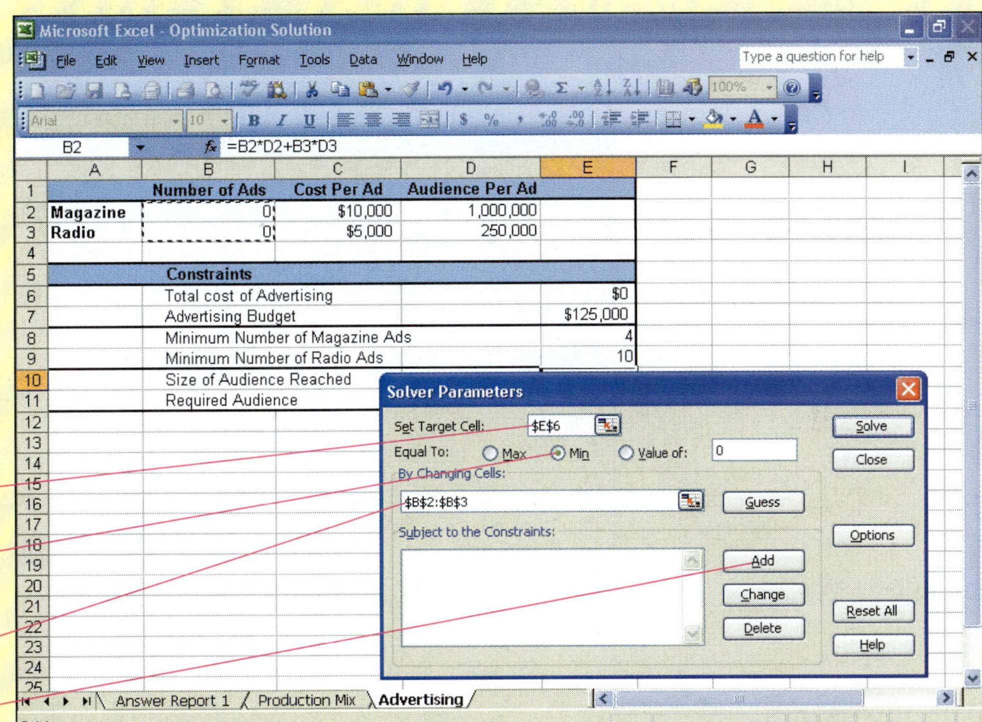

(b) Set the Target and Adjustable Cells (step 2)

FIGURE B.6 Hands-on Exercise 2 (*continued*)

REVIEW THE TERMINOLOGY

Solver is an optimization technique that allows you to maximize or minimize the value of an objective function, such as profit or cost, respectively. The formula to compute the objective function is stored in the target cell within the worksheet. Other cells in the worksheet contain the variables or adjustable cells. Another set of cells contains the value of the available resources or constraints. This type of optimization problem is referred to as linear programming.

Step 3: Enter the Constraints

- You should see the Add Constraint dialog box in Figure B.6c with the insertion point (a flashing vertical line) in the Cell Reference text box.
  - Click in **cell E6** (the cell containing the total cost of advertising).
  - The <= constraint is selected by default.
  - Click in the text box to contain the value of the constraint, then click **cell E7** to enter the cell reference in the Add Constraint dialog box. Click **Add**.
- You will see a new (empty) Add Constraint dialog box, which enables you to enter additional constraints. Use pointing to enter each of the constraints shown below. (Solver converts each reference to an absolute reference.)
  - Enter the constraint **E10>=E11**. Click **Add**.
  - Enter the constraint **B2>=E8**. Click **Add**.
  - Enter the constraint **B3>=E9**. Click **OK** since this is the last constraint.

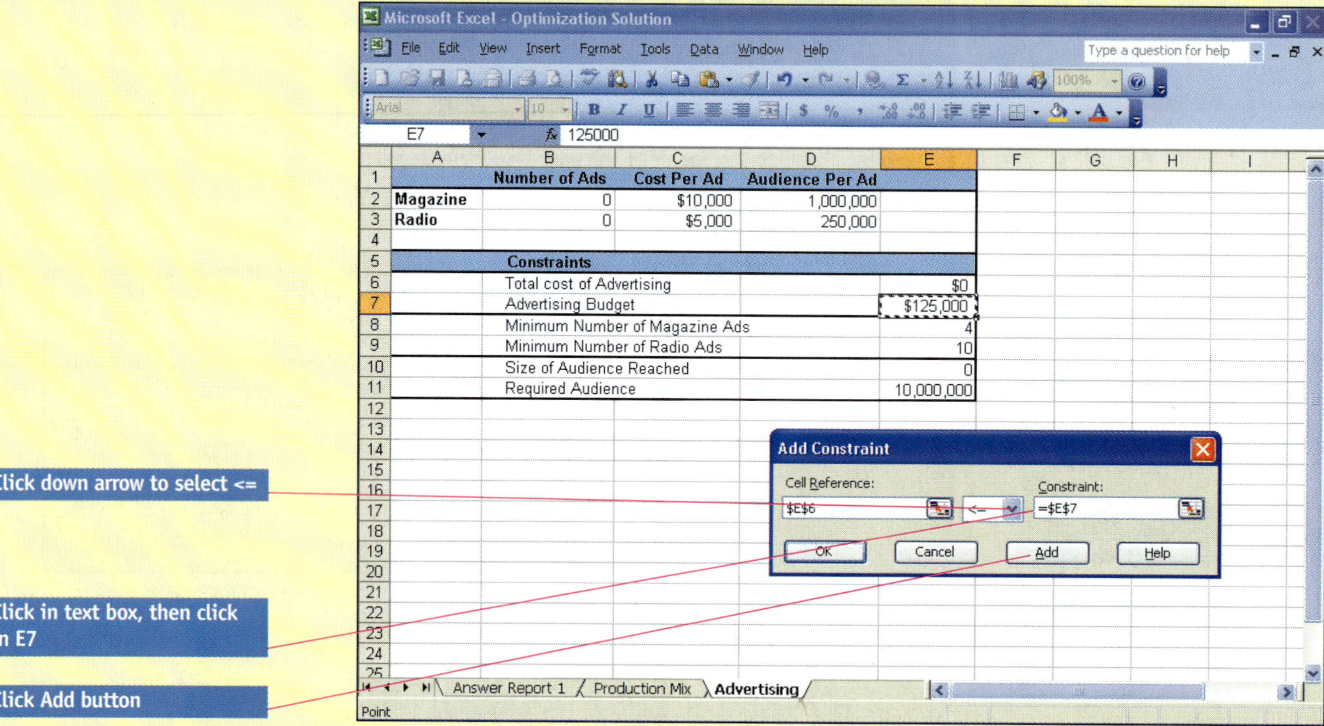

(c) Enter the Constraints (step 3)

FIGURE B.6 Hands-on Exercise 2 (*continued*)

SHOW ITERATION RESULTS

Solver uses an iterative (repetitive) approach in which each iteration (trial solution) is one step closer to the optimal solution. It may be interesting, therefore, to examine the intermediate solutions, especially if you have a knowledge of optimization techniques, such as linear programming. Click the Options command button in the Solver Parameters dialog box, check the Show Iterations Results box, click OK to close the Solver Options dialog box, then click the Solve command button in the usual fashion. A Show Trial Solutions dialog box will appear as each intermediate solution is displayed in the worksheet. Click Continue to move from one iteration to the next until the optimal solution is reached.

Step 4: Solve the Problem

- Check that the contents of the Solver Parameters dialog box match those in Figure B.6d. (The constraints appear in alphabetical order rather than the order in which they were entered.)
- Click the **Solve button** to solve the problem. The Solver Results dialog box appears and indicates that Solver has arrived at a solution.
- The option button to Keep Solver Solution is selected by default. Click **OK** to close the Solver Results dialog box and display the solution.
- Save the workbook.

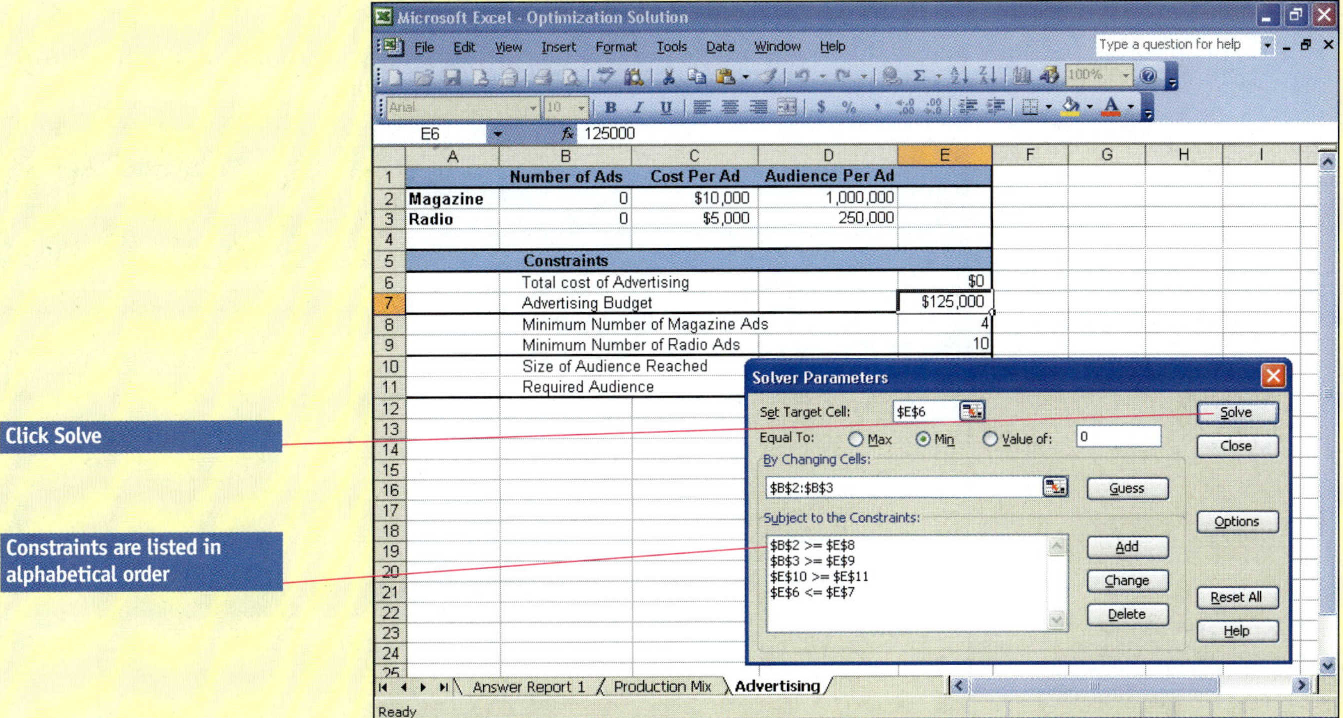

(d) Solve the Problem (step 4)

FIGURE B.6 Hands-on Exercise 2 (*continued*)

USE POINTING TO ENTER CELL FORMULAS

A cell reference can be typed directly into a formula, or it can be entered more easily through pointing. To use pointing, select (click) the cell to contain the formula, type an equal sign to begin entering the formula, then click (or move to) the cell containing the value to be used. Type any arithmetic operator to place the cell reference into the formula, then continue pointing to additional cells. Press the Enter key (instead of typing an arithmetic operator) to complete the formula.

Step 5: Impose an Integer Constraint

- The number of magazine ads in the solution is 7.5 as shown in Figure B.6e. This is a noninteger number, which is reasonable in the context of Solver but not in the "real world" as one cannot place half an ad.
- Pull down the **Tools menu**. Click **Solver** to once again display the Solver Parameters dialog box. Click the **Add button** to display the Add Constraint dialog box in Figure B.6e.
- The insertion point is already positioned in the Cell Reference text box. Click and drag to select **cells B2 through B3**. Click the **drop-down arrow** in the Constraint list box and click **int** (for integer).
- Click **OK** to accept the constraint and close the Add Constraint dialog box.
- The Solver Parameters dialog box appears on your monitor with the integer constraint added. Click **Solve** to solve the problem.

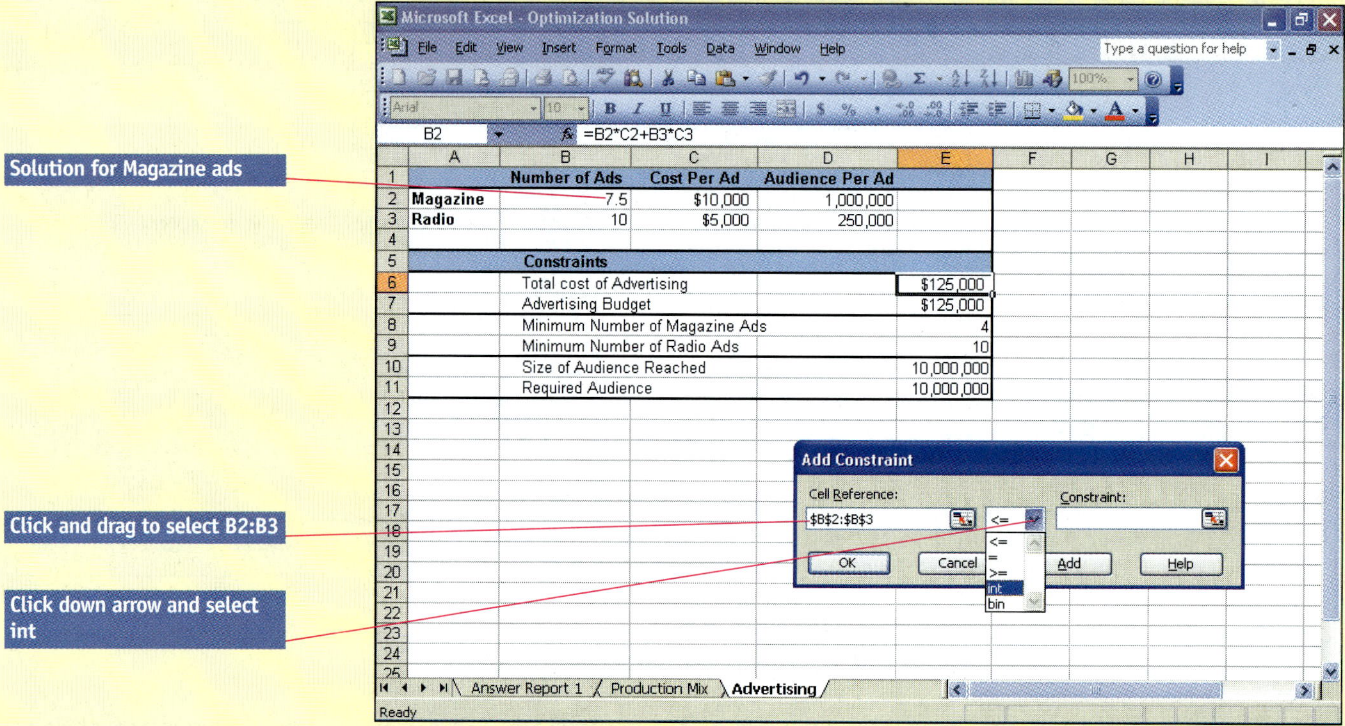

(e) Impose an Integer Constraint (step 5)

FIGURE B.6 Hands-on Exercise 2 (*continued*)

DO YOU REALLY NEED AN INTEGER SOLUTION?

It seems like such a small change, but specifying an integer constraint can significantly increase the amount of time required for Solver to reach a solution. The examples in this chapter are relatively simple and did not take an inordinate amount of time to solve. Imposing an integer constraint on a more complex problem, however, may challenge your patience as Solver struggles to reach a solution.

Step 6: The Infeasible Solution

- You should see the dialog box in Figure B.6f, indicating that Solver could *not* find a solution that satisfied the existing constraints. This is because the imposition of the integer constraint would raise the number of magazine ads from 7.5 to 8, which would increase the total cost of advertising to $130,000, exceeding the budget of $125,000.
- The desired audience can still be reached but only by relaxing one of the binding constraints. You can, for example, retain the requisite number of magazine and radio ads by increasing the budget. Alternatively, the budget can be held at $125,000, while still reaching the audience by decreasing the required number of radio ads.
- Click **Cancel** to exit the dialog box and return to the worksheet.

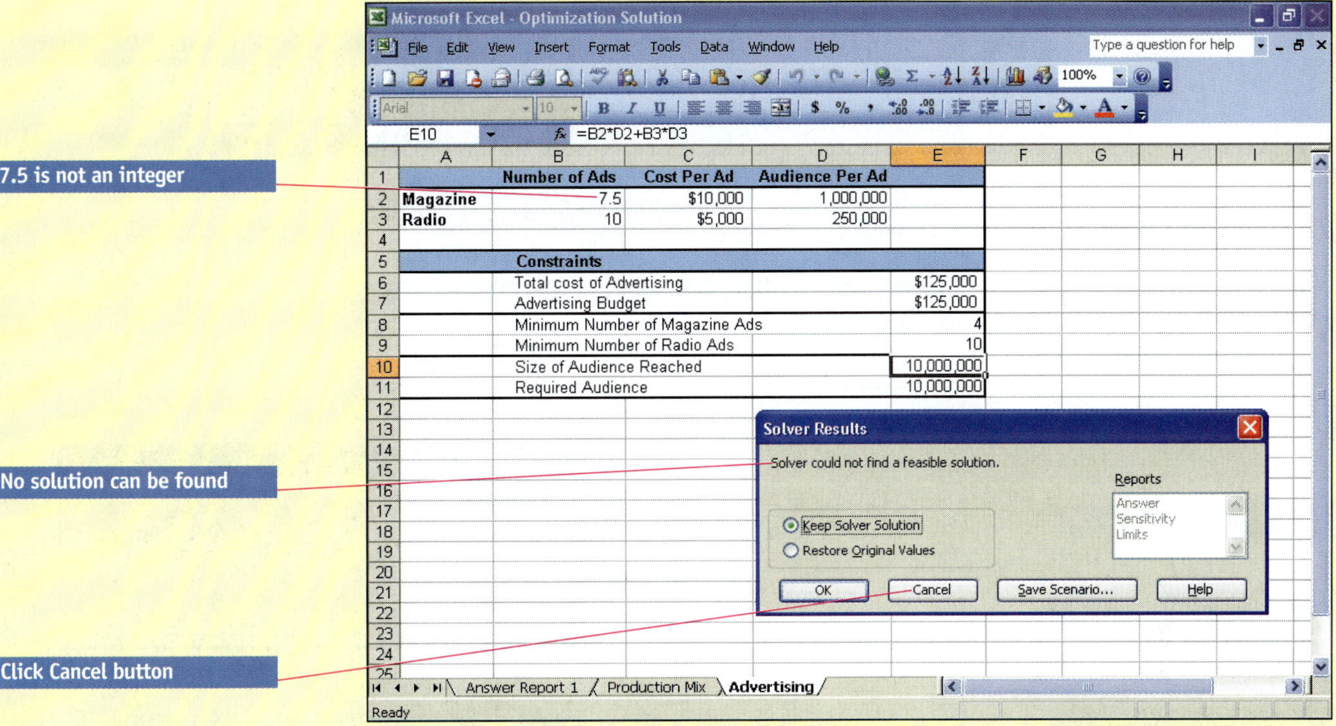

(f) The Infeasible Solution (step 6)

FIGURE B.6 Hands-on Exercise 2 (*continued*)

UNABLE TO FIND A SOLUTION

Solver is a powerful tool, but it cannot do the impossible. Some problems simply do not have a solution because the constraints may conflict with one another, and/or because the constraints exceed the available resources. Should this occur, and it will, check your constraints to make sure they were entered correctly. If Solver is still unable to reach a solution, it will be necessary to relax one or more of the constraints.

Step 7: Relax a Constraint

- Click in **cell E9** (the cell containing the minimum number of radio ads). Enter **9** and press **Enter**.
- Pull down the **Tools menu**. Click **Solver** to display the Solver Parameters dialog box. Click **Solve**. This time Solver finds a solution as shown in Figure B.6g.
- Click **Answer** in the Reports list box, then click **OK** to generate the report. You will see the report being generated, after which the Solver Results dialog box closes automatically.
- Click the **Answer Report 2 worksheet tab** to view the report. Add your name to the report, boldface your name, print the answer report, and submit it to your instructor.
- Save the workbook.

Click in E9 and enter 9

A solution was found

Click Answer

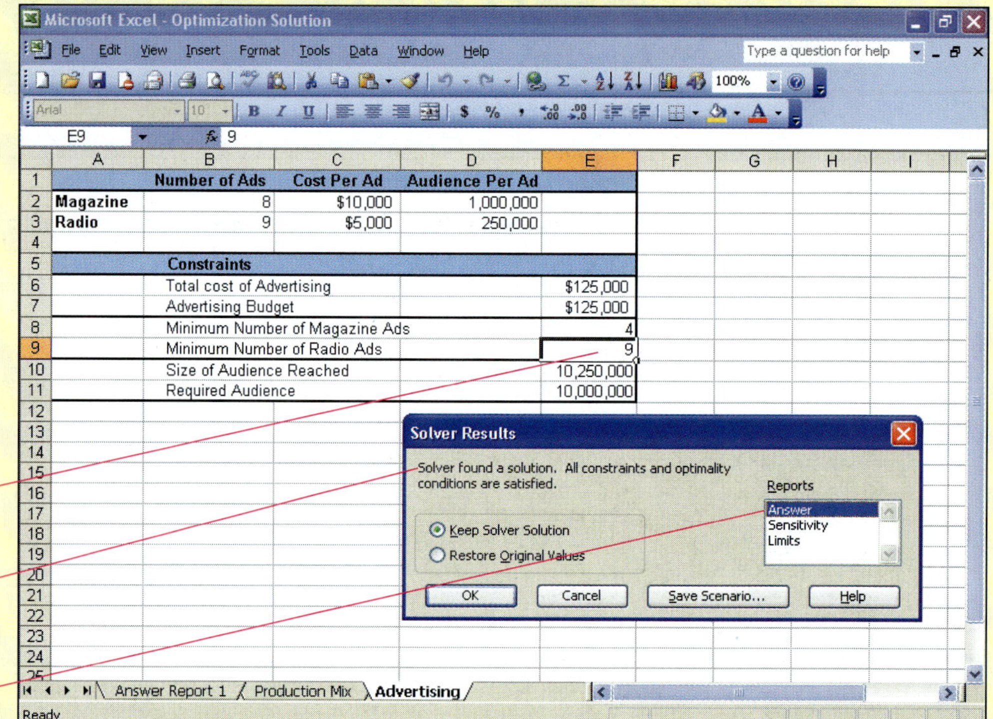

(g) Relax a Constraint (step 7)

FIGURE B.6 Hands-on Exercise 2 (*continued*)

SENSITIVITY, BINDING, AND NONBINDING CONSTRAINTS

A sensitivity report shows the effect of increasing resources associated with the binding and nonbinding constraints within the optimization problem. A binding constraint has a limiting effect on the objective value; that is, relaxing a binding constraint by increasing the associated resource will improve the value of the objective function. Conversely, a nonbinding constraint does not have a limiting effect, and increasing its resource has no effect on the value of the objective function.

Step 8: Add the Documentation Worksheet

- This step creates a documentation worksheet similar to the one in Chapter 6. Pull down the **Insert menu** and click the **Worksheet command**.
- Double click the **tab** of the newly inserted worksheet. Enter **Documentation** as the new name and press **Enter**. If necessary, click and drag the worksheet tab to move it to the beginning of the workbook.
- Enter the descriptive entries in **cells A3, A4, and A6** as shown in Figure B.6h. Use boldface as shown. Increase the width of column A.
- Enter your name in **cell B3**. Enter **=Today( )** in **cell B4**. Press **Enter**. Click the **Left Align button** to align the date as shown in the figure.
- Increase the width of column B, then click in **cell B6** and enter the indicated text. Do not press the Enter key until you have completed the entry.
- Click in **cell B6**, then pull down the **Format menu** and click the **Cells command** to display the Format Cells dialog box. Click the **Alignment tab**, click the box to **Wrap Text**, then click **OK**.
- Point to **cell A6**, then click the **right mouse button** to display a shortcut menu. Click **Format Cells** to display the Format Cells dialog box. If necessary, click the **Alignment tab**, click the **drop-down arrow** in the Vertical list box, and select **Top**. Click **OK**.
- Click in **cell A1**. Enter **Solver—An Optimization Technique**. Change the font size to **18**. Click and drag to select **cells A1** and **B1**. Click the **Merge and Center button** to center the title across cells A1 and B1.
- Complete the entries in the remainder of the worksheet. Check the worksheet for spelling. Save the workbook. Print the documentation worksheet.

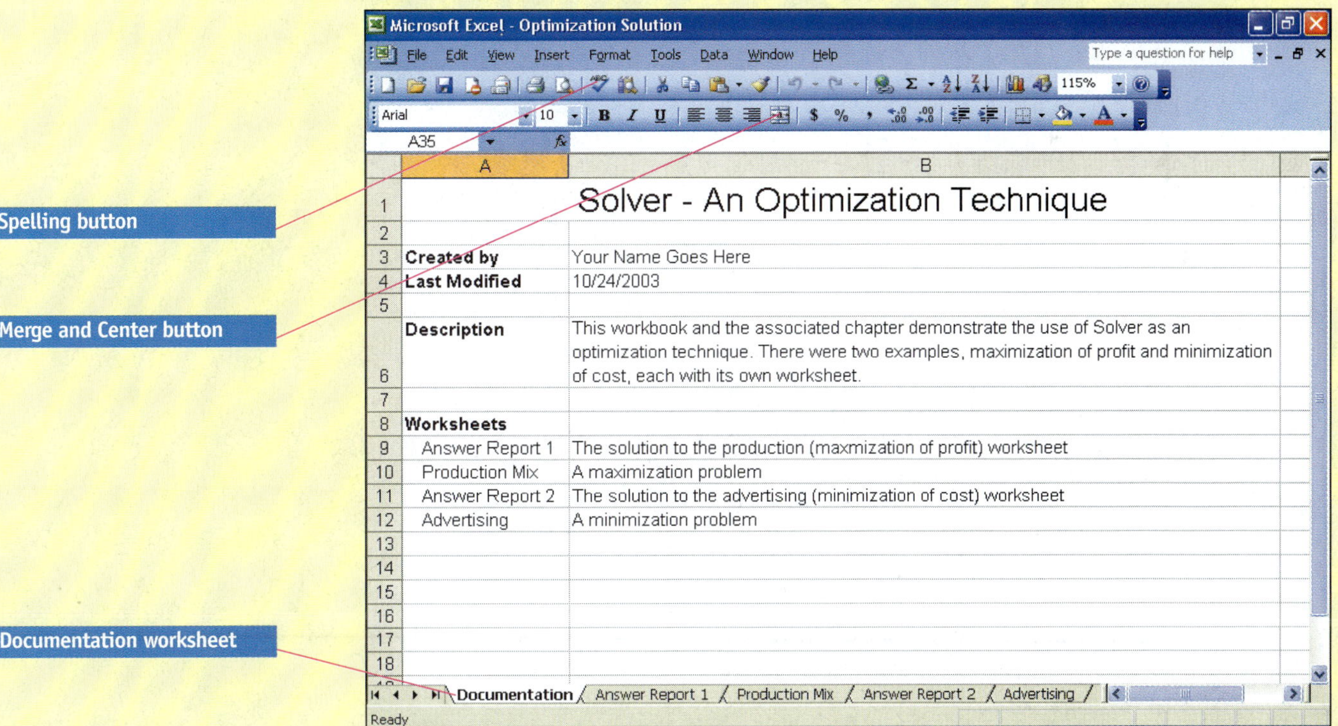

(h) Add the Documentation Worksheet (step 8)

FIGURE B.6 Hands-on Exercise 2 (*continued*)

SUMMARY

Solver is an optimization and resource allocation tool that helps you achieve a desired goal, such as maximizing profit or minimizing cost. The information required by Solver is entered through the Solver Parameters dialog box, which is divided into three sections: the target cell, the adjustable cells, and the constraints.

The target cell identifies the goal (or objective function), which is the cell whose value you want to maximize, minimize, or set to a specific value. The adjustable cells are the cells whose values are changed until the constraints are satisfied and the target cell reaches its optimum value. The constraints specify the restrictions. Each constraint consists of a comparison containing a cell or cell range on the left, a relational operator, and a numeric value or cell reference on the right.

The Solver Options dialog box lets you specify how Solver will attempt to find a solution. The Max Time and Iterations entries determine how long Solver will work on finding a solution. If either limit is reached before a solution is found, Solver will ask whether you want to continue. The default settings of 100 seconds and 100 iterations are sufficient for simpler problems, but may not be enough for complex problems with multiple constraints.

KEY TERMS

CHAPTER

1

Getting Started with Microsoft® Windows® XP

OBJECTIVES

After reading this chapter you will:

1. Describe the Windows desktop.
2. Use the Help and Support Center to obtain information.
3. Describe the My Computer and My Documents folders.
4. Differentiate between a program file and a data file.
5. Download a file from the Exploring Office Web site.
6. Copy and/or move a file from one folder to another.
7. Delete a file, and then recover it from the Recycle Bin.
8. Create and arrange shortcuts on the desktop.
9. Use the Search Companion.
10. Use the My Pictures and My Music folders.
11. Use Windows Messenger for instant messaging.

hands-on exercises

1. WELCOME TO WINDOWS XP
   Input: None
   Output: None
2. DOWNLOAD PRACTICE FILES
   Input: Data files from the Web
   Output: Welcome to Windows XP (a Word document)
3. WINDOWS EXPLORER
   Input: Data files from exercise 2
   Output: Screen Capture within a Word document
4. INCREASING PRODUCTIVITY
   Input: Data files from exercise 3
   Output: None
5. FUN WITH WINDOWS XP
   Input: None
   Output: None

CASE STUDY

UNFORESEEN CIRCUMSTANCES

Steve and his wife Shelly have poured their life savings into the dream of owning their own business, a "nanny" service agency. They have spent the last two years building their business and have created a sophisticated database with numerous entries for both families and nannies. The database is the key to their operation. Now that it is up and running, Steve and Shelly are finally at a point where they could hire someone to manage the operation on a part-time basis so that they could take some time off together.

Unfortunately, their process for selecting a person they could trust with their business was not as thorough as it should have been. Nancy, their new employee, assured them that all was well, and the couple left for an extended weekend. The place was in shambles on their return. Nancy could not handle the responsibility, and when Steve gave her two weeks' notice, neither he nor his wife thought that the unimaginable would happen. On her last day in the office Nancy "lost" all of the names in the database—the data was completely gone!

Nancy claimed that a "virus" knocked out the database, but after spending nearly $1,500 with a computer consultant, Steve was told that it had been cleverly deleted from the hard drive and could not be recovered. Of course, the consultant asked Steve and Shelly about their backup strategy, which they sheepishly admitted did not exist. They had never experienced any problems in the past, and simply assumed that their data was safe. Fortunately, they do have hard copy of the data in the form of various reports that were printed throughout the time they were in business. They have no choice but to manually reenter the data. ■

Your assignment is to read the chapter, paying special attention to the information on file management. Think about how Steve and Shelly could have avoided the disaster if a backup strategy had been in place, then summarize your thoughts in a brief note to your instructor. Describe the elements of a basic backup strategy. Give several other examples of unforeseen circumstances that can cause data to be lost.

WELCOME TO WINDOWS® XP

Windows® XP is the newest and most powerful version of the Windows operating system. It has a slightly different look than earlier versions, but it maintains the conventions of its various predecessors. You have seen the Windows interface many times, but do you really understand it? Can you move and copy files with confidence? Do you know how to back up the Excel spreadsheets, Access databases, and other documents that you work so hard to create? If not, now is the time to learn.

We begin with an introduction to the desktop, the graphical user interface that lets you work in intuitive fashion by pointing at icons and clicking the mouse. We identify the basic components of a window and describe how to execute commands and supply information through different elements in a dialog box. We stress the importance of disk and file management, but begin with basic definitions of a file and a folder. We also introduce Windows Explorer and show you how to move or copy a file from one folder to another. We discuss other basic operations, such as renaming and deleting a file. We also describe how to recover a deleted file (if necessary) from the Recycle Bin.

Windows XP is available in different versions. Windows ***XP Home Edition*** is intended for entertainment and home use. It includes a media player, new support for digital photography, and an instant messenger. Windows ***XP Professional Edition*** has all of the features of the Home Edition plus additional security to encrypt files and protect data. It includes support for high-performance multiprocessor systems. It also lets you connect to your computer from a remote station.

The login screen in Figure 1 is displayed when the computer is turned on initially and/or when you are switching from one user account to another. Several individuals can share the same computer. Each user, however, retains his or her individual desktop settings, individual lists of favorite and recently visited Web sites, as well as other customized Windows settings. Multiple users can be logged on simultaneously, each with his or her programs in memory, through a feature known as ***fast user switching***.

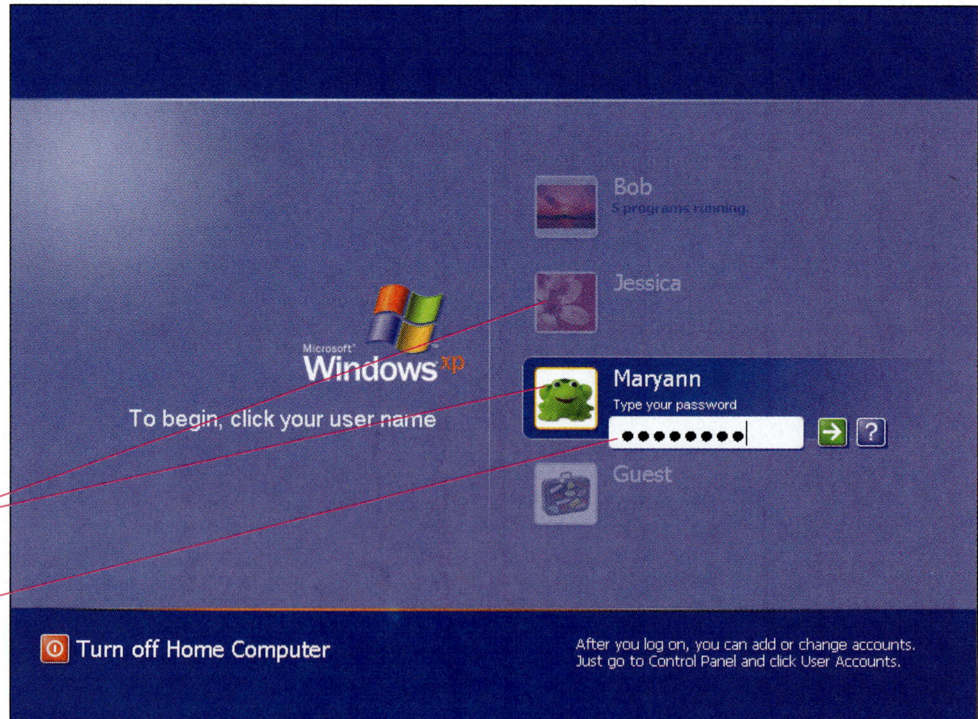

FIGURE 1 Windows XP Login

Windows XP, as well as all previous versions of Windows, creates a working environment for your computer that parallels the working environment at home or in an office. You work at a desk. Windows operations take place on the ***desktop***. There are physical objects on a desk such as folders, a dictionary, a calculator, or a phone. The computer equivalents of those objects appear as icons (pictorial symbols) on the desktop. Each object on a real desk has attributes (properties) such as size, weight, and color. In similar fashion, Windows assigns properties to every object on its desktop. And just as you can move the objects on a real desk, you can rearrange the objects on the Windows desktop.

Windows XP has a new interface, but you can retain the look and feel of earlier versions as shown in Figure 2. The desktop in Figure 2a uses the default ***Windows XP theme*** (the wallpaper has been suppressed), whereas Figure 2b displays the "same" desktop using the ***Windows Classic theme***. The icons on either desktop are used to access specific programs or other functions.

The ***Start button***, as its name suggests, is where you begin; it works identically on both desktops. Click the Start button to see a menu of programs and other functions. The Windows XP ***Start menu*** in Figure 2a is divided into two columns. The column on the left displays the most recently used programs for easy access, whereas the column on the right contains a standard set of entries. It also shows the name of the individual who is logged into the computer. The ***Classic Start menu*** in Figure 2b contains only a single column. (Note the indication of the Windows XP Professional operating system that appears at the left of the menu.)

Do not be concerned if your desktop is different from ours. Your real desk is arranged differently from those of your friends, just as your Windows desktop will also be different. Moreover, you are likely to work on different systems—at school, at work, or at home; what is important is that you recognize the common functionality that is present on all desktops.

Look now at Figure 2c, which displays an entirely different desktop, one with four open windows that is similar to a desk in the middle of a working day. Each window in Figure 2c displays a program or a folder that is currently in use. The ability to run several programs at the same time is known as ***multitasking***, and it is a major benefit of the Windows environment. Multitasking enables you to run a word processor in one window, create a spreadsheet in a second window, surf the Internet in a third window, play a game in a fourth window, and so on. You can work in a program as long as you want, then change to a different program by clicking its window.

The ***taskbar*** at the bottom of the desktop contains a button for each open window, and it enables you to switch back and forth between the open windows by clicking the appropriate button. A ***notification area*** appears at the right end of the taskbar. It displays the time and other shortcuts. It may also provide information on the status of such ongoing activities as a printer or Internet connection.

The desktop in Figure 2d is identical to the desktop in Figure 2c except that it is displayed in the Windows Classic theme. The open windows are the same, as are the contents of the taskbar and notification area. The choice between the XP theme or Windows Classic (or other) theme is one of personal preference.

Moving and Sizing a Window

A window can be sized or moved on the desktop through appropriate actions with the mouse. To ***size a window***, point to any border (the mouse pointer changes to a double arrow), then drag the border in the direction you want to go—inward to shrink the window or outward to enlarge it. You can also drag a corner (instead of a border) to change both dimensions at the same time. To ***move a window*** while retaining its current size, click and drag the title bar to a new position on the desktop.

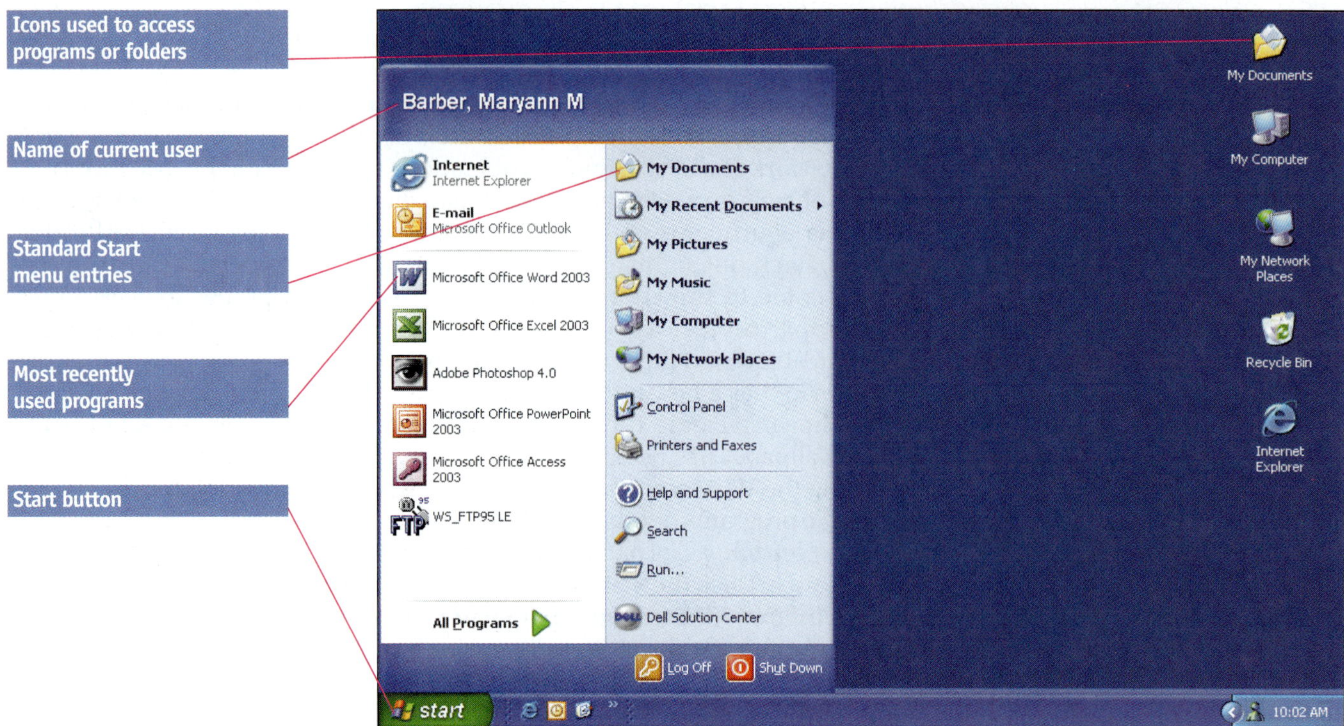

(a) Windows XP Theme and Start Menu

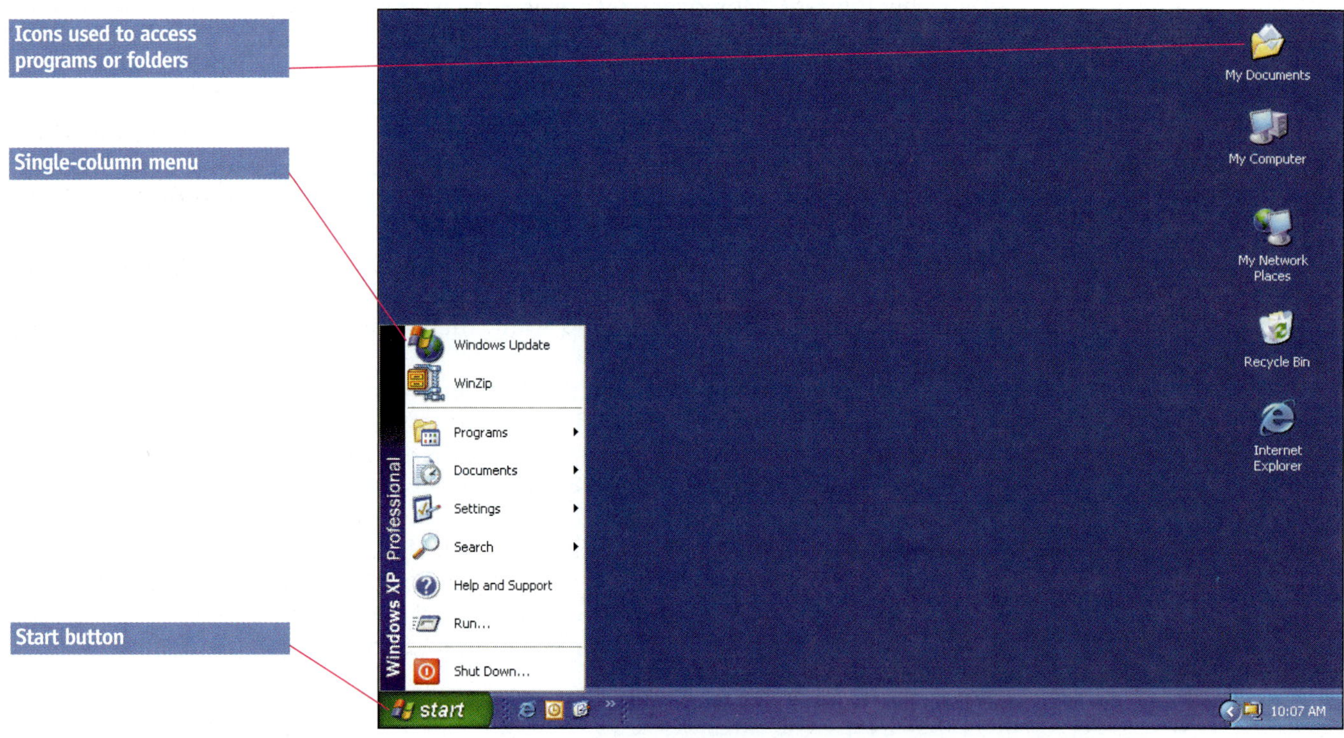

(b) Windows Classic Theme and Start Menu

FIGURE 2 The Desktop and Start Menu

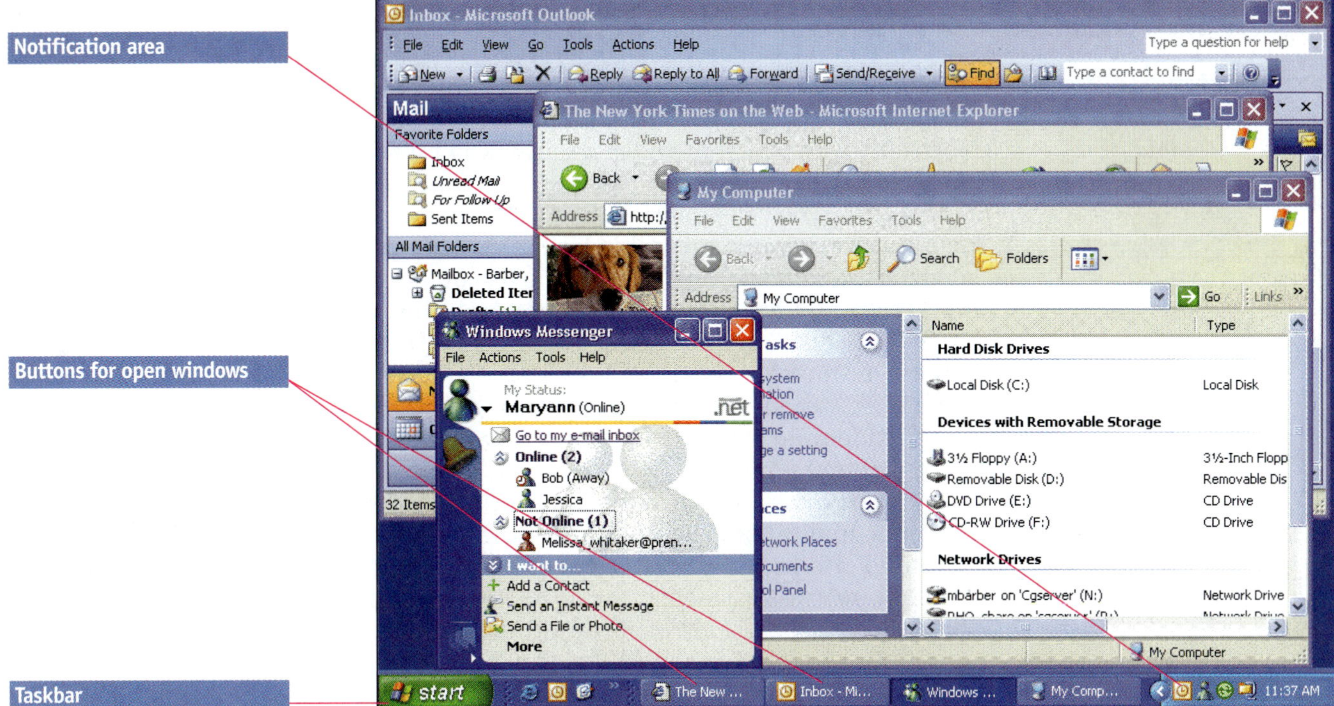

(c) Windows XP Theme

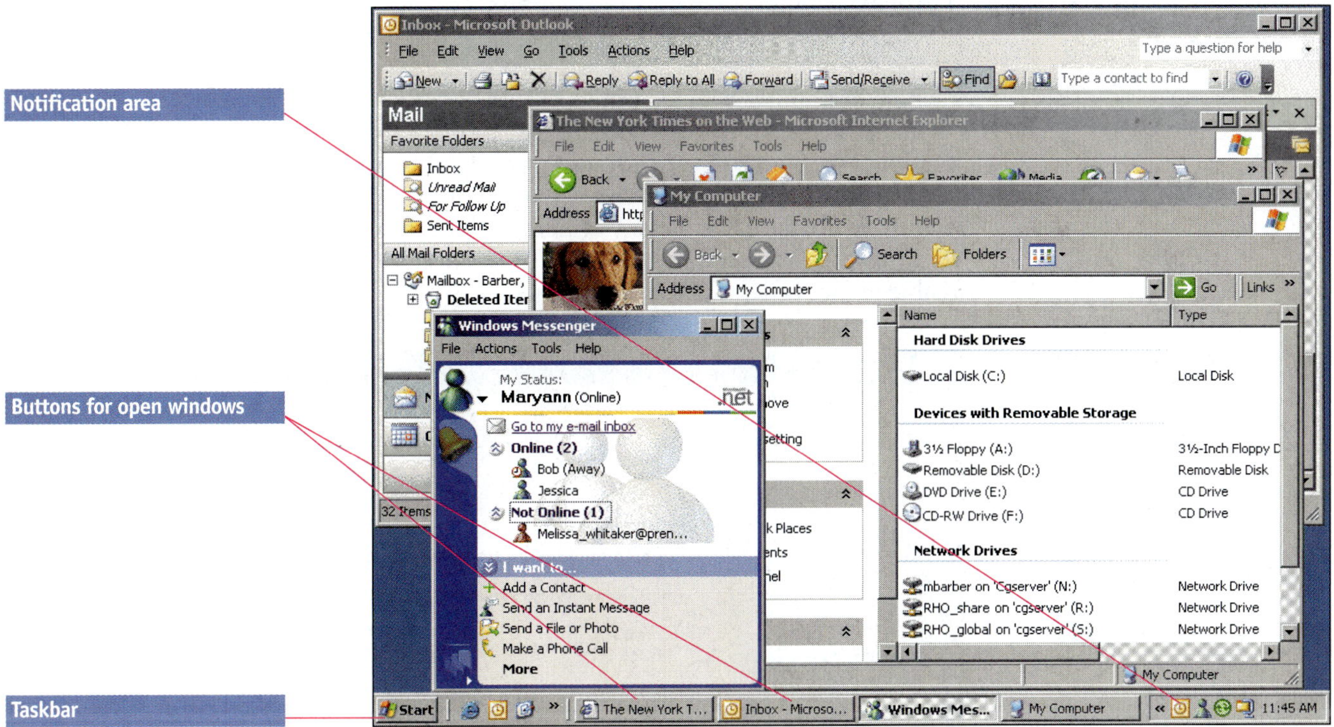

(d) Windows Classic Theme

FIGURE 2 The Desktop and Start Menu (*continued*)

ANATOMY OF A WINDOW

All Windows applications share a common user interface and possess a consistent command structure. This means that every Windows application works essentially the same way, which provides a sense of familiarity from one application to the next. In other words, once you learn the basic concepts and techniques in one application, you can apply that knowledge to every other application.

The ***My Computer folder*** in Figure 3 is used to illustrate basic technology. This folder is present on every system, and its contents depend on the hardware of the specific computer. Our system, for example, has one local disk, a floppy drive, a removable disk (an Iomega Zip® drive), a DVD drive, and a CD-RW (recordable) drive. Our intent at this time, however, is to focus on the elements that are common to every window. A ***task pane*** (also called a task panel) is displayed at the left of the window to provide easy access to various commands that you might want to access from this folder.

The ***title bar*** appears at the top of every window and displays the name of the folder or application. The icon at the extreme left of the title bar identifies the window and also provides access to a control menu with operations relevant to the window, such as moving it or sizing it. Three buttons appear at the right of the title bar. The ***Minimize button*** shrinks the window to a button on the taskbar, but leaves the window in memory. The ***Maximize button*** enlarges the window so that it takes up the entire desktop. The ***Restore button*** (not shown in Figure 3) appears instead of the Maximize button after a window has been maximized, and restores the window to its previous size. The ***Close button*** closes the window and removes it from memory and the desktop.

The ***menu bar*** appears immediately below the title bar and provides access to pull-down menus. One or more ***toolbars*** appear below the menu bar and let you execute a command by clicking a button, as opposed to pulling down a menu. The ***status bar*** at the bottom of the window displays information about the window as a whole or about a selected object within a window.

A vertical (or horizontal) ***scroll bar*** appears at the right (or bottom) border of a window when its contents are not completely visible and provides access to the unseen areas. The vertical scroll bar at the right of the task panel in Figure 3 implies that there are additional tasks available that are not currently visible. A horizontal scroll bar does not appear since all of the objects in the My Computer folder are visible at one time.

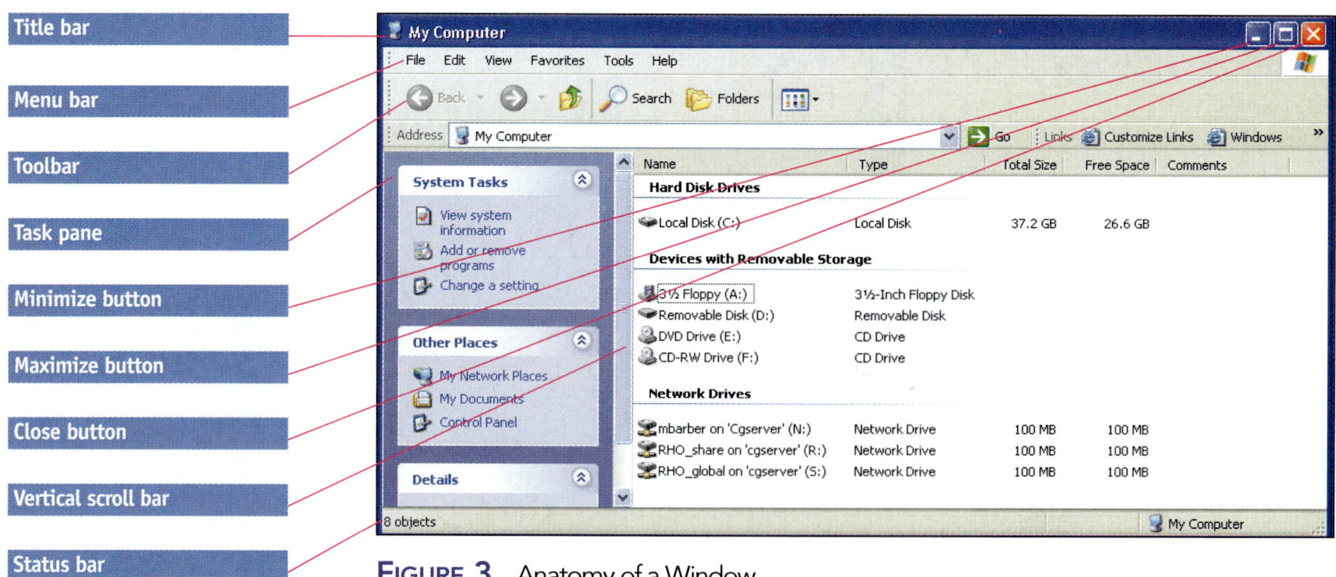

FIGURE 3 Anatomy of a Window

Pull-down Menus

The menu bar provides access to ***pull-down menus*** that enable you to execute commands within an application (program). A pull-down menu is accessed by clicking the menu name or by pressing the Alt key plus the underlined letter in the menu name; for example, press Alt+V to pull down the View menu. (You may have to press the Alt key to see the underlines.) Figure 4 displays three pull-down menus that are associated with the My Computer folder.

Commands within a menu are executed by clicking the command or by typing the underlined letter. Alternatively, you can bypass the menu entirely if you know the equivalent shortcuts shown to the right of the command in the menu (e.g., Ctrl+X, Ctrl+C, or Ctrl+V to cut, copy, or paste as shown within the Edit menu). A dimmed command (e.g., the Paste command in the Edit menu) means the command is not currently executable, and that some additional action has to be taken for the command to become available.

An ellipsis (. . .) following a command indicates that additional information is required to execute the command; for example, selection of the Format command in the File menu requires the user to specify additional information about the formatting process. This information is entered into a dialog box (discussed in the next section), which appears immediately after the command has been selected.

A check next to a command indicates a toggle switch, whereby the command is either on or off. There is a check next to the Status Bar command in the View menu of Figure 4, which means the command is in effect (and thus the status bar will be displayed). Click the Status Bar command and the check disappears, which suppresses the display of the status bar. Click the command a second time and the check reappears, as does the status bar in the associated window.

A bullet next to an item, such as Icons in the View menu, indicates a selection from a set of mutually exclusive choices. Click a different option within the group—such as Thumbnails—and the bullet will move from the previous selection (Icons) to the new selection (Thumbnails).

An arrowhead after a command (e.g., the Arrange Icons by command in the View menu) indicates that a submenu (also known as a cascaded menu) will be displayed with additional menu options.

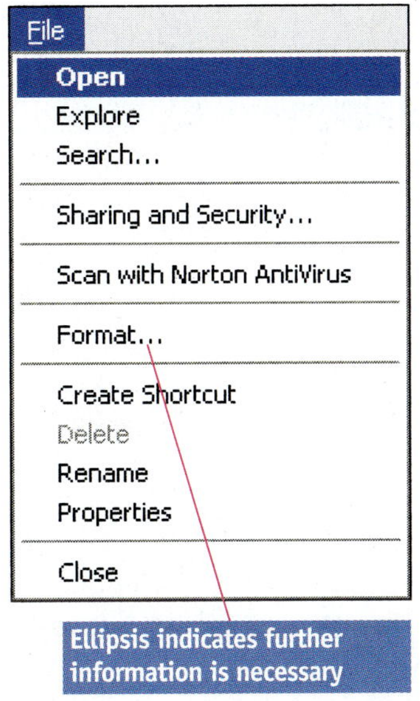

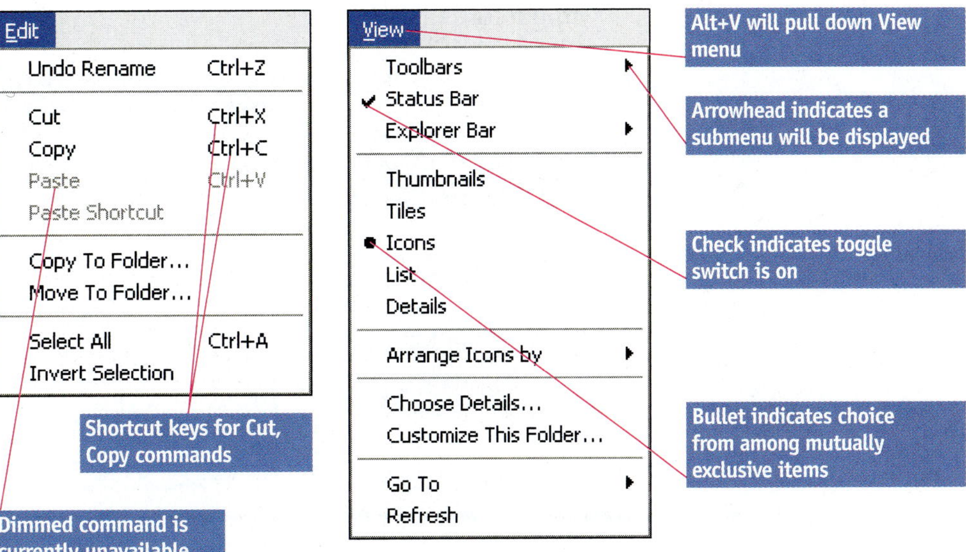

FIGURE 4 Pull-down Menus

Dialog Boxes

A ***dialog box*** appears when additional information is necessary to execute a command. Click the Print command in Internet Explorer, for example, and you are presented with the Print dialog box in Figure 5, requesting information about precisely what to print and how. The information is entered into the dialog box in different ways, depending on the type of information that is required. The tabs at the top of the dialog box provide access to different sets of options. The General tab is selected in Figure 5.

Option (radio) buttons indicate mutually exclusive choices, one of which *must* be chosen, such as the page range. In this example you can print all pages, the selection (if it is available), the current page (if there are multiple pages), or a specific set of pages (such as pages 1–4), but you can choose *one and only one* option. Any time you select (click) an option, the previous option is automatically deselected.

A ***text box*** enters specific information such as the pages that will be printed in conjunction with selecting the radio button for pages. A ***spin button*** is another way to enter specific information such as the number of copies. Click the up or down arrow to increase or decrease the number of pages, respectively. You can also enter the information explicitly by typing it into a spin box, just as you would a text box.

Check boxes are used instead of option buttons if the choices are not mutually exclusive or if an option is not required. The Collate check box is checked, whereas the Print to file box is not checked. Individual options are selected and cleared by clicking the appropriate check box, which toggles the box on and off. A ***list box*** (not shown in Figure 5) displays some or all of the available choices, any one of which is selected by clicking the desired item.

The ***Help button*** (a question mark at the right end of the title bar) provides help for any item in the dialog box. Click the button, then click the item in the dialog box for which you want additional information. The Close button (the X at the extreme right of the title bar) closes the dialog box without executing the command.

All dialog boxes also contain one or more ***command buttons***, the function of which is generally apparent from the button's name. The Print button in Figure 5, for example, initiates the printing process. The Cancel button does just the opposite and ignores (cancels) any changes made to the settings, then closes the dialog box without further action.

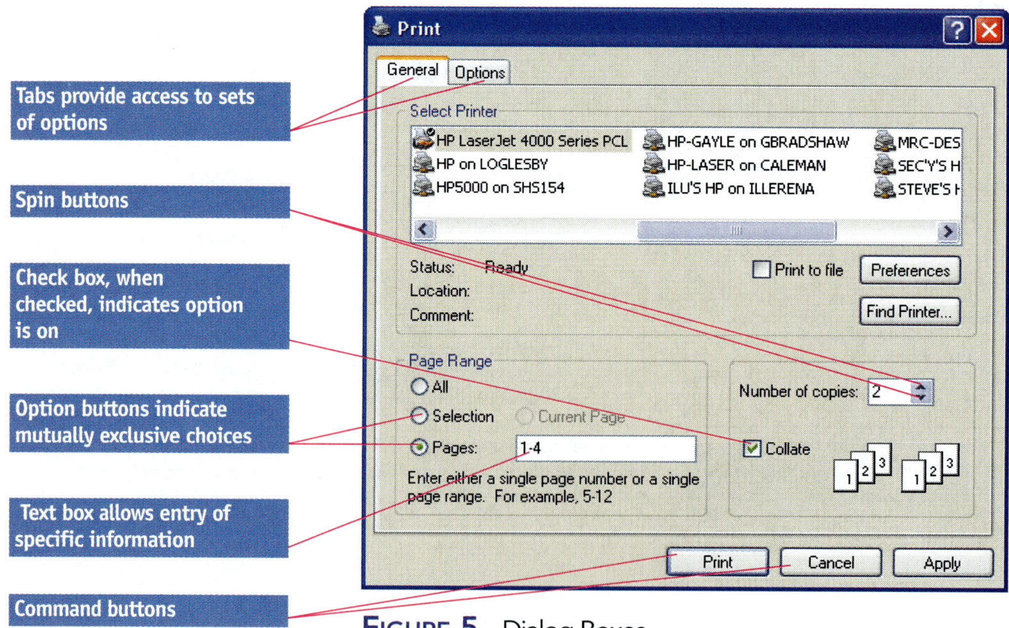

FIGURE 5 Dialog Boxes

HELP AND SUPPORT CENTER

The ***Help and Support Center*** combines such traditional features as a search function and an index of help topics. It also lets you request remote help from other Windows XP users, and/or you can access the Microsoft Knowledge base on the Microsoft Web site. Click the Index button, type the keyword you are searching for, then double click the subtopic to display the associated information in the right pane. The mouse is essential to Windows, and you are undoubtedly familiar with its basic operations such as pointing, clicking, and double clicking. Look closely, however, at the list of subtopics in Figure 6 and you might be surprised at the amount of available information. Suffice it to say, therefore, that you will find the answer to almost every conceivable question if only you will take the trouble to look.

The toolbar at the top of the window contains several buttons that are also found in ***Internet Explorer 6.0***, the Web browser that is built into Windows XP. The Back and Forward buttons enable you to navigate through the various pages that were viewed in the current session. The Favorites button displays a list of previously saved (favorite) help topics from previous sessions. The History button shows all pages that were visited in this session.

The Support button provides access to remote sources for assistance. Click the Support button, then click the link to ask a friend to help, which in turn displays a Remote Assistance screen. You will be asked to sign in to the Messenger service (Windows Messenger is discussed in more detail in a later section). Your friend has to be running Windows XP for this feature to work, but once you are connected, he or she will be able to view your computer screen. You can then chat in real time about the problem and proposed solution. And, if you give permission, your friend can use his or her mouse and keyboard to work on your computer. Be careful! It is one thing to let your friend see your screen. It is quite a leap of faith, however, to give him or her control of your machine.

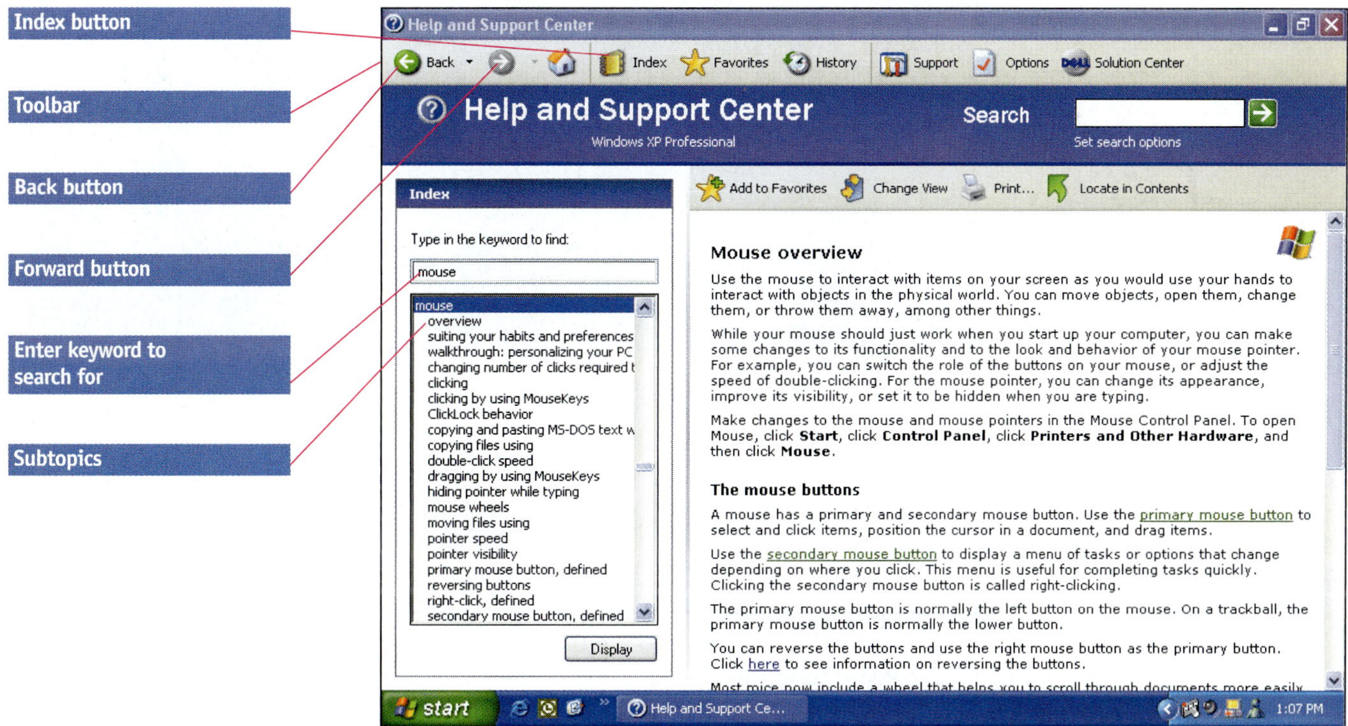

FIGURE 6 Help and Support Center

hands-on exercise

1 Welcome to Windows XP

Objective To log on to Windows XP and customize the desktop; to open the My Computer folder; to move and size a window; to format a floppy disk and access the Help and Support Center. Use Figure 7 as a guide.

Step 1: Log On to Windows XP

- Turn on the computer and all of the peripheral devices. The floppy drive should be empty prior to starting your machine.
- Windows XP will load automatically, and you should see a login screen similar to Figure 7a. (It does not matter which version of Windows XP you are using.) The number and names of the potential users and their associated icons will be different on your system.
- Click the icon for the user account you want to access. You may be prompted for a password, depending on the security options in effect.

Click icon for user account to be accessed

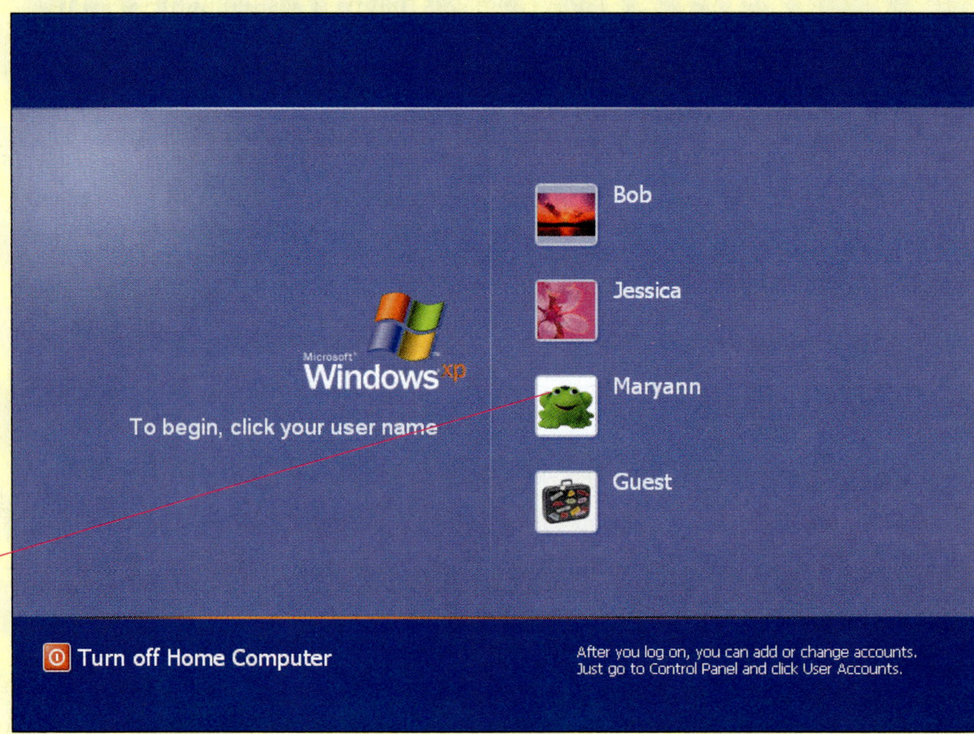

(a) Log On to Windows XP (step 1)

FIGURE 7 Hands-on Exercise 1

USER ACCOUNTS

The available user names are created automatically during the installation of Windows XP, but you can add or delete users at any time. Click the Start button, click Control Panel, switch to the Category view, and select User Accounts. Choose the desired task, such as creating a new account or changing an existing account, then supply the necessary information. Do not expect, however, to be able to modify user accounts in a school setting.

Step 2: Choose the Theme and Start Menu

- Check with your instructor to see if you are able to modify the desktop and other settings at your school or university. If your network administrator has disabled these commands, skip this step and go to step 3.
- Point to a blank area on the desktop, click the **right mouse button** to display a context-sensitive menu, then click the **Properties command** to open the Display Properties dialog box. Click the **Themes tab** and select the **Windows XP theme** if it is not already selected. Click **OK**.
- We prefer to work without any wallpaper (background picture) on the desktop. **Right click** the desktop, click **Properties**, then click the **Desktop tab** in the Display Properties dialog box. Click **None** as shown in Figure 7b, then click **OK**. The background disappears.
- The Start menu is modified independently of the theme. **Right click** a blank area of the taskbar, click the **Properties command** to display the Taskbar and Start Menu Properties dialog box, then click the **Start Menu tab**.
- Click the **Start Menu option button**. Click **OK**.

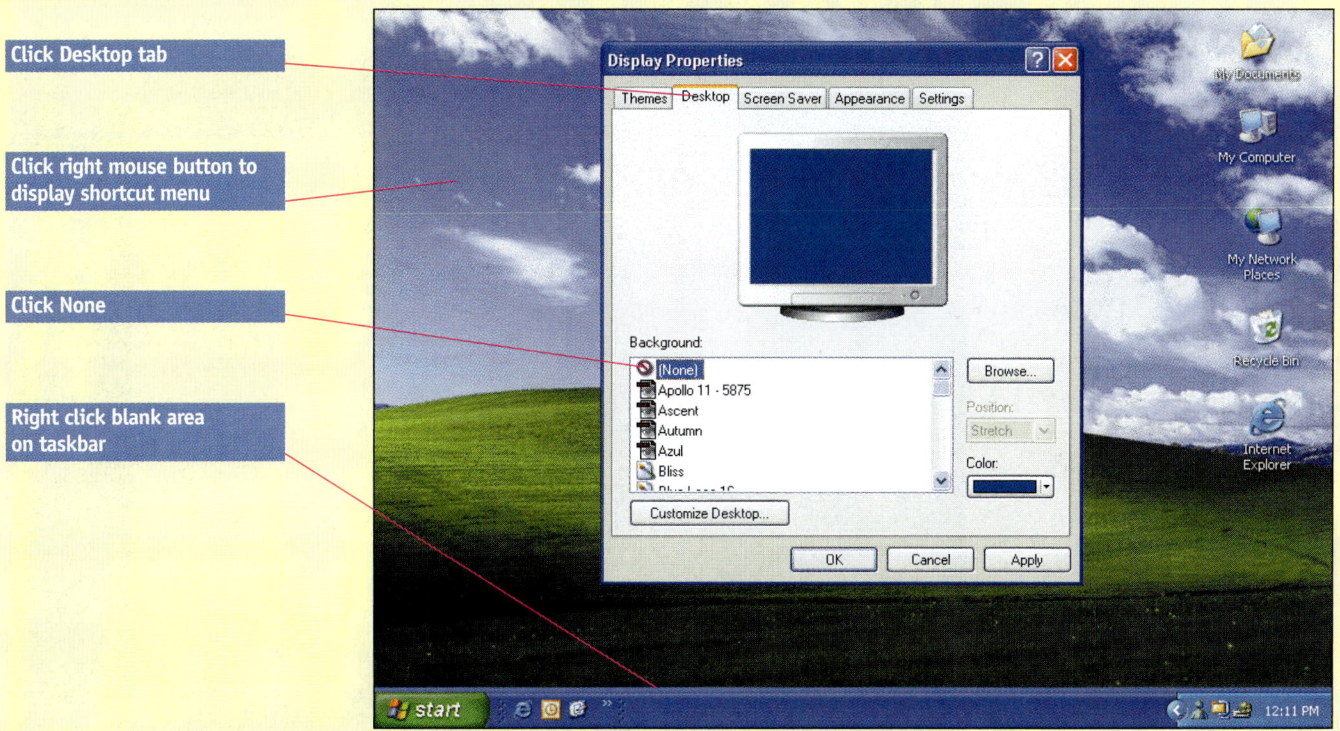

(b) Choose the Theme and Start Menu (step 2)

FIGURE 7 Hands-on Exercise 1 (*continued*)

IMPLEMENT A SCREEN SAVER

A screen saver is a delightful way to personalize your computer and a good way to practice with basic commands in Windows XP. Right click a blank area of the desktop, click the Properties command to open the Display Properties dialog box, then click the Screen Saver tab. Click the down arrow in the Screen Saver list box, choose the desired screen saver, then set the option to wait an appropriate amount of time before the screen saver appears. Click OK to accept the settings and close the dialog box.

Step 3: Open the My Computer Folder

- Click the **Start button** to display a two-column Start menu that is characteristic of Windows XP. Click **My Computer** to open the My Computer folder. The contents of your window and/or its size and position on the desktop will be different from ours.
- Pull down the **View menu** as shown in Figure 7c to make or verify the following selections. (You have to pull down the View menu each time you make an additional change.)
  - The **Status Bar command** should be checked. The Status Bar command functions as a toggle switch. Click the command and the status bar is displayed; click the command a second time and the status bar disappears.
  - Click the **Tiles command** to change to this view. Selecting the Tiles view automatically deselects the previous view.
- Pull down the **View menu**, then click (or point to) the **Toolbars command** to display a cascaded menu. If necessary, check the commands for the **Standard Buttons** and **Address Bar**, and clear the other commands.
- Click the **Folders button** on the Standard Buttons toolbar to toggle the task panel on or off. End with the task panel displayed as shown in Figure 7c.

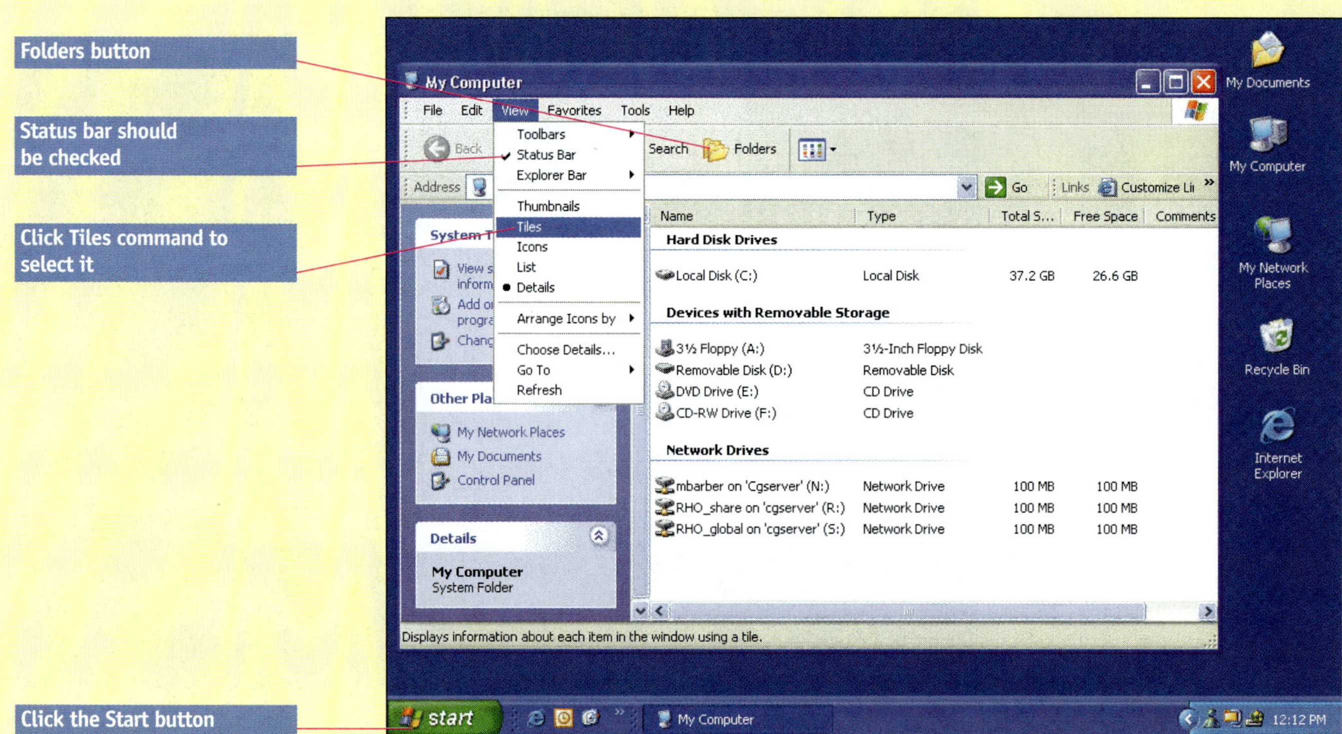

(c) Open the My Computer Folder (step 3)

FIGURE 7 Hands-on Exercise 1 (*continued*)

DESIGNATING THE DEVICES ON A SYSTEM

The first (usually only) floppy drive is always designated as drive A. (A second floppy drive, if it were present, would be drive B.) The first hard (local) disk on a system is always drive C, whether or not there are one or two floppy drives. Additional local drives, if any, such as a zip (removable storage) drive, a network drive, a CD and/or a DVD, are labeled from D on.

Step 4: Move and Size a Window

- Move and size the My Computer window on your desktop to match the display in Figure 7d.
  - To change the width or height of the window, click and drag a border (the mouse pointer changes to a double arrow) in the direction you want to go; drag the border inward to shrink the window or outward to enlarge it.
  - To change the width and height at the same time, click and drag a corner rather than a border.
  - To change the position of the window, click and drag the title bar.
- Click the **Minimize button** to shrink the My Computer window to a button on the taskbar. My Computer is still active in memory although its window is no longer visible. Click the **My Computer button** on the taskbar to reopen the window.
- Click the **Maximize button** so that the My Computer window expands to fill the entire screen. Click the **Restore button** (which replaces the Maximize button and is not shown in Figure 7d) to return the window to its previous size.
- Practice these operations until you can move and size a window with confidence.

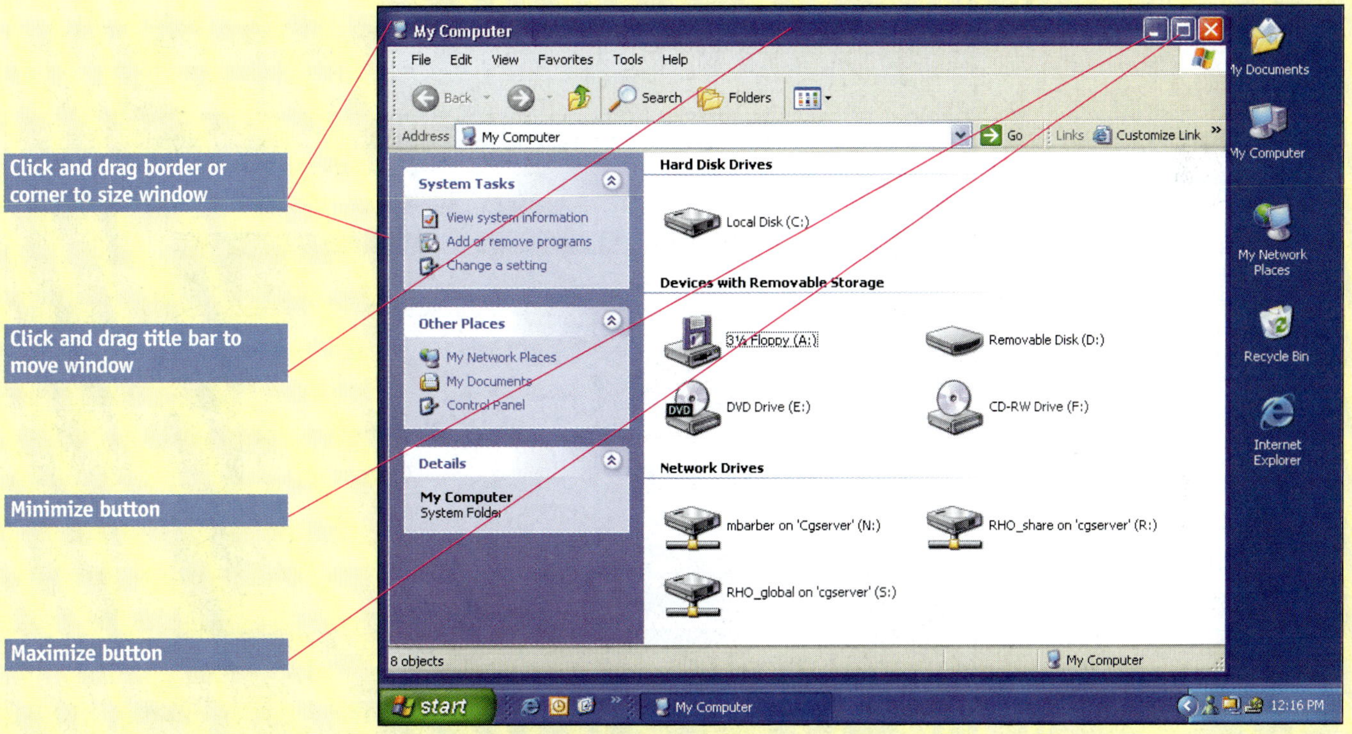

(d) Move and Size a Window (step 4)

FIGURE 7 Hands-on Exercise 1 (*continued*)

MINIMIZING VERSUS CLOSING AN APPLICATION

Minimizing a folder or an application leaves the object open in memory and available at the click of the appropriate button on the taskbar. Closing it, however, removes the object from memory, which also causes it to disappear from the taskbar. The advantage of minimizing an application or folder is that you can return to it immediately with the click of the mouse. The disadvantage is that too many open applications will eventually degrade the performance of a system.

Step 5: Capture a Screen

- Prove to your instructor that you have sized the window correctly by capturing the desktop that currently appears on your monitor. Press the **Print Screen key** to copy the current screen display to the **clipboard**, an area of memory that is available to every application.
- Nothing appears to have happened, but the screen has in fact been copied to the clipboard and can be pasted into a Word document. Click the **Start button**, click the **All Programs command**, then start **Microsoft Word** and begin a new document.
- Enter the title of your document (I Did My Homework) followed by your name as shown in Figure 7e. Press the **Enter key** two or three times to leave blank lines after your name.
- Pull down the **Edit menu** and click the **Paste command** (or click the **Paste button** on the Standard toolbar) to copy the contents of the clipboard into the Word document.
- Print this document for your instructor. There is no need to save this document. Exit Word.

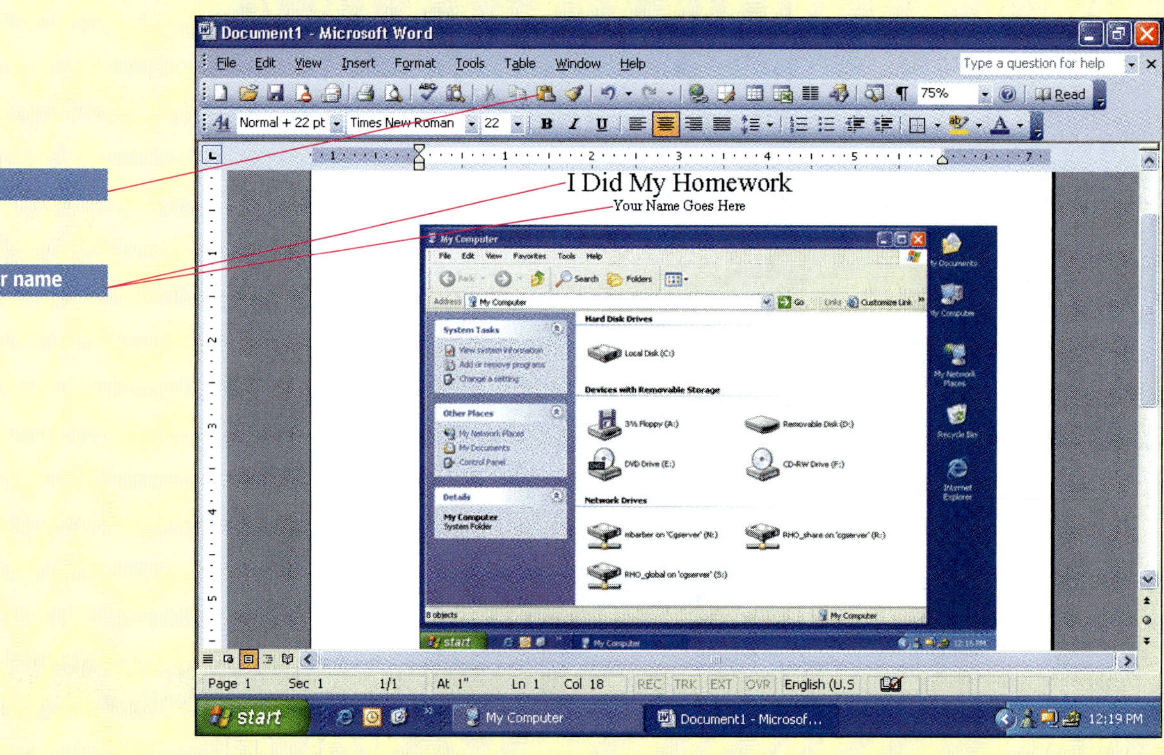

(e) Capture a Screen (step 5)

FIGURE 7 Hands-on Exercise 1 (*continued*)

THE FORMAT PICTURE COMMAND

Use the Format Picture command to facilitate moving and/or sizing an object within a Word document. Right click the picture to display a context-sensitive menu, then click the Format Picture command to display the associated dialog box. Click the Layout tab, choose any layout other than Inline with text, and click OK. You can now click and drag the picture to position it elsewhere within the document.

Step 6: Format a Floppy Disk

- Place a floppy disk into drive A. Select (click) **drive A** in the My Computer window, then pull down the **File menu** and click the **Format command** to display the Format dialog box in Figure 7f.
  - Set the **Capacity** to match the floppy disk you purchased (1.44MB for a high-density disk and 720KB for a double-density disk. The easiest way to determine the type of disk is to look for the label HD or DD, respectively.).
  - Click the **Volume label text box** if it's empty, or click and drag over the existing label if there is an entry. Enter a new label (containing up to 11 characters), such as **Bob's Disk**.
  - You can check the **Quick Format box** if the disk has been previously formatted, as a convenient way to erase the contents of the disk.
- Click the **Start button,** then click **OK**—after you have read the warning message—to begin the formatting operation. The formatting process erases anything that is on the disk, so be sure that you do not need anything on the disk.
- Click **OK** after the formatting is complete. Close the dialog box, then save the formatted disk for the next exercise. Close the My Computer window.

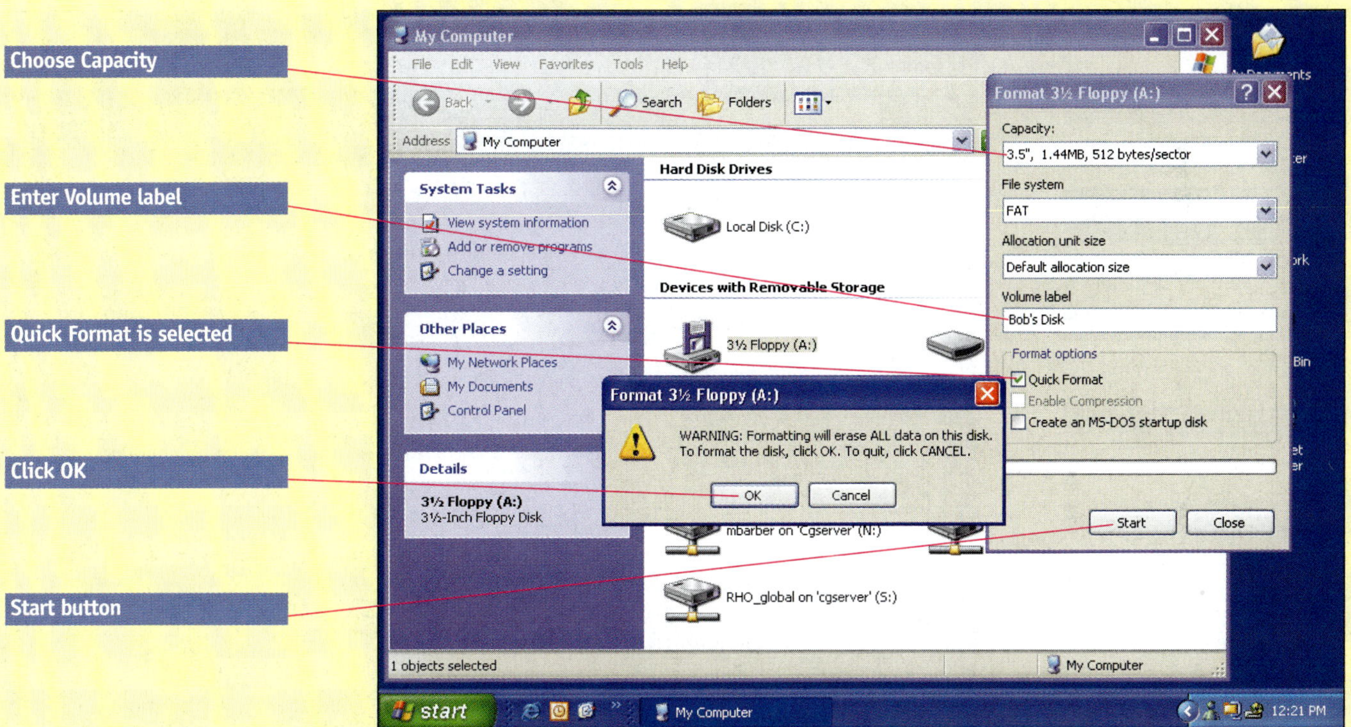

(f) Format a Floppy Disk (step 6)

FIGURE 7 Hands-on Exercise 1 (*continued*)

THE DEMISE OF THE FLOPPY DISK

You may be surprised to discover that your system no longer has a floppy disk drive, but it is only the latest victim in the march of technology. Long-playing records have come and gone. So too have 8-track tapes and the laser disk. The 3½-inch floppy disk has had a long and successful run, but it, too, is slated for obsolescence with Dell's recent announcement that it will no longer include a floppy drive as a standard component in desktop systems. Still, the floppy disk will "live forever" in the Save button that has the floppy disk as its icon.

Step 7: The Help and Support Center

- Click the **Start button**, then click the **Help and Support command** to open the Help and Support Center. Click the **Index button** to open the index pane. The insertion point moves automatically to the text box where you enter the search topic.
- Type **help**, which automatically moves you to the available topics within the index. Double click **central location for Help** to display the information in the right pane as shown in Figure 7g.
- Toggle the display of the subtopics on and off by clicking the plus and minus sign, respectively. Click the **plus sign** next to Remote Assistance, for example, and the topic opens. Click the **minus sign** next to Tours and articles, and the topic closes.
- Right click anywhere within the right pane to display the context-sensitive menu shown in Figure 7g. Click the **Print command** to print this information for your instructor.
- Close the Help and Support window.

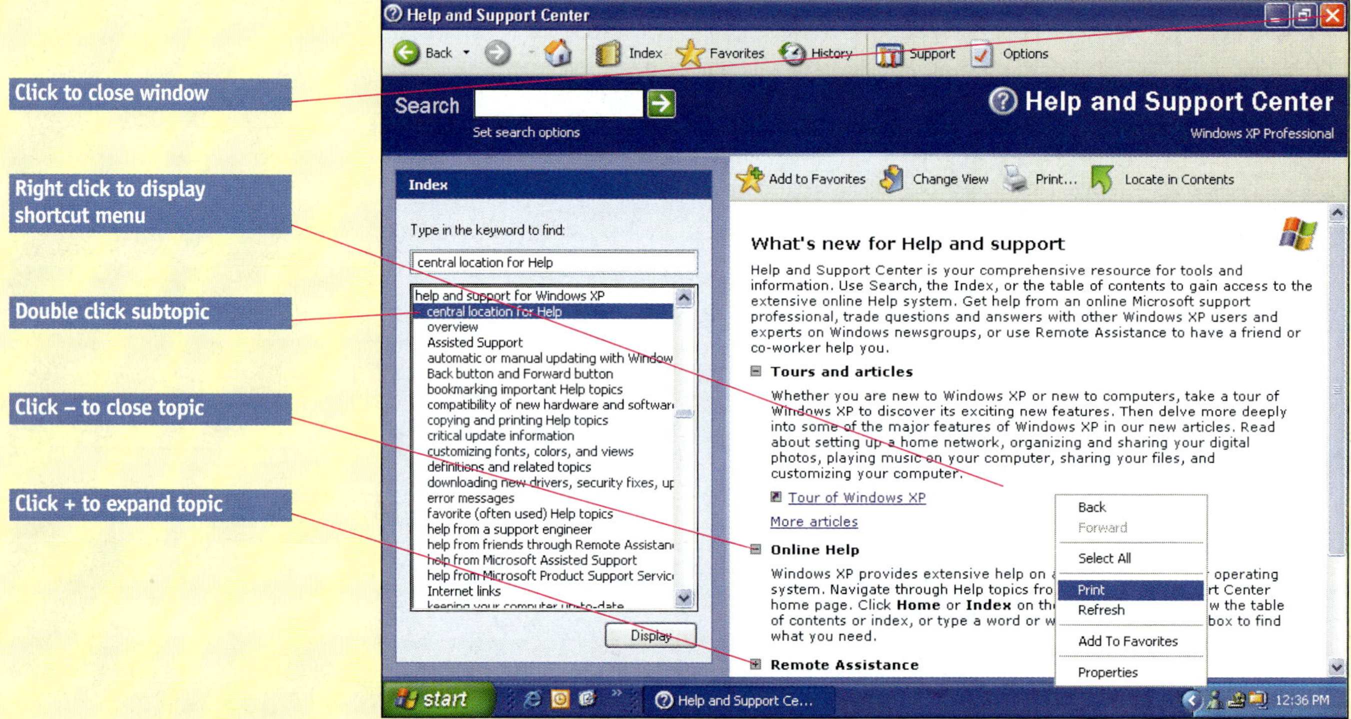

(g) The Help and Support Center (step 7)

FIGURE 7 Hands-on Exercise 1 (*continued*)

THE FAVORITES BUTTON

Do you find yourself continually searching for the same information? If so, you can make life a little easier by adding the page to a list of favorite help topics. Start the Help and Support Center, use the Index button to display the desired information in the right pane, and then click the Add to Favorites button to add the topic to your list of favorites. You can return to the topic at any time by clicking the Favorites button at the top of the Help and Support window, then double clicking the bookmark.

Step 8: Log (or Turn) Off the Computer

- It is very important that you log off properly, as opposed to just turning off the power. This enables Windows to close all of its system files and to save any changes that were made during the session.
- Click the **Start button** to display the Start menu in Figure 7h, then click the **Log Off button** at the bottom of the menu. You will see a dialog box asking whether you want to log off or switch users.
  - Switching users leaves your session active. All of your applications remain open, but control of the computer is given to another user. You can subsequently log back on (after the new user logs off) and take up exactly where you left off.
  - Logging off ends your session, but leaves the computer running at full power. This is the typical option you would select in a laboratory setting at school.
- To turn the computer off, you have to log off as just described, then select the **Turn Computer Off command** from the login screen. Welcome to Windows XP!

Click Log Off

Click Start button

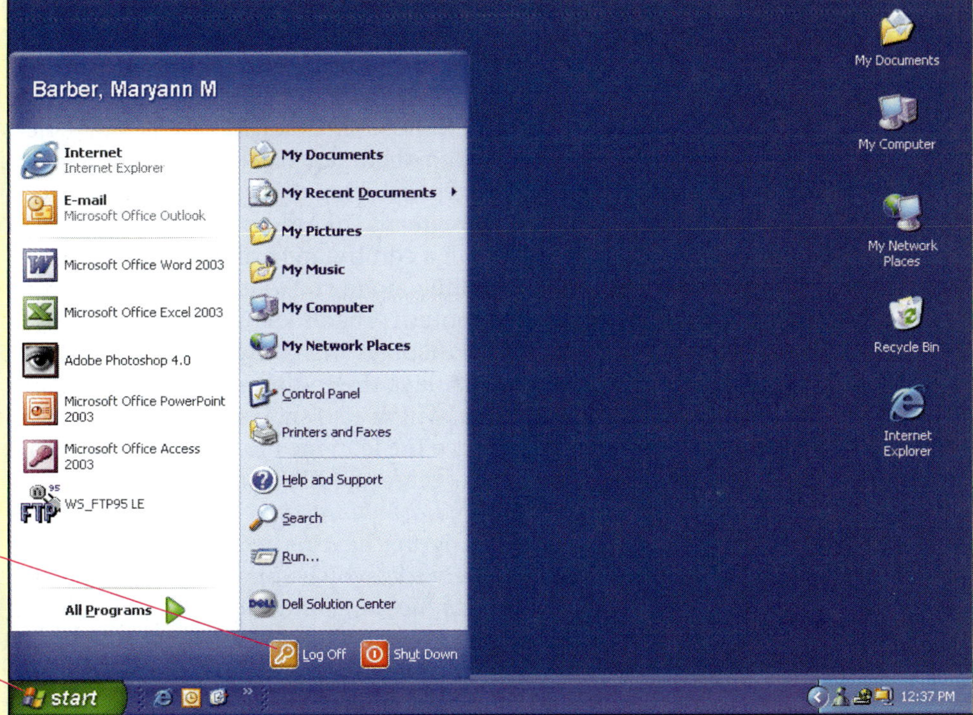

(h) Log (or Turn) Off Computer (step 8)

FIGURE 7 Hands-on Exercise 1 (*continued*)

THE TASK MANAGER

The Start button is the normal way to exit Windows. Occasionally, however, an application may "hang"—in which case you want to close the problem application but continue with your session. Press Ctrl+Alt+Del to display the Windows Task Manager dialog box, then click the Applications tab. Select the problem application (it will most likely say "not responding"), and click the End Task button. This capability is often disabled in a school setting.

A ***file*** is a set of instructions or data that has been given a name and stored on disk. There are two basic types of files, ***program files*** and ***data files***. Microsoft Word and Microsoft Excel are examples of program files. The documents and workbooks that are created by these programs are data files. A program file is executable because it contains instructions that tell the computer what to do. A data file is not executable and can be used only in conjunction with a specific program. In other words, you execute program files to create and/or edit the associated data files.

Every file has a ***filename*** that identifies it to the operating system. The filename can contain up to 255 characters and may include spaces and other punctuation. (Filenames cannot contain the following characters: \, /, :, *, ?, “, <, >, and |.) We find it easier, however, to restrict the characters in a filename to letters, numbers, and spaces, as opposed to having to remember the special characters that are not permitted.

Files are kept in ***folders*** to better organize the thousands of files on a typical system. A Windows folder is similar to an ordinary manila folder that holds one or more documents. To continue the analogy, an office worker stores his or her documents in manila folders within a filing cabinet. Windows stores its files in electronic folders that are located on a disk, CD-ROM, or other device.

Many folders are created automatically by Windows XP, such as the My Computer or My Documents folders that are present on every system. Other folders are created whenever new software is installed. Additional folders are created by the user to hold the documents he or she creates. You might, for example, create a folder for your word processing documents and a second folder for your spreadsheets. You could also create a folder to hold all of your work for a specific class, which in turn might contain a combination of word processing documents and spreadsheets. The choice is entirely up to you, and you can use any system that makes sense to you. A folder can contain program files, data files, or even other folders.

Figure 8 displays the contents of a hypothetical folder with nine documents. Figure 8a displays the folder in ***Tiles view***. Figure 8b displays the same folder in ***Details view***, which also shows the date the file was created or last modified. Both views display a file icon next to each file to indicate the ***file type*** or application that was used to create the file. *Introduction to E-mail*, for example, is a PowerPoint presentation. *Basic Financial Functions* is an Excel workbook.

The two figures have more similarities than differences, such as the name of the folder (*Homework*), which appears in the title bar next to the icon of an open folder. The Minimize, Restore, and Close buttons are found at the right of the title bar. A menu bar with six pull-down menus appears below the title bar. The Standard Buttons toolbar is below the menu, and the Address bar (indicating the drive and folder) appears below the toolbar. Both folders also contain a task pane that provides easy access to common tasks for the folder or selected object.

Look closely and you will see that the task panes are significantly different. This is because there are no documents selected in Figure 8a, whereas the *Milestones in Communications* document is selected (highlighted) in Figure 8b. Thus, the File and Folder Tasks area in Figure 8a pertains to folders in general, whereas the available tasks in Figure 8b are pertinent to the selected document. The Details areas in the two task panes are also consistent with the selected objects and display information about the Homework folder and selected document, respectively. A status bar appears at the bottom of both windows and displays the contents of the selected object.

The last difference between the task panes reflects the user's preference to open or close the Other Places area. Click the upward chevron in Figure 8a to suppress the display and gain space in the task pane, or click the downward chevron in Figure 8b to display the specific links to other places. The task pane is new to Windows XP and did not appear in previous versions of Windows.

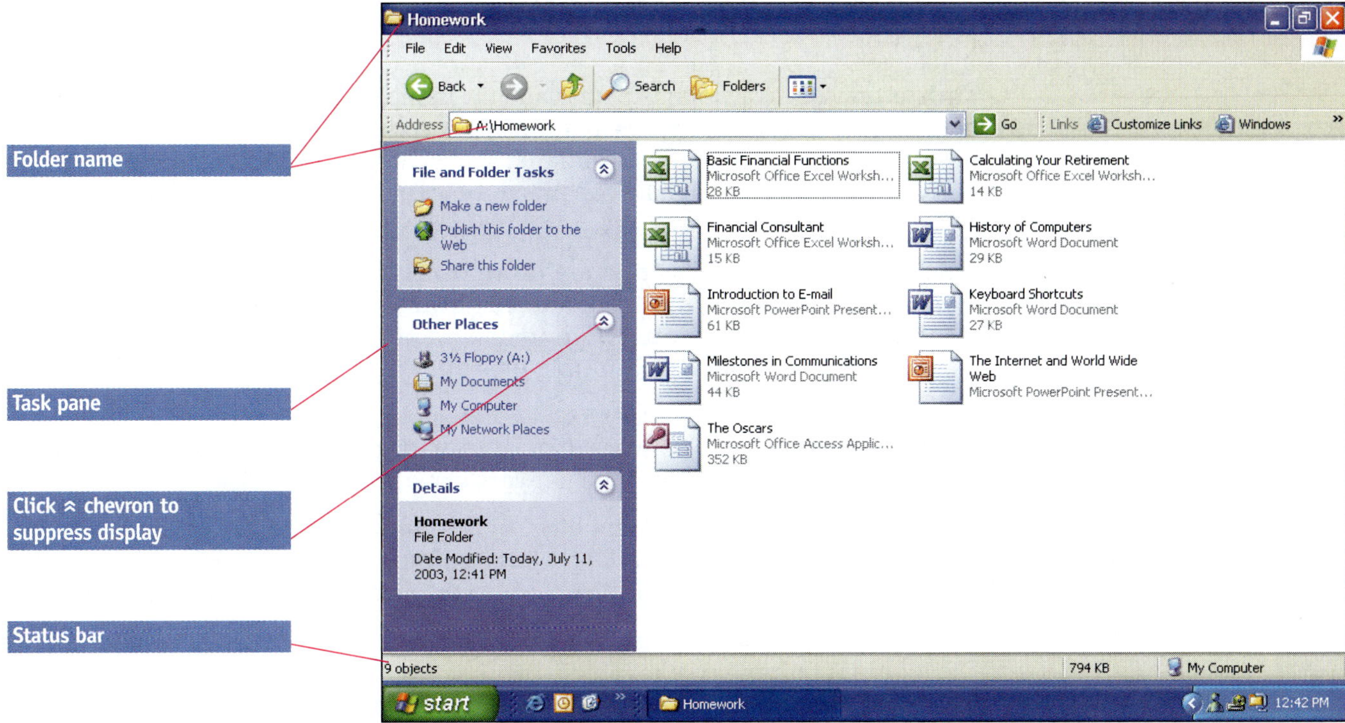

(a) Tiles View

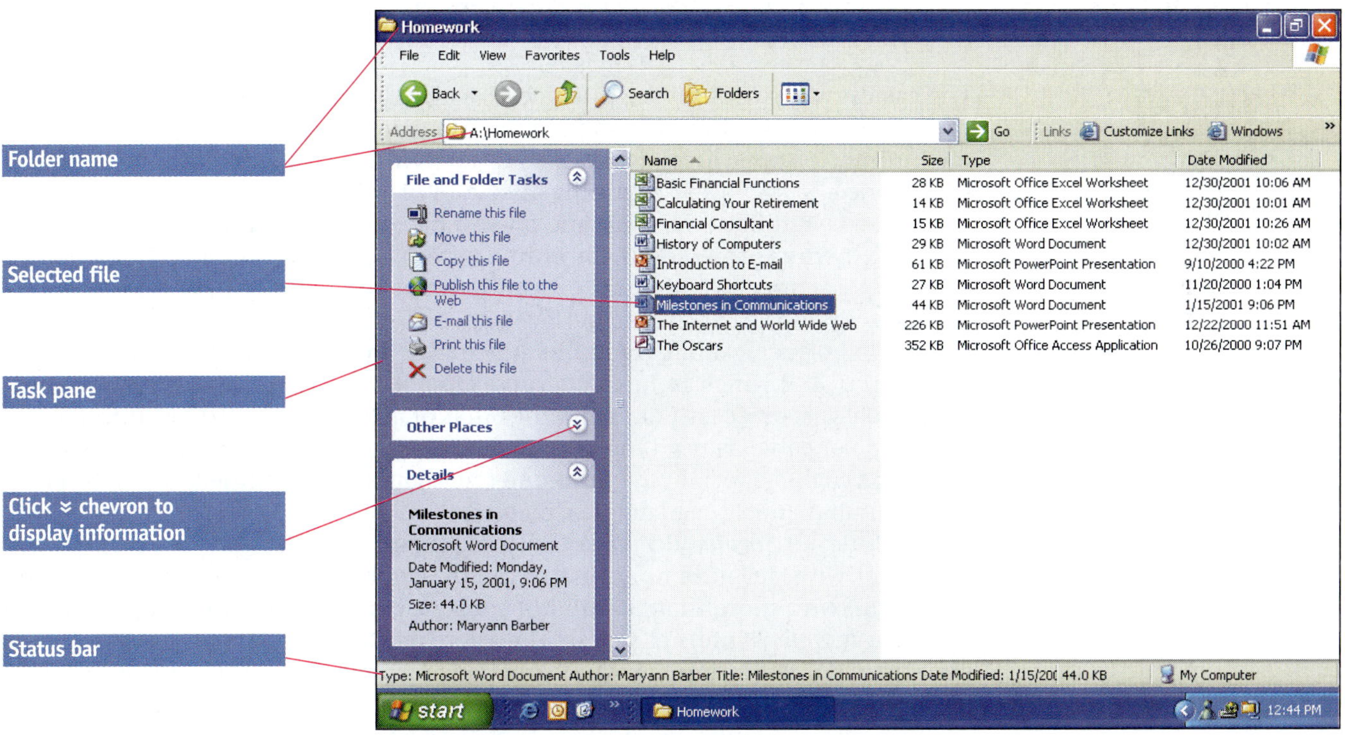

(b) Details View

FIGURE 8 Files and Folders

THE EXPLORING OFFICE PRACTICE FILES

There is only one way to master disk and file management and that is to practice at the computer. To do so requires that you have a series of files with which to work. We have created these files for you, and we use the files in the next two hands-on exercises. Your instructor will make the practice files available to you in different ways:

- The files can be downloaded from our Web site at www.prenhall.com/grauer. Software and other files that are downloaded from the Internet are typically compressed (made smaller) to reduce the amount of time it takes to transmit the file. In essence, you will download a single ***compressed file*** and then uncompress the file into multiple files onto a local drive as described in the next hands-on exercise.
- The files may be on a network drive at your school or university, in which case you can copy the files from the network drive to a floppy disk.
- There may be an actual "data disk" in the computer lab. Go to the lab with a floppy disk, then use the Copy Disk command (on the File menu of My Computer when drive A is selected) to duplicate the data disk and create a copy for yourself.

It doesn't matter how you obtain the practice files, only that you are able to do so. Indeed, you may want to try different techniques to gain additional practice with Windows XP. Note, too, that Windows XP provides a ***firewall*** to protect your computer from unauthorized access while it is connected to the Internet. (See exercise 2 at the end of the chapter.)

CONNECTING TO THE INTERNET

The easiest way to obtain the practice files is to download the files from the Web, which requires an Internet connection. There are two basic ways to connect to the Internet—from a local area network (LAN) or by dialing in. It's much easier if you connect from a LAN (typically at school or work) since the installation and setup have been done for you, and all you have to do is follow the instructions provided by your professor. If you connect from home, you will need a modem, a cable modem, or a DSL modem, and an Internet Service Provider (or ISP).

A ***modem*** is the hardware interface between your computer and the telephone system. In essence, you instruct the modem, via the appropriate software, to connect to your ISP, which in turn lets you access the Internet. A cable modem provides high-speed access (20 to 30 times that of an ordinary modem) through the same type of cable as used for cable TV. A DSL modem also provides high-speed access through a special type of phone line that lets you connect to the Internet while simultaneously carrying on a conversation.

An ***Internet Service Provider*** is a company or organization that maintains a computer with permanent access to the Internet. America Online (AOL) is the largest ISP with more than 30 million subscribers, and it provides a proprietary interface as well as Internet access. The Microsoft Network (MSN) is a direct competitor to AOL. Alternatively, you can choose from a host of other vendors who provide Internet access without the proprietary interface of AOL or MSN.

Regardless of which vendor you choose as an ISP, be sure you understand the fee structure. The monthly fee may entitle you to a set number of hours per month (after which you pay an additional fee), or it may give you unlimited access. The terms vary widely, and you should shop around for the best possible deal. Price is not the only consideration, however. Reliability of service is also important. Be sure that the equipment of your provider is adequate so that you can obtain access whenever you want.

hands-on exercise

2 Download the Practice Files

Objective To download a file from the Web and practice basic file commands. The exercise requires a formatted floppy disk and access to the Internet. Use Figure 9 as a guide.

Step 1: **Start Internet Explorer**

- Click the **Start button**, click the **All Programs command**, and then click **Internet Explorer** to start the program. If necessary, click the **Maximize button** so that Internet Explorer takes the entire desktop.
- Click anywhere within the **Address bar**, which automatically selects the current address (so that whatever you type replaces the current address). Enter **www.prenhall.com/grauer** (the http:// is assumed). Press **Enter**.
- You should see the Exploring Office Series home page as shown in Figure 9a. Click the book for **Office 2003**, which takes you to the Office 2003 home page.
- Click the **Student Downloads tab** (at the top of the window) to go to the Student Download page.

Enter www.prenhall.com/grauer in Address bar

Click book for Office 2003

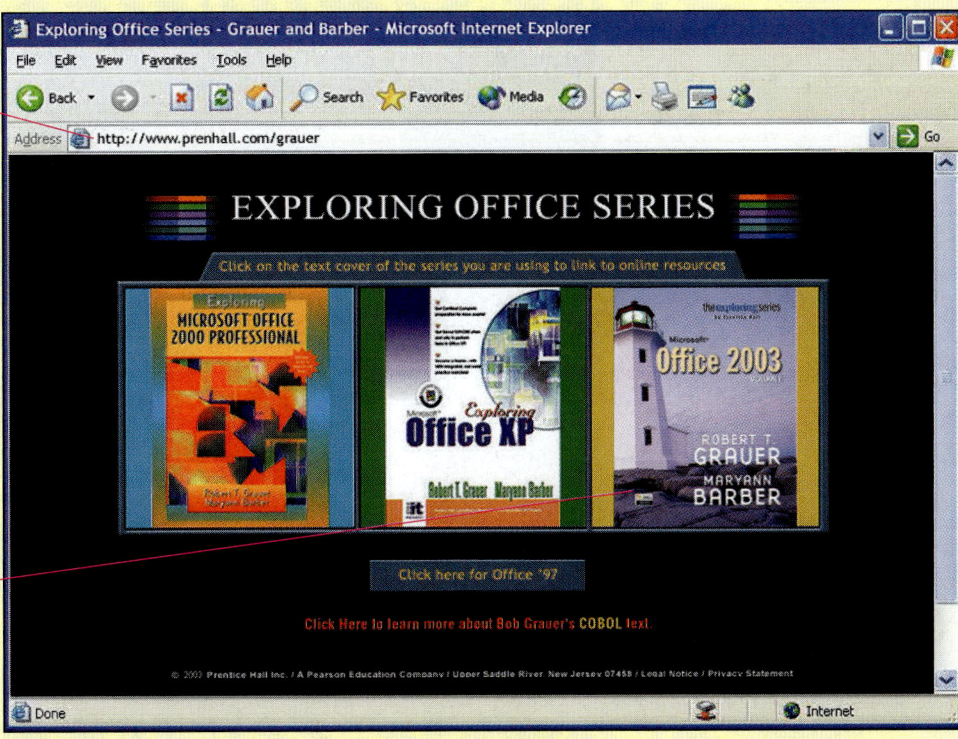

(a) Start Internet Explorer (step 1)

FIGURE 9 Hands-on Exercise 2

A NEW INTERNET EXPLORER

The installation of Windows XP automatically installs a new version of Internet Explorer. Pull down the Help menu and click the About Internet Explorer command to display the current release (version 6.0). Click OK to close the About Internet Explorer window.

Step 2: Download the Practice Files

- You should see the Student Download page in Figure 9b. Place the formatted floppy disk from the first exercise in drive A. Be sure there are no files on this disk.
- Scroll down the page until you see the link to the student data disk for **Windows XP**. Click the link to download the practice files.
- You will see the File Download dialog box, asking what you want to do. Click the **Save button** to display the Save As dialog box. Click the **drop-down arrow** on the Save in list box, and select (click) **drive A**.
- Click **Save** to download the file. The File Download window may reappear and show you the status of the downloading operation as it takes place.
- If necessary, click **Close** when you see the dialog box indicating that the download is complete. Minimize Internet Explorer.

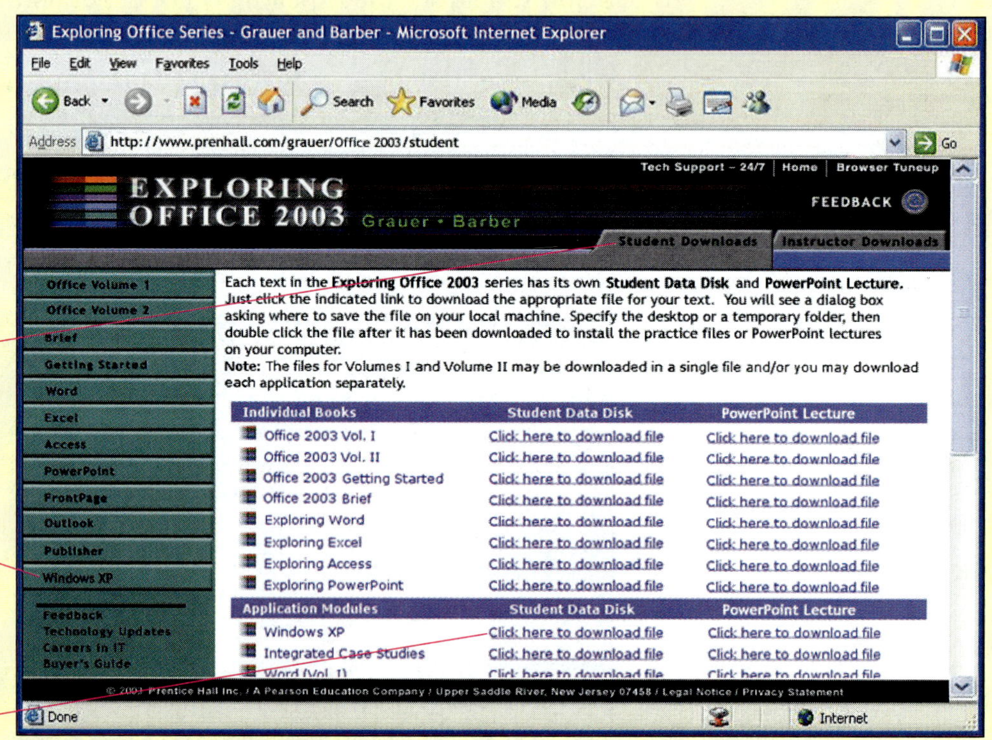

(b) Download the Practice Files (step 2)

FIGURE 9 Hands-on Exercise 2 (*continued*)

EXPLORE OUR WEB SITE

The Exploring Office Series Web site offers an online study guide (multiple-choice, true/false, and matching questions) for each individual textbook to help you review the material in each chapter. You can take practice quizzes by yourself and/or e-mail the results to your instructor. These online study guides are available via the tabs in the left navigation bar. You can return to the Student Download page at any time by clicking the tab toward the top of the window and/or you can click the link to Home to return to the home page for the Office 2003 Series. And finally, you can click the Feedback button at the top of the screen to send a message directly to Bob Grauer.

Step 3: Install the Practice Files

- Click the **Start button**, then click the **My Computer command** on the menu to open the My Computer folder. If necessary, click the Maximize button so that the My Computer window takes up the entire desktop. Change to the **Details view**.
- Click the icon for **drive A** to select it. The description of drive A appears at the left of the window. Double click the icon for **drive A** to open this drive. The contents of the My Computer window are replaced by the contents of drive A as shown in Figure 9c.
- Double click the **XPData file** to install the practice files, which displays the dialog box in Figure 9c. When you have finished reading, click **OK** to continue the installation and display the WinZip Self-Extractor dialog box.
- Check that the Unzip To Folder text box specifies **A:** to extract the files to the floppy disk. Click the **Unzip button** to extract (uncompress) the practice files and copy them onto the designated drive.
- Click **OK** after you see the message indicating that the files have been unzipped successfully. Close the WinZip dialog box.

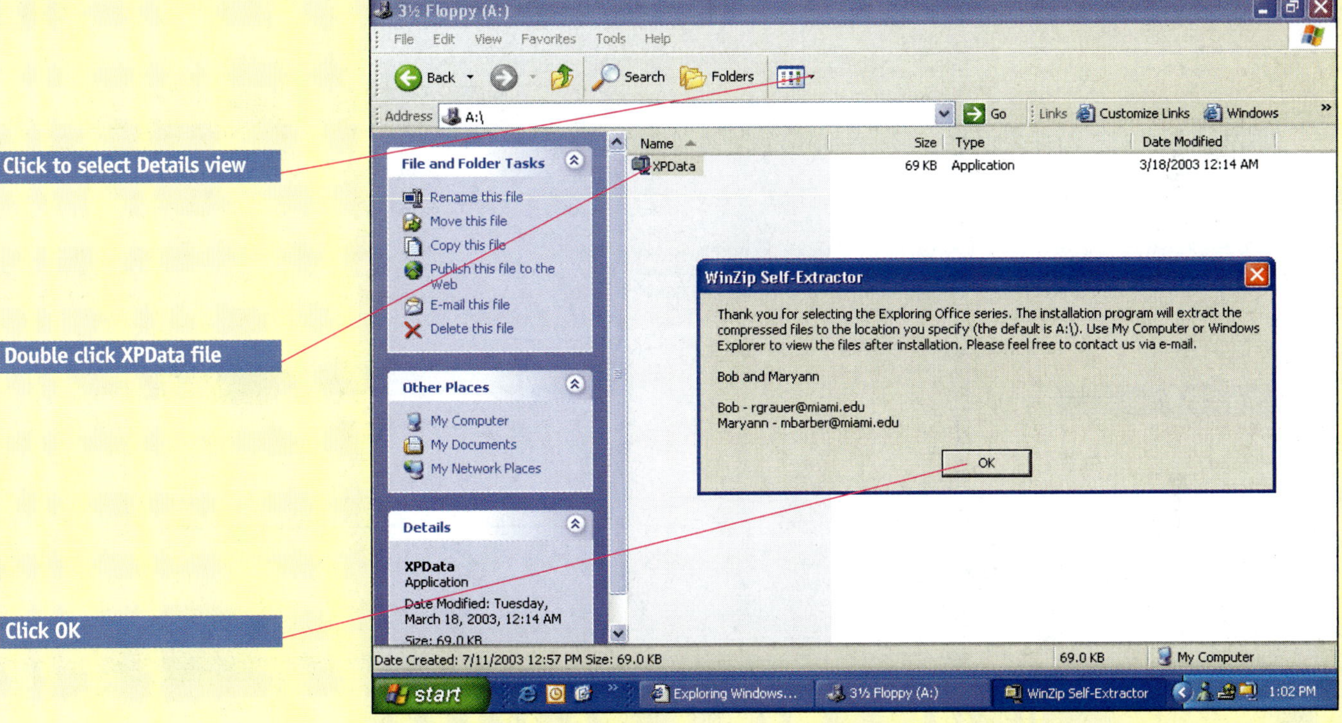

(c) Install the Practice Files (step 3)

FIGURE 9 Hands-on Exercise 2 (*continued*)

DOWNLOADING A FILE

Software and other files are typically compressed (made smaller) to reduce the amount of storage space the files require on disk and/or the time it takes to download the files. In essence, you download a compressed file (which may contain multiple individual files), then you uncompress (expand) the file on your local drive to access the individual files. After the file has been expanded, it is no longer needed and can be deleted.

Step 4: Delete the Compressed File

- The practice files have been extracted to drive A and should appear in the Drive A window. If you do not see the files, pull down the **View menu** and click the **Refresh command**.
- If necessary, pull down the **View menu** and click **Details** to change to the Details view in Figure 9e. You should see a total of eight files in the drive A window. Seven of these are the practice files on the data disk. The eighth file is the original file that you downloaded earlier. This file is no longer necessary, since it has been already been expanded.
- Select (click) the **XPData file**. Click the **Delete this file command** in the task pane (or simply press the **Del key**). Pause for a moment to be sure you want to delete this file, then click **Yes** when asked to confirm the deletion as shown in Figure 9d.
- The XPData file is permanently deleted from drive A. (Items deleted from a floppy disk or network drive are not sent to the Recycle bin, and cannot be recovered.)

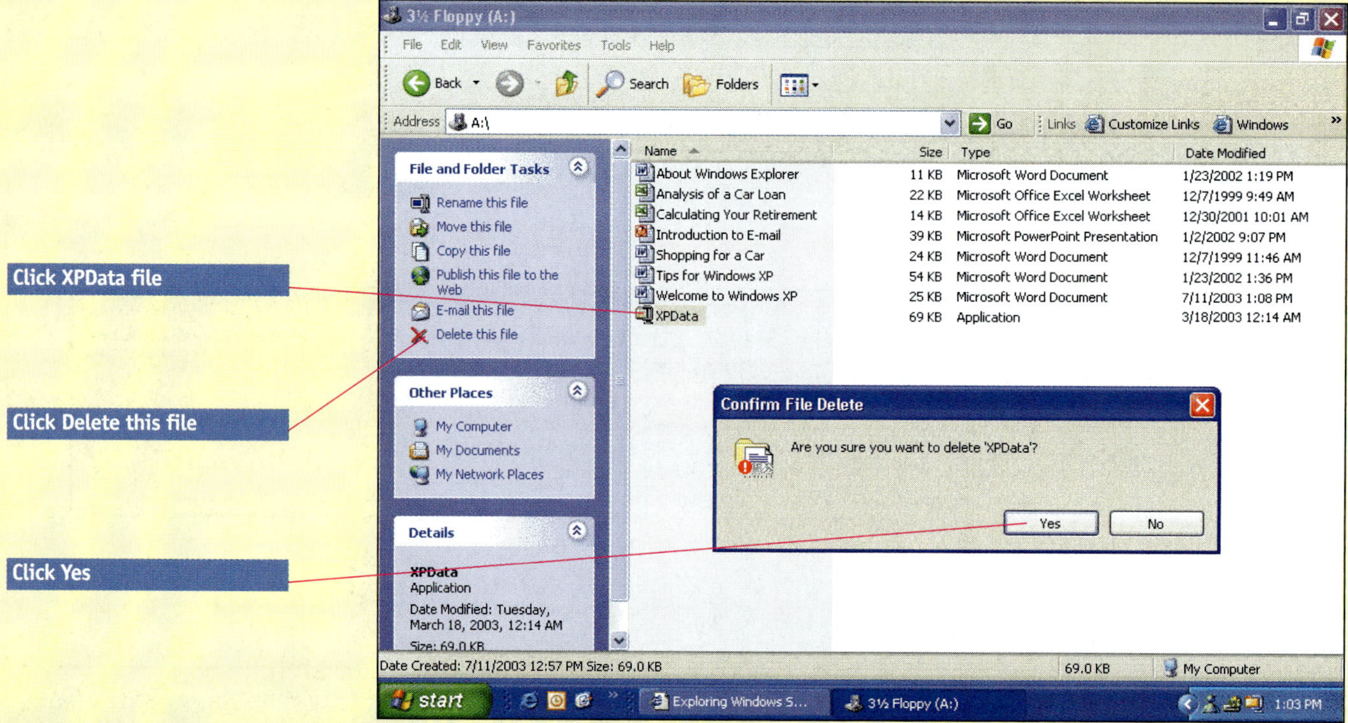

(d) Delete the Compressed File (step 4)

FIGURE 9 Hands-on Exercise 2 (*continued*)

SORT BY NAME, DATE, FILE TYPE, OR SIZE

The files in a folder can be displayed in ascending or descending sequence, by name, date modified, file type, or size, by clicking the appropriate column heading. Click Size, for example, to display files in the order of their size. Click the column heading a second time to reverse the sequence; that is, to switch from ascending to descending, and vice versa. Click a different column heading to display the files in a different sequence.

Step 5: Modify a Document

- Double click the **Welcome to Windows XP** document from within My Computer to open the document as shown in Figure 9e. (The document will open in the WordPad accessory if Microsoft Word is not installed on your machine.)
- Maximize the window for Microsoft Word. Read the document, and then press **Ctrl+End** to move to the end of the document. Do not be concerned if your screen does not match ours exactly.
- Add the sentence shown in Figure 9e, press the **Enter key** twice, then type your name. Click the **Save button** on the Standard toolbar to save the document.
- Pull down the **File menu**, click the **Print command**, and click **OK** (or click the **Print button** on the Standard toolbar) to print the document and prove to your instructor that you did the exercise.
- Pull down the **File menu** and click **Exit** to close Microsoft Word. You should be back in the My Computer folder.

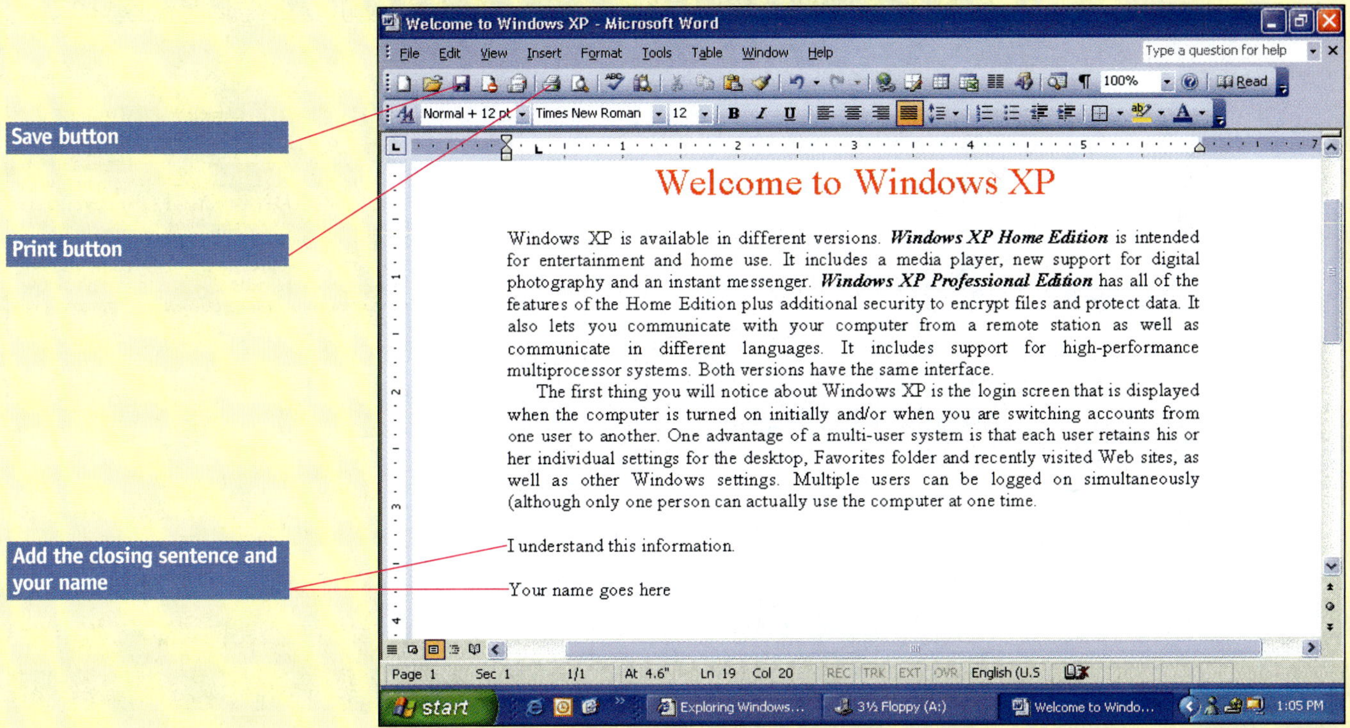

(e) Modify a Document (step 5)

FIGURE 9 Hands-on Exercise 2 (*continued*)

THE DOCUMENT, NOT THE APPLICATION

The Windows operating system is document oriented, which means that you are able to think in terms of the document rather than the application that created it. You can still open a document in traditional fashion, by starting the application that created the document, then using the File Open command in that program to retrieve the document. It's often easier, however, to open the document from within a folder by double clicking its icon. Windows will start the associated application and then open the document for you.

Step 6: Create a New Folder

- Look closely at the date and time that are displayed next to the Welcome to Windows XP document in Figure 9f. It should show today's date and the current time (give or take a minute) because that is when the document was last modified. Your date will be different from ours.
- Look closely and see that Figure 9f also contains an eighth document, called "Backup of Welcome to Windows XP." This is a backup copy of the original document that will be created automatically by Microsoft Word if the appropriate options are in effect. (See the boxed tip below.)
- Click **a blank area** in the right pane to deselect the Welcome to Windows XP document. The commands in the File and Folder Tasks area change to basic folder operations.
- Click the command to **Make a New folder**, which creates a new folder with the default name "New Folder". Enter **New Car** as the new name. You will move files into this folder in step 7.

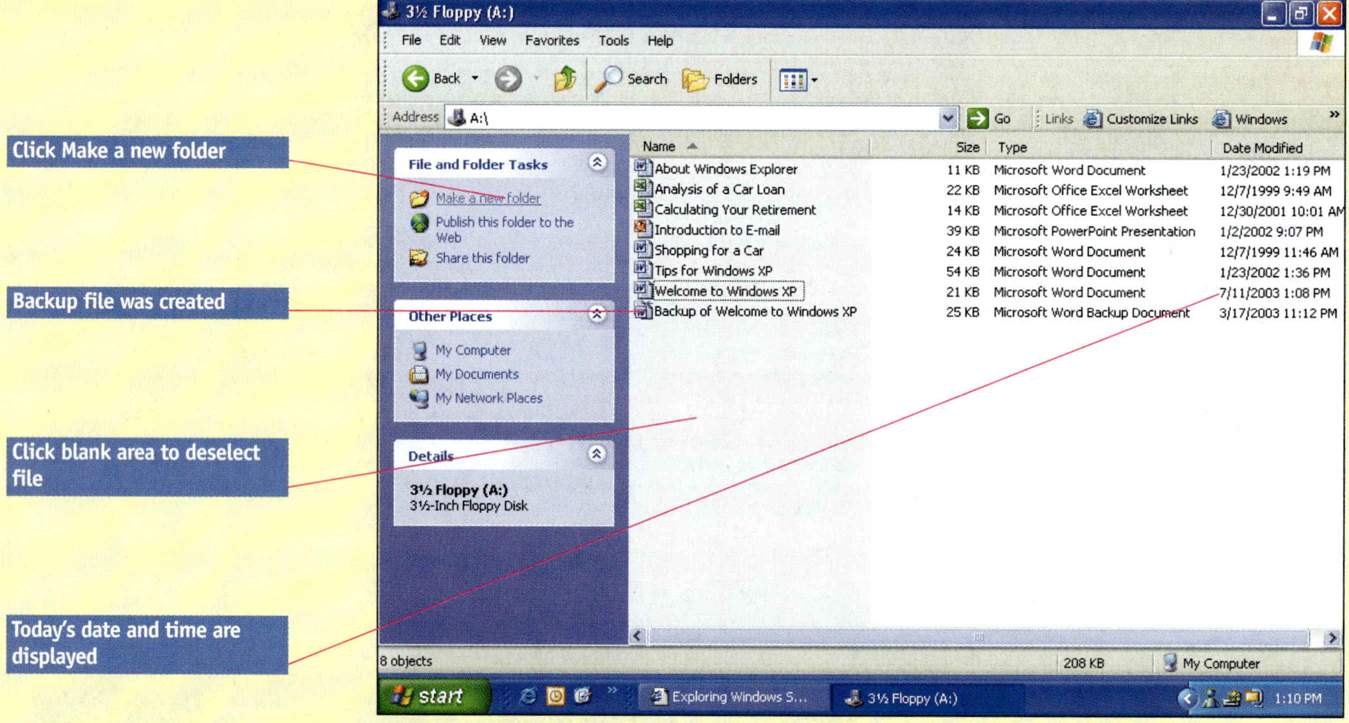

(f) Create a New Folder (step 6)

FIGURE 9 Hands-on Exercise 2 (*continued*)

USE WORD TO CREATE A BACKUP COPY

Microsoft Word enables you to automatically keep the previous version of a document as a backup copy. The next time you are in Microsoft Word, pull down the Tools menu, click the Options command, click the Save tab, then check the box to Always create backup copy. Every time you save a file from this point on, the previously saved version is renamed "Backup of document," and the document in memory is saved as the current version. The disk will contain the two most recent versions of the document, enabling you to retrieve the previous version if necessary.

Step 7: Move the Files

- There are different ways to move a file from one folder to another. The most basic technique is to
  - Select (click) the **Analysis of a Car Loan** workbook to highlight the file, then click the **Move this file command** in the task pane.
  - You will see the Move Items dialog box in Figure 9g. Click the plus sign (if it appears) next to the 3½ floppy disk to expand the disk and view its folders. Click the **New Car folder**, then click the **Move button**.
  - The selected file is moved to the New Car folder and the dialog box closes. The Analysis of a Car Loan document no longer appears in the right pane of Figure 9g because it has been moved to a new folder.
- If the source and destination folders are both on the same drive, as in this example, you can simply click and drag the file to its new destination. Thus, click and drag the **Shopping for a Car** Word document to the New Car folder. Release the mouse when the file is directly over the folder to complete the move.
- Double click the **New Car folder** to view the contents of this folder, which should contain both documents. The Address bar now says A:\New Car.

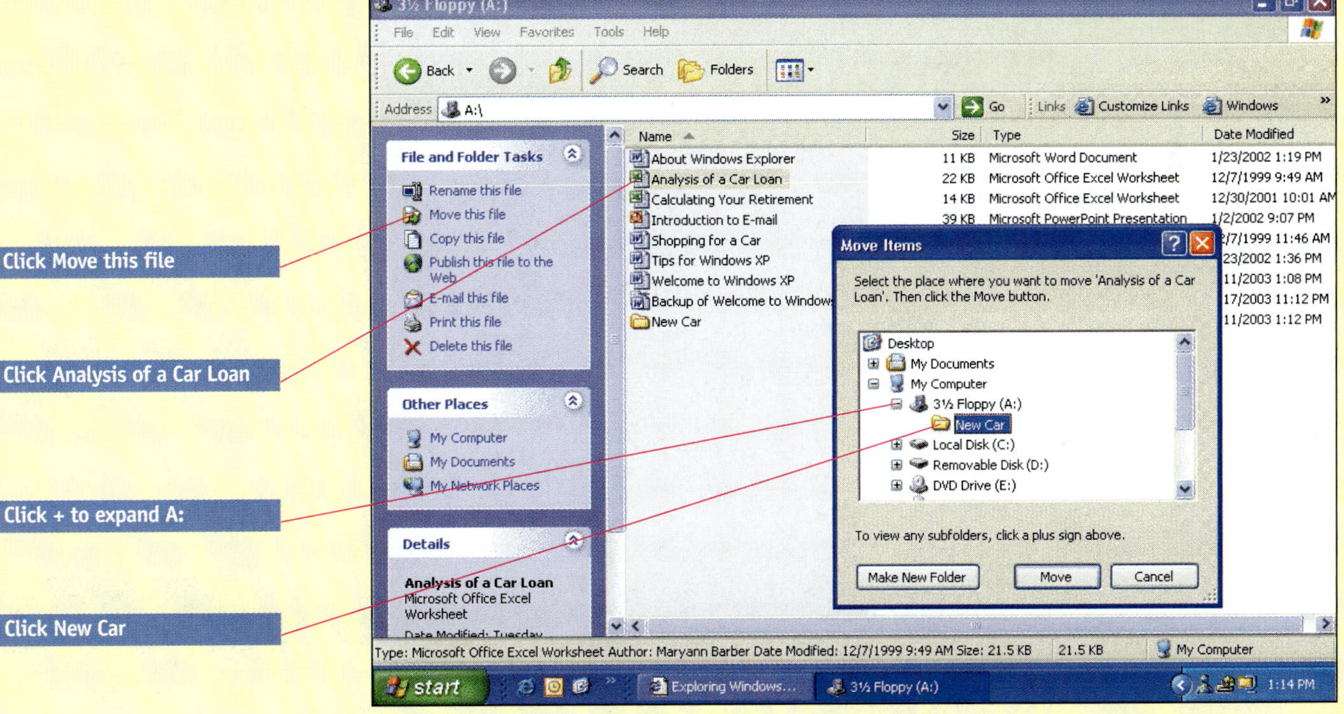

(g) Move the Files (step 7)

FIGURE 9 Hands-on Exercise 2 (*continued*)

THE PLUS AND MINUS SIGNS

Any drive, be it local or on the network, may be expanded or collapsed to display or hide its folders. A minus sign indicates that the drive has been expanded and that its folders are visible. A plus sign indicates the reverse; that is, the device is collapsed and its folders are not visible. Click either sign to toggle to the other. Clicking a plus sign, for example, expands the drive, then displays a minus sign next to the drive to indicate that the folders are visible. Clicking a minus sign has the reverse effect.

Step 8: A Look Ahead

- Click the **Folders button** to display a hierarchical view of the devices on your computer as shown in Figure 9h. This is the same screen that is displayed through Windows Explorer, a program that we will study after the exercise.
- The Folders button functions as a toggle switch; click the button a second time and the task pane (also called task panel) returns. Click the **Folders button** to return to the hierarchical view.
- The New Car folder is selected (highlighted) in the left pane because this is the folder you were working in at the previous step. The contents of this folder are displayed in the right pane.
- Click the icon for the **3½ floppy drive** to display the contents of drive A. The right pane displays the files on drive A as well as the New Car folder.
- Close the My Computer folder. Close Internet Explorer. Log off if you do not want to continue with the next exercise at this time.

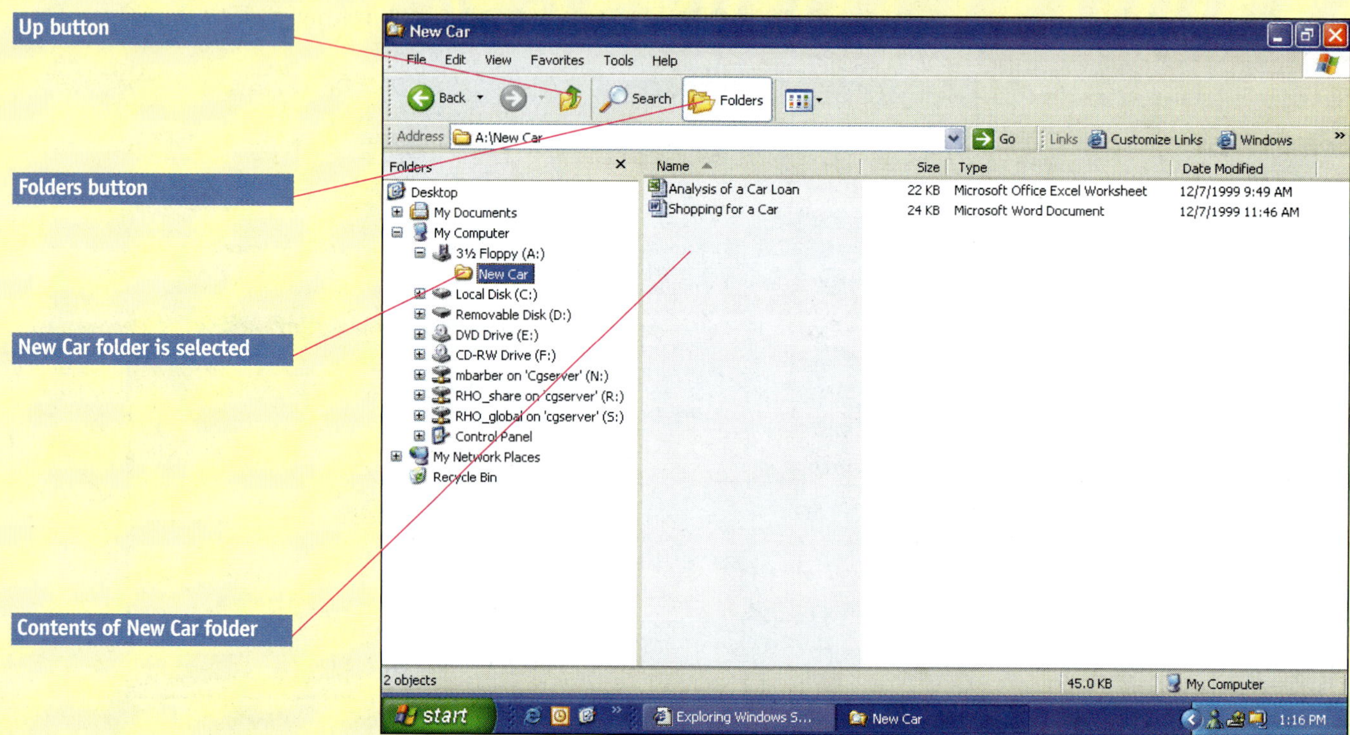

(h) A Look Ahead (step 8)

FIGURE 9 Hands-on Exercise 2 *(continued)*

NAVIGATING THE HIERARCHY

Click the Up button on the Standard Buttons toolbar to move up one level in the hierarchy in the left pane and display the associated contents in the right pane. Click the Up button when you are viewing the New Car folder, for example, and you are returned to drive A. Click the Up button a second time and you will see the contents of My Computer. Note, too, how the contents of the Address bar change each time you view a different folder in the right pane.

Windows Explorer is a program that displays a hierarchical (tree) structure of the devices on your system. Consider, for example, Figure 10a, which displays the contents of a hypothetical Homework folder as it exists on our computer. The hierarchy is displayed in the left pane, and the contents of the selected object (the Homework folder) are shown in the right pane. The advantage of viewing the folder in this way (as opposed to displaying the task pane) is that you see the location of the folder on the system; that is; the Homework folder is physically stored on drive A.

Let's explore the hierarchy in the left pane. There is a minus sign next to the icon for drive A to indicate that this drive has been expanded and thus you can see its folders. Drive C, however, has a plus sign to indicate that the drive is collapsed and that its contents are not visible. Look closely and you see that both drive A and drive C are indented under My Computer, which in turn is indented under the desktop. In other words, the desktop is at the top of the hierarchy and it contains the My Computer folder, which in turn contains drive A and drive C. The desktop also contains a My Documents folder, but the plus sign next to the My Documents folder indicates the folder is collapsed. My Computer, on the other hand, has a minus sign and you can see its contents, which consist of the drives on your system as well as other special folders (Control Panel and Shared Documents).

Look carefully at the icon next to the Homework folder in the left pane of the figure. The icon is an open folder, and it indicates that the (Homework) folder is the active folder. The folder's name is also shaded, and it appears in the title bar. Only one folder can be active at one time, and its contents are displayed in the right pane. The Milestones in Communications document is highlighted (selected) in the right pane, which means that subsequent commands will affect this document, as opposed to the entire folder. If you wanted to work with a different document in the Homework folder, you would select that document. To see the contents of a different folder, such as Financial Documents, you would select (click) the icon for that folder in the left pane (which automatically closes the Homework folder). The contents of the Financial Documents folder would then appear in the right pane.

You can create folders at any time just like the Homework and Financial Documents folders that we created on drive A. You can also create folders within folders; for example, a correspondence folder may contain two folders of its own, one for business correspondence and one for personal letters.

Personal Folders

Windows automatically creates a set of personal folders for every user. These include the ***My Documents folder*** and the ***My Pictures folder*** and ***My Music folder*** within the My Documents folder. The My Documents folder is collapsed in Figure 10a, but it is expanded in Figure 10b, and thus its contents are visible. The My Music folder is active, and its contents are visible in the right pane.

Every user has a unique set of personal folders, and thus Windows has to differentiate between the multiple "My Documents" folders that may exist. It does so by creating additional folders to hold the documents and settings for each user. Look closely at the Address bar in Figure 10b. Each back slash indicates a new folder, and you can read the complete path from right to left. Thus, the My Music folder that we are viewing is contained in My Documents folder within Maryann's folder, which in turn is stored in a Documents and Settings folder on drive C.

Fortunately, however, Windows does the housekeeping for you. All you have to do is locate the desired folder—for example, My Music or My Pictures—in the left pane, and Windows does the rest. ***Personal folders*** are just what the name implies—"personal," meaning that only one person has access to their content. Windows also provides a ***Shared Documents folder*** for files that Maryann may want to share with others.

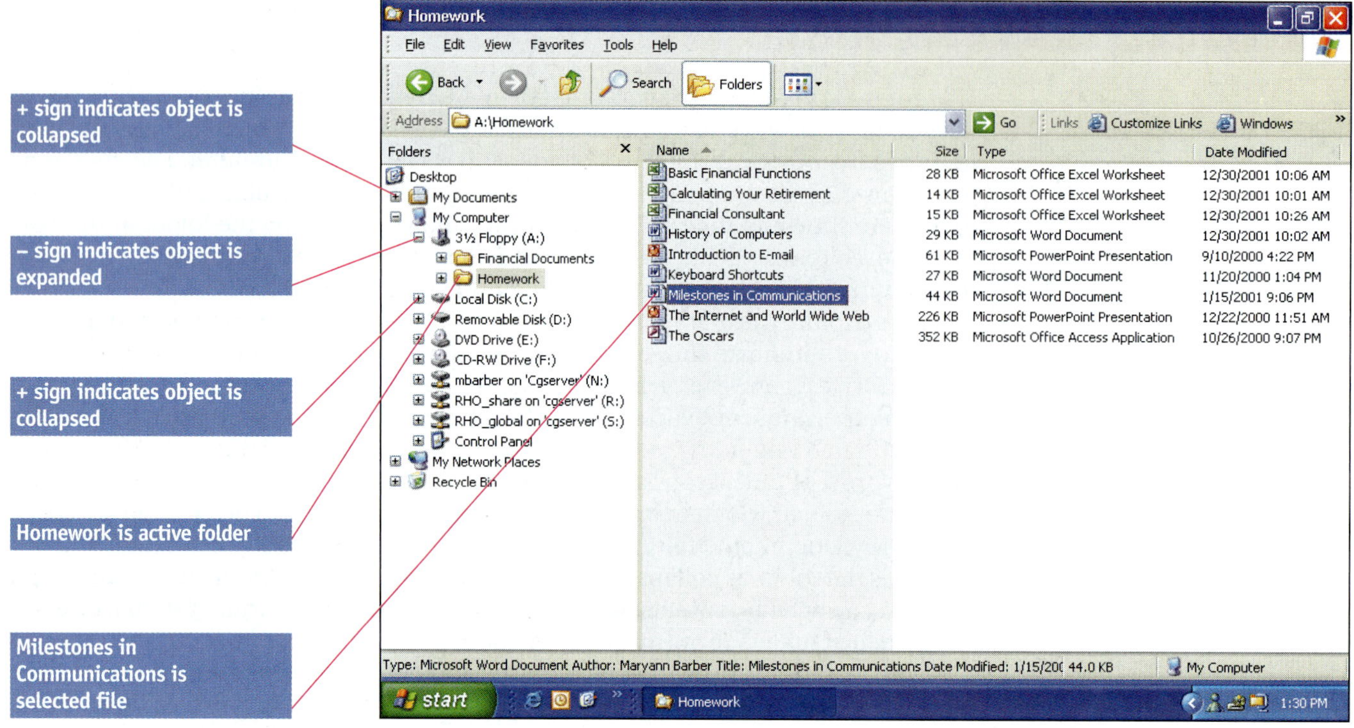

(a) Homework Folder

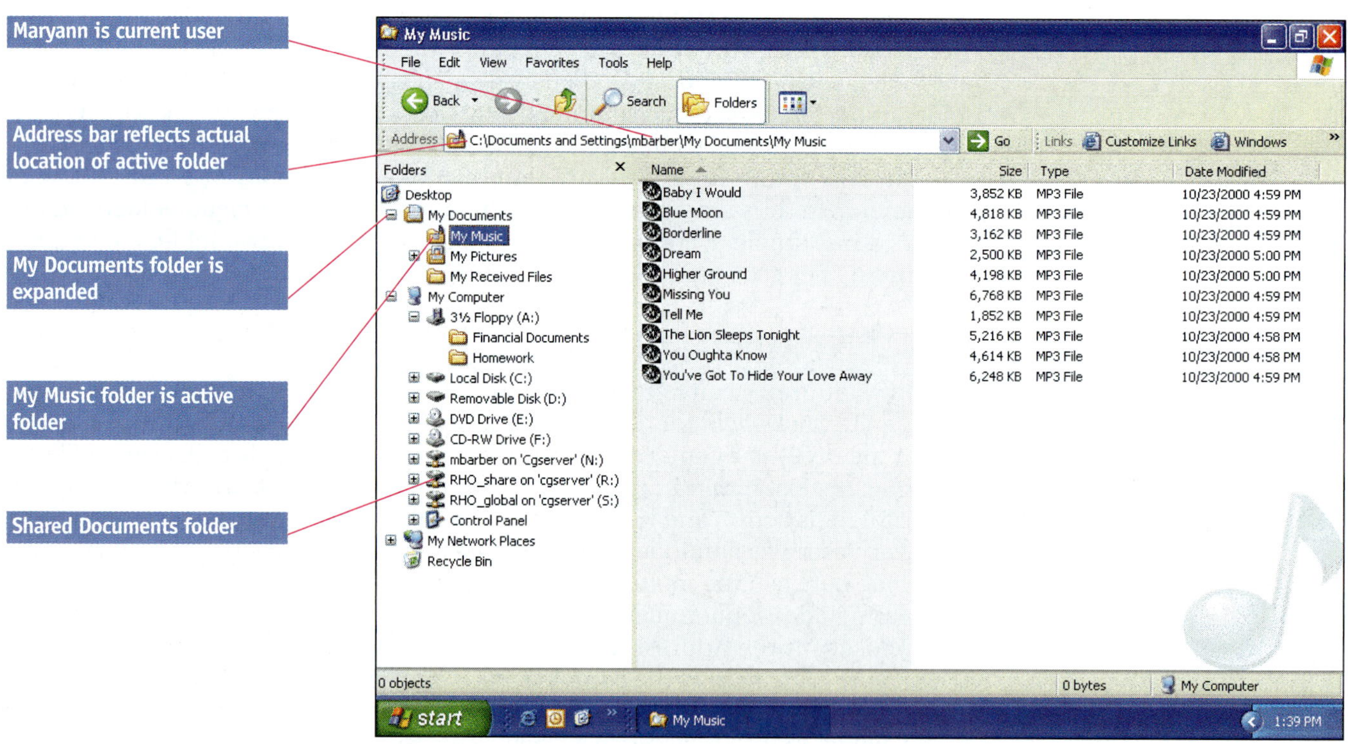

(b) My Music Folder

FIGURE 10 Windows Explorer

Moving and Copying a File

The essence of file management is to ***move*** and ***copy a file*** or folder from one location to another. This can be done in different ways. The easiest is to click and drag the file icon from the source drive or folder to the destination drive or folder, within Windows Explorer. There is one subtlety, however, in that the result of dragging a file (i.e., whether the file is moved or copied) depends on whether the source and destination are on the same or different drives. Dragging a file from one folder to another folder on the same drive moves the file. Dragging a file to a folder on a different drive copies the file. The same rules apply to dragging a folder, where the folder and every file in it are moved or copied, as per the rules for an individual file.

This process is not as arbitrary as it may seem. Windows assumes that if you drag an object (a file or folder) to a different drive (e.g., from drive C to drive A), you want the object to appear in both places. Hence, the default action when you click and drag an object to a different drive is to copy the object. You can, however, override the default and move the object by pressing and holding the Shift key as you drag.

Windows also assumes that you do not want two copies of an object on the same drive, as that would result in wasted disk space. Thus, the default action when you click and drag an object to a different folder on the same drive is to move the object. You can override the default and copy the object by pressing and holding the Ctrl key as you drag. It's not as complicated as it sounds, and you get a chance to practice in the hands-on exercise, which follows shortly.

Deleting a File

The ***Delete command*** deletes (erases) a file from a disk. The command can be executed in different ways, most easily by selecting a file, then pressing the Del key. It's also comforting to know that you can usually recover a deleted file, because the file is not (initially) removed from the disk, but moved instead to the Recycle Bin, from where it can be restored to its original location. Unfortunately, files deleted from a floppy disk are not put into the Recycle Bin and hence cannot be recovered.

The ***Recycle Bin*** is a special folder that contains all files that were previously deleted from any hard disk on your system. Think of the Recycle Bin as similar to the wastebasket in your room. You throw out (delete) a report by tossing it into a wastebasket. The report is gone (deleted) from your desk, but you can still get it back by taking it out of the wastebasket as long as the basket wasn't emptied. The Recycle Bin works the same way. Files are not deleted from the hard disk per se, but moved instead to the Recycle Bin from where they can be restored to their original location. (The protection afforded by the Recycle Bin does not extend to files deleted from a floppy disk.)

Backup

It's not a question of *if* it will happen, but *when*—hard disks die, files are lost, or viruses may infect a system. It has happened to us and it will happen to you, but you can prepare for the inevitable by creating adequate backup *before* the problem occurs. The essence of a ***backup strategy*** is to decide which files to back up, how often to do the backup, and where to keep the backup.

Our strategy is very simple—back up what you can't afford to lose, do so on a daily basis, and store the backup away from your computer. You need not copy every file, every day. Instead, copy just the files that changed during the current session. Realize, too, that it is much more important to back up your data files than your program files. You can always reinstall the application from the original disks or CD, or if necessary, go to the vendor for another copy of an application. You, however, are the only one who has a copy of the term paper that is due tomorrow. Once you decide on a strategy, follow it, and follow it faithfully!

hands-on exercise

3 Windows Explorer

Objective Use Windows Explorer to move, copy, and delete a file; recover a deleted file from the Recycle Bin. Use Figure 11 as a guide.

Step 1: Create a New Folder

- Place the floppy disk from the previous exercise into drive A. Click the **Start Button**, click the **All Programs command**, click **Accessories**, then click **Windows Explorer**. Click the **Maximize button**.
- Expand or collapse the various devices on your system so that My Computer is expanded, but all of the devices are collapsed.
- Click (select) **drive A** in the left pane to display the contents of the floppy disk. You should see the New Car folder that was created in the previous exercise.
- Point to a blank area anywhere in the **right pane**, click the **right mouse button**, click the **New command**, then click **Folder** as the type of object to create.
- The icon for a new folder will appear with the name of the folder (New Folder) highlighted. Type **Windows Information** to change the name. Press **Enter**.

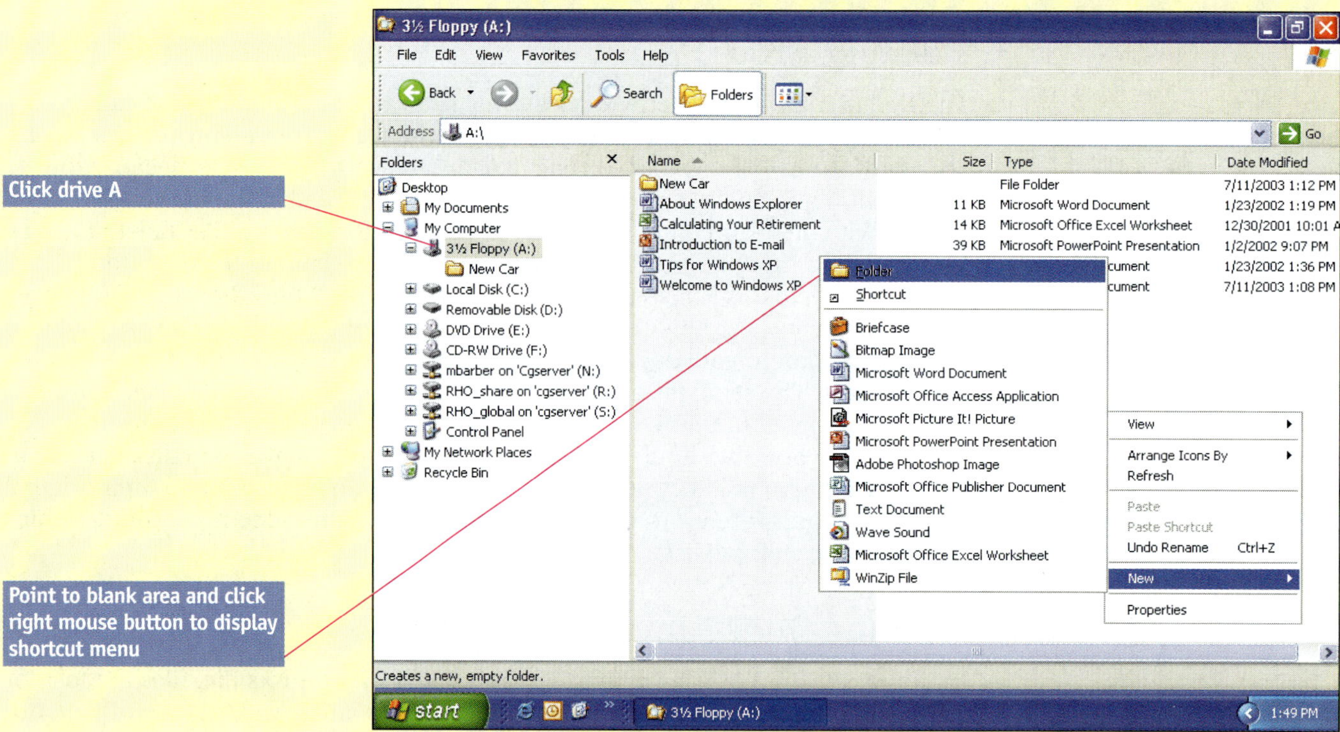

(a) Create a New Folder (step 1)

FIGURE 11 Hands-on Exercise 3 (*continued*)

THE RENAME COMMAND

Right click the file or a folder whose name you want to change to display a context-sensitive menu, and then click the Rename command. The name of the folder will be highlighted with the insertion point at the end of the name. Enter (or edit) the new (existing) name and press Enter.

Step 2: Move the Files

- If necessary, change to the **Details view** and click the **plus sign** next to drive A to expand the drive as shown in Figure 11b. Note the following:
  - The left pane shows that drive A is selected. The right pane displays the contents of drive A (the selected object in the left pane). The folders are shown first and appear in alphabetical order. If not, press the **F5 (Refresh) key** to refresh the screen.
  - There is a minus sign next to the icon for drive A in the left pane, indicating that it has been expanded and that its folders are visible. Thus, the folder names also appear under drive A in the left pane.
- Click and drag the **About Windows Explorer** document in the right pane to the **Windows Information folder** in the left pane, to move the file into that folder.
- Click and drag the **Tips for Windows XP** and the **Welcome to Windows XP** documents to move these documents to the **Windows Information folder**.
- Click the **Windows Information folder** in the left pane to select the folder and display its contents in the right pane. You should see the three files that were just moved.
- Click the **Up button** to return to drive A.

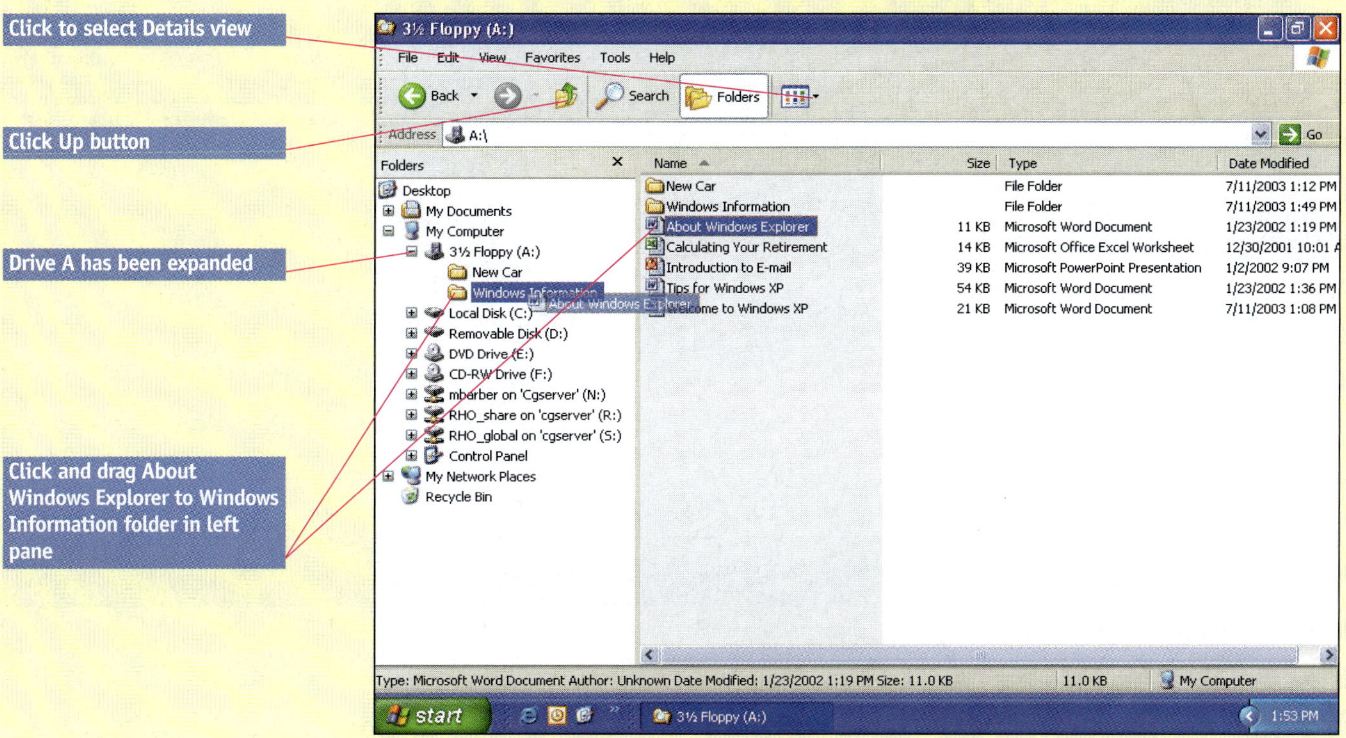

(b) Move the Files (step 2)

FIGURE 11 Hands-on Exercise 3 (*continued*)

SELECT MULTIPLE FILES

Selecting (clicking) one file automatically deselects the previously selected file. You can, however, select multiple files by clicking the first file, then pressing and holding the Ctrl key as you click each additional file. Use the Shift key to select multiple files that are adjacent to one another by clicking the icon of the first file, then pressing and holding the Shift key as you click the icon of the last file.

Step 3: Copy a Folder

- Point to the **Windows Information folder** in the right pane, then **right click and drag** this folder to the **My Documents folder** (on drive C) in the left pane. Release the mouse to display a context-sensitive menu.
- Click the **Copy Here command** as shown in Figure 11c.
  - You may see a Copy files message box as the individual files within the Windows Information folder are copied to the My Documents folder.
  - If you see the Confirm Folder Replace dialog box, it means that you (or another student) already copied these files to the My Documents folder. Click the **Yes to All button** so that your files replace the previous versions in the My Documents folder.
- Click the **My Documents folder** in the left pane. Pull down the **View menu** and click the **Refresh command** (or press the **F5 key**) so that the hierarchy shows the newly copied folder. (Please remember to delete the Windows Information folder from drive C at the end of the exercise.)

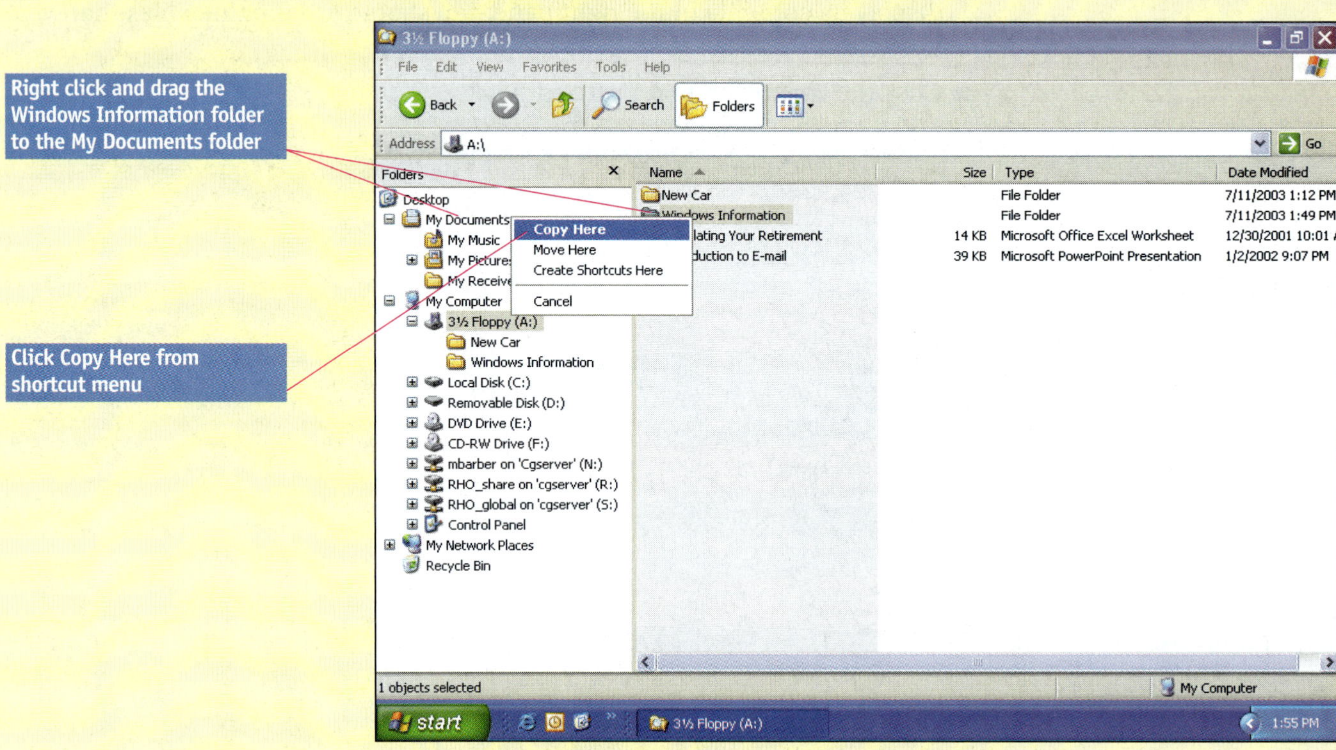

(c) Copy a Folder (step 3)

FIGURE 11 Hands-on Exercise 3 (*continued*)

RIGHT CLICK AND DRAG

The result of dragging a file with the left mouse button depends on whether the source and destination folders are on the same or different drives. Dragging a file to a folder on a different drive copies the file, whereas dragging the file to a folder on the same drive moves the file. If you find this hard to remember, and most people do, click and drag with the right mouse button to display a context-sensitive menu asking whether you want to copy or move the file. This simple tip can save you from making a careless (and potentially serious) error. Use it!

Step 4: Modify a Document

- Click the **Windows Information folder** within the My Documents folder to make it the active folder and to display its contents in the right pane. Change to the **Details view**.
- Double click the **About Windows Explorer** document to start Word and open the document. Do not be concerned if the size and/or position of the Microsoft Word window are different from ours. Read the document.
- If necessary, click inside the document window, then press **Ctrl+End** to move to the end of the document. Add the text shown in Figure 11d.
- Pull down the **File menu** and click **Save** to save the modified file (or click the **Save button** on the Standard toolbar). Pull down the **File menu** and click **Exit** to exit from Microsoft Word.
- Pull down the **View menu** and click the **Refresh command** (or press the **F5 key**) to update the contents of the right pane. The date and time associated with the About Windows Explorer document (on drive C) have been changed to indicate that the file has been modified.

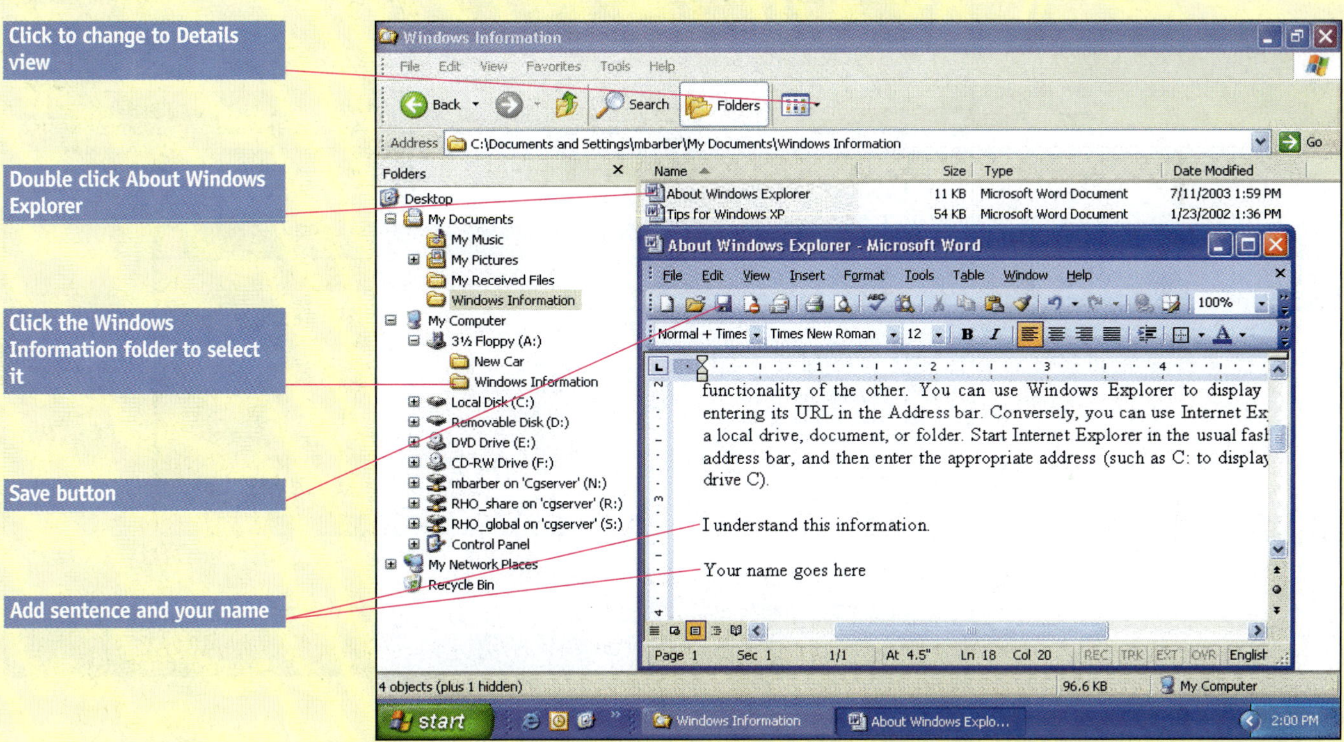

(d) Modify a Document (step 4)

FIGURE 11 Hands-on Exercise 3 (*continued*)

KEYBOARD SHORTCUTS

Most people begin with the mouse, but add keyboard shortcuts as they become more proficient. Ctrl+B, Ctrl+I, and Ctrl+U are shortcuts to boldface, italicize, and underline, respectively. Ctrl+X (the X is supposed to remind you of a pair of scissors), Ctrl+C, and Ctrl+V correspond to Cut, Copy, and Paste, respectively. Ctrl+Home and Ctrl+End move to the beginning or end of a document. These shortcuts are not unique to Microsoft Word, but are recognized in virtually every Windows application.

Step 5: Copy (Back up) a File

- Verify that the **Windows Information folder** (on drive C) is the active folder, as denoted by the open folder icon. Click and drag the icon for the **About Windows Explorer** document from the right pane to the **Windows Information folder** on **drive A** in the left pane.
- You will see the message in Figure 11e, indicating that the folder (on drive A) already contains a file called About Windows Explorer and asking whether you want to replace the existing file.
- Click **Yes** because you want to replace the previous version of the file on drive A with the updated version from the My Documents folder.
- You have just backed up a file by copying the About Windows Explorer document from a folder on drive C to the disk in drive A. In other words, you can use the floppy disk to restore the file to drive C should anything happen to it.
- Keep the floppy disk in a safe place, away from the computer.

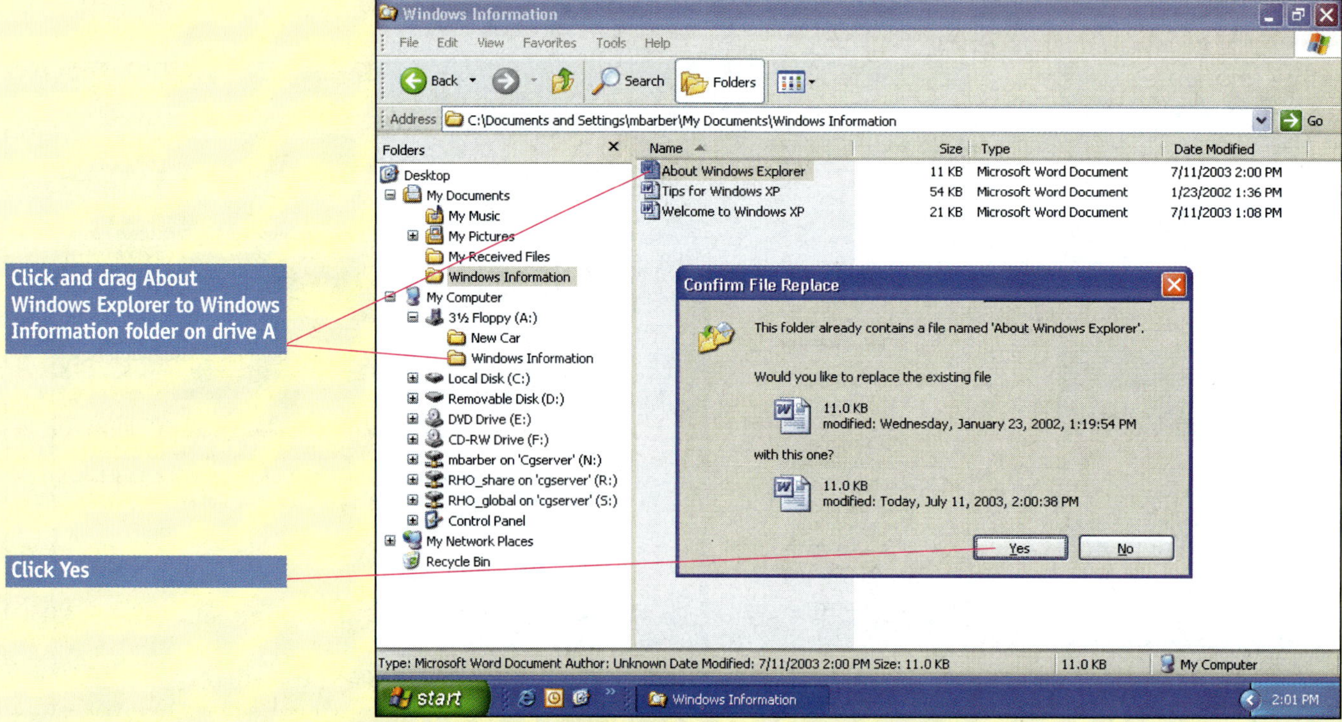

(e) Copy (Back up) a File (step 5)

FIGURE 11 Hands-on Exercise 3 (*continued*)

THE MY DOCUMENTS FOLDER

The My Documents folder is created by default with the installation of Windows XP. There is no requirement that you store your documents in this folder, but it is convenient, especially for beginners who may lack the confidence to create their own folders. The My Documents folder is also helpful in a laboratory environment where the network administrator may prevent you from modifying the desktop and/or from creating your own folders on drive C, in which case you will have to use the My Documents folder.

Step 6: Delete a Folder

- Select (click) **Windows Information folder** within the My Documents folder in the left pane. Pull down the **File menu** and click **Delete** (or press the **Del key**).
- You will see the dialog box in Figure 11f, asking whether you are sure you want to delete the folder and send its contents to the Recycle Bin, which enables you to restore the folder at a later date.
- Click **Yes** to delete the folder. The folder disappears from drive C. Note that you have deleted the folder and its contents.
- Now pretend that you do not want to delete the folder. Pull down the **Edit menu**. Click **Undo Delete**.
- The deletion is cancelled and the Windows Information folder reappears in the left pane. If you do not see the folder, pull down the **View menu** and click the **Refresh command** (or press the **F5 key**).

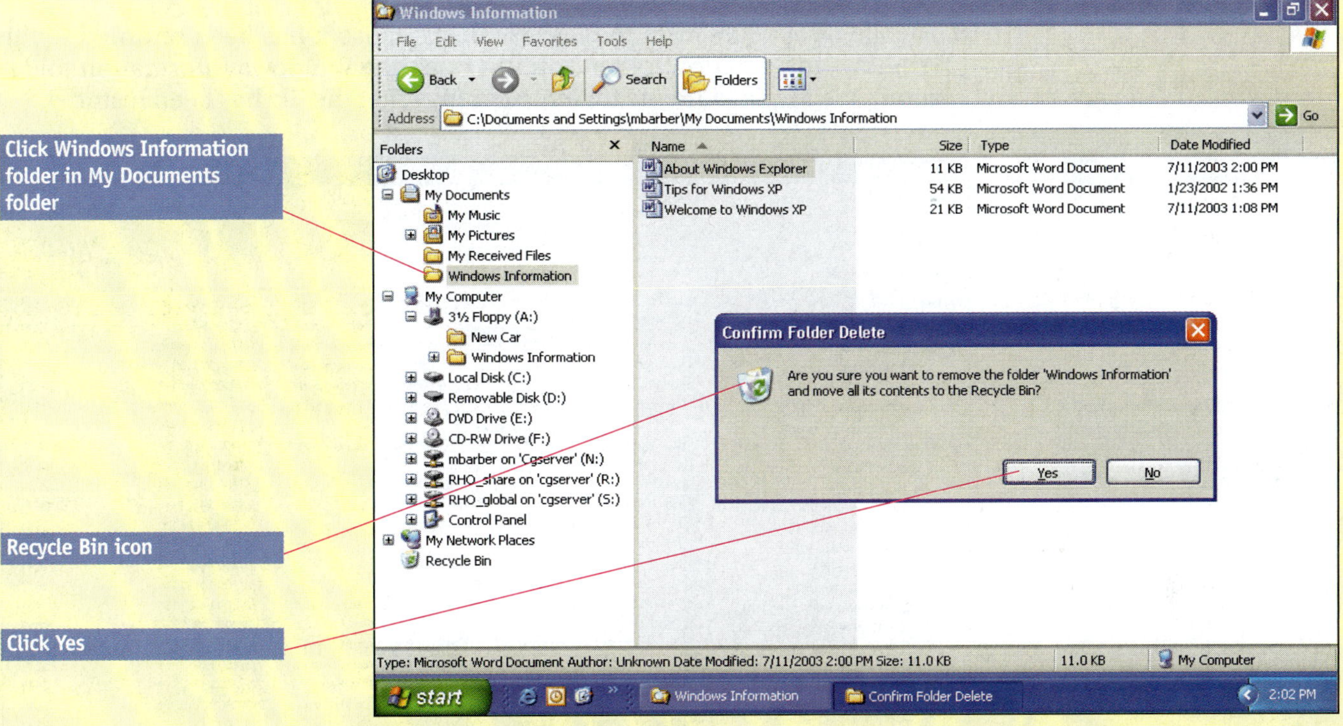

(f) Delete a Folder (step 6)

FIGURE 11 Hands-on Exercise 3 (*continued*)

CUSTOMIZE WINDOWS EXPLORER

Increase or decrease the size of the left pane within Windows Explorer by dragging the vertical line separating the left and right panes in the appropriate direction. You can also drag the right border of the various column headings (Name, Size, Type, and Modified) in the right pane to increase or decrease the width of the column and see more or less information in that column. And best of all, you can click any column heading to display the contents of the selected folder in sequence by that column. Click the heading a second time and the sequence changes from ascending to descending and vice versa.

Step 7: The Recycle Bin

- If necessary, select the **Windows Information folder** within the My Documents folder in the left pane. Select (click) the **About Windows Explorer** file in the right pane. Press the **Del key**, then click **Yes** when asked to delete the file.
- Click the **down arrow** in the vertical scroll bar in the left pane until you can click the icon for the **Recycle Bin**.
- The Recycle Bin contains all files that have been previously deleted from the local (hard) disks, and hence you will see a different number of files than those displayed in Figure 11g.
- Change to the **Details view**. Pull down the **View menu**, click (or point to) **Arrange Icons by**, then click **Date Deleted** to display the files in this sequence. Execute this command a second time (if necessary) so that the most recently deleted file appears at the top of the window.
- Right click the **About Windows Explorer** file to display the context-sensitive menu in Figure 11g, then click the **Restore command**.
- The file disappears from the Recycle bin because it has been returned to the Windows Information folder. You can open the Windows Information folder within the My Documents folder to confirm that the file has been restored.

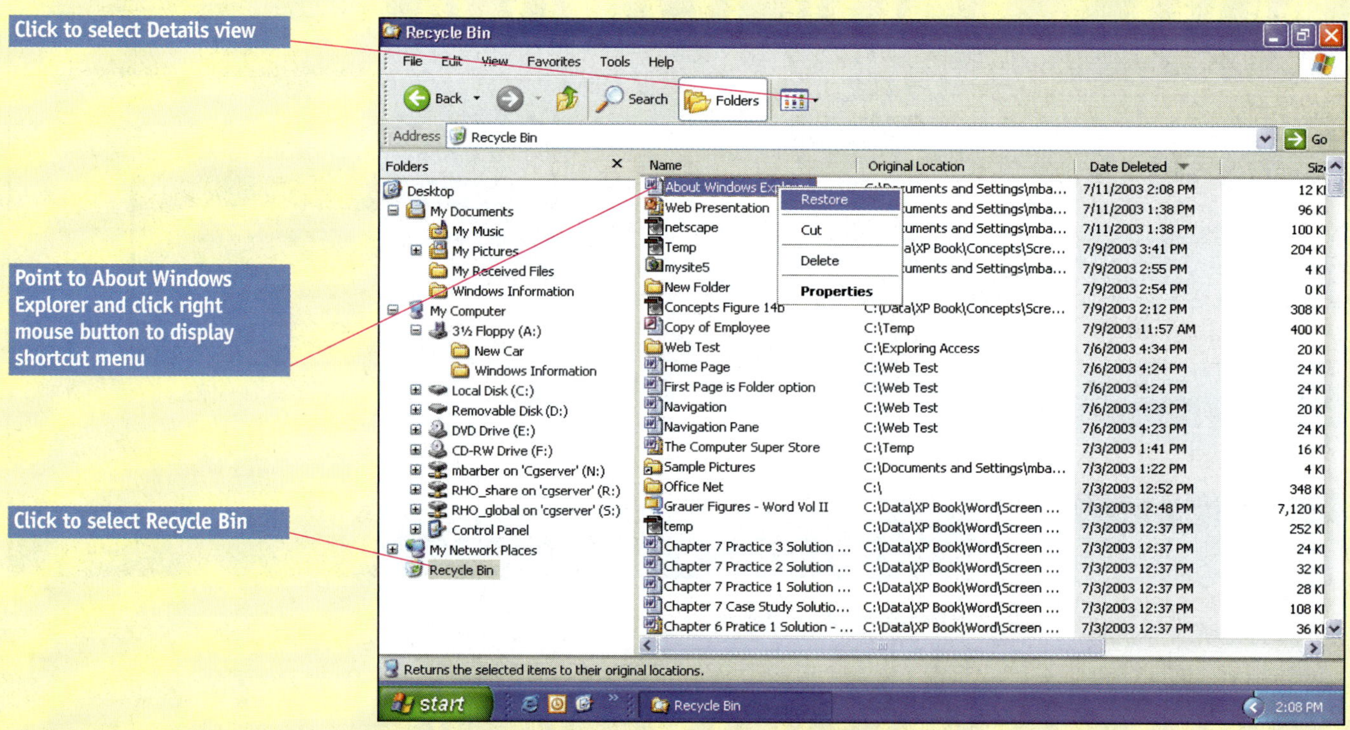

(g) The Recycle Bin (step 7)

FIGURE 11 Hands-on Exercise 3 (*continued*)

TWO WAYS TO RECOVER A FILE

The Undo command is present in Windows Explorer. Thus, you do not need to resort to the Recycle Bin to recover a deleted file provided you execute the Undo command immediately (within a few commands) after the Delete command was issued. Some operations cannot be undone (in which case the Undo command will be dimmed), but Undo is always worth a try.

Step 8: The Group By Command

- Select (click) the **Windows Information folder** on drive A. You should see the contents of this folder (three Word documents) in the right pane.
- Pull down the **View menu**, (click or) point to the **Arrange Icons by command**, then click the **Show in Groups command** from the cascaded menu.
- You see the same three files as previously, but they are displayed in groups according to the first letter in the filename. Click the **Date Modified** column, and the files are grouped according to the date they were last modified.
- The Show in Groups command functions as a toggle switch. Execute the command and the files are displayed in groups; execute the command a second time and the groups disappear.
- Select (click) the icon for **drive A** in the left pane to display the contents of drive A. You should see two folders and two files. Pull down the **View menu**, (click or) point to the **Arrange Icons by command**, and then click the **Show in Groups command** from the cascaded menu.
- Change to the **Details view**. Click the **Type column** to group the objects by folder and file type.

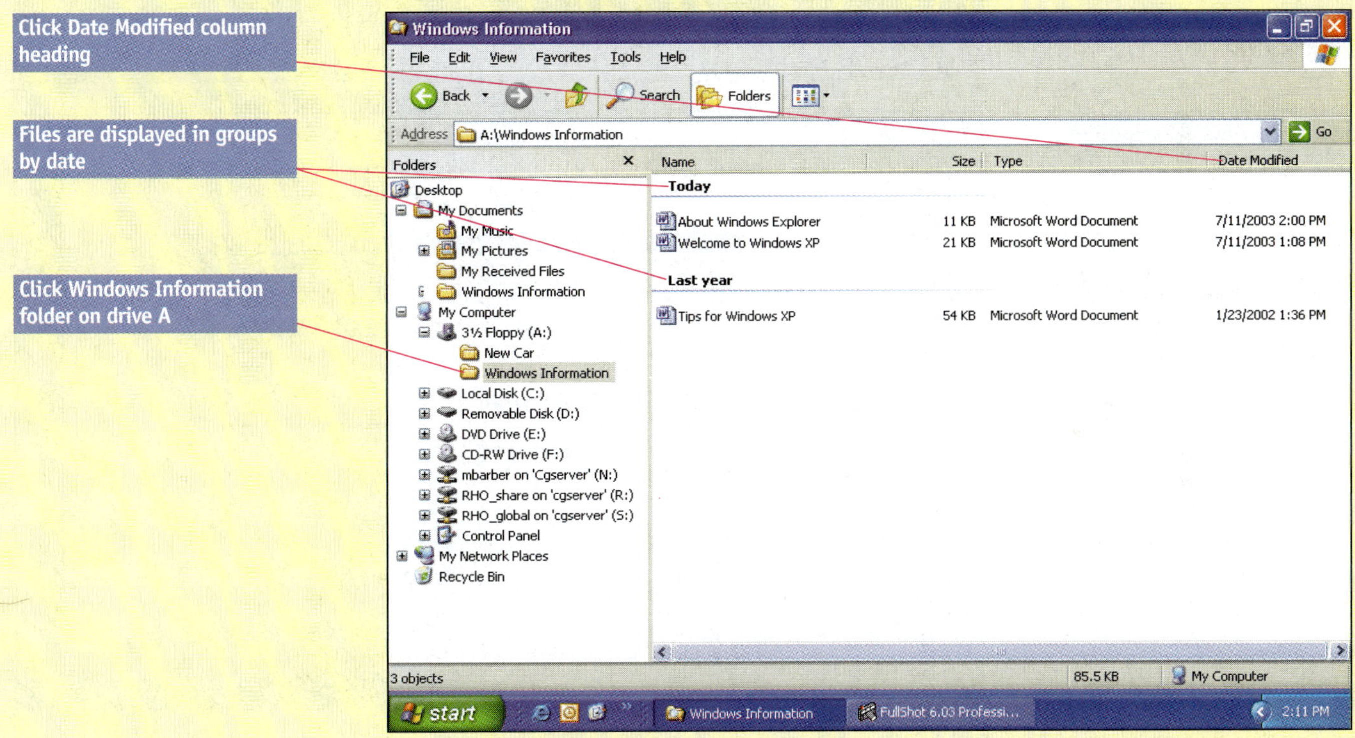

(h) The Group By Command (step 8)

FIGURE 11 Hands-on Exercise 3 (*continued*)

KEEP THE VIEW

Once you set the desired view in a folder, you may want to display every other folder according to those parameters. Pull down the Tools menu, click the Folder Options command, and click the View tab. Click the button to Apply to All folders, then click Yes when prompted to confirm. Click OK to close the Folder Options dialog box. The next time you open another folder, it will appear in the same view as the current folder.

Step 9: Complete the Exercise

- Prove to your instructor that you have completed the exercise correctly by capturing the screen on your monitor. Press the **Print Screen key**. Nothing appears to have happened, but the screen has been copied to the clipboard.
- Click the **Start button**, click the **All Programs command**, then start Microsoft Word and begin a new document. Enter the title of your document, followed by your name as shown in Figure 11i. Press the **Enter key** two or three times.
- Pull down the **Edit menu** and click the **Paste command** (or click the **Paste button** on the Standard toolbar) to copy the contents of the clipboard into the Word document.
- Print this document for your instructor. There is no need to save this document. Exit Word.
- Delete the **Windows Information folder** from the My Documents folder as a courtesy to the next student. Close Windows Explorer.
- Log off if you do not want to continue the next exercise at this time. (Click the **Start button**, click **Log Off**, then click **Log Off** a second time to end your session.)

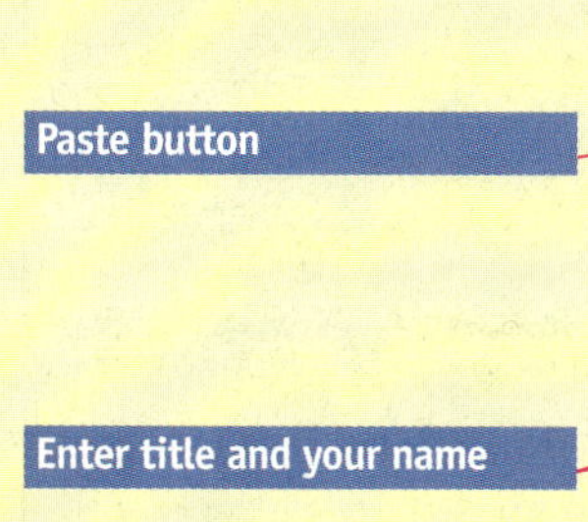

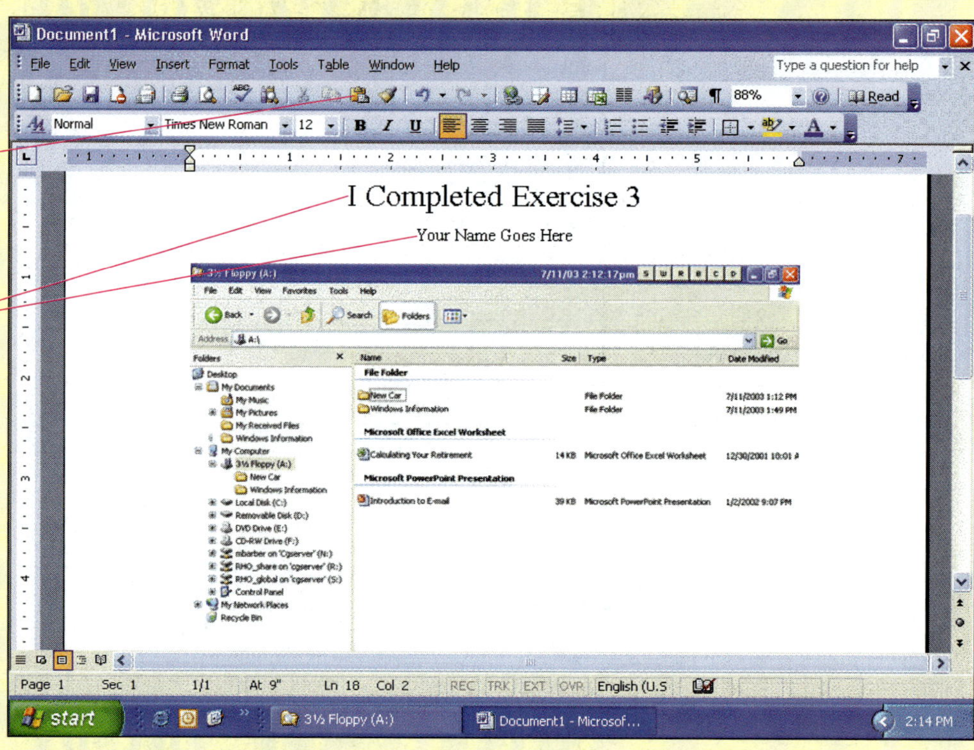

(i) Complete the Exercise (step 9)

FIGURE 11 Hands-on Exercise 3 (*continued*)

SWITCHING USERS VERSUS LOGGING OFF

Windows XP gives you the choice of switching users or logging off. Switching users leaves all of your applications open, but it relinquishes control of the computer to another user. This lets you subsequently log back on (after the new user logs off) and take up exactly where you were. Logging off, on the other hand, closes all of your applications and ends the session, but it leaves the computer running at full power and available for someone else to log on.

INCREASING PRODUCTIVITY

You have learned the basic concepts of disk and file management, but there is so much more. Windows XP has something for everyone. It is easy and intuitive for the novice, but it also contains sophisticated tools for the more knowledgeable user. This section describes three powerful features to increase your productivity. Some or all of these features may be disabled in a school environment, but the information will stand you in good stead on your own computer.

The Control Panel

The ***Control Panel*** affects every aspect of your system. It determines the appearance of your desktop, and it controls the performance of your hardware. You can, for example, change the way your mouse behaves by switching the function of the left and right mouse buttons and/or by replacing the standard mouse pointers with animated icons that move across the screen. You will not have access to the Control Panel in a lab environment, but you will need it at home whenever you install new hardware or software. You should be careful about making changes, and you should understand the nature of the new settings before you accept any of the changes.

The Control Panel in Windows XP organizes its tools by category as shown in Figure 12. Point to any category and you see a Screen Tip that describes the specific tasks within that category. The Appearance and Themes category, for example, lets you select a screen saver or customize the Start menu and taskbar. You can also switch to the Classic view that displays every tool in a single screen, which is consistent with all previous versions of Windows.

The task pane provides access to the ***Windows Update*** function, which connects you to a Web site where you can download new device drivers and other updates to Windows XP. You can also configure your system to install these updates automatically as they become available. Some updates, especially those having to do with Internet security, are absolutely critical.

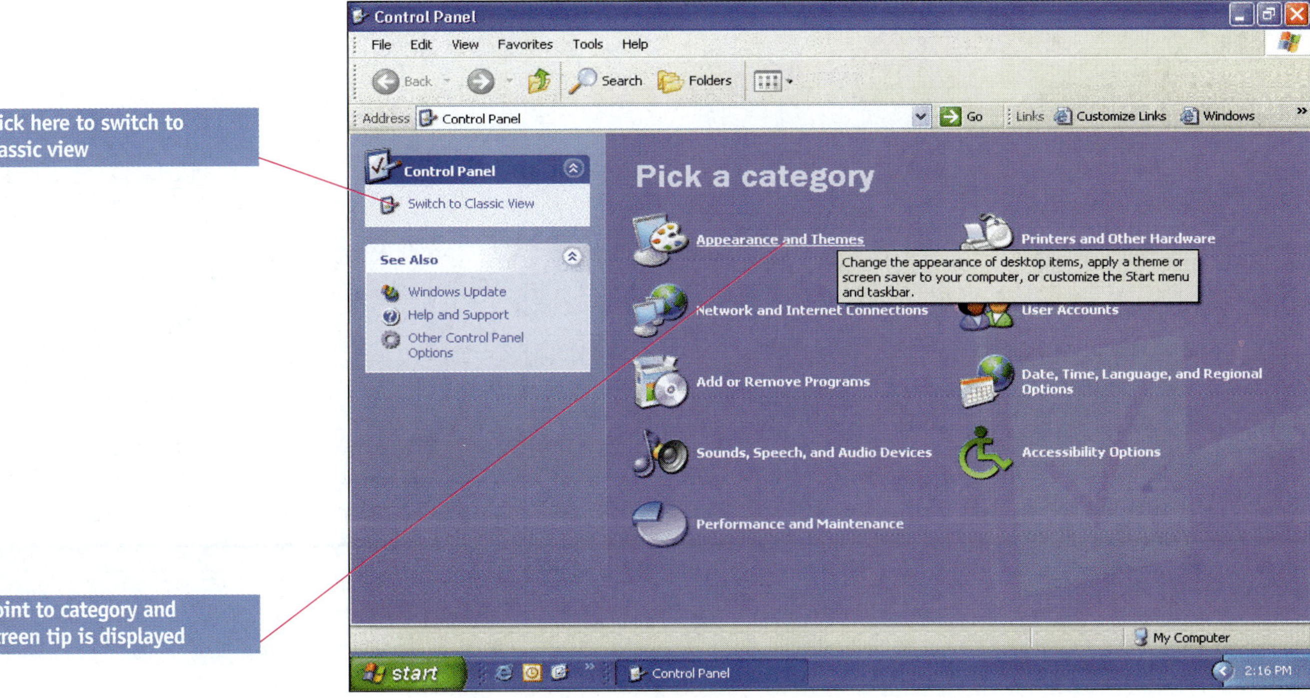

FIGURE 12 The Control Panel

Shortcuts

A ***shortcut*** is a link to any object on your computer, such as a program, file, folder, disk drive, or Web page. Shortcuts can appear anywhere, but are most often placed on the desktop or on the Start menu. The desktop in Figure 13 contains a variety of shortcuts, each of which contains a jump arrow to indicate a shortcut icon. Double click the shortcut to Election of Officers, for example, and you start Word and open this document. In similar fashion, you can double click the shortcut for a Web page (Exploring Windows Series), folder, or disk drive (drive A) to open the object and display its contents.

Creating a shortcut is a two-step process. First, you use Windows Explorer to locate the object such as a file, folder, or disk drive. Then you select the object, use the right mouse button to drag the object to the desktop, and then click the Create Shortcut command from the context-sensitive menu. A shortcut icon will appear on the desktop with the phrase "shortcut to" as part of the name. You can create as many shortcuts as you like, and you can place them anywhere on the desktop or in individual folders. You can also right click a shortcut icon after it has been created to change its name. Deleting the icon deletes the shortcut and not the object.

Windows XP also provides a set of predefined shortcuts through a series of desktop icons that are shown at the left border of the desktop in Figure 13. Double click the My Computer icon, for example, and you open the My Computer folder. These desktop icons were displayed by default in earlier versions of Windows, but not in Windows XP. They were added through the Control Panel as you will see in our next exercise.

Additional shortcuts are found in the ***Quick Launch toolbar*** that appears to the right of the Start button. Click any icon and you open the indicated program. And finally, Windows XP will automatically add to the Start menu shortcuts to your most frequently used programs. Desktop shortcuts are a powerful technique that will increase your productivity by taking you directly to a specified document or other object.

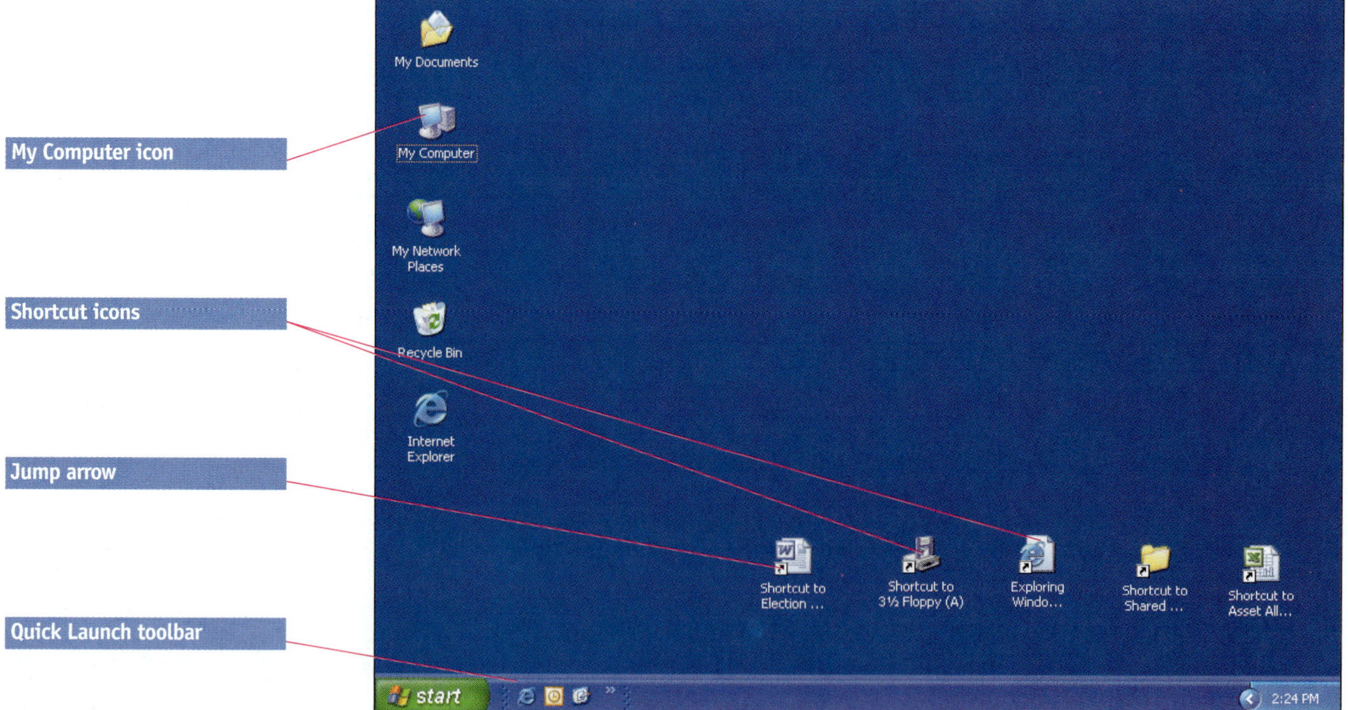

FIGURE 13 Desktop with Shortcuts

The Search Companion

Sooner or later you will create a file, and then forget where (in which folder) you saved it. Or you may create a document and forget its name, but remember a key word or phrase in the document. Or you may want to locate all files of a certain file type—for example, all of the sound files on your system. The ***Search Companion*** can help you to solve each of these problems and is illustrated in Figure 14.

The Search Companion is accessed from within any folder by clicking the Search button on the Standard Buttons toolbar to open the search pane at the left of the folder. You are presented with an initial search menu (not shown in Figure 14) that asks what you want to search for. You can search your local machine for media files (pictures, music, or video), documents (such as spreadsheets or Word documents), or any file or folder. You can also search the Help and Support Center or the Internet.

Once you choose the type of information, you are presented with a secondary search pane as shown in Figure 14. You can search according to a variety of criteria, each of which will help to narrow the search. In this example we are looking for any document on drive C that has "Windows" as part of its filename and further, contains the name "Maryann" somewhere within the document. The search is case sensitive. This example illustrates two important capabilities, namely that you can search on the document name (or part of its name) and/or its content.

Additional criteria can be entered by expanding the chevrons for date and size. You can, for example, restrict your search to all documents that were modified within the last week, the past month, or the last year. You can also restrict your search to documents of a certain size. Click the Search button after all of the criteria have been specified to initiate the search. The results of the search (the documents that satisfy the search criteria) are displayed in the right pane. You can refine the search if it is unsuccessful and/or you can open any document in which you are interested. The Search Companion also has an indexing service to make subsequent searches faster.

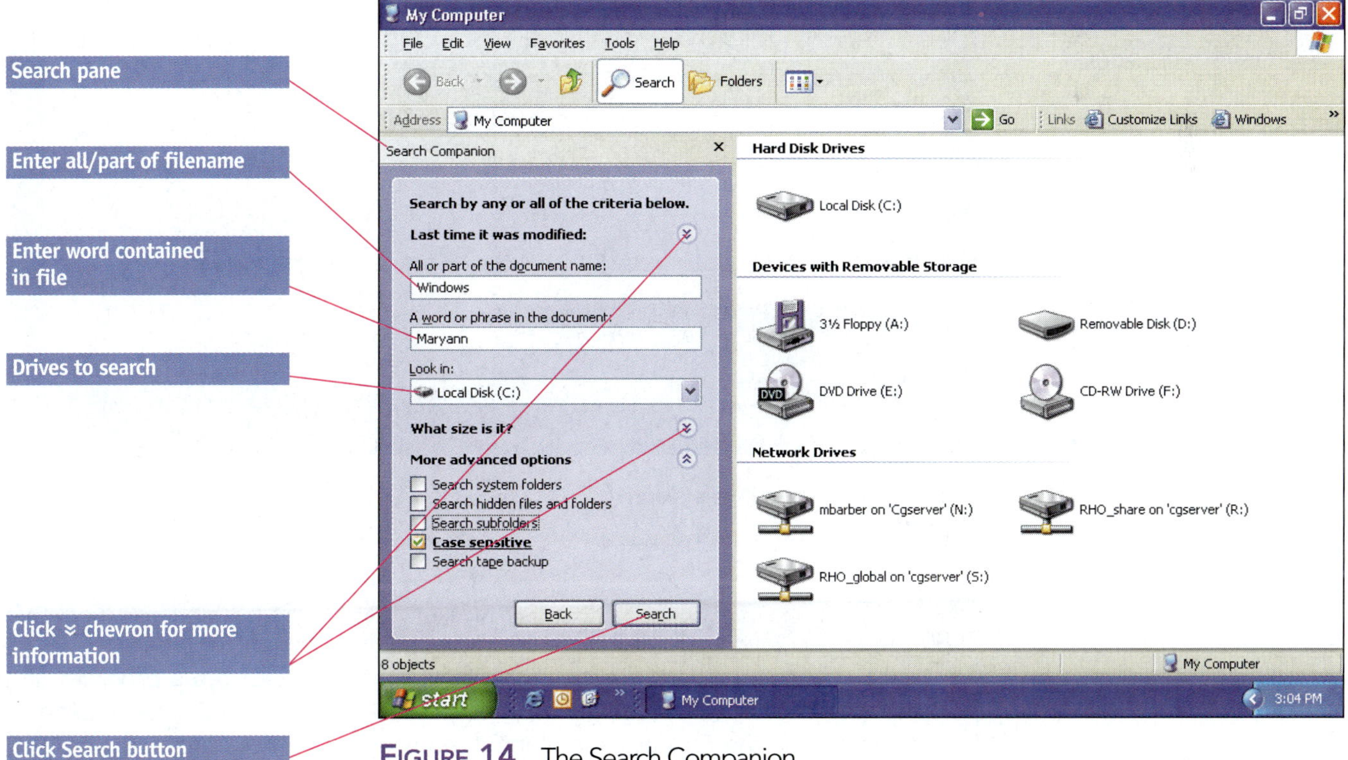

FIGURE 14 The Search Companion

hands-on exercise

4 Increasing Productivity

Objective To create and use shortcuts; to locate documents using the Search Companion; to customize your system using the Control Panel; to obtain a passport account. The exercise requires an Internet connection. Use Figure 15 as a guide.

Step 1: Display the Desktop Icons

- Log on to Windows XP. Point to a blank area on the desktop, click the **right mouse button** to display a context-sensitive menu, then click the **Properties command** to open the Display Properties dialog box in Figure 15a.
- Click the **Desktop tab** and then click the **Customize Desktop button** to display the Desktop Items dialog box.
- Check the boxes to display all four desktop icons. Click **OK** to accept these settings and close the dialog box, then click **OK** a second time to close the Display Properties dialog box.
- The desktop icons should appear on the left side of your desktop. Double click any icon to execute the indicated program or open the associated folder.

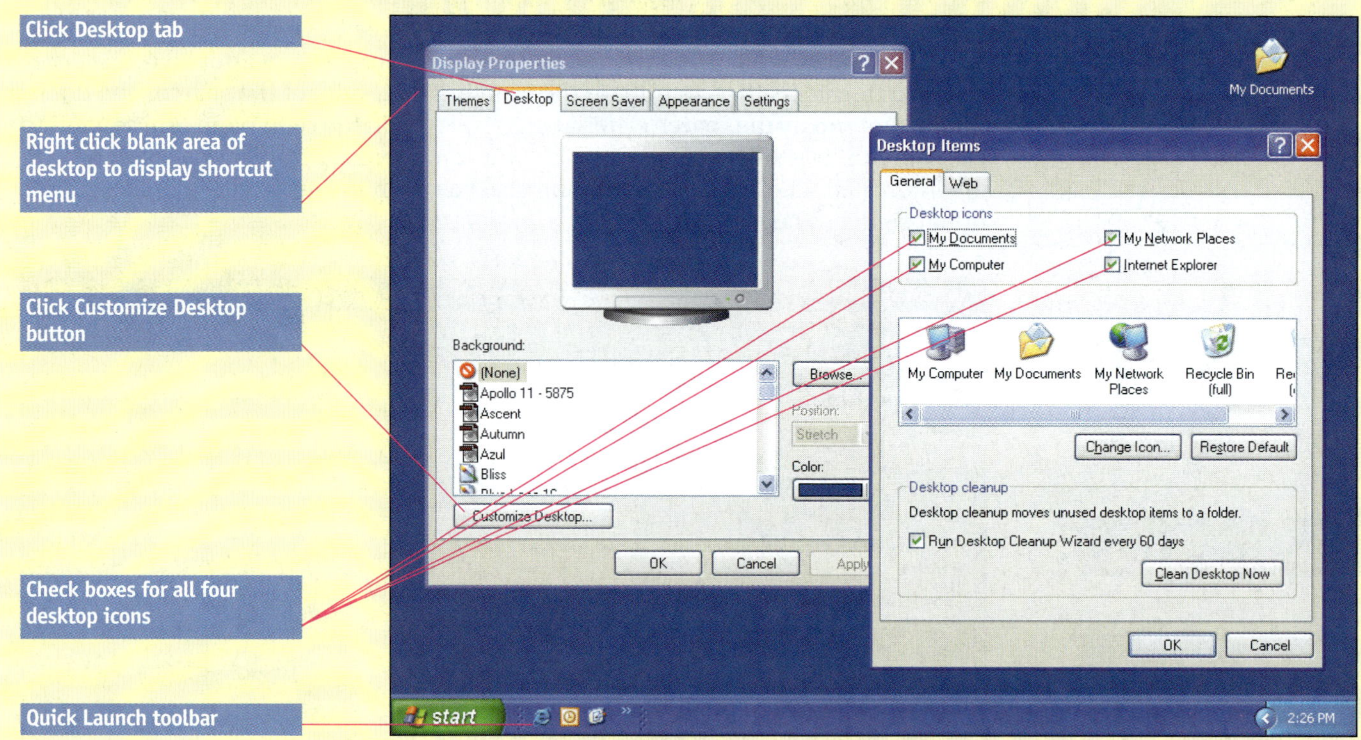

(a) Display the Desktop Icons (step 1)

FIGURE 15 Hands-on Exercise 4

THE QUICK LAUNCH TOOLBAR

The Quick Launch toolbar is a customizable toolbar that executes a program or displays the desktop with a single click. Right click a blank area of the taskbar, point to (or click) the Toolbars command, then check the Quick Launch toolbar to toggle its display on or off.

Step 2: Create a Web Shortcut

- Start Internet Explorer. You can double click the newly created icon at the left of the desktop, or you can single click its icon in the Quick Launch toolbar. Click the **Restore button** so that Internet Explorer is not maximized, that is, so that you can see a portion of the desktop.
- Click in the Address bar and enter the address **www.microsoft.com/windowsxp** to display the home page of Windows XP. Now that you see the page, you can create a shortcut to that page.
- Click the **Internet Explorer icon** in the Address bar to select the entire address, point to the Internet Explorer icon, then click and drag the icon to the desktop (you will see a jump arrow as you drag the text). Release the mouse to create the shortcut in Figure 15b.
- Prove to yourself that the shortcut works. Close Internet Explorer, and then double click the shortcut you created. Internet Explorer will open, and you should see the desired Web page. Close (or minimize) Internet Explorer since you do not need it for the remainder of the exercise.

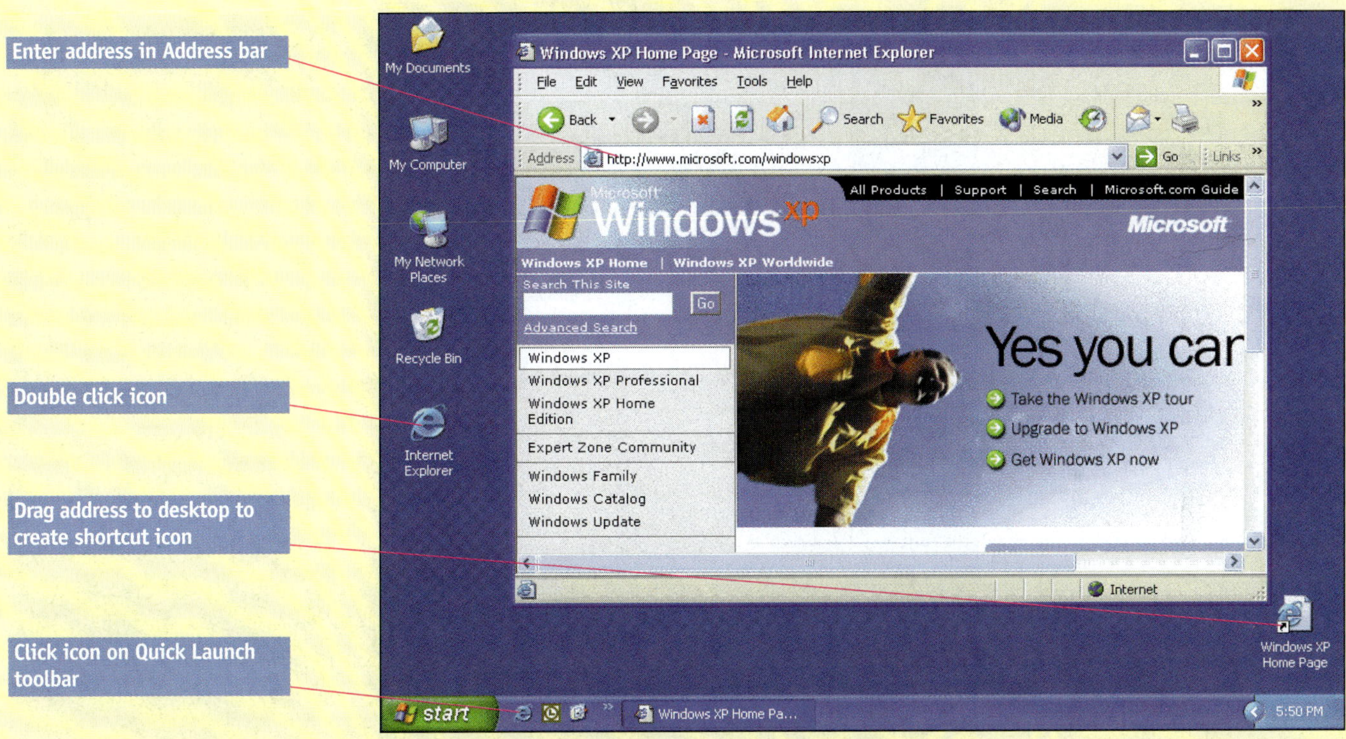

(b) Create a Web Shortcut (step 2)

FIGURE 15 Hands-on Exercise 4 (*continued*)

WORKING WITH SHORTCUTS

You can work with a shortcut icon just as you can with any other icon. To move a shortcut, drag its icon to a different location on the desktop. To rename a shortcut, right click its icon, click the Rename command, type the new name, then press the enter key. To delete a shortcut, right click its icon, click the Delete command, and click Yes in response to the confirming prompt. Deleting a shortcut deletes just the shortcut and not the object to which the shortcut refers.

Step 3: Create Additional Shortcuts

- Double click the **My Computer icon** to open this folder. Place the floppy disk from hands-on exercise 3 into the floppy drive. Double click the icon for **drive A** to display the contents of the floppy disk as shown in Figure 15c.
- The contents of the Address bar have changed to A:\ to indicate the contents of the floppy disk. You should see two folders and two files.
- Move and size the window so that you see a portion of the desktop. Right click and drag the icon for the **Windows Information folder** to the desktop, then release the mouse. Click the **Create Shortcuts Here command** to create the shortcut.
- Look for the jump arrow to be sure you have created a shortcut (as opposed to moving or copying the folder). If you made a mistake, right click a blank area of the desktop, then click the **Undo command** to reverse the unintended move or copy operation.
- Right click and drag the icon for the **PowerPoint presentation** to the desktop, release the mouse, and then click the **Create Shortcuts Here command**.

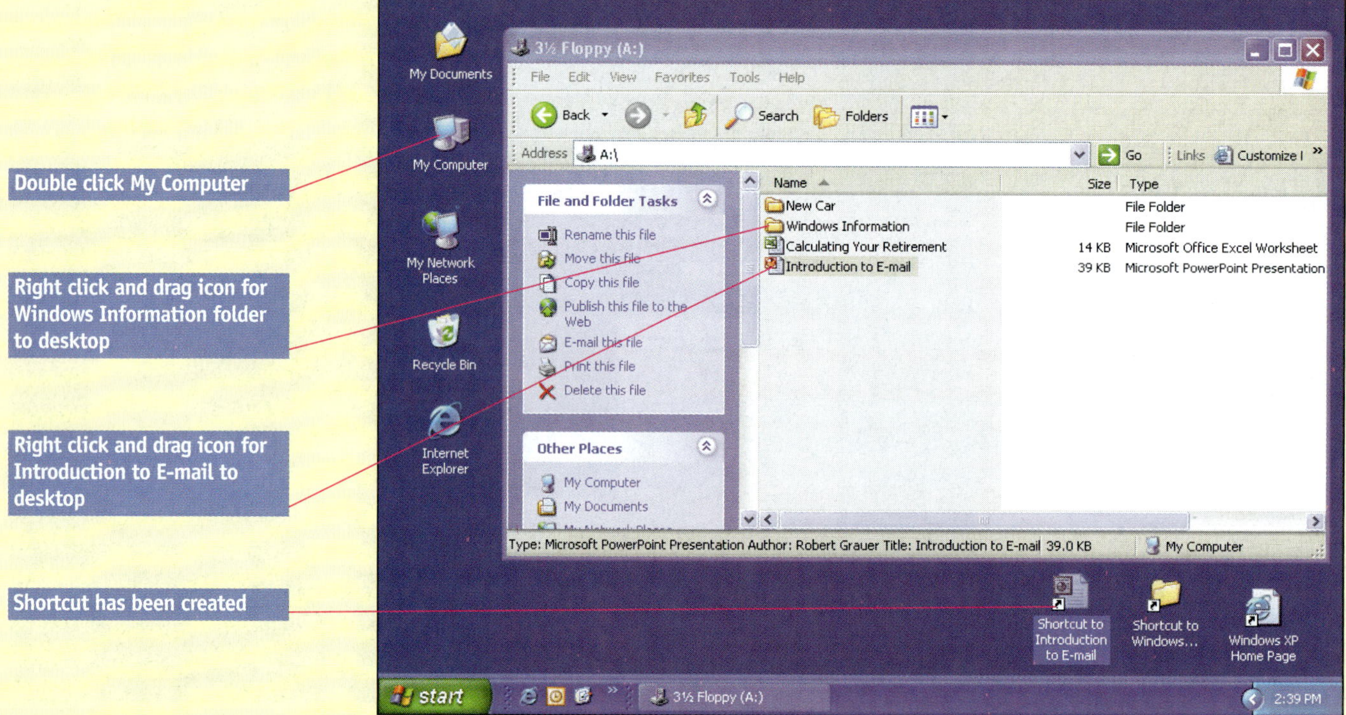

(c) Create Additional Shortcuts (step 3)

FIGURE 15 Hands-on Exercise 4 (*continued*)

THE ARRANGE ICONS COMMAND

The most basic way to arrange the icons on your desktop is to click and drag an icon from one place to another. It may be convenient, however, to have Windows arrange the icons for you. Right click a blank area of the desktop, click (or point to) the Arrange Icons by command, then click Auto Arrange. All existing shortcuts, as well as any new shortcuts, will be automatically aligned along the left edge of the desktop. Execute the Auto Arrange command a second time to cancel the command, and enable yourself to manually arrange the icons.

Step 4: Search for a Document

- Maximize the My Computer window. Click the **Search button** on the Standard Buttons toolbar to display the Search pane. The button functions as a toggle switch. Click the button and the Search pane appears. Click the button a second time and the task pane replaces the Search Companion.
- The initial screen (not shown in Figure 15d) in the Search Companion asks what you are searching for. Click **Documents (word processing, spreadsheet, etc.)**.
- You may be prompted to enter when the document was last modified. Click the option button that says **Don't Remember**, then click **Use advanced search options**. You should see the screen in Figure 15d.
- Enter the indicated search criteria. You do not know the document name and thus you leave this text box blank. The other criteria indicate that you are looking for any document that contains "interest rate" that is located on drive A, or in any subfolder on drive A.
- Click the **Search button** to initiate the search. You will see a Search dialog box to indicate the progress of the search, after which you will see the relevant documents.

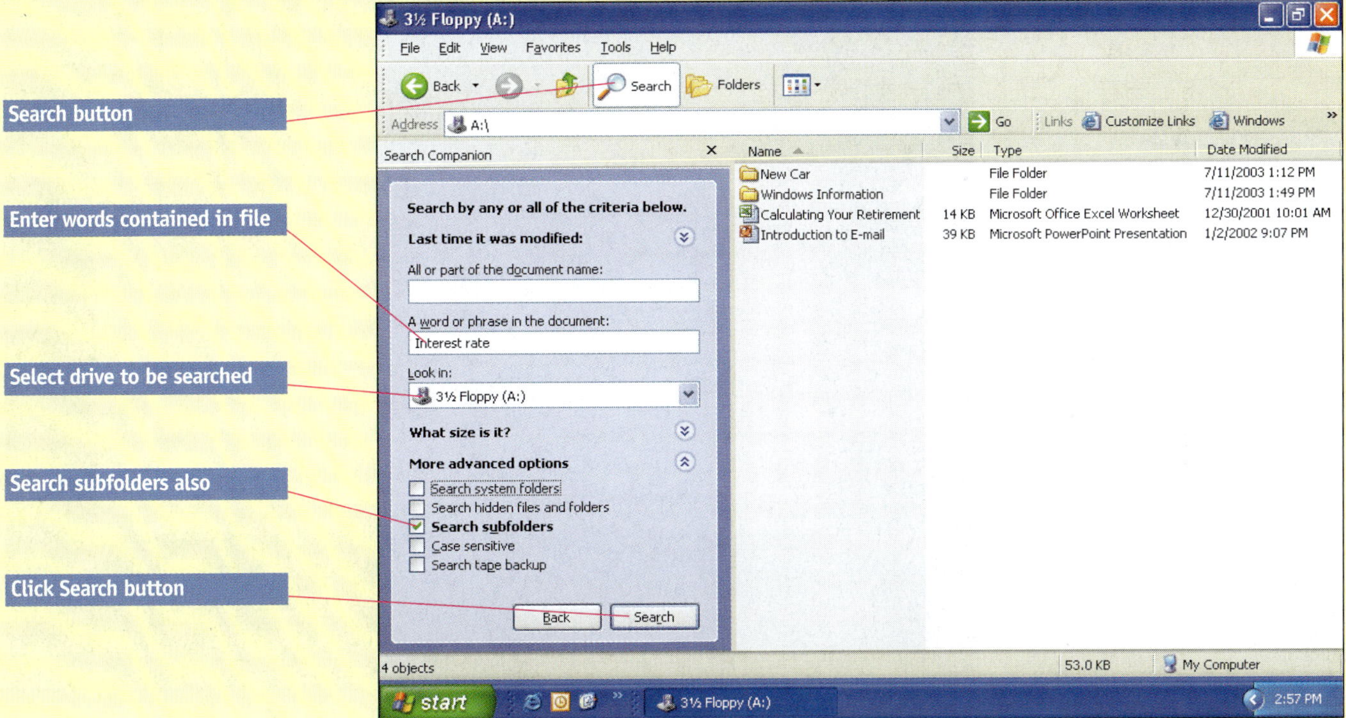

(d) Search for a Document (step 4)

FIGURE 15 Hands-on Exercise 4 (*continued*)

YOU DON'T NEED THE COMPLETE FILENAME

You can enter only a portion of the filename, and the Search Companion will still find the file(s). If, for example, you're searching for the file "Marketing Homework," you can enter the first several letters such as "Marketing" and Windows will return all files whose name begins with the letters you've entered—for example, "Marketing Homework" and "Marketing Term Paper."

Step 5: Search Results

- The search should return two files that satisfy the search criteria as shown in Figure 15e. Click the **Views button** and select **Tiles view** if you want to match our figure. If you do not see the same files, it is for one of two reasons:
  - You did not specify the correct search criteria. Click the **Back button** and reenter the search parameters as described in step 4. Repeat the search.
  - Your floppy disk is different from ours. Be sure to use the floppy disk as it existed at the end of the previous hands-on exercise.
- Click the **Restore button** so that you again see a portion of the desktop. Right click and drag the **Calculating Your Retirement** workbook to the desktop to create a shortcut on the desktop.
- Close the Search Results window, close the My Documents window, then double click the newly created shortcut to open the workbook.
- Retirement is a long way off, but you may want to experiment with our worksheet. It is never too early to start saving.
- Exit Excel when you are finished.

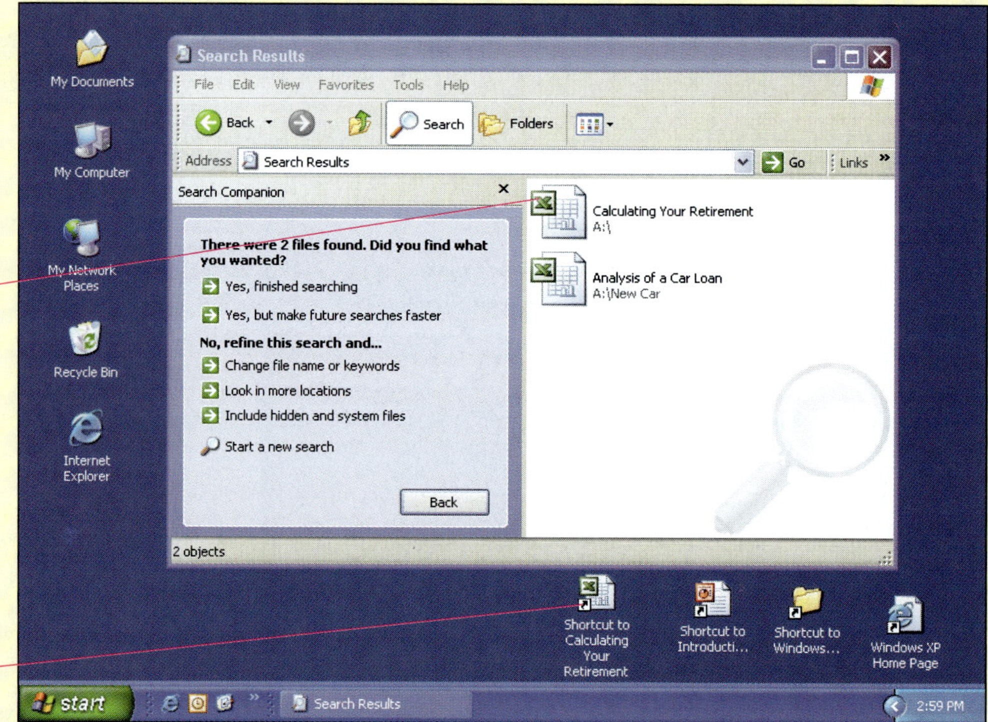

(e) Search Results (step 5)

FIGURE 15 Hands-on Exercise 4 (*continued*)

SHORTCUT WIZARD

Shortcuts can be created in many ways, including the use of a wizard. Right click a blank area of the desktop, click (or point) to the New command, then choose Shortcut to start the wizard. Enter the Web address in the indicated text box (or click the Browse button to locate a local file). Click Next, then enter the name for the shortcut as it is to appear on the desktop. Click the Finish button to exit the wizard. The new shortcut should appear on the desktop.

Step 6: Open the Control Panel Folder

- Click the **Start button**, then click **Control Panel** to open the Control Panel folder. Click the command to **Switch to Classic View** that appears in the task pane to display the individual icons as shown in Figure 15f. Maximize the window.
- Double click the **Taskbar and Start Menu icon** to display the associated dialog box. Click the **Taskbar tab**, then check the box to **Auto-hide the taskbar.** Your other settings should match those in Figure 15f. Click **OK** to accept the settings and close the dialog box.
- The taskbar (temporarily) disappears from your desktop. Now point to the bottom edge of the desktop, and the taskbar reappears. The advantage of hiding the taskbar in this way is that you have the maximum amount of room in which to work; that is, you see the taskbar only when you want to.
- Double click the **Fonts folder** to open this folder and display the fonts that are installed on your computer. Change to the **Details view**.
- Double click the icon of any font other than the standard fonts (Arial, Times New Roman, and Courier New) to open a new window that displays the font. Click the **Print button**. Close the Font window.

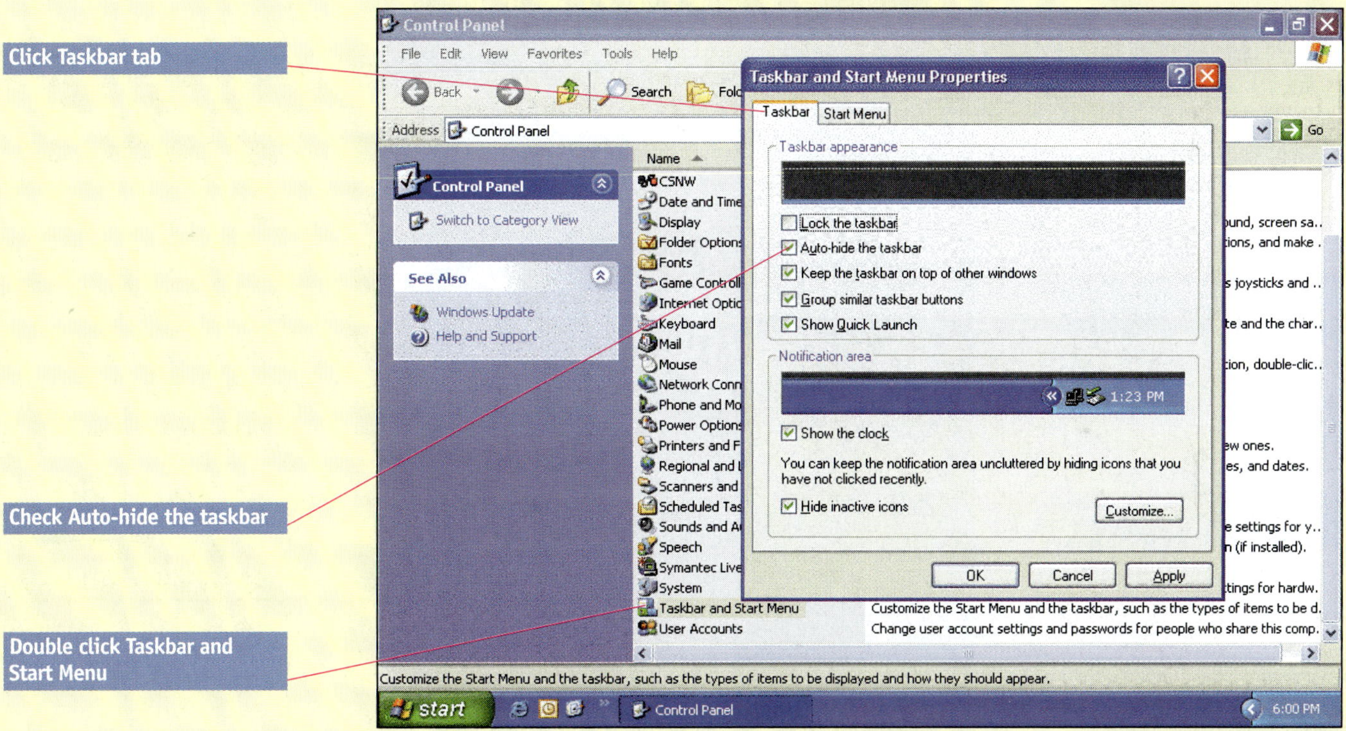

(f) Open the Control Panel Folder (step 6)

FIGURE 15 Hands-on Exercise 4 (*continued*)

MODIFY THE START MENU

Click and drag a shortcut icon to the Start button to place the shortcut on the Start menu. It does not appear that anything has happened, but the shortcut will appear at the top of the Start menu. Click the Start button to display the Start menu, then press the Esc key to exit the menu without executing a command. You can delete any item from the menu by right clicking the item and clicking the Unpin from the Start menu command.

Step 7: Obtain a .NET Passport

- Click the **Back button** to return to the Control Panel, then double click the **User Accounts icon** in the Control Panel folder. Maximize the User Accounts window so that it takes the entire desktop.
- Click the icon corresponding to the account that is currently logged to display a screen similar to Figure 15g. Click the command to **Set up my account to use a .NET passport**. You will see the first step in the Passport Wizard.
- Click the link to **View the privacy statement**. This starts Internet Explorer and goes to the .NET Passport site on the Web. Print the privacy agreement. It runs nine pages, but it contains a lot of useful information.
- Close Internet Explorer after you have printed the agreement. You are back in the Passport Wizard. Click **Next** to continue.
- Follow the instructions on the next several screens. You will be asked to enter your e-mail address and to supply a password. Click **Finish** when you have reached the last screen.
- You will receive an e-mail message after you have registered successfully. You will need your passport in our next exercise when we explore Windows Messenger and the associated instant messaging service.

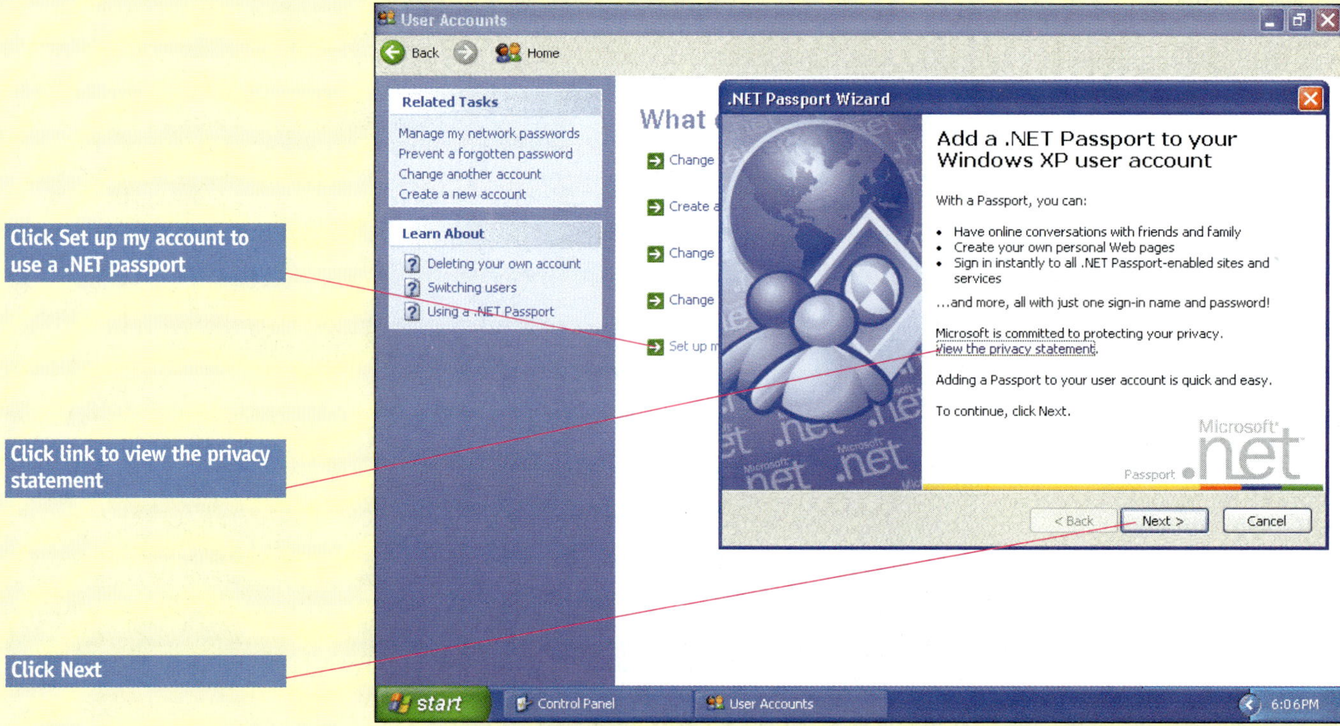

(g) Obtain a .NET Passport (step 7)

FIGURE 15 Hands-on Exercise 4 (*continued*)

UPDATING YOUR PASSPORT

You can modify the information in your passport profile at any time. Open the Control Panel, click User Accounts, select your account, then click the command to Change Your .NET passport. You can change your password, change the question that will remind you about your password should you forget it, and/or change the information that you authorize the passport service to share with others.

Step 8: Windows Update

- Close the User Accounts window to return to the Control Panel folder. Click the link to **Windows Update** to display a screen similar to Figure 15h.
- Click the command to **Scan for updates**. (This command is not visible in our figure.) This command will take several seconds as Windows determines which (if any) updates it recommends. Our system indicates that there are no critical updates but that additional updates are available.
- Click the link(s) to review the available updates. You do not have to install the vast majority of available updates. It is essential, however, that you install any updates deemed critical. One critical update appeared shortly after the release of Windows XP and closed a hole in the operating system that enabled hackers to break into some XP machines.
- Click the link to **View installation history** to see which updates were previously installed. Print this page for your instructor.
- Close the Update window. Log off the computer if you do not want to continue with the next exercise at this time.

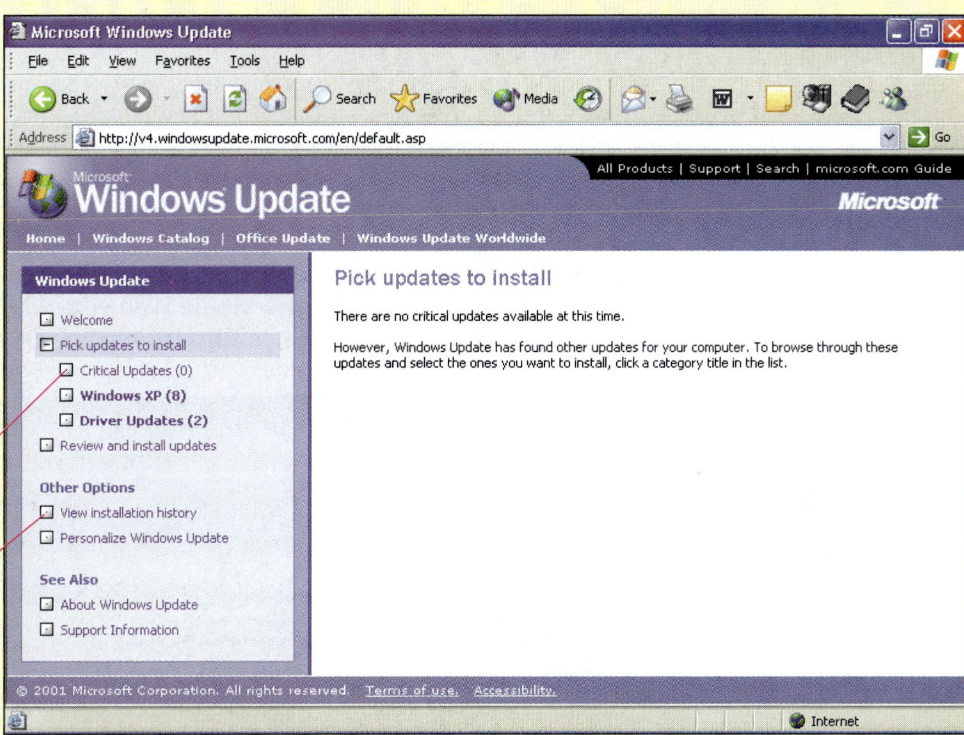

(h) Windows Update (step 8)

FIGURE 15 Hands-on Exercise 4 (*continued*)

THE SHOW DESKTOP BUTTON

The Show Desktop button or command minimizes every open window and returns you immediately to the desktop. You can get to this command in different ways, most easily by clicking the Show Desktop icon on the Quick Launch toolbar. The button functions as a toggle switch. Click it once and all windows are minimized. Click it a second time and the open windows are restored to their position on the desktop.

FUN WITH WINDOWS XP

The "XP" in Windows XP is for the experience that Microsoft promises individuals who adopt its operating system. Windows XP makes it easy to enjoy music and video, work with ***digital photographs***, and chat with your friends. This section describes these capabilities and then moves to a hands-on exercise in which you practice at the computer. All of the features are available on your own machine, but some may be disabled in a laboratory setting. It's not that your professor does not want you to have fun, but listening to music or engaging in instant messaging with your friends is not practical in a school environment. Nevertheless, the hands-on exercise that follows enables you to practice your skills in disk and file management as you work with multiple files and folders.

Windows Media Player

The ***Windows Media Player*** combines the functions of a radio, a CD, or DVD player, and an information database into a single program. It lets you listen to radio stations anywhere in the world, play a CD, or watch a DVD movie (provided you have the necessary hardware). You can copy selections from a CD to your computer, organize your music by artist and album, and then create a customized ***playlist*** to play the music in a specified order. The playlist may include as many songs from as many albums as you like and is limited only by the size of your storage device. The Media Player will also search the Web for audio or video files and play clips from a favorite movie.

The buttons at the left of the Media Player enable you to switch from one function to the next. The Radio Tuner button is active in Figure 16, and the BBC station is selected. Think of that—you are able to listen to radio stations from around the world with the click of a button. The Media Guide button connects you to the home page of the Windows Media Web site, where you can search the Web for media files and/or play movie clips from your favorite movies.

FIGURE 16 Windows Media Player

Digital Photography

Windows XP helps you to organize your pictures and share them with others. The best place to store photographs is in the My Pictures folder or in a subfolder within this folder as shown in Figure 17. The complete path to the folder appears in the Address bar and is best read from right to left. Thus, you are looking at pictures in the Romance Folder, which is in the My Pictures folder, which in turn is stored in a My Documents folder. Remember that each user has his or her unique My Documents folder, so the path must be further qualified. Hence, you are looking at the My Documents folder, within a folder for Jessica (one of several users), within the Documents and Settings folder on drive C. The latter folder maintains the settings for all of the users that are registered on this system.

The pictures in Figure 17 are shown in the ***Thumbnails view***, which displays a miniature image of each picture in the right pane. (Other views are also available and are accessed from the View menu or Views button.) The Picture Tasks area in the upper right lists the functions that are unique to photographs. You can view the pictures as a slide show, which is the equivalent of a PowerPoint presentation without having to create the presentation. You can print any picture, use it as the background on your desktop, or copy multiple pictures to a CD, provided you have the necessary hardware. You can also order prints online. You choose the company; select print sizes and quantities, supply the billing and shipping information, and your photographs are sent to you.

One photo is selected (BenWendy) in Figure 17, and the associated details are shown in the Details area of the task pane. The picture is stored as a JPG file, a common format for photographs. It was created on January 21, 2002.

The File and Folder Tasks area is collapsed in our figure, but you can expand the area to gain access to the normal file operations (move, copy, and delete). You can also e-mail the photograph from this panel. Remember, too, that you can click the Folders button on the Standard Buttons toolbar to switch to the hierarchical view of your system, which is better suited to disk and file management.

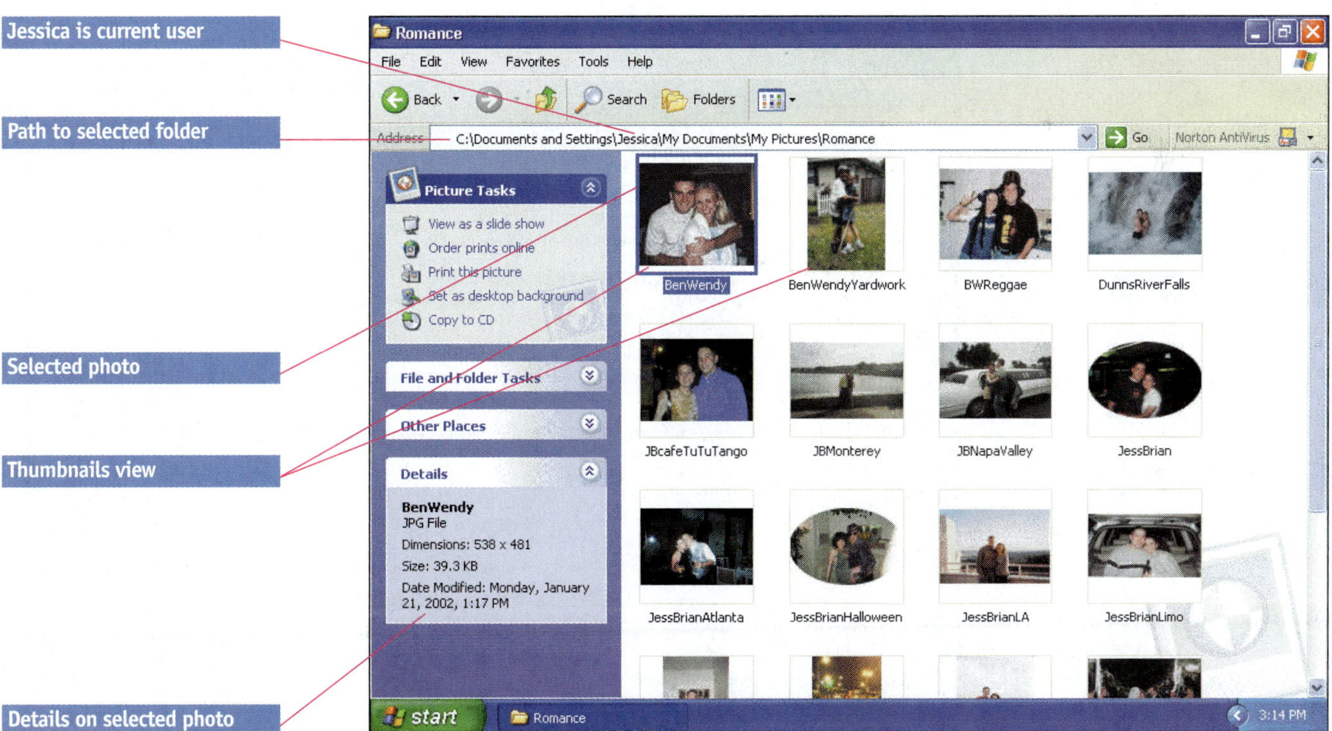

FIGURE 17 Working with Pictures

Windows Messenger

Windows Messenger is an instant messaging system in which you chat with friends and colleagues over the Internet. (It is based on the same technology as the "buddies list" that was made popular by America Online.) You need an Internet connection, a list of contacts, and a ***Microsoft passport*** that is based on your e-mail address. The passport is a free Microsoft service that enables you to access any passport-enabled Internet site with a single user name and associated password. (Step 7 in the previous hands-on exercise described how to obtain a passport.)

You can initiate a conversation at any time by monitoring the contacts list to see who is online and starting a chat session. Up to four people can participate in the same conversation. It is easy, fun, and addictive. You know the instant someone signs on, and you can begin chatting immediately. The bad news, however, is that it is all too easy to chat incessantly when you have real work to do. Hence you may want to change your status to indicate that you are busy and unable to participate in a conversation.

Figure 18 displays a conversation between Maryann and Bob. The session began when Maryann viewed her contact list, noticed that Bob was online, and started a conversation. Each person enters his or her message at the bottom of the conversation window, and then clicks the Send button. Additional messages can be sent without waiting for a response. Emoticons can be added to any message for effect. Note, too, the references to the file transfer that appear within the conversation, which are the result of Maryann clicking the command to send a file or photo, then attaching the desired file.

Windows Messenger is more than just a vehicle for chatting. If you have speakers and a microphone, you can place phone calls from your computer without paying a long distance charge. The most intriguing feature, however, is the ability to ask for remote assistance, whereby you can invite one of your contacts to view your desktop as you are working in order to ask for help. It is as if your friend were in the room looking over your shoulder. He or she will see everything that you do and can respond immediately with suggestions.

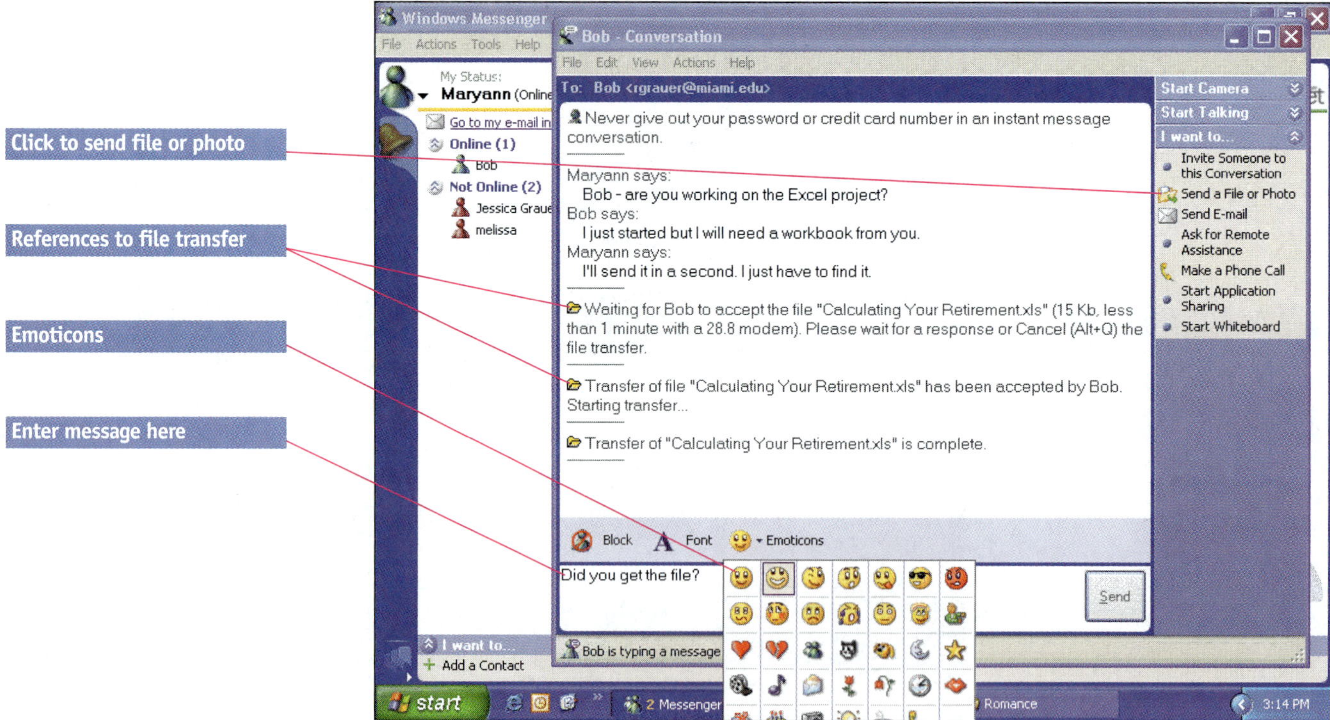

FIGURE 18 Windows Messenger

hands-on exercise

5 Fun with Windows XP

Objective To use Windows Media Player, work with photographs, and experiment with Windows Messenger. Check with your professor regarding the availability of the resources required for this exercise. Use Figure 19.

Step 1: Open the Shared Music Folder

- Start Windows Explorer. Click the **Folders button** to display the tree structure. You need to locate some music to demonstrate the Media Player.
- The typical XP installation includes some files within the Shared Documents folder. Expand the My Computer folder to show the **Shared Documents folder**, expand the **Shared Music folder**, and then open the **Sample Music folder** as shown in Figure 19a.
- Point to any file (it does not matter if you have a different selection of music) to display the ScreenTip describing the music. Double click the file to start the Media Player and play the selected music.

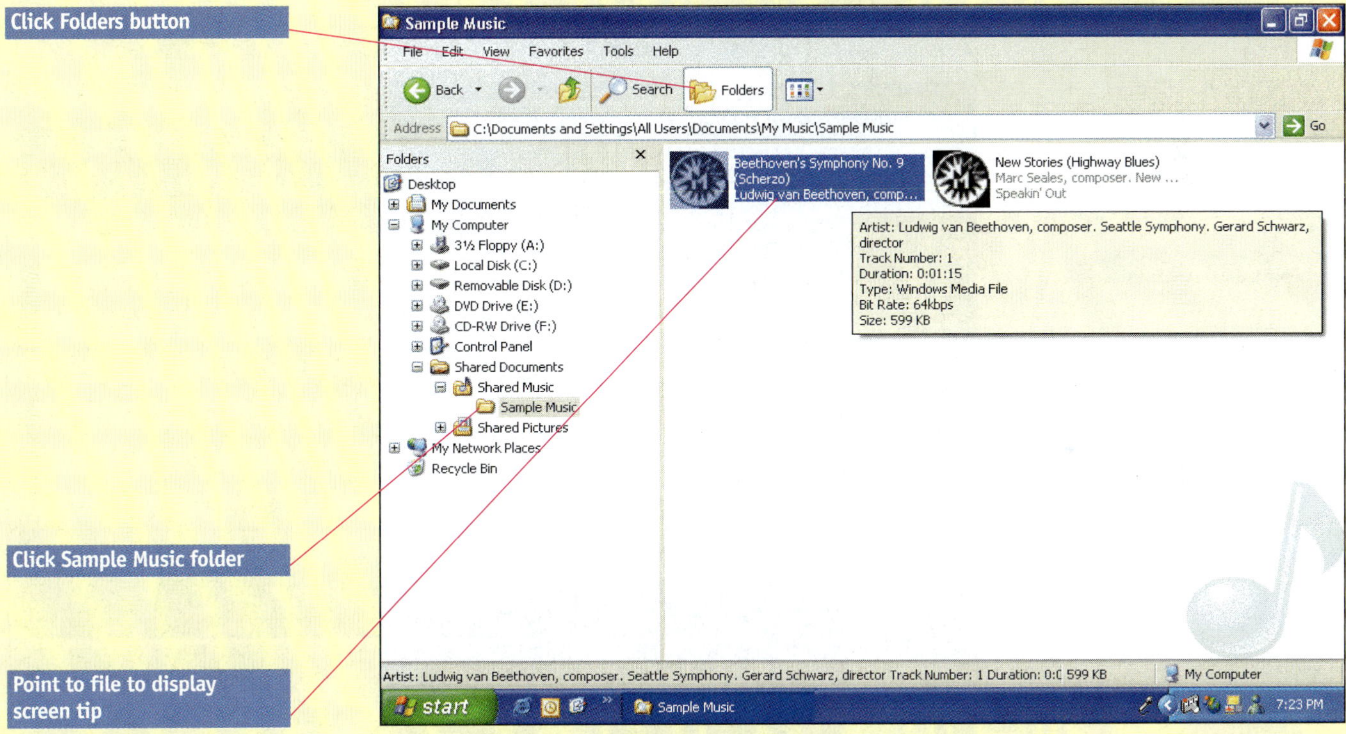

(a) Open the Shared Music Folder (step 1)

FIGURE 19 Hands-on Exercise 5

SHARED FOLDERS VERSUS PERSONAL FOLDERS

Windows XP automatically creates a unique My Documents folder for every user, which in turn contains a unique My Pictures folder and My Music folder within the My Documents folder. These folders are private and cannot be accessed by other users. Windows also provides a Shared Documents folder that is accessible to every user on a system.

Step 2: Listen to the Music

- You should hear the music when the Windows Media Player opens in its own window as shown in Figure 19b. The controls at the bottom of the window are similar to those on any CD player.
  - You can click the **Pause button**, then click the **Play button** to restart the music at that point.
  - You can click the **Stop button** to stop playing altogether.
  - You can also drag the slider to begin playing at a different place.
- You can also adjust the volume as shown in Figure 19b. Double click the **Volume Control icon** in the notification area at the right of the taskbar to display the Volume Control dialog box. Close this window.
- Click the **Radio Tuner button** at the side of the Media Player window. The system pauses as it tunes into the available radio stations.
- Select a radio station (e.g., **BBC World**) when you see the list of available stations, then click the **Play button** after you choose a station.
- You will see a message at the bottom of the window indicating that your computer is connecting to the media, after which you will hear the radio station.

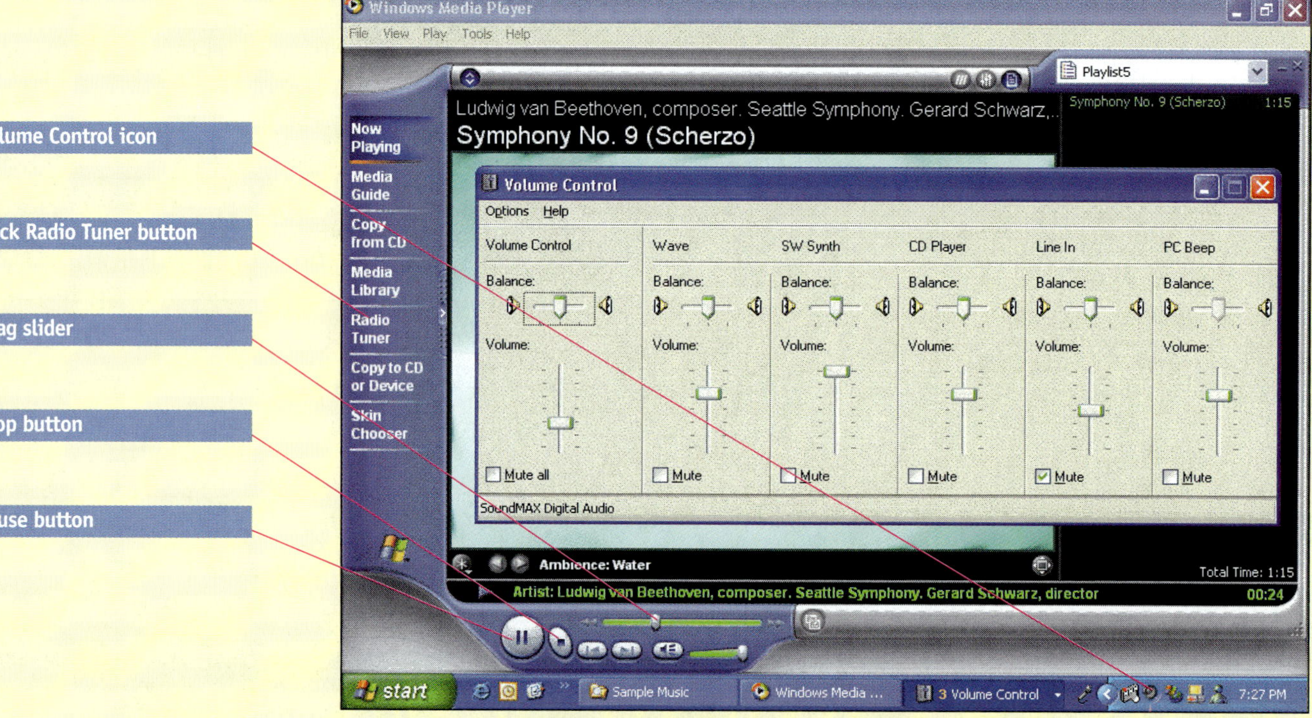

(b) Listen to the Music (step 2)

FIGURE 19 Hands-on Exercise 5 (*continued*)

OTHER MEDIA PLAYERS

If you double click a music (MP3) file, and a program other than Windows Media starts to play, it is because your system has another media player as its default program. You can still use the Windows Media Player, but you will have to start the program explicitly from the Start menu. Once the Media Player is open, pull down the File menu and click the Open command, then select the music file you want to play.

Step 3: Create a Playlist

- Click the **Media Library button** at the side of the Media player to display the media files that are currently on your computer.
  - The left pane displays a tree structure of your media library. Thus, you click the plus or minus sign to collapse or expand the indicated folder.
  - The right pane displays the contents of the selected object (the My Music playlist) in Figure 19c.
- Do not be concerned if your media library is different from ours. Click the **New playlist button**, enter **My Music** as the name of the new list, and click **OK**.
- Click the newly created playlist in the left pane to display its contents in the left pane. The playlist is currently empty.
- Start **Windows Explorer**. Open the **My Music Folder** within the My Documents folder. If necessary, click the **Restore button** to move and size Windows Explorer so that you can copy documents to the Media library.
- Click and drag one or more selections from the My Music folder to the right pane of the Media library to create the playlist. Close Windows Explorer.
- Click the **down arrow** in the list box at the upper right of the Media Gallery and select the My Music playlist to play the songs you have selected.

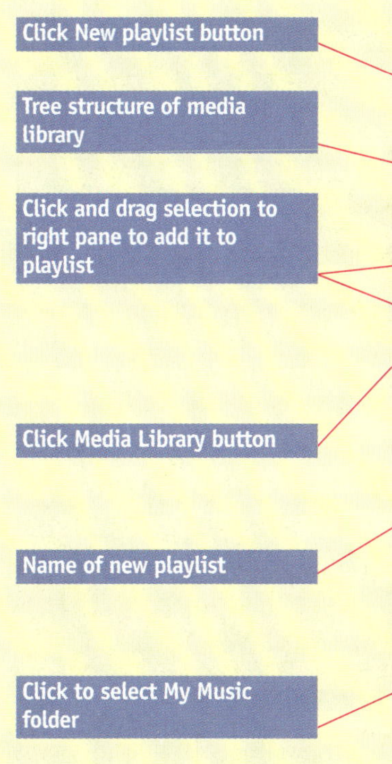

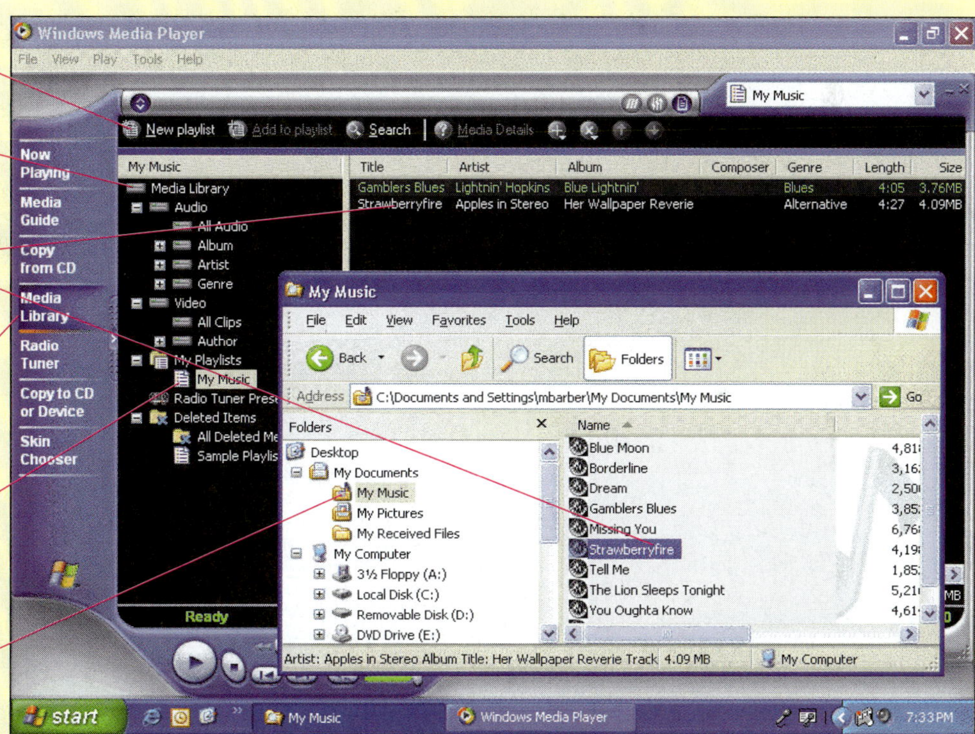

(c) Create a Playlist (step 3)

FIGURE 19 Hands-on Exercise 5 *(continued)*

THE MEDIA GUIDE

Click the Media Guide button at the left of the Media Player to display the home page of the Windows Media Site. You can also get there by starting Internet Explorer and entering windowsmedia.com in the Address bar. Either way, you will be connected to the Internet and can search the Web for media files and/or play clips from your favorite movie.

Step 4: Create a Pictures Folder

- You can use your own pictures, or if you don't have any, you can use the sample pictures provided with Windows XP. Start (or maximize) Windows Explorer. Open the **My Pictures folder** within the **My Documents folder**.
- Do not be concerned if the content of your folder is different from ours. Our folder already contains various subfolders with different types of pictures in each folder.
- Click the **Views button** and change to the **Thumbnails view**. This view is especially useful when viewing folders that contain photographs because (up to four) images are displayed on the folder icon.
- Right click anywhere in the right pane to display a context-sensitive menu as shown in Figure 19d. Click **New**, and then click **Folder** as the type of object to create.
- The icon for a new folder will appear with the name of the folder (New Folder) highlighted. Enter a more appropriate name (we chose **Romance** because our pictures are those of a happy couple), and press **Enter**.
- Copy your pictures from another folder, a CD, or floppy disk to the newly created folder.

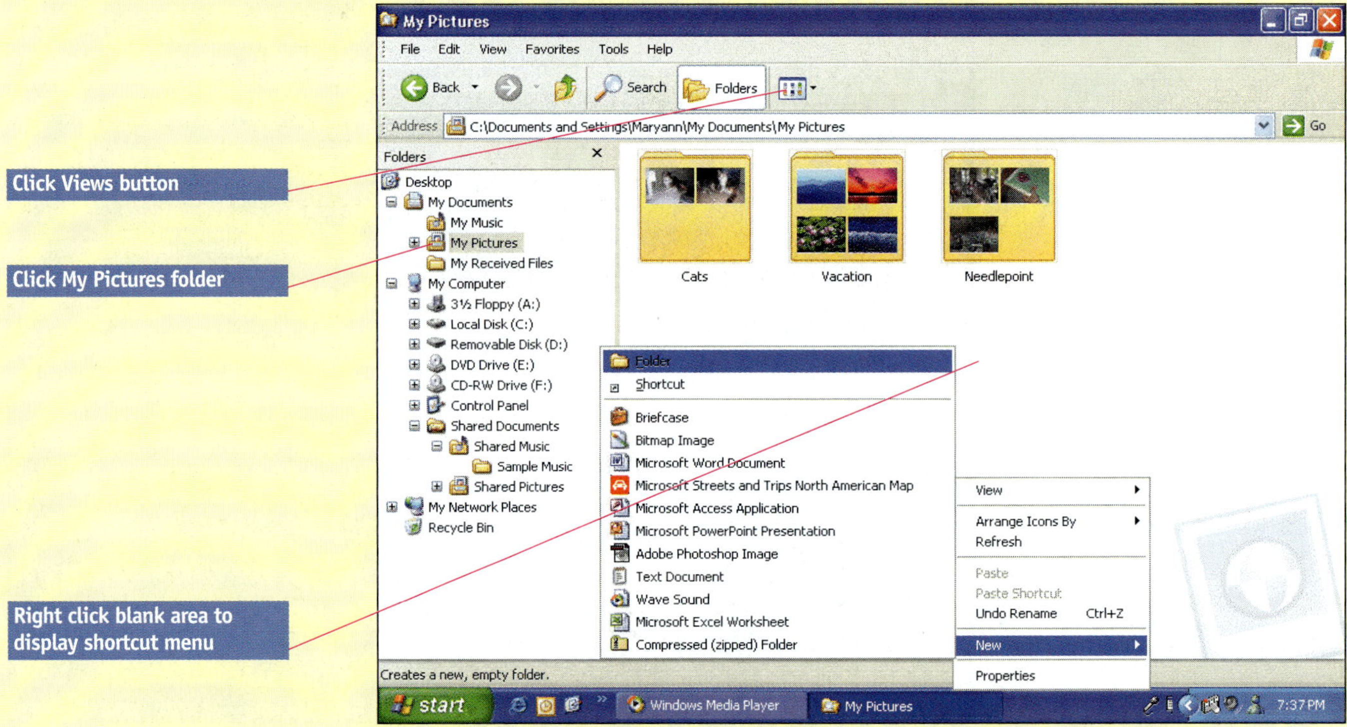

(d) Create a Pictures Folder (step 4)

FIGURE 19 Hands-on Exercise 5 (*continued*)

DESIGN GALLERY LIVE

The Microsoft Design Gallery is an excellent source of photographs and other media. Start Internet Explorer and go to the Design Gallery at dgl.microsoft.com. Enter the desired topic in the Search for text box, indicate that you want to search everywhere, and specify that the results should be photos. Download one or more of the photos that are returned by the search and use those pictures to complete this exercise.

Step 5: Display Your Pictures

- Double click the newly created folder to display its contents. Click the **Folders button** to display the Windows Explorer task pane, as opposed to the hierarchy structure. Click the **Views button** and change to the **Filmstrip view** as shown in Figure 19e.
- Click the **Next Image** or (**Previous Image**) **button** to move from one picture to the next within the folder. If necessary, click the buttons to rotate pictures clockwise or counterclockwise so that the pictures are displayed properly within the window.
- Click the command to **View as a slide show**, then display your pictures one at a time on your monitor. This is a very easy way to enjoy your photographs. Press the **Esc key** to stop.
- Choose any picture, then click the command to **Print this picture** that appears in the left pane. Submit this picture to your instructor.
- Choose a different picture and then click the command to **Set as desktop background**. Minimize Windows Explorer.

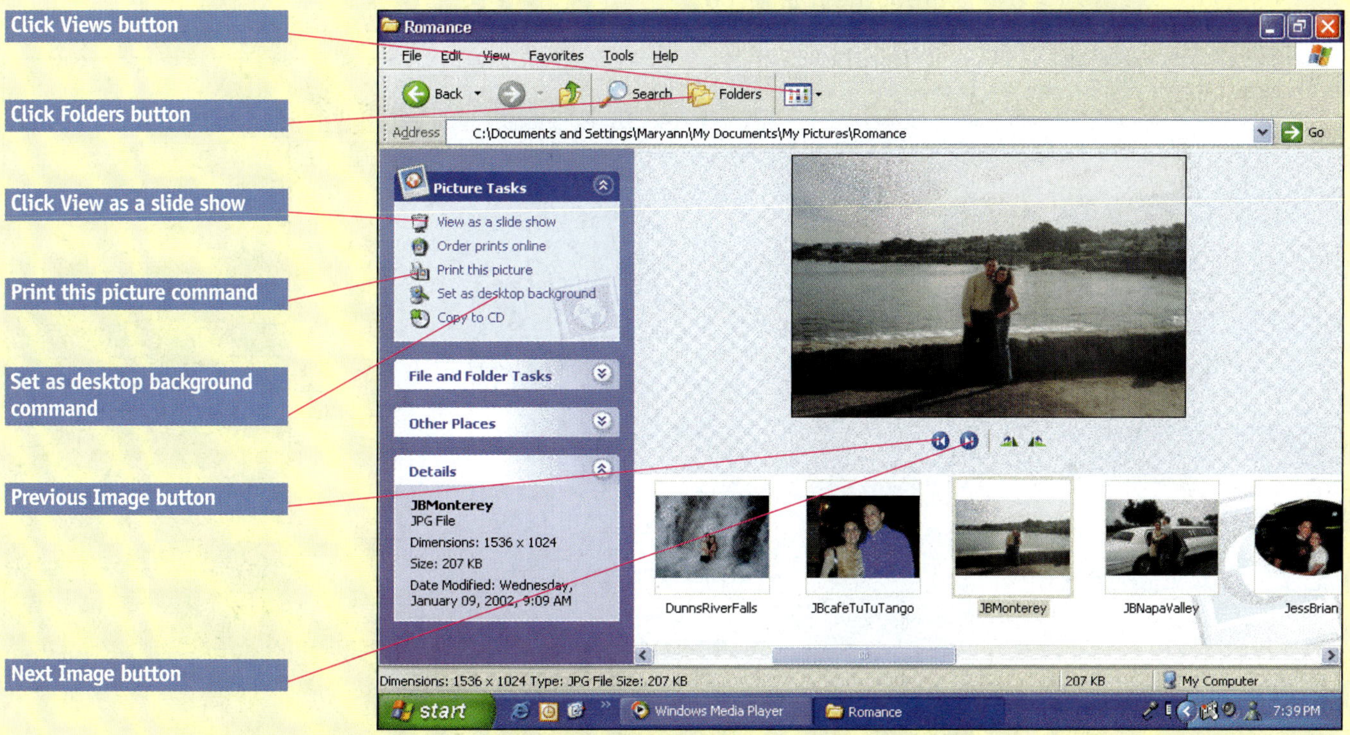

(e) Display Your Pictures (step 5)

FIGURE 19 Hands-on Exercise 5 (*continued*)

CHANGE THE VIEW

Click the down arrow next to the Views button on the Standard toolbar to change the way files are displayed within a folder. The Details view provides the most information and includes the filename, file type, file size, and the date that the file was created or last modified. (Additional attributes are also possible.) Other views are more visual. The Thumbnails view displays a miniature image of the file and is best used with clip art, photographs, or presentations. The Filmstrip view is used with photographs only.

Step 6: Customize the Desktop

- Your desktop should once again be visible, depending on which (if any) applications are open. If you do not see the desktop, right click a blank area of the taskbar, then click the **Show Desktop command**.
- You should see the picture you selected earlier as the background for your desktop. The picture is attractive (you chose it), but it may be distracting.
- To remove the picture, **right click** the background of the desktop and click the **Properties command** to display the Display Properties dialog box in Figure 19f.
- Click the **Desktop tab**, then click **None** in the Background list box. Click **OK** to accept this setting and close the dialog box. The picture disappears.
- Regardless of whether you keep the background, you can use your pictures as a screen saver. Redisplay the Display Properties dialog box. Click the **Screen Saver tab** in the Display Properties box, then choose **My Picture Slideshow** from the screen saver list box.
- Wait a few seconds and the picture within the dialog box will change, just as it will on your desktop. Click **OK** to accept the screen saver and close the Display Properties dialog box.

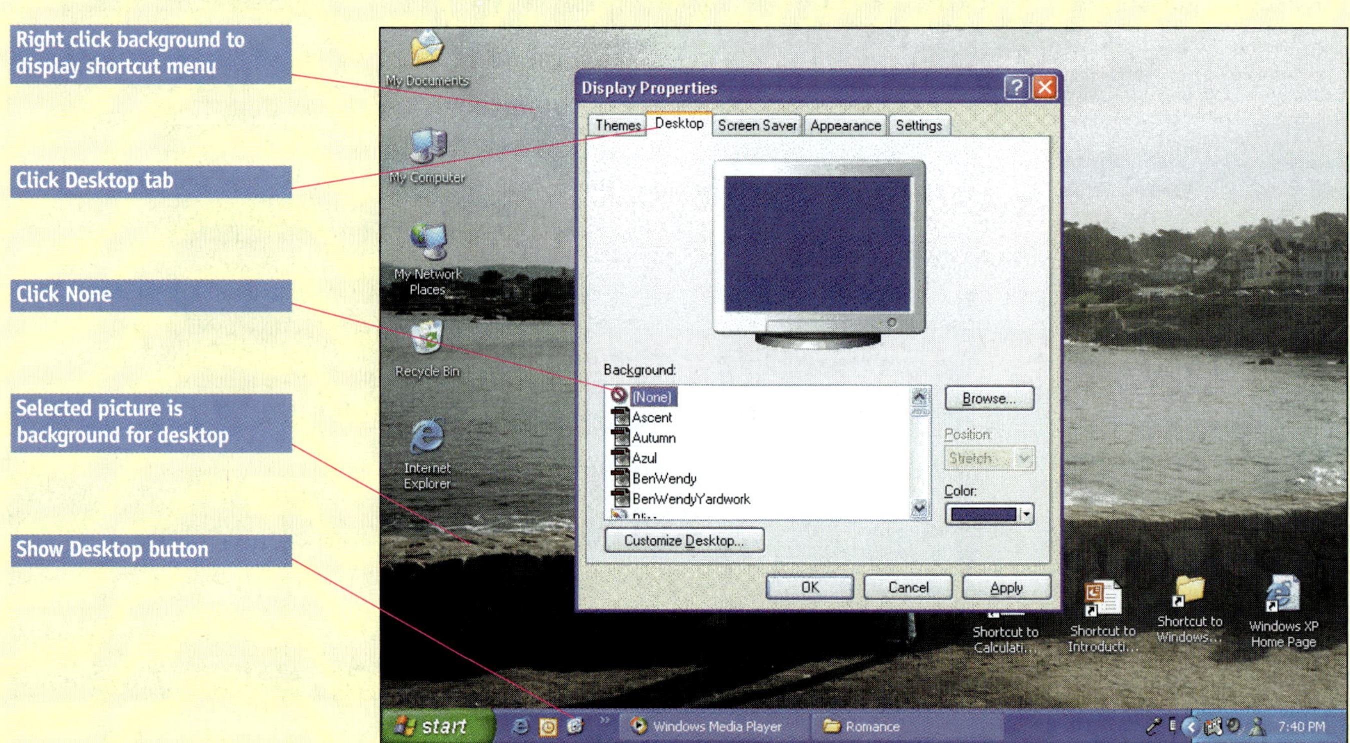

(f) Customize the Desktop (step 6)

FIGURE 19 Hands-on Exercise 5 (*continued*)

CHANGE THE RESOLUTION

The resolution of a monitor refers to the number of pixels (picture elements or dots) that are displayed at one time. The higher the resolution, the more pixels are displayed, and hence you see more of a document at one time. You can change the resolution at any time. Right click the desktop, click the Properties command to show the Display Properties dialog box, then click the Settings tab. Drag the slider bar to the new resolution, then click OK.

Step 7: Start Windows Messenger

- You need a passport to use Windows Messenger. Double click the **Windows Messenger icon** in the notification area of the taskbar to sign in.
- Maximize the Messenger window. You will see a list of your existing contacts with an indication of whether they are online.
- Add one or more contacts. Pull down the **Tools menu**, click the command to **Add a Contact**, then follow the onscreen instructions. (The contact does not have to have Windows XP to use instant messaging.)
- Double click any contact that is online to initiate a conversation and open a conversation window as shown in Figure 19g.
- Type a message at the bottom of the conversation window, then click the **Send button** to send the message. The text of your message will appear immediately on your contact's screen. Your friend's messages will appear on your screen.
- Continue the conversation by entering additional text. You can press the **Enter key** (instead of clicking the **Send button**) to send the message. You can also use **Shift + enter** to create a line break in your text.

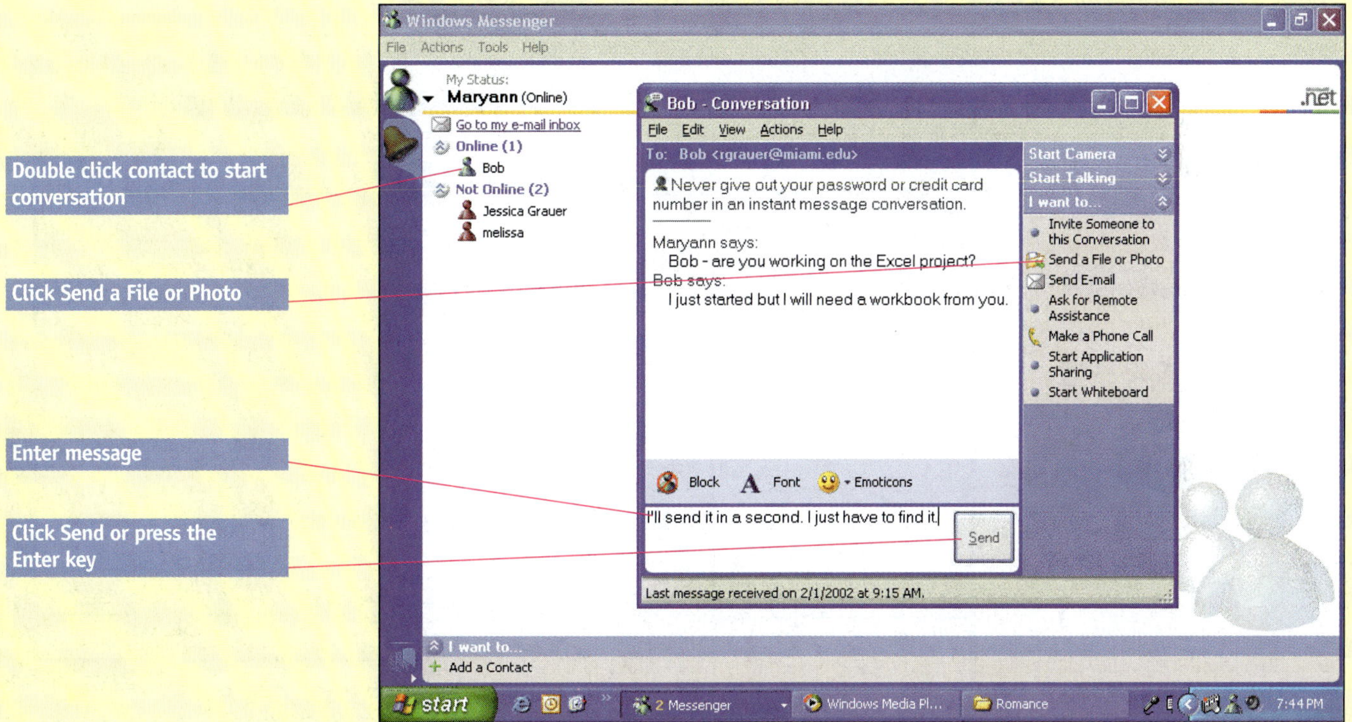

(g) Start Windows Messenger (step 7)

FIGURE 19 Hands-on Exercise 5 (*continued*)

CHANGE YOUR STATUS

Anyone on your contact list knows immediately when you log on; thus, the larger your contact list, the more likely you are to be engaged in idle chitchat when you have real work to do. You can avoid unwanted conversations without being rude by changing your status. Click the down arrow next to your name in the Messenger window and choose a different icon. You can appear offline or simply indicate that you are busy. Either way you will be more likely to get your work done.

Step 8: Attach a File

- Click the command to **Send a File or Photo**, which displays the Send a File dialog box in Figure 19h. It does not matter which file you choose, since the purpose of this step is to demonstrate the file transfer capability.
- A series of three file transfer messages will appear on your screen. Windows Messenger waits for your friend to accept the file transfer, then it indicates the transfer has begun, and finally, that the transfer was successful.
- Click the command to **Invite someone to this conversation** if you have another contact online. You will see a second dialog box in which you select the contact.
- There are now three people in the conversation. (Up to four people can participate in one conversation.) Your friends' responses will appear on your screen as soon as they are entered.
- Send your goodbye to end the conversation, then close the conversation window to end the chat session. You are still online and can participate in future conversations.
- Close Windows Messenger. You will be notified if anyone wants to contact you.

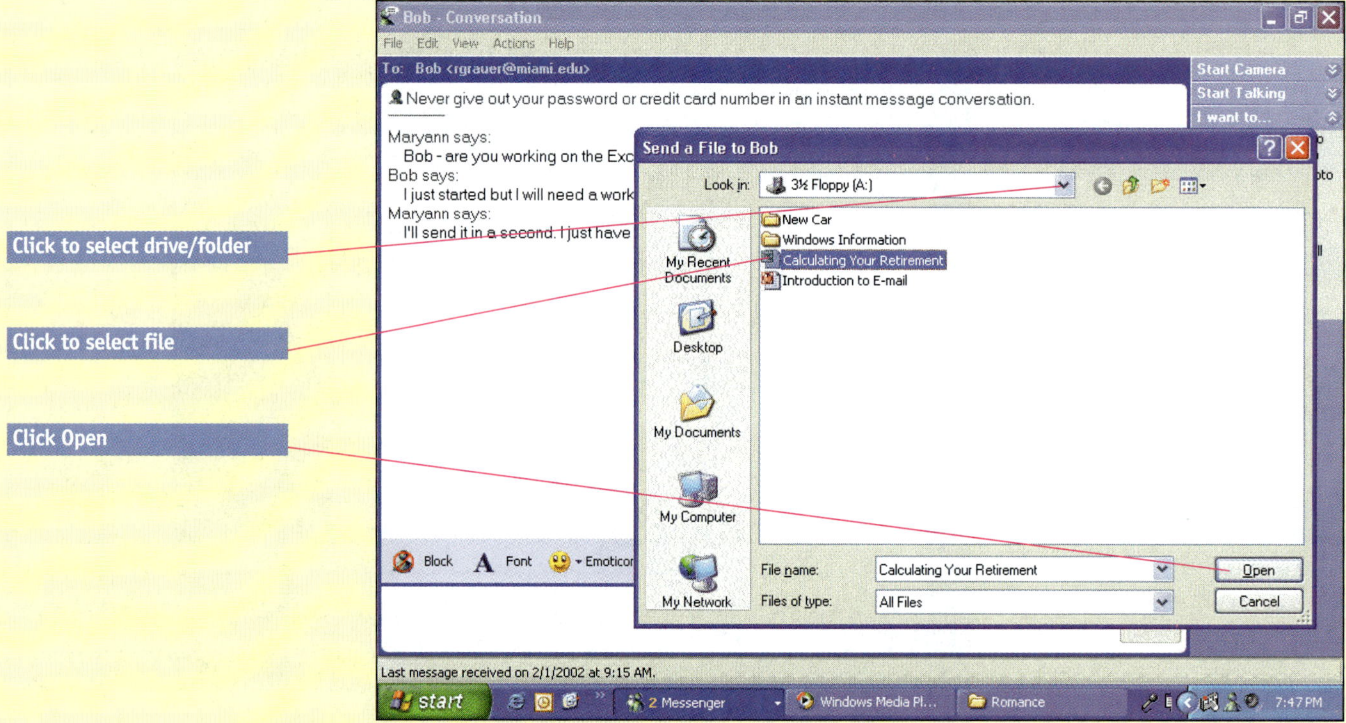

(h) Attach a File (step 8)

FIGURE 19 Hands-on Exercise 5 (*continued*)

E-MAIL VERSUS INSTANT MESSAGING

E-mail and instant messaging are both Internet communication services, but there are significant differences. E-mail does not require both participants to be online at the same time. E-mail messages are also permanent and do not disappear when you exit your e-mail program. Instant messaging, however, requires both participants to be online. Its conversations are not permanent and disappear when you end the session.

Step 9: Ask for Assistance

- Your contacts do not require Windows XP to converse with you using Windows Messenger. Windows XP is required, however, to use the remote assistance feature.
- Click the **Start button**, then click the **Help and Support command** to display the home page of the Help and Support Center. Click the **Support button**, then click the command to **Ask a friend to help**.
- A Remote Assistance screen will open in the right pane. Click the command to **Invite someone to help**, which will display your contact list as shown in Figure 19i. You can choose any contact who is online, or you can enter the e-mail address of someone else.
- You will see a dialog box indicating that an invitation has been sent. Once your friend accepts the invitation, he or she will be able to see your screen. A chat window will open up in which you can discuss the problem you are having. Close the session when you are finished.
- Pull down the **File menu** and click the command to **Sign out**. The Windows Messenger icon in the notification will indicate that you have signed out.

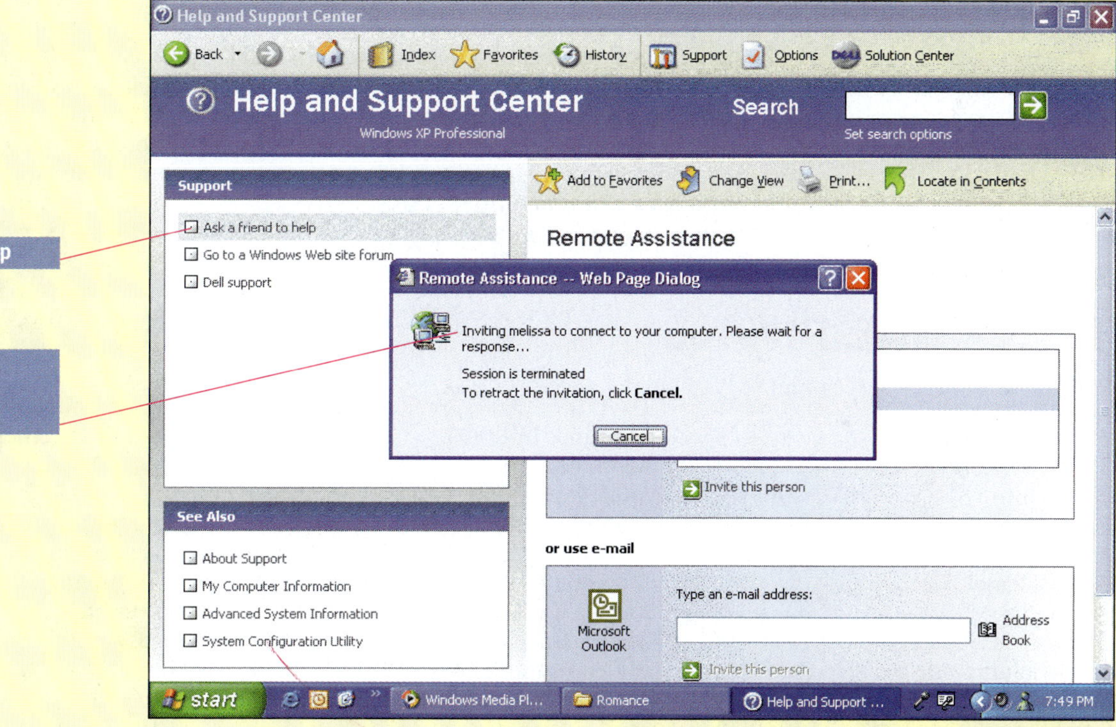

(i) Ask for Assistance (step 9)

FIGURE 19 Hands-on Exercise 5 *(continued)*

SUPPORT ONLINE

Microsoft provides extensive online support in a variety of formats. Start at the Windows XP home page (www.microsoft.com/windowsxp), then click the Support button to see what is available. You will be able to search the Microsoft Knowledge Base for detailed information on virtually any subject. You can also post questions and participate in threaded discussions in various newsgroups. Support is available for every Microsoft product.

SUMMARY

Windows XP is the newest and most powerful version of the Windows operating system. It has a slightly different look than earlier versions, but it maintains the conventions of its predecessors. All Windows operations take place on the desktop. Every window contains the same basic elements, which include a title bar, a Minimize button, a Maximize or Restore button, and a Close button. All windows may be moved and sized. The taskbar contains a button for each open program and enables you to switch back and forth between those programs by clicking the appropriate button. You can obtain information about every aspect of Windows through the Help and Support Center.

A file is a set of data or set of instructions that has been given a name and stored on disk. There are two basic types of files, program files and data files. A program file is an executable file, whereas a data file can be used only in conjunction with a specific program. Every file has a filename and a file type.

Files are stored in folders to better organize the hundreds (or thousands) of files on a disk. A folder may contain program files, data files, and/or other folders. Windows automatically creates a set of personal folders for every user. These include the My Documents folder and the My Pictures folder and My Music folder within the My Documents folder. Windows also provides a Shared Documents folder that can be accessed by every user. The My Computer folder is accessible by all users and displays the devices on a system.

Windows Explorer facilitates every aspect of disk and file management. It presents a hierarchical view of your system that displays all devices and, optionally, the folders on each device. Any device may be expanded or collapsed to display or hide its folders.

Windows XP contains several tools to help you enjoy your system. The Windows Media Player combines the functions of a radio, CD player, DVD player, and an information database into a single program. Windows Messenger is an instant messaging system in which you chat with friends and colleagues over the Internet.

The Control Panel affects every aspect of your system. It determines the appearance of your desktop and it controls the performance of your hardware. A shortcut is a link to any object on your computer, such as a program, file, folder, disk drive, or Web page. The Search Companion enables you to search for a file according to several different criteria.

KEY TERMS

- Backup strategy ... 31
- Check box ... 8
- Classic Start menu ... 3
- Close button ... 6
- Command button ... 8
- Compressed file ... 20
- Control Panel ... 41
- Copy a file ... 31
- Data file ... 18
- Delete command ... 31
- Desktop ... 3
- Details view ... 18
- Dialog box ... 8
- Digital photographs ... 52
- Fast user switching ... 2
- File ... 18
- File type ... 18
- Filename ... 18
- Filmstrip view ... 59
- Firewall ... 20
- Folder ... 18
- Help and Support Center ... 9
- Help button ... 8
- Internet Explorer 6.0 ... 9
- Internet Service Provider ... 20
- List box ... 8
- Maximize button ... 6
- Menu bar ... 6
- Microsoft passport ... 54
- Minimize button ... 6
- Modem ... 20
- Move a file ... 31
- Move a window ... 3
- Multitasking ... 3
- My Computer folder ... 6
- My Documents folder ... 29
- My Music folder ... 29
- My Pictures folder ... 29
- Notification area ... 3
- Option button ... 8
- Personal folders ... 29
- Playlist ... 52
- Program file ... 18
- Pull-down menu ... 7
- Quick Launch toolbar ... 42
- Radio button ... 8
- Recycle Bin ... 31
- Rename command ... 32
- Restore button ... 6
- Scroll bar ... 6
- Search Companion ... 43
- Shared Documents folder ... 29
- Shortcut ... 42
- Size a window ... 3
- Spin button ... 8
- Start button ... 3
- Start menu ... 3
- Status bar ... 6
- Task pane ... 6
- Taskbar ... 3
- Text box ... 8
- Thumbnails view ... 53
- Tiles view ... 18
- Title bar ... 6
- Toolbar ... 6
- Windows Classic theme ... 3
- Windows Explorer ... 29
- Windows Media Player ... 52
- Windows Messenger ... 54
- Windows Update ... 41
- Windows® XP ... 2
- Windows XP theme ... 3
- XP Home Edition ... 2
- XP Professional Edition ... 2

MULTIPLE CHOICE

1. Which of the following is true regarding a dialog box?
   (a) Option buttons indicate mutually exclusive choices
   (b) Check boxes imply that multiple options may be selected
   (c) Both (a) and (b)
   (d) Neither (a) nor (b)

2. Which of the following is the first step in sizing a window?
   (a) Point to the title bar
   (b) Pull down the View menu to display the toolbar
   (c) Point to any corner or border
   (d) Pull down the View menu and change to large icons

3. Which of the following is the first step in moving a window?
   (a) Point to the title bar
   (b) Pull down the View menu to display the toolbar
   (c) Point to any corner or border
   (d) Pull down the View menu and change to large icons

4. Which button appears immediately after a window has been maximized?
   (a) The Close button
   (b) The Minimize button
   (c) The Maximize button
   (d) The Restore button

5. What happens to a window that has been minimized?
   (a) The window is still visible but it no longer has a Minimize button
   (b) The window shrinks to a button on the taskbar
   (c) The window is closed and the application is removed from memory
   (d) The window is still open but the application has been removed from memory

6. What is the significance of a faded (dimmed) command in a pull-down menu?
   (a) The command is not currently accessible
   (b) A dialog box appears if the command is selected
   (c) A Help window appears if the command is selected
   (d) There are no equivalent keystrokes for the particular command

7. The Recycle Bin enables you to restore a file that was deleted from
   (a) Drive A
   (b) Drive C
   (c) Both (a) and (b)
   (d) Neither (a) nor (b)

8. Which of the following was suggested as essential to a backup strategy?
   (a) Back up all program files at the end of every session
   (b) Store backup files at another location
   (c) Both (a) and (b)
   (d) Neither (a) nor (b)

9. A shortcut may be created for
   (a) An application or a document
   (b) A folder or a drive
   (c) Both (a) and (b)
   (d) Neither (a) nor (b)

10. What happens if you click the Folders button (on the Standard Buttons toolbar in the My Computer folder) twice in a row?
    (a) The left pane displays a task pane with commands for the selected object
    (b) The left pane displays a hierarchical view of the devices on your system
    (c) The left pane displays either a task pane or the hierarchical view depending on what was displayed prior to clicking the button initially
    (d) The left pane displays both the task pane and a hierarchical view

... continued

multiple choice

11. The Search Companion can

(a) Locate all files containing a specified phrase
(b) Restrict its search to a specified set of folders
(c) Both (a) and (b)
(d) Neither (a) nor (b)

12. Which views display miniature images of photographs within a folder?

(a) Tiles view and Icons view
(b) Thumbnails view and Filmstrip view
(c) Details view and List view
(d) All views display a miniature image

13. Which of the following statements is true?

(a) A plus sign next to a folder indicates that its contents are hidden
(b) A minus sign next to a folder indicates that its contents are hidden
(c) A plus sign appears next to any folder that has been expanded
(d) A minus sign appears next to any folder that has been collapsed

14. Ben and Jessica are both registered users on a Windows XP computer. Which of the following is a *false statement* regarding their personal folders?

(a) Ben and Jessica each have a My Documents folder
(b) Ben and Jessica each have a My Pictures folder that is stored within their respective My Documents folders
(c) Ben can access files in Jessica's My Documents folder
(d) Jessica cannot access files in Ben's My Documents folder

15. When is a file permanently deleted?

(a) When you delete the file from Windows Explorer
(b) When you empty the Recycle Bin
(c) When you turn the computer off
(d) All of the above

16. What happens if you (left) click and drag a file to another folder on the same drive?

(a) The file is copied
(b) The file is moved
(c) The file is deleted
(d) A shortcut menu is displayed

17. How do you shut down the computer?

(a) Click the Start button, then click the Turn Off Computer command
(b) Right click the Start button, then click the Turn Off Computer command
(c) Click the End button, then click the Turn Off Computer command
(d) Right click the End button, then click the Turn Off Computer command

18. Which of the following can be accomplished with Windows Messenger?

(a) You can chat with up to three other people in the conversation window
(b) You can place telephone calls (if you have a microphone and speaker) without paying long-distance charges
(c) You can ask for remote assistance, which enables your contact to view your screen as you are working
(d) All of the above

ANSWERS

1. c	**7.** b	**13.** a
2. c	**8.** b	**14.** c
3. a	**9.** c	**15.** b
4. d	**10.** c	**16.** b
5. b	**11.** c	**17.** a
6. a	**12.** b	**18.** d

PRACTICE WITH WINDOWS XP

1. **Two Different Views:** The document in Figure 20 is an effective way to show your instructor that you understand the My Computer folder, the various views available, the task pane, and the hierarchy structure. It also demonstrates that you can capture a screen for inclusion in a Word document. Proceed as follows:
   a. Open the My Computer folder, click the Views button, and switch to the Tiles view. Click the Folders button to display the task pane. Size the window as necessary so that you will be able to fit two folders onto a one-page document as shown in Figure 20.
   b. Press and hold the Alt key as you press the Print Screen key to copy the My Computer window to the Windows clipboard. (The Print Screen key captures the entire screen. Using the Alt key, however, copies just the current window.) Click the Start menu, click Programs, and then click Microsoft Word to start the program. Maximize the window.
   c. Enter the title of the document, press Enter, and type your name. Press the Enter key twice in a row to leave a blank line.
   d. Pull down the Edit menu. Click the Paste command to copy the contents of the clipboard to the document. Press the Enter key to add a figure caption, then press the Enter key two additional times.
   e. Click the taskbar to return to the My Computer folder. Change to the Details view. Click the Folders button to display the hierarchy structure, as opposed to the task pane. Expand My Computer in the left pane, but collapse all of the individual devices. Press Alt+Print Screen to capture the My Computer folder in this configuration.
   f. Click the taskbar to return to your Word document. Press Ctrl+V to paste the contents of the clipboard into your document. Enter an appropriate caption below the figure. Save the completed document and print it for your instructor.

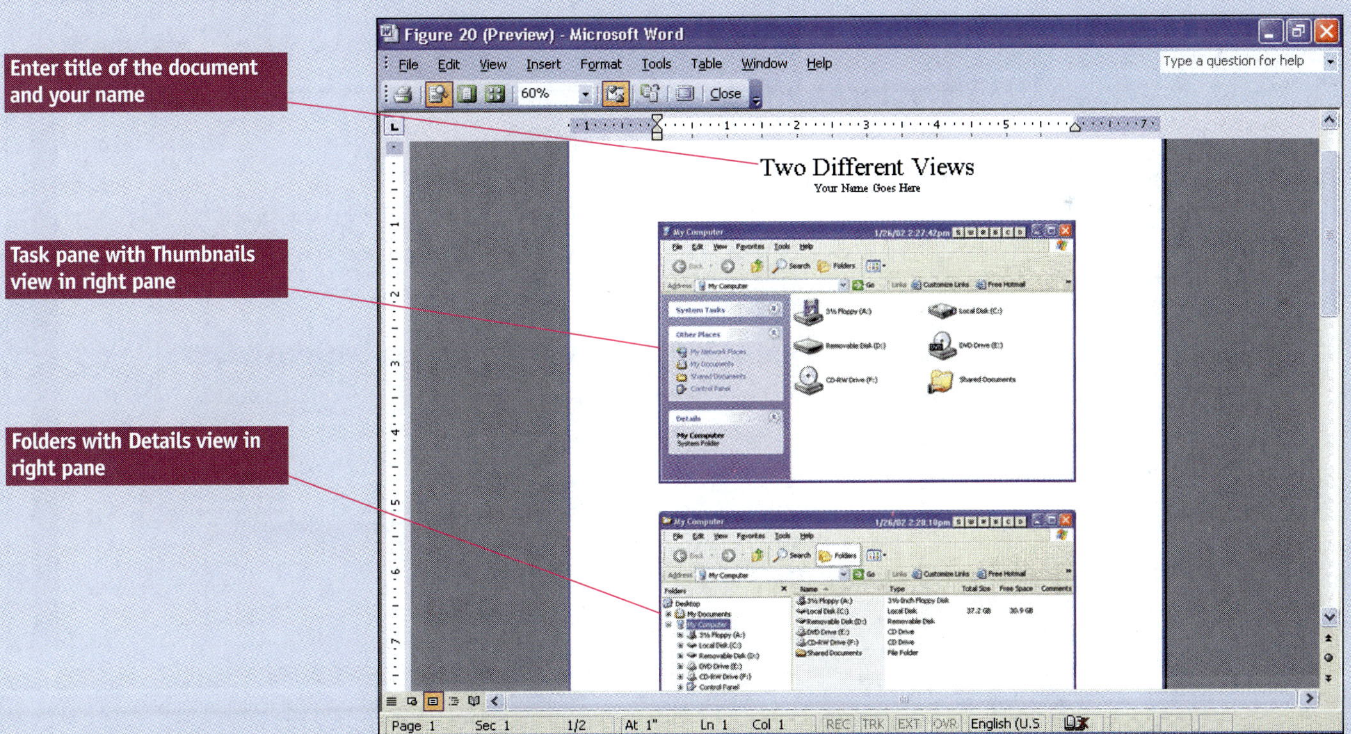

FIGURE 20 Two Different Views (exercise 1)

2. **Network Connections:** The document in Figure 21 displays the network connections on our system as well as the status of one of those connections. Your assignment is to create the equivalent document for your computer. Proceed as follows:
   a. Open the Control Panel, switch to the Classic view, then double click the Network Connections icon to display the Network Connections folder. (You can also get to this folder from My Computer, by clicking the link to My Network Places, and then clicking Network Connections from within the Network Tasks area.)
   b. Maximize the Network Connections folder so that it takes the entire desktop. Change to the Tiles view. Click the Folders button to display the task pane. Select (click) a connection, then click the link to View status of the connection, to display the associated dialog box.
   c. Press the Print Screen key to print this screen. Start Microsoft Word and open a new document. Press the Enter key several times, then click the Paste button to copy the contents of the clipboard into your document.
   d. Press Ctrl+Home to return to the beginning of the Word document, where you can enter the title of the document and your name. Compose a paragraph similar to the one in our figure that describes the network connections on your computer. Print this document for your instructor.
   e. Experiment with the first two network tasks that are displayed in the task pane. How difficult is it to set up a new connection? How do you set a firewall to protect your system from unauthorized access when connected to the Internet? How do you establish a home or small office network?
   f. Use the Help and Support Center to obtain additional information. Print one or two Help screens for your instructor.

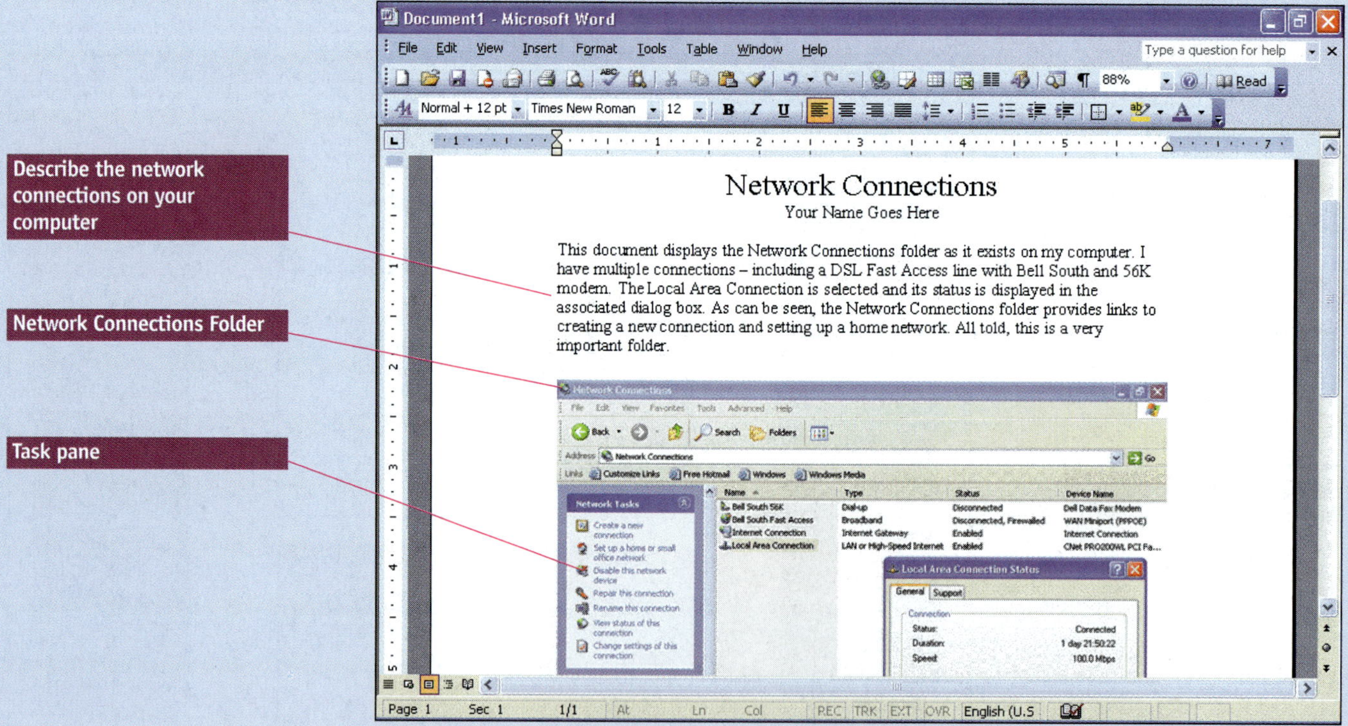

FIGURE 21 Network Connections (exercise 2)

3. **Create Your Own Folders:** Folders are the key to the Windows storage system. Folders can be created at any time and in any way that makes sense to you. The My Courses folder in Figure 22, for example, contains five folders, one folder for each class you are taking. In similar fashion, the Correspondence folder in this figure contains two additional folders according to the type of correspondence. Proceed as follows:
   a. Place the floppy disk from hands-on exercise 3 into drive A. Start Windows Explorer. Click the Folders button to display the hierarchy structure in the left pane. Change to the Details view.
   b. Create a Correspondence folder on drive A. Create a Business folder and a Personal folder within the Correspondence folder.
   c. Create a My Courses folder on drive A. Create a separate folder for each course you are taking within the My Courses folder. The names of your folders will be different from ours.
   d. Pull down the View menu, click the Arrange Icons by command, and click the command to Show in Groups. Click the Date Modified column header to group the files and folders by date. The dates you see will be different from the dates in our figure.
   e. The Show in Groups command functions as a toggle switch. Execute the command, and the files are displayed in groups; execute the command a second time, and the groups disappear. (You can change the grouping by clicking the desired column heading.)
   f. Use the technique described in problems 1 and 2 to capture the screen in Figure 22 and incorporate it into a document. Add a short paragraph that describes the folders you have created, then submit the document to your instructor.

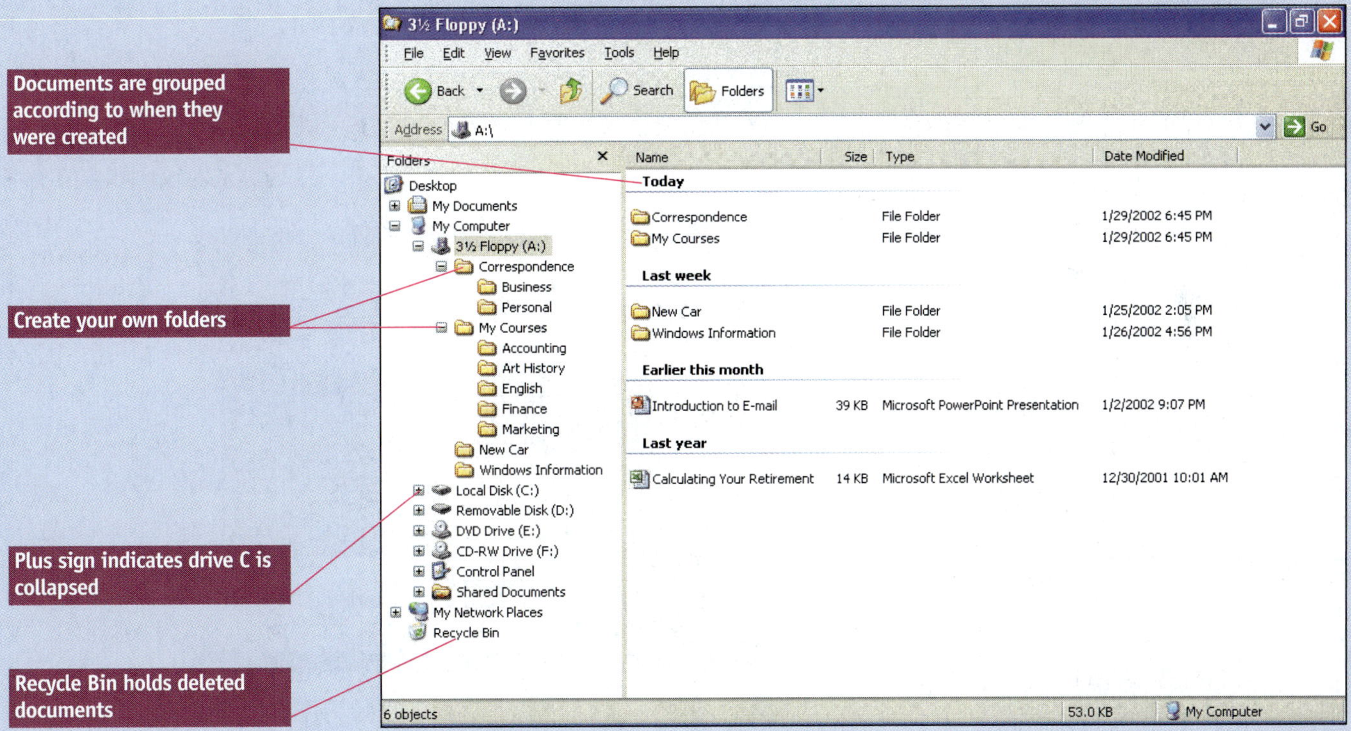

FIGURE 22 Create Your Own Folders (exercise 3)

4. **What's New in Windows XP:** Anyone, whether an experienced user or a computer novice, can benefit from a quick overview of new features in Windows XP. Click the Start button, click Help and Support, and then click the link to What's New in Windows XP. Click the second link in the task pane (taking a tour or tutorial), select the Windows XP tour, and choose the desired format. We chose the animated tour with animation, music, and voice narration.
   a. Relax and enjoy the show as shown in Figure 23. The task bar at the bottom of the figure contains three buttons to restart the show, exit, or toggle the music on and off. Exit the tutorial when you are finished. You are back in the Help and Support window, where you can take a tour of the Windows Media Player. Try it. Click the Close button at the upper right of any screen or press Escape to exit the tour. Write a short note to your instructor with comments about either tour.
   b. Return to the Help and Support Center and find the topic, "What's New in Home Networking." Print two or three subtopics that describe how to create a home network. Does the task seem less intimidating after you have read the information?
   c. Locate one or more topics on new features in digital media such as burning a CD or Windows Movie Maker. Print this information for your instructor.
   d. Return once again to the Help and Support Center to explore some of the other resources that describe new features in Windows XP. Locate the link to Windows News Groups, and then visit one of these newsgroups online. Locate a topic of interest and print several messages within a threaded discussion. Do you think newsgroups will be useful to you in the future?
   e. You can also download a PowerPoint presentation by the authors that describes new features in Windows XP. Go to www.prenhall.com/grauer, click the text for Office XP, then click the link to What's New in Windows XP, from where you can download the presentation.

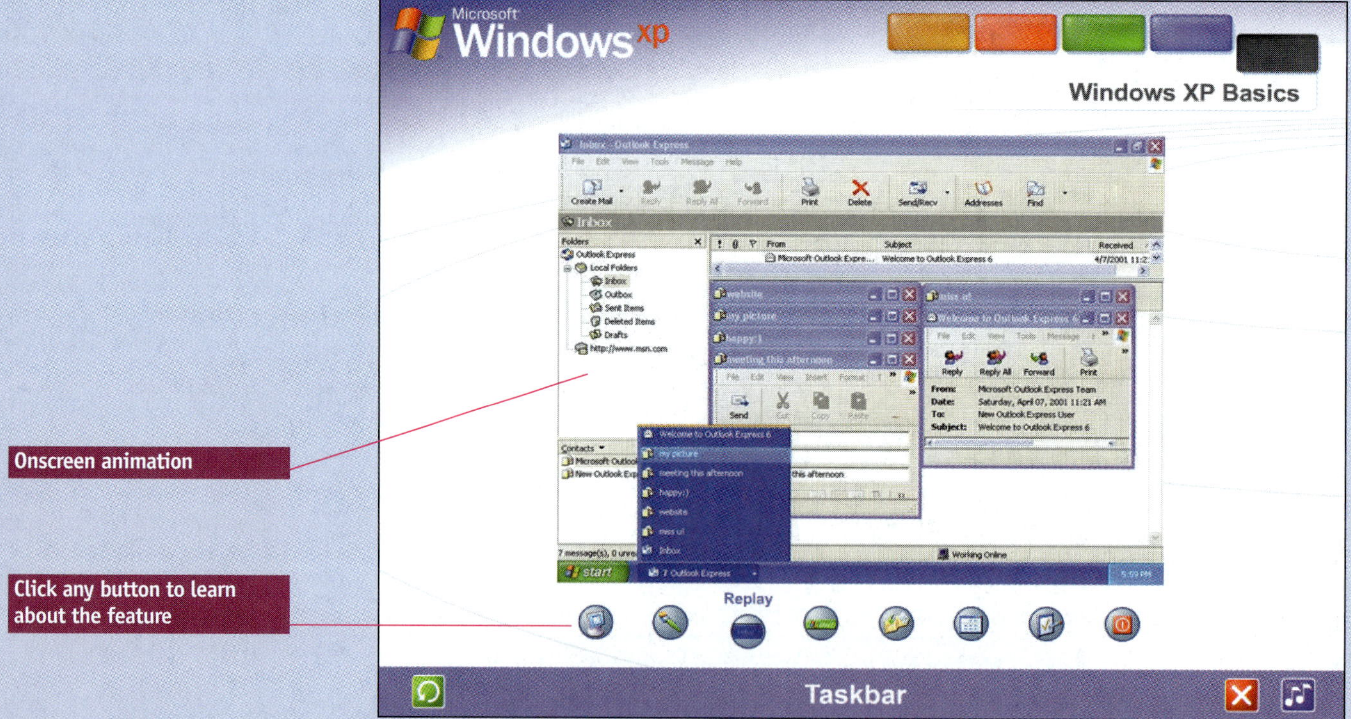

FIGURE 23 What's New in Windows XP (exercise 4)

5. **Keyboard Shortcuts:** Almost every command in Windows can be executed in different ways, using either the mouse or the keyboard. Most people start with the mouse and add keyboard shortcuts as they become more proficient. There is no right or wrong technique, just different techniques, and the one you choose depends entirely on personal preference. If, for example, your hands are already on the keyboard, it is faster to use the keyboard equivalent if you know it.

   There is absolutely no need to memorize these shortcuts, nor should you even try. A few, however, have special appeal and everyone has favorites. You are probably familiar with general Windows shortcuts such as Ctrl+X, Ctrl+C, and Ctrl+V to cut, copy, and paste, respectively. (The X is supposed to remind you of a pair of scissors.) Ctrl+Z is less well known and corresponds to the Undo command. You can find additional shortcuts through the Help command.

   a. Use the Help and Support Center to display the information in Figure 24, which shows the available shortcuts within a dialog box. Two of these, Tab and Shift+Tab, move forward and backward, respectively, from one option to the next within the dialog box. The next time you are in a physician's office or a dentist's office, watch the assistant as he or she labors over the keyboard to enter information. That person will typically type information into a text box, then switch to the mouse to select the next entry, return to the keyboard, and so on. Tell that person about Tab and Shift+Tab; he or she will be forever grateful.

   b. The Help and Support Center organizes the shortcuts by category. Select the Natural keyboard category (not visible in Figure 24), then note what you can do with the ⊞ key. Press the ⊞ key at any time, and you display the Start menu. Press ⊞+M and you minimize all open windows. There are several other, equally good shortcuts in this category.

   c. Select your five favorite shortcuts in any category, and submit them to your instructor. Compare your selections to those of your classmates. Do you prefer the mouse or your newly discovered shortcuts?

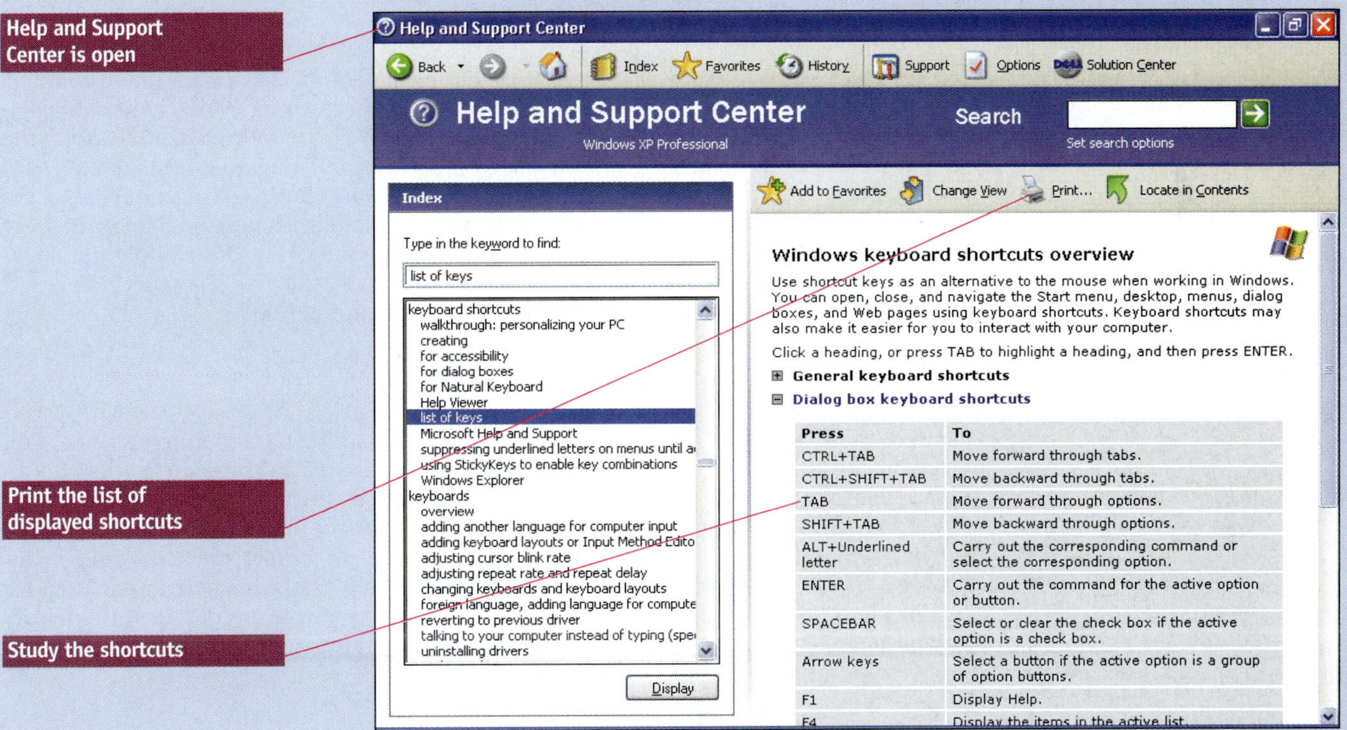

FIGURE 24 Keyboard Shortcuts (exercise 5)

MINI CASES

Planning for Disaster

Do you have a backup strategy? Do you even know what a backup strategy is? You had better learn, because sooner or later you will wish you had one. You will erase a file, be unable to read from a floppy disk, or worse yet, suffer a hardware failure in which you are unable to access the hard drive. The problem always seems to occur the night before an assignment is due. The ultimate disaster is the disappearance of your computer, by theft or natural disaster. Describe, in 250 words or less, the backup strategy you plan to implement in conjunction with your work in this class.

Tips for Windows XP

Print the *Tips for Windows XP* document that was downloaded as one of the practice files in the hands-on exercises. This document contains many of the boxed tips that appeared throughout the chapter. Read the document as a review and select five of your favorite tips. Create a new document for your instructor consisting of the five tips you selected. Add a cover page titled, "My Favorite Tips." Include your name, your professor's name, and a reference to the Grauer/Barber text from where the tips were taken.

File Compression

You've learned your lesson and have come to appreciate the importance of backing up all of your data files. The problem is that you work with large documents that exceed the 1.44MB capacity of a floppy disk. Accordingly, you might want to consider the acquisition of a file compression program to facilitate copying large documents to a floppy disk in order to transport your documents to and from school, home, or work. You can download an evaluation copy of the popular WinZip program at www.winzip.com. Investigate the subject of file compression and submit a summary of your findings to your instructor.

The Threat of Virus Infection

A computer virus is an actively infectious program that attaches itself to other programs and alters the way a computer works. Some viruses do nothing more than display an annoying message at an inopportune time. Most, however, are more harmful, and in the worst case, erase all files on the disk. Use your favorite search engine to research the subject of computer viruses to answer the following questions. When is a computer subject to infection by a virus? What precautions does your school or university take against the threat of virus infection in its computer lab? What precautions, if any, do you take at home? Can you feel confident that your machine will not be infected if you faithfully use a state-of-the-art anti-virus program that was purchased in June 2002?

Your First Consultant's Job

Go to a real installation such as a doctor's or attorney's office, the company where you work, or the computer lab at school. Determine the backup procedures that are in effect, then write a one-page report indicating whether the policy is adequate and, if necessary, offering suggestions for improvement. Your report should be addressed to the individual in charge of the business, and it should cover all aspects of the backup strategy; that is, which files are backed up and how often, and what software is used for the backup operation. Use appropriate emphasis (for example, bold italics) to identify any potential problems. This is a professional document (it is your first consultant's job), and its appearance should be perfect in every way.

CHAPTER 1

Getting Started with VBA: Extending Microsoft Office 2003

OBJECTIVES

After reading this chapter you will:

1. Describe the relationship of VBA to Microsoft Office 2003.
2. Explain how to create, edit, and run a VBA procedure.
3. Use the MsgBox statement and InputBox function.
4. Explain how to debug a procedure by stepping through its statements.
5. Use the If. . . Then. . .Else statement to implement a decision.
6. Explain the Case statement.
7. Create a custom toolbar.
8. Describe several statements used to implement a loop.
9. Describe event-driven programming.

hands-on exercises

1. INTRODUCTION TO VBA
   Input: None
   Output: VBA workbook
2. DECISION MAKING
   Input: VBA workbook
   Output: VBA workbook
3. LOOPS AND DEBUGGING
   Input: VBA workbook
   Output: VBA workbook
4. EVENT-DRIVEN PROGRAMMING
   Input: VBA workbook; Financial Consultant workbook
   Output: VBA workbook; Financial Consultant workbook
5. EVENT-DRIVEN PROGRAMMING
   Input: VBA Switchboard and Security database
   Output: VBA Switchboard and Security database

CASE STUDY
ON-THE-JOB TRAINING

Your first job is going exceedingly well. The work is very challenging and your new manager, Phyllis Simon, is impressed with the Excel workbooks that you have developed thus far. Phyllis has asked you to take it to the next level by incorporating VBA procedures into future projects. You have some knowledge of Excel macros and have already used the macro recorder to record basic macros. You are able to make inferences about the resulting code, but you will need additional proficiency in VBA to become a true expert in Excel.

The good news is that you work for a company that believes in continuing education and promotes from within. Phyllis has assigned you to a new interdepartmental team responsible for creating high-level Excel applications that will be enhanced through VBA. Moreover, you have been selected to attend a week-long seminar to learn VBA so that you can become a valued member of the team. The seminar will be held in San Diego, California, where there is a strong temptation to study sand and surf rather than VBA. Thus, Phyllis expects you to complete a series of VBA procedures upon your return—just to be sure that you were not tempted to skip class and dip your toes in the water. ■

Your assignment is to read the VBA primer at the end of the text and focus on the first three hands-on exercises that develop the syntax for basic VBA statements—MsgBox, InputBox, decision making through If/Else and Case statements, and iteration through the For . . . Next and Do Until statements. You will then open the partially completed *VBA Case Study—On-the-Job Training*, start the VBA editor, and then complete the tasks presented in the procedures in Module1. (The requirements for each procedure appear as comments within the procedure.) Add a command button for each macro to the Excel workbook, and then print the worksheet and a copy of the completed module for your instructor. Last, but not least, create a suitable event procedure for closing the workbook.

INTRODUCTION TO VBA

Visual Basic for Applications (VBA) is a powerful programming language that is accessible from all major applications in Microsoft Office XP. You do not have to know VBA to use Office effectively, but even a basic understanding will help you to create more powerful documents. Indeed, you may already have been exposed to VBA through the creation of simple macros in Word or Excel. A ***macro*** is a set of instructions (i.e., a program) that simplifies the execution of repetitive tasks. It is created through the ***macro recorder*** that captures commands as they are executed, then converts those commands into a VBA program. (The macro recorder is present in Word, Excel, and PowerPoint, but not in Access.) You can create and execute macros without ever looking at the underlying VBA, but you gain an appreciation for the language when you do.

The macro recorder is limited, however, in that it captures only commands, mouse clicks, and/or keystrokes. As you will see, VBA is much more than just recorded keystrokes. It is a language unto itself, and thus, it contains all of the statements you would expect to find in any programming language. This lets you enhance the functionality of any macro by adding extra statements as necessary—for example, an InputBox function to accept data from the user, followed by an If . . . Then . . . Else statement to take different actions based on the information supplied by the user.

This supplement presents the rudiments of VBA and is suitable for use with any Office application. We begin by describing the VBA editor and how to create, edit, and run simple procedures. The examples are completely general and demonstrate the basic capabilities of VBA that are found in any programming language. We illustrate the MsgBox statement to display output to the user and the InputBox function to accept input from the user. We describe the For . . . Next statement to implement a loop and the If . . . Then . . . Else and Case statements for decision making. We also describe several debugging techniques to help you correct the errors that invariably occur. The last two exercises introduce the concept of event-driven programming, in which a procedure is executed in response to an action taken by the user. The material here is application-specific in conjunction with Excel and Access, but it can be easily extended to Word or PowerPoint.

One last point before we begin is that this supplement assumes no previous knowledge on the part of the reader. It is suitable for someone who has never been exposed to a programming language or written an Office macro. If, on the other hand, you have a background in programming or macros, you will readily appreciate the power inherent in VBA. VBA is an incredibly rich language that can be daunting to the novice. Stick with us, however, and we will show you that it is a flexible and powerful tool with consistent rules that can be easily understood and applied. You will be pleased at what you will be able to accomplish.

VBA is a programming language, and like any other programming language its programs (or procedures, as they are called) are made up of individual statements. Each ***statement*** accomplishes a specific task such as displaying a message to the user or accepting input from the user. Statements are grouped into ***procedures***, and procedures, in turn, are grouped into ***modules***. Every VBA procedure is classified as either public or private. A ***private procedure*** is accessible only from within the module in which it is contained. A ***public procedure***, on the other hand, can be accessed from any module.

The statement, however, is the basic unit of the language. Our approach throughout this supplement will be to present individual statements, then to develop simple procedures using those statements in a hands-on exercise. As you read the discussion, you will see that every statement has a precise ***syntax*** that describes how the statement is to be used. The syntax also determines the ***arguments*** (or parameters) associated with that statement, and whether those arguments are required or optional.

THE MSGBOX STATEMENT

The ***MsgBox statement*** displays information to the user. It is one of the most basic statements in VBA, but we use it to illustrate several concepts in VBA programming. Figure 1a contains a simple procedure called MsgBoxExamples, consisting of four individual MsgBox statements. All procedures begin with a ***procedure header*** and end with the ***End Sub statement***.

The MsgBox statement has one required argument, which is the message (or prompt) that is displayed to the user. All other arguments are optional, but if they are used, they must be entered in a specified sequence. The simplest form of the MsgBox statement is shown in example 1, which specifies a single argument that contains the text (or prompt) to be displayed. The resulting message box is shown in Figure 1b. The message is displayed to the user, who responds accordingly, in this case by clicking the OK button.

Example 2 extends the MsgBox statement to include a second parameter that displays an icon within the resulting dialog box as shown in Figure 1c. The type of icon is determined by a VBA ***intrinsic*** (or predefined) ***constant*** such as vbExclamation, which displays an exclamation point in a yellow triangle. VBA has many such constants that enable you to simplify your code, while at the same time achieving some impressive results.

Example 3 uses a different intrinsic constant, vbInformation, to display a different icon. It also extends the MsgBox statement to include a third parameter that is displayed on the title bar of the resulting dialog box. Look closely, for example, at Figures 1c and 1d, whose title bars contain "Microsoft Excel" and "Grauer/Barber", respectively. The first is the default entry (given that we are executing the procedure from within Microsoft Excel). You can, however, give your procedures a customized look by displaying your own text in the title bar.

Procedure header

End Sub statement

```
Public Sub MsgBoxExamples()
'This procedure was written by John Doe on 6/10/2003

    MsgBox "Example 1 - VBA is not difficult"
    MsgBox "Example 2 - VBA is not difficult", vbExclamation
    MsgBox "Example 3 - VBA is not difficult", vbInformation, "Grauer/Barber"
    MsgBox "Example 4 - VBA is not difficult", , "Your name goes here"

End Sub
```

(a) VBA Code

Message only

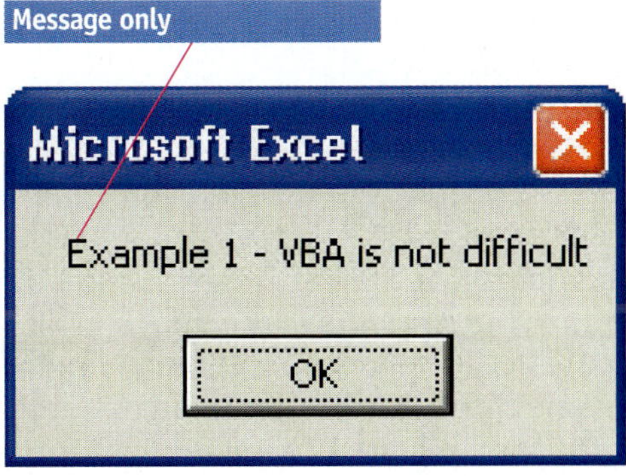

(b) Example 1—One Argument

Icon is displayed

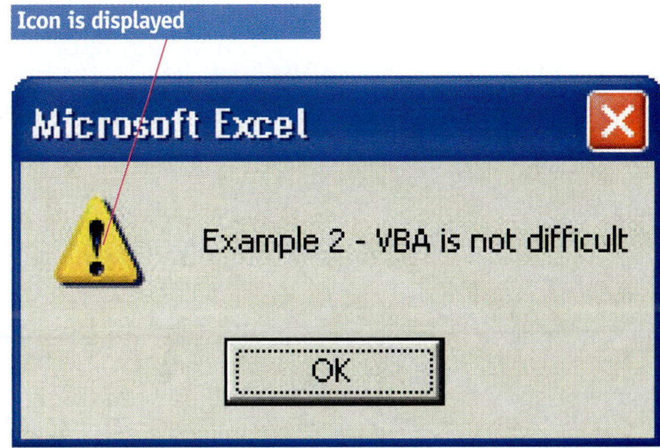

(c) Example 2—Two Arguments

FIGURE 1 The MsgBox Statement

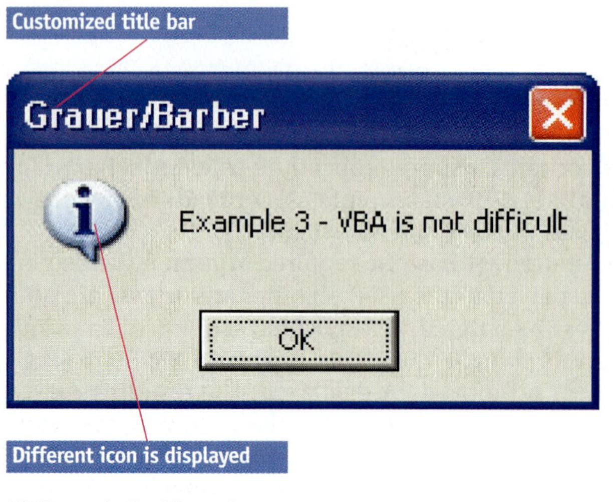

(d) Example 3—Three Arguments

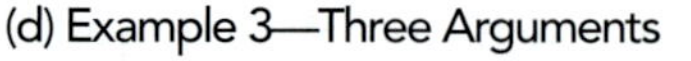

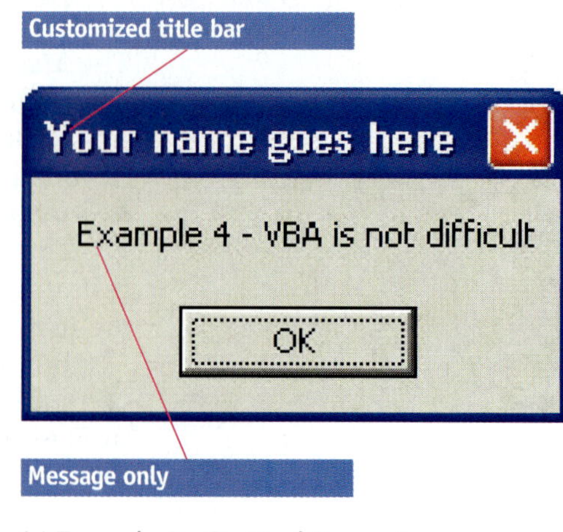

(e) Example 4—Omitted Parameter

FIGURE 1 The MsgBox Statement (*continued*)

Example 4 omits the second parameter (the icon), but includes the third parameter (the entry for the title bar). The parameters are positional, however, and thus the MsgBox statement contains two commas after the message to indicate that the second parameter has been omitted.

THE INPUTBOX FUNCTION

The MsgBox statement displays a prompt to the user, but what if you want the user to respond to the prompt by entering a value such as his or her name? This is accomplished using the ***InputBox function***. Note the subtle change in terminology in that we refer to the InputBox *function*, but the MsgBox *statement*. That is because a function returns a value, in this case the user's name, which is subsequently used in the procedure. In other words, the InputBox function asks the user for information, then it stores that information (the value returned by the user) for use in the procedure.

Figure 2 displays a procedure that prompts the user for a first and last name, after which it displays the information using the MsgBox statement. (The Dim statement at the beginning of the procedure is explained shortly.) Let's look at the first InputBox function, and the associated dialog box in Figure 2b. The InputBox function displays a prompt on the screen, the user enters a value ("Bob" in this example), and that value is stored in the variable that appears to the left of the equal sign (strFirstName). The concept of a variable is critical to every programming language. Simply stated, a ***variable*** is a named storage location that contains data that can be modified during program execution.

The MsgBox statement then uses the value of strFirstName to greet the user by name as shown in Figure 2c. This statement also introduces the ampersand to ***concatenate*** (join together) two different character strings, the literal "Good morning", followed by the value within the variable strFirstName.

The second InputBox function prompts the user for his or her last name. In addition, it uses a second argument to customize the contents of the title bar (VBA Primer in this example) as can be seen in Figure 2d. Finally, the MsgBox statement in Figure 2e displays both the first and last name through concatenation of multiple strings. This statement also uses the ***underscore*** to continue a statement from one line to the next.

VBA is not difficult, and you can use the MsgBox statement and InputBox function in conjunction with one another as the basis for several meaningful procedures. You will get a chance to practice in the hands-on exercise that follows shortly.

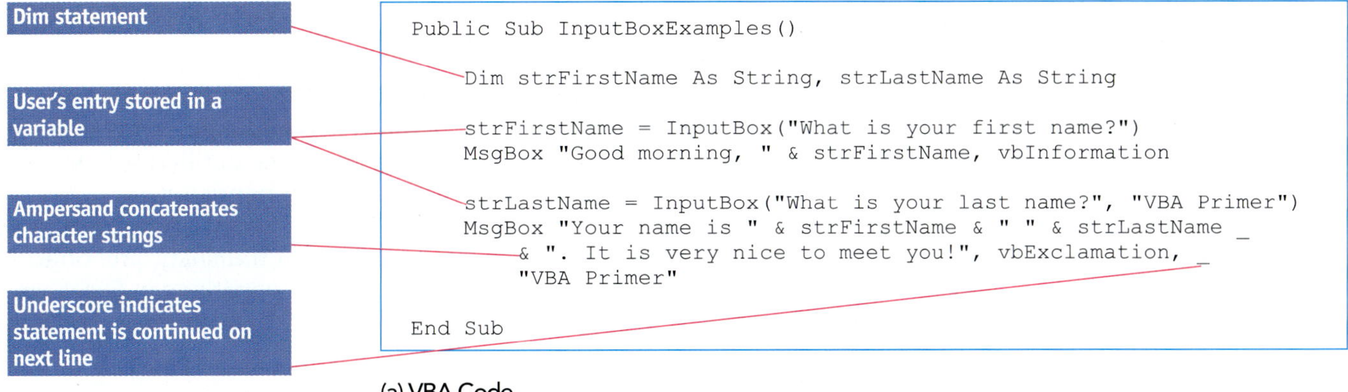

(a) VBA Code

(b) InputBox

(c) Concatenation

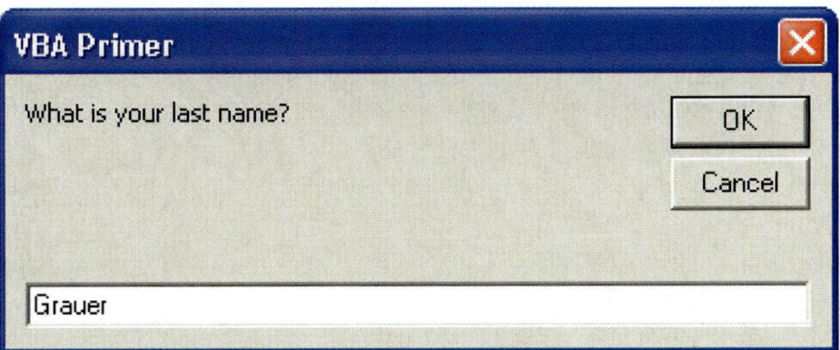

(d) Input Box Includes Argument for Title Bar

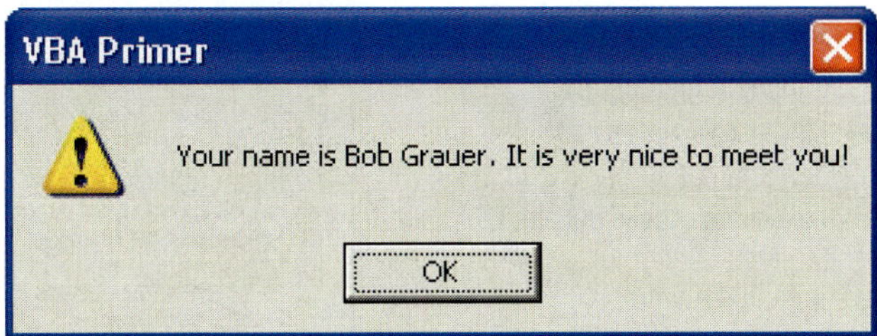

(e) Concatenation and Continuation

FIGURE 2 The InputBox Function

Declaring Variables

Every variable must be declared (defined) before it can be used. This is accomplished through the ***Dim*** (short for Dimension) ***statement*** that appears at the beginning of a procedure. The Dim statement indicates the name of the variable and its type (for example, whether it will hold characters or numbers), which in turn reserves the appropriate amount of memory for that variable.

A variable name must begin with a letter and cannot exceed 255 characters. It can contain letters, numbers, and various special characters such as an underscore, but it cannot contain a space or the special symbols !, @, &, $, or #. Variable names typically begin with a prefix to indicate the type of data that is stored within the variable such as "str" for a character string or "int" for integers. The use of a prefix is optional with respect to the rules of VBA, but it is followed almost universally.

THE VBA EDITOR

All VBA procedures are created using the ***Visual Basic editor*** as shown in Figure 3. You may already be familiar with the editor, perhaps in conjunction with creating and/or editing macros in Word or Excel, or event procedures in Microsoft Access. Let's take a moment, however, to review its essential components.

The left side of the editor displays the ***Project Explorer***, which is similar in concept and appearance to the Windows Explorer, except that it displays the objects associated with the open document. If, for example, you are working in Excel, you will see the various sheets in a workbook, whereas in an Access database you will see forms and reports.

The VBA statements for the selected module (Module1 in Figure 3) appear in the code window in the right pane. The module, in turn, contains declarations and procedures that are separated by horizontal lines. There are two procedures, MsgBoxExamples and InputBoxExamples, each of which was explained previously. A ***comment*** (nonexecutable) statement has been added to each procedure and appears in green. It is the apostrophe at the beginning of the line, rather than the color, that denotes a comment.

The ***Declarations section*** appears at the beginning of the module and contains a single statement, ***Option Explicit***. This option requires every variable in a procedure to be explicitly defined (e.g., in a Dim statement) before it can be used elsewhere in the module. It is an important option and should appear in every module you write.

The remainder of the window should look reasonably familiar in that it is similar to any other Office application. The title bar appears at the top of the window and identifies the application (Microsoft Visual Basic) and the current document (VBA Examples.xls). The right side of the title bar contains the Minimize, Restore, and Close buttons. A menu bar appears under the title bar. Toolbars are displayed under the menu bar. Commands are executed by pulling down the appropriate menu, via buttons on the toolbar, or by keyboard shortcuts.

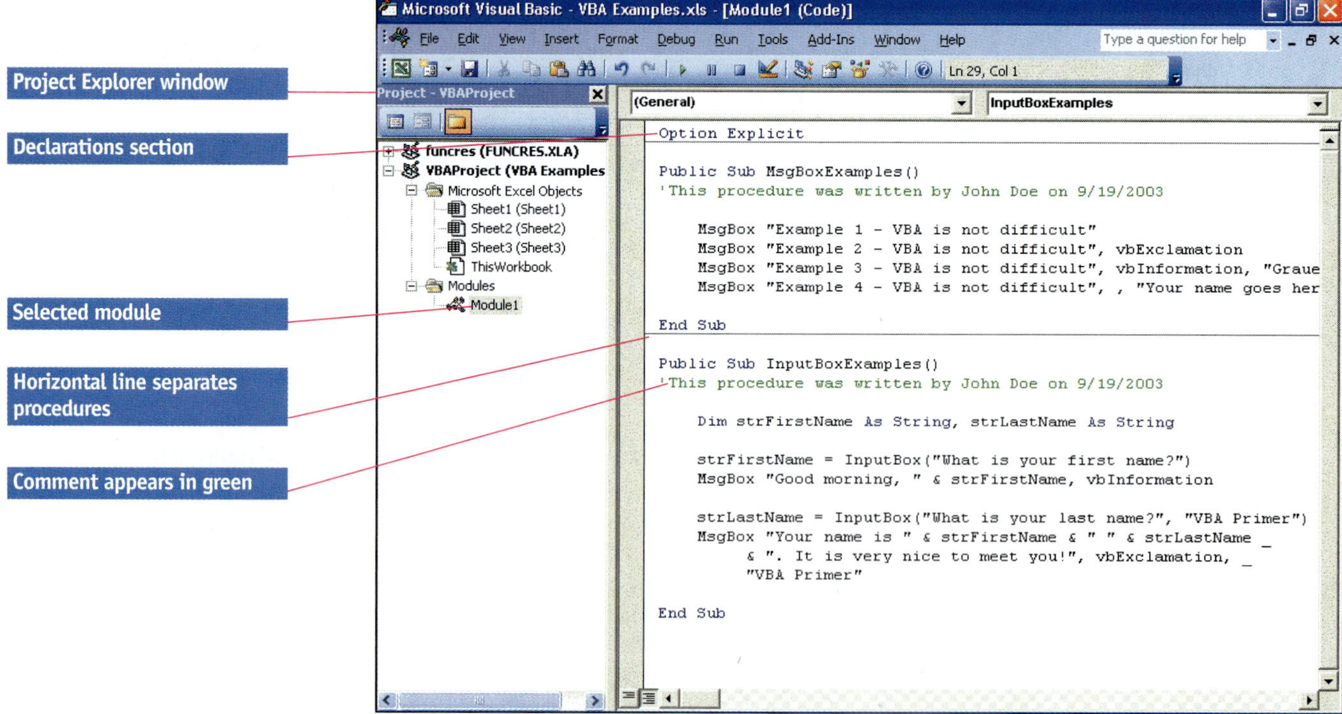

FIGURE 3 The VBA Editor

hands-on exercise

1 Introduction to VBA

Objective To create and test VBA procedures using the MsgBox and InputBox statements. Use Figure 4 as a guide in the exercise. You can do the exercise in any Office application.

Step 1a: Start Microsoft Excel

- We suggest you do the exercise in either Excel or Access (although you could use Word or PowerPoint just as easily). Go to step 1b for Access.
- Start **Microsoft Excel** and open a new workbook. Pull down the **File menu** and click the **Save command** (or click the **Save button** on the Standard toolbar) to display the Save As dialog box. Choose an appropriate drive and folder, then save the workbook as **VBA Examples**.
- Pull down the **Tools menu**, click the **Macro command**, then click the **Visual Basic Editor command** as shown in Figure 4a. Go to step 2.

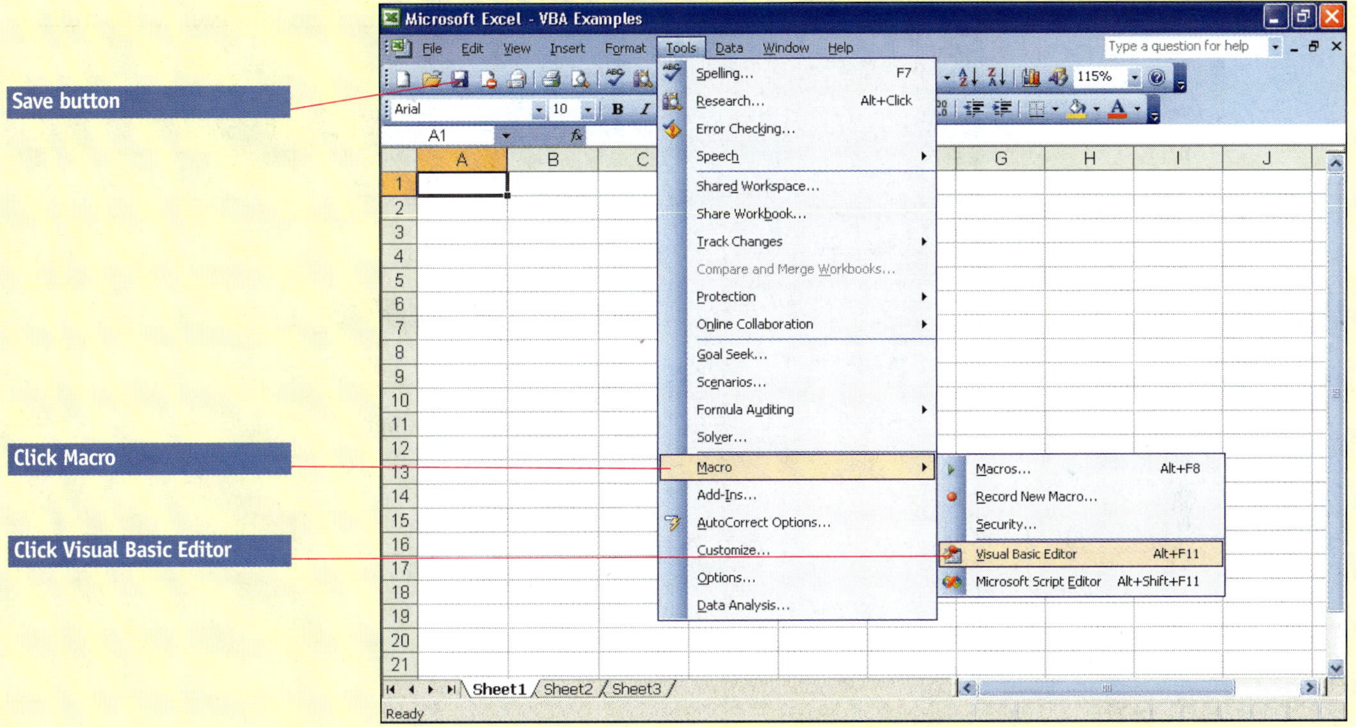

(a) Start Microsoft Excel (step 1a)

FIGURE 4 Hands-on Exercise 1

Step 1b: Start Microsoft Access

- Start **Microsoft Access** and choose the option to create a **Blank Access database**. Save the database as **VBA Examples**.
- Pull down the **Tools menu**, click the **Macro command**, then click the **Visual Basic Editor command**. (You can also use the **Alt+F11** keyboard shortcut to open the VBA editor without going through the Tools menu.)

Step 2: Insert a Module

- You should see a window similar to Figure 4b, but Module1 is not yet visible. Close the Properties window if it appears.
- If necessary, pull down the **View menu** and click **Project Explorer** to display the Project Explorer pane at the left of the window. Our figure shows Excel objects, but you will see the "same" window in Microsoft Access.
- Pull down the **Insert menu** and click **Module** to insert Module1 into the current project. The name of the module, Module1 in this example, appears in the Project Explorer pane.
- The Option Explicit statement may be entered automatically, but if not, click in the code window and type the statement **Option Explicit**.
- Pull down the **Insert menu** a second time, but this time select **Procedure** to display the Add Procedure dialog box in Figure 4b. Click in the **Name** text box and enter **MsgBoxExamples** as the name of the procedure. (Spaces are not allowed in a procedure name.)
- Click the option buttons for a **Sub procedure** and for **Public scope**. Click **OK**. The sub procedure should appear within the module and consist of the Sub and End Sub statements.

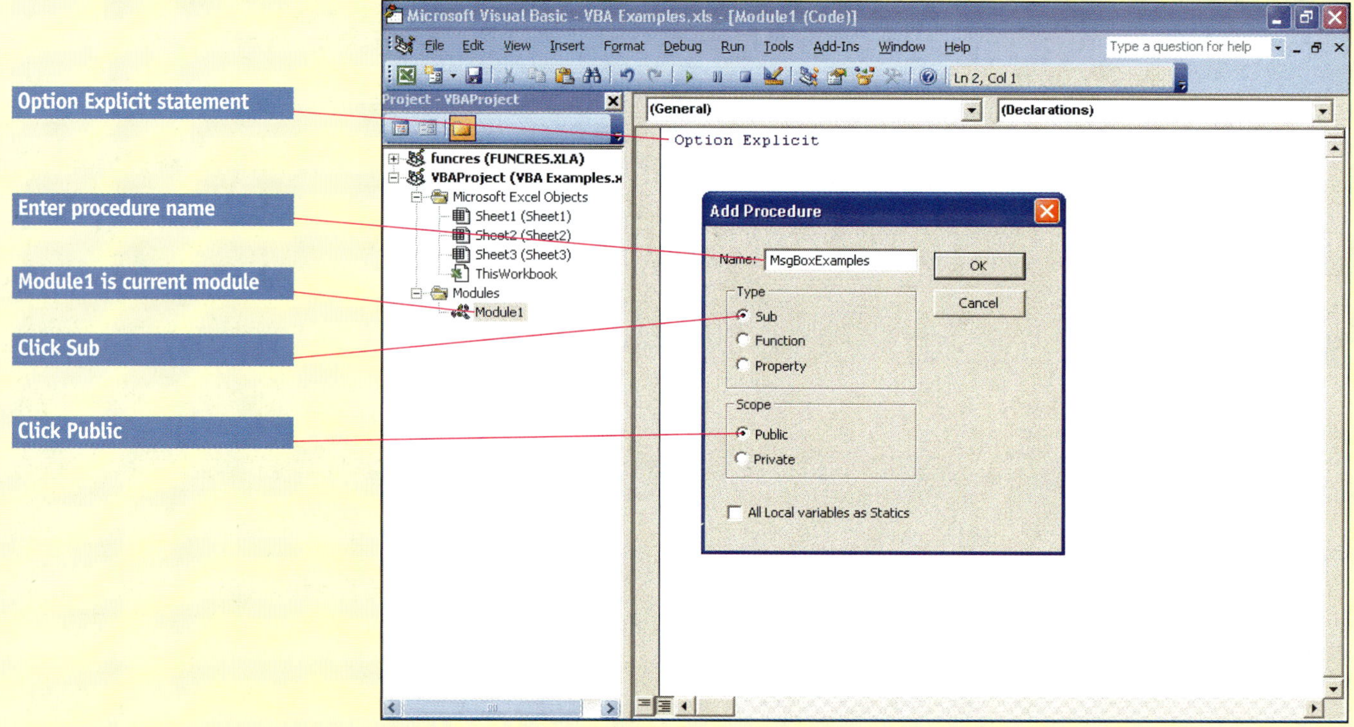

(b) Insert a Module (step 2)

FIGURE 4 Hands-on Exercise 1 (*continued*)

THE OPTION EXPLICIT STATEMENT

The Option Explicit statement is optional, but if it is used it must appear in a module before any procedures. The statement requires that all variables in the module be declared explicitly by the programmer (typically with a Dim, Public, or Private statement), as opposed to VBA making an implicit assumption about the variable. It is good programming practice and it should be used every time.

Step 3: The MsgBox Statement

- The insertion point (the flashing cursor) appears below the first statement. Press the **Tab key** to indent the next statement. (Indentation is not a VBA requirement, but is used to increase the readability of the statement.)
- Type the keyword **MsgBox**, then press the **space bar**. VBA responds with Quick Info that displays the syntax of the statement as shown in Figure 4c.
- Type a **quotation mark** to begin the literal, enter the text of your message, **This is my first VBA procedure**, then type the closing **quotation mark**.
- Click the **Run Sub button** on the Standard toolbar (or pull down the **Run menu** and click the **Run Sub command**) to execute the procedure.
- You should see a dialog box, containing the text you entered, within the Excel workbook (or other Office document) on which you are working.
- After you have read the message, click **OK** to return to the VBA editor.

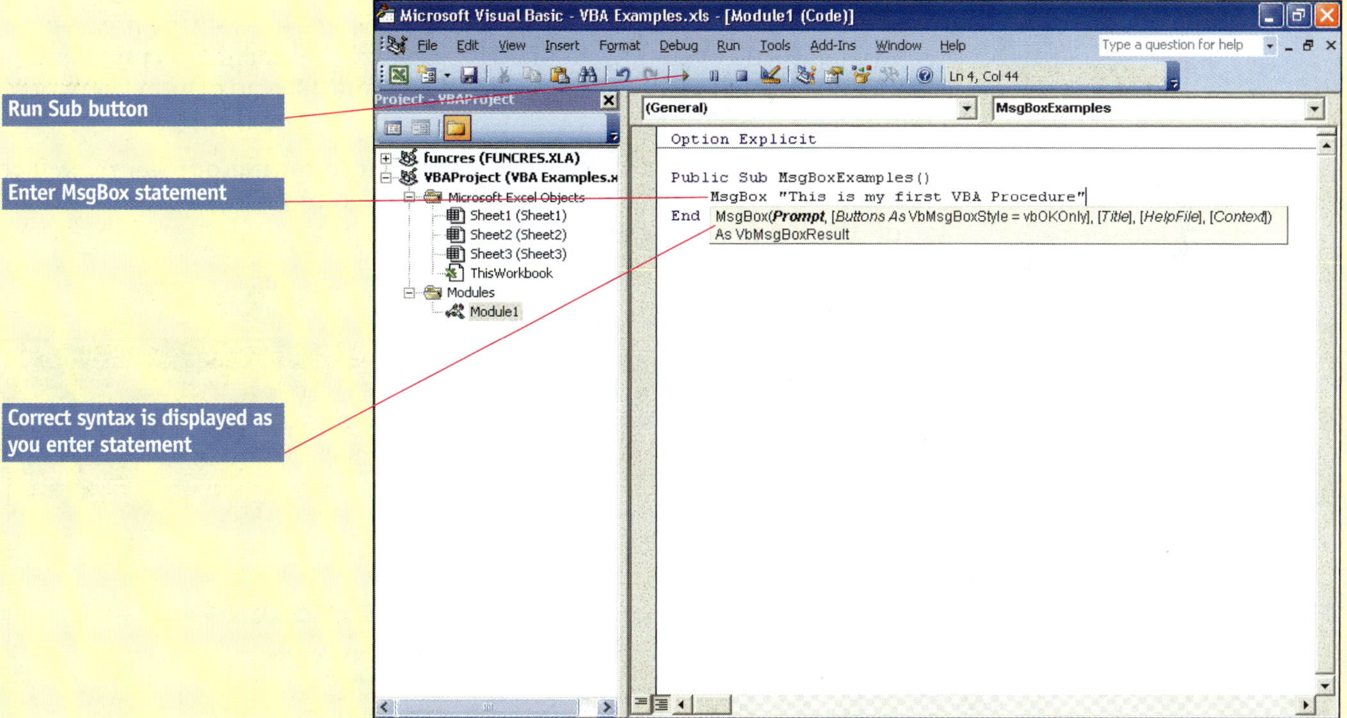

(c) The MsgBox Statement (step 3)

FIGURE 4 Hands-on Exercise 1 (*continued*)

QUICK INFO—HELP WITH VBA SYNTAX

Press the space bar after entering the name of a statement (e.g., MsgBox), and VBA responds with a Quick Info box that displays the syntax of the statement. You see the arguments in the statement and the order in which those arguments appear. Any argument in brackets is optional. If you do not see this information, pull down the Tools menu, click the Options command, then click the Editor tab. Check the box for Auto Quick Info and click OK.

Step 4: Complete the Procedure

- You should be back within the MsgBoxExamples procedure. If necessary, click at the end of the MsgBox statement, then press **Enter** to begin a new line. Type **MsgBox** and press the **space bar** to begin entering the statement.
- The syntax of the MsgBox statement will appear on the screen. Type a **quotation mark** to begin the message, type **Add an icon** as the text of this message, then type the closing **quotation mark**. Type a **comma**, then press the **space bar** to enter the next parameter.
- VBA automatically displays a list of appropriate parameters, in this case a series of intrinsic constants that define the icon or command button that is to appear in the statement.
- You can type the first several letters (e.g., **vbi**, for vbInformation), then press the **space bar**, or you can use the **down arrow** to select **vbInformation** and then press the **space bar**. Either way you should complete the second MsgBox statement as shown in Figure 4d. Press **Enter**.
- Enter the third MsgBox statement as shown in Figure 4d. Note the presence of the two consecutive commas to indicate that we omitted the second parameter within the MsgBox statement. Enter your name instead of John Doe where appropriate. Press **Enter**.
- Enter the fourth (and last) MsgBox statement following our figure. Select **vbExclamation** as the second parameter, type a **comma**, then enter the text of the title bar, as you did for the previous statement.
- Click the **Save button** to save the changes to the module.

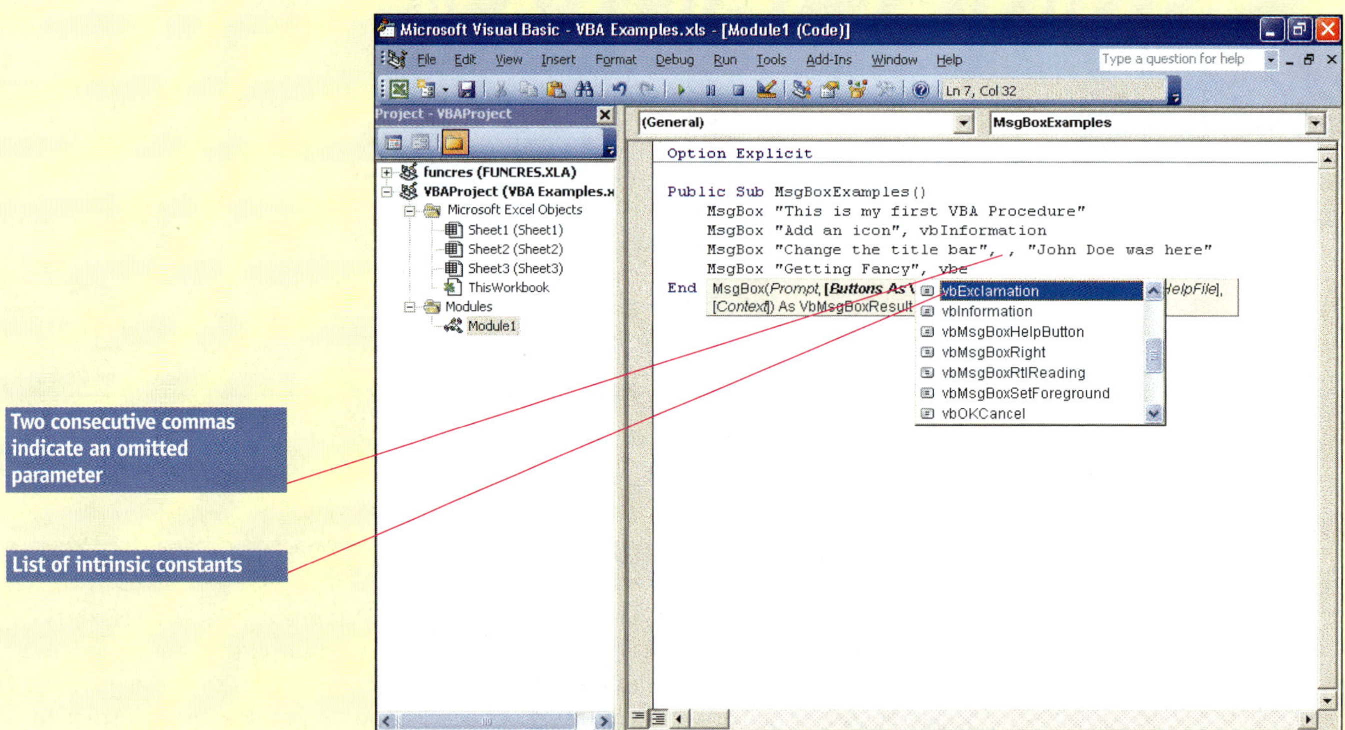

(d) Complete the Procedure (step 4)

FIGURE 4 Hands-on Exercise 1 (*continued*)

Step 5: Test the Procedure

- It's convenient if you can see the statements in the VBA procedure at the same time you see the output of those statements. Thus we suggest that you tile the VBA editor and the associated Office application.
- Minimize all applications except the VBA editor and the Office application (e.g., Excel).
- Right click the taskbar and click **Tile Windows Horizontally** to tile the windows as shown in Figure 4e. (It does not matter which window is on top. (If you see more than these two windows, minimize the other open window, then right click the taskbar and retile the windows.)
- Click anywhere in the VBA procedure, then click the **Run Sub button** on the Standard toolbar.
- The four messages will be displayed one after the other. Click **OK** after each message.
- Maximize the VBA window to continue working.

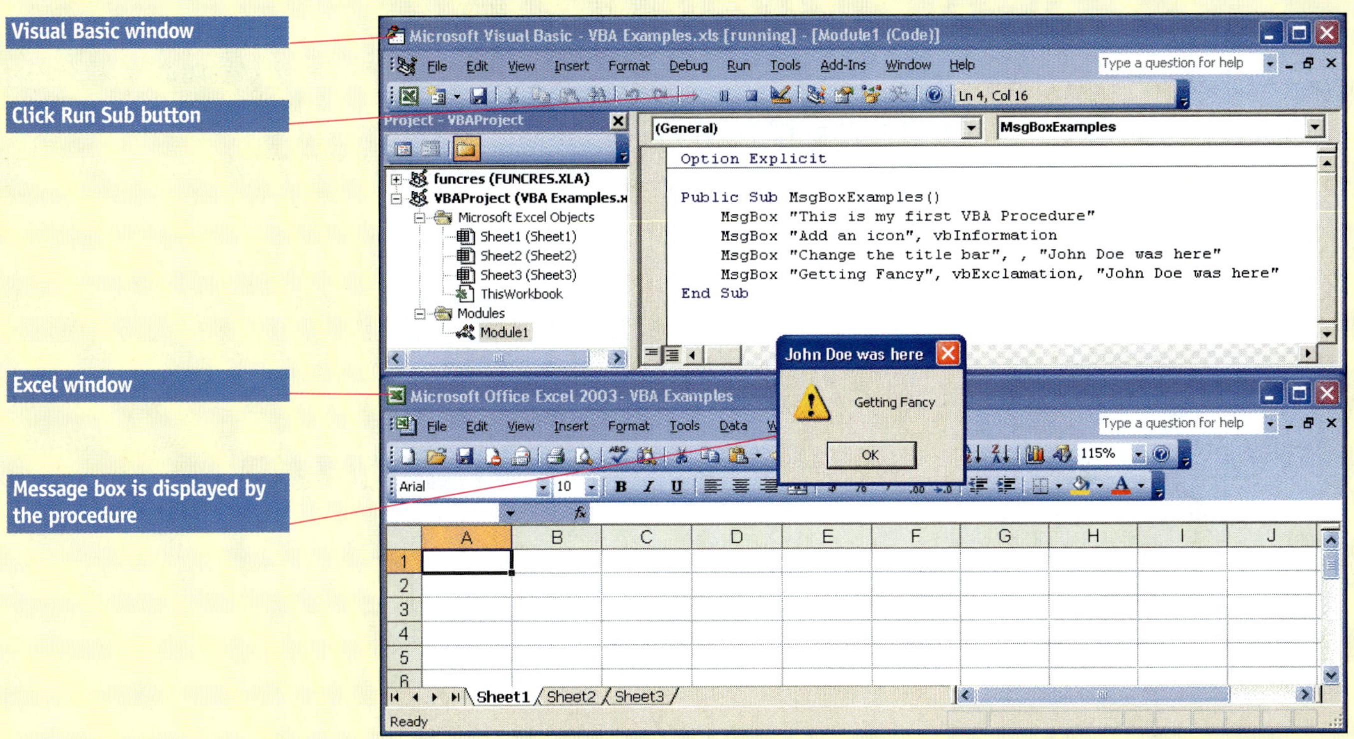

(e) Test the Procedure (step 5)

FIGURE 4 Hands-on Exercise 1 (*continued*)

HIDE THE WINDOWS TASKBAR

You can hide the Windows taskbar to gain additional space on the desktop. Right click any empty area of the taskbar to display a context-sensitive menu, click Properties to display the Taskbar properties dialog box, and if necessary click the Taskbar tab. Check the box to Auto Hide the taskbar, then click OK. The taskbar disappears from the screen but will reappear as you point to the bottom edge of the desktop.

Step 6: Comments and Corrections

- All VBA procedures should be documented with the author's name, date, and other comments as necessary to explain the procedure. Click after the procedure header. Press the **Enter key** to leave a blank line.
- Press **Enter** a second time. Type an **apostrophe** to begin the comment, then enter a descriptive statement similar to Figure 4f. Press **Enter** when you have completed the comment. The line turns green to indicate it is a comment.
- The best time to experiment with debugging is when you know your procedure is correct. Go to the last MsgBox statement and delete the quotation mark in front of your name. Move to the end of the line and press **Enter**.
- You should see the error message in Figure 4f. Unfortunately, the message is not as explicit as it could be; VBA cannot tell that you left out a quotation mark, but it does detect an error in syntax.
- Click **OK** in response to the error. Click the **Undo button** twice, to restore the quotation mark, which in turn corrects the statement.
- Click the **Save button** to save the changes to the module.

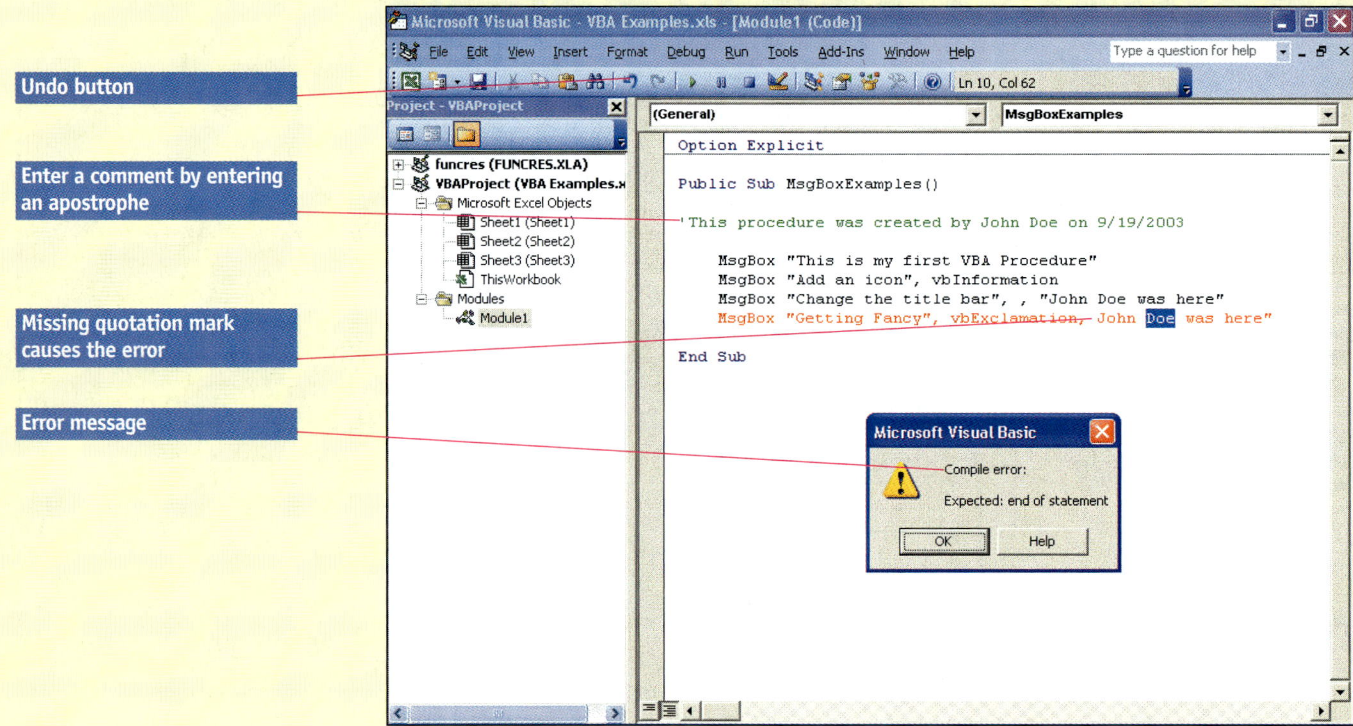

(f) Comments and Corrections (step 6)

FIGURE 4 Hands-on Exercise 1 (*continued*)

RED, GREEN, AND BLUE

Visual Basic for Applications uses different colors for different types of statements (or a portion of those statements). Any statement containing a syntax error appears in red. Comments appear in green. Keywords, such as Sub and End Sub, appear in blue.

Step 7: Create a Second Procedure

- Pull down the **Insert menu** and click **Procedure** to display the Add Procedure dialog box. Enter **InputBoxExamples** as the name of the procedure. (Spaces are not allowed in a procedure name.)
- Click the option buttons for a **Sub procedure** and for **Public scope**. Click **OK**. The new sub procedure will appear within the existing module below the existing MsgBoxExamples procedure.
- Enter the statements in the procedure as they appear in Figure 4g. Be sure to type a space between the ampersand and the underscore in the second MsgBox statement. Click the **Save button** to save the procedure before testing it.
- You can display the output of the procedure directly in the VBA window if you minimize the Excel window. Thus, **right click** the Excel button on the taskbar to display a context-sensitive menu, then click the **Minimize command**. There is no visible change on your monitor.
- Click the **Run Sub button** to test the procedure. This time you see the Input box displayed on top of the VBA window because the Excel window has been minimized.
- Enter your first name in response to the initial prompt, then click **OK**. Click **OK** when you see the message box that says "Hello".
- Enter your last name in response to the second prompt and click **OK**. You should see a message box similar to the one in Figure 4g. Click **OK**.
- Return to the VBA procedure to correct any mistakes that might occur. Save the module.

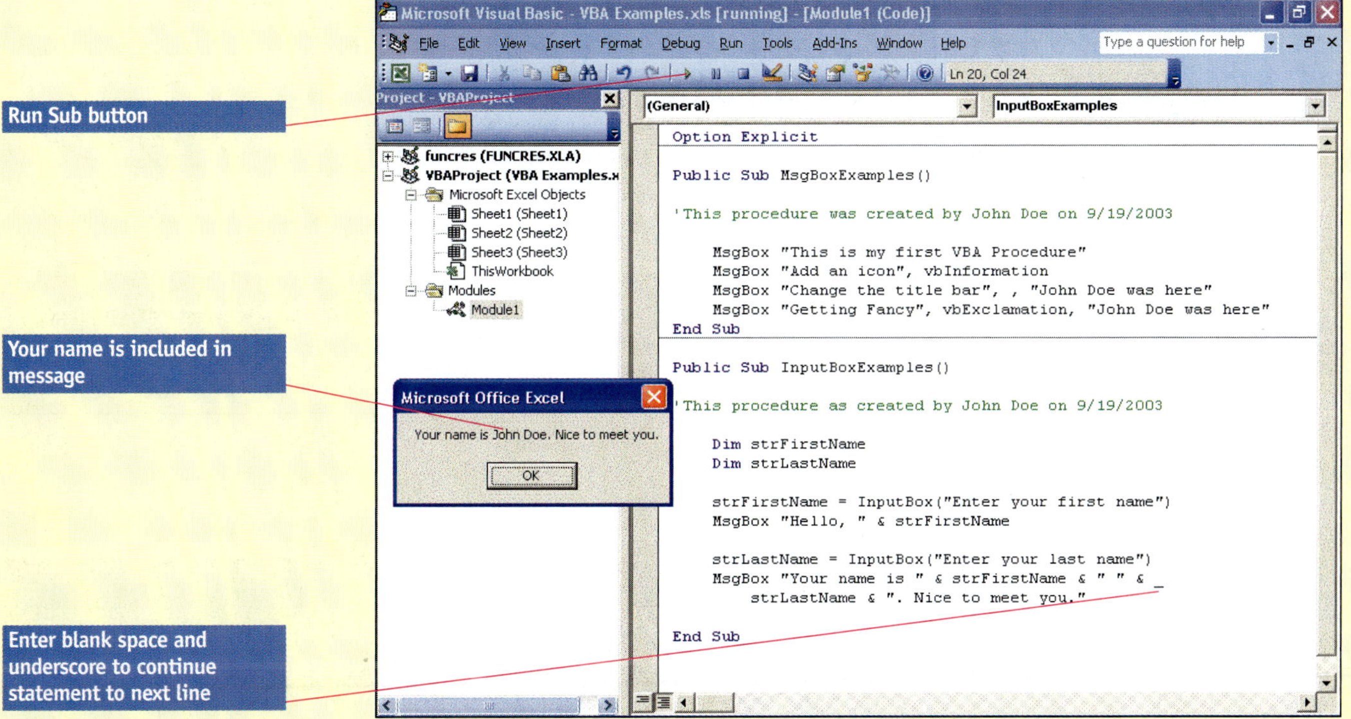

(g) Create a Second Procedure (step 7)

FIGURE 4 Hands-on Exercise 1 (*continued*)

Step 8: Create a Public Constant

- Click after the Options Explicit statement and press **Enter** to move to a new line. Type the statement to define the constant, **ApplicationTitle**, as shown in Figure 4h, and press **Enter**.
- Click anywhere in the MsgBoxExamples procedure, then change the third argument in the last MsgBox statement to ApplicationTitle. Make the four modifications in the InputBoxExamples procedure as shown in Figure 4h.
- Click anywhere in the InputBoxExamples procedure, then click the **Run Sub button** to test the procedure. The title bar of each dialog box will contain a descriptive title corresponding to the value of the ApplicationTitle constant.
- Change the value of the ApplicationTitle constant in the General Declarations section, then rerun the InputBoxExamples procedure. The title of every dialog box changes to reflect the new value.
- Save the procedure. Do you see the advantage of defining a title in the General Declarations section?

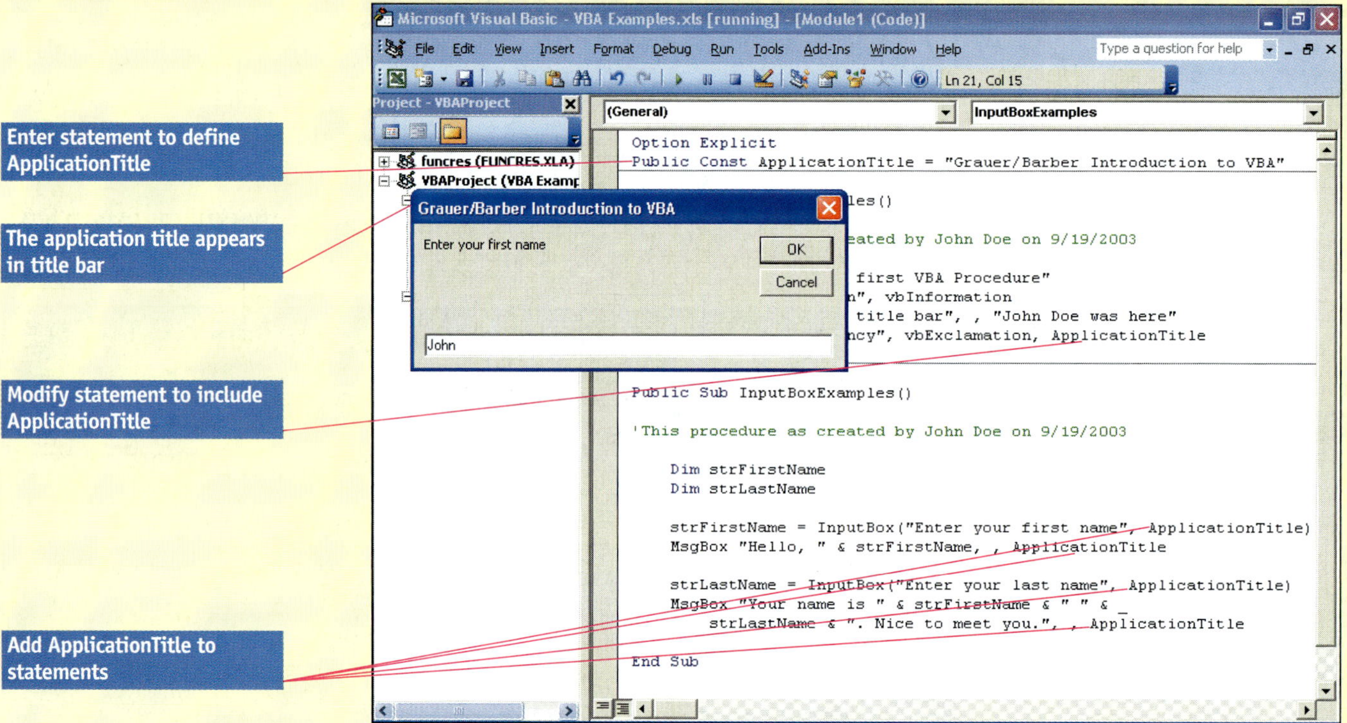

(h) Create a Public Constant (step 8)

FIGURE 4 Hands-on Exercise 1 (*continued*)

CONTINUING A VBA STATEMENT—THE & AND THE UNDERSCORE

A VBA statement can be continued from one line to the next by typing a space at the end of the line to be continued, typing the underscore character, then continuing on the next line. You may not, however, break a line in the middle of a literal (character string). Thus, you need to complete the character string with a closing quotation mark, add an ampersand (as the concatenation operator to display this string with the character string on the next line), then leave a space followed by the underscore to indicate continuation.

Step 9: Help with VBA

- You should be in the VBA editor. Pull down the **Help menu** and click the **Microsoft Visual Basic Help command** to open the Help pane.
- Type **Input Box function** in the Search box, then click the arrow to initiate the search. The results should include a hyperlink to InputBox function. Click the **hyperlink** to display the Help screen in Figure 4i.
- Maximize the Help window, then explore the information on the InputBox function to reinforce your knowledge of this statement.
  - ❑ Click the **Print button** to print this page for your instructor.
  - ❑ Click the link to **Example** within the Help window to see actual code.
  - ❑ Click the link to **See Also**, which displays information about the MsgBox statement.
- Close the Help window, but leave the task pane open. Click the **green** (back) **arrow** within the task pane to display the Table of Contents for Visual Basic Help, then explore the table of contents.
  - ❑ Click any closed book to open the book and "drill down" within the list of topics. The book remains open until you click the icon a second time to close it.
  - ❑ Click any question mark icon to display the associated help topic.
- Close the task pane. Pull down the **File menu** and click the **Close and Return to Microsoft Excel command** (or click the **Close button** on the VBA title bar) to close the VBA window and return to the application. Click **Yes** if asked whether to save the changes to Module1.
- You should be back in the Excel (or Access) application window. Close the application if you do not want to continue with the next exercise at this time.
- Congratulations. You have just completed your first VBA procedure. Remember to use Help any time you have a question.

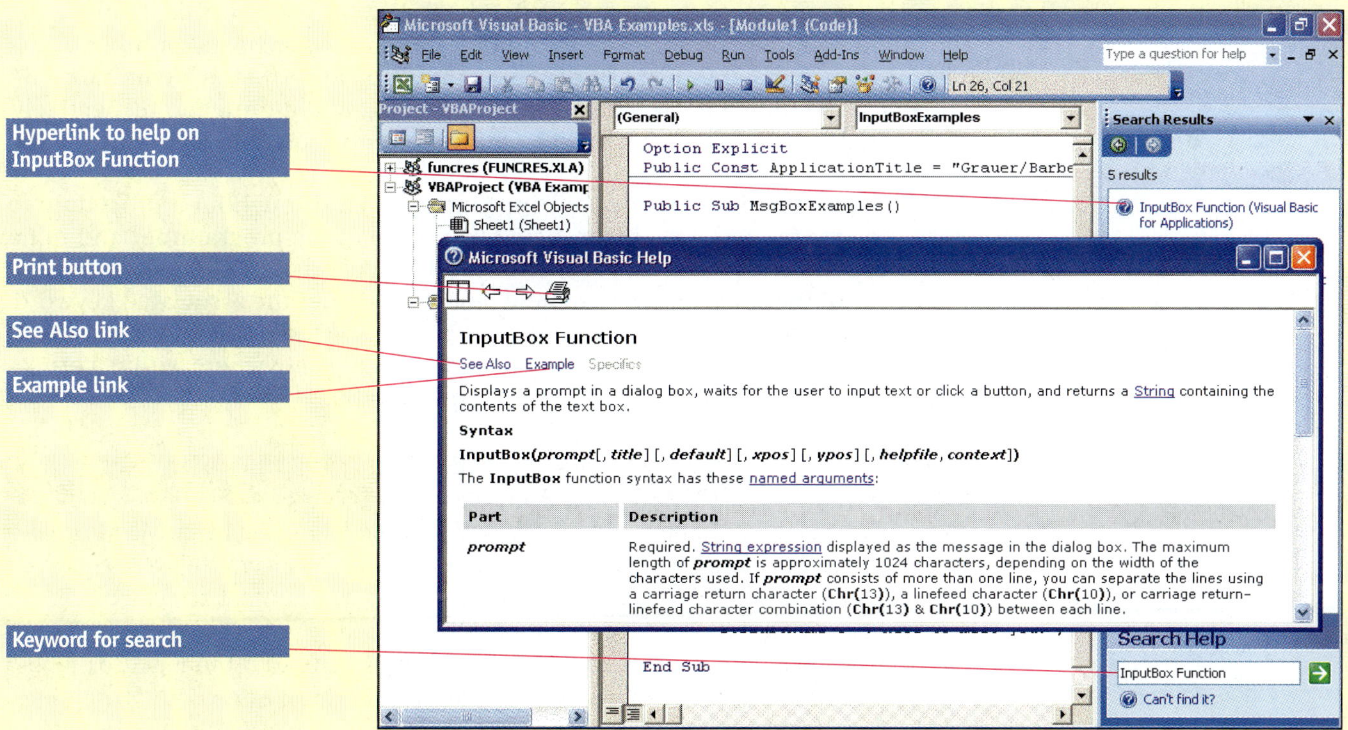

(i) Help with VBA (step 9)

FIGURE 4 Hands-on Exercise 1 (*continued*)

IF . . . THEN . . . ELSE STATEMENT

The ability to make decisions within a program, and then execute alternative sets of statements based on the results of those decisions, is crucial to any programming language. This is typically accomplished through an ***If statement***, which evaluates a condition as either true or false, then branches accordingly. The If statement is not used in isolation, however, but is incorporated into a procedure to accomplish a specific task as shown in Figure 5a. This procedure contains two separate If statements, and the results are displayed in the message boxes shown in the remainder of the figure.

The InputBox statement associated with Figure 5b prompts the user for the name of his or her instructor, then it stores the answer in the variable strInstructorName. The subsequent If statement then compares the user's answer to the literal "Grauer". If the condition is true (i.e., Grauer was entered into the input box), then the message in Figure 5c is displayed. If, however, the user entered any other value, then the condition is evaluated as false, the MsgBox is not displayed, and processing continues with the next statement in the procedure.

The second If statement includes an optional ***Else clause***. Again, the user is asked for a value, and the response is compared to the number 50. If the condition is true (i.e., the value of intUserStates equals 50), the message in Figure 5d is displayed to indicate that the response is correct. If, however, the condition is false (i.e., the user entered a number other than 50), the user sees the message in Figure 5e. Either way, true or false, processing continues with the next statement in the procedure. That's it—it's simple and it's powerful, and we will use the statement in the next hands-on exercise.

You can learn a good deal about VBA by looking at existing code and making inferences. Consider, for example, the difference between literals and numbers. ***Literals*** (also known as ***character strings***) are stored differently from numbers, and this is manifested in the way that comparisons are entered into a VBA statement. Look closely at the condition that references a literal (strInstructorName = "Grauer") compared to the condition that includes a number (intUserStates = 50). The literal ("Grauer") is enclosed in quotation marks, whereas the number (50) is not. (The prefix used in front of each variable, "str" and "int", is a common VBA convention to indicate the variable type—a string and an integer, respectively. Both variables are declared in the Dim statements at the beginning of the procedure.)

Note, too, that indentation and spacing are used throughout a procedure to make it easier to read. This is for the convenience of the programmer and not a requirement for VBA. The If, Else, and End If keywords are aligned under one another, with the subsequent statements indented under the associated keyword. We also indent a continued statement, such as a MsgBox statement, which is typically coded over multiple lines. Blank lines can be added anywhere within a procedure to separate blocks of statements from one another.

THE MSGBOX FUNCTION—YES OR NO

A simple MsgBox statement merely displays information to the user. MsgBox can also be used as a function, however, to accept information from the user such as clicking a Yes or No button, then combined with an If statement to take different actions based on the user's input. In essence, you enclose the arguments of the MsgBox function in parentheses (similar to what is done with the InputBox function), then test for the user response using the intrinsic constants vbYes and vbNo. The statement, If MsgBox("Are you having fun?", vbYesNo)=vbYes asks the user a question, displays Yes and No command buttons, then tests to see if the user clicked the Yes button.

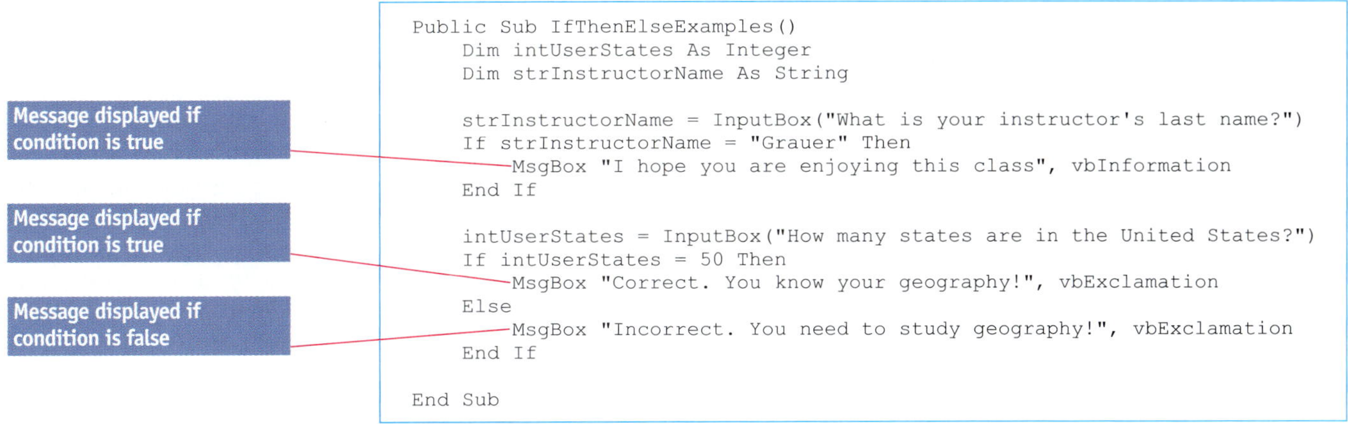


```
Public Sub IfThenElseExamples()
    Dim intUserStates As Integer
    Dim strInstructorName As String

    strInstructorName = InputBox("What is your instructor's last name?")
    If strInstructorName = "Grauer" Then
        MsgBox "I hope you are enjoying this class", vbInformation
    End If

    intUserStates = InputBox("How many states are in the United States?")
    If intUserStates = 50 Then
        MsgBox "Correct. You know your geography!", vbExclamation
    Else
        MsgBox "Incorrect. You need to study geography!", vbExclamation
    End If

End Sub
```

(a) VBA Code

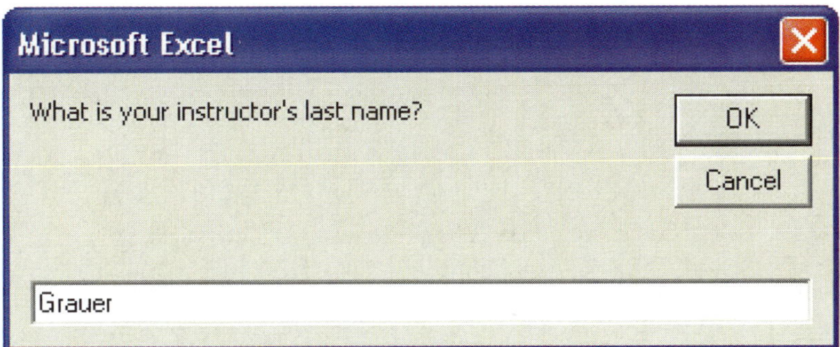

(b) InputBox Prompts for User Response

(c) Condition Is True

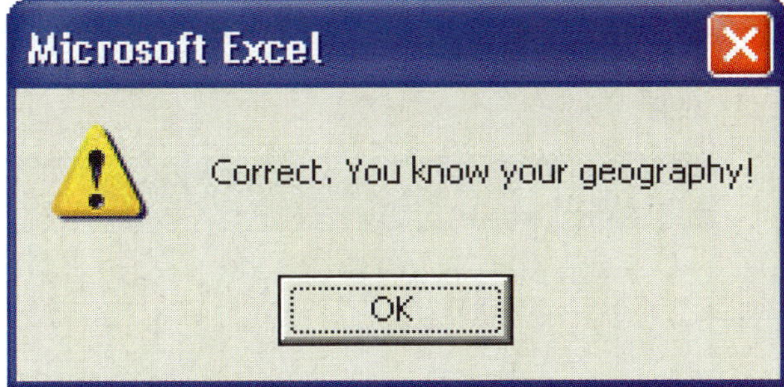

(d) Answer Is Correct (condition is true)

(e) Answer Is Wrong (condition is false)

FIGURE 5 The If Statement

CASE STATEMENT

The If statement is ideal for testing simple conditions and taking one of two actions. Although it can be extended to include additional actions by including one or more ElseIf clauses (If . . . Then . . . ElseIf . . . ElseIf . . .), this type of construction is often difficult to follow. Hence the ***Case statement*** is used when multiple branches are possible.

The procedure in Figure 6a accepts a student's GPA, then displays one of several messages, depending on the value of the GPA. The individual cases are evaluated in sequence. (The GPAs must be evaluated in descending order if the statement is to work correctly.) Thus, we check first to see if the GPA is greater than or equal to 3.9, then 3.75, then 3.5, and so on. If none of the cases is true, the statement following the Else clause is executed.

Note, too, the format of the comparison in that numbers (such as 3.9 or 3.75) are not enclosed in quotation marks because the associated variable (sngUserGPA) was declared as numeric. If, however, we had been evaluating a string variable (such as, strUserMajor), quotation marks would have been required around the literal values (e.g., Case Is = "Business", Case Is = "Liberal Arts", and so on.) The distinction between numeric and character (string) variables is important.

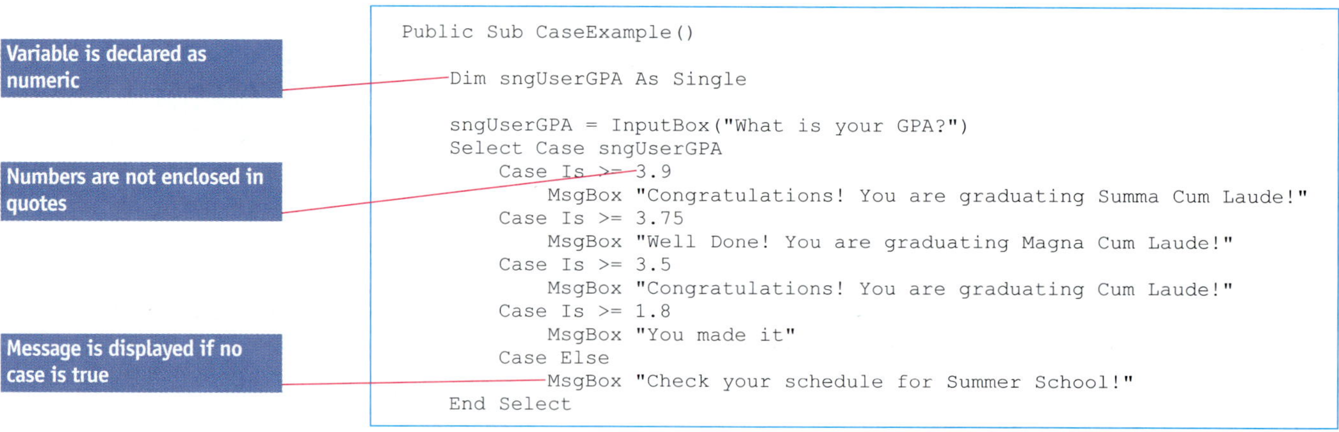


```
Public Sub CaseExample()

    Dim sngUserGPA As Single

    sngUserGPA = InputBox("What is your GPA?")
    Select Case sngUserGPA
        Case Is >= 3.9
            MsgBox "Congratulations! You are graduating Summa Cum Laude!"
        Case Is >= 3.75
            MsgBox "Well Done! You are graduating Magna Cum Laude!"
        Case Is >= 3.5
            MsgBox "Congratulations! You are graduating Cum Laude!"
        Case Is >= 1.8
            MsgBox "You made it"
        Case Else
            MsgBox "Check your schedule for Summer School!"
    End Select
```

(a) VBA Code

(b) Enter the GPA

Microsoft Excel

Congratulations! You are graduating Cum Laude!

OK

(c) Third Option Is Selected

FIGURE 6 The Case Statement

CUSTOM TOOLBARS

A VBA procedure can be executed in several different ways. It can be run from the Visual Basic editor by pulling down the Run menu and clicking the Run Sub button on the Standard toolbar, or using the F5 function key. It can also be run from within the Office application (Word, Excel, or PowerPoint, but not Access), by pulling down the Tools menu, clicking the Macro command, then choosing the name of the macro that corresponds to the name of the procedure.

Perhaps the best way, however, is to create a ***custom toolbar*** that is displayed within the application as shown in Figure 7. (A custom menu can also be created that contains the same commands as the custom toolbar.) The toolbar has its own name (Bob's Toolbar), yet it functions identically to any other Office toolbar. You have your choice of displaying buttons only, text only, or both buttons and text. Our toolbar provides access to four commands, each corresponding to a procedure that was discussed earlier. Click the Case Example button, for example, and the associated procedure is executed, starting with the InputBox statement asking for the user's GPA.

A custom toolbar is created via the Toolbars command within the View menu. The new toolbar is initially big enough to hold only a single button, but you can add, move, and delete buttons following the same procedure as for any other Office toolbar. You can add any command at all to the toolbar; that is, you can add existing commands from within the Office application, or you can add commands that correspond to VBA procedures that you have created. Remember, too, that you can add more buttons to existing office toolbars.

Once the toolbar has been created, it is displayed or hidden just like any other Office toolbar. It can also be docked along any edge of the application window or left floating as shown in Figure 7. It's fun, it's easy, and as you may have guessed, it's time for the next hands-on exercise.

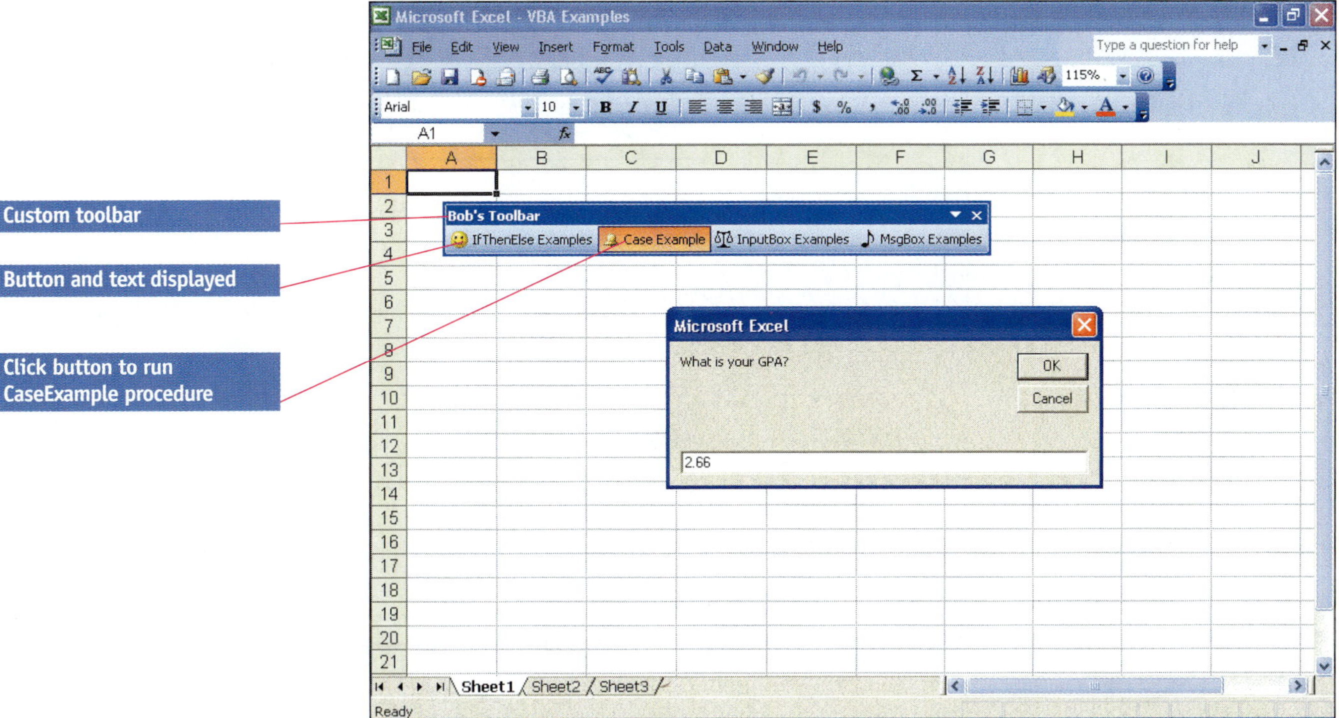

FIGURE 7 Custom Toolbars

hands-on exercise

2 Decision Making

Objective To create procedures with If . . . Then . . . Else and Case statements, then create a custom toolbar to execute those procedures. Use Figure 8 as a guide in the exercise.

Step 1: Open the Office Document

- Open the **VBA Examples workbook** or Access database from the previous exercise. The procedure differs slightly, depending on whether you are using Access or Excel.
  - In Access, you simply open the database.
  - In Excel you will be warned that the workbook contains a macro as shown in Figure 8a. Click the button to **Enable Macros**.
- Pull down the **Tools menu**, click the **Macro command**, then click the **Visual Basic Editor command**. You can also use the **Alt+F11** keyboard shortcut to open the VBA editor without going through the Tools menu.

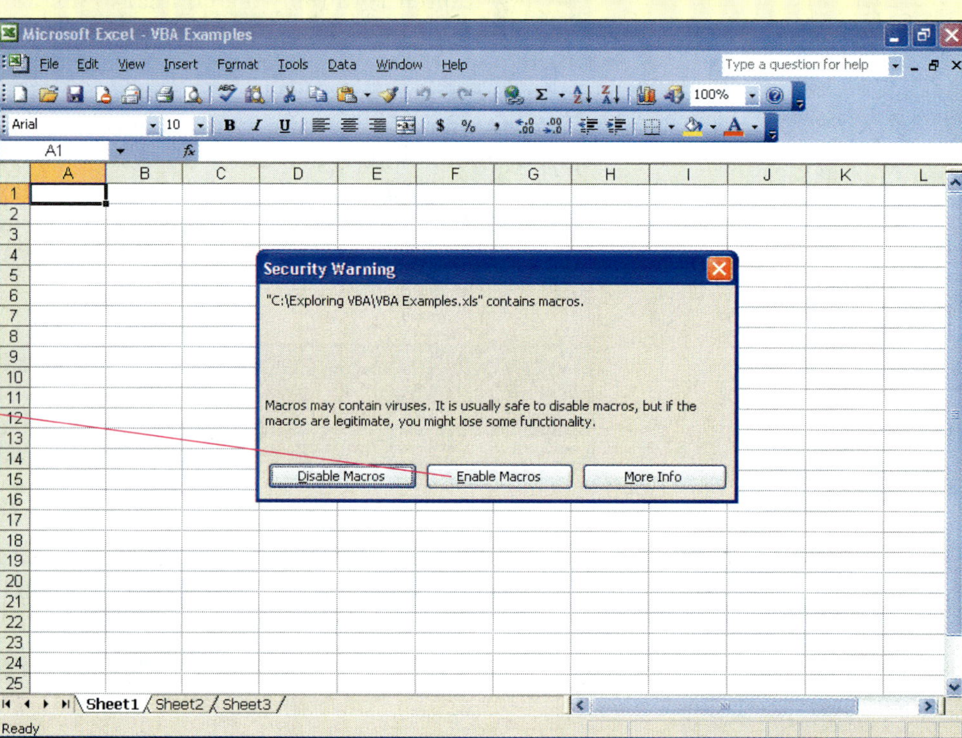

(a) Open the Office Document (step 1)

FIGURE 8 Hands-on Exercise 2

MACRO SECURITY

A computer virus could take the form of an Excel macro; thus, Excel will warn you that a workbook contains a macro, provided the security option is set appropriately. Pull down the Tools menu, click the Options command, click the Security tab, and then set the Macro Security to either High or Medium. High security disables all macros except those from a trusted source. Medium security gives you the option to enable macros. Click the button only if you are sure the macro is from a trusted source.

Step 2: Insert a New Procedure

- You should be in the Visual Basic editor as shown in Figure 8b. If necessary, double click **Module1** in the Explorer Window to open this module. Pull down the **Insert menu** and click the **Procedure command** to display the Add Procedure dialog box.
- Click in the **Name** text box and enter **IfThenElseExamples** as the name of the procedure. Click the option buttons for a **Sub procedure** and for **Public scope**. Click **OK** to create the procedure.
- The Sub procedure should appear within the module and consist of the Sub and End Sub statements as shown in Figure 8b.
- Click within the newly created procedure, then click the **Procedure View button** at the bottom of the window. The display changes to show just the current procedure.
- Click the **Save button** to save the module with the new procedure.

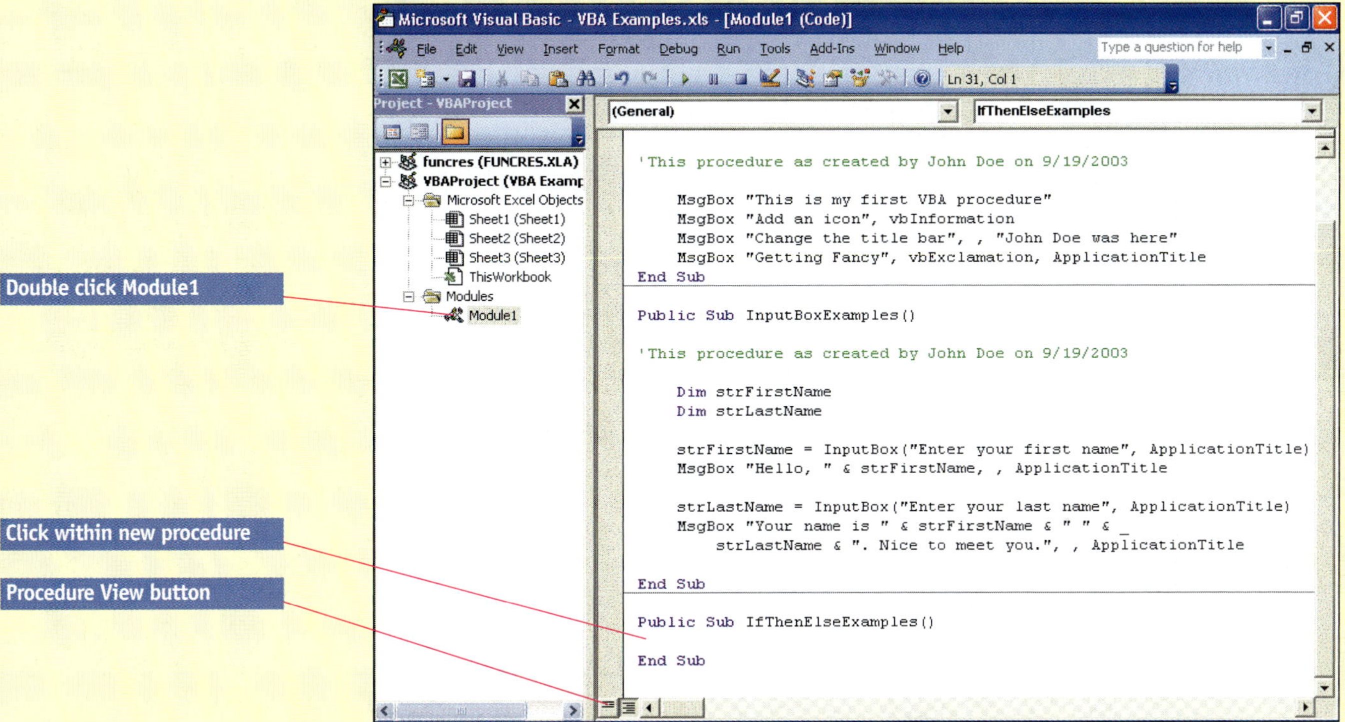

(b) Insert a New Procedure (step 2)

FIGURE 8 Hands-on Exercise 2 (*continued*)

PROCEDURE VIEW VERSUS FULL MODULE VIEW

The procedures within a module can be displayed individually, or alternatively, multiple procedures can be viewed simultaneously. To go from one view to the other, click the Procedure View button at the bottom of the window to display just the procedure you are working on, or click the Full Module View button to display multiple procedures. You can press Ctrl+PgDn and Ctrl+PgUp to move between procedures in either view.

Step 3: Create the If . . . Then . . . Else Procedure

- Enter the IfThenElseExamples procedure as it appears in Figure 8c, but use your instructor's name instead of Bob's. Note the following:
  - The Dim statements at the beginning of the procedure are required to define the two variables that are used elsewhere in the procedure.
  - The syntax of the comparison is different for string variables versus numeric variables. String variables require quotation marks around the comparison value (e.g., strInstructorName = "Grauer"). Numeric variables (e.g., intUserStates = 50) do not.
  - Indentation and blank lines are used within a procedure to make the code easier to read, as distinct from a VBA requirement. Press the **Tab key** to indent one level to the right.
  - Comments can be added to a procedure at any time.
- Save the procedure.

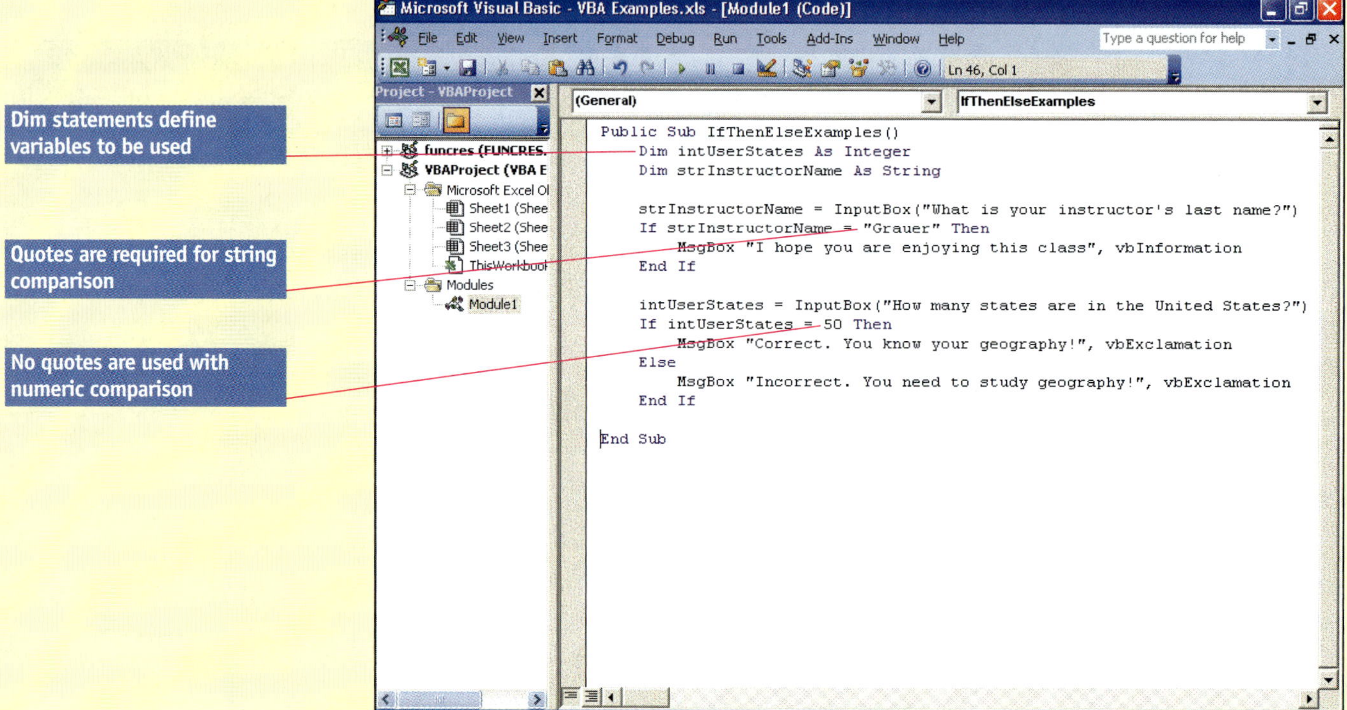

(c) Create the If . . . Then . . . Else Procedure (step 3)

FIGURE 8 Hands-on Exercise 2 (*continued*)

THE COMPLETE WORD TOOL

It's easy to misspell a variable name within a procedure, which is why the Complete Word tool is so useful. Type the first several characters in a variable name (such as "intU" or "strI" in the current procedure), then press Ctrl+Space. VBA will complete the variable name for you, provided that you have already entered a sufficient number of letters for a unique reference. Alternatively, it will display all of the elements that begin with the letters you have entered. Use the down arrow to scroll through the list until you find the item, then press the space bar to complete the entry.

Step 4: Test the Procedure

- The best way to test a procedure is to display its output directly in the VBA window (without having to switch back and forth between that and the application window). Thus, right click the Excel button on the taskbar to display a context-sensitive menu, then click the **Minimize command**.
- There is no visible change on your monitor. Click anywhere within the procedure, then click the **Run Sub button**. You should see the dialog box in Figure 8d.
- Enter your instructor's name, exactly as it was spelled within the VBA procedure. Click **OK**.
- You should see a second message box that hopes you are enjoying the class. This box will be displayed only if you spell the instructor's name correctly. Click **OK**.
- You should see a second input box that asks how many states are in the United States. Enter **50** and click **OK**. You should see a message indicating that you know your geography. Click **OK** to close the dialog box.
- Click the **Run Sub button** a second time, but enter a different set of values in response to the prompts. Misspell your instructor's name, and you will not see the associated message box.
- Enter any number other than 50, and you will be told to study geography.
- Continue to test the procedure until you are satisfied it works under all conditions. We cannot overemphasize the importance of thorough testing!

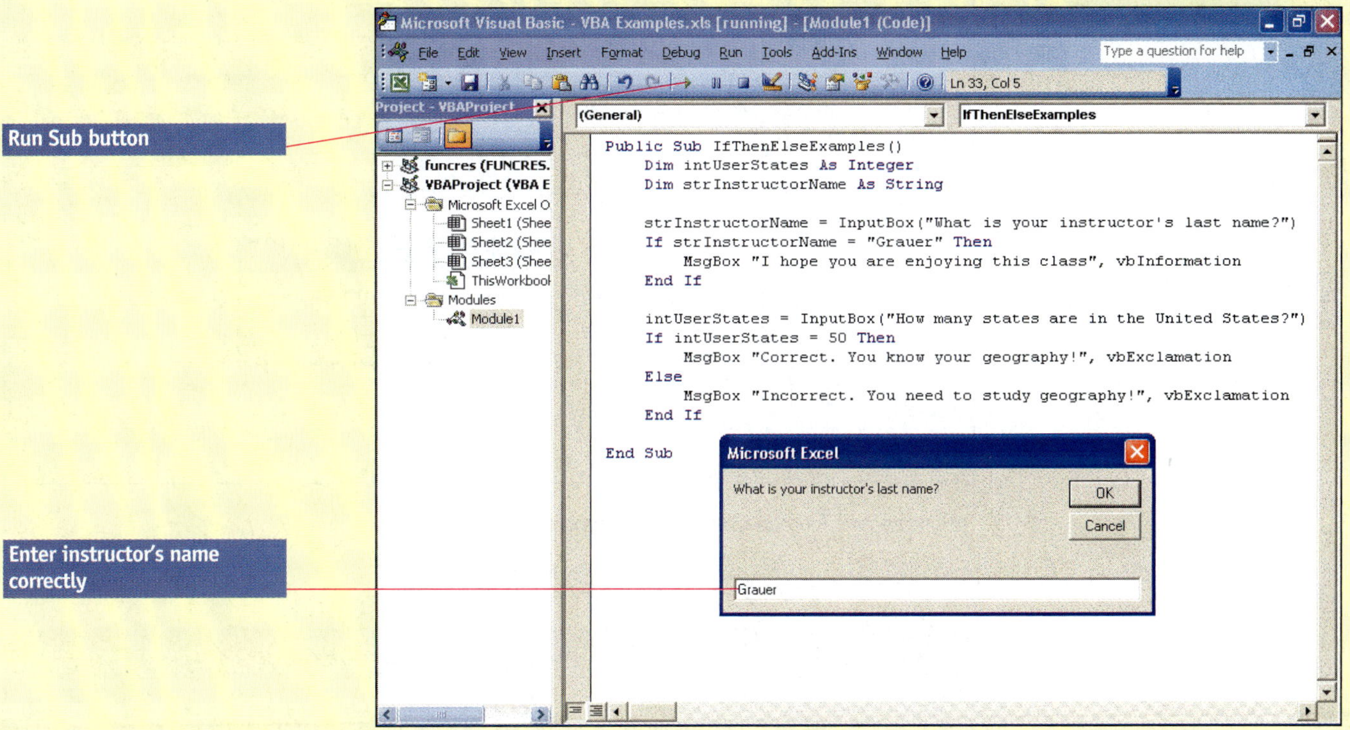

(d) Test the Procedure (step 4)

FIGURE 8 Hands-on Exercise 2 (*continued*)

Step 5: Create and Test the CaseExample Procedure

- Pull down the **Insert menu** and create a new procedure called **CaseExample**, then enter the statements exactly as they appear in Figure 8e. Note:
  - The variable sngUserGPA is declared to be a single-precision floating-point number (as distinct from the integer type that was used previously). A floating-point number is required in order to maintain a decimal point.
  - The GPA must be tested in descending order if the statement is to work correctly.
  - You may use any editing technique with which you are comfortable. You could, for example, enter the first case, copy it four times in the procedure, then modify the copied text as necessary.
  - The use of indentation and blank lines is for the convenience of the programmer and not a requirement of VBA.
- Click the **Run Sub button**, then test the procedure. Be sure to test it under all conditions; that is, you need to run it several times and enter a different GPA each time to be sure that all of the cases are working correctly.
- Save the procedure.

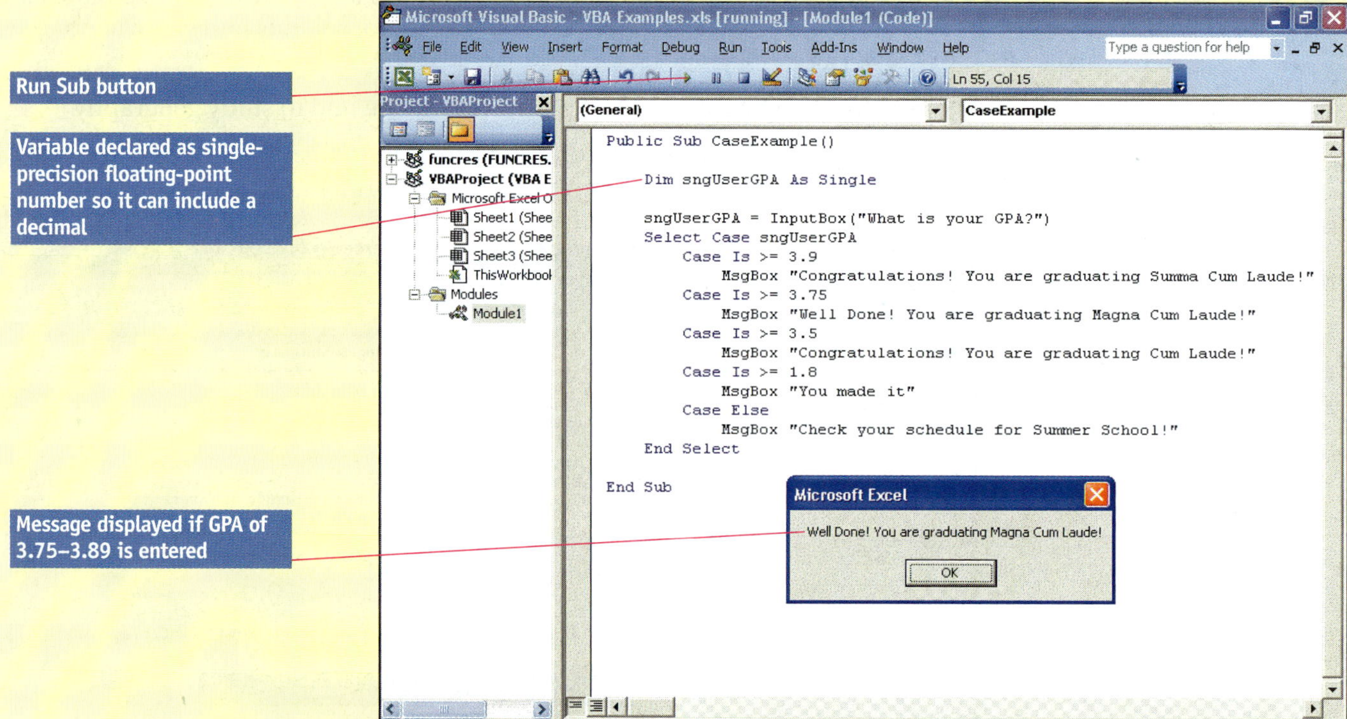

(e) Create and Test the CaseExample Procedure (step 5)

FIGURE 8 Hands-on Exercise 2 (*continued*)

RELATIONAL OPERATORS

The condition portion of an If or Case statement uses one of several relational operators. These include =, <, and > for equal to, less than, or greater than, respectively. You can also use >=, <=, or <> for greater than or equal to, less than or equal to, or not equal. This is basic, but very important, information if you are to code these statements correctly.

Step 6: Create a Custom Toolbar

- Click the **View Microsoft Excel** (or **Access**) **button** to display the associated application window. Pull down the **View menu**, click (or point to) the **Toolbars command**, then click **Customize** to display the Customize dialog box in Figure 8f. (Bob's toolbar is not yet visible.) Click the **Toolbars tab**.
- Click the **New button** to display the New Toolbar dialog box. Enter the name of your toolbar—e.g., **Bob's toolbar**—then click **OK** to create the toolbar and close the New Toolbar dialog box.
- Your toolbar should appear on the screen, but it does not yet contain any buttons. If necessary, click and drag the title bar of your toolbar to move the toolbar within the application window.
- Toggle the check box that appears next to your toolbar within the Customize dialog box on and off to display or hide your toolbar. Leave the box checked to display the toolbar and continue with this exercise.

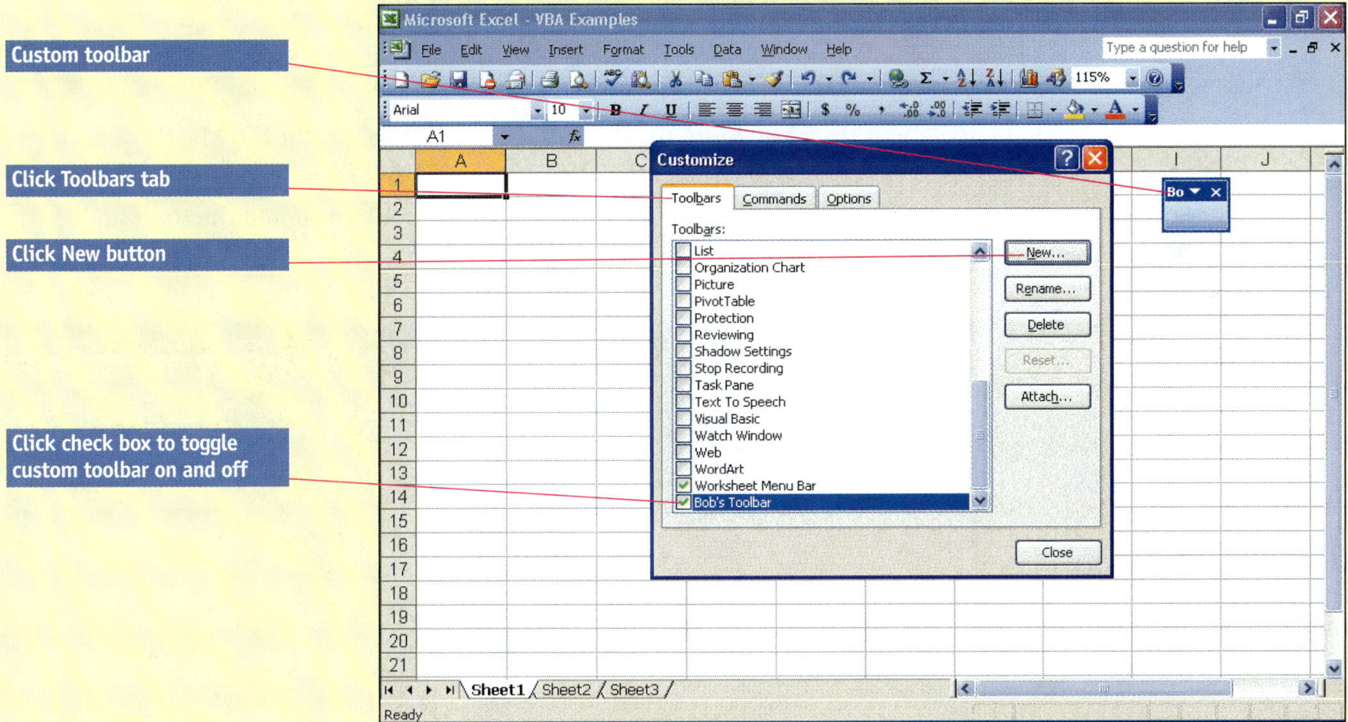

(f) Create a Custom Toolbar (step 6)

FIGURE 8 Hands-on Exercise 2 (*continued*)

FIXED VERSUS FLOATING TOOLBARS

A toolbar may be docked (fixed) along the edge of the application window, or it can be displayed as a floating toolbar anywhere within the window. You can switch back and forth by dragging the move handle of a docked toolbar to move the toolbar away from the edge. Conversely, you can drag the title bar of a floating toolbar to the edge of the window to dock the toolbar. You can also click and drag the border of a floating toolbar to change its size.

Step 7: Add Buttons to the Toolbar

- Click the **Commands tab** in the Customize dialog box, click the **down arrow** in the Categories list box, then scroll until you can select the **Macros category**. (If you are using Access and not Excel, you need to select the **File category**, then follow the steps as described in the boxed tip on the next page.)
- Click and drag the **Custom button** to your toolbar and release the mouse. A "happy face" button appears on the toolbar you just created. (You can remove a button from a toolbar by simply dragging the button from the toolbar.)
- Select the newly created button, then click the **Modify Selection command button** (or right click the button to display the context-sensitive menu) in Figure 8g. Change the button's properties as follows:
  - Click the **Assign Macro command** at the bottom of the menu to display the Assign Macro dialog box, then select the **IfThenElseExamples macro** (procedure) to assign it to the button. Click **OK**.
  - Click the **Modify Selection button** a second time.
  - Click in the **Name Textbox** and enter an appropriate name for the button, such as **IfThenElseExamples**.
  - Click the **Modify Selection button** a third time, then click **Text Only (Always)** to display text rather than an image.
- Repeat this procedure to add buttons to the toolbar for the MsgBoxExamples, InputBoxExamples, and CaseExample procedures that you created earlier.
- Close the Customize dialog box when you have completed the toolbar.
- Save the workbook.

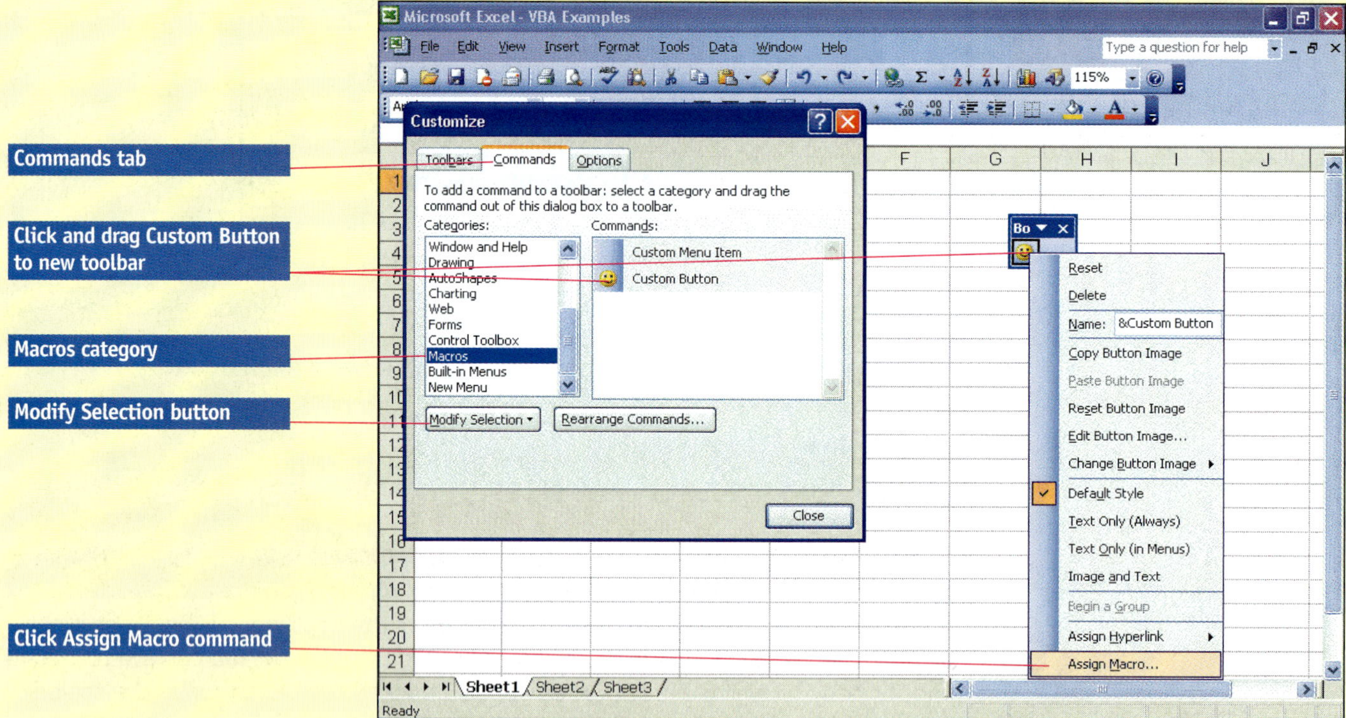

(g) Add Buttons to the Toolbar (step 7)

FIGURE 8 Hands-on Exercise 2 (*continued*)

Step 8: Test the Custom Toolbar

- Click any command on your toolbar as shown in Figure 8h. We clicked the **InputBoxExamples button**, which in turn executed the InputBoxExamples procedure that was created in the first exercise.
- Enter the appropriate information in any input boxes that are displayed. Click **OK**. Close your toolbar when you have completed testing it.
- If this is not your own machine, you should delete your toolbar as a courtesy to the next student. Pull down the **View menu**, click the **Toolbars command**, click **Customize** to display the Customize dialog box, then click the **Toolbars tab**. Select (highlight) the toolbar, then click the **Delete button** in the Customize dialog box. Click **OK** to delete the button. Close the dialog box.
- Exit Office if you do not want to continue with the next exercise.

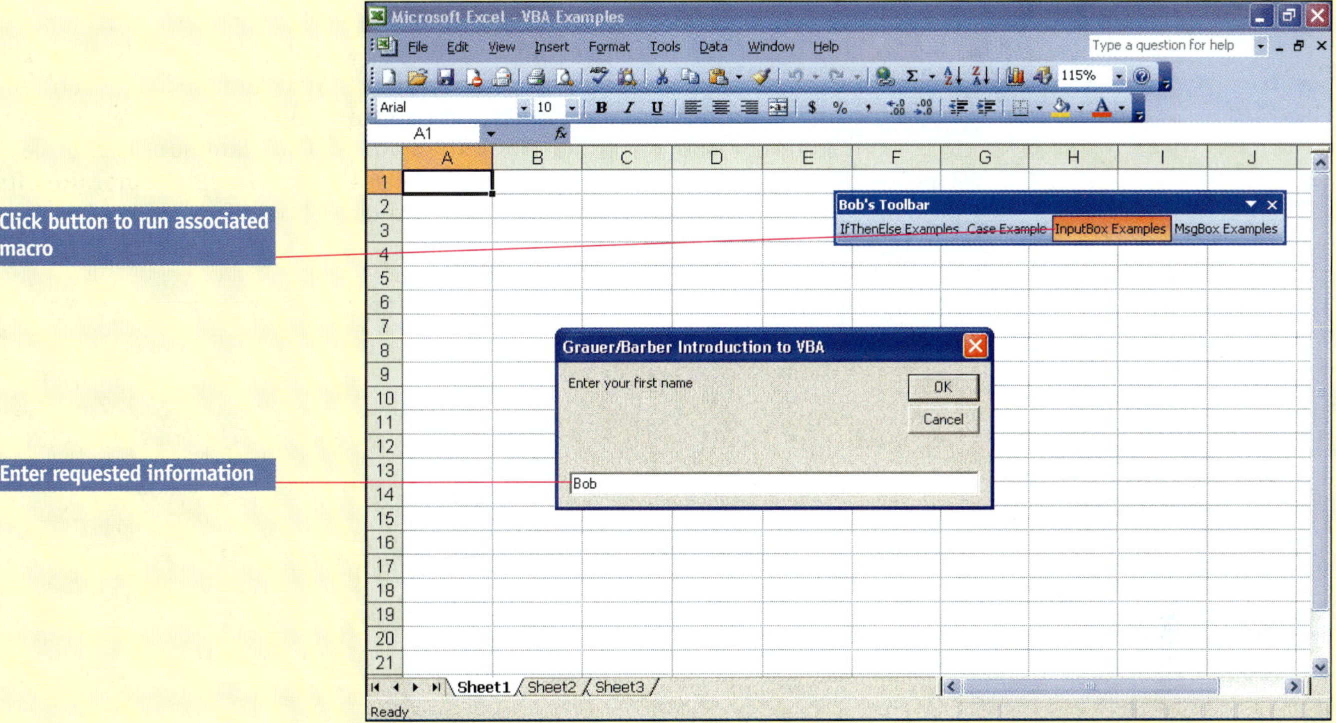

(h) Test the Custom Toolbar (step 8)

FIGURE 8 Hands-on Exercise 2 (*continued*)

ACCESS IS DIFFERENT

The procedure to add buttons to a custom toolbar in Access is different from the procedure in Excel. Pull down the View menu, click the Toolbars command, then click the Customize command. Select the File category within the Customize dialog box, then click and drag the Custom command to the newly created toolbar. Select the command on the toolbar, then click the Modify Selection command button in the dialog box. Click Properties, click the On Action text box, then type the name of the procedure you want to run in the format, =procedurename(). Close the dialog boxes, then press Alt+F11 to return to the VBA editor. Change the keyword "Sub" that identifies the procedure to "Function". Return to the database window, then test the newly created toolbar.

FOR . . . NEXT STATEMENT

The ***For . . . Next statement*** executes all statements between the words For and Next a specified number of times, using a counter to keep track of the number of times the statements are executed. The statement, For intCounter = 1 to N, executes the statements within the loop N times.

The procedure in Figure 9 contains two For . . . Next statements that sum the numbers from 1 to 10, counting by 1 and 2, respectively. The Dim statements at the beginning of the procedure declare two variables, intSumofNumbers to hold the sum and intCounter to hold the value of the counter. The sum is initialized to zero immediately before the first loop. The statements in the loop are then executed 10 times, each time incrementing the sum by the value of the counter. The result (the sum of the numbers from 1 to 10) is displayed after the loop in Figure 9b.

The second For . . . Next statement increments the counter by 2 rather than by 1. (The increment or step is assumed to be 1 unless a different value is specified.) The sum of the numbers is reset to zero prior to entering the second loop, the loop is entered, and the counter is initialized to the starting value of 1. Each subsequent time through the loop, however, the counter is incremented by 2. Each time the value of the counter is compared to the ending value, until it (the counter) exceeds the ending value, at which point the For . . . Next statement is complete. Thus the second loop will be executed for values of 1, 3, 5, 7, and 9. After the fifth time through the loop, the counter is incremented to 11, which is greater than the ending value of 10, and the loop is terminated.

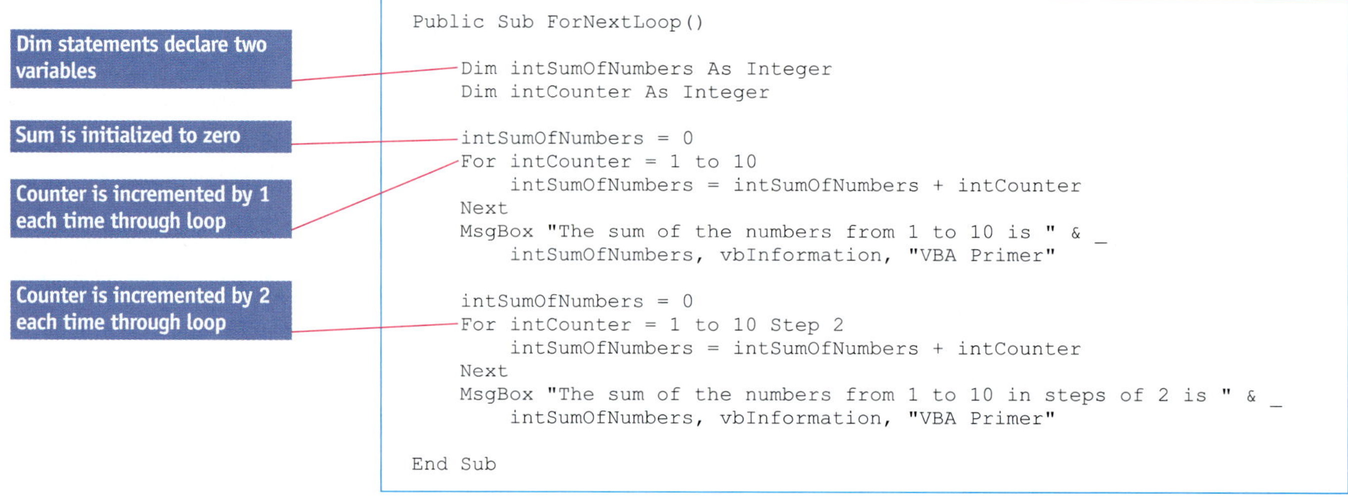


```
Public Sub ForNextLoop()

    Dim intSumOfNumbers As Integer
    Dim intCounter As Integer

    intSumOfNumbers = 0
    For intCounter = 1 to 10
        intSumOfNumbers = intSumOfNumbers + intCounter
    Next
    MsgBox "The sum of the numbers from 1 to 10 is " & _
        intSumOfNumbers, vbInformation, "VBA Primer"

    intSumOfNumbers = 0
    For intCounter = 1 to 10 Step 2
        intSumOfNumbers = intSumOfNumbers + intCounter
    Next
    MsgBox "The sum of the numbers from 1 to 10 in steps of 2 is " & _
        intSumOfNumbers, vbInformation, "VBA Primer"

End Sub
```

(a) VBA Code

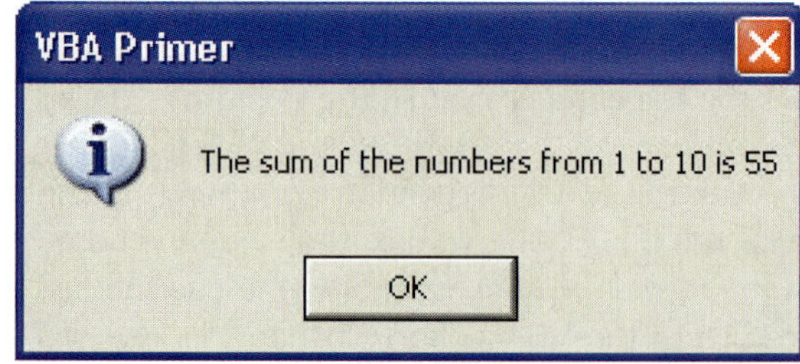

(b) In Increments of 1

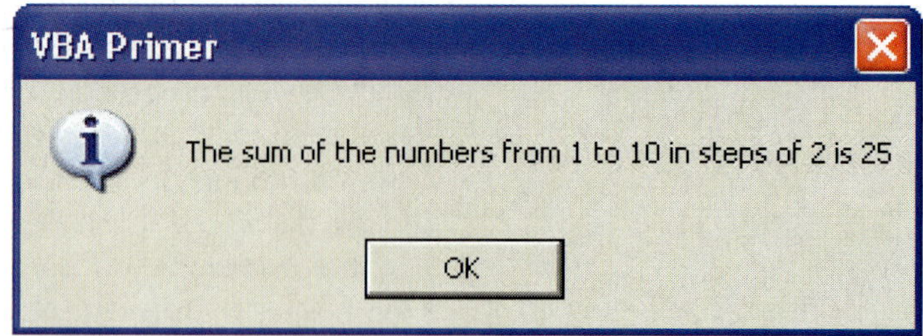

(c) In Increments of 2

FIGURE 9 For . . . Next Loops

DO LOOPS

The For . . . Next statement is ideal when you know in advance how many times you want to go through a loop. There are many instances, however, when the number of times through the loop is indeterminate. You could, for example, give a user multiple chances to enter a password or answer a question. This type of logic is implemented through a Do loop. You can repeat the loop as long as a condition is true (Do While), or until a condition becomes true (Do Until). The choice depends on how you want to state the condition.

Regardless of which keyword you choose, Do While or Do Until, two formats are available. The difference is subtle and depends on whether the keyword (While or Until) appears at the beginning or end of the loop. Our discussion will use the Do Until statement, but the Do While statement works in similar fashion.

Look closely at the procedure in Figure 10a, which contains two different loops. In the first example the Until condition appears at the end of the loop, which means the statements in the loop are executed, and then the condition is tested. This ensures that the statements in the loop will be executed at least once. The second loop, however, places the Until condition at the beginning of the loop, so that it (the condition) is tested prior to the loop being executed. Thus, if the condition is satisfied initially, the second loop will never be executed. In other words, there are two distinct statements ***Do . . . Loop Until*** and ***Do Until . . . Loop***. The first statement executes the loop, then tests the condition. The second statement tests the condition, then enters the loop.

Until appears at end of loop

Until appears at beginning of loop

```
Public Sub DoUntilLoop()

    Dim strCorrectAnswer As String, strUserAnswer As String

    strCorrectAnswer = "Earth"

    Do
        strUserAnswer = InputBox("What is the third planet from the sun?")
    Loop Until strUserAnswer = strCorrectAnswer
    MsgBox "You are correct, earthling!", vbExclamation

    strUserAnswer = InputBox("What is the third planet from the sun?")
    Do Until strUserAnswer = strCorrectAnswer
        strUserAnswer = InputBox("Your answer is incorrect. Try again.")
    Loop
    MsgBox "You are correct, earthling!", vbExclamation

End Sub
```

(a) (VBA Code)

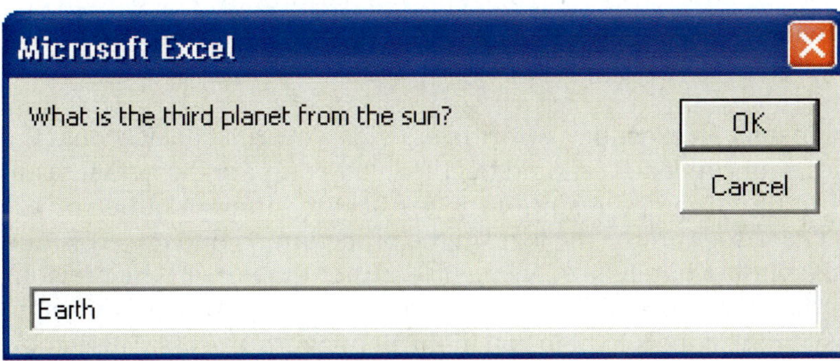

(b) Input the Answer

Microsoft Excel

You are correct, earthling!

OK

(c) Correct Response

FIGURE 10 Do Until Loops

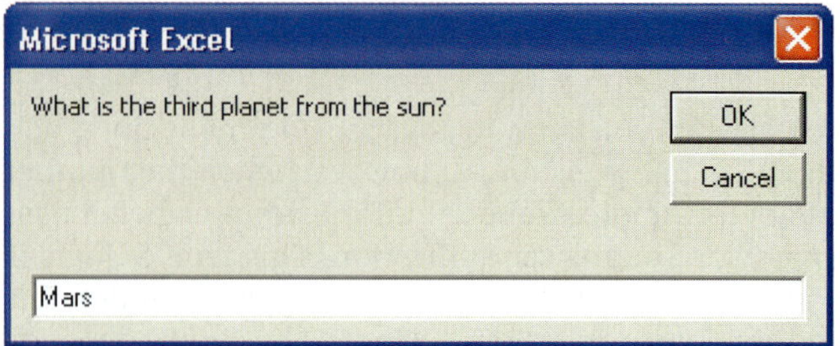

(d) Wrong Answer Initially

(e) Second Chance

FIGURE 10 Do Until Loops (*continued*)

It's tricky, but stay with us. In the first example the user is asked the question within the loop, and the loop is executed repeatedly until the user gives the correct answer. In the second example the user is asked the question outside of the loop, and the loop is bypassed if the user answers it correctly. The latter is the preferred logic because it enables us to phrase the question differently, before and during the loop. Look carefully at the difference between the InputBox statements and see how the question changes within the second loop.

DEBUGGING

As you learn more about VBA and develop more powerful procedures, you are more likely to make mistakes. The process of finding and correcting errors within a procedure is known as ***debugging*** and it is an integral part of programming. Do not be discouraged if you make mistakes. Everyone does. The important thing is how quickly you are able to find and correct the errors that invariably occur. We begin our discussion of debugging by describing two types of errors, ***compilation errors*** and ***execution*** (or ***run-time***) ***errors***.

A compilation error is simply an error in VBA syntax. (Compilation is the process of translating a VBA procedure into machine language, and thus a compilation error occurs when the VBA editor is unable to convert a statement to machine language.) Compilation errors occur for many reasons, such as misspelling a keyword, omitting a comma, and so on. VBA recognizes the error before the procedure is run and displays the invalid statement in red together with an associated error message. The programmer corrects the error and then reruns the procedure.

Execution errors are caused by errors in logic and are more difficult to detect because they occur without any error message. VBA, or for that matter any other programming language, does what you tell it to do, which is not necessarily what you want it to do. If, for example, you were to compute the sales tax of an item by multiplying the price by 60% rather than 6%, VBA will perform the calculation and simply display the wrong answer. It is up to you to realize that the results of the procedure are incorrect, and you will need to examine its statements and correct the mistake.

So how do you detect an execution error? In essence, you must decide what the expected output of your procedure should be, then you compare the actual result of the procedure to the intended result. If the results are different, an error has occurred, and you have to examine the logic in the procedure to find the error. You may see the mistake immediately (e.g., using 60% rather than 6% in the previous example), or you may have to examine the code more closely. And as you might expect, VBA has a variety of tools to help you in the debugging process. These tools are accessed from the ***Debug toolbar*** or the ***Debug menu*** as shown in Figure 11 on the next page.

The procedure in Figure 11 is a simple For . . . Next loop to sum the integers from 1 to 10. The procedure is correct as written, but we have introduced several debugging techniques into the figure. The most basic technique is to step through the statements in the procedure one at a time to see the sequence in which the statements are executed. Click the ***Step Into button*** on the Debug toolbar to enter (step into) the procedure, then continue to click the button to move through the procedure. Each time you click the button, the statement that is about to be executed is highlighted.

Another useful technique is to display the values of selected variables as they change during execution. This is accomplished through the ***Debug.Print statement*** that displays the values in the ***Immediate window***. The Debug.Print statement is placed within the For . . . Next loop so that you can see how the counter and the associated sum change during execution.

As the figure now stands, we have gone through the loop nine times, and the sum of the numbers from 1 to 9 is 45. The Step Into button is in effect so that the statement to be executed next is highlighted. You can see that we are back at the top of the loop, where the counter has been incremented to 10, and further, that we are about to increment the sum.

The ***Locals window*** is similar in concept except that it displays only the current values of all the variables within the procedure. Unlike the Immediate window, which requires the insertion of Debug.Print statements into a procedure to have meaning, the Locals window displays its values automatically, without any effort on the part of the programmer, other than opening the window. All three techniques can be used individually, or in conjunction with one another, as the situation demands.

We believe that the best time to practice debugging is when you know there are no errors in your procedure. As you may have guessed, it's time for the next hands-on exercise.

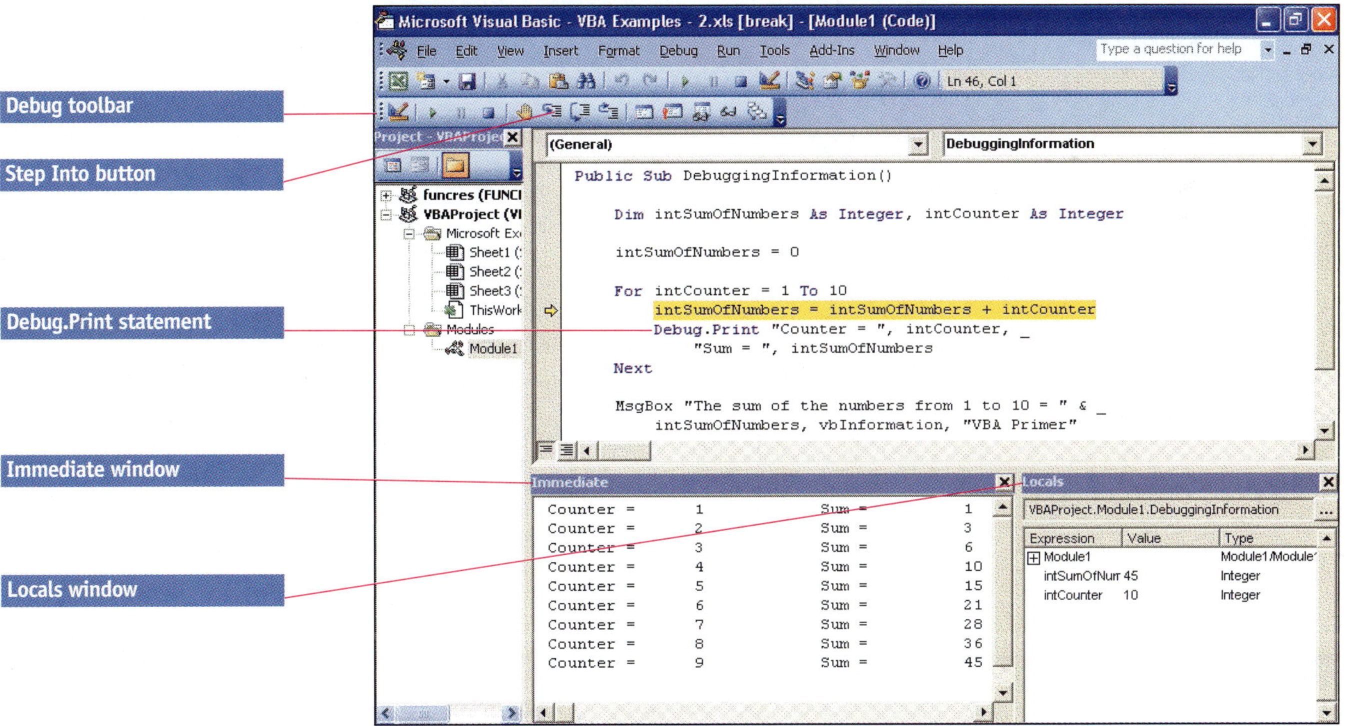

FIGURE 11 Debugging

hands-on exercise

3 Loops and Debugging

Objective To create a loop using the For . . . Next and Do Until statements; to open the Locals and Immediate windows and illustrate different techniques for debugging. Use Figure 12 as a guide in the exercise.

Step 1: Insert a New Procedure

- Open the **VBA Examples workbook** or the Access database from the previous exercise. Either way, pull down the **Tools menu**, click the **Macro command**, then click **Visual Basic editor** (or use the **Alt+F11** keyboard shortcut) to start the VBA editor.
- If necessary, double click **Module1** within the Project Explorer window to open this module. Pull down the **Insert menu** and click the **Procedure command** to display the Add Procedure dialog box.
- Click in the **Name** text box and enter **ForNextLoop** as the name of the procedure. Click the option buttons for a **Sub procedure** and for **Public scope**. Click **OK** to create the procedure.
- The Sub procedure should appear within the module and consist of the Sub and End Sub statements as shown in Figure 12a.
- Click the **Procedure View button** at the bottom of the window as shown in Figure 12a. The display changes to show just the current procedure, giving you more room in which to work.
- Save the module.

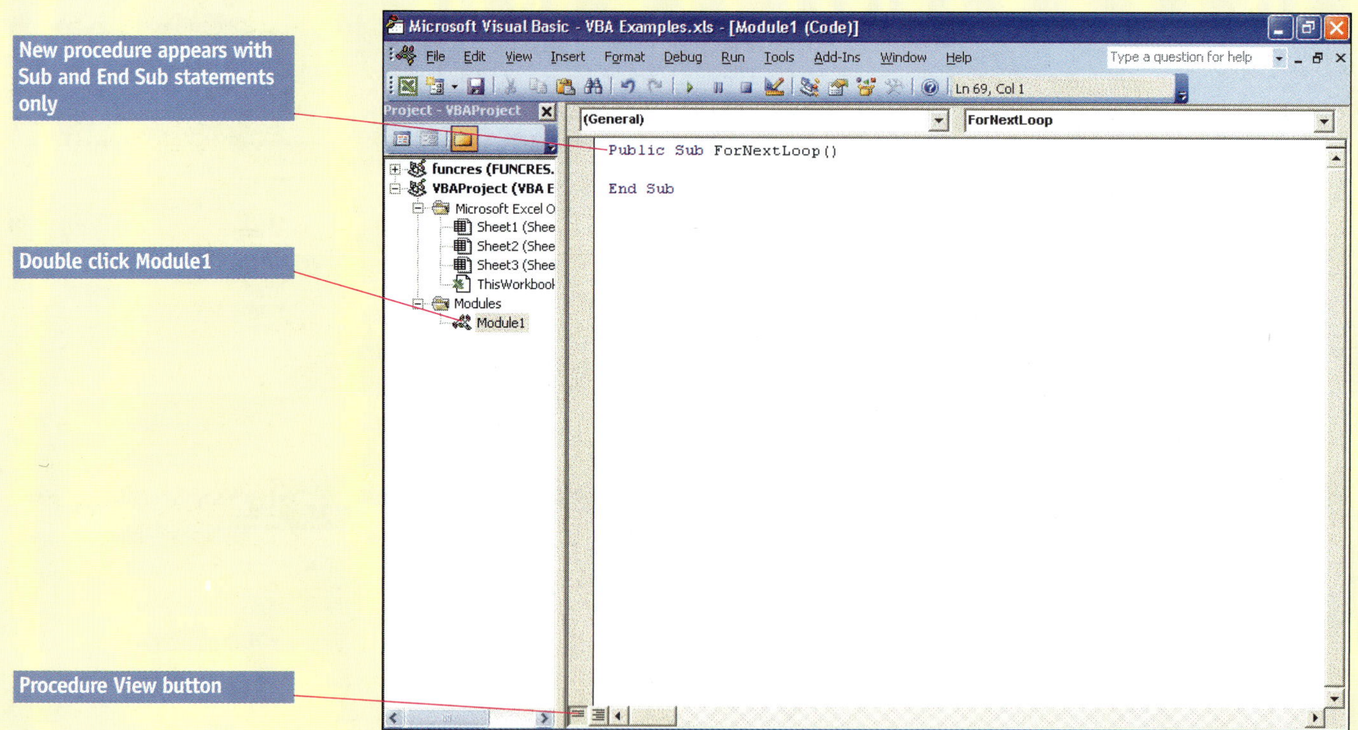

(a) Insert a New Procedure (step 1)

FIGURE 12 Hands-on Exercise 3

Step 2: Test the For . . . Next Procedure

- Enter the procedure exactly as it appears in Figure 12b. Note the following:
  - A comment is added at the beginning of the procedure to identify the author and the date.
  - Two variables are declared at the beginning of the procedure, one to hold the sum of the numbers and the other to serve as a counter.
  - The sum of the numbers is initialized to zero. The For . . . Next loop varies the counter from 1 to 10.
  - The statement within the For . . . Next loop increments the sum of the numbers by the current value of the counter. The equal sign is really a replacement operator; that is, replace the variable on the left (the sum of the numbers) by the expression on the right (the sum of the numbers plus the value of the counter.
  - Indentation and spacing within a procedure are for the convenience of the programmer and not a requirement of VBA. We align the For and Next statements at the beginning and end of a loop, then indent all statements within a loop.
  - The MsgBox statement displays the result and is continued over two lines as per the underscore at the end of the first line.
  - The ampersand concatenates (joins together) the text and the number within the message box.
- Click the **Save button** to save the module. Right click the **Excel button** on the Windows taskbar to display a context-sensitive menu, then click the **Minimize command**.
- Click the **Run Sub button** to test the procedure, which should display the MsgBox statement in Figure 12b. Correct any errors that may occur.

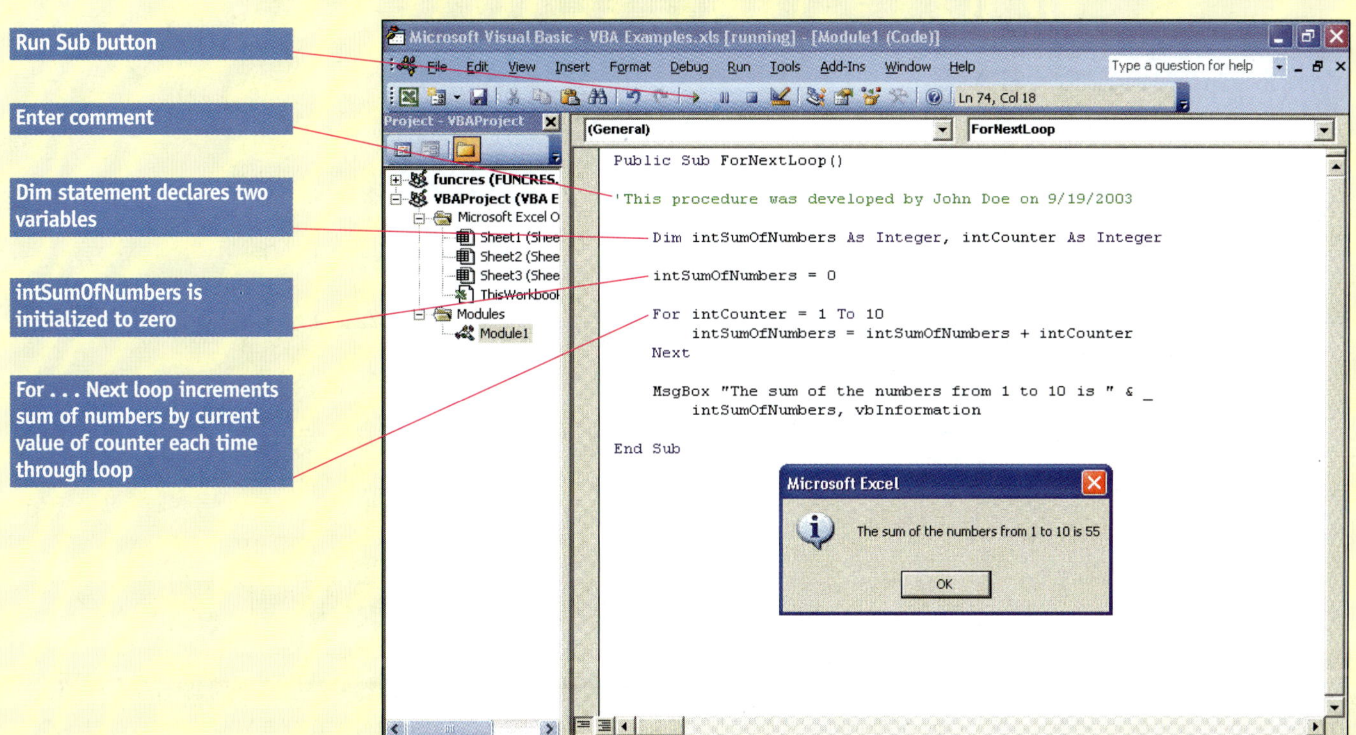

(b) Test the For . . . Next Procedure (step 2)

FIGURE 12 Hands-on Exercise 3 (*continued*)

Step 3: **Compilation Errors**

- The best time to practice debugging is when you know that the procedure is working properly. Accordingly, we will make some deliberate errors in our procedure to illustrate different debugging techniques.
- Pull down the **View menu**, click the **Toolbars command**, and (if necessary) toggle the Debug toolbar on, then dock it under the Standard toolbar.
- Click on the statement that initializes intSumOfNumbers to zero and delete the "s" at the end of the variable name. Click the **Run Sub button**.
- You will see the message in Figure 12c. Click **OK** to acknowledge the error, then click the **Undo button** to correct the error.
- The procedure header is highlighted, indicating that execution is temporarily suspended and that additional action is required from you to continue testing. Click the **Run Sub button** to retest the procedure.
- This time the procedure executes correctly and you see the MsgBox statement indicating that the sum of the numbers from 1 to 10 is 55. Click **OK**.

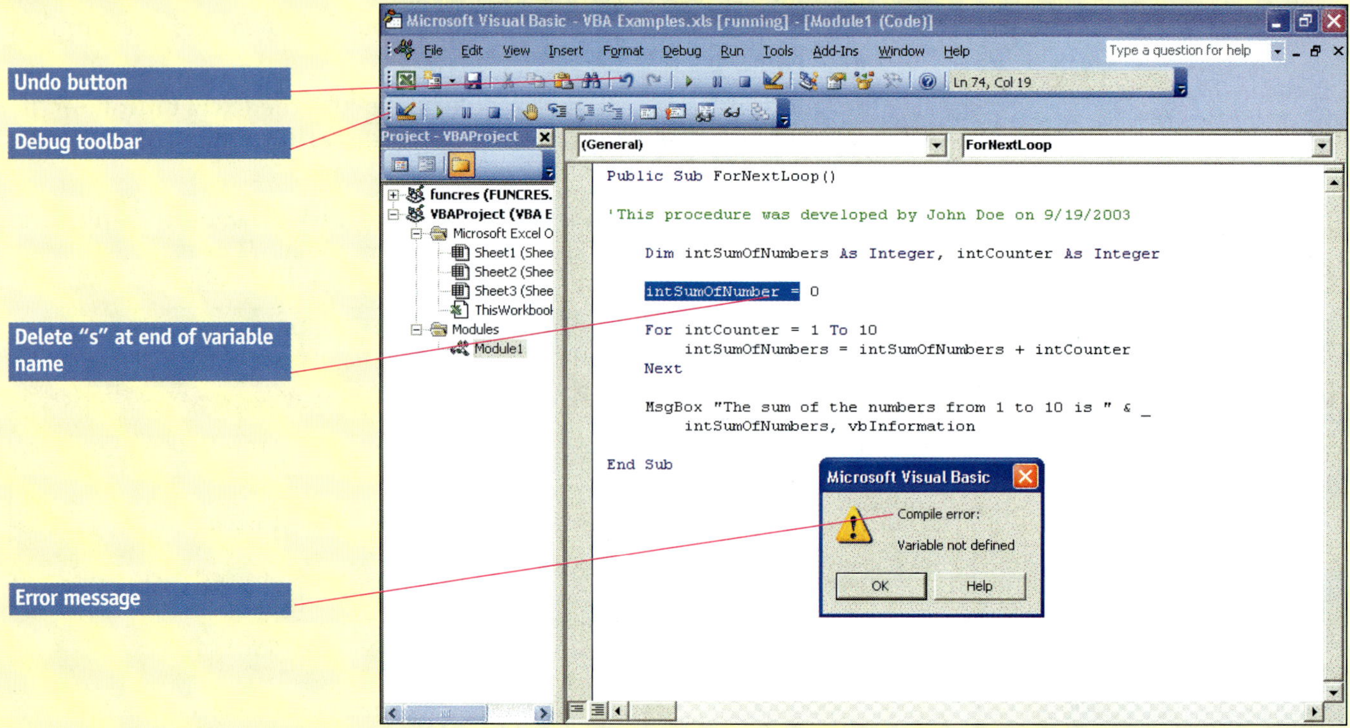

(c) Compilation Error (step 3)

FIGURE 12 Hands-on Exercise 3 (*continued*)

USE HELP AS NECESSARY

Pull down the Help menu at any time (or press the F1 key) to access the VBA Help facility to explore at your leisure. Use the Print command to create hard copy. (You can also copy the help text into a Word document to create your own reference manual.) The answers to virtually all of your questions are readily available if only you take the time to look.

Step 4: Step through a Procedure

- Pull down the **View menu** a second time and click the **Locals Window command** (or click the **Locals Window button** on the Debug toolbar).
- If necessary, click and drag the top border of the Locals window to size the window appropriately as shown in Figure 12d.
- Click anywhere within the procedure. Pull down the **Debug menu** and click the **Step Into command** (or click the **Step Into button** on the Debug toolbar). The first statement (the procedure header) is highlighted, indicating that you are about to enter the procedure.
- Click the **Step Into button** (or use the **F8** keyboard shortcut) to step into the procedure and advance to the next executable statement. The statement that initializes intSumOfNumbers to zero is highlighted, indicating that this statement is about to be executed.
- Continue to press the **F8 key** to step through the procedure. Each time you execute a statement, you can see the values of intSumOfNumbers and intCounter change within the Locals window. (You can click the **Step Out button** at any time to end the procedure.)
- Correct errors as they occur. Click the **Reset button** on the Standard or Debug toolbars at any time to begin executing the procedure from the beginning.
- Eventually you exit from the loop, and the sum of the numbers (from 1 to 10) is displayed within a message box.
- Click **OK** to close the message box. Press the **F8 key** a final time, then close the Locals window.
- Do you see how stepping through a procedure helps you to understand how it works?

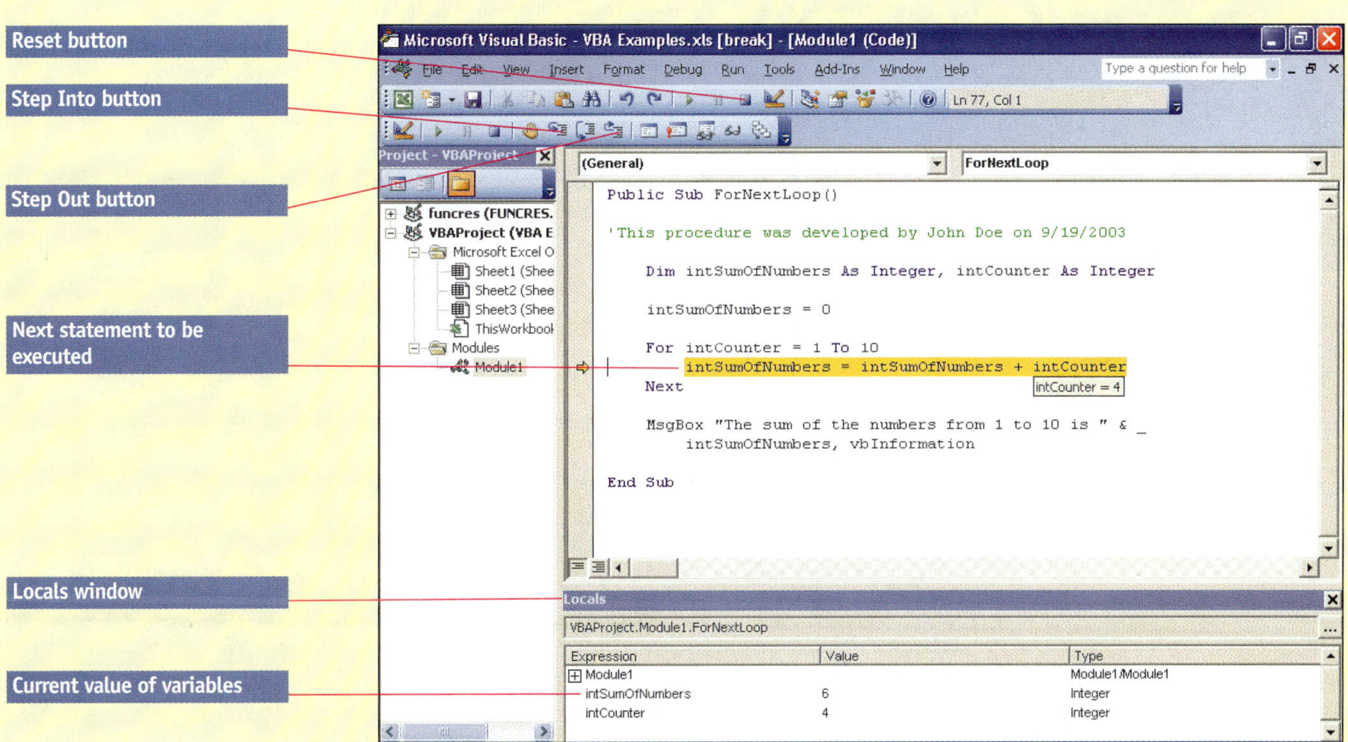

(d) Step through a Procedure (step 4)

FIGURE 12 Hands-on Exercise 3 (*continued*)

Step 5: The Immediate Window

- You should be back in the VBA window. Click immediately to the left of the Next statement and press **Enter** to insert a blank line. Type the **Debug.Print** statement exactly as shown in Figure 12e. (Click **OK** if you see a message indicating that the procedure will be reset.)
- Pull down the **View menu** and click the **Immediate Window command** (or click the **Immediate Window button** on the Debug toolbar). The Immediate window should be empty, but if not, you can click and drag to select the contents, then press the **Del key** to clear the window.
- Click anywhere within the For . . . Next procedure, then click the **Run Sub button** to execute the procedure. You will see the familiar message box indicating that the sum of the numbers is 55. Click **OK**.
- You should see 10 lines within the Immediate window as shown in Figure 12e, corresponding to the values displayed by the Debug.Print statement as it was executed within the loop.
- Close the Immediate window. Do you see how displaying the intermediate results of a procedure helps you to understand how it works?

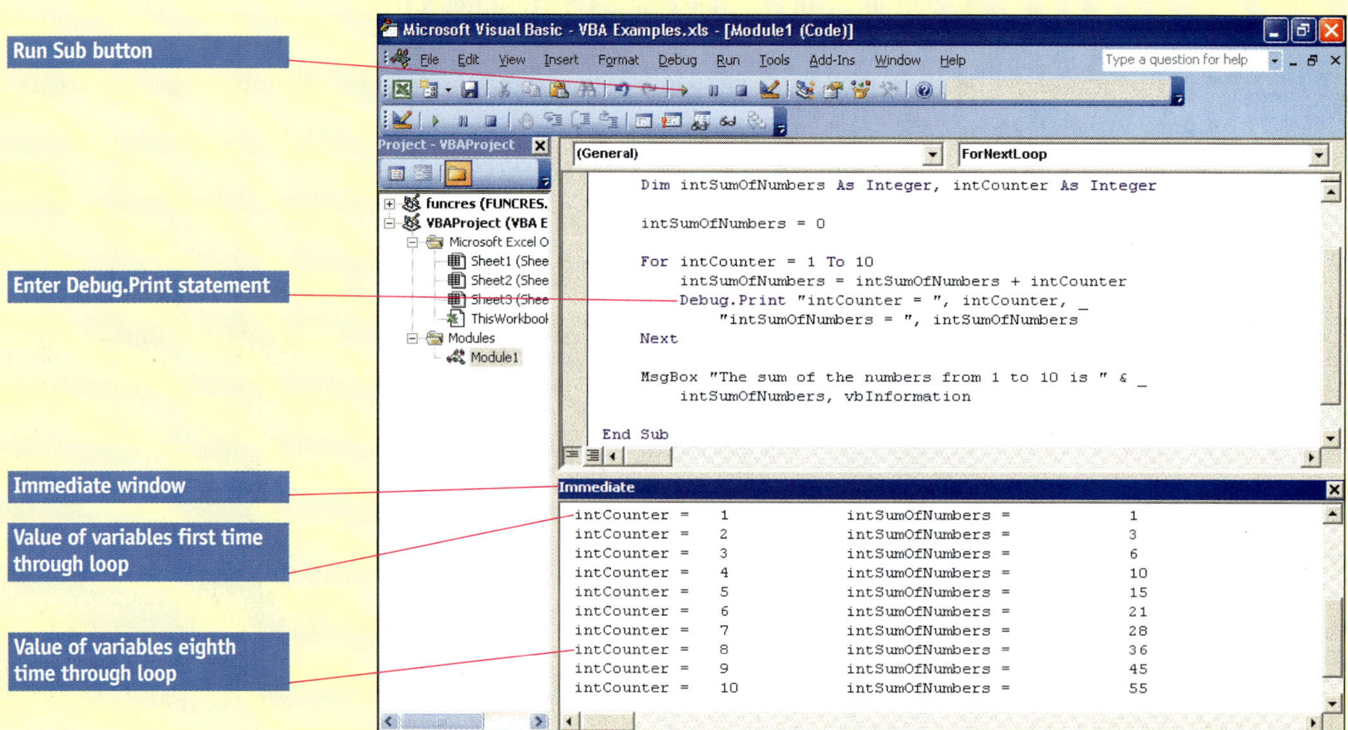

(e) The Immediate Window (step 5)

FIGURE 12 Hands-on Exercise 3 (*continued*)

INSTANT CALCULATOR

Use the Print method (action) in the Immediate window to use VBA as a calculator. Press Ctrl+G at any time to display the Immediate window. Click in the window, then type the statement Debug.Print, followed by your calculation, for example, Debug.Print 2+2, and press Enter. The answer is displayed on the next line in the Immediate window.

Step 6: A More General Procedure

- Modify the existing procedure to make it more general—for example, to sum the values from any starting value to any ending value:
  - Click at the end of the existing Dim statement to position the insertion point, press **Enter** to create a new line, then add the second **Dim statement** as shown in Figure 12f.
  - Click before the For statement, press **Enter** to create a blank line, press **Enter** a second time, then enter the two **InputBox statements** to ask the user for the beginning and ending values.
  - Modify the For statement to execute from **intStart** to **intEnd** rather than from 1 to 10.
  - Change the MsgBox statement to reflect the values of intStart and intEnd, and a customized title bar. Note the use of the ampersand and the underscore, to indicate concatenation and continuation, respectively.
- Click the **Save button** to save the module.

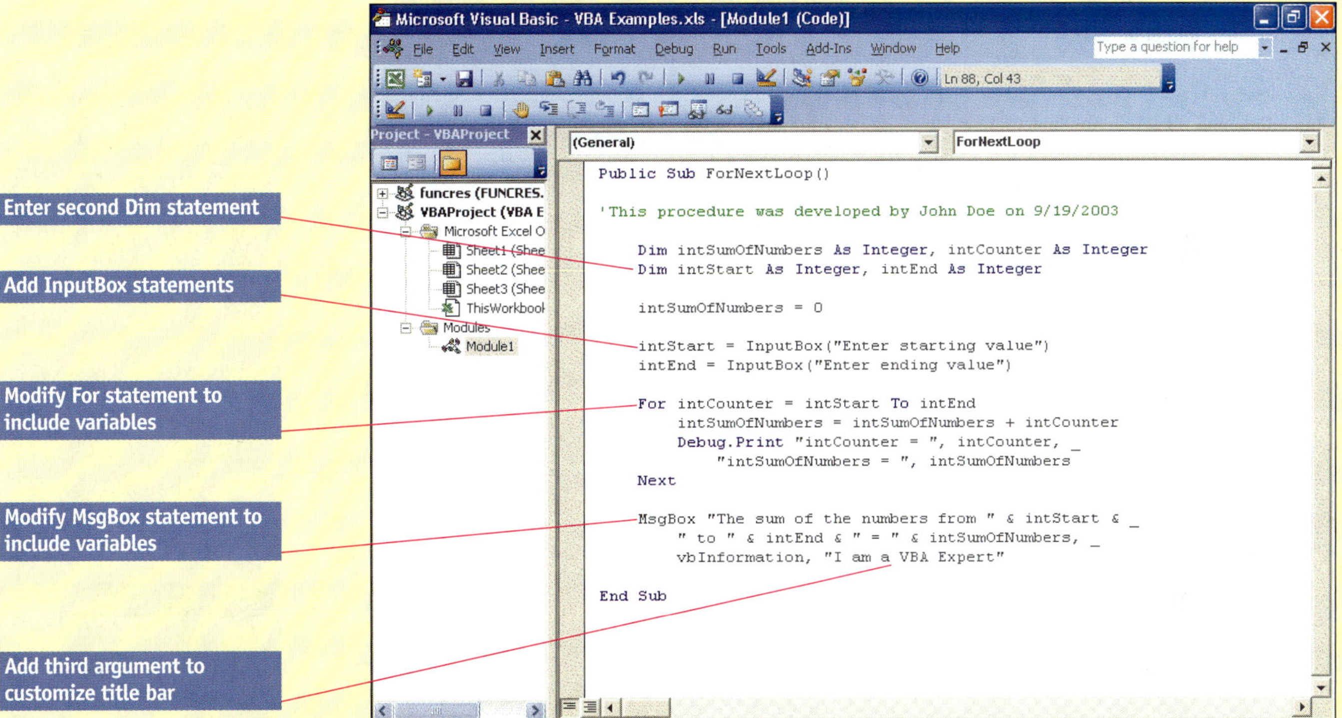

(f) A More General Procedure (step 6)

FIGURE 12 Hands-on Exercise 3 (*continued*)

USE WHAT YOU KNOW

Use the techniques acquired from other applications such as Microsoft Word to facilitate editing within the VBA window. Press the Ins key to toggle between the insert and overtype modes as you modify the statements within a VBA procedure. You can also cut, copy, and paste statements (or parts of statements) within a procedure and from one procedure to another. The Find and Replace commands are also useful.

Step 7: Test the Procedure

- Click the **Run Sub button** to test the procedure. You should be prompted for a beginning and an ending value. Enter any numbers you like, such as 10 and 20, respectively, to match the result in Figure 12g.
- The value displayed in the MsgBox statement should reflect the numbers you entered. For example, you will see a sum of 165 if you entered 10 and 20 as the starting and ending values.
- Look carefully at the message box that is displayed in Figure 12g. Its title bar displays the literal "I am a VBA expert", corresponding to the last argument in the MsgBox statement.
- Note, too, the spacing that appears within the message box, which includes spaces before and after each number. Look at your results and, if necessary, modify the MsgBox statement so that you have the same output. Click **OK**.
- Save the procedure.

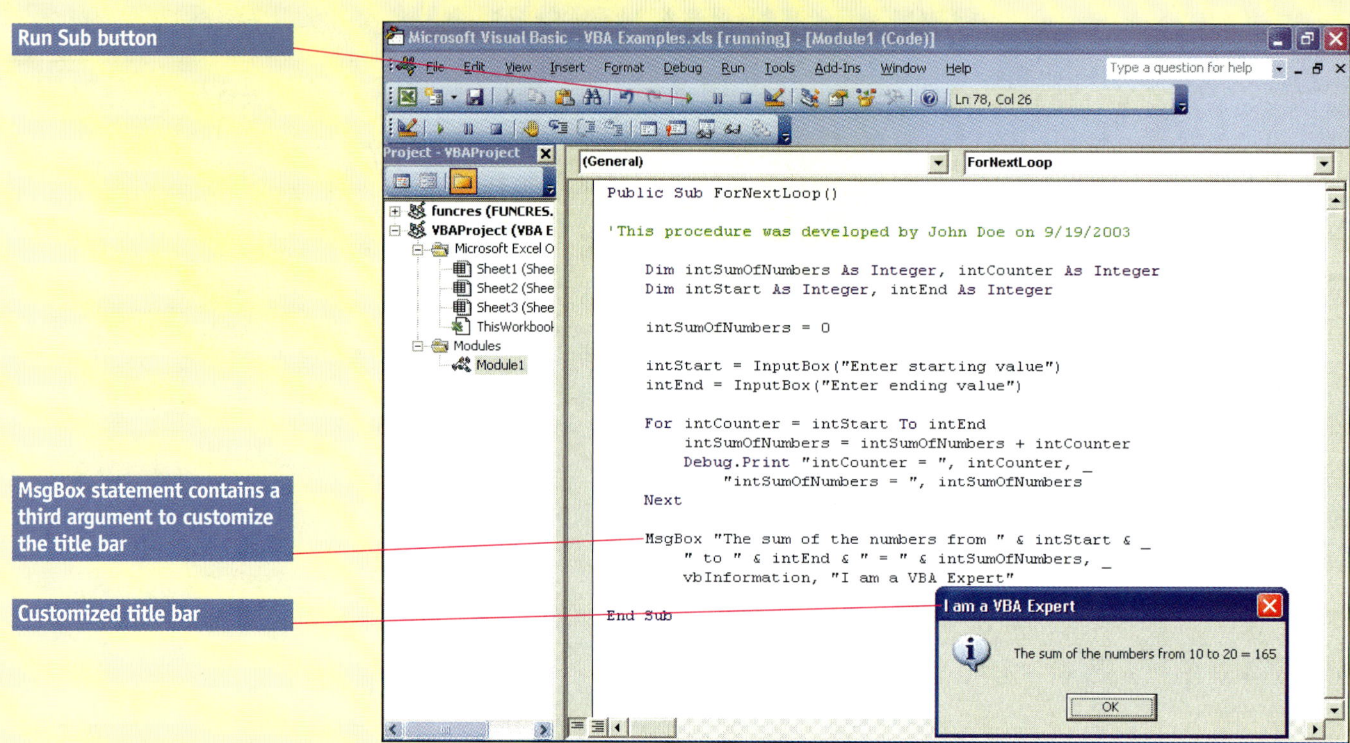

(g) Test the Procedure (step 7)

FIGURE 12 Hands-on Exercise 3 (*continued*)

CHANGE THE INCREMENT

The For . . . Next statement can be made more general by supplying an increment within the For statement. Try For intCount = 1 To 10 Step 2, or more generally, For intCount = intStart to intEnd Step intStepValue. "Step" is a Visual Basic keyword and must be entered that way. intCount, intEnd, and intStepValue are user-defined variables. The variables must be defined at the beginning of a procedure and can be initialized by requesting values from the user through the InputBox statement.

Step 8: Create a Do Until Loop

- Pull down the **Insert menu** and click the **Procedure command** to insert a new procedure called **DoUntilLoop**. Enter the procedure as it appears in Figure 12h. Note the following:
  - Two string variables are declared to hold the correct answer and the user's response, respectively.
  - The variable strCorrectAnswer is set to "Earth", which is the correct answer for our question.
  - The initial InputBox function prompts the user to enter his/her response to the question. A second InputBox function appears in the loop that is executed if and only if the user enters the wrong answer.
  - The Until condition appears at the beginning of the loop, so that the loop is entered only if the user answers incorrectly. The loop executes repeatedly until the correct answer is supplied.
  - A message to the user is displayed at the end of the procedure after the correct answer has been entered.
- Click the **Run Sub button** to test the procedure. Enter the correct answer on your first attempt, and you will see that the loop is never entered.
- Rerun the procedure, answer incorrectly, then note that a second input box appears, telling you that your answer was incorrect. Click **OK**.
- Once again you are prompted for the answer. Enter **Earth**. Click **OK**. The procedure ends.
- Save the procedure.

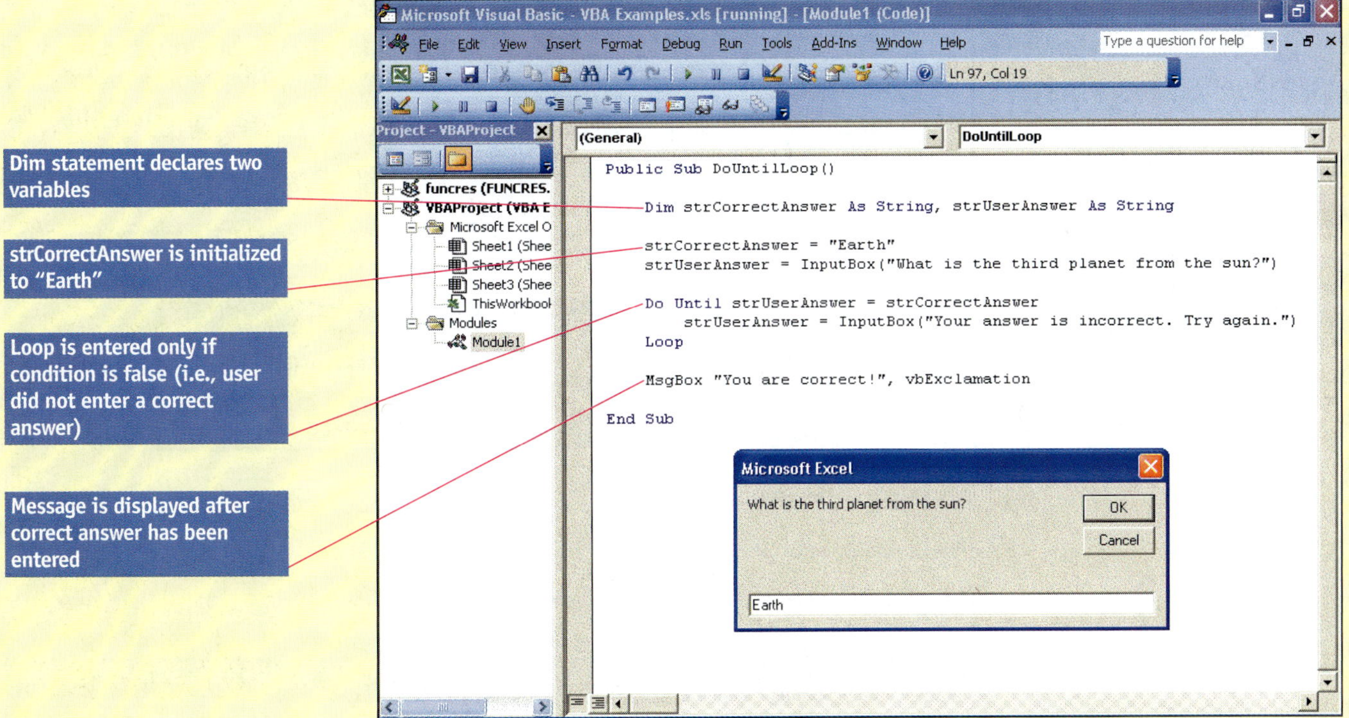

(h) Create a Do Until Loop (step 8)

FIGURE 12 Hands-on Exercise 3 (*continued*)

Step 9: A More Powerful Procedure

- Modify the procedure as shown in Figure 12i to include the statements to count and print the number of times the user takes to get the correct answer.
  - The variable intNumberOfAttempts is declared as an integer and is initialized to 1 after the user inputs his/her initial answer.
  - The Do loop is expanded to increment intNumberOfAttempts by 1 each time the loop is executed.
  - The MsgBox statement after the loop is expanded prints the number of attempts the user took to answer the question.
- Save the module, then click the **Run Sub button** to test the module. You should see a dialog box similar to the one in Figure 12i. Click **OK**. Do you see how this procedure improves on its predecessor?
- Pull down the **File menu** and click the **Print command** to display the Print dialog box. Click the option button to print the current module for your instructor. Click **OK**.
- Close the Debug toolbar. Exit Office if you do not want to continue with the next hands-on exercise at this time.

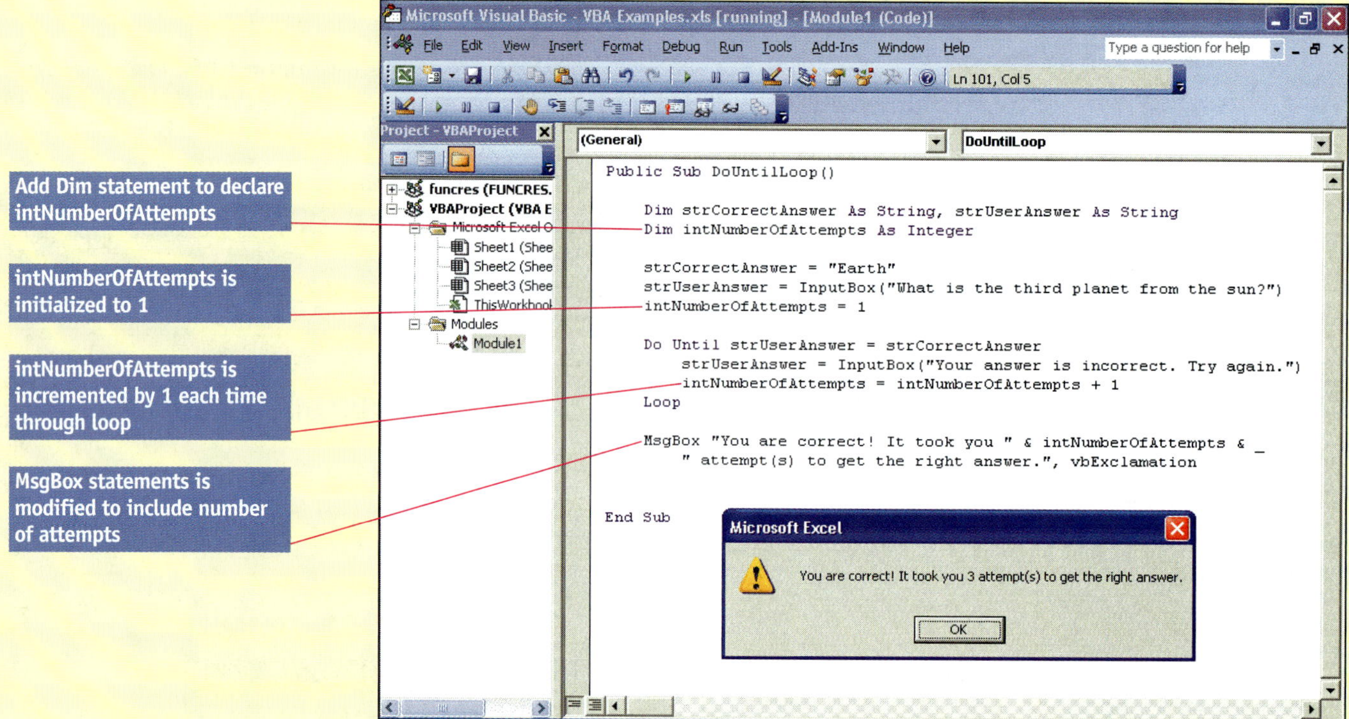

(i) A More Powerful Procedure (step 9)

FIGURE 12 Hands-on Exercise 3 (*continued*)

IT'S NOT EQUAL, BUT REPLACE

All programming languages use statements of the form N = N + 1, in which the equal sign does not mean equal in the literal sense; that is, N cannot equal N + 1. The equal sign is really a replacement operator. Thus, the expression on the right of the equal sign is evaluated, and that result replaces the value of the variable on the left. In other words, the statement N = N + 1 increments the value of N by 1.

PUTTING VBA TO WORK (MICROSOFT EXCEL)

Our approach thus far has focused on VBA as an independent entity that can be run without specific reference to the applications in Microsoft Office. We have covered several individual statements, explained how to use the VBA editor to create and run procedures, and how to debug those procedures, if necessary. We hope you have found the material to be interesting, but you may be asking yourself, "What does this have to do with Microsoft Office?" In other words, how can you use your knowledge of VBA to enhance your ability in Microsoft Excel or Access? The answer is to create ***event procedures*** that run automatically in response to events within an Office application.

VBA is different from traditional programming languages in that it is event-driven. An ***event*** is defined as any action that is recognized by an application such as Excel or Access. Opening or closing an Excel workbook or an Access database is an event. Selecting a worksheet within a workbook is also an event, as is clicking on a command button on an Access form. To use VBA within Microsoft Office, you decide which events are significant, and what is to happen when those events occur. Then you develop the appropriate event procedures.

Consider, for example, Figure 13, which displays the results of two event procedures in conjunction with opening and closing an Excel workbook. (If you are using Microsoft Access instead of Excel, you can skip this discussion and the associated exercise, and move to the parallel material for Access that appears after the next hands-on exercise.) The procedure associated with Figure 13a displays a message that appears automatically after the user executes the command to close the associated workbook. The procedure is almost trivial to write, and consists of a single MsgBox statement. The effect of the procedure is quite significant, however, as it reminds the user to back up his or her work after closing the workbook. Nor does it matter how the user closes the workbook—whether by pulling down the menu or using a keyboard shortcut—because the procedure runs automatically in response to the Close Workbook event, regardless of how that event occurs.

The dialog box in Figure 13b prompts the user for a password and appears automatically when the user opens the workbook. The logic here is more sophisticated in that the underlying procedure contains an InputBox statement to request the password, a Do Until loop that is executed until the user enters the correct password or exceeds the allotted number of attempts, then additional logic to display the worksheet or terminate the application if the user fails to enter the proper password. The procedure is not difficult, however, and it builds on the VBA statements that were covered earlier.

The next hands-on exercise has you create the two event procedures that are associated with Figure 13. As you do the exercise, you will gain additional experience with VBA and an appreciation for the potential event procedures within Microsoft Office.

HIDING AND UNHIDING A WORKSHEET

Look carefully at the workbooks in Figures 13a and 13b. Both figures reference the identical workbook, Financial Consultant, as can be seen from the title bar. Look at the worksheet tabs, however, and note that two worksheets are visible in Figure 13a, whereas the Calculations worksheet is hidden in Figure 13b. This was accomplished in the Open workbook procedure and was implemented to hide the calculations from the user until the correct password was entered.

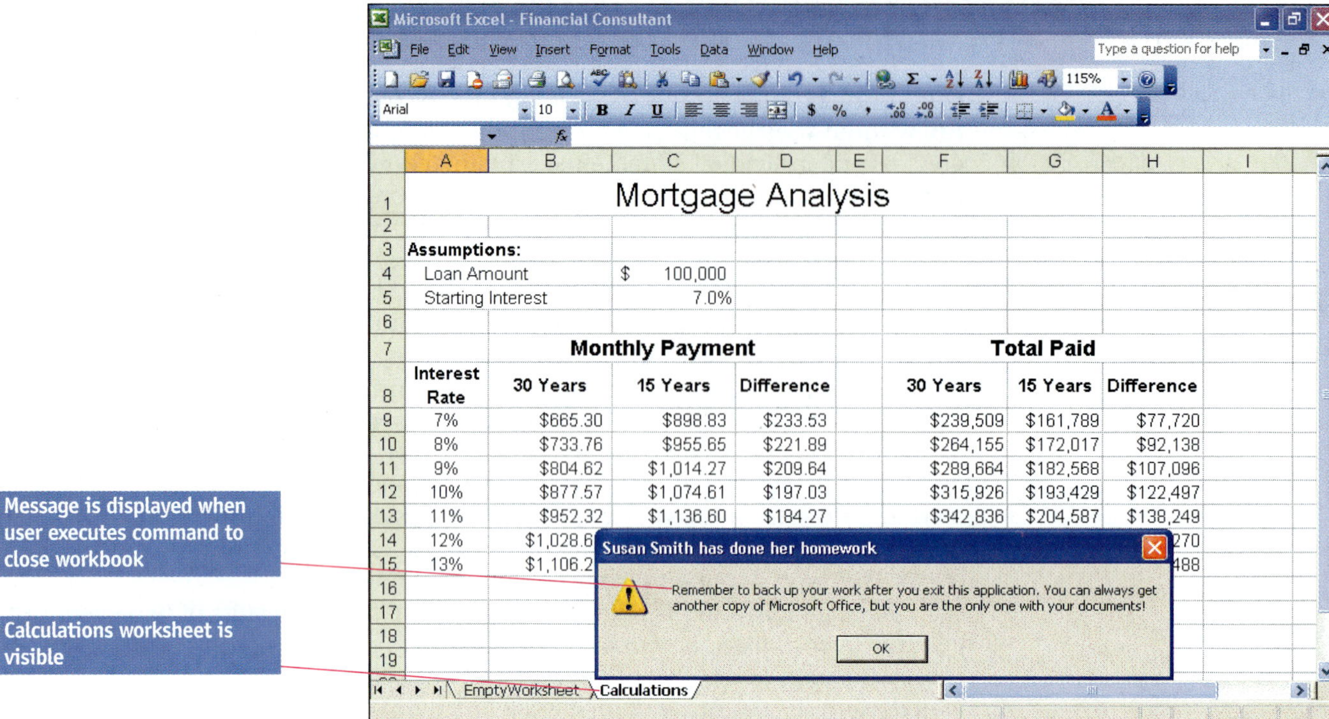

		Mortgage Analysis					
Assumptions:							
Loan Amount		$ 100,000					
Starting Interest		7.0%					
	Monthly Payment				Total Paid		
Interest Rate	30 Years	15 Years	Difference		30 Years	15 Years	Difference
7%	$665.30	$898.83	$233.53		$239,509	$161,789	$77,720
8%	$733.76	$955.65	$221.89		$264,155	$172,017	$92,138
9%	$804.62	$1,014.27	$209.64		$289,664	$182,568	$107,096
10%	$877.57	$1,074.61	$197.03		$315,926	$193,429	$122,497
11%	$952.32	$1,136.60	$184.27		$342,836	$204,587	$138,249
12%	$1,028.6						270
13%	$1,106.2						488

(a) Message to the User (Close Workbook event)

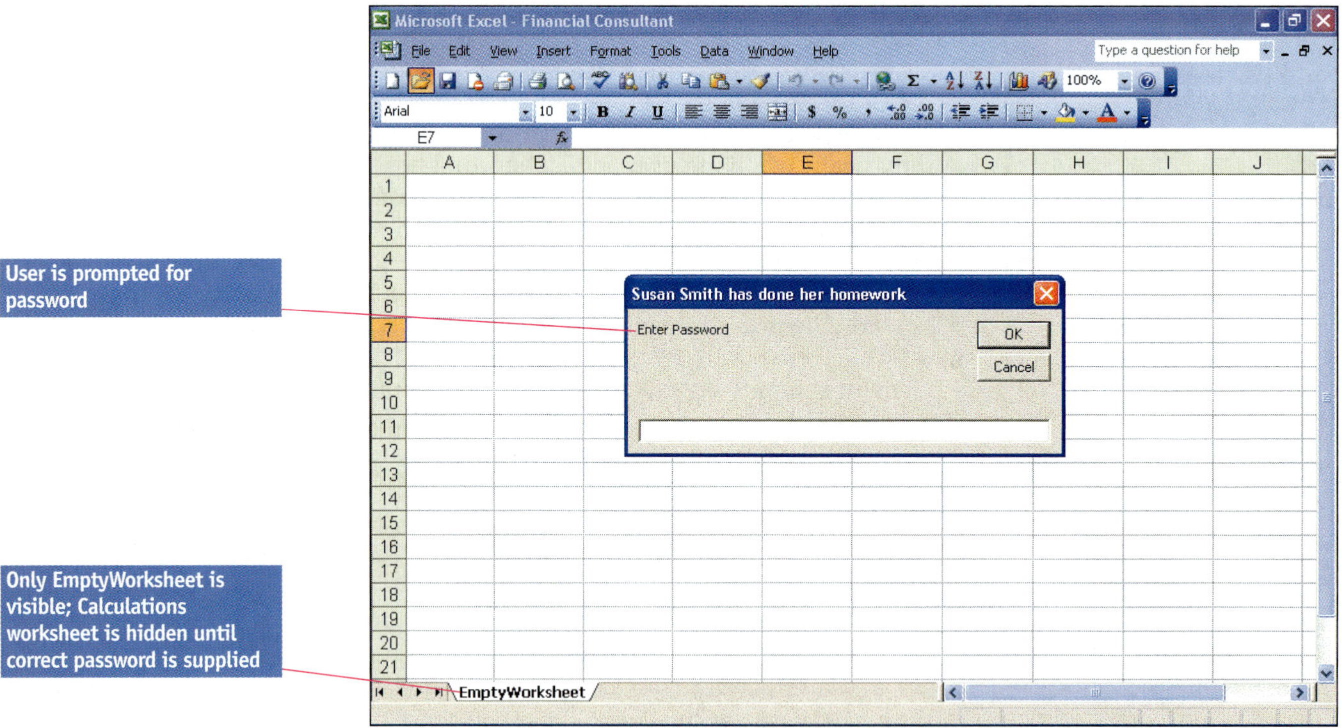

(b) Password Protection (Open Workbook event)

FIGURE 13 Event-Driven Programming

4 Event-Driven Programming (Microsoft Excel)

Objective To create an event procedure to implement password protection that is associated with opening an Excel workbook; to create a second event procedure that displays a message to the user upon closing the workbook. Use Figure 14 as a guide in the exercise.

Step 1: Create the Close Workbook Procedure

- Open the **VBA Examples workbook** you have used for the previous exercises and enable the macros. If you have been using Access rather than Excel, start Excel, open a new workbook, then save the workbook as **VBA Examples**.
- Pull down the **Tools menu**, click the **Macro command**, then click the **Visual Basic Editor command** (or use the **Alt+F11** keyboard shortcut).
- You should see the Project Explorer pane as shown in Figure 14a, but if not, pull down the **View menu** and click the **Project Explorer**. Double click **ThisWorkbook** to create a module for the workbook as a whole.
- Enter the **Option Explicit statement** if it is not there already, then press **Enter** to create a new line. Type the statement to declare the variable, **ApplicationTitle**, using your name instead of Susan Smith.
- Click the **down arrow** in the Object list box and select **Workbook**, then click the **down arrow** in the Procedure list box and select the **BeforeClose event** to create the associated procedure. (If you choose a different event by mistake, click and drag to select the associated statements, then press the **Del key** to delete the procedure.)
- Enter the comment and MsgBox statement as it appears in Figure 14a.
- Save the procedure.

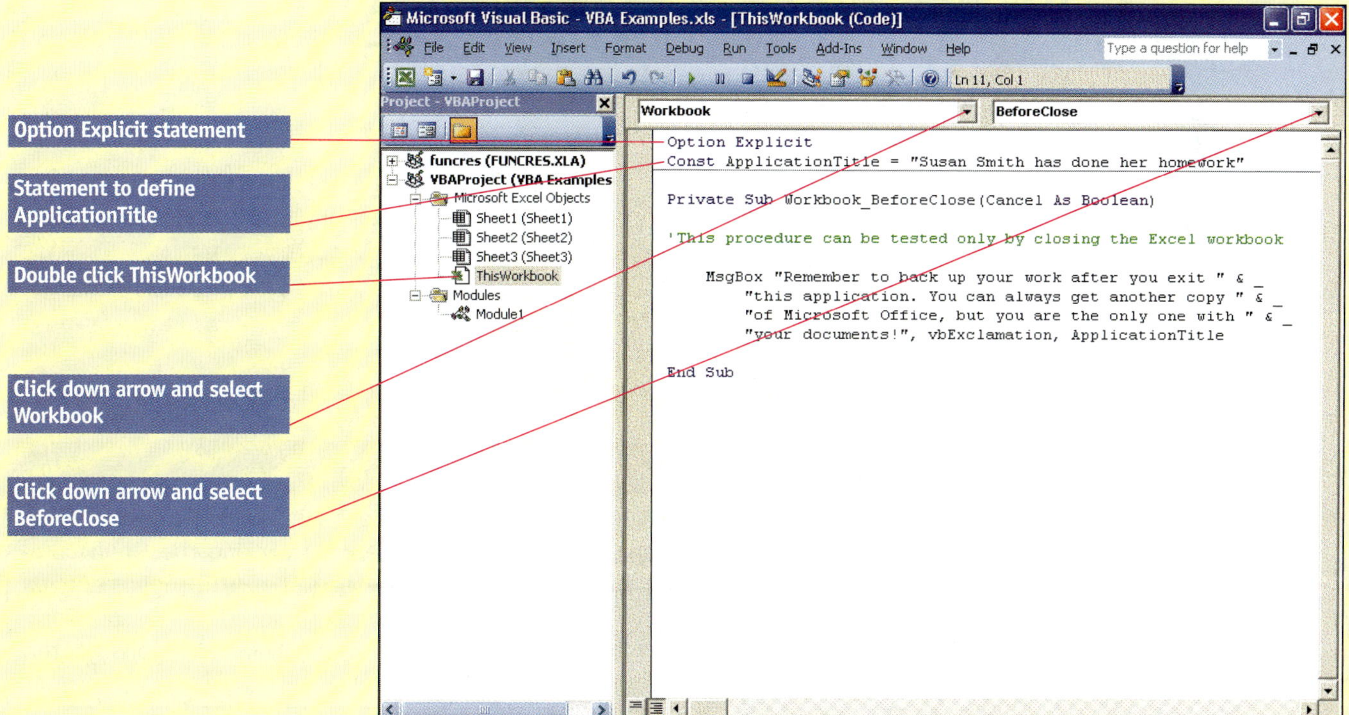

(a) Create the Close Workbook Procedure (step 1)

FIGURE 14 Hands-on Exercise 4

Step 2: Test the Close Workbook Procedure

- Click the **View Microsoft Excel button** on the Standard toolbar or on the Windows taskbar to view the Excel workbook. The workbook is not empty; that is, it does not contain any cell entries, but it does contain multiple VBA procedures.
- Pull down the **File menu** and click the **Close command**, which runs the procedure you just created and displays the dialog box in Figure 14b. Click **OK** after you have read the message, then click **Yes** if asked to save the workbook.
- Pull down the **File menu** and reopen the **VBA Examples workbook**, enabling the macros. Press **Alt+F11** to return to the VBA window to create an additional procedure.
- Double click **ThisWorkbook** from within the Project Explorer pane to return to the BeforeClose procedure and make the necessary corrections, if any.
- Save the procedure.

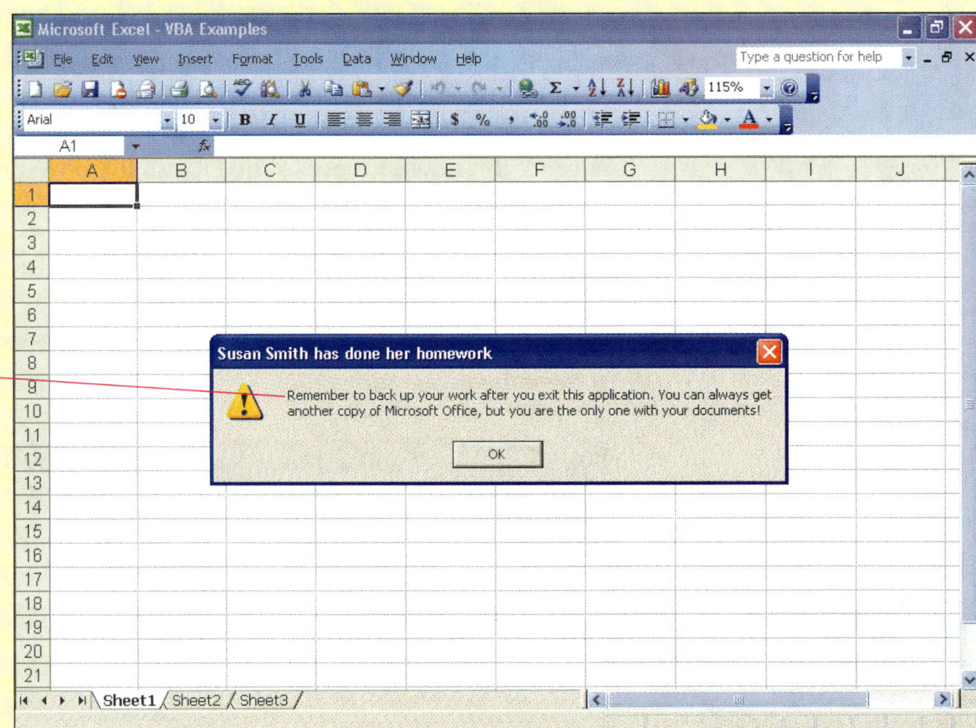

(b) Test the Close Workbook Procedure (step 2)

FIGURE 14 Hands-on Exercise 4 (*continued*)

THE MOST RECENTLY OPENED FILE LIST

One way to open a recently used workbook is to select the workbook directly from the File menu. Pull down the File menu, but instead of clicking the Open command, check to see if the workbook appears on the list of the most recently opened workbooks located at the bottom of the menu. If so, just click the workbook name, rather than having to make the appropriate selections through the Open dialog box.

Step 3: Start the Open Workbook Event Procedure

- Click within the Before Close procedure, then click the **Procedure View button** at the bottom of the Code window. Click the **down arrow** in the Procedure list box and select the **Open event** to create an event procedure.
- Enter the VBA statements as shown in Figure 14c. Note the following:
  - Three variables are required for this procedure—the correct password, the password entered by the user, and the number of attempts.
  - The user is prompted for the password, and the number of attempts is set to 1. The user is given two additional attempts, if necessary, to get the password correct. The loop is bypassed, however, if the user supplies the correct password on the first attempt.
- Minimize Excel. Save the procedure, then click the **Run Sub button** to test it. Try different combinations in your testing; that is, enter the correct password on the first, second, and third attempts. The password is case-sensitive.
- Correct errors as they occur. Click the **Reset button** at any time to begin executing the procedure from the beginning. Save the procedure.

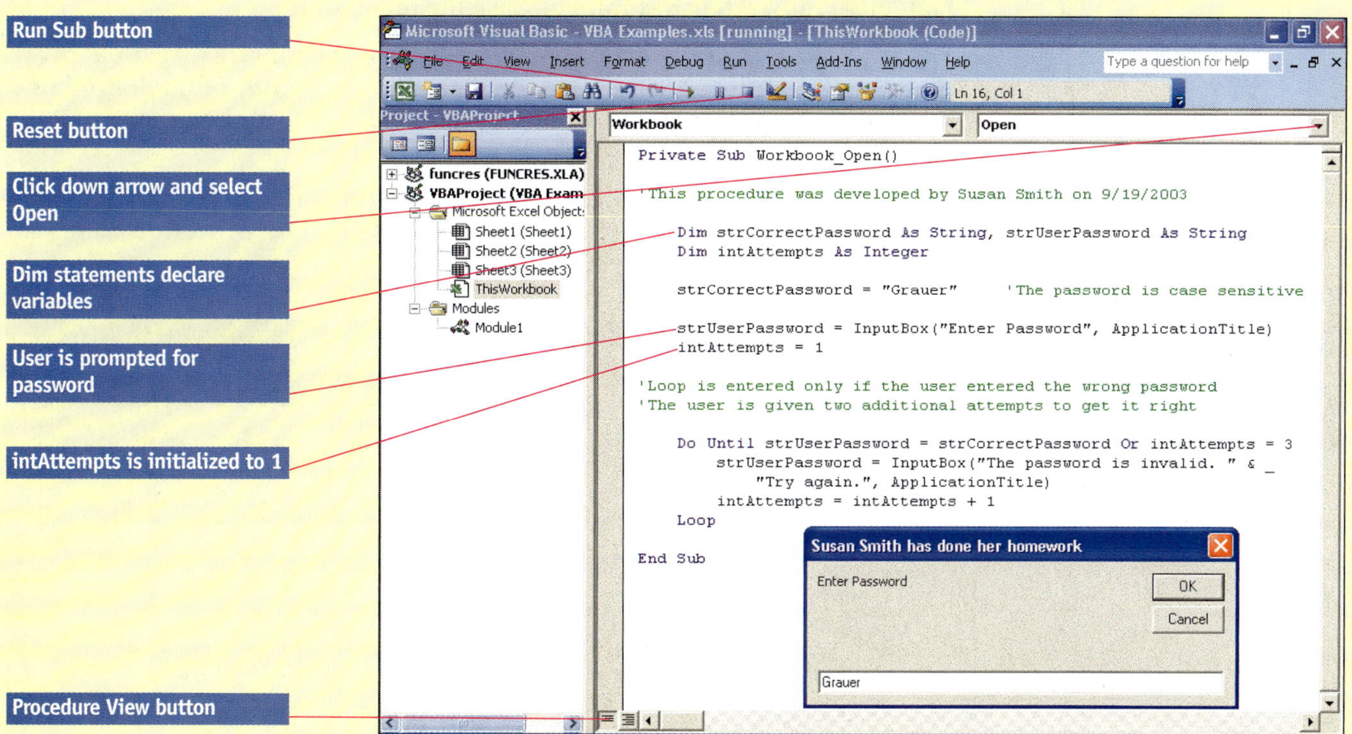

(c) Start the Open Workbook Event Procedure (step 3)

FIGURE 14 Hands-on Exercise 4 (*continued*)

THE OBJECT AND PROCEDURE BOXES

The Object box at the top of the code window displays the selected object such as an Excel workbook, whereas the Procedure box displays the name of the events appropriate to that object. Events that already have procedures appear in bold. Clicking an event that is not bold creates the procedure header and End Sub statements for that event.

Step 4: Complete the Open Workbook Event Procedure

- Enter the remaining statements in the procedure as shown in Figure 14d. Note the following:
  - The If statement determines whether the user has entered the correct password and, if so, displays the appropriate message.
  - If, however, the user fails to supply the correct password, a different message is displayed, and the workbook will close due to the **Workbooks.Close statement** within the procedure.
  - As a precaution, put an apostrophe in front of the Workbooks.Close statement so that it is a comment, and thus it is not executed. Once you are sure that you can enter the correct password, you can remove the apostrophe and implement the password protection.
- Save the procedure, then click the **Run Sub button** to test it. Be sure that you can enter the correct password (**Grauer**), and that you realize the password is case-sensitive.
- Delete the apostrophe in front of the Workbooks.Close statement. The text of the statement changes from green to black to indicate that it is an executable statement rather than a comment. Save the procedure.
- Click the **Run Sub button** a second time, then enter an incorrect password three times in a row. You will see the dialog box in Figure 14d, followed by a message reminding you to back up your workbook, and then the workbook will close.
- The first message makes sense, the second does not make sense in this context. Thus, we need to modify the Close Workbook procedure when an incorrect password is entered.

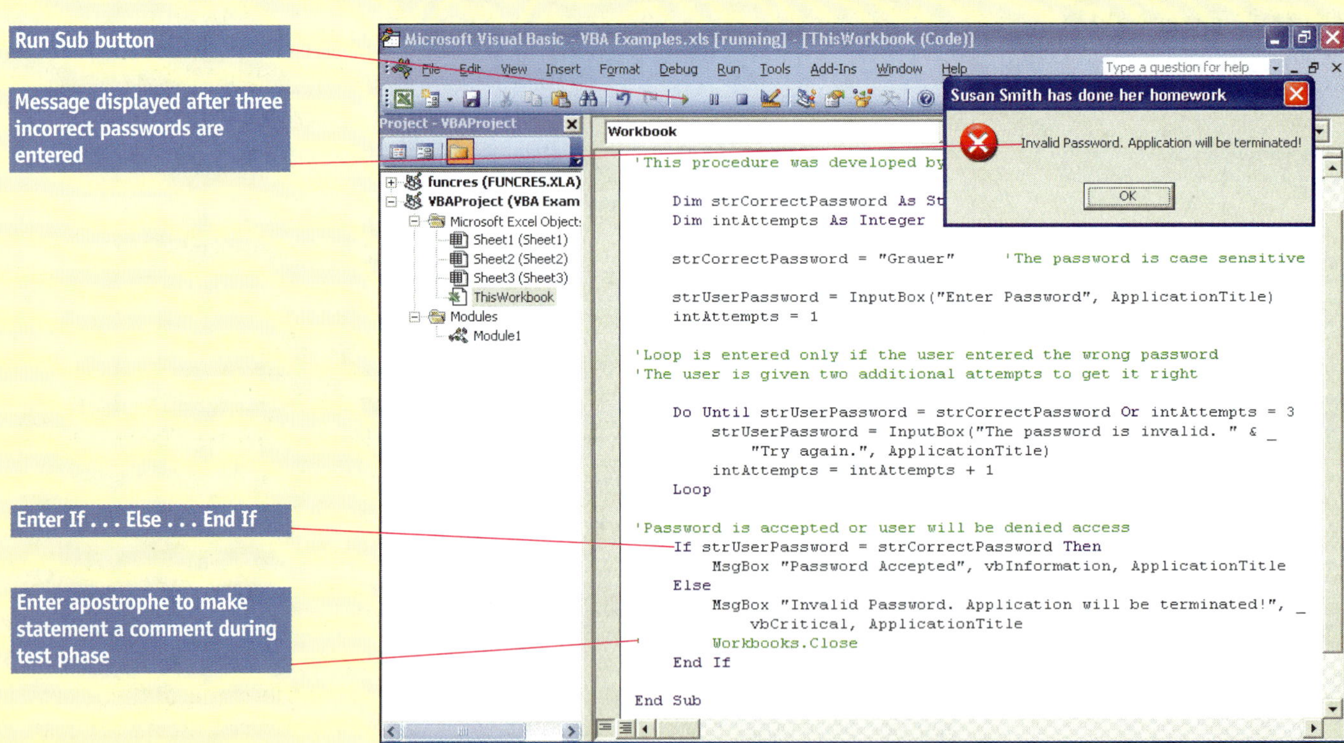

(d) Complete the Open Workbook Event Procedure (step 4)

FIGURE 14 Hands-on Exercise 4 (*continued*)

Step 5: Modify the Before Close Event Procedure

- Reopen the **VBA Examples workbook**. Click the button to **Enable Macros**.
- Enter the password, **Grauer** (the password is case-sensitive), press **Enter**, then click **OK** when the password has been accepted.
- Press **Alt+F11** to reopen the VBA editor, and (if necessary) double click **ThisWorkbook** within the list of Microsoft Excel objects.
- Click at the end of the line defining the ApplicationTitle constant, press **Enter**, then enter the statement to define the **binNormalExit** variable as shown in Figure 14e. (The statement appears initially below the line ending the General Declarations section, but moves above the line when you press Enter.)
- Modify the BeforeClose event procedure to include an If statement that tests the value of the binNormalExit variable as shown in Figure 14e. You must, however, set the value of this variable in the Open Workbook event procedure as described in step 6.
- Save the procedure.

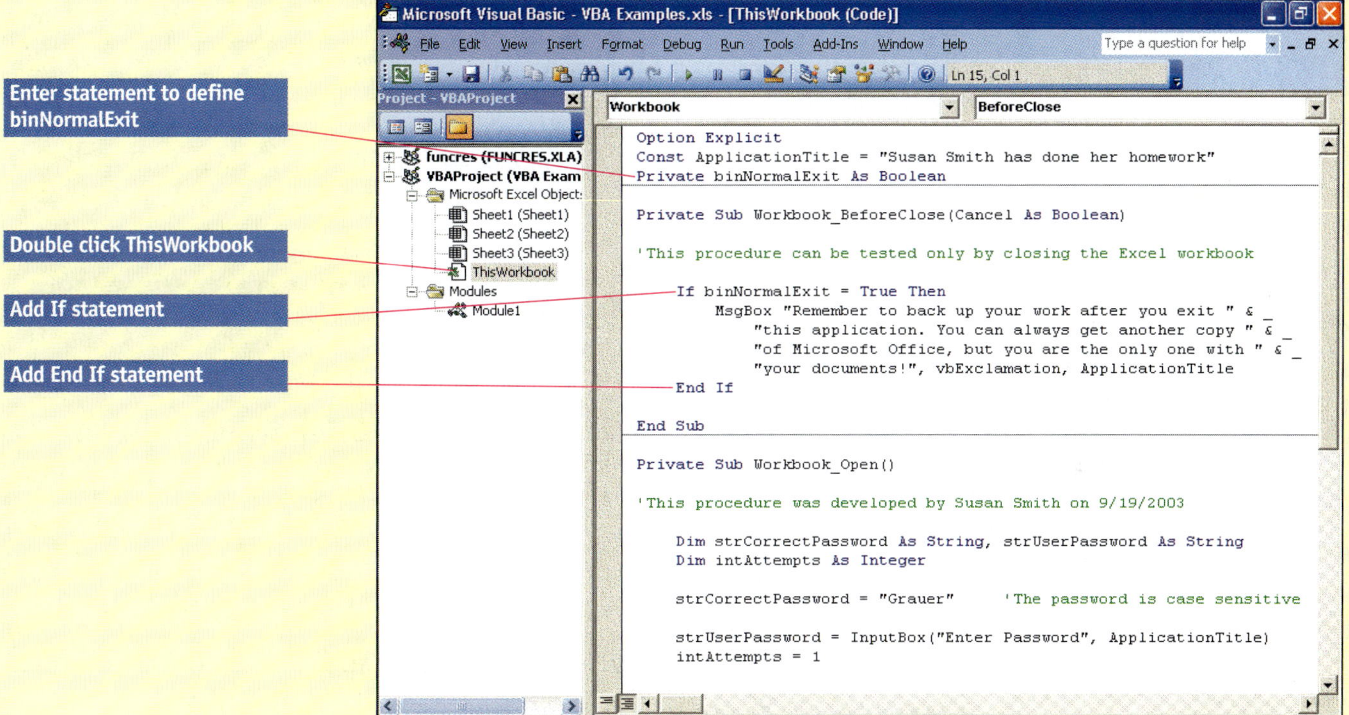

(e) Modify the Before Close Event Procedure (step 5)

FIGURE 14 Hands-on Exercise 4 (*continued*)

SETTING A SWITCH

The use of a switch (binNormalExit, in this example) to control an action within a procedure is a common programming technique. The switch is set to one of two values according to events that occur within the system, then the switch is subsequently tested and the appropriate action is taken. Here, the switch is set when the workbook is opened to indicate either a valid or invalid user. The switch is then tested prior to closing the workbook to determine whether to print the closing message.

Step 6: Modify the Open Workbook Event Procedure

- Scroll down to the Open Workbook event procedure, then modify the If statement to set the value of binNormalExit as shown in Figure 14f:
  - Take advantage of the Complete Word tool to enter the variable name. Type the first few letters, "**binN**", then press **Ctrl+Space**, and VBA will complete the variable name.
  - The indentation within the statement is not a requirement of VBA per se, but is used to make the code easier to read. Blank lines are also added for this purpose.
  - Comments appear throughout the procedure to explain its logic.
  - Save the modified procedure.
- Click the **Run Sub button**, then enter an incorrect password three times in a row. Once again, you will see the dialog box indicating an invalid password.
- Click **OK**. This time you will not see the message reminding you to back up your workbook. The workbook closes as before.

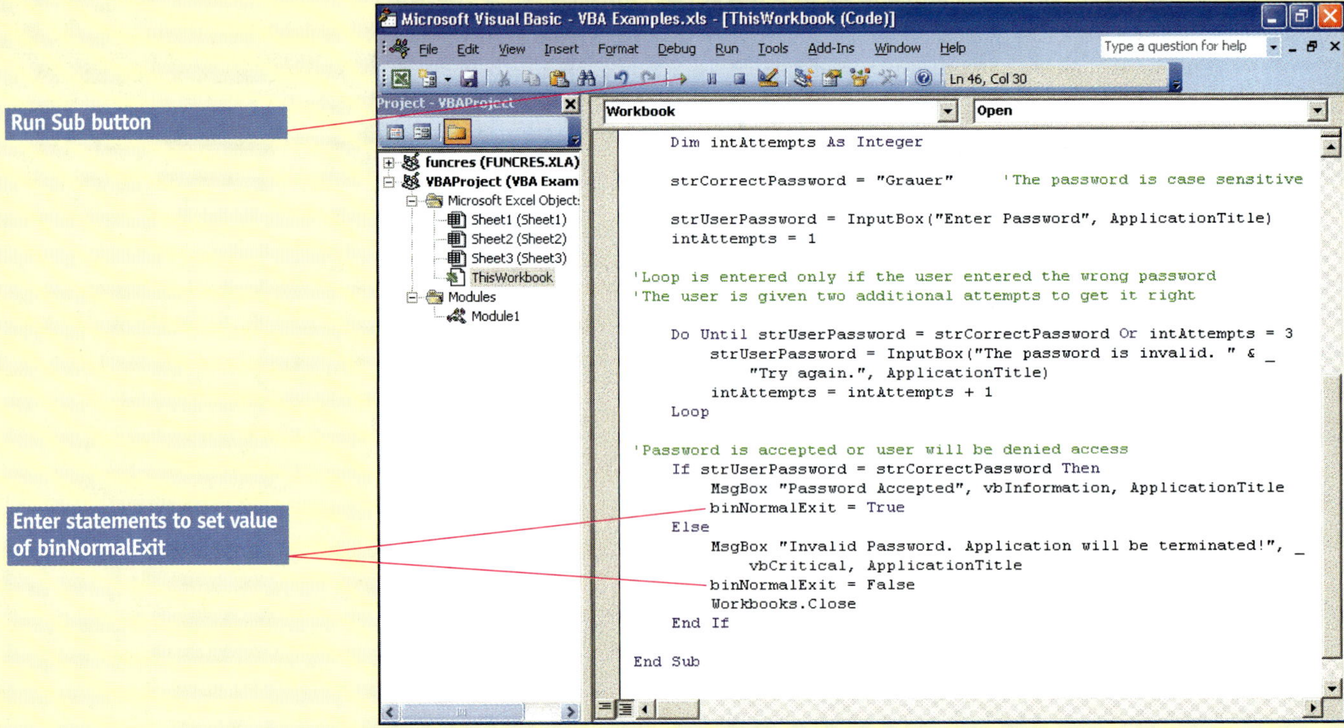

(f) Modify the Open Workbook Event Procedure (step 6)

FIGURE 14 Hands-on Exercise 4 (*continued*)

TEST UNDER ALL CONDITIONS

We cannot overemphasize the importance of thoroughly testing a procedure, and further, testing it under all conditions. VBA statements are powerful, but they are also complex, and a misplaced or omitted character can have dramatic consequences. Test every procedure completely at the time it is created, while the logic of the procedure is fresh in your mind.

Step 7: Open a Second Workbook

- Reopen the **VBA Examples workbook**. Click the button to **Enable Macros**.
- Enter the password, **Grauer**, then press **Enter**. Click **OK** when you see the second dialog box telling you that the password has been accepted.
- Pull down the **File menu** and click the **Open command** (or click the **Open button** on the Standard toolbar) and open a second workbook. We opened a workbook called **Financial Consultant**, but it does not matter which workbook you open.
- Pull down the **Window menu**, click the **Arrange command**, click the **Horizontal option button**, and click **OK** to tile the workbooks as shown in Figure 14g. The title bars show the names of the open workbooks.
- Pull down the **Tools menu**, click **Macro**, then click **Visual Basic editor**.

Financial Consultant workbook

VBA Examples workbook

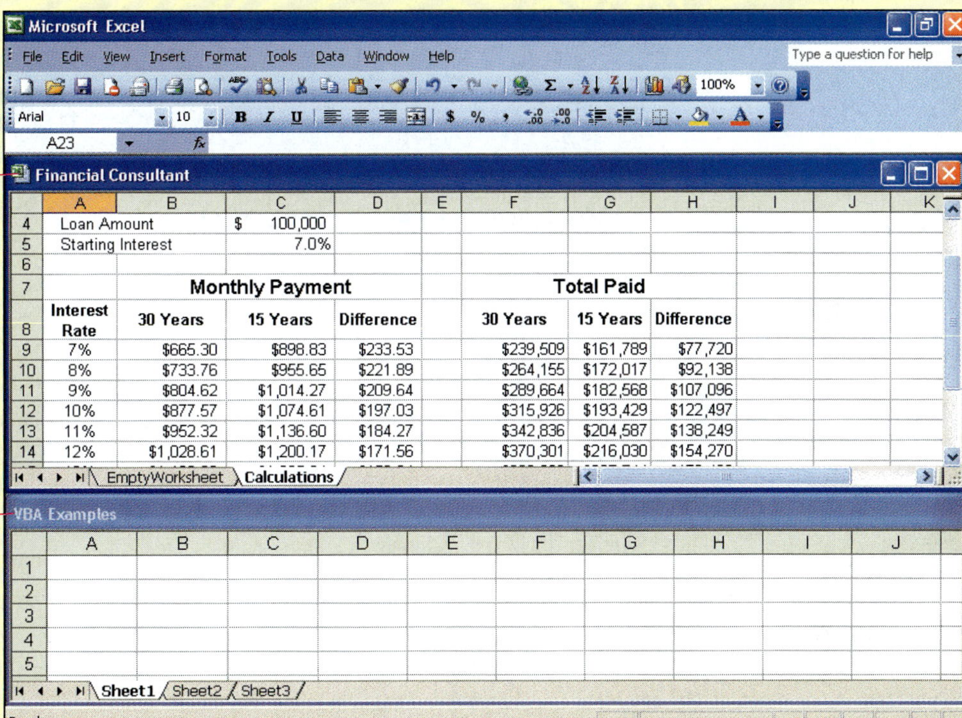

(g) Open a Second Workbook (step 7)

FIGURE 14 Hands-on Exercise 4 (*continued*)

THE COMPARISON IS CASE-SENSITIVE

Any literal comparison (e.g., strInstructorName = "Grauer") is case-sensitive, so that the user has to enter the correct name and case for the condition to be true. A response of "GRAUER" or "grauer", while containing the correct name, will be evaluated as false because the case does not match. You can, however, use the UCase (uppercase) function to convert the user's response to uppercase, and test accordingly. In other words, UCase(strInstructorName) = "GRAUER" will be evaluated as true if the user enters "Grauer" in any combination of upper- or lowercase letters.

Step 8: Copy the Procedure

- You should be back in the Visual Basic editor as shown in Figure 14h. Copy the procedures associated with the Open and Close Workbook events from the VBA Examples workbook to the other workbook, Financial Consultant.
  - Double click **ThisWorkbook** within the list of Microsoft Excel objects under the VBA Examples workbook.
  - Click and drag to select the definition of the ApplicationTitle constant in the General Declarations section, the binNormalExit definition, plus the two procedures (to open and close the workbook) in their entirety.
  - Click the **Copy button** on the Standard toolbar.
  - If necessary, expand the Financial Consultant VBA Project, then double click **ThisWorkbook** with the list of Excel objects under the Financial Consultant workbook. Click underneath the **Option Explicit command**.
  - Click the **Paste button** on the Standard toolbar. The VBA code should be copied into this module as shown in Figure 14h.
- Click the **Save button** to save the module.

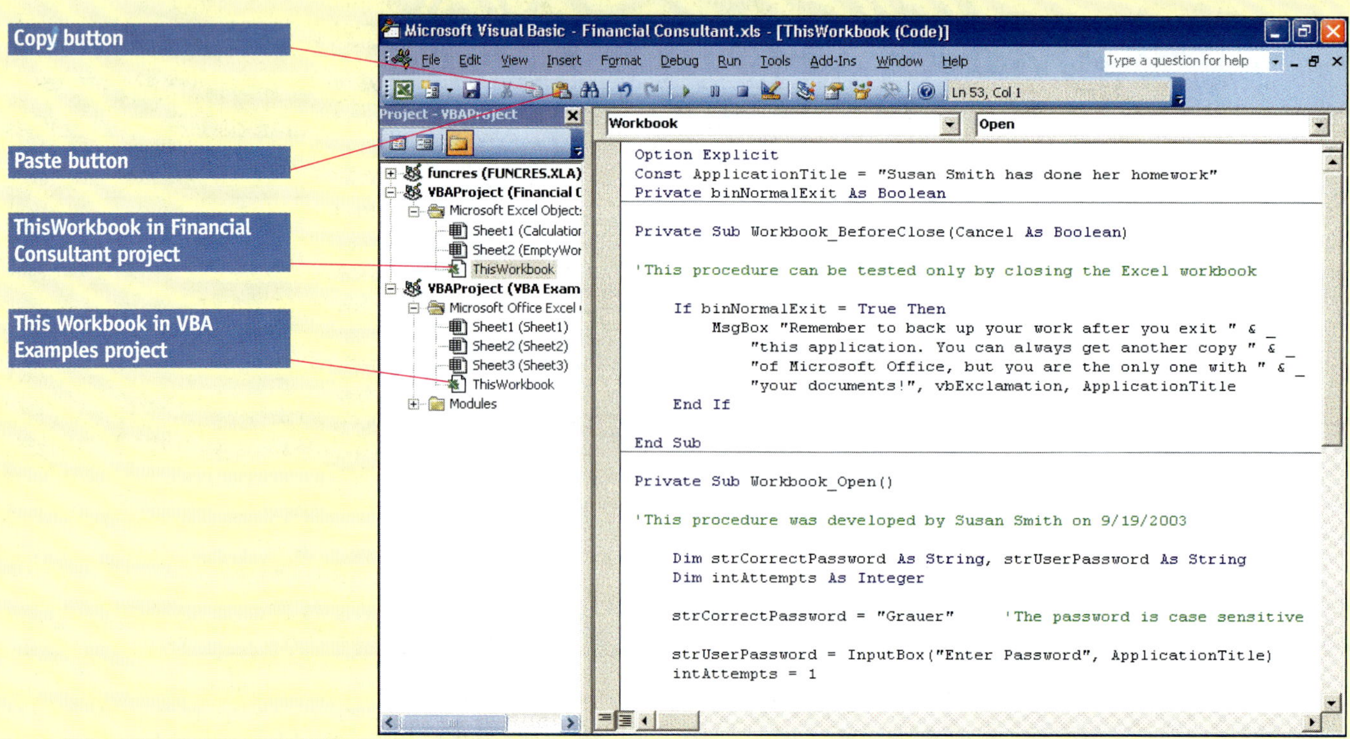

(h) Copy the Procedure (step 8)

FIGURE 14 Hands-on Exercise 4 (*continued*)

THE VISIBLE PROPERTY

The Calculations worksheet sheet should be hidden until the user enters the correct password. This is accomplished by setting the Visible property of the worksheet to false at the beginning of the Open Workbook event procedure, then setting it to true after the correct password has been entered. Click in the Open Workbook event procedure after the last Dim statement, press Enter, then enter the statement Sheet1.Visible = False to hide the Calculations worksheet. Scroll down in the procedure (below the MsgBox statement within the If statement that tests for the correct password), then enter the statement Sheet1.Visible = True followed by the statement Sheet1.Activate to select the worksheet.

Step 9: Test the Procedure

- Click the **View Microsoft Excel button** on the Standard toolbar within the VBA window (or click the **Excel button** on the Windows taskbar) to view the Excel workbook. Click in the window containing the Financial Consultant workbook (or whichever workbook you are using), then click the **Maximize button.**
- Pull down the **File menu** and click the **Close command**. (The dialog box in Figure 14i does not appear initially because the value of binNormalExit is not yet set; you have to open the workbook to set the switch.) Click **Yes** if asked whether to save the changes to the workbook.
- Pull down the **File menu** and reopen the workbook. Click the button to **Enable Macros**, then enter **Grauer** when prompted for the password. Click **OK** when the password has been accepted.
- Close this workbook, close the **VBA Examples workbook**, then pull down the **File menu** and click the **Exit command** to quit Excel.

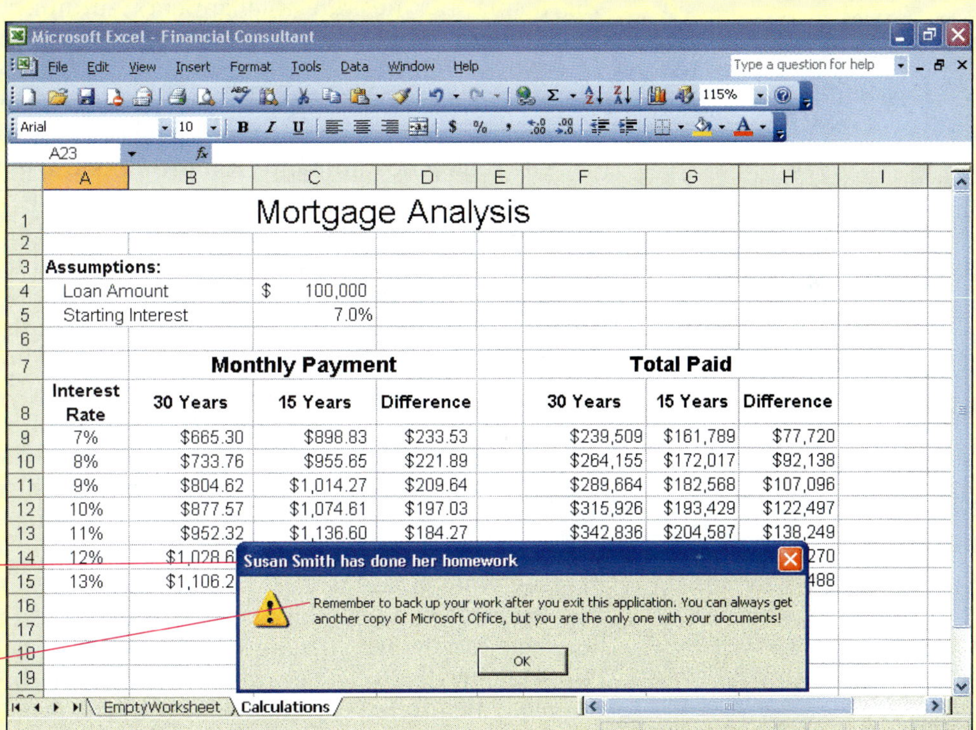

(i) Test the Procedure (step 9)

FIGURE 14 Hands-on Exercise 4 (*continued*)

SCREEN CAPTURE

Prove to your instructor that you have completed the hands-on exercise correctly by capturing a screen, then pasting the screen into a Word document. Do the exercise until you come to the screen that you want to capture, then press the PrintScreen key at the top of the keyboard. Click the Start button, start Word, and open a Word document, then pull down the Edit menu and click the Paste command to bring the captured screen into the Word document. Right click the screen within the Word document, click the Format Picture command, click the Layout tab, and select the Square layout. Click OK to close the dialog box. You can now move and size the screen within the document.

PUTTING VBA TO WORK (MICROSOFT ACCESS)

The same VBA procedure can be run from multiple applications in Microsoft Office, despite the fact that the applications are very different. The real power of VBA, however, is its ability to detect events that are unique to a specific application and to respond accordingly. An event is defined as any action that is recognized by an application. Opening or closing an Excel workbook or an Access database is an event. Selecting a worksheet within a workbook is also an event, as is clicking on a command button on an Access form. To use VBA within Microsoft Office, you decide which events are significant, and what is to happen when those events occur. Then you develop the appropriate ***event procedures*** that execute automatically when the event occurs.

Consider, for example, Figure 15, which displays the results of two event procedures in conjunction with opening and closing an Access database. (These are procedures similar to those we created in the preceding pages in conjunction with opening and closing an Excel workbook.) The procedure associated with Figure 15a displays a message that appears automatically after the user clicks the Switchboard button to exit the database. The procedure is almost trivial to write, and consists of a single MsgBox statement. The effect of the procedure is quite significant, however, as it reminds the user to back up his or her work. Indeed, you can never overemphasize the importance of adequate backup.

The dialog box in Figure 15b prompts the user for a password and appears automatically when the user opens the database. The logic here is more sophisticated in that the underlying procedure contains an InputBox statement to request the password, a Do Until loop that is executed until the user enters the correct password or exceeds the allotted number of attempts, then additional logic to display the switchboard or terminate the application if the user fails to enter the proper password. The procedure is not difficult, however, and it builds on the VBA statements that were covered earlier.

The next hands-on exercise has you create the event procedures that are associated with the database in Figure 15. The exercise references a switchboard, or user interface, that is created as a form within the database. The switchboard displays a menu that enables a nontechnical person to move easily from one object in the database (e.g., a form or report) to another.

The switchboard is created through a utility called the Switchboard Manager that prompts you for each item you want to add to the switchboard, and which action you want taken in conjunction with that menu item. You could do the exercise with any database, but we suggest you use the database we provide to access the switchboard that we created for you. The exercise begins, therefore, by having you download a data disk from our Web site.

EVENT-DRIVEN VERSUS TRADITIONAL PROGRAMMING

A traditional program is executed sequentially, beginning with the first line of code and continuing in order through the remainder of the program. It is the program, not the user, that determines the order in which the statements are executed. VBA, on the other hand, is event-driven, meaning that the order in which the procedures are executed depends on the events that occur. It is the user, rather than the program, that determines which events occur, and consequently which procedures are executed. Each application in Microsoft Office has a different set of objects and associated events that comprise the application's object model.

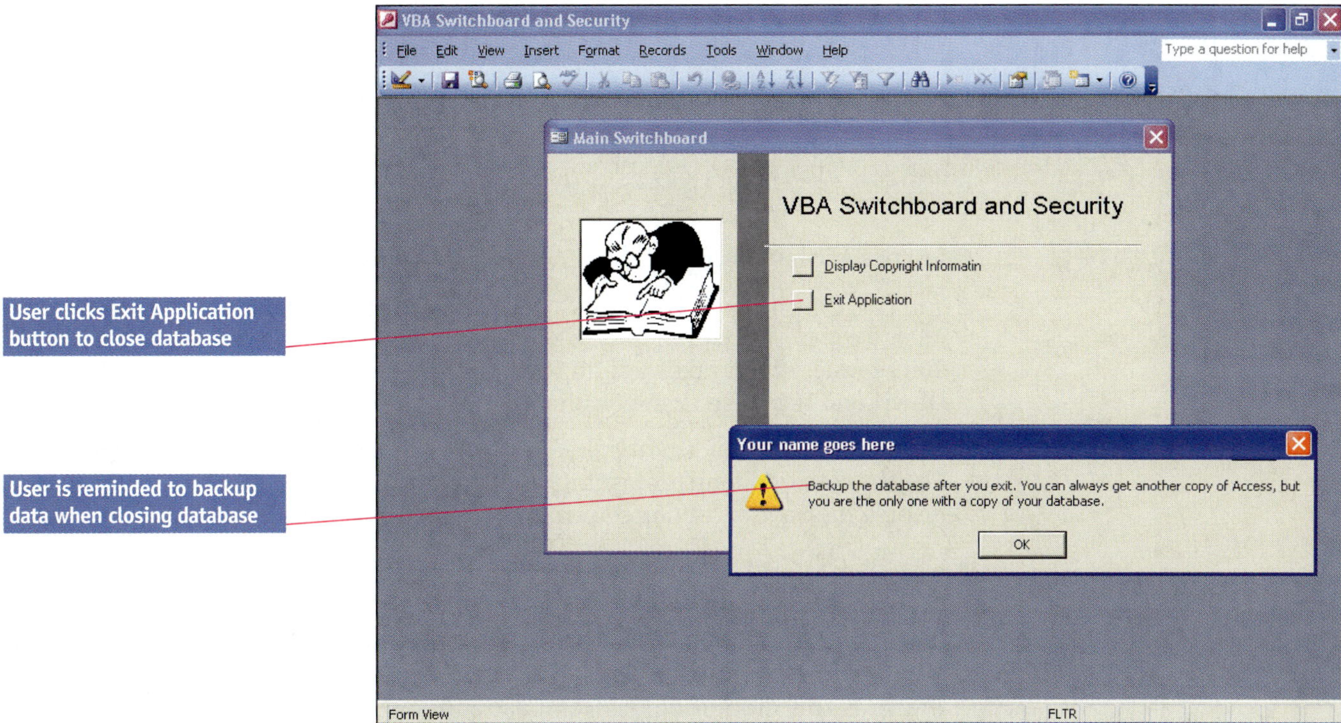

(a) Reminder to the User (Exit Application event)

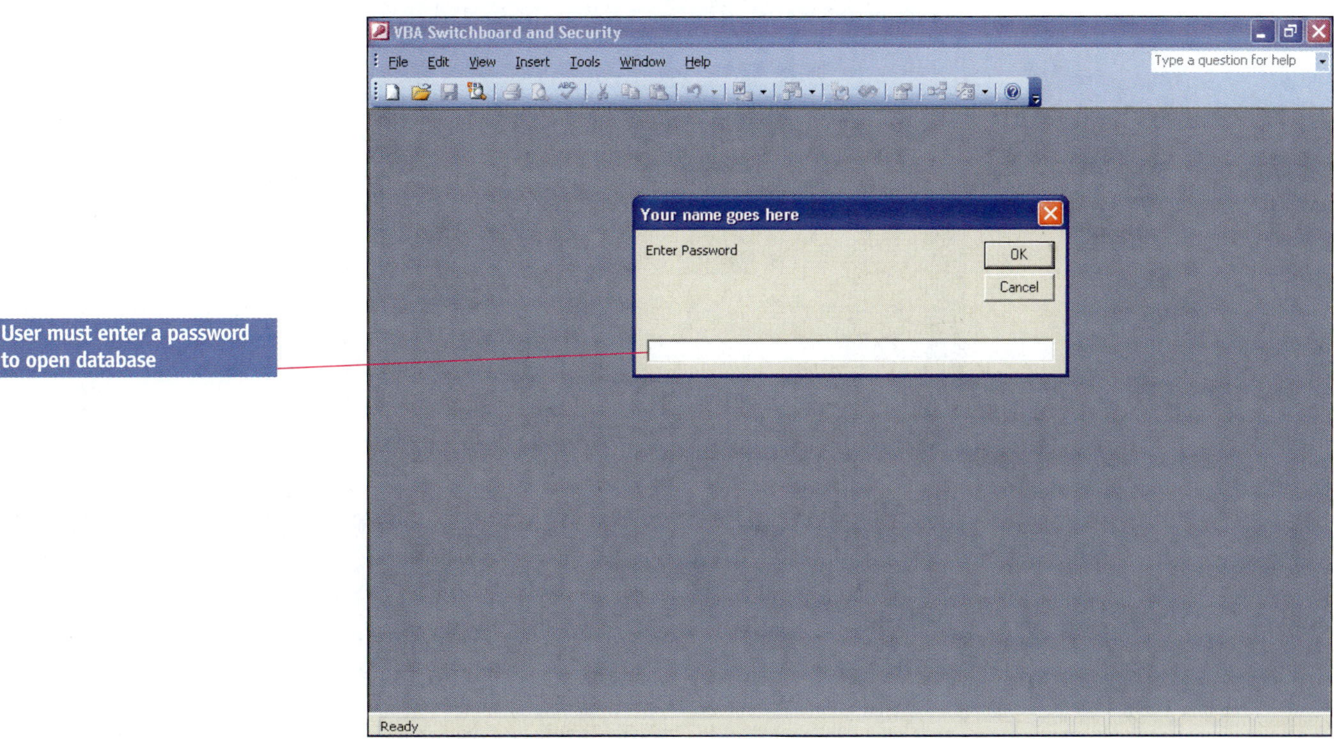

(b) Password Protection (Open Form event)

FIGURE 15 Event-Driven Programming (Microsoft Access)

hands-on exercise

5 Event-Driven Programming (Microsoft Access)

Objective To implement password protection for an Access database; to create a second event procedure that displays a message to the user upon closing the database. Use Figure 16 as a guide in the exercise.

Step 1: Open the Access Database

- You can do this exercise with any database, but we suggest you use the database we have provided. Go to **www.prenhall.com/grauer**, click the **Office 2003 book**, which takes you to the Office 2003 home page. Click the **Student Download tab** to go to the Student Download page.
- Scroll until you can click the link for **Getting Started with VBA**. You will see the File Download dialog box asking what you want to do. Click the **Save button** to display the Save As dialog box, then save the file on your desktop.
- Double click the file after it has been downloaded and follow the onscreen instructions to expand the self-extracting file that contains the database.
- Go to the newly created **Exploring VBA folder** and open the **VBA Switchboard and Security database**. Click the **Open button** when you see the security warning. You should see the Database window in Figure 16a.
- Pull down the **Tools menu**, click the **Macro command**, then click the **Visual Basic Editor command**. Maximize the VBA editor window.

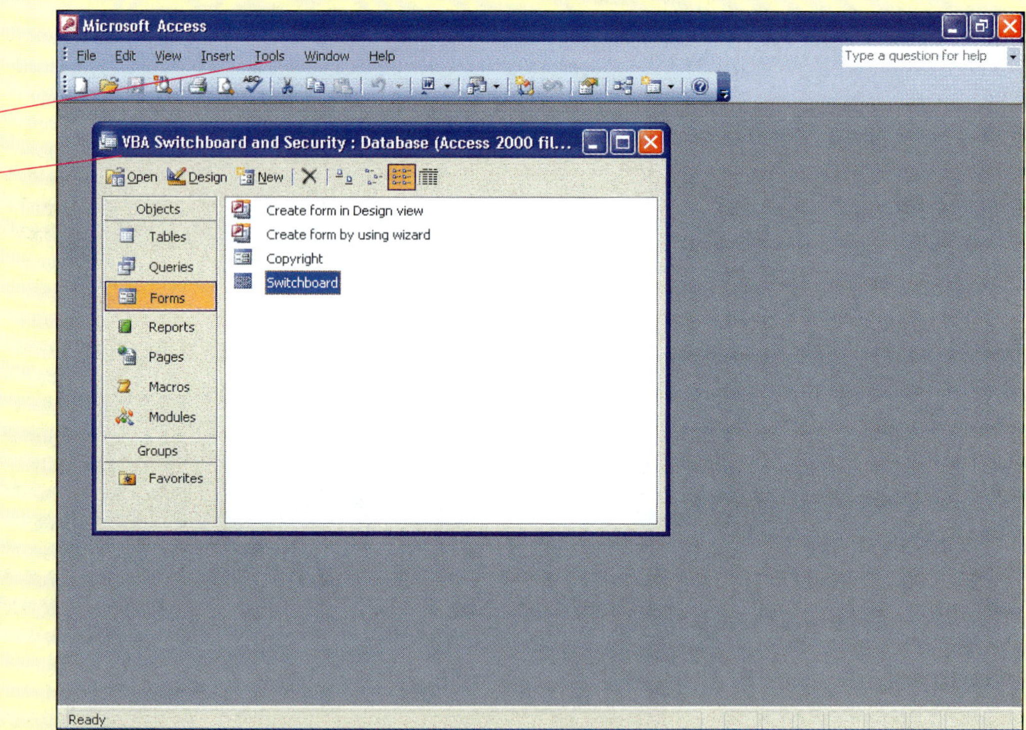

(a) Open the Access Database (step 1)

FIGURE 16 Hands-on Exercise 5

Step 2: Create the ExitDatabase Procedure

- Pull down the **Insert menu** and click **Module** to insert Module1. Complete the **General Declarations section** by adding the Option Explicit statement (if necessary) and the definition of the ApplicationTitle constant as shown in Figure 16b.
- Pull down the **Insert menu** and click **Procedure** to insert a new procedure called **ExitDatabase**. Click the option buttons for a **Sub procedure** and for **Public scope**. Click **OK**.
- Complete the ExitDatabase procedure by entering the **MsgBox** and **DoCmd.Quit** statements. The DoCmd.Quit statement will close Access, but it is entered initially as a comment by beginning the line with an apostrophe.
- Click anywhere in the procedure, then click the **Run Sub button** to test the procedure. Correct any errors that occur, then when the MsgBox displays correctly, **delete the apostrophe** in front of the DoCmd.Quit statement.
- Save the module. The next time you execute the procedure, you should see the message box you just created, and then Access will be terminated.

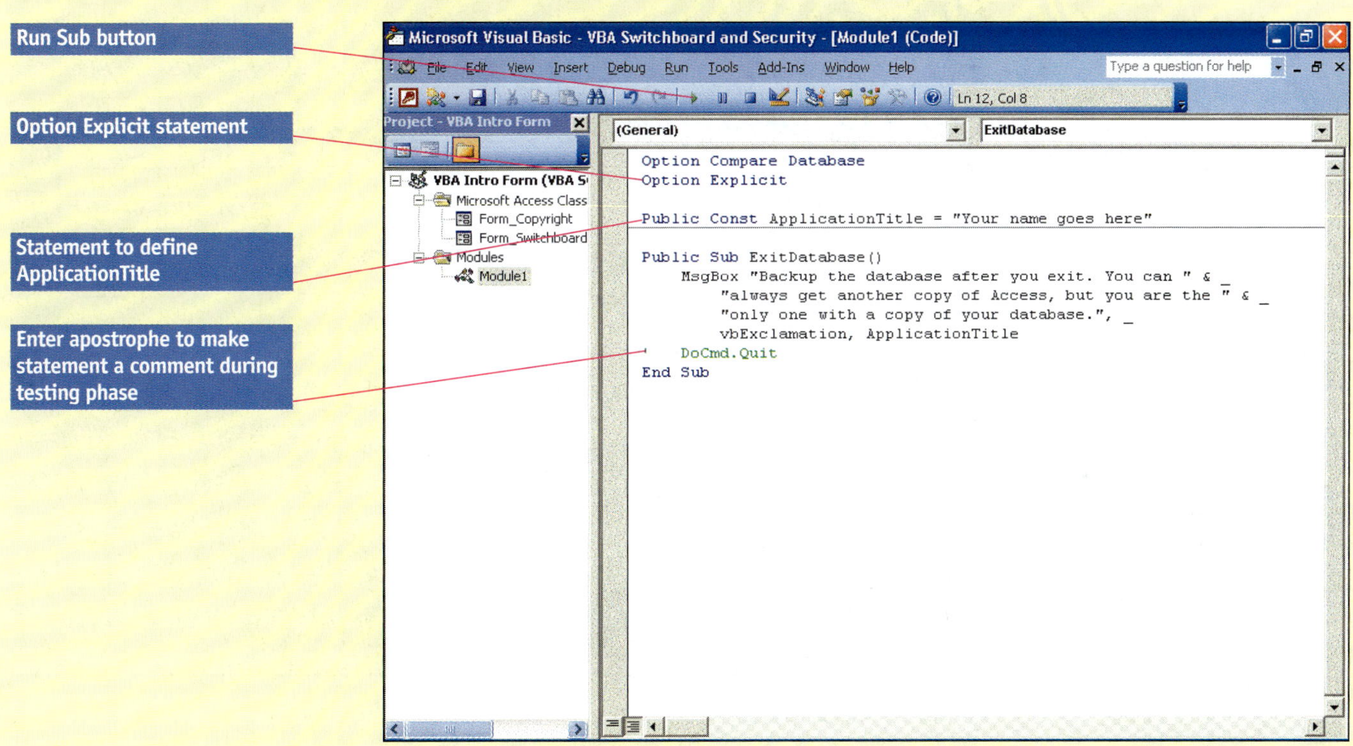

(b) Create the ExitDatabase Procedure (step 2)

FIGURE 16 Hands-on Exercise 5 (*continued*)

CREATE A PUBLIC CONSTANT

Give your application a customized look by adding your name or other identifying message to the title bar of the message and/or input boxes that you use. You can add the information individually to each statement, but it is easier to declare a public constant from within a general module. That way, you can change the value of the constant in one place and have the change reflected automatically throughout your application.

Step 3: Modify the Switchboard

- Click the **View Microsoft Access button** on the Standard toolbar within the VBA window to switch to the Database window (or use the **F11** keyboard shortcut).
- Pull down the **Tools menu**, click the **Database Utilities command**, then choose **Switchboard Manager** to display the Switchboard Manager dialog box in Figure 16c.
- Click the **Edit button** to edit the Main Switchboard and display the Edit Switchboard Page dialog box. Select the **&Exit Application command** and click its **Edit button** to display the Edit Switchboard Item dialog box.
- Change the command to **Run Code**. Enter **ExitDatabase** in the Function Name text box. Click **OK**, then close the two other dialog boxes.
- The switchboard has been modified so that clicking the Exit button will run the VBA procedure you just created.

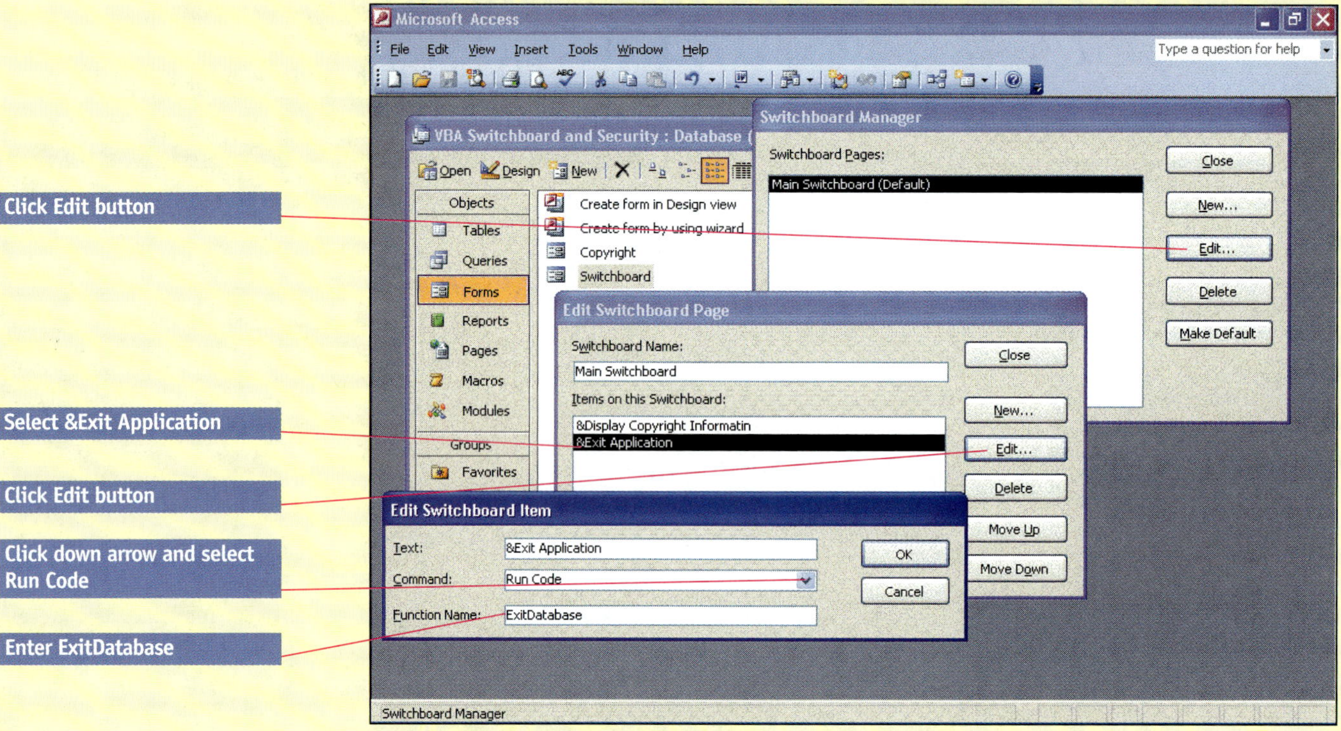

(c) Modify the Switchboard (step 3)

FIGURE 16 Hands-on Exercise 5 (*continued*)

CREATE A KEYBOARD SHORTCUT

The & has special significance when used within the name of an Access object because it creates a keyboard shortcut to that object. Enter "&Exit Application", for example, and the letter E (the letter immediately after the ampersand) will be underlined and appear as "Exit Application" on the switchboard. From there, you can execute the item by clicking its button, or you can use the Alt+E keyboard shortcut (where "E" is the underlined letter in the menu option).

Step 4: Test the Switchboard

- If necessary, click the **Forms button** in the Database window. Double click the **Switchboard form** to open the switchboard as shown in Figure 16d. The switchboard contains two commands.
- Click the **Display Copyright Information command** to display a form that we use with all our databases. (You can open this form in Design view and modify the text to include your name, rather than ours. If you do, be sure to save the modified form, then close it.)
- Click the **Exit Application command** (or use the **Alt+E** keyboard shortcut). You should see the dialog box in Figure 16d, corresponding to the MsgBox statement you created earlier. Click **OK** to close the dialog box.
- Access itself will terminate because of the DoCmd.Quit statement within the ExitDatabase procedure. (If this does not happen, return to the VBA editor and remove the apostrophe in front of the DoCmd statement.)

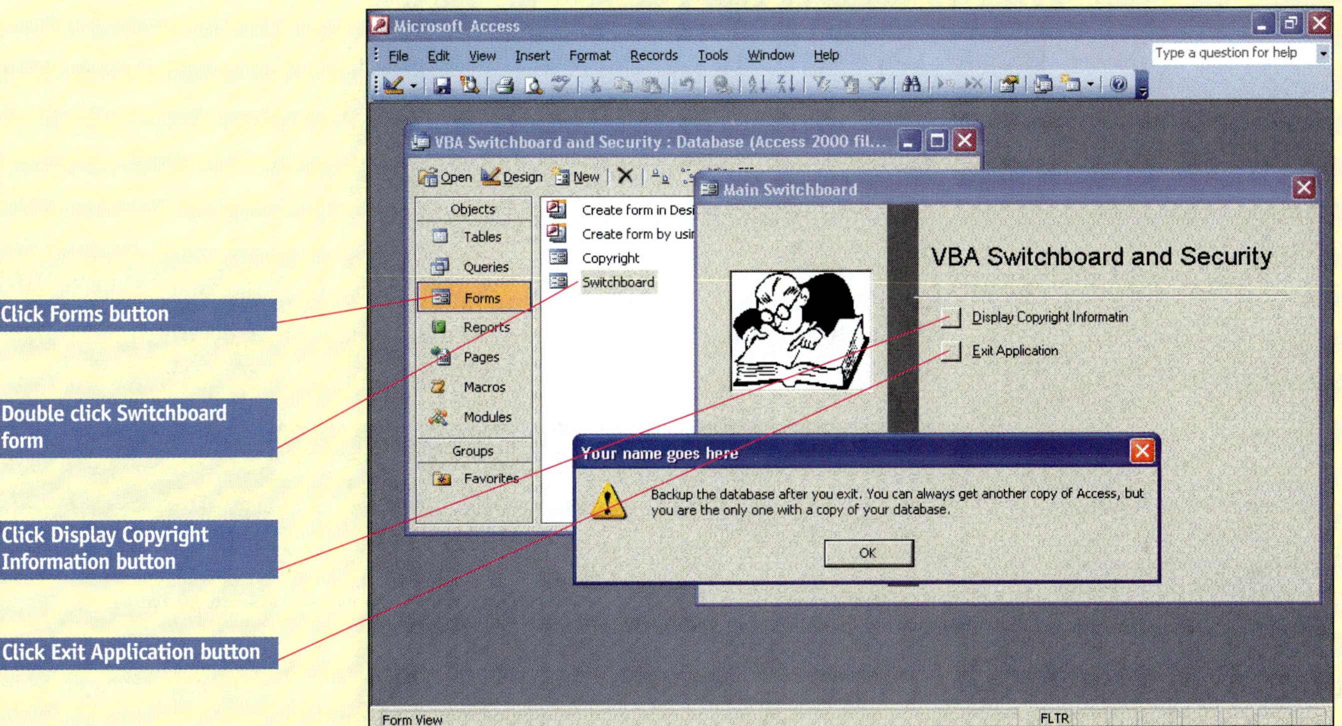

(d) Test the Switchboard (step 4)

FIGURE 16 Hands-on Exercise 5 (*continued*)

BACK UP IMPORTANT FILES

It's not a question of *if* it will happen, but *when*—hard disks die, files are lost, or viruses may infect a system. It has happened to us, and it will happen to you, but you can prepare for the inevitable by creating adequate backup before the problem occurs. The essence of a backup strategy is to decide which files to back up (your data), how often to do the backup (whenever it changes), and where to keep the backup (away from your computer). Do it!

Step 5: Complete the Open Form Event Procedure

- Start Access and reopen the **VBA Switchboard and Security database**. Press **Alt+F11** to start the VBA editor.
- Click the **plus sign** next to Microsoft Office Access Class objects, double click the module called **Form_Switchboard**, then look for the partially completed **Form_Open procedure** as shown in Figure 16e.
- The procedure was created automatically by the Switchboard Manager. You must, however, expand this procedure to include password protection. Note the following:
  - Three variables are required—the correct password, the password entered by the user, and the number of attempts.
  - The user is prompted for the password, and the number of attempts is set to 1. The user is given two additional attempts, if necessary, to get the correct password.
  - The If statement at the end of the loop determines whether the user has entered the correct password, and if so, it executes the original commands that are associated with the switchboard. If, however, the user fails to supply the correct password, an invalid password message is displayed and the **DoCmd.Quit** statement terminates the application.
  - We suggest you place an **apostrophe** in front of the statement initially so that it becomes a comment, and thus it is not executed. Once you are sure that you can enter the correct password, you can remove the apostrophe and implement the password protection.
- Save the procedure. You cannot test this procedure from within the VBA window; you must cause the event to happen (i.e., open the form) for the procedure to execute. Click the **View Microsoft Access button** on the Standard toolbar to return to the Database window.

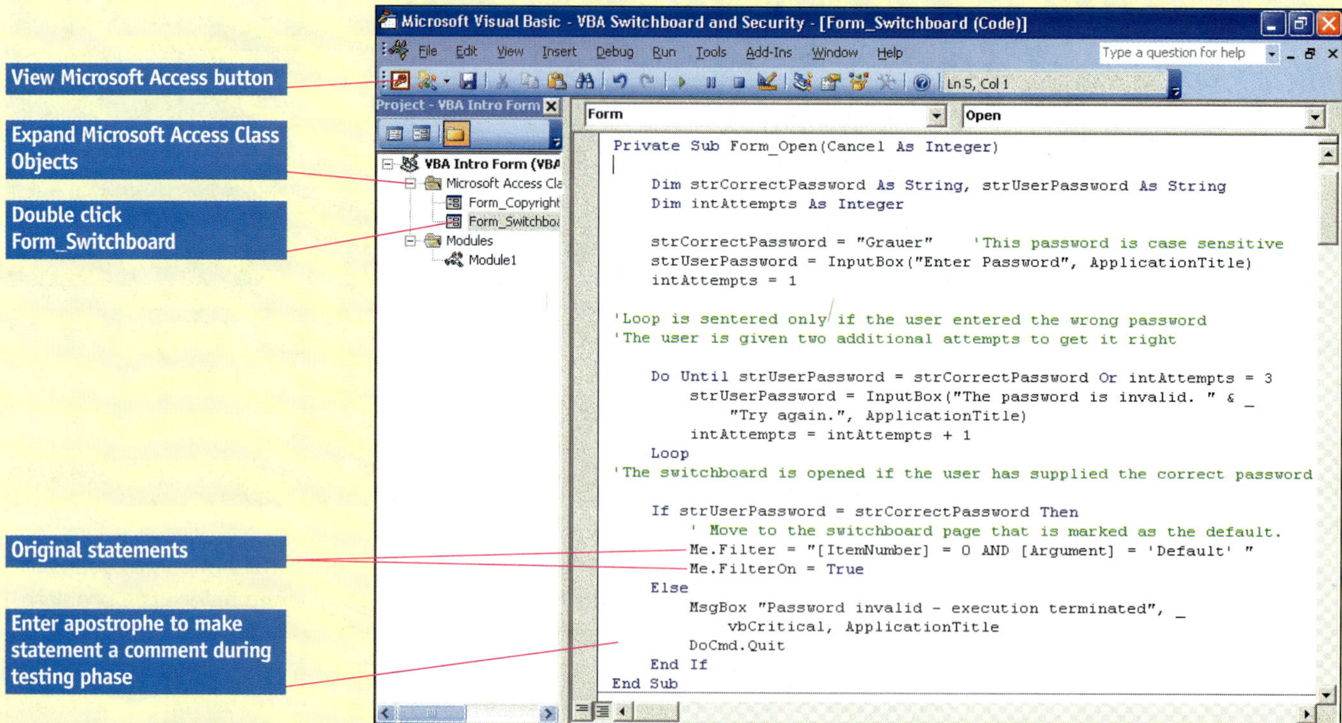

(e) Complete the Open Form Event Procedure (step 5)

FIGURE 16 Hands-on Exercise 5 (*continued*)

Step 6: Test the Procedure

- Close all open windows within the Access database except for the Database window. Click the **Forms button**, then double click the **Switchboard form**.
- You should be prompted for the password as shown in Figure 16f. The password (in our procedure) is **Grauer**.
- Test the procedure repeatedly to include all possibilities. Enter the correct password on the first, second, and third attempts to be sure that the procedure works as intended. Each time you enter the correct password, you will have to close the switchboard, then reopen it.
- Test the procedure one final time, by failing to enter the correct password. You will see a message box indicating that the password is invalid and that execution will be terminated. Termination will not take place, however, because the DoCmd.Quit statement is currently entered as a comment.
- Press **Alt+F11** to reopen the VBA editor. Open the **Microsoft Access Class Objects folder** and double click on **Form_Switchboard**. Delete the apostrophe in front of the DoCmd.Quit statement. The text of the statement changes from green to black to indicate that it is an executable statement. Save the procedure.

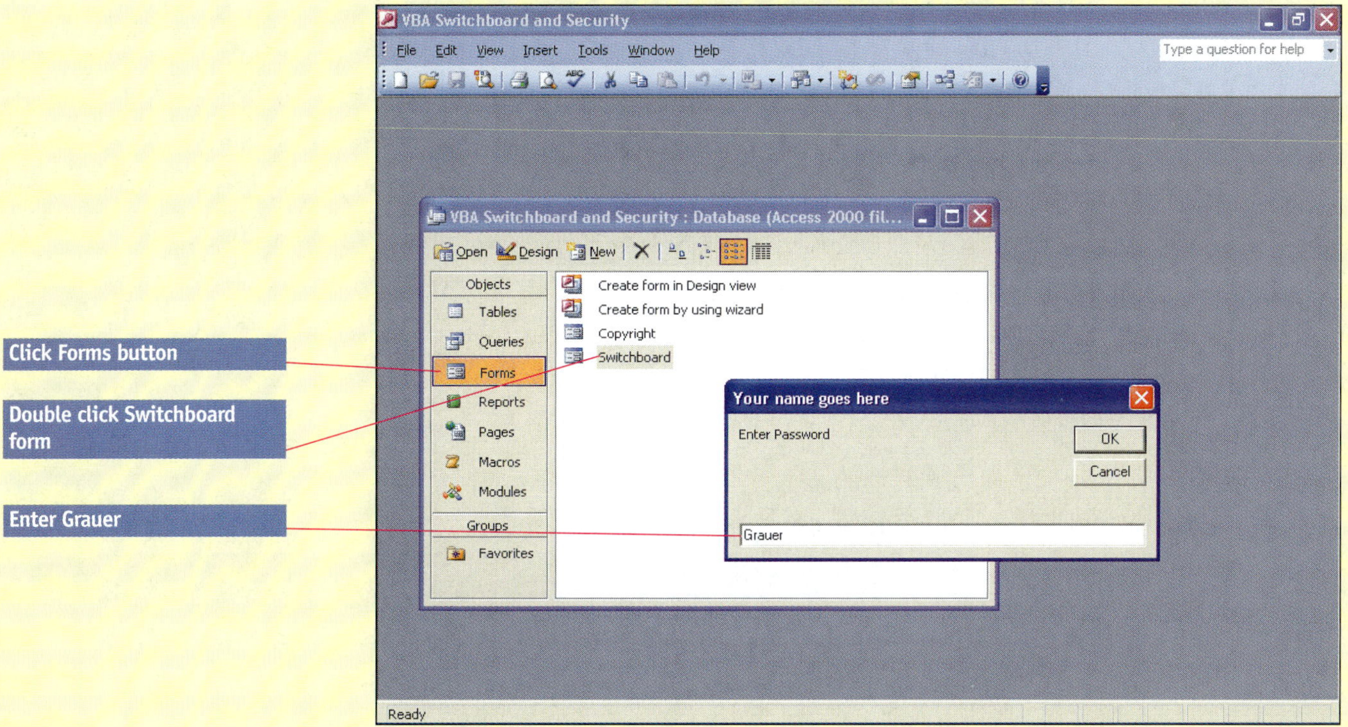

(f) Test the Procedure (step 6)

FIGURE 16 Hands-on Exercise 5 (*continued*)

TOGGLE COMMENTS ON AND OFF

Comments are used primarily to explain the purpose of VBA statements, but they can also be used to "comment out" code as distinct from deleting the statement altogether. Thus, you can add or remove the apostrophe in front of the statement, to toggle the comment on or off.

Step 7: Change the Startup Properties

- Click the **View Microsoft Access button** on the VBA Standard toolbar to return to the Database window.
- Close all open windows except the Database window. Pull down the **Tools menu** and click **Startup** to display the Startup dialog box as shown in Figure 16g.
- Click in the **Application Title** text box and enter the title of the application, **VBA Switchboard and Security** in this example.
- Click the **drop-down arrow** in the Display Form/Page list box and select the **Switchboard form** as the form that will open automatically in conjunction with opening the database.
- Clear the check box to display the Database window. Click **OK** to accept the settings and close the dialog box.
- The next time you open the database, the switchboard should open automatically, which in turn triggers the Open Form event procedure that will prompt the user to enter a password.

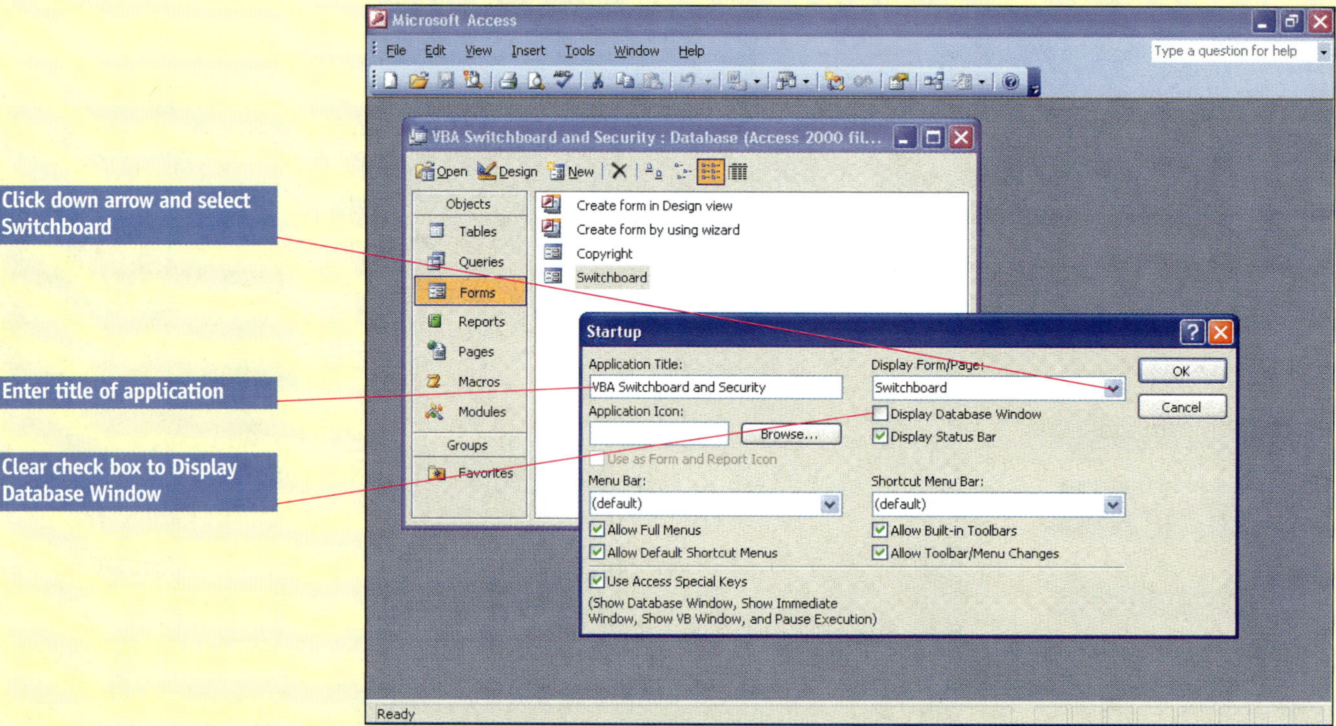

(g) Change the Startup Properties (step 7)

FIGURE 16 Hands-on Exercise 5 (*continued*)

HIDE THE DATABASE WINDOW

Use the Startup property to hide the Database window from the novice user. You avoid confusion and you may prevent the novice from accidentally deleting objects in the database. Of course, anyone with some knowledge of Access can restore the Database window by pulling down the Window menu, clicking the Unhide command, then selecting the Database window from the associated dialog box. Nevertheless, hiding the Database window is a good beginning.

Step 8: Test the Database

- Close the database, then reopen the database to test the procedures we have created in this exercise. The sequence of events is as follows:
  - ❑ The database is loaded and the switchboard is opened but is not yet visible. The Open Form procedure for the switchboard is executed, and you are prompted for the password as shown in Figure 16h.
  - ❑ The password is entered correctly and the switchboard is displayed. The Database window is hidden, however, because the Startup Properties have been modified.
- Click the **Exit Application command** (or use the **Alt+E** keyboard shortcut). You will see the message box reminding you to back up the system, after which the database is closed and Access is terminated.
- Reopen the database. This time, however, you are to enter the wrong password three times in a row. You should see a message indicating that the execution was terminated due to an invalid password.
- Testing is complete and you can go on to add the other objects to your Access database. Congratulations on a job well done.

Enter password

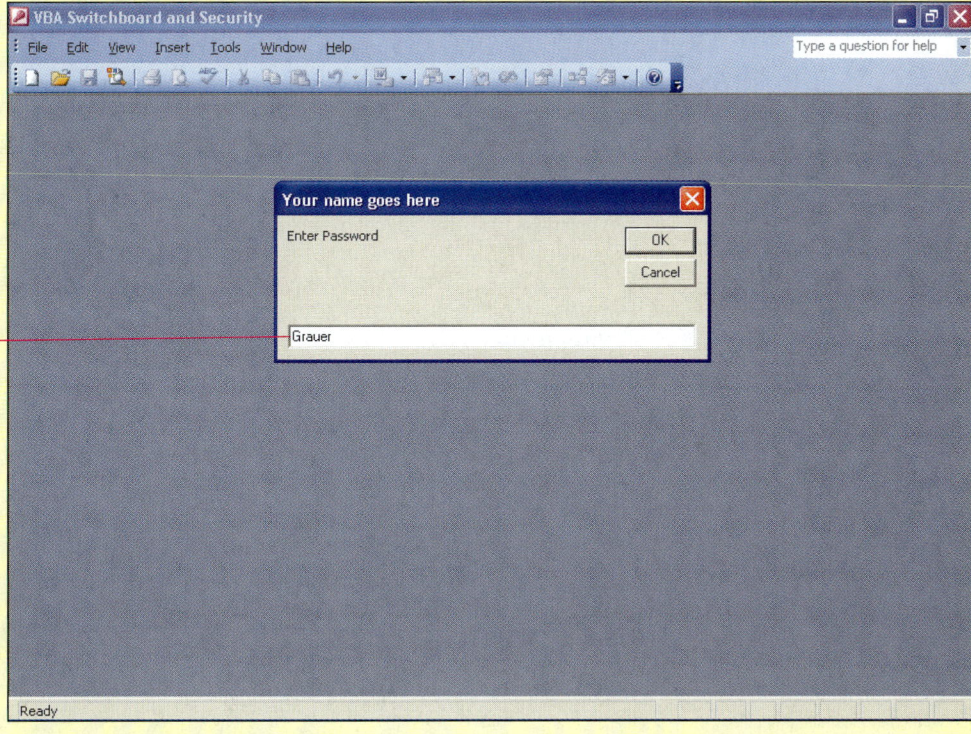

(h) Test the Database (step 8)

FIGURE 16 Hands-on Exercise 5 (*continued*)

RESTORING HIDDEN MENUS AND TOOLBARS

You can use the Startup property to hide menus and/or toolbars from the user by clearing the respective check boxes. A word of caution, however—once the menus are hidden, it is difficult to get them back. Start Access, pull down the File menu, and click Open to display the Open dialog box, select the database to open, then press and hold the Shift key when you click the Open button. This powerful technique is not widely known.

SUMMARY

Visual Basic for Applications (VBA) is a powerful programming language that is accessible from all major applications in Microsoft Office XP. A VBA statement accomplishes a specific task such as displaying a message to the user or accepting input from the user. Statements are grouped into procedures, and procedures in turn are grouped into modules. Every procedure is classified as either private or public.

The MsgBox statement displays information to the user. It has one required argument, which is the message (or prompt) that is displayed to the user. The other two arguments—the icon that is to be displayed in the dialog box and the text of the title bar—are optional. The InputBox function displays a prompt to the user requesting information, then it stores that information (the value returned by the user) for use later in the procedure.

Every variable must be declared (defined) before it can be used. This is accomplished through the Dim (short for Dimension) statement that appears at the beginning of a procedure. The Dim statement indicates the name of the variable and its type (for example, whether it will hold a character string or an integer number), which in turn reserves the appropriate amount of memory for that variable.

The ability to make decisions within a procedure, then branch to alternative sets of statements is implemented through the If . . . Then . . . Else or Case statements. The Else clause is optional, but may be repeated multiple times within an If statement. The Case statement is preferable to an If statement with multiple Else clauses.

The For . . . Next statement (or For . . . Next loop as it is also called) executes all statements between the words For and Next a specified number of times, using a counter to keep track of the number of times the loop is executed. The Do . . . Loop Until and/or Do Until . . . Loop statements are used when the number of times through the loop is not known in advance.

VBA is different from traditional programming languages in that it is event-driven. An event is defined as any action that is recognized by an application, such as Excel or Access. Opening or closing an Excel workbook or an Access database is an event. Selecting a worksheet within a workbook is also an event, as is clicking on a command button on an Access form. To use VBA within Microsoft Office, you decide which events are significant, and what is to happen when those events occur. Then you develop the appropriate event procedures.

KEY TERMS

MULTIPLE CHOICE

1. Which of the following applications in Office XP has access to VBA?
   (a) Word
   (b) Excel
   (c) Access
   (d) All of the above

2. Which of the following is a valid name for a VBA variable?
   (a) Public
   (b) Private
   (c) strUserFirstName
   (d) int Count Of Attempts

3. Which of the following is true about an If statement?
   (a) It evaluates a condition as either true or false, then executes the statement(s) following the keyword "Then" if the condition is true
   (b) It must contain the keyword Else
   (c) It must contain one or more ElseIf statements
   (d) All of the above

4. Which of the following lists the items from smallest to largest?
   (a) Module, procedure, statement
   (b) Statement, module, procedure
   (c) Statement, procedure, module
   (d) Procedure, module, statement

5. Given the statement, MsgBox "Welcome to VBA", "Bob was here", which of the following is true?
   (a) "Welcome to VBA" will be displayed within the resulting message box
   (b) "Welcome to VBA" will appear on the title bar of the displayed dialog box
   (c) The two adjacent commas will cause a compilation error
   (d) An informational icon will be displayed with the message

6. Where are the VBA procedures associated with an Office document stored?
   (a) In the same folder, but in a separate file
   (b) In the Office document itself
   (c) In a special VBA folder on drive C
   (d) In a special VBA folder on the local area network

7. The Debug.Print statement is associated with the:
   (a) Locals window
   (b) Immediate window
   (c) Project Explorer
   (d) Debug toolbar

8. Which of the following is the proper sequence of arguments for the MsgBox statement?
   (a) Text for the title bar, prompt, button
   (b) Prompt, button, text for the title bar
   (c) Prompt, text for the title bar, button
   (d) Button, prompt, text for the title bar

9. Which of the following is a true statement about Do loops?
   (a) Placing the Until clause at the beginning of the loop tests the condition prior to executing any statements in the loop
   (b) Placing the Until clause at the end of the loop executes the statements in the loop, then it tests the condition
   (c) Both (a) and (b)
   (d) Neither (a) nor (b)

10. Given the statement, For intCount = 1 to 10 Step 3, how many times will the statements in the loop be executed (assuming that there are no statements in the loop to terminate the execution)?
    (a) 10
    (b) 4
    (c) 3
    (d) Impossible to determine

... continued

multiple choice

11. Which of the following is a *false* statement?

(a) A dash at the end of a line indicates continuation
(b) An ampersand indicates concatenation
(c) An apostrophe at the beginning of a line signifies a comment
(d) A pair of quotation marks denotes a character string

12. What is the effect of deleting the apostrophe that appears at the beginning of a VBA statement?

(a) A compilation error will occur
(b) The statement is converted to a comment
(c) The color of the statement will change from black to green
(d) The statement is made executable

13. Which of the following If statements will display the indicated message if the user enters a response other than "Grauer" (assuming that "Grauer" is the correct password)?

(a) If strUserResponse <> "Grauer" Then MsgBox "Wrong password"
(b) If strUserResponse = "Grauer" Then MsgBox "Wrong password"
(c) If strUserResponse > "Grauer" Then MsgBox "Wrong password"
(d) If strUserResponse < "Grauer" Then MsgBox "Wrong password"

14. Which of the following will execute the statements in the loop at least once?

(a) Do . . . Loop Until
(b) Do Until ..... Loop
(c) Both (a) and (b)
(d) Neither (a) nor (b)

15. The copy and paste commands can be used to:

(a) Copy statements within a procedure
(b) Copy statements from a procedure in one module to a procedure in another module within the same document
(c) Copy statements from a module in an Excel workbook to a module in an Access database
(d) All of the above

16. Which of the following is true about indented text in a VBA procedure?

(a) The indented text is always executed first
(b) The indented text is always executed last
(c) The indented text is rendered a comment and is never executed
(d) None of the above

17. Which statement will prompt the user to enter his or her name and store the result in a variable called strUser?

(a) InputBox.strUser
(b) strUser = MsgBox("Enter your name")
(c) strUser = InputBox("Enter your name")
(d) InputBox("Enter strUser")

18. Given that strUser is currently set to "George", the expression "Good morning, strName" will return:

(a) Good morning, George
(b) Good morning, strName
(c) Good morning George
(d) Good morning strName

ANSWERS

1. d	**7.** b	**13.** a
2. c	**8.** b	**14.** a
3. a	**9.** c	**15.** d
4. c	**10.** b	**16.** d
5. a	**11.** a	**17.** c
6. b	**12.** d	**18.** b

Index

D

E

F

G

H

K

L

M

N

P

R

S

T

U

V

W

Z